A PRACTICAL APPROACH TO
PLANNING LAW

A PRACTICAL APPROACH TO
PLANNING LAW

FOURTEENTH EDITION

Dr Ashley Bowes
LLB, PhD, BARRISTER
Cornerstone Barristers, Gray's Inn, London

OXFORD
UNIVERSITY PRESS

OXFORD
UNIVERSITY PRESS

Great Clarendon Street, Oxford, OX2 6DP,
United Kingdom

Oxford University Press is a department of the University of Oxford.
It furthers the University's objective of excellence in research, scholarship,
and education by publishing worldwide. Oxford is a registered trade mark of
Oxford University Press in the UK and in certain other countries

© Ashley Bowes 2019

The moral rights of the author have been asserted

Twelfth Edition published in 2012
Thirteen Edition published in 2014
Fourteenth Edition published in 2019

Impression: 28

All rights reserved. No part of this publication may be reproduced, stored in
a retrieval system, or transmitted, in any form or by any means, without the
prior permission in writing of Oxford University Press, or as expressly permitted
by law, by licence or under terms agreed with the appropriate reprographics
rights organization. Enquiries concerning reproduction outside the scope of the
above should be sent to the Rights Department, Oxford University Press, at the
address above

You must not circulate this work in any other form
and you must impose this same condition on any acquirer

Crown copyright material is reproduced under Class Licence
Number C01P0000148 with the permission of OPSI
and the Queen's Printer for Scotland

Published in the United States of America by Oxford University Press
198 Madison Avenue, New York, NY 10016, United States of America

British Library Cataloguing in Publication Data
Data available

Library of Congress Control Number: 2019937069

ISBN 978–0–19–883325–3

Printed and bound by
CPI Group (UK) Ltd, Croydon, CR0 4YY

Links to third party websites are provided by Oxford in good faith and
for information only. Oxford disclaims any responsibility for the materials
contained in any third party website referenced in this work.

The Town Clerk's Views

In a few years this country will be looking
As uniform and tasty as its cooking.
Hamlets which fail to pass the planners' test
Will be demolished. We'll rebuild the rest
To look like Welwyn mixed with Middle West.
All fields we'll turn to sports grounds, lit at night
From concrete standards by fluorescent light:
And over all the land, instead of trees,
Clean poles and wire will whisper in the breeze.
We'll keep one ancient village just to show
What England once was when the times were slow—
Broadway for me. But here I know I must
Ask the opinion of our National Trust.
And ev'ry old cathedral that you enter
By then will be an Area Culture Centre.
Instead of nonsense about Death and Heaven
Lectures on civic duty will be given;
Eurhythmic classes dancing round the spire,
And economics courses in the choir.
So don't encourage tourists. Stay your hand
Until we've really got the country plann'd.

John Betjeman, 1948*

---

* Reproduced by permission of John Murray (Publishers) Limited.

PREFACE

I was honoured to be asked to revise this long-running introductory work to planning law, originally conceived by Professor Victor Moore and last revised in 2013 by my friend and colleague on the *Journal of Planning & Environment Law* Editorial Board, Professor Michael Purdue. The task of following these two giants of the planning world has been made all the more daunting by the sad death of Professor Moore in 2017 and by my realizing that the first edition of this work, in October 1987, was produced when I was celebrating my first birthday. As before, the structure has remained loyal to Professor Moore's original conception.

The last six years since the previous edition has seen a number of new pieces of primary legislation, including the Self-Build and Custom Housebuilding Act 2015, Housing and Planning Act 2016, and the Neighbourhood Planning Act 2017. These pieces of legislation have introduced wholly new concepts, such as permission in principle and self-build housing, as well as extending the existing powers for the Secretary of State in plan-making, including neighbourhood plan-making. The well-used Development Management Procedure and General permitted Development Orders were re-cast in 2015 and the Environmental Impact Assessment and Habitats Regulations re-cast in 2017.

In 2018, the Government issued a revised version of the National Planning Policy Framework, to which tehnical amendments were made in 2019. The meaning and implications of this document (and its predecessor issued shortly before the previous edition) has dominated the litigation in the courts in the years which have followed, and has even reached the Supreme Court in *Hopkins Homes Ltd v Secretary of State for Communities & Local Government* [2017] UKSC 37; [2017] 1 WLR 1865 (considered in Chapter 11).

The Supreme Court has also been busy revisiting some fundamental principles of the planning system, including the duty to give reasons for the grant of planning permission in *R (CPRE Kent) v Dover District Council* [2017] UKSC 79; [2018] 1 WLR 108 (considered in Chapter 11), the interpretation of planning permissions in *Trump International Golf Scotland Ltd v Scottish Ministers* [2015] UKSC 74; [2016] 1 WLR 85, the interaction of planning permission with private law nuisance in *Coventry v Lawrence* [2014] UKSC 46; [2015] AC 106 (both considered in Chapter 15), the lawful scope of planning obligations in *Aberdeen City and Shire District Development Planning Authority v Elsick Development Co Ltd* [2017] UKSC 66; [2017] PTSR 1413 (considered in Chapter 17), as well as the

Preface

interpretation of the obligations under the EIA, Habitats, and SEA Directives in *R (Champion) v North Norfolk District Council* [2015] UKSC 52; [2015] 1 WLR 3710 (considered in Chapter 12), and *R (Buckinghamshire CC) v Secretary of State for Transport* [2014] UKSC 3; [2014] 1 WLR 324 (considered in Chapter 13).

At the point of finalization of this edition, the terms on which the United Kingdom is to leave the European Union remain unclear. However, the Government's intention is that the obligations under the EIA, SEA, and Habitats Directives are to be preserved after the UK's withdrawal, and has published draft Regulations, under the terms of the European Union (Withdrawal) Act 2018, to preserve those obligations. Accordingly, there remains a full and up-to-date consideration of these regimes, including recent CJEU decisions such as *Gemeinde Altrip v Land Rheinland-Pfalz* [2014] PTSR 311, *People Over Wind v Teoranta* [2018] PTSR 1668, and *Grace & Sweetman v An Bord Pleanala* [2018] Env LR 37 within Chapters 12, 13, and 26 of this edition.

Since the previous edition, the Planning Court has been formed in April 2014. Much (but not all) planning litigation is now heard within this specialist list within the Queen's Bench Division. The Court is led by the Planning Liaison Judge (presently Mr Justice Holgate) and has its own forms and timetables, as well as specialist Administrative Court Judges with planning expertise. This reform, together with the diligence of the Planning Liaison Judges, has undoubtedly improved the efficiency of planning litigation at first instance. Additionally, the appointment of Lord Justice Lindblom to the Court of Appeal in July 2015 has ensured that planning law continues to have a champion at the appellate level, following the retirement of Sir Jeremy Sullivan in September 2015.

I have attempted to state the law as it stood at 1 January 2019.

Dr Ashley Bowes
Cornerstone Barristers,
Gray's Inn,
London.
1 January 2019.

PREFACE TO THE FIRST EDITION

Given the large number of excellent books available on the subject of planning law, some excuse is obviously needed to justify this new addition to existing literature.

The invitation to write a book of no more than 350 pages, including appendices, on the subject and without the use of footnotes, proved to be a challenge impossible to resist.

In the pages that follow therefore, I have tried to prune what is an extremely difficult and complex subject down to its basic principles. I have attempted to describe planning law and its administration in both simple and practical terms, and resisted the temptation to stray too far into technical details or to refer to judicial decisions which have made occasional departures from those basic principles.

Two aspects, however, must be drawn to the reader's attention. First, limitations of space has meant this book does not deal with the law and practice in Scotland, which, although substantially similar to that for England and Wales, has a number of significant differences. Secondly, the book has anticipated the bringing into force of the changes made to the law by the planning provisions of the Housing and Planning Act 1986. It is expected, however, that the provisions of the Act not yet in force will be brought into force by commencement order before the year has run its course.

Lastly, after years of promise, a new General Development Order is expected to be promulgated shortly. But as anyone interested in the use and development of land will know, if a publication in this subject were to await the translation of all proposals into reality, no books on planning law would be published at all.

October 1987

CONTENTS—SUMMARY

Table of Cases — xxiii
Table of Legislation and Other Instruments — xlix
List of Abbreviations — lxv

1. Historical Introduction — 1
2. Planning Organization — 13
3. The Evolution of Development Plans — 47
4. Development Plans: Their Legal Significance After the Planning and Compulsory Purchase Act 2004 — 57
5. Definition of Development 1: Operational Development — 83
6. Definition of Development 2: Material Change of Use — 107
7. The Need for Planning Permission 1: General Permitted Development Order; Local Development Orders — 155
8. The Need for Planning Permission 2: Cases of Doubt — 181
9. Applications for Planning Permission 1: Pre-Submission Requirements — 189
10. Applications for Planning Permission 2: Procedure on Receipt of Applications by the Local Planning Authority — 209
11. Determinations of Applications for Planning Permission — 227
12. Environmental Impact Assessment — 281
13. Strategic Environmental Assessment — 317
14. Conditions — 329
15. The Construction, Scope, Effect, and Life of a Planning Permission — 365
16. Development by the Crown, Statutory Undertakers, and Local Authorities; Public Works Orders — 387
17. Planning Agreements; Planning Obligations; and The Community Infrastructure Levy — 401
18. Appeals; Statutory Review; Judicial Review; The Ombudsman — 423
19. Human Rights — 471
20. Enforcement of Planning Control — 479

Contents—Summary

21. Listed Buildings and Conservation Areas	533
22. Ancient Monuments and Areas of Archaeological Importance	575
23. Minerals	581
24. The Control of Outdoor Advertisements	593
25. Trees, Hedgerows, and High Hedges	605
26. Conservation of Natural Habitats and Protected Species and Biodiversity	615
27. Remedies for Adverse Planning Decisions	623
28. Nationally Significant Infrastructure Projects	631
29. Town and Village Greens	645
Index	665

CONTENTS

Table of Cases	xxiii
Table of Legislation and Other Instruments	xlix
List of Abbreviations	lxv

1. HISTORICAL INTRODUCTION

A	THE GROWTH OF PUBLIC CONTROL OVER LAND USE	1.01
B	LATER LEGISLATIVE LANDMARKS	1.21
C	THE LOCALISM ACT 2011 AND SUBSEQUENT REFORM	1.27

2. PLANNING ORGANIZATION

A	THE SECRETARY OF STATE	2.03
B	LOCAL PLANNING AUTHORITIES	2.64
C	GREATER LONDON	2.98

3. THE EVOLUTION OF DEVELOPMENT PLANS

A	HISTORICAL INTRODUCTION TO DEVELOPMENT PLANS	3.01
B	DEVELOPMENT PLANS PREPARED UNDER THE 1947 ACT (FIRST GENERATION PLANS)	3.05
C	DEVELOPMENT PLANS PREPARED UNDER THE 1968 ACT (SECOND GENERATION PLANS)	3.11
D	CHANGES TO THE 1968 DEVELOPMENT PLANS SYSTEM	3.26
E	DEVELOPMENT PLANS PREPARED UNDER THE 2004 ACT (THIRD GENERATION PLANS)	3.29
F	THE LOCALISM ACT 2011 AND THE ABOLITION OF THE REGIONAL STRATEGIES	3.34

4. DEVELOPMENT PLANS: THEIR LEGAL SIGNIFICANCE AFTER THE PLANNING AND COMPULSORY PURCHASE ACT 2004

A	SUSTAINABLE DEVELOPMENT AND COMMUNITY INVOLVEMENT	4.03
B	THE SURVEY	4.12
C	LOCAL DEVELOPMENT SCHEMES	4.17
D	THE LOCAL DEVELOPMENT FRAMEWORK	4.22
E	LOCAL DEVELOPMENT DOCUMENTS AND NEIGHBOURHOOD PLANS	4.26
F	PREPARATION OF DEVELOPMENT PLAN DOCUMENTS	4.45
G	THE INDEPENDENT EXAMINATION OF DEVELOPMENT PLAN DOCUMENTS	4.49
H	THE BINDING NATURE OF INSPECTORS' REPORTS	4.56
I	POWERS OF THE SECRETARY OF STATE WITH REGARD TO LOCAL DEVELOPMENT DOCUMENTS	4.59
J	MISCELLANEOUS PROVISIONS OF PART 2	4.60
K	LEGAL CHALLENGES TO DEVELOPMENT PLANS	4.67
L	DEVELOPMENT PLANS: THEIR LEGAL SIGNIFICANCE	4.77
M	TRANSITIONAL PROVISIONS: TRANSFERRING FROM THE OLD SYSTEM TO THE NEW SYSTEM	4.86
N	WALES: REGIONAL FUNCTIONS AND LOCAL DEVELOPMENT	4.90

5. DEFINITION OF DEVELOPMENT 1: OPERATIONAL DEVELOPMENT

A	NEED FOR PLANNING PERMISSION	5.01
B	DEFINITION OF DEVELOPMENT	5.02
C	OPERATIONAL DEVELOPMENT	5.11

6. DEFINITION OF DEVELOPMENT 2: MATERIAL CHANGE OF USE

A	MATERIAL CHANGE OF USE	6.02
B	USES EXCLUDED FROM DEVELOPMENT	6.10
C	USES INCLUDED WITHIN DEVELOPMENT	6.92

D	ADVERTISING	6.100
E	INTENSIFICATION	6.104
F	THE PLANNING UNIT, AND PRIMARY OR DOMINANT AND ANCILLARY USES	6.115
G	INTERRUPTION AND ABANDONMENT OF A USE	6.143
H	SUBDIVISION OF A PLANNING UNIT	6.163

7. THE NEED FOR PLANNING PERMISSION 1: GENERAL PERMITTED DEVELOPMENT ORDER; LOCAL DEVELOPMENT ORDERS

A	TOWN AND COUNTRY PLANNING (GENERAL PERMITTED DEVELOPMENT) ORDER	7.05
B	GENERAL CONSIDERATIONS	7.06
C	FURTHER CONSIDERATION OF SOME OF THE PARTS	7.24
D	LOCAL DEVELOPMENT ORDERS	7.58
E	NEIGHBOURHOOD DEVELOPMENT ORDERS	7.63
F	PERMISSION IN PRINCIPLE	7.69

8. THE NEED FOR PLANNING PERMISSION 2: CASES OF DOUBT

A	CERTIFICATE OF LAWFULNESS OF PROPOSED USE OR DEVELOPMENT (CLOPUD)	8.02
B	ACTION FOR A DECLARATION	8.09
C	CARRYING OUT AN ACTIVITY WITHOUT ASCERTAINING WHETHER IT NEEDS PERMISSION	8.17

9. APPLICATIONS FOR PLANNING PERMISSION 1: PRE-SUBMISSION REQUIREMENTS

A	CONTENT AND FORM	9.01
B	OUTLINE PLANNING PERMISSION AND PERMISSION IN PRINCIPLE	9.13
C	NOTIFICATION OF OWNERS	9.30
D	FEES FOR PLANNING APPLICATIONS	9.50
E	TWIN-TRACKING	9.57

F	CONSULTATIONS WITH THE LOCAL PLANNING AUTHORITY	9.59
G	CONSULTATIONS BY APPLICANT	9.63
H	THE PLANNING REGISTER	9.64

10. APPLICATIONS FOR PLANNING PERMISSION 2: PROCEDURE ON RECEIPT OF APPLICATIONS BY THE LOCAL PLANNING AUTHORITY

A	ACKNOWLEDGMENT OF RECEIPT OF APPLICATION	10.01
B	POWER TO DECLINE TO DETERMINE APPLICATIONS	10.10
C	PUBLICITY FOR PLANNING APPLICATIONS	10.26
D	NOTIFICATION REQUIREMENTS	10.41
E	CONSULTATION	10.48
F	DEVELOPMENT NOT IN ACCORDANCE WITH THE PROVISIONS OF THE DEVELOPMENT PLAN	10.56
G	AMENDMENT OF APPLICATIONS	10.61

11. DETERMINATIONS OF APPLICATIONS FOR PLANNING PERMISSION

A	DELEGATION	11.01
B	ESTOPPEL BY REPRESENTATION	11.15
C	DETERMINATION OF A PLANNING APPLICATION	11.27

12. ENVIRONMENTAL IMPACT ASSESSMENT

A	INTRODUCTION	12.01
B	PROJECTS REQUIRING ENVIRONMENTAL IMPACT ASSESSMENT	12.06
C	JUDICIAL CHALLENGE	12.42

13. STRATEGIC ENVIRONMENTAL ASSESSMENT

A	INTRODUCTION	13.01
B	DETERMINATIONS OF THE RESPONSIBLE AUTHORITY	13.11
C	PREPARATION OF ENVIRONMENTAL REPORT	13.14

14. CONDITIONS

A	THE GENERAL POWER	14.05
B	SPECIFIC POWERS TO IMPOSE CONDITIONS	14.36
C	CHALLENGING AN INVALID CONDITION	14.69
D	EFFECT OF AN INVALID CONDITION	14.70
E	REMOVING CONDITIONS PREVIOUSLY ATTACHED	14.76
F	RETROSPECTIVE PLANNING APPLICATIONS	14.78
G	DURATION OF PLANNING PERMISSIONS	14.81

15. THE CONSTRUCTION, SCOPE, EFFECT, AND LIFE OF A PLANNING PERMISSION

A	CONSTRUCTION OF A PLANNING PERMISSION	15.01
B	SCOPE OF A PLANNING PERMISSION	15.16
C	EFFECT OF A PLANNING PERMISSION	15.28
D	PUBLIC RIGHTS OF WAY AND DEVELOPMENT	15.40
E	INTERFERENCE WITH EASEMENTS AND OTHER INTERESTS OR RIGHTS	15.41
F	PLANNING AND HIGHWAYS	15.42
G	PLANNING PERMISSION AND ACTIONS IN NUISANCE	15.47
H	PLANNING PERMISSION AND ACTIONS FOR NEGLIGENCE	15.53
I	PLANNING PERMISSION AND ACTIONS IN DECEIT	15.58
J	LIFE OF A PLANNING PERMISSION	15.63

16. DEVELOPMENT BY THE CROWN, STATUTORY UNDERTAKERS, AND LOCAL AUTHORITIES; PUBLIC WORKS ORDERS

A	THE CROWN	16.01
B	STATUTORY UNDERTAKERS	16.05
C	LOCAL AUTHORITIES	16.10
D	PUBLIC WORKS ORDERS	16.30

17. PLANNING AGREEMENTS; PLANNING OBLIGATIONS; AND THE COMMUNITY INFRASTRUCTURE LEVY

A	INTRODUCTION AND ENABLING POWERS	17.01
B	PLANNING OBLIGATIONS	17.17
C	PLANNING OBLIGATIONS (THE DETAILED REGIME)	17.21
D	CREATION OF PLANNING OBLIGATIONS	17.25
E	MODIFICATION AND DISCHARGE OF PLANNING OBLIGATIONS	17.32
F	APPEALS	17.37
G	AMENDMENT OF PLANNING OBLIGATIONS	17.39
H	THE SECRETARY OF STATE'S POLICY	17.40
I	REFORMING PLANNING CONTRIBUTIONS	17.60
J	THE COMMUNITY INFRASTRUCTURE LEVY	17.63

18. APPEALS; STATUTORY REVIEW; JUDICIAL REVIEW; THE OMBUDSMAN

A	APPEALS	18.01
B	NATURAL JUSTICE OR FAIRNESS	18.17
C	WRITTEN REPRESENTATION PROCEDURE	18.39
D	HEARINGS	18.44
E	LOCAL INQUIRIES	18.49
F	MAJOR INFRASTRUCTURE PROJECTS	18.64
G	TIME WITHIN WHICH THE SECRETARY OF STATE IS REQUIRED TO TAKE DECISIONS	18.70
H	POWER TO CORRECT DECISION LETTERS	18.73
I	AWARD OF COSTS	18.79
J	STATUTORY REVIEW	18.93
K	JUDICIAL REVIEW	18.117
L	THE REQUIREMENT OF STANDING	18.121
M	THE NEED FOR EXPEDITION	18.124
N	THE PLANNING COURT AND THE CRIMINAL JUSTICE AND COURTS ACT 2015	18.127
O	THE REMEDY	18.130
P	THE ROLE OF THE OMBUDSMAN	18.131

19. HUMAN RIGHTS
A	THE HUMAN RIGHTS ACT 1998	19.01

20. ENFORCEMENT OF PLANNING CONTROL
A	INTRODUCTION	20.01
B	PLANNING CONTRAVENTION NOTICES	20.07
C	ADDITIONAL RIGHTS OF ENTRY ON PROPERTY	20.13
D	TEMPORARY STOP NOTICES	20.17
E	ENFORCEMENT NOTICES	20.25
F	ISSUE OF ENFORCEMENT NOTICES	20.40
G	CONTENT OF ENFORCEMENT NOTICES	20.56
H	APPEALS AGAINST ENFORCEMENT NOTICES	20.70
I	STOP NOTICES	20.109
J	BREACH OF CONDITION NOTICES	20.138
K	INJUNCTIONS	20.152
L	REVERSION TO EARLIER USE	20.168
M	CERTIFICATES OF LAWFULNESS OF EXISTING USE OR DEVELOPMENT (CLEUDS) AND CERTIFICATES OF LAWFULNESS OF PROPOSED USE OR DEVELOPMENT (CLOPUDS)	20.169

21. LISTED BUILDINGS AND CONSERVATION AREAS
A	INTRODUCTION	21.01
B	LISTED BUILDINGS	21.02
C	WHAT CAN BE LISTED	21.23
D	THE PROTECTION	21.45
E	BUILDINGS IN ECCLESIASTICAL USE AND MONUMENTS	21.49
F	LISTED BUILDING CONSENT	21.56
G	LISTED BUILDING ENFORCEMENT NOTICES	21.77
H	LISTED BUILDING PURCHASE NOTICES	21.93
I	CERTIFICATES OF IMMUNITY	21.94
J	LISTED BUILDINGS IN NEED OF REPAIR	21.98
K	BUILDING PRESERVATION NOTICES	21.113

L	CONSERVATION AREAS	21.130
M	RECENT CHANGES	21.149

22. ANCIENT MONUMENTS AND AREAS OF ARCHAEOLOGICAL IMPORTANCE

A	SCHEDULED MONUMENTS	22.02
B	ANCIENT MONUMENTS	22.08
C	AREAS OF ARCHAEOLOGICAL IMPORTANCE	22.11
D	PROTECTION UNDER PLANNING LEGISLATION	22.13

23. MINERALS

A	INTRODUCTION	23.01
B	OLD MINING PERMISSIONS	23.03
C	MINING PERMISSIONS GRANTED BETWEEN 1948 AND 1982	23.13
D	INTERPRETATION OF MINING PERMISSIONS	23.32

24. THE CONTROL OF OUTDOOR ADVERTISEMENTS

A	INTRODUCTION	24.01
B	DEEMED CONSENT	24.15
C	EXPRESS CONSENT	24.22
D	AREAS OF SPECIAL CONTROL (ASC)	24.25
E	FLY-POSTING	24.31
F	DEVELOPMENT AND THE DISPLAY OF ADVERTISEMENTS	24.37

25. TREES, HEDGEROWS, AND HIGH HEDGES

A	THE PROTECTION OF TREES	25.01
B	COMPENSATION	25.19
C	THE PROTECTION OF HEDGEROWS	25.20
D	THE CONTROL OF HIGH HEDGES	25.34

26. CONSERVATION OF NATURAL HABITATS AND PROTECTED SPECIES AND BIODIVERSITY

A	THE HABITATS REGULATIONS 2017	26.02
B	CASE LAW	26.13

27. REMEDIES FOR ADVERSE PLANNING DECISIONS

A	COMPENSATION FOR RESTRICTIONS ON DEVELOPMENT	27.01
B	COMPENSATION FOR THE REVOCATION OR MODIFICATION OF PLANNING PERMISSIONS UNDER SECTION 97 OF THE 1990 ACT	27.08
C	COMPENSATION FOR DISCONTINUANCE OF A USE OR THE ALTERATION OR REMOVAL OF BUILDINGS OR WORKS UNDER SECTION 102 OF THE 1990 ACT	27.14
D	PURCHASE NOTICES	27.16

28. NATIONALLY SIGNIFICANT INFRASTRUCTURE PROJECTS

A	ALTERNATIVE METHODS OF DETERMINING MAJOR PROJECTS	28.09
B	NATIONALLY SIGNIFICANT INFRASTRUCTURE PROJECTS	28.13

29. TOWN AND VILLAGE GREENS

A	INTRODUCTION	29.01
B	RIGHT TO APPLY	29.07
C	DEFINITION	29.15
D	PROCEDURE	29.37
E	POST-REGISTRATION RIGHTS	29.41
F	RECTIFICATION	29.46

Index   665

TABLE OF CASES

INTERNATIONAL CASES

Court of Justice of the European Union (CJEU)

Ecologistas en Accion-CODA v Ayuntamiento de Madrid [2009] PTSR 458.......12.45, 12.47
Grace & Sweetman v An Bord Pleanala [2018] Env LR 37......................... 26.16
Gemeinde Altrip v Land Rheinland-Pfalz [2014] PTSR 311........................ 12.50
People Over Wind & Sweetman v Coillte Teoranta [2018] PTSR 1668 ....12.22, 26.15–26.16, 26.24
Sweetman and ors v An Bord Pleanála (Case C-258/11) [2014] PTSR 1092............. 26.24
Waddenzee case (Case C-127/02) [2004] ECR-1 7405............................ 26.24

European Court of Human Rights

Bryan v United Kingdom [1996] JPL 386 (ECHR) 19.04, 19.10
Buckley v United Kingdom [1996] JPL 1018 (ECHR)............................. 19.05
Chapman v United Kingdom (2001) 33 EHRR 329............................... 19.06

DOMESTIC CASES

Scotland

Archid Architecture and Interior Design v Dundee City Council [2013] CSOH 137,
    [2014] JPL 336... 11.13
David Lowe & Sons Ltd v Musselburgh Corporation 1974 SLT 5 .... 14.27
Lafarge Redland Aggregates Ltd v Scottish Ministers 2001 SC 298................... 19.13
Lakin v Secretary of State for Scotland 1988 SLT 780............................. 2.26
Noble Organisation Ltd v Falkirk DC 1994 SLT 100 .... 10.14
Simpson v Edinburgh Corporation 1961 SLT 17 ....4.81–4.82

United Kingdom

Aberdeen City Council & Shire Strategic Development Planning Authority v
    Elsick Development Company Ltd [2017] UKSC 66; [2017] PTSR 1413 .... 11.47
Adams & Wade Ltd v Minister of Housing and Local Government
    (1965) 18 P & CR 60 ....27.28–27.29
Adamson v Paddico (267) Limited and Taylor v Betterment Properties (Weymouth)
    Limited [2014] UKSC 7; [2014] AC 1072 ....29.48, 29.50
Adargh Glass Ltd v Chester City Council [2009] EWHC 745; [2009] Env LR 34 .... 20.29
Addison Lee Ltd v Westminster City Council [2012] EWHC 152 (Admin);
    [2012] JPL 969 .... 24.15
ADT Auctions Ltd v Secretary of State for the Environment, Transport, and the
    Regions (2000 WL 389632) 26.18
Agecrest Ltd v Gwynedd CC [1998] JPL 325................................... 14.107
Ahern and Brentwood Borough Council v Secretary of State for the Environment
    [1996] 72 P. & C.R. 61... 11.68
Ahmed v Secretary of State for Communities and Local Government [2013] EWHC
    2084 (Admin); [2014] 2 P & CR 11..................................... 20.92

Table of Cases

Alderson v Secretary of State for the Environment [1984] JPL 429 .... 14.26
Alfonso Dilieto v Ealing LBC [1998] PLCR 212 .... 20.150–20.151
Allen v Secretary of State for the Environment and Reigate and Banstead BC [1990] JPL 340 .... 6.37
Allnatt London Properties Ltd v Middlesex CC (1964) 15 P & CR 288 ..... 14.31, 14.33, 14.72
Alnwick DC v Secretary of State for the Environment, Transport, and the Regions
 [1999] JPL B190 .... 11.50
Alnwick DC v Secretary of State for the Environment, Transport, and the Regions
 [2000] JPL 473 .... 2.46, 2.49, 2.51
Amalgamated Investment & Property Co Ltd v John Walker & Sons Ltd [1976] JPL 308 .... 21.120
Amstel Group Corporation Ltd v Secretary of State for Communities and Local
 Government [2018] EWHC 633 (Admin) 17.55
Anglia Building Society v Secretary of State for the Environment [1984] JPL 175 .... 11.79
Arun District Council v First Secretary of State [2006] EWCA Civ 1172;
 [2007] 1 WLR 523 .... 20.30
Ashbridge Investments Ltd v Minister of Housing and Local Government
 [1965] 1 WLR 1320 .... 18.103
Ashdown Forest Economic Development LLP v SSCLG, Wealden District Council
 [2014] EWHC 406 (Admin)... 26.24
Ashdown Forest Economic Development LLP v Wealden District Council & Anor
 [2015] EWCA Civ 681; [2016] PTSR 78 .... 13.28, 26.24
Ashley v Secretary of State for Communities and Local Government [2012]
 EWCA Civ 559; [2012] JPL 1235... 18.43
Associated Provincial Picture Houses Ltd v Wednesbury Corporation
 [1948] 1 KB 223 .... 11.59, 12.20, 12.28, 12.42, 12.47, 13.28, 14.28, 14.108,
  15.23, 15.45–15.46, 17.14, 17.16, 17.44, 17.51, 17.53,
  18.85, 18.103–18.104, 18.106–18.107, 18.109, 21.130
Attorney General ex rel Sutcliffe v Calderdale Borough Council (1982) 46 P & CR 399 .... 7.23
Attorney-General v Bastow [1957] 1 QB 514 .... 20.152
Attorney-General v Howard United Reform Church Trustees, Bedford [1976] AC 363 .... 21.51
Attorney-General v Smith [1958] 2 QB 173 .... 20.153
Attorney-General v Taff-Ely BC (1981) 42 P & CR 1; (1979) 39 P & CR 223 (CA) 11.12
Aylesbury Vale District Council v Florent, Florent and Oxford Gun Company
 [2007] EWHC 724 (QB); [2008] JPL 70 .... 20.166

Bagshaw v Wyre Borough Council [2014] EWHC 508 (Admin) 26.04
Balco Transports Services Ltd v Secretary of State for the Environment (No 2)
 [1986] JPL 123 .... 27.18
Bambury v Hounslow LBC [1966] 2 QB 204 .... 20.52
Barchester Healthcare Ltd v Secretary of State for Communities and Local
 Government [2010] EWHC 2784 (Admin); [2011] JPL 544 .... 6.80
Barker v Hambleton DC [2012] EWCA Civ 610; [2013] PTSR 41 .... 4.71
Barlow v Secretary of State for Communities and Local Government [2019] EWHC 146 .... 18.37
Barnett v Secretary of State [2009] EWCA Civ 476 .... 15.13
Barratt Developments Plc v City of Wakefield Council [2010] EWCA Civ. 897 .... 4.72
Barvis Ltd v Secretary of State for the Environment (1971) 22 P & CR 710 ..... 5.18–5.19, 5.22
Basildon District Council and ors v Equality and Human Rights Commission
 [2009] EWCA Civ 13; [2009] JPL 1074..................................... 20.167
BDW Trading Ltd (t/a David Wilson Homes) (Central, Mercia and West Midlands) v
 Secretary of State for Communities and Local Government [2016] EWCA Civ 493;
 [2017] PTSR 1337 .... 11.38
Beach v Secretary of State for the Environment and the Regions and Runnymede BC
 [2001] EWHC Admin 381; [2002] JPL 185................................... 6.135
Beaulieu Property Management v Secretary of State for the Environment
 (1997) EGCS 129.. 11.64
Bedfordshire CC v Central Electricity Generating Board [1985] JPL 43 .... 20.154

Table of Cases

Bellway Urban Renewal Southern v Gillespie [2003] EWCA Civ 400; [2003] Env LR 30 .... 12.19
Belmont Farm Ltd v Minister of Housing and Local Government
   [1962] 13 P & CR 417 ....6.46, 7.50
Bendles Motors Ltd v Bristol Corporation [1963] 1 WLR 247 (Div Court) 6.02, 6.115
Berkeley v Secretary of State for the Environment [2001] 2 AC 603 .... 12.28, 12.48–12.49
Bernard Wheatcroft Ltd v Secretary of State for the Environment [1982] JPL 37 ....15.17,
                                                                                                 15.19, 15.23–15.24, 15.26
Betterment Properties (Weymouth) Limited v Dorset CC [2012] EWCA Civ 250;
   [2012] 2 P & CR 3 .... 29.22
Bibb v Bristol CC [2011] EWHC 3057 .... 11.48
Binning Property Corp Ltd v Secretary of State for Housing, Communities and Local
   Government [2019] EWCA Civ 250.. 20.101
Birmingham Corporation v Minister of Housing and Local Government [1964] 1 QB 178 .... 6.107
Bloor Homes (East Midlands) Ltd v Secretary of State for Communities and Local
   Government [2014] EWHC 754 (Admin); [2017] PTSR 1283 .... 18.104
Blum v Secretary of State for the Environment [1987] JPL 278 ....6.08, 6.112
Blythe Valley District Council v Persimmon Homes (North East) Ltd [2008]
   EWCA Civ 861; [2009] JPL 335.. 4.54
Boddington v British Transport Police [1999] 2 AC 143........................... 20.151
Boggis v. Natural England [2009] EWCA Civ 1061 .... 26.24
Bovis Homes Ltd v New Forest District Council [2002] EWHC 483 (Admin)........... 19.19
Bowen-West v Secretary of State for Communities and Local Government
   [2012] EWCA Civ 321; [2012] Env LR 321...............................12.20, 12.47
Bracking v Secretary of State for Work and Pensions [2013] EWCA Civ 1345;
   [2014] Eq LR 60 .... 11.51
Brazil (Concrete) Ltd v Amersham RDC (1967) 18 P & CR 396..................... 6.121
Breckland DC v Secretary of State for the Environment (1992) 65 P & CR 34........... 15.23
Brenda Wilkinson v Rossendale BC [2002] EWHC 1204 (Admin); [2003] JPL 82 .... 14.79
Britannia (Cheltenham) Ltd v Secretary of State for the Environment and Tewkesbury
   [1978] JPL 554 .... 10.61
British Airports Authority Plc v Secretary of State for Transport, Local Government
   and the Regions [2002] EWHC 1920 (Admin); [2003] JPL 610................. 12.44
British Airports Authority v Secretary of State for Scotland [1980] JPL 260 ....14.16, 14.29
British Railways Board v Secretary of State for the Environment [1994] JPL 32 .... 14.46
British Telecommunications plc and Bloomsbury Land Investments v Gloucester City
   Council [2001] EWHC Admin 1001; [2002] 2 P & CR 33 .....10.61, 12.16–12.17, 12.19
Britton v Secretary of State for the Environment [1997] JPL 617 .... 5.25
Broads Authority v Secretary of State for the Environment, Transport, and the
   Regions and David Phillips Investments Ltd [2001] PLCR 66..................... 8.03
Broadview Energy Developments Ltd v Secretary of State for Communities and
   Local Government [2016] EWCA Civ 562; [2016] JPL 1207.................... 18.38
Brown v First Secretary of State [2003] EWCA Civ 665; [2003] JPL 1536.............. 21.77
Broxbourne Borough Council v Secretary of State for the Environment [1980] QB 1..... 20.188
Buckinghamshire CC v Callingham [1952] 2 QB 515 .... 5.15
Buglife v Thurrock Thames Gateway Development Corporation [2008] EWHC
   475 (Admin); [2008] Env LR 31.. 26.18
Bullock v Secretary of State for the Environment and Malvern Hills DC [1980] JPL 461 ... 25.04
Burdle v Secretary of State for the Environment [1972] 1 WLR 1207 (Div Court).....6.130, 6.134
Burford v Secretary of State for Communities and Local Government
   [2017] EWHC 1493 (Admin); [2017] JPL 1300.............................6.15, 7.24
Burhill Estates Ltd v Woking BC [1995] JPL 147.................................... 8.14
Burridge v Breckland DC [2013] EWCA Civ 228 ....12.46–12.47
Burroughs Day v Bristol City Council [1996] 1 PLR 78.............................. 5.39
Butler v Derby City Council [2005] EWHC 2835 QBD (Admin)..................... 24.10
Buxton v Minister of Housing and Local Government [1961] 1 QB 278 .... 18.57

Table of Cases

Cadbury Schweppes Pension Trust Ltd v Secretary of State for the Environment
  [1990] EGCS 86 .... 18.28
Calder Gravel Ltd v Kirklees MBC (1989) 60 P & CR 322 .... 23.04
Calverton Parish Council v Nottingham City Council [2015] EWHC 1078 (Admin) 4.05
Calverton Parish Council v Nottingham City Council [2015] EWHC 503 (Admin);
  [2015] PTSR 1130 .... 18.97
Cambridge City Council v Secretary of State for the Environment (1991) 89 LGR 1015 .... 5.50
Cambridge City Council v Secretary of State for the Environment (1992) 64 P & CR 257 .... 5.76
Camden LBC v McDonald's Restaurants Ltd (1992) 65 P & CR 423 .... 15.68
Cardiff City Council v National Assembly for Wales and Malik [2006] EWHC
  1412 (Admin); [2007] 1 P & CR 9 .... 14.123
Cardiff Rating Authority v Guest Keen Baldwin Iron and Steel Co Ltd [1949] 1 KB 385 .... 5.19
Carpet Decor (Guildford) Ltd v Secretary of State for the Environment [1981] J.P.L. 806 .... 15.13
Carpets of Worth Ltd v Wyre Forest DC (1991) 62 P & CR 334 (CA) 11.57
Carter Commercial Development Ltd v Secretary of State for the Environment
  [2002] EWHC 1200 (Admin) 15.13
Carter Commercial Developments v Secretary of State [2002] EWCA Civ 1994 .... 15.13
Catesby Estates Ltd v Steer [2018] EWCA Civ 1697; [2018] JPL 1375 .... 21.01
Cawley v Secretary of State for the Environment [1990] JPL 742 .... 6.62
Centre 21 v Secretary of State for the Environment [1986] JPL 915 .... 18.103
Chalfont St Peter Parish Council v Chiltern District Council
  [2014] EWCA Civ 1393 .... 13.25
Cheshire CC v Woodward [1962] 2 QB 126 .... 5.16–5.18, 5.22
Chesterton Commercial (Bucks) Ltd v Wokingham DC [2018] EWHC 1795 (Admin);
  [2018] JPL 1347 .... 10.24
Church Commissioners v Secretary of State for the Environment (1995) 71 P & CR 73 ..... 6.128
City and District Council of St Albans v Secretary of State for Communities and Local
  Government [2009] EWHC 1280 (Admin); [2010] 1 JPL 70 .... 13.23
City of Bradford Metropolitan Council v Secretary of State for the Environment
  [1986] JPL 598 (CA) 14.21–14.22
City of Edinburgh Council v Secretary of State for Scotland [1997] 3 PLR 71 .... 21.31
City of Edinburgh v Secretary of State for Scotland [1997] 1 WLR 1447 (HL) 11.36, 11.38,
                                                                    11.41, 18.106
City of London Corporation v Secretary of State for the Environment
  (1971) 23 P & CR 169 .... 6.91
CJ Holder v Gedling Borough Council v Mr John Nigel and ors [2014] EWCA Civ 599 ... 11.81
Clarke v Minister of Housing and Local Government (1966) 18 P & CR 82
  (Div Court) 6.108, 6.146
Clarke v Secretary of State for the Environment (1992) 65 P & CR 85 .... 7.49
Clive Payne v the National Assembly for Wales and Caerphilly County Borough
  Council [2006] EWHC 597 (Admin); [2007] JPL 117 .... 20.78
Clyde & Co v Secretary of State for the Environment [1977] JPL 521 ...... 11.92, 11.94, 11.97
Coghurst Wood Leisure Park Limited v Secretary of State for Transport, Local Government,
  and the Regions [2002] EWHC 1091 (Admin); [2003] JPL 206 .... 11.20, 11.23
Coleshill & District Investment Co Ltd v Minister of Housing and Local Government
  [1969] 1 WLR 746 .... 5.42, 5.61, 5.75–5.76
Colley v Canterbury City Council [1992] JPL 925 .... 27.19
Collis Radio Ltd v Secretary of State for the Environment [1975] JPL 221 .... 11.78–11.79
Commercial Land Ltd v Secretary of State for Transport, Local Government, and the
  Regions and Royal Borough of Kensington and Chelsea [2002] EWHC 1264 (Admin) 14.97
Connors v Reigate and Banstead BC [2000] JPL 1178 (CA) 20.160
Cooper Estates Strategic Land Ltd v Royal Tunbridge Wells Borough Council
  [2017] EWHC 224 (Admin) 4.38
Copeland BC v Secretary of State for the Environment (1976) 31 P & CR 403 .... 20.57
Cotterell v Secretary of State for the Environment [1991] JPL 1155 .... 18.34

Table of Cases

Covent Garden Community Association Ltd v Greater London Council
  [1981] JPL 183 .... 11.136–11.137, 11.140, 18.122
Coventry v Lawrence [2014] UKSC 13; [2014] AC 822............................. 15.52
Cox v First Secretary of State [2003] EWHC 1290 Admin 11.25
CPRE (Kent) v Dover District Council [2017] UKSC 79; [2018] 1 WLR 108...........11.05,
                                                                  11.29–11.30, 12.40
Crawford-Brunt v Secretary of State for Communities and Local Government
  [2015] EWHC 3580 (Admin); [2016] JPL 573............................. 18.99
Cresswell v Pearson (1998) 75 P & CR 404 .... 20.136
Croke v Secretary of State for Communities and Local Government [2019] EWCA Civ 54....18.98
Crowborough Parish Council v Secretary of State for the Environment
  [1981] JPL 281 (Div Court) 6.43
Croydon LBC v Gladden [1994] JPL 723........................... 6.29, 14.56, 20.160
Croydon LBC v Secretary of State for the Environment [2000] PLCR 171.............. 18.48
CSSU v Minister for the Civil Service [1985] AC 374 .... 11.22

Daniel Platt Ltd v Secretary of State for the Environment and Staffordshire CC
  [1996] JPL 349 .... 14.106
Dartford Borough Council v Secretary of State for Communities and Local Government
  [2016] EWCA Civ 141; [2017] PTSR 737 .... 4.85
David Gate v Secretary of State for Transport [2013] EWHC 2937 ....28.34, 28.37
David Lewis v Three Rivers DC [2013] EWHC 3250 (Admin); [2014] JPL 636 .... 20.113
David Saxby v Secretary of State for the Environment and Westminster City Council
  [1998] JPL 1132... 8.12
Debenhams plc v Westminster City Council [1987] AC 396 ....21.28–21.30, 21.32, 21.34
Delta and Design and Engineering Ltd v Secretary of State for the Environment and
  South Cambridgeshire DC [2000] JPL 726............................14.17, 14.19
Derbyshire Dales D C v Secretary of State for Communities and Local Government
  [2010] EWHC 1729 (Admin); [2010] 1 P & CR 19........................... 11.88
Devonshire CC v Allens Caravans (Estates) Ltd (1962) 14 P & CR 440 (Div Court)....... 6.08
Dignity Funerals Ltd v Breckland DC [2017] EWHC 1492 (Admin).................. 11.45
Dill v Secretary of State for Communities and Local Government
  [2018] EWCA Civ 2619 .... 21.24
Distinctive Properties (Ascot) Ltd v Secretary of State for Communities and Local
  Government [2015] EWCA Civ 1250; [2016] 1 WLR 1839..................... 25.04
Distinctive Properties (Ascot) Ltd v Secretary of State for Communities and Local
  Government [2015] EWHC 729 (Admin); [2015] JPL 1083 .... 20.80
DLA Delivery Ltd v Baroness Cumberlege of Newick [2018] EWCA Civ 1305 .... 11.66
DLA Delivery v. Lewes District Council [2015] EWHC 2311 .... 26.24
Dorset CC v Secretary of State for the Environment, Transport, and the Regions and
  Rothchild Estates Ltd [1999] JPL 633....................................... 23.22
Duffy v Secretary of State [1981] JPL 811.. 6.134
Duguid v Secretary of State for the Environment, Transport and the Regions
  (2001) 82 P & CR 6 .... 20.97
Dunnett Investments Ltd v Secretary of State for Communities and Local Government
  [2017] EWCA Civ 192; [2017] JPL 848........................... 6.91, 7.14, 15.15
Dunoon Developments Ltd v Secretary of State for the Environment [1992] J.P.L. 936 .... 15.13
Dunster Properties Ltd v First Secretary of State [2007] EWCA Civ 236 .... 11.65
Dyason v Secretary of State for the Environment and Chiltern DC [1998] JPL 778 .... 18.45, 18.48
Dyer v Dorset CC [1989] QB 346 (CA)................................. 6.12, 6.14–6.15

Ealing LBC v Ryan [1965] 2 QB 486.. 6.94
Earthline Ltd v West Berkshire Council [2003] JPL 715 (CA) 23.01
East Barnet UDC v British Transport Commission [1962] 2 QB 484
  (Div Court).. 6.03, 6.09, 6.116, 11.114

East Dumbartonshire Council v Secretary of State for Scotland and MacTaggart &
  Mickel Ltd [1999] 1 PLR 53 ....14.101–14.102
East Hampshire DC v SLV Building Products Ltd [1996] (Lands Tribunal) 20.146
East Northamptonshire District Council v Secretary of State for Communities and
  Local Government [2014] EWCA Civ 137; [2015] 1 WLR 45 .... 21.58
East Staffordshire Borough Council v Secretary of State for Communities and
  Local Government [2017] EWCA Civ 893; [2017] PTSR 88 .... 11.40, 11.58, 11.120
EC Gransden & Co Ltd v Secretary of State for the Environment
  (1987) 54 P & CR 361 .... 11.56
EC Gransden & Co Ltd v Secretary of State for the Environment (1987) 54 P & CR 86 ... 11.55
ECC Construction Ltd v Secretary of State for the Environment [1995] JPL 322 .... 11.128
Elliot v Secretary of State for Communities and Local Government [2012] EWHC 1574;
  [2013] Env LR 5 .... 26.23
Ellis v Secretary of State for Communities and Local Government [2009]
  EWHC 634 (Admin); [2010] 1 P & CR 21 .... 20.185
Elsick Development Co Ltd v Aberdeen City & Shire Strategic Development
  Planning Authority [2017] UKSC 66; [2017] PTSR 1413 ....14.07, 17.58
Emin v Secretary of State for the Environment [1989] JPL 909 .... 6.20
Enfield LBC v Secretary of State for the Environment [1975] JPL 155 .... 4.82
English v Dedham Vale Properties Ltd [1978] 1 WLR 93 .... 9.48
Ensign Group Ltd v First Secretary of State [2006] EWHC 255 .... 4.73
Errington v Minister of Health [1935] 1 KB 249 (CA) 18.18
Esdell Caravan Parks Ltd v Hemel Hempstead RDC [1966] 1 QB 895 (CA) 6.106
Essex CC v Ministry of Housing and Local Government (1967) 18 P & CR 531 ..... 2.15, 28.10
Essex Water Co v Secretary of State for the Environment [1989] JPL 914 .... 6.141
Etheridge v Secretary of State for the Environment and Torbay BC [1984] JPL 340 ...... 14.114
Evans v Basingstoke and Deane BC [2013] JPL 229 .... 14.34

F G Whitley & Sons Co Ltd v Secretary of State for Wales
  [1990] JPL 678 .... 14.103, 14.106, 14.108
F Lucas & Sons Ltd v Dorking & Horley RDC (1964) 62 LGR 491 .... 14.121
Fairmount Investments Ltd v Secretary of State for the Environment
  [1976] 1 WLR 1255 ....18.19, 18.103
Fawcett Properties v Buckingham County Council [1961] A.C. 636............. 14.06, 14.14,
                                                                14.25–14.26, 15.13
Fayrewood Fish Farms Ltd v Secretary of State for the Environment [1984] JPL 267 .... 5.61, 5.78
Fidler v First Secretary of State for the Environment and Reigate and Banstead BC
  [2003] EWHC 2003 (Admin); [2004] 1 PLR 1 .... 20.38
Fidler v Secretary of State for Communities and Local Government [2010]
  EWHC 143 (Admin); [2010] JPL 915 .... 20.29
Finlay v Secretary of State for the Environment [1983] JPL 802 .... 11.107
Finney v Welsh Ministers [2018] EWHC 3073 .... 14.77
First Secretary of State v Chelmsford BC [2003] EWHC 2800 (Admin); [2004] JPL 1074 ..... 20.29
Fisher v Wychavon DC [2001] JPL 694 .... 14.75
Forest of Dean DC v Secretary of State for the Environment [1995] JPL B184 .... 6.08
Fowles v Heathrow Airport Limited [2008] EWHC 219 (Ch) 20.136
Fox Strategic Land and Property Ltd v Secretary of State for Communities and
  Local Government [2013] 1 P & CR 6 .... 18.104
Fox v First Secretary of State [2003] EWHC 887 (Admin) 6.44
Fox v Secretary of State [1993] JPL 448 .... 18.35
Frackman v Secretary of State for Communities and Local Government
  [2018] EWCA Civ 9; [2018] Env LR 18 ....11.155, 12.67
Friends Provident Life and Pensions Ltd v the Secretary of State for Transport,
  Local Government and the Regions and ors [2002] JPL 958 .... 19.17
Fuller v Secretary of State for the Environment [1987] 2 EGLR 189 .... 6.134

Table of Cases

Furmston v Secretary of State for the Environment [1983] JPL 49 .... 18.26
Fyson v Buckinghamshire CC [1958] 1 WLR 634 .... 6.144, 6.146

G Percy Trentham Ltd v Gloucestershire CC [1966] 1 WLR 506 .... 6.120–6.121
Gabbitas v Secretary of State for the Environment [1985] JPL 630 .... 20.177
Garland v Ministry of Housing and Local Government [1968] 20 P & CR 93............. 7.21
Gateshead MBC v Secretary of State for the Environment
   (1993) 67 P & CR 179 .... 11.147, 11.156
Geall v Secretary of State for the Environment [1999] JPL 909...................... 18.07
George Wimpey & Co Ltd v New Forest DC [1979] JPL 313 .... 14.37
George Wimpey & Co Ltd v Secretary of State for the Environment [1978] JPL 776 ...... 11.49
Georgiou v Enfield LBC [2004] LGR 497 .... 16.24
Gerber v Wiltshire Council [2016] EWCA Civ 84; [2016] 1 WLR 2593 .... 18.124
Gill v Secretary of State for the Environment [1985] JPL 710........................ 6.39
Gillingham BC v Medway (Chatham) Dock Co Ltd [1993] QB 343 .... 15.47–15.48
Gladman Developments Ltd v Secretary of State for Communities and Local
   Government [2017] EWHC 2768 (Admin); [2018] Env LR 15 .... 11.155
Gladman Developments Ltd v Secretary of State for Communities and Local
   Government [2017] EWHC 2768 (Admin); [2018] PTSR 616 .... 14.48, 18.111
Glamorgan CC v Carter [1963] 1 WLR 1 (Div Court)........................... 6.104
Good v Epping Forest DC [1994] JPL 372..................................... 17.16
Goremsandu v Secretary of State for Communities and Local Government
   [2015] EWHC 2194 (Admin).. 20.136
Government of the Republican of France v Royal Borough of Kensington & Chelsea
   [2017] EWCA Civ 429; [2017] 1 WLR 3206................................. 15.14
Grampian Regional Council v City of Aberdeen DC (1984) 47 P & CR 633 ...... 14.42, 14.44–14.48
Granada Theatres Ltd v Secretary of State for the Environment [1976] JPL 96 ...... 11.91, 18.23
Granada Theatres Ltd v Secretary of State for the Environment [1981] JPL 278 .... 11.93
Gravesham BC v Secretary of State for the Environment (1982) 47 P & CR 142 .... 7.23
Greater London Council v Secretary of State for the Environment [1986] JPL 193........ 11.84,
   11.86–11.87
Gregory v Camden LBC [1966] 1 WLR 899 .... 10.58
Greyfort Properties v Secretary of State for Communities and Local Government
   [2011] EWCA Civ 908... 14.109
Griffiths v Secretary of State for the Environment [1983] 2 AC 51 .... 18.97
Guildford RDC v Penny [1959] 2 QB 112..................................... 6.104

Haddow v Secretary of State for the Environment (1998) 95(7) LSG 33................ 15.56
Hall & Co Ltd v Shoreham-by-Sea UDC [1964] 1 WLR 240 (CA) 14.21, 14.71
Hall & Co Ltd v Shoreham-by-Sea UDC was MJ Shanley Ltd v Secretary of State
   for the Environment [1982] JPL 380...................................... 14.23
Hall v Lichfield DC, noted at [1979] JPL 426 .... 6.155
Hallam Land Management Ltd v Secretary of State for Communities and Local
   Government [2018] EWCA Civ 1808; [2019] JPL 63................... 11.122–11.123
Hambledon & Chiddingfold Parish Councils v Secretary of State for the
   Environment [1976] JPL 502 .... 18.22
Hammond v Secretary of State for the Environment and Maldon DC
   [2001] EWHC Admin 1172... 20.108
Hancock v Secretary of State for the Environment (1988) 55 P & CR 216............... 7.52
Handoll and Suddick v Warner, Goodman & Streat, Cook, and East Lindsey DC
   [1995] JPL 930 .... 14.104–14.105
Hanily v Minister of Local Government and Planning [1952] 2 QB 444 .... 9.31
Harding v Secretary of State for the Environment [1984] JPL 503 .... 7.50
Harrods v Secretary of State for the Environment, Transport, and the Regions and the Royal
   Borough of Kensington and Chelsea [2002] EWCA Civ 412; [2002] JPL 1258 .... 6.27, 6.127

Table of Cases

Hart District Council v Secretary of State for Communities and Local Government
 [2008] EWHC 1204 (Admin); [2008] 2 P & CR 16.....................26.14–26.15
Hartley v Minister of Housing and Local Government [1970] 1 QB 413...............6.148,
 6.151–6.152, 6.154
Haven Leisure Ltd v Secretary of State for the Environment and
 North Cornwall DC [1994] JPL 148..11.67
Health and Safety Executive v Wolverhampton City Council [2010] EWCA Civ 892......11.50
Health and Safety Executive v Wolverhampton City Council [2012] UKSC 34;
 [2012] 1 WLR 2264...2.49, 11.50
Heard v Broadland DC [2012] EWHC 344 (Admin); [2012] Env LR 23...............13.25
Hedley Byrne & Co v Heller & Partners Ltd [1964] AC 465........................15.54
Henry Boot Homes Ltd v Bassetlaw DC [2002] EWCA Civ 983; [2003] 1 P & CR 23....11.23
Hertfordshire CC v Secretary of State for Communities and Local Government and
 Metal and Waste Recycling Ltd [2012] EWCA Civ 1473......................6.114
Hewlett v Secretary of State for the Environment [1985] JPL 404......................7.30
Hidderley v Warwickshire CC (1963) 14 P & CR 134 (Div Court)....................6.06
High Peak BC v Secretary of State for the Environment [1981] JPL 366................14.93
Hillingdon LBC v Guinea Enterprises Ltd (and 15 others) [1997] JPL B11.............20.161
Hillingdon LBC v Secretary of State for Communities and Local Government
 [2018] EWHC 845 (Admin)..17.79
Hillingdon v Secretary of State for Communities and Local Government
 [2008] EWHC 198 (Admin)..20.188
Hoare v Vale of White Horse DC [2017] EWHC 1711 (Admin).....................4.42
Hopkins Developments Ltd v Secretary of State for Communities and Local
 Government [2014] EWCA Civ 470; [2014] PTSR 1145......................18.37
Hopkins Developments v First Secretary of State and North Wiltshire DC
 [2007] JPL 1056..11.150
Hopkins Homes Ltd v Secretary of State for Communities and Local Government
 [2017] UKSC 37; [2017] 1 WLR 1865...........4.10, 4.85, 11.40–11.41, 11.54–11.55,
 11.121, 18.109
Hotak v London Borough of Southwark [2015] UKSC 30; [2016] AC 811.............11.51
Hoveringham Gravels Ltd v Secretary of State for the Environment
 [1975] QB 754 (CA)..11.49, 22.15
Howard v Secretary of State for the Environment [1975] QB 235.....................20.72
Hudson v Secretary of State for the Environment [1984] JPL 258....................18.24
Hughes v Secretary of State for the Environment, Transport, and the Regions
 [1999] JPL 83...6.160
Hunter v Canary Wharf Ltd [1996] 1 All ER 482.................................15.49

I'm Your Man Ltd v Secretary of State for the Environment [1999] PLCR 109...........14.49
Iddenden v Secretary of State for the Environment [1972] 1 WLR 1433.................5.47
In Charles Church Developments Ltd v South Northamptonshire DC [2000] PLCR 40....4.76
In Re Findlay [1985] AC 318..11.45
Inland Revenue Commissioners v National Federation of Self Employed and
 Small Business [1982] AC 617..2.42
International Traders Ferry Ltd v Adur DC [2004] EWCA Civ 288; [2004] 2 PLR 106...20.120
Ioannou v Secretary of State for Communities and Local Government [2014] EWCA
 Civ 1432; [2015] 1 P & CR 10...20.74

Jackson v Secretary of State for Communities and Local Government
 [2015] EWCA Civ 1246; [2016] QB 811...................................20.32
James Iday Pension Trustees Ltd v First Secretary of State [2006] EWCA Civ 1387........8.03
James Stewart's Application v Planning Appeals Commission, Re 2003 [NI 149].........19.19
James v Brecon CC (1963) 15 P & CR 20..5.15
James v Secretary of State for the Environment (1990) 61 P & CR 234 (Div Court).......6.13

James v Secretary of State for Wales [1966] 1 WLR 135 . . . . .6.105–6.106, 10.03, 10.05
Jarmain v Secretary of State for the Environment, Transport and the Regions
    [2000] JPL 1063 . . . . 20.37
Jelson Ltd v Derby City Council [2000] JPL 203 . . . . 17.30
Jennings Motors Ltd v Secretary of State for the Environment [1980] JPL 521 . . . . . .15.35–15.36
Jillings v Secretary of State for the Environment [1984] JPL 32. . . . . 6.126
JJ Gallagher Ltd v Cherwell District Council [2016] EWCA Civ 1007;
    [2016] 1 WLR 5126 . . . . 4.76
John & Joseph Davenport v Hammersmith & Fulham LBC [1999] JPL 1112 . . . . .14.40, 20.147
John Kennelly Sales Ltd v Secretary of State for the Environment [1994] 1 PLR 10 . . . . 20.96
John Taylor v Secretary of State for Wales [1985] JPL 792. . . . . 18.112
Johnson v Secretary of State for Communities and Local Government
    [2007] EWHC 1839 (Admin). 15.27
Jones v Mordue [2015] EWCA Civ 1243; [2016] 1 WLR 2682 . . . . 21.58
Jones v NHS Property Services Ltd and Lancashire County Council v Secretary of
    State for Environment, Food and Rural Affairs [2018] EWCA Civ 721;
    [2018] 2 P & CR 15 . . . . 29.17–29.18, 29.34, 29.36, 29.40
Jones v Secretary of State for Wales (1990) 88 LGR 942 . . . . .14.45–14.47
Jones v Stockport MBC (1985) 50 P & CR 299 . . . . 7.49
Jory v Secretary of State for Transport, Local Government, and the Regions and Asia House
    and Westminster City Council [2002] EWHC 2724 (Admin); [2003] JPL 549 . . . . . . 18.43

Kalra v Secretary of State for the Environment [1996] JPL 850. . . . . 6.66
Kane v New Forest DC [2001] EWCA Civ 878; [2002] 1 WLR 312 . . . . 15.57
Kaur v Secretary of State for the Environment [1990] JPL 814 . . . . 20.95
Kebbel Developments Ltd v Leeds City Council [2018] EWCA Civ 450;
    [2018] 1 WLR 4625 . . . . 4.39
Keenan v Woking Borough Council [2017] EWCA Civ 438; [2018] PTSR 697. . . . . 7.17
Kennedy v Secretary of State for Wales [1996] 1 PLR 97. . . . . 21.40
Kensington & Chelsea RLBC v C G Hotels [1981] JPL 190 . . . . 5.37
Kensington and Chelsea RBC v Secretary of State for the Environment
    [1981] JPL 50 (Div Court) 6.110
Kent CC v Batchelor (1976) 33 P & CR 185 (CA). 25.04
Kent CC v Kingsway Investments (Kent) Ltd [1971] AC 72. . . . . 14.73
Kent CC v Secretary of State for the Environment [1995] JPL 610. . . . . 21.70
Kestrel Hydro v Secretary of State for Communities and Local Government
    [2016] EWCA Civ 784 . . . . 20.64
Kettering BC v Perkins [1999] JPL 166. . . . . 20.163
Kingston upon Thames RBC v National Solus Sites Ltd [1994] JPL 251 . . . . 24.05
Kingston-upon-Thames RLBC v Secretary of State for the Environment
    [1973] 1 WLR 1549 . . . . 14.33
Kingswood DC v Secretary of State for the Environment [1988] JPL 248. . . . . 18.115
Kinnersley Engineering Ltd v Secretary of State for the Environment, Transport
    and the Regions [2001] JPL 1082 . . . . 20.98
Kirklees MBC v Wickes Building Supplies Ltd [1993] AC 227. . . . . 20.164
Kirklees MDC v Angus Heron [2011] EWHC 2393 (Admin); [2012] JPL 466 . . . . 20.130
Kirkman v Secretary of State for Wales [1995] EGCS 127 . . . . 14.89
Knott v Secretary of State for the Environment and Caradon DC [1997] JPL 713 . . . . 14.61
Kyte v Secretary of State for the Environment [1997] CLY 4093. . . . . 11.85

Ladbroke (Rentals) Ltd v Secretary of State for the Environment [1981] JPL 427. . . . 11.49, 11.146
Laing Homes Ltd v Secretary of State for Transport, Local Government, and
    the Regions [2003] JPL 559. . . . . 11.84
Lamb Properties Ltd v Secretary of State for the Environment [1983] JPL 303. . . . . 6.75
Lambert v West Devon BC [1997] JPL 735 . . . . 15.54

Table of Cases

Larkin v Basildon DC [1980] JPL 407 ... 7.29
Lawrence v Fen Tigers Ltd [2014] UKSC 13; [2014] AC 822 ... 11.152
Lawson Builders Ltd v Secretary of State for Communities and Local Government
  [2015] EWCA Civ 122; [2015] PTSR 1324 ... 14.77
Leisure Great Britain plc v Isle of Wight CC [2000] PLCR 88 ... 14.108
Lever Finance Ltd v Westminster (City) LBC [1971] 1 QB 222 (CA) ... 11.15
Lewis Thirkwell v Secretary of State for the Environment [1978] JPL 844 ... 9.16
Lipsen v Secretary of State for the Environment [1976] P & CR 95 (Div Court) ... 20.62
Lisle-Mainwaring v Carol [2017] EWCA Civ 1315; [2018] JPL 194 ... 11.103
London Borough of Havering v Secretary of State for the Environment
  (1983) 45 P & CR 258 ... 20.136
London Borough of Lambeth v Secretary of State for Communities and
  Local Government [2018] EWCA Civ 844; [2018] 2 P & CR 17 ... 14.77, 15.14
London Parachuting Ltd v Secretary of State for the Environment
  (1985) 52 P & CR 376 ... 20.102
London Residuary Body v Lambeth LBC [1990] 1 WLR 744 ... 11.97
London Residuary Body v Secretary of State for the Environment [1988] JPL 637 (CA) ... 6.58
Lord Luke v Minister of Housing and Local Government [1968] 1 QB 172 ... 18.62–18.63
Lough v First Secretary of State [2004] 1 WLR 2557 ... 19.12

M J Shanley v Secretary of State for the Environment [1982] JPL 380 and
  Marie Finlay v Secretary of State [1983] JPL 802 ... 18.110
Mackman v Secretary of State for Communities and Local Government
  [2015] EWCA Civ 716; [2016] Env LR 6 ... 12.21
Maidstone BC v Mortimer (1980) 43 P & CR 67 (Div Court) ... 25.06
Main v Secretary of State for Communities and Local Government
  (1998) 77 P & CR 300) ... 20.188
Main v Secretary of State for the Environment, Transport and the Regions
  (1999) 77 P & CR 300 ... 6.127
Main v Swansea City Council [1985] JPL 558 ... 9.46
Malvern Hills DC v Secretary of State for the Environment (1983) 46 P & CR 58 (CA) ... 20.123
Malvern Hills DC v Secretary of State for the Environment [1982] JPL 439 ... 14.95
Manchester City Council v McLoughlin (2000) The Times, 5 April 2000 ... 20.69
Manchester City Council v Secretary of State for the Environment [1988] JPL 774 ... 18.85
Manning v Secretary of State for the Environment [1976] JPL 634 ... 15.07
Mansell v Tonbridge & Malling Borough Council [2017] EWCA Civ 1314;
  [2018] JPL 176 ... 11.07, 11.68
Mansi v Elstree DC (1964) 15 P & CR 153 ... 20.96
Manydown Co Ltd v Basingstoke and Deane Borough Council
  [2012] EWHC 977 (Admin); [2012] JPL 1188 ... 4.74
Marie Finlay v Secretary of State [1983] JPL 802 ... 18.110
Marshall v Nottingham Corporation [1960] 1 WLR 707 (Div Court) ... 6.09
Maximus Networks Ltd v Secretary of State for Communities and Local Government
  [2018] EWHC 1933 (Admin) ... 9.11
McAlpine v Secretary of State for the Environment [1995] 1 PLR 16 ... 6.14
McCarthy v Secretary of State for Communities and Local Government and South
  Cambridgeshire [2006] EWHC 3287 ... 11.81
McCarthy v Secretary of State for the Environment, Transport and the Regions
  [1999] JPL 993 ... 20.59
McClean Homes (East Anglia) Ltd v Secretary of State for the Environment, Transport,
  and the Regions and Chelmsford BC [1999] PLCR 372 ... 9.19
McDaid v Clydebank DC [1984] JPL 579 ... 20.47
Medway Council v Secretary of State for Communities and Local Government
  [2016] EWHC 644 (Admin) ... 17.36
Menston Action Group v City of Bradford MDC [2016] EWCA Civ 796 ... 14.20

Table of Cases

Miaris v Secretary of State for Communities and Local Government
  [2016] EWCA Civ 75; [2016] JPL 784 .... 20.74
Miles v the National Assembly for Wales [2007] EWHC 10 (Admin) 20.183
Miller-Mead v Minister of Housing and Local Government [1963] 2 QB 196 (CA) 7.40,
  15.03–15.04, 20.76, 20.93
Millington v Secretary of State for the Environment, Transport, and the Regions
  [2000] JPL 297 .... 6.42
Ministry of Defence v Wiltshire County Council (1995) 4 All ER 931 .... 29.17
Mitchell v Secretary of State for the Environment [1994] EGCS 111 .... 11.127–11.128
MMF (UK) Ltd v Secretary of State for Communities and Local Government
  [2010] EWHC 3686 (Admin); [2011] JPL 1067 .... 9.15
Monomart (Warehouses) Ltd v Secretary of State for the Environment [1977] JPL 524 ..... 6.78
Moore (Moore v Secretary of State for Communities and Local Government
  [2013] JPL 192) 6.07
Moore v Secretary of State (1999) 77 P & CR 114 .... 20.30
Moore v Secretary of State for the Environment, Transport, and the Regions
  [1998] JPL 877 (CA) 6.07
Munnich v Godstone RDC [1966] 1 WLR 427 .... 20.41
Murfitt v Secretary of State for the Environment (1980) 40 P & CR 254 .... 20.64
Murphy v Brentwood District Council [1991] 1 AC 398 .... 15.53
Murrell v Secretary of State for Communities and Local Government
  [2010] EWCA Civ 1367; [2012] 1 P & CR 6 .... 7.18

National Anti-Vivisection Society v First Secretary of State [2004] EWHC 2074 (Admin) 18.111
Nelsovil v Minister of Housing and Local Government [1962] 1 WLR 404 (Div Court) ... 20.80
New Forest DC v Secretary of State for the Environment [1984] JPL 178 .... 11.111
New Windsor v Mellor [1975] Ch 380, CA 29.41
Newark & Sherwood District Council v Secretary of State for Communities and
  Local Government [2013] EWHC 2162 (Admin) 15.14
Newbury DC v Secretary of State for the Environment [1981] AC 578 ..... 11.19, 14.07–14.08,
  14.12, 14.16–14.18, 14.20, 14.24, 15.33–15.34, 17.14, 17.44, 17.50
Newcastle upon Tyne City Council v Secretary of State for Communities
  and Local Government [2009] EWHC 3469 (Admin); [2010] JPL 904 .... 9.07
Newport BC v Secretary of State for Wales [1997] JPL 650 .... 24.09
Newport BC v Secretary of State for Wales [1998] JPL 377 (CA) 11.106
Newsmith Stainless Ltd v Secretary of State for the Environment, Transport and the
  Regions (Practice Note) [2001] EWHC Admin 74 .... 18.104
Nicholson v Secretary of State for the Environment and Maldon District Council
  (1998) 76 P & CR 191 .... 20.185
No Adastral New Town Ltd v Suffolk Coastal DC [2015] EWCA Civ 88;
  [2015] Env LR 28 .... 13.27
Norfolk CC v Secretary of State for the Environment [1973] 1 WLR 400 .... 11.11
Norman Brunt v Secretary of State for Communities and Local Government
  [2018] EWHC 2910 (Admin) 18.99
North Cornwall DC v Secretary of State for the Environment Transport and the
  Regions [2002] EWHC 2318 (Admin); [2003] 1 P & CR 25 .... 7.39
North Devon D C v Ludgate [2009] JPL 1659 .... 6.46
North Devon DC v the First Secretary of State [2003] EWHC 157 (Admin);
  [2004] 1 P & CR 38 .... 6.86
North Norfolk District Council v Secretary of State for Housing, Communities
  and Local Government [2018] EWHC 2076 (Admin) 18.12
North Warwickshire BC v Secretary of State for the Environment
  [1984] JPL 435 (Div Court) 6.45
North Wiltshire District Council v Secretary of State for the Environment
  (1992) 65 P & CR 137 .... 11.62–11.64, 18.104

Northampton BC v First Secretary of State [2005] EWHC 168 (Admin) 15.13
Northavon DC v Secretary of State for the Environment [1990] JPL 579. . . . . 6.161
Northumberland CC v Secretary of State for the Environment [1989] JPL 700 . . . . 11.143
Nottingham CC and Brostowe BC v Secretary of State for the Environment, Transport,
 and the Regions [1999] EGCS 35 . . . . 11.44
Nottingham City Council v Calverton Parish Council [2015] EWHC 503 (Admin),
 [2015] PTSR 1130 . . . . 4.71
Nottinghamshire County Council v Secretary of State for the Environment, Transport,
 and the Regions [2002] JPL 161 . . . . 11.101
Nourish v Adamson [1998] JPL 859 (Div Court) 20.142

Oakimber Ltd v Elmbridge BC (1991) 62 P & CR 594 . . . . 15.12
O'Brien v South Cambridgeshire DC [2016] EWHC 36 (Admin); [2016] JPL 656 . . . . 10.22
Oldham MBC v Roland Bardsley (Builders) Ltd [1996] JPL B119 . . . . 14.106
Oxfordshire County Council v Oxford City Council [2004] EWHC 12 (Ch);
 [2004] Ch 253. . . . . 29.20, 29.26, 29.30, 29.31, 29.41, 29.43
Oxted Residential Ltd v Tandridge District Council [2016] EWCA Civ 414 . . . . 4.72

Paddico (267) Ltd v Kirklees Borough Council [2012] EWCA Civ 262;
 [2012] 2 P & CR 1 . . . . 29.17, 29.47
Paddico (267) Ltd v Kirklees Metropolitan Council [2011] EWHC 1606 (Ch) 29.34
Palisades Investments Ltd v Secretary of State for the Environment [1993] 3 PLR 49 . . . . 6.65
Palm Developments Ltd v Secretary of State for Communities and Local Government
 [2009] EWHC 220 (Admin); [2009] 2 P & CR 16. . . . . 25.04
Palmer v Herefordshire Council [2016] EWCA Civ 1061. . . . . 11.07, 11.29
Panton and Farmer v Secretary of State for the Environment, Transport, and the
 Regions and Vale of White Horse DC [1999] JPL 461 . . . . 20.179, 20.181
Paramaguru v Ealing LBC [2018] EWHC 373 (Admin) 6.86
Parkes v Secretary of State for the Environment [1978] 1 WLR 1308 (CA). 6.01
Peak Park Joint Planning Board v Secretary of State for the Environment [1980] JPL 114 . . . . 14.34
Peake v Secretary of State for Wales (1971) 22 P & CR 889 (Div Court) 6.109, 6.110
Pêche d'Or Investments v Secretary of State for the Environment [1996] JPL 311 . . . . 7.31
Perrin v Northampton BC [2007] EWCA Civ 1353; [2008] 1 WLR 1307. . . . . 25.05
Persimmon Homes Teeside Ltd v R (on the application of Lewis)
 [2008] EWCA Civ 746 . . . . 16.28
Petticoat Lane Rentals Ltd v Secretary of State for the Environment
 [1971] 1 WLR 1112 . . . . 15.28, 15.31–15.32, 15.38
Pilkington v Secretary of State for the Environment [1973] 1 WLR 1527 . . . . 15.63–15.64, 15.66
Pioneer Aggregates (UK) Ltd v Secretary of State for the Environment
 [1985] AC 132 . . . . 15.38, 15.64, 15.67
Pitman et al v the Secretary of State for the Environment [1989] JPL 831 (CA) 6.48
Porter v Magill [2002] 2 AC 257. . . . . 16.23, 16.28
Porter v Secretary of State for Transport [1996] 3 All ER 693 (CA). 20.107
Postwood Developments Ltd v Secretary of State for the Environment [1992] JPL 823 . . . . 11.67
Poundstretcher v Secretary of State for the Environment [1988] 3 PLR 69 . . . . 11.80
Poyser and Mills' Arbitration, Re [1964] 2 QB 467. . . . . 18.57, 18.103
Prengate Properties Ltd v Secretary of State for the Environment [1973] JPL 313. . . . . 7.34
Preston New Road Action Group v Secretary of State for Communities and Local
 Government [2018] EWCA Civ 9; [2018] Env LR 18 . . . . 18.37
Prossor v Minister of Housing and Local Government (1968) 67 LGR 109
 (Div Court). 15.30–15.31, 15.33
Pyrford Properties Ltd v Secretary of State for the Environment (1978) 36 P & CR 28 . . . . 18.63
Pyx Granite Co Ltd v Ministry of Housing and Local Government
 [1958] 1 QB 554. . . . . 14.06, 14.13
Pyx Granite Co Ltd v Ministry of Housing and Local Government [1960] AC 260 . . . . 8.09

Table of Cases

R v Aylesbury Vale DC, ex parte Chaplin (1998) 76 P & CR 207 .... 11.30
R v Ashford DC [1998] P.L.C.R. 12 .... 15.13
R v Bassetlaw DC, ex p G A N Oxby [1997] JPL 576 .... 2.40
R v Bassetlaw DC, ex p Oxby [1998] PLCR 283 .... 11.14
R v Beaconsfield Magistrates, ex p South Buckinghamshire DC
    (1993) 157 JP 1073 (Div Court) 20.131–20.132
R v Berkshire CC, ex p Wokingham DC [1997] JPL 461 .... 2.96
R v Bradford-on-Avon UDC, ex p Boulton [1964] 1 WLR 1136 .... 9.44, 9.46
R v Bristol CC, ex p Anderson [2000] PLCR 104 .... 14.12
R v Broadlands DC, St Matthew Society Ltd and Peddars Way Housing Association,
    ex p Dove, Harpley, and Wright [1998] JPL B84 .... 11.105
R v Bromley LBC, ex p Sinclair [1991] 3 PCR 60 .... 6.86
R v Canterbury CC, ex p Springimage Ltd [1995] JPL 20 .... 16.26
R v Canterbury City Council, ex p Halford [1992] 2 PLR 137 .... 21.130
R v Caradon DC, ex p Knott (2000) 80 P & CR 154 .... 14.64
R v Cardiff CC, ex p Sears Group Properties Ltd [1998] PLSCS 92 .... 15.46
R v Carlisle City Council, ex p Cumbrian Co-operative Society Ltd
    [1986] JPL 206 .... 10.60, 11.84, 11.86
R v Chung Tak Lam v Borough of Torbay [1998] PLCR 30 .... 15.55–15.56
R v City of London Corporation and Royal Mutual Insurance Society, ex parte
    Mystery of the Barbers (1997) 73 P & CR 59 .... 15.41
R v Commissioner for Local Administration, ex p Liverpool CC
    [2001] 1 All ER 462 (CA) 18.138
R v Cotswold DC, ex p Barrington Parish Council [1997] EGCS 66 .... 18.122
R v Coventry City Council, ex p Arrowcroft Group plc [2001] PLCR 113 .... 14.77
R v Doncaster MDC, ex p British Railways Board [1987] JPL 444 .... 16.14
R v Durham CC and Lafarge Redland Aggregates Ltd, ex p Lowther
    [2002] JPL 197 (CA) 5.07
R v Durham CC and Sherburn Stone Company Limited, ex p Huddleston
    [2000] JPL 1125 .... 12.53, 23.26
R v Ealing LBC, ex p Zainuddin [1995] JPL 925 .... 14.35, 20.149
R v East Sussex CC, ex p Reprotech (Pebsham) Ltd [2002] UKHL 8;
    [2003] 1 WLR 348 .... 11.18, 11.20–11.22
R v Epping Forest BC, ex p Philcox [2000] PLCR 57 .... 20.187
R v Essex CC, ex p Tarmac Roadstone Holdings Ltd [1998] JPL B23 .... 11.50
R v Flintshire CC, ex p Somerfield Stores Ltd [1998] EGCS 53 .... 14.107
R v Foreign Secretary, ex p World Development Movement Ltd [1995] 1 WLR 386 ..... 18.121
R v Gillingham BC, ex p Parham Ltd [1988] JPL 336 (Div Court) 17.14
R v Greenwich LBC, ex p Patel (1985) 51 P & CR 282 .... 20.46–20.47
R v Hammersmith and Fulham London Borough Council, ex p Burkett
    [2002] UKHL 23; [2002] 1 WLR 1593 .... 18.125, 23.26
R v Hillingdon LBC, ex p Royco Homes Ltd [1974] QB 720 .... 14.09, 14.21
R v Inland Revenue Commissioners, ex p National Federation of Self-Employed
    and Small Businesses Ltd [1982] AC 619 .... 18.121
R v Inspectorate of Pollution, ex p Greenpeace Ltd (No 2) [1994] 4 All ER 329 (CA) 18.122
R v Kuxhaus [1988] QB 631 (CA) 20.102, 21.83
R v Lambeth LBC, ex p Sharp [1987] JPL 440 (CA) 16.13–16.14
R v Leominster DC, ex p Antique Country Buildings Ltd [1988] JPL 554 ..... 21.79, 21.81
R v Leominster DC, ex p Pothecary [1998] JPL 335 (CA) 8.21
R v Local Commissioner for Administration, ex p Bradford MDC [1979] QB 287 ...... 18.134
R v London Borough of Tower Hamlets, ex p Barrett Homes Ltd [2000] JPL 1050 ...... 11.129
R v Mendip District Council, ex parte Fabre (2000) 80 P. & C.R. 500 .... 11.07
R v Merton LBC, ex p Barker [1998] JPL 440 .... 17.39
R v Minister of Housing and Local Government, ex p Chichester RDC
    [1960] WLR 587 (Div Court) 27.18

Table of Cases

R v Newbury DC and Newbury and District Agricultural Society, ex p Chievely
  Parish Council [1999] PLCR 51 .... 9.18
R v Newbury DC, ex p Stevens (1992) 65 P & CR 438 .... 9.17
R v North Lincolnshire Council, ex p Horticulture and Garda Products Sales
  (Humberside) Ltd [1998] Env LR 295 .... 23.23
R v North Somerset DC and Pioneer Aggregates (UK) Ltd, ex p Garnett
  [1997] JPL 1015 .... 18.122
R v North Yorkshire CC, ex p Brown [2000] 1 AC 397 .... 12.52, 12.56
R v North Yorkshire County Council, ex p Brown [1999] JPL 616 .... 23.05, 23.08, 23.24
R v Oldham MBC and Pugmanor Properties Ltd, ex p Foster [2000] JPL 111 .... 23.19
R v Oxfordshire County Council ex p Sunningwell [2000] 1 AC 335 ...... 29.02, 29.04–29.05,
                                                                29.19, 29.21, 29.23, 29.28
R v Peak District National Park Authority, ex p Blacklow Industries Ltd [2000] JPL 290 ... 23.09
R v Plymouth City Council, ex p Plymouth and South Devon Co-operative Society
  (1994) 67 P & CR 78 .... 17.41, 17.50
R v Plymouth City Council, ex p Plymouth and South Devon Co-operative Society
  [1993] JPL 1099 .... 17.16
R v Poole Borough Council, ex p Beebee [1991] JPL 643 .... 11.54
R v Restormel BC, ex p Parkyn and Corbett [2000] JPL 1211; [2001] JPL 1415 (CA) 2.53
R v Richmond upon Thames LBC, ex p McCarthy & Stone (Developments) Ltd
  [1992] 2 AC 48 .... 9.60
R v Rochdale MBC, ex p Milne (2001) 81 P & CR 365 .... 11.43, 12.60, 12.62
R v Rochdale MBC, ex p Tew [2000] JPL 54 .... 12.58, 23.26
R v Rochdale Metropolitan Borough Council, Ex p Milne (No 2) (2000) 81 P & CR 27 ... 11.38
R v Royal County of Berkshire, ex p Mangnall [1985] JPL 258 .... 11.82, 11.86
R v Secretary of State for the Environment ex p Billson [1999] QB 374 .... 29.24
R v Secretary of State for the Environment, ex p Bath and North Somerset DC
  [1999] 1 WLR 1759 .... 18.07
R v Secretary of State for the Environment, ex p Bilton (1975) 31 P & CR 154 .... 14.114
R v Secretary of State for the Environment, ex p Corby BC [1995] JPL 115 .... 14.116
R v Secretary of State for the Environment, ex p David Baber [1996] JPL 1032 ..... 11.63–11.64
R v Secretary of State for the Environment, ex p Hillingdon LBC [1986] 1 WLR 807 ..... 11.02
R v Secretary of State for the Environment, ex p Kirkstall Valley Campaign
  [1996] 3 All ER 304 .... 16.27
R v Secretary of State for the Environment, ex p North Norfolk DC [1994] EGCS 131 .... 18.91
R v Secretary of State for the Environment, ex p Rose Theatre Trust Co [1990] 1 QB 504 .... 22.21
R v Secretary of State for the Environment, ex p Slough BC [1995] JPL 135 .... 15.12
R v Secretary of State for the Environment, ex p Wakefield MBC (1998) 75 P & CR 78 ... 18.92
R v Secretary of State for the Environment, Transport, and the Regions, ex p Borough
  of Kirklees [1999] JPL 882 .... 18.55
R v Secretary of State for the Environment, Transport, and the Regions, ex p Carter
  Commercial Developments Ltd [1999] PLCR 125 .... 2.26
R v Secretary of State for Wales, ex p City and County of Swansea [1999] JPL 524 .... 21.99
R v Sevenoaks DC, ex p Terry [1985] 3 All ER 226 .... 16.19, 16.22, 16.26
R v Sheffield City Council ex p Russell (1994) 68 P&CR 331 .... 20.188
R v Somerset CC, ex p Morris & Perry (Gurney Slade Quarry) Ltd [2000] 2 PLCR 117 ... 23.10
R v South Northamptonshire DC, ex p Crest Homes plc [1995] JPL 200 (CA) 17.29
R v Southwark LBC, ex p Murdoch (1990) 155 JP 163 .... 20.112
R v St Edmundsbury BC, ex p Investors in Industry Commercial Properties Ltd
  [1985] 1 WLR 1168 (Div Court) 10.58, 10.60, 14.74, 16.21
R v Staffordshire County Council, ex p Alfred McAlpine Homes Ltd
  [2002] EWHC 76 (Admin); [2002] 2 PLR 1 .... 29.32
R v Suffolk County Council, ex parte Steed (1998) 75 P & CR 102 .... 29.05
R v Surrey CC, ex p Oakimber Ltd [1995] EGCS 120 .... 21.131
R v Swale BC, ex p the Royal Society for the Protection of Birds [1991] JPL 39 ..... 12.42–12.43

R v Swale Borough Council ex p RSPB [1991] PLR 6. . . . . 12.46
R v Swansea City Council, ex p Elitestone Ltd (1993) 66 P & CR 422. . . . . 5.20
R v Tandridge DC, ex p Mohamed Al Fayed [1999] JPL 825 . . . . 11.108
R v Teesside Development Corporation, ex p William Morrison plc and Redcar
 and Cleveland BC [1998] JPL 23 . . . . 2.76
R v Teignbridge DC, ex p Teignmouth Quay Co Ltd [1995] 2 PLR 1. . . . . 20.12
R v Thanet DC and Kent International Airport plc, ex p Tapp and Britton
 [2002] PLCR 88 . . . . 8.03
R v Thanet District Council ex p Tapp [2001] EWCA Civ 559. . . . . 20.188
R v Thurrock BC, ex p Tesco Stores Ltd [1994] JPL 328. . . . . 6.63
R v Vale of Glamorgan DC, ex p Adams [2001] JPL 93 . . . . 11.118
R v Wakefield MDC, ex p Pearl Assurance plc [1997] JPL B131. . . . . 11.54
R v Warwickshire CC, ex p Powergen plc [1998] JPL 131. . . . . .15.43, 15.46
R v Waveney DC, ex p Bell [2001] PLCR 292 . . . . 12.61
R v Wealden DC, ex p Charles Church (South East) Ltd [1989] JPL 837. . . . . 17.15
R v Wells Street Metropolitan Stipendiary Magistrate, ex p Westminster City Council
 [1986] 1 WLR 1046 (Div Court) 21.48
R v West Oxfordshire DC, ex p Pearce Homes Ltd [1986] JPL 523 . . . . 15.09
R v Westminster City Council, ex p Monahan [1990] 1 QB 87 . . . . .11.134, 11.143
R v Wicks [1997] 2 All ER 801. . . . . 20.150
R v Yeovil BC, ex p Trustees of Elim Pentecostal Church, Yeovil (1971) 23 P & CR 39 . . . . 11.09
R (Adesina) v Nursing and Midwifery Council [2013] EWCA Civ 818 . . . . 18.98
R (Adlard) v the Secretary of State for Transport, Local Government, and the
 Regions [2002] JPL 1379 . . . . .19.17–19.18
R (Aggregate Industries UK Ltd) v English Nature [2003] Env LR 3 . . . . 19.17
R (Akester) v. DEFRA [2010] EWHC 232 (Admin). 26.24
R (Anne-Marie Goodman) v London Borough of Lewisham and Big Yellow Property
 Company Ltd [2003] EWCA Civ 140; [2003] Env LR 140 . . . . 12.09
R (Banghard) v Bedford Borough Council [2017] EWHC 2391 (Admin);
 [2018] PTSR 1050 . . . . .10.23, 10.25
R (Barkas) v North Yorkshire County Council [2014] UKSC 31; [2015] AC 195. . . . . . . .29.21,
 29.26–29.28, 29.45
R (Barker) v Bromley LBC [2006] UKHL 52; [2007] 1 AC 470. . . . . 12.63, 12.66–12.67
R (Bateman) v South Cambridgeshire District Council [2011] EWCA Civ 157 . . . . 12.21
R (Beresford) v Sunderland City Council [2003] UKHL 60; [2004] 1 AC 889. . . . . .29.22–29.27
R (Bleaklow Industries) v Secretary of State for Communities and Local Government
 [2009] EWCA Civ 206 . . . . 15.13
R (Blewett) v Derbyshire CC [2003] EWHC 2775 (Admin); [2004] Env LR 29 . . . . 12.29
R (Carlton-Conway) v Harrow LBC [2002] EWCA Civ 927; [2002] JPL 1216. . . . . 11.04
R (Champion) v North Norfolk District Council [2015] UKSC 52;
 [2015] 1 WLR 3710 . . . . .26.14, 26.24
R (Cheltenham Builders) v South Gloucestershire District Council
 [2003] EWHC 2803 (Admin); [2004] 4 PLR 95 . . . . .29.18, 29.30
R (Flint) v South Gloucestershire Council [2016] EWHC 2180 (Admin); [2017] JPL 310 . . . . . 20.188
R (Fox Strategic Land and Property Ltd) v Chorley BC [2014] EWHC 1179 (Admin);
 [2014] JPL 1152. . . . . 17.67
R (Giordano Ltd) v London Borough of Camden [2018] EWHC 3417. . . . . 17.79
R (Gregan and ors) v Hartlepool BC and Able UK Ltd [2003] EWHC 3278 (Admin). 8.15
R (Hall Hunter Partnership) v First Secretary of State [2006] EWHC 3482 (Admin);
 [2007] 2 P & CR 5. . . . . 7.39
R (Hampton Bishop Parish Council) v Herefordshire Council [2015] 1 WLR 2367. . . . . . . 11.38
R (Hart Aggregates Ltd) v Hartlepool Borough Council [2005] EWHC 840 (Admin) 14.109
R (Hart District Council) v. SSCLG [2008] 2 P&CR 16 . . . . 26.24
R (Hillingdon LBC) v Secretary of State for Transport [2017] EWHC 121 (Admin);
 [2017] 1 WLR 2166 . . . . 28.13

R (Holborn Studios Ltd) v Hackney LBC [2017] EWHC 2823;
  [2017] PTSR 997 .... 10.62
R (Hossack) v Kettering BC and English Churches Housing Group
  [2002] EWCA Civ 886; [2003] 2 P & CR 34 .... 6.85
R (Hourhope Ltd) v Shropshire Council [2015] EWHC 518 (Admin);
  [2015] PTSR 933 .... 17.79
R (Howells) v Secretary of State for Communities and Local Government
  [2009] EWHC 2757 (Admin); [2010] JPL 741 .... 20.94
R (I'm Your Man Ltd) v North Somerset Council [2004] EWHC 342 (Admin);
  [2004] 4 PLR 1 .... 6.28
R (Innovia Cellophane Ltd) v Infrastructure Planning Commission [2011] EWHC
  2883 (Admin); [2012] PTSR 1132 .... 28.34, 28.37
R (Jones) v Mansfield District Council [2003] EWCA Civ 1408; [2004] Env L.R. 21 ..... 12.21
R (Judge) v First Secretary of State [2005] EWCA Civ 1155 .... 21.81
R (Langton) v Secretary of State for Communities and Local Government
  [2018] EWHC 2190 (Admin) 26.16
R (Lewis) v Redcar & Cleveland Borough Council [2010] UKSC 11;
  [2010] 2 AC 70 .... 29.19, 29.21–29.22, 29.28–29.29, 29.32, 29.41
R (Lynes and Lynes) v West Berkshire DC [2002] EWHC 1828 (Admin);
  [2003] JPL 1137 .... 20.77
R (Medway DC) v Secretary of State for Transport, Local Government and the Regions
  [2002] EWHC 2516 (Admin); [2003] JPL 583 .... 26.13
R (Mid Counties Co-Operative) v Forest of Dean [2013] EWHC 1908 (Admin) 11.66
R (Midcounties Co-operative Limited) v Wyre Forest DC [2010] EWCA Civ 841 .... 15.13
R (Morge) v Hampshire CC [2011] UKSC 2; [2011] 1 WLR 268 .... 26.20, 26.22–26.23
R (Mountcook Land Ltd) v Westminster City Council [2003] EWCA Civ 1346;
  [2017] PTSR 1166 .... 11.102–11.103
R (Mynydd y Gwynt) v. Secretary of State for Business Energy and Industrial
  Strategy [2016] EWHC 2581 .... 26.24
R (Newhaven Port & Properties Ltd) v East Sussex County Council
  [2012] EWHC 647 (Admin); [2012] 3 WLR 709 .... 29.28–29.31
R (Newhaven Port & Properties Ltd) v East Sussex County Council
  [2013] EWCA Civ 673; [2014] QB 282 .... 29.10
R (Noble Organisation Ltd) v Thanet District Council [2005] ECWA Civ 782;
  [2006] Env. L.R.8 .... 12.21
R (North Wiltshire) v Cotswold District Council [2009] EWHC 3702 (Admin) 20.188
R (on the application of Abdul Wakil) v Hammersmith and Fulham LBC
  [2012] EWHC 1411 (QB); [2013] Env LR 3 .... 4.28
R (on the application of Adlard and ors) v Secretary of State for Environment,
  Transport, and the Regions [2002] EWCA Civ 757; [2002] 1 WLR 2515 .... 2.29
R (on the application of Alconbury Developments Ltd) v Secretary of State for the
  Environment, Transport, and the Regions; R (on the application of Holding &
  Barnes) v Secretary of State for the Environment, Transport and the Regions;
  Secretary of State for the Environment, Transport, and the Regions v Legal and
  General Society Ltd [2001] 2 WLR 1389 .... 19.08–19.09, 19.11, 19.15, 19.22
R (on the application of Allaway) v Oxfordshire County Council
  [2016] EWHC 2677 (Admin) 29.20
R (on the application of Alpha Plus Group Ltd) v Royal Borough of Kensington
  and Chelsea [2007] EWHC 2840 (Admin) 15.38
R (on the application of Arndale Properties Ltd) v Worcester City Council
  [2008] JPL 1583 .... 21.130
R (on the application of Baker) v Bath and North East Somerset District Council
  [2009] EWHC 595 (Admin); [2010] 1 P & CR 4 .... 12.08
R (on the application of Baker) v Secretary of State for Communities and Local Government
  and Bromley London Borough [2008] EWCA Civ 141; [2009] PTSR 809 .... 11.52

R (on the application of Bateman) v South Cambridgeshire District Council
 [2011] EWCA Civ 157 .... 12.20
R (on the application of Beronstone Ltd) v First Secretary of State and Chiltern DC
 [2006] EWHC 2391 (Admin) 5.79, 6.50
R (on the application of Bewley Homes Plc) v Waverley Borough Council
 [2017] EWHC 1776 (Admin); [2017] PTSR 423 .... 4.38
R (on the application of Birchall Gardens LLP) v Hertfordshrie County Council
 [2016] EWHC 2794 (Admin); [2017] Env LR 17 .... 12.21
R (on the application of Brent LBC) v Secretary of State for Communities and
 Local Government [2008] EWHC 1991 (Admin) 14.98
R (on the application of Buckinghamshire CC) v Secretary of State for Transport
 [2014] UKSC 3; [2014] 1 WLR 324 .... 13.06
R (on the application of Buckley) v Bath & North East Somerset Council
 [2018] EWHC 1551 (Admin); [2018] JPL 1231 .... 11.53
R (on the application of Cairns) v Hertfordshire County Council
 [2018] EWHC 2050 (Admin) 12.22
R (on the application of Cala Homes (South) Ltd) v Secretary of State for Communities
 and Local Government [2011] EWCA Civ 639; [2011] 2 EGLR 75 .... 3.34, 11.61
R (on the application of Carroll) v South Somerset District Council
 [2008] EWHC 104 (Admin) 11.14
R (on the application of Catt) v Brighton & Hove City Council [2007] EWCA
 Civ 298; [2007] Env LR 32 .... 12.51
R (on the application of Chalfont St Peter Parish Council) v Chiltern District Council
 [2013] EWHC 1877 (Admin) 4.75
R (on the application of Champion) v North Norfolk District Council
 [2015] UKSC 52; [2015] 1 WLR 3710 .... 12.50–12.51
R (on the application of Cherkley Campaign Ltd) v Mole Valley District Council
 [2014] EWCA Civ 567 .... 4.89, 11.39
R (on the application of Christopher Mellor) v Secretary of State for Communities
 and Local Government [2009] EWCA Civ. 1201 .... 12.25
R (on the application of CK Properties (Theydon Bois) Ltd) v Epping Forest District
 Council [2018] EWHC 1649 (Admin) 4.74
R (on the application of Clear Channel UK Ltd) v Hammersmith and Fulham LBC
 [2009] EWCA Civ 2142; [2010] JPL 751 .... 24.15
R (on the application of Cooper Estates Strategic Land Ltd) v Wiltshire Council
 [2018] EWHC 1704 (Admin) 29.13
R (on the application of Copeland) v Tower Hamlets LBC [2010] EWHC 1845
 (Admin); [2011] JPL 40 .... 11.48
R (on the application of Cotham School) v Bristol City Council [2018] EWHC
 1022 (Admin) 29.22, 29.36
R (on the application of Crematoria Management Ltd) v Welwyn Hatfield BC
 [2018] EWHC 382 (Admin) 12.09
R (on the application of Crownhall Estates) v Chichester District Council
 [2016] EWHC 73 (Admin) 4.38
R (on the application of Cummins) v Camden LBC [2001] EWHC Admin 116 .... 19.17
R (on the application of Daws Hill Neighbourhood Forum) v Wycombe District
 Council [2014] EWCA Civ 228; [2014] 1WLR 1362 .... 4.35
R (on the application of Dillner) v Sheffield City Council [2016] EWHC 945 (Admin);
 [2016] Env LR 31 .... 5.67
R (on the application of DLA Delivery Ltd) v Lewes District Council
 [2017] EWCA Civ 58; [2017] PTSR 949 .... 4.39
R (on the application of Evans) v Secretary of State for Communities and Local
 Government [2013] EWCA Civ 114; [2013] JPL 1027 .... 12.20, 12.28
R (on the application of Friends of the Earth) v Welsh Ministers [2015] EWHC
 776 (Admin); [2016] Env LR 1 .... 13.26

R (on the application of Gladman Developments Ltd) v Aylesbury Vale District Council
[2014] EWHC 4323 (Admin); [2015] JPL 656. .... 4.39
R (on the application of Gleeson Developments Limited) v Secretary of State for
Communities and Local Government [2014] EWCA Civ 1118;
[2014] PTSR 1226 .... 11.13, 18.16
R (on the application of Goodman) v London Borough of Lewisham and the Big
Yellow Property Company [2003] EWCA Civ 140; [2003] Env LR 28 .... 12.42
R (on the application of Goring-on-Thames Parish Council) v South Oxfordshire
District Council [2018] EWCA Civ 860 .... 12.50
R (on the application of Hall Hunter Partnership) v First Secretary of State and
Waverley BC and ors [2006] EWHC 3482 .... 5.28
R (on the application of Harbidge) v Secretary of State for Communities and
Local Government [2012] EWHC 1128 (Admin) 20.33
R (on the application of Harris) v Haringey LBC [2010] EWCA Civ 703;
[2011] PTSR 931 .... 11.52
R (on the application of Harvey) v Mendip District Council [2017] EWCA Civ 1784;
[2018] JPL 419 .... 9.21
R (on the application of High Peak Spar Ltd) v Secretary of State for Communities
and Local Government [2009] EWHC 3719 (Admin) 23.32
R (on the application of Hockley) v Essex County Council [2013] EWHC 4051 (Admin) 12.20
R (on the application of Howsmoor Developments Ltd and ors) v South
Gloucestershire Council [2008] EWHC 262 (Admin) 13.22
R (on the application of HS2 Action Alliance Ltd) v Secretary of State for Transport
[2014] EWCA Civ 1578; [2015] PTSR 1025 .... 13.06
R (on the application of IM Properties Ltd) v Lichfield District Council
[2014] EWHC 2440 (Admin); [2014] PTSR 1484 .... 4.74
R (on the application of Islam) v Secretary of State for Communities and Local
Government [2012] EWHC 1314 (Admin) 5.21
R (on the application of Issacs) v Secretary of State for Communities and Local
Government [2009] EWHC 557 .... 11.52–11.53
R (on the application of John Childs) v First Secretary of State and Test Valley BC
[2005] EWHC 2368; [2006] JPL 1326 .... 6.113
R (on the application of Jones) v Mansfield DC [2003] EWHC 7 (Admin) 12.15
R (on the application of Jones) v Mansfield District Council [2004] Env. L.R. 21 .... 12.20
R (on the application of Kabbell Developments Ltd) v Secretary of State
(2004, unreported) 11.24
R (on the application of Kathro) v Rhondda Cynon Taff CBC [2002] PLCR 304 .... 19.16
R (on the application of Khatun) v Newham LBC [2005] EWCA Civ 55; [2005] QB 37 ... 11.45
R (on the application of Khodari) v Kensington & Chelsea LBC [2017] EWCA Civ 333;
[2018] 1 WLR 584 .... 17.25
R (on the application of KPJR Management Company Ltd) v London Borough
of Richmond [2018] EWHC 84 (Admin); [2018] JPL 838 .... 6.142, 8.10
R (on the application of Kverndal) v London Borough of Hounslow Council
[2015] EWHC 3084 (Admin) 11.68
R (on the application of Lambrou) v Secretary of State for Communities and
Local Government [2013] EWHC 325 (Admin); [2014] JPL 538 .... 20.39
R (on the application of Larkfleet Ltd) v South Kesteven DC [2015] EWCA Civ
887; [2016] Env LR 4 .... 12.46–12.47
R (on the application of Lebus) v South Cambridgeshire DC [2002] EWHC
Admin 2009 .... 12.17, 12.19
R (on the application of Leckhampton Green Land Action Group Ltd) v Tewkesbury
Borough Council [2017] EWHC 198 (Admin); [2017] Env LR 28 .... 11.06
R (on the application of Lewis) v Redcar and Cleveland Borough Council
[2007] EWHC 3166 (Admin); [2008] JPL 1156 .... 26.17

xl

R (on the application of Lichfield Securities Ltd) v Lichfield DC and Christopher
   JN Williams [2001] PLCR 519 .... 17.57
R (on the application of Loader) v Rother District Council [2016] EWCA Civ 795 .... 11.07
R (on the application of Loader) v Secretary of State for Communities and Local
   Government [2012] EWCA Civ 869; [2013] PTSR 406 .... 12.15, 12.20
R (on the application of Luton Borough Council) v Central Bedfordshire Council
   [2015] EWCA Civ 537; [2015] 2 P & CR 19 .... 11.45, 11.88
R (on the application of Mansfield District Council) v Secretary of State for Housing,
   Communities and Local Government [2018] EWHC 1794 (Admin);
   [2018] JPL 1334 .... 17.35
R (on the application of Marshall) v East Dorset District Council
   [2018] EWHC 226 (Admin) 7.17
R (on the application of Maynard) v Chiltern District Council
   [2015] EWHC 3817 (Admin) 4.42
R (on the application of Mellor) v Secretary of State for Communities and Local
   Government [2010] Env LR 18 .... 12.20
R (on the application of Millgate Developments Ltd) v Wokingham BC
   [2011] EWCA Civ 1062; [2012] JPL 258 .... 17.37, 17.55
R (on the application of Milton Keynes Council) v Secretary of State for Communities
   and Local Government [2011] EWHC 1060 (Admin) 7.37
R (on the application of Morge) v Hampshire County Council [2011] UKSC 2 .... 11.07
R (on the application of Nestwood Homes Developments Ltd) v South Holland
   District Council [2014] EWHC 863 (Admin); [2014] BLGR 354 .... 18.142
R (on the application of Newey) v South Hams District Council
   [2018] EWHC 1872 (Admin) 11.05
R (on the application of Newhaven Port & Properties Ltd) v East Sussex County
   Council [2015] UKSC 7; [2015] AC 1547 .... 29.35–29.36
R (on the application of North Norfolk Planning Watch Ltd) v North Norfolk
   District Council [2017] EWHC 3345 (Admin); [2018] PTSR 768 .... 9.05
R (on the application of O'Brien and O'Brien) v Basildon DC [2006] EWHC 1346 ...... 19.21
R (on the application of Oakley) v South Cambridgeshire District Council
   [2017] EWCA Civ 71; [2017] 1 WLR 3765 .... 11.29–11.30
R (on the application of Ortona Ltd) v Secretary of State for Communities and
   Local Government [2008] EWHC 3207 (Admin); [2009] JPL 1033 .... 18.30
R (on the application of Oxfordshire & Buckinghamshire Mental Health NHS
   Foundation Trust) v Oxfordshire County Council [2010] EWHC 530 (Admin) 29.33
R (on the application of Oyston Estates Ltd) v Fylde Borough Council
   [2017] EWHC 3086 (Admin) 4.42
R (on the application of Payne) v Secretary of State for Communities and
   Local Government [2011] JPL 767 .... 18.56
R (on the application of Persimmon Homes Ltd) v Secretary of State for the
   Communities and Local Government [2007] EWHC 1985 (Admin) 2.29, 11.87
R (on the application of Plant) v Lambeth LBC [2016] EWHC 3324 (Admin);
   [2017] PTSR 453 .... 11.45
R (on the application of Prideaux) v Buckingham CC [2013] EWHC 1054;
   [2013] Env LR 32 .... 26.23
R (on the application of Reid) v Secretary of State for Transport, Local Government
   and the Regions [2002] EWHC 2174 .... 20.98
R (on the application of Richardson) v North Yorkshire County Council
   [2003] EWCA Civ 1860; [2004] 1 WLR 1920 .... 12.40
R (on the application of Romer) v London Borough of Haringey [2006]
   EWHC 3480 (Admin); [2007] JPL 1354 .... 20.39
R (on the application of Save Woolley Valley Action Group Limited) v Bath and
   North East Somerset Council [2012] EWHC 2161 (Admin); [2013] Env LR 8 .... 5.29

R (on the application of Seamus Gavin) v London Borough of Haringey and Anor
  [2003] EWHC 2591 (Admin)..10.36
R (on the application of Sellars) v Basingstoke and Deane BC [2013]
  EWHC 3673 (Admin); [2014] JPL 643 ....20.185
R (on the application of Shasha) v Westminster City Council [2016] EWHC
  3283 (Admin); [2017] PTSR 306 ....11.05
R (on the application of Skipton Properties Ltd) v Craven District Council
  [2017] EWHC 534 (Admin); [2017] JPL 825............................4.28
R (on the application of Smith) v Secretary of State for Communities and Local
  Government [2012] EWHC 963 (Admin); [2012] JPL 975 ....11.61
R (on the application of Springhall) v Richmond LBC [2006] EWCA Civ 19 ....11.04
R (on the application of St Albans District Council) v Secretary of State for Communities
  and Local Government [2017] EWHC 1751 (Admin) 3.35
R (on the application of Stavrinidies) v Secretary of State for Communities and
  Local Government [2010] EWHC 3479 (Admin); [2011] JPL 922..................7.23
R (on the application of Stonegate Homes Ltd) v Horsham District Council
  [2016] EWHC 2512..4.42
R (on the application of Tendring District Council) v Secretary of State for Communities
  and Local Government [2008] EWHC 2122 (Admin); [2009] JPL 350 ....6.80
R (on the application of The Garden and Leisure Group Ltd) v North Somerset
  Council [2003] EWHC 1605 (Admin); [2004] 1 P & CR 39.....................17.35
R (on the application of the Government of the Republic of France) v Royal Borough
  of Kensington & Chelsea [2017] EWCA Civ 429; [2017] 1 WLR 3206...........21.152
R (on the application of Thornton Hall Hotel Ltd) v Wirral MBC [2018]
  EWHC 560 (Admin); [2018] PTSR 954...............................18.124
R (on the application of TW Logistics) v Tendring District Council
  [2013] EWCA Civ 9; [2013] 2 P & CR 9...............................4.85
R (on the application of Usk Valley Conservation Group) v Brecon Beacons National
  Park Authority [2010] 2 P & CR 14.................................2.49, 11.50
R (on the application of Vetterlein) v Hampshire CC and Hampshire Waste Services
  Ltd [2002] PLCR 289...19.13
R (on the application of Welcome Break Group Ltd) v Stroud District Council
  [2012] EWHC 140..17.55
R (on the application of Wells) v Secretary of State for Transport Local Government
  and the Regions [2004] Env LR 27 ....12.57
R (on the application of West Berkshire District Council) v Secretary of State
  for Communities and Local Government [2016] EWCA Civ 441;
  [2016] 1 WLR 3923 ....11.42, 11.54–11.55
R (on the application of Whitmey) v Commons Commissioners [2004] EWCA
  Civ 951; [2005] QB 282..29.38
R (on the application of Williams) v Powys County Council [2017] EWCA Civ 427......11.07
R (on the application of Winchester City Council) v Secretary of State for the
  Communities and Local Government [2007] EWHC 2303 (Admin);
  [2008] 1 P & CR 15) 6.73
R (on the application of Woolley Action Group) v Bath and North East Somerset
  Council [2012] EWHC 2161 (Admin) 5.23
R (on the application of Woolley) v Cheshire East BC [2009] EWHC 1227 (Admin);
  [2010] Env LR 5...26.21
R (on the application of Working Title Films Ltd) v Westminster City Council
  [2016] EWHC 1855 (Admin).......................................17.55
R (on the application of Wright) v Forest of Dean District Council [2017] EWCA
  Civ 2102; [2018] JPL 672..11.47
R (on the application of) Hadfield v Secretary of State for Transport, Local Government,
  and the Regions [2002] EWHC 1226 (Admin)............................2.28

R (Orbital Shopping Park Swindon Limited) v Swindon BC [2016] EWHC
448 (Admin); [2016] PTSR 736 .... 17.79
R (Perrett) v Secretary of State for Communities and Local Government [2009]
EWCA Civ 1365; [2010] 2 All ER 578.. 20.104
R (Rapose) v London Borough of Wandsworth [2010] EWHC 3126 (Admin);
[2011] JPL 600 .... 20.136
R (Redrow Homes Ltd) v First Secretary of State and South Gloucestershire Council
[2003] EWHC 304 (Admin)... 9.20
R (Royal Borough of Kensington & Chelsea) v Secretary of State for Communities
and Local Government [2016] EWHC 1785 (Admin) 6.97
R (SAVE Britain's Heritage) v Secretary of State for Communities and Local
Government [2011] EWCA Civ 334; [2011] PTSR 1140.................. 5.55, 21.148
R (Save Britain's Heritage) v Secretary of State for Communities and Local Government
[2018] EWCA Civ 2137; [2019] 1 WLR 929 .... 2.27
R (Scott Jones) v North Warwickshire BC [2001] PLCR 509 .... 11.84
R (Seamus Gavin) v Haringey LBC and Wolseley Centres Ltd [2003] EWHC
2591 (Admin) 10.40
R (Shropshire Council) v Secretary of State for Communitie and Local Government
[2019] EWHC 16 (Admin)... 17.79
R (Vue Entertainment Ltd) v City of York Council [2017] EWHC 588 (Admin)......... 14.77
R (Wall) v Brighton and Hove DC [2004] EWHC 2582 .... 18.08
R (West Berkshire District Council) v Secretary of State for Communities and
Local Government [2016] EWCA Civ 441; [2016] 1 WLR 3923 .... 2.59
R (Wilson) v Wychavon DC and anor [2007] EWCA Civ 52.......................... 20.19
R F W Coppen (Trustees of the Thames Ditton Lawn Tennis Club) v K J Bruce-Smith
[1998] JPL 1077 .... 5.64
Ralls v Secretary of State for the Environment [1998] JPL 444 .... 6.140
Rambridge v Secretary of State for the Environment [1997] 74 P & CR 126 .... 7.31
Ramsay v Secretary of State for the Environment and Suffolk DC [1998] JPL 60.......... 7.41
Ramsay v Secretary of State for the Environment, Transport, and the Regions and
Suffolk Coastal DC [2000] JPL 1123 .... 7.44
Rann v Secretary of State for the Environment [1980] JPL 109....................... 6.54
Rastrum v Secretary of State for Communities and Local Government
[2009] EWCA Civ 1340 .... 14.109
Ratcliffe v Secretary of State for the Environment [1975] JPL 728 .... 5.63
Rawlings v Secretary of State for the Environment and Tandridge DC
(1990) 60 PCR 413... 6.137
Rhodes v Minister of Housing and Local Government [1963] 1 WLR 208............... 11.83
Richardson Development Ltd v Birmingham City Council [1999] JPL 1001 .... 21.32
Richmond LBC v Secretary of State for the Environment, Transport, and the Regions
and Richmond Churches Housing Trust [2001] JPL 84 .... 6.97
Richmond upon Thames LBC v Secretary of State for the Environment [1984] JPL 24 .... 17.10
Richmond-upon-Thames LBC v Secretary of State for the Environment (1978) 37 P & CR 151.... 21.70
Riordan Communications Ltd v South Bucks DC [2000] JPL 594.................... 14.102
RMC Management Services Ltd v Secretary of State for the Environment
(1972) 222 EG 1593... 11.73
Robbins v Secretary of State for the Environment [1989] 1 WLR 201 .... 21.103
Rockhold Ltd v Secretary of State for the Environment [1986] JPL 130 .... 18.29
Roger Lethem v Secretary of State and Worcester City Council [2003] JPL 332.......... 11.157
Rugby Football Union v Secretary of State for the Environment, Transport, Local
Government, and the Regions [2002] EWCA Civ 169; [2003] JPL 96 .... 6.90
Rugby School Governors v Secretary of State for the Environment [1975] JPL 97 .... 11.90
Runnymede DC v Harwood [1994] JPL 724 .... 20.160
Ryeford Homes Ltd v Sevenoaks DC [1990] JPL 36................................... 15.53

Table of Cases

Sage v Secretary of State for the Environment, Transport and the Regions and
    Maidstone BC [2003] UKHL 22; [2003] 1 WLR 983....................20.26, 20.29
Sainsburys Supermarkets Ltd v First Secretary of State [2005] EWCA Civ 520...........11.42
Salvatore Cumbo v Secretary of State for the Environment [1992] JPL 366 ....6.40
Sample (Warkworth) Ltd v Alnwick DC (1984) 48 P & CR 474 ....20.123
Save Britain's Heritage v Number 1 Poultry Ltd [1991] 1 WLR 153(CA)..........18.58, 21.70
Save Historic Newmarket Ltd v Forest Heath DC [2011] EWHC 606 (Admin);
    [2011] JPL 1233 ....13.24
Scarborough BC v Adams [1983] JPL 673 ....20.41
Schimizu (UK) Ltd v Westminster City Council [1997] JPL 523 ....21.04–21.05, 21.25
Scrivener v Minister of Housing and Local Government (1966) 18 P & CR 357 ....6.56
Sea & Land Power & Energy Ltd v Secretary of State for Communities and Local
    Government [2012] EWHC 1419 (QB).......................................18.104
Second City (South West) Ltd v Secretary of State for the Environment
    (1990) 61 P & CR 498 ....18.27
Secretary of State for Communities and Local Government v Bleaklow Industries Ltd
    [2009] EWCA Civ 206; [2009] 2 P & CR 21................................23.32
Secretary of State for Communities and Local Government v Bovale and
    Herefordshire DC [2009] EWCA Civ 171; [2009] 1 WLR 2274 ....18.116
Secretary of State for Communities and Local Government v Hopkins Homes Ltd
    [2017] UKSC 37; [2017] 1 WLR 1865..2.59
Secretary of State for the Environment v Edwards [1994] 1 PLR 62 ....11.87–11.88
Secretary of State for the Environment, Transport, and the Regions v Skerritts
    of Nottingham [2000] JPL 789..6.15, 21.29
Secretary of State for the Environment, Transport, and the Regions v Thurrock BC
    [2002] EWCA Civ 226; [2002] 2 PLR 43......................20.179–20.182, 20.184
Seddon Properties Ltd v Secretary of State for the Environment
    (1981) 42 P & CR 26...18.103–18.104
Sevenoaks DC v First Secretary of State [2004] EWHC 771 (Admin)..................15.13
Shepherd v Secretary of State for the Environment and Three Rivers DC
    [1997] JPL 764 ....7.34
Simmons v Secretary of State for the Environment [1985] JPL 253 ....18.25
Simplex GE (Holdings) Ltd v Secretary of State for Communities and Local
    Government [2017] PTSR 1041 ....18.114
Sinclair-Lockhart's Trustees v Central Land Board (1950) 1 P & CR 195...............6.12
Skerritts of Nottingham Ltd v Secretary of State for the Environment, Transport,
    and the Regions [2000] PLR 102...5.21
Slough Estates plc v Welwyn Hatfield DC [1996] 2 PLR 50..........................15.58
Slough Estates v Slough Borough Council [1971] A.C. 958 ....15.06, 15.13
Smith v Secretary of State for the Environment [1983] JPL 462 ....14.57
Smyth v. Secretary of State for Communities and Local Government
    [2015] EWCA Civ 174 ....26.24
Somak Travel v Secretary of State for the Environment (1988) 55 P & CR 250 ....20.64
Somerford Parish Council v Cheshire East Borough Council
    [2016] EWHC 619 (Admin)..29.39
Sosmo Trust v Secretary of State for the Environment [1983] JPL 806 ....11.50
South Buckinghamshire DC v Secretary of State for the Environment and
    Berkeley Homes Ltd [1999] JPL 1340......................................11.99
South Buckinghamshire District Council v Porter (No 2) [2004] UKHL 33;
    [2004] 1 WLR 1953 ....4.38, 11.30, 18.58
South Bucks DC v Porter (No 1) [2003] UKHL 26 ....19.13
South Bucks DC v Porter [2002] 1 WLR 139....................................20.132
South Bucks DC v Porter [2003] AC 558...............................11.119, 20.165
South Bucks DC v Secretary of State for the Environment [1989] JPL 351..............7.45
South Bucks District Council v Porter (No 2) [2004] 1 WLR 1953 ....18.104

Table of Cases

South Cambridgeshire DC v Flynn [2006] EWHC 1320 .20.132, 20.162
South Hams District Council v Halsey [1996] JPL 761 . . . . 20.76
South Lakeland DC v Secretary of State for the Environment [1992] 2 AC 141 . . . . 21.137
South Lakeland DC v Secretary of State for the Environment and Rowbotham
   [1991] JPL 440 . . . . 11.116
South Northamptonshire Council v Secretary of State for the Environment
   (1995) 70 P & CR 224 . . . . 2.27
South Oxfordshire DC v Secretary of State for the Environment [1981] JPL 359 . . . . 14.94
South Oxfordshire DC v Secretary of State for the Environment [1995] JPL 213 . . . . 11.141
South Oxfordshire DC v Secretary of State for the Environment, Transport, and
   the Regions [2000] PLCR 315. . . . . 6.27
South Somerset District Council v Secretary of State for the Environment
   (Practice Note) [2017] PTSR 1075; (1992) 66 P & CR 83 . . . . 18.104
South Staffordshire DC v Secretary of State for the Environment [1987] JPL 635 . . . . 15.37
Southwark LBC v ML Frow [1989] JPL 645. . . . . 20.155
Sovmots Investments Ltd v Secretary of State for the Environment [1979] AC 144 . . . . 11.49
Sparkes v Secretary of State for the Environment, Transport and the Regions
   [2000] PLCR 279 . . . . 20.63
St Albans DC v Secretary of State for the Environment [1993] JPL 374 . . . . .11.35, 11.66
St Vincent Housing Association v Secretary of State for Communities and Local
   Government [2011] EWHC 3339 (Admin); [2012] JPL 845 . . . . 25.01
Staffordshire CC v NGR Land Developments Limited and Roberts [2003] JPL 56. . . . . 15.66
Staffordshire CC v Riley [2002] PLCR 75. . . . . 14.102
Staffordshire Moorlands DC v Cartwright (1991) 63 P & CR 285 . . . . 15.12
Stainer v Secretary of State for the Environment [1994] JPL 44 . . . . 18.97
Steeples v Derbyshire County Council [1985] 1 WLR 256 . . . . 16.13
Steinberg v Secretary of State for the Environment (1988) 58 P & CR 453 . . . . . .21.134–21.136
Stephens v Cuckfield RDC [1959] 1 QB 516 . . . . 6.13
Stevens v Bromley LBC [1972] Ch 400. . . . . .20.41, 20.120
Stringer v Minister of Housing and Local Government [1970] 1 WLR 1281 . . . . . 11.46, 11.70, 11.73
Sullivan v Warwick DC and Wilson Bowden Developments Ltd and English Heritage
   [2003] EWHC 606 (Admin); [2003] JPL 1545. . . . . 21.05
Sumner v Secretary of State for Communities and Local Government
   [2010] EWHC 372 (Admin); [2010] JPL 1014. . . . . 20.31
Swale Borough Council v First Secretary of State [2005] EWCA Civ 1568;
   [2006] JPL 886 . . . . 20.182
Sykes v Secretary of State for the Environment [1981] JPL 285. . . . . 6.44

Tameside MBC v Secretary of State for the Environment [1984] JPL 180. . . . . 11.112
Tandridge DC v Verrechia [2000] QB 318 . . . . 20.76
Tarmac Heavy Building Materials Ltd UK v Secretary of State for the Environment,
   Transport, and the Regions [2000] PLCR 157. . . . . 14.20
Taylor v Betterment Properties (Weymouth) Ltd [2012] EWCA Civ 250;
   [2012] 2 P & CR 3 . . . . 29.02
Taylor Wimpey UK Ltd and Beazer Homes Reigate Ltd v Crawley Borough Council
   [2008] EWHC 2644 . . . . 4.73
Telford & Wrekin Borough Council v Secretary of State for Communities and
   Local Government [2013] EWHC 1638 (Admin) Turner 17.55
Telford & Wrekin Council v Secretary of State for Communities and Local
   Government [2013] EWHC 79 (Admin) 15.13
Telford and Wrekin [2013] JPL 832 . . . . 14.35
Tesco Stores Ltd v Dundee City Council [2012] UKSC 13;
   [2012] PTSR 983 . . . . 4.85, 11.38, 11.43, 18.104, 18.108
Tesco Stores Ltd v Secretary of State for the Environment
   [1995] 1 WLR 759 (HL). 11.54, 11.59, 17.45, 17.51, 17.53, 18.104–18.105

Table of Cases

Tewkesbury BC v Keeley [2004] EWHC 2594 (QB) 5.23
Thames Heliports plc v London Borough of Tower Hamlets (1997) 74 P & CR 164 .... 5.10,
6.08, 8.10
Thomas v Bridgend CBC [2012] JPL 25 .... 19.18
Thrasyvoulou v Secretary of State for the Environment [1990] 2 AC 273 .... 20.105, 20.108
Tidman v Reading BC [1994] 3 PLR 72 .... 9.62
Tidswell v Secretary of State for the Environment [1977] JPL 104 .... 7.40
Tiviot Way Investments Ltd v Secretary of State for Communities and Local
   Government [2016] JPL 171 .... 11.38
Topdeck Holdings Ltd v Secretary of State [1991] JPL 961 .... 18.110
Trillium (Prime) Property GP Ltd v Tower Hamlets LBC [2011] EWHC 146 (Admin) ... 21.130
Trott v Broadland District Council [2011] EWCA Civ 301 .... 20.78
Trump International Golf Club Scotland Ltd v Scottish Ministers [2015] UKSC 74;
   [2016] 1 WLR 85 .... 15.14
Trustees of the Castelly-Mynach Estate v Secretary of State for Wales [1985] JPL 40 .... 6.159
Trustees of Walton on Thames Charities v Walton and Weighbridge District Council
   (1970) 21 P. & C. R. 411 .... 15.13
Trusthouse Forte Hotels Ltd v Secretary of State for the Environment
   (1986) 53 P & CR 293 .... 11.83
TW Logistics Ltd v Essex County Council [2018] EWCA Civ 2172;
   [2018] 3 WLR 1926 .... 29.36, 29.45

Unex Dumpton Ltd v Secretary of State for the Environment [1990] JPL 344 .... 21.135
University of Bristol v North Somerset CC [2013] EWHC 231 (Admin); [2013] JPL 940 ...... 3.35

Vickers-Armstrong v Central Land Board (1957) 9 P & CR 33 .... 6.118, 6.120

W H Tolley & Son Ltd v Secretary of State for the Environment (1998) 75 P & CR 533 .... 11.158
Wain v Secretary of State for the Environment (1981) 44 P &CR 289 .... 27.18
Wakelin v Secretary of State for the Environment [1978] JPL 769 .... 6.167, 6.169
Wallington v Secretary of State for Wales [1991] JPL 942 .... 6.18, 6.21–6.24, 6.30
Walsall BC v Secretary of State for Communities and Local Government
   [2013] EWCA Civ 370; [2013] JPL 1183 .... 20.101
Walsall MBC v Secretary of State for Communities and Local Government
   [2012] EWHC 1756 .... 7.18
Walters v Secretary of State for Wales [1979] JPL 171 .... 11.50
Waltham Forest LBC v Oakmesh Ltd and Family Mosaic Housing
   [2009] EWHC 1688; [2010] JPL 249 .... 17.30
Walton v Scottish Ministers [2012] UKSC 44; [2013] PTSR 51 .... 12.49–12.50, 18.99
Wandsworth LBC v Secretary of State for Transport, Local Government, and the
   Regions and BT Cellnet [2003] EWHC 622 .... 11.20
Wansdyke DC v Secretary of State for the Environment [1992] JPL 1168 .... 11.143
Ward v Secretary of State for the Environment [1990] JPL 347 .... 21.136
Watermead Parish Council v Aylesbury Vale District Council [2017] EWCA Civ 152 ..... 11.07
Watson v Croft Promo-Sport [2009] EWCA Civ 15 .... 15.52
Watts v Secretary of State for the Environment [1991] JPL 719 .... 21.29
Wealden DC v. SSCLG [2016] EWHC 247 (Admin) 26.24
Wealden District Council v Secretary of State for Communities and Local Government
   [2017] EWHC 351 (Admin); [2017] Env LR 31 .... 26.24
Wealdon DC v Nelson James Krushandal [1999] JPL 174 .... 20.163
Wealdon DC v Secretary of State for the Environment and Colin Day [1988] JPL 268 ..... 6.38
Webber v Minister of Housing and Local Government (1967) 19 P & CR 1 .... 6.147
Welton v North Cornwall DC (CA, 17 July 1996) 15.54
Welwyn Hatfield Council v Secretary of State for Communities and Local
   Government [2011] UKSC 15; [2011] 2 AC 304 .... 20.29, 20.31–20.32

xlvi

Table of Cases

Wendy Fair Markets Ltd v Secretary of State for Communities and Local Government
[1996] JPL 649 .... 20.101
Wessex Regional Health Authority v Salisbury DC [1984] JPL 344 .... 15.18
West Bowers Farm Products v Essex CC (1985) P & CR 368 (CA) 5.06, 5.07
West Midlands Probation Committee v Secretary of State for the Environment
[1998] JPL 388 (CA)... 11.104
Western Fish Products Ltd v Penwith DC (1979) 38 P & CR 7 .... 11.16, 11.19
Westminster Bank Ltd v Minister of Housing and Local Government [1971] AC 508 ..... 11.49
Westminster City Council v British Waterways Board
[1985] AC 676 .... 6.141, 11.96–11.97, 11.100
Westminster City Council v Great Portland Estates plc [1985] AC 661 .... 11.113, 11.115
Westminster City Council v Jones [1981] JPL 750 .... 20.154
Westminster City Council v Secretary of State for Communities and Local
Government [2015] EWCA Civ 482....................................... 6.114
Westminster City Council v Secretary of State for the Environment and Aboro
[1983] JPL 602 .... 20.59
Westminster Renslade Ltd v Secretary of State for the Environment [1983] JPL 454 ...... 17.08
Wheeler v JJ Saunders Ltd [1995] JPL 619....................................... 15.48
White v Herefordshire Council [2007] EWCA Civ 1207 .... 27.30
White v Secretary of State for the Environment (1989) 58 P & CR 281 (CA) 6.161
Wiggins v Secretary of State for the Environment, Transport, and the Regions and
Slough BC [2001] PLCR 365 .... 15.39
William Blossom v Derbyshire CC [2011] EWHC 2566 (Admin); [2012] JPL 443 .... 12.15
William Davis Ltd v Charnwood Borough Council [2017] EWHC 3006 (Admin);
[2017] JPL 549 .... 4.28
William Walton v Scottish Ministers [2012] UKSC 44; [2012] PTSR 51................ 26.23
Williams v Minister of Housing and Local Government
(1967) 18 P & CR 514.................................. 6.36, 6.122, 6.126–6.127
Wilson v West Sussex CC [1963] 2 QB 764 .... 15.04
Wimpey Homes Holdings Ltd v Secretary of State [1993] JPL 919.................... 17.29
Windsor & Maidenhead RBC v Brandrose Investments Ltd [1983] 1 WLR 509 .... 17.13
Windsor and Maidenhead RBC v Secretary of State for the Environment
[1988] JPL 410 .... 21.07
Winfield v Secretary of State for Communities and Local Government
[2012] EWCA Civ 1415; [2013] 1 WLR 948 .... 24.15
Wingrove v Stratford on Avon District Council [2015] EWHC 287 (Admin);
[2015] PTSR 708 .... 10.22
Winterburn v Bennett [2016] EWCA Civ 482; [2017] 1 WLR 646.................... 29.22
Winters v Secretary of State for Communities and Local Government
[2017] EWHC 357 (Admin); [2017] PTSR 568.................................. 7.17
Winton v Secretary of State for the Environment [1984] JPL 188..................... 6.168
Wipperman v Barking LBC (1965) 17 P & CR 225................... 6.132, 6.151, 6.153
Wivenhoe Port Ltd v Colchester BC [1985] JPL 396 .... 15.11
Wood-Robinson v Secretary of State for the Environment and Wandsworth LBC
[1998] JPL 976... 11.76
Wycombe DC v Williams [1995] 3 PLR 19 .... 14.105

Young v Secretary of State for the Environment [1983] JPL 677 (CA) 20.168

Zurich Assurance Ltd v Westminster City Council [2014] EWHC 758 (Admin) 4.53

PRIVY COUNCIL

Beau Songe Developments Ltd v United Basalt Products Ltd [2018] UKPC 1 .... 4.85

TABLE OF LEGISLATION AND OTHER INSTRUMENTS

TABLE OF STATUTES

Acquisition of Land Act 1981 ....18.67, 28.05
Administration of Justice Act 1969
   s 12 ....18.129
Agricultural Land (Removal of Surface
   Soil) Act 1953 ....20.01
Airports Act 1986............ 18.67, 28.05
Ancient Monuments and Archaeological
   Areas Act 1979 .... 15.09,
                     22.02, 22.08–22.20
   s 1 ....21.21–21.22, 22.02
   s 2 ....22.03
   s 3 ....22.04
   s 5(1) 22.05
   s 12 ....22.10
   s 33 ....22.11
   s 35 ....22.11
   s 42(4) 22.12
   s 61(7) 22.01
Anti-Social Behaviour Act 2003
   s 43 ....24.33
   Pt 8 ....25.35
Caravan Sites and Control of
   Development Act 1960 ....10.03
Civil Aviation Act 1982 .... 18.67, 28.05
Commons Act 1876
   s 29 .... 29.01, 29.44
Commons Act 2006 .....29.01, 29.06, 29.26
   s 15 .... 29.07, 29.09–29.11,
                  29.13–29.14, 29.35
   s 15(4) 29.10
   s 15A 29.12
   s 15A(2) 29.12
   s 15C 29.13
   s 19 ....29.46
   Sch 1A 29.13–29.14
   Sch 1B 29.13–29.14
Commons Registration Act 1965 ..... 29.01,
                        29.03, 29.33
   s 10 ....29.41
   s 14 ....29.46
   s 22 ....29.30
Compensation Act 1973
   s 19(3) 19.18

Control of Pollution Act 1974 ....11.146
Countryside and Rights of Way
   Act 2000 .... 29.06, 29.33
Criminal Justice and Courts Act 2015 ....4.68,
                       18.123, 18.129
Development Land Tax Act 1976 ....1.16
Enterprise and Regulation Reform
   Act 2013 .... 1.30, 21.08, 21.27, 21.149
   s 60(2) 21.150
   s 60(3) 21.151
   s 61 ....21.152
Environment Act 1995 ... 1.23, 2.67, 11.154,
                   18.13, 23.21–23.22
   s 63 ....2.68
   s 96 .... 23.01, 23.15
   s 97 ....25.20
   Sch 13 .... 23.09, 23.15, 23.16, 23.18, 23.24
   Sch 13, para 9(1) 23.25
   Sch 14 ....23.15, 23.20, 23.24
   Sch 14, para 6(1) 23.25
Environmental Protection
   Act 1990 .... 11.146–11.147
Equality Act 2010
   s 149 ....11.51
   s 149(1) 11.51
European Communities Act 1972 .....12.03
   s 2(2) 23.24
European Union (Withdrawal
   Act) 2018 ....12.03, 13.03, 26.02
Forestry Act 1967 ....25.04
   s 15 ....25.05
   s 198 ....25.05
General Rate Act 1967 .... 21.28, 21.27
Government of Wales Act 1998 ... 1.23, 2.06
Government of Wales Act 2006 ... 2.06, 4.91
Greater London Authority
   Act 1999 .... 1.23, 2.98
Greater London Authority Act 2007 ....2.98
Growth and Infrastructure
   Act 2013 ....1.28–1.29, 7.59, 17.36,
                       29.06, 29.11
   s 1 ....2.19, 2.54, 10.01
   s 2 ....18.92
   s 4(1) 7.02

Growth and Infrastructure Act 2013 (*cont.*)
  s 6 ....7.57
  s 7 ....17.36
  s 10 ....23.20
  s 16 ....29.13
  s 16(4) 29.14
  s 16(5) 29.14
  s 26 ....28.15
  s 35 ....28.15
  s 60 ....7.02
  s 61B(7A) 7.57
  Sch 3 ....23.20
Highways Act 1980 ....5.68
  s 278 ....15.42–15.46, 17.59
Historic Buildings and Ancient
  Monuments Act 1953
  Pt I 21.133
Housing Act 1957 ....18.19
Housing Act 1985
  s 12(1) 29.26
Housing Act 1988
  s 62 ....2.88
  s 67 ....2.88
Housing Act 2004 ....6.82
Housing and Planning Act 1986 ...2.81,
                            6.87, 21.52
Housing and Planning Act 2016 ...1.32, 4.40,
                            4.59, 7.67, 9.25
  ss 203–206 ....15.41
Housing and Regeneration Act 2008 ....2.77
Housing, Town Planning etc Acts
  of 1909–1925 ....27.02
Housing, Town Planning etc
  Act 1909 .... 1.06, 1.09
  s 54 .... 1.02, 1.03
Housing, Town Planning etc
  Act 1919 ....1.03
Human Rights Act 1998 ....1.23, 2.29,
           11.119, 19.01–19.02, 19.12,
           19.13, 19.22, 20.132, 20.165
  s 1 ....7.61
  s 6 ....20.165
  s 6(1) 19.01
Inclosure Act 1857
  s 12 .... 29.01, 29.44
Land Commission Act 1967 ....1.16
Land Compensation Act 1961 ....4.84
  s 5 ....27.10, 27.15, 27.38
  s 31 ....27.36
Law of Property Act 1925
  s 84 ....17.32
  s 193 ....29.24
Law of Property (Miscellaneous Provisions)
  Act 1989
  s 2 ....17.30

Leasehold Reform, Housing and Urban
  Development Act 1993
  Pt III 2.75
  s 170 ....2.75
Legal Aid, Sentencing and Punishment
  of Offenders Act 2012 .... 20.113,
                         20.129, 25.08
Licensing Act 1964...............11.157
Local Democracy Economic Development
  and Construction Act 2009 ....3.34, 4.01
  s 70 ....3.32
Local Government Act 1972
  s 101 .... 11.01, 16.25
  s 111 .... 29.38–29.39
  s 122 ....20.153, 29.25, 29.43
  s 250(5) 18.79, 18.90
Local Government Act 1974 .... 18.131,
                         18.134, 18.137
Local Government Act 1985 ... 3.04, 3.14–3.15
Local Government Act 1992 ... 2.65, 3.04, 3.16
Local Government Act 2002
  Pt 3 ....16.29
Local Government Act 2003
  s 98 ....9.61
Local Government and Planning
  (Amendment) Act 1981 ....20.81
Local Government, Planning and
  Land Act 1980 .... 2.72, 2.75
  Pt XVI 2.70
  s 149 ....2.71–2.72, 11.53
  s 179 ....2.78
  Sch 32 .... 2.78–2.79
Local Land Charges Act 1975.........17.31
Localism Act 2011 .... 1.27, 2.94, 2.100,
           3.34–3.36, 4.01, 4.33, 4.60, 7.61,
           7.65, 17.71, 17.74, 18.68, 20.02,
                    24.35, 25.08, 28.07
  Ch 5 ....16.29
  s 25 ....16.29
  s 111 ....4.21
  s 112 ....4.56
  s 116 ....7.04
  s 122 ....9.63
  s 122(2) 9.63
  s 123 ....10.22, 20.73, 20.89
  s 124 ....20.32
  s 125 ....20.126
  s 127(1) 24.35
  s 128 ....28.19
  s 129 ....28.19
  s 130 ....28.13, 28.21, 28.23
  s 131 ....28.16
  s 138(8) 28.30
  s 140 ....28.32

Table of Legislation and Other Instruments

s 143 ....11.145	s 55 ....28.26
Sch 11 ....7.65	s 60 ....28.26
Sch 13 ....28.19	s 61 ....28.27
Sch 13 para 10(1) 28.25	s 65 ....28.27
London Local Authorities Act 1995 ....24.06	s 87 ....28.29
London Olympic Games and Paralympic	s 88 ....28.28
Games Act 2006 ....2.74	s 90 ....28.29
Minister of Town and Country Planning	s 91 ....28.29
Act 1943 ....2.03	s 92 ....28.17
Ministers of the Crown Act 1975 ....2.04	s 93 ....28.29
National Parks and Access to the	s 98 ....28.29
Countryside Act 1949	s 102 ....28.30
s 21 ....25.24	s 104(3) 28.20
Natural Environment and Rural	s 104(7) 28.20
Communities Act 2006	s 106 ....28.20, 28.30
s 40 ....26.19	s 114 ....29.13
s 78 ....26.20	s 115(1) 28.34, 28.36
Neighbourhood Planning	s 118 ....28.35
Act 2017 .... 1.33, 4.40, 4.43–4.44	s 120 ....28.17, 28.32
Norfolk and Suffolk Broads Act 1988 ....2.90	s 122 ....28.33
Open Spaces Act 1906	s 123 ....28.34
s 10 ....29.25	s 160 ....28.36
Parliamentary Commissioner	s 161 ....28.36
Act 1967 ....18.131, 18.134, 18.137	s 169 ....28.36
Pipelines Act 1962 ....28.15	s 182 ....4.48
Planning Act 2008 ....1.26, 1.29, 4.29, 7.12,	s 185 ....4.76
9.56, 10.13, 10.21, 15.52, 17.24,	s 190 ....10.63
17.64, 17.68, 17.72, 18.06, 18.39,	s 205 ....17.63
18.69, 18.75, 25.17, 28.13, 28.07	s 208(3), (4) 17.64
Pt I 28.24	s 209 ....17.64
s 5 .... 28.13, 28.20	s 211 ....17.66
s 5(5) 28.20	s 211(2) 17.66
s 6 .... 28.13, 28.22	s 212 ....17.67
s 6A 28.21	s 223 ....17.54
s 6A(3) 28.21	Sch 5 ....28.32
s 7 .... 28.13, 28.21	Planning and Compensation Act 1991 ...1.18,
s 8 .... 28.13, 28.21	1.22, 2.20, 2.94, 4.83, 5.08, 5.50–5.51,
s 9 .... 28.13, 28.23	5.69, 10.10, 10.26, 10.28, 11.33,
s 12 ....28.21	12.03, 12.55, 16.13, 16.15, 17.01,
s 12(3), (4) 28.21	18.83, 20.07, 20.13, 20.26, 20.33,
s 13(1) 28.13	20.58, 20.67, 20.101, 20.103,
s 14 ....28.15	20.113, 20.116, 20.118, 20.121,
ss 15–30 ....28.15	20.124, 20.127, 20.128, 20.140,
s 32 ....28.18	20.159, 20.169, 21.45, 21.46,
s 32(2) 28.18	21.82, 21.83–21.85, 21.92, 23.04,
s 32(3) 28.18	23.05, 23.06, 23.12–23.13,
s 33 .... 28.16, 28.18	23.20, 23.24, 24.24, 27.05
s 35 ....28.15	Pt I 20.03
s 35ZA 28.15	s 12 ....17.22
ss 42–44 ....28.24	s 14 ....5.70
s 47 ....28.24	s 15 ....12.03
s 48 ....29.13	s 22 .... 12.52, 12.54, 12.56,
s 49 ....28.24	16.04, 23.04, 23.05, 23.08
s 51 ....28.25	s 22(2) 23.05
Pt VI 28.26	s 22(3) 23.05

Planning and Compensation Act 1991 (cont.)
  s 24 .... 24.07
  s 25 .... 21.83
  s 26 .... 4.83
  Sch 2 .... 12.52, 16.04, 23.04, 23.05
  Sch 2, para 2(1)(a) 23.05
  Sch 2, para 2(1)(c) 23.05
  Sch 2, para 2(2) 23.05, 23.25
  Sch 2, para 2(4)(b) 23.05
  Sch 2, para 2(6) 23.10
  Sch 2, para 2(6)(b) 23.05
  Sch 2, para 3(2) 23.05
  Sch 3 .... 21.85, 21.86
Planning and Compulsory Purchase
  Act 1990 .... 2.86
Planning and Compulsory Purchase
  Act 1991 .... 3.26
Planning and Compulsory Purchase
  Act 2004 .... 1.23–1.24, 2.20, 2.72,
    2.86, 2.94, 3.04, 3.32–3.33, 4.01–4.02,
      4.22, 4.31, 4.51, 4.69, 4.79, 4.84,
      4.86–4.87, 5.35, 9.08, 9.11, 9.13, 9.53,
        10.08, 10.11, 10.14, 10.20, 12.62,
        14.81, 14.118, 14.120, 16.04, 17.62,
        20.02, 20.06, 21.62, 23.11, 24.24
  Pt 1 .... 4.87
  Pt 2 .... 4.12, 4.59, 4.65, 4.87
  s 13 .... 4.14
  s 13(1) 4.12
  s 13(2) 4.12
  s 13(3) 4.13
  s 14 .... 4.14
  s 14(3), (4) 4.15
  s 14A 9.26
  s 15 .... 4.17–4.18, 4.21
  s 17 .... 4.45
  s 17(1)(a) 4.25
  s 17(7) 29.13
  s 17(7)(a) 4.23
  s 18(3) 4.11
  s 18A 11.36
  s 19 .... 4.48
  s 19(2) 4.48
  s 19(3) 4.11, 4.29
  s 20 .... 4.49, 4.56
  s 21 .... 2.20, 4.59
  s 23 .... 4.56
  s 23(2) 29.13
  s 23(3) 29.13
  s 25 .... 4.62
  s 26 .... 4.63
  s 27 .... 4.59
  ss 28–31 .... 4.64
  s 33 .... 4.65
  s 33A 3.35, 4.16
  s 35 .... 4.66
  s 36 .... 4.66
  s 37(3) 4.26
  s 37(6) 11.34
  s 38 .... 2.98, 4.77, 4.87, 4.88
  s 38(2)(c) 4.34
  s 38(3) 4.45
  s 38(3A) 4.43
  s 38(6) 4.26, 4.34, 4.84, 4.89, 7.74,
      11.34–11.36, 11.38–11.40, 11.44,
      11.121, 14.89, 20.40, 21.70, 24.02
  s 38A 4.35, 29.13
  s 38A(3) 4.36, 29.13
  s 38B 4.37
  s 38C(5) 4.36, 7.66
  s 39 .... 4.04, 4.05
  s 40 .... 7.56
  s 42 .... 9.02
  s 43 .... 10.18
  ss 46–48 .... 17.61
  s 49 .... 5.35
  s 50 .... 10.09
  s 51 .... 14.83, 14.110
  s 52 .... 20.17
  s 54 .... 10.53
  s 55 .... 18.70
  ss 56–59 .... 18.73
  Pt 6 .... 4.90
  s 61C 7.60
  Pt 7 .... 16.02
  s 113 ... 4.67, 4.69, 4.72, 4.74–4.76, 18.129
  s 113(2) 4.70
  s 121 .... 4.87
  Sch A2 .... 4.44
  Sch 2 .... 18.70
  Sch 8 .... 4.79, 4.88, 29.13
  Sch 8, para 1(3) 4.89
Planning (Consequential Provisions)
  Act 1990 .... 1.21
Planning etc (Scotland) Act 2006 .... 2.05
Planning (Hazardous Substances)
  Act 1990 .... 1.21, 1.22, 9.05, 9.53,
                              16.02, 16.37
Planning (Listed Buildings and
  Conservation Areas) Act 1990 .... 1.21,
      2.31, 9.53, 9.56, 10.47, 11.35, 16.02,
      21.02, 21.08–21.09, 21.83, 21.91–21.92
  s 1 .... 5.48, 21.09, 21.22, 21.51
  s 1(4) 21.09
  s 1(5) 21.23–21.24, 21.27
  s 1(5)(a) 21.25, 21.29, 21.32
  s 3 .... 21.50, 21.113
  s 4 .... 21.50

Table of Legislation and Other Instruments

s 6	21.95
s 7	21.45, 21.50
s 8	21.50, 21.57
s 8(3)	21.73
s 9	21.45, 21.50–21.51, 21.116
s 10	21.60
s 10(3)	21.62
s 10(4)	21.61
s 13	21.67, 21.68
s 15	21.67
s 15(5)	21.65
s 16(1)	21.71
s 16(2)	21.58, 21.70
s 16(3)	21.71
s 17(1)	21.71
s 17(2)	21.60
s 17(3)	21.71
s 18(1), (2)	21.72
s 19	21.63
s 20(2)	21.70
s 20A	10.09
s 21	18.06
s 21(3)	21.76
s 26A	21.150
s 26B	21.150
s 26C	21.151
s 26D	21.151
s 29	21.117
ss 32–37	21.93
s 38	21.77
s 39(3)	21.83
s 43	21.116
s 47	21.50, 21.101
s 48	21.95, 21.105
s 49	21.107
s 50	21.108
s 54	21.50, 21.98
s 55	21.99
s 57	2.75
s 59	21.50
s 60(1)–(3)	21.52
s 60(1), (2)	21.50
s 60(5), (6)	21.52
s 61	21.22
s 65	21.84, 21.86
s 65(5)	21.86
s 65(3A)	21.84–21.85
s 66(1)	21.58
s 67	2.88, 10.43, 10.45
s 69	17.13, 21.130
s 71	21.133
s 72	21.133, 21.142
s 73	2.75, 2.88, 10.45, 21.143
s 74	21.50, 21.148
s 75	21.50
s 88	21.92
s 88A	21.92
s 89	18.79
s 91(1)	21.25
Planning (Wales) Act 2015	2.06, 4.91, 29.06
Political Parties, Elections, and Referendums Act 2000	24.12
Public Health Act 1875	
s 164	29.25
Race Relations Act 1976	
s 71(1)	11.52
Railways Act 1993	16.43
s 8	28.15
Rent Act 1968	14.10
s 2	14.10
Scotland Act 1998	1.23, 2.05
Self-Build and Custom Housebuilding Act 2015	1.31, 11.160
Senior Courts Act 1981	
s 16	20.101
s 31	18.118, 18.121, 18.123
s 31(2A)	18.123, 12.50
s 31(2A)(a)	18.123
s 31(2A)(b)	18.123
s 31(2B)	18.123
s 31(3D)	18.123
s 31(3E)	18.123
s 31(4)	18.123
s 31(6)	18.124
Town and Country Planning Act 1932	1.07, 27.02
s 34	17.01
Town and Country Planning Act 1947	1.04, 1.13–1.14, 1.16–1.19, 2.20, 3.04–3.05, 3.07–3.08, 6.118, 6.146, 11.33, 17.01, 23.03, 27.03
Town and Country Planning Act 1953	1.16
Town and Country Planning Act 1968	1.04, 3.04, 3.10, 3.11, 5.32–5.33, 20.43, 20.171, 27.28, 28.09
Town and Country Planning Act 1971	3.10, 3.11
s 22(2)(a)	7.30
s 22(2)(f)	6.169
s 29	11.56, 11.97
s 29(1)	11.97, 14.43
s 52	17.01–17.04, 17.07, 17.13, 17.16, 17.19, 17.21, 17.32, 17.39
s 209(1)	14.43
s 277	21.140
s 277(8)	21.134–21.138, 21.140
s 287	11.57

Town and Country Planning
Act 1990 . . . . 1.21–1.22, 1.24, 2.06,
2.13, 2.64, 2.90, 2.93–2.94, 2.98,
3.10–3.11, 3.24–3.26, 3.27, 3.28, 4.44,
4.79, 4.80, 5.03, 5.16, 5.26, 5.61, 5.63,
5.77, 6.01, 8.12, 8.19, 9.53, 9.56, 9.60,
10.14, 11.33, 12.02, 14.57, 14.61, 14.81,
16.02, 16.04, 16.06, 16.13, 17.01, 17.68,
18.06, 18.13, 18.39, 18.83, 18.93, 18.96,
20.05, 20.13, 20.16, 20.26, 20.32,
20.54, 20.58, 20.67, 20.117, 20.118,
20.121, 21.25, 23.01, 24.02, 24.06,
24.10, 24.24, 24.31, 26.09
s 1(4) 23.01
s 2 . . . . .2.67
s 2(2) 11.162
s 2A(2) 11.161
s 4A 2.68
s 6(1) 2.79
s 8 . . . . .2.89
s 8A 2.75
s 26H 21.152
Pt II 3.15, 4.83
s 31(6) 3.24
s 48 . . . . .21.112
s 51 . . . . .2.35
s 54 . . . . .21.112
s 54A 4.83, 4.84, 11.34,
11.35, 11.101, 18.141
Pt III 2.71, 2.75, 2.88, 5.59, 7.12,
7.59, 15.63, 20.97, 21.73, 24.37, 26.06
s 55 . . . . 5.02, 5.50, 5.67, 5.70, 5.76,
6.97, 8.10, 14.04, 21.03, 25.01, 28.18
s 55(1) 5.02, 5.08, 5.28, 5.31, 5.33,
5.38–5.39, 5.78–5.79, 6.96, 20.26
s 55(1A) 5.08, 5.12, 5.40
s 55(2)–(2B) 5.30
s 55(2)–(5) .5.08
s 55(2) 6.95, 20.27, 20.28
s 55(2)(a)–(c) 5.08, 5.51
s 55(2)(a)–(f) 6.53
s 55(2)(a) 5.30–5.33, 5.35, 6.23, 7.30
s 55(2)(b) 5.65–5.66
s 55(2)(c) 5.65
s 55(2)(d) 5.08, 6.10–6.11, 6.16,
6.18, 6.20–6.21, 6.22, 6.30, 6.33
s 55(2)(e) 5.08, 6.10, 6.33
s 55(2)(f) 2.13, 5.08, 6.10, 6.33, 6.87
s 55(2)(g) 5.08, 5.51, 21.121
s 55(2A), (2B) 5.08, 5.35
s 55(3) 5.08, 6.92
s 55(3)(a) 6.87, 6.92–6.93, 6.97
s 55(3)(b) 6.92, 6.98
s 55(3)(b)(i) 5.25
s 55(4) 5.08, 5.73, 23.01
s 55(4A) 5.08, 5.70
s 55(5) 5.08, 6.100, 6.102
s 56 . . . . 2.86, 14.90, 14.98, 14.103
s 56(4) 14.90, 14.93–14.94
s 57(1) 5.01, 7.01
s 57(2) 14.57
s 57(4) 20.168
s 58A 7.67, 9.25
s 59 . . . . 2.15, 21.151, 28.10, 29.13
s 59(3) 7.02
s 59A 7.67, 9.25, 21.151
s 60 . . . . 7.02, 21.151
s 60(1) 7.02
s 61A 7.56, 12.30, 21.151
s 61A(2) 29.13
ss 61B–61D 7.56, 21.151
s 61E 7.61
s 61F 4.35
s 61G 4.35
s 61K 4.37
s 61N(1)–(3) 4.42
s 61W 9.63
s 61X 9.63
s 61Y 9.63
s 62 . . . . .9.02, 9.07, 9.63
s 62(3) 9.07
ss 62A–62C 2.19
s 64 . . . . 5.44, 6.43, 11.18, 20.169
s 65 . . . . 9.33, 10.28, 18.09, 23.01
s 65(1) 29.13
s 65(6) 9.44
s 69 . . . . .9.64
s 70 . . . . 11.56, 11.97, 18.10, 29.13
s 70(1) . . . 11.27, 14.02, 14.07, 14.40, 14.43
s 70(2) . . . 4.80, 7.74, 11.31, 11.38, 11.40,
11.45, 11.54, 11.71, 11.101,
11.145, 17.16, 17.44
s 70(2)(aza) .4.40
s 70(2)(c) .11.45
s 70A 10.12, 10.17
s 70B 10.18
s 70C 10.22–10.25
s 71A 12.03
s 72(1) 18.10
s 72(1)(a) .14.37
s 72(1)(b) 14.49, 14.53
s 72(3) 14.58, 14.60
s 72(4) 14.60
s 73 . . . . .9.09, 10.39, 11.18, 11.24,
14.76–14.77, 14.80, 14.116, 14.118
s 73A . . . 8.20, 14.78–14.80, 14.86, 21.73
s 73(4) 14.116, 14.117
s 73(5) 14.118
s 74(1)(b) .10.56
s 74(1B) 2.99

s 75(1) 14.61, 15.67	s 106 . . . . .1.28, 5.59, 11.24, 11.133,
s 75(2) 5.03, 14.68	11.141, 12.62, 14.22, 15.09, 15.42,
s 75(3) 5.04, 14.68	17.01–17.03, 17.21–17.22, 17.25–17.26,
s 76A 10.13, 10.19	17.29, 17.30–17.31, 17.39, 17.42,
s 77 . . . . 2.24, 2.26, 2.32, 9.65, 10.13,	17.54, 17.56–17.57, 17.59,
12.27, 16.08, 18.96, 19.08	18.141–18.142, 22.17, 26.09
s 78 . . . . 2.21, 7.71, 8.06, 9.17, 9.41,	s 106A . . . 17.01, 17.22–17.23, 17.33, 17.35
10.02, 10.05, 10.19, 11.162, 12.27,	s 106B 17.01, 17.22–17.23, 17.37
18.02–18.04, 18.06, 18.12, 18.21,	ss 106BA–106BC 17.36
18.50, 18.94, 18.96, 19.08, 21.75	s 107 . . . . .2.44, 2.49, 7.11, 15.63,
s 78(2) 10.13	27.08, 27.11
s 78A 10.08	s 108 . . . . .7.11, 27.11–27.12
s 79 . . . . .11.13, 18.01, 19.08	s 114 . . . . 27.04, 27.06
s 79(1) 11.162	s 115 . . . . 15.63, 27.14
s 79(1)(b) 15.27	s 116 . . . . .23.01
s 79(2) 18.12	Pt V 27.04
s 79(3) 18.12	Pt VI 4.84, 21.93
s 79(6) 18.10	ss 137–140 . . . . .27.16
s 79(6A) 18.11	s 141 . . . . 18.96, 27.16
s 80 . . . . .11.13	s 142 . . . . 27.16, 27.29
s 81 . . . . .11.13	s 143 . . . . 27.16, 27.34
s 82 . . . . .2.79, 2.81, 11.13	s 143(8) 27.36
s 83 . . . . 2.81, 11.13	ss 144–148 . . . . .27.16
s 84 . . . . 2.81, 11.13	Pt VII 20.01, 20.03, 20.75, 20.189
s 85 . . . . .2.81, 2.86, 11.13	s 171A 20.66, 20.138
s 86 . . . . 2.81, 11.13	s 171A(1) 20.25, 20.56
s 87 . . . . 2.81, 11.13	s 171A(2) 20.25
s 87(1) 21.132	s 171B 20.31, 20.33, 20.66
ss 88–90 . . . . .11.13	s 171B(2) 20.30
s 90(1) 16.09, 16.10	s 171B(4) 20.38, 20.39
s 90(2A) 16.47, 16.49–16.50, 29.13	s 171B(4)(b) .20.36
s 91 . . . . .11.13, 14.60,	s 171C 20.07, 20.66, 20.121
14.82, 14.115, 14.119, 15.63	s 171C(1) 20.07
s 92 . . . . 11.13, 14.60, 14.115,	s 171C(2) 20.07
14.118, 14.119, 15.63	s 171C(3) 20.07
s 92(2) 14.110	s 171C(4) 20.10
s 93 . . . . 11.13, 14.60	s 171C(5) 20.08
s 93(4) 14.88	s 171D 20.07, 20.66
s 94 . . . . . .2.23, 2.86, 11.13, 14.60, 14.120	s 171D(1) 20.09
s 95 . . . . .11.13, 14.60, 18.96	s 171D(3) 20.09
s 95(4) 14.121	s 171E. 20.17, 20.66
s 95(5) 14.121, 14.123, 14.124	s 171E(3)(c) .20.17
s 96. . . . . .11.13	s 171F 20.17–20.18, 20.66
s 96A 10.63, 11.13	s 171G 20.17, 20.66
s 97 . . . . 2.23, 2.44, 2.49, 4.84, 11.13,	s 171H 20.17, 20.66
15.63, 18.96, 27.11, 27.40	s 172 . . . . .20.40, 20.66, 20.73
s 98. . . . . .11.13	s 172(1) 4.84
s 99. . . . . .11.13	s 172(2) 20.40–20.41,
s 100 . . . . . .2.35–2.36, 2.53, 11.13, 15.63	20.47, 20.48, 20.71
s 101 . . . . .28.09	s 172(3) 20.49, 20.51, 20.54
s 101(4) 11.09	s 172A 20.126
s 102 . . . . .2.23, 4.84, 6.01, 11.50,	s 173. . . . . .20.66
18.96, 27.40	s 173(1) 20.56
s 104 . . . . 2.35–2.36	s 173(2) 20.58
s 105 . . . . .23.01	s 173(3), (4) .20.60

lv

Table of Legislation and Other Instruments

Town and Country Planning Act 1990 (*cont.*)
- s 173(5) 20.60
- s 173(8) 20.50
- s 173(9) 20.65, 20.73
- s 173(11) 20.62
- s 173A...........................20.66
- s 173A(1) 20.68
- s 174 ....2.22, 18.06, 20.41, 20.66, 20.73, 20.82, 20.88, 20.91, 20.102, 20.150
- s 174(1) 20.70, 20.71
- s 174(2) 14.63, 20.73, 20.75, 20.76
- s 174(2)(a)–(d) 20.39
- s 174(2)(a) 20.89, 20.105
- s 174(2)(b) 20.105
- s 174(2)(c) 20.87, 20.105
- s 174(2)(d) 20.87, 20.105, 20.177
- s 174(2)(e) 20.87, 20.105
- s 174(3) 20.79
- s 174(4) 20.82, 20.83
- s 174(5) 20.82, 20.83
- s 175.............................20.66
- s 175(1) 20.82
- s 175(4) 21.83
- s 175(1)(a), (b) 20.83
- s 175(1)(d) 20.83
- s 175(3) 20.86
- s 175(4) 20.55, 20.102
- s 176.............................20.66
- s 176(1) 20.91, 20.94
- s 176(3) 20.83
- s 176(5) 20.43
- s 177 .... 18.96, 20.66, 20.88, 20.90
- s 177(5) 9.55, 20.89
- s 178 .... 19.21, 20.124
- s 178(1) 20.46
- s 178(4) 20.125
- s 179 ....20.126–20.127, 20.159
- s 179(3) 20.77
- s 179(5) 20.131
- s 179(6)–(8) 20.44–20.46
- s 180 .... 20.135–20.137
- s 181(1) 20.133, 20.136
- s 181(2) 20.97
- s 183 ....20.111
- s 183(1) 20.111
- s 183(2) 20.111
- s 183(4) 20.115
- s 183(5) 20.117
- s 183(6) 20.115
- s 186 ....14.96
- s 186(2) 20.120
- s 186(5) 20.121
- s 187 ....20.114
- s 187(1) 20.113
- s 187A 20.140–20.141, 20.159
- s 187A(1), (2) 20.141
- s 187A(7) 20.143
- s 187A(11) 20.148
- s 187B 19.13, 20.159, 20.160, 20.163, 20.165–20.166
- s 188 ....20.128
- s 191 ...... 2.23, 8.02, 8.04, 8.07, 11.20, 20.23, 20.169, 20.88, 21.152
- s 191(1) 20.173
- s 191(2) 20.174
- s 191(3) 20.174–20.175
- s 191(4) 20.175–20.176
- s 191(5) 20.178
- s 191(6) 20.178
- s 192 .... 2.23, 5.24, 8.02–8.04, 8.07–8.09, 8.12–8.13, 11.18, 11.20, 20.169, 20.189, 21.152, 25.17
- s 192(2)–(6) 25.17
- s 192(7) 25.17
- s 193 ....8.04, 20.169, 25.17
- s 194.............................20.169
- s 195 ....18.06, 18.96, 20.169
- s 196.............................20.169
- s 196A 20.13–20.14, 20.16
- s 196B 20.13, 20.16
- s 196B(1) 20.15
- s 196C 20.13, 20.16
- s 196D 21.136
- s 197 ....25.01
- s 198 .... 18.96, 25.02
- s 200 ....25.05
- s 201 ....25.13
- s 202A 25.17–25.18
- ss 202B–202G 25.17
- s 206 .... 25.05, 25.08
- s 206(1) 25.08
- s 206(4) 25.08
- s 206(4C), (4D) 25.08
- s 208 ....2.23
- s 211 ....21.146
- s 220 ....2.23, 24.01, 24.06
- s 221 .... 24.01, 24.25
- s 221(5) 18.96
- s 222 .... 6.101, 24.01, 24.37
- s 223.............................24.01
- s 224 ....24.01, 24.04, 24.06
- s 224(3) 24.04
- s 224(5) 24.32
- s 225 ....24.01, 24.06, 24.33
- s 225(3)–(5) 24.06
- s 225A 24.35
- s 225C 24.35

Table of Legislation and Other Instruments

s 225E 24.35
s 225F 24.36
s 226 . . . . .4.84
s 228 . . . . .17.49
s 237 . . . . 15.41, 15.43–15.44
s 237(1) 15.41
s 237(4) 15.41
s 247 . . . . .15.40
s 247(1) 14.43
s 257 . . . . .15.39
s 262(1) 16.05
s 263 . . . . .16.08
s 278 . . . . .9.65
s 284 . . . . 4.69, 27.31
s 284(1) 18.94
s 285 . . . . .20.44–20.46, 20.130
s 285(1) 20.75
s 287 . . . . .4.76
s 288 . . . . .8.06, 9.11, 11.70, 11.86,
12.48, 18.29, 18.94, 18.96,
18.98–18.100, 18.116–18.118,
18.129, 20.101, 25.13, 27.31
s 288(1) 18.95
s 288(4B) 18.97
s 288(4C) .18.129
s 288(5) 18.113
s 288(9) 18.100
s 289 . . . . 6.07, 20.100, 18.102,
18.129, 20.101
s 289(6) 20.101
s 289(4A) 20.55, 20.103
s 293A 29.13
s 303 . . . . .9.50
s 303(2) 9.55
s 316 . . . . .16.11
s 316(6) 16.12
s 319A 18.39
s 319A(6) 18.12
s 320(2) 18.79
s 324 . . . . .20.07
s 327A 9.11
s 330 . . . . 20.07, 20.121
s 333 . . . . .2.12
s 336 . . . . .5.25
s 336(1) 5.02–5.03, 5.14, 5.31, 5.41,
5.46, 5.50, 5.61, 5.68, 5.72, 6.35,
6.45–6.46, 20.41, 21.23, 24.07, 24.10
Sch 1 . . . . 12.03, 23.01
Sch 1, para 1 .2.95
Sch 1, para 7(1) 10.51
Sch 2 . . . . .12.03
Sch 3 . . . . .21.107, 27.38–27.39
Sch 3, para 1 . . . 14.91, 27.10, 27.20, 27.39

Sch 3, para 2 . . . 14.91, 27.10, 27.20, 27.39
Sch 4A, para 1 . . . . .29.13
Sch 4B 4.36, 7.66
Sch 4B, para 4(1) 29.13
Sch 4B, paras 7–10 . . . . .4.38
Sch 4B, para 12 . . . . .4.40
Sch 4B, para 13 . . . . .4.40
Sch 4B, para 13B 4.40
Sch 4C 7.65
Sch 5, para 1 . . . . 15.63, 23.01
Sch 5, para 2 . . . . .23.01
Sch 5, paras 3–6 . . . . .23.01
Sch 6 . . . . .18.79
Sch 6, para 3(1) 18.16
Sch 8 . . . . .25.17
Sch 9, para 1 . . . . .18.96
Sch 9, para 3 . . . . 18.96, 23.01
Sch 9, para 4 . . . . 18.96, 23.01
Sch 9, para 5 . . . . .23.01
Sch 9, para 6 . . . . 18.96, 23.01
Sch 9, paras 7–10 . . . . .23.01
Town and Country Planning
    Act 2004 .25.16
s 27 . . . . .29.13
s 54 . . . . .29.13
Town and Country Planning (Minerals)
    Act 1981 . . . . . . 5.73–5.74, 23.01–23.02,
23.12–23.14, 23.16
Town and Country Planning
    (Scotland) Act 1972
s 26(1) 14.43
s 198(1) 14.42–14.43
Town and Country Planning (Scotland)
    Act 1992 .10.14
Transport and Works Act 1992 . . . .16.49, 18.128
Pt I 16.33, 28.11
s 1 . . . . 16.34, 16.47
s 2 . . . . .16.34
s 3 . . . . 16.35, 16.47
s 5 . . . . .16.36
s 6 . . . . .29.13
s 7 . . . . .16.38
s 9 . . . . 16.40, 16.42, 16.46, 29.12
s 10 . . . . .16.39
s 11 . . . . .16.39
Sch 1 . . . . .16.36
Tribunals and Inquiries Act 1992 . . . . .18.100
s 9 . . . . .18.21
Water Resources Act 1991 . . . . 11.146, 12.08
Wildlife and Countryside Act 1981
s 28 . . . . 2.82, 25.24
s 29 . . . . .2.82
s 41(3) 7.20

lvii

TABLE OF STATUTORY INSTRUMENTS

Ancient Monuments (Class Consents) Order 1994, SI 1994/1381 ....22.04
Civil Procedure Rules 1998, SI 1998/3132 .... 18.90, 18.127
  Pt 8 ....18.116
  PD 8C 18.116
  Pt 54 ....18.118, 18.121, 18.124
  r 54.5 ....18.126
  r 54.5(5) 18.119
  r 54.12(7) 18.119
  Section II 18.127
  r 54.22(2) 18.128
Commons (Registration of Town of Village Greens) (Interim Arrangements) (England) Regulations 2007, SI 2007/457
  reg 6(4) 29.37
Commons Registration (England) Regulations 2014, SI 2014/3038
  reg 36(3)(a) 29.40
Community Infrastructure Levy Regulations 2010, SI 2010/948 ....17.63, 17.69–17.70, 17.77
  reg 40 ....17.79
  reg 67 ....17.79
  reg 122 ....17.55
  reg 122(2) 17.54
Community Infrastructure Levy (Amendment) (England) Regulations 2019 ....17.81
Conservation of Habitats and Species Regulations 2017, SI 2017/1012 ....26.02, 26.19, 26.21, 26.24
  reg 9(3) 26.20, 26.22
  reg 43 ....26.20
  reg 63 ....26.03, 26.14, 26.16
  reg 64 ....26.05
  reg 70 ....26.06
  reg 71 ....26.07
  reg 72 ....26.09
  reg 75 ....26.10
  reg 75(a) 26.11
  reg 76 ....26.11
  reg 77 .... 26.10–26.11
  regs 80–83 ....26.12
Conservation (Natural Habitats etc) Regulations 1994, SI 1994/2716
  reg 48 ....26.17
Control of Advertisement Regulations 1992, SI 1992/662 .... 24.05, 24.31
Ecclesiastical Exemption (Listed Buildings and Conservation Areas) Order 1994, SI 1994/1771 ....21.54
Ecclesiastical Exemption (Listed Buildings and Conservation Areas) Order 2010, SI 2010/1176 ....21.55
Environmental Assessment of Certain Plans and Programmes Regulations 2004, SI 2004/1633 ....4.27, 13.03, 13.06, 13.09, 13.16, 13.19
  reg 4 ....13.18
  Pt 2 ....13.23
  reg 5 ....13.13
  reg 5(1)–(3) 13.05
  reg 8 ....13.07, 13.19, 13.22
  reg 9 ....13.11
  reg 9(1) 13.12
  reg 10 ....13.12
  Pt 3 ....13.13–13.14, 13.16
  reg 12 .... 4.75, 13.22
  reg 12(2) 13.14
  reg 12(3) 13.14–13.15
  Pt 4 ....13.20
  reg 17 ....13.15
  Sch 1 ....13.11
  Sch 2, paras 1–10 ....13.15
Environmental Assessments and Miscellaneous Planning (Amendment) (EU Exit) Regulations 2018, SI 2018/1232 .... 12.03, 13.03
Environmental Impact Assessment (Mineral Permissions and Amendment) (England) Regulations 2008, SI 2008/1556 ....23.29
Environmental Information Regulations 2004, SI 2004/3391 ....12.34
Environmental Permitting (England and Wales) Regulations 2010, SI 2010/675 ...... 12.08
  reg 5(2)(b), (c) 12.08
  reg 5(4) 12.08
  Pt 2 ....12.08
Hedgerows Regulations 1997, SI 1997/1160 ....25.20
  reg 3 ....25.23
  reg 5(6) 25.30
  regs 7–16 ....25.33
  Sch 1, Part II 25.32
  Sch 4 ....25.26
High Hedges (Appeals) (England) Regulations 2005, SI 2005/711 .... 25.39
Infrastructure Planning (Applications: Prescribed Forms and Procedure) Regulations 2009, SI 2009/2264 ... 28.24
Infrastructure Planning (Environmental Impact Assessment) Regulations 2017, SI 2017/572 ....28.24
  Pt IX 23.24

Table of Legislation and Other Instruments

Infrastructure Planning (Interested Parties and Miscellaneous Provisions) Regulations 2015, SI 2015/462 ...28.30
Neighbourhood Planning (General) Regulations 2012, SI 2012/637 ....4.36
Neighbourhood Planning (Prescribed Dates) Regulations 2012, SI 2012/2030 ...4.41
Neighbourhood Planning (Referendums) Regulations 2012, SI 2012/2031 ...4.41
Openness of Local Government Bodies Regulation 2014, SI 2014/2095
   reg 7 ....11.05
Planning (Listed Buildings) (Certificates of Lawfulness of Proposed Works) (England) Regulations 2014, SI 2014/552 ....21.152
Planning (Listed Buildings and Conservation) (Amendment) (England) Regulations 2015, SI 2015/809 ....10.43
Planning (Listed Buildings and Conservation Areas) (Heritage Partnership Agreements) (England) Regulations 2014, SI 2014/550 ...21.150
Planning (Listed Buildings and Conservation Areas) (Wales) Regulations 2012, SI 2012/793 ....21.08
Planning (Listed Buildings and Conservation Areas) Regulations 1990, SI 1990/1519 ......10.43, 21.08, 21.60, 21.72
   reg 5 ....21.143
   reg 5A 10.43
Planning (Local Listed Building) (Consent Orders) (Procedure) (England) Regulations 2014, SI 2014/551 ....21.151
Town and Country Planning (Appeals) (Written Representation Procedure) (England) Regulations 2000, SI 2000/1628 ....18.100
Town and Country Planning (Assessment of Environmental Effects) Regulations 1988, SI 1988/1199...8.08, 12.42, 12.58
Town and Country Planning (Assessment of Environmental Effects) Regulations 2011, SI 2011/139 ....11.154
Town and Country Planning (Brownfield Land Register) Regulations 2017, SI 2017/403 ....9.26
   Pt 2 ....9.27
   reg 3 ....7.68
   reg 4 ....9.29
   reg 14 ....9.29
Town and Country Planning (Compensation for Restrictions on Mineral Working and Mineral Waste Depositing) Regulations 1997, SI 1997/1111 ...23.01
Town and Country Planning (Consultation) (England) Direction 2009 ... 2.34, 10.56
Town and County Planning (Control of Advertisements) (England) Regulations 2007, SI 2007/783 ......18.100, 24.01, 24.03, 24.05, 24.33, 24.34, 24.37
   reg 1(3) 24.12
   reg 2(1) 24.21
   reg 3(1) 24.02
   reg 3(4) 24.02
   reg 4 ....24.12
   Pt 2 ....24.12
   reg 6 .... 24.15, 24.22
   reg 7 ....24.19
   reg 8 ....24.21
   Pt 3 ....24.12
   reg 14 ....24.22
   Pt 4 ....21.147
   reg 30 ....24.04
   Sch 1 ....24.12
   Sch 1, Classes A–I 24.12
   Sch 2 ....24.17
   Sch 3 ....24.15
   Sch 3, Classes 1–16 ....24.15
   Sch 3, Class 12 ....24.19
   Sch 3, Class 13 .... 24.19, 24.23
   Sch 3, Class 14 ....24.23
Town and Country Planning (Demolition—Description of Buildings) Direction 1995 ....5.62
Town and Country Planning (Demolition—Description of Buildings) Direction 2014 ....5.52
   para 2(1)(a)–(d) 5.55
   para 3(1)(b) 5.53
   para 3(2) 5.53
Town and Country Planning (Determination of Appeals by Appointed Persons) (Prescribed Classes) Regulations 1997, SI 1997/420 ....18.13
Town and Country Planning (Determination of Appeal Procedure) (Prescribed Period) (England) Regulations 2009, SI 2009/454 ...18.39
Town and Country Planning (Determination by Inspectors) (Inquiries Procedure) (England) Rules 2000, SI 2000/1625 ...... 18.37, 18.50–18.51, 18.57
   r 4(1) 18.53
   r 5(1) 18.53
   r 6(1) 18.53
   r 6 (3) 18.53

Town and Country Planning
(Determination by Inspectors)
(Inquiries Procedure) (England)
Rules 2000, SI 2000/1625 (*cont.*)
   r 6(5), (6) 18.53
   r 7 .... 18.53–18.54
   r 10 .... 18.54–18.55
   r 11(1), (2) 18.56
   r 12 ....18.56
   r 14 ....18.56
   r 15 ....18.56
   r 16 ....18.56
   r 17(1) 18.56
   r 17(2)(b) 18.56
   r 18 ....18.57
   r 19 ....18.57
Town and Country Planning (Development
   Management Procedure) Order 2010,
   SI 2010/2184 .... 10.16,
                     10.28, 10.33, 21.64
   art 2 .... 10.32, 10.35
   art 2(1) 10.31
   art 3 ....5.35
   art 10 ....10.63
   art 15 .... 10.28–10.29, 10.36, 10.40, 10.47
   art 15(2) 10.30, 10.47, 10.57
   art 15(4) 10.31, 10.36
   art 15(5) 10.34
   art 15(6) 10.37
   art 15(7) 10.35
   art 18 .... 10.41, 10.48, 21.126
   art 18(2) 10.42
   art 18(7) 10.38
   art 20 ....10.39
   art 22 ....10.53
   art 23 ....10.54
   art 24 ....10.46
   art 25 ....10.42
   art 32 ....10.56
   art 34 ....10.02
   Sch 1 ....10.02
   Sch 3 .... 10.30–10.31, 10.34
   Sch 4 .... 10.41, 10.48
   Sch 4 para (s) 21.129
   Sch 8 ....8.03
Town and Country Planning
   (Development Management
   Procedure) (England) Order 2015,
   SI 2015/595 .... 2.13, 2.33, 9.02,
         9.07, 9.16, 9.35, 9.38, 18.09, 21.64
   Pt 1 .... 9.65, 12.36
   art 2 ....9.14
   art 2(1) 9.15, 18.41
   Pt 2 ....9.65
   art 5 ....9.16

art 8 ....12.64
art 9 ....9.09
art 9(3) 9.09
art 10(3) 2.99
art 13 .... 9.33, 9.38
art 14 ....9.38
art 15 ....12.36
art 16 ....12.36
art 18 .... 12.34, 21.126
art 18(4) 2.32
art 20 ....14.119
art 31 .... 2.31–2.32
art 33(1)(b) 9.42
art 35 .... 11.08, 11.28
art 36 ....18.06
art 37 ....18.06
art 37(8) 18.41
art 40 ....9.65
Sch 2 ....9.34
Sch 3 ....12.36
Sch 4 .... 7.72, 12.34
Sch 4 para (s) 21.126
Town and Country Planning (Development
   Plan) (England) Regulations 1999,
   SI 1999/3280 .... 3.11, 3.24
Town and Country Planning (Development
   Plans) (England) Direction 1981 ... 10.58
Town and Country Planning (Development
   Plans and Consultation) (Departures)
   Direction 1999 ...... 10.56, 10.58–10.59
Town and Country Planning (Enforcement)
   (Inquiries Procedure) (England) Rules
   2002, SI 2002/2686 ..... 18.100, 20.86
Town and Country Planning (Enforcement
   Notices and Appeals) Regulations 2002,
   SI 2002/2682 .... 18.100, 20.83
   reg 4 ....20.66
Town and Country Planning (Environmental
   Impact Assessment) (Amendment)
   (England) Regulations 2008,
   SI 2008/2093 ....12.66
Town and Country Planning (Environmental
   Impact Assessment) (England)
   Regulations 2017, SI 2017/571 .... 5.67,
         12.01, 12.05–12.06, 12.16–12.17,
         12.42, 12.48, 12.50, 12.52, 12.58,
            12.60, 12.62, 12.66, 23.29
   reg 2(1) 12.05, 12.34, 12.38
   reg 3 .... 11.159, 12.38
   reg 4(2) 12.05
   reg 5(5)(a) 12.25
   reg 6 ....12.26
   reg 6(1) 12.24
   reg 15 .... 12.32, 23.31
   reg 16 ....23.31

Table of Legislation and Other Instruments

reg 18(3) 12.05
reg 18(3)(a)–(d) 12.05
reg 19 . . . . .12.34
reg 23 . . . . .12.35
reg 26(1) 12.38
reg 26(1)(a) .12.38
reg 29(2) 12.39
reg 30 . . . . 11.28, 12.40
reg 30(1)(d) 12.39
reg 35, 36 . . . . .12.41
reg 58 . . . . .12.39
Sch 1 . . . . 5.60, 5.67, 7.16, 7.56
Sch 2 . . . . . 5.60, 5.67, 7.16, 12.06, 12.08,
        12.26, 12.27, 12.28, 12.30–12.31,
        12.43, 12.46, 12.59–12.60, 12.65
Sch 3 . . . . 12.25, 12.59
para 3(h) 12.22
Sch 4, paras 1–8 . . . . .12.05
Town and Country Planning
    (Environmental Impact
    Assessment) (England and Wales)
    (Amendment) Regulations 2000,
    SI 2000/2867 . . . . 23.24, 23.27
Town and Country Planning
    (Environmental Impact
    Assessment) (England and
    Wales) Regulations 1999,
    SI 1999/293 . . . . . . 18.53, 23.24, 23.29,
                                    23.30–23.31
reg 10 . . . . .23.30
reg 11 . . . . .23.31
Town and Country Planning
    (Environmental Impact
    Assessment) (England and
    Wales) Regulations 2011,
    SI 2011/1824 . . . . . . .2.85, 12.21, 16.38
Sch 1 . . . . .12.06
paras 1–12 .12.08
para 13 . . . . .12.08
para 21 . . . . .12.08
Sch 2 . . . . 12.12–12.14
para 10(b) 12.13
Sch 3 . . . . .12.12
Sch 4 . . . . .12.05
Town and Country Planning
    (Environmental Impact
    Assessment) (Wales) Regulations
    2017, SI 2017/567 . . . . .12.01
Town and Country Planning (Fees for
    Applications, Deemed Applications
    and Site Visits) (England) Regulations
    2012, SI 2012/2920 . . . . .9.51
Town and Country Planning General
    Development Order 1977, SI 1977/289
    Class 1.3 . . . . .6.20
Town and Country Planning General
    Development Order 1988,
    SI 1988/1813
art 3(1) 8.10
Sch 2, Pt I, Class E 6.14
Sch 2, Pt IV, Class B 8.10
Town and Country Planning
    (General Development Procedure)
    Order 1995, SI 1995/419 . . . . 7.05,
                                    10.36, 18.53
art 2(3) 21.128
art 8(4)(a) 10.36
Sch 1, Class I(1) 7.29
Town and Country Planning (General
    Development Procedure)
    (Amendment) (England) Order
    2009, SI 2009/453 . . . . .14.119
Town and Country Planning (General
    Permitted Development) Order 1995,
    SI 1995/418 . . . . 7.41, 10.17, 10.39,
                            16.09, 16.10, 21.121
art 2(3) 21.145
art 4 . . . . .5.57, 6.50,
                        7.06–7.11, 7.45, 21.144
Sch 2, Pt 1 . . . . 7.26–7.27
Sch 2, Pt 1, Classes A–H 7.27
Sch 2, Pt 1, Class A 7.29
Sch 2, Pt 1, Class A1(a)–(h) 7.29
Sch 2, Pt 1, Class A2 . . . . .7.29
Sch 2, Pt 1, Class E 7.31
Sch 2, Pt 1, Class F 7.28
Sch 2, Pt 1, Class H 7.32
Sch 2, Pt 2, Class A 7.33–7.34
Sch 2, Pt 2, Class B 7.33–7.34
Sch 2, Pt 2, Class C 7.33
Sch 2, Pt 2, Class D 7.33
Sch 2, Pt 2, Class E 7.33
Sch 2, Pt 2, Class F 7.33
Sch 2, Pt 3, Classes A–V 7.36
Sch 2, Pt 3, Classes M–V 7.37
Sch 2, Pt 3, Class V, para W 7.37
Sch 2, Pt 4 . . . . 7.38, 7.44–7.46
Sch 2, Pt 4, Class A 7.38–7.39
Sch 2, Pt 4, Class B . 7.38, 7.40, 7.43, 7.46
Sch 2, Pt 4, Class C 7.38
Sch 2, Pt 4, Class CA 7.38
Sch 2, Pt 4, Class D 7.38
Sch 2, Pt 6 . . . . 7.47, 7.52
Sch 2, Pt 6, Class A 7.47–7.49, 7.51
Sch 2, Pt 6, Class A.1(c) 7.52
Sch 2, Pt 6, Class B 7.47–7.48, 7.51
Sch 2, Pt 6, Class C 7.47
Sch 2, Pt 6, Class D.1(1) 7.52
Sch 2, Pt 6, Class E 7.53
Sch 2, Pt 11, Class A 8.08

Town and Country Planning (General
  Permitted Development) Order 1995,
  SI 1995/418 (cont.)
  Sch 2, Pt 16 .... 7.54
  Sch 2, Pt 17, Class A 8.08
  Sch 2, Pt 31 .... 21.148
Town and Country Planning (General
  Permitted Development) (Amendment)
  (England) Order 2010,
  SI 2010/654 .... 7.10
Town and Country Planning (General
  Permitted Development) (Amendment)
  (England) Order 2013,
  SI 2013/1101 .... 21.148
Town and Country Planning (General
  Permitted Development Order)
  (England) Order 2015,
  SI 2015/596 ..... 2.13, 2.14, 5.56, 6.34,
        6.52, 7.05, 7.06, 7.13, 7.16–7.17,
        7.20–7.25, 12.30–12.31, 21.148
  art 2(3) 7.20
  art 3 .... 25.27
  art 3(1) 7.13
  art 3(4) 7.12–7.13
  art 3(5) 7.15
  art 4 .... 7.06
  art 4(1), (2) 7.09
  art 10(2)(1) 2.99
  Sch 2 .... 7.06
  Sch 2, Pts 1–19 .... 7.05
  Sch 2, Pt 1 .... 6.51, 7.06, 7.13, 7.23
  Sch 2, Pt 1, Class A 7.19, 7.23
  Sch 2, Pt 1, Class B 7.23
  Sch 2, Pt 2 .... 6.51
  Sch 2, Pt 3 .... 7.35
  Sch 2, Pt 3, Class R 7.17
  Sch 2, Pt 3, Class V, para W(3) 7.17
  Sch 2, Pt 6 .... 5.71, 6.46, 7.17
  Sch 2, Pt 9 .... 5.66, 5.67
  Sch 2, Pt 11, Class B 5.54
  Sch 2, Pt 17, Classes K, KA 7.06
  Sch 2, Pt 17, Class M 7.06
  Sch 2, Pt 31 .... 5.55–5.56
  Sch 3, para 1(13) 7.10
Town and Country Planning
  General Regulations 1976,
  SI 1976/1419 .... 16.11, 16.13
Town and Country Planning
  General Regulations 1992,
  SI 1992/1492 .... 16.11, 16.13
  regs 9, 10 .... 16.25
Town and Country Planning General
  (Amendment) Regulations 1998,
  SI 1998/2800 .... 16.25

Town and Country Planning (Green Belt)
  Direction 2005 .... 2.34
Town and Country Planning (Hearings
  Procedure) (England) Rules 2000,
  SI 2000/1626 .... 18.44
  r 12(1), (2) 18.44
Town and Country Planning (Inquiries
  Procedure) (England) Rules 2000,
  SI 2000/1624 .... 18.50, 18.59,
                18.100, 18.101, 18.103,
  r 17 .... 18.60
  r 17(5) 18.60
Town and Country Planning
  (Inquiries Procedure) Rules 1974,
  SI 1974/419 .... 18.103
Town and Country Planning (Local
  Development) (England)
  (Amendment) Regulations 2009,
  SI 2009/401 .... 4.19
Town and Country Planning (Local
  Planning) (England) Regulations 2012,
  SI 2012/767 .... 4.12, 4.19, 4.31
  reg 5 .... 4.24, 4.26
  reg 5(1)(a)(iv) 4.28
  reg 5(2) 4.25
  reg 9(1)(a) 4.47
  reg 10A 4.16
  Part 5 .... 4.29
  reg 19 .... 4.74
Town and Country Planning (Mayor of
  London) Order 2008, SI 2008/580 ... 2.99
Town and Country Planning (Permission
  in Principle) Order 2017,
  SI 2017/402
  art 5D 7.69
  art 5V 7.71
Town and Country Planning (Permission
  in Principle) Order 2017,
  SI 2017/1309 .... 9.27
  art 5B 9.29
Town and Country Planning (Playing Fields)
  (England) Direction 1998 .... 2.33
Town and Country Planning (Residential
  Development on Greenfield Land)
  (England) Direction 2000 .... 2.33
Town and Country Planning (Shopping
  Development) (England and Wales)
  (No 2) Direction 1993 .... 2.33
Town and Country Planning (Temporary
  Stop Notice) (England) (Revocation)
  Regulations 2013, SI 2013/830 ... 20.18
Town and Country Planning (Temporary
  Stop Notices) (England) Regulations
  2005, SI 2005/206 .... 20.18

Town and Country Planning (Timetable
 for Decisions) (England) Order 2005,
 SI 2005/205 . . . . .18.70
Town and Country Planning (Tree
 Preservation) (England) Regulations
 2012, SI 2012/605 . . . . .25.09
 Pt 6 . . . . .25.19
 reg 24(4) 25.19
Town and Country Planning (Trees)
 Regulations 1999,
 SI 1999/1892 . . . . .25.04
 Pt III 21.146
Town and Country Planning (Use Classes)
 Order 1987, SI 1987/764 . . . .2.13, 2.14,
  6.09, 6.54–6.56, 6.77, 6.91, 6.120–6.122,
  6.135, 6.136, 6.169, 7.35, 15.13, 15.15
 art 2 . . . . 6.73, 6.79
 art 2(3) 7.37
 art 3(1) 6.169
 art 3(6) 6.57, 6.79
 art 4 . . . . .6.87
 Sch. 6.54, 6.79
 Sch, Class A1 . . . . . . .2.46, 2.99, 6.62, 6.63,
  6.65, 6.78, 6.128, 7.36, 11.157, 15.69
 Sch, Class A1(a)–(k) 6.59
 Sch, Class A2 . . . . .2.99, 6.61,
  6.64–6.67, 6.72, 7.36, 15.69
 Sch, Class A2(a) 6.64
 Sch, Class A2(b) 6.64, 6.66
 Sch, Class A2(c) 6.64, 6.66
 Sch, Class A3 . . . . .2.99, 6.68,
  6.128, 7.36, 11.157, 15.69
 Sch, Class A4 . . . . .2.99, 6.69, 7.36
 Sch, Class A5 . . . . . . 2.99, 6.61, 6.70, 7.36
 Sch, Class B1 . . . . 2.99, 6.66, 6.72,
  6.74–6.76, 7.36
 Sch, Class B2 . . . . . . 2.99, 6.76–6.77, 7.36
 Sch, Classes B3–B7 . . . . .6.77
 Sch, Class B8 . . . . .2.99, 6.78, 7.36
 Sch, Class C1 . . . . 2.99, 6.79
 Sch, Class C2 . . . . .2.99, 6.80, 6.86
 Sch, Class C2A 6.81
 Sch, Class C3 . . . . .6.80, 6.82,
  6.84–6.85, 6.87, 7.36
 Sch, Class C3(a) 6.82–6.83
 Sch, Class C3(b) 6.86
 Sch, Class C4 . . . . . . 6.82–6.84, 6.86, 7.36
 Sch, Class D1 . . . . 2.99, 6.88
 Sch, Class D2 . . . . .2.99, 6.89, 7.36
 Sch, Class D2(b) 6.90
 Sch, Class D2(e) 6.90
Town and Country Planning (Use Classes)
 (Amendment) (England) Order 2010,
 SI 2010/653 . . . . .6.82

Town and Country Planning (Windscale and
 Calder Works) Special Development
 Order 1978, SI 1978/523 . . . . .2.17
Town and Country Planning (Written
 Representation Procedure) (England)
 Regulations 2009, SI 2009/452 . . . 18.40
 Pt 1 . . . . .18.41
 reg 2(1) 18.41
 Pt 2 . . . . .18.42
Transport and Works (Applications and
 Objections Procedure) (England and
 Wales) Rules 2006, SI 2006/1466 . . . 16.38
Transport and Works (Inquiry Procedure)
 Rules 1992, SI 1992/2817 . . . . . . .16.39

EU LEGISLATION

Directives

Directive 75/442/EEC on Waste
 Annex IIA 6.57
Directive 79/409/EEC on the
 Conservation of Wild Birds 13.15,
  26.01–26.02
Directive 85/337/EEC on the
 Assessment of the Effects of Certain
 Public and Private Projects on the
 Environment 12.48, 12.52, 12.56,
  13.01–13.02, 13.04, 23.08
 art 2(1) 12.45, 12.64
 art 4(2) 12.64
 Annex I 13.05, 13.13
 Annex II 13.05, 13.13
Directive 91/271/EEC on Urban
 Waste Water Treatment
 art 2, point (6) 12.07
Directive 91/689/EEC on
 Hazardous Waste 6.57
Directive 92/43/EC on the Conservation
 of Natural Habitats and of Wild
 Fauna and Flora . . . 13.14, 26.01, 26.02,
  26.20–26.21, 26.24
 art 6 . . . . 13.05, 13.13
 art 6(3) 26.15, 26.24
 art 6(4) 26.16
 art 7 . . . . 13.05, 13.13
 art 12 . . . . .26.19
 art 12(1) 26.19, 26.22
 art 16(1) 26.19
Directive 97/11/EC amending
 Directive 85/337/ EEC on the
 Assessment of the Effects of Certain
 Public and Private Projects on the
 Environment 13.05

Directive 97/62/EC adapting to Technical and Scientific Progress Directive 92/43/ EEC on the Conservation of Natural Habitats and of Wild Fauna and Flora .13.05
Directive 2001/42/EC on the Environmental Assessment of Plans and Programmes 4.30, 4.75, 13.01–13.02, 13.09, 13.10, 13.21
   art 3(2) 13.05
   art 5 . . . . .13.24
   art 5(1) 13.24
Directive 2008/98/EC on Waste and Repealing certain Directives
   Annex I 12.07
   art 3(2) 12.07
Directive 2009/31/EC on the Geological Storage of Carbon Dioxide 12.07–12.08

Directive 2011/92/EU on the Assessment of the Effects of Certain Public and Private Projects on the Environment. 12.01

INTERNATIONAL LEGISLATION

Aarhus Convention 1998 . . . . 12.26, 12.28, 12.40
European Convention on Human Rights 1950 . . . . 1.23, 19.03, 19.07, 19.11, 19.13, 19.19
   art 6 . . . . 19.01, 19.04, 19.10, 19.13, 19.15–19.18, 20.166
   art 6(1) 19.01, 19.04, 19.08
   art 8 . . . . 19.01, 19.05–19.06, 19.11–19.13, 20.165, 29.10
   art 8(1) 19.06
   art 14 . . . . .20.19
   First Protocol, art 1 . . . 19.01, 19.11–19.12, 20.166, 29.10

LIST OF ABBREVIATIONS

ASCs	areas of special control
CILs	Community Infrastructure Levies
CLEUD	Certificate of lawfulness of existing use or development
CLOPUD	Certificate of lawfulness of proposed use or development
DMPO	Development Management Procedure Order
EPS	European Protected Species
GPDO	General Permitted Development Order
HATs	Housing action trusts
IDOs	interim development orders
LDO	local development order
MPAs	mineral planning authorities
MPGs	Minerals Planning Guidance notes
NPPF	National Planning Policy Framework
NPS	national policy statement
PPGs	Planning Policy Guidance Notes
PPSs	Planning Policy Statements
ROMPs	Registration of Old Mining (or Mineral) Permissions
RPGs	regional planning guidance
SACs	Special Areas of Conservation
SPAs	Special Protection Areas
SPZs	Simplified planning zones
STOL	short take-off and landing
UCO	Use Classes Order
UDCs	urban development corporations
UDPs	unitary development plans

1

HISTORICAL INTRODUCTION

A. THE GROWTH OF PUBLIC CONTROL OVER LAND USE	1.01	C. THE LOCALISM ACT 2011 AND SUBSEQUENT REFORM		1.27
B. LATER LEGISLATIVE LANDMARKS	1.21			

A. THE GROWTH OF PUBLIC CONTROL OVER LAND USE

Before there existed any public control over the use and development of land, landowners were free to use land in any way they wished, subject only to any limitations in the grant under which they held the land and to obligations placed upon them at common law. In essence, therefore, provided an owner acted within the limitation of his estate or interest and committed no nuisance or trespass against his neighbour's property, he was free to use his land for the purpose for which it was economically best suited. Today, most societies require not only that this freedom be restricted for the public good, but also that the use to which land is put should be determined by the long-term interests of the community as a whole rather than as a consequence of the incidence and spread of individual land ownership. **1.01**

Although by as early as the middle of the 19th century, public health legislation in Great Britain had been passed to remedy the worst effects of insanitary housing conditions, it was not until 1909 that an attempt was made to deal with more general land use problems such as the separation of incompatible uses or the lack of amenity land. The Housing, Town Planning etc Act 1909 was primarily concerned with housing in that it gave wide powers to local authorities to build new houses and to clear existing substandard housing. Section 54 of that Act, however, gave local authorities the power to prepare schemes: **1.02**

> as respects any land which is in course of development or appears likely to be used for building purposes, with the general object of securing proper sanitary conditions,

amenity, and convenience in connection with the laying out and use of the land, and of any neighbouring lands.

Here was the beginning of planning law. Yet from the start it was plagued by a number of problems, many of which have recurred and remained unresolved to the present day.

1.03 Section 54 of the 1909 Act was discretionary in that local authorities were not required to prepare schemes, merely empowered to do so. The Housing, Town Planning etc Act 1919 attempted to remedy that defect by requiring the council of every borough or urban district with a population of over 20,000 to prepare schemes for land in the course of development or likely to be used for building purposes. Despite the fact that in 1919 Parliament set a time limit for the preparation of these schemes, the time limit had to be extended on a number of occasions as authorities found that the formidable task of preparing schemes could not be accomplished within the time set for so doing.

1.04 Although in 1919 the time taken to prepare schemes may have been exacerbated by the shortage of people possessing the necessary technical skills, the problem of delay has never been satisfactorily resolved. Under the Town and Country Planning Act 1947, local planning authorities were required within three years to submit to the Minister a development plan for their area. Most authorities found they were unable to do so within that period. Then, under the Town and Country Planning Act 1968, although no time limit was laid down for the submission of structure plans to the Secretary of State, it took some 14 years before the last structure plan was submitted to him for approval. Similar delay problems have applied with regard to the preparation, alteration, or replacement of all subsequent types of development plan.

1.05 Unfortunately for the planning process, development pressures often build up faster than planners can plan. Hence the more outdated a development plan may be, the less relevant it becomes to making decisions about the use and development of land and the greater the pressure on authorities to rely on other material considerations than the development plan and to make land use decisions on an individual and ad hoc basis.

1.06 Another problem with the 1909 Act was that before a scheme could be implemented it had to be approved by central government and an opportunity given to people to object to its provisions. The difficulty in this area has always been that democracy and speed rarely go hand in hand, and if the public are to be given the right to influence the content of the scheme or plan, the preparation and approval or adoption process is by that much delayed. Later legislation has continued to give the public the right to be consulted when a development plan is being prepared and to object to policies in the plan before its final adoption or approval.

1.07 The third problem to arise under early planning legislation came to be known as the compensation/betterment problem. Planning control can affect property values for better or worse, and the problem that needed to be solved was how to treat those whose land had either decreased in value (the compensation aspect), or increased in value (the betterment aspect) due to a scheme. The early legislation allowed local authorities to recover from owners 50 per cent of any increase in the value of land due to the making of a scheme. At the same time, it gave owners a right to receive compensation from the authority for any decrease in the value of their land. Under the Town and Country Planning Act 1932, the amount of betterment which a local authority could recover from owners was increased from 50 to 75 per cent. In addition, however, the owner was given the right to require payment to be deferred until he had actually realized the increased value through the sale of the land or its development. If this did not happen within five years as regards land zoned for industrial or commercial purposes, or 14 years in any other case, no betterment at all was payable.

1.08 The operation of these financial provisions proved disastrous. A local authority wishing to control the development of land in its area might find itself faced with a heavy liability for compensation which it would have difficulty in meeting unless it was also prepared to allow some development in the area. On the other hand, a local authority not wishing to restrict development in its area might hope to obtain a considerable sum by way of betterment from owners, without any liability to pay compensation. As it turned out, however, the collection of betterment proved to be almost impossible, mainly because of the lapsing provisions previously referred to.

1.09 The failure to deal satisfactorily with the financial consequences of land use planning meant the failure of land use planning itself. It has been estimated that after more than a quarter of a century of effort the number of schemes which were prepared and approved under the 1909 Act and subsequent legislation could be counted on the fingers of one hand!

1.10 The advent of the Second World War presented an opportunity to consider whether a more effective system for the control of land use could be found. The opportunity had been taken to set up a number of bodies charged with investigating particular facets of the land-use system. The three main reports produced by this exercise were the Barlow Report, the Scott Report, and the Uthwatt Report.

The Barlow Report This was the report of the Royal Commission on the Distribution of Industrial Population (Cmd 6153). Set up in 1937, it was to inquire into the causes of the geographical distribution of the industrial population, and to consider the social, economic, and strategic disadvantages resulting from the concentration of industry and industrial population in cities and regions. It was also to consider what methods should be taken to counteract them.

The report advocated the dispersal of industry from congested urban areas and the progressive redevelopment of those areas wherever necessary.

The Scott Report   This was a report of a Committee on Land Utilisation in Rural Areas (Cmd 6378). The Committee was asked to consider the problems of piecemeal development of agricultural land and the unrestricted development of the coastline.

The Uthwatt Report   This report, perhaps the most influential of the three, was by the Expert Committee on Compensation and Betterment (Cmd 6386) under the chairmanship of Uthwatt J. The main feature of this report was an examination of the problem of compensation and betterment. In so doing it identified the twin concepts of shifting value and floating value.

1.11 The idea behind the concept of shifting value was that planning control does not reduce the total sum of land values, but merely redistributes it by increasing the value of some land whilst decreasing the value of other land. Because of this it was possible for one authority to find itself paying compensation for restrictions on development, whilst a neighbouring authority could recover betterment because of those restrictions. The lesson to be learnt, therefore, was that financial arrangements to deal with the compensation/betterment problem could not be dealt with at a local level.

1.12 The idea behind the concept of floating values was that potential value is by nature speculative. Development may take place on land parcel A or parcel B. The prospect floats over both parcels. The value of any parcel of land is obtained by estimating whether the development is likely to take place on one parcel of land or on another. Where planning restrictions are imposed on land and owners are given the right to claim compensation for any loss so caused, they will tend to assume that but for those restrictions the floating value would settle on their land, rather than on the land of their neighbours. The result was that owners claiming compensation would tend to overestimate the prospect of the development taking place on their land, so that in total, all claims for compensation over an area could far exceed the actual loss of development value suffered.

1.13 All three reports contributed significantly to the system of land-use control established by the Town and Country Planning Act 1947. The Act came into effect on 1 July 1948. The essential features of that Act were as follows:

(a) It created local planning authorities and required each authority to prepare a development plan for its area indicating the manner in which it proposed land in its area should be used, whether by development or otherwise, and the ways in which any such development should be carried out.

(b) All land was made subject to planning control, not just land within a scheme prepared by the authority. As a result, apart from minor development, any person wishing to develop land had first to obtain express planning permission to do so

from the local planning authority. In deciding whether to grant or refuse permission, the authority was to be guided by the provisions of the development plan.
(c) Wide powers were given to local planning authorities to deal with development carried out without planning permission.
(d) Wide powers were given to local planning authorities to secure the preservation of trees and buildings of architectural or historic interest and to control the display of advertisements.
(e) If a person was granted planning permission for any development falling outside the existing use of his land, he had to pay a development charge to the state equal to the value of that permission.
(f) If a person was refused planning permission for such development, no compensation was paid for that refusal.
(g) To compensate landowners affected by (e) and (f) above who may perhaps have purchased their land before the Act came into force at a price reflecting its value for development, the Act set up a fund of £300 million. Any owner who could prove that his land had depreciated as a result of the 1947 Act could make a claim against the fund for the difference between the value of the land for existing use purposes and its value on the assumption the Act had not been passed. Payments from the fund were to be made in 1954.

1.14 It will be seen that the financial provisions of the Act ((e) to (g) above) attempted to solve the problems examined by the Uthwatt Committee. The sum of £300 million was an estimate of the total development value of land nationally, and claims against the fund were, if necessary, to be scaled down, so that in total they added up to that sum.

1.15 Furthermore, since the fund was administered by central government, local planning authorities were left free to make planning decisions without any regard to the economic or financial consequences of so doing.

1.16 Most of the financial provisions of the 1947 Act have now been dismantled. In particular, the Town and Country Planning Act 1953 abolished the development charge. Although further attempts were made by the Land Commission Act 1967 and the Development Land Tax Act 1976 to recoup for the community part of the development value of land which would otherwise accrue to the owner, no special tax on development value now exists, although an owner may be liable to pay capital gains tax on such value if he realizes a capital gain on the disposal of his land. One further point should be noted. Today, developers may be required to contribute to some of the external costs borne by the community as a result of their proposals, through the use of what is known as planning obligations and the new Community Infrastructure Levy.

1.17 It will be remembered that the 1947 legislation contained no provision for the payment of compensation to a landowner refused planning permission for development which fell outside the existing use of his land. When the development charge was abolished in 1953, it was decided to maintain that rule, so that in general since the 1947 Act no compensation has been payable for any loss incurred by the refusal of planning permission for such development, or indeed for the grant of planning permission made subject to conditions.

1.18 This general rule, however, was subject to one exception. An owner could claim compensation if he or his successors in title could show the existence of a claim made under the 1947 Act against the £300 million fund in respect of loss suffered as a result of the Act. In such rare cases, the compensation was limited to the amount of the claim or the amount of the loss due to the planning decision, whichever was less. Even this exception, however, has now been abolished. The Planning and Compensation Act 1991 repealed almost all existing statutory provisions providing for the payment of compensation for adverse planning decisions.

1.19 With regard to the non-financial provisions of the 1947 Act however, the elements of the system established at that time have withstood the passage of time. Although numerous changes and improvements have been made to the statutory provisions since that date, the basic scheme of the legislation remains the same.

1.20 Among the many changes made to this basic scheme since 1947 mention might be made of:

(a) a number of major reorganizations of local government, which have led to changes in the number and size of local planning authorities and their respective functions;
(b) a fundamental change to the development plan system;
(c) the progressive strengthening of the provisions for enforcing planning control, and of the provisions relating to the preservation of buildings of special architectural or historic interest;
(d) the introduction of environmental impact assessments in making decisions about major development proposals.

Yet despite the continued reverence of the law to the basic elements of the system as introduced in 1947, the law has become not only more complex, but also considerably more disparate in its application. Today, quite apart from the normal technicalities of the law and its procedures, a landowner wishing to develop his land may have additionally to consider such matters as: whether his land is within a simplified planning zone, a national park, an Area of Outstanding Natural Beauty, a conservation area, or a site of special scientific interest; what plan or plans constitute the development plan for the area; whether the development proposed is permitted under a special development order, a general development order, a local development order or a neighbourhood development order; whether the proposed development is subject to environmental impact assessment; and whether there is a building on the land of special architectural or historic interest, or a tree protected by a tree preservation order, or the land contains a scheduled monument.

B. LATER LEGISLATIVE LANDMARKS

Town and Country Planning legislation was first consolidated in 1962, and then again in 1971. However, this consolidation legislation continued to be subject to frequent amendment. So much so, that in 1989, the Government decided to ask the Law Commission to consolidate the legislation yet again. It was decided that the consolidation should involve four separate Acts of Parliament. Consolidation of legislation does not normally involve changes in the substance of the law. In this case, however, the opportunity was taken to correct a number of anomalies and inconsistencies of a technical nature. Subject to these changes however, the Acts restated the then existing law. The four Acts, which all received the Royal Assent on 24 May 1990, were: **1.21**

(a) the Town and Country Planning Act 1990. This Act consolidated certain enactments relating to town and country planning;
(b) the Planning (Listed Buildings and Conservation Areas) Act 1990. This Act consolidated certain enactments in relation to special controls in respect of buildings and areas of special architectural or historic interest;
(c) the Planning (Hazardous Substances) Act 1990. This Act consolidated certain enactments relating to special controls in respect of hazardous substances;
(d) the Planning (Consequential Provisions) Act 1990. This Act made provision for repeals, consequential amendments, transitional and transitory matters, and savings in connection with the consolidation of enactments in the Acts mentioned above.

With the exception of the Planning (Hazardous Substances) Act 1990, most of the provisions of the Acts came into force on 24 August 1990. Hereinafter, in this text, the main Act, the Town and Country Planning Act 1990, will often be referred to simply as 'the 1990 Act'. **1.22**

These reforms were followed up by the Planning and Compensation Act 1991 which received the Royal Assent on 25 July 1991. It amended the law relating to both planning and to compulsory acquisition procedure and to the assessment of compensation for the compulsory acquisition of land.

Significant post-1991 changes to planning legislation have been made by the following Acts: **1.23**

Environment Act 1995 This Act created the Environment Agency for England and Wales and a Scottish Environment Protection Agency, along with other measures to improve the protection and management of the environment.

In the land-use field, the Act made provision for the existing National Park boards to be wound up and replaced by new National Park authorities, which are now the local planning authority for the area of the Park. In addition, the Act provided for an initial review and updating of mineral planning permissions granted in the 1950s, 1960s, and 1970s, and the periodic review of all mineral planning permissions thereafter.

Scotland Act 1998 and the Government of Wales Act 1998 These Acts began a process whereby many of the planning powers previously exercised by the Parliament of the United Kingdom on a national basis were transferred to the Scottish Parliament or to the National Assembly for Wales.

Human Rights Act 1998 This Act, which came into force on 2 October 2000, incorporated into domestic law the provisions of the European Convention on Human Rights. Its provisions are dealt with in Chapter 19.

Greater London Authority Act 1999 This Act established a Mayor and a Greater London Assembly for the Greater London Area, and contained wide powers which gave the Mayor a major role in the determination of planning applications for the more important development proposals in the London Area.

Planning and Compulsory Purchase Act 2004 This Act received the Royal Assent on 13 May 2004. Its provisions were based on a consultation paper issued by the Government in December 2001 entitled *Delivering a Fundamental Change*. The Act introduced important changes to many areas of planning law, including changes to the development plan system and to planning control. Changes to the development plan system included the creation and use of regional spatial strategies and local development schemes to replace existing development plans. Changes to the planning control system embraced the abolition of crown immunity; changes to the basis of planning obligations; a restriction on the practice of twin-tracking; a requirement that development be commenced within three years; a strengthening of enforcement provisions; and the beginning of a new process for the handling of decisions on major infrastructure projects.

1.24 Some of the provisions of the 2004 Act are 'free-standing', in the sense that they contain provisions additional to those found in the Town and Country Planning Act 1990. Other provisions of the 2004 Act however, have operated by repealing or amending, or by the substitution of existing provisions in the 1990 Act.

The Planning Act 2008

1.25 The Government published, on 21 May 2007, a White Paper (Cm 7120) *Planning for a Sustainable Future*, proposing further major reforms to legislation. The proposed reforms included the following:

- the publication of a new national policy framework setting out how the country's key infrastructure needs will be met in the next 10–25 years;

- the provision of a clearer inquiry system with more expertise, led by an independent commission able to take decisions on individual projects;
- the imposition of a legal requirement on developers to consult the public and other key parties;
- an expansion of free access to planning advice;
- an extension of permitted development rights to cover minor household development such as conservatories, small-scale extensions, and microgeneration devices like solar panels;
- the provision of simpler information requirements for applications for planning permission, and the introduction of a fast track appeals system.

The Planning Act 2008 gave effect to most of the above reforms that required primary legislation. One of the most important provisions of the Act was the establishment of a new corporate body called the Infrastructure Planning Commission and the creation of one single consent regime for all nationally significant infrastructure proposals. The second important provision of the Act enabled the creation of a new Community Infrastructure Levy, to sit alongside planning obligations and planning contributions, whereby owners and developers can contribute wholly or partly towards the cost of infrastructure required to support the development which they are proposing. These topics are dealt with in Chapters 17 and 28 respectively. **1.26**

C. THE LOCALISM ACT 2011 AND SUBSEQUENT REFORM

The 2011 Act abolished the 'regional strategies' which used to form part of the development plan. Instead a new duty is imposed on local authorities and other public bodies to work together on planning issues. A new form of 'neighbourhood planning' has been set up by which local communities can draw up a neighbourhood development plan and grant full or outline planning permission for new homes and businesses. Linked to this is a community right to build as the Act provides that a community organization, formed by members of the local community, will be able to bring forward development proposals, providing they meet minimum criteria and can demonstrate local support through a referendum. The Act then introduces a new requirement for developers to consult local communities before submitting planning applications for very large developments, strengthens enforcement rules and reforms the community infrastructure levy and other local finance considerations. The law regarding the way local plans are made has also been changed with limitations on the powers of Inspectors to rewrite policies. In the case of nationally significant infrastructure projects the Infrastructure Planning Commission has been abolished and the final decisions are now to be made by the Secretary of State. **1.27**

Historical Introduction

The Growth and Infrastructure Act 2013

1.28 The Growth and Infrastructure Act 2013 makes the following changes to the planning system:

- creation of an option to make planning applications directly to the Secretary of State when a local planning authority has been designated as not performing adequately;
- broadening of the powers of the Secretary of State to award costs between the parties at planning appeals;
- imposition of limits on the powers that local planning authorities have to require information with planning applications;
- allowing for the reconsideration of economically unviable affordable housing requirements contained in s 106 agreements;
- restrictions on the rights to apply for land proposed for development to be registered as a town or village green.

1.29 The main objective of the Act is to promote growth and facilitate the provision of infrastructure and it clarifies the position of variations and replacements of pre-Planning Act consents under the Planning Act 2008. The Act also enables the Secretary of State to direct that business and commercial projects of national significance can be considered under the nationally significant infrastructure regime contained in the Planning Act 2008. The Mayor of London is given the power to delegate decisions concerning planning applications of potential strategic importance.

The Enterprise and Regulation Reform Act 2013

1.30 The Enterprise and Regulation Reform Act 2013 makes important changes to the law concerning Listed Buildings and Conservation Areas. The need to obtain Conservation Area Consent for the demolition of an unlisted building in a conservation area in England has been removed and instead such works require planning permission. With regard to the listing of buildings, the Act allows for certain structures or objects to be specifically excluded from the listing and for specific features of a building to be identified as lacking architectural merit. There is also provision for the entering of 'heritage partnerships' under which agreements can be entered by owners and planning authorities as to the works that can be carried out to the listed building. Similarly, the Act allows the Secretary of State to make Listed Building Consent Orders and for local planning authorities to make Local Listed Building Consent Orders authorizing particular works for the alteration or extension of listed buildings in England. There is also provision for certificates of lawfulness (setting out works to a listed building which can be carried out without Listed Building Consent) and certificates of immunity (that buildings will not be listed for at least five years).

Self-Build and Custom Housebuilding Act 2015

1.31 The Act imposes a duty on relevant authorities to maintain a register of individuals (either acting alone or organized into groups) who have expressed an interest in acquiring a serviced plot of land in order to build a house for such an individual to occupy as a home.

Housing and Planning Act 2016

1.32 The Act introduces changes to the neighbourhood planning process as well as providing the Secretary of State with wider powers to intervene in the plan-making process. The Act also introduces the new concept of 'Permission in Principle'.

Neighbourhood Planning Act 2017

1.33 The Act makes further provision for neighbourhood plans, clarifying the status of emerging plans. Provision is also made to amend neighbourhood plans without the need for starting the process from scratch. The Act also places the 'no scheme' rule in the CPO process on a statutory footing.

2

PLANNING ORGANIZATION

A. THE SECRETARY OF STATE	2.03	C. GREATER LONDON	2.98
B. LOCAL PLANNING AUTHORITIES	2.64		

From its very beginning in 1909, planning legislation has given to local authorities direct power and responsibility for the carrying on of the day-to-day administration of land-use control. Central government's role in the administration of planning began as, and has since remained, the supervision and co-ordination of the way in which those powers and responsibilities are exercised. **2.01**

There are, of course, many bodies with a role to play in the field of town and country planning. Basically, however, planning organization has two main tiers: a central government tier under the mantle of the Secretary of State, and a local government tier in the shape of local planning authorities. **2.02**

A. THE SECRETARY OF STATE

Nowhere in the law is there to be found any general statement of the responsibilities of the Secretary of State. The duty imposed on a predecessor, the Minister of Town and Country Planning, which was set out in the Minister of Town and Country Planning Act 1943, 'of securing consistency and continuity in the framing and execution of a national policy with respect to the use and development of land throughout England and Wales', was repealed in 1970. One should shed no tears. The duty imposed was too vague and too wide to be legally enforceable. It did represent, however, a statement of the political responsibility of that Minister to Parliament; and in that same sense, the statement, though now unwritten, describes the political responsibility of the Secretary of State. **2.03**

Under our governmental system there is more than one Secretary of State. Yet in law the office is one and indivisible, so that any Secretary of State may exercise the **2.04** powers of any other. The functions of any particular Secretary of State however are normally allocated to each by Order in Council made under the Ministers of the Crown Act 1975. In this way, since May 2006 the Secretary of State responsible for planning has been the Secretary of State for Communities and Local Government.

2.05 The position is otherwise with regard to Scotland and Wales. Under the Scotland Act 1998, Scotland now has a separate Parliament and its own executive. Under the Act the Scottish Parliament is given power to make primary legislation within its own area of competence, an area which includes both town and country planning and the environment. The Scottish Parliament is also able to decide policy so that, over a period of time, Scottish planning law and practice may diverge substantially from the traditionally unified approach which has characterized United Kingdom planning law since its inception. Where there has been divergence (see eg the Planning etc (Scotland) Act 2006), limitation of space in this edition prevents its consideration.

2.06 The position in Wales is also different. The Government of Wales Act 1998 established not a Welsh Parliament, but a National Assembly for Wales. Unlike the Scottish Parliament, the National Assembly was not then given the power to amend primary legislation. As with Scotland, however, the Assembly was given the power to make and amend subordinate or secondary legislation, but the power was limited of course to those areas of government for which the Assembly was responsible. Here, as in Scotland, those areas include town and country planning and the environment. In essence, therefore, the decisions which were previously made by the Secretary of State for Wales in relation to those areas were transferred to the National Assembly for Wales. These decisions of course not only include the making of policy, but such matters as the determination of appeals under the Town and Country Planning Act 1990. However, as a result of the Government of Wales Act 2006, following an affirmative referendum on March 2011, the Welsh Assembly has 'primary' legislative power to enable it to pass legislation on town and country planning and the Planning (Wales) Act 2015 came into force on 6 June 2015. As a result, the law on planning in Wales, although still based on the English model, is becoming increasingly distinctive.

2.07 As far as England is concerned, the Secretary of State is presently assisted in the exercise of his powers and functions by one Minister of State and five Parliamentary Under-Secretaries of State, each with special responsibilities for specific aspects of environmental matters.

2.08 These arrangements, however, are political arrangements allowing for the sharing of departmental responsibilities between a number of Ministers in the same Department of State. They in no way affect the particular powers and functions which in law are placed exclusively upon the Secretary of State.

2.09 Following the creation of a new Department of National Heritage in 1992, responsibility for the listing of historic buildings in England passed to another Secretary of State, the Secretary of State for National Heritage. In 1997, this title was changed to the Secretary of State for Culture, Media, and Sport. Control over works to historic buildings, however, remains the responsibility of the Secretary of State for Communities and Local Government. The Secretary of State for Culture, Media, and Sport, however, has responsibility for scheduling ancient monuments and granting scheduled monument consents; repair notices and associated compulsory purchase orders; and policy, procedures, and reserve powers in respect of the designation of conservation areas.

2.10 The organization of planning administration places the Secretary of State at the apex of a pyramid of power. Despite many attempts made over the years to shift more of the responsibility for planning decisions from central to local government, planning organization remains a hierarchy of centralized pontification, with the Secretary of State the supreme central pontiff. So it is that, however small a parcel of land may be, the final say in determining the use to which that land can be put is given, in law, to the Secretary of State.

2.11 Governmental powers and duties are broadly analysed as being of three kinds, namely legislative, administrative, and judicial. So too, may the powers and duties of the Secretary of State under planning legislation be analysed.

Legislative powers

2.12 Despite the length of the 1990 Act, many of its provisions are no more than general statements of principle. The Secretary of State, however, is given power by the Act to fill in the detail by making regulations or orders. Under s 333 of the 1990 Act, the power to make regulations and many of the more important orders are exercisable by statutory instrument. The use of this power is subject to varying degrees of parliamentary control or scrutiny. Statutory instruments are normally required to be laid before Parliament for a period of 40 days. The more important statutory instruments also require an 'affirmative resolution' of both Houses of Parliament during that period before they come into effect. With others, the statutory instrument comes into effect automatically, unless during that period either House of Parliament passes a 'negative resolution' preventing it from doing so. Finally, some statutory instruments have merely to be laid before Parliament, thus avoiding any more formal parliamentary control.

2.13 Under the 1990 Act, most statutory instruments containing *regulations* are subject to the negative resolution procedure. So too are most statutory instruments containing a *development order*. Most other statutory instruments containing orders, however, including the important Town and Country Planning (Use Classes) Order, have merely to be laid before Parliament. Three of the main statutory instruments made by the Secretary of State are as follows:

(a) *Town and Country Planning (Use Classes) Order 1987*. This Order specifies 15 'use Classes' for the purpose of s 55(2)(f) of the 1990 Act. Its significance is that where buildings or other land are used for a purpose within any of the classes specified in the Order, the use of the buildings or other land for any purpose within the same class is not to be taken to involve development. The Order is hereafter referred to as the Use Classes Order or the UCO.

(b) *Town and Country Planning (General Permitted Development) Order 2015 (GPDO).* The main purpose of this Order is to grant planning permission for certain classes of development without the need to make an application to the local planning authority for an express grant of planning permission. In many cases, the permission given by the Order is subject to extensive conditions and limitations. Development specified in the Order is commonly referred to as 'permitted development'. This Order is hereafter referred to as the General Permitted Development Order or the GPDO. It should be noted that in Wales a slightly different version applies.

(c) *Town and Country Planning (Development Management Procedure) (England) Order 2015 (DMPO).* This Order specifies the procedures connected with planning applications, appeals to the Secretary of State, and related matters so far as these are not laid down in the 1990 Act or elsewhere. It also deals with the maintenance of registers of planning applications, applications for certificates of lawful use or development, and other related matters. This Order is hereafter referred to as the Development Management Procedure Order or the DMPO.

2.14 The power of the Secretary of State to make these orders, though subject to varying degrees of parliamentary control, shows the extent of his legislative power. By reducing the number of 'Classes' in the Use Classes Order, or by extending the content of a Use Class, he can reduce the number of activities which constitute development and therefore require planning permission. By widening the scope of the development permitted by the GPDO, he can remove activities which constitute development from the general control of local planning authorities. Recent changes have reduced markedly the number of planning applications made to local planning authorities for householder development.

2.15 The Secretary of State also has power under s 59 of the 1990 Act to make a special development order. Unlike a general development order which will normally apply to all land, a special development order grants planning permission only for the development of the land specified in the order. Although the power has been used sparingly, its scope can be illustrated by the case of *Essex CC v Ministry of Housing and Local Government* (1967) 18 P & CR 531. In this case an order was made under s 59 to grant planning permission for the development of Stansted for the site of the third London airport. This was challenged on the grounds that the Minister had taken into account further questions of fact, and it was claimed that in accordance with the rules of natural justice the Minister was not entitled to make an order until he had received and considered representations made to him on the new facts. In granting the application to strike out, the court held that the power of the Minister to make a special development order under the section was a purely *administrative legislative power*, for the exercise of which he is responsible to nobody except Parliament, and that no duty was imposed on him to act judicially before making an order under the section. What the court was here recognizing was that the decision to grant planning permission by a special development order was an administrative act, but one exercised by the Minister in a legislative form.

2.16 Mention should also be made of the following bizarre, but perfectly legal, use of the Secretary of State's power to grant planning permission by special development order.

2.17 In 1977 an application for planning permission was made to construct an oxide fuel reprocessing plant at Windscale (now known as Sellafield) in Cumbria. Because of the public concern over the proposed development, the Secretary of State 'called in' the application for his own decision rather than leave the decision to be made by the local planning authority. Then, following a public local inquiry into the application and objections made to it, the Inspector recommended that, subject to conditions, the application should be granted. Normally, the Secretary of State would have done no more than decide whether or not to accept his Inspector's recommendation. In this instance, however, he considered that Parliament should be able to express a view on the proposed development. He decided, therefore, to refuse the application for planning permission. In so doing, he avoided any objections which might arise as a result of his quasi-judicial role in the planning process. The parliamentary debate was then able to take place without giving rise to an obligation on the Secretary of State to reopen the inquiry if fresh evidence was forthcoming during the course of the debate. The Secretary of State then granted, by special development order (Town and Country Planning (Windscale and Calder Works) Special Development Order 1978, SI 1978/523), planning permission for the very same development which he had earlier refused, with the parliamentary debate taking place on a 'prayer' against the order.

2.18 A somewhat different procedure was followed, however, with regard to the decision on an application by the Central Electricity Generating Board to build a nuclear power station at Sizewell, in Essex. After receiving the report of the Inspector, both Houses of Parliament were given an opportunity to debate the report and the issues involved. In the debate in the House of Commons, the Secretary of State made it clear that he was there to listen to the views which would be expressed and that he had no intention of commenting or making observations on the report. Shortly after the debate had been held the Secretary of State proceeded to grant planning permission for the development proposed in the application.

Administrative powers

2.19 Although local planning authorities are the primary bodies responsible for the day-to-day administration of planning, the Secretary of State has wide power to ensure that they act in accordance with his general policy. He also has wide powers to enable him to supervise and co-ordinate their individual activities. Section 1 of the Growth and Infrastructure Act 2013 has also provided applicants with the option of applying to the Secretary of State directly for planning permission if a council has been designated by the Secretary of State as not performing adequately in determining applications. This process is set out in new ss 62A to 62C which have been inserted into the 1990 Act. In addition, he provides general guidance and advice to local planning authorities on how they should exercise their powers.

2.20 One of the basic documents through which the Secretary of State exercises general policy control is the development plan for an area. Under the 1947 legislation he was required to approve all development plans prepared by local planning authorities. When structure and local plans were introduced in 1968, he was required to approve only the structure plan part, which he could do in whole or in part and with or without modifications or reservations. Then, following the Planning and Compensation Act 1991, planning authorities were given the power to *adopt* all development plans. The Secretary of State's policy control over structure plans, however, was maintained by a requirement that, in formulating the general policies to be included in a structure plan, the authority must have regard to specified matters including 'any regional or strategic planning guidance given by the Secretary of State to assist them in the preparation of the plan'. The power given to local planning authorities to adopt their own development plans, leaving the Secretary of State with selective powers to secure compliance with his policies, did not produce the effect intended. In particular, the system failed to make provision for the large increase in residential development which the Secretary of State wished to see. Accordingly, the Planning and Compulsory Purchase Act 2004 ended the earlier relaxation of the Secretary of State's general power of control by giving him the power to direct changes to a local planning authority's local development scheme and to approve the authority's local development documents (see Chapter 4). He also has powers under s 21 of the 2004 Act to direct a local planning authority to modify a development plan document if he considers it to be unsatisfactory and to call in the plan or part of it for his own decision.

2.21 The powers of the Secretary of State also extend to determining appeals made under s 78 of the 1990 Act against the refusal by a local planning authority to grant planning permission, or against a decision to grant planning permission subject to conditions. In the year 2012/13, the Secretary of State (or an Inspector acting on his behalf) determined almost 20,500 planning appeals under the provisions of s 78 of the 1990 Act.

2.22 The Secretary of State is also required under s 174 of the 1990 Act to determine appeals made against enforcement notices served by local planning authorities; and in doing so, he may uphold, quash, or vary the enforcement notice, and may, in appropriate circumstances, grant planning permission for the development to which the notice relates.

2.23 Under the 1990 Act, the Secretary of State determines appeals against decisions of local planning authorities in many other areas, including decisions relating to certificates of lawfulness of existing use or development (s 191), certificates of lawfulness of proposed use or development (s 192), the display of advertisements (s 220), and the cutting down, topping, or lopping of trees the subject of a tree preservation order (s 208). He may also be required to confirm orders made by local planning authorities revoking or modifying a planning permission previously granted (s 97), orders requiring a use of land to be discontinued or the alteration or removal of buildings or works (s 102), and notices requiring that development begun but not completed should be completed (s 94).

2.24 Under s 77 of the 1990 Act, the Secretary of State may by a direction (which he may decide to withdraw) 'call in' applications for planning permission for his own determination, rather than allow them to be determined by the local planning authority. The power is used very selectively.

2.25 The guidelines for the exercise of the Secretary of State's call in power are set out in a number of sources. On 16 June 1999, in answer to a parliamentary question, the then Minister Richard Caborn in what became known as the 'Caborn Principles' stated that:

Such cases may include, for example, those which in his opinion:

- may conflict with national policies on important matters;
- may have significant long-term impact on economic growth and meeting housing needs across a wider area than a single local authority;
- could have significant effects beyond their immediate locality;
- give rise to substantial cross-boundary or national controversy;
- raise significant architectural and urban design issues; or
- may involve the interests of national security or of foreign Governments.

However, each case will continue to be considered on its individual merits.

These criteria were last amended in a Written Statement on 26 October 2012 to include applications which 'may have significant long-term impact on economic growth and meeting housing needs across a wider area than a single local authority'.

2.26 The power of the Secretary of State to call in a planning application under s 77 is unfettered, subject, of course, to its being exercised having regard to all material considerations and not being perverse. In *Lakin v Secretary of State for Scotland* 1988 SLT 780, the Secretary of State decided not to call in one of two competing applications for the development of a superstore in Stirling. It was recognized that only one of the two would succeed; and in the other an appeal to the Secretary of State was pending. The Scottish courts considered that in not calling in the application for his own decision the Secretary of State was effectively determining its planning merits and this was both improper and unfair. However, in *R v Secretary of State for the Environment, Transport, and the Regions, ex p Carter Commercial Developments Ltd* [1999] PLCR 125, the Secretary of State decided to call in just one of two competing planning applications. In an action seeking judicial review of that decision the High Court held that the Secretary of State could so proceed so long as he had regard to the implications for the consideration of any other proposals, as one of the relevant considerations in his decision. The application was refused.

2.27 In *South Northamptonshire Council v Secretary of State for the Environment* (1995) 70 P & CR 224, the Court of Appeal held that the Secretary of State did not have to give reasons for not calling in an application, though it recognized that in practice he normally would do so. However, in *R (Save Britain's Heritage) v Secretary of State for Communities and Local Government* [2018] EWCA Civ 2137; [2019] 1 WLR 929 the Court of Appeal held that the Secretary of State had created a legitimate expectation by the publication of a Green Paper in December 2001 and subsequent review in March 2010, promising that the Minister would give reasons for either call-in or non-intervention. The Court rejected the argument that the Minister was under a common law duty to provide reasons, although Coulson LJ and Singh LJ disagreed as to whether a 'procedural discretion' (which does not affect anyone's rights) could ever give rise to a common law duty to supply reasons.

2.28 In *R (on the application of) Hadfield v Secretary of State for Transport, Local Government, and the Regions* [2002] EWHC 1226 (Admin) Sullivan J refused an application for judicial review of a decision by the Secretary of State to call in an application for planning permission to use buildings as a dwellinghouse. The land was within the green belt and the planning officer had recommended refusal. The Council, however, did not accept that recommendation and resolved that permission be granted. As a result, the application was referred to the Secretary of State as a 'departure application', and he then decided to call it in.

2.29 In *R (on the application of Adlard and others) v Secretary of State for Environment, Transport, and the Regions* [2002] EWCA Civ 757; [2002] 1 WLR 2515, the Court of Appeal refused to grant an application for judicial review of a decision of the Secretary of State not to call in an application for the redevelopment of Fulham Football Ground. It had been unsuccessfully argued that, under the Human Rights Act 1998, objectors to the development were entitled as of right to an oral hearing given that it was a very major development with important consequences for local people. Subsequently, a number of other legal challenges to the decision of the Secretary of State not to call in an application for planning permission based upon human rights grounds have also failed. Perhaps the latest word in this area of law is to be found in the decision of Sullivan J in R *(on the application of Persimmon Homes Ltd) v Secretary of State for the Communities and Local Government* [2007] EWHC 1985 (Admin). There the claimant unsuccessfully sought judicial review of the Secretary of State's decision not to call in an application for planning permission for a large development on the southeastern side of Banbury. The claimant alleged that in so deciding he had, inter alia, wrongly taken into account the planning merits of the proposed development. This was not a case, as in Lakin, of two rival sites for the same development. In giving judgment Sullivan J considered that it was no part of the Secretary of State's duty in deciding whether to call in an application for his own decision to consider the merits of the application. He considered that in deciding whether to call in the application, he was entitled to carry out a preliminary assessment of the 'planning merits' of the application to the extent that it was necessary to do so, in order to enable him to make a judgment on whether the proposed development might conflict with national policy or raise issues of more than local importance.

2.30 Specific instances where the Secretary of State has exercised his call-in power have included proposals for development at Windscale (mentioned above), the redevelopment of Spitalfields Market, Stamford Bridge football stadium, proposals for the construction of an aerodrome for use by short take-off and landing (STOL) aircraft on land in the London Docklands, and later, proposals to extend the runway and to install runway approach lighting. More recently, he called in for his own decision the application by the British Airports Authority to build a fifth terminal at London (Heathrow) Airport.

2.31 In addition to the power to call in applications for planning permission for his own decision, the Secretary of State also has power under the Planning (Listed Buildings and Conservation Areas) Act 1990 to call in for his own decision applications made to the local planning authority for listed building consent. Associated with the Secretary of State's power to call in applications for his own determination, is his power under Art 31 of the DMPO, to give a direction to local planning authorities restricting their power to grant planning permission for development, either indefinitely or for a specified period of time. Such directions are made with regard either to a class of application or to an application for a specific site. The purpose of the power appears to be to protect the Secretary of State's right to call in the application by giving him time to consider whether or not he should in fact exercise that power. A direction so given, however, does not take away the power of the local planning authority to refuse to grant planning permission for the development proposed. Occasionally too, the power is used to safeguard land from development, where the land is needed for further public works such as roads or other transport facilities.

2.32 In addition, under the DMPO, Art 18(4), the Secretary of State may give directions to a local planning authority requiring the authority to consult with any person or body named in the direction before granting planning permission. The authority named in the direction may well be the Secretary of State. In this way the body consulted is formally made aware of particular planning applications. In cases where the Secretary of State is required to be consulted, he may decide to use his powers either to give a direction to the local planning authority under Art 31, or decide to call in the application for his own decision under s 77.

2.33 An example of the exercise by the Secretary of State of his powers under the DMPO has been the requirement that local planning authorities consult him on any applications for development comprising gross shopping floor space of 20,000 square metres or more and prohibiting the grant of planning permission for such development until at least 21 days after the consultation. Consultation is not required, however, where the local planning authority decides to refuse the application. The relevant direction, the Town and Country Planning (Shopping Development) (England and Wales) (No 2) Direction 1993, was earlier contained as an Annex to Circular 15/93. Other examples are the Town and Country Planning (Playing Fields) (England) Direction 1998 (proposals for the development of playing fields against the advice of the Sports Council) and the Town and Country Planning (Residential Development on Greenfield Land) (England) Direction 2000 (proposals for the development of land on a greenfield site comprising the provision of 150 houses or flats or of houses or flats on 5 hectares).

2.34 Other directions issued by the Secretary of State include the Town and Country Planning (Green Belt) Direction 2005, contained in the Annex to Circular 11/05 in relation to inappropriate development in the green belt which would involve the construction of a building or buildings with a floor space of more than 1,000 square metres, or any other development which, by reason of its scale or nature or location, would have a significant impact on the openness of the green belt. A further Direction contained in Circular 04/2006 required a local planning authority to notify the Secretary of State of any application for major development in a 'flood risk area' for which the authority is minded to grant permission against the advice on flood risk grounds of the Environment Agency. Most of the directions issued by the Secretary of State in the past have been contained in Circulars issued by him as and when the need for him to be informed of specific types of planning application have arisen. Information as to the various types of development referred to in those directions was thus to be found in a number of source documents. In April 2009 it was decided to cancel and replace the provisions of a number of past directions in relation to England, and for them to be collected together in a single document. This has been done in Circular 02/09, the Town and Country Planning (Consultation) (England) Direction which covers many of the previous directions and requires consultation with the Secretary of State for defined Green Belt development, development outside town centres, World

Heritage Site development, playing field development, or flood risk area development. With the publication of the online Planning Practice Guidance Suite, circulars giving guidance were cancelled on 6 March 2014 but the 2009 Direction has been expressly saved.

2.35 Mention should also be made of the Secretary of State's wide default powers (eg under s 51 of the 1990 Act in relation to development plans, and ss 100 and 104 in connection with the revocation of planning permission and the discontinuance of a use). Although default powers have been rarely exercised, the powers under ss 100 and 104 allow him to impose a particular course of action on a local planning authority. In 1991, the Secretary of State issued a direction that planning permission granted by Wealden District Council for a dwellinghouse be revoked after two previous applications for similar developments on the same site had been refused by the Council and, on appeal, by the Secretary of State.

2.36 Later in the autumn of 1992, the Secretary of State decided to hold an administrative inquiry into the operation of the planning system by North Cornwall District Council. The terms of reference of the inquiry were 'to consider the issues which have been raised about the administration of the planning system in North Cornwall and to make recommendations on any desirable changes in the formulation of policy or in procedures'. Quite separately from the setting up of this inquiry, the Secretary of State also announced he was considering whether it would be expedient for him to exercise his powers under ss 100 and 104 of the 1990 Act to make orders revoking two planning permissions previously granted by the Council and/or requiring the discontinuance of use or the removal of buildings or works. The action arose because of a number of complaints made about the lack of consistency in planning decisions made by North Cornwall District Council. The Council had been criticized by the Local Government Ombudsman over particular planning decisions, and the District Auditor had also made criticisms in a public interest report. Such criticisms had been the subject of wider public comment with the showing of a Channel 4 TV programme 'Cream Teas and Concrete' in December 1991, which had featured specific cases.

2.37 The report of the inquiry set up by the Secretary of State and published towards the end of 1993, found that the North Cornwall District Council had granted planning permission for sporadic development in the open countryside on an inconsistent basis and contrary to national planning guidance and approved policies in the county structure plan. The report also criticized inappropriate decisions by the Council and its committees, the lack of formally adopted policies, inadequate publicity arrangements, and a number of procedural problems. Following this concern and the resulting inquiry, the Secretary of State in August 1993 exercised his power to revoke a planning permission granted for a farmer's retirement house in North Cornwall as being contrary to planning policy, and in another case took steps to require the carrying out of landscaping and further works to the exterior of an agricultural dwelling in order to minimize its effect on an Area of Outstanding Natural Beauty.

2.38 It seems, however, that the grant of planning permission for development contrary to planning policy guidance had occurred in areas other than North Cornwall. Following criticism by the Commission for Local Administration in Wales and the Welsh Affairs Select Committee of the House of Commons of similar practices by local planning authorities in the principality, the Secretary of State for Wales thought it appropriate to write to all Welsh local planning authorities to remind them of the need to be fair and consistent in the treatment of planning applications.

2.39 Some local planning authorities have been able to recognize their own shortcomings. In 1995, Bassetlaw District Council appointed an independent expert to investigate concerns relating to a number of planning matters which centred on planning permissions granted by the Council against officer advice, almost all of which appeared to involve a single developer. His report (the Phelps report), which was accepted by the Council, contained recommendations which included a call for the planning committee to resign en bloc to restore confidence in the planning system and programmed training for committee members into how the planning system works and the implications for them of national, regional, and county guidance.

2.40 The Bassetlaw report had an interesting sequel. In December 1996, the High Court in *R v Bassetlaw DC, ex p G A N Oxby* [1997] JPL 576, refused an application to quash two decisions of the District Council to grant planning permission for the development of two sites identified in the report, made on the alleged basis that the decisions were affected by fraud and/or bias. The application had been brought by the Leader of the Council in conjunction with the respondent Council, following the Council's consideration of the Phelps report.

2.41 At the outset of the case, three preliminary points had been taken, namely whether the Leader of the Council had a sufficient interest; whether there was an alternative remedy available to the Council; and whether the application had been made out of time.

2.42 With regard to the first point, Popplewell J, after reviewing the case law and relevant literature on standing, held that the law had moved on since the well-known case of *Inland Revenue Commissioners v National Federation of Self Employed and Small Business* [1982] AC 617 (the 'Mickey Mouse' case), and he was, therefore, prepared to accept that the applicant, as a council tax payer, had sufficient standing to bring the proceedings.

2.43 With regard to the last point, Popplewell J held that although it was not incumbent upon the Council to start judicial review proceedings until 14 March 1996 when it had received the report of the Phelps inquiry, in not submitting the application for judicial review until 21 June 1996 and having regard to the length of time since planning permission had been granted, the application had not been made promptly.

2.44 It is on the second preliminary point however, that the judgment raised issues of greater importance. After referring to the powers available to the District Council under ss 97 and 107 of the 1990 Act to revoke planning permission, Popplewell J held that the effect of the application for judicial review was to circumvent those statutory provisions, and he felt it would be quite wrong in this instance to allow the matter to proceed in that way given that there was an alternative remedy which the Council could pursue. One of the many factors which may have influenced this decision was that the landowners themselves were innocent of any fraud or bias that may have been present in the decision to grant planning permission.

2.45 The Court of Appeal ([1999] PLCR 283), however, took a somewhat different view. Whilst upholding the decision of Popplewell J that the leader of the Council had sufficient *locus standi* to bring the proceedings, the Court of Appeal found that there had been no undue delay and that what delay there was was marginal. More importantly, the court reversed Popplewell J's finding that judicial review should not lie to quash the Council's decisions. In the court's view it was legitimate and proper for the Council to seek to have the planning permissions set aside without the payment of compensation. According to the court, it would be wrong for the landowners to enjoy the benefit if they should not have received it in the first place. They had no legitimate grievance in being deprived of what they should never have had.

2.46 Two of the most recent and significant examples of the use made by the Secretary of State of his power to revoke or modify a planning permission which resulted in a legal challenge occurred in the cases of *Alnwick District Council and Restormel Borough Council. In Alnwick DC v Secretary of State for the Environment, Transport, and the Regions* [2000] JPL 473 the High Court refused an application by the District Council to quash the Secretary of State's decision, made on the recommendations of his Inspector, to make an order modifying a grant of planning permission which the Council had given for development contrary to the provisions of the development plan, by the deletion from it of Class A1 retail use.

2.47 The District Council's main argument was that in deciding to make the order, the Secretary of State had misdirected himself in law in holding that the obligation on the Council to pay compensation was a factor he was obliged to ignore in deciding whether it was expedient to modify the permission.

2.48 In dismissing the argument, Richards J held that insofar as the financial consequences of modification did not relate to the use and development of land, they were not capable of amounting to a material consideration. He also considered that the Council's argument that the payment of compensation would jeopardize proposed leisure facilities was a consideration that was too remote, and that the Council had not elaborated or supported it by any detailed evidence.

2.49 However, in *R (on the application of Usk Valley Conservation Group) v Brecon Beacons National Park Authority* [2010] EWHC 71 (Admin); [2010] 2 P & CR 14, Ouseley J refused to follow Richards J. He held that a local planning authority's decision to take enforcement rather than discontinuance action on the basis that no compensation was payable in respect of the former was entirely lawful. He considered that it would be extraordinary for Parliament to require a decision, which could have large adverse financial consequences, to be taken by a public body which could at no stage lawfully consider those consequences, however great or disproportionate the cost. It is submitted that similarly, when considering the use of his default powers, the Secretary of State should take into account the financial consequences. The Supreme Court has resolved this tension in the case law by siding with the reasoning of Richards J in *Alnwick*, finding in *The Health and Safety Executive v Wolverhampton City Council* [2012] UKSC 34; [2012] 1 WLR 2264 that regard must be had to compensation which might be payable under s 107 when considering whether to exercise powers under s 97.

2.50 It will be recalled that where the Secretary of State exercises his power to revoke or modify, it is in the nature of a default power. The Secretary of State's policy with regard to the exercise of that power was set out on his behalf in the House of Commons on 20 December 1989 where it was said:

> ... My Rt. Hon. Friend's practice has been to use this power only rarely. He has taken the view that the power should be used only if the original decision is judged to be grossly wrong, so that damage is likely to be done to the wider public interest ...

2.51 In the *Alnwick* case, the District Council had argued that the Secretary of State had misapplied that policy by failing to look at the consequences of the grossly wrong decision for the wider public interest. Dismissing that argument also, Richards J held that the words 'so that' were words of explanation rather than consequence. Accordingly, the finding that the damage to the wider public interest lay in the harm to Alnwick's vitality and viability as a shopping centre was a proper application of the Secretary of State's policy.

2.52 As a result, the District Council became liable to pay compensation to Safeway Stores plc, who had purchased the site subsequent to the grant of the permission. The sum was thought likely to be substantial; probably in excess of £4m. It is understood, however, that through an agreement whereby the landowner who had sold the land to Safeway Stores agreed to buy the land back at the same price that it had been sold for and the meeting by the Council's insurers of Safeway's legal costs, the liability of the District Council was minimal.

2.53 The other more recent and significant example of the use by the Secretary of State of his powers under s 100 of the 1990 Act to revoke or modify a planning permission occurred in March 2000, where he modified a planning permission for B1, B2, B8, and non-food retail use granted by Restormel Borough Council, by deleting from the planning permission the reference to the non-food retail use. It was accepted by the Inspector appointed to hold an inquiry into the proposed order that this grant was grossly wrong as it was in conflict with both the relevant policies and provisions of the development plan and with national policy guidance in the then PPG 6 and PPG 13. In addition, she found that the development would materially harm the vitality and viability of nearby established shopping centres. These findings and the Inspector's conclusion that the decision to grant permission was grossly wrong, were accepted by the Secretary of State. There then followed a challenge not to the Secretary of State's decision, but to the original grant of planning permission which had been made in May 1997. The action, *R v Restormel BC, ex p Parkyn and Corbett*, was brought by the chairman of the Council's planning and building control committee on behalf of the Council, and by another councillor acting in his capacity as elector and council tax payer. In the High Court ([2000] JPL 1211), the challenge to the grant of permission was rejected on the grounds, inter alia, of the long delay in applying for judicial review and bearing in mind that any challenge brought by the Council before the decision on the modification order would have been so lacking in merit that it would have failed. This decision was upheld by the Court of Appeal. The developers then sought compensation from the Council for the loss resulting from the modification of the permission. In August 2004, compensation of £1,586,000 was awarded to the developers by the Lands Tribunal.

2.54 Section 1 of the Growth and Infrastructure Act 2013 has introduced a very important provision which provides applicants for planning permission with the option of applying directly to the Secretary of State if a local planning authority has been designated as not performing adequately in determining planning applications. This in effect allows the Secretary of State to take over the development control functions of the authority.

2.55 In order to inform local planning authorities and others about his policies and to lessen the need for him to use the powers he possesses (eg by keeping to a minimum the number of appeals made to him from decisions of local planning authorities), the Secretary of State has issued policy guidance in the form of Planning Policy Statements (PPSs), Planning Policy Guidance Notes (PPGs) Circulars, White Papers, and other minor policy statements. The importance to local planning authorities and others who are concerned with the use and development of land of knowing the Secretary of State's policy on major planning policies cannot be overestimated. The form and content of this policy has varied over the years and has recently been fundamentally revised.

2.56 In 1988, the Secretary of State first began to issue PPGs to provide guidance on general and specific aspects of planning policy and Minerals Planning Guidance notes (MPGs) to provide advice on the control of minerals development. The aim of PPGs and MPGs was intended to provide concise and practical guidance on planning policies, in a clear and accessible form. Since 1988, the role of Departmental Circulars has been restricted to giving advice on legislation and procedures. More recently PPGs began to be replaced by Planning Policy Statements.

2.57 In December 2010 the Government announced that it considered that the current suite of planning policy statements and guidance notes was too centralist in its approach, and too long and cumbersome for councils and developers to use effectively. There was no over- arching integrated statement of the Government's priorities for the country and the role which planning can play in delivering those priorities. Therefore, the Government has produced a simple national planning policy framework (NPPF) setting out their priorities for the planning system in England in a single, concise document covering all major forms of development proposals handled by local authorities. Most of the national planning policies set out in PPSs, MPSs (Mineral Planning Statements), PPGs and MPGs have been integrated into this single document. The main exception are policies on minerals where PPS10 *Planning for Sustainable Waste Management* is to be revised and annexed to the National Waste Management Plan. Until that Plan is finalized, the Statement will remain in force. However, local authorities preparing waste plans should have regard to policies in the National Planning Policy Framework. Annex 3 to the NPPF (2012) set out the following documents which were replaced by the NPPF (2012):

1. Planning Policy Statement: *Delivering Sustainable Development* (31 January 2005)
2. Planning Policy Statement: *Planning and Climate Change—Supplement to Planning Policy Statement 1* (17 December 2007)
3. Planning Policy Guidance 2: *Green Belts* (24 January 1995)
4. Planning Policy Statement 3: *Housing* (9 June 2011)
5. Planning Policy Statement 4: *Planning for Sustainable Economic Growth* (29 December 2009)
6. Planning Policy Statement 5: *Planning for the Historic Environment* (23 March 2010)
7. Planning Policy Statement 7: *Sustainable Development in Rural Areas* (3 August 2004)
8. Planning Policy Guidance 8: *Telecommunications* (23 August 2001)
9. Planning Policy Statement 9: *Biodiversity and Geological Conservation* (16 August 2005)
10. Planning Policy Statement 12: *Local Spatial Planning* (4 June 2008)
11. Planning Policy Guidance 13: *Transport* (3 January 2011)

12. Planning Policy Guidance 14: *Development on Unstable Land* (30 April 1990)
13. Planning Policy Guidance 17: *Planning for Open Space, Sport and Recreation* (24 July 2002)
14. Planning Policy Guidance 18: *Enforcing Planning Control* (20 December 1991)
15. Planning Policy Guidance 19: *Outdoor Advertisement Control* (23 March 1992)
16. Planning Policy Guidance 20: *Coastal Planning* (1 October 1992)
17. Planning Policy Statement 22: *Renewable Energy* (10 August 2004)
18. Planning Policy Statement 23: *Planning and Pollution Control* (3 November 2004)
19. Planning Policy Guidance 24: *Planning and Noise* (3 October 1994)
20. Planning Policy Statement 25: *Development and Flood Risk* (29 March 2010)
21. Planning Policy Statement 25 Supplement: *Development and Coastal Change* (9 March 2010)
22. Minerals Policy Statement 1: *Planning and Minerals* (13 November 2006)
23. Minerals Policy Statement 2: *Controlling and Mitigating the Environmental Effects of Minerals Extraction in England. This includes its Annex 1: Dust and Annex 2: Noise* (23 March 2005—Annex 1: 23 March 2005 and Annex 2: 23 May 2005)
24. Minerals Planning Guidance 2: *Applications, Permissions and Conditions* (10 July 1998)
25. Minerals Planning Guidance 3: *Coal Mining and Colliery Spoil Disposal* (30 March 1999)
26. Minerals Planning Guidance 5: *Stability in Surface Mineral Workings and Tips* (28 January 2000)
27. Minerals Planning Guidance 7: *Reclamation of Minerals Workings* (29 November 1996)
28. Minerals Planning Guidance 10: *Provision of Raw Material for the Cement Industry* (20 November 1991)
29. Minerals Planning Guidance 13: *Guidance for Peat Provision in England* (13 July 1995)
30. Minerals Planning Guidance 15: *Provision of Silica Sand in England* (23 September 1996)
31. Circular 05/2005: *Planning Obligations* (18 July 2005)
32. Government Office London Circular 1/2008: *Strategic Planning in London* (4 April 2008)
33. Letter to Chief Planning Officers: *Town and Country Planning (Electronic Communications) (England) Order 2003* (2 April 2003)
34. Letter to Chief Planning Officers: *Planning Obligations and Planning Registers* (3 April 2002)
35. Letter to Chief Planning Officers: *Model Planning Conditions for development on land affected by contamination* (30 May 2008)
36. Letter to Chief Planning Officers: *Planning for Housing and Economic Recovery* (12 May 2009)

37. Letter to Chief Planning Officers: *Development and Flood Risk—Update to the Practice Guide to Planning Policy Statement 25* (14 December 2009)
38. Letter to Chief Planning Officers: *Implementation of Planning Policy Statement 25 (PPS25)—Development and Flood Risk* (7 May 2009)
39. Letter to Chief Planning Officers: *The Planning Bill—delivering well designed homes and high quality places* (23 February 2009)
40. Letter to Chief Planning Officers: *Planning and Climate Change—Update* (20 January 2009)
41. Letter to Chief Planning Officers: *New powers for local authorities to stop 'garden- grabbing'* (15 June 2010)
42. Letter to Chief Planning Officer: *Area Based Grant: Climate Change New Burdens* (14 January 2010)
43. Letter to Chief Planning Officers: *The Localism Bill* (15 December 2010)
44. Letter to Chief Planning Officers: *Planning policy on residential parking standards, parking charges, and electric vehicle charging infrastructure* (14 January 2011)

2.58 Wales has its own planning policy guidance notes, such as Planning Policy (Wales) and Planning Guidance (Wales) Unitary Development Plans.

2.59 The policy contained in Policy Statements and Guidance Notes constituted a material consideration which local planning authorities, and indeed the Secretary of State himself, had to take into account in exercising their planning powers and the same must apply to the National Planning Policy Framework. It is unclear the extent to which the previous policy documents such as the Planning Policy Statements, now replaced, still constitute material considerations. This aspect is dealt with in Chapter 11. Occasionally, significant planning policy changes may be announced through statements made by the Secretary of State in Parliament. As to the legal status of national policy see: *Secretary of State for Communities and Local Government v Hopkins Homes Ltd* [2017] UKSC 37; [2017] 1 WLR 1865. As to the process for promulgating new policy, see *R (West Berkshire District Council) v Secretary of State for Communities and Local Government* [2016] EWCA Civ 441; [2016] 1 WLR 3923.

The new Planning Practice Guidance Suite

2.60 As previously indicated, the Secretary of State also issues Circulars. Those often contain the Secretary of State's views on the meaning and effect of new legislation as well as giving policy guidance. Although they are helpful to an understanding of the law, they are not authoritative interpretations of the law, the courts being the only body having the power to do this.

2.61 In October 2012, the Government asked Lord Taylor of Goss Moor to review the 7,000 or more pages of existing planning practice guidance that had been issued by Governments over the years. Much of this guidance had become out of date and the Government accepted his main recommendation that the 7,000 or so pages should be reduced to a single Planning Practice document and perhaps more importantly that this document should be a web-based live resource hosted on a single site as a coherent up-to-date guidance suite. On 6 March 2014 this website called the Planning Practice Guidance Suite was opened. The new guidance is set out as a series of questions which then provide a connection to the relevant part of the National Planning Policy Framework. The planning practice guidance is to be updated as needed and users can sign up for e-mail alerts on any changes, or view these revisions directly on the site. The online resource is at: planningguidance.planningportal.gov.uk.

Judicial powers

Although as stated above, the interpretation of the law is a matter for the courts, the Secretary of State has power in specific situations to make preliminary determinations of law. In dealing with an appeal against an enforcement notice, for example, he may have to decide whether the activity enforced against is development and thus a breach of planning control. He also has power to determine whether or not a particular activity constitutes development in dealing with an appeal made to him against a determination made by a local planning authority as to whether or not a proposed activity would be lawful. These matters are essentially matters of law, in which the person affected and the local planning authority may either decide to accept the Secretary of State's determination or to challenge it in the courts. **2.62**

Although the occasions when the Secretary of State acts judicially may be few, he frequently has to act in a quasi-judicial capacity. It is now established law that in dealing with such matters as appeals from the decisions of local planning authorities, the Secretary of State is acting in a quasi-judicial capacity and thus bound to observe the rules of natural justice. These rules provide considerable procedural safeguards for the parties involved in the appeal. The matter is dealt with more fully in Chapter 18. **2.63**

B. LOCAL PLANNING AUTHORITIES

County planning authorities and district planning authorities

In some parts of England the powers conferred by the 1990 Act on the local planning authority are exercisable by two local authorities, namely by the county council as the county planning authority for its area and by the district council as the district planning authority for its area. This dual responsibility for the exercise of planning powers, however, is absent in large parts of the country including Greater London and the metropolitan areas. Following the abolition of **2.64** the Greater London Council and the metropolitan county councils on 1 April 1986, the only local authorities with power to act as the local planning authority in those areas are the London boroughs and the metropolitan districts respectively.

2.65 Furthermore, the dual responsibility which previously existed in many other parts of England has been curtailed further as a result of changes to the structure of local government brought about by the Local Government Act 1992. That Act has now led to the dismemberment of much of the two-tier system of local government in England and the replacement of many authorities by newly created 'unitary authorities', each exercising within its own area the planning powers previously exercised separately by the county council as county planning authority and the district council as district planning authority for the area.

2.66 The division of responsibility between the county planning authority and the district planning authority where a two-tier system of local government still exists is discussed later.

Joint planning boards

2.67 In order to provide cohesion in the administration of planning functions over a wider area than that administered by a single county or district planning authority, s 2 of the 1990 Act allows the Secretary of State to constitute a joint board as the county planning authority for the areas or parts of the areas of any two or more counties, or as the district planning authority for the areas or parts of the areas of any two or more districts. Under the section, such boards are bodies corporate, with perpetual succession and a common seal. It is believed that joint boards have been established in England on only two occasions. In 1973, the Lake District Special Planning Board and the Peak Park Joint Planning Board were created to administer planning functions in the areas of the respective national parks. Both Boards were wound up on 1 April 1997, following the creation of new National Park authorities for each national park under the Environment Act 1995 (see below).

National Park authorities

2.68 The Environment Act 1995, s 63, gives the Secretary of State power to establish, for any National Park, a 'National Park authority' to carry out, in relation to the Park, the functions conferred on such an authority by or under the Act. By virtue of s 4A of the 1990 Act the National Park authority for a Park is made the sole planning authority for the area of the Park. Accordingly, functions conferred by or under the planning Acts on a planning authority (including the preparation and maintenance of development plans and development control) have, in relation to the Park, become functions of the National Park authority and not of any other authority.

2.69 Acting under these powers, the Secretary of State established in 1996 National Park Authorities for the following National Parks: Dartmoor, Exmoor, Lake District, Northumberland, North Yorkshire Moors, Peak District, and Yorkshire Dales. The new National Park Authorities assumed their full planning functions on 1 April 1997. In Wales, National Park Authorities have been established for National Parks at Brecon Beacons, the Pembrokeshire Coast, and Snowdonia, and those authorities assumed full planning functions on 1 April 1996. A more recent addition to the list has been the creation of a national park for the South Downs, which came into full operation in April 2011.

Urban development corporations

2.70 Under Part XVI of the Local Government, Planning and Land Act 1980, the Secretary of State was empowered, subject to approval by both Houses of Parliament, to make orders designating urban development areas and to set up urban development corporations (UDCs) to secure the regeneration of those areas. The criteria adopted for the selection of such areas were the level of unemployment, the amount of derelict and vacant land, and the extent to which public sector funds would be likely to lever private sector investment to regenerate the area. Under the Act, UDCs had general powers to acquire, hold, manage, reclaim, and dispose of land, to carry out building and other operations, and to provide services and infrastructure.

2.71 Under s 149 of the 1980 Act, the Secretary of State could, by order, provide that a UDC should be the local planning authority for the whole or any portion of its area, for such purposes of Part III of the 1971 Act (now Part III of the 1990 Act) (ie development control functions), and in relation to such kinds of development, as may be prescribed. Once such an order had been made, the UDC became for the purposes of Part III of the 1990 Act the local planning authority for the area in place of any authority that would otherwise be the local planning authority for that area, in relation to such kinds of development as are specified in the order.

2.72 The Planning and Compulsory Purchase Act 2004 has amended the 1980 Act to allow any member of the Board of the UDC, a committee or subcommittee of members, or a member of the Board's staff, to exercise planning functions conferred on the UDC by s 149 of the 1980 Act. Accordingly, a UDC can now delegate planning functions in the same way as any other local planning authority is able to do.

2.73 In the past, UDCs were set up in many areas, including London Docklands; Liverpool Merseyside; the Black Country; Greater Manchester (Trafford Park); Tyne and Wear; Teesside; Cardiff Bay; Central Manchester; Leeds; Sheffield; Wolverhampton; Bristol; Birmingham Heartlands; Plymouth; and Thurrock. Unlike enterprise zones, no fixed life was set for UDCs, and in the last few years all of these have been progressively wound up, so that planning powers have now been returned to the appropriate local authority for each area.

2.74 A recent variation in the type of authority created to deal with regeneration was the establishment by the London Olympic Games and Paralympic Games Act 2006 of the Olympic Delivery Authority. The Authority, which is a corporate body, is charged under the Act with delivering the public sector obligations (such as the necessary venues and infrastructure) required for the 2012 Games. Under the Act, the Authority is given the same planning powers as those of a UDC.

Homes England

2.75 Part III of the Leasehold Reform, Housing and Urban Development Act 1993 established, as a body corporate, the Urban Regeneration Agency. In practice, the Agency preferred to be known as English Partnerships. The Agency's main object was to secure the regeneration of land in England which was suitable for regeneration and which was vacant or unused; in an urban area and underused or ineffectively used; or was contaminated, derelict, neglected, or unsightly. The Agency was given wide powers, which included a power to acquire, hold, manage, reclaim, improve, develop, redevelop, and dispose of land. Under s 170 of the 1993 Act, the Secretary of State was given power to designate urban regeneration areas, which were intended to be similar to urban development areas designated under the Local Government, Planning and Land Act 1980 (see 2.70), save that the regeneration of the area was to be carried out by the Urban Regeneration Agency rather than a specially created UDC. Where the Secretary of State exercised the power to make a designation order, the order could provide that the Agency should be the local planning authority for the whole or any part of the designated area for such purposes of Part III of the 1990 Act and ss 57 and 73 of the Planning (Listed Buildings and Conservation Areas) Act 1990 as may be specified in the order; and in relation to such kinds of development as may be so specified. Under a new s 8A of the 1990 Act, where a designation order transferred any of the planning functions mentioned above to the Agency, the body which would otherwise be the local planning authority for the area in question could no longer exercise those functions. A recent example of the use by the Secretary of State of his power under the Act occurred in 2004 with the transfer of the powers of the local planning authority to the Urban Regeneration Agency for designated areas in Milton Keynes.

2.76 In exercising functions as a local planning authority, the Agency was required to act objectively in carrying them out. In a case involving a UDC, *R v Teesside Development Corporation, ex p William Morrison plc and Redcar and Cleveland BC* [1998] JPL 23, a grant of planning permission by the Corporation was quashed because it had allowed its functions as a regeneration agency to dominate if not dictate the performance of its planning functions, to the extent that it failed to make any objective judgment on the planning merits in breach of policies in the structure plan for the area. The same considerations, it seems, would apply to the carrying out of planning functions by the Urban Regeneration Agency or its successor body, the Homes and Communities Agency.

2.77 The Housing and Regeneration Act 2008 abolished the Urban Regeneration Agency and created the Homes and Communities Agency. The objects of the new Agency include improving the supply and quality of housing in England, securing the regeneration or development of land or infrastructure in England, and contributing to sustainable development and good design. Its creation brings together the functions of the Urban Development Agency (on whose powers the powers of the new body are modelled substantially) and the Housing Corporation. Although the Agency has no planning powers as of right, the Secretary of State may by designation order confer on the Agency planning functions exercisable in a designated area, including the power to determine planning applications. The Agency was renamed Homes England on 11 January 2018.

Enterprise zone authorities

2.78 Under s 179 of and Sch 32 to the Local Government, Planning and Land Act 1980, the Secretary of State is given power to designate, by order, an area of land as an enterprise zone. Enterprise zones were originally conceived as experimental. The hope was that by removing certain tax burdens and by relaxing or speeding up a number of administrative controls, private sector industrial and commercial activity within the zones would be encouraged.

2.79 Schedule 32 provides that each enterprise zone should be administered by an enterprise zone authority. Furthermore, s 6(1) of the 1990 Act provides that an order made under Sch 32 may provide that the enterprise zone authority shall be the local planning authority for the area for such purposes of the Planning Acts, and in relation to such kinds of development as may be prescribed by the order. The order may also provide that the enterprise zone authority shall be the local planning authority for the area covered by the scheme to the extent mentioned in the order, to the exclusion of the body which would otherwise be the local planning authority for the area. As far as planning control is concerned, s 82 of the 1990 Act provides that the adoption or approval of a simplified planning scheme has effect to grant in relation to the zone, planning permission for development specified in the scheme or for development of any class so specified. Hence an express application for planning permission is not necessary for such development.

2.80 The Schedule also provides that the designation order should specify the period for which the area is to remain an enterprise zone. So far, all the designation orders have limited the life of the zone to 10 years from the date of the order. On 7 February 2014 it was announced that 25 new enterprise zones were to be designated. They will be subject to 'radically simplified planning approaches' and the Government envisages that Local Development Orders (LDOs) will be the primary mechanism for achieving this. LDOs, which require public consultation and the approval of the Secretary of State, can be used to exempt certain development identified in local development documents from the need for planning permission.

Simplified planning zones

2.81 The Housing and Planning Act 1986 gave local planning authorities power to designate simplified planning zones in their area. The power is now to be found in ss 82 to 87 of the 1990 Act. Simplified planning zones (SPZs) are an extension of the planning regime which had been pioneered in enterprise zones. By granting planning permission for development specified in the SPZ scheme, developers know with certainty the precise type of development that can be carried out within the zone without having to make (and pay for) a planning application. This secures that the work, expense, and delay associated with the preparation, making, processing, and determination of applications for planning permission are thereby saved.

2.82 SPZs cannot be set up in national parks, conservation areas, the Broads, Areas of Outstanding Natural Beauty, land identified in a development plan as part of a green belt, or land forming part of an area of special scientific interest under ss 28 or 29 of the Wildlife and Countryside Act 1981.

2.83 The adoption or approval of an SPZ scheme operates to grant in relation to the zone, or to any part of it specified in the scheme, planning permission for the development specified in the scheme or for the development of any class so specified.

2.84 Schemes may be either general or specific. A general scheme will grant a general or wide permission for almost all types of development, but list exceptions where an application for planning permission will be required. A specific scheme will identify the specific type or types of development permitted and any limitations imposed. An application for planning permission would then have to be made for any development not specified in the scheme.

2.85 Planning permission cannot be granted by an SPZ scheme for development for which an environmental impact assessment is required under the Town and Country Planning (Environmental Impact Assessment) (England and Wales) Regulations 2011, SI 2011/1824. There is nothing to prevent Sch 2 development being included within an SPZ, but such development can only be granted permission by the SPZ provided the development has been the subject of a 'screening opinion' or a direction by the Secretary of State that it is not development requiring environmental impact assessment (see Chapter 12).

2.86 Section 85 of the 1990 Act, as amended by the Planning and Compulsory Purchase Act 1990 and the 2004 Act, provides that an SPZ scheme shall take effect on the date of its adoption or approval or the date specified in the scheme, and be for 10 years or such date as is specified in the scheme. At the end of that period the scheme, and the planning permission it grants, will cease to have effect. If, however, at the end of that period, development authorized by the permission has been begun, it may be completed. If it has been begun but completion is unreasonably delayed, the authority may serve a completion notice under the provisions of s 94 of the 1990 Act. The provisions of s 56 of the 1990 Act apply in determining when development authorized by an SPZ scheme has been begun. (These provisions are dealt with later in Chapter 14.)

2.87 The policy relating to SPZs was set out in PPG 5: *Simplified Planning Zones*. However, this was replaced by PPS 4: *Planning for Sustainable Economic Growth* in 2009, and this in turn was replaced by the NPPF. The NPPF does not mention SPZs specifically, however it does suggest that planning can be simplified in particular areas.

In addition, the government is establishing 'enterprise zones' in Local Enterprise Partnerships areas. LEPs are able to bid for enterprise zones. Amongst other things, enterprise zones include simplified planning procedures. This is generally done through the use of Local Development Orders, to allow certain developments without the need for planning permission.

Housing action trusts (HATs)

2.88 Under s 62 of the Housing Act 1988, the Secretary of State is given power to establish housing action trusts (HATs). The purpose of these trusts is to secure the improvement of local authority housing stock which may be transferred to them in their area, and then hand them over to other owners and managers. Most HATs have been given a life span of 10 years. Under s 67 of that Act, the Secretary of State may, by order, provide that for such purposes of Part III of the 1990 Act (development control) and ss 67 and 73 of the Planning (Listed Buildings and Conservation Areas) Act 1990 (publicity for applications for planning permission affecting the settings of listed buildings or conservation areas), and in relation to such kinds of development as may be specified in the order, a housing action trust shall be the local planning authority for the whole or part of its area.

2.89 Under s 8 of the 1990 Act, where such an order is made, the trust is to be the local planning authority for such area, in place of any authority which would otherwise be the local planning authority for that area in relation to the development as is specified in the order. Since 1988 six HATs were established but all have been now wound up.

Broads Authority

2.90 Under the Norfolk and Suffolk Broads Act 1988, a Broads Authority was established with a general duty to manage the Broads for the purposes of conserving and enhancing the natural beauty of the Broads; to promote the enjoyment of the Broads by the public; and to protect the interests of navigation. Under the 1990 Act, the Broads Authority is made the sole planning authority for the Broads.

Local nature partnerships

2.91 Local nature partnerships have been set up by the Department for Environment, Food & Rural Affairs and are partnerships of a broad range of local organizations, businesses, and people who aim to help bring about improvements in their local natural environment.

Division of planning powers between the county planning authority and the district planning authority

2.92 Bodies that may be a local planning authority within an area are thus county councils, district councils, joint planning boards, National Park authorities, urban development corporations, Homes and Communities Agency, enterprise zone authorities, housing action trusts, and the Broads Authority. The main functions of local planning authorities are two-fold: namely the preparation and maintenance of a development plan or a local development scheme and local development documents for their area; and development control, which includes such matters as the determination of applications for planning permission and the service of enforcement notices.

2.93 In those parts of the country where there is both a county planning authority and a district planning authority for an area, the basic scheme of the 1990 legislation is to distribute planning powers and functions in the area between the two main authorities in the following way.

2.94 Development plans and local development schemes

(a) The position under the 1990 Act was that the county planning authority was required to prepare and maintain a structure plan for its area. In addition, the county planning authority, as the mineral planning authority for the county, was required to prepare a minerals local plan for its area. Furthermore, under a provision introduced by the Planning and Compensation Act 1991, the county planning authority was required to prepare a waste local plan, either separately or as part of a joint waste and minerals local plan.

The Planning and Compulsory Purchase Act 2004 phases out structure plans which were to be replaced by regional strategies as revised by the Regional Planning Boards. However, the regional strategies and the Regional Planning Boards have in their turn been abolished by the Localism Act 2011. Waste and mineral local plans are also being phased out and replaced by a waste and minerals local development scheme prepared by county planning authorities, together with local development documents prepared in accordance with the scheme.

(b) Under the 1990 Act, a district planning authority was required to prepare a local plan where there was a structure plan covering its area. Where the district planning authority is a unitary authority, it would normally prepare a unitary development plan. In such cases, that authority was also responsible for preparing waste and minerals plans. Under the Planning and Compulsory Purchase Act 2004 local plans as such are now being phased out and replaced by a local development framework prepared by the district planning authority, together with local development documents prepared in accordance with the scheme. The Localism Act 2011 has limited the discretion of planning Inspectors to insert their own wording into the development plan documents which are contained in the local development framework.

Development control 2.95

(a) A county planning authority is mainly responsible for development control functions within its area in respect of 'county matters'. County matters are defined in para 1 of Sch 1 to the 1990 Act and are confined to the winning and working of minerals and related matters, the operational development of land partly within and partly outside National Parks, and waste.

A problem has arisen in relation to applications for planning permission which include both a county matter and a non-county matter. Which tier of local planning authority has the jurisdiction to determine such an application? In *R v Berkshire CC, ex p Wokingham DC* [1997] JPL 461, Beldam LJ (in the Court of Appeal) held that the test to be applied was whether in substance an application for permission to develop land was a county matter, whilst Potter LJ held the test to be whether the content of the application was such that, having regard to the proposed overall user of the site in question, that part of the application which related to a county matter formed a substantial element of it. Accordingly, the court refused to rule that Berkshire County Council had no jurisdiction to determine an application for planning permission for a waste recycling and transfer station together with buildings for light industrial use. It was also held, obiter, that the words of the statute did not permit an application to be treated as two or more separate applications to be determined by different authorities, because to sever could cause an administrative nightmare. 2.96

(b) The district planning authority will normally be responsible for all other development control functions within its area. Development control includes not only the determination of applications for planning permission and related matters, but also the enforcement of planning control.

2.97 Recent statistics show that around 470,000 applications for planning permission and related consents were made to district planning authorities in England in 2017/18, as against around 923 applications made to county planning authorities. Most of that latter number related to applications for mineral development and the deposit of waste.

C. GREATER LONDON

2.98 The Greater London Authority Act 1999 established a Greater London Assembly for the Greater London Area for the purpose of promoting economic and social development in Greater London and the improvement of the environment in the area. The Act also provided that Greater London should have a directly elected Mayor, with the power to exercise any of the important functions of the Authority on its behalf. In effect therefore, the decision-making power of the Assembly was confined to the approval of the budget and the making of certain key appointments. In particular, the Act requires that the Mayor should prepare and keep under review a 'spatial development strategy' for the Greater London Area. The spatial development strategy contains the Mayor's general policies for the use and development of land in Greater London, which are thus similar to the regional spatial strategies prepared for the rest of the country under the Planning and Compulsory Purchase Act 2004 but which have now been abolished. Under s 38 of the 2004 Act, the Mayor's spatial development strategy is part of the development plan for the Greater London Area along with development plan documents which have been adopted or approved by the London boroughs or the City of London Corporation. Neither the Mayor nor the Greater London Assembly are a local planning authority for their area although the Mayor may be directed to be the local planning authority for the Greater London Area in specific cases. The London boroughs and the City of London Corporation remain the sole planning authorities for their areas, though in preparing their development plan documents they are required to have regard to the Mayor's spatial development strategy. The powers of the Mayor were further strengthened by the Greater London Authority Act 2007. It amended the provisions of the 2004 Act to require local planning authorities in Greater London to send a copy of their draft local development scheme to the Mayor, who may direct that changes be made to it. The Mayor is also given the power to direct the local planning authority to prepare a revision to its local development scheme. A further important amendment to the 1990 Act gives the Mayor power to direct that planning applications which are of potential strategic importance be determined by him in place of the local planning authority. Where the Mayor does determine such an application and grants planning permission, he is given the power to enforce its terms. The Mayor may, however, if he grants planning permission for the development, provide that any subsequent applications in connection with it, such as an application for approval of reserved matters, be dealt with by the local planning authority. It should also be noted that where the Mayor gives a direction, he may also determine any connected applications for listed building consent, conservation consent, or hazardous substances consent.

The Mayor is also a statutory consultee for a specific range of applications for planning permission having potential strategic importance and, in such cases, he has the power under s 74(1B) of the 1990 Act to direct the refusal of planning permission. That power is available to the Mayor if he believes that to grant the application would be contrary to his spatial development strategy or prejudicial to its implementation, or otherwise contrary to good strategic planning in Greater London. If the Mayor should direct the refusal of such an application, and the developer is dissatisfied with the decision, the developer may have no choice but to appeal against the refusal to the Secretary of State. However, the Secretary of State has the power to issue a direction prohibiting a local planning authority from implementing a direction from the Mayor in prescribed circumstances or during prescribed periods. Many of the powers of the Mayor depend upon an application for planning permission being a PSI application, namely an application defined in the Schedule to the Town and Country Planning (Mayor of London) Order 2008, SI 2008/580 as any application for planning permission for development which the local planning authority considers falls within a category set out in the Order. The type of development there defined includes the following. **2.99**

Large scale development

Category 1A

1. Development which comprises or includes the provision of more than 150 houses, flats, or houses and flats.

Category 1B

1. Development (other than development which only comprises the provision of houses, flats, or houses and flats) which comprises or includes the erection of a building or buildings—
   (a) in the City of London and with a total floorspace of more than 100,000 square metres;
   (b) in Central London (other than the City of London) and with a total floorspace of more than 20,000 square metres; or
   (c) outside Central London and with a total floorspace of more than 15,000 square metres.

Category 1C

1. Development which comprises or includes the erection of a building of one or more of the following descriptions—
   (a) the building is more than 25 metres high and is adjacent to the River Thames;

(b) the building is more than 150 metres high and is in the City of London;
(c) the building is more than 30 metres high and is outside the City of London.

Category 1D

1. Development which comprises or includes the alteration of an existing building where—
   (a) the development would increase the height of the building by more than 15 metres; and
   (b) the building would, on completion of the development, fall within a description set out in paragraph 1 of Category 1C.

Major infrastructure

Category 2A

1. Development which comprises or includes mining operations where the development occupies more than 10 hectares.

Category 2B

1. Waste development to provide an installation with capacity for a throughput of more than—
   (a) 5,000 tonnes per annum of hazardous waste; or
   (b) 50,000 tonnes per annum of waste produced outside the land in respect of which planning permission is sought.
2. Waste development where the development occupies more than one hectare.

Category 2C

1. Development to provide—
   (a) an aircraft runway;
   (b) a heliport (including a floating heliport or a helipad on a building);
   (c) an air passenger terminal at an airport;
   (d) a railway station or a tram station;
   (e) a tramway, an underground, surface or elevated railway, or a cable car;
   (f) a bus or coach station;
   (g) an installation for a use within Class B8 (storage or distribution) of the Schedule to the Use Classes Order where the development occupies more than 4 hectares;
   (h) a crossing over or under the River Thames; or
   (i) a passenger pier on the River Thames.
2. Development to alter an air passenger terminal to increase its capacity by more than 500,000 passengers per year.

3. Development for a use which includes the keeping or storage of buses or coaches where—
   (a) it is proposed to store 70 or more buses or coaches or buses and coaches; or
   (b) the part of the development that is to be used for keeping or storing buses or coaches or buses and coaches occupies more than 0.7 hectares.

Category 2D

2. Waste development which does not accord with one or more provisions of the development plan in force in the area in which the application site is situated and which falls into one or more of these sub-categories—
   (a) it occupies more than 0.5 hectares;
   (b) it is development to provide an installation with a capacity for a throughput of more than—
      (i) 2,000 tonnes per annum of hazardous waste; or
      (ii) 20,000 tonnes per annum of waste.

Development which may affect strategic policies

Interpretation

1. In this Part, land shall be treated as used for a particular use if—
   (a) it was last used for that use; or
   (b) it is allocated for that use in—
      (i) the development plan in force in the area in which the application site is situated;
      (ii) proposals for such a plan; or
      (iii) proposals for the alteration or replacement of such a plan.

Category 3A

1. Development which is likely to—
   (a) result in the loss of more than 200 houses, flats, or houses and flats (irrespective of whether the development would entail also the provision of new houses or flats); or
   (b) prejudice the residential use of land which exceeds 4 hectares and is used for residential use.

Category 3B

1. Development—
   (a) which occupies more than 4 hectares of land which is used for a use within Class B1 (business), B2 (general industrial) or B8 (storage or distribution) of the Use Classes Order; and
   (b) which is likely to prejudice the use of that land for any such use.

Category 3C

1. Development which is likely to prejudice the use as a playing field of more than 2 hectares of land which—
   (a) is used as a playing field at the time the relevant application for planning permission is made; or
   (b) has at any time in the five years before the making of the application been used as a playing field.
2. In paragraph 1 'playing field' has the same meaning as in article 10(2)(1) of the GDPO (consultation before the grant of permission).

Category 3D

1. Development—
   (a) on land allocated as Green Belt or Metropolitan Open Land in the development plan, in proposals for such a plan, or in proposals for the alteration or replacement of such a plan; and
   (b) which would involve the construction of a building with a floorspace of more than 1,000 square metres or a material change in the use of such a building.

Category 3E

1. Development—
   (a) which does not accord with one or more provisions of the development plan in force in the area in which the application site is situated; and
   (b) comprises or includes the provision of more than 2,500 square metres of floorspace for a use falling within any of the following classes in the Use Classes Order—
       (i) class A1 (retail);
       (ii) class A2 (financial and professional);
       (iii) class A3 (food and drink);
       (iv) class A4 (drinking establishments);
       (v) class A5 (hot food takeaways);
       (vi) class B1 (business);
       (vii) class B2 (general industrial);
       (viii) class B8 (storage and distribution);
       (ix) class C1 (hotels);
       (x) class C2 (residential institutions);
       (xi) class D1 (non-residential institutions);
       (xii) class D2 (assembly and leisure).

Category 3F

1. Development for a use, other than residential use, which includes the provision of more than 200 car parking spaces in connection with that use.

Category 3G

1. Development which—
    (a) involves a material change of use;
    (b) does not accord with one or more provisions of the development plan in force in the area in which the application site is situated,
    (c) where the application site is used or designed to be used wholly or mainly for the purpose of treating, keeping, processing, recovering or disposing of refuse or waste materials; and
    (d) the application site—
        (i) occupies more than 0.5 hectares; or
        (ii) contains an installation with a capacity for a throughput of more than 2,000 tonnes per annum of hazardous waste; or
        (iii) contains an installation with a capacity for a throughput of more than 20,000 tonnes per annum of waste.

Category 3H

1. Development which—
    (a) comprises or includes the provision of houses, flats or houses and flats;
    (b) does not accord with one or more provisions of the development plan in force in the area in which the application site is situated; and
    (c) is on a site that is adjacent to land used for treating, keeping, processing, recovering or disposing of refuse or waste materials with a capacity for a throughput of more than—
        (i) 2,000 tonnes per annum of hazardous waste; or
        (ii) 20,000 tonnes per annum of waste.

Category 3I

1. Development which—
    (a) involves a material change of use;
    (b) does not accord with one or more provisions of the development plan in force in the area in which the application site is situated; and
    (c) is either—
        (i) on a site that is used for keeping or storing 70 or more buses or coaches or buses and coaches; or
        (ii) on a site on which an area of over 0.7 hectares is used for keeping or storing buses or coaches or buses and coaches.

Development on which the Mayor must be consulted by virtue of a direction of the Secretary of State

Category 4

1. Development in respect of which the local planning authority is required to consult the Mayor by virtue of a direction given by the Secretary of State under article 10(3) of the DMPO.

2.100 The Localism Act 2011 has given new housing and regeneration powers to the Greater London Assembly, abolished the London Development Agency, limited the powers of the Homes and Communities Agency to outside London and given the Mayor enabling powers to designate development corporations.

3

THE EVOLUTION OF DEVELOPMENT PLANS

A. HISTORICAL INTRODUCTION TO DEVELOPMENT PLANS	3.01	D. CHANGES TO THE 1968 DEVELOPMENT PLANS SYSTEM	3.26
B. DEVELOPMENT PLANS PREPARED UNDER THE 1947 ACT (FIRST GENERATION PLANS)	3.05	E. DEVELOPMENT PLANS PREPARED UNDER THE 2004 ACT (THIRD GENERATION PLANS)	3.29
C. DEVELOPMENT PLANS PREPARED UNDER THE 1968 ACT (SECOND GENERATION PLANS)	3.11	F. THE LOCALISM ACT 2011 AND THE ABOLITION OF THE REGIONAL STRATEGIES	3.34

A. HISTORICAL INTRODUCTION TO DEVELOPMENT PLANS

Development plans play a vital part in the system for the control of development. They constitute the main backcloth against which applications for planning permission are determined and decisions are made on whether or not to issue an enforcement notice to terminate unauthorized development. The strength of the development plan system is that it ensures that there is both a rational and a consistent basis for making those decisions. **3.01**

It should be emphasized that although development plans may play a dominant part in the way in which development control is exercised they are not entirely prescriptive. They do not, for example, absolutely guarantee that an application for planning permission for development which conforms to the provisions of the development plan for an area will necessarily be granted, or that development which does not accord with the development plan will not be granted. **3.02**

Development plans, however, have a further and important purpose, namely the co-ordination of those factors which influence the scale, location, and timing of **3.03** the development or redevelopment of land, particularly with regard to the extent and availability of the necessary infrastructure.

3.04 Although the primary purpose of development plans has remained fairly constant from the first moment an obligation was placed on local planning authorities to prepare them following the Town and Country Planning Act 1947, their form and content has undergone considerable change. Between 1948 and 2004 there have been three different generations of development plans, each of which was able to influence the way in which development control functions under the Planning Acts were exercised. The three generations of development plans have been:

(a) development plans prepared under provisions originally contained in the Town and Country Planning Act 1947;
(b) development plans prepared under provisions originally contained in the Town and Country Planning Act 1968, comprising structure plans and local plans and, later, unitary development plans prepared under the provisions originally contained in the Local Government Act 1985 following upon the dissolution in April 1986 of the Greater London Council and the Metropolitan County Councils. In many areas of the country where further unitary authorities were created following the reorganization of local government under the Local Government Act 1992 authorities have been required to prepare unitary development plans in preference to maintaining a structure and local plan;
(c) development plans prepared under the provisions of the 2004 Act.

B. DEVELOPMENT PLANS PREPARED UNDER THE 1947 ACT (FIRST GENERATION PLANS)

3.05 The Town and Country Planning Act 1947 provided that as soon as may be after the appointed day (1 July 1948), each local planning authority should carry out a survey of its area and, within three years, or such extended period as the Minister might allow, submit to him a report of the survey together with a development plan for its area. The purpose of the survey was to assemble and collate information about the area to form the basis for the preparation of the authority's plan for that area.

3.06 The purpose of the old-style development plan was to indicate the manner in which the local planning authority proposed that land in its area should be used, whether by the carrying out thereon of development or otherwise, and the stages by which such development should be carried out. In addition, the Act provided that a plan might in particular define the sites of proposed roads, public and other buildings and works, airfields, parks, pleasure grounds, nature reserves, and open spaces, or allocate areas of land for use for agricultural, residential, industrial, or other purposes of any class specified in the plan. The development plan could also define as an area of comprehensive development, an area which in the opinion of the authority should be developed as a whole for the purposes of dealing with extensive war damage, bad layout, or obsolete development, or for the purpose of relocating population or industry or replacing open space in the course of the development or redevelopment of an area. The statutory basis for the old-style development plans has now been removed and such plans are now part of history.

The 1947 Act, however, recognized the ever-changing nature of land-use planning by imposing on each local planning authority a duty, once in every five years, to carry out a fresh survey of its area, and to submit to the Minister a report of the survey, together with proposals for any alterations or additions to the plan which appeared to it to be required. After 1968, these plans could not be amended without the Secretary of State's approval. **3.07**

Defects of the 1947 development plans system

By the mid-1960s, it had become clear that the development plan system established under the 1947 Act was failing to meet current needs. One of the main difficulties was that the content of the old-style development plans had been based on two assumptions: that the population would remain stable; and that there would be little growth in the volume of motor traffic. In fact, both these assumptions proved to be false. An increase in the population which followed the end of the Second World War had led to an increase in the demand for hospitals, schools, and housing. An increase in the standard of living in the same period had led to an increase in the number of motor vehicles using the roads, to a need for investment in a new road programme to accommodate those vehicles, and thus to the growth of development pressure on land where it had never previously existed. In theory at least, it should have been possible for the old-style development plans to be amended to accommodate the changes that were then taking place. In practice, however, this proved to be impossible because of the rapid pace of change and the law's requirement that the same administrative procedures be followed for proposals to amend development plans as were required for their original preparation. **3.08**

In addition, however, the old-style development plans had a further and more fundamental defect. The plans concentrated on land use, and did so in excessive detail. The concentration took place at the expense of many other factors which help to shape the environment but also require to be integrated into land-use planning, such as national investment programmes and social and economic objectives. Indeed, in retrospect it seems unlikely that a single statutory document would ever be able to perform both functions adequately. **3.09**

Against this background, in 1964 the Government set up a Planning Advisory Group comprising officers of local government, the professions, and departments concerned to advise it on the future of the development plan system. Its report, **3.10**

The Future of Development Plans, published in 1965, recommended the gradual adoption of a new 'two-tier' development plan system. Most of the report's recommendations were given effect in the Town and Country Planning Act 1968, and later consolidated, first in the Town and Country Planning Act 1971, and then in the 1990 Act.

C. DEVELOPMENT PLANS PREPARED UNDER THE 1968 ACT (SECOND GENERATION PLANS)

3.11 The statutory provisions relating to the two-tier development plan system were introduced by the Town and Country Planning Act 1968 and continued in legislative force by the Town and Country Planning Acts of 1971 and 1990 and the associated Town and Country Planning (Development Plan) (England) Regulations 1999. The essence of the system was the creation of a single development plan for an area but one having two tiers, namely, a structure plan tier and a local plan tier, with each tier performing a different but related function.

3.12 The purpose of the structure plan tier of the development plan was that it should sketch general lines of development in an area with a broad brush. Basically, structure plans were concerned with land use, but dealt with it in terms of policies applicable to the major land uses such as employment, housing, education, and recreation, and, in particular, transport policy and lines of communication within the area and in relation to neighbouring areas. Structure plans set out policies and proposals of structural or strategic importance for an area. They also provided important links between national economic and social planning and local land-use planning. Because structure plans dealt with policies and proposals for a wide area in very general terms, they did not deal with individual properties or show the precise boundaries of areas where particular policies apply.

3.13 Local plans, on the other hand, were much more detailed than their parent structure plan. They dealt with local issues, but within the context of the policies set out in the structure plan. They developed and applied the policies of the structure plan in force for the area, and showed how these policies related to precisely defined areas of land. Local plans also provided the basis for the exercise of a local planning authority's development control functions. In addition, by allocating sites for particular purposes, they formed the basis on which the development or redevelopment of an area could proceed.

3.14 Following the abolition of the Greater London Council and the Metropolitan County Councils by the Local Government Act 1985, the existing two-tier system of local planning authorities in Greater London and the metropolitan areas of England was reduced to one, so that, as from 1 April 1986, the London boroughs and the metropolitan districts began to exercise all the functions of the local planning authority in their areas.

The Local Government Act 1985 also provided for the introduction in the Greater London and metropolitan areas of new 'unitary development plans' (UDPs). The authority for these plans was contained in Part II of the 1990 Act. Each local planning authority in those areas was required to prepare a UDP for their area. **3.15**

Later, following a much wider reorganization of local government structure by the Local Government Act 1992, which created unitary authorities in many other areas of the country, the Secretary of State was given power to direct a unitary authority to prepare a unitary development plan for its area. The essence of the UDP was that it was prepared in two parts. Part I contained the authority's general policies for its area, whilst Part II formulated those policies in detail. In essence the two parts were comparable respectively with the structure plan part and the local plan part of the development plan introduced in 1968. With a UDP, however, both parts were prepared and adopted by a single local planning authority. **3.16**

Defects of the 1968 development plans system

Although work had begun by 1971 on the preparation of the first structure plans, it was not until 1985, some 14 years later, that all the 82 'first-generation' structure plans which were to cover England and Wales had been approved. Subsequently, local (county) planning authorities were engaged in preparing alterations to structure plans; and in some cases, their complete replacement. **3.17**

According to the Department of the Environment in 1986, one of the main reasons for the slowness in preparing and approving structure plan proposals was that many of the written statements and explanatory memoranda were much longer than they actually needed to be. **3.18**

Another difficulty causing delay in the preparation and approval of structure plans was a widespread tendency for local planning authorities to include policies in them that had little or nothing to do with land-use planning or the physical environment. Examples of irrelevant policies in structure plans submitted for approval included those relating to building design standards, storage of cycles, the development of co-operatives, racial or sexual disadvantage, standards of highway maintenance, parking charges, the location of picnic sites, and so-called 'nuclear-free zones'. In all these cases, approval by the Secretary of State was delayed by the need to delete or modify these proposals from the submitted structure plan. **3.19**

As far as local plans were concerned, by 1986 many local plans had not been adopted, the average time being taken between the deposit and the adoption of local plans being about 20 months. Although the Secretary of State regarded many local plans as too detailed and containing policies unrelated to the purposes of development plans, the main reason for delay in the adoption of local plans was **3.20** seen as the length and complexity of the procedures for preparing them and the relationship between local plans and structure plans.

3.21 The defects of the 1968 development plan system led local planning authorities to begin to rely on non-statutory plans and policies to guide development in their areas, rather than take the formal steps of altering an existing development plan or preparing a new one. The result was that the public were denied the right to object to these plans and policies as they were not subject to the rigours of an independent examination in public or to a public local inquiry.

3.22 Yet another difficulty was that there was little regional input into the content of plans, particularly structure plans. To deal with this problem, the Government introduced regional planning guidance (RPGs). For a number of years the first stage in the transmission of a national land-use policy to local land-use decision-taking was this guidance. According to a former Planning Policy Guidance Note:

> RPGs sets out broad strategic policies at the regional level where there are matters which, though not of national scope, apply across regions or parts of regions and need to be considered on a scale wider than the area of a single strategic planning authority.

3.23 The main purpose of an RPG was to provide a regional spatial strategy within which local authority development plans and local transport plans could be prepared. They provided a broad development strategy for the region over a 15- to 20-year period and identified the scale and distribution of provision for new housing and priorities for the environment, transport, infrastructure, economic development, agriculture, minerals, and waste treatment and disposal.

3.24 The importance of RPGs in guiding and informing local planning authorities in the preparation of development plans was underpinned by statute. By s 31(6) of the Town and Country Planning Act 1990, authorities were required to have regard to RPGs in formulating the general policies contained in structure plans. Corresponding duties were imposed in relation to unitary development plans and local plans by the 1990 Act and the Town and Country Planning (Development Plan) (England) Regulations 1999. Thus, the guidance in an RPG could be a material consideration in the consideration of individual planning decisions.

3.25 It is important to note, however, that the preparation and formulation of RPGs was not governed by statutory provisions. The procedures followed were in fact non-statutory. This non-statutory procedure mirrored to a great extent the statutory procedures laid down by the 1990 Act and regulations made thereunder for the preparation of structure plans. The procedure involved the preparation of draft regional planning guidance by the Regional Planning Body in consultation with the relevant Government Regional Offices and major stakeholders. Then followed its publication; the consideration of written representations; the holding of an examination in public before an independent panel, and a report by the panel to the Secretary of State; publication of a further version of the RPG; further consultation; and eventually the issue of the RPG in its final form.

D. CHANGES TO THE 1968 DEVELOPMENT PLANS SYSTEM

The Government eventually decided to make a number of legislative changes to the development plan system pending wider reform. As the 1990 Act was basically a consolidation act, the changes thought necessary were made to the 1990 Act by the Planning and Compulsory Purchase Act 1991. **3.26**

In particular, the Act required county councils to prepare a *single* structure plan to cover the work of their area (insofar as they had not already done so). In addition, county councils were given power to adopt their own structure plans instead of sending them to the Secretary of State for his approval. **3.27**

The Act also updated the discretionary power given to every local planning authority in a non-metropolitan area to prepare a *single* local plan covering the whole of its area with a mandatory requirement to do so. The authority was also given power to adopt its own local plan. Another important change was to give the Secretary of State greater control over the *content* of structure and local plans. Finally, a duty was placed on mineral planning authorities (see Chapter 23) to prepare a 'minerals local plan' containing the authority's detailed policies for its area in respect of the winning and working of minerals. Likewise, the Act also introduced a new statutory requirement for local planning authorities to prepare a 'waste local plan' to contain policies in respect of development involving the deposit of refuse or waste materials in its area. **3.28**

E. DEVELOPMENT PLANS PREPARED UNDER THE 2004 ACT (THIRD GENERATION PLANS)

In a consultation paper, *Delivering a Fundamental Change*, published in December 2001, the Government proposed a more far-reaching reform of the development plan system. The Government's main criticism of the existing system centred on the role of local plans. According to the consultation paper, the system of local plans was over-complex; they were often inconsistent with policies set out at national or regional levels; they were too long; preparation was slow and expensive; and they contained too many policies. As a result, they were failing their users. Furthermore, preparation of local plans was being overtaken by new local authority policies and programmes such as community strategies and regeneration and neighbourhood renewal initiatives. **3.29**

3.30 Accordingly, the Government decided to fundamentally reform the development plan system. The proposal was to abolish all structure plans, local plans, and unitary development plans with a new single level of plan to be known as the Local Development Plan Framework. This Framework would consist of:

- a statement of core policies setting out the local authority's vision and strategy in promoting and controlling development throughout its area;
- more detailed action plans for further smaller local areas of change such as urban extensions, town centres, and neighbourhoods undergoing renewal; and
- a map showing the areas of change for which action plans were to be prepared and existing designations, such as conservation areas.

3.31 The consultation paper criticized the local development plan public local inquiry system, at which objections to the plan could be heard, as often time-consuming and adversarial. So this too was to be reformed.

3.32 On 18 July 2002, the Government reaffirmed the intention to proceed with the abolition of structure plans and the replacement of local and unitary development plans with a Local Development Framework. It also announced that regional planning guidance was to be replaced by a statutory regional spatial strategy. These proposals were given effect to in the Planning and Compulsory Purchase Act 2004 ('the 2004 Act'). The Act itself does not use the term 'Local Development Framework' but in practice the term covers the whole portfolio of documents relating to local development plans. One of the objectives of the new system was to speed up the preparation and amendment of development plans by breaking up the plan into separate components which then could be amended separately when necessary. It should be noted that s 70 of the Local Democracy Economic Development and Construction Act 2009 subsumed regional spatial strategies and regional economic strategies into regional strategies.

3.33 With the passing of the 2004 Act, the existing system of development plans have begun to be gradually phased out. Accordingly, the law and procedures relating to that system have ceased to be relevant to the development plan system introduced by the 2004 Act. Whilst the earlier provisions may still have some lingering significance, no detailed discussion of them has been included in this book.

F. THE LOCALISM ACT 2011 AND THE ABOLITION OF THE REGIONAL STRATEGIES

3.34 The Localism Act 2011 ('the 2011 Act') has abolished the regional planning tier by the removal of regional strategies and the bodies responsible for maintaining those strategies. That previous attempt by the Coalition Government to revoke the regional strategies by executive action ignited a flurry of litigation. Those cases culminated in *R (on the application of Cala Homes (South) Ltd) v Secretary of State* *for Communities and Local Government* [2011] EWCA Civ 639; [2011] 2 EGLR 75 which examined the scope of the Secretary of State's discretion under the 2009 Act, on which see further: A Bowes, 'Revocation of Regional Strategies: A State Frontier Rolled Back too Soon? Cala Homes (South) Ltd v Secretary of State for Communities and Local Government [2010] EWHC 2866 (Admin)' [2011] 2 JPL 137.

The gap left between the Local Development Plan Framework and the National Plan has been filled by a new duty under on local authorities and other bodies to co-operate with each other in relation to planning of sustainable development, inserted at s 33A of the Planning and Compulsory Purchase Act 2004 by the Localism Act 2011. The objective is to ensure constructive and active engagement to maximize effective working on sustainable development and use of land, in particular in connection with strategic infrastructure. This duty came into effect on 15 November 2011 and is not retrospective; see *University of Bristol v North Somerset CC* [2013] EWHC 231 (Admin); [2013] JPL 940. A recent consideration of the duty can be found within the judgment of Sir Ross Cranston in *R (on the application of St Albans District Council) v Secretary of State for Communities and Local Government* [2017] EWHC 1751 (Admin). A review of the case law prior to the *St Albans* case can be found within C Howell Williams QC and M Murphy, 'The Call of Duty' [2016] 10 JPL 957, the authors drew-out six main conclusions from the case law and Inspector's reports, at 970–971: **3.35**

- First, local planning authorities must do more than mere consultation. There must be engagement on a constructive, active, and ongoing basis. They must at least consider whether or not to prepare agreements on joint approaches and joint local development documents.
- Secondly, they must focus on outcomes. The duty requires cooperation in maximizing the effectiveness of plan preparation. Moreover, examination Inspectors will look at the results of any engagement.
- Thirdly, local planning authorities should address the requirements of the duty to cooperate as they apply to the circumstances of their area at an early stage in the plan-making process.
- Fourthly, even though the duty is not a duty to agree, local planning authorities should make every effort to reach agreement.
- Fifthly, local planning authorities should ensure that there is a robust evidence-based approach to the carrying out of the duty (including records of meetings and progress). Statements of common ground and memoranda of understanding might assist, but it is the substance of those documents that will matter. The demonstration of compliance with the duty to cooperate is not a box-ticking exercise.
- Sixthly, local planning authorities should not assume that cooperative engagement with other authorities is not necessary in the post-submission examination

stage; it will remain a relevant and potentially important consideration particularly in the context of the policies in the NPPF.

3.36 The Act also amends the process by which development plan documents are adopted so that the local planning authority has more power over the final content of the plans and is not completely bound by the report of the Inspector who has examined the submitted plans.

4

DEVELOPMENT PLANS: THEIR LEGAL SIGNIFICANCE AFTER THE PLANNING AND COMPULSORY PURCHASE ACT 2004

A. SUSTAINABLE DEVELOPMENT AND COMMUNITY INVOLVEMENT	4.03	H. THE BINDING NATURE OF INSPECTORS' REPORTS	4.56
B. THE SURVEY	4.12	I. POWERS OF THE SECRETARY OF STATE WITH REGARD TO LOCAL DEVELOPMENT DOCUMENTS	4.59
C. LOCAL DEVELOPMENT SCHEMES	4.17		
D. THE LOCAL DEVELOPMENT FRAMEWORK	4.22	J. MISCELLANEOUS PROVISIONS OF PART 2	4.60
E. LOCAL DEVELOPMENT DOCUMENTS AND NEIGHBOURHOOD PLANS	4.26	K. LEGAL CHALLENGES TO DEVELOPMENT PLANS	4.67
F. PREPARATION OF DEVELOPMENT PLAN DOCUMENTS	4.45	L. DEVELOPMENT PLANS: THEIR LEGAL SIGNIFICANCE	4.77
G. THE INDEPENDENT EXAMINATION OF DEVELOPMENT PLAN DOCUMENTS	4.49	M. TRANSITIONAL PROVISIONS: TRANSFERRING FROM THE OLD SYSTEM TO THE NEW SYSTEM	4.86
		N. WALES: REGIONAL FUNCTIONS AND LOCAL DEVELOPMENT	4.90

The Planning and Compulsory Purchase Act 2004 introduced a sea change from the development plan system of the past. The new system provided for the replacement of the non-statutory regional guidance, structure plans, local plans, waste plans, mineral plans, and unitary development plans by regional spatial strategies and local development documents. As stated earlier, the Local Democracy Economic Development and Construction Act 2009 renamed the regional spatial strategies as regional strategies but basically retained the same system. The Localism Act 2011 has however swept away the whole system of regional strategies

4.01

and regional authorities and replaced them simply with a duty on local authorities to co-operate.

4.02 The provisions in the Act for the introduction of the new system allowed for structure plans to be 'saved' (ie continued in force) for a period of three years from the date of commencement of the Act, unless within that period revisions to the regional strategy were expressed to replace structure plan policies in whole or in part or the Secretary of State by direction had extended the three-year period to such policies as are specified in the direction. With regard to local plans, the Secretary of State by regulations, may require that within a prescribed period, local planning authorities submit to him a timetable for the preparation of local development documents over the following three years. Local plans may also be 'saved' during the three-year period but subject to replacement of policies in the plans by approved development plan documents. In some cases after the three-year period has ended the Secretary of State may continue policies in the local plan which are compliant with an authority's local development framework (see para 4.67).

A. SUSTAINABLE DEVELOPMENT AND COMMUNITY INVOLVEMENT

4.03 Before going into the detail of the present system of development plans it is necessary to explain two underlying principles. The first is the principle of sustainable development.

4.04 Section 39 of the 2004 Act requires persons or bodies responsible for exercising any function in relation to local development documents, to exercise that function with the objective of contributing to the achievement of sustainable development.

4.05 For a number of years planning policy guidance has contained a number of specific references to this concept. It has now received express statutory recognition in s 39. For an analysis of s 39 and its relationship to the references to 'sustainable development' in the National Planning Policy Framework (NPPF), see the analysis by Jay J in *Calverton Parish Council v Nottingham City Council* [2015] EWHC 1078 (Admin).

4.06 The idea behind the expression is the wish to ensure that everybody enjoys a better quality of life both now and in the future. A widely used definition of the term is that drawn up by the World Commission on Environment and Development in 1987, as being 'development that meets the needs of the present without compromising the ability of future generations to meet their own needs'.

4.07 A commitment to the concept of sustainable development was established in May 1999 with the publication by the Government of *A Better Quality of Life— a Strategy for Sustainable Development for the UK* (Cmnd 4345). That strategy identified four broad objectives all of which have to be achieved at the same time. They are:

— social progress which recognizes the needs of everyone;
— effective protection of the environment;
— the prudent use of natural resources; and
— maintenance of high and stable levels of economic growth and employment.

4.08 How the Government expects the objective of sustainability to be achieved is set out in the NPPF which states:

> 7. The purpose of the planning system is to contribute to the achievement of sustainable development. At a very high level, the objective of sustainable development can be summarised as meeting the needs of the present without compromising the ability of future generations to meet their own needs.
> 8. Achieving sustainable development means that the planning system has three overarching objectives, which are interdependent and need to be pursued in mutually supportive ways (so that opportunities can be taken to secure net gains across each of the different objectives):
>   a) an economic **objective**—to help build a strong, responsive and competitive economy, by ensuring that sufficient land of the right types is available in the right places and at the right time to support growth, innovation and improved productivity; and by identifying and coordinating the provision of infrastructure;
>   b) a social **objective**—to support strong, vibrant and healthy communities, by ensuring that a sufficient number and range of homes can be provided to meet the needs of present and future generations; and by fostering a well-designed and safe built environment, with accessible services and open spaces that reflect current and future needs and support communities' health, social and cultural well-being; and
>   c) an environmental **objective**—to contribute to protecting and enhancing our natural, built and historic environment; including making effective use of land, helping to improve biodiversity, using natural resources prudently, minimizing waste and pollution, and mitigating and adapting to climate change, including moving to a low carbon economy.
> 9. These objectives should be delivered through the preparation and implementation of plans and the application of the policies in this Framework; they are not criteria against which every decision can or should be judged. Planning policies and decisions should play an active role in guiding development towards sustainable solutions, but in doing so should take local circumstances into account, to reflect the character, needs and opportunities of each area.

The presumption in favour of sustainable development

4.09 The National Policy Planning Framework also sets out a new presumption in favour of sustainable development as follows:

> 11. Plans and decisions should apply a presumption in favour of sustainable development.

For plan-making this means that:
a) plans should positively seek opportunities to meet the development needs of their area, and be sufficiently flexible to adapt to rapid change;
b) strategic policies should, as a minimum, provide for objectively assessed needs for housing and other uses, as well as any needs that cannot be met within neighbouring areas, unless:
   i. the application of policies in this Framework that protect areas or assets of particular importance provides a strong reason for restricting the overall scale, type or distribution of development in the plan area; or
   ii. any adverse impacts of doing so would significantly and demonstrably outweigh the benefits, when assessed against the policies in this Framework taken as a whole.

For **decision-taking** this means:
c) approving development proposals that accord with an up-to-date development plan without delay; or
d) where there are no relevant development plan policies, or the policies which are most important for determining the application are out-of-date, granting permission unless:
   i. the application of policies in this Framework that protect areas or assets of particular importance provides a clear reason for refusing the development proposed; or
   ii. any adverse impacts of doing so would significantly and demonstrably outweigh the benefits, when assessed against the policies in this Framework taken as a whole.

4.10 Removing much controversy from the original NPPF, the revised version has a closed list of policies which 'provide a clear reason for refusing permission'. These are set out within footnote 6 as policies relating to 'habitats sites (and those sites listed in paragraph 176) and/or designated as Sites of Special Scientific Interest; land designated as Green Belt, Local Green Space, an Area of Outstanding Natural Beauty, a National Park (or within the Broads Authority) or defined as Heritage Coast; irreplaceable habitats; designated heritage assets (and other heritage assets of archaeological interest referred to in footnote 63); and areas at risk of flooding or coastal change.' Removing further uncertainty left by Lord Gill's judgment in *Hopkins Homes Ltd v Secretary of State for Communities and Local Government* [2017] UKSC 37; [2017] 1 WLR 1865 at [85], the revised NPPF makes clear that such policies do not include those within the development plan itself, just those within the NPPF. Similarly, footnote 7 defines 'out of date' as including:

> for applications involving the provision of housing, situations where the local planning authority cannot demonstrate a five year supply of deliverable housing sites (with the appropriate buffer, as set out in paragraph 73); or where the Housing Delivery Test indicates that the delivery of housing was substantially below (less than 75% of) the housing requirement over the previous three years.

Community involvement

4.11 Section 18 of the 2004 Act requires the local planning authority to prepare a statement of community involvement and once adopted the preparation of other local development documents must comply with the statement of community involvement; see ss 18(3) and 19(3).

B. THE SURVEY

4.12 Part 2 of the 2004 Act and the Local Planning Regulations contain the provisions relating to local development. The present regulations are the Town and Country Planning (Local Development) (England) Regulations 2012 (SI 2012/767). In order to provide for the proper planning of an area by the local planning authority, the authority is required by s 13(1) of the Act to keep under review the matters which may be expected to affect the development of their area or the planning of its development. Section 13(2) sets out that these matters include:

(a) the principal physical, economic, social, and environmental characteristics of the area of the authority;
(b) the principal purposes for which land is used in the area;
(c) the size, composition, and distribution of the population of the area;
(d) the communications, transport system, and traffic of the area;
(e) any other considerations which may be expected to affect those matters; and
(f) such other matters as may be prescribed or as the Secretary of State (in a particular case) may direct.

Section 13(3) further provides that the matters also include: **4.13**

(a) any changes which the authority thinks may occur in relation to any other matter; and
(b) the effect such changes are likely to have on the development of the authority's area or on the planning of such development.

4.14 This section 13 duty is imposed on district councils, unitary districts, and the London boroughs. Under s 14, however, a county council is placed under a similar duty for any part of its area for which there is also a district council.

4.15 Note too that subsections (3) and (4) of s 14 of the 2004 Act also allow county councils if required by regulations made by the Secretary of State to keep such matters under review that may not necessarily relate to a county matter. That extension to the role of the county council is intended to enable the county to become involved in joint working arrangements with the district councils through a joint committee structure.

4.16 From 6 April 2018, a local planning authority is under a statutory duty to review its local plan and statement of community involvement, every five years from the date of adoption see: reg 10A of the Town and Country Planning (Local Development Planning) (England) Regulations 2012. Guidance on how to conduct a review is to be found within the PPG under the 'Plan Making' section. There is no express requirement for consultation although, there is an uncertainty whether a plan review amounts to 'an activity which supports' 'the preparation of development plan documents' which would engage the duty to cooperate with other planning authorities under s 33A of the Planning and Compulsory Purchase Act 2004. Whilst the language of s 33A is not entirely clear-cut, it would appear that plan reviews are a step prior to the scope of s 33A and that it is only where a review indicates changes to the plan are required that the duty to cooperate kicks in. The point is however likely to be tested in the courts given the controversial question of meeting unmet need between authorities in a market area.

C. LOCAL DEVELOPMENT SCHEMES

4.17 Section 15 of the Act requires local planning authorities to submit to the Secretary of State a local development scheme. Once prepared, the scheme is required to be kept under review by the authority, and revised as appropriate. Note that in areas where the county council is a local planning authority, a duty is placed on the county council to submit minerals and waste development schemes.

4.18 The purpose of the local development scheme is to provide a public statement of the local planning authority's programme for the production of local development documents. It thus enables the public to find out what the local planning authority is proposing to do and where, and when and at what stage it can expect to be involved in the planning process. The matters to be included in local development schemes are set out in s 15 of the Act and online in the PPG (12-009-20140306) as follows:

> This must specify (among other matters) the documents which, when prepared, will comprise the Local Plan for the area. It must be made available publicly and kept up-to-date. It is important that local communities and interested parties can keep track of progress. Local planning authorities should publish their Local Development Scheme on their website.

4.19 The Town and Country Planning (Local Development) (England) (Amendment) Regulations 2009, SI 2009/401 (now consolidated into the 2012 Regulations) removed the duty on local planning authorities to specify supplementary planning documents and statements of community involvement in a local development scheme. Furthermore, they no longer have to prepare a suitability appraisal report for their supplementary planning documents, nor submit the sustainability appraisal to the Secretary of State for examination. However, it should be noted that the Supplementary Planning Documents will need a Strategic Environmental Assessment if they set the framework for future development.

The documents required to be prepared by local development schemes therefore fall into two groups, namely documents which will be development plan documents, and other 'non-development plan' documents. The former is by far the most important (see later at para 4.26). **4.20**

Central government control over the content of a local development scheme used to be ensured by requiring its submission to the Secretary of State. However, s 111 of the 2011 Act has amended s 15 of the 2004 Act so that there is no longer a requirement to submit the local development scheme to the Secretary of State. However, the Secretary of State retains powers to direct changes but will only be able to use them for the purpose of ensuring effective plan coverage. **4.21**

D. THE LOCAL DEVELOPMENT FRAMEWORK

Although the term local development framework is not used in the 2004 Act, elsewhere the term is used to refer to the system by which local and unitary development plans are to be replaced by the creation of local development documents. The term was used in para 1.4 of the first PPS12 where it was explained in the following way: **4.22**

> The local development framework will be comprised of local development documents, which include development plan documents, that are part of the statutory development plan and supplementary planning documents which expand policies set out in a development plan document or provide additional detail. The local development framework will also include the statement of community involvement, the local development scheme, and the annual monitoring report. Furthermore, local planning authorities should also include any local development orders and or simplified planning zones, which have been adopted. The local development framework, together with the regional spatial strategy, provides the essential framework for planning in the local authority's area.

The NPPF now describes the local development documents as a 'local plan':

> The plan for the future development of the local area, drawn up by the local planning authority in consultation with the community. In law this is described as the development plan documents adopted under the Planning and Compulsory Purchase Act 2004. Current core strategies or other planning policies, which under the regulations would be considered to be development plan documents, form part of the Local Plan. The term includes old policies which have been saved under the 2004 Act.

Section 17(7)(za) of the 2004 Act provides that regulations may prescribe what descriptions of documents are to be prepared as local development documents. **4.23**

4.24 Regulation 5 of the 2012 Regulations prescribes the documents which must be prepared as local development documents as:

    (a) any document prepared by a local planning authority containing statements of one or more of the following:
        (i) the development and use of land which the local planning authority wish to encourage during any specified period;
        (ii) the allocation of sites for a particular type of development or use;
        (iii) any environmental, social, design and economic objectives which are relevant to the attainment of the development or use of land which the local planning authority wishes to encourage during any specified period;
        (iv) development management and site allocation policies which are intended to guide the determination of planning applications;
    (b) a document of the description mentioned in para (a) which contains policies applying to sites or areas by reference to an Ordnance Survey map.

4.25 Regulation 5(2) of the 2012 Regulations also prescribes that the descriptions of other documents prescribed for the purposes of s 17(1)(a) which, if prepared, must be specified as Local Development Documents in a local development scheme, are as follows:

    (a) any document which:
        (i) relates only to part of the area of the local planning authority;
        (ii) identifies that area as an area of significant change or special conservation; and
        (iii) contains the authority's policies in relation to the area; and
    (b) any other document which includes a site allocation policy.

E. LOCAL DEVELOPMENT DOCUMENTS AND NEIGHBOURHOOD PLANS

4.26 The non-statutory local development framework is comprised of local development documents some of which will be statutory 'development plan' documents. This distinction is very important as development plan documents are those documents which are to form part of the authority's development plan once they have been subject to independent review. As such, under s 38(6) of the 2004 Act, where, in making a determination, regard must be had to the development plan, the determination must be made in accordance with the plan unless material considerations indicate otherwise (see Chapter 11). Section 37(3) simply defines a development plan document as 'a local development document which is specified as a development plan document in the local development scheme'. Regulation 5 of the Town and Country Planning (Local Planning) (England) Regulations 2012 (SI 2012/767) explains which documents are development plan documents, however, as will be explained below, the Regulations are not straightforward.

Supplementary planning documents

4.27 Supplementary planning documents may be included in a local development documents file. These documents can provide further details of policies and proposals in a development plan document. They may take the form of design guides, area development briefs, or other documents supplementing policies which are in a development plan document. What they cannot do is avoid the need to include policies and proposals which should be included within a development plan document. They must also be consistent with national planning policies and contain a reasoned justification of the policies. The 2004 Regulations define a supplementary planning document as a local development document which is not a development plan document or a statement of community involvement. So, it should be emphasized that supplementary planning documents are not subject (as are development plan documents) to independent examination, and they do not form part of the statutory development plan for the area.

4.28 In *R (on the application of Abdul Wakil) v Hammersmith and Fulham LBC* [2012] EWHC 1411 (QB); [2013] Env LR 3, Wilkie J held that a document which purported to be a Supplementary Planning Document was in substance an Action Area Plan and as such a Development Plan Document and should have been subject to independent assessment by the Secretary of State. The scope to adopt Supplementary Planning Documents has been much reduced since the decision of *R (on the application of Skipton Properties Ltd) v Craven District Council* [2017] EWHC 534 (Admin); [2017] JPL 825 in which Jay J held at [93] that reg 5(1)(iv) should be read disjunctively, thus any SPD which concerns 'development management ... policies' or 'site allocation policies' and which is 'intended to guide the determination of applications for planning permission' is likely to need to be prepared as a Development Plan Document, subject to independent examination and sustainability appraisal. Jay J's judgment was followed by Gilbart J in *William Davis Ltd v Charnwood Borough Council* [2017] EWHC 3006 (Admin); [2017] JPL 549. Indeed, following that case law a planning authority may well be left wondering what can go into an SPD at all. Jay J's observation in *Skipton* at [94] that the Regulations should be revised appears therefore very sensible.

4.29 The process of preparing and adopting a supplementary planning document therefore differs substantially from that required for development plan documents. The local planning authority is required to publish the draft supplementary planning document which no longer has to be accompanied by an appraisal of sustainability but, under s 19(3) of the 2004 Act as amended by the 2008 Act, the authority must comply with the statement of community involvement. Once the local planning authority has made such representations in the draft supplementary planning document and made changes considered appropriate, the authority may proceed to adoption. The 2012 Regulations (Part 5) contain provisions with regard to public participation in the preparation of supplementary planning guidance before its adoption.

4.30 Mention should also be made of the need for local development documents to comply with strategic environmental assessment now required under Council Directive 2001/42 EC (see Chapter 13).

4.31 The procedure leading to the adoption of a local development plan document is contained in the Act and in the Regulations.

4.32 The Regulations contain detailed provisions relating to the procedures for pre-submission consultation, pre-submission public participation, the making of representations, the submission of documents and information to the Secretary of State, and the handling by the authority of any representations made. Given below are the main features of this process.

Neighbourhood development plans

4.33 The Localism Act 2011 created a new concept, the 'neighbourhood development plan'. The PPG (41-001-20140306) explains these as follows:

> Neighbourhood planning gives communities direct power to develop a shared vision for their neighbourhood and shape the development and growth of their local area. They are able to choose where they want new homes, shops and offices to be built, have their say on what those new buildings should look like and what infrastructure should be provided, and grant planning permission for the new buildings they want to see go ahead. Neighbourhood planning provides a powerful set of tools for local people to ensure that they get the right types of development for their community where the ambition of the neighbourhood is aligned with the strategic needs and priorities of the wider local area.

4.34 The revolutionary aspect of these new creatures was to make them a part of the statutory development plan, see s 38(2)(c) of the Planning and Compulsory Purchase Act 2004, and thus they were clothed with the statutory priority of s 38(6) of the 2004 Act. It also meant that neighbourhood development plans (or simply neighbourhood plans) attained the same status as the local plan for the area. It is for these reasons that neighbourhood plans have attracted a good deal of attention from the courts since the first plans were adopted in 2013. The concept of neighbourhood plans was part of the 2010–2015 Coalition Government's 'Localism Agenda' explained by J Stanton, 'The Big Society and Community Development: Neighbourhood Planning under the Localism Act' (2014) 16(4) Env L Rev 262 and A Bowes, 'Rise of the Neighbourhood Triffids' [2011] 4 JPL 386.

4.35 By s 38A of the Planning and Compulsory Purchase Act 2004 'any qualifying body' may initiate the process to 'make' a neighbourhood plan. A qualifying body is a parish council or 'any organisation or body designated as a neighbourhood forum, authorised for the purposes of a neighbourhood development plan to act in relation to a neighbourhood area' (commonly known as a 'neighbourhood forum'). The local planning authority is empowered to authorize an organization or body to act in relation to a given 'neighbourhood area' by s 61F of the Town and Country Planning Act 1990 subject to the criteria therein. Section 61G of the Town and Country Planning Act 1990 deals with 'neighbourhood area', however aside from designating the area of a parish council as a single neighbourhood area the discretion on the planning authority is wide. As the Court of Appeal held in *R (on the application of Daws Hill Neighbourhood Forum) v Wycombe District Council* [2014] EWCA Civ 228; [2014] 1 WLR 1362, s 61G confers a 'broad discretion' on the planning authority. Hence in that case, it was open to the planning authority to refuse to include, within a neighbourhood area, two large strategic sites. See further: A Bowes, 'Determining a "Neighbourhood Area"—Plan-Led Paradigm or Broad Discretion?' [2013] 8 JPL 926.

4.36 By s 38A(3) of the Planning and Compulsory Purchase Act 2004, Sch 4B to the Town and Country Planning Act 1990 has effect to prescribe the procedure for promoting, examining, and making a neighbourhood development plan, subject to the modifications at s 38C(5) of the Planning and Compulsory Purchase Act 2004. The Neighbourhood Planning (General) Regulations 2012 (SI 2012/637) provide further detail on the procedure to designate neighbourhood areas and forums as well as detail on the preparation of neighbourhood plans.

4.37 Section 38B of the Planning and Compulsory Purchase Act 2004 provides that a neighbourhood plan must (i) specify the period it is to have effect, (ii) does not relate to 'excluded development' as defined at s 61K of the 1990 Act and (iii), must not relate to more than one neighbourhood area.

4.38 Paragraphs 7 to 10 of Sch 4B to the 1990 Act makes provision for independent examination of neighbourhood plans. There has been extensive case law on the examination of neighbourhood plans. The statutory question as to whether it is 'appropriate' for the plan to proceed to referendum is different to whether a local plan is 'sound', the neighbourhood plan process is a lighter touch, see: *R (on the application of Crownhall Estates) v Chichester District Council* [2016] EWHC 73 (Admin). The High Court held in *R (on the application of Bewley Homes Plc) v Waverley Borough Council* [2017] EWHC 1776 (Admin); [2017] PTSR 423 that the standard of examiner's reasons was not that set out in the speech of Lord Brown in *South Buckinghamshire DC v Porter (No 2)* [2004] UKHL 33; [2004] 1 WLR 1953. Lang J held it was an inquisitorial rather than an adversarial process. Ouseley J came to a similar conclusion in the context of examining local plans in *Cooper Estates Strategic Land Ltd v Royal Tunbridge Wells Borough Council* [2017] EWHC 224 (Admin).

4.39 The requirement that the plan be in 'general conformity' with the 'strategic policies' of the local plan was considered in *Kebbell Developments Ltd v Leeds City Council* [2018] EWCA Civ 450; [2018] 1 WLR 4625, upholding a decision to proceed to referendum in spite of 'a degree of tension' between the neighbourhood plan and the local plan. In *R (on the application of DLA Delivery Ltd) v Lewes District Council* [2017] EWCA Civ 58; [2017] PTSR 949, the Court of Appeal rejected the submission that a neighbourhood plan could not come forward ahead of an up-to-date local plan. Similarly, in *R (on the application of Gladman Developments Ltd) v Aylesbury Vale District Council* [2014] EWHC 4323 (Admin); [2015] JPL 656, the High Court found that a neighbourhood plan could make site allocations even where there was no present development plan document setting out the strategic policies for housing.

4.40 The planning authority is not, however, bound to accept the examiner's recommendations. Paragraphs 12 to 13 of Sch 4B to the 1990 Act gives the authority a discretion to reject the examiner's recommendations. However, in recognition of a number of instances where local authorities were rejecting recommendations, Parliament inserted a new para 13B into Sch 4B through the Housing and Planning Act 2016, which enables the Secretary of State to intervene. The Neighbourhood Planning Act 2017 makes it explicit that a planning authority is required to have regard to a post-examination neighbourhood plan by inserting a new s 70(2)(aza) into the Town and Country Planning Act 1990.

4.41 Upon making a neighbourhood plan, the planning authority must hold a referendum. The rules for holding a referendum are set out in the Neighbourhood Planning (Referendums) Regulations 2012 (SI 2012/2031) and Neighbourhood Planning (Prescribed Dates) Regulations 2012 (SI 2012/2030).

4.42 By s 61N of the Town and Country Planning Act 1990 a legal challenge can be brought at three stages in the process of making a neighbourhood plan: (i) the decision to proceed to referendum (s 61N(2)), (ii) the conduct of the referendum (s 61N(3)), and (iii) the decision to make or decline to make a plan following referendum (s 61N(1)). These staged provisions have raised difficult questions about whether a claim is in time. Some of the early cases took a relaxed view to a challenge raising issues which could have been brought at an earlier point, see, for example, *R (on the application of Maynard) v Chiltern District Council* [2015] EWHC 3817 (Admin) and *R (on the application of Stonegate Homes Ltd) v Horsham District Council* [2016] EWHC 2512. However, in *Hoare v Vale of White Horse DC* [2017] EWHC 1711 (Admin), the High Court held that a challenge under s 61N(2) could not result in the quashing of the plan after the local planning authority had made it since s 61N(1) provides that only a claim brought within the post-making six-week period may do that. A further claim should have been brought under s 61N(1) to do that or an interim injunction obtained to prevent the plan being made, see at [181]–[186] per John Howell QC. In *R (on the application of Oyston Estates Ltd) v Fylde Borough Council* [2017] EWHC 3086 (Admin) Kerr J held that a legal error could only be raised at the step it occurred. In that case, the court held that an alleged unlawful failure to follow the examiner's recommendation and to carry out an appropriate assessment had to be challenged when the decision was made to hold a referendum rather than when the plan was made.

4.43 The neighbourhood plan becomes part of the statutory development plan once it is 'made' by the planning authority or, from 19 July 2017, the plan has passed referendum but the planning authority has not yet 'made' the plan see: s 38(3A) of the Planning and Compulsory Purchase Act 2004 (added by the Neighbourhood Planning Act 2017).

4.44 The Neighbourhood Planning Act 2017 also introduced a provision for neighbourhood plans to be modified. The procedure for modification is now set out at Sch A2 to the Town and Country Planning Act 1990. Guidance on updates to a neighbourhood plan are provided within the PPG (41-084-20180222 to 41-086-20180222).

F. PREPARATION OF DEVELOPMENT PLAN DOCUMENTS

4.45 Section 17 of the 2004 Act specifies the documents which must be specified in a local development scheme. The local development scheme must, inter alia, specify which of those documents are to be development plan documents. These are documents which require a formal scrutiny and appraisal process. Thereafter, they form, by virtue of s 38(3) of the 2004 Act, part of the development plan for the area.

4.46 Development plan documents are spatial planning documents, so that in preparing them local authorities are not just to be concerned with physical aspects of location and land use, but also economic, social, and environmental matters.

4.47 An adopted policies map must be prepared to accompany all development plan documents. Regulation 9(1)(a) provides that the adopted policies map must be on an Ordnance Survey base and illustrate geographically the policies contained in the adopted development plan. Where the adopted policies map consists of text and maps, the text prevails if the map and text conflict. Being a separate development plan document, it must be revised as new development plan documents are prepared.

4.48 Section 19(2) of the 2004 Act provides that in preparing local development documents the local planning authority must have regard to national policies and advice contained in guidance issued by the Secretary of State. Section 182 of the Planning Act 2008 has inserted a new provision into s 19 of the 2004 Act which requires development plan documents to contribute to the mitigation of, and adaption to, climate change.

G. THE INDEPENDENT EXAMINATION OF DEVELOPMENT PLAN DOCUMENTS

4.49 On completion of the pre-submission consultation process required by the authority's community involvement policies, s 20 of the 2004 Act requires that the development plan document should be submitted for independent examination. For that purpose, two copies of the development plan document must be sent to the Planning Inspectorate, along with:

(a) the report of the sustainability proposal;
(b) any supporting technical documents such as urban capacity studies and housing needs surveys; and
(c) a copy of the statement of community involvement and a statement of compliance.

4.50 The local planning authority should at that same time publish a notice that the development plan document has been submitted for independent examination and invite representations to be made within a specified period of six weeks. Where the representations include proposals for alternative site allocations, the authority should publish them and invite representations. All representation on a development plan document that seeks changes to it should specify precisely the changes being sought.

4.51 The purpose of the examination is to determine whether the development plan document satisfies the requirements of the Act with regard to its preparation, and is sound. The Act does not define the term 'sound' but according to the NPPF it is considered to be as follows:

> 35. Local plans and spatial development strategies are examined to assess whether they have been prepared in accordance with legal and procedural requirements, and whether they are sound. Plans are 'sound' if they are:
> a) Positively prepared—providing a strategy which, as a minimum, seeks to meet the area's objectively assessed needs; and is informed by agreements with other authorities, so that unmet need from neighbouring areas is accommodated where it is practical to do so and is consistent with achieving sustainable development;
> b) Justified—an appropriate strategy, taking into account the reasonable alternatives, and based on proportionate evidence;
> c) Effective—deliverable over the plan period, and based on effective joint working on cross-boundary strategic matters that have been dealt with rather than deferred, as evidenced by the statement of common ground; and
> d) Consistent with national policy—enabling the delivery of sustainable development in accordance with the policies in this Framework.'

4.52 In *Barrett Developments Plc v Wakefield Metropolitan Borough Council* [2010] EWCA Civ 897; [2011] JPL 48, Carnwath LJ held of the term 'sound' at [11] and [33]:

> 11. I would emphasise that this guidance, useful though it may be, is advisory only. Generally it appears to indicate the Department's view of what is required to make a strategy 'sound', as required by the statute. Authorities and inspectors must have regard to it, but it is not prescriptive. Ultimately it is they, not the Department, who are the judges of 'soundness'. Provided that they reach a conclusion which is not 'irrational' (meaning 'perverse'), their decision cannot be questioned in the courts. The mere fact that they may not have followed the policy guidance in every respect does not make the conclusion unlawful.
>
> 33. ... As I have said, 'soundness' was a matter to be judged by the inspector and the Council, and raises no issue of law, unless their decision is shown to have been 'irrational', or they are shown to have ignored the relevant guidance or other considerations which were necessarily material in law.

4.53 That approach remains relevant in the post-NPPF world, see: *Zurich Assurance Ltd v Westminster City Council* [2014] EWHC 758 (Admin) per Sales J at [114].

4.54 In *Blythe Valley District Council v Persimmon Homes (North East) Ltd* [2008] EWCA Civ 861; [2009] JPL 335 the Court of Appeal quashed part of a development plan because it was inconsistent with national policy. The problem had arisen because national policy had changed during the course of preparation of the core strategy. The Court of Appeal also held that the Inspector holding the examination had wrongly taken the approach that there was a presumption that the policy was sound unless evidence was produced demonstrating the contrary. This mistake was understandable in that PPS12 used to state that there was such a presumption. Keene LJ pointed out that the legislation contains no such presumption. The last version of PPS12 stated at para 4.49 that 'The starting point for the examination is the assumption that the local authority has submitted *what it considers to be* a sound plan' and the wording of the NPPF equally states that the local authority should submit a plan which they consider to be sound; see para 35 of the NPPF.

4.55 The examination will be carried out by 'a person appointed by the Secretary of State'. This will normally be an Inspector drawn from the Planning Inspectorate. Any person who made representations seeking to change the development plan document must be given the opportunity to appear before and be heard by that person. At the conclusion of the examination, the person appointed must make recommendations and give reasons for those recommendations.

H. THE BINDING NATURE OF INSPECTORS' REPORTS

4.56 Unlike the position under the pre-2004 Act system where a local planning authority was not obliged to accept an Inspector's proposed modifications to a local plan, under the post-2004 Act system the modifications proposed by the Inspector following examination of a development plan document were binding on the authority. This was probably the most controversial feature of the development plan reforms. Section 23 of the 2004 Act provides that the authority has power to adopt a development plan document as originally prepared where the person carrying out the examination so recommends. The authority also has power to adopt a development plan document with modifications if the person carrying out the examination has recommended the modifications. Otherwise subject only to intervention by the Secretary of State, the authority was not given any choice in the matter and had to proceed to adopt the development plan as soon as practical or start the process again. Section 112 of the Localism Act 2011 amends s 20 so that the Inspector must recommend adoption where the Inspector considers it would be reasonable to conclude that the document satisfies the statutory requirements and can be considered sound. Otherwise the Inspector must recommend non-adoption, giving reasons for doing so. Section 112 also amends s 23 so that the local planning authorities do not have to implement the Inspector's recommendations.

4.57 Where the Inspector has not recommended adoption, the authority will be able to adopt after following the Inspector's modifications and, if asked, the Inspector must recommend modifications. More importantly the authority can make their own modifications and resubmit the draft document to the Inspector for examination. Also, the authority can adopt the document having made 'non-material' changes. There is also now a power for the authority to withdraw a development plan document at any time before its adoption.

4.58 Once adopted, the local development plan document then becomes part of the local development framework and part of the development plan for the area.

I. POWERS OF THE SECRETARY OF STATE WITH REGARD TO LOCAL DEVELOPMENT DOCUMENTS

4.59 Section 21 of the 2004 Act gives the Secretary of State wide powers of intervention in the preparation of local development documents. If he considers a document to be unsatisfactory, he may at any time before it is adopted direct the local planning authority to modify it in accordance with the direction. With regards to any development plan document, he has the additional power to direct that it should be submitted to him for his approval. It should also be noted that under s 27 of the 2004 Act, the Secretary of State is given wide power to prepare or revise a development plan document if he considers those functions are not being properly carried out by the local planning authority themselves. He also has a power to direct that a plan be withdrawn. The Housing and Planning Act 2016 inserted further powers of intervention for the Secretary of State and Mayor of London into Part 2 of the Planning and Compulsory Purchase Act 2004. These included (i) a power to direct amendment of local development schemes, (ii) a power to give a direction to an examiner of a local planning document, and (iii) amendments of the pre-existing power of intervention.

J. MISCELLANEOUS PROVISIONS OF PART 2

(a) Withdrawal

4.60 A local planning authority may now withdraw a local development document at any time before adoption, even where a development plan document has been submitted for independent examination. The Localism Act 2011 has removed the requirement that the Inspector had to recommend or the Secretary of State direct withdrawal.

(b) Adoption

4.61 A local planning authority may adopt a local development document that is not a local development plan document either as originally prepared or as modified to take into account representations made in relation to the document or any other relevant matter.

(c) Revocation

4.62 The Secretary of State may at any time revoke a local development plan at the request of the local planning authority. He may also prescribe the descriptions of local development documents which may be revoked by the authority themselves (s 25).

(d) Revision

4.63 A local planning authority may at any time prepare a revision of a local development document, and indeed must do so if the Secretary of State directs it to do so and in accordance with any timetable as he directs. It must also revise a local development document if an enterprise zone scheme is created within the area of the authority, or an existing enterprise zone scheme is modified (s 26).

(e) Joint committees

4.64 Sections 28–31 of the Act deal with the setting up of arrangements for two or more local planning authorities to prepare jointly a local development document. It also provides for the establishment of joint committees of one or more local planning authorities and one or more county councils in relation to any area of the county council for which there is a district council.

(f) Urban development corporations

4.65 Section 33 allows the Secretary of State to direct that Part 2 of the Act shall not apply to the area of an urban development corporation, in which case the local planning authority will not be required to prepare a local development scheme for that area.

(g) Implementation

4.66 Section 35 requires local planning authorities to report annually to the Secretary of State on the implementation of their local development scheme and whether the policies in the local development documents are being achieved. Finally, s 36 enables the Secretary of State to make regulations in connection with the exercise by any person of functions under the Act.

K. LEGAL CHALLENGES TO DEVELOPMENT PLANS

4.67 Under the provisions of s 113 of the 2004 Act a person may challenge the validity of the following strategies, plans, and documents:

(a) the Wales Spatial Plan;
(b) a development plan document;
(c) a local development plan;
(d) a revision of a document mentioned in paras (a), (b), or (c) above;
(e) the Mayor of London's spatial development strategy; or
(f) an alteration or replacement of the spatial development strategy, and anything falling within paras (a) to (g) is referred to as a 'relevant document'.

4.68 However, following an amendment inserted by the Criminal Justice and Courts Act 2015, since 26 October 2016, permission of the High Court has been required prior to bringing a challenge.

4.69 This section in effect applies to the various plans and documents introduced by the 2004 Act and provides a similar protection from legal challenge to that given to the pre-2004 development plans by s 284 of the 1990 Act. Accordingly, the grounds of challenge by an aggrieved person under s 113 are limited to two, namely applications made to the High Court on the ground that:

(a) the document is not within the appropriate power; and
(b) a procedural requirement has not been complied with.

It may also be necessary for the applicant to show that his interests have been substantially prejudiced by a failure to comply with a procedural requirement which relates to the application, publication, or approval of a relevant document.

4.70 A further limitation on the use of this power is that the person aggrieved must make the application within six weeks of the 'relevant date' so that after the six-week period has passed it is no longer possible to challenge the validity of a strategy, plan, or document. This is because subsection 2 of s 113 provides that a 'relevant document' (as defined above) must not be questioned in any legal proceedings insofar as is provided by the provisions of the section.

4.71 The 'relevant date' is expressed to be the date the National Assembly for Wales approves the Wales Spatial Plan (or a revision of it); the date of adoption by the local planning authority of a development plan document or its approval by the Secretary of State (as the case may be); and the date of adoption by a local planning authority in Wales of a local development plan or its approval by the National Assembly for Wales (as the case may be); and the date when the Mayor of London publishes the spatial development strategy (or an alteration or replacement of it). This wording was held by the Court of Appeal in *Barker v Hambleton DC* [2012] EWCA Civ 610; [2013] PTSR 41 to mean that time ran from that date and not from the following day after the date of approval or adoption. If the court office is closed on the day time expires, *Nottingham City Council v Calverton Parish Council* [2015] EWHC 503 (Admin), [2015] PTSR 1130 holds that the period is treated as ending on the next working day.

4.72 On any application to the High Court under this section the court has power to quash wholly or partly the plan or document either generally or insofar as it affects the property of the applicant. The High Court also has the power, by interim order, wholly or partly to suspend the operation of the plan or document until final determination of the proceedings. In *Oxted Residential Ltd v Tandridge District Council* [2016] EWCA Civ 414 Lindblom LJ explained of the scope of statutory review under s 113 at [27]:

> Challenges such as this to the adoption of a development plan document by a local planning authority will seldom succeed. That is largely because the task of testing the soundness of a development plan document is not a task for the court. It lies squarely within the realm of planning judgment, exercised within the relevant statutory scheme and in the light of relevant policy and guidance. Under section 113 of the 2004 Act the court's role is to review that exercise of judgment, on traditional public law grounds. The question here—as it was, for example, in *Grand Union Investments*—is whether the local planning authority's adoption of the plan under challenge, following the recommendation of the inspector who conducted the examination, was perverse—that is to say that the adoption of the plan was beyond the range of reasonable judgment. As Carnwath L.J., as he then was, said in *Barratt Developments Plc v City of Wakefield Council* [2010] EWCA Civ. 897 (in paragraph 11 of his judgment), provided the inspector and the local planning authority reach a conclusion on soundness that is not 'irrational' (meaning 'perverse'), their decision cannot be questioned in the courts. Soundness, said Carnwath L.J. (at paragraph 33), was a 'matter to be judged by the inspector and the Council, and raises no issue of law, unless their decision is shown to have been "irrational", or they are shown to have ignored the relevant guidance or other considerations, which were necessarily material in law'.

4.73 One of the first legal challenges to the post-2004 development plan system occurred in *Ensign Group Ltd v First Secretary of State* [2006] EWHC 255, where the High Court quashed part of a regional spatial strategy because of errors (admitted by the Secretary of State) contained in a strategy document.

See also *Taylor Wimpey UK Ltd and Beazer Homes Reigate Ltd v Crawley Borough Council* [2008] EWHC 2644 where there was a successful challenge to an adopted core strategy.

4.74 In *Manydown Co Ltd v Basingstoke and Deane Borough Council* [2012] EWHC 977 (Admin); [2012] JPL 1188 Lindblom J held that s 113 did not preclude challenges to prior steps to the submission of a development plan document. On the other hand, in *R (on the application of IM Properties Ltd) v Lichfield District Council* [2014] EWHC 2440 (Admin); [2014] PTSR 1484 Patterson J held that an authority's decision to endorse main modification to a development plan at examination was precluded from challenge by s 113. In *R (on the application of CK Properties (Theydon Bois) Ltd) v Epping Forest District Council* [2018] EWHC 1649 (Admin), Supperstone J held that a decision to conduct a reg 19 consultation and thereafter submit a plan to the Secretary of State was not ousted by s 113. Interestingly, Lang J when granting permission in the *CK Properties* case restrained the Council from submitting the plan to the Secretary of State for examination.

4.75 Legal challenges under s 113 appear to have focused on the discharge of the duty in reg 12 of the Environmental Assessment of Certain Plans and Programmes Regulations 2004 (SI 2004/1633) (Transposing Directive 2001/42/EC Assessment of the Effects of Certain Plans and Programmes on the Environment). Namely that the Inspector (and subsequently the LPA) failed to adequately assess the reasonable alternatives to the spatial strategy set out in the adopted DPD, or failed to investigate an adequate number of reasonable alternatives, or failed to properly assess them or provide adequate reasons for rejecting them, see, for example: *R (on the application of Chalfont St Peter Parish Council) v Chiltern District Council* [2013] EWHC 1877 (Admin). For a further discussion on the 2004 Regulations and the obligations of reg 12, see Chapter 13.

4.76 If part of a plan is quashed by the court, the question arises as to whether the previous stages in the plan-making process which have not been challenged and quashed should remain valid. Is the local planning authority required to start the whole plan-making process again from the beginning in relation to that part, or can it proceed again to the adoption stage in order to comply with the court's order in the light of all the information then available? The court has no power to amend the plan. In *Charles Church Developments Ltd v South Northamptonshire DC* [2000] PLCR 40, in a case concerning the former system of development plans the High Court held that the term 'plan' in s 287 of the 1990 Act comprised the plan both in draft and adopted form, so that where part of a local plan is quashed, it has the effect of quashing that part of the plan both in draft and as adopted. However, changes made to s 113 by s 185 of the Planning Act 2008 have given more flexibility by giving powers to the court to remit the relevant document with directions as to the action to be taken, on which see the analysis of the Court of Appeal of the Judge's exercise of those powers in *JJ Gallagher Ltd v Cherwell District Council* [2016] EWCA Civ 1007; [2016] 1 WLR 5126.

L. DEVELOPMENT PLANS: THEIR LEGAL SIGNIFICANCE

Section 38 of the Planning and Compulsory Purchase Act provides that the development plan for any area in England (other than Greater London) shall be the development plan documents (taken as a whole) that have been adopted or approved in relation to that area. With regard to Greater London, the development plan is to be the spatial development strategy, and the development plan documents (taken as a whole) that have been adopted or approved in relation to that area. The section applies this definition of the development plan to other relevant legislation. **4.77**

The section provides that where regard has to be had to the development plan in any determination made under the Planning Acts, the determination must be made in accordance with the plan unless material considerations indicate otherwise. Additionally, the section provides that where there is a conflict in a development plan between any one policy and another, the conflict should be resolved in favour of the policy contained in the last document to be adopted, approved, or published (as the case may be). **4.78**

It should be noted that as the new development plan system envisaged by the 2004 Act begins to be introduced, special transitional provisions apply to the relevance of development plans effective under the 1990 Act. This is dealt with in Sch 8 to the 2004 Act, and is referred to in para 4.60. **4.79**

The end product of the plan-making process is to provide, as far as possible, a concise statement of the policy framework within which development in any area is to be promoted or controlled. This aim is reflected in a number of statutory provisions found in the 1990 Act and elsewhere which require the decision-maker to have regard to the provisions of the development plan. The main provisions are: **4.80**

(a) In dealing with applications for planning permission, s 70(2) of the 1990 Act requires that the local planning authority 'shall have regard to the provisions of the development plan, insofar as material to the application, and to any other material considerations'.

The precise meaning of the phrase 'shall have regard to the provisions of the development plan' has been judicially considered on a number of occasions. In *Simpson v Edinburgh Corporation* 1961 SLT 17, Lord Guest said that the expression 'shall have regard to' did not in his view mean 'slavishly adhere to'. According to his **4.81**

Lordship, the phrase requires the local planning authority to consider the development plan, but it does not oblige it to follow it. He went on:

> In view of the nature and purpose of a development plan ... I should have been surprised to find an injunction on the planning authority to follow it implicitly, and I do not find anything in the Act to suggest this was intended ... It was also pointed out that if the phrase was mandatory, then the addition of the words 'to any other material considerations' ... would, if the development plan and other material considerations were inconsistent, face the planning authority with an impossible task of reconciling the two ... The [local] planning authority are to consider all the material considerations, of which the development plan is one.

4.82 The view expressed by Lord Guest in *Simpson v Edinburgh Corporation* was considered and followed in *Enfield LBC v Secretary of State for the Environment* [1975] JPL 155, where Melford Stevenson J refused to quash a grant of planning permission given by the Secretary of State for industrial development in the green belt contrary to the provisions of the development plan which he had approved. The Court held that the words 'have regard to' did not make adherence to the plan mandatory.

4.83 The Planning and Compensation Act 1991 altered the significance of this provision. Section 26 of the 1991 Act provided that the following provision should be added at the end of Part II of the 1990 Act

> s 54A. Where, in making any determination under the planning Acts, regard is to be had to the development plan, the determination shall be made in accordance with the plan unless material considerations indicate otherwise.

4.84 The effect of this provision is discussed further in Chapter 11. It should be noted, however, that s 54A was repealed by the Planning and Compulsory Purchase Act 2004, and replaced by s 38(6) of that Act which states '... the determination must be made in accordance with the plan unless material considerations indicate otherwise'. The substitution of the word 'must' for 'shall' could be interpreted as giving more force to the policies in the development plan but this is doubtful.

(b) Where planning permission for development is necessary and has not been obtained, s 172(1) of the 1990 Act requires the local planning authority, in considering whether to issue an enforcement notice requiring the breach to be remedied, to have 'regard to the provisions of the development plan and to any other material considerations'.

(c) In considering whether to revoke or modify a permission granted for development on an application made under Part III of the 1990 Act, s 97 of the Act requires the local planning authority to have regard 'to the development plan and to any other material considerations'.

(d) In considering whether to make an order requiring discontinuance of the use of land or the removal or alteration of buildings or works, s 102 of the 1990 Act requires the local planning authority to have regard 'to the development plan and to any other material considerations'.

(e) In exercising powers under s 226 of the 1990 Act to compulsorily acquire land in connection with development and for other planning purposes, a local authority is required, in considering whether land is suitable for development, redevelopment, or improvement, to have regard, inter alia, 'to the provisions of the development plan, so far as material' and to any other considerations which would be material for the purposes of determining an application for planning permission for development on the land.

(f) The interests of owner-occupiers of land may be 'blighted' when an indication has been given in a development plan that land may be required for some public purpose. In such cases, Part VI of the 1990 Act allows the owners of certain interests in land so affected to serve 'blight notices' on the appropriate authority requiring the authority to purchase their interests.

(g) Where land is being acquired by a public authority for some public purpose, the compensation paid for the interest acquired is normally based on its market value. In order to assist in the determination of that value, the Land Compensation Act 1961 provides that the parties may assume that, were it not for the acquisition, planning permission would have been granted for development of a specific kind. Some of these assumptions about planning permission depend directly upon the provisions of the development plan.

4.85 As to the interpretation of the meaning of development plans, in a landmark judgment, the Supreme Court held in *Tesco Stores v Dundee CC* [2012] UKSC 13; [2012] PTSR 983 that the meaning of planning policy is a question of law. Lord Reed held that policies should be interpreted objectively, in accordance with the language used, read always in their proper context, see: [17]–[19]. However, the public are entitled to rely on a document as it stands without having to engage in 'forensic archeology' by trawling through supporting documents which informed the plan's production in order to work out its meaning, see: *R (on the application of TW Logistics) v Tendring District Council* [2013] EWCA Civ 9; [2013] 2 P & CR 9. The Supreme Court has approved the extension of the *Tesco* objective approach to the construction of the provisions of the NPPF in *Hopkins Homes Ltd v Secretary of State for Communities and Local Government* [2017] UKSC 37; [2017] 1 WLR 1865 and, in *Dartford Borough Council v Secretary of State for Communities and Local Government* [2016] EWCA Civ 141; [2017] PTSR 737 Lewison LJ at [23] applied the *TW Logistics* principle to construing the NPPF, rejecting the submission that regard should be had to a Written Ministerial Statement to interpret its provisions. Interestingly, the Privy Council has also extended the *Tesco* doctrine to Mauritius in *Beau Songe Developments Ltd v United Basalt Products Ltd* [2018] UKPC 1, on which see A Bowes, 'The Tesco Doctrine Extends to Paradise' [2018] 5 JPL 489. The 'objective' approach has not been without criticism however, see, for example, M Bedford QC. 'Tesco Stores Ltd v Dundee CC: A Form of Non-Statutory Fiction?' [2017] 9 JPL 914. In *Solo Retail Ltd v Tandridge DC* [2019] EWHC 489 (Admin) Lieven J held that the *Tesco* doctrine did not extend to the interpretation of the PPG, on which see further, A Bowes 'Interpreting and appling the Planning Practice Guidance' [2019] 6 JPL 537.

M. TRANSITIONAL PROVISIONS: TRANSFERRING FROM THE OLD SYSTEM TO THE NEW SYSTEM

4.86 The Government's main objectives underlying the arrangements made in the 2004 Act for transferring to the new system of development plans were to move as quickly as possible from the old system of regional planning guidance, structure plans, local plans, waste and minerals plans, and unitary development plans to a system of regional spatial strategies and local development documents and in addition, to maintain continuity in the development plan system as a framework for the exercise of development control until the new system has been introduced.

4.87 The Act received Royal Assent on 13 May 2004. Section 121 of the Act enables the Secretary of State to bring the provisions of the Act into force on such day as he appoints. The key date in these transitional arrangements, therefore, was the date when Parts 1 and 2 of the Act and s 38 (definition of development plan) were brought into effect, namely 28 September 2004. Because of the slow progress in adopting development plan documents these transitional arrangements have become of increasing importance.

4.88 The transitional arrangements are contained in Sch 8 to the Act. The provisions are elaborate and complicated. The Schedule provides that with one minor exception, whatever constitutes the development plan in an area at the date of commencement of s 38 of the Act retains that development plan status. This status, however, will only survive for whatever is the earlier of:

(a) the end of a period of 3 years from the commencement of the Act;
(b) the day when in relation to an old policy, a new policy which expressly replaces it is published, adopted, or approved.

It should be noted here that an old policy referred to above is one which immediately before the commencement of s 38 formed part of the development plan for the area. A new policy is one that is contained in an alteration or replacement of a spatial development strategy or in a development plan document. It should also be noted that local development documents cannot replace saved policies as they do not form part of a development plan. The three-year period has of course now elapsed but development plans can still be saved if the Secretary of State so directs.

4.89 So the policies in the old-style plans which were adopted before 28 September 2004 no longer have effect after 27 September 2007 unless they have been saved by Direction of the Secretary of State under Sch 8, para 1(3) of the 2004 Act (such Directions will in practice be issued by regional Government Offices usually with a covering letter). The policies which have been saved by a Direction remain in effect until they are expressly replaced by a new policy which has been published and is adopted or approved. In agreeing to extend saved policies, the Government Office will expect local planning authorities to replace them promptly by policies in development plan documents. It was held in *R (on the application of Cherkley Campaign Ltd) v Mole Valley DC* [2014] EWCA Civ 567 that where a policy was saved, when interpreting or implementing the saved policies, regard could and should be had to any descriptive or explanatory matter to aid the construction of the policy. However, it is only the words in the policy box to which the presumption at s 38(6) of the 2004 Act applies and the supporting text cannot add additional policy hurdles or trump the words of the policy.

N. WALES: REGIONAL FUNCTIONS AND LOCAL DEVELOPMENT

4.90 The provisions of Part 6 of the 2004 Act provide for the National Assembly for Wales to prepare a Wales Spatial Plan setting out such of the policies of the National Assembly as it thinks appropriate in relation to the use and development of land in Wales. The basic pattern of development plans (including the single tier of local government and the uniform pattern of unitary development plans introduced in 1994) is to be retained but reformed. Under the provisions of Part 6, every local planning authority is required to prepare a development plan to be known as a local development plan, and to review it and revise it as necessary. The local planning authority will be required to have regard to the Wales Spatial Plan in preparing their local development plan. Part 6 also provides for the independent examination of local development plans, and procedures for their preparation have been simplified. If the Assembly thinks that a development plan is unsatisfactory, it may at any time before adoption direct it to be modified giving reasons.

4.91 The Government of Wales Act 2006 provides for the Assembly to have full legislative authority on all devolved matters (which include planning) if this is approved by a Welsh Referendum. Such a referendum was approved in early 2011 which means that the Welsh system of development plans is very likely to continue to be different from the English one. This has now come to pass in the Planning (Wales) Act 2015.

5

DEFINITION OF DEVELOPMENT 1: OPERATIONAL DEVELOPMENT

A. NEED FOR PLANNING PERMISSION	5.01	C. OPERATIONAL DEVELOPMENT	5.11
B. DEFINITION OF DEVELOPMENT	5.02		

A. NEED FOR PLANNING PERMISSION

5.01 Section 57(1) of the 1990 Act provides that, subject to the following provisions of that section, 'planning permission is required for the carrying out of any development of land'. This planning permission may be granted following the determination of an express application for permission made to the local planning authority for the area in which the land is situated. In other cases, however, it is not necessary for an express application to be made. This is because planning permission for the development in question may have been granted by a development order, which may be a special, local, neighbourhood, or general order (such development is generally known as 'permitted' development), or by some other specific statutory provision (as in the case of enterprise zones or simplified planning zones), or be deemed to have been granted under other provisions of the Act (as in the case of the display of certain advertisements), or authorized by some private Act of Parliament.

B. DEFINITION OF DEVELOPMENT

5.02 The term 'development' is central to the power of local planning authorities to control the use and development of land. It is defined in s 55 and in s 336(1) (the interpretation section) of the 1990 Act. Section 55(1) contains the central core of the definition and provides that development may take one of two forms, namely, 'the carrying out of building, engineering, mining or other operations in, on, over or under land' or 'the making of any material change in the use of any buildings or other land'.

5.03 The scheme of the Act is to keep these two forms of development separate and distinct. So, in order to prevent confusion which might otherwise arise between the two forms by way of overlap, s 336(1) of the 1990 Act provides that the expression 'use' in relation to land, 'does not include the use of land for the carrying out of any building or other operations thereon'. Hence, any planning permission granted solely for the making of a material change in the use of land or buildings will not authorize the carrying out of an operation on the land in order to secure the better enjoyment of that new use. On the other hand, the Act recognizes that the enjoyment of a building erected under a grant of planning permission will almost inevitably involve a change in the use of the land on which the building has been erected. Accordingly, s 75(2) of the 1990 Act provides that:

> Where planning permission is granted for the erection of a building, the grant of permission may specify the purposes for which the building may be used.

5.04 Section 75(3) then goes on to say:

> If no purpose is so specified, the permission shall be construed as including permission to use the building for the purpose for which it is designed.

5.05 The two forms of development, namely, a building, engineering, mining, or other operation and a material change of use, are often referred to as two limbs in order to emphasize their related but independent characteristics. The first limb is often referred to as 'operational development'.

5.06 The fact that the two forms of development are kept separate and distinct, however, does not entirely exclude the possibility of a single process comprising both operational development and a material change of use. In *West Bowers Farm Products v Essex CC* (1985) P & CR 368 (CA), Nourse LJ said:

> The planning legislation is not impressed by the indivisibility of single processes. It cares only for their effects. A single process might for planning purposes amount to two activities. Whether it did so or not was a question of fact and degree. If it involved two activities, each of substance, so that *one is not merely ancillary to the other*, then both required permission [author's emphasis].

5.07 The *West Bowers* case is, however, exceptional. There the owners were carrying out operations on farmland consisting of digging a reservoir to contain water for agricultural irrigation. This operation constituted an 'engineering operation requisite for the use of land for the purpose of agriculture'. In the course of digging the reservoir the owners were extracting and selling huge quantities of gravel which constituted 'the use of land for the winning and working of minerals', a different class of development. The owners needed planning permission and the issue was on what basis to make the application. If the application related 'solely' to engineering operations requisite to the use of the land for agricultural purposes, no fee had to be paid, nor did the application need to be advertised. The local planning authority, however, contended successfully that the owner was also using the land for the winning and working of minerals. Thus, in the *West Bowers* case the one individual process had two physical aspects, each of which fell into a different specific category. As was subsequently explained in *R v Durham CC and Lafarge Redland Aggregates Ltd, ex p Lowther* [2001] EWCA Civ 781; [2002] Env. LR 13 it is correct to analyse the *West Bowers* case as involving two separate and sequential activities. In the *West Bowers* case there were two aspects of one activity, each of which had different consequences according to the express terms of the planning regulations, so that each had to be separately considered.

5.08 Although the core of the definition is contained in s 55(1) and (1A) of the 1990 Act, it is qualified by important provisions contained in subsections (2) to (5) of that section. Subsection (2) lists three operations (paras (a) to (c)), three uses (paras (d) to (f)), and then one further operation (para (g) added to the subsection by the Planning and Compensation Act 1991), which are not to be taken to involve the development of land. Subsections (2A) and (2B) disapply certain operations which affect only the interior of a building which would otherwise fall within para (a). Subsection (3) lists two uses which, for the avoidance of doubt, are declared to involve a material change of use. Subsection (4) amplifies the meaning of the term mining operations; subsection (4A) brings certain fish-farming activities within the definition of development; and subsection (5) provides that the display of certain advertisements shall constitute a material change of use.

5.09 The courts have continually and consistently stated that whether activities amount to development is a question of fact and degree for the planning authorities; that is the local planning authorities and the Secretary of State. So, while the courts lay down authoritative statements as to the meaning of the statutory definition, the application of the words to particular circumstances is for the planning authorities. The courts will therefore normally only overturn determinations as to whether an activity amounts to development if the decision reveals an error of law.

5.10 Thus in *Thames Heliports plc v London Borough of Tower Hamlets* (1997) 74 P & CR 164 the Court of Appeal refused to make a declaration as to whether the use of the River Thames as a heliport would amount to development as a material change of use. Schiemann LJ stated that:

> [M]any questions in planning law depend on an evaluation of facts which the legislation has entrusted initially and primarily to the planning authorities including the Secretary of State. In general in this type of case the court's jurisdiction is invoked after the decision has been made by a planning authority when it is sought to control the legality of the decision.

C. OPERATIONAL DEVELOPMENT

5.11 As already stated, the first limb of the definition of development is the 'carrying out of building, engineering, mining or other operations in, on, over or under land'.

Building operations

5.12 Subsection (1A) of s 55 of the Act provides that the term 'building operations' includes:

(a) demolition of buildings;
(b) rebuilding;
(c) structural alterations of or additions to buildings; and
(d) other operations normally undertaken by a person carrying on business as a builder.

5.13 Two points about this definition should be noted. First, the use of the word 'includes' shows that the words that follow it are not exhaustive of its meaning; secondly and somewhat surprisingly, the erection of an entirely new building is not specifically mentioned as being within the term. It seems fairly clear, however, that such activity must fall within the concluding clause of the definition as being work normally undertaken by a person carrying on business as a builder.

Buildings

5.14 As recognized in the definition given to the words 'building operations', the work done will normally involve work to a 'building'. The meaning of the word 'building', therefore, may also be relevant to the question of whether a particular activity constitutes development. 'Building' is defined in s 336(1) to include 'any structure or erection, and any part of a building, as so defined, but does not include plant or machinery comprised in a building'. The word 'building', therefore, has been given in this context a wider meaning than is normally given to it in everyday parlance. It will thus include 'erections' which may not normally be regarded as 'buildings'.

5.15 As might be expected, therefore, a number of significant judicial decisions have been made on its precise meaning and application. In *Buckinghamshire CC v Callingham* [1952] 2 QB 515 the Court of Appeal held that the model village and railway at Bekonscot near Beaconsfield was a structure or erection, and therefore a building within the meaning of that word. In *James v Brecon CC* (1963) 15 P & CR 20, however, it was held that a battery of six swing-boats erected at a fairground was not a structure or erection. An important factor in that decision was that the entire battery could be dismantled by six men in no more than half an hour. Thus, in determining whether a structure or erection exists, factors likely to be considered dominant by the courts are size permanence and physical

Operational Development

attachment. That much seems clear from two of the more important judicial decisions made in this area.

In *Cheshire CC v Woodward* [1962] 2 QB 126, a coal merchant installed a coal hopper and conveyor equipment in his coal yard without first obtaining a grant of planning permission to do so. The hopper, which was some 16 to 20 feet in height and mounted on wheels, traversed and delivered coal to stationary lorries beneath. An enforcement notice was then served on behalf of the county council alleging a breach of planning control and requiring the removal of the hopper and conveyor. The coal merchant appealed to the Minister against the enforcement notice and the Minister, after holding an inquiry, accepted the recommendation of the Inspector and quashed the notice. The council then appealed to the High Court on the point of law that the Minister had erred in holding that the installation was not development. In dismissing the appeal, Lord Parker CJ said: **5.16**

> ... the Act is referring to any structure or erection which can be said to form part of the realty, and to change the physical character of the land.

It seems, however, that an object may be affixed to land and not be a building, or not be affixed to land and be a building. According to Lord Parker CJ in *Cheshire CC v Woodward*: **5.17**

> The mere fact that something is erected in the course of a building operation which is affixed to the land does not determine the matter. Equally, as it seems to me, the mere fact that it can be moved and is not affixed does not determine the matter ... There is no one test; you look at the erection, equipment, plant, whatever it is, and ask: in all the circumstances is it to be treated as part of the realty? So here ... one must look at the whole circumstances, including what is undoubtedly extremely relevant, the degree of permanency with which it is affected.

The decision in *Cheshire CC v Woodward* was later considered by the courts in *Barvis Ltd v Secretary of State for the Environment* (1971) 22 P & CR 710. In that case the appellant company had erected at its depot a mobile crane normally used by it for erecting precast concrete structures on contract sites. The crane was some 89 feet high and ran on a steel track permanently fixed in concrete. The crane could be dismantled in sections and re-erected, but took several days to do so. The local planning authority maintained that the erection constituted development and served an enforcement notice on the appellant requiring its removal. Following an appeal, the notice was upheld by the Secretary of State. The appellant company then challenged the decision of the Secretary of State in the High Court. It maintained that the crane was intended to be moved on and off land as requirements demanded; that it was not fixed to the land, nor did it form part of the realty. Furthermore, its degree of permanence was slight and had not altered the physical character of the land. Dismissing the appeal, Bridge J said he did not wish in the slightest degree to question the validity or usefulness of the tests propounded in *Cheshire CC v Woodward*, which he considered it might be necessary **5.18** to apply in a borderline case. He felt, however, that here it was not necessary to apply the tests propounded in that case. One must ask, he said:

> ... was the crane, when erected, a 'building' within the definition ...? 'Building' includes any structure or erection. If, as a matter of impression, one looks objectively at this enormous crane, it seems to me impossible to say that it did not amount to a structure or erection.
>
> ... in my judgment, this crane was not the less a structure or erection by reason of its limited degree of mobility on rails on the site, nor by reason of the circumstance that at some future date, uncertain when it was erected, the appellants contemplated that it would be dismantled ...

He also added that if the crane was a building as defined he would want a great deal of persuading that the erection of it had not amounted to a building or other operation.

5.19 The *Barvis* case is the strongest authority for the view that the key elements in deciding whether something is a building or not are size, permanence, and physical attachment to the land. Indeed, this approach is at one with that taken by the court in a rating case, *Cardiff Rating Authority v Guest Keen Baldwin Iron and Steel Co Ltd* [1949] 1 KB 385, where the three factors identified in deciding what constituted a structure were size, permanence, and physical attachment.

5.20 In *R v Swansea City Council, ex p Elitestone Ltd* (1993) 66 P & CR 422, the question arose whether chalets were buildings and therefore capable of being protected from demolition by conservation area status. The Court of Appeal considered the chalets were buildings and that the degree of permanence was a highly material factor in so deciding. Other significant factors may, however, be size and composition by component parts, as where a structure results from the assembly on site of the various parts which go to make it up.

5.21 The relevance of permanence as a factor to be considered can be seen in *Skerritts of Nottingham Ltd v Secretary of State for the Environment, Transport, and the Regions* [2000] PLR 102. There a question arose as to whether the erection of a marquee every year to remain on site between February and October amounted to a building operation. An enforcement notice served by the local planning authority requiring its removal had been upheld on appeal by an Inspector acting on behalf of the Secretary of State. The marquee measured 40 metres by 17 metres with a ridge height of 5 metres. Its erection required several people to work for several days. The 16 feet of metal portal frames sat on square metal plates spiked into the soil beneath. This, together with internal bracing and its considerable weight, held the marquee in place. Inside the marquee was a timber floor, supported by metal ground beams resting on the land. The Inspector had concluded, as a matter of fact and degree, that the marquee was a building owing to its dimensions, its permanence (rather than its fleeting nature); and the secure nature of its anchorage. Accordingly, since the marquee was a building operation, Skerritts were carrying out building operations every year when it was erected. Skerritts then appealed successfully to the High Court on the question of the Inspector's approach to permanence. Reinstating the decision of the Inspector, however, the Court of Appeal rejected the argument by Skerritts that the annual removal of the marquee deprived it of the quality of permanence. Permanence in this context does not necessarily connote a state of affairs which is to continue forever or continuously. The term, according to the court, carried with it a degree of flexibility between temporary on the one hand and everlasting on the other, and it did not mean that an object had to be on the land for 365 days in the year. To hold otherwise would mean that any object, however large and well-constructed, which was built in such a way that it could be dismantled and removed annually for a short time, would be outside planning control. Rather similarly in *R (on the application of Islam) v Secretary of State for Communities and Local Government* [2012] EWHC 1314 (Admin) the High Court upheld a decision of an Inspector that the setting up of two large umbrellas constituted development as building operations: the umbrellas were fixed and permanent.

5.22 Despite what was said in *Cheshire CC v Woodward* and *Barvis Ltd v Secretary of State for the Environment*, one can envisage many situations in which the question of whether or not an object is a structure or erection will be finely balanced and where it may be difficult to decide on which side the scales should be brought down.

5.23 More recently, the High Court held in *Tewkesbury BC v Keeley* [2004] EWHC 2594 (QB), that a mobile shed was not a structure or erection falling within the definition of a building. The court accepted that in none of the cases to which it had been referred had a structure been held to be a building which was mobile to the extent of having wheels so that it could be freely moved about on site. This accords with the view the courts have taken with regard to the position of caravans. So, the placing of caravans on land will not be a building operation, but it may well be development as a material change of use. Then in *R (on the application of Woolley Action Group) v Bath and North East Somerset Council* [2012] EWHC 2161 (Admin) Lang J quashed a decision of a local planning authority where, in coming to its decision that the setting up of poultry sheds did not amount to building operations, the authority had failed to consider important factors and had wrongly considered that because the actions were not those normally carried out by a builder they could not be building operations.

5.24 It should be remembered here that the decision-making processes in the planning law field allows the Secretary of State, in determining such matters as appeals against enforcement notices or the refusal of an authority to issue a certificate of lawfulness of a proposed use or development under s 192 of the 1990 Act, to make an initial determination on whether or not a particular activity constitutes development. Although this is a determination on a point of law, landowners and local planning authorities may be willing to accept his decision and be reluctant to pursue the matter further by challenging his decision in the courts. Hence, the Secretary of State's decision in a particular case is in fact often final, especially as the courts regard such judgments as primarily a matter of fact and degree for the planning authorities.

5.25 In that capacity, he has held that such things as a carport, a portakabin, a slide (erected on a pier at a seaside resort), a plastic tree (erected in the children's playing area in the grounds of a public house), a steel frame supporting a polythene cover over a swimming-pool, a model railway track, a radio mast, and a large area of timber decking in the grounds of a hotel were structures or erections and thus within the definition of a building. More recently, Inspectors have held that plastic tunnels assembled on agricultural land to protect growing stock from wind and rain constituted an operation within s 55(3)(b)(i) of the 1990 Act: see below (Refs: APP/Y2620/4/04/1142007 and APP/R/3650/C/64/11602/3). In another case, an Inspector held that the erection in the garden of a public house of three large umbrellas, attached together with canvas side shades, each of which was in a concrete footing fell within the definition of a building in s 336 of the 1990 Act (Ref: APP/H5390/C/03/1128513). It has also been held by an Inspector that a large stainless steel sculpture mounted on a cross-shaped metal framework amounted to a building operation and its replacement by a similar sculpture that had sliding spring bolts so that it was removable equally was development (Ref: APP/ K5600/X/10/2140909 and [2011] JPL 822). On the other hand, an Inspector has held that the installation of a free-standing cash dispensing machine on a garage forecourt was not a building operation (Ref: APP/22830/C/06/2009917) and the Secretary of State has held that the erection of benders (a woven timber framework covered with tarpaulins and anchored down by posts driven into the ground and sealed with turf sods) used for the purpose of human habitation, constituted not operational development but a material change of use. This last decision was later upheld by the High Court in *Britton v Secretary of State for the Environment* [1997] JPL 617. For a very useful example of the application of the principles, see Ministerial decision reported at [2011] JPL 978.

5.26 From a practical point of view, in considering operational development, it should be borne in mind that the General Permitted Development Order grants planning permission for such minor matters as the erection or construction of gates, fences, walls, or other means of enclosure. However, this is not in itself conclusive proof that in law minor work of this kind necessarily constitutes a building operation: the content of an order made under the Act cannot be used to try to discover the meaning of the Act itself.

5.27 A problem in this area of control concerned the extent to which the placing of cloches or polytunnels on agricultural land during the growing season amounts to a building operation and is subject therefore to planning control. The reason this is done is to enhance yields or to encourage earlier harvesting.

5.28 The problem was raised in *R (on the application of Hall Hunter Partnership) v First Secretary of State and Waverley BC and ors* [2006] EWHC 3482. In this case the appellants had erected extensive polytunnels on their fruit farm. The evidence was that one acre of polytunnels took 45 man-hours to erect and 35 man-hours to dismantle. The leg supports for the tunnels were screwed into the ground by machine, which was also used to bend straight lengths of metal into arcs to create covering loops. The height of the tunnels varied according to the crop planted, and could be as high as 4 metres. The tunnels could also vary in width from 5.5 metres to 8 metres and in length from 50 metres to 400 metres. Furthermore, the tunnels would remain in one particular location for between three and seven months in any one year. The local planning authority had served enforcement notices on the appellants requiring the polytunnels to be removed. Following a dismissal of an appeal against the notices by an Inspector appointed by the Secretary of State, the appellants claimed that the Inspector had erred in law in concluding that the polytunnels were development within the meaning of s 55(1) of the 1990 Act. Dismissing their appeal, Sullivan J, in the High Court, held that the Inspector's assessment of the factual material was entirely in accord with the legal principles to be applied. He had considered all the circumstances, and in particular the three factors of size, degree of physical attachment, and permanence.

5.29 The circumstances in which polytunnels are erected on agricultural land will of course, vary enormously. One polytunnel may differ significantly from another, yet each may have to be considered separately against the three factors that determine whether or not their placing constitutes development. The judgment of Solomon might be required, see, for example, the erroneous approach of the planning authority to poultry units identified by Lang J in *R (on the application of Save Woolley Valley Action Group Limited) v Bath and North East Somerset Council* [2012] EWHC 2161 (Admin); [2013] Env LR 8.

Building operations which are not development

5.30 Mention was made earlier that s 55(2) to (2B) of the 1990 Act specifies a number of operations and uses which are not to be taken to involve the development of land. The operation mentioned in para (a) of s 55(2) is:

> the carrying out for the maintenance, improvement or other alteration of any building of works which—
> (i) affect only the interior of the building, or
> (ii) do not materially affect the external appearance of the building,
> and are not works for making good war damage or works begun after 5th December 1968 for the alteration of a building by providing additional space in it underground.

5.31 This provision makes it clear that it is not development to remove, say, an internal wall of a building. The provision however, is sometimes misunderstood. There are many activities which may affect only the interior of a building or do not materially affect its external appearance. These activities will not constitute development, not because of the provisions in s 55(2)(a) but because the work involved does not constitute a building operation. In other words, one must first consider whether the work involved falls within the meaning of development as defined in ss 55(1) and 336(1). If it does, one has then to consider whether it is excluded from that definition by being an activity which falls within s 55(2)(a). Thus, it is not development to replace a broken pane of glass in the window of a dwellinghouse. The reason is that it is not an operation as defined in ss 55(1) and 336(1), and the fact that the replacement does not materially affect the external appearance of the building is not relevant.

5.32 The value of following this approach is best seen with regard to the concluding provision in s 55(2)(a), namely the words 'and are not ... works begun after 5th December 1968 for the alteration of a building by providing additional space in it underground'. These words were introduced into the law by the Town and Country Planning Act 1968. The need to do so arose from the wishes of a provincial department store to extend its premises. Because policy and site limitations respectively prevented the store from extending either upwards or outwards it decided to obtain the additional space it needed by excavating downwards. On the completion of the work and the opening of the store's household basement the additional custom generated by the extension caused considerable congestion in the surrounding streets.

5.33 The work done by the store was not within the definition of development and the local planning authority was powerless to prevent it. Although it constituted a building operation (and possibly also an engineering operation) under s 55(1), it was excluded from the definition of development by virtue of being work for the alteration of a building which affected only its interior. During the passage of the 1968 Act through Parliament, the opportunity was taken to close this lacuna in the law by, as it were, excluding that exclusion for the future. Thus, after 5 December 1968, the work carried out by the store would have required planning permission. Such work would be a building operation, and one to which the exclusive provisions of para (a) of s 55(2) would not apply.

5.34 Another problem with this exclusion was to arise when changes were made to Government policy with regard to retail development. It became clear that the creation in an existing retail store of additional internal floor space to be used for that purpose was not affected by the changes made in 1968, since the additional space was not being created below ground. So that, for example, the erection of a mezzanine floor within retail buildings and its use for that purpose would not normally require planning permission. Where a local planning authority wished to control such additions, only a condition imposed in the original grant of permission which limited the amount of floor space to be used within the building for retail purposes could do so. Few permissions did that.

5.35 Amendments made by the Planning and Compulsory Purchase Act 2004 now enable the Secretary of State to remedy that mischief. Section 49 of the 2004 Act added new subsections 2A and 2B to s 55 of the 1990 Act by allowing the Secretary of State by a development order to specify 'any circumstances or description of circumstances in which [s 55] subsection 2 [is] not to apply to operations mentioned in para (a) of that subsection, which [would] have the effect of increasing the gross floor space of the building by such amount or percentage amount as is so specified'. Furthermore, it was provided in s 55(2B) that when a development order is made under this amendment, it may make different provision for different purposes. The power was used in 2006 and can now be found in art 3 of the Town and Country Planning Development Management Procedure Order 2010. Its effect is that increases of internal floor space, such as mezzanine floors exceeding 200 square metres in buildings used for retail sales and including buildings used as retail warehouse clubs (other than for the sale of hot food), are not excluded from the definition of development and will thus require planning permission.

5.36 The question of whether or not carrying out works for the maintenance, improvement, or other alteration of a building materially affects the external appearance of the building is one which will normally be determined by the local planning authority or, on appeal, by the Secretary of State. In two rare cases, however, the question has come to be determined by the courts.

5.37 In *Kensington & Chelsea RLBC v C G Hotels* [1981] JPL 190 the owners of a west London hotel installed floodlights without planning permission. The local planning authority then served an enforcement notice requiring their removal. Some of the floodlights were attached to the basement area of the hotel; others simply stood under their own weight on first floor balconies but were not attached to the building other than by the electricity supply cable.

5.38 The owners of the hotel had appealed to the Secretary of State and an Inspector, acting on his behalf, had concluded that there was no breach of planning control and quashed the notice. In dismissing an appeal against the decision of the Secretary of State, the Divisional Court held that assuming, without actually deciding, that the installation of floodlights constituted development within s 55(1) of the 1990 Act, the placing of electric cables and floodlights in position and the fixing of some of them to the building, did not 'materially affect the external appearance of the building'. If the external appearance of the building had been materially affected, it was caused by the running of electricity through the cables, not by the positioning and fixing of the floodlights.

5.39 More positive help as to the interpretation of this provision has now been given by the High Court in *Burroughs Day v Bristol City Council* [1996] 1 PLR 78, where the occupiers of a building proposed an alteration to the roof of the building and replacement of windows to the front elevation in order to accommodate the installation of a lift in the building. A question then arose as to whether the occupiers were entitled to compensation for the refusal of listed building consent to carry out those works under statutory provisions which have now been repealed. That in turn required a consideration of whether the work was development under s 55(1) of the 1990 Act. The court held that in interpreting the words of the provision and in applying them to particular facts, the following points should be taken into account, namely:

(a) what had to be affected was the 'external appearance of the building, not the "exterior" of the building'. The use of the word 'appearance' meant that it was not sufficient for the external surface of a building to be affected by the proposed alteration. The alteration had to be one which affected the way in which the exterior of the building could be seen by an observer outside the building;
(b) the external appearance of the building had to be 'materially' affected. That effect must be more than *de minimis*;
(c) whether the effect of the alteration was 'material' must depend in part on the degree of visibility; and
(d) the effect on the external appearance must be judged for its materiality in relation to the building as a whole and not by reference to a part of a building taken in isolation.

The old problem of demolition

5.40 The problem of whether or not the demolition of a building *simpliciter* constitutes development has for many years been uncertain yet important. 'Building operations', it may be recalled, is defined in s 55(1A) to include 'demolition of buildings; rebuilding; structural alterations of or additions to buildings; and other operations normally undertaken by a person carrying on business as a builder'.

5.41 Prior to the 1991 Act, the definition of building operations (previously found in s 336(1) of the Act) did not include 'demolition of buildings' and this led to much uncertainty.

5.42 The leading case in this area was without doubt that of *Coleshill & District Investment Co Ltd v Minister of Housing and Local Government* [1969] 1 WLR 745. The facts are particularly crucial to the decision. A site had consisted of six separate buildings used during the last war as an ammunition depot. Four of the buildings had been used as magazines, the other two for the storage of explosives. Around each building was a blast wall 9 feet in height. Against each wall and on its outside was a sloping embankment of rubble and soil extending out about 8 feet from the base. The functional relationship between the wall with its embankment and the buildings which it surrounded is only too self-evident.

5.43 There was no dispute between the parties that the original use having been discontinued, the six buildings had an existing use for storage purposes. The appellant company wished to remove the embankments and walls. As a first step it started to remove the embankments. Following complaints by residents, the local planning authority served an enforcement notice on the company requiring it to cease the removal. The company, having taken the view that this activity did not constitute development and that no planning permission was necessary, appealed against the enforcement notice to the Minister, who refused to grant planning permission for the development and upheld the notice.

5.44 The company had also wished to demolish the walls. It therefore applied to the local planning authority, under what was then s 64 of the 1990 Act, for a determination whether that operation would constitute development. Having heard nothing from the authority within the period prescribed for doing so, the company appealed to the Minister against non-determination of its application. The Minister then determined that the removal of the walls would constitute development and that planning permission was required. Thus, by two separate procedural routes, the Minister had given a decision that the removal of the embankments and walls constituted development. In the High Court the company again contended that an act of demolition was not development. The case eventually reached the House of Lords. Their Lordships thought that the question of whether demolition was or was not development was a neat and arresting question, but not one that needed to be answered on the facts of the case. According to their Lordships, the true path of enquiry was not to crystal-gaze or to ask hypothetical questions. One had to see exactly what had been done, and then see whether it came within the statutory definition of development. They pointed out that it was unnecessary (and possibly misleading) to give work a single label like demolition, and then try to apply the definition to that label. Their Lordships were clearly right. Nothing is to be gained by asking, for example, whether renovation, or repair, or rehabilitation constitutes development.

5.45 The House of Lords went on to find that the Minister had made no error of law in holding:

(a) that the blast walls and embankments were an integral part of the buildings and that the removal of the blast walls would constitute a building operation; and
(b) that the removal of the embankments was an engineering operation.

5.46 The decision proved difficult to interpret. There was no doubt that an important feature of the case was the upholding of the Minister's finding that the blast walls and embankments formed an integral part of the buildings. Hence it was inevitable that their removal would constitute development, since a building operation was then defined in s 336(1) to include 'structural alterations . . . to buildings'.

5.47 The decision thus raised the important question of whether or not it would be development to remove the whole of a building or a building complex. Leaving aside the possibility that its removal might constitute an engineering operation (see para 5.61) it is difficult to see how, if the whole of a building were demolished, it could be said to be 'a rebuilding operation, a structural alteration or an addition to a building'. It could be, however, that the courts would regard that activity as an 'other operation normally undertaken by a person carrying on business as a builder'. No one, it seems, could be sure. There was an obiter statement which suggested that, unless the total removal of a building constituted an engineering operation, the work would not be regarded as development. In *Iddenden v Secretary of State for the Environment* [1972] 1 WLR 1433 the appellant had demolished a Nissen hut and workshop and erected in its place a new building. The local planning authority had served an enforcement notice upon him requiring him to demolish the new building which had been erected without planning permission. Iddenden claimed that the notice was invalid because it did not also require him to re-erect the buildings he had demolished. It was held that the local planning authority had a discretion to decide what steps were required to restore the land to its condition before the development took place. It could if it wished, decide that all that was necessary was the pulling down of the new building. That effectively disposed of the appellant's argument. For good measure, however, Lord Denning MR added that: 'Whilst some demolition operations may be development … the demolition of buildings such as these was not.' In other words, it was not a breach of planning control to remove these old buildings.

5.48 The difficulty of knowing whether or not the law regarded the *total* demolition of a building as development had important consequences for development control. The demolition of a building sometimes took place in order to remove an impediment to the grant of planning permission for the redevelopment of the land on which the building stood. Planning permission, for example, might be refused for the redevelopment of land with an existing community use such as shops and theatres, because of a desire to retain those uses; and this even though the redevelopment proposal was in accordance with the provisions of the development plan for the area. If the shops and theatres are first demolished, no valid reason would then exist for the refusal of the permission. Nowhere was this more of a problem than with regard to buildings having some architectural or historical interest, but which were not considered to possess such special qualities as to warrant their inclusion in the statutory list of buildings (called listed buildings) kept by the Secretary of State under the provisions of s 1 of the Planning (Listed Buildings and Conservation Areas) Act 1990. The significance of this was that if the buildings were within the list they could not be demolished without listed building consent to do so first being obtained. A somewhat similar rule applied to the demolition, without conservation area consent, of a non-listed building situated within a conservation area. It often happens that once an application for planning permission is made for redevelopment of land on which there stands a building which, although not listed, has some architectural or historical interest, the application will generate suggestions that the building has sufficient special qualities to warrant it being added to the list, and so subject to the special protection which is given to listed buildings. If it is added, the prospect of obtaining listed building consent for its demolition to enable the redevelopment to go ahead is not likely to be high. It follows, therefore, that in these situations there is pressure on landowners and developers to first demolish the building and then make an application for planning permission for the redevelopment of the land on which it stood. In this way no one is alerted to the possibility that an important building would be lost to the public heritage if planning permission was granted, and by the time the public is alerted, it has already been lost.

5.49 In past years, further concern was expressed over the wanton demolition of existing houses, prior to the submission of an application for planning permission for residential development of the land on which the houses stood with a much higher housing density. In addition, concern was also expressed at the method of demolition and that, once completed, sites were not always cleared of debris and rubble, nor were sites fenced to prevent damage to amenity. In a consultation paper issued in 1989 by the Secretary of State, various ways to deal with this problem were canvassed.

5.50 As it so happened, the Secretary of State's consideration of the views expressed by consultees was quickly overtaken by events. In *Cambridge City Council v Secretary of State for the Environment* (1991) 89 LGR 1015, Mr David Widdicombe QC, sitting in the High Court as a Deputy Judge, described the question whether demolition was development within the Act as 'a question which like a ghost has haunted planning law for many years ... The time has now come when the ghost must be laid to rest'. He then went on to hold that the demolition of houses was a 'building operation' being (as per the definition in s 336(1)) an 'other operation normally undertaken by a person carrying on business as a builder'. Although an appeal against that decision was subsequently allowed by the Court of Appeal (1992) 90 LGR 275, the Government decided after the High Court decision to include a provision in the Planning and Compensation Act 1991 to amend the definition of building operations, then contained in s 336(1) of the 1990 Act, to include the 'demolition of buildings' and to include that definition in the body of s 55.

The current position with demolition

5.51 It was not the intention of the Government that the demolition of every type of building should be development and therefore require planning permission. Accordingly, the 1991 Act amendment gave the Secretary of State power to make directions enabling him to provide that the demolition of particular types of building was not to involve development. Thus, the following new para (g) was added to the three operations listed in s 55(2) (in paras (a) to (c)) which are *not* to be taken to involve development:

> ... the demolition of any description of building specified in a direction given by the Secretary of State to local planning authorities generally or to a particular local authority.

5.52 The Secretary of State has since issued the Town and Country Planning (Demolition—Description of Buildings) Direction 2014. The effect of the Direction is to provide that the demolition of the following types of building shall *not* be taken to involve development of land:

(a) any building the cubic content of which, measured externally, does not exceed 50 cubic metres;
(b) the whole or any part of any gate, fence, wall or other means of enclosure (except in a conservation area).

5.53 It should be noted that for the purposes of the Direction, the term 'building' does not include part of a building except within para 3(1)(b) and 3(2).

5.54 It should be noted that demolition of certain types of building is permitted development in the circumstances set out in Class B, Part 11, Sch 2 of the Town and Country Planning (General Permitted Development Order) (England) Order 2015 (SI 2015/596). Notably, from 23 May 2017, pubs (Use Class A4) are excluded from the permitted development tolerance.

5.55 In *R (SAVE Britain's Heritage) v Secretary of State for Communities and Local Government* [2011] EWCA Civ 334; [2011] PTSR 1140 the Court of Appeal ruled that demolition is a project within the Environmental Impact Assessment Directive and so capable of requiring an environmental impact assessment. It was therefore held that, paras 2(1)(a)–(d) of the Demolition Direction (set out at 5.52) are unlawful and so the first four categories of demolition require planning permission in addition to any other consent. However, such acts of demolition will attract permitted development rights under Part 31 of the General Permitted Development Order in the same way as the demolition of dwellinghouses and of buildings adjoining dwellinghouses are permitted development. This process does enable environmental impact screening to take place and for an environmental statement to be required where necessary. This process is explained below.

5.56 The remaining control over demolition is intended in the main to apply to the demolition of dwellinghouses and of buildings adjoining dwellinghouses. However, because the demolition of most dwellinghouses does not justify the full application of these new controls, the Secretary of State has, with one important exception, exercised his power in relation to the General Permitted Development Order to include as permitted development the demolition of all buildings which are not already excluded from control by the Direction described above. With that one exception, namely, where a building has been made unsafe or uninhabitable, either through deliberate action or neglect by anyone having an interest in the land on which the building stands and the building can be made secure through temporary repairs or support, the demolition of a dwellinghouse or of a building adjoining a dwellinghouse is permitted without the need for express planning permission by virtue of Part 31 of Sch 2 to the Order. Before such permitted development rights may be used, however, the Order provides that the developer must first apply to the local planning authority for a determination of whether the prior approval of the authority is required as to the *method* of the proposed demolition and any proposed restoration of the site. The authority is then given 28 days to consider the matter. If the developer is not notified within the 28-day period that prior approval is required, he may proceed to demolish the building in accordance with the details submitted by him to the authority in his application for the determination. If, on the other hand, the authority requires prior approval to be obtained before demolition, the only remedy available to the developer is to seek that prior approval and then, if approval should not be given, to appeal to the Secretary of State.

The purpose of this prior-approval requirement is to give local planning authorities the opportunity to regulate the details of demolition and restoration of the site in order to minimize the impact of that activity on local amenity. It must be emphasized, however, that the need to seek prior approval does not in fact prevent demolition from taking place once the prior-approval process has been negotiated. In order to do that, there must be in place an Art 4 direction (see Chapter 6), withdrawing the permitted development right. **5.57**

Refusal of approval cannot be based on the absence of an approved scheme of redevelopment. At the application for approval stage, demolition is not an issue. It is concerned solely with details of the method of demolition and the restoration of the site. Approval could be withheld, for example, if the demolition proposals did not include measures to protect trees, the erection of fencing on the perimeter of the land to provide a safe and secure environment during demolition, an undertaking not to carry out site burning, a provision relating to hours of work, the removal of demolition rubble, and an undertaking to level the site and to leave it clean and tidy and clear of all hazards on completion of the demolition. **5.58**

It should be noted too that the prior-approval procedure does not apply where demolition is: **5.59**

(a) urgently necessary in the interests of health or safety, provided that the developer gives a written justification for the demolition to the local planning authority as soon as reasonably practicable after the demolition has taken place;
(b) on land which is the subject of planning permission, for the redevelopment of the land granted on an application or deemed to be granted under Part III of the Act;
(c) required or permitted to be carried out by or under any enactment (eg as the result of an enforcement notice); or
(d) required to be carried out by virtue of a relevant obligation (eg a s 106 agreement).

The above changes do not affect the need to obtain planning permission for the partial demolition of a building which is generally regarded as a 'structural **5.60** alteration' to a building. Furthermore, demolition of a building may still constitute an engineering operation. Also, where the proposed development falls within Sch 1 or 2 of the Environmental Impact Assessment Regulations, permitted development rights can only apply if a screening opinion or direction has been adopted that environmental impact assessment is not required. Otherwise, where a proposed demolition is likely to have significant effects on the environment, the permitted development rights are withdrawn. The developer will then have to apply for planning permission and an environmental impact assessment would have to be carried out.

Engineering operations

5.61 The 1990 Act gives little guidance on the meaning of the expression 'engineering operations' save that s 336(1) provides that it includes 'the formation or laying out of means of access to highways'. It will be recalled that in *Coleshill & District Investment Co Ltd v Minister of Housing and Local Government* [1969] 1 WLR 746, the House of Lords found that the Minister had not erred in law in holding the removal of an embankment to be an engineering operation. In this case it was shown that the removal of the embankment would require many lorries to be used over a prolonged period to transport the debris away from the site. On the other hand, the removal of a mere shovelful of earth from one spot to another is unlikely to be considered an engineering operation. Somewhere in between lies the demarcation line that separates an activity which is not an engineering operation from one which is. The meaning of the term had earlier received little judicial consideration. The absence of judicial guidance led at one time to much uncertainty and inconsistency in cases where the term had to be applied. In 1983, however, the meaning of the term was clarified by the decision in *Fayrewood Fish Farms Ltd v Secretary of State for the Environment* [1984] JPL 267, in which the High Court had to consider whether the excavation and removal of topsoil for the purpose of extracting underlying gravel constituted an 'engineering operation'. The Secretary of State had thought that it did. In remitting the matter back to the Secretary of State with the opinion of the court, Mr David Widdicombe QC, sitting as a Deputy High Court Judge, accepted that the Secretary of State was basically right to hold that engineering operations called for engineering skills, but that he had gone too far in requiring that there had to be a 'specific project which is of sufficient predetermined size and shape that a conception of the finished project can be illustrated on a plan or drawing'. In his view, the term 'engineering operations' should be given its ordinary meaning in the English language. It must mean, he said, 'operations of the kind usually undertaken by engineers, ie, operations calling for the skills of an engineer'. These would normally be civil engineers, but could be traffic engineers or other specialist engineers who applied their skills to land. It did not mean, he said, 'that an engineer must actually be engaged on the project, simply that it was the kind of operation on which an engineer could be employed, or which would be within his purview'.

5.62 In the exercise of his appellate functions, the Secretary of State has held that the removal of part of an embankment supporting a railway bridge and the deposit of subsoil and topsoil on land constituted an engineering operation [1983] JPL 615. In another decision (Ref: APP/Q3 115/X/04/1149901), an Inspector held that the demolition of a bridge carrying a disused railway line over a road was not development, since the bridge was a building within the Demolition of Buildings Direction 1995. However, the alteration to the contours of the adjacent embankment abutting the bridge was an engineering operation requiring planning permission.

5.63 Although the deposit of refuse or waste materials on land is regarded by the 1990 Act as being, if anything, a material change of use, it was suggested by the High Court in *Ratcliffe v Secretary of State for the Environment* [1975] JPL 728 that the deposit of refuse could amount to an 'engineering operation'.

5.64 In *R F W Coppen (Trustees of the Thames Ditton Lawn Tennis Club) v K J Bruce-Smith* [1998] JPL 1077, the Court of Appeal held that, contrary to the finding of the High Court, the proposed breaking up and digging out of tennis courts was more aptly considered to be an engineering or other operation than demolition and a building operation.

5.65 Whatever the meaning of the term 'engineering operation' its compass is limited by the provisions in paras (b) and (c) of s 55(2) of the 1990 Act, the two remaining operations specified in that subsection as not to be taken to involve the development of land. The provisions are as follows:

(b) the carrying out on land within the boundaries of a road by a highway authority of any works required for the maintenance or improvement of the road, but in the case of any such works which are not exclusively for the maintenance of the road, not including any works which may have significant adverse effects on the environment; and
(c) the carrying out by a local authority or statutory undertakers of any works for the purpose of inspecting, repairing or renewing any sewers, mains, pipes, cables, or other apparatus, including the breaking open of any street or other land for that purpose.

5.66 As regards the activity mentioned in para (b), it should be remembered that, particularly in country areas, the boundaries of a road may frequently be much wider than that part of the road which is actually 'made up'. This provision may enable the local highway authority, therefore, to make important alterations to the line of a road by such activities as ironing out a curve or removing old walls and hedges, without the need to apply for planning permission to do so. This freedom from planning control is compounded by a provision in the General

Definition of Development 1: Operational Development

Permitted Development Order. Part 9 of the Order grants planning permission for the carrying out by a local highway authority:

(a) on land within the boundaries of a road, of any works required for the maintenance or improvement of the road, where such works involve development by virtue of s 55(2)(b) of the Act; or

(b) on land outside but adjoining the boundary of an existing highway, of works required for or incidental to the maintenance or improvement of the highway.

Although the local highway authority would, unless it already owned adjacent land, have to purchase it from the owner before being able to avail itself of the permission granted by the order, the two provisions taken together give a wide latitude to highway authorities to alter the layout of a road without the public being able to influence its proposals.

5.67 The problem has been ameliorated to some extent by the amendments made to s 55 and Part 9 of the General Permitted Development Order (and incorporated in this text above) by the Environmental Impact Assessment Regulations 2017. The result is that such development may form part of or be Sch 1 or Sch 2 development and require environmental impact assessment, or otherwise have adverse environmental effects and therefore require an express grant of planning permission. For a recent discussion on the ability to undertake works in the highway and the interaction with the EIA Regulations 2017, see: *R (on the application of Dillner) v Sheffield City Council* [2016] EWHC 945 (Admin); [2016] Env LR 31.

5.68 It will be recalled that s 336(1) provides that engineering operations includes 'the formation or laying out of means of access to highways'. It would seem, therefore, that the simple driving of a vehicle onto the highway from adjoining land without more, such as the laying of hardcore or the removal of a hedge, is not in itself an engineering operation. However, under the Highways Act 1980 the highway authority has power to erect fences or posts to prevent access to the highway from adjacent land.

5.69 Prior to the Planning and Compensation Act 1991, doubts also existed about the extent to which fish farming constituted development, and thus an activity subject to development control.

5.70 Section 14 of the 1991 Act inserted into s 55 of the 1990 Act a new subsection (4A) to bring fish tanks (cages) in inland waters within the definition of development. The new subsection (4A) provides:

Where the placing or assembly of any tank in any part of any inland waters for the purpose of fish farming there would not, apart from this sub-section, involve development of the land below, this Act shall have effect as if the tank resulted from carrying out engineering operations over that land; and in this sub-section—

'fish farming' means the breeding, rearing or keeping of fish or shellfish (which includes any kind of crustacean and mollusc);

'inland waters' means waters which do not form part of the sea or of any creek, bay or estuary or of any river as far as the tide flows; and

'tank' includes any cage and any other structure for use in fish farming.

5.71 Allied to the decision to make the placing or assembly of fish tanks development, Part 6 of Sch 2 to the General Permitted Development Order provides that such activity should be permitted development under the Order when carried out on land outside national parks. However, under the Order, a person wishing to exercise such permitted development 'rights' must give prior notice to the local planning authority. This prior-notification procedure allows the local planning authority to decide within a period of 28 days whether or not it wishes to make the activity subject to its prior approval. If the authority does so decide, it allows it to exercise control over the siting and appearance of the development.

Mining operations

5.72 As originally enacted the definition of development contained no definition of the term 'mining operations'. In s 336(1), however, minerals are defined to include 'all minerals and substances in or under land of a kind ordinarily worked for removal by underground or surface working, except that it does not include peat cut for purposes other than sale'.

5.73 The Town and Country Planning (Minerals) Act 1981 amended the definition of development by adding a new provision. This is now contained in s 55(4) which states:

For the purposes of this Act mining operations include—
(a) the removal of material of any description—
   (i) from a mineral-working deposit;
   (ii) from a deposit of pulverised fuel ash or other furnace ash or clinker; or
   (iii) from a deposit of iron, steel or other metallic slags; and
(b) the extraction of minerals from a disused railway embankment.

5.74 The 1981 Act was passed after the Government had considered the report of the Stevens Committee on Planning Control over Mineral Workings. Concern was there expressed about whether the definition of development, and particularly mining operations, was wide enough to include the recovery of material originally removed or extracted from the land and then deposited on it, such as a slagheap from a coal mine or a coal deposit on a railway line. The amendment made to the definition of development by the 1981 Act makes clear that this and other like activities over which there was similar doubt now fall within that definition.

Other operations

5.75 It is clear that there must be some restriction on the words 'other operations'. As was pointed out by the House of Lords in *Coleshill & District Investment Co Ltd v Minister of Housing and Local Government* [1969] 1 WLR 746, the use of the words 'building, engineering, mining or other operations' makes it clear that not every operation constitutes development since to hold otherwise would be to render the words 'building, engineering and mining' superfluous. Their Lordships also pointed out that since 'mining' operations differed substantially from 'building' operations, it was not possible for a single genus to fit all three words. Accordingly, 'other operations' could not be construed *ejusdem generis*. Their Lordships all agreed, however, that there must be some restriction on the meaning of 'other operations'; that it must be construed by reference to building, engineering, and mining, and that the maxim *noscitur a sociis* might apply even though it is not *ejusdem generis*. Lord Pearson also suggested that although no single genus would fit all three preceding words, it was possible that there were three separate genera, and that 'other operations' would connote an activity similar to 'building operations', or to 'engineering operations', or to 'mining operations'.

5.76 In *Cambridge City Council v Secretary of State for the Environment* (1992) 64 P & CR 257, the Court of Appeal, having concluded that there had been no evidence before the Deputy Judge upon which he had been entitled to make a finding of fact that the demolition of houses constituted work normally undertaken by a person who carried on business as a builder, went on to consider whether the work constituted an 'other operation' on land. On the basis of authority (ie the *Coleshill* decision), the Court of Appeal concluded that it did not. The court emphasized that 'other' operations in s 55 of the 1990 Act did not mean all other operations; and that other operations had to be '... at least of a constructive character, leading to an identifiable and positive result' or be '... similar to building operations or to engineering operations'.

5.77 Because of the wide definition given in the Act to the words building, engineering, and mining, there has been little further judicial consideration of the meaning of the term 'other operations'. However, a number of examples of findings of other operations have been contained in ministerial decisions given on appeal.

5.78 When making decisions on appeal in this area, it is not uncommon for the Secretary of State (or the Inspector) to confine himself to a statement that the activity which he is considering is or is not development; or, at best, to confine himself to a reference to one of the specific operations listed in s 55(1). In one ministerial decision, however, the Inspector held that the deposit of waste materials on land for the purpose of raising the level of the land to make it suitable for agricultural use was not a building or engineering operation, but an 'other operation' for which planning permission was required: [1982] JPL 741. That decision, however, was made before the Inspector had the benefit of the judgment in *Fayrewood Fish Farms Ltd v Secretary of State for the Environment* [1984] JPL 267. Had that been available, he might well have held that the deposit in question was an engineering operation.

5.79 In another ministerial decision reported at [1985] JPL 129 it was held that the installation of a protective grille over a shop window and door was an 'other operation' within the meaning of s 55(1) of the 1990 Act. In a later decision in 1996 (unreported), a golf club had constructed a further tee to their golf course, which had an existing nine-hole capacity, in order to enable golfers more conveniently to use the course for a full 18 holes. The Inspector rejected the local planning authority's contention that the construction works constituted an 'engineering operation', but held instead that the works amounted to an 'other operation' within the definition in s 55(1). More recently, an Inspector held that freestanding parasols (with heaters installed) in a sunken base were works falling within the definition of 'other operations' (Ref: APP/R1038/C/03/1136482). In another case, *R (on the application of Beronstone Ltd) v First Secretary of State and Chiltern DC* [2006] EWHC 2391 (Admin), reference was made, without judicial criticism, to a finding of an Inspector that the placing of 554 wooden stakes into the ground to define and mark out boundaries and extent of 40 plots of land was an 'other operation'.

6

DEFINITION OF DEVELOPMENT 2: MATERIAL CHANGE OF USE

A. MATERIAL CHANGE OF USE	6.02	F. THE PLANNING UNIT, AND PRIMARY OR DOMINANT AND ANCILLARY USES	6.115
B. USES EXCLUDED FROM DEVELOPMENT	6.10		
C. USES INCLUDED WITHIN DEVELOPMENT	6.92	G. INTERRUPTION AND ABANDONMENT OF A USE	6.143
D. ADVERTISING	6.100	H. SUBDIVISION OF A PLANNING UNIT	6.163
E. INTENSIFICATION	6.104		

6.01 The term 'material change of use' is not defined in the 1990 Act. Its meaning has to be ascertained, therefore, by reference to the many cases in which the courts have had to consider its significance. In *Parkes v Secretary of State for the Environment* [1978] 1 WLR 1308 (CA), Lord Denning MR said that 'operations' comprised activities which resulted in some physical alteration to the land, which had some degree of permanence to the land itself; whereas 'use' comprised activities which are done in, alongside, or on the land but which did not interfere with the actual physical characteristics of the land. Accordingly, he held that, for the purposes of serving a discontinuance order under what is now s 102 of the 1990 Act, the sorting, processing, and disposal of scrap materials was a 'use' of land.

A. MATERIAL CHANGE OF USE

6.02 It must be emphasized that the activity which constitutes the second limb of the term 'development' is not merely a 'change of use' but a 'material change of use'. The attitude of the courts to the question of whether or not a change of use is material is that it is largely a matter of fact and degree for the local planning authority to decide, and they will only interfere if the decision is one to which the authority could not reasonably have come. In *Bendles Motors Ltd v Bristol Corporation* [1963] 1 WLR 247 an application for planning permission had been

Definition of Development 2: Material Change of Use

made to the local planning authority for permission to erect an egg-vending machine on the forecourt of garage premises. After permission had been refused, the owners of the garage proceeded nevertheless to erect the machine on the forecourt. The machine measured some 6 feet in height, 2 feet 7 inches deep, and 2 feet 7 inches wide. Since it was both free-standing and gravity-fed, it could not be considered to be operational development. The local planning authority had served an enforcement notice requiring the removal of the machine and, on appeal, the Minister had upheld the notice. The owners then appealed to the High Court against the Minister's decision on a point of law.

6.03 The Minister had upheld the enforcement notice on the ground that the stationing of the egg-vending machine on the site involved a change of use of the land on which it stood and that its introduction on the site involved a material change of use of the land, since the use of the machine was in the nature of a 'shop use', in that it attracted customers not necessarily concerned with the motoring service provided by the garage. In dismissing the appeal Lord Parker CJ quoted his own words in *East Barnet UDC v British Transport Commission* [1962] 2 QB 484 (Div Court):

> It is a question of fact and degree in every case and ... the court is unable to interfere with a finding ... on such a matter unless it must be said that they could not properly have reached that conclusion. That was dealing with a case stated from justices, but in my judgment the same is true of an appeal from the Minister himself. This court can only interfere if satisfied that it is a conclusion that he could not, properly directing himself as to the law, have reached.

Later, the Lord Chief Justice went on to say:

> I confess that at first sight, and indeed at last sight, I am somewhat surprised that it can be said that the placing of this small machine on this large forecourt can be said to change the use of these premises in a material sense from that of a garage and petrol filling station by the addition of a further use. It is surprising, and it may be, if it was a matter for my own personal judgment, that I should feel inclined to say that the egg-vending machine was *de minimis*; but it is not a question of what my opinion is on that matter, it is for the Minister to decide.

6.04 It is submitted that this was clearly a sensible decision. The court held that the Minister had not erred in law in holding that the change of use from a garage and petrol filling- station, to a garage, petrol filling-station, and 'shop use' was material. Had the Lord Chief Justice given precedence to his personal feelings, it would have been difficult for the local planning authority to control a later installation on the forecourt of other types of vending machines. Furthermore, if the garage and petrol filling-station use were then to be abandoned, a change to an exclusively shop use would have been achieved. On the other hand, it has to be accepted that in practice a small amount of sales of retail goods may be incidental to a main petrol filling use and so would not amount to a material change.

6.05 The case demonstrates that whether or not a change of use is material is a question of fact and degree in every case for decision by the local planning authority, or on appeal by the Secretary of State. It also demonstrates that a material change of use may occur not only where a change is made from, say, use A to use B, but also where a change is made from use A to use A and B by the addition of a further use.

6.06 The same approach was followed in *Hidderley v Warwickshire CC* (1963) 14 P & CR 134 (Div Court), where the installation of an egg-vending machine on farm land adjacent to a lay-by on a public road was held to constitute a material change of use.

6.07 In this area it is important to bear in mind two cardinal principles. First, that the assessment of facts and matters of planning judgment have always been regarded as exclusively for the decision-maker. Secondly, the courts have a limited ability to intervene, as indicated by Nourse LJ in *Moore v Secretary of State for the Environment, Transport, and the Regions* [1998] JPL 877 (CA), where he said at p 70:

> A question of fact and degree, although it is a question of fact, involves the application of a legal test. If the Secretary of State applies the correct test, the court, on an appeal under section 289, can only interfere with his decision if the facts found are incapable of supporting it. If, on the other hand, he applies an incorrect test, then the court can interfere and itself apply the correct test to the facts found.

In another case with the name *Moore* (*Moore v Secretary of State for Communities and Local Government* [2012] EWCA Civ 1202; [2013] JPL 192), Sullivan LJ (giving the judgment of the Court of Appeal) held that whether a change from the use of a property as a family dwellinghouse to a commercial letting as holiday accommodation, amounted to a material change of use was a matter of fact and degree and depended on particular circumstances of the use for holiday accommodation. So, whether a use of a dwellinghouse for commercial holiday lettings was a material change of use would depend on the particular nature of the commercial holiday letting. In this case the Court of Appeal held that the Inspector had not erred in law in holding that where an eight-bedroom house had been occupied by a family, the use by large groups of up to 18 people for short periods was a material change of use.

6.08 Another question that has arisen is whether, when determining whether a change of use is material, it is proper to consider the effect of the change on adjacent land. Some early cases indicated that it was. However, it seemed sensible to consider the change merely in relation to the planning unit in question; and to consider the off-site effects that the change would bring as relevant to the question of whether planning permission should be granted. But it is otherwise. In *Devonshire CC v Allens Caravans (Estates) Ltd* (1962) 14 P & CR 440 (Div Court), Lord Parker said:

> The materiality to be considered is a materiality from the planning point of view and, in particular, the question of amenities.

In the same case, Gorman J said:

> It seems to me that one of the criteria for determining what is a material change may well be in effect the planning of the neighbourhood.

A later case is *Blum v Secretary of State for the Environment* [1987] JPL 278 which has a more explicit passage on the relevance of off-site effects. Simon Brown J said:

> The Inspector here had plainly addressed himself, as he was in law obliged to do, to the character of the use. He did so in large part, but not in fact exclusively, by reference to the extent to which the additional use of the premises as a riding school intensified certain aspects of the activity both on and off site. He referred to the additional staff required, the additional facilities required, and he observed that there would be more horse activity, more horse traffic, more rides out, more car traffic, more car parking. Not exclusively, though, because he also referred to the introduction of a sanded paddock which had been provided on site for instructional purposes. True, that in itself had not been felt by the planning authority to amount to a material change of use; but that could not prevent their having regard to it in assessing the overall impact of the introduction of the new use on the overall character of the use of the land.

Both cases and the statements made in them were considered with approval by David Widdicombe QC sitting as a Deputy High Court Judge in *Forest of Dean DC v Secretary of State for the Environment* [1995] JPL B184. In that case the Secretary of State's decision in respect of an enforcement notice relating to a change of use of a caravan park from holiday use to permanent residential use was remitted to him because the Inspector had failed to take into account the relevance of off-site effects in determining whether a material change of use had occurred. Then in *Thames Heliport v Tower Hamlets LBC* (1997) 74 P & CR 164 Glidewell LJ held that in considering whether a material change had taken place the decision-maker had to ask whether anything had changed on the land which is capable of being material from an environmental point of view and that this must be looked at from the point of view of human beings likely to be affected by the change which has occurred. This does have the consequence that there can be an overlap between the factors that determine whether development has taken place and whether, if so, planning permission should be granted.

6.09 It is also clear that certain changes in the use of land will not be material. This is because in determining whether any activity constitutes a change of use, it is the character of the use which has to be considered, not the particular purpose of a particular occupier. In *East Barnet UDC v British Transport Commission* [1962] 2 QB 484 the Divisional Court refused to interfere with the decision of justices (who had quashed enforcement notices served on the company) that to use land as a transit depot for the handling and storage of crated motor vehicles, following upon the use of the land for the storage and distribution of coal, did not constitute development. In expressing the view that what really had to be considered was the character of the use of the land, not the particular purpose of a particular occupier, Lord Parker CJ quoted with approval a statement by Glyn-Jones J in *Marshall v Nottingham Corporation* [1960] 1 WLR 707 (Div Court) where he said:

> The mere fact that a dealer in the course of his business begins to deal in goods in which he had not dealt before does not necessarily involve a change, still less a material change, in his use of the land or premises where the business is carried on. A dealer in musical instruments might 50 years ago have begun to deal in gramophones or phonographs, as I suppose they would then have been called; and then in the course of time in radio sets and later in television sets. A dealer in electrical appliances, as demand changed and fresh appliances were invented, might have successively added vacuum cleaners, refrigerators, washing machines and the like to his stock-in-trade, and he too might have begun to deal in radio and television sets. Each of them may have ceased to sell goods formerly sold for which there is no longer an adequate demand. Yet neither, in my view, has thereby altered the use he is making of his premises.

The position may be far less clear, however, where a retail business is carried on but a change takes place in the type of business, as might occur, for example, where the business of a baker is substituted for that of a butcher. Fortunately, for most practical purposes the problem is dissolved by the existence of the Use Classes Order (see para 6.57).

B. USES EXCLUDED FROM DEVELOPMENT

Whatever may be the meaning of the term 'material change of use', its scope is restricted by paras (d) to (f) of s 55(2) of the 1990 Act, in which three uses are expressly stated *not* to involve the development of land. The three uses are: **6.10**

(d) A use incidental to the enjoyment of a dwellinghouse.
(e) A use for agriculture or forestry.
(f) A change of use within the same use Class.

Use incidental to the enjoyment of a dwellinghouse

By s 55(2)(d) of the 1990 Act, 'the use of any buildings or other land within the curtilage of a dwellinghouse for any purpose incidental to the enjoyment of the dwellinghouse as such' is not to be taken to involve development of the land. **6.11**

Under this provision, it is not a material change of use to convert, say, a henhouse into a workshop or an outhouse to provide additional sleeping accommodation for one's family. The provision refers, however, to the *use of* buildings or other land, so that if the occupier finds it necessary to carry out operational development for the better enjoyment of that use, planning permission will be needed for that operation. The paragraph also refers to the use of any buildings or other land within the '*curtilage*' of a dwellinghouse. Precisely what constitutes the curtilage **6.12** may not always be clear. The definition of the term most usually referred to is that given in a Scottish case of *Sinclair-Lockhart's Trustees v Central Land Board* (1950) 1 P & CR 195, as:

> ground which is used for the comfortable enjoyment of a house ... and thereby as an integral part of the same, although it has not been marked off or enclosed in any way. It is enough that it serves the purposes of the house ... in some necessary or reasonably useful way.

It has also been held in *Dyer v Dorset CC* [1989] QB 346 (CA) that the definition in the *Oxford English Dictionary* is adequate for most purposes. That definition is:

> a small court, yard, garth or piece of ground attached to a dwellinghouse and forming one enclosure with it, or so regarded by the law; the area attached to and containing a dwellinghouse and its outbuildings.

6.13 It seems from *Stephens v Cuckfield RDC* [1959] 1 QB 516, however, that land may be a garden but not be within a curtilage. In *James v Secretary of State for the Environment* (1990) 61 P & CR 234 (Div Court), it was held that there are three criteria for determining whether land is within the curtilage of a building, namely:

(a) physical layout;
(b) ownership, past, and present;
(c) use or function, past, and present.

6.14 In the case of *McAlpine v Secretary of State for the Environment* [1995] 1 PLR 16 (concerning the interpretation of the word 'curtilage' in the General Development Order 1988, Sch 2, Part 1, Class E) following the decision in *Dyer* it was said that 'curtilage is constrained to a small area about a building, it is not necessary for there to be physical enclosure but the land needs to be regarded in law as part of one enclosure with the house, and overall the term has a restrictive meaning'.

6.15 However the criteria for defining a curtilage have now been restated by the Court of Appeal in *Secretary of State for the Environment, Transport, and the Regions v Skerritts of Nottingham* [2000] JPL 789, where it was held that although the decision in *Dyer* was plainly correct, the court in that case had gone further than was necessary in expressing the view that the curtilage of a building must always be small, or that the notion of smallness was inherent in the expression. No piece of land could ever be within the curtilage of more than one building, and if houses were built to a density of 20 or more to an acre, the curtilage of each house could be extremely restricted. But as was said in *Dyer*, the definition of a curtilage in relation to a building must remain a question of fact and degree in each case. In this case, the Court of Appeal held that the curtilage of a large building was likely to extend to what were, or had in the past been, in the context of ownership and function, ancillary buildings. The law on 'curtilage' was helpfully reviewed by Supperstone J in *Burford v Secretary of State for Communities and Local Government* [2017] EWHC 1493 (Admin).

6.16 Possibly the most important part of para (d) of s 55(2), however, is the last two words. The requirement is that use must be incidental to the enjoyment of the dwellinghouse 'as such', ie as a dwellinghouse. Hence to use land within the curtilage of a dwellinghouse for the parking of a commercial vehicle used for business purposes is not within this provision, although as a matter of fact and degree such a use might not be considered to be material. This is an area of particular difficulty where a person uses outbuildings or a room in a dwellinghouse to carry on a hobby or an activity having a business or commercial element. Artists' studios and the giving of music lessons are classic examples of this problem. The use of outbuildings for mending cloth, carrying on a tailoring business or dog breeding, the use of a room for a nursing agency, and the use of a kitchen to prepare sandwiches and salads for local firms, have all been held by the Secretary of State to constitute development.

6.17 In all these cases it is necessary for the authority to look at the nature and scale of the hobby or non-domestic use being carried on, and then to judge whether as a matter of fact and degree a further use has been added to the existing dwellinghouse use. It seems that an activity carried out by the occupier of a dwellinghouse is not automatically incidental to the enjoyment of the dwellinghouse as such merely because it is a hobby; it has to be a use incidental to the enjoyment of the dwellinghouse, as opposed to the enjoyment of the occupier.

6.18 The application of the provision in s 55(2)(d) was considered by the Court of Appeal in *Wallington v Secretary of State for Wales* [1991] JPL 942, where a challenge was made to a decision by an Inspector appointed by the Secretary of State to uphold an enforcement notice which had alleged the making of a material change in the use of a dwellinghouse by the addition of a further, wholly non-commercial use, namely the keeping within the curtilage of the dwellinghouse of some 44 dogs. It was argued on behalf of the appellant that in applying s 55(2)(d), the Inspector had regarded the question as being whether as a matter of fact and degree it was '*reasonable*' to regard the relevant activity as the use of the premises for a purpose incidental to the enjoyment of the dwelling as such. It was claimed that to apply an objective test of reasonableness was erroneous, since it would place an unjustifiable restriction on an enthusiast who had an eccentric hobby of his own.

6.19 In rejecting the argument and dismissing the appeal, Slade LJ, in the Court of Appeal, held that the Inspector had been entitled to have regard to what people *normally* do in dwellinghouses to decide whether, as a matter of fact and degree on the one hand, (a) the keeping of 40 or more dogs should be regarded as reasonably incidental to the enjoyment of the dwellinghouse, or on the other hand (b) the number of dogs kept exceeded what could reasonably be so regarded.

6.20 The court also made reference to a decision of Sir Graham Eyre QC, sitting as a Deputy High Court Judge, in *Emin v Secretary of State for the Environment*

[1989] JPL 909. That decision concerned the criteria set down in Class 1.3 of then General Development Order 1977, which dealt with development within the curtilage of a dwellinghouse 'required for a purpose incidental to the enjoyment of the dwellinghouse as such', although a distinction might be drawn between the wording of that order and of s 55(2)(d), which does not include the word 'required'. Nevertheless, according to Slade LJ, certain observations of Sir Graham Eyre were helpful and apposite in the present case, where he had said (at p 913):

> The fact that such a building had to be required for a purpose associated with the enjoyment of a dwellinghouse could not rest solely on the unrestrained whim of him who dwelt there but connoted some sense of reasonableness in all the circumstances of the particular case. That was not to say that the arbiter could impose some hard objective test so as to frustrate the reasonable aspirations of a particular owner or occupier so long as they were sensibly related to his enjoyment of the dwelling. The word 'incidental' connoted an element of subordination in land use terms in relation to the enjoyment of the dwellinghouse itself.

6.21 According to Farquharson LJ in the Court of Appeal in the *Wallington* case, in approaching the question of whether a use was for a purpose incidental to the enjoyment of a dwellinghouse, it was sensible to consider what would be the normal use of a dwellinghouse, although this was not determinative of the question. In his view, consideration of whether the use was subjective or objective merely complicated matters. In his judgment, the word 'incidental' meant subordinate in land-use terms to the enjoyment of a dwellinghouse as a dwellinghouse. In considering whether a use came within s 55(2)(d), one had to have regard to such things as where the dwellinghouse was situated, its size and how much ground was included in its curtilage, the nature and scale of the activity said to be incidental to enjoyment of the dwellinghouse as such, and the disposition and character of the occupier. He might also have added that in the case of dogs, their breed and prolixity to barking would also be relevant considerations.

6.22 It will be seen that the judgments in the *Wallington* case do not make clear the precise criteria to be applied in determining whether a use falls within para (d) of s 55(2). Slade LJ appeared to favour taking an objective view of whether an activity was incidental, whereas Farquharson LJ clearly thought little help was to be gained by considering any subjective/objective dichotomy.

6.23 Since the keeping of 44 dogs in the *Wallington* case was held to be outside the provisions of s 55(2)(a), the question that arises is how many dogs a person may keep in order to come within the paragraph. In the *Wallington* case the Inspector had expressly accepted that to impose any specific limiting number would be 'arbitrary'; but had gone on, in order to be sure not to over-enforce, to agree with the planning authority that the requirement section of the enforcement notice should enable up to six dogs to be kept on the premises without the need for planning permission.

6.24 In a later ministerial decision, an Inspector upheld an enforcement notice alleging a material change of use within the curtilage of a dwellinghouse by the keeping of dogs, and requiring that the number kept at the premises at any one time should be reduced to not more than three. The Inspector, who had the benefit of having seen the decision in the *Wallington* case, considered that the main issue was whether the continued keeping of the dogs (which over the years had varied between six and eight excluding puppies) would be likely to be harmful to the amenities which occupiers of neighbouring houses would reasonably be expected to enjoy. Although the Inspector considered that the figure of three dogs cited in the notice as the number which would be acceptable might be regarded as arbitrary, the number was not inappropriate to a normal domestic situation, even allowing for the fact that this figure might be exceptional when not every household had dogs.

6.25 In yet another ministerial decision, [1993] JPL 901, an Inspector again upheld an enforcement notice which had required that the number of dogs kept within the curtilage of a dwellinghouse be reduced to not more than three. The property in question was a two-bedroom mid-terrace property with a small front garden and a hard-surfaced yard area to the rear. In his decision letter, the Inspector considered it important to distinguish between the enjoyment of the dwellinghouse as such and the enjoyment of the occupier. Put another way, the occupier of a dwellinghouse might well be enjoying himself in some way which was not related to the dwellinghouse *as a dwelling*. In this particular case, for example, the evidence showed that the occupation of the dwellinghouse had been given over to a very large degree to the keeping of animals associated with an animal welfare charity.

6.26 Another (but unreported) ministerial decision, involved the keeping of nine German shepherd dogs at a small semi-detached house with modest curtilage located in an urban estate of similar houses in Banbury. The Inspector's view was that the house appeared to have been given over to the dogs, to the point where the interior accommodation looked more suited to housing dogs than people; and he found that the garden was largely given over to dog runs and kennels. In his view, the scale of the dog keeping in relation to the modest size of this suburban property went well beyond that which may be considered incidental to the enjoyment of the dwelling.

6.27 Mention should also be made of *South Oxfordshire DC v Secretary of State for the Environment, Transport, and the Regions* [2000] PLCR 315, where the Deputy Judge upheld a decision by an Inspector that the use of land around a dwellinghouse for the landing and taking off of helicopters was a use incidental to the enjoyment of the dwellinghouse taking into account the nature of the house and the purposes of the helicopter use, namely as a personal means of transport for the owner and members of his family. This case might be contrasted with

Harrods v Secretary of State (see para 6.127), though it may be noted that the question at issue there was not whether the activity carried on was a use incidental to the enjoyment of a dwellinghouse as such, but whether the activity was within the existing use of the land. There the Court of Appeal refused to interfere with a finding by the Secretary of State that the introduction of a helicopter use to the roof of a department store amounted to a material change in the use of the store. The court considered that the correct approach was to consider on general principles whether there had been a material change of use. Here one had to concentrate not on what was incidental to a particular shop (Harrods) bearing in mind its particular mode of operation, but to see what activities were reasonably incidental to shops in general.

6.28 That principle was followed in *R (I'm Your Man Ltd) v North Somerset Council* [2004] EWHC 342 (Admin); [2004] 4 PLR 1, where the High Court held that the local planning authority had been entitled to decide that the use of land at a helicopter museum for helicopter 'air experience' flights, with passengers who were visitors to the museum and helicopter flights to and from the museum with or without passengers who were visitors to the museum, were incidental to the primary use of land as a museum which did not constitute a material change of use. Whether this was a change of use was a question of fact and degree for the authority to decide.

6.29 In judicial decisions relating to uses incidental to the enjoyment of a dwellinghouse as such, a noteworthy case is *Croydon LBC v Gladden* [1994] JPL 723. There the Court of Appeal upheld an enforcement notice served by the local planning authority that placing a replica Spitfire aeroplane in the garden of a dwellinghouse was not a use incidental to the enjoyment of the dwellinghouse as such. The court held that the concept of what was incidental to such enjoyment included an element of reasonableness. It could not rest solely on the unrestrained whim of the occupier, and no one could regard it as reasonable to keep a replica Spitfire as incidental to the enjoyment of the dwellinghouse. The court also considered that any pleasure, however exquisite, derived from defying the local authority was not enjoyment of the dwellinghouse as such.

6.30 Another issue that has arisen is whether land within the curtilage of a dwellinghouse can be used by the owner as a private burial ground for himself and his family without the need to apply for planning permission. In a ministerial decision, [1994] JPL 305, a Scottish inquiry reporter held that it could be so used. The reporter made no mention of the Scottish provision equivalent to s 55(2)(d) of the 1990 Act, it being unlikely, following the decision in the *Wallington* case, to be a use incidental to the enjoyment of the dwellinghouse as such. The reporter held, however, that since the proposed project would involve the digging of only a very limited number of graves (by hand), it would not amount to an 'engineering or other operation'; and since there would be no change in the surface land use, nor any upstanding physical features resulting from the intending burials, it could not be said that the proposal amounted to a 'material change of use'.

6.31 In a later ministerial decision reported at [1996] JPL 1083, the Secretary of State held that a proposal to dig two trenches for the burial of two bodies within the curtilage of a dwellinghouse did not constitute development. In that case there was no intention to mark the site with a headstone or memorial and it was proposed to level the site after interment. The Secretary of State decided that the proposed activity could not be regarded as incidental to the enjoyment of the dwellinghouse as such on the basis that that use could not be regarded as a normal element of residential use. However, since the burial site would after interment be indistinguishable from its surroundings, the small area of land affected was within a general residential curtilage, and the scale of the proposal was small, he had concluded as a matter of fact and degree that any change in the character of the planning unit was '*de minimis*' and that no change of use had occurred.

6.32 In the past few years there has been a growing interest in the number of certificates of lawful use issued by local planning authorities for non-commercial burials on private land where operational development is not considered significant. So, whether planning permission is required in order to be buried in the garden of a dwellinghouse is a question of fact and degree in every case, taking into consideration the nature of any memorial to be erected on the site. Quite apart from planning law considerations, however, any death must be registered with the Registrar of Births and Deaths and a certificate of disposal obtained, and objections may be raised to the burial by environmental health officers if there is a risk of danger to public health, having regard to such matters as having a sufficient depth of soil on top of the body, the height of the water table, and the distance from watercourses.

Use for agriculture or forestry

6.33 The second of the three uses listed in paras (d) to (f) of s 55(2) which are expressly stated *not* to involve the development of land is:

> (e) the use of any land for the purposes of agriculture or forestry (including afforestation) and the use for any of those purposes of any building occupied together with land so used.

6.34 Again the provision refers to the *use* of land for the purposes of agriculture or forestry, so operational development on land used for agriculture or forestry is not within the exclusion. Certain operational development on land used for those purposes is, however, permitted development under the General Permitted Development Order.

6.35 Some disputes have arisen about whether particular activities fall within this exemption. Section 336(1) of the 1990 Act provides that 'agriculture' includes horticulture, fruit growing, seed growing, dairy farming, the breeding and keeping of livestock (including any creature kept for the production of food, wool skins, or fur, or for the purpose of its use in the farming of land), the use of land as grazing land, meadow land, osier land, market gardens and nursery grounds, and the use of land for woodlands where that use is ancillary to the farming of land for other agricultural purposes.

6.36 There have been many cases where the courts have had to consider this agriculture or forestry exclusion: in *Williams v Minister of Housing and Local Government* (1967) 18 P & CR 514 the owner of a nursery garden used a timber building situated on the land as a retail shop selling produce grown on the land. When he started to sell produce grown elsewhere, the local planning authority issued an enforcement notice which the Minister subsequently upheld. The High Court there agreed with the Minister that the use of land for agriculture necessarily includes the selling of produce grown on the land, but that the selling of products grown elsewhere was not an agricultural use.

6.37 In *Allen v Secretary of State for the Environment and Reigate and Banstead BC* [1990] JPL 340 the court declined to interfere with an Inspector's judgment that a material change of use had occurred where the revenue from the sale of imported plants reached about 10 per cent of total turnover.

6.38 In *Wealdon DC v Secretary of State for the Environment and Colin Day* [1988] JPL 268, the Court of Appeal upheld the decision of an Inspector to quash an enforcement notice requiring the removal of a caravan placed upon agricultural land for the purpose of providing a weatherproof place for the storage and mixing of cattle food and to provide shelter for Mr Day, on the ground that the caravan was used for animal feed preparation and shelter and as such was ancillary to the agricultural use of the land.

6.39 In *Gill v Secretary of State for the Environment* [1985] JPL 710 the High Court held that the occasional killing of animals which had been reared and bred on a farm might be within the normal use of land used for agricultural purposes, but that the wholesale slaughter of large numbers of foxes, kept on land for the purpose of producing skins or furs, was not within the definition of agriculture.

6.40 In *Salvatore Cumbo v Secretary of State for the Environment* [1992] JPL 366, the High Court refused to interfere with the decision of an Inspector that the establishment on a farm of a cheese-making business would be outside the realms of wholly agricultural use and be in the nature of a mixed farming and manufacturing use for which planning permission was necessary.

6.41 In two ministerial decisions, the view has been expressed that the breeding of rats, mice, guinea pigs, or gerbils to provide food for snakes and reptiles is not agricultural use; and that to constitute an agricultural use creatures being bred had to contribute directly or indirectly to the human food chain.

6.42 In a more recent judicial decision, *Millington v Secretary of State for the Environment, Transport, and the Regions* [2000] JPL 297 the Court of Appeal had to decide whether the Secretary of State was right in considering an enforcement notice appeal, to proceed on the basis that where land is used for the creation of a new product (wine), from produce grown on the land (grapes), the land was therefore no longer being used for the purposes of agriculture and as such not exempt from planning control. The court considered the Secretary of State had not been right. According to the court:

> the proper approach to the root question in this case is ... to consider whether what the Millingtons were doing can, having regard to ordinary and reasonable practice, be regarded as ordinarily incidental to the growing of grapes for wine included in the general term agriculture, ancillary to normal farming activities, reasonably necessary to make the product marketable or disposable to profit or whether it had come to the stage where the operations cannot reasonably be said to be consequential on the agricultural operations of producing crops.

Since the Secretary of State had not adopted that approach, the enforcement notice was remitted back to him to make a new decision in the light of the court's judgment.

6.43 In *Crowborough Parish Council v Secretary of State for the Environment* [1981] JPL 281 (Div Court), it was held that the use of land for allotments was an agricultural use falling within the definition of agriculture and that in determining an appeal against what was then called a s 64 determination, the Secretary of State had erred in law in holding otherwise.

6.44 In *Sykes v Secretary of State for the Environment* [1981] JPL 285, the Divisional Court had to consider whether the use of land for grazing horses was within the definition of agriculture. The Secretary of State had held that it was, and his view was supported by the court. The case raises, however, important issues with regard to the use of land for what is sometimes referred to as 'horsiculture'. This usually refers to the practice of keeping horses on land for horse-riding purposes. If the land is used intensively for that purpose the horses may need to be supplied with extra food. In such cases the question to be asked is: what use is being made of the land? Is it for the purpose of grazing? If not, then the activity may amount to a material change of use. Donaldson LJ said:

> If ... horses are being kept on the land and are being fed wholly or primarily by other means so that such grazing as they do is completely incidental and perhaps achieved merely because there are no convenient ways of stopping them doing it, then plainly the land is not being used for grazing but merely being used for keeping the animals.

It follows, therefore, that land will not normally be treated as being used for the 'grazing' of horses and thus an agricultural use, if the horses are primarily kept on it for some other purpose such as recreation or exercise when the grazing is seen as completely incidental and inevitable. It would be otherwise, however, if little or no extra food was provided for horses kept on the land, but which were being used for riding or associated activities elsewhere, such as on adjacent bridleways. *Sykes* was considered in *Fox v First Secretary of State* [2003] EWHC 887 (Admin) in which Sullivan J declined to quash an Inspector's decision that land was not being used for grazing, rather keeping horses.

6.45 Another significant case on the definition of agriculture was *North Warwickshire BC v Secretary of State for the Environment* [1984] JPL 435 (Div Court), where it was held that the use of a *building* for the purposes of agriculture also fell within the paragraph. The paragraph refers to the use of land for the purposes of agriculture 'and the use for any of those purposes of any building occupied together with land so used'. The court considered that because the definition of land in s 336(1) of the 1990 Act meant 'any corporeal hereditament, including a building', the two phrases had to be construed disjunctively. This means that the agricultural use of a building is not development even though the agricultural use is in no way dependent upon the land on which the building stands. If this decision is correct, it would be possible to convert a disused building in suburbia into a chicken farm without the change amounting to development.

6.46 It should be noted that the statutory definition of agriculture in s 336(1) of the 1990 Act does not include any requirement that the activity should be carried on in connection with a trade or business, or that it should be profitable, viable, or sustainable. This is in marked contrast to the definition of 'agricultural land' for the purposes of permitted development rights under Part 6 of Sch 2 to the General Permitted Development Order where the land must be used for the purposes of a trade or business. The ministerial decision of *North Devon D C v Ludgate* [2009] JPL 1659 considers the question of whether fish farming is an agricultural use. It would seem clear that the breeding of fish for the object of providing food must be an agricultural use, as even if fish are not livestock as such, they must come within the definition of a creature kept for the production of food. As Lord Parker pointed out in *Belmont Farm Ltd v Minister of Housing and Local Government* [1962] 13 P & CR 417, the inclusion in the term livestock of 'including any creature kept for the production of food, wool, skins or fur, or for the purpose of its use in the farming of land' was clearly intended to include bees, possibly pheasants and fish. However, the crucial factor is whether the fish are kept for the production of food. If they are bred for other purposes such as sport or recreation it is not an agricultural use. So, as the Inspector pointed out, just as there can be different types of horse (the recreational horse and the farming horse) there can be different types of fish. In the particular case in question the fish were bred primarily to stock sporting lakes which needed a supply of fish.

Leisure plots

As the restrictive nature of planning control became clearer in the post-war period, a practice developed whereby owners of land in certain parts of the country sought to obtain a greater profit from their land than that obtained from its agricultural use, by selling small parcels to others, the sales often being accompanied by suggestions that the parcels could be used for a variety of leisure purposes. Areas particularly affected included the Thames Estuary and the New Forest. The purchasers of each parcel were likely to be town dwellers, who believed that they might in future be able to build on the land or use it for camping or for siting a caravan. **6.47**

In the late 1970s and the early 1980s, the Minister responsible for planning held on appeals from decisions of local planning authorities that a change from agricultural use to leisure use amounted to a material change of use. In *Pitman et al v the Secretary of State for the Environment* [1989] JPL 831 (CA), leisure plots were defined as pieces of land where leisure activities were carried on with some degree of frequency, and leisure activities were defined as activities which people carry on in their free time for the primary purpose of pleasure or amusement rather than the acquisition of money or money's worth; the court gave the examples of enjoying the view and the sunshine. It upheld the decision that the change of use from agriculture to use as leisure plots was a material change. **6.48**

There is now some evidence that a resumption of the practice of farmers and others subdividing land into small plots and then selling them (sometimes over the internet) to unsuspecting purchasers, is still taking place. **6.49**

In the case of *R (on the application of Beronstone Ltd) v First Secretary of State and Chiltern DC* [2006] EWHC 2391 (Admin), the High Court dismissed an appeal from the decision of an Inspector to uphold an enforcement notice served by the local planning authority. The notice had required the removal of a number of 'fence posts' which had been erected on land within an Area of Outstanding Natural Beauty without planning permission. The contravention of planning control had involved the erection of 554 wooden stakes driven into the ground at about 4 metres apart. The posts were regularly spaced across open ground in a grid-like pattern. They sought to define and mark out the boundaries and extent of about 40 separate plots of land, together with a network of access bays. In addition, the top of the marker stakes had been painted differently to distinguish between those defining access ways and those defining the plots. At an earlier stage, the local planning authority, fearful that permitted development rights might be relied on to allow for the laying out of some means of enclosure, had made an Art 4 direction removing that possibility. The enforcement notice successfully alleged **6.50**

Definition of Development 2: Material Change of Use

that this amounted to 'other operations' not a material change of use but the case illustrates the problem.

Extensions to gardens of dwellinghouses

6.51 Under the present law the extension of a domestic garden to include adjacent land may well constitute a material change of use requiring planning permission. This situation commonly arises where land being used for agricultural purposes is incorporated with land forming part of the curtilage of a dwellinghouse. The problem for planning control with this situation is that unless challenged the landowner would benefit from permitted development rights in Parts 1 and 2 of Sch 2 to the General Permitted Development Order over a much larger curtilage, thus enabling him to erect porches, garden sheds, tennis courts, garages, and oil tanks on the 'added' land, and to fence the boundary of the larger residential curtilage without the need for an express grant of planning permission.

6.52 In November 1996, the Government expressed sympathy with the concern felt that the requirement to obtain planning permission for extensions to domestic gardens amounted to an unnecessary burden. In a consultation paper then issued, the Government invited views on a proposal to include the extension of a garden of a dwellinghouse onto adjoining land as permitted development under the General Permitted Development Order. In June 1997, however, the Government decided not to proceed with the implementation of this proposal.

Change of use within the same use Class

6.53 The third of the three uses listed in paras (a) to (f) of s 55(2) which is expressly stated *not* to involve the development of land is:

> (f) in the case of buildings or other land which are used for a purpose of any class specified in an order made by the Secretary of State under this section, the use of the buildings or other land or, subject to the provisions of the order, of any part thereof for any other purpose of the same class.

6.54 The relevant order is now the Town and Country Planning (Use Classes) Order 1987, which came into force on 1 June 1987. It replaced a previous order which had not been substantially changed since it was introduced in 1948. The 1987 Order, as subsequently amended, now specifies in a Schedule to the Order, 15 different Classes of use for the purposes of para (f), so that a change of use within the same use Class is not to be taken to involve the development of land. It should be noted that the effect of the Use Classes Order is to specify that a change of use which results in the old and the new uses falling within the same use Class is not development. It does not specify that a change of use involving a change from one use Class to some other use Class is necessarily development. Whether or not it is depends upon whether a material change of use has taken place. This was made clear in *Rann v Secretary of State for the Environment* [1980] JPL 109. The Use Classes Order is thus a liberalizing measure freeing certain activities from planning control. It does not seek to restrict activities by making them subject to planning control when they would otherwise not be so.

6.55 The concept of the Use Classes Order requires that it be applied to a single definable use of land or building and not to a composite use, unless of course any other uses are ancillary to the single dominant use.

6.56 The Order is divided into four parts, which correspond broadly with (a) shopping area uses; (b) other business and industrial uses; (c) residential uses; and (d) social and community uses of a non-residential kind. This classification makes it more likely that a change of use from one part of the order to another will be regarded as a material change of use, particularly where the different uses have sharply contrasting environmental effects. This would accord with the approach in *Scrivener v Minister of Housing and Local Government* (1966) 18 P & CR 357 in which it was held that the division of the old Use Classes Order 1963 into 'light', 'general', and 'special' industrial uses classified such uses according to the extent to which they caused nuisance or inconvenience in the neighbourhood.

6.57 It should be noted that not all uses of buildings or other land are allocated to a particular Class in the Order. Those uses not allocated to a particular Class are known as *sui generis*. Indeed, Art 3(6) of the Order specifically identifies a number of uses not included in any Class of the Order. They are the use of buildings or other land:

(a) as a theatre;
(b) as an amusement arcade or centre, or a funfair;
(c) as a launderette;
(d) for the sale of fuel for motor vehicles;
(e) for the sale or display for sale of motor vehicles;
(f) for a taxi business or business for the hire of motor vehicles;
(g) as a scrapyard, or a yard for the storage or distribution of minerals, or the breaking of motor vehicles;
(h) for any work registrable under the Alkali, etc, Works Regulation Act 1906;
(i) as a hostel;
(j) as a waste disposal installation for the incineration, chemical treatment (as defined in Annex IIA to Directive 75/442/EEC under heading D9), or landfill of waste to which Directive 91/689/EEC applies;
(k) as a retail warehouse club being a retail club where goods are sold, or displayed for sale, only to persons who are members of that club;
(l) as a night-club; or
(m) as a casino.

(Special additional provisions apply to building or other land situated in Wales.)

6.58 There are no doubt many other uses that can be regarded as *sui generis*. In *London Residuary Body v Secretary of State for the Environment* [1988] JPL 637 (CA) it was held that London's County Hall did not fall within the office use Class of the Order as its office use was incidental to the primary 'London governmental use' to which the building had been put. A significant feature of the County Hall case was that the building had a high public profile as the seat of a local government function with a considerable amount of public involvement and access. That decision was considered in a later ministerial decision [2003] JPL 920, where the question arose as to whether a building occupied by the Public Trust Office could be used for general office work without the need for planning permission. The Inspector held that it could so be used, on the ground that the use by the Public Trust Office led to no involvement of, or access for, members of the general public. Other *sui generis* uses could also include, for example, the use of buildings or other land for the storage of minerals, use as a hostess bar, or the provision of accommodation for asylum seekers.

Part A—Shopping area uses

Class A1. Shops

6.59 Under this heading, the Order lists, in paras (a) to (k), the following specified uses:

(a) for the retail sale of goods other than hot food;
(b) as a post office;
(c) for the sale of tickets or as a travel agency;
(d) for the sale of sandwiches or other cold food for consumption off the premises;
(e) for hairdressing;
(f) for the direction of funerals;
(g) for the display of goods for sale;
(h) for the hiring out of domestic or personal goods or articles;
(i) for the washing or cleaning of clothes or fabrics on the premises;
(j) for the reception of goods to be washed, cleaned, and repaired; and
(k) as an internet cafe, where the primary purpose of the premises is to provide facilities for enabling members of the public to access the internet,

where the sale, display, or services is to visiting members of the public.

6.60 Hence, for example, a butcher's shop can become a travel agent or hairdresser and remain within the same use Class.

6.61 Building societies are included in Class A2 (financial and professional services); and shops for the sale of hot food in Class A5 (food and drink) (see below).

6.62 In *Cawley v Secretary of State for the Environment* [1990] JPL 742 it was held that the scope of Class A1 is restricted to retail uses which take place in a building and not on open land. This is because the heading of the Class 'Shops' necessarily refers to buildings. So, the use of open land for retail sales is a *sui generis* use.

6.63 In one high-profile case, *R v Thurrock BC, ex p Tesco Stores Ltd* [1994] JPL 328, it was necessary to consider the scope of the phrase 'visiting members of the public'. A retailer named Costco had been granted planning permission to operate a warehouse club selling a limited selection of products within a wide range of product categories only to members of the club who had paid a subscription and were within categories of person specified by Costco. Tesco argued that the development was essentially a retail use on an industrial and commercial site which would be contrary to the authority's development plan policy which sought to promote wholesale cash and carry warehousing on the site but to exclude retail uses within Class A1 which would affect the vitality and viability of existing shopping centres. As a *sui generis* use, it was neither a warehouse use nor a retail use. In refusing Tesco's application for judicial review of the grant of planning permission, Schiemann J held that if there was a restriction on persons who were able to enter and buy then the premises were not prima facie properly described as being used for the sale of goods to visiting members of the public. Hence, the use did not fall within Class A1.

Class A2. Financial and professional services

6.64 This Class is intended to provide flexibility in the use of buildings for a sector of the economy which is rapidly expanding, particularly that part which needs to be accommodated in shop-type premises in a shopping area. It embraces use for the provision of:

(a) financial services;
(b) professional services (other than health or medical services); or
(c) any other services (including use as a betting office) which it is appropriate to provide in a shopping area,

where the services are provided principally to visiting members of the public.

6.65 This Class includes use by banks, building societies, betting shops, accountants, architects, surveyors, mortgage and insurance brokers, and law centres. Since membership of this Class depends also upon services being provided primarily to visiting members of the public, barristers' chambers do not come within it. In *Palisades Investments Ltd v Secretary of State for the Environment* [1993] 3 PLR 49 the High Court upheld an Inspector's finding that a business of selling currency came within Class A2 rather than Class A1.

6.66 In *Kalra v Secretary of State for the Environment* [1996] JPL 850, the Court of Appeal had to consider the question of whether use of land as a solicitors' office was an A2 use or a B1 (Business Use) or whether some were one and some were the other. Staughton LJ there addressed the difficulty for planning authorities in resolving the problem. He pointed out that Class A2 required the provision of services principally to visiting members of the public. It was, he said, like the difference between an 'on-licence' and an 'off-licence' for the sale of wines and spirits. The practice of some solicitors would currently not be an 'on-licence' practice, where services were provided by letter or telephone or fax or e-mail. But some solicitors did provide services principally to visiting members of the public, so it is a matter of fact whether a solicitor's office is covered by the definition and much will depend upon the level of pedestrian flow. Quite apart from considering the differences between an A2 use and a B1 use, the court found that in upholding the refusal of a local planning authority to grant planning permission for a change of use of a retail shop to a solicitors' office (within Class A2), the Inspector had not applied the correct tests. In particular, he had erred in holding that to be within Class A2(b) the use had also to be a use which was appropriate to provide in a shopping area, a requirement which applied only to uses within Class A2(c). In a subsequent redetermination of the appeal, the Secretary of State granted the planning permission the applicant had sought.

6.67 The requirement that the services must be provided primarily to visiting members of the public is always likely to cause difficulty. Access by the public to financial institutions or professional offices may not be constant and the Order does not lay down a prescribed level of access. A bank, for example, may be a building mainly for internal administration of trust accounts with little public access. It would appear not to be a use within Class A2 and any change by the bank to use for normal banking services used by the public may constitute a material change of use.

Class A3. Restaurants and cafes

6.68 Use for the sale of food and drink for consumption on the premises.

Class A4. Drinking establishments

6.69 Use as a public house, wine-bar, or other drinking establishment.

Class A5. Hot food takeaways

6.70 Use for the sale of hot food for consumption off the premises.

6.71 Problems sometimes arise with regard to restaurants which provide a 'takeaway' food service or a baker's shop which allows customers to take away hot drinks or eat sandwiches etc, on the premises. In such cases in order to categorize the particular use Class into which the establishment should fall, it is usual to consider the primary purpose of the relevant unit. In such cases, a consideration of the relevant 'turnover' for each part of the unit's sales becomes relevant.

Part B—Other business and industrial uses

Class B1. Business

6.72 This Class embraces use for any of the following purposes:

(a) as an office other than a use within Class A2 (financial and professional services);

(b) for research and development of products or processes; or
(c) for any industrial process,

being a use which can be carried out in any residential area without detriment to the amenity of that area by reason of noise, vibration, smell, fumes, smoke, soot, ash, dust, or grit.

6.73 There has been much litigation over the term 'industrial process' despite the term being defined in Art 2 of the Use Classes Order (see in particular *R (on the application of Winchester City Council) v Secretary of State for the Communities and Local Government* [2007] EWHC 2303 (Admin); [2008] 1 P & CR 15).

6.74 This Class brings together many of the uses which in the previous order were found in the office and light industry classes which now no longer exist. The Class also includes other uses broadly similar in their environmental impact, such as the use of buildings for the manufacture of computer hardware and software, computer research and development, consultancy and after-sales services, micro-engineering, biotechnology, and pharmaceutical research, development, and manufacture.

6.75 An important qualification, however, is that to come within the Class, the use has to be one which can be carried out in any residential area without detriment to the amenity of that area by reason of noise, vibration, smell, fumes, smoke, soot, ash, dust, or grit. In *Lamb Properties Ltd v Secretary of State for the Environment* [1983] JPL 303, when faced with a similar test under a previous class, McCullough J held that it is irrelevant whether the area in which the use is actually carried out is already heavily polluted or is or is not a residential area. The test would seem to be whether the use would normally be detrimental to a hypothetical residential area.

Class B2. General industrial

6.76 This Class includes any use for the carrying on of an industrial process, other than one which falls within Class B1 (the Business Class).

6.77 When the Order was made in 1987 it contained Classes B3 to B7 described as 'Special industrial groups A to E' but they have since been repealed. The uses previously within those Classes are now all contained within Class B2.

Class B8. Storage or distribution

6.78 This Class comprises buildings and other land used for storage or as a distribution centre. Retail warehouses, where the main purpose is the sale of goods direct to members of the public visiting the premises fall within the Shops Use Class (A1), even though a limited part of the building may be used for storage. This would follow from the decision of the High Court in *Monomart (Warehouses) Ltd v Secretary of State for the Environment* [1977] JPL 524 in which it was held that a warehouse is not a building in which retail selling is the principal activity carried on, so that sales are acceptable only on a scale which is incidental to the main permitted use. A feature of this Class is that uses within it may be conducted entirely on open land.

Part C—Residential uses

Class C1. Hotels

6.79 This Class includes use as a hotel, boarding house and guest house, but does not include the use of a building as a hotel, boarding, or guest house where a significant element of care is provided. Article 2 of the Order provides a definition of the word 'care'. Until April 1994, 'hostels' were included in this particular use Class. Because of the threat to the amenity of tourist areas from the use made of the freedom to change the use of premises from that of a hotel to a hostel without the need to obtain planning permission, it was decided to exclude hostels from the Class; and also to provide that a hostel was not included within *any* class of the Schedule to the Order. In short, use as a hostel became a *sui generis* use under Art 3(6) of the Order.

Class C2. Residential institutions

6.80 The uses contained in this Class are the use for the provision of residential accommodation and care to people in need of care (other than a use within Class C3 (dwellinghouses)); the use as a hospital or nursing home; and use as a residential school, college, or training centre. The term 'nursing home' has been widely construed in *R (on the application of Tendring District Council) v Secretary of State for Communities and Local Government* [2008] EWHC 2122 (Admin); [2009] JPL 350, where it was said that the term was a wide one and there were no bright lines to be drawn between hospitals, nursing homes, and residential homes as in Class C2, so that the use of a building as a home for specialist mental health treatment could reasonably be described in ordinary language as a nursing home even though it was possible to describe it as a hospital and/or a residential care home. In *Barchester Healthcare Ltd v Secretary of State for Communities and Local Government* [2010] EWHC 2784 (Admin); [2011] JPL 544 it was accepted that the term 'residential development' in a policy in a development plan could include a Class C2 use.

Class C2A. Secure residential institutions

6.81 Use for the provision of secure residential accommodation, including use as a prison, young offenders' institution, detention centre, secure training centre, custody centre, short-term holding centre, secure hospital, secure local authority accommodation, or use as a military barracks.

Classes C3. Dwellinghouses and C4. Houses in multiple occupation

6.82 As a consequence of the Town and Country Planning Amendment (England) Order 2010 Class C3 now consists of three parts. These are the use as a single dwellinghouse (whether or not as a sole or main residence) by:

(a) a single person or by people to be regarded as forming a single household as defined by the Housing Act 2004 (basically a 'family');
(b) those living together as a single household and receiving care, and

(c) those living together as a single household who do not fall within the C4 definition of a house in multiple occupation.

In the case of Class C3(a) there is no restriction on the number of residents but in the other two categories there must be no more than six people.

Class C4 is a new Class created by the amendment Order and covers small shared houses or flats occupied by between three and six unrelated individuals who share basic amenities. This use is basically where tenanted living accommodation is occupied by persons as their only or main residence, who are not related or living together as a single household but who share one or more basic amenities. This change came into force on 6 April 2010. It is therefore similar to C3(a) with the important difference that while the persons are sharing facilities, they are not living together as a single household. The limit of six persons means that where seven or more persons are sharing facilities (what may be termed a large house or flat in multiple occupation) this is not covered by C4 and is *sui generis*. **6.83**

The grouping together of the uses in Class C3 means that it is not development when a dwellinghouse occupied by a family or a single person is used as a small community care house providing support for disabled and mentally disabled people, provided that all the residents live together as a single household and that they number no more than six including resident staff. Similarly, other groups of people, up to a maximum of six, such as students, not necessarily related to each other, may live in a dwellinghouse on a communal basis, so long as they do so as a single household. Sharing a communal living-room, toilet facilities, kitchen, etc, sharing the cost of electricity, gas, and telephone by the occupiers, a common doorbell, the common purchase and consumption of food, may all be evidence indicating that persons are living together as a single household. On the other hand, the creation of C4 means that (provided it is a material change of use) a change from Class C3 to Class C4 (or vice versa) requires planning permission but, as will be seen, such changes are now made permitted development. **6.84**

The interpretation of terms in Class C3 of the Order has given rise to a certain amount of litigation. In *R (Hossack) v Kettering BC and English Churches Housing Group* [2002] EWCA Civ 886; [2003] 2 P & CR 34 the Court of Appeal had to consider, with regard to Class C3, the nature of the relationship required between residents before they could be said to be 'living together as a single household'. The court considered that the fact that the residents had been brought together because of a common need for 'accommodation, support and resettlement' was not necessarily determinative of their status. There were, according to the court, no certain indicia the presence or absence of any of which was by itself conclusive. **6.85**

In *North Devon DC v the First Secretary of State* [2003] EWHC 157 (Admin); [2004] 1 P & CR 38, the High Court had to consider whether a dwelling used for providing care for two children fell within Class C2 or Class 3(b) of the Order. **6.86**

The evidence was that two non-resident staff were on duty at all times in the dwelling and that the children were under continuous supervision by a team of six or eight adult carers who operated in 8-hour shifts. The court held that notwithstanding *R v Bromley LBC, ex p Sinclair* [1991] 3 PCR 60 which had held otherwise, Class C3(b) required at least one non-residential carer, together with of course those who were being cared for. The use here more properly fell within Class C2. It was said that the concept of living together as a household meant a proper functioning household had to exist, and in the context of this case, meant that the children and a carer had to reside in the premises. In *Paramaguru v Ealing LBC* [2018] EWHC 373 (Admin) the High Court held that children under the age of 18 fell within the definition of 'residents' for the purposes of Class C4. Moreover, Supperstone J held that save as for the exemption of self-contained flats explained in Class C4, HMO should be given the same meaning in both housing and planning legislation.

6.87 The Housing and Planning Act 1986 amended the provisions of para (f) of what is now s 55(2) to make it clear that, subject to the provisions of the Order, planning permission is not required where premises are subdivided provided that both the existing and proposed use fall within the same use Class. Article 4 of the Order, however, provides that this general rule shall not apply in the case of a building used as a dwellinghouse (Class C3). The benefit of this exclusion, therefore, is not available wherever a dwellinghouse is subdivided. This accords with the special provision found in subsection (3)(a) of s 55 of the 1990 Act.

Part D—Social and community uses of a non-residential kind

Class D1. Non-residential institutions

6.88 The common element in the uses included in this Class is that the buildings are visited by members of the public on a non-residential basis. It includes use as a crèche, school, church, museum, public library reading room, and as a law court.

Class D2. Assembly and leisure

6.89 Uses in this Class include places of mass assembly, such as cinemas and concert halls (but not theatres and casinos which are *sui generis*), bingo and dance halls, and all indoor and outdoor sports and recreations, not involving motorized vehicles or firearms.

6.90 The Court of Appeal has held that the use of land as a concert hall (Class D2(b)) must necessarily be restricted to buildings with the degree of enclosure required to function as such; hence, the use of land at Twickenham rugby stadium could not be held to be within that use category (*Rugby Football Union v Secretary of State for the Environment, Transport, Local Government, and the Regions* [2002] EWCA Civ 169; [2003] JPL 96). Furthermore, it was held that the holding of concerts did not fall within Class D2(e), use as an 'area for ... outdoor sports or recreation'. The Class made a distinction between watching and playing. Concert performances were neither sport nor recreation; recreation required some physical effort from those involved.

Ousting the ambit of the Use Classes Order

In *City of London Corporation v Secretary of State for the Environment* (1971) 23 P & CR 169, it was accepted that a local planning authority and the Secretary of State could grant planning permission subject to a condition that restricted the rights which would otherwise be available under the Use Classes Order. The court upheld as valid the grant of planning permission to use premises as an employment agency, but subject to a condition that the premises should be used 'as an employment agency and for no other purpose'. In *Dunnett Investments Ltd v Secretary of State for Communities and Local Government* [2017] EWCA Civ 192; [2017] JPL 848 the Court of Appeal reviewed what a planning authority needed to say in a condition to remove the benefit of the Use Classes Order. Hickenbottom LJ (giving judgment of the Court) held that a condition which provided that the property could be used for 'no other purpose whatsoever, without express planning consent from the Local Planning Authority first being obtained' was sufficiently clear to exclude the operation of the Use Classes Order. The High Court's approach in *Dunnett* (upheld by the Court of Appeal) has not however been without criticism, see: B Garbett, 'Implied Conditions in Planning: Are we Losing the Way?' [2017] 1 JPL 2 in which the author suggests guidance should be provided to replace that removed with the revocation of Circular 11/95 in 2014. **6.91**

C. USES INCLUDED WITHIN DEVELOPMENT

Subsection (3) of s 55 of the 1990 Act specifies two uses (in paras (a) and (b)), which, for the avoidance of doubt, are declared to involve a material change of use: namely, use of a single dwellinghouse as two or more separate dwellinghouses and the deposit of refuse and waste material. **6.92**

Use of a single dwellinghouse as two or more separate dwellinghouses

By s 55(3)(a) of the 1990 Act: **6.93**

> ... the use as two or more separate dwellinghouses of any building previously used as a single dwellinghouse involves a material change in the use of the building and of each part of it which is so used.

This provision is intended to bring under planning control the use of houses for multiple occupation. The utility of the provision, however, has been much restricted by the decision of the Divisional Court of the Queen's Bench Division in *Ealing LBC v Ryan* [1965] 2 QB 486. Multiple occupation, it seems, is in itself **6.94** not enough to fall within this provision. Here, the court had to consider the application of the provision to a dwellinghouse part of which had been let out to an old lady and to another family. An enforcement notice had been served sometime earlier requiring the respondent to discontinue the use of the house as two or more separate dwellings. On the failure to comply with the notice, the respondent had been prosecuted by the local planning authority for non-compliance with it, but acquitted by the justices. On an appeal by the authority by way of case stated, the court, in upholding the decision of the justices that there had been no breach of planning control, considered that the important phrase in the provision was the term 'separate dwellinghouses'. According to Ashworth J:

> ... a house may well be occupied by two or more persons, who are to all intents and purposes living separately, without that house being thereby used as separate dwellings.

In other words, people may live separately under one roof without occupying separate dwellings. His lordship then went on to say that in considering whether these were separate dwellings:

> The existence or absence of any form of physical reconstruction is a relevant factor; another is the extent to which the alleged separate dwellings can be regarded as separate in the sense of being self-contained and independent of other parts of the same property.

6.95 It should be remembered here that work for the maintenance, improvement, or other alteration of a building which affects only the interior of the building, or which does not materially affect its external appearance, is itself not development by virtue of s 55(2) of the 1990 Act.

6.96 As a result of this case, local planning authorities have sought to control multiple occupation through other means, and in particular by alleging that there has been material change of use under s 55(1) of the 1990 Act.

6.97 Section 55(3)(a) of the 1990 Act deals with the use of a single dwellinghouse as two or more separate dwellinghouses. No similar provision applies to the use of two or more separate dwellinghouses as a single dwellinghouse. Whether or not this change of use is a material change of use has not been entirely free from doubt. In *Richmond LBC v Secretary of State for the Environment, Transport, and the Regions and Richmond Churches Housing Trust* [2001] JPL 84, the High Court held that if a change of use gave rise to a planning consideration, for example, the effects on the residential character of the area, a strain on the welfare services, or a reduction in the stock of private accommodation available for renting, they were all relevant factors to be taken into account in considering whether or not the change amounted to a material change of use. The position is that whereas the conversion of a single dwellinghouse is by express statutory provision a material change of use, the reverse situation is a question of fact and degree for the decision-maker. And if a particular use fulfils a legitimate or recognized planning purpose, it is relevant to the decision to be made. That approach was followed by Holgate J in *R (Royal Borough of Kensington & Chelsea) v Secretary of State for Communities and Local Government* [2016] EWHC 1785 (Admin) at [7], who summarized the legal principles as follows:

(1) A planning purpose is one which relates to the character of the use of land;
(2) Whether there would be a material change in the use of land or buildings falling within the definition of 'development' in section 55 of TCPA 1990 depends upon whether there would be a change in the character of the use of land;
(3) The extent to which an existing use fulfils a proper planning purpose is relevant in deciding whether a change from that use would amount to a material change of use. Thus, the need for a land use such as housing or a type of housing in a particular area is a planning purpose which relates to the character of the use of land;
(4) Whether the loss of an existing use would have a significant planning consequence(s), even where there would be no amenity or environmental impact, is relevant to an assessment of whether a change from that use would represent a material change of use;
(5) The issues in (2) and (4) above are issues of fact and degree for the decision maker and are only subject to challenge on public law grounds;
(6) Whether or not a planning policy addresses a planning consequence of the loss of an existing use is relevant to, but not determinative of, an issue under (4) above.

Deposit of refuse and waste material

By s 55(3)(b) of the 1990 Act: **6.98**

... the deposit of refuse or waste materials on land involves a material change in its use, notwithstanding that the land is comprised in a site already used for that purpose, if
(i)   the superficial area of the deposit is extended; or
(ii) the height of the deposit is extended and exceeds the level of the land adjoining the site.

It seems reasonably clear that under the first part of this provision, the deposit of refuse or waste materials on land constitutes development. But the paragraph may also be important, not for what it says, but for what it does not say. The implication of the second part of the provision is that if a hole in the ground is already being lawfully used for the deposit of refuse or waste, any further deposit of waste or refuse in that same hole does not involve development of the land unless the limitations mentioned above are exceeded. **6.99**

D. ADVERTISING

Subsection (5) of s 55 of the 1990 Act contains a special provision with regard to the display of certain advertisements: **6.100**

Without prejudice to any regulations made under the provisions of this Act relating to the control of advertisements, the use for the display of advertisements of any external part of a building which is not normally used for that purpose shall be treated for the purposes of this section as involving a material change in the use of that part of the building.

6.101 With reference to this provision, s 222 of the 1990 Act provides that where the display of advertisements in accordance with the regulations relating to the control of advertisements involves the development of land, planning permission for that development shall be deemed to be granted, so that no application for planning permission is necessary. Note however, that if the erection of an advertisement affects the character of a listed building to which it is attached, listed building consent will be required.

6.102 Under the regulations for the display of advertisements, the person responsible can be prosecuted if he displays an advertisement without 'consent'. The purpose of s 55(5), therefore, seems to be to give a local planning authority alternative methods of proceeding in cases where an advertisement is displayed on an external part of a building not normally used for that purpose, without advertising consent for its display having been granted. In such a case, the authority may proceed either by way of an enforcement notice for breach of planning control, or by prosecution for breach of the advertising regulations.

6.103 The use of an enforcement notice to control the unlawful display of advertisements as opposed to prosecution may have advantages. Enforcement action can be quick and inexpensive if there are multi-advertisements. In such a case, prosecution of each separate advertiser may take much longer and be more costly. In addition, under the provisions relating to advertisements, there is no power whereby the local planning authority can physically remove them. It is of course, possible, though probably unnecessary, for the authority to pursue both proceedings.

E. INTENSIFICATION

6.104 The question whether the intensification of a use constitutes a material change of use has until quite recently given rise to much uncertainty, misunderstanding, and ambivalence. In one of the early cases, *Guildford RDC v Penny* [1959] 2 QB 112, the Court of Appeal refused to interfere with the finding of justices that an increase in the number of caravans in a field from 8 to 27 was not development. In this case the court was prepared to concede that intensification could be relevant to the question of whether there had been a material change of use, but thought that whether or not it was relevant depended upon the particular circumstances of the particular case. The court gave as an example the Oval cricket ground being used to provide a greater number of cricket pitches with contemporaneous playing on each pitch, or an increase of housing estate density. Later, in *Glamorgan CC v Carter* [1963] 1 WLR 1 (Div Court), the court had to consider whether planning permission was needed for a caravan use commenced before 1 July 1948. The question of intensification was raised before the court and in the course of his judgment Salmon J said:

> Although I do not express any concluded view on the point, I very much doubt whether intensification of use—... confining what I say to this caravan site—could be a material change of user. Once it is established that the whole site is used as a caravan site, it does not seem to me that the use is materially changed by bringing a larger number of caravans upon the site.

The early cases in this area continued to be dominated by caravans. In *James v Secretary of State for Wales* [1966] 1 WLR 135, the Court of Appeal recognized that an intensification of an existing use could be a material change of use. In referring to this aspect, Lord Denning MR said: 'I think that a considerable increase in the number of caravans would be a material change of use.' Russell LJ said: 'I would agree that ... it is possible in law for the Minister to consider that the use of land for stationing ... three other caravans is a material change of use. One swallow does not make a summer.' The latter phrase was a colourful reference to the fact that a grant of planning permission to station one caravan on land did not entitle the owner to add any more. **6.105**

Yet another caravan case was in issue in *Esdell Caravan Parks Ltd v Hemel Hempstead RDC* [1966] 1 QB 895 (CA). In dealing with the question of intensification, Lord Denning MR said: **6.106**

> ... I doubt very much whether the occupier could increase from 24 to 78 without permission. An increase in intensity of that order may well amount to a material change of use—see the recent case of *James v Secretary of State for Wales*.

He then went on to assume that a material change of use had not taken place.

Perhaps the first important non-caravan case was *Birmingham Corporation v Minister of Housing and Local Government* [1964] 1 QB 178. There the local planning authority had served enforcement notices alleging the making of a material change in the use of two houses, from use as single dwellinghouses to use as houses let in lodgings, and directing that the latter use should cease. At the inquiry into the appeal the Inspector had the assistance of a legal assessor, who advised him that, because of shared facilities in one of the houses, it could not be said that there were within it separate dwellinghouses; and that as regards the other house, while it was used intensively, in the matter of residential use, intensification of use did not amount per se to a material change of use. Acting on this legal advice the Inspector concluded that what was alleged in the enforcement notices did not constitute development. The Minister accepted the Inspector's recommendation and quashed the enforcement notices, whereupon the local planning authority appealed to the High Court against the decision of the Minister. Allowing the appeal, Lord Parker CJ said that in his judgment the Minister had erred in law in saying that because the houses remained residential, in the sense of a dwellinghouse in which people lived, there could not be a **6.107** material change of use. In his opinion, the case should go back to the Minister with the opinion of the court and it would then be for him to find whether what had taken place in each of the houses amounted to a material change in their use, despite the fact that they both remained dwellinghouses. The Minister would take into consideration the use to which they were put; that private dwellinghouses were being used for multiple paying occupation, or that houses which had been used for private families were now being used for gain by the letting out of rooms.

6.108 It will be seen, therefore, that a house may have a residential use both before and after the making of a material change of use. In considering how this can be so, it may be possible to divide up a single genus of residential use into various species of residential use, so that even though a general residential user remains, the change from a private dwellinghouse to multiple paying occupation may nevertheless constitute development. One should note that although the Inspector in his recommendation, and the Minister in his decision, both used the phrase 'intensification', the term is not used in Lord Parker's judgment. The decision did not justify, therefore, the proposition that intensification may constitute development. What happened here was that there was a change (which could be considered to be material) in the *character* of the residential use. This approach was borne out in the later case of *Clarke v Minister of Housing and Local Government* (1966) 18 P & CR 82. On 1 July 1948, the lodge of a large private house had been occupied by a gardener employed in connection with the commercial exploitation of the garden attached to the house. In September 1948, the lodge was sold and used as a private residence. In 1953, the house was converted into a hotel, and in 1963 the lodge was bought and used for the purpose of accommodating waiters employed by the hotel. The district council, acting as agents for the local planning authority, thereupon served an enforcement notice on the occupier alleging that there had been a material change in the use of the lodge to a use for the purpose of providing living accommodation for the hotel staff. The occupier appealed to the Minister who, in dismissing the appeal, accepted the 'conclusion' of the Inspector that a material change in the use of the lodge had taken place in 1963, from that of a use by a single family into that of multiple occupation by staff of the hotel. In dismissing an appeal to the High Court from the decision of the Minister, Lord Parker CJ said:

> I see no reason to criticise the Minister's decision ... It seems to me that he was perfectly entitled to say here that there was a single family unit occupation before; that that ceased and that the change to staff accommodation was a material change of use. It is a case, as it seems to me, that does not involve a change by intensification, but by reason of totally different character of the user. I cannot see anything in law which prevented the Minister from saying that there was a change, and that that was a material change from the planning point of view.

6.109 Perhaps the only case decided on the basis that an intensification of use per se involved a material change of use is *Peake v Secretary of State for Wales* (1971)

22 P & CR 889 (Div Court). The case involved the part-time use of a garage in a garden for the repair by the owner of his car and occasionally his friends' cars. When the owner became redundant from his employment, he started repairing cars on a full-time basis. It was held that a change in activity from part-time to full-time could not of itself amount to a material change of use, but that the Secretary of State was entitled to conclude on the facts that there had been a change in the use of the garage for repair work by reason of the intensification of use. Clearly, the court was right to hold that there had been development. But it was not the intensification of the use that amounted to development. What had taken place was a change in the character of the use, from that of premises used as a dwellinghouse with ancillary private garage, to that of premises used as a dwellinghouse and a commercial garage.

Perhaps the greatest contribution made to the understanding of this area of law was made by Donaldson LJ in *Kensington and Chelsea RBC v Secretary of State for the Environment* [1981] JPL 50 (Div Court). Here, the Borough Council had served an enforcement notice alleging a material change in the use of a garden adjacent to a restaurant for the purposes of a restaurant. On appeal, the Inspector had decided that the planning unit comprised the restaurant and the garden, so there was no breach of planning control in using the garden as ancillary to the restaurant. The Borough Council did not appeal from that part of the Inspector's decision, but it complained that the Inspector had erred by failing to consider the Council's alternative argument that there had been a material change of use by intensification of the restaurant use. In dismissing the appeal, Donaldson LJ is reported to have said: **6.110**

> Similarly, in *Peake's* case, the original use of the planning unit had been as a private garage. What had been objected to in the enforcement notice had been the use of the premises as a commercial garage. In a sense the vice of changing a private garage into a commercial garage was that one had far more cars coming and going. In that sense it might be said to be intensification, but half the trouble in this case (and perhaps in other cases) was that the word 'intensification' had a perfectly clear meaning in ordinary language. It had a wholly different meaning in the mouths of planners. In ordinary language, intensification meant more of the same thing or possibly a denser composition of the same thing. In planning language, intensification meant a change to something different. It was much too late no doubt to suggest that the word 'intensification' should be deleted from the language of planners, but it had to be used with very considerable circumspection, and it had to be clearly understood by all concerned that intensification which did not amount to a material change of use was merely intensification and not a breach of planning control.

He (Donaldson LJ) hoped that, where possible, those concerned with planning would get away from the term and try to define what was the material change of use by reference to the terminus a quo and terminus ad quem. Indeed, if the planners were incapable of formulating what was the use after 'intensification' and what was the use before 'intensification', then there had been no material change of use.

6.111 The intensification of a use, therefore, may act as a catalyst of a material change. But for that to take place, there must be a change in the character of the use. For that change to take place, one ought to be able to give a name to the use before the change, and a name to the use after the change, and they must be of an essentially different character.

6.112 The settled nature of this principle in planning law was recognized by Simon Brown J in *Blum v Secretary of State for the Environment* [1987] JPL 278, where he said:

> It is well recognised in law that the issue whether or not there had been a material change of use fell to be considered by reference to the character of the use of land. It is equally well recognised that intensification was capable of being of such a nature and degree as itself to affect the character of the land and its use and thus give rise to a material change of use. Mere intensification, if it fell short of changing the character of the use, would not constitute a material change.

6.113 An advantage of the test suggested by Donaldson LJ is that it gives certainty to a question which in many cases would be uncertain. It may, however, be too rigid a test to apply in every case. In *R (on the application of John Childs) v First Secretary of State and Test Valley BC* [2005] EWHC 2368; [2006] JPL 1326 James Goudie QC (sitting as a Deputy High Court Judge) decided that a single increase in the number of caravans from four to eight at a time on land in an area virtually devoid of any development at all, involved a change in the character of the land and amounted to development.

6.114 More recently, in *Hertfordshire CC v Secretary of State for Communities and Local Government and Metal and Waste Recycling Ltd* [2012] EWCA Civ 1473, the Court of Appeal affirmed the basic principle of the need to show a change in character and held that a change which has resulted in adverse impacts is not therefore a material change if there has not been a change in the character of the use. Finally, in *Westminster City Council v Secretary of State for Communities and Local Government* [2015] EWCA Civ 482 the Court of Appeal followed *Hertfordshire*, but left open the question of the correct baseline against which to assess the change of use at [35], ie was it the immediate previous use or was it any lawful use to which the land could be put at that time prior to the change?

F. THE PLANNING UNIT, AND PRIMARY OR DOMINANT AND ANCILLARY USES

6.115 Problems occasionally arise as to the precise geographical area to be considered in determining whether the carrying out of a new activity on land constitutes a material change of use. The smaller the area to be considered, the greater the justification for holding that, as a matter of fact and degree, the new activity involves the development of land. The problem was demonstrated in *Bendles Motors Ltd v Bristol Corporation* [1963] 1 WLR 247 (Div Court) (the case of the free-standing, gravity-fed, egg-vending machine, see para 6.02). There, counsel for the garage owners had claimed that the Minister had made a fatal error in considering only the 9 square feet upon which the egg-vending machine stood, and that in considering whether the change was material, he should have considered the premises as a whole. The evidence showed, however, that though the Minister had looked at the 9 square feet in considering whether there had been a change of use, he had in fact looked at the total area of the garage forecourt in considering whether the change was material. Hence the Minister's approach had disclosed no error of law.

6.116 An early case on the planning unit was that of *East Barnet UDC v British Transport Commission* [1962] 2 QB 484. In that case the court had to consider whether there had been a material change of use when land previously used as a coal depot was used for the handling and storage of crated motor vehicles. The land in question had been divided into seven distinct parcels, of which only six had been used as a coal depot, whilst the seventh had remained unoccupied. It was argued on behalf of the local planning authority that because the vacant parcel had been unoccupied, it was impossible to say that no material change of use had taken place. Dismissing that argument, Lord Parker CJ said:

> Whatever unit one considers in these cases is always a matter of difficulty, but looked at as a matter of common sense in the present case it seems to me that this [ie the vacant parcel] was merely an unused part of the unit in question.

6.117 Almost side by side with the development of the law relating to the planning unit has been the development of the principle that land may have a dominant or primary use, to which other uses may be subservient or ancillary. Hence, in determining the use of buildings or land, it may be that regard should be had to a larger unit of which the building or land in question is merely a part. So that if land and buildings are together used for a single dominant or primary purpose, it is that purpose which determines the character of the use of the whole unit, without regard to any ancillary uses to which individual parts of the unit may be put.

6.118 One of the earliest cases to address this problem was *Vickers-Armstrong v Central Land Board* (1957) 9 P & CR 33, where the Court of Appeal had to consider whether a claim for loss of development value under the Town and Country Planning Act 1947 could be made in respect of a building which, although situated within the company's aviation works complex, had been used for administrative purposes. It was agreed by both parties that the highest value that could be placed on the administrative building was its value for use as a general industrial building, and that, if planning permission would have been required before it could have been used for that purpose, the loss of development value would have been £15,000. If, on the other hand, planning permission would not have been required, no loss of development value would have occurred. Crucial to the resolution of this dispute, therefore, was the nature of the use to which the administrative block had been put. If the use was that of a general industrial building, planning permission would not be required to change to that use. If, however, its use was that of general offices, planning permission would be required. The Court of Appeal, upholding the decision of the Lands Tribunal, held that the appellant's works 'as a whole' had been used for general industrial purposes and that the use of the administrative block was incidental to that main purpose. Hence, the owner had suffered no loss of development value.

6.119 It seems from this decision, therefore, that once the planning unit has been established, the character of the primary use which is carried on in the unit colours the character of every part of that unit, notwithstanding that some parts of it may be devoted entirely to some incidental or ancillary use. An example may be taken of a factory complex, comprising a factory where the main manufacturing processes are carried on, a car park for employees' cars, a canteen or refectory, and a sports ground for recreational use by employees. The unit has a primary (industrial) use, to which the other uses are all ancillary. It follows that the occupier of the unit may change the location of those ancillary uses without any material change of use being involved. Any operational development, of course, will need planning permission but, subject to that, planning permission will not be needed if the occupier of that unit decides that the location of the car park and sports ground should be exchanged: he might also decide that owing to the additional demand for car-parking spaces, the sports ground should also be used for that purpose. This too would not be development, so long as the ancillary car-parking use remains a use ancillary to the dominant 'industrial' use. Should that ancillary use, however, itself become dominant (as would happen if the owner of the factory complex allowed members of the general public to use the car park), a change of use would have occurred from that of industrial use, to that of industrial use and car-parking.

6.120 It has to be said that the implications of the *Vickers-Armstrong* case were not at first generally recognized. It was, after all, a case more concerned with compensation for the loss of development rights than with the application of general principles of planning law. It was not until 1966 in *G Percy Trentham Ltd v Gloucestershire CC* [1966] 1 WLR 506 that the principle in the *Vickers-Armstrong* case was first considered to be of more general application. The facts involved a site which comprised a farmhouse, a farmyard, and farm buildings. Prior to its purchase by building and civil engineering contractors, the farm buildings had been used to house tractors and livestock associated with the farm. After purchase, the farm buildings were used by the contractors for the storage of building materials. Since planning permission to use the land for that purpose had not been granted, the local planning authority sought its discontinuance by an enforcement notice served on the building contractors. The notice alleged that a material change of use had taken place from agricultural purposes (namely, the storage of farm machinery) to the storage of plant and machinery of building contractors. On appeal against the notice and in the courts, the contractors had argued that, by virtue of the then Use Classes Order, planning permission for the change was not required. They claimed that the use of the buildings and other land for the storage of tractors and for the storage of building materials, both fell within the then Class X of the Order, which spoke of 'use as a wholesale warehouse or repository for any purpose'. Accordingly, no development had taken place. Dismissing this argument, the Court of Appeal held that a repository was a place where goods are stored as part of a storage business, so that the term did not cover the use of farm buildings to store tractors where the storage was ancillary to the use of the farm. But then, after having decided the issue in narrow terms in favour of the local planning authority, the Court of Appeal went further in holding that, looked at in isolation, even if the buildings did constitute a repository or warehouse, they could not be severed from the rest of the farmhouse buildings. The court thought that, in considering the Use Classes Order, it was necessary to look at the whole of the unit being used, the whole area on which a particular activity was carried on, including uses incidental to, or included in, the activity. The court gave, as an example, a baker's shop with a flour store and a dwellinghouse above in one unit, which could be changed into a butcher's shop with a meat store and dwellinghouse above without the need for planning permission. In this case, it was clear that the planning unit being considered comprised the farmhouse, farm buildings, and yard, and in no sense could the unit be regarded as a warehouse or repository.

6.121 Buttressed by a further decision of the Court of Appeal in *Brazil (Concrete) Ltd v Amersham RDC* (1967) 18 P & CR 396, where the court followed the principles it had enunciated earlier in *G Percy Trentham Ltd v Gloucestershire CC*, it became settled law that in order to see whether a change of use was permitted under the Use Classes Order, regard should be had to the whole area in which a particular activity is carried on and the primary purpose for which the whole area is used. The character of the user is then determined by that primary purpose and not by any ancillary uses.

6.122 The question that then remained to be answered was whether a similar principle applied in cases where the Use Classes Order was not in issue. In *Williams v Minister of Housing and Local Government* (1967) 18 P & CR 514, the Queen's Bench Divisional Court decided that it did.

6.123 Williams owned a nursery garden and made his living by selling, from a timber building which was situated in one corner, fruit, vegetables, and flowers grown in the garden. Then, in order to give his customers a wider choice of produce, he purchased from a market imported fruit such as bananas, oranges, and lemons and placed them on sale alongside the homegrown produce. The local planning authority thereupon served an enforcement notice on Williams which, as subsequently upheld by the Minister, alleged the carrying out of development by the use of the timber building as a retail shop without planning permission and prohibiting the use of the building as a shop, except for the sale of indigenous agricultural produce grown on the land.

6.124 On appeal, the Minister took the view that the building should not be looked at in isolation and that the building and garden should be taken as a whole. He then proceeded to uphold the notice on the ground that the established use of the building was restricted to the sale of agricultural produce grown on the land and was a use incidental to the use of the premises as a nursery and market garden; and that the sale of imported fruit had effected a change in the character of the use to that of a greengrocer's shop, which constituted a material change of use.

6.125 The Divisional Court refused to interfere with the Minister's decision, taking the view that he had acted correctly in looking at the premises as a whole. The court held that the primary use of the premises was agriculture, the use of the timber building for selling produce was ancillary to that use, and that the Minister was entitled to find that although the quantitative change was small, a change which involved selling fruit not grown on the premises constituted a material change of use. In the *Williams* case it was not entirely clear what percentage of total sales was accounted for by imported fruit. A figure of 10 per cent was mentioned, however; and it seems that anything less than that order of proportion will tend to be regarded as *de minimis* and insignificant from a planning point of view.

6.126 There is now a well-established principle that the right to use land for some dominant or primary purpose includes the right to use it for any purpose which is ancillary to that primary or dominant purpose. The addition of an ancillary use, therefore, cannot be a material change of use. Neither can the substitution of one ancillary use for another. But if an ancillary use becomes a primary use, a material change of use may have taken place. This is seen not only in *Williams v Minister of Housing and Local Government* but also in *Jillings v Secretary of State for the Environment* [1984] JPL 32. There, land and buildings in the Norfolk Broads had been used for boat-hire purposes, but included an ancillary use of boat manufacture. Later the manufacturing of boats increased to such an extent that it had become a primary purpose. Instead of the land being used for boat-hire purposes, it was being used for a dual purpose of boat-hire and the manufacture of boats for sale. As one use had now given way to two, the Divisional Court had no qualms about upholding the validity of an enforcement notice alleging that a material change of use had taken place.

6.127 If a use of land or buildings is not incidental or ancillary to the primary use, then if the use is material, planning permission will be required even if that use is small, see: *Main v Secretary of State for the Environment, Transport and the Regions* (1999) 77 P & CR 300. That is subject to the principle that *de minimis* uses can be dismissed, see: *Williams v Minister of Housing and Local Government* (1967) 18 P & CR 514 per Widgery J at 518. In *Harrods v Secretary of State for the Environment, Transport, and the Regions and the Royal Borough of Kensington* *and Chelsea* [2002] EWCA Civ 412; [2002] JPL 1258, the Secretary of State had refused on appeal an application for a lawful development certificate for the proposed use of the existing roof of Harrods department store for helicopter landing, solely for the use of the owner of the store in connection with his position of chairman and his work in directing the day-to-day operations of the store. The Secretary of State had regard in making his decision to the 'ordinary and reasonable practice' or to what was 'normally done' at inner city department stores. The Court of Appeal refused to interfere with the Secretary of State's decision. It held that the Secretary of State was entitled to come to the conclusion that introducing a helicopter pad on the roof of Harrods would constitute material change in the use of the store.

6.128 In developing the above principles, the courts have often had to consider the precise boundaries of the planning unit. Take, for example, a block of flats or a mega-shopping centre where a number of shops are located within the shopping centre. Is the planning unit the whole building or is each individual flat or centre a planning unit? In *Church Commissioners v Secretary of State for the Environment* (1995) 71 P & CR 73, it was held that a shop in the MetroCentre in Gateshead constituted an individual planning unit so that planning permission was required to change the use from Class A1 to A3.

6.129 Similarly, where a motorway services area includes a variety of shops providing a range of facilities for travellers such as eating areas, general shops, and an amusement arcade, each individual shop may constitute a separate planning unit, so that a change of use from any unit to a betting office would involve a change of use and, if material, require planning permission.

6.130 In many cases the question may pose something of a conundrum. On the one hand, one is looking at the planning unit in order to determine its use. On the other, one is looking at the use in order to determine the planning unit. Fortunately, some important guidelines in resolving this problem were given by Bridge J (as he then was) in *Burdle v Secretary of State for the Environment* [1972] 1 WLR 1207 (Div Court). His Lordship had been involved as counsel in many cases concerning disputes about the planning unit. As a judge, he used this opportunity to set out firm guidelines for its determination. According to his Lordship there were three criteria for determining the correct planning unit:

(a) Whenever it is possible to recognize a single main purpose of the occupier's use of his land to which secondary activities are incidental or ancillary, the whole unit of occupation should be considered.
(b) Even though the occupier carries on a variety of activities and it is not possible to say that one is incidental or ancillary to another, the entire unit of occupation should be considered.
(c) Where there are two or more physically separate and distinct uses, occupied as a single unit but for substantially different and unrelated purposes, each

area used for a different main purpose (together with its incidental and ancillary activities) ought to be considered a separate planning unit.

6.131 Bridge J recognized that deciding which of the three categories applied to the circumstances of a particular case at any given time might be difficult. On this he said:

> Like the question of material change of use, it must be a question of fact and degree. There may indeed be an almost imperceptible change from one category to another. Thus, for example, activities initially incidental to the main use of an area of land may grow in scale to a point where they convert the single use to a composite use and produce a material change of use of the whole. Again, activities once properly regarded as incidental to another use or as part of a composite use may be so intensified in scale and physically concentrated in a recognisably separate area that they produce a new planning unit the use of which is materially changed. It may be a useful working rule to assume that the unit of occupation is the appropriate planning unit, unless and until some smaller unit can be recognised as the site of activities which amount in substance to a separate use both physically and functionally.

6.132 In propounding the first criterion, Bridge J had in mind the commonest situation of all, where an occupier carries on a single dominant use on the land he occupies. With regard to the second criterion, Bridge J had in mind the situation that existed in *Wipperman v Barking LBC* (1965) 17 P & CR 225, where an occupier of land was using it for a number of unrelated and different purposes, none of which was ancillary to any other and which were not confined to any particular location on the land. Furthermore, it was not possible to identify any particular part of the land as the site of any particular primary use. In such cases, the planning unit is the entire area of occupation with the whole unit being used for a number of planning purposes.

6.133 With regard to the third criterion, Bridge J had in mind the situation where an occupier of land was using it for a number of unrelated and different purposes but it was possible to identify the particular part of the site where each purpose was carried on. In such cases it would be right to divide the unit of occupation into as many different planning units as there were different purposes carried on.

6.134 Despite the guidelines given in the *Burdle* case, problems continue to arise in particular cases. In *Fuller v Secretary of State for the Environment* [1987] 2 EGLR 189, land was being farmed by the appellant as an agricultural unit. The holding, however, comprised a widely scattered number of farms, some as much as 8 miles apart. A question arose as to whether the Secretary of State in upholding an enforcement notice, was correct in holding that the agricultural unit comprised a number of separate planning units. Dismissing an appeal against the Secretary of State's decision, Stuart-Smith J held that there was clearly material evidence upon which he could come, as a question of fact and degree, to the conclusion he did. According to his Lordship, the Secretary of State had been right to regard the physical separation of the farms as an important consideration, but not the only one. In so finding, he quoted with approval from the judgment of Glidewell J in *Duffy v Secretary of State* [1981] JPL 811 where he said:

> In my judgment when buildings lie on opposite sides of a road, at some distance from each other, separated by other properties, that geographical separation must be a major, and may be the main factor in deciding whether they form one planning unit.

An interesting issue may arise where an occupier uses his land for a variety of uses, none of which is incidental or ancillary to any other. If he then proceeds to add another use to those which are already carried on, is there a requirement that in determining whether there has been a material change in the use of the land, one has merely to consider the addition of that use without regard to its effect on existing uses; or must that effect be considered against the totality of the existing uses? In *Beach v Secretary of State for the Environment and the Regions and Runnymede BC* [2001] EWHC Admin 381; [2002] JPL 185, Ouseley J stated the correct approach: **6.135**

> In my judgment, the law is as follows: where in respect of one planning unit a use comprises A, B and C together is joined by use D, there is a change of use, which may or may not be a material change of use to uses A, B, C. But whether there is a material change of use or not involves a comparison of uses A, B and C with uses A, B, C and D. If the change does involve a material change of use, it is to a new use which comprises both the old and the new uses, whether they are separate uses within the one planning unit or mixed or composite uses within the one planning unit. If, as time goes on, another use is added so that the use being carried on is A, B, C, D, plus now E, the same issues arise. Whether a material change of use has occurred is to be judged by whether the uses A, B, C, D and E are materially different in planning terms from the use A, B, C and D. If it is, it is a new use again comprising old and new uses. Uses A, B and C are not treated as distinct uses unaffected by the additional uses unless they are carried out in a distinct planning use. That is not the issue that arises here.

A question may sometimes arise as to whether the Use Classes Order has any application to a mixed or composite use of land. In conceptual terms the Use Classes Order would appear to relate to single uses, which suggests that the Order has no application to a component part of a mixed use, unless of course the component part can be identified as being carried on within its own planning unit. **6.136**

Another question that may arise is whether a single planning unit can cover an area of land in the separate occupation of two or more people. Within the context of an enforcement notice, it was held in *Rawlings v Secretary of State for the Environment and Tandridge DC* (1990) 60 PCR 413, that the selection of the appropriate planning unit was essentially a matter of fact and degree, and that the Secretary of State had not erred in dismissing (through his Inspector) an appeal against an enforcement notice in respect of a piece of land which had been divided into small plots for occupation by caravan dwellers. **6.137**

6.138 More recently in a ministerial decision reported at [1996] JPL 429, an enforcement notice had alleged:

> a change of use of part of a beach for the sale and display of sundry beach goods including surfboards and wetsuits, and for the sale of hot dogs and ice-creams, other than in accordance with permitted rights.

6.139 Whilst recognizing that the identification of the correct planning unit was often assisted by the coincidence of ownership, occupation, and user, the Inspector found that rather than determining the planning unit by reference to the area of land occupied by the recipient of the notice, it was as a matter of fact and degree proper to regard the unit as including, 'the entire beach, including the area devoted to car parking'.

6.140 In another recent case, *Ralls v Secretary of State for the Environment* [1998] JPL 444, the Court of Appeal upheld a decision of an Inspector to treat as one planning unit a total of five parcels of land, some of which were not contiguous and whose unity of ownership was not present. The Inspector had found that the coordinated pattern of land use for the holding of a market in excess of 14 days in any calendar year overcame the physical separation of the various land parcels and their separate occupancy. In this case, the appellant had owned all five parcels prior to his disposal of some of the parcels, including one to his mother. The court emphasized that what was the proper planning unit was essentially a matter of fact and degree for the decision-maker, and that occupation and ownership were not conclusive.

6.141 With regard to the concept of dominant and ancillary uses, it should be noted that this can only apply to activities within the same planning unit. In *Westminster City Council v British Waterways Board* [1985] AC 676, Lord Bridge of Harwich said:

> The concept of a single planning unit used for one main purpose to which other uses carried on within the unit are ancillary is a familiar one in planning law. But it is a misapplication of this concept to treat the use or uses of a single planning unit as ancillary to activities carried on outside the unit altogether.

Also, in *Essex Water Co v Secretary of State for the Environment* [1989] JPL 914, Sir Graham Eyre QC said 'treating the use of a single planning unit as ancillary to activities carried on outside the unit altogether is a misapplication of the concept'.

6.142 There is a useful recent review of the authorities on 'planning unit' by Lang J in *R (on the application of KPJR Management Company Ltd) v London Borough of Richmond* [2018] EWHC 84 (Admin); [2018] JPL 838. The case concerned the unusual circumstances of a floating marina on the River Thames, to which a number of the moored boats had been used for residential occupation as houseboats. The planning authority decided that the entire marina was a single planning unit and that it had established a mixed residential and leisure use as a whole by more than 10 years' unauthorized use, notwithstanding that only a portion of the moorings had been in residential use for that time period. Upon the claimant's challenge, the Judge found that the relevant planning unit was squarely a judgment for the planning authority to decide and that they had not left out of account relevant considerations in arriving at that decision.

G. INTERRUPTION AND ABANDONMENT OF A USE

6.143 If a use of land or buildings is temporarily discontinued, the resumption of that use is not development. If, however, a use is permanently discontinued, it would appear that the revival of that use is development.

6.144 One of the earliest cases to consider the interruption or temporary discontinuance of a use was *Fyson v Buckinghamshire CC* [1958] 1 WLR 634. The facts were that from 1943 to 1949, land within the county had been used for storage purposes. From 1949 to 1956, the land was not used at all, except for a brief period of four months from the end of 1953 to March 1954. In 1956, the land was once again used for storage purposes. Subsequently, an enforcement notice was served on behalf of the local planning authority requiring the use of the land for storage purposes to be discontinued, on the ground that in 1956 a material change had been made in the use of the land without planning permission. The authority claimed that the previous storage use was discontinued in 1949, and that when the land was once again used for storage in 1956 a new use had been instituted.

6.145 On appeal to the magistrates' court, the justices found as a question of fact that no material change in the use of the land had taken place since 1948, so that no planning permission was required to carry on the storage use in 1956. On an appeal from the decision of the justices, the Divisional Court held that they were fully entitled to come to that decision. The court pointed out that since 1943 there had never been a use of the land by anyone except for a storage use; and that all that had happened was a rather long interruption of the storage use without any change having taken place.

6.146 Although *Fyson v Buckinghamshire CC* shows that a use of land may survive a physical interruption of that use, the courts soon began to suggest that there might be situations where a use of land could be lost through the process of abandonment. In *Clarke v Minister of Housing and Local Government* (1966) 18 P & CR 82 (Div Court) a lodge in the garden of a large house was occupied successively by a gardener engaged in the commercial exploitation of the house, as a single family dwelling having no connection with the house, and lastly as residential accommodation for waiters employed at the house, which by then had been converted into a hotel. In upholding the validity of an enforcement notice in relation to the last of these three uses the court held that a change of occupation from that of a single family unit to staff accommodation was a change to a different character of use, and that, accordingly, there had been a material change of use. The occupier, however, had also contended that one had the right in law to go back to the use of the lodge as it existed on 1 July 1948 (the appointed day under the Town and Country Planning Act 1947), namely its use by a servant engaged in the exploitation of the garden attached to the house; and he claimed that there was no difference in use between that activity and that of waiters employed in the exploitation, not of the garden, but of the hotel. The court held that it was questionable whether there could be a right to revert back to the use of land as it existed on 1 July 1948, but that even assuming the user of the lodge on that date was that of user by a servant, that use had been wholly abandoned when it began to be used as a private residence.

6.147 The notion of abandonment was again referred to in *Webber v Minister of Housing and Local Government* (1967) 19 P & CR 1. Here the appellant owned and occupied a four-acre field which since 1960 had been used for a variety of seasonal activities. Between Easter and the end of September the field was used for camping. Between September and Easter, it was used for grazing livestock, except on Saturdays when it was used as a football pitch. In addition, the field was used somewhat infrequently for local events such as flower shows. In September 1965, shortly before the campers were due to depart for the winter, the local planning authority served an enforcement notice on the appellant requiring him to remove all tents, caravans, and Dormobiles from the land within 28 days. Now before 1968, if an authority had allowed four years to pass without serving an enforcement notice, it was then too late for the authority to put a stop to the contravening use. The appellant maintained that since he had been using the land in the same way since 1960, it was no longer open to the authority to take enforcement action. The local planning authority, however, maintained that a change of use was being made twice a year, from grazing to camping and then from camping back to grazing, and that since planning permission had not been obtained for the latest change of use from grazing to camping (which had taken place only six months previously), the enforcement notice could not be challenged on the ground that it had not been served within four years. The Court of Appeal held that the purpose for which land is normally used had to be ascertained by looking at its use from year to year over a considerable period of time. Here the normal use of the field was for two purposes, namely, camping in summer and grazing in winter. So long as that continued, there could not be a material change of use. Hence the seasonal change of use from grazing to camping was not a change that required planning permission. But having thus disposed of the matters in contention, Lord Denning MR, went on to suggest that if the normal use of the land were to be abandoned for a time, the resumption of it afterwards would require planning permission.

6.148 The concept of abandonment was finally recognized by the Court of Appeal in the celebrated case of *Hartley v Minister of Housing and Local Government* [1970]

1 QB 413. The facts were that prior to 1961, land had been used for the dual purpose of a petrol filling station and for the display and sale of cars. In March of that year a Mr Fisher purchased the property and until his death a few months later continued to use the land for both purposes. After his death, his widow, Mrs Fisher, ran the business with the help of her 19-year-old son. Because he lacked experience in the business, however, Mrs Fisher did not allow her son to sell cars. Together, they continued to use the land for the business of a petrol filling station only, until finally disposing of the land to Hartley in 1965. Immediately the new purchaser, in addition to continuing the petrol filling station business, resumed the business of the display and sale of cars. Thereupon the local planning authority served an enforcement notice on Hartley, alleging a material change of use of the land without planning permission and requiring him to cease that use. On appeal to the Minister against the notice, the Minister found that by 1965 the use of the land for the purpose of car sales had been abandoned and that the present use of the site was that of a petrol filling station only. On that ground the Minister held the enforcement notice to be valid.

Hartley then appealed to the High Court, and from there to the Court of Appeal, which held that the Minister was entitled to find that the use for car selling had been abandoned and that once a use has been abandoned, it could not be resurrected without planning permission. Lord Denning MR said: **6.149**

> ... when a man ceases to use a site for a particular purpose and lets it remain unused for a considerable time, then the proper inference may be that he has abandoned the former use. Once abandoned, he cannot start to use the site again, unless he gets planning permission: and this is so, even though the new use is the same as the previous one.

According to Lord Denning, whether the cessation of a use amounted to abandonment depended on the circumstances. If land remained unused for a considerable time, in such circumstances that a reasonable man might conclude that the previous use had been abandoned, it was open to the local planning authority or the Minister to do so as well. As regards the date for determining whether or not a use had been abandoned, Lord Denning thought that the material time for doing so was when the new use was started. **6.150**

A number of points can be made with regard to this decision. First, although it was concerned with the abandonment of one of two dual uses and its subsequent resumption, the same reasoning would clearly apply to the abandonment and subsequent resumption of a single use of land. Secondly, the recognition that it is possible to abandon a use means that, where it does occur, the land could be left with no planning use at all, other than its use for some purpose such as agriculture or forestry, which does not involve its development. Thirdly, although planning permission is required to resume an abandoned use, it is not also required for the abandonment of the use. In *Hartley's* case it was unsuccessfully argued that there could be no material change of use between a 'nil' use of land (ie after **6.151**

Definition of Development 2: Material Change of Use

abandonment) and the resumption of the previous use for car sales, unless there was a similar but opposite material change of use when the use of the land for car sales ceased. That point was dealt with forcibly by Widgery LJ who said:

> No one can make a man continue with a branch of his business if he does not wish and no one is going to interpret this legislation as though it gave a local authority that power.

That statement echoed what his Lordship (then Widgery J) had said in the Divisional Court in *Wipperman v Barking LBC* (1965) 17 P & CR 225. In that case the planning history of the land involved the following three stages:

Stage 1	1958 to 1961	Land used for: (a) Storage of farming materials. (b) Storage of building materials. (c) Residential caravan by person engaged in building and fencing work.
Stage 2	1961 to 1962	Land used for: (a) Storage of farming materials. (b) Storage of building materials. (c) Car-breaking and the storage of car parts.
Stage 1	1962 to date of enforcement notice	Wipperman and Buckingham, trading as Five Star Conservatories, go into occupation, give up the car-breaking use, and use the whole of the land for storage of materials used in the manufacture of conservatories and house extensions.

It will be seen that the caravan use in stage 1 had given way to a car-breaking use in stage 2; and that the car-breaking use in stage 2 had given way to a storage use in stage 3.

6.152 The court had to consider the validity of an enforcement notice which had alleged that a material change of use had taken place between stages 2 and 3. The court said that if it had merely been a case of suspension of the car-breaking use with the storage use being maintained at its former intensity, no material change of use would have occurred. The reason for this is that merely to cease one of a number of component activities in a composite use of land did not in itself amount to a material change of use. This was the very same principle which was accepted again by the Court of Appeal in *Hartley v Minister of Housing and Local Government* [1970] 1 QB 413 when it expressed the view that the abandonment of a use would not amount to a material change of use.

6.153 With regard to the actual validity of the enforcement notice in *Wipperman v Barking LBC* (1966) 17 P & CR 225, the court held that although the car-breaking use had been suspended, the storage use had not been maintained at its former intensity. Instead, it had taken over the whole of the unit including that part previously used for car-breaking. So, as a matter of law, it seems that where there is a site with a number of component uses, there can be a material change of use if one component is allowed to absorb the entire site to the exclusion of the other use or uses. It should, of course, be pointed out that in such cases the material change of use would result not from the intensification of that one component use but from the fact that the absorption of the entire site by that component use to the exclusion of the others has resulted in a change in the character of the use.

6.154 One further matter to be considered in relation to abandonment is the circumstances when abandonment will be held to have taken place. According to Lord Denning MR in the *Hartley* case, it is open to the local planning authority or the Minister to conclude that a use has been abandoned if land has remained unused for a considerable time in such circumstances that a reasonable man might conclude that it had been abandoned. It is submitted that in considering whether a use has been abandoned one has also to consider the intention of the party concerned, and in subsequent decisions in this area this is a factor to which much weight has been given.

6.155 In *Hall v Lichfield DC*, noted at [1979] JPL 426, a woman had lived in a cottage since at least 1935. In 1961 she had entered hospital as a voluntary patient, where she remained until her death in 1974, apart from occasional visits to the cottage, the last of them in 1968. The deceased's sister and niece had been correctly advised by the council that if they removed the furniture from the cottage it would not attract rates. This they had duly done, but without informing the deceased for fear of upsetting her. Their intention at all times had been to return the furniture to the cottage if the deceased were ever to recover sufficiently to be able to live there again on her own, which had been her hope. Shortly after the deceased's death, the property was put on the market (though not sold) as a result of which doubts had been raised by the council about the lawful use of the property.

6.156 As might be envisaged, the cottage was in a dilapidated condition. It was also situated in a green belt. The view of the authority was that planning permission was necessary before residential use of the property could be resumed, and it appeared that this was not likely to be granted. The authority also took the view that because of the state of the cottage, even if residential use had not been abandoned, any works of renovation would constitute a rebuilding operation and require planning permission.

6.157 Counsel advising the personal representatives took the view that in order to prevent any confusion arising between questions relating to residential use of the property and those relating to structural alterations, it was appropriate to seek a declaration that the residential use of the cottage had not been abandoned and that there was an existing right to occupy it for that purpose. That declaration was duly granted.

6.158 That approach has also been followed in decisions made by the Secretary of State on appeal. In one such case the local planning authority had made a determination that the resumption of residential use would constitute a material change of use [1980] JPL 759. The owner of the property in question had vacated the property and, whilst empty, the property had been vandalized. The owner, however, had taken the trouble to board up the premises and had reported the vandalism to the police. Allowing the appeal against the authority's determination, the Minister held that the owner had not disclosed a firm intention to abandon the residential use of the property and he in turn granted a declaration that the resumption of residential use would not constitute development.

6.159 It seems, however, that the intention of the party concerned is just one of the factors, albeit a very important factor, which has to be taken into account. In *Trustees of the Castelly-Mynach Estate v Secretary of State for Wales* [1985] JPL 40, the Queen's Bench Divisional Court, in considering the validity of a determination that the resumption for residential use of a disused derelict house required planning permission, gave judicial acknowledgment to the submission of counsel that, in deciding whether a use had been abandoned, it was necessary to consider four factors: (a) the physical condition of the building; (b) the period of non-use; (c) whether there had been any other intervening use; and (d) evidence regarding the owner's intention.

6.160 In *Hughes v Secretary of State for the Environment, Transport, and the Regions* [1999] JPL 83, the Court of Appeal emphasized that in considering the issue of abandonment, it was necessary to have regard to all the relevant circumstances and that it would be wrong to elevate the intentions of an owner to a paramount status, or conversely to subordinate other relevant considerations to that of intention. Although intention was relevant, the court said that it could not be decisive, because at the end of the day the test must be the view to be taken by a reasonable man with knowledge of all the relevant circumstances.

6.161 The doctrine of abandonment continues to be affirmed by the courts. Other judicial decisions include *White v Secretary of State for the Environment* (1989) 58 P & CR 281 (CA) and *Northavon DC v Secretary of State for the Environment* [1990] JPL 579.

6.162 In a rather similar way the implementation of a grant of planning permission or the beginning of new planning history can mean that established uses have been extinguished and cannot be continued. This is discussed in Chapter 15 under the heading 'Effect of a Planning Permission'.

H. SUBDIVISION OF A PLANNING UNIT

6.163 Except in those rare cases where a personal planning permission has been granted, planning law is concerned with the use of land, not generally with the identity of the person who occupies or owns it. It follows that if a large parcel of land used for a particular purpose is divided into smaller parcels, and each parcel is conveyed to a number of different purchasers, those purchasers should be able to continue to use the land for that same purpose without the need for planning permission.

6.164 This principle, however, may not apply where land which is used for both a dominant and ancillary purpose is divided into two and each part sold, so that one purchaser acquires that part of the land used for the primary purpose and the other purchaser acquires that part used for the ancillary purpose.

6.165 In principle, it would seem that the purchaser of the part of the land previously used for the ancillary purpose cannot continue to use it for that purpose without first obtaining planning permission since he has converted what was previously an ancillary use into a dominant use. The position may not be entirely clear, however, as regards the position of the purchaser of the part of the land previously used for the dominant purpose. What was previously a dominant purpose continues to be a dominant purpose despite the change of ownership, which should suggest that no development has occurred.

6.166 It is, of course, a problem not confined to the subdivision of a planning unit consequent upon the sale of part of the unit. The problem can also arise (though less commonly so) where the owner divides up a unit without selling any part. Unfortunately, the law on this issue is less clear.

6.167 These issues have been considered by the courts on two known occasions. In *Wakelin v Secretary of State for the Environment* [1978] JPL 769, a large house set in its own grounds had been used as a single family unit. Planning permission was then granted for the erection in the grounds of garages and additional residential accommodation subject to a condition that it should only be occupied by a close relative or member of the household staff of the main house. The additional buildings were later converted into self-contained flats, and the question then arose whether the change to separate occupancy amounted to a material change of use. The Court of Appeal thought it did. According to Lord Denning MR, the division of a large planning unit into two separate units was beyond question a material change of use. Browne LJ also considered that on the facts there had been a material change of use, but he did not think it necessary to decide whether the creation of a new planning unit out of an existing unit would *always* amount to a material change of use.

6.168 In *Winton v Secretary of State for the Environment* [1984] JPL 188, a building formerly used to make breeze-blocks had been divided into two. One part was then used for metal working; the other part for car conversions. The local planning authority then served separate enforcement notices in relation to each part alleging a material change of use without permission. The appellants appealed to the Secretary of State against the notices and he, after an inquiry, concluded that when the new uses were instituted, there was, as a matter of fact and degree, in each case a material change of use from the permitted use. Nevertheless, he quashed the notices on the ground that planning permission should be granted for a limited period. The appellants then appealed to the High Court to quash the Secretary of State's decision. Dismissing the appeal, the High Court held that although the mere subdivision of a single planning unit into two separate planning units did not of itself amount to development, whether the subdivision amounted to a material change of use was a matter of fact and degree, which in the normal circumstances of an appeal to him was a matter exclusively for the Secretary of State to decide.

6.169 It should be noted that the appellants also argued that since the uses both before and after the subdivision fell within the same use Class, by virtue of the then s 22(2)(f) of the 1971 Act and Art 3(1) of the Order, no development had taken place. This argument the High Court rejected on the grounds that to hold otherwise could mean that a large factory complex with a multiplicity of separate uses but within the same Class could be subdivided into smaller units without development being involved, and that this would be inconsistent with the approach to development control indicated in the *Wakelin* case. It should be noted, however, that Parliament has now intervened in relation to uses falling within the same use Class of the Use Classes Order. Except in the case of dwellinghouses, planning permission is not required where premises are subdivided, so long as both the old and the new use fall within the same use Class. The provision does not, of course, affect the law as it relates to the subdivision of a planning unit outside the Use Classes Order.

7

THE NEED FOR PLANNING PERMISSION 1: GENERAL PERMITTED DEVELOPMENT ORDER; LOCAL DEVELOPMENT ORDERS

A. TOWN AND COUNTRY PLANNING (GENERAL PERMITTED DEVELOPMENT) ORDER	7.05	D. LOCAL DEVELOPMENT ORDERS	7.58
		E. NEIGHBOURHOOD DEVELOPMENT ORDERS	7.63
B. GENERAL CONSIDERATIONS	7.06	F. PERMISSION IN PRINCIPLE	7.69
C. FURTHER CONSIDERATION OF SOME OF THE PARTS	7.24		

7.01 Section 57(1) of the 1990 Act provides that, subject to the provisions of the section, planning permission is required for the carrying out of any development of land. Planning permission may be granted in three main ways, namely by development order without the need for any application to be made, by a deemed grant of planning permission, or as the result of an express application for planning permission made to the local planning authority.

7.02 A development order is made by the Secretary of State. It may be a special development order or a general development order. Section 59(3) provides that a development order may be either:

(a) as a general order applicable, except so far as the order otherwise provides, to all land; or

(b) as a special order applicable only to such land or descriptions of land as may be specified in the order.

Section 60(1) of the 1990 Act provides that planning permission granted by a development order may be granted either unconditionally or subject to such conditions or limitations as may be specified in the order. Section 4(1) of the Growth and Infrastructure Act 2013 amends s 60 so that where the order grants permitted development for a change of use, the order may specify matters which require the approval of the LPA or the Secretary of State. This gives flexibility so that the operation of the order can vary according to the circumstances.

7.03 Examples of the use made by the Secretary of State to grant planning permission by special development order have been given in Chapter 2.

7.04 Section 116 of the Localism Act 2011 ('the 2011 Act') has introduced a new kind of development order—the neighbourhood development order. This breaks new ground by devolving the power to initiate the making of development orders to parish councils and local community groups called a 'neighbourhood forum'.

A. TOWN AND COUNTRY PLANNING (GENERAL PERMITTED DEVELOPMENT) ORDER

7.05 The current Order (SI 2015/596) came into effect on 15 April 2015. It replaced and re-enacted with amendments part of the General Development Order 1995 which was then repealed. The 2015 Order specifies in Sch 2, in 19 separate Parts, various classes of development which may be undertaken upon land without the permission of the local planning authority or the Secretary of State. Each Part may itself include a number of Classes of development. Development falling within the Classes is known as 'permitted development'. In considering the application of development control procedures it may be necessary to refer to the Order. The Parts are as follows:

Part
1. Development within the curtilage of a dwellinghouse.
2. Minor operations.
3. Changes of use.
4. Temporary buildings and uses.
5. Caravan sites and recreational camp sites.
6. Agricultural and forestry
7. Non-domestic extensions, alternations etc.
8. Transport related development.
9. Development relating to roads.
10. Repairs to services.
11. Heritage and demolition.
12. Development by local authorities.
13. Water and sewage.
14. Renewable energy.
15. Power related development.
16. Communications.
17. Mining and minerals exploration.
18. Miscellaneous development.
19. Development by the Crown or for national security purposes.

B. GENERAL CONSIDERATIONS

Before considering in more detail the application of the GPDO, a number of important general points should be borne in mind, any of which may have the effect of rendering the Order inapplicable in particular circumstances. **7.06**

Under Art 4 of the Order, if either the Secretary of State or the local planning authority is satisfied that it is expedient that development described in any Part, Class, or paragraph in Sch 2, other than Class K, KA or M of Part 17 should not be carried out unless permission is granted for it on an application, he or they may give a direction that the planning permission granted by the Order shall not apply. A direction so made is referred to as an 'Article 4 direction'. Where such a direction has been made, its effect is to require an application for planning permission to be made for the development specified in the direction, which, if the development were to take place elsewhere, would not be required. Article 4 directions are commonly found in conservation areas, nearly half of the total number of directions currently in force covering residential properties in such areas. In such areas, if no directions existed, the extension of a dwellinghouse (within the prescribed limits) would be permitted development under Part 1 of Sch 2. The owner could, therefore, build an extension which was out of character with the dwellinghouse and any surrounding buildings. If an Article 4 direction has been made in relation to that development, the owner must apply for express planning permission to build the extension, and the local planning authority would be able to refuse permission or otherwise secure (eg through conditions) that the proposed extension is in harmony with the surrounding buildings. **7.07**

Article 4 directions are also commonly used in rural areas to prevent damage to vulnerable areas from the indiscriminate siting of buildings; from the subdivision of agricultural land; or from temporary uses such as car boot sales and motor sports. **7.08**

In procedural terms there are two main types of Article 4 directions which are: **7.09**

— non-immediate directions (permitted development rights are only withdrawn upon confirmation of the direction by the local planning authority following local consultation); and
— immediate directions (where permitted development rights are withdrawn with immediate effect, but must be confirmed by the local planning authority following local consultation within six months, or else the direction will lapse).

There are certain permitted development rights that cannot be withdrawn by any Article 4 direction (these are specified in Art 4(1) and (2) of the GPDO). These exemptions are to ensure permitted development rights related to national concerns, safety, or maintenance work for existing facilities cannot be withdrawn. **7.10**

Immediate directions can only be used to withdraw a small number of permitted development rights.

7.11 The role of the Secretary of State has been changed in England by the Town and Country Planning (General Permitted Development) (Amendment) (England) Order 2010 which came into force on 6 April 2010. Whereas before the Secretary of State had to confirm certain Article 4 directions, it is now for local planning authorities to confirm all Article 4 directions (except those made by the Secretary of State) in the light of local consultation (see Sch 3). The Secretary of State does however retain a power for 'cancelling or modifying' any direction made by a local planning authority, see Sch 3, para 1(13) of the GPDO.

7.12 One of the problems with the making of an Article 4 direction is that if an application for planning permission is made for development covered by the direction, the refusal of permission or a grant subject to conditions other than those previously imposed by the Order, may allow the landowner affected to claim compensation under ss 107 and 108 of the 1990 Act for abortive expenditure, or other loss or damage directly attributable to the withdrawal of the 'permitted development rights'. Although claims are fairly rare, where they are made substantial sums may be involved.

7.13 An amendment to this right to compensation has now been made by the Planning Act 2008, which provides that where planning permission granted by a development order is withdrawn by the issue of a direction, compensation would be payable only if an application for planning permission for that development formerly permitted by that order is made within 12 months of the direction taking effect (see paras 27.12 and 27.13). This condition is to ensure that a right to compensation does not exist in perpetuity just because the development refused was once permitted development.

7.14 Article 3(4) of the Order provides that nothing in the Order shall operate to permit development contrary to any condition imposed by any planning permission granted or deemed to be granted under Part III of the Act otherwise than by the Order.

7.15 Local planning authorities and the Secretary of State not infrequently impose conditions on the grant of planning permission to restrict the scope of development which would otherwise be permitted under the Order. For example, a grant of planning permission for residential development may contain the following condition:

> Pursuant to Art 3(4) of the Town and Country Planning General Permitted Development Order 2015, the provisions of Art 3(1) and Part 1 of Schedule 2 to the said Order (relating to development within the curtilage of a dwellinghouse) shall not apply to any dwellinghouse to which this permission relates and no such development within the curtilage of any such dwellinghouse shall be carried out without the permission of the local planning authority being first obtained.

The reason for these conditions is often that the local planning authority in granting permission for the development may feel that it has allowed the maximum possible development of the site and has no wish to see the landowner, having implemented the planning permission, now use his permitted development 'rights' to enlarge the size of the building. The condition is thus often imposed to restrict the amount of site coverage by buildings in relation to the size of the plot.

7.16 It should be noted, however, that for permitted development rights to be withdrawn on a grant of planning permission, clear wording is required, see: *Dunnett Investments Ltd v Secretary of State for Communities and Local Government* [2017] EWCA Civ 192; [2012] JPL 848.

7.17 Under Art 3(5) of the Order permitted development rights may only be exercised in relation to an existing use or building if the use or the construction of the building is lawful (Art 3(5)).

7.18 Development is not permitted under the Order if an application for planning permission for that development would be for a project listed in Sch 1 or Sch 2 to the Town and Country Planning (Environmental Impact Assessment) Regulations 2017 and thus be subject to environmental assessment.

7.19 In a number of cases before permitted development rights can be exercised, the developer must first apply to the local planning authority for a determination of whether the authority's 'prior approval' is required (see, for example, the controversial Part 3, Class R 'agricultural buildings to a flexible commercial use'). Prior approval cannot be given where the building works have already begun, see: *Winters v Secretary of State for Communities and Local Government* [2017] EWHC 357 (Admin); [2017] PTSR 568. Where the authority determines that prior approval is not required, or no determination is made by the authority within the time specified for doing so in the relevant Part of the Order, the developer may then proceed to exercise those permitted development rights, it does not however permit the proposed development to take place if it is outside the relevant PD tolerances themselves, see: *Keenan v Woking Borough Council* [2017] EWCA Civ 438; [2018] PTSR 697. Furthermore, in *R (on the application of Marshall) v East Dorset District Council* [2018] EWHC 226 (Admin) Lang J held at [44] that:

> a local planning authority does not have power under the prior approval provisions of the GPDO, or indeed any other provision of the GPDO, to determine whether or not the proposed development comes within the description of the relevant class in the GPDO.

> This decision concerned the application of Part 6 of the GPDO, whereas the provisions of Part 3 (Class V, para.W(3)), for example, do appear to contemplate consideration as to whether the proposed development falls within the PD tolerances and so it might be that Lang J went too far to say such a determination is precluded by *any* provision of the GPDO.

7.20 A failure to seek prior approval from the local planning authority will mean that the development will be in breach of planning control and permitted development rights will not apply. In cases where the authority refuses approval for the proposed development there is a right of appeal to the Secretary of State. It was held by the Court of Appeal in *Murrell v Secretary of State for Communities and Local Government* [2010] EWCA Civ 1367; [2012] 1 P & CR 6 that the time limits will be applied strictly. It was also held that an application for a determination as to whether prior approval is necessary, does not need to be in any particular form and does not need to be accompanied by anything more than a written description of the proposed development and of the materials to be used and a plan indicating the site, together with the required fee. So, a request by the local planning authority for an amended application did not stop time from running even though the applicant did submit another application. As a result, once 28 days had elapsed from the date that the authority received the application, there was no need for prior approval and the developer could take advantage of the permitted development rights. It is crucial that the notification is received before the time limit has expired. In *Walsall MBC v Secretary of State for Communities and Local Government* [2012] EWHC 1756 it was held that absence of proof that the notification was received in time would not be determinative. There was a presumption that the letter had been correctly posted on the date by which it would be delivered in time by the ordinary course of post. However, this presumption can be rebutted if the contrary is proved.

7.21 Some of the development which is permitted under the Order (eg Part 1, Class A—the enlargement, improvement, or other alteration of a dwellinghouse) has a size restriction or a tolerance related to the size of the original building. 'Original' is defined in the Order as meaning, in relation to a building existing on 1 July 1948, as existing on that date; and in relation to a building built on or after 1 July 1948, as so built. The effect of this is that if, say, a dwellinghouse has been erected under a grant of planning permission in 1970, the size of the permitted development is calculated in relation to the size of the curtilage around the dwellinghouse as then built. An owner cannot, therefore, claim the benefit of 'permitted development rights' to extend the dwellinghouse, and then once extended claim further permitted development rights calculated on the basis of the dwellinghouse as extended. He may, however, extend a dwellinghouse on more than one occasion, so long as in total the size of all the extensions taken together does not exceed the tolerances permitted by the Order.

7.22 The extent of the permitted development which is allowed by the Order has been modified in a number of special cases. This is particularly so in relation to what is called Art 2(3) land. This is defined in the Order as land within a National Park, an Area of Outstanding Natural Beauty, a conservation area, an area specified by the Secretary of State for the purposes of s 41(3) of the Wildlife and Countryside Act 1981, the Broads, and a World Heritage Site. In various parts to the Order, the development permitted where the land is Art 2(3) land is more restricted than in other cases. This is because of the need to exercise greater control over minor development in highly sensitive areas.

7.23 It should be remembered that where the development carried out exceeds that permitted by the Order, the breach of planning control is not just the excess beyond what is permitted by the Order, but the whole of the development carried out. Unless the excess is considered by the local planning authority to be *de minimis*, the whole of the development may become subject to enforcement action. In *Garland v Ministry of Housing and Local Government* [1968] 20 P & CR 93, the Court of Appeal held that once the cubic capacity permitted under the Order had been exceeded, demolition of the entire structure could be required and not simply that part of the extension which fell outside the permitted capacity. The court considered that specified limits to the size of development permitted formed part of the definition of permitted development.

C. FURTHER CONSIDERATION OF SOME OF THE PARTS

7.24 This section considers only selected Classes of permitted development. Many of the Classes are subject to detailed limits on such matters as size, height, proximity to curtilage boundaries, and in some cases external appearance. If those limits are not met the development will not be permitted by the Order. Reference to the Order is therefore essential when reading the text.

Part 1—Development within the curtilage of a dwellinghouse

7.25 Many of the Classes of permitted development set out in Part 1 of Sch 2 (particularly Classes A and B) are so detailed that many problems of interpretation and application have arisen. For example, it is not always a simple matter to decide whether or not a building is actually a dwellinghouse. In *Gravesham BC v Secretary of State for the Environment* (1982) 47 P & CR 142 it was said, 'whether a building was or was not a "dwelling-house" … was a question of fact; that a distinctive characteristic of a dwellinghouse was its ability to afford to those who used it the facilities required for day-to-day private domestic existence …'. It should be noted too that the definition of a dwellinghouse in the Order does not include a building containing one or more flats, or a flat contained within such a building. So the definition of a dwellinghouse for the purposes of GPDO is very technical and in *R (on the application of Stavrinidies) v Secretary of State for Communities and Local Government* [2010] EWHC 3479 (Admin); [2011] JPL 922 it was held that in deciding whether premises are a dwellinghouse the decision-maker should make clear whether the term flat is being used in the way as defined in the GPDO or in some other way. The term 'curtilage' was considered by the Court of Appeal in *Attorney General ex rel Sutcliffe v Calderdale Borough Council* (1982) 46 P & CR 399 per Stephenson LJ at 407:

> Three factors have to be taken into account in deciding whether a structure (or object) is within the curtilage of a listed building ... whatever may be the strict conveyancing interpretation of the ancient and somewhat obscure word 'curtilage'. They are (1) the physical 'layout' of the listed building and the structure, (2) their ownership, past and present, (3) their use or function, past and present. Where they are in common ownership and one is used in connection with the other, there is little difficulty in putting a structure near a building or even some distance from it into its curtilage.

7.26 Whilst the Court of Appeal was considering the term in the listed building context, Supperstone J applied those criteria to the GPDO in *Burford v Secretary of State for Communities and Local Government* [2017] EWHC 1493 (Admin); [2017] JPL 1300 at [38].

7.27 In 2008 the Government decided to make important changes to permitted development rights by enlarging the power of landowners to extend their homes without the need to apply for express planning permission. The change was duly implemented by an amendment made to the GPDO from 1 October 2008 and are now incorporated into the 2015 Order.

7.28 The change was mainly achieved by substituting a new Part 1 of Sch 2 to the 1995 order. The crucial change made was that where previously the right to extend was limited by the size of the enlargement relative to the size of the original dwellinghouse, the new provision gives a right to extend a dwellinghouse to 50 per cent of the total area of the curtilage of the dwellinghouse (excluding the ground area of the original building).

7.29 Part 1 is the Part most frequently used in day-to-day development control. It contains eight Classes of permitted development from Class A to Class H, as set out below:

Class A	The enlargement, improvement, or other alteration of a dwellinghouse. Some of the tolerances within Class A are time limited.
Class B	The enlargement of a dwellinghouse consisting of an addition or alteration to its roof.
Class C	Any other alteration to the roof of a dwellinghouse.
Class D	The erection or construction of a porch outside any external door of a dwelling- house.
Class E	The provision within the curtilage of a dwellinghouse of (a) any building or enclosure, swimming, or other pool required for a purpose incidental to the enjoyment of the dwellinghouse as such, or the maintenance, improvement, or other alteration of such a building or enclosure; or (b) a container used for domestic heating purposes for the storage of oil or liquid petroleum gas.
Class F	(a) the provision within the curtilage of a dwellinghouse of a hard surface for any purpose incidental to the enjoyment of the dwellinghouse as such; or (b) the replacement in whole or in part of such a surface.
Class G	The installation, alteration, or replacement of a chimney, flue, or soil and vent pipe on a dwellinghouse.
Class H	The installation, alteration, or replacement of a microwave antenna on a dwellinghouse or within the curtilage of a dwellinghouse.

7.30 Class F imposes a requirement that the provision of a hard surface within the curtilage of a dwellinghouse under permitted development rights, needs to be made of 'porous materials' or a run off provided to a permeable or porous area within the curtilage of the dwellinghouse. This requirement could help to prevent flooding.

Other matters

7.31 It will be seen that Class A permits the enlargement, improvement, or other alteration of a dwellinghouse, as long as the work does not infringe the limitations set out in A1 (paras (a) to (h)), or A2. A particular problem which sometimes arises with the application of Class A, is where an owner begins to repair or renovate a disused or dilapidated dwellinghouse in a piecemeal fashion over a prolonged period of time. The question then is whether the owner is 'improving' the dwelling and is thus within the Class, or whether he is re-erecting the dwellinghouse by stages so as to embrace its entirety and thus be outside the Class. In *Larkin v Basildon DC* [1980] JPL 407, the appellant rebuilt all the four external walls of a dwellinghouse in two distinct stages. This involved first pulling down and rebuilding two walls of the dwellinghouse and then subsequently rebuilding another two walls. The appellant contended that the works were permitted development under Class I (1) of what was then Sch 1 to the General Development Order as the 'enlargement, improvement or other alteration' of a dwellinghouse. The Divisional Court considered that whether the activities with which they were concerned amounted to improvement or rebuilding depended almost entirely on matters of fact and degree. It concluded that the Secretary of State's decision that the original building had virtually ceased to exist and the operations amounted to the construction of a new dwelling and did not therefore come within the Class was valid.

7.32 In *Hewlett v Secretary of State for the Environment* [1985] JPL 404 an enforcement notice was served by the local planning authority in respect of the works carried out to a very small building which had only three walls. This work apparently involved jacking up the roof, then undertaking certain operations to the walls in turn, and then at a later stage working on the roof itself. The appeal was based on the Town and Country Planning Act 1971, s 22(2)(a) which was the forerunner to s 55(2)(a) of the 1990 Act. It was submitted that the operations amounted to the 'maintenance, improvement or other alteration' of the building not materially affecting the external appearance. The Court of Appeal held, inter alia, that improvement works of rebuilding done to a building, albeit in stages, amounted to the erection of a new building and not the original building in an improved form and that this was a matter of fact and degree for the Secretary of State to decide.

7.33 Problems have also occurred in relation to Class E. This Class typically includes garages, garden sheds, domestic stores, or games rooms to be used by residents.

The Need for Planning Permission 1

In *Pêche d'Or Investments v Secretary of State for the Environment* [1996] JPL 311, it was held that whether a building fell within Class E was a matter of fact and degree in every case. In this case the provision of a study room was not excluded from the Class. In *Rambridge v Secretary of State for the Environment* [1997] 74 P & CR 126, however, it was held that the Class did not include buildings designed for primary residential accommodation or additions to basic living accommodation, such as bedrooms or kitchens. In other words, the building is only permitted if it is required for a purpose incidental to the enjoyment of the dwellinghouse.

7.34 There have been frequent changes to Class H of Part I. The present position is that the Class permits the installation, alteration, or replacement of satellite antennas on a dwellinghouse, or within the curtilage of a dwellinghouse, subject to certain limits and conditions. There are, however, a number of limitations on the availability of this permission, including those relating to number of antennas, cubic capacity, the position where installed, and whether or not located on designated land.

Part 2—Minor operations

7.35 Part 2 contains three classes of permitted development as set out below.

Class A	The erection, construction, maintenance, improvement, or alteration of a gate, fence, wall, or other means of enclosure. The 2013 Amendment Order has increased allowances for schools.
Class B	The formation, laying out, and construction of a means of access to a highway which is not a trunk road or a classified road, where that access is required in connection with development permitted by any class in this Schedule (other than by Class A of this Part).
Class C	The painting of the exterior of any building or work.
Class D	The installation, alteration or replacement, within an area lawfully used for off-street parking, of an electrical outlet mounted on a wall for recharging electric vehicles.
Class E	The installation, alteration or replacement, within an area lawfully used for off-street parking, of an upstand with an electrical outlet mounted on it for recharging electric vehicles.
Class F	The installation, alteration or replacement on a building of a closed circuit television camera to be used for security purposes.

7.36 In *Prengate Properties Ltd v Secretary of State for the Environment* [1973] JPL 313 it was held with regard to Class A that a wall was not authorized unless it had some actual function of enclosure. So, a free-standing wall in the middle of a garden would not be covered. Then in *Shepherd v Secretary of State for the Environment and Three Rivers DC* [1997] JPL 764, the High Court held that Class B was not confined to the formation of a means of access to a highway which was adjacent to the land on which the permitted development was to take place. The right was available under the Class even where there was intervening

Part 3—Changes of use

As has been seen under the Town and Country Planning (Use Classes) Order 1987 a change of use within the same use Class does not involve the development of land. A change of use between two use Classes, however, will only constitute development if it involves a material change of use. If it does constitute a material change of use Part 3 of the GPDO builds on the Use Classes Order by granting permitted development for certain changes from one use class to another. **7.37**

The use Classes affected by this Part of the Order are: **7.38**

PART A
  A1 Shops.
  A2 Financial and professional services.
  A3 Restaurants and cafes.
  A4 Drinking establishments.
  A5 Hot food takeaways.
PART B
  B1 Businesses.
  B2 General Industrial.
  B8 Storage or distribution.
PART C
  C3 Dwellinghouses.
  C4 Houses of Multiple Occupation.
PART D
  D2 Assembly and leisure.

Under Classes A to V in Part 3 of the General Permitted Development Order, the following unilateral changes between different use Classes are permitted development.

Class A	Development consisting of a change of use of a building from a use falling within Class A3 (restaurants and cafes), A5 (hot food takeaways) of the Schedule to the Use Classes Order, to a use falling within Class A1 (shops) or Class A2 (financial and professional services) of that Schedule.
Class AA	Development consisting of a change of use of a building and any land within its curtilage— (a) from a use falling within Class A4 of the Schedule to the Use Classes Order to a use falling within Class A4 (drinking establishments) with a use falling within Class A3 (restaurants and cafes) ("drinking establishments with expanded food provision"); and (b) from a use as a drinking establishment with expanded food provision to a use falling within Class A4 (drinking establishments).

Class B	Development consisting of a change of use of a building from a use falling within Class A5 (hot food takeaways) of the Schedule to the Use Classes Order, to a use falling within Class A3 (restaurants and cafes) of that Schedule.

Class C	Development consisting of—
	(a) a change of use of a building from a use—
	   (i) falling within Class A1 (shops) or Class A2 (financial and professional services) of the Schedule to the Use Classes Order,
	   (ii) as a betting office or pay day loan shop, or
	   (iii) as a casino,
	to a use falling within Class A3 (restaurants and cafes) of the Schedule to the Use Classes Order, or (b) development referred to in paragraph (a) together with building or other operations for the provision of facilities for—
	   (i) ventilation and extraction (including the provision of an external flue), and
	   (ii) the storage of rubbish,
	reasonably necessary to use the building for a use falling within Class A3 (restaurants and cafes) of that Schedule.

Class D	Development consisting of a change of use of a building and any land within its curtilage from a use falling within Class A1 (shops) of the Schedule to the Use Classes Order, to use falling within Class A2 (financial and professional services) of that Schedule.
Class E	Development consisting of a change of use of a building with a display window at ground floor level from— (a) a use falling within Class A2 (financial and professional services) of the Schedule to the Use Classes Order, or (b) a use as a betting office or a pay day loan shop, to a use falling within Class A1 (shops) of the Schedule to the Use Classes Order.
Class F	Development consisting of a change of use of a building from a use as a betting office or a pay day loan shop to a use falling within Class A2 (financial and professional services) of the Schedule to the Use Classes Order.

Class G	Development consisting of a change of use of a building—
	(a) from a use for any purpose within Class A1 (shops) of the Schedule to the Use Classes Order, to a mixed use for any purpose within Class A1 (shops) of that Schedule and as up to 2 flats;
	(b) from a use for any purpose within Class A1 (shops) of the Schedule to the Use Classes Order, to a mixed use for any purpose within Class A2 (financial and professional services) of that Schedule and as up to 2 flats;
	(c) from a use—
	   (i) for any purpose within Class A2 (financial and professional services) of the Schedule to the Use Classes Order, or
	   (ii) as a betting office or a pay day loan shop,
	to a mixed use for any purpose within Class A2 (financial and professional services) of that Schedule and as up to 2 flats;
	(d) where that building has a display window at ground floor level, from a use—
	   (i) for any purpose within Class A2 (financial and professional services) of the Schedule to the Use Classes Order, or,
	   (ii) as a betting office or a pay day loan shop,
	to a mixed use for any purpose within Class A1 (shops) of the Schedule to the Use Classes Order and as up to 2 flats;
	(e) from a use as a betting office or a pay day loan shop to a mixed use as a betting office or a pay day loan shop and as up to 2 flats.

Class H Development consisting of a change of use of a building—
(a) from a mixed use for any purpose within Class A1 (shops) of the Schedule to the Use Classes Order and as up to 2 flats, to a use for any purpose within Class A1 (shops) of that Schedule;
(b) from a mixed use for any purpose within Class A1 (shops) of the Schedule to the Use Classes Order and as up to 2 flats, to a use for any purpose within Class A2 (financial and professional services) of that Schedule;
(c) from a mixed use—
  (i) for any purpose within Class A2 (financial and professional services) of the Schedule to the Use Classes Order and as up to 2 flats,
  (ii) as a betting office or pay day loan shop and as up to 2 flats,
to a use for any purpose within Class A2 (financial and professional services) of that Schedule;
(d) where that building has a display window at ground floor level, from a mixed use for any purpose—
  (i) within Class A2 (financial and professional services) of the Schedule to the Use Classes Order and as up to 2 flats, or
  (ii) as a betting office or pay day loan shop and as up to 2 flats,
to a use for any purpose within Class A1 (shops) of the Schedule to the Use Classes Order;
(e) from a mixed use as a betting office or pay day loan shop and as up to 2 flats to a use as a betting office or pay day loan shop.

Class I Development consisting of a change of use of a building—
(a) from any use falling within Class B2 (general industrial) or B8 (storage or distribution) of the Schedule to the Use Classes Order, to a use for any purpose falling within Class B1 (business) of that Schedule;
(b) from any use falling within Class B1 (business) or B2 (general industrial) of the Schedule to the Use Classes Order, to a use for any purpose falling within Class B8 (storage or distribution) of that Schedule.

Class J Development consisting of a change of use of a building from a use—
(a) falling within Class A1(shops) or Class A2(financial and, professional services) of the Schedule to the Use Classes Order
(b) as a betting office or pay day loan shop, to a use falling within Class D2(assembly and leisure) of that Schedule.

Class K Development consisting of a change of use of a building from a use as a casino to a use falling within Class D2(assembly and leisure) of the Schedule to the Use Classes Order.

Class L Development consisting of a change of use of a building—
(a) from a use falling within Class C4(houses in multiple occupation) of the Schedule to the Use Classes Order, to a use falling within Class C3 (dwellinghouses) of that Schedule;
(b) from a use falling within Class C3(dwellinghouses) of the Schedule to the Use Classes Order, to a use falling within Class C4 (houses in multiple occupation) of that Schedule.

The validity of these changes by statutory instrument was challenged in *R (on the application of Milton Keynes Council) v Secretary of State for Communities and Local Government* [2011] EWHC 1060 (Admin) where it was argued that the statutory instruments should be quashed because there had been a failure to consult directly with local planning authorities before deciding to make the changes. However,

7.39

this challenge was rejected and the decision has been upheld by the Court of Appeal; [2011] EWCA Civ 1575.

Class M	Development is not permitted by Class M if—
	(a) the building was not used for one of the uses referred to in Class M(a)—
	   (i) on 20th March 2013, or
	   (ii) in the case of a building which was in use before that date but was not in use on that date, when it was last in use;
	(b) permission to use the building for a use falling within Class A1 (shops) or Class A2 (financial and professional services) of the Schedule to the Use Classes Order has been granted only by this Part;
	(c) the cumulative floor space of the existing building changing use under Class M exceeds 150 square metres;
	(d) the development (together with any previous development under Class M) would result in more than 150 square metres of floor space in the building having changed use under Class M;
	(e) the development would result in the external dimensions of the building extending beyond the external dimensions of the existing building at any given point;
	(f) the development consists of demolition (other than partial demolition which is reasonably necessary to convert the building to a use falling within Class C3 (dwellinghouses) of the Schedule to the Use Classes Order); or
	(g) the building is—
	   (i) on article 2(3) land;
	   (ii) in a site of special scientific interest;
	   (iii) in a safety hazard area;
	   (iv) in a military explosives storage area;
	   (v) a listed building; or
	   (vi) a scheduled monument.

Class N	Development consisting of—
	(a) a change of use of a building and any land within its curtilage from a use as—
	   (i) an amusement arcade or centre, or
	   (ii) a casino,
	to a use falling within Class C3(dwellinghouses) of the Schedule to the Use Classes Order; or
	(b) development referred to in paragraph (a) together with building operations reasonably necessary to convert the building referred to in paragraph (a) to a use falling within Class C3(dwellinghouses) of that Schedule.

Class O	Development consisting of a change of use of a building and any land within its curtilage from a use falling within Class B1(a)(offices) of the Schedule to the Use Classes Order, to a use falling within Class C3(dwellinghouses) of that Schedule.
Class P	Development consisting of a change of use of a building and any land within its curtilage from a use falling within Class B8(storage or distribution centre) of the Schedule to the Use Classes Order to a use falling within Class C3(dwellinghouses) of that Schedule.
Class Q	Development consisting of— (a) a change of use of a building and any land within its curtilage from a use as an agricultural building to a use falling within Class C3(dwellinghouses) of the Schedule to the Use Classes Order; or (b) development referred to in paragraph (a) together with building operations reasonably necessary to convert the building referred to in paragraph (a) to a use falling within Class C3(dwellinghouses) of that Schedule.

Class R	Development consisting of a change of use of a building and any land within its curtilage from a use as an agricultural building to a flexible use falling within Class A1(shops), Class A2(financial and professional services), Class A3(restaurants and cafes), Class B1(business), Class B8(storage or distribution), Class C1(hotels) or Class D2(assembly and leisure) of the Schedule to the Use Classes Order.
Class S	Development consisting of a change of use of a building and any land within its curtilage from a use as an agricultural building to use as a state-funded school or a registered nursery.
Class T	Development consisting of a change of use of a building and any land within its curtilage from a use falling within Class B1(business), Class C1(hotels), Class C2(residential institutions), Class C2A(secure residential institutions) or Class D2(assembly and leisure) of the Schedule to the Use Classes Order, to use as a state-funded school or a registered nursery.
Class U	Development consisting of a change of use of land from a use permitted by Class T to the previous lawful use of the land.
Class V	Development consisting of a change of use of a building or other land from a use permitted by planning permission granted on an application, to another use which that permission would have specifically authorised when it was granted.

The procedure for seeking prior approval under Part 3 is set out within Class V, paragraph W.

Part 4—Temporary buildings and uses

This Part of Sch 2 to the Order contains the following two Classes: 7.40

Class A	The provision on land of buildings, moveable structures, works, plant, or machinery required temporarily in connection with and for the duration of operations being or to be carried out on, in, under, or over that land or on land adjoining that land.
Class B	The use of any land for any purpose for not more than 28 days in total in any calendar year, of which not more than 14 days in total may be for the purposes of (a) the holding of a market; (b) motor car and motorcycle racing including trials of speed, and practising for these activities, and the provision on the land of any moveable structure for the purposes of the permitted use.
Class C	The use of a building and any land within its curtilage as a state-funded school for 2 academic years.
Class CA	provision of a temporary state-funded school on previously vacant commercial land
Class D	The use of a building from use Classes A1, A2, A3, A5, B1, D1, and D2 to either use Class A1, A2, A3, or B1. The change is only authorized for a continuous period of two years and there is an upper limit of 150 square metres.

Under Class A of this Part, a builder's hut, used for administrative purposes on a construction site during the course of building operations, would be permitted development during the period of construction. In *R (Hall Hunter Partnership) v First Secretary of State* [2006] EWHC 3482 (Admin); [2007] 2 P & CR 5 Sullivan J held that the word operations only included 'operational development' and the permitted development rights did not apply to activities which in lay terms might 7.41

amount to operations but in planning law amounted to a use of land. However, in an earlier decision, *North Cornwall DC v Secretary of State for the Environment Transport and the Regions* [2002] EWHC 2318 (Admin); [2003] 1 P & CR 25, Sullivan J emphasized that because of its temporary nature there was no reason to adopt a restrictive interpretation to this Class and he found that it permitted the provision of a temporary structure on the forecourt of a shop to enable retail sales to take place while building works were being carried out.

7.42 Class B of Part 4 permits the use of land for certain temporary purposes. The permission does not apply, however, where the land in question is a building or is within the curtilage of a building, or to the use of land as a caravan site. Also, the right does not apply when a person intends that it is to be carried out for longer than the permitted 28 or 14 days. In *Tidswell v Secretary of State for the Environment* [1977] JPL 104 an enforcement notice had been served requiring the discontinuance of land for use as a market. At the time of service of the notice, the contravening development had operated for a total of nine Sundays, but the use of the land for that purpose on Sundays had continued after service of the notice for at least another nine months. By the date of the appeal, the use had continued far beyond the Order limits (every Sunday from 23 June 1974 until 15 April 1975, ie 37 Sundays in 1974 and 15 in 1975). The Queen's Bench Divisional Court upheld the Secretary of State's view that the benefit of the Order was not available to the appellant. In this case all the evidence suggested that the use was not a temporary use but a permanent one. The decision upheld the validity of the enforcement notice served after use of the land as a market for the first nine Sundays. In upholding the enforcement notice, Forbes J quoted Upjohn LJ in *Miller-Mead v Minister of Housing and Local Government* [1963] 2 QB 196 (CA), 231 where he said, 'a permanent user for a purpose not permitted and a temporary casual user up to 28 days in any one year are quite different things'. It would therefore seem that even if the use was restricted to 28 or 14 days each year it would not be covered if it was intended to keep up this intermittent use in future years and so make it a permanent intermittent use. However, this interpretation would seem to go against the literal wording.

7.43 In deciding whether or not a change of use is to a temporary casual use or to a permanent intermittent use, it may be relevant to consider the use in the light of the way in which the land is likely to be used in practice. In *Ramsay v Secretary of State for the Environment and Suffolk DC* [1998] JPL 60 it was held in a challenge to the refusal by the Secretary of State on appeal to grant a lawful development certificate for 'the use of land for vehicular sports and leisure activities on not more than 28 days in any calendar year' that he was entitled to conclude that the use was a permanent, intermittent use which was not permitted by the GPDO. The site had retained throughout the year the physical features of the use on a permanent basis, eg rope around the track enclosures, moveable huts used for the collection of entry fees, and the sale of refreshments to spectators, vehicle track, and tyres. It had all the hallmarks of a permanent, if intermittent, change of use.

7.44 Subsequently, however, the appellants applied for and were granted a lawful development certificate in respect of the earlier operational development of the land, namely, 'the creation of a circuit or track by mechanical excavation and raising the banks and jumps on formerly level or graded field or meadow'. The certificate thus established the lawful existence of the physical changes that had been made.

7.45 Thereafter, the appellants sought a lawful development certificate in identical terms to that which they had applied for earlier and which had been refused. The evidence again was that between each use of the land for vehicle sports and leisure activities, the land continued to be used for the grazing of sheep. The application for that certificate was again refused by the Secretary of State on the ground that the proposed use was a permanent use falling outside Part 4 of Class B of the Schedule.

7.46 In *Ramsay v Secretary of State for the Environment, Transport, and the Regions and Suffolk Coastal DC* [2000] JPL 1123, the Court of Appeal quashed the Secretary of State's decision, holding that if the physical changes were allowed to take place and they did not prevent the normal permanent use from continuing for most of the year (in this case agricultural) there was no reason in principle why rights under Part 4 should not be available for another use which did not take place for more than 28 days of the year. The court emphasized that the critical factors were the duration of the proposed use of the land and the reversion in between times to its normal use.

7.47 In *South Bucks DC v Secretary of State for the Environment* [1989] JPL 351, the Court of Appeal held that the effect of Part 4 was to grant as many planning permissions as there were changes of use, so that where land was used at intervals of one week for a Sunday market, a change of use occurred every time the market was held. The significance of this decision is that it enables the local planning authority to issue an Article 4 direction withdrawing the permitted development rights, even where the landowner has begun to use the 'temporary permission' but not exhausted it completely. In effect, therefore, the provision does not grant a single permission for temporary use of land for each calendar year. It allows the landowner to make up to 28 changes of use for the same activity, on each of the days permitted in any year.

7.48 In 1992, the Government considered whether further control should be introduced over the temporary use of land for clay pigeon shooting, markets and car boot sales, war games, and the use of land by helicopters landing and taking-off. When being carried out, these activities may generate excessive traffic and noise, causing concern to local residents in the area. Again, in January 2002, the Government once more sought views on whether any changes were desirable to this Part of the Order. It decided however, that no changes would be made to any of the existing provisions in Part 4. It will be seen that Part 4 now restricts these activities on land to the following specified frequencies in any one calendar year:

	On SSIs, residential curtilage or a caravan site	Elsewhere
Markets	14 days	14 days
Motor sports	nil	14 days
Clay pigeon shooting	nil	28 days
War games	nil	28 days
All others (including helicopters)	28 days	28 days

It should be noted that Class B does not allow the use of land for the display of advertisements.

Part 6—Agricultural and Forestry

7.49 This part of Sch 2 gives permitted development rights for the following four Classes of development:

Class A	The carrying out on agricultural land comprised in an agricultural unit of 5 hectares or more in area of— (a) works for the erection, extension or alteration of a building; or (b) any excavation or engineering operations, which are reasonably necessary for the purposes of agriculture within that unit.
Class B	The carrying out on agricultural land comprised in an agricultural unit, of not less than 0.4 but less than 5 hectares in area, of development consisting of— (a) the extension or alteration of an agricultural building; (b) the installation of additional or replacement plant or machinery; (c) the provision, rearrangement or replacement of a sewer, main, pipe, cable or other apparatus; (d) the provision, rearrangement or replacement of a private was (e) the provision of a hard surface; (f) the deposit of waste; or (g) the carrying out of any of the following operations in connection with fish farming, namely, repairing ponds and raceways; the installation of grading machinery, aeration equipment or flow meters and any associated channel; the dredging of ponds; and the replacement of tanks and nets, where the development is reasonably necessary for the purposes of agriculture within the unit.
Class C	The winning and working on land held or occupied with land used for the purposes of agriculture of any minerals reasonably necessary for agricultural purposes within the agricultural unit of which it forms part.

7.50 Under these provisions, the development allowed on agricultural land is divided. In particular, in Class A the permitted development is restricted to agricultural units of 5 hectares or more, subject to a minimum size of one hectare where the development would be carried out on a separate parcel of land within and forming part of that larger unit. Class B permitted development is restricted to agricultural land comprised in an agricultural unit with an area of 0.4 hectares or more, but less than 5 hectares in area. It should be noted that under both Class A and B it may be necessary, before exercising permitted development rights, to first apply to the local planning authority for a determination as to whether the authority's prior approval is required for certain details of the development proposed. In particular, the provisions for prior notification apply where it is proposed to erect, extend, or alter an agricultural building. If the authority gives notice that prior approval is needed for such development, the applicant is required by the Schedule to display a site notice on or near the land on which the proposed development is to be carried out, leaving the notice in position for not less than 21 days in the 28 days from the date on which the local planning authority gave notice to the applicant.

The development rights permitted by Class A of Part 6 of Sch 2 apply only to building operations 'reasonably necessary for the purposes of agriculture within that unit'. In *Clarke v Secretary of State for the Environment* (1992) 65 P & CR 85 it was held that to qualify as permitted development, the buildings did not have to be reasonably necessary for the particular agricultural enterprise being undertaken on the unit at the time the buildings were erected; they simply have to be reasonably necessary for, and designed for, the purposes of agriculture within that unit. It is essentially a question of fact and degree, to be decided with regard to the circumstances prevailing at the date when the building was erected, and relating to the particular building on the particular unit. It seems that this assessment can refer to the future intended agricultural use of the land since there is no requirement that the building should be intended to accommodate only an existing use (*Jones v Stockport MBC* (1985) 50 P & CR 299). **7.51**

For a building to be permitted development, it has to be designed for the purposes of agriculture. According to *Belmont Farms Ltd* (1962) 13 P & CR 417, this relates to its physical appearance and layout. In *Harding v Secretary of State for the Environment* [1984] JPL 503, it was said that design related to appearance rather than function 'to ensure that buildings in the countryside should look like farm buildings and not dwelling houses'. **7.52**

Another provision should be particularly noted. Development under Classes A and B is not permitted by the Order if it involves the provision of accommodation for livestock or the storage of slurry and sewerage sludge within 400 metres of the curtilage of a 'protected building'. The purpose of the provision is to maintain a 'cordon sanitaire' between livestock and livestock slurry and nearby residential accommodation. The permitted development rights apply to buildings to house microgeneration equipment, hydro turbines, biomass boilers and anaerobic digestion systems and to store associated waste and fuel as long as the fuel or waste is produced on the farm or by the boiler or system. **7.53**

7.54 Finally, Part 6 does not permit development if 'it would consist of, or include, the erection, extension or alteration of a dwelling' (Class A.1(c)). There was originally some uncertainty whether a farmhouse and its curtilage can be counted in the 5 ha of the agricultural unit. However, in *Hancock v Secretary of State for the Environment* (1988) 55 P & CR 216 Glidewell LJ held at 222 that:

> the Secretary of State was wrong in law in finding that the farmhouse and garden area were incapable of being land used for agriculture. No doubt, whether any particular house is or is not 'used for agriculture' is a question of fact and degree, applying the criteria laid down in the two cited cases. In any event, what I must do is to send the case back to the Secretary of State. But it seems to me inconceivable that, applying those criteria, any decision other than that this farmhouse and garden is agricultural land would be impossible.

The *Hancock* judgment has been given effect by para D.1(1) which provides:

> agricultural unit' means agricultural land which is occupied as a unit for the purposes of agriculture, including—
> (a) any dwelling or other building on that land occupied for the purpose of farming the land by the person who occupies the unit, or
> (b) any dwelling on that land occupied by a farmworker

Forestry (Part 6 cont)

7.55 Part 6 also gives permitted development rights to certain operational development carried out on land used for forestry, as follows:

Class E	The carrying out on land used for the purposes of forestry, including afforestation, of development reasonably necessary for those purposes consisting of— (a) works for the erection, extension or alteration of a building; (b) the formation, alteration or maintenance of private ways; (c) operations on that land, or on land held or occupied with that land, to obtain the materials required for the formation, alteration or maintenance of such ways; (d) other operations (not including engineering or mining operations)

Part 16—Communications

7.56 Part 16 covers the installation, alteration, or replacement of any telecommunication apparatus, the use of land in an emergency for a period not exceeding six months to station and operate moveable telecommunication apparatus required for the replacement of unserviceable telecommunication apparatus, including the provision of moveable structures on the land for the purposes of that use, or development ancillary to radio equipment housing. Restrictions placed on the availability of permitted development rights include the height of the relevant apparatus and its distance from a highway.

7.57 An important condition which the operator is required to comply with relates to the requirement of a 56-day prior-notification procedure where the development consists of the installation, alteration, or replacement of a mast, an antenna and radio equipment housing, including most ground-based masts up to 15 metres in height. Under this procedure the developer is required to give prior notification of what is proposed to the local planning authority and the owner of the land. The authority then has 56 days to determine the application. If it fails to do so, the authority is deemed to have granted approval for the development proposed.

D. LOCAL DEVELOPMENT ORDERS

Introduction

Section 40 of the Planning and Compulsory Purchase Act 2004 introduced a new procedure to allow for the making of local development orders by local planning authorities. It inserted into the 1990 Act four new sections, ss 61A to 61D, the purpose of which is to give local planning authorities a discretionary power to extend the permitted development rights given by the GPDO. As with the GPDO, it removes the need for an application to be made for planning permission for development specified in the Order. A local development order (LDO) differs from the GPDO in that whereas with the GPDO permitted development rights are set out at national level, with an LDO those rights are set locally. However, an LDO may only be made to implement policies contained in a local development plan document or a local development plan. The permission granted by an LDO may relate to all land within the area of the authority, or to any part of it, or to a site specified in the order. For example, the restriction of an LDO to a particular site may assist in the regeneration of an employment area or an industrial estate. The permission granted by the order may be granted either unconditionally or subject to such conditions or limitations as are specified in the order. The new s 61A of the 1990 Act, however, provides that an order may specify any area or a Class of development for which an order cannot be made. For example, an authority may choose to restrict the scope of an LDO by directing that the order shall not apply to a particular development. Furthermore, there are a number of specific statutory restrictions preventing an authority from making an LDO, such as where the development would affect a listed building or have an adverse effect on the setting of a listed building, development is likely to have a significant effect on a European site and which is not directly connected with or necessary to the management of the site, and for development of a type specified in Sch 1 of the Environmental Impact Assessment Regulations. When preparing an LDO, a local planning authority must produce a concise statement justifying why it should be made. This statement must include a description of the development which would be permitted, a statement of policies which the LDO would implement, and a plan or statement identifying the land to which the LDO applies. **7.58**

The provisions used to allow the Secretary of State, at any time before the local planning authority adopted an LDO, to direct that the order be submitted to him **7.59** for approval and then to reject or modify the order. Section 6 of the Growth and Infrastructure Act 2013 has abolished these powers and a new s 61B(7A) simply requires a local planning authority to submit a copy of a local development order to the Secretary of State after the order has been adopted.

Preparation of an LDO

7.60 Local planning authorities are being encouraged to make an LDO at the same time as the development plan document to which it relates. This is because the authority will then be able to carry out the consultation requirements for both at the same time and reduce the overall resource cost of preparation. Unlike a development plan document, however, the LDO does not require independent testing and is not subject to the binding nature of an Inspector's report. When preparing an LDO the authority must produce a concise statement justifying why it should be made. This is to be known as a statement of reasons and must include a description of the development which would be permitted by the order, a statement of the policies which the LDO would implement, and a plan or statement identifying the land to which the LDO is to apply. The authority must also comply with the same publicity and consultation requirements as are required for the production of a development plan document. In addition, it must also consult anybody who would have been a statutory consultee for an application for planning permission for the development in question.

7.61 The Act requires local planning authorities to place LDOs and their statement of reasons on a new Part III to the planning register. Thereafter, the local planning authority must report annually to the Secretary of State on the extent to which the LDO is achieving its purpose.

Completion of development after revision of revocation of order

7.62 With regard to all development orders, whether local, general, or specific, the new s 61C of the 2004 Act provides that a development order or a local development order may include provisions which permit the completion of development if the planning permission is withdrawn after the development is started but before it is completed. This provision will therefore apply where planning permission granted by the order is withdrawn or if the order is amended so that it ceases to grant planning permission for the development or materially changes any condition or limitation to which the permission was subject.

E. NEIGHBOURHOOD DEVELOPMENT ORDERS

7.63 The Localism Act 2011 ('the 2011 Act') inserts a new s 61E into the 1990 Act which empowers either a parish council or a neighbourhood forum to initiate the process for making a neighbourhood development order. It also places a duty on local planning authorities to make a neighbourhood development order, if there is a referendum vote in favour of the order, except when the making of the order would be incompatible with any European Community obligation or any of the rights under the European Convention on Human Rights referred to in s 1 of the Human Rights Act 1998. The Act also confers powers on the Secretary of State to make regulations about the procedure to be followed by a local planning authority where they intended to refuse to make a neighbourhood development order despite a 'yes' vote in a referendum. For example, requirements to consult before making a final decision could be imposed, as well as requirements for a local planning authority to give notice that they propose to refuse to an order.

7.64 The Secretary of State and a local planning authority (with the consent of the Secretary of State) can revoke a neighbourhood development order.

7.65 The neighbourhood development orders can grant either site-specific planning permission or grant planning permissions that relate to all or part of a neighbourhood area. However, there are restrictions on the kind of development, for example, mining related development is excluded. Conditions can be imposed on the permitted development.

7.66 When exercising the power to designate a local neighbourhood area, local authorities must consider whether it should be designated a business area. If it is designated as a business area, businesses are entitled to a parallel referendum. So, there will be two referendums (one of residents and one of non-domestic rate payers) and the local planning authority is then not obliged to adopt the proposed neighbourhood development area unless both referenda are in support of the proposal.

7.67 It should be noted that the Act also creates a particular type of neighbourhood development order called a community right to build order which authorizes community-led specific development. Details of the provisions are set out in Sch 4C to the Town and Country Planning Act 1990 inserted by Sch 11 to the 2011 Act. Community organizations can apply for such an order which sets out how the provisions in respect of neighbourhood development orders apply to such an application.

7.68 The procedure for making a neighbourhood development order is set out at Sch 4B to the Town and Country Planning Act 1990. A detailed discussion of the procedure for the making of a neighbourhood development order is contained in Chapter 4 under 'neighbourhood development plans' as the statutory process is the same (with minor modifications set out within s 38C(5) of the Planning and Compulsory Purchase Act 2004).

F. PERMISSION IN PRINCIPLE

7.69 The Housing and Planning Act 2016 introduces, by inserting ss 58A and 59A into the Town and Country Planning Act 1990, an alternative way of obtaining planning permission for housing-led development which separates the consideration of matters of principle for proposed development from the technical detail of the development. The 'permission in principle' consent route has two stages: the first stage (or permission in principle stage) establishes whether a site is suitable in principle and the second ('technical details consent') stage is when the detailed development proposals are assessed. The PPG explains that non-residential development may also be given permission in principle providing housing occupies the majority of the floorspace of the overall scheme.

7.70 By reg 3 of the Town and Country Planning (Brownfield Land Register) Regulations 2017 (SI 2017/403) each local planning authority in England must maintain a 'brownfield land register', consisting of land which meets the four criteria within reg 4, which are (i) the land has an area of at least 0.25 hectares or is capable of supporting at least 5 dwellings, (ii) the land is suitable for residential development, (iii) the land is available for residential development, and (iv) residential development of the land is achievable. In most cases this has not been an especially difficult obligation for planning authorities, considering the pre-existing obligation to demonstrate a five-year period of deliverable housing sites which involves a similar survey of land within their areas.

7.71 The planning authority may grant 'permission in principle' either by (i) granting permission in response to a valid application (the requirements of which are set out within art 5D of the Town and Country Planning (Permission in Principle) Order 2017 (SI 2017/402)) (for a default period of three years), or by entering the site onto Part 2 of its brownfield land register (for a default period of five years). There are certain types of development for which permission in principle cannot be granted, these are: householder development, winning and working of minerals, EIA development or Habitats development (meaning that which alone or in combination with others is 'likely to have a significant effect on a European site or a European offshore marine site'). Major development cannot be granted via application, only by entering it on Part 2 of the register. Development on land not defined as 'previously developed' can only be granted by application. Moreover, allocations within the neighbourhood plan do not give rise to a permission in principle. Grants of permission in principle cannot be subject to conditions but there is nothing to stop a planning authority indicating what they would like to see come forward by way of a technical details application.

7.72 Once permission in principle has been obtained, the second stage is known as the 'technical details consent' stage. Technical details consent is required before development can proceed, it is obtained by submitting a valid application in accordance with a live permission in principle. A valid application consists of (i) a completed application form, (ii) which complies with the national information requirements, (iii) the correct application fee, and (iv) the provision of the local information requirements. Technical details applications, in line with permission in principle applications, are determined in accordance with the development plan unless material considerations indicate otherwise. Such applications must be determined 'as quickly as possible' and in any event, ten weeks for major development, 16 weeks for development subject to an EIA, and five weeks in all other cases. By contrast to a permission in principle, conditions may be attached to the grant of a technical details consent.

7.73 There is no right of appeal where a local planning authority decides not to enter a site in Part 2 of a brownfield land register and trigger the grant of permission in principle. A person with an interest in a site has the option of submitting a planning application to the local planning authority. There is a right of appeal under s 78 of the Town and Country Planning Act 1990, where a local planning authority refuses permission in principle upon receipt of a valid application. The procedure is set out within art 5V of the 2017 Order. Similarly, an applicant can appeal a refusal to grant technical details consent.

7.74 Consultation must be undertaken before sites can be granted permission in principle by either application or placement on Part 2 of the brownfield land register. The details of which bodies need to be consulted is set out within Sch 4 of the Development Management Order 2015. Similarly, consultation must take place prior to granting technical details consent.

7.75 Full guidance on the application and determination process is set out within the PPG 'Permission in Principle' section, para 58-001-20180615 onwards.

7.76 The lacuna within the permission in principle regime must be that there is no obligation upon the planning authority to move land onto Part 2 of its brownfield land register and thus grant consent. Whilst there is a policy obligation upon planning authorities to 'regularly review' sites on Part 1 to see if they are suitable to move to Part 2 (PPG 58-010-20180615) there is no hard-edged duty to move suitable sites into Part 2. Furthermore, by s 70(2) of the Town and Country Planning Act 1990 and s 38(6) of the Planning and Compulsory Purchase Act 2004, a planning authority must determine an application of permission in principle in accordance with the provisions of the development plan, unless material considerations indicate otherwise. All in all, the provisions are unlikely to radically transform the prospects of the speed at which development consent be obtained, see the observations by A Bowes, 'Brownfield Land Registers and Permission in Principle' [2017] JPL 661 at 662 and A Samuels, 'The Brownfield Land Register and the Implications' [2018] JPL 978, who said at 980 that: '[t]he brownfield land register may turn out to be an ineffective bureaucratic burden, adding little to the awareness of land potentially capable of adding to the housing stock'.

8

THE NEED FOR PLANNING PERMISSION 2: CASES OF DOUBT

A. CERTIFICATE OF LAWFULNESS OF PROPOSED USE OR DEVELOPMENT (CLOPUD) 8.02	C. CARRYING OUT AN ACTIVITY WITHOUT ASCERTAINING WHETHER IT NEEDS PERMISSION 8.17
B. ACTION FOR A DECLARATION 8.09	

Given the complexities of the definition of development and the difficulties which may arise in deciding whether in any particular case proposed development is permitted development, landowners may be in doubt about whether they need to make an express application for planning permission to the local planning authority before carrying out some activity. In most circumstances there is an opportunity to put the matter beyond doubt. **8.01**

A. CERTIFICATE OF LAWFULNESS OF PROPOSED USE OR DEVELOPMENT (CLOPUD)

Under s 192 of the 1990 Act, if any person wishes to ascertain whether: **8.02**

(a) any proposed use of buildings or other land; or
(b) any operations proposed to be carried out in, on, over or under land,

would be lawful, he may make an application for the purpose to the local planning authority specifying the land and describing the use or operations in question. Then, if the local planning authority is satisfied on the information provided that the use or operations described in the application would be lawful if instituted or begun at the time of the application, it must issue a certificate to that effect; and in any other case it must refuse the application. A certificate may be issued therefore if the proposed use or operation does not constitute development or if it does but the development is 'permitted development' under the GPDO, or the carrying out of it would be in accordance with an existing planning permission.

The certificate procedure enables people to ascertain whether specified operations or activities stated in the application would be lawful under planning law. It cannot be used to ask the question 'what is or what would be' lawful on the land. As already stated, s 192 deals with the lawfulness of a *proposed* use or development. It should be distinguished from s 191 which deals with the lawfulness of an *existing* use or development.

8.03 In seeking a certificate under s 192 the onus of proof is on the applicant, who will need to describe his proposal in sufficient detail and with sufficient precision to enable the authority to make its decision. It was held by the Court of Appeal in *R v Thanet DC and Kent International Airport plc, ex p Tapp and Britton* [2002] PLCR 88 that it was not open to a local planning authority to require an application for a s 192 certificate to be modified. (This is in contrast to the position under s 191 where that power exists.) The local planning authority may instead refuse the application and suggest the applicant amend the description of the proposed development in a fresh application. In another case, *Broads Authority v Secretary of State for the Environment, Transport, and the Regions and David Phillips Investments Ltd* [2001] PLCR 66, it was held that an application under s 192 could be granted even if it related to a grant of planning permission requiring the submission of further details, such as is required in the case of an outline planning permission. Section 192 is couched in mandatory terms and has to be complied with. If the certificate is not in the prescribed form as set out in Sch 8 to the Development Management Procedure Order 2010 (DMPO), it will not comprise a valid certificate. In *James Iday Pension Trustees Ltd v First Secretary of State* [2006] EWCA Civ 1387, the Court of Appeal held that in issuing a certificate under s 192 headed 'Permission for Development' the planning authority had failed to master the strict requirements of the section.

8.04 Section 193 of the 1990 Act contains various provisions to enable the form of application and the procedure for dealing with applications for both ss 191 and 192 certificates to be prescribed by development order, for a certificate to be issued in respect of whole or part of the land specified in any application, for applications to be entered in the planning register, for certificates to be revoked if based on an application containing a falsehood in some material particular, and for offences to be created where a person gives false information in order to obtain a certificate. A certificate issued under the section must specify the land to which it relates; describe the use or operations in question (by specific use class if appropriate); give reasons for determining the use or operation to be lawful; and specify the date of the application for the certificate.

8.05 The section also provides that the lawfulness of any use or operations for which a certificate is in force shall be conclusively presumed unless there is a material change before the use is instituted or the operations begun, in any of the matters relevant to determining such lawfulness.

8.06 In dealing with an application the local planning authority has no discretion, since it is making a determination of law based on proposed facts. If the applicant is aggrieved by the determination of the local planning authority, he may appeal to the Secretary of State under s 78 of the 1990 Act, and from his determination to the High Court under s 288.

8.07 An important limitation to the scope of a s 192 certificate procedure is that it is not available where the proposed activity has already been carried out. In such a case the owner may elect to do nothing, and then if an enforcement notice is served, appeal against it to the Secretary of State on the ground that the matters alleged in the notice do not constitute a breach of planning control. It appears also that although a local planning authority has jurisdiction under ss 191 and 192 of the 1990 Act to determine whether planning permission is or may be required, there is no equivalent to this in relation to listed building consent.

8.08 The provision in s 192 allowing 'any person' to apply for a certificate is intended to allow the procedure to be used by prospective purchasers of land in addition to owners. It does, however, also allow other interested parties to do so, as happened in a somewhat unique case involving Railtrack plc (Ref: APP/X/98/X/5210/3059). The issue was whether planning permission was necessary to remodel the existing main railway lines between Euston station and the Primrose Hill tunnels, Camden. In order to settle the matter, objecting residents (even though they considered that the proposed works did not constitute permitted development) applied for a certificate. Railtrack considered that an application for planning permission to carry out the work was unnecessary, since the proposed works constituted permitted development by virtue of Class A of Part 11 and Class A of Part 17 of Sch 2 to the Town and Country Planning (General Permitted Development) Order 1995. Local residents thought otherwise, on the ground that permitted development rights had no application where the development was such as to require environmental assessment by virtue of the Town and Country Planning (Assessment of Environmental Effects) Regulations 1988, SI 1988/1199. They maintained that the works proposed by Railtrack required such an assessment, so that the development could only be lawful if express planning permission was granted. To help resolve the issue, the residents applied for a certificate under s 192. The local planning authority, however, failed to determine the application within the required 8-week period, resulting in the residents appealing to the Secretary of State against non-determination. At the subsequent public inquiry, Railtrack adopted the role of appellants, with the residents acting as a major interested party and being in the position of asking the Secretary of State to dismiss their own appeal. In the event the Secretary of State determined that the proposed work did not require environmental assessment, whereupon he issued a certificate that the proposed works were lawful as being permitted under the General Permitted Development Order.

B. ACTION FOR A DECLARATION

8.09 In *Pyx Granite Co Ltd v Ministry of Housing and Local Government* [1960] AC 260, the House of Lords decided that as an alternative to seeking a determination under planning legislation that no planning permission was required for a particular activity on land, a landowner could by way of an originating summons apply to the courts for a declaration to the same effect. The right to use this alternative has now long since been removed and any advantage it may have had is now provided for by the landowner's right to apply for a certificate under s 192. An action for a declaration, however, may be used in order to determine the scope of a planning permission.

8.10 In one case, *Thames Heliport v Tower Hamlets LBC* (1997) 74 P & CR 164, an application for a number of declarations was sought by way of originating summons to determine whether planning permission was needed for a vessel floating but not moored in the tidal River Thames for the purpose of enabling helicopters to transport passengers more quickly between London (Heathrow) Airport and the City. Declarations were also sought on whether, if planning permission was required for that activity, the 28 days' use permitted under the then General Development Order 1988, Art 3(1) and Sch 2, Part IV, Class B, applied to each of the 20 different sites on the river where the helicopters might take off and land, or was restricted to the whole length of the tidal River Thames on which that activity might take place. The decision of the High Court was that planning permission was required and that the 28 days' permitted use would cover the whole of the tidal river. On appeal, however, the Court of Appeal was only prepared to grant a declaration (and duly did so) that the use of the vessel for the purposes stated *could* constitute a material change of use of the River Thames for the purposes of s 55 of the 1990 Act. The position of houseboats and changes of use was considered by Lang J in *R (on the application of KP JR Management Co Ltd) v Richmond-upon-Thames LBC* [2018] EWHC 84 (Admin); [2018] JPL 838. Mindful that the question of whether a change of use is material or not was one of fact and degree which Parliament had entrusted to the local planning authorities, the court declined to grant a declaration that the use of the River Thames for the purposes stated *would* constitute a material change of use.

8.11 The Court of Appeal also refused to make a declaration with regard to the question of whether the 28 days' permitted use covered the whole of the tidal River Thames or a lesser stretch of it. In the court's view the extent of permitted development rights depended upon the determination of the appropriate planning unit. This again was a question of fact and degree to be determined by the local planning authority. The court felt that it would be inappropriate to attempt to use the mechanism of securing a declaration from the court, so as to inhibit the decision-takers primarily entrusted with the task of deciding those matters from forming their own view.

8.12 Following that decision, it is clear that an application for planning permission does not include either expressly or by implication, a request that the authority should determine whether or not planning permission is required for what has been applied for. This was confirmed in *David Saxby v Secretary of State for the Environment and Westminster City Council* [1998] JPL 1132, where it was held that it would no longer be consistent with the scheme under the 1990 Act for an applicant to be able to require the local planning authority to determine whether planning permission was required as part of a planning application. Should the applicant require a binding determination of the issue he should apply for a certificate of lawful use under s 192 of the 1990 Act.

8.13 There is now no doubt that although the courts will normally decline to answer the question, 'Is the activity proposed development?' (since the s 192 procedure should be available to answer that question), they will consider whether or not planning permission has been granted for particular development or what is actually authorized by the permission.

8.14 In *Burhill Estates Ltd v Woking BC* [1995] JPL 147, the Court of Appeal granted a declaration that an outline permission for development, which involved work on a listed barn, was a valid permission capable of being implemented notwithstanding the destruction of the barn in a severe gale.

8.15 In *R (Gregan and ors) v Hartlepool BC and Able UK Ltd* [2003] EWHC 3278 (Admin), an application was made to quash a decision by the Council that planning permission granted in 2002 to Able UK Ltd provided permission for a site on the north bank of Seaton Channel (which runs into the River Tees at Teesmouth) to be used for 'dismantling and refurbishment of ships'. The action had been brought to halt by the dismantling and recycling of a number of ships at the site which had formed part of the US National Defense Reserve Fleet. The first of these ships had in fact already set off from the United States under tow to cross the Atlantic.

8.16 The High Court heard that the words 'marine structure' used in the earlier grant of planning permission to describe the activity which would be carried on at the site was not wide enough to include the term 'ships'. However, because the Council's decision was not a grant of planning permission but merely an informal expression of the view of an officer of the Council, the court could not make an order quashing the 'decision'. Instead, it granted a declaration that the earlier permission did not allow the dismantling and refurbishment of ships.

C. CARRYING OUT AN ACTIVITY WITHOUT ASCERTAINING WHETHER IT NEEDS PERMISSION

8.17 There may be advantages but also considerable disadvantages in going ahead with an activity without ascertaining whether it requires planning permission, bearing in mind the power of the local planning authority to take enforcement action in respect of any breach of planning control. From a cost point of view, it should be recognized that operational development is expensive to carry out and, in the event of an enforcement action being taken, it is expensive to have to reinstate the land to its former condition. A change of use, on the other hand, can often be carried out, and if necessary the earlier use reinstated, at much less cost.

8.18 Another difference however, is with regard to the application of the four-year and 10-year rules. Enforcement action cannot be taken in respect of operational development unless served within four years of it being carried out. As regards the making of a material change of use, however, enforcement action against the contravening development may normally not be taken more than 10 years after it has been carried out (see para 20.33).

8.19 A major, but perhaps unknown factor in this area is not only the question of whether the local planning authority would take enforcement action in respect of the contravening development, but whether if action were taken, it would be upheld by the Secretary of State on appeal. There is no doubt that where there is evidence of a breach of planning control, a local planning authority is duty bound to consider taking enforcement action, but does not have to do so. The 1990 Act provides that an authority 'may' issue an enforcement notice where it 'appears to it that there has been a breach of planning control' and 'it is expedient to do so', having regard to the development plan and other material considerations.

8.20 This is an aspect of planning law which affects not only those in doubt about whether they must make an express application for planning permission, but also those who are in no doubt that it does but who nevertheless develop without it. The position is that before serving an enforcement notice, a local planning authority will often ask the owner to submit an application for planning permission under s 73A of the 1990 Act in respect of development carried out before the date of the application. This procedure enables the local planning authority to publicize the application and listen to the views of third parties on the development which has already taken place, and then to weigh up the strength of opposition to that development before deciding whether to grant or refuse permission. Where the decision taken is to refuse permission, the authority will normally also take a decision to issue an enforcement notice in respect of the development. When an application is made for planning permission for development already carried out, however, the owner may be able to show that the environmental effects of the development are not as bad as might have been anticipated, or the authority may consider that the development already carried out can be made more acceptable by the imposition of conditions and accordingly grant retrospective planning permission subject to those conditions.

8.21 The local planning authority's position has been admirably explained by Schiemann LJ in *R v Leominster DC, ex p Pothecary* [1998] JPL 335 (CA) at 345 where he said:

> It is not rare that buildings are put up without the appropriate planning permission. Sometimes there is no planning objection at all. Sometimes there is an insuperable objection. There are many situations between the two ends of what is a continuum. There are situations where the authority would not have given permission for the development if asked for permission for precisely that which has been built, but the development is not so objectionable that it is reasonable to require it to be pulled down. To require this would be a disproportionate sanction for the breach of the law concerned. That is why Parliament has imposed the requirement of expediency. What weight the authority gives to the existence of the building is a matter for the authority. There are policy reasons ... for not giving much weight to the existence of a building put up without the necessary planning permission, but these will not prevail in every case ... [T]here can ... be cases where the authority can say that, while it would not have granted the permission for that precise building there, it is not expedient to require it to be pulled down. Circumstances vary infinitely.

9

APPLICATIONS FOR PLANNING PERMISSION 1: PRE-SUBMISSION REQUIREMENTS

A. CONTENT AND FORM	9.01	E. TWIN-TRACKING	9.57
B. OUTLINE PLANNING PERMISSION AND PERMISSION IN PRINCIPLE	9.13	F. CONSULTATIONS WITH THE LOCAL PLANNING AUTHORITY	9.59
C. NOTIFICATION OF OWNERS	9.30	G. CONSULTATIONS BY APPLICANT	9.63
D. FEES FOR PLANNING APPLICATIONS	9.50	H. THE PLANNING REGISTER	9.64

A. CONTENT AND FORM

Until fairly recently there was no standard form prescribed for the making of an application for planning permission. Each local planning authority could provide its own form for doing so. This led to a variation in the amount of information required by each authority, and was a concern for large-scale developers, such as volume house builders, where development projects could involve applications being made to many different local planning authorities. **9.01**

This has now been changed by the creation of a Standard Application Form. Section 42 of the Planning and Compulsory Purchase Act 2004 substituted a new s 62 to replace the old s 62 in the 1990 Act. Under the new section the Secretary of State was given the power to prescribe the form for the making of applications for planning permission and related planning matters. These requirements are now to be found in the Town and Country Planning (Development Management Procedure) (England) Order 2015 (the DMPO). **9.02**

In addition to the provision of a standard application form, a further amendment created a requirement for local planning authorities to validate applications before **9.03** beginning to consider them. This validation is intended to clarify the information required by the authority at that stage.

9.04 The Standard Application Form is now the only method of making the vast majority of applications for planning permission.

9.05 The Standard Application Form cannot be used for applications for mining operations or the use of land for mineral-working deposits or for applications for hazardous substance consent under the Planning (Hazardous Substances) Act 1990. Although, in *R (on the application of North Norfolk Planning Watch Ltd) v North Norfolk District Council* [2017] EWHC 3345 (Admin); [2018] PTSR 768 the Deputy Judge found that use of the Standard Application Form for demolition of an unlisted building in a conservation area (which had its own specialist form) did not rob the planning authority of jurisdiction to determine the application, see [66].

9.06 The Standard Application Form can be accessed by the applicant directly, through the Planning Portal via the following link: <http://www.planningportal.gov.uk>, or via a local planning authority link to the planning portal on its website. An application can also be made on a paper version of the form provided by the local planning authority.

9.07 With regard to the validation of planning applications, the first stage is for the local planning authority to ensure that all the necessary supporting information has been correctly provided with the application. The DMPO provides a mandatory list of national requirements for all applications in a form for each application type. In addition, the Standard Application Form will specify additional information required by the local planning authority and shown on a local list on the local planning authority's website. To this end the Ministry of Housing, Communities and Local Government has issued a recommended list of local requirements from which local planning authorities may, if they wish, choose their specific local requirements to be included in their local lists. Then, if the local planning authority is satisfied it has received an application that complies with both the mandatory national requirements specified in the DMPO and its published local list it can proceed to register it as a valid application and to its consideration and determination. In *Newcastle upon Tyne City Council v Secretary of State for Communities and Local Government* [2009] EWHC 3469 (Admin); [2010] JPL 904 it was held that an application was valid if it contained the particulars or evidence required by a local planning authority under s 62(3) and therefore invalid if it did not. It was also held that it was for the authority to decide if particular information is necessary and its view cannot be overturned by the Secretary of State on appeal, though he could decide if the application was otherwise valid. However, s 5 of the Growth and Infrastructure Act 2013 has now placed limits on the information that can be required. A new provision in s 62 requires that information requests must be reasonable having regard to the nature and scale of the proposed development. It must also be reasonable to think that the subject matter of the information will be material to the determination of the application.

9.08 Other changes made by the 2004 Act include a provision for a development order to require applications for planning permission for such development as is specified in the order to be accompanied by such of the following as specified below:

(a) a statement about the design principles and concepts that have been applied to the development;
(b) a statement about how issues relating to access to the development have been dealt with.

9.09 Article 9 of the DMPO now provides that a design and access statement must accompany most planning applications, whether they be for outline planning permission or for full planning permission. They are not required, however, for certain applications for planning permission including for:

- development of land without compliance with conditions previously attached made pursuant to s 73 of the 1990 Act;
- a material change in the use of land or buildings;
- engineering or mining operations;
- development of an existing dwellinghouse, or development within the curtilage of a dwellinghouse for any purpose incidental to the enjoyment of the dwellinghouse, where no part of that dwellinghouse or curtilage is within a designated area. 'Designated area' means a National Park, site of special scientific interest, conservation area, Area of Outstanding Natural Beauty, World Heritage Site, and the Broads.

According to Art 9(3) of the DMPO, a design and access statement shall:

(a) explain the design principles and concepts that have been applied to the development;
(b) demonstrate the steps taken to appraise the context of the development and how the design of the development takes that context into account;
(c) explain the policy adopted as to access, and how policies relating to access in relevant local development documents have been taken into account;
(d) state what, if any, consultation has been undertaken on issues relating to access to the development and what account has been taken of the outcome of any such consultation; and
(e) explain how any specific issues which might affect access to the development have been addressed.

9.10 The design and access statement is a short report to accompany and support a planning application to illustrate the process that has led to the development proposal, and to explain and justify the proposal in a structured way. According to the PPG (14-029-20140306) the statement should 'provide a framework for applicants to explain how the proposed development is a suitable response to the site and its setting, and demonstrate that it can be adequately accessed by prospective users. Design and Access Statements can aid decision-making by enabling local planning authorities and third parties to better understand the analysis that has underpinned the design of a development proposal'. They should also allow local communities, access groups, amenity groups, and other stakeholders to involve themselves more directly in the planning process without needing to interpret plans that can be technical and confusing. In doing so, it should also help to increase certainty for people affected by development proposals and improve trust between communities, developers, and planners.

9.11 Lastly, the 2004 Act introduced a new s 327A into the 1990 Act. This provides that the local planning authority must not entertain an application if it fails to comply with any provision in the law which imposes a requirement as to the form or manner in which an application is made; or the form or content of any document or other matter which accompanies the application. This provision could have the consequence that the distinction between mandatory and directory requirement no longer applies and any failure would make the application invalid. However, the case law has re-stated the discretion on the part of the Court not to quash a permission where the application failed to comply with the requirements of the DMPO, notwithstanding s 327A. Dove J summarized the position in *Maximus Networks Ltd v Secretary of State for Communities and Local Government* [2018] EWHC 1933 (Admin) at [24]:

> Whether as part of an application for judicial review or, as here, as part of an application under section 288 of the 1990 Act, the court will always retain a discretion as to whether or not to grant relief. Section 327A of the 1990 Act makes clear that the local planning authority has no discretion to waive or overlook failures to comply with the requirements provided by the legislation for the proper formulation of an application. By implication it makes clear that if a local planning authority were to do so that would amount to an error of law justifying the court's intervention. However, the court will always retain a residual discretion as to whether or not to grant relief in the form of quashing the planning permission, a discretion which will be exercised bearing in mind a wide range of considerations.

9.12 The amendments made by the 2004 Act provide like powers to prescribe the form of applications for consents required under tree preservation orders, for the display of advertisements, and for work to listed buildings and in conservation areas.

B. OUTLINE PLANNING PERMISSION AND PERMISSION IN PRINCIPLE

9.13 Where the permission sought is for the erection of a building, and the applicant so desires, an application may be made for 'outline planning permission'. An application for outline planning permission can only be made where the permission sought is for the erection of a building. It is not available for other forms of development. However, it seems that the outline procedure may properly be used to cover operational development carried out on what might be called an ancillary basis along with the construction of a building. For example, an application for outline planning permission for a supermarket might include development of a car park to serve the development. The purpose in allowing an application for outline planning permission to be made is that it gives a prospective developer the opportunity to find out at an early stage, and before he has incurred substantial cost, whether or not a proposal is likely to be approved by the local planning authority. When such an application is made the applicant need not submit details of any proposed 'reserved matters' at this stage.

An *application* for outline planning permission may result in the *grant* of outline planning permission (as opposed to what is often referred to as 'full' planning permission). An outline planning permission is defined in Art 2 of the DMPO to mean: **9.14**

> ... planning permission for the erection of a building, subject to a condition requiring the subsequent approval of the local planning authority with respect to one or more reserved matters ...

Reserved matters in relation to an outline planning permission, or an application for such permission means: any of the following matters in respect of which details have not been given in the application:

(a) access;
(b) appearance;
(c) landscaping;
(d) layout; and
(e) scale.

Article 2(1) of the DMPO contains definitions of each of the above reserved matters in the following terms: **9.15**

— *access*—the accessibility to and within the site, for vehicles, cycles, and pedestrians in terms of the positioning and treatment of access and circulation routes and how these fit into the surrounding access network;
— *appearance*—the aspects of a building or place within the development which determine the visual impression the building or place makes, including the external built form of the development, its architecture, materials, decoration, lighting, colour, and texture;
— *landscaping*—the treatment of land (other than buildings) for the purpose of enhancing or protecting the amenities of the site and the area in which it is situated and includes screening by fences, walls, or other means, earthworks, the laying out or provision of gardens, courts or squares, water features, sculpture, or public art, and the provision of other amenity features;

— *layout*—the way in which buildings, routes, and open spaces within the development are provided, situated, and orientated in relation to each other and to buildings and spaces outside the development; and
— *scale*—the height, width, and length of each building proposed within the development in relation to its surroundings.

In *MMF (UK) Ltd v Secretary of State for Communities and Local Government* [2010] EWHC 3686 (Admin); [2011] JPL 1067 it was held by the High Court that an Inspector had erred in law in an appeal against a refusal to grant approval for reserved matters by confusing 'Scale' with 'Appearance'. It was held that 'Scale' and 'Appearance' were concerned with two different aspects of a building. The size of a building was concerned with relationship with other buildings and was a question of scale. How the building was designed within that overall shape concerned its appearance. That could involve a consideration of its relationship with other buildings, but if so, it was applying a different criterion to one of scale.

9.16 The requirements of submission for an outline application have been scaled back in the 2015 Order, with only minimal requirements now at Art 5. However, the PPG (14-034-20140306) explains that the following is required:

> information about the proposed use or uses, and the amount of development proposed for each use, is necessary to allow consideration of an application for outline planning permission.

No development may commence until all reserved matters have been approved. It is well-settled case law that the grant of outline permission constitutes a commitment by the local planning authority to the principle of the development, thus preventing the authority from refusing to approve any reserved matter on grounds which go to the principle of the development (*Lewis Thirkwell v Secretary of State for the Environment* [1978] JPL 844). In granting outline planning permission, therefore, the local planning authority has committed itself to the form of development which is comprised in the permission subject only to the subsequent approval of those specified reserved matters. A local planning authority, however, may consider that it is unable to determine an application for outline planning permission independently of any reserved matters. This view is frequently taken with regard to applications for the erection of buildings in conservation areas. In such cases, the local planning authority can require the applicant to submit further details with regard to all the reserved matters or any of them before proceeding to consider the development proposal.

9.17 Although outline planning permission is a permission granted subject to a condition requiring approval of reserved matters, it was held in *R v Newbury DC, ex p Stevens* (1992) 65 P & CR 438 that, contrary to previous doubts, the authority had the power under s 78 of the 1990 Act to impose a condition on the grant of approval of a reserved matter, even though that aspect had not been mentioned in the outline permission, so long as the condition did not derogate from the outline permission already granted. Accordingly, it would be within the powers of a local planning authority, for example, to remove permitted development rights at the reserved matters stage.

9.18 The courts have had to consider several matters relating to the scope and effect of outline planning permissions. In *R v Newbury DC and Newbury and District Agricultural Society, ex p Chievely Parish Council* [1999] PLCR 51, the Court of Appeal held it to be unlawful for a local planning authority to grant outline planning permission with a reserved matters condition where details of the reserved matters had already been given in the outline application. Furthermore, the court went on to consider whether (as had been suggested in the High Court) density was a reserved matter, on the ground that, 'external appearance', 'means of access', or 'landscaping' were not appropriate to govern the scale of development. The court decided that if a local planning authority wished to limit, at the outline stage, the scale of the development, it must do so by an appropriate condition. So too, an outline application which specifies the floor area commits the applicant to development on that scale, subject to minimal changes and to such adjustments as can reasonably be attributed to siting, design, and external appearance.

9.19 One question the courts have had to consider is what considerations are relevant in determining an application for approval of reserved matters. In *McClean Homes (East Anglia) Ltd v Secretary of State for the Environment, Transport, and the Regions and Chelmsford BC* [1999] PLCR 372, the Deputy Judge, Mr George Bartlett QC, put it this way:

> In such cases the principle of the development is established by the grant of outline planning permission, so that the parties, applicant and planning authority, have moved from the question of whether any development of the type proposed may be acceptable to the question of the form that the development should take. That there is at least one such form that is acceptable is implicit in the grant of planning permission.

It is also implicit, therefore, that some forms of development will not be acceptable. Whether any precise form of development is acceptable or non-acceptable at the reserved matters stage must, of course, depend upon the provisions of the current development plan and any other material considerations. Although the courts do not appear so far to have expressly considered the question, material considerations would include the provisions of any development plan which has been amended since the outline planning permission was granted, together with those other material considerations existing at the time the application for approval of reserved matters is determined. This is subject, however, to the overriding requirement that the consideration of any new policies at the detailed application stage does not enable the local planning authority to derogate from the principle of the development already established by the grant of outline permission.

9.20 In *R (Redrow Homes Ltd) v First Secretary of State and South Gloucestershire Council* [2003] EWHC 304 (Admin) the Secretary of State, in determining an appeal on an application for approval of reserved matters, had sought to impose a condition that the site 'shall be used by public service vehicles only'. The High Court quashed the determination because the condition would have the effect of modifying the grant of outline planning permission which had imposed no restriction as to the particular types of traffic able to use the access.

9.21 In *R (on the application of Harvey) v Mendip District Council* [2017] EWCA Civ 1784; [2018] JPL 419 the Court of Appeal held that reservation of 'scale' at the outline stage would not enable the local authority a discretion to restrict the number of units at the reserved matters stage, see: Sales LJ at [41].

9.22 It should also be borne in mind that the definition of the words 'reserved matters' is exclusive and does not include any other matters. Thus, a condition in an outline planning permission which provides for subsequent approval by the local planning authority of mitigation measures or the substitution of other land, is not a reserved matter.

9.23 The Government has long accepted that the use of outline planning permission has significant faults. In particular it allows the 'redlining' on a map of an area or development site for a particular use or uses with few details of the development being shown. In such circumstances local communities are given little opportunity to influence the details of the proposed development. For developers too, there is the problem that if an environmental impact assessment is required for the development, an outline planning permission may not provide sufficient detail to comply with the relevant regulations (see Chapter 12).

9.24 In the consultation paper, *Delivering a Fundamental Change*, published in December 2001, the Government floated the idea of replacing outline planning permissions with a system whereby a developer might obtain a certificate or a statement of development principles from the local planning authority that it has the authority's agreement to work up a detailed scheme against parameters determined by the agreement. Any formal application would subsequently be submitted in detail and the existence of the certificate would weigh heavily in the determination of planning permission. This proposal was contained in the Planning and Compulsory Purchase Bill but was dropped because of opposition from the building industry.

9.25 The Housing and Planning Act 2016 introduced a new concept of 'permission in principle' by inserting new ss 58A and 59A into the Town and Country Planning Act 1990. This provides for a new route for obtaining planning permission for 'housing-led' development which separates the principle of development from technical details consent.

9.26 New s 14A of the Planning and Compulsory Purchase Act 2004 empowers the Secretary of State to require (by subordinate legislation) local authorities to maintain a register of land of a prescribed description. The Secretary of State has prescribed the land to be maintained on the register by the Town and Country Planning (Brownfield Land Register) Regulations 2017 (SI 2017/403).

9.27 Permission in principle can be obtained either by the local planning authority granting permission in principle upon a valid application, on which see: Town and Country Planning (Permission in Principle) Order 2017 (SI 2017/1309). Alternatively, permission in principle may be granted by the planning authority entering a site upon Part 2 of its Brownfield Register.

9.28 Following a grant of permission in principle, the site must receive a grant of technical details consent before development can proceed. The granting of technical details consent has the effect of granting planning permission for the development. Technical details consent can be obtained following submission of a valid application to the local planning authority. An application for technical details consent must be in accordance with the permission in principle that is specified by the applicant.

9.29 There are certain types of land and development for which permission in principle cannot be granted, these are set out at Art 5B of the Permission in Principle Order (above) and regs 4 and 14 of the Brownfield Register Regulations (above). These exclusions include EIA development and the winning and working of minerals. Detailed guidance on the permission in (principle and technical details regime is available in the PPG (58-049-20180615 onwards).

C. NOTIFICATION OF OWNERS

9.30 It is sometimes said that anyone can make an application for planning permission. If this be so, the prospect that a beggar might apply for planning permission for the redevelopment of land be it in Bermondsey or Belgravia (if he can afford the fee to do so) is unlikely to raise much enthusiasm with the local planning authority for the area. The consideration of applications for planning permission is a time-consuming business for local planning authorities. Nevertheless, applications for planning permission have been made by persons with little capacity to implement the permission should it be granted. In 1980, the British Airports Authority, which owned a number of airports in England, made an application for outline planning permission to extend the airport capacity of Stansted Airport. The Town and Country Planning Association's view was that the expansion of airport capacity in the South East would be better accommodated by building a new airport at Maplin Sands in Essex. In order that consideration should be given to this at the same time as the proposed development at Stansted, the Association applied for planning permission (which was subsequently withdrawn) for that development. Furthermore, the local authority within whose area Stansted was located, the Uttlesford District Council, thought that a better solution to the expansion of Stansted was an expansion of the terminal facilities at London Heathrow Airport. Accordingly, the District Council submitted an application to the local planning authority for the Heathrow area for the building of a fifth passenger terminal complex at the airport. Both that application and the application submitted by the British Airports Authority were then called in by the Secretary of State for his own decision and treated for all practical purposes as one.

9.31 Although it is probably incorrect to say that anyone can apply for planning permission, it is not necessary that the applicant should have any present interest in the land that is the subject of the application. In *Hanily v Minister of Local Government and Planning* [1952] 2 QB 444, where a third party had applied for and been granted planning permission to develop land without the knowledge of the owner of the land, the High Court thought that anybody who genuinely hoped to acquire an interest in the land could properly apply for planning permission.

9.32 Whatever the applicant's position, however, if he is not the owner of an interest in every part of the land to which the application relates, he has been required since 1962 to give notice of the application to the holders of certain interests in the land.

9.33 Under s 65 of the 1990 Act and Art 13 of the DMPO it is provided that:
(1) … an applicant for planning permission shall give requisite notice of the application to any person (other than the applicant) who on the prescribed date is an owner of the land to which the application relates, or a tenant—
(a) by serving the notice on every such person whose name and address is known to him; and
(b) where he has taken reasonable steps to ascertain the names and addresses of every such person, but has been unable to do so, by local advertisement after the prescribed date.

9.34 The 'prescribed date' under the article is defined as being 'the day 21 days before the date of the application', and the 'requisite notice' means 'notice in the appropriate form as set out in Sch 2 to the Order'.

9.35 Under the Order, the applicant or the person applying on his behalf is required to serve on an owner or tenant of any land to which the application relates, notice that he is applying to the local planning authority for planning permission for development, details of which must be specified. The notice must also inform the owner of the land or tenant, that if he wishes to do so he may make representations about the application to the local planning authority within 21 days of service of the notice.

9.36 For the purpose of these provisions the term 'owner' means the estate owner in respect of the fee simple or a leasehold interest the unexpired term of which is not less than seven years. Where a leasehold interest exists in land, therefore, an applicant who owns the freehold interest in the land to which the application relates will not be required to give specific notice to the owner of any leasehold interests with less than seven years to run. If, on the other hand, the applicant is himself the owner of a leasehold interest then, irrespective of the length of his term, he must give specific notice of his application to the freeholder.

9.37 In addition, if any of the land to which the application relates is or forms part of an agricultural holding, specific notice must be given to the tenant thereof, irrespective of the length of his interest. The purpose in giving notice of an application to the tenant of an agricultural holding, whatever his interest, is that the tenant may lose his security of tenure if the landlord can show that he wishes to put the land to some non-agricultural use.

9.38 The effect of the Order is to require applicants not only to notify owners and agricultural tenants of a planning application they intend to submit in relation to the owner's or tenant's land, but also requires the applicant to certify (see Art 14), in a form published by the Secretary of State or in a form substantially to the like effect, that the notification requirements in Art 13 have been satisfied. The Standard Application Form sets out four possible types of certificate. The four certificates, only one of which is required to be submitted with the application for planning permission, are as follows.

9.39 *Certificate A* This certificate states that on the day 21 days before the date of the accompanying application nobody, except the applicant, was the owner (as earlier defined) of any part of the land to which the application relates.

Certificate B This certificate states that the applicant has given the requisite notice to everyone else who, on the day 21 days before the date of the accompanying application, was the owner (as earlier defined) of any part of the land to which the application relates. The certificate further requires the applicant to list the owners to whom notice has been given, the address at which notice was served and the date of service.

Certificate C This certificate applies where the applicant is able to discover and give notice to some but not *all* persons owning an interest in the land. It states that the applicant is unable to issue certificate A or B; also that the applicant has given the requisite notice to persons (who must be specified) who on the day 21 days before the date of the application were owners (as earlier defined) to which the application relates.

As well as listing the names of owners notified, along with their addresses at which they were served and the date notice was served, the certificate must also state that the applicant has taken all reasonable steps open to him (which must be specified) to find out the names and addresses of the *other* owners of the land or of a part of it, but that he has been unable to do so. The steps taken must include publication in a newspaper circulating in the locality in which the land is situated.

Certificate D This certificate applies where the applicant is unable to discover the names of *any* of the persons owning an interest in the land. It states that the owner is unable to give certificate A; also that he has taken the reasonable steps open to him (which must be specified and include publication of notice of the application in a newspaper circulating in the locality), to find out the names and addresses of everyone else who on the day 21 days before the date of the application was the owner (as earlier defined) of any part of the land to which the application relates, but that he has been unable to do so.

9.40 It should be noted that a further certificate must be given (in addition to certificates A to D) stating either that none of the land to which the application relates is, or is part of, an agricultural holding or that the applicant has given the requisite notice to every person who on the day 21 days before the date of the application was a tenant of an agricultural holding on all or part of the land to which the application relates.

9.41 The above procedures also apply to any appeal made to the Secretary of State under s 78 of the 1990 Act. Furthermore, under the Order, the above procedures apply to applications for planning permission for development consisting of the winning and working of minerals, but with some variations.

9.42 There is no point in giving an owner notice of an application to develop land in which he has an interest, unless he is also given the opportunity to make representations with regard to the development proposed. Hence, Art 33(1)(b) of the Order provides that where a certificate contains a statement that notice of the application has been given to another, the local planning authority shall take in account representations made within 21 days of the date when notice was given.

9.43 It should be noted that, other than for certificate A, the procedure merely requires the applicant to state in a certificate that notice of the application has been given to the appropriate persons. Under the Order, authorities are required to notify their decisions to the applicants, but apart from notifying owners and agricultural tenants who have made representations on any application for planning permission affecting their land, there is no statutory requirement for authorities to notify their decision to other parties. The system does not guarantee that the applicant has actually given notice and, because acknowledgment of the authority's decision is restricted, the owner of an interest in the land may remain unaware that an application has been made. In practice it is known that the certificate procedure does not work particularly well, particularly where applications are submitted by an agent on behalf of the applicant.

9.44 It seems that non-compliance with these provisions may have a variable effect. Section 65(6) provides that if a person issues a certificate which purports to comply with any requirements imposed by virtue of the section and contains a statement which he knows to be false or misleading in a material particular—or recklessly issues a certificate which purports to comply with any such requirement and contains a statement which is false or misleading in a material particular—he shall have committed an offence and be liable on summary conviction to a fine not exceeding level 5 on the standard scale. Of more importance than any criminal sanction, however, is the effect of a certificate containing a false, misleading, or inaccurate statement on any planning permission which has been granted. In *R v Bradford-on-Avon UDC, ex p Boulton* [1964] 1 WLR 1136, an application was made for an order of *certiorari* to quash a grant of planning permission for residential development. A certificate which had been signed on behalf of the applicant, stated that he was the owner of the fee simple in the land. In fact, the applicant was not the owner of the fee simple. He had been negotiating for the purchase of the land from the owner, who was in fact privy to the application. Refusing to grant the order sought, the Divisional Court held that, on the true construction of the statutory provisions, a planning authority had jurisdiction to entertain an application for planning permission if it was accompanied by a genuine certificate in the approved terms signed by the applicant, and that a factual error in the certificates did not deprive the authority of that jurisdiction.

9.45 One factor which seemed to influence the decision was that a grant of planning permission runs with the land and is relied on by subsequent purchasers. If a purchaser was to be required to investigate whether the certificate submitted with the application was correct in its factual averments before being able to rely on the grant, the conveyancing difficulties would be formidable.

9.46 Following the *Bradford-on-Avon* case it was generally recognized, though with some reluctance, that the grant of planning permission would survive any factual error in the content of a certificate, at least as long as there was no actual dishonesty. The later case of *Main v Swansea City Council* [1985] JPL 558, however, has done much to clarify the position. In this case outline planning permission had been granted for residential development. The certificate which had accompanied the application stated that notice of the application had been given to all other owners of land, namely, the City Council. It transpired that the land the subject of the application also included land owned by a person whose identity was unknown, and that the certificate did not specify that notice of the development had been published in a local newspaper circulating in the locality as was required. The appropriate certificate was thus certificate C, not B which had been submitted. The applicant had applied for judicial review to quash the grant of planning permission. The Court of Appeal held that in considering the failure of the applicant to comply with the statutory requirements, one had to look not only at the nature of the failure, but also at such matters as the identity of the applicant for relief, the lapse of time before proceedings were taken, and the effect on other parties and on the public. In this case the court had no doubt that the defect in the certificates was sufficient to enable it to strike down the subsequent grant of planning permission in certain circumstances, as where, for example, a prompt application had been made by the owner of the non-council owned land. Although the defects were not such as to render the grant a nullity, the court held that it had discretion whether to grant the relief sought. In refusing to exercise that discretion in favour of the applicant, the court took into account the fact that, throughout the period between the grant of the outline permission and the approval of reserved matters (over three years), the applicant had not objected; that the scheme which had been approved did not involve the development of the land not owned by the City Council; and that the Secretary of State in full knowledge of the position had not sought relief. It was too late, therefore, for the applicant to obtain the necessary relief to quash the permission and with it the subsequent approval of reserved matters.

9.47 Although the courts are now able, in the exercise of their discretion, to give relief to a claimant where there is an error in the certificate submitted, in an appropriate case a remedy in private law may be available.

9.48 In *English v Dedham Vale Properties Ltd* [1978] 1 WLR 93, the prospective purchaser of a parcel of land submitted an application for planning permission to develop the land in the vendors' names and without their authority. The application, which was subsequently granted, was signed by an employee of the prospective purchaser stating himself to be the vendors' agent. The accompanying certificate described the applicants (ie the vendors) as the estate owners in fee simple of the land to which the application related. The certificate would in fact have been accurate had it been made with the vendors' authority. Without that authority, however, the application should have been accompanied by a certificate stating that the vendors had been given notice of the making of the application.

9.49 In making the application, the purchaser's employee had asked that the decision notice be sent to him at the purchaser's address. Hence the vendors remained ignorant of the application for planning permission and of its subsequent grant and, whilst still unaware, conveyed the land in question to the purchaser for a price lower than they would have done had they known the true position. As a result, the surviving vendor (one having died) brought an action against the purchaser claiming, inter alia, damages for fraudulent misrepresentation in regard to the prospects of obtaining planning permission, and an account of the profits which had accrued to the purchasers as a result of the grant. In the Chancery Division it was held by Slade J that whilst there had not been any misrepresentation by the purchaser as to the prospect of obtaining planning permission and he was therefore absolved from any charge of fraud, he was accountable to the vendors for the profit he had received as a result of making the planning application. This was because, in relation to the application, he had assumed the character of self-appointed agent of the vendors, thereby placing himself in a fiduciary relationship with them; and he had failed to disclose to them the fact that the application had been made. Slade J also held that where, during the course of negotiations for a contract for the sale and purchase of a property, the proposed purchaser, in the name of and purportedly as agent for the vendor but without the vendor's consent or authority, took some action in regard to the property such as making a planning application, which, if it had been disclosed to the vendor might reasonably have been likely to influence him in deciding whether or not to conclude a contract, a fiduciary relationship arose between the two parties which gave rise to a duty on the purchaser to disclose to the vendor before the conclusion of the contract what he had done as the vendor's purported agent; and, in the event of non-disclosure, the purchaser was liable to account to the vendor for any profit he made in the course of the purported agency, unless the vendor had consented to his retaining the profit.

D. FEES FOR PLANNING APPLICATIONS

Under s 303 of the 1990 Act, the Secretary of State may make regulations for the payment of a fee to local planning authorities in respect of applications made to them for any permission, consent, approval, determination, or certificate. **9.50**

The current regulations are the Town and Country Planning (Fees for Applications, Deemed Applications and Site Visits) (England) Regulations 2012 (SI 2012/2920), as recently amended. The latest amendment was in 2017. Guidance on the fees regime is set out in the PPG (22-001-20180615 onwards). The regime covers a wide range of activity and provides, inter alia, for fees to be payable where an application is made for planning permission, for a certificate of lawful use or development, for the approval of reserved matters, for consent to the display of advertisements, and on a deemed application for planning permission which arises when an appeal is made against an enforcement notice. **9.51**

The fees charged are based on broad categories of development and are designed to relate the fee to the approximate cost of dealing with applications for the different kinds of development. These costs cover the whole development control process from the validation of the application and its registration, through to the issue of the decision letter. **9.52**

Before the 2004 Act, the power of the Secretary of State to prescribe a fee payable to a local planning authority related only to an authority's handling of planning applications. The Planning and Compulsory Purchase Act 2004 amended the provision to widen the scope of the Secretary of State's power to enable him to provide for the payment of charges and fees relating to any other function of local planning authorities under the 1990 Act, the Planning (Listed Building and Conservation Areas) Act 1990, and the Planning (Hazardous Substances) Act 1990. **9.53**

9.54 The Secretary of State has used this increased power to charge fees to require them to be paid in respect of site visits by local planning authorities to mining and landfill sites, in order to monitor compliance with conditions in planning permissions to which they are subject.

9.55 The new (substituted) subsection (2) of s 303 now enables the appropriate authority (being the Secretary of State in England or the Welsh Ministers in Wales) to make provision in regulations for the whole of the fee which is payable when an applicant appeals under s 177(5) of the 1990 Act against an enforcement notice to be paid to either the local planning authority, the appropriate authority, or both the local planning authority and the appropriate authority.

9.56 The Planning Act 2008 also inserted into the Town and Country Planning Act 1990 a new power which allows the Secretary of State to make provision, by way of regulations, for the payment of a fee for appeals made under the Town and Country Planning Act 1990 and the Planning (Listed Building and Conservation Areas) Act 1990. The fee is to be payable by the appellant and the regulations may set out, in particular, when the fee should be paid, how the fee should be calculated and by whom, the circumstances under which an appeal fee may be refunded, and the effect of either paying or not paying the fee.

E. TWIN-TRACKING

9.57 With some of the more important development proposals, it was not uncommon for a developer to submit two identical or near identical applications for planning permission for the same development. The purpose of this was that if the local planning authority has not determined either application for planning permission within the prescribed period of eight weeks for doing so, the developer could exercise his right to appeal to the Secretary of State against non-determination of one of the applications. The authority could then determine that other application and, if refused, the developer knew that he had a place in the appeal queue in respect of the earlier application. It allowed the authority and developer to continue to negotiate over the second application. If the authority subsequently granted planning permission for the development on the second application, the developer could then withdraw his appeal against non-determination of the first.

9.58 The use of twin-tracking by developers has now been much reduced by giving local planning authorities power to refuse to determine applications for planning permission where the application is intended to put pressure on the authority to grant it. This is dealt with in Chapter 10.

F. CONSULTATIONS WITH THE LOCAL PLANNING AUTHORITY

9.59 It is common practice to hold discussions with the local planning authority before formally submitting an application for planning permission. Paragraph 39 NPPF provides that

> Early engagement has significant potential to improve the efficiency and effectiveness of the planning application system for all parties. Good quality pre-application discussion enables better coordination between public and private resources and improved outcomes for the community.

The value of this is that, in the course of such discussions, proposals can be adapted to ensure that they better reflect community aspirations and that applications are complete and address all the relevant issues. Local planning authorities and applicants should, it is considered, take a positive attitude towards early engagement in pre-application discussions so that formal applications can be dealt with in a more certain and speedy manner and the quality of decisions can be better assured.

9.60 The House of Lords had held that where pre-planning application discussions are held with the local planning authority, the authority had no power to make a charge for so doing, see: *R v Richmond upon Thames LBC, ex p McCarthy & Stone (Developments) Ltd* [1992] 2 AC 48.

9.61 The effect of this decision has now been reversed. Section 98 of the Local Government Act 2003 gives local authorities the power to charge for pre-planning application consultations.

9.62 If informal planning advice is given to a member of the public by officers of a local planning authority, no general duty of care exists to make the authority liable to the person advised if the advice is negligent. In *Tidman v Reading BC* [1994] 3 PLR 72, the High Court dismissed an action brought by a member of the public who claimed he had been given negligent advice as to the need for planning permission for land he was trying to sell and had not been advised on the steps he could take to clarify the position. Negligent advice by a local planning authority may, however, be the subject of a complaint to the Local Government Ombudsman alleging maladministration. Many such complaints have succeeded and have resulted in authorities making ex gratia payments to those affected.

G. CONSULTATIONS BY APPLICANT

9.63 Section 122 Localism Act 2011 breaks new ground by requiring, when implemented by development order, prospective developers to consult local communities before submitting applications for certain developments. A new s 61W is inserted into the Town and Country Planning Act 1990 which requires any person who intends to apply for planning permission for development of a prescribed description first to consult the local community and any specified persons, so that they may collaborate or comment. The prospective developer must have regard to any advice that the local planning authority may have provided. A new s 61X then requires the developer to have regard to any comments or responses generated by the consultation undertaken in accordance with s 61W, when deciding whether to make any changes to their proposals before submitting their planning applications. A new s 61Y enables the Secretary of State to set out further provisions as to how the consultation required under s 61W should be undertaken in practice. Subsection (2) of s 1 22 amends s 62 of the Town and Country Planning Act 1990 so that an account of the consultation undertaken in accordance with s 61W must accompany any planning application for development to which the new duty applies, in order to make it valid.

H. THE PLANNING REGISTER

9.64 Under s 69 of the 1990 Act, every local planning authority must keep in such manner as may be prescribed by development order, a register containing such information as may be prescribed with respect to applications for planning permission made to the authority. The register must be kept available for inspection by members of the public at all reasonable hours.

9.65 Under Art 40 of the DMPO, the register of applications for planning permission is to be kept in two parts. Part 1 must contain a copy of every application for planning permission and of any application for approval of reserved matters submitted to the authority and not finally disposed of, together with copies of plans and drawings submitted with them. Part 2 must contain in respect of every application for planning permission:

(a) a copy (which may be photographic or in electronic form) of the application and of plans and drawings submitted in relation thereto;
(b) particulars of any direction given under the Act or the Order in respect of the application;
(c) the decision (if any) of the local planning authority in respect of the application, including details of any conditions subject to which permission was granted, the date of such decision, and the name of the local planning authority;
(d) the reference number, the date, and effect of any decision of the Secretary of State in respect of the application, whether on appeal or on a reference under s 77 of the 1990 Act; and
(e) the date of any subsequent approval (whether approval of reserved matters or any other approval required) given in relation to the application;

(f) & (g) a copy (which may be photographic or in electronic form) of any planning obligation or s 278 agreement entered into in connection with any decision in respect of the application or taken into account when the decision was made;
(g) particulars of any modification to or discharge of any planning obligation or s 278 agreement included in the register in accordance with (f) and (g).

Other registers keep details of such matters as environmental impact assessment statements, simplified planning zone schemes, enforcement notices, and stop notices. Under the 1990 Act, the registers must be kept open for public inspection at all reasonable times. **9.66**

10

APPLICATIONS FOR PLANNING PERMISSION 2: PROCEDURE ON RECEIPT OF APPLICATIONS BY THE LOCAL PLANNING AUTHORITY

A. ACKNOWLEDGMENT OF RECEIPT OF APPLICATION	10.01	E. CONSULTATION	10.48
B. POWER TO DECLINE TO DETERMINE APPLICATIONS	10.10	F. DEVELOPMENT NOT IN ACCORDANCE WITH THE PROVISIONS OF THE DEVELOPMENT PLAN	10.56
C. PUBLICITY FOR PLANNING APPLICATIONS	10.26	G. AMENDMENT OF APPLICATIONS	10.61
D. NOTIFICATION REQUIREMENTS	10.41		

A. ACKNOWLEDGMENT OF RECEIPT OF APPLICATION

10.01 An application for planning permission is made to the authority with responsibility for determining the application. In the case of a non-metropolitan area with a two-tier division of planning responsibility, most applications fall to be determined by the district planning authority for the area in which the land is situated. If the application relates to a county matter, application must be made to the county planning authority for the area. In those areas where the local planning authority is a unitary authority, all applications are made to the unitary authority for the area. Section 1 of the Growth and Infrastructure Act 2013 has also provided applicants with the option of applying to the Secretary of State if a council has been designated as not performing adequately in determining applications.

10.02 On receipt of the application, the local planning authority is required to validate the application and then to send an acknowledgment to the applicant in the terms (or substantially in the terms) set out in Sch 1 to the Development Management Procedure Order (DMPO or the Order). A requirement of Art 34 of the Order is that the authority shall notify the applicant of its decision on the application within eight weeks from the date on which the application was received. Where the application relates to major development (see para 10.32) the eight-week period is extended to 13 weeks. Furthermore, where the development requires environmental impact assessment, the period is 16 weeks. All of these periods can be extended where agreed in writing between the applicant and the local planning authority. If notice of the decision has not been given by the appropriate date, the applicant is entitled to treat the non-determination as a refusal of the application and may appeal to the Secretary of State in accordance with s 78 of the 1990 Act within a further period of six months.

10.03 The precise effect of the provision that the authority shall give notice of its decision within the prescribed period was considered by the Court of Appeal in *James v Secretary of State for Wales* [1966] 1 WLR 135. Under the special provisions of the Caravan Sites and Control of Development Act 1960, where express planning permission for the use of land as a caravan site had not previously been given, an application for a site licence under the Act also operated as an application for planning permission. Then if, within six months of the application having been made, express planning permission had not been given, permission for the use of the land as a caravan site was deemed to have been given.

10.04 James claimed that by virtue of these provisions he had deemed permission for the use of his land as a caravan site without restriction. The authority maintained, however, that an express planning permission for a restricted number of caravans had previously been granted, so that James could not claim the benefit for any larger number. James thereupon contended, but unsuccessfully, that since the express planning permission had not been given within two months of the application, the permission was, therefore, null and void. In his judgment, which examined the effect of the requirement to give notice of the decision within the prescribed period, Lord Denning MR said:

> The grant or refusal of permission after two months is not void, but at most voidable. If a planning authority allow more than two months to go by, and then *give* permission, with or without conditions, the permission is good. At any rate it is good, if it is accepted and acted upon. Or if an appeal is made against it, for it is then too late to avoid it. If a planning authority allow more than two months to go by, and then *refuse* permission, the party aggrieved can appeal against the refusal. Alternatively he can treat the failure to determine within two months as a refusal and appeal on that ground. If he does not appeal, he cannot afterwards say that the grant or refusal was bad because it was made after the two months.

10.05 The two-month period mentioned by Lord Denning in the *James* case has now been reduced to the eight weeks mentioned earlier. It is a decision of some importance. Unless the applicant has appealed against non-determination of the planning application, it enables the local planning authority to grant a valid planning permission after the eight-week period has expired; but it also gives the applicant the option of either implementing the permission or appealing against any conditions which it might contain. If planning permission is refused after the eight-week period, the applicant may appeal against the refusal. If no decision has been given by the end of the period of eight weeks, the applicant can appeal against non-determination of his application under s 78 of the 1990 Act. If he does so, this deprives the authority of the power to take a decision upon it.

10.06 Local planning authorities have for many years determined about 65 per cent of applications for planning permission within the statutory eight-week period. This percentage is now beginning to rise. One of many reasons why they fail to determine more within that period is the obligation placed upon them to consult with or notify others with regard to different kinds of application.

10.07 As was said in 10.05 above, when a local planning authority fails to determine an application for planning permission within the prescribed period, the applicant may appeal to the Secretary of State against non-determination. The general position is that once the appeal has been made, the local planning authority loses jurisdiction to determine the application, despite the fact that the authority might subsequently be in a position to do so itself.

10.08 The Planning and Compulsory Purchase Act 2004 made a limited amendment to this position by inserting a new s 78A in the 1990 Act. The purpose of this new section, when fully implemented, will be to allow a short additional period of time (which is to be prescribed by development order) in which the local planning authority can still issue a decision even though an appeal against non-determination has been made. During that short period following the lodging of the appeal, a local planning authority and the Secretary of State will both have jurisdiction to determine the application. If the local planning authority refuses planning permission, the appeal against non-determination becomes an appeal against refusal. In such a case the Secretary of State must give the appellant the opportunity to revise the grounds of appeal and to change any option he has chosen relating to the procedure on appeal. If the authority grants permission subject to conditions, the applicant may proceed with the appeal against the grant of planning permission subject to conditions or revise the grounds of appeal. The period of dual jurisdiction when set is likely to be two to three weeks after the eight-week deadline.

10.09 Section 50 also provides for a similar provision to be inserted as s 20A in the Planning (Listed Buildings and Conservation Areas) Act 1990.

B. POWER TO DECLINE TO DETERMINE APPLICATIONS

Power to decline to determine repeat applications

10.10 Before the Planning and Compensation Act 1991, a local planning authority could not refuse to determine an application for planning permission. Every application had to be considered on its merits, despite the fact that the merits may have already been considered and rejected on a previous application made for the same or similar development. It was thought that by making repeat applications for the same development, developers sought to wear down the resistance of local planning authorities and neighbours to the proposed development, so that planning permission for it would eventually be granted.

10.11 Until the 2004 Act, the powers of a planning authority were limited and only allowed it to decline to determine applications for planning permission where a similar application had been refused by the Secretary of State within the previous two years. That power has been extended by the 2004 Act to give planning authorities greater control over how they deal with repeat applications.

10.12 The provisions are now to be found in a new s 70A of the 1990 Act. The power to decline to determine applications under the section is limited to those cases where a 'similar application' has been made. An application will be 'similar' to another if (and only if) the local planning authority thinks that the development and the land to which the applications relate are the same or substantially the same. In addition, the power to decline requires there to have been no significant change in the relevant considerations since the relevant event. The relevant considerations are the development plan so far as material to the application, and any other material consideration. The relevant event is the date of refusal of a similar application or the dismissal of the appeal as the case may be.

10.13 Where the above circumstances apply, a local planning authority may refuse to determine a relevant application if any of the following three situations exist:

(a) within a period of two years ending with the date on which a relevant application is received the Secretary of State has refused a similar application referred to him under ss 76A or 77 (called in applications);

(b) within a period of two years ending with the date on which a relevant application is received the Secretary of State has dismissed an appeal against the refusal of a similar application or an appeal made under s 78(2) (ie for non-determination) in respect of a similar application;

(c) within a period of two years ending with the date on which a relevant application is received the local planning authority has refused *more than one* similar application and there has been no appeal to the Secretary of State against any such refusal.

The Planning Act 2008 has further amended these provisions so that they also apply where the earlier application is a deemed application arising from an enforcement appeal. The Act also amends these provisions to ensure that a local planning authority is not prevented from exercising its powers to decline to determine an application by the fact that an appeal has been made but has been withdrawn before being determined.

10.14 There is no right of appeal to the Secretary of State should the applicant consider the planning authority to have no grounds for refusing to consider a relevant application. The only remedy is to seek judicial review of the authority's decision. This would have to be on the usual grounds. In effect, the applicant would have to show that the planning authority took into account irrelevant considerations, or failed to have regard to a material consideration, or that its decision was perverse. So far, few such challenges appear to have been made. In a Scottish case, *Noble Organisation Ltd v Falkirk DC* 1994 SLT 100, the court had to consider a similar provision in the Town and Country Planning (Scotland) Act 1992 to that in the 1990 Act before the changes made to them by the 2004 Act. It failed because the Court held that on the facts, the repeat application was similar to the first and that the amendments it made to the first application were merely cosmetic.

10.15 The planning authority is given a power to decline repeat applications, not a duty to do so. It does not have to. Being discretionary in nature, the planning authority may decide to determine any repeat application. PPG (14-058-20140306) states:

> The purpose of these powers is to inhibit the use of 'repeat' applications that the local planning authority believes are submitted with the intention of, over time, wearing down opposition to proposed developments.

It continues that planning authorities have a discretion

> to entertain 'repeat' planning applications where they are satisfied that a genuine attempt has been made to overcome the planning objections which led to rejection of the previous proposal or there has been a material change in circumstances.

One can envisage a number of situations where the repeat application is not intended to wear down the opposition. It may be, for example, that the applicants believe that objections to their development proposals can be dissipated by the offer of further planning obligations.

10.16 If the planning authority declines to determine a repeat application, the authority must under the DMPO, give notice of that fact to the applicant. This should be done within the eight-week period allowed under the DMPO for the determination of planning applications. If not, the applicant will retain the right to appeal to the Secretary of State against non-determination of the appeal.

10.17 The previous power was limited to applications for planning permission. The new s 70A to the 1990 Act applies equally to applications for listed building consent, applications for conservation area consent, and application for prior approval of the local planning authority for development permitted under the GPDO.

Power to decline to determine overlapping applications

10.18 Section 43 of the 2004 Act also introduced into the 1990 Act a new s 70B which gives local planning authorities the power to decline to proceed with the processing of an application where a similar application is under consideration by the authority. Here an application is similar to another application if the local planning authority thinks that the development and the land to which it relates are the same or substantially the same.

10.19 This power will be available where *any* of the following conditions apply in relation to a similar application:

(i) a similar application is under consideration by the local planning authority and the determination period for that application has not expired;
(ii) a similar application is under consideration by the Secretary of State (either by way of call in under s 76A or on appeal under s 78) and the Secretary of State has not issued his decision; or
(iii) a similar application has been granted by the local planning authority, has been refused by it or has not been determined by the authority within the determination period (this will normally be eight weeks), and the time within which an appeal could be made to the Secretary of State under s 78 has not expired.

10.20 The new provisions have been extended by the 2004 Act to apply also to applications for listed building and conservation area consent. Furthermore, the Secretary of State has power to prescribe by order classes of development to which, or circumstances in which, the new provision is not to apply.

10.21 The Planning Act 2008 has now amended these provisions further so that the powers also relate to applications received on the same day. A further amendment to these provisions applies them to deemed applications arising from an enforcement appeal.

Power to decline retrospective planning applications

10.22 Section 123 of the Localism Act 2011 inserts a new s 70C into the 1990 Act. This section provides that a local planning authority may decline to determine a planning application where the development has already been completed, if an enforcement notice has been issued in relation to any part of the development. The purpose of the provision has been explained in two cases. First, in *Wingrove* *v Stratford on Avon District Council* [2015] EWHC 287 (Admin); [2015] PTSR 708 Cranston J held at [30] that:

> The legislative history of section 70C demonstrates that Parliament's intention was to provide a tool to local planning authorities to prevent retrospective planning applications being used to delay enforcement action being taken against a development. It seems to me that there is a legislative steer in favour of exercising the discretion, especially since an enforcement notice can be appealed and the planning merits thereby canvassed. Since delay is the bugbear against which the section is directed, a claimant's actual motives to use a retrospective planning application to delay matters is clearly a consideration in favour of a decision to invoke section 70C.

Lewis J held in *O'Brien v South Cambridgeshire DC* [2016] EWHC 36 (Admin); [2016] JPL 656 at [72]:

> The purpose underlying the legislative provisions is that an applicant for permission for an unauthorised development cannot insist on more than one determination of the underlying planning merits of that development.

10.23 The scope of s 70C was considered in *R (Banghard) v Bedford Borough Council* [2017] EWHC 2391 (Admin); [2018] PTSR 1050 by Nathalie Lieven QC (sitting as a Deputy Judge). Although the planning authority had a wide discretion and there was necessarily an element of planning judgment in whether the development for which permission was being sought involved 'any part of the matters specified' in the enforcement notice as constituting the breach of planning control alleged, on the facts of that case the learned judge did not see how it could properly be said that the permission sought for a storage building was part of the breach of planning control in the enforcement notice, namely the erection of a dwelling house: 'The fact that some part of the building is the same and it is on the same footprint is not sufficient to mean that part of the matters is those specified in the EN'. At [30] the Deputy Judge held however that:

> There may of course be cases where the developer fails to appeal, as happened in Wingrove, and s.70C can still be used. But in such cases the developer had a full opportunity to a fair process and did not avail himself of it. There may also be cases where the developer makes a very minor change from what was considered in the enforcement appeal, whether in terms of a minor change to the nature of the use applied for, or a minor change to the built form. In those circumstances it will be open to the local planning authority to rely on s.70C. Such a decision will indeed involve the exercise of planning judgement by the authority.

10.24 The latest consideration of s 70C is by Martin Rodger QC (sitting as a Deputy High Court Judge) in *Chesterton Commercial (Bucks) Ltd v Wokingham DC* [2018] EWHC 1795 (Admin); [2018] JPL 1347. The Deputy Judge held that the focus of s 70C at [67] and [69] was as follows:

> 67. First, s.70C is not concerned with the existence of differences between two developments, but with the existence of similarities. The statutory language requires an assessment of whether granting the planning permission sought would involve granting permission for *any part* of the matters specified in the enforcement notice.

The fact that granting the application would also involve granting permission for matters which were not specified in the enforcement notice, or that it would not involve granting permission for other matters which were specified in the notice, are nothing to the point when considering whether the power to decline to determine the application is engaged. The extent of any differences may be very relevant to the exercise of the local planning authority's discretion, but that is a later stage of the exercise.

69. Secondly, the statutory objective of stopping applicants who have undertaken development in breach of planning control from gaming the system by tactical appeals and retrospective applications is not achieved by asking only whether the planning merits of a proposal have already been determined. The applicant cannot have multiple 'bites at the cherry', but nor can he decline the cherry when it is available to be bitten, and insist on biting it on a later occasion.

10.25 The Deputy Judge disagreed with the suggestion of Nathalie Lieven QC in *Banghard* that s 70C is restricted to a case of a 'very minor change', finding at [72] that such a construction was 'at odds with the reference in s.70C to "planning permission for … any part of the matter specified in the enforcement notice"'.

C. PUBLICITY FOR PLANNING APPLICATIONS

10.26 Prior to the Planning and Compensation Act 1991, publicity for planning applications was limited to a number of special situations, such as applications described as 'bad neighbour' development. There was no general duty placed on local planning authorities to give publicity to an application for planning permission, the matter being regarded as being purely a matter between the applicant and the local planning authority as guardian of the public interest. Some local planning authorities, however, adopted a policy of consulting with third parties such as neighbours where, in the opinion of the authority, the proposed development would be likely to affect them adversely. There was no statutory requirement that this should be done, but it was regarded by many a local planning authority as a feature of good administration.

10.27 If a local planning authority had a policy of notifying third parties of an application, the failure to do so did not give rise to any legal consequence. A complaint might be made, however, to the Local Government Ombudsman, who could hold that an authority's failure to comply with its own policy in this regard amounted to maladministration. If it could be shown that the complainant had suffered injustice as a result of that maladministration, the report of the Local Government Ombudsman could result in a remedy being provided by the local planning authority. Sometimes this has led to an authority making a payment to the complainant which reflected the depreciation in the value of his property caused by the development carried out.

10.28 The position in England was radically altered by the Planning and Compensation Act 1991. By that Act, the Secretary of State was given power in a new s 65 of the 1990 Act to make provision by development order requiring notice to be given of any application for planning permission. At the same time, the Government expressed a wish to extend publicity requirements to cover all types of application. This is now achieved in the Development Management Procedure Order, under which responsibility for the publication of planning applications is imposed on the local planning authority. Guidance on the publicity duties of authorities is provided in the PPG 'Determining a planning application' section. The relevant statutory provisions are found in Art 15 of the DMPO, which provides:

> An application for planning permission shall be publicised by the local planning authority to which the application is made in the manner prescribed by this article.

10.29 The article requires three different levels of publicity according to the nature of the development applied for, namely, development of a kind specified in Art 15, major development, and other development not falling under either of these two heads.

Development specified in Article 15

10.30 Article 15(2) of the Order provides that in the case of an application for planning permission for development which:

(a) is accompanied by an environmental statement;
(b) does not accord with the provisions of the development plan;
(c) would affect a public right of way,

the publicity given to the application shall be by giving the requisite notice (in the form set out in Sch 3 to the Order or in a form substantially to the like effect) by the display of a site notice in at least one place on or near the land to which the application relates for not less than 21 days, *and* by publishing the notice in a newspaper circulating in the locality in which the land to which the application relates is situated.

Major development

10.31 Under Art 15(4) of the Order, in the case of an application for planning permission other than a para 1A or 2 application, if the development proposed is major development the application shall be publicized by giving notice (in the form set out in Sch 3 to the Order) by a site display (which is defined by Art 2(1) as the posting of the notice by firm affixture to some object sited and displayed in such a way as to be easily visible and legible by members of the public) in at least one place on or near the land to which the application relates for not less than 21 days. The alternative is to serve the notice on any owner or occupier of any land adjoining the land to which the application relates. In addition to these alternatives, a notice must also be published in a newspaper circulating in the locality in which the land to which the application relates is situated.

10.32 Article 2 defines 'major' development as development involving any one or more of the following:

(a) the winning and working of minerals or the use of land for mineral working deposits;
(b) waste development;
(c) the provision of dwellinghouses where—
 (i) the number of dwellinghouses to be provided is ten or more; or
 (ii) the development is to be carried out on a site having an area of 0.5 hectares or more and it is not known whether the development falls within para (c)(i);
(d) the provision of a building or buildings where the floor space to be created by the development is 1,000 square metres or more; or
(e) development carried out on a site having an area of one hectare or more.

10.33 As indicated earlier, the Order no longer contains a list of developments classified as 'bad neighbour'. It is considered, however, that applications for certain types of development may warrant the wider publicity now accorded to 'major development' as described above.

Other development

10.34 In the case of development not falling within 10.27 or 10.28 above, Art 15(5) of the Order provides that the application for planning permission shall be published by displaying the requisite notice (in the form set out in Sch 3 to the Order) by posting a site notice in at least one place on or near the land to which the application relates for not less than 21 days, *or* serving the notice on any owner or occupier of any land adjoining the land to which the application relates.

All applications must be published on local planning authority websites

10.35 Article 15(7) of the DMPO requires local planning authorities to publish the following information on their websites:

(a) address of application;
(b) description of the proposed development;
(c) in the case of EIA development accompanied by an ES, that ES;
(d) date by which representations should be made;
(e) where and when copies of applications, maps, etc are available for public inspection;
(f) how representations can be made; and that
(g) where representations are made on householder applications (as defined in Art 2), in the event of an appeal, those representations may also be used for appeal purposes and there will be no further opportunity to comment.

Summary

The following is a summary of the above publicity requirements for planning applications under the provisions of Art 15. **10.36**

Nature of development	Publicity required
Development where application accompanied by an environmental statement	Advertisement in a local newspaper *and* site Information on website
Development involving a departure notice from the development plan	
Development affecting a public right of way	
Minor development	Advertisement in local newspaper *and* either site notice *or* neighbour notification Information on website
Major development	Site notice or neighbour notification Information on website

It will be seen that there is a choice with both major development and minor development, of giving publicity by either site notice or neighbour notification. The local planning authority has a choice. As Richards J said in the case of *R (on the application of Seamus Gavin) v London Borough of Haringey and Anor* [2003] EWHC 2591 (Admin):

> I have substantial doubts as to whether article 8(4)(a) [now Art 15(4)] imposes on a local planning authority an obligation to consider which of the two methods is best calculated to give notice of the application to those likely to be interested in the application. On the face of it, either of those methods is equally valid in every case: the relevant judgment has already been made by the Secretary of State, who, in making the 1995 Order, has formed the view that the purpose of ensuring that sufficient notice is given will be sufficiently achieved by a combination of (a) either of those methods plus (b) local advertisement.

It should be noted that in all cases where a site notice is required or given, Art 15(6) provides that the local planning authority is not to be treated as having failed to comply with that requirement if the notice is, without fault or intention of the authority, removed, obscured, or defaced before the period of 21 days has elapsed, if the authority have taken reasonable steps for its protection and, if need be, replacement. **10.37**

Furthermore, Art 18(7) of the Order provides that the local planning authority should take into account any representations made within 21 days from the date notice of the application is given or 14 days from the date any advertisement appeared in a local newspaper, and that the local planning authority shall not determine an application for planning permission until the expiration of those periods. **10.38**

10.39 The 2015 Order adds an additional requirement to consult before the grant of permission pursuant to s 73 of the 1990 Act or the grant of a replacement permission subject to a new time limit, see: Art 20.

10.40 It seems that the failure to comply with Art 15 could be a sufficient reason for the courts to quash a grant of planning permission, so long as the claimant for relief could show that he had been substantially prejudiced by the failure, and his application was made timeously (see *R (Seamus Gavin) v Haringey LBC and Wolseley Centres Ltd* [2003] EWHC 2591 (Admin)).

D. NOTIFICATION REQUIREMENTS

Development affecting highways

10.41 Under Art 18 and Sch 4 of the DMPO, the local planning authority is required to notify the Secretary of State of applications for planning permission for development which consists of or includes the formation, laying out, or alteration of any access to or from any part of certain categories of trunk roads.

Parish and community councils

10.42 Under Art 25 of the DMPO where a Parish Council are notified under the above provisions, they must 'as soon as practicable' notify the local planning authority who are determining the application whether they propose to make any representations about the manner in which the application should be determined, and must make any representations to that authority within 21 days of the notification to them of the application. By Art 18(2) the planning authority may not determine the application prior to being notified that the parish council do not wish to make representations, representations are made by that council or 21 days has elapsed. The planning authority must take into account any representations received from the parish council.

Development affecting the setting of a listed building

10.43 Under s 67 of the Planning (Listed Buildings and Conservation Areas) Act 1990, the Secretary of State is given power to prescribe the publicity to be given to an application for planning permission where the local planning authority considers the development would affect the setting of a listed building. This has been done by the Planning (Listed Buildings and Conservation) (Amendment) (England) Regulations 2015, SI 2015/809 which amend the Planning (Listed Buildings and Conservation Areas) Regulations 1990 by inserting a new reg 5A. This requires that in such cases the authority must publish in a local newspaper circulating in the locality in which the land is situated, and display on or near the land for not less than seven days, a notice indicating the nature of the development in question and naming a place where a copy of the application and all other plans and documents submitted with it can be seen.

10.44 Here, the local planning authority may have to take two independent decisions. First, to decide if the proposed development would, if granted, affect the setting of a listed building. If so, the application must be given publicity. Secondly, and after publicity has been given to the application and any representations received taken into account, to decide whether planning permission should be granted.

Development affecting the character or appearance of a conservation area

10.45 Section 73 gives the Secretary of State similar power to that of s 67 in relation to the effect of a listed building under the same regulations where the authority considers the development would affect the character or appearance of a conservation area. The local planning authority must publish, in a local newspaper circulating in the locality in which the land is situated and for not less than seven days display on or near the land, a notice indicating the nature of the development in question and naming a place where a copy of the application can be seen.

Applications falling within the jurisdiction of a county planning authority

10.46 Under Art 24 of the DMPO, a county planning authority must, in relation to a county matter, give the district planning authority an opportunity to make recommendations about the manner in which applications for planning permission, applications for certificates of lawfulness of existing use, or development, certificates of lawfulness of proposed use, or development and the approval of reserved matters should be determined by the county.

Duplication of publicity and notice requirements

10.47 The provisions of Art 15 of the DMPO, referred to earlier, may result in a degree of overlapping or duplication with other statutory requirements, or indeed within the article itself. For example, 'major' development may also require an environmental assessment, and the article applies different publicity requirements to each. Again, the publicity for development which is not specified within Art 15(2) (para 1A and 2 applications) and is not major development may be different from the publicity required under the Planning (Listed Buildings and Conservation Areas) Act 1990 in respect of applications for development affecting the character or appearance of a conservation area or the setting of a listed building. Clearly, in order to be within the law, the more demanding of the publicity requirements should be followed.

E. CONSULTATION

10.48 The provisions of Art 18 and Sch 4 of the DMPO allow for the views of various specialist bodies to be obtained on particular types of development. It is an important provision which provides that, before granting planning permission for certain specified types of development, a local planning authority should consult with named authorities or persons. For example, where the development would involve the manufacture, processing, keeping, or use of a hazardous substance likely to lead to a notifiable quantity of such substance, the authority is required to consult with the Health and Safety Executive. So, for example, in a case involving a proposal to develop the site of the former Staveley Central Station for residential purposes, the Secretary of State, in dismissing an appeal against the refusal of the local planning authority to grant planning permission, had regard to the view of the Health and Safety Executive that the potential hazards arising from the proximity of the site to land presently being used for the manufacture and storage of highly flammable liquids precluded the use of the site for housing.

10.49 Of more general application is the requirement to consult with the local highway authority where the development involves the formation, laying out, or alteration of any means of access to a highway; and with Natural England where the development is not development for agricultural purposes and is not in accordance with the provisions of the development plan and would involve the loss of not less than 20 hectares of grades 1, 2, or 3a agricultural land.

10.50 Where consultation is required, the consultee must normally be given at least 14 days' notice to make representations, which must be taken into account by the local planning authority before they determine the application.

10.51 Note too that a county planning authority must also be consulted on applications for planning permission for a limited range of development now set out in Sch 1, para 7(1) of the 1990 Act.

Consultation responses

10.52 Because no statutory timescale has ever been imposed on bodies required to be consulted within which responses are to be made, much of the delay in determining planning applications has been laid at the door of statutory consultees, some of whom are statutory bodies, others non-statutory. This has now been changed.

10.53 Section 54 of the Planning and Compulsory Purchase Act 2004 introduced a provision which requires that persons or bodies required to be consulted by the Secretary of State or local planning authority (as the case may be) before the grant of any planning permission, approval, or consent required under the Planning

Acts, must respond to the consultation request within a prescribed period. The new provision applies also to consultation by any person prior to an application for permission, approval, or consent. The provision enables the Secretary of State to prescribe, by development order, under s 54 of the 2004 Act, the new consultation requirements which trigger the duty to respond, and the period within which each statutory consultee must reply. The section allows the Secretary of State to prescribe the procedures to be followed; the information to be provided by the consultee; and the requirements of the substantive response which the provisions require the consultee to provide. This is now set out in Art 22 of the DMPO. The provisions do not change the right of bodies like parish councils and the national amenity societies to be notified of planning applications. The deadline for response is 21 days after the date on which the statutory consultee receives the consultation. This period may be extended by agreement between both parties.

Article 23 requires statutory consultees to report to the Secretary of State on their compliance with the duty to respond within a prescribed period, and prescribes the content of the report. **10.54**

The report must show the number of consultation requests received, the number that were responded to within the prescribed period, and (if appropriate) a summary of reasons why the statutory deadline has not been met in all cases. **10.55**

F. DEVELOPMENT NOT IN ACCORDANCE WITH THE PROVISIONS OF THE DEVELOPMENT PLAN

Section 74(1)(b) of the 1990 Act authorizes the local planning authority, in such cases and subject to such conditions as may be prescribed by a development order, or by directions given by the Secretary of State thereunder, to grant planning permission which does not accord with the provisions of the development plan. In addition, Art 32 of the DMPO authorizes local planning authorities to grant permission for development not in accordance with the development plan in such cases and subject to such conditions as may be prescribed by directions given by the Secretary of State. No express authorization has ever been required for a grant of planning permission for development not in accordance with the development plan. However, it must be taken that these provisions are directed at laying down special procedures where an application is contrary to the plan. The Town and Country Planning (Development Plans and Consultation) (Departures) Directions 1999, which were issued as Annex 1 to Circular 07/99, used to require special consultation for certain departures but these were revoked by the Town and Country Planning (Consultation) (England) Direction 2009. This new Direction introduces a new requirement for local planning authorities to refer applications where they are minded to grant planning permission in circumstances **10.56** where English Heritage has objected on the grounds that a proposed development could have an adverse impact on the outstanding universal value, integrity, authenticity and significance of a World Heritage Site or its setting, including any buffer zone or its equivalent, and has not withdrawn its objection. Under the new direction local planning authorities must still inform the Secretary of State if they intend to approve an application that includes the following types of development:

- in the Green Belt;
- of a large retail, office or leisure use outside a town centre;
- leading to the loss of a playing field;
- in a flood risk area.

10.57 It should, be noted that departure applications are subject to the statutory publicity required under Art 15(2) of the DMPO (see para 10.29).

10.58 An important question raised in the past has been the precise consequences that flow from a failure to comply with the Directions. Does a failure to do so render the subsequent grant of planning permission void? In an old case, *Gregory v Camden LBC* [1966] 1 WLR 899, it was held that a neighbour did not possess the necessary standing to challenge a grant of planning permission for development which involved a departure from the development plan, but had been granted without compliance with the procedure required by the Direction. In a later case, *R v St Edmundsbury BC, ex p Investors in Industry Commercial Properties Ltd* [1985] 1 WLR 1168, an application was made to the High Court for judicial review to quash outline planning permission granted to J Sainsbury plc for the erection of a supermarket on land in Bury St Edmunds town centre. One of the many grounds for challenge alleged that there had been a defect in the statutory advertisement required by the then Town and Country Planning (Development Plans) (England) Direction 1981, in that it had not included any reference to the fact that the application conflicted with the development plan. It was contended by the applicants for judicial review that the requirements of the Direction were mandatory and a condition precedent to the grant of a valid planning permission. Rejecting that contention, Stocker J thought that to construe the Direction as mandatory would involve difficulties likely to lead to practical and commercial problems. He had no doubt that the words 'in the opinion of the local planning authority' did require that proper consideration be given to the problem, but it seemed to him inappropriate for a Direction, the breach of which involved the proposition that planning permission granted was void, should be regarded as mandatory since this might involve investigating the committee's opinion and whether such opinion was based upon full and proper consideration. The words themselves suggest that a directive and procedural order, rather than a mandatory one, arose.

10.59 After expressing the view that the absence of information in the statutory advertisement had had no effect because a wide section of the public were aware that the development would involve a departure from the town map, Stocker J went on to say that if he was wrong in his conclusion that the Direction was a procedural one, and not mandatory involving a condition precedent, he would, in the exercise of discretion, not have made an order for judicial review on this ground.

10.60 The approach of Stocker J in *R v St Edmundsbury BC* was followed later by Macpherson J in *R v Carlisle City Council, ex p Cumbrian Co-operative Society Ltd* [1986] JPL 206, where it was held that a failure to comply with the Direction did not invalidate the grant of a deemed planning permission by the local planning authority for development of a superstore on a site owned by the authority.

G. AMENDMENT OF APPLICATIONS

10.61 It is common practice for an application for planning permission to be amended by agreement following negotiations between the applicant and the authority's planning officer. In *Britannia (Cheltenham) Ltd v Secretary of State for the Environment and Tewkesbury* [1978] JPL 554 it was recognized that it was competent for the applicants and planning authority to agree a variation of an application at any time up to the determination of the application. 'To take any other view,' it was said, 'would fly in the face of everyday practice and make the planning machine even more complicated than it is.' In *British Telecommunications plc v Gloucester CC* [2001] EWHC Admin 1001, the limitations on this practice were recognized. As Elias J remarked:

> It is inevitable in the process of negotiating with officers and consulting with the public, that proposals will be made or ideas emerge which will lead to a modification of the original planning application. It is plainly in the public interest that proposed developments should be improved in this way. If the law were too quick to compel applicants to go through all the formal stages of a fresh application, it would inevitably deter developers from being receptive to sensible proposal for change ... I would add that of course the interests of the public must also be fully protected when an amendment is under consideration.

10.62 In the view of the High Court, where the change proposed is substantial, the procedure cannot be used to sidestep the rights of third parties or in circumstances where statutory requirements (eg for consultation) have not been complied with. Detailed consideration of the procedural obligations upon a planning authority in accepting amendments, as distinct from the power to do so, was illuminated in the judgment of John Howell QC (sitting as a Deputy Judge) in *R (Holborn Studios Ltd) v Hackney LBC* [2017] EWHC 2823; [2017] PTSR 997 at [79]–[80]:

> 79 In considering whether it is unfair not to re-consult, in my judgment it is necessary to consider whether not doing so deprives those who were entitled to be consulted on the application of the opportunity to make any representations that, given the nature and extent of the changes proposed, they may have wanted to make on the application as amended.

80 I do not accept that the test for whether re-consultation is required if an amendment is proposed to an application for planning permission is whether it involves a 'fundamental change' and involves a 'substantial difference' to the application or whether it results in a development that is in substance different from that applied for. These are three potentially different tests that have been suggested as stating the substantial constraint on what changes are impermissible. Depending on how each is interpreted, it is possible that the test would indicate re-consultation was not required when fairness would require it. As I have explained, even if the proposed amendment was not of any these types, a person may still have representations that he or she may want to make about the changes, given their nature and extent, if given the opportunity. In my judgment it is preferable to ask what fairness requires in the circumstances.

10.63 Section 190 of the Planning Act 2008 inserts a new s 96A into the 1990 Act. It introduces an express power into the Act to provide for a local planning authority to make a change to a planning permission if it is satisfied the change is not material. The express legislative power includes the power to impose new conditions and to remove or alter existing conditions. The power may be exercised only on an application made by or on behalf of a person with an interest in the land to which the planning permission relates. Article 10 of the DMPO sets out the procedure for making such an application.

11

DETERMINATIONS OF APPLICATIONS FOR PLANNING PERMISSION

A. DELEGATION	11.01	C. DETERMINATION OF	
B. ESTOPPEL BY		A PLANNING APPLICATION	11.27
REPRESENTATION	11.15		

A. DELEGATION

Under s 101 of the Local Government Act 1972, a local authority may arrange for the discharge of any of its functions by a committee, a subcommittee, an officer of the authority, or by any other local authority. **11.01**

In *R v Secretary of State for the Environment, ex p Hillingdon LBC* [1986] 1 WLR 807, it was held that a committee meant more than one person, so that a local authority has no power to delegate any of its functions to any individual member of the authority. To overcome this difficulty, however, many local planning authorities have made delegation arrangements authorizing an officer of the council (such as the Chief Planning Officer) to exercise functions on the council's behalf but only after consultation with a particular member of the council (such as the chairman of the planning committee). **11.02**

Every local planning authority has arrangements whereby their planning control functions are delegated to a committee. Most local planning authorities have also made arrangements for the discharge of many of their functions by an officer of the authority. Current statistics show that about 90 per cent of all planning decisions are determined by officers under schemes of delegation, without reference to a committee. The actual scope of an officer's delegated powers will, like all delegated arrangements, depend upon the terms of the particular scheme of delegation. Frequently those arrangements give an officer power to decide applications for planning permission which do not conflict with the development plan or other planning policies of the authority. In many cases the scale or size **11.03** of the development proposed may also be relevant to whether the delegation of authority is available.

11.04 In *R (Carlton-Conway) v Harrow LBC* [2002] EWCA Civ 927; [2002] JPL 1216 the Court of Appeal quashed the decision of the authority's Chief Planning Officer to use his delegated power to grant planning permission for a residential extension. The terms of delegation provided that the officer could determine all applications other than those where 'approval of development is recommended and written objection or objections have been received, except where the proposals do not conflict with agreed policies, standards and guidelines'. It was claimed that the development proposed did conflict with the authority's agreed policies and should therefore have been decided by the appropriate committee of the authority. The Court of Appeal agreed that the development proposed was not the kind of case to which the delegation applied. The court held that the complexities present in the proposals were such that a planning officer could not reasonably act on the exception and the only rational decision would have been to refer it to the next meeting of the planning committee. According to Pill LJ, 'When [as here] there are real issues as to the meaning of planning policies and as to their application to the facts of the case, reference to the appropriate committee was required.' In *R (on the application of Springhall) v Richmond LBC* [2006] EWCA Civ 19, the Court of Appeal, affirming a decision of the High Court, held that the *Carlton-Conway* case did not compel the same result where there was no such uncertainty about the applicable planning policies and the facts to which they had to be applied.

11.05 Since 6 August 2014, decisions made by an officer of the Council must be accompanied by a written record providing, amongst other things, the reasons for the decision, see: reg 7 of the Openness of Local Government Bodies Regulation 2014 (SI 2014/2095). However, it was not until the decision of the High Court in *R (on the application of Shasha) v Westminster City Council* [2016] EWHC 3283 (Admin); [2017] PTSR 306 that it became widely understood that the 2014 Regulations applied to planning decisions. The correctness of that position was confirmed in the judgment of Lord Carnwath JSC in *CPRE (Kent) v Dover District Council* [2017] UKSC 79; [2018] 1 WLR 108 at [30]. In *R (on the application of Newey) v South Hams District Council* [2018] EWHC 1872 (Admin) Garnham J found the obligation to supply reasons in accordance with the 2014 Regulations extended to the discharge of a planning condition (in that case, a construction methodology condition).

11.06 In cases where planning functions are not delegated to an officer but are exercised by a committee or a subcommittee of the authority, the role of officers will be to ensure that all considerations material to the decision to be made are brought to the attention of the committee or subcommittee together with (in most cases) a recommendation as to how the application should be dealt with. The Local

Government Ombudsman has rightly advised local authorities that any report to a committee should provide all the material that members need to make an informed decision. The report should be in clear terms and should cover as necessary the relevant law and policy; sufficient and accurate information to enable members to understand the issues to be considered or determined; a summary of the outcome of any consultation or seeking of advice; a reference to all the considerations which have to be taken into account; the identification of possible approaches which could be adopted; the reasons for any recommendations; and an analysis of any financial or other significant implications which are relevant. As Holgate J held in *R (on the application of Leckhampton Green Land Action Group Ltd) v Tewkesbury Borough Council* [2017] EWHC 198 (Admin); [2017] Env LR 28 at [51]:

> the purpose of an officer's report is not to decide the issues or issues (as in the case of an Inspector's decision letter), but to inform the members of considerations relevant to the merits of a planning application .... an officer's report does not necessarily have to rehearse well-known principles of national and local planning policy. Such a report identifies matters which, in the judgment of the officer, he or she considers should be included for consideration by the members. It is trite law that the report need not indicate to the members what conclusions they should draw upon a particular issue or even on the planning application itself. The report may leave that to the members. Although the members are expected to have read the officers' report beforehand, their decision-making process is not confined to the contents of that report. The members are entitled to contribute their own opinions and reasoning to the process and in their meeting they may well debate the merits of a proposal'

The question of the material the committee should have available to it before reaching its decision has, however, been subject to a number of judicial decisions. Happily, these principles have been summarized by Lindblom LJ in *Mansell v Tonbridge & Malling Borough Council* [2017] EWCA Civ 1314; [2018] JPL 176 at [42]: **11.07**

> (2) The principles are not complicated. Planning officers' reports to committee are not to be read with undue rigour, but with reasonable benevolence, and bearing in mind that they are written for councillors with local knowledge (see the judgment of Baroness Hale of Richmond in *R. (on the application of Morge) v Hampshire County Council* [2011] UKSC 2 , at paragraph 36, and the judgment of Sullivan J., as he then was, in *R. v Mendip District Council, ex parte Fabre* (2000) 80 P. & C.R. 500 , at p.509). Unless there is evidence to suggest otherwise, it may reasonably be assumed that, if the members followed the officer's recommendation, they did so on the basis of the advice that he or she gave (see the judgment of Lewison L.J. in *Palmer v Herefordshire Council* [2016] EWCA Civ 1061, at paragraph 7). The question for the court will always be whether, on a fair reading of the report as a whole, the officer has materially misled the members on a matter bearing upon their decision, and the error has gone uncorrected before the decision was made. Minor or inconsequential errors may be excused. It is only if the advice in the officer's report is such as to misdirect the members in a material way—so that, but for the flawed advice it was given, the committee's decision would or might have

been different—that the court will be able to conclude that the decision itself was rendered unlawful by that advice.

(3) Where the line is drawn between an officer's advice that is significantly or seriously misleading—misleading in a material way—and advice that is misleading but not significantly so will always depend on the context and circumstances in which the advice was given, and on the possible consequences of it. There will be cases in which a planning officer has inadvertently led a committee astray by making some significant error of fact (see, for example *R. (on the application of Loader) v Rother District Council* [2016] EWCA Civ 795), or has plainly misdirected the members as to the meaning of a relevant policy (see, for example, *Watermead Parish Council v Aylesbury Vale District Council* [2017] EWCA Civ 152). There will be others where the officer has simply failed to deal with a matter on which the committee ought to receive explicit advice if the local planning authority is to be seen to have performed its decision-making duties in accordance with the law (see, for example, *R. (on the application of Williams) v Powys County Council* [2017] EWCA Civ 427). But unless there is some distinct and material defect in the officer's advice, the court will not interfere.

11.08 The need for officers' reports to include all information on relevant considerations relating to the application is underlined by the Town and Country Planning (Development Management Procedure) (England) Order 2015 (SI 2015/595). Article 35 of which requires that reasons are given for the imposition of conditions and for the refusal of planning permission. Furthermore, in cases of EIA development, reasons must be given for the grant of planning permission and, as discussed later in this chapter, reasons may be required as an obligation under the common law, for the grant of planning permission in non-EIA cases.

11.09 As with the exercise of all delegated power, the actions of the delegatee, acting within the four corners of his power, will bind the delegator. Furthermore, where power to discharge functions has been delegated to another, the donor of the power is usually free to withdraw that power before it has been exercised. Under s 101(4), where a power to discharge a function has been delegated to a committee, a subcommittee, or an officer, this does not prevent the authority or the committee (as the case may be) discharging the function themselves. In *R v Yeovil BC, ex p Trustees of Elim Pentecostal Church, Yeovil* (1971) 23 P & CR 39 the Church had made an application for planning permission. The minutes of the planning committee of the Council recorded its decision that 'the town clerk be authorized to approve the application subject to [certain] conditions when evidence of an agreement about the car-parking facilities has been received'. At a subsequent meeting the planning committee, after having heard evidence that the development would be detrimental to the amenities of the area, changed its mind and decided to refuse the application. The applicant thereupon applied for an order of *mandamus* requiring the authority to issue conditional planning consent for the development, contending that the committee had already committed itself, and that as all that remained was for the town clerk to issue notices of approval, the Council was in no position to change its mind.

11.10 The High Court held that, on the facts, there was no question of planning permission having been granted at any time before the town clerk had expressed a view with regard to the adequacy of any evidence presented to him. Moreover, the Council had delegated the final determination of the application to the town clerk, and unless and until he had made such determination within the authority granted to him, no question of planning permission having been granted arose; and the clerk not having finally determined the matter before the later committee meeting, it was open to the Council to change its mind and to withdraw its provisional approval and refuse the application.

11.11 Officers of the local planning authorities also exercise many functions of a magisterial nature, as where they transmit to the applicant the decision made by the local planning authority. In *Norfolk CC v Secretary of State for the Environment* [1973] 1 WLR 400, a company made an application for planning permission to build an extension to a factory. The planning committee refused the application. Then, by mistake, the planning officer sent a notice to the applicant saying planning permission had been granted. As soon as the mistake was discovered the Council sent a letter to the applicant apologizing, together with a proper notice of refusal. The company immediately cancelled, without penalty, an order for new machinery. But it continued to maintain that it had the benefit of a valid planning permission. In order to bring matters to a head, the company commenced development. This enabled the Council to serve an enforcement notice against which the company appealed to the Secretary of State. He duly proceeded to quash the notice, so the Council appealed to the High Court against that decision. Allowing the appeal, the court held that the Council was entitled to serve the enforcement notice because the officer concerned only had authority to transmit to the applicant the decision of the planning committee. He had no authority himself to make a decision on the planning application so that the notice given by him could not be regarded as a grant of planning permission.

11.12 A similar approach was taken in *Attorney-General v Taff-Ely BC* (1981) 42 P & CR 1. In this rather complicated case, in 1975, Co-operative Retail Services Ltd (CRS) applied for planning permission to develop land as a superstore. A few months later, Sir Robert McAlpine Ltd (with Tesco stores in mind) applied for planning permission to develop other land for the same purpose just half a mile away from the CRS site. It was clear that only one of the two applications could be granted and that it was the Tesco site that was favoured by the local planning authority. Accordingly, it refused planning permission for the CRS site. On the very same day, the authority considered and adopted a recommendation of a subcommittee of its planning committee that planning permission be granted for the development of the Tesco site. A dispute then arose as to the exact status of the subcommittee's decision. CRS took the view that it had merely expressed the authority's preliminary views on the application, prior to discussions taking place between the authority and the Mid-Glamorgan County Council which was the county planning authority for the area. Tesco's agents, however, took the view that the action of the subcommittee constituted a grant of planning permission for the development, and threatened the authority that if it did not issue the grant it would bring an action for *mandamus* to compel it to do so and for damages for the loss it had suffered. After a threat of legal action, the town clerk issued a grant of planning permission. In an action for a declaration the Court of Appeal ((1979) 39 P & CR 223) held that on the true construction of the relevant minutes of the planning subcommittee the local planning authority had not resolved to grant planning permission for the development. Furthermore, since the town clerk could only transmit to the applicant the decision of the local planning authority, the authority could not ratify what was in fact a nullity. On appeal to the House of Lords, the decision of the Court of Appeal was upheld.

11.13 In *Archid Architecture and Interior Design v Dundee City Council* [2013] CSOH 137, [2014] JPL 336 the Scottish Court of Session (Outer House) held that once a permission is issued, a planning authority has no power to withdraw that permission, even if issued in error. The point was considered again by the Court of Appeal in *R (on the application of Gleeson Developments Limited) v Secretary of State for Communities and Local Government* [2014] EWCA Civ 1118; [2014] PTSR 1226. Sullivan LJ held at [22] and [24]:

> 22. If a planning permission has been granted, whether on appeal by the Secretary of State or by an appointed person, or on an application for planning permission by a local planning authority, there is no power to 'withdraw' that planning permission on the basis that there has been an administrative error at some stage in the decision-making process. Once granted, a planning permission may be revoked only under the procedure contained in ss.97–100 of the Act ...

> 24. A planning permission confers a substantive right, often a very valuable substantive right, and it is therefore by its very nature irrevocable, save under the procedure which is contained in ss.79–100 of the Act which make provision for compensation.

11.14 Where a decision has been issued in error, the proper course for a planning authority is for a rate payer (often a member of the authority) to bring a judicial review of the decision, see: *R v Bassetlaw DC, ex parte Oxby* [1998] PLCR 283 and *R (on the application of Carroll) v South Somerset District Council* [2008] EWHC 104 (Admin).

B. ESTOPPEL BY REPRESENTATION

11.15 An issue which once bedevilled planning law was the extent to which a representation made by an officer of a local planning authority could bind the authority. The long-established principle was that a public authority could not be stopped from exercising statutory powers by the representations of an officer. From 1967 however, a number of exceptions began to be made to that principle. In *Lever Finance Ltd v Westminster (City) LBC* [1971] 1 QB 222 (CA) Lord Denning MR said:

> I know that there are authorities which say a public authority cannot be estopped ... from doing its public duty ... But those statements must now be taken with considerable reserve. There are many matters which public authorities can now delegate to their officers. If an officer, acting within the scope of his ostensible authority, makes a representation on which another acts, then a public authority may be bound by it, just as much as a private concern would be.

11.16 The judgment of Lord Denning was thereafter taken at its face value, particularly by the Secretary of State in dealing with appeals against enforcement notices. Almost any representation made by an officer within the scope of his ostensible authority was regarded as capable of binding the authority. The doctrine of estoppel was poised to run wild and duly did so. That in turn led to extreme caution by the officers of local planning authorities in giving advice and guidance to prospective applicants for planning permission. Eventually, the judgment of a strong Court of Appeal in *Western Fish Products Ltd v Penwith DC* (1979) 38 P & CR 7 was able to limit the situations where representations by officers of an authority might bind the authority.

11.17 Thereafter, it seemed that for an authority to be bound by the actions of an officer, there needed to be some evidence to justify that assumption, such as a previous course of conduct indicating that the officer had ostensible authority to commit the authority.

11.18 The whole basis of estoppel in public law, however, and indeed the extent to which there are exceptions to the general principle that public authorities cannot be estopped from performing their statutory duties was raised again by judgment of the House of Lords in *R v East Sussex CC, ex p Reprotech (Pebsham) Ltd* [2002] UKHL 8; [2003] 1 WLR 348. The case was concerned, inter alia, with the question of whether a resolution of a committee of the local planning authority to agree to amend a condition subject to which an earlier planning permission had been granted, could be inferred as a determination under s 64 of the Town and Country Planning Act 1990 (a section now replaced by s 192). The Court of Appeal considered it could be. The House of Lords thought otherwise, holding that it was impossible to say that a conditional resolution to grant planning permission (under s 73 of the Act) which itself did not bind the authority, could by implication constitute a binding determination under s 64.

11.19 On the general question of estoppel in public law, Lord Hoffmann said:

> I think that it is unhelpful to introduce private law concepts of estoppel into planning law. As Lord Scarman pointed out in *Newbury DC v Secretary of State for the Environment* [1981] 578, at 616, estoppels bind individuals on the ground that it would be unconscionable for them to deny what they have represented or agreed.

But these concepts of private law should not be extended into 'the public law of planning control, which binds everyone'.

Later, he said:

> It is true that in early cases ... Lord Denning MR used the language of estoppel in relation to planning law. At that time the public law concepts of abuse of power and legitimate expectation were very undeveloped and no doubt the analogy of estoppel seemed useful. In *Western Fish* the Court of Appeal tried its best to reconcile these invocations of estoppel with the general principle that a public authority cannot be estopped from exercising a statutory discretion or performing a public duty. But the results did not give universal satisfaction ... *It seems to me that in this area, public law has already absorbed whatever is useful from the moral values which underlie the private law concept of estoppel and the time has come for it to stand upon its own two feet.* (author's emphasis)

11.20 Commenting upon the judgment of the House of Lords in the *Reprotech* case, Richards J in *Coghurst Wood Leisure Park Limited v Secretary of State for Transport, Local Government, and the Regions* [2002] EWHC 1091 (Admin) said:

> It is obvious that the judgments in [Powergen and] Reprotech mark an important change in direction in this area of planning law. Looked at together, they emphasise not just the need to apply public law concepts rather than private law concepts but also the importance attached in public law to a statutory body's powers and duties and to the wider public interest. It cannot be assumed that exceptions previously found to exist will still apply. Substantial reappraisal is required.

Again, in *Wandsworth LBC v Secretary of State for Transport, Local Government, and the Regions and BT Cellnet* [2003] EWHC 622, the High Court held that following the approach of the House of Lords in *Reprotech* there would now be no extra statutory jurisdiction to allow a planning appeal simply on the grounds of estoppel. It follows that though planning officers are generally helpful in giving advice and offering opinions, if a binding decision is required a formal application must be made under what are now ss 191 or 192 of the 1990 Act.

11.21 Whatever the ramifications may be of the House of Lords decision in *Reprotech*, the giving of misleading advice may nevertheless be a ground for making a complaint to the Local Government Ombudsman. In one report (No 627/H/80) the planning officer of a local planning authority had told a prospective purchaser of land during discussions that he could see no objection to the erection of a two-storey building on the land. The prospective purchaser acted on that advice and completed the purchase. Then, the planning officer, contrary to his earlier advice, recommended to the authority that planning permission be granted only for a bungalow. After a finding by the Local Government Ombudsman of injustice suffered as a result of maladministration, the local planning authority made an *ex gratia* payment of £2,000 to the complainant to compensate him for his loss.

11.22 Concurrently with the demise of estoppel as a principle to be applied in planning law by the judgment of the House of Lords in the *Reprotech* case, attention has turned to the question of whether another principle of public law, namely that of legitimate expectation, can be used to achieve the same result. A legitimate expectation may be said to occur where a public body leads someone to believe that a certain practice or a particular situation exists or may come about. As was said in the public law case of *CSSU v Minister for the Civil Service* [1985] AC 374, a legitimate expectation may arise 'either from an express promise given on behalf of a public authority or from the existence of a regular practice which the claimant can reasonably expect to continue'.

11.23 The approach taken by the courts as expressed in *Coghurst Wood Leisure v Secretary of State* [2002] EWHC 1091 (Admin); [2003] JPL 206 is to accept that whilst situations may occur in planning law where the principle of legitimate expectation might apply, it is likely to be very rare. In *Henry Boot Homes Ltd v Bassetlaw DC* [2002] EWCA Civ 983; [2003] 1 P & CR 23 it was unsuccessfully claimed that the local planning authority, in approving an application for the approval of reserved matters and subsequently, had conducted itself in such a way as to give rise to a legitimate expectation on the part of the developer that it would not be prevented from developing the site pursuant to the outline planning permission, despite the fact that it had not complied with the relevant conditions in the outline permission prior to the commencement of operations. In effect, what the claimant was seeking was a non-statutory variation of a condition. Giving judgment against it, Keane LJ said:

> The interests of third parties and the public in such matters also greatly reduce the potential for a legitimate expectation, such as is contended for in the present appeal, to arise. One of the reasons is that it is difficult to see how a legitimate expectation, said to derive from the conduct of the local authority, could operate so as to prevent an interested third party from questioning whether development has validly begun and whether the planning permission is still extant....
>
> Mr Lowe invited us to say that legitimate expectation could never operate so as to enable the developer to begin development validly and effectively in breach of condition. I am not prepared to adopt so absolute a proposition. It is possible that circumstances might arise where it was clear that there was no third party or public interest in the matter and a court might take the view that a legitimate expectation could then arise from the local planning authority's conduct or representations. But, as was said in the *Coghurst Wood* case, one suspects that such cases will be very rare.

11.24 In another recent case, *R (Kabbell Developments Ltd) v Secretary of State* (2004 unreported) the Court of Appeal accepted that once a s 106 obligation had been entered into, the landowners who had entered into it (and their successors) had a legitimate expectation that an application for outline planning permission for residential development (which the s 106 objection was intended to facilitate) would be granted. The court, however, held that in this case if the time for submission of an application for approval of reserved matters had expired (in considering an application under s 73 of the Act for some later date for submission) there was no legitimate expectation that it would be granted. The only legitimate expectation the landowners would have was that the application would be dealt with in accordance with legal principles and the provisions of the Act. In other words, in determining the application for approval of reserved matters, an authority would take into account all material considerations, including any changes in planning policy since that grant of the outline planning permission and the fact that since the grant the developer may have already fulfilled his duty under the s 106 obligation.

11.25 In *Cox v First Secretary of State* [2003] EWHC 1290 Admin, the High Court accepted that a grievance as a result of misleading advice given unintentionally could not properly amount to a legitimate expectation such as to warrant a grant of planning permission, though it might well found a justified complaint to the Local Government Ombudsman.

11.26 It is possible, however, that the courts may take a more sympathetic view towards the application of legitimate expectations in procedural aspects of planning law, as by for example requiring that persons should be consulted where there has been a promise to do so, or where there is an established practice of doing so.

C. DETERMINATION OF A PLANNING APPLICATION

11.27 Section 70(1) of the Town and Country Planning Act 1990 provides that where an application is made to a local planning authority for planning permission:

(a) … they may grant planning permission, either conditionally or subject to such conditions as they think fit; or
(b) they may refuse planning permission.

11.28 Reasons must be given for the refusal of planning permission and, where permission is granted, for the imposition of conditions, see: Art 35 of the Town and Country Planning (Development Management Procedure) (England) Order 2015 (SI 2015/595). Where the permission amounts to 'EIA Development' reasons must also be stated for the grant of permission, see: reg 30 of the Town and Country Planning (Environmental Impact Assessment) Regulations 2017 (SI 2017/571).

11.29 Since 2013 there has been no statutory duty to supply reasons for the grant of planning permission in non-EIA cases. In *Dover District Council v CPRE (Kent)* [2017] UKSC 79; [2018] 1 WLR 108 however, the Supreme Court held that in some cases, a duty to give reasons for the grant of planning permission arose outside the statutory obligations as a requirement of the common law. Although *CPRE* concerned a case governed by the EIA Regulations, and thus the planning authority were under a duty to supply reasons anyway, the Supreme Court upheld the decision of the Court of Appeal in *R (on the application of Oakley) v South Cambridgeshire District Council* [2017] EWCA Civ 71; [2017] 1 WLR

3765 which was not a case concerning EIA Development and so it is safe to say the Court's reasoning is of general application. Lord Carnwath JSC who gave the judgment of the Court in *CPRE* found the duty to supply reasons was necessary in some cases in order to ensure the planning authority had arrived at a rational decision on relevant grounds at [68]. In short, the remedy of judicial review would be hollow if objectors were not able to know the basis on which a decision had been taken. Both *CPRE* and *Oakley* were in a sense, easy cases. They both concerned departures from recommendations of officers, as such the planning authority could not rely on the reasoning in the officer's report as the basis of the decision (see *Palmer* above). The permissions issued in both cases represented substantial departures from the development plan.

11.30 Unhelpfully, their Lordships in *CPRE* provided no particular guidance as to when the duty would arise beyond the observations at [59] that 'typically' the duty to supply reasons for the grant of permission would arise in cases such as *CPRE* and *Oakley*. That raises the question whether, on a less significant scheme, the duty would arise. Elias LJ in *Oakley* appeared to continence that no duty to supply reasons would arise where it was obvious on the publicly available material that the committee 'merely balanced the interests differently' at [65]. Moreover, neither in *Oakley* or *CPRE*, was there any suggestion that the decision in *R v Aylesbury Vale DC, ex parte Chaplin* (1998) 76 P & CR 207, based on such reasoning, was wrongly decided. Indeed, Sales LJ affirmed that approach in *Oakley* at [71]. That might well be because the purpose of imposing a duty to supply reasons is to reveal any error of law so as to 'make effective the right to challenge the decision by judicial review' (see Lord Carnwath JSC in *CPRE* at [51]), thus provided it is possible to infer that the decision was rational, based on relevant material, the duty is not likely to arise. However, the best advice therefore appears to be that where permission is granted contrary to the advice within an officer's report, clear reasons are supplied in the minutes, setting out how the committee grappled with the relevant policy tests and what factors they took into account which justified coming to a different view to their professional officers. The standard of reasoning is that set out in *South Buckinghamshire District Council v Porter (No 2)* [2004] UKHL 33; [2004] 1 WLR 1953 per Lord Brown at [36].

11.31 Section 70(2) of the 1990 Act provides that the local planning authority, in dealing with an application for planning permission, 'shall have regard to the provisions of the development plan, so far as material to the application, and to any other material considerations'. For the meaning of the term 'development plan', see Chapters 3 and 4.

11.32 As stated earlier, the courts have held that the expression 'shall have regard to the provisions of the development plan', does not require that the plan should be slavishly adhered to. As long as the development plan was considered, an authority has been able to base their decision on 'other material considerations'. The provisions have enabled local planning authorities and the Secretary of State, as a matter of policy during the 1980s when development plans were beginning to get out of date, to give rather less weight to the provisions of the development plan than had formerly been the case.

11.33 When the term 'material considerations' was first introduced into the law by the Town and Country Planning Act 1947, the intention was probably to allow local planning authorities, when determining applications for planning permission, to have regard to any amendments the authority were proposing to make to the approved development plan. In other words, the term was seen mainly as an adjunct to the preceding phrase, 'the provisions of the development plan'. The position was altered, however, as a result of a provision inserted into the 1990 Act by the Planning and Compensation Act 1991, which gave the development plan a place of primacy over other material considerations in the exercise by local planning authorities of their development control functions.

11.34 That provision is now to be found at s 38(6) of the Planning and Compulsory Purchase Act 2004, which now provides as follows:

> If regard is to be had to the development plan for the purpose of any determination to be made under the planning Acts the determination must be made in accordance with the plan unless material considerations indicate otherwise.

Compared with the provision found in s 54A, the significant change made by s 37(6) is the substitution of the word *shall* and its replacement with the word *must*. It is not clear whether the change from 'shall' to 'must' was meant to increase the status of the development plan. It seems unlikely but the change removes any doubt that there is a presumption in favour of the plan.

11.35 The s 54A provision has been considered by the courts on a number of occasions and their decisions on the meaning of that section will equally apply to the new s 38(6). In *St Albans DC v Secretary of State for the Environment* [1993] JPL 374, the effect of s 54A was considered. The Deputy Judge, Mr David Widdicombe QC, after accepting as common ground that the section had no relevance to applications for consent to the demolition of a listed building under the Planning (Listed Buildings and Conservation Areas) Act 1990, felt it was clear that s 54A did set up a presumption in favour of the development plan, but for its rebuttal it was sufficient if there were 'material considerations which indicate otherwise'.

11.36 The effect of the Scottish equivalent of England's s.38(6) was considered by the House of Lords in *City of Edinburgh v Secretary of State for Scotland* [1997] 1 WLR 1447. In that case their Lordships made it quite clear that the provision gave rise to a presumption in favour of the plan. As Lord Clyde said at 1458:

> By virtue of section 18A the development plan is no longer simply one of the material considerations. Its provisions, provided that they are relevant to the particular application, are to govern the decision unless there are material considerations which indicate that in the particular case the provisions of the plan should not be

followed. If it is thought to be useful to talk of presumptions in this field, it can be said that there is now a presumption that the development plan is to govern the decision on an application for planning permission. It is distinct from what has been referred to in some of the planning guidance, such as for example in paragraph 15 of the Planning Policy Guidance Notes PPG1 (January 1988), as a presumption but what is truly an indication of a policy to be taken into account in decision-making. By virtue of section 18A if the application accords with the development plan and there are no material considerations indicating that it should be refused, permission should be granted. If the application does not accord with the development plan it will be refused unless there are material considerations indicating that it should be granted. One example of such a case may be where a particular policy in the plan can be seen to be outdated and superseded by more recent guidance. Thus, the priority given to the development plan is not a mere mechanical preference for it. There remains a valuable element of flexibility. If there are material considerations indicating that it should not be followed then a decision contrary to its provisions can properly be given.

Their Lordships went on, however, to say that the presumption was in essence one of fact; it still left the assessment of the facts and the weighing of the considerations in the hands of the decision-maker. As Lord Hope said at 1450:

> The only questions for the court are whether the decision taker had regard to the presumption, whether the other considerations which he regarded as material were relevant considerations to which he was entitled to have regard and whether, looked at as a whole, his decision was irrational. It would be a mistake to think that the effect of [section 18A] was to increase the power of the court to intervene in decisions about planning control.

11.37 The function of the court, therefore, was to see whether the decision taker had regard to the presumption, not to assess whether the decision-maker gave enough weight to it where there were other material considerations indicating that the determination should not be made in accordance with the development plan.

11.38 The speeches of their Lordships in *City of Edinburgh* have been applied to English law and considered a number of times. The authorities were recently summarized by Lindblom LJ in *BDW Trading Ltd (t/a David Wilson Homes) (Central, Mercia and West Midlands) v Secretary of State for Communities and Local Government* [2016] EWCA Civ 493; [2017] PTSR 1337 at [21]:

- First, the s 38(6) duty is a duty to make a decision (or 'determination') by giving the development plan priority, but weighing all other material considerations in the balance to establish whether the decision should be made, as the statute presumes, in accordance with the plan (see Lord Clyde's speech in the *City of Edinburgh Council case* [1997] 1 WLR 1447 , 1458–1459.
- Secondly, therefore, the decision-maker must understand the relevant provisions of the plan, recognizing that they may sometimes pull in different directions: see Lord Clyde's speech in the *City of Edinburgh Council* case, at 1459D–F, the judgments of Lord Reed JSC and Lord Hope of Craighead DPSC in *Tesco*

Stores Ltd v Dundee City Council (Asda Stores Ltd intervening) [2012] PTSR 983, respectively at paras 19 and 34, and the judgment of Sullivan J in *R v Rochdale Metropolitan Borough Council, Ex p Milne (No 2)* (2000) 81 P & CR 27, paras 48–50.

- Thirdly, s 38(6) does not prescribe the way in which the decision-maker is to go about discharging the duty. It does not specify, for all cases, a two-stage exercise, in which, first, the decision-maker decides 'whether the development plan should or should not be accorded its statutory priority', and secondly, 'if he decides that it should not be given that priority it should be put aside and attention concentrated upon the material factors which remain for consideration': see Lord Clyde's speech in the *City of Edinburgh Council* case, at 1459–1460.
- Fourthly, however, the duty can only be properly performed if the decision-maker, in the course of making the decision, establishes whether or not the proposal accords with the development plan as a whole: see *R (Hampton Bishop Parish Council) v Herefordshire Council* [2015] 1 WLR 2367, para 28, per Richards LJ and *Tiviot Way Investments Ltd v Secretary of State for Communities and Local Government* [2016] JPL 171, paras 27–36, per Patterson J.
- And fifthly, the duty under s 38(6) is not displaced or modified by government policy in the NPPF. Such policy does not have the force of statute. Nor does it have the same status in the statutory scheme as the development plan. Under s 70(2) of the 1990 Act and s 38(6) of the 2004 Act, its relevance to a planning decision is as one of the other material considerations to be weighed in the balance: see the *Hampton Bishop Parish Council* case, para 30, per Richards LJ.

11.39 It should however be noted that the s 38(6) duty bites only on the words in the policy box and not on the supporting text, which serves only as an 'aid to interpretation' and cannot add new policy tests or 'trump' the wording in the policy box, see: *R (on the application of Cherkley Campaign Ltd) v Mole Valley District Council* [2014] EWCA Civ 567 per Richards LJ at [16] and [21].

11.40 The introduction in March 2012 of the National Planning Policy Framework, drafted in notably more directional and unqualified terms than previous planning policy, has given rise to a sizeable amount of case law, especially concerning its interaction with the statutory duty at s 38(6) and the 'presumption in favour of sustainable development' (now at para 11 of the NPPF). This interaction was addressed by the Supreme Court in *Hopkins Homes Ltd v Secretary of State for Communities and Local Government* [2017] UKSC 37; [2017] 1 WLR 1865, on which see further: A Bowes, 'The NPPF and the Statutory Code' [2017] 8 JPL 785. Lord Carnwath JSC held at [21] that:

> The Framework itself makes clear that as respects the determination of planning applications (by contrast with plan-making in which it has statutory recognition), it is no more than 'guidance' and as such a 'material consideration' for the purposes of section 70(2) of the 1990 Act … It cannot, and does not purport to, displace

the primacy given by the statute and policy to the statutory development plan. It must be exercised consistently with, and not so as to displace or distort, the statutory scheme.

The correct approach to the application of the presumption in favour of sustainable development in the development management context was explained by the Court of Appeal in *East Staffordshire Borough Council* v *Secretary of State for Communities and Local Government* [2017] EWCA Civ 893; [2018] PTSR 88 per Lindblom LJ at [22]–[23].

The House of Lords held in *City of Edinburgh* that decision-takers are not obliged to always follow the development plan. The situation on the ground may have changed significantly since the plan was adopted. Accordingly, as Lord Clyde held in *City of Edinburgh,* the weight a decision-taker attaches to a conflict with the development plan may vary, for example where 'a particular policy in the plan can be seen to be outdated and superseded by more recent guidance' or, as Lord Carnwath JSC held in *Hopkins* at [55], the situation has changed on the ground. Seen in that light, there is nothing unlawful about a decision-taker reducing the weight to policies which restrict the supply of housing in circumstances where there is a shortfall in the supply of housing land. How much weight a decision-taker gives to policies superseded by more recent guidance or overtaken by events on the ground is a matter of planning judgment for them. **11.41**

A decision is not therefore bound to follow more recent guidance over policies in the development plan. Thus, in *R (on the application of West Berkshire Council)* v *Secretary of State for Communities and Local Government* [2016] EWCA Civ 441; [2016] 1 WLR 3923 the Court of Appeal held that a policy which required that affordable housing contributions should not be sought from residential schemes of ten or fewer units was not unlawful because, notwithstanding the mandatory terms in which it was drafted, the decision-taker always retained a flexibility whether to depart from the provisions of the development plan in light of more recent government policy. Moreover, Sedley LJ observed in *Sainsburys Supermarkets Ltd v First Secretary of State* [2005] EWCA Civ 520 at [16] that national policy is 'not a rule but a guide'. See further on the effect of *West Berkshire*: A Bowes, 'Affordable Housing and Vacant Building Credit' [2016] 9 JPL 847 and 'Affordable Housing on Small Sites Post R. (on the application of West Berkshire DC) v Secretary of State for Communities and Local Government' [2017] 1 JPL 1 commenting on the Planning Inspectorate decision (APP/K3605/W/16/3146699). **11.42**

Development plans often contain exceptions, qualifications, overlapping, or even contradictory policies and issues on which value judgments have to be made. In *R v Rochdale MBC, ex p Milne* (2001) 81 P & CR 365, Sullivan J said: **11.43**

> It is not at all that unusual for development plan policies to pull in different directions. A proposed development may be in accord with development plan policies which, for example, encourage development for employment purposes, and yet be

contrary to policies which seek to protect open countryside. In such cases there may be no clear cut answer to the question: is this proposal in accordance with the plan? The local planning authority has to make a judgment bearing in mind such factors as the importance of the policies which are complied with or infringed, and the extent of compliance or breach.

Those *obiter* views were expressly approved in *Tesco Stores Ltd v Dundee City Council* [2012] UKSC 13; [2012] PTSR 983 by Lord Hope at [34].

11.44 It should also be emphasized that a development plan in course of preparation is only a material consideration, and does not become part of the development plan for the purpose of s 38(6) until it is adopted, or in the case of a neighbourhood development plan, at the point at which it passes referendum and as the planning authority have not resolved not to make the plan. The point was recognized in *Nottingham CC and Brostowe BC v Secretary of State for the Environment, Transport, and the Regions* [1999] EGCS 35 by Sullivan J when he said:

> But there is a clear difference, in my judgment, between a statutory obligation to determine an appeal in accordance with Development Plan policies unless material considerations indicate otherwise, and an obligation to have regard to emerging policies as material considerations, even if the emerging policies are accorded considerable weight.

Other material considerations

11.45 In determining applications for planning permission, the decision-maker is also under a duty to have regard to 'any other material considerations' see: s 70(2)(c) of the Town and Country Planning Act 1990. In general public law, it is for the decision-maker to decide (i) whether to take account of a given material consideration and (ii) how far to go in obtaining information relating to that consideration, subject to intervention by the court only on irrationality grounds, see: *In Re Findlay* [1985] AC 318 per Lord Scarman at 333–334; *R (on the application of Khatun) v Newham LBC* [2005] EWCA Civ 55; [2005] QB 37 per Laws LJ at [34]–[35], summarized in *R (on the application of Plant) v Lambeth LBC* [2016] EWHC 3324 (Admin); [2017] PTSR 453 per Holgate J at [62]. It has occasionally been suggested that s 70(2) of the 1990 Act alters the correctness of that proposition in the determination of planning applications, such that a decision-maker is obliged to have regard to *every* material consideration, see, for example, the submission in *Dignity Funerals Ltd v Breckland DC* [2017] EWHC 1492 (Admin) at [76]. However, the prevailing view is that *Re Findlay* is binding authority and is equally applicable to planning cases, see: *R (on the application of Luton Borough Council) v Central Bedfordshire Council* [2015] EWCA Civ 537; [2015] 2 P & CR 19 per Sales LJ at [71] That is also the prevailing view in the commentary, see: R Williams, 'From CREEDNZ to Cumberlege: A Review of the Law on Material Considerations' [2017] 12 JPL 1358 and J Findlay QC and A Bowes, 'Are All Considerations Equal? A Muse on Materiality' [2016] 5 JPL 443.

Determination of a Planning Application

Whatever the genesis of the term may have been, it is now recognized to have a much wider connotation and can cover social and economic considerations. In *Stringer v Minister of Housing and Local Government* [1970] 1 WLR 1281, Cooke J, in upholding a decision to refuse planning permission for development which would have interfered with the working of the Jodrell Bank telescope, said:

11.46

> It may be conceded at once that the material considerations to which the Minister is entitled and bound to have regard in deciding the appeal must be considerations of a planning nature. I find it impossible, however, to accept the view that such considerations are limited to matters relating to amenity ... it seems to me that any consideration which relates to the use and development of land is capable of being a planning consideration.

However, the scope is not limitless, as the Court of Appeal held when rejecting as 'immaterial' a donation to the local community of the proportion of the turnover derived from the operation of a wind turbine in *R (on the application of Wright) v Forest of Dean District Council* [2017] EWCA Civ 2102; [2018] JPL 672. Hickenbottom LJ held at [28(ii)]:

11.47

> For a consideration to be material, it must have a planning purpose (i.e. it must relate to the character or the use of land, and not be solely for some other purpose no matter how well-intentioned and desirable that purpose may be); and it must fairly and reasonably relate to the permitted development (i.e. there must be a real—as opposed to a fanciful, remote, trivial or *de minimis*—connection with the development).

In the context of planning obligations, the Supreme Court affirmed those principles in *Aberdeen City Council & Shire Strategic Development Planning Authority v Elsick Development Company Ltd* [2017] UKSC 66; [2017] PTSR 1413 per Lord Hodge at [28]. It should, however, be noted that the Supreme Court has granted permission to appeal in *Wright* (2 May 2018 per Lords Wilson, Carnwath, and Lloyd-Jones) and so further clarification of the law might well be forthcoming.

The wide scope of material considerations is well illustrated by the decision of Cranston J in *R (on the application of Copeland) v Tower Hamlets LBC* [2010] EWHC 1845 (Admin); [2011] JPL 40 where he held that promoting social objectives could be a material consideration and that therefore the need to promote healthy eating can be a material consideration. In considering an application for a fastfood takeaway, the planning committee had been wrongly told that the potential effect on healthy eating by the proximity of a school to the proposed takeaway could not be taken into account and so their grant of planning permission was quashed. While it is for the courts to determine whether a factor in law is capable of being a material consideration, the weight to be given to the consideration is essentially a matter for the local planning authority or the Secretary of State. Indeed, it is for the LPA or the Secretary of State to determine whether in a particular set of circumstances a consideration is in fact material. In *Bibb v Bristol CC* [2011] EWHC 3057 Ouseley J held that the impact on planning permission

11.48

A of granting planning permission B could be material if the LPA had to accept the factual premise that without the grant of planning permission B permission A would not be implemented.

11.49 Among the matters commonly regarded as relating to the use and development of land are the siting of buildings, their number, area, height, mass, design, and external appearance; means of access; landscaping; impact on neighbouring land; availability of infrastructure; traffic considerations; and communications.

The following are other examples of considerations held by the courts to be material:

(a) The safeguarding of land required for a road-widening scheme (*Westminster Bank Ltd v Minister of Housing and Local Government* [1971] AC 508).
(b) The protection of an ancient monument (*Hoveringham Gravels Ltd v Secretary of State for the Environment* [1975] QB 754).
(c) The likelihood of the proposed development being carried out (*Sovmots Investments Ltd v Secretary of State for the Environment* [1979] AC 144).
(d) The risk of flooding to neighbouring landowners (*George Wimpey & Co Ltd v Secretary of State for the Environment* [1978] JPL 776).
(e) Disturbance or annoyance to neighbouring occupiers from a casino (*Ladbroke (Rentals) Ltd v Secretary of State for the Environment* [1981] JPL 427).

11.50 The wide definition of what can be a material consideration means that the courts have more often laid down what can be capable of being a material consideration than what cannot. However, the following are some examples of considerations held by the courts not to be material:

(a) The question of whether development was economically worthwhile (*Walters v Secretary of State for Wales* [1979] JPL 171). However, although the financial viability of development may not be a material consideration, in *Sosmo Trust v Secretary of State for the Environment* [1983] JPL 806 it was held that the lack of financial viability could be material where a failure to grant planning permission for development would result in a building being left unoccupied and derelict. Finance may also be material where funds are being provided by development being allowed contrary to the development plan, in order to enable development which is not contrary to the plan to proceed (enabling development).
(b) In *R v Essex CC, ex p Tarmac Roadstone Holdings Ltd* [1998] JPL B23, the High Court held that a planning permission the sole or primary purpose of which was to legitimize a previous breach so as to make lawful that which was not lawful, did not relate to the development's planning merits. If something were brought to the attention of an authority as being in breach of planning laws, the authority's duty was to consider in the circumstances of the case whether any form of enforcement was appropriate. It was not lawful for the authority, instead

of doing that, to decide to confer a mantle of legality upon what has been done by a further grant of planning permission, and for no perceptible reason other than to confer such a mantle.

(c) The cost to a local planning authority of modifying or revoking a planning permission or of issuing a discontinuance order (after some disagreement in the lower courts) has been held by the Supreme Court to be capable of being considered by the planning authorities. Indeed, Lord Carnwath (who gave the only reasoned judgment in *Health and Safety Executive v Wolverhampton City Council* [2012] UKSC 34; [2012] 1 WLR 2264) stated that the public authorities would generally be bound to consider the cost, where the cost might not be proportionate to the public interest served by the order, as in *Alnwick DC v Secretary of State for the Environment, Transport, and the Regions* [1999] JPL B190. But this was doubted by Ouseley J in *R (on the application of Usk Valley Conservation Group) v Brecon Beacons National Park Authority* [2010] 2 P & CR 14 in a case concerning a discontinuance order under s 102 of the 1990 Act and in *Health and Safety Executive v Wolverhampton City Council* [2010] EWCA Civ 892 Sullivan LJ (supported by Longmore LJ) approved of Ouseley's decision, though Pill LJ thought that *Alnwick* had been rightly decided.

By s 149(1) of the Equality Act 2010 a public authority in the exercise of its functions must: (a) eliminate discrimination, harassment, victimization, and any other conduct that is prohibited by or under this Act; (b) advance equality of opportunity between persons who share a relevant protected characteristic and persons who do not share it; and (c) foster good relations between persons who share a relevant protected characteristic and persons who do not share it. The requirements of s 149 are summarized by McCombe LJ in *Bracking v Secretary of State for Work and Pensions* [2013] EWCA Civ 1345; [2014] Eq LR 60 at [26] which were in turn approved by Lord Neuberger PSC in *Hotak v London Borough of Southwark* [2015] UKSC 30; [2016] AC 811 at [73]. **11.51**

In *R (on the application of Baker) v Secretary of State for Communities and Local Government and Bromley London Borough* [2008] EWCA Civ 141; [2009] PTSR 809, it was said that the previous duty under s 71(1) of the Race Relations Act 1976 duty is not a duty to eliminate unlawful racial discrimination or to promote equality of opportunity and good relations between different persons of different racial groups, but a duty to have regard to the need to achieve these goals. In the *Baker* case and in *R (on the application of Issacs) v Secretary of State for Communities and Local Government* [2009] EWHC 557 it was held that reference does not have to be specifically made to s 71(1) as long as the decision-maker has had substantive due regard to the relevant statutory needs. However, in *R (on the application of Harris) v Haringey LBC* [2010] EWCA Civ 703; [2011] PTSR 931 the Court of Appeal held that, where there is clear evidence that the development raises issues of equality and good race relations, there needs to be actual analysis **11.52** of that material in the light of the specific statutory duties. In *Harris* there had been no such analysis.

11.53 A recent consideration of the s 149 duty in the planning context is to be found in *R (on the application of Buckley) v Bath & North East Somerset Council* [2018] EWHC 1551 (Admin); [2018] JPL 1231. Lewis J found that the planning authority had failed to have due regard to the impact on elderly and disabled person of granting permission which might have led to the demolition of their existing homes, arising from a regeneration scheme. Lewis J distinguished the planning policy at issue in *Isaacs* at [33] on the basis that:

> That guidance focused on a particular group, gypsies and travellers, recognised the specific problems and disadvantages that that group faced and considered how to address the need to provide sites where they could live. Policy H8 is a more general policy dealing with affordable housing regeneration schemes

Government policies

11.54 Just as draft development plans can be material consideration, so too can government policies be material considerations. In *Hopkins*, Lord Carnwath JSC identified the source of the Minister's power to promulgate planning policy, holding at [19] that it derived 'expressly or by implication, from the planning Acts which give him overall responsibility for oversight of the planning system', his Lordship rejected the suggestion made by Laws LJ, that the power stemmed from Prerogative in *R (on the application of West Berkshire District Council) v Secretary of State for Communities and Local Government* [2016] EWCA Civ 441; [2016] 1 WLR 3923 at [12]. It is important to recognize that government policy cannot change what is or what is not a material consideration, which is a matter for the courts, see: *Tesco Stores Ltd v Secretary of State for the Environment* [1995] 1 WLR 759 per Lord Hoffmann at 780. In this sense government publications are material considerations in that they are the source of the Government's views on what are legally material considerations, as when a policy might set out the weight to be given to the protection of amenities as opposed to economic growth. In this regard Schiemann J (as he then was) in *R v Poole Borough Council, ex p Beebee* [1991] JPL 643, pointed out that planning Circulars are full of broad statements with many presumptions, many of which are mutually irreconcilable, so that in a particular case one may have to give way to another. That statement is even more apposite to apply to Planning Policy Guidance Notes and Planning Policy Statements. Given the language used in s 70(2) of the 1990 Act and the original intent behind the use of the words 'other material considerations' it is not surprising that government policy should lie fairly and squarely within that term. The main vehicles for the articulation of government policy used to be Planning Policy Guidance Notes and Planning Policy Statements, and these will always be a material consideration in making development control decisions at least until they are withdrawn. But, as it was said in *R v Wakefield MDC, ex p Pearl Assurance plc* [1997] JPL B131,

PPGs are not delegated legislation and do not have the force of statutes. They are 'guidelines not tramways. They do not purport to deal definitively with every situation which may arise.' He went on to say that whether a piece of guidance amounts as a matter of law to a material consideration has to be judged by reference to the content of the particular case. It followed, therefore, that part of a PPG which amounts to a material consideration in one case may not necessarily be a material consideration in every case, though certain elements of the guidance may be of universal application.

11.55 It must be borne in mind too, that a Guidance Note or Statement can in no way remove from the local planning authority or Secretary of State the obligation to consider the development plan for the area, which must always be pre-eminent (see above discussion of *Hopkins* and *West Berkshire* cases). Furthermore, in *EC Gransden & Co Ltd v Secretary of State for the Environment* (1987) 54 P & CR 86, Woolf J (as he then was) made it clear that a policy statement in a Guidance Note or Circular cannot turn what would otherwise be a material planning consideration into an irrelevant consideration. But it seems from that case that a Guidance Note or Circular can decide that more weight should be given to one or to some material considerations than to others, though the authority would not act ultra vires if it preferred some other weighting.

11.56 In *EC Gransden & Co Ltd v Secretary of State for the Environment* (1987) 54 P & CR 361, Woolf J set out *in extenso* the proper approach to policy considerations at that time embodied in Circulars. He said (at pp 93–4):

> ... it seems to me, first of all, that any policy, if it is to be a policy which is a proper policy for planning purposes, must envisage that in exceptional circumstances the Minister has the right to depart from that policy. If the situation was otherwise ... it would be an improper attempt to curtail the discretion which is provided by the Act, which indicates that in determining planning applications regard is not only to be had to the provisions of the development plan so far as material, but also to any other material considerations.
>
> What then is the significance of the inspector having failed to follow the policy? Does that mean that this court has to quash his decision? The situation, as I see it, is as follows: first, section 29 [now s 70] lays down what matters are to be regarded as material, and the policy cannot make a matter which is otherwise a material consideration an irrelevant consideration. Secondly, if the policy is a lawful policy, that is to say if it is not a policy which is defective because it goes beyond the proper role of a policy by seeking to do more than indicate the weight which should be given to relevant considerations, then the body determining an application must have regard to the policy. Thirdly, the fact that a body has to have regard to the policy does not mean that it needs necessarily to follow the policy. However, if it is going to depart from the policy, it must give clear reasons for ... not doing so in order that the recipient of its decision will know why the decision is being made as an exception to the policy and the grounds upon which the decision is taken. Fourthly, in order to give effect to the approach which I have just indicated it is essential that the policy is properly understood by the determining body. If the body making the decision fails

to properly understand the policy, then the decision will be as defective as it would be if no regard had been paid to the policy. Fifthly, if proper regard, in the manner in which I have indicated, is not given to the policy, then this court will quash the decision unless the situation is one of those exceptional cases where the court can be quite satisfied that the failure to have proper regard to the policy has not affected the outcome in that the decision would in any event have been the same.

11.57 The materiality of Circulars and Planning Policy Guidance Notes was also considered in *Carpets of Worth Ltd v Wyre Forest DC* (1991) 62 P & CR 334 (CA), where Purchas LJ said:

> I must consider the status of these documents. They are not issued under statutory authority. 'Prescribed' considerations involve regulations made by the Secretary of State under section 287 of the 1971 Act and are therefore subject to resolution of each House of Parliament. Ministerial circulars as published or as summarised in PPGs have therefore no formal statutory force and should therefore not be treated as such for any purpose. This includes in my judgment the manner in which they should be construed and/or applied. They constitute announcements of the current ministerial planning policy. The only statutory obligation upon the local planning authority is 'to have regard to them'. They are in no way bound by them.

Then later he said:

> Although the local authority is not bound by the policy circulars, it should observe them and depart from them only if there are clear reasons, which should be stated, for so doing.

11.58 Although it is a requirement of the law that in order for a decision-maker to have regard to a policy or to determine an application in accordance with it the policy must be properly understood, the court's role is limited to construing the policy in question, leaving the decision-maker to apply the policy to the planning issues as a matter of fact. The Government has revoked most of the PPSs, PPGs and MPGs and replace them with the new National Planning Policy Framework (NPPF). The NPPF must equally have the status of a material consideration and so the presumption in favour of sustainable development contained in the NPPF must be a material consideration. As to the interpretation and application of the term 'sustainable development' in the NPPF, see: *East Staffordshire Borough Council v Secretary of State for Communities and Local Government* [2017] EWCA Civ 893; [2017] PTSR 88 per Lindblom LJ at [22].

11.59 It is important also to emphasize that the law makes a clear distinction between the question of whether something is or is not a material consideration, and the weight which should be given to it. As Lord Hoffmann said in *Tesco Stores Ltd v Secretary of State for the Environment* [1995] 1 WLR 759 at 780:

> The former is a question of law and the latter is a question of planning judgment, which is entirely a matter for the planning authority. Provided that the planning authority has regard to all material considerations, it is at liberty (provided that it does not lapse into *Wednesbury* irrationality) to give them whatever weight the planning authority thinks fit or no weight at all. The fact that the law regards something as

a material consideration therefore involves no view about the part, if any, which it should play in the decision-making process.

11.60 A case in practice where a problem commonly occurs as to the weight to be given to a material consideration is when a development plan is being prepared but has not yet been formally adopted (or approved). The precise weight to be given to the emerging development plan is, of course, a matter for the decision-maker. If an application for planning permission would, if granted, prejudice the outcome of the development plan process, that may amount to a case for refusing the application on the grounds of prematurity.

11.61 Also in *R (on the application of Cala Homes (South) Ltd v Secretary of State for Communities and Local Government* [2011] EWCA Civ 639 it was accepted that the intention of the Government to abolish regional strategies in the Localism Bill was capable of being a material consideration although until the regional strategies were actually abolished, they still formed part of the policies in the development plan. Sullivan LJ held that as the prospective change in planning policy was a material consideration, the intention to effect this change in policy said much about the weight to be given to prospective change. He indicated that the weight to be given was strengthened as it becomes more certain that the regional strategies would be abolished by Act of Parliament. Also, a prospective change to Government policy can be a material consideration even if the policy has not yet been formally withdrawn. In *R (on the application of Smith) v Secretary of State for Communities and Local Government* [2012] EWHC 963 (Admin); [2012] JPL 975 the Minister had announced that Circular 1/2006 dealing with Gypsy Sites was to be revoked. On appeal against an enforcement notice the Minister in dismissing the appeal had stated that he had given less weight to the circular. It was held that as a matter of principle a prospective change to policy was capable of being a material consideration.

Previous appeal decisions

11.62 In *North Wiltshire DC v Secretary of State for the Environment* (1992) 65 P & CR 137, the Court of Appeal held that it was indisputable that a previous appeal decision concerning the same application site was a material consideration in determining a subsequent application for the development of the same site. The reason is the need for like cases to be decided in a like manner so that there is consistency in the appellate process. In his judgment Mann LJ said:

> Consistency is self-evidently important to both developers and development control authorities. But it is also important for the purpose of securing public confidence in the operation of the development control system. I do not suggest and it would be wrong to do so, that like cases *must* be decided alike. An Inspector must always exercise his own judgment. He is therefore free upon consideration to disagree with the judgment of another but before doing so he ought to have regard to the importance of consistency and to give his reasons for departure from the previous decision.

To state that like cases should be decided alike presupposes that the earlier case is alike and is not distinguishable in some relevant respect. If it is distinguishable then it usually will lack materiality by reference to consistency, although it may be material in some other way. Where it is indistinguishable then ordinarily it must be a material consideration. A practical test for the inspector is to ask himself whether, if I decide this case in a particular way, am I necessarily agreeing or disagreeing with some critical aspect of the decision in the previous case?

11.63 The *North Wiltshire* case concerned an earlier decision on the same site. In *R v Secretary of State for the Environment, ex p David Baber* [1996] JPL 1032, the Court of Appeal had to consider an earlier appeal decision on a site that was different from but close to the second appeal site. There, Glidewell LJ referred to the test proposed by Mann LJ in *North Wiltshire* and continued:

> He [Glidewell LJ] suggested that the test which the inspector ought to have posed to himself was slightly different. It was: a previous decision having been drawn to my attention, do I take the view that it may well be sufficiently closely related to the matters in issue in my appeal that I ought to have regard to it and either follow it or distinguish it?

11.64 In *Beaulieu Property Management v Secretary of State for the Environment* (1997) EGCS 129 it was accepted that the decision-maker, and ultimately the court, must first determine that the first appeal decision is 'alike and not distinguishable in some relevant respect' (*North Wiltshire*) or 'sufficiently closely related to the matters in issue' (*Baber*) such that it was a material consideration. If it was material, then the decision-maker is under a duty to give reasons if his decision departs from the previous decision. A failure to give reasons could lead to the court quashing a decision if there was substantial prejudice to the applicant.

11.65 In *Dunster Properties Ltd v First Secretary of State* [2007] EWCA Civ 236, an Inspector differed from the view taken by a previous Inspector as to the effect of proposed development on the character or appearance of a conservation area. The second Inspector made no comment on why he took a different view from the first Inspector, other than to state that each case should be judged on its own merits. This was considered by the Court of Appeal to be inadequate, which duly quashed the second Inspector's decision.

11.66 In the early days, the principle was based on the need for consistency through the appellate process. It was only a question of time before the principle was extended to the decision-making power of local planning authorities, see: *R (Mid Counties Co-Operative) v Forest of Dean* [2013] EWHC 1908 (Admin) per Stewart J at [16]. Quite apart from the need for consistency, the need to have regard to previous decisions can be important elsewhere particularly where land has the benefit of a previous planning permission which has not been implemented and a new development proposal has to be considered, the argument being that implementation of a new planning permission would be better than the implementation of an old permission. A recent review (and arguably an extension) of the consistency

Determination of a Planning Application

principle is to be found in the judgment of Lindblom LJ *DLA Delivery Ltd v Baroness Cumberlege of Newick* [2018] EWCA Civ 1305 at [34]:

- First, because consistency in planning decision-making is important, there will be cases in which it would be unreasonable for the Secretary of State not to have regard to a previous appeal decision bearing on the issues in the appeal he is considering. This may sometimes be so even though none of the parties has relied on the previous decision or brought it to the Secretary of State's attention (para 100). And it may be necessary in those circumstances, in the interests of fairness, to give the parties an opportunity to make further representations in the light of the previous decision.
- Secondly, the court should not attempt to prescribe or limit the circumstances in which a previous decision can be a material consideration. It may be material, for example, because it relates to the same site, or to the same or a similar form of development on another site to which the same policy of the development plan relates, or to the interpretation or application of a particular policy common to both cases (see para 92 of Holgate J's judgment in *St Albans City and District Council*).
- Thirdly, the circumstances in which it can be unreasonable for the Secretary of State to fail to take into account a previous appeal decision that has not been brought to his notice by one of the parties will vary. But in tackling this question, it will be necessary for the court to consider whether the Secretary of State was actually aware, or ought to have been aware, of the previous decision and its significance for the appeal now being determined (paras 100, 101, and 105 of the judgment). As the judge said, '[before] the close of the "adversarial" part of the proceedings, the Secretary of State and his inspectors can normally rely, not unreasonably, on participants to draw attention to any relevant decision[, but] that does not mean that they are never required to make further enquiries about any matter, including about other ... decisions that may be significant' (para 101).

11.67 This gives rise to what has been called the fall-back principle, and it requires the decision-maker in determining the second application for planning permission to have regard to the merits of the previous decision and the reasons for it. Recent examples of the operation of this rule occurred in *Postwood Developments Ltd v Secretary of State for the Environment* [1992] JPL 823, and *Haven Leisure Ltd v Secretary of State for the Environment and North Cornwall DC* [1994] JPL 148. This latter case is one authority for the proposition that not only has the existence of the 'previous' planning permission to be shown, but also that the permission is likely to be implemented if permission for the later development is refused.

11.68 The principles of fallback were recently summarized by the Court of Appeal in *Mansell v Tonbridge & Malling BC* [2017] EWCA Civ 1314 per Lindblom LJ at [27] as follows:

   (1) Here, as in other aspects of the law of planning, the court must resist a prescriptive or formulaic approach, and must keep in mind the scope for a lawful exercise of planning judgment by a decision-maker.

(2) The relevant law as to a 'real prospect' of a fallback development being implemented was applied by this court in Samuel Smith Old Brewery (see, in particular, paragraphs 17 to 30 of Sullivan L.J.'s judgment, with which the Master of the Rolls and Toulson L.J. agreed; and the judgment of Supperstone J. in R. (on the application of Kverndal) v London Borough of Hounslow Council [2015] EWHC 3084 (Admin) , at paragraphs 17 and 42 to 53). As Sullivan L.J. said in his judgment in Samuel Smith Old Brewery, in this context a 'real' prospect is the antithesis of one that is 'merely theoretical' (paragraph 20). The basic principle is that '... for a prospect to be a real prospect, it does not have to be probable or likely: a possibility will suffice' (paragraph 21). Previous decisions at first instance, including Ahern and Brentwood Borough Council v Secretary of State for the Environment [1996] 72 P. & C.R. 61 must be read with care in the light of that statement of the law, and bearing in mind, as Sullivan L.J. emphasized, '... "fall back" cases tend to be very fact-specific' (ibid.). The role of planning judgment is vital. And '[it] is important ... not to constrain what is, or should be, in each case the exercise of a broad planning discretion, based on the individual circumstances of that case, by seeking to constrain appeal decisions within judicial formulations that are not enactments of general application but are themselves simply the judge's response to the facts of the case before the court' (paragraph 22).

(3) Therefore, when the court is considering whether a decision-maker has properly identified a 'real prospect' of a fallback development being carried out should planning permission for the proposed development be refused, there is no rule of law that, in every case, the 'real prospect' will depend, for example, on the site having been allocated for the alternative development in the development plan or planning permission having been granted for that development, or on there being a firm design for the alternative scheme, or on the landowner or developer having said precisely how he would make use of any permitted development rights available to him under the GPDO. In some cases that degree of clarity and commitment may be necessary; in others, not. This will always be a matter for the decision-maker's planning judgment in the particular circumstances of the case in hand.

Protection of private interests

11.69 It is constantly said that the object of planning control is to restrict private development in the public interest and not in the private interest. Examples of public-interest matters include acceptable standards of privacy, adequate daylight or sunlight, and freedom from excessive noise. The preservation of open views, however, is a private interest which the law is not intended to protect. Occasionally, of course, public and private interests overlap.

11.70 Although it is not the proper function of planning law to protect private interests, in the course of protecting the public interest a landowner may obtain a benefit which he would not otherwise enjoy. In *Stringer v Minister of Housing and Local Government* [1970] 1 WLR 1281, the director of the Nuffield Radio Astronomy Laboratories, which operated the Jodrell Bank radio telescope, sought to persuade the local planning authority that in considering applications for planning permission in the surrounding area, it should have regard to the efficient operation of the telescope. It appeared that the efficiency of the telescope was affected by electrical sparks and other forms of disturbance which emanated from terrestrial sources in the neighbourhood, since those sources produced signals similar to the signals the telescope received from outer space. The danger of interference from such things as radios, televisions, and motor vehicles, however, diminished the more distant they were from the telescope. So, the local planning authority, the rural district council, and the University of Manchester (which owned the telescope) entered into an agreement whereby the local planning authority undertook to discourage development within a certain radius of the station. Stringer became a victim of this agreement. His application for planning permission was refused on the ground that, if granted, the development would interfere with the efficient running of the telescope. His appeal against the refusal to the Minister was dismissed. Stringer then appealed to the High Court under what is now s 288 of the 1990 Act for an order quashing the Minister's decision.

11.71 The court held that the agreement between the local planning authority and the University was null and void because its intention was to bind the local planning authority to disregard considerations which it was required to have regard to under what is now s 70(2) of the 1990 Act. The agreement breached the basic principle that a public authority cannot by contract bind itself to disregard its statutory duties. The court went on, however, to consider that the Minister's decision was valid. The Minister had not been party to the improper agreement and had not bound himself to follow any particular course of action. In determining the appeal, which included the determination of the planning application as if it were made to him *de novo*, the Minister was entitled to have a policy with regard to the proposed development and here that policy was to discourage development in the vicinity of the telescope. As long as that policy was not followed blindly so as to exclude the consideration by him of all material considerations, his decision could not be faulted.

11.72 Faced with the likely success of that argument, however, Stringer also argued that the Minister had taken into account a consideration which was not material, namely the private interests of Jodrell Bank radio telescope. Dismissing that argument, Cooke J held that the term 'material considerations' was not limited to considerations of amenity and that in a proper case might take into account private interests as well as public interests. The fact that the proposed development would interfere with the operation of the telescope was a material consideration in determining the application.

11.73 The decision was followed shortly after in *RMC Management Services Ltd v Secretary of State for the Environment* (1972) 222 EG 1593. The company had applied to the High Court to quash a decision of the Secretary of State dismissing an appeal from a refusal by the local planning authority to grant planning permission for the erection of a ready-mixed concrete batching plant. The reason given for the dismissal of the appeal was that the development would generate an abnormal level of airborne abrasive dust which would affect the operations of four neighbouring establishments. The four establishments had been attracted to that area by the relatively clean air needed to carry on their high-precision engineering work. The company alleged that in so deciding the Secretary of State was seeking to protect the extraordinary requirements of adjacent occupiers in the use and enjoyment of their land at the expense of and to the detriment of the company in the use and enjoyment of its land. It was not disputed that the proposed use would have been normal for an industrial estate and that it would not have given rise to an actionable nuisance by escape of dust, even if carried out in a residential area. In refusing the application Bristow J adopted the language of Cooke J in *Stringer v Minister of Housing and Local Government* [1970] 1 WLR 1281, where he said:

> 'In principle, it seems to me that any consideration which relates to the use and development of land is capable of being a planning consideration. Whether a particular consideration falling within that broad class is material in any given case will depend upon the circumstances.'

11.74 In dealing with the application before him, Bristow J thought that the Secretary of State was entitled to ask himself whether the proposed development was compatible with the proper and desirable use of other land in the area. In his view the risk to the four special clean-air neighbours was a planning consideration which the Secretary of State was entitled to consider and right to consider material.

11.75 So the fact that the special interests of adjoining occupiers of land in clean air was protected gave them (as a side effect) a benefit under planning law they would not have enjoyed at common law.

11.76 Although it is clear law that planning control is concerned only with the public interest, where private rights are being interfered with the proper question to ask is whether the public interest requires that the interests of that party should be considered. In *Wood-Robinson v Secretary of State for the Environment and Wandsworth LBC* [1998] JPL 976, the applicant had been refused planning permission for the construction of a dwellinghouse within the curtilage of a block of flats. On appeal the Inspector had upheld the refusal, holding that although the proposed development would not have an adverse effect on the surrounding locality, it would have an adverse effect on the amenity of local residents. Refusing to quash the decision of the Secretary of State, the High Court held that it was legitimate for the Secretary of State to take into account the effects on local residential amenity.

Creation of a precedent

11.77 The courts have accepted the principle that although land may be suitable for the development proposed, the local planning authority may refuse planning permission for that development if to grant it would be likely to lead to a proliferation of applications for similar development, which the authority would then find it difficult to refuse. Such a situation would be even more likely if a permission were granted in breach of a policy without any good reason, leading to other applications being made equally devoid of good reason.

11.78 In *Collis Radio Ltd v Secretary of State for the Environment* [1975] JPL 221, the owners of a warehouse, who had used it for storing electrical goods, began to use it to carry on a cash and carry business. The local planning authority had served an enforcement notice on the owners requiring them to cease and to restore the land to its former user. The Secretary of State dismissed the owners' appeal against the notice on the ground, inter alia, that while the development on the appeal site was unlikely to have a particularly harmful effect on the existing shopping centres, a proliferation of such developments might well do. The owners appealed to the Secretary of State against the notice solely on the ground that 'planning permission ought to be granted' for the development. Their appeal to the court against the Secretary of State's decision to uphold the enforcement notice was based on the ground that, if planning permission were to be granted, the effect of possible future developments of the type enforced against was not a material consideration. In dismissing the appeal, Lord Widgery CJ said that it was of great importance when considering a single planning application to ask what the consequences in the locality would be and what side effects would flow if permission were granted. Insofar as planning permission for the one site was judged by the Secretary of State in the light of the consequences for other sites, no error of law had been disclosed. It seems, however, that something more than a mere assertion or generalized concern is needed. There must be evidence to indicate that if planning permission were granted, it would make it more difficult to refuse other planning applications for similar development which may have damaging effects.

11.79 The decision of the Divisional Court in *Collis Radio Ltd v Secretary of State for the Environment* was followed in *Anglia Building Society v Secretary of State for the Environment* [1984] JPL 175, where planning permission for a change of use from retailing to that of a building society branch office was refused on the ground that to grant the permission would create a precedent that might adversely affect the authority's planning policy for the area, which was to preserve primary shopping areas and to resist non-retail uses except in exceptional cases. Here, although the presence of building society offices in the area was not in itself objectionable, other building societies might use the grant of permission as a lever to establish offices in the area, and this would have led to a dilution of the predominantly retailing character of the area.

11.80 In *Poundstretcher v Secretary of State for the Environment* [1988] 3 PLR 69, Deputy Judge David Widdicombe QC, in a well-known statement, said:

> Be that as it may, in the present case the inspector clearly did rely on precedent. I accept Mr Hobson's proposition that where precedent is relied on, mere fear or generalised

concern is not enough. There must be evidence in one form or another for the reliance on precedent. In some cases the facts may speak for themselves. For instance, in the common case of the rear extension of one of a row or terrace of dwellings, it may be obvious that other owners in the row are likely to want extensions if one is permitted. Another clear example is sporadic development in the countryside.

11.81 In addition, a grant of planning permission, even for a limited period, may be considered to be a precedent for other similar development, including even unauthorized development (see *McCarthy v Secretary of State for Communities and Local Government and South Cambridgeshire* [2006] EWHC 3287). An interesting example is *CJ Holder v Gedling Borough Council v Mr John Nigel and ors* [2014] EWCA Civ 599 where the planning committee in determining an application for a wind turbine was wrongly given the impression that precedent was of no materiality whatsoever.

Existence of alternative sites

11.82 The operation of the planning control system relies heavily on the local planning authority responding to development proposals made by individual landowners or developers for individual sites. Hence, as a matter of principle, it would seem that the question of alternative sites ought not to be a material consideration in determining whether planning permission should be given for the development of the land the subject of the application. The courts, however, have been reluctant to follow that approach. In *R v Royal County of Berkshire, ex p Mangnall* [1985] JPL 258, the applicant sought judicial review to quash a grant of planning permission for the extraction of sand given in favour of a neighbouring landowner on the ground that the authority had failed to have proper regard to the existence of an alternative site. It was alleged that before granting planning permission, the authority should have made a comparative evaluation of both sites. According to Nolan J, there was no hard-and-fast rule governing the evaluation of alternative sites, but the statutory duty to have regard to material considerations would, in certain cases, more easily recognized than defined, require the consideration of another possible site than that for which permission was sought. In his judgment, there were serious environmental disadvantages in allowing the development of the neighbouring land. He thought that here the requirement to 'have regard to the provisions of the development plan ... and to any other material considerations', could not be complied with unless the authority had regard to the merits or demerits of the other site, but that it was reading too much into the section to say that an equal evaluation of that site was required. Since it was shown that the authority had in fact considered the merits of the alternative site, the application for judicial review failed.

11.83 It seems, therefore, that the merits or demerits of an alternative site *can* be a material consideration, but that the authority is under no duty to evaluate the alternative site in the same way as it must do with the application site. This seems reasonable, since there would be no practical way of securing that without the submission of a planning application for the development of the alternative site. An early case, *Rhodes v Minister of Housing and Local Government* [1963] 1 WLR 208, established that there is no duty on the local planning authority to 'root around' to see whether there may be an alternative site. On the other hand, it was said in *Trusthouse Forte Hotels Ltd v Secretary of State for the Environment* (1986) 53 P & CR 293 that it 'may be possible for the authority to decide in certain cases that a particular need can be satisfied elsewhere than on the appeal site even though no other specific sites are identified and established as preferable alternatives'.

The law was summarized by Simon Brown LJ in that case (and was quoted with approval by Laws LJ in the Court of Appeal in *R (Scott Jones) v North Warwickshire BC* [2001] PLCR 509 and by Richards J in *Laing Homes Ltd v Secretary of State for Transport, Local Government, and the Regions* [2003] EWHC 1967 (Admin); [2003] JPL 559) in the following terms: **11.84**

(1) Land (irrespective of whether it is owned by the applicant for planning permission) may be developed in any way which is acceptable for planning purposes. The fact that other land exists (whether or not in the applicant's ownership) upon which the development would be yet more acceptable for planning purposes would not justify the refusal of planning permission upon the application site.
(2) Where, however, there are clear planning objections to development upon a particular site then it may well be relevant and indeed necessary to consider whether there is a more appropriate alternative site elsewhere. This is particularly so when the development is bound to have significant adverse effects and where the major argument advanced in support of the application is that the need for the development outweighs the planning disadvantages inherent in it.
(3) Instances of this type of case are developments, whether of national or regional importance, such as... airports, coalmining, petro-chemical plants, nuclear power stations and gypsy encampments...
(4) In contrast to the situations envisaged above are cases where development permission is being sought for dwellinghouses, offices (see the *GLC* case itself) and superstores (at least in the circumstances of and *R v Carlisle City Council and the Secretary of State for the Environment, ex p Cumbrian Co-operative Society Ltd*). [See para 11.86 below.]
(5) There may be cases where, even although they contain the characteristics referred to above, nevertheless it could properly be regarded as unnecessary to go into questions of comparability. This would be so particularly if the environmental impact was relatively slight and the planning objections were not especially strong.

11.85 Later, Pill LJ in the Court of Appeal in *Kyte v Secretary of State for the Environment* [1997] CLY 4093 opined:

> When considering possible alternative sites, there can be no universally applicable rule as to the area to be considered or the range of detail of inquiry required... Potentially the exercise upon alternative sites is an exercise without limits.

11.86 An early example of the difficulties in this area was seen in *R v Carlisle City Council, ex p Cumbrian Co-operative Society Ltd* [1986] JPL 206 where Macpherson J held that on an application to consider the use of land as a superstore there was no need for the authority to consider *in detail* the merits of alternative sites. Precisely when the merits or demerits of an alternative site can be material was not exhaustively spelt out in the *Mangnall* case. Some help in this area, however, has been given in *Greater London Council v Secretary of State for the Environment* [1986] JPL 193. Here, Cable Cross Projects Ltd had applied to the London Docklands Development Corporation for planning permission for office development. The Secretary of State had called in the application and an Inspector, after holding an inquiry, had recommended that permission be refused. The Secretary of State, however, after considering the Inspector's report, had decided to grant permission. The local council then appealed unsuccessfully to the High Court under what is now s 288 of the 1990 Act for an order to quash the Secretary of State's decision. One of the grounds of challenge was that the Secretary of State had failed to have regard to a material consideration by not examining other comparable sites. In the Court of Appeal, Oliver LJ thought that there were cases where a comparable site had to be a material consideration; an obvious example was an airport. Without seeking to lay down a test for every case, because definition was always dangerous in these circumstances, he thought it might be that:

> ... comparability was appropriate generally to cases having the following characteristics: first of all, the presence of a clear public convenience, or advantage, in the proposal under consideration; secondly, the existence of inevitable adverse effects or disadvantages to the public or to some section of the public in the proposal; thirdly, the existence of an alternative site for the same project which would not have those effects, or would not have them to the same extent; and fourthly, a situation in which there could only be one permission granted for such development, or at least only a very limited number of permissions.

11.87 This criteria for the materiality of the relative merits of the application sites and other sites was endorsed in the case of *R (on the application of Persimmon Homes Ltd) v Secretary of State for Communities and Local Government* [2007] EWHC 1985 (Admin) and the earlier case of *Secretary of State for the Environment v Edwards* [1994] IPLR 62. In *Edwards* a number of applications had been made for planning permission for the construction of roadside service areas on different sites along an improved trunk road. All had been refused by the local planning authority and appeals were pending. In one case the appeal was by the written representation procedure but another applicant had elected for a planning inquiry and requested that all the appeals be considered at the same inquiry. The Secretary of State had refused this request and the appeal by written representation went ahead before an Inspector and succeeded. However, the High Court quashed the Inspector's decision because he should have taken account of the alternative proposals: the case had the four characteristics set out in *Greater London Council v Secretary of State for the Environment*. An appeal by the Secretary of State from the decision of the High Court was subsequently dismissed by the Court of Appeal. That decision has been reported at [1994] 1 PLR 62.

11.88 In *Derbyshire Dales D C v Secretary of State for Communities and Local Government* [2010] EWHC 1729 (Admin); [2010] 1 P & CR 19 Carnwath LJ drew a distinction between the case where it was argued that the decision-maker had erred in law by taking an alternative site into consideration, and where the error was the failure to take into account an alternative site. In the latter case Carnwath argued that it was necessary to find some legal principle which *compelled* the decision-maker to have regard to alternative sites and not merely *empowered* him to do so. He pointed out that he had only been referred to one case (*Secretary of State for the Environment v Edwards* [1994] 1 PLR 62) where it was held that there had been a failure to have regard to alternative sites and in this case alternative sites had been identified and were before the Secretary of State on appeal. Carnwath went on to make clear that a requirement to have regard to alternative sites only applied when it was a matter of legal obligation (because it was 'obviously material'). This will be more difficult to prove than the case where alternative sites are taken into account when it will only be necessary to show that it is permissible. However, in both cases it would seem that the evaluation as to whether it is 'relevant or at least permissible' rather than 'relevant and indeed necessary' is a matter of planning judgement on the particular facts. Carnwath LJ's analysis in *Derbyshire Dales* was endorsed by the Court of Appeal in *R (on the application of Luton Borough Council) v Central Bedfordshire Council* [2015] EWCA Civ 537; [2015] 2 P & CR 19 at [71].

Risk of piecemeal development

11.89 It seems that if a landowner makes an application for planning permission to develop only part of his land, there may be circumstances where the authority would be justified in refusing permission until such time as the landowner has indicated to the authority his proposals for the remainder of his land.

11.90 In *Rugby School Governors v Secretary of State for the Environment* [1975] JPL 97, the school had applied for planning permission to develop part of the school estate. The local planning authority had decided to deal with it on the ground that piecemeal development of the estate was bad planning practice and that individual applications should await a master plan, the preparation of which had been agreed earlier with the applicants. The school then appealed to the Secretary of State against non-determination of the application by the authority, who directed that it be determined by an Inspector. He dismissed the appeal. The school then applied to quash his decision on the ground that the Inspector had, while purporting to give a considered refusal, failed to determine the appeal or that he had taken into account irrelevant considerations. Refusing the application, Willis J held that by his endorsement of the authority's policy, the Secretary of State could not be said to have failed to comply with his statutory obligation to determine the appeal. He also held that given the background, it would require special circumstances to justify permitting an individual application to proceed in advance of agreement on a master plan. It should be noted that here the authority should have decided, like the Inspector on behalf of the Secretary of State, to refuse the application instead of deciding not to determine it.

Preservation of existing uses

11.91 One of the first cases to consider the relevance of the existing use of land as a material consideration in determining an application for planning permission for the development of the land was *Granada Theatres Ltd v Secretary of State for the Environment* [1976] JPL 96. There, the owners of a cinema applied for planning permission to change its use to that of a bingo and social club. Following the refusal of the application, the owners appealed to the Secretary of State who, mainly as a result of a petition by children for the retention of the cinema, dismissed the appeal. The application to quash that decision was based on the grounds that the Secretary of State had taken a mistaken view that the refusal of the permission would ensure the continued use of the building as a cinema and that he had acted contrary to the rules of natural justice in that he had taken into account the petition without giving the applicants an opportunity to comment on it. On both those grounds the Secretary of State consented to the decision being quashed by the court.

11.92 In *Clyde & Co v Secretary of State for the Environment* [1977] JPL 521 planning permission had been granted to erect a building, the western half of which was to be used for offices, the eastern half to be used as dwellings. The applicants proceeded to build and occupy the western half, but the eastern half was not completed. The applicants then made a further application to change the permitted use of the eastern half from residential to office use. The application was refused, and an appeal to the Secretary of State against the refusal was not upheld. The applicants then applied to the High Court for the decision to be quashed on the ground that the Secretary of State had erred in law in basing his decision on the ground that the loss of residential accommodation ought to be resisted. The Divisional Court granted the application, but this was reversed by the Court of Appeal which restored the Secretary of State's decision. The Court of Appeal held that the Secretary of State's ground for refusal was not wrong in law. Housing need was a material consideration, and if permission for office use was refused, there was at least a fair chance that the building would be used for housing rather than be allowed to stand empty.

11.93 The next important case to be considered by the courts was *Granada Theatres Ltd v Secretary of State for the Environment* [1981] JPL 278. Here the applicants owned a cinema in Chichester where trade had declined to such an extent that it had become the second most unprofitable cinema in the Granada group. The company had applied for planning permission to change the use of the cinema to another bingo and social club. On refusal of the application, the applicants had appealed to the Secretary of State, but without any success. In his decision letter the Secretary of State had said that he did not regard as material the alleged demerits such as they might be of bingo as an activity, and he had not been influenced by unfavourable comments made about it in connection with the appeal. He did, however, consider public demand for the retention of a cinema facility in Chichester on the one hand and for the introduction of commercial bingo on the other as well as the availability of alternative suitable premises and ways and means of providing these facilities. He accepted that, notwithstanding the expression of public opinion in favour of retaining the cinema, the appellant company faced difficulties in running the cinema as it stood, but the company had already given some thought to the possibility of finding an alternative use which would still incorporate a cinema element. He also accepted that the proposed change of use to bingo was likely to be much more profitable than the present use. However, he concluded that it might well be that a cinema and bingo operation or a multi-unit cinema were not the only possibilities, and despite the appellant's declared intention of closing the present cinema soon, the Secretary of State could not rule out the hope that, as the Inspector had suggested, an increased interest in the cinema or further examination of alternative ways of using the building could yet result in the retention of a viable cinema facility. He therefore rejected the appeal.

11.94 In an action to quash the Secretary of State's decision, Forbes J, referring to the decision in *Clyde & Co v Secretary of State for the Environment*, confessed to being surprised that it should have been necessary for there to be an authority for the proposition that in a change of use case the desirability of preserving the existing use was a material consideration, because it seemed to him so self-evident a proposition. According to Forbes J, however, there could be situations where the question of desirability of retaining the existing use was not material. If all the parties agreed that the continuation of an existing use was undesirable, one need not consider the question of desirability further. It was a concluded question. But where there was a dispute between the parties about whether an existing use should be retained or not, it seemed to him inevitable that the desirability of retaining it was a material question. Here, the sole issue for the Secretary of State to decide was whether there was a possibility, a reasonable possibility perhaps, that the existing use would be preserved if planning permission was refused. Forbes J decided that it was reasonable for the Secretary of State to come to that conclusion and so refused to interfere with his decision.

11.95 The tests so far applied by the courts in considering the relevance of an existing use in determining planning applications had been whether, if permission were refused, there would be a 'fair chance' or 'a possibility' or 'a reasonable possibility' that the existing use would continue.

11.96 In *Westminster City Council v British Waterways Board* [1985] AC 676 however, the House of Lords held that the preservation of an existing use which had been temporarily suspended could not afford a ground of refusal of planning permission for an otherwise acceptable change of use, unless it could be shown that the refusal might lead to a resumption of the suspended use. In dealing with the question of resumption, Lord Bridge of Harwich thought that the 'fair chance' test was, on the facts, an unnecessarily lax criterion. In his view, in a contest between the planning merits of two competing uses, to justify the refusal of permission for use B on the sole ground that use A ought to be preserved, it must be necessary at least to show 'a balance of probabilities' that if permission is refused for use B, the land in dispute will be effectively put to use A.

11.97 In another case, *London Residuary Body v Lambeth LBC* [1990] 1 WLR 744, the House of Lords in allowing an appeal from a decision of the Court of Appeal, held that in exercising powers under s 29 of the 1971 Act (s 70 of the 1990 Act), a local planning authority was not bound to apply between two uses a competing needs test of whether in planning terms the desirability of preserving the existing use outweighs the merits of the proposed new use. After considering the cases of *Clyde & Co v Secretary of State* [1977] JPL 521 and *Westminster City Council v British Waterways Board* [1985] AC 676, Lord Keith of Kinkel said:

> In my opinion nothing in either the *Clyde* case or in the *Westminster Council* case is properly to be interpreted as laying down that the competing needs test exists as a matter of law. Such a proposition would involve putting an unwarranted gloss on the language of s 29(1) of the 1971 Act. The most that can be extracted from the two cases is that the desirability of preserving an existing use of land is a material consideration to be taken into account under that subsection, provided there is a reasonable probability that such use will be preserved if permission for the new use is refused. If the Court of Appeal is right, it must follow that the presumption in favour of development can in law only receive effect where other planning considerations for or against a proposed use are evenly balanced. Such a straitjacket cannot properly be imposed on the Secretary of State. It must be left to him, in the exercise of a reasonable discretion, to form his own judgment whether any planning objections are of sufficient importance to overcome the presumption. This was the view taken, in my opinion correctly, by Simon Brown J. It should be kept in mind that in the case of many individual planning applications, for example to build a single house somewhere in the country, there is no question of it being possible to prove a need for the development. There may, however, be some planning objection to it which is not of very great weight. In such a situation it must surely be open to the

determining authority to decide that the presumption may properly receive effect and to grant planning permission.

11.98 Whether or not there is a 'reasonable probability' or perhaps 'a realistic prospect' that an existing use will be preserved will depend on the individual facts of each case. Factors like the institution of a new use in breach of planning control, the demolition of a building in which an old use took place, a sustained period of disuse, and evidence that the old use ceased because it was not economically viable to carry it on and is unlikely to be resurrected, remain of great evidential value in determining the future use of a parcel of land.

11.99 In *South Buckinghamshire DC v Secretary of State for the Environment and Berkeley Homes Ltd* [1999] JPL 1340, it was said that it was not sufficient for the decision-maker to rely on a theoretical possibility that an authorized use may be resumed. He had to assess the possibility that it would and give it appropriate weight.

11.100 The test laid down in the *British Waterways Board* case has in the past been exclusively related to the existing use of land, and the principle has been enunciated in that specific context. The question may also be posed, however, as to whether or not the same or a similar test was to be applied to competing future uses. That question could have important consequences for development control generally. Land may be considered by a local planning authority to be suitable for, say, future educational needs, yet it has to consider an application for planning permission to develop the land for housing. Attempts are often made to safeguard land for particular purposes, and faced with an application for a competing use for that land, the 'balance of probabilities' test would, as far as the future use of the land is concerned, be likely to require more speculation than if the test was applied to the preservation of an existing use.

11.101 One case which has considered this issue is *Nottinghamshire County Council v Secretary of State for the Environment, Transport, and the Regions* [2002] JPL 161. There the High Court held that if a judgment was made, whether through the development plan process or outside it, that it appeared desirable to preserve the option of using a piece of land for a purpose seen to be of benefit to the public interest for the country or the local community, this was, in principle, a material planning consideration for the purposes of ss 70(2) and 54A of the Act. The weight given to that consideration would vary hugely from case to case. Each case would turn on its own merits. Therefore, in considering whether to grant planning permission for a proposal which would pre-empt the possibility of the desirable future use, the relative desirability of the two uses would have to be weighed. In striking the balance, the likelihood of the desirable use actually coming about was doubtless a highly material consideration. However, there was no warrant to put a gloss on the wide statutory discretion by imposing the prohibition that the desirability of the future use could only be a material consideration if it had a 51 per cent probability of coming about.

11.102 The issue was again considered in *R (Mountcook Land Ltd) v Westminster City Council* [2003] EWCA Civ 1346; [2017] PTSR 1166. There the Court of Appeal accepted that it would be irrational to have regard to an alternative proposal, and stated that for some other use to be a material consideration, there had to be a likelihood or real possibility of that other use being achieved. Auld LJ summarized the position thus at [30]:

(1) in the context of planning control, a person may do what he wants with his land provided his use of it is acceptable in planning terms;
(2) there may be a number of alternative uses from which he could choose, each of which would be acceptable in planning terms;
(3) whether any proposed use is acceptable in planning terms depends on whether it would cause planning harm judged according to relevant planning policies where there are any;
(4) in the absence of conflict with planning policy and/or other planning harm, the relative advantages of alternative uses on the application site or of the same use on alternative sites are normally irrelevant in planning terms;
(5) where ... an application proposal does not conflict with policy, otherwise involves no planning harm and, as it happens, includes some enhancement, any alternative proposals would normally be irrelevant;
(6) even in exceptional circumstances where alternative proposals might be relevant, inchoate or vague schemes and/or those that are unlikely or have no real possibility of coming about would not be relevant or, if they were, should be given little or no weight.

11.103 The *Mount Cook* test was considered by the Court of Appeal in *Lisle-Mainwaring v Carol* [2017] EWCA Civ 1315; [2018] JPL 194 and permission to appeal to the Supreme Court was refused on 5 February 2018. The correct approach would now appear to be settled.

The fears of residents

11.104 In *West Midlands Probation Committee v Secretary of State for the Environment* [1998] JPL 388 (CA), the Court of Appeal held that the commission of criminal offences and anti-social behaviour by occupiers of proposed development could be a material consideration in the determination of applications for planning permission if it was intimately connected with the development. In that case planning permission which had been sought for a bail and probation hostel, had been refused on appeal because of the crime and disorder committed by the hostel's residents. The evidence had been that this was connected with the use of the land and did not arise out of the isolated and idiosyncratic behaviour of particular residents.

11.105 Another case which considered how far residents' fears are a material consideration in determining applications for planning permission is *R v Broadlands DC, St Matthew Society Ltd and Peddars Way Housing Association, ex p Dove, Harpley, and Wright* [1998] JPL B84. There, planning permission had been granted for a change of use from a hotel to a hostel, a bed group home with staff flats, and a number of one-bedroom flats. An officer had reported to the relevant subcommittee that determined the application, that a common thread running through letters of objection to the proposed development suggested '... that the occupants of the development will be unemployed, unemployable, anti-social and morally unstable, thereby posing a security risk to persons in the locality'. The officer went on to say that concern over the nature and character of the potential residents of the proposed development was not a land and planning issue. In refusing an application for judicial review of the Council's decision, the High Court held that the officer's advice had been erroneous, and that the anti-social behaviour of the residents of the proposed hostel was a land-use consideration and material to planning. However, the applicants had been unable to show that the subcommittee had not taken the residents' fears into account in arriving at their decision.

11.106 What is not clear from the case law in this area is the extent to which it must be shown that residents' fears are justified. Even if their fears were unjustified, the case of *Newport BC v Secretary of State for Wales* [1998] JPL 377 (CA) has established that they might still be a material consideration, though in that situation the decision-maker is likely to accord those fears much less than he would otherwise do. It has also been recognized that the planning system does not operate on the basis that development can proceed only if harm can be guaranteed never to occur. Furthermore, the system requires the decision-maker to have regard to other systems of statutory control that exist to deal with situations likely to generate residents' fears.

11.107 Lastly, it seems that local planning authorities should not make moral judgments on the way in which property may be used if planning permission is to be granted. In *Finlay v Secretary of State for the Environment* [1983] JPL 802, the Secretary of State had dismissed an appeal against an enforcement notice which had alleged an unauthorized use of a house as a private members' club. The club was known for showing sexually explicit films to members. In his decision letter the Secretary of State had referred to the fact that this could alter the environmental character of the area by introducing a use detrimental to residential amenities. In dismissing a challenge to the Secretary of State's decision, the High Court held that far from making any moral judgment on the type of films shown, he was making a planning judgment on whether the showing of such films adversely affected the local environment.

11.108 In *R v Tandridge DC, ex p Mohamed Al Fayed* [1999] JPL 825, objections had been made by the appellant to a grant of planning permission for the erection of a radio telephone base station tower on nearby land. The High Court, whilst accepting that there had been a flaw in the Council's decision-making process in not consulting the Health and Safety Executive before granting permission, refused to exercise its discretion to quash the grant. In the Court of Appeal, [2000]

JPL 604, Schiemann LJ recognized as common ground '... that the existence of objectively unjustified fears in the locality can, in some circumstances, be a legitimate factor for a local planning authority to take into account when deciding a planning application'. He then went on to dismiss the appeal from the decision of the High Court.

11.109 Fears relating to health may be particularly aroused where a telecommunications code systems operator seeks to erect an antenna close to residential or educational property. Advice on the provision of such equipment is currently contained in PPG8 Telecommunications. The Government has accepted that emissions from mobile phone base stations should meet the International Commission on Non-Ionizing Radiation Protection (ICNIRP) guideline for public exposure. Any planning application should be accompanied by a Declaration of Conformity indicating that the equipment and installation are designed to be in full compliance with the ICNIRP public exposure guidelines. Government guidance in PPG8 indicates that where the guideline is met it should not be necessary to consider further the health aspects of such schemes and concerns about them.

Personal circumstances of the applicant

11.110 Although in practice the personal circumstances of an applicant do occasionally result in his obtaining a favourable decision from the local planning authority, the legal authority for this practice is not of long standing.

11.111 In *New Forest DC v Secretary of State for the Environment* [1984] JPL 178, a Mr Clarke was the owner of a bungalow built with an occupancy condition restricting its use to past or present employees of an adjacent hotel, or to agricultural or forestry workers. He had made a number of applications for planning permission to use the bungalow without the occupancy condition and, save for the last, all had been refused. Finally, the Secretary of State had granted planning permission on appeal. The local planning authority claimed in the Queen's Bench Division that the Secretary of State had wrongly taken into account Mr Clarke's financial circumstances and that this was not a material consideration. Rejecting that argument, Taylor J held that it was proper to take into account personal circumstances and personal hardship where matters might be very evenly balanced, and to consider the effect the decision might have on the individual applicant. Obviously, such a consideration could only be peripheral to the main planning issues which had to be taken into account.

11.112 In *Tameside MBC v Secretary of State for the Environment* [1984] JPL 180 it again was held that the Secretary of State was entitled to take personal hardship into account.

11.113 The consideration of personal circumstances, but only on a marginal basis, was given the seal of the highest judicial authority in *Westminster City Council* *v Great Portland Estates plc* [1985] AC 661. In that case the respondent company had challenged both the industrial and the office policies contained in the Westminster City local plan. With regard to industrial development, the general policy was that applications for planning permission for new industrial floor space and the creation of new industrial employment were to be encouraged. That general policy was modified in the case of applications for planning permission to rehabilitate or redevelop existing industrial premises. In these cases the authority's general policy was supplanted where considered necessary to maintain the continuation of industrial uses important to the diverse character, vitality, and functioning of Westminster. There the policy was to be to protect 'specific industrial activities' from redevelopment. The respondent company challenged this latter aspect as being outside the purposes of planning law. The essence of the company's argument was that the protection of specified industrial activities was not a policy concerned with the development and use of land, but one concerned with the protection of particular users of land. It was irrelevant, it was claimed, to have regard in this way to the interests of individual occupiers.

11.114 In rejecting the challenge to the authority's industrial policy, Lord Scarman, giving the only speech, but one concurred in by all the other Law Lords, adopted the general principle enunciated by Lord Parker CJ in *East Barnet UDC v British Transport Commission* [1962] 2 QB 484 (Div Court) that in considering whether there had been a change of use, 'what is really to be considered is the character of the use of the land, not the particular purposes of a particular occupier'. It was a logical process, Lord Scarman thought, to extend the ambit of that statement to the formulation of planning policies and proposals. However, like all generalizations, he said, the statement of Lord Parker had its own limitations. Personal circumstances of the occupier, personal hardship, and the difficulties of business which are of value to the community were not to be ignored in the administration of planning control.

11.115 A good example of the application of *Westminster City Council v Great Portland Estates plc* [1985] AC 661 with somewhat unusual consequences is seen in decisions involving listed buildings in the Lake District. In December 1987, the South Lakeland District Council became aware that original windows in a row of listed terrace houses at Nos 1, 3, and 4 Eastside, The Square, Burton-in-Kendal, had been replaced by modern casement windows without listed building consent. Following a decision by the authority to take enforcement action to remedy the breaches of control, the owner of No 3 submitted an application for listed building consent to retain the new windows. On appeal to the Secretary of State, an Inspector allowed the appeal and granted the retrospective listed building consent applied for.

11.116 In *South Lakeland DC v Secretary of State for the Environment and Rowbotham* [1991] JPL 440, the local planning authority then sought unsuccessfully to challenge that decision in the High Court, which held, inter alia, that the Inspector had not erred in regarding the personal circumstances of the elderly applicant, namely the costs and disruption which would be caused by having to put back the original windows and the loss of the comfort an aged resident would derive from double glazing, as material factors to be taken into account in applying planning legislation. The High Court also made it clear (as had the Inspector in his decision letter) that the granting of the consent afforded no precedent in relation to other pending cases.

11.117 Accordingly, the local planning authority then proceeded to take listed building enforcement action against the owners of Nos 1 and 4 Eastside. Both owners appealed against the notice to the Secretary of State. The same Inspector in both cases concluded that the replacement windows were inappropriate and upheld the notices. In one of them, personal circumstances were advanced by the appellant but discounted by the Inspector. In both cases reference was made to replacement windows installed at No 3 Eastside with now listed building consent. On this aspect the Inspector said:

> ... the fact that inappropriate windows have been granted consent at No 3 makes it more, and not less, important to ensure that appropriate windows are installed elsewhere in the front façade. Consequently, I find no merit in the suggestion that, for uniformity, inappropriate windows should be installed in all the windows of the front elevation of Nos 1–4.

Following the decision, the elderly occupant of No 3, whose personal circumstances were crucial to the decision to grant listed building consent, vacated the premises, which were then put up for sale.

11.118 A more recent case on personal circumstances was *R v Vale of Glamorgan DC, ex p Adams* [2001] JPL 93, where a grant of planning permission to convert and change the use of three barns to residential use was quashed because members of the local planning committee had not been advised that 'personal circumstances of an occupier, personal hardship, and the difficulties of business which are of value to the community' were capable of being material considerations even if to give effect to them would involve an exception from general policy. The application to quash had been made by a tenant farmer of the land who risked losing his security of tenure if planning permission were to be granted.

11.119 It should also be noted that the variety of circumstances that might be described as 'personal' is probably extremely wide. As the House of Lords in *South Bucks DC v Porter* [2003] UKHL 26; [2003] 2 AC 558 recognized, there is now an overlap between the requirements of the Human Rights Act 1998 and decisions made previously by domestic courts in this area.

Housing land supply

11.120 Paragraph 73 of the NPPF requires that local planning authorities identify and update annually a supply of specific deliverable sites sufficient to provide a minimum of five years' worth of housing. The automatic policy consequence of a failure to demonstrate a five years' supply of housing is that the so-called 'tilted balance' in paragraph 11 of the NPPF is engaged (via footnote 7). That is to say the decision-taker should grant permission unless the application of policies in the NPPF provides a clear reason for refusal (on which see *East Staffordshire BC v Secretary of State for Communities and Local Government* [2017] EWCA Civ 893, [2018] PTSR 88 per Lindblom LJ at [22]) or the adverse consequences 'significantly and demonstrably' outweigh the benefits of granting permission.

11.121 Paragraph 11 of the NPPF (and the 'tilted balance') is however a presumption of policy and does not (nor could not) displace the statutory priority afforded to the development plan by s 38(6) of the Planning and Compulsory Purchase Act 2004. Rather, the purpose is to seek to influence the exercise of the discretion within the structure of s 38(6), as Lord Gill explained in *Hopkins Homes Ltd v Secretary of State for Communities and Local Government* [2017] UKSC 37; [2017] 1 WLR 1865 at [83]:

> If a planning authority that was in default of the requirement of a five years' supply were to continue to apply its environmental and amenity policies with full rigour, the objective of the Framework could be frustrated. The purpose of paragraph 49 is to indicate a way in which the lack of a five years' supply of sites can be put right. It is reasonable for the guidance to suggest that in such cases the development plan policies for the supply of housing, however recent they may be, should not be considered as being up to date.

11.122 However, whether the shortfall in the supply of housing justifies determining a given application for permission otherwise than in accordance with the provisions of the development plan remains a planning judgment for the decision-taker. The NPPF is silent on the weight to attach to policies which restrict the supply of housing (eg countryside policies) in circumstances where there is not a five-year supply, however Lindblom LJ gave some guidance as to considerations the planning decision-taker might take into account in that respect in *Hallam Land Management Ltd v Secretary of State for Communities and Local Government* [2018] EWCA Civ 1808; [2019] JPL 63 at [51]:

> the policies .... of the NPPF do not specify the weight to be given to the benefit, in a particular proposal, of reducing or overcoming a shortfall against the requirement for a five-year supply of housing land. This is a matter for the decision-maker's planning judgment, and the court will not interfere with that planning judgment except on public law grounds. But the weight given to the benefits of new housing development in an area where a shortfall in housing land supply has arisen is likely to depend on factors such as the broad magnitude of the shortfall, how long it is likely to persist, what the local planning authority is doing to reduce it, and how much of it the development will meet.

11.123 It follows that a proposal for housing development in the open countryside is likely to stand greater prospects of success if the scale of housing shortfall is great and the steps being made to make up the shortfall (eg by a local plan review or new local plan) are at an early stage, than if the shortfall in the supply of housing is small and the planning authority has taken proactive steps to make up the shortfall of housing. Accordingly, whilst it is not necessary to identify the exact level of land supply, a planning decision-taker determining an application for housing development where there is accepted to be a land supply shortfall needs to 'identify at least the broad magnitude of any shortfall in the supply of housing land' per Lindblom LJ in *Hallam Land* at [52].

11.124 There is a further discussion on the relevance of a five-year supply and the application of paragraph 11 of the NPPF (formerly paragraph 14 of the NPPF) in the following articles: A Bowes, 'The NPPF and the Statutory Code' [2017] JPL 785; A Bowes, 'Further Clarification of NPPF Para.14' [2017] JPL 1071; S Choongh and P Cairnes, 'The Element of Planning Discretion in the Context of an Up-To-Date Plan: The Implications of the Barwood case' [2018] JPL 129; and A Bowes, 'The Effects of a Lack of a Five-Year Supply' [2018] JPL 1198.

Affordable housing

11.125 One issue on which there could be a much clearer and more authoritative statement of the law concerns the basis on which a local planning authority has the power to promote the provision of 'affordable housing'. The present position however, is that the power to provide affordable housing is firmly established in both law and government housing policy.

11.126 The difficulty has been that the policy may conflict with the principle that planning seeks to control the character of the use of land not the particular purpose of a particular occupier, although it has always been accepted that personal circumstances may be a material consideration.

11.127 Some light was shone on this conflict by *Mitchell v Secretary of State for the Environment* [1994] EGCS 111. The local planning authority had a policy 'to resist proposals for the conversion into self-contained accommodation of houses in multiple occupation meeting a known and established need'. The authority had failed to determine an application for permission to change the use of a house in multiple occupation into self-contained flats and there was an appeal to the Secretary of State, who applied the authority's policy and dismissed the appeal. The High Court had then quashed the Secretary of State's decision on the ground that the authority's policy was not a material consideration which could be taken into account. An appeal by the Secretary of State against that decision however, was upheld by the Court of Appeal. The Court held that 'material considerations' were not confined to questions of amenity and environmental impact. The need for housing in a particular area could be a material consideration. No sensible distinction could be drawn between a need for housing generally and a need for a particular type of housing, whether defined in terms of cost, tenure, or otherwise. The fact that the need might be dictated by considerations of cost or type was irrelevant.

11.128 In the *Mitchell* case the local planning authority's policy had been contained in its draft Unitary Development Plan. In *ECC Construction Ltd v Secretary of State for the Environment* [1995] JPL 322, the High Court followed that decision, but went further in holding that although it was not necessary for the need for affordable housing to be included in formulated policies, it could arise by implication. The decision is thus authority for the proposition that the absence of affordable housing in a development proposal could render the development unacceptable.

11.129 Again, in *R v London Borough of Tower Hamlets, ex p Barrett Homes Ltd* [2000] JPL 1050 the High Court refused to grant an application for a declaration that supplementary planning guidance which required the provision of affordable housing was unlawful and must not be taken into account as a material consideration in determining a planning permission application.

11.130 The NPPF directs local planning authorities in planning housing provision to plan for a full range of market housing. In particular, they must take into account the need to deliver 'low-cost housing' as part of the general housing mix. It should be noted that the term low-cost housing, which has previously been used to describe one aspect of affordable housing, is now excluded from that definition.

11.131 'Affordable housing' is now within the Glossary to the NPPF. It includes 'affordable housing for rent', 'starter homes', 'discounted market sales housing', and 'other affordable routes to home ownership'.

11.132 A key ingredient of affordable housing is that it should include provision for the houses to remain at an appropriate price for future eligible households or, if that restriction is lifted, the subsidy to be recycled for alternative housing provision.

11.133 The procedure for providing affordable housing usually takes the form of the developer entering into a s 106 agreement, whereby either the land is transferred to a housing association, charitable organization, or similar body; or by the developers themselves undertaking the role of registered social landlords and managing the units as affordable housing then and in the future; or through an agent such as a housing association. The obligation is also likely to deal with the mix of the affordable housing, nomination rights, occupancy criteria, location, and provision to ensure that the affordable housing remains affordable. It will also ensure that the housing remains permanently affordable for successive occupiers. In some circumstances, a local planning authority may accept from the developer a financial contribution to enable the authority to provide the affordable housing elsewhere than on the site for which planning permission is being sought.

Enabling development and financial considerations

11.134 In *R v Westminster City Council, ex p Monahan* [1990] 1 QB 87, the Court of Appeal made clear that 'any other material considerations' could properly include 'financial considerations'. In this case an application had been made to the High

Court for judicial review to quash a grant of planning permission and various consents for the demolition of a number of listed and unlisted buildings as part of a development scheme to improve the facilities at the Royal Opera House, Covent Garden. The main purpose of the scheme had been the redevelopment of the Opera House, but this could only proceed if permission were also granted for adjacent commercial development which would provide the funds needed to improve the Opera House. But for this essential link, planning policy would have dictated that planning permission would not have been granted for the commercial development alone. In the courts the appellants claimed unsuccessfully that the local planning authority had taken into account a consideration that was not material, namely the generation of finance from part of the proposed development to be used for the benefit of the Opera House; and had failed to consider a material consideration, namely that if finance was a material consideration, they had not considered other sources of finance available to the Opera House not involving the commercial development.

11.135 Upholding the decision of the High Court, the Court of Appeal held that financial constraints on the economic viability of a desirable planning development are unavoidable facts of life in an imperfect world, and virtually all planning decisions involve some kind of balancing exercise. Provided that the ultimate determination of a planning decision is based on planning grounds and not on some ulterior motive and that it is not irrational, there is no basis for holding it invalid in law solely on the ground that it has taken account of, and adjusted itself to, the financial realities of the overall situation. The meaning of 'material consideration' in the Town and Country Planning Act has been circumscribed in wide terms and these do not exclude financial considerations from being treated as material in appropriate cases. Hence, the financing of the development scheme was capable of being a material consideration, as it related to the use and development of land.

11.136 It is probable that the *Covent Garden* case has led to an increase in the number of cases where it is claimed that any detriment suffered by a grant of permission for part of a development scheme contrary to established policy, would be more than offset by the benefit to be gained from other aspects of the scheme if the whole were to be allowed to proceed.

11.137 In a number of later ministerial decisions the '*Covent Garden* influence' can be seen. The first decision granted planning permission for the erection of eight houses in the walled kitchen garden of Croome Court, Worcester, a Grade 1 listed building, the construction of which was begun in 1751 by 'Capability' Brown, and was now unoccupied and in need of restoration. The Inspector found that the proposed development would be contrary to the policies of the approved structure plan for the area so that the proposal should normally fail. However, he accepted the applicant's contention that if the development were permitted the profit realized from the sale of eight building plots would generate enough cash to enable restoration of the house to proceed. At the inquiry, the parties had favoured a planning agreement to achieve this. In the event, this did not prove possible, so the Inspector dealt with it by conditions.

11.138 In another decision, the Secretary of State had to consider whether to grant planning permission to Wates Homes Ltd for the erection, inter alia, of a superstore at Broadlands, Hampshire. The applicants argued that by permitting the development, sufficient funds would be generated to secure the restoration and future maintenance of Broadlands House and surrounding estate, which included no less than 50 listed buildings.

11.139 In dismissing the appeal, the Secretary of State considered that whilst it was reasonable to take that into account, he could not agree with the Inspector's judgment that the needs of this historic house could justify the introduction of an inappropriate and intensive form of development, with all its attendant disturbance into a countryside area contrary to structure plan policies.

11.140 This decision raises the question of whether, if one is to take advantage of the *Covent Garden* approach, there has to be a functional link between the proposed development and the land to be benefited by it, or for both to be on the same site. In this instance, the site of the proposed development was approximately two miles from Broadlands House itself.

11.141 Another example of enabling development is a 1994 ministerial decision, where planning permission was given for a 36-hole golf course with clubhouse and car-parking on land at Mapledurham Estate, Mapledurham, near Reading, in an Area of Outstanding Natural Beauty. A significant reason for so doing was that some of the listed buildings in the estate's ownership were in need of urgent repair, and the income from the proposed golf course would enable a 20-year programme of repairs to be undertaken. The decision was later challenged unsuccessfully in the High Court in *South Oxfordshire DC v Secretary of State for the Environment* [1995] JPL 213 on grounds which included an allegation that the method chosen for securing that the programme of repairs would be undertaken (a s 106 agreement) was a nullity.

11.142 Again, in a ministerial decision [1995] JPL 654, planning permission was granted for the construction of an education centre and car-parking spaces at Paignton Zoo, and for the construction of a 65,000 square foot food retail store on adjoining land. Although the Secretary of State accepted that the proposals involved a degree of conflict with certain development plan policies, he considered the benefits from the new development carried greater weight. Those benefits were that the future viability of the zoo would be ensured by allowing it to upgrade facilities which would be to the advantage of tourism and avoid the job losses which would result from closing the zoo.

11.143 Apart from *R v Westminster City Council, ex p Monahan*, other cases where the courts have recognized the principle of enabling development as a material consideration include *Northumberland CC v Secretary of State for the Environment* [1989] JPL 700 and *Wansdyke DC v Secretary of State for the Environment* [1992] JPL 1168.

11.144 Before granting planning permission a local planning authority must ensure that all material considerations are taken into account. Within the context of enabling development it was suggested by the High Court in *R v West Dorset DC, ex p Searle* (unreported, 21 February 2000), that although an authority may consider that before granting planning permission an independent evaluation or assessment of the financial appraisal submitted by the developer was a necessary tool by which to judge the appropriateness of the proposed development, there was no necessity for the authority to go that far. Latham J concluded that on the evidence before him, the authority was within its rights to conclude that the benefits of proceeding with the applicant's proposals as they stood outweighed the planning detriments: in this case the restoration of a Grade II* listed building. On appeal, the Court of Appeal [1999] JPL 331 upheld the decision of Latham J by a majority.

11.145 So, while there is some doubt over whether in determining the making of revocation or discontinuance orders, the local planning authority is entitled to take into account the costs of paying compensation (see para 11.48), it seems settled law that a financial benefit or disadvantage to a local planning authority as a result of a grant or refusal of planning permission is not a material consideration for the purposes of s 70(2) of the 1990 Act. However, this may have to be reconsidered in the light of s 143 of the Localism Act 2011. Section 143 amends s 70(2) providing that, as well as the development plan and other material considerations, the local planning authority shall have regard to any local finance considerations, so far as material to the application. 'Local finance considerations' are defined as:

(a) a grant or other financial assistance that has been, or will or could be, provided to a relevant authority by a Minister of the Crown, or
(b) sums that a relevant authority has received, or will or could receive, in payment of Community Infrastructure Levy.

The explanatory notes to the Act state that it is not intended to change the current position about what lawfully can or must be taken into account in the determination of a planning application or to ascribe any particular weight to 'local finance considerations'. The amendment is said to be simply clarificatory. The crucial word as always is 'material' and whether the prospect of getting a 'new homes bonus' by granting planning permission will be material even if the monies will not be spent in a way that is not directly related to the development being proposed.

Planning and pollution control

11.146 Pollution controls in the United Kingdom are exercised through a range of organizations and a variety of mechanisms, including licensing and authorization procedures which are applied to processes and substances which can have potentially harmful effects on the environment. In the past few years, a substantial body of new legislation such as the Control of Pollution Act 1974, the Environmental Protection Act 1990, and the Water Resources Act 1991 have considerably extended the scope and effectiveness of pollution controls. The relation between planning and pollution control, however, is not particularly clear. An early case, *Ladbroke (Rentals) Ltd v Secretary of State for the Environment* [1981] JPL 427, established that disturbance or annoyances caused to other occupiers of land is a relevant planning consideration regardless of powers to control the source under other legislation.

11.147 The problem was discussed in the case of *Gateshead MBC v Secretary of State for the Environment* (1993) 67 P & CR 179. The Northern Regional Hospital Authority had applied to the local planning authority for outline planning permission for a clinical waste incinerator which had been refused. On appeal to the Secretary of State by the Health Authority, an Inspector had concluded that whilst an appropriate plant could be built to meet the various standards relating to emission limits laid down by HM Inspectorate of Pollution under the Environmental Protection Act 1990, the effect on air quality and agriculture in the locality was insufficiently defined, and that public disquiet about environmental pollution could not be sufficiently allayed to make the proposed development acceptable. Accordingly, he recommended to the Secretary of State that planning permission for the incinerator should be refused. The Secretary of State, however, declined to accept the recommendation and granted permission for the development on the grounds first, that the Secretary of State could not lawfully abdicate his planning responsibilities to the Environmental Protection Act 1990 regime; secondly, that there was no evidence on which he could be satisfied that controls under that regime would be adequate and thirdly, that if he could not properly be satisfied that these concerns could be dealt with under that regime, it followed that the proposal would not comply with structure plan requirements for the consequences in terms of environmental impact to be acceptable.

11.148 In an unsuccessful application to the High Court to quash the Secretary of State's decision, it was held that the environmental impact of emissions into the atmosphere was a material consideration in determining planning applications, but so too was the existence of pollution controls. After remarking that any attempt to draw a demarcation line between the two forms of control was not helpful, Jeremy Sullivan QC (then a Deputy Judge) went on to say:

> At one extreme there will be cases where the evidence at the planning stage demonstrates that potential pollution problems have been substantially overcome, so that

any reasonable person will accept that the remaining details can sensibly be left to the EPA authorisation process.

At the other extreme, there may be cases where the evidence of environmental problems is so damning at the planning stage that any reasonable person would refuse planning permission, saying, in effect, there is no point in trying to resolve these very grave problems through the EPA process. Between these two extremes there will be a whole spectrum of cases disclosing pollution problems of different types and differing degree of complexity and gravity.

11.149 This judgment was subsequently upheld by the Court of Appeal [1994] 1 PLR 85.

It seems, therefore, that the weight to be given to environmental issues and the power to control them under pollution legislation in determining applications for planning permission is a matter for the particular decision-maker, be it local planning authority or Secretary of State. In appropriate cases local planning authorities can decide to leave pollution control to pollution control authorities; but they are not obliged as a matter of law to do so.

11.150 The NPPF makes it clear that planning control and pollution control are separate but complementary procedures, with both being designed to protect the environment from the potential harm caused by development and other operations, but with different objectives. In *Hopkins Developments v First Secretary of State and North Wiltshire DC* [2006] EWHC 2823; [2007] Env. LR 14 it was held that an Inspector was entitled to refuse permission because of the dust that would be caused, notwithstanding the fact that mitigating conditions would be imposed on emissions by the necessary planning and pollution control permit.

11.151 It is clear that the scope of the planning regime for protecting the environment is wider than that of the pollution control regime. For example, Her Majesty's Inspectors of Pollution are not likely to pay regard to the effect of noxious emissions on the development potential of an area, or to consider whether in any particular case the location of a particular process would make the area less attractive for securing its regeneration.

11.152 It should also be remembered that the controls exercised under the regulatory pollution regime exist to prevent or mitigate harm from what are called 'prescribed processes'. Any grant of planning permission for development involving such processes in no way inhibits Inspectors of Pollution from refusing to authorize that process where they consider it would cause demonstrable harm. That point is well illustrated by the Supreme Court's decision in *Lawrence v Fen Tigers Ltd* [2014] UKSC 13; [2014] AC 822 in which the Court held (Lord Carnwath JSC dissenting) that planning permission could not be relied upon as a defence to a nuisance claim.

11.153 Where the development would not involve an authorization requirement under pollution control, it would seem that local planning authorities still have some latitude to invoke the planning regime for amenity reasons. For example, it would seem acceptable for a local planning authority to seek to control through the planning system a shop for the sale of hot food to be located in a residential area, irrespective of whether the effects of that development on the living conditions of neighbours would be susceptible to control as being a statutory nuisance.

With regard to pollution control, it should be noted that Her Majesty's Inspectorate of Pollution, the National Rivers Authority, and Waste Regulation Authorities are now part of the Environment Agency set up by the Environment Act 1995. The Agency has indicated that it will become involved with land-use planning in the following ways: **11.154**

(i) responding to consultations by local planning authorities under the Town and Country Planning (Assessment of Environmental Effects) Regulations 2011;
(ii) responding to requests from developers for information relating to their applications under the Regulations at (i) above;
(iii) responding to consultation on planning applications;
(iv) responding and providing input to the preparation of development plans;
(v) responding to general enquiries about proposed developments; and
(vi) providing technical advice to the Government at regional or national level in response to requests for information about the significance of any likely pollution from a proposed development.

The issue was considered recently in the context of hydrocarbon exploration projects (often involving a process known as fracturing but more commonly known as 'fracking'). In *Frackman v Secretary of State for Communities and Local Government* [2018] EWCA Civ 9; [2018] Env LR 18 the Court of Appeal rejected an argument that the Secretary of State had acted irrationally by assuming other pollution control mechanisms would operate effectively in line with the policy advice in the NPPF. However, in *Gladman Developments Ltd v Secretary of State for Communities and Local Government* [2017] EWHC 2768 (Admin); [2018] Env LR 15 Suppersone J rejected an argument that air quality management at a national level was akin to a 'pollution control regime' such as to permit an inspector to leave that consideration out of account in a planning appeal. **11.155**

Planning and licensing control

The decision in the *Gateshead* case (see para 11.142) suggests that the notion that the operation of planning law ought not to attempt to replicate the law on pollution and other environmental controls is essentially one of planning policy and practice than of law. The existence of alternative statutory means of controlling pollution continues to be therefore in law, a material consideration for authorities to take into account in dealing with applications for development which would also be subject to those other forms of statutory control, such as licensing control. **11.156**

In *Roger Lethem v Secretary of State and Worcester City Council* [2002] EWHC 1549 (Admin); [2003] JPL 332, the High Court refused an application to quash a decision by an Inspector to dismiss an appeal against a refusal by the local **11.157** planning authority to grant planning permission for a change of use of premises from a use within Class A1 of the Use Classes Order to a café/bar within use Class A3. The applicants unsuccessfully contended that the Inspector erred in failing to recognize that the objections he found to aspects of the proposed café/bar were matters that fell to be dealt with under the Licensing Act 1964, and would not, therefore, justify a refusal of planning permission.

Consolidation of undesirable uses

11.158 Uses which are undesirable in a particular area can only be required to cease if the local planning authority is prepared to serve a discontinuance order in respect of the use and to pay compensation for loss suffered as a result. Where, however, undesirable uses exist it has been held that a local planning authority can refuse planning permission for development of the site if to grant permission would perpetuate and consolidate the use being carried on the land. For example, where a person carries on as an established use the business of storage and haulage of plant hire on open land, he might apply for planning permission to construct a building in which to carry out that activity. The authority may then refuse planning permission in the hope that the use will diminish or cease altogether. The principle was recognized in *W H Tolley & Son Ltd v Secretary of State for the Environment* (1998) 75 P & CR 533, where it was stated:

> The concept of consolidation of an undesirable use is familiar in planning. As I understand it, it implies not ... an increase or an intensification in the current use, but a strengthening of the features that support it, thus making it less likely that the use will diminish in intensity or be replaced by a less undesirable use. By refusing planning permission for a development which it considers would consolidate the existing undesirable use, the planning authority seek to preserve the prospect of its diminution or replacement.

Environmental information

11.159 Under reg 3 of the Town and Country Planning (Environmental Impact Assessment) Regulations 2017 (SI 2017/571), a local planning authority or the Secretary of State must not grant planning permission for any development to which the Regulations apply, unless it has first taken into consideration any environmental information. This area of law is dealt with in the next chapter.

Self-Build and Custom Housebuilding

11.160 The Self-build and Custom Housebuilding Act 2015 allows individuals wishing to build their own home to register their interest in acquiring a suitable plot of land with the relevant authority. Specifically, the Act makes provision for:

> a) relevant authorities to maintain a register of people who are seeking to acquire a serviced plot in their area in order that they may build houses for them to occupy as homes; and

b) certain authorities (broadly, local authorities) to have regard to the demand for custom build housing as evidenced by the registers when exercising certain functions including those relating to planning and housing.

11.161 Section 2A(2) of the Act creates a new duty upon 'an authority to which this section applies'

must give suitable development permission in respect of enough serviced plots of land to meet the demand for self-build and custom housebuilding in the authority's area arising in each base period.

11.162 Whilst the Secretary of State (or an Inspector appointed on his behalf) is not mentioned at s 2(2), it would appear that the duty must extend to the Secretary of State determining planning appeals under s 78 of the Town and Country Planning Act 1990 because s 79(1) of the 1990 Act provides that the Secretary of State 'may deal with the application as if it had been made to him in the first instance'.

12

ENVIRONMENTAL IMPACT ASSESSMENT

| A. INTRODUCTION | 12.01 | C. JUDICIAL CHALLENGE | 12.42 |
| B. PROJECTS REQUIRING ENVIRONMENTAL IMPACT ASSESSMENT | 12.06 | | |

A. INTRODUCTION

12.01 A requirement for the environmental impact assessment (EIA) of certain major development projects was a result of the first direct impact of European Community law on domestic town and country planning law. Originally promulgated in 1985, Council Directive 'The Assessment of the Effect of Certain Public and Private Projects on the Environment' is now in a recast form, as Directive 2011/92/EU. The terms of which have been implemented in England and Wales by the Town and Country Planning (Environmental Impact Assessment) Regulations 2017 (SI 2017/571 in England) and (SI 2017/567 in Wales). This chapter will however focus on the English Regulations. There are in fact many sets of statutory provisions which implement different parts of the Directive, dealing with such matters as afforestation projects, highways, harbour works, land drainage, fish farming, and electricity and pipeline works. Where the procedure for the approval of projects requiring environmental impact assessment under the Directive is dealt with under other legislation (eg highways under the Highways Acts), separate subordinate legislation has been introduced. These, however, fall outside the scope of this chapter.

12.02 The present Regulations apply to applications for development that require planning permission under the 1990 Act and to local authorities in the exercise of their enforcement functions.

12.03 Most of the regulations governing EIA were introduced under powers given to Ministers by the European Communities Act 1972. During the passage of the Planning and Compensation Act 1991 through Parliament, however, the Government accepted the view that as regards planning legislation there should be some direct statutory authority for the implementation of the European Community Directive. In addition, it considered that there was an argument for extending environmental impact assessment to types of project beyond those specifically required by the Directive. Accordingly, s 15 of the 1991 Act inserted a new s 71A into the 1990 Act to give the Secretary of State power to make regulations about the consideration to be given, before planning permission for development is granted, of the likely environmental effects of the proposed development. He can thus at any time enlarge the classes of development for which EIA may be required. He did in fact do so in 1994, when he amended the Regulations to add privately financed toll roads to Sch 1 and wind generators, motorway service areas, and coast protection works to Sch 2. Following the amendment of the Directive in 1997 that amendment has now been repealed, the development mentioned having been subsumed within the EIA Regulations. The departure of the United Kingdom from the European Union in 2019 is not (at least in the short-term) anticipated by the Government to change the operation of the EIA regime. This is because the Government has published the Environmental Assessments and Miscellaneous Planning (Amendment) (EU Exit) Regulations 2018 (SI 2018/1232), under the provisions of the European Union (Withdrawal Act) 2018, which is intended to ensure the EIA regime 'will continue to operate as [it] did before the date we leave the EU'.

12.04 'Environmental Impact Assessment' can be seen as 'a technique for the systematic compilation of expert quantitative analysis and qualitative assessment of a project's environmental effects, and the presentation of results in a way which enables the importance of the predicted results, and the scope for modifying or mitigating them, to be properly evaluated by the relevant decision-making body before a planning application decision is taken'.

12.05 In order to understand the procedures that have to be followed, it is important to understand the following terms, the last two of which are expressed in legal terms in reg 2(1):

(a) *Environmental impact assessment* is essentially a process. It is the whole process required to reach a decision on whether or not to allow the project to proceed. Environmental assessment involves the presentation, collection, publication, and assessment of environmental information on the environmental effects of a project, and also the final judgment upon it. An important part of that process is the submission of an environmental statement.

(b) *Environmental information* means the environmental statement, including any further information and any other information, any representations made by

Schedule 4 Information for Inclusion in Environmental Statements

anybody recognized by the Regulations to be invited to make representations, and any representations duly made by any other person about the environmental effects of the development.

(c) *Environmental statement* is the information which must be provided by the developer in conjunction with his application for planning permission for the project.

According to reg 18(3) an environmental statement is a statement which includes 'at least'

(a) a description of the proposed development comprising information on the site, design, size and other relevant features of the development;
(b) a description of the likely significant effects of the proposed development on the environment;
(c) a description of any features of the proposed development, or measures envisaged in order to avoid, prevent or reduce and, if possible, offset likely significant adverse effects on the environment;
(d) a description of the reasonable alternatives studied by the developer, which are relevant to the proposed development and its specific characteristics, and an indication of the main reasons for the option chosen, taking into account the effects of the development on the environment;
(e) a non-technical summary of the information referred to in sub-paragraphs (a) to (d); and
(f) any additional information specified in Schedule 4 relevant to the specific characteristics of the particular development or type of development and to the environmental features likely to be significantly affected.

A new requirement in the 2017 Regulations is that statement is prepared by 'competent experts' and a statement setting out their expertise.

SCHEDULE 4 INFORMATION FOR INCLUSION IN ENVIRONMENTAL STATEMENTS

PART I

1. Description of the development, including in particular
   (a) a description of the location of the development;
   (b) a description of the physical characteristics of the whole development, including, where relevant, requisite demolition works, and the land-use requirements during the construction and operational phases;
   (c) a description of the main characteristics of the operational phase of the development (in particular any production process), for instance, energy demand and energy used, nature and quantity of the materials and natural resources (including water, land, soil and biodiversity) used;

(d) an estimate, by type and quantity, of expected residues and emissions (such as water, air, soil and subsoil pollution, noise, vibration, light, heat, radiation and quantities and types of waste produced during the construction and operation phases.
2. A description of the reasonable alternatives (for example in terms of development design, technology, location, size and scale) studied by the developer, which are relevant to the proposed project and its specific characteristics, and an indication of the main reasons for selecting the chosen option, including a comparison of the environmental effects.
3. A description of the relevant aspects of the current state of the environment (baseline scenario) and an outline of the likely evolution thereof without implementation of the development as far as natural changes from the baseline scenario can be assessed with reasonable effort on the basis of the availability of environmental information and scientific knowledge.
4. A description of the factors specified in regulation 4(2) likely to be significantly affected by the development: population, human health, biodiversity (for example fauna and flora), land (for example land take), soil (for example organic matter, erosion, compaction, sealing), water (for example hydromorphological changes, quantity and quality), air, climate (for example greenhouse gas emissions, impacts relevant to adaptation), material assets, cultural heritage, including architectural and archaeological aspects, and landscape.
5. A description of the likely significant effects of the development on the environment resulting from a number of specified aspects.
6. A description of the forecasting methods or evidence, used to identify and assess the significant effects on the environment, including details of difficulties (for example technical deficiencies or lack of knowledge) encountered compiling the required information and the main uncertainties involved.
7. A description of the measures envisaged to avoid, prevent, reduce or, if possible, offset any identified significant adverse effects on the environment and, where appropriate, of any proposed monitoring arrangements (for example the preparation of a post-project analysis). That description should explain the extent, to which significant adverse effects on the environment are avoided, prevented, reduced or offset, and should cover both the construction and operational phases.
8. A description of the expected significant adverse effects of the development on the environment deriving from the vulnerability of the development to risks of major accidents and/or disasters which are relevant to the project concerned.
9. A non-technical summary of the information provided under paragraphs 1 to 8
10. A reference list detailing the sources used for the descriptions and assessments included in the environmental statement.

B. PROJECTS REQUIRING ENVIRONMENTAL IMPACT ASSESSMENT

The Regulations apply to two separate lists of development projects: 12.06

(a) 'Schedule 1 development', for which EIA is mandatory;
(b) 'Schedule 2 development', for which EIA is required if the particular project is considered likely to give rise to significant effects on the environment by virtue of factors such as its nature, size, or location or to development located wholly or partly in a 'sensitive area'.

Schedule 1 development

The following types of development require EIA in every case: 12.07

The carrying out of development to provide any of the following:

1. Crude-oil refineries (excluding undertakings manufacturing only lubricants from crude oil) and installations for the gasification and liquefaction of 500 tonnes or more of coal or bituminous shale per day.
2. (a) Thermal power stations and other combustion installations with a heat output of 300 megawatts or more; and
   (b) Nuclear power stations and other nuclear reactors (except research installations for the production and conversion of fissionable and fertile materials, whose maximum power does not exceed 1 kilowatt continuous thermal load).
3. (a) Installations for the reprocessing of irradiated nuclear fuel.
   (b) Installations designed—
      (i) for the production or enrichment of nuclear fuel;
      (ii) for the processing of irradiated nuclear fuel or high-level radioactive waste;
      (iii) for the final disposal of irradiated nuclear fuel;
      (iv) solely for the final disposal of radioactive waste; or
      (v) solely for the storage (planned for more than 10 years) of irradiated nuclear fuels or radioactive waste in a different site than the production site.
4. (a) Integrated works for the initial smelting of cast-iron and steel;
   (b) Installations for the production of non-ferrous crude metals from ore, concentrates, or secondary raw materials by metallurgical, chemical, or electrolytic processes.
5. Installations for the extraction of asbestos and for the processing and transformation of asbestos and products containing asbestos—
   (a) for asbestos-cement products, with an annual production of more than 20,000 tonnes of finished products;

(b) for friction material, with an annual production of more than 50 tonnes of finished products; and

(c) for other uses of asbestos, utilization of more than 200 tonnes per year.

6. Integrated chemical installations, that is to say, installations for the manufacture on an industrial scale of substances using chemical conversion processes, in which several units are juxtaposed and are functionally linked to one another and which are—

(a) for the production of basic organic chemicals;

(b) for the production of basic inorganic chemicals;

(c) for the production of phosphorous-, nitrogen-, or potassium-based fertilizers (simple or compound fertilizers);

(d) for the production of basic plant health products and of biocides;

(e) for the production of basic pharmaceutical products using a chemical or biological process;

(f) for the production of explosives.

7. (a) Construction of lines for long-distance railway traffic and of airports with a basic runway length of 2,100 metres or more;

(b) Construction of motorways and express roads;

(c) Construction of a new road of four or more lanes, or realignment and/or widening of an existing road of two lanes or less so as to provide four or more lanes, where such new road, or realigned and/or widened section of road would be 10 kilometres or more in a continuous length.

8. (a) Inland waterways and ports for inland-waterway traffic which permit the passage of vessels of over 1,350 tonnes;

(b) Trading ports, piers for loading and unloading connected to land and outside ports (excluding ferry piers) which can take vessels of over 1,350 tonnes.

9. Waste disposal installations for the incineration, chemical treatment (as defined in Annex I to Directive 2008/98/EC of the European Parliament and of the Council of 19 November 2008 on waste under heading D9), or landfill of hazardous waste as defined in Article 3(2) of that Directive.

10. Waste disposal installations for the incineration or chemical treatment (as defined in Annex I to Directive 2008/98/EC under heading D9) of non-hazardous waste with a capacity exceeding 100 tonnes per day.

11. Groundwater abstraction or artificial groundwater recharge schemes where the annual volume of water abstracted or recharged is equivalent to or exceeds 10 million cubic metres.

12. (a) Works for the transfer of water resources, other than piped drinking water, between river basins where the transfer aims at preventing possible shortages of water and where the amount of water transferred exceeds 100 million cubic metres per year;

(b) In all other cases, works for the transfer of water resources, other than piped drinking water, between river basins where the multi-annual

average flow of the basin of abstraction exceeds 2,000 million cubic metres per year and where the amount of water transferred exceeds 5 per cent of this flow.
13. Waste water treatment plants with a capacity exceeding 150,000 population equivalent as defined in Art 2 point (6) of Council Directive 91/271/EEC.
14. Extraction of petroleum and natural gas for commercial purposes where the amount extracted exceeds 500 tonnes per day in the case of petroleum and 500,000 cubic metres per day in the case of gas.
15. Dams and other installations designed for the holding back or permanent storage of water, where a new or additional amount of water held back or stored exceeds 10 million cubic metres.
16. Pipelines for the transport of gas, oil, or chemicals with a diameter of more than 800 millimetres and a length of more than 40 kilometres.
17. Installations for the intensive rearing of poultry or pigs with more than—
    (a) 85,000 places for broilers or 60,000 places for hens;
    (b) 3,000 places for production pigs (over 30 kg); or
    (c) 900 places for sows.
18. Industrial plants for—
    (a) the production of pulp from timber or similar fibrous materials;
    (b) the production of paper and board with a production capacity exceeding 200 tonnes per day.
19. Quarries and open-cast mining where the surface of the site exceeds 25 hectares, or peat extraction where the surface of the site exceeds 150 hectares.
20. Construction of overhead electrical power lines with a voltage of 220 kV or more and a length of more than 15 km.
21. Installations for storage of petroleum, petrochemical or chemical products with a capacity of 200,000 tonnes or more.
22. Storage sites pursuant to Directive 2009/31/EC of the European Parliament and of the Council of 23 April 2009 on the geological storage of carbon dioxide.
23. Installations for the capture of carbon dioxide streams for the purposes of geological storage pursuant to Directive 2009/31/EC from installations referred to in this Schedule, or where the total yearly capture of carbon dioxide is 1.5 megatonnes or more.
24. Any change to or extension of development listed in this Schedule where such a change of extension itself meets the thresholds, if any, or description of development set out in this Schedule.

Schedule 2 development

12.08 The following types of development ('Schedule 2 development') require EIA if likely to have significant effects on the environment by virtue of nature, size, or location. The schedule sets out against each description of development the threshold or criteria for the purpose of classifying whether such development is within the schedule. Schedule 2 development, however, may also include development which, whilst listed in column 1 below, is located wholly or in part in a 'sensitive area'. In such cases, the threshold and criteria mentioned in column 2 do not apply to the development. 'Sensitive areas' are defined to include such cases as Sites of Special Scientific Interest, National Parks, Areas of Outstanding Natural Beauty, Scheduled Monuments, World Heritage Sites, and European sites.

Description of development and applicable thresholds and criteria for the purposes of the definition of 'Schedule 2 Development'

1. In the table below—
   'area of the works' includes any area occupied by apparatus, equipment, machinery, materials, plant, spoil heaps, or other facilities or stores required for construction or installation; 'controlled waters' has the same meaning as in the Water Resources Act 1991; 'floorspace' means the floorspace in a building or buildings.
2. The table below sets out the descriptions of development and applicable thresholds and criteria for the purpose of classifying development as Sch 2 development.

SCHEDULE 2

Column 1	Column 2
Description of development	Applicable thresholds and criteria

The carrying out of development to provide any of the following—

1. *Agriculture and aquaculture*	
(a) Projects for the use of uncultivated land or semi-natural areas for intensive agricultural purposes;	The area of the development exceeds 0.5 hectare.
(b) Water management projects for agriculture, including irrigation and land drainage projects;	The area of the works exceeds one hectare.
(c) intensive livestock installations (unless included in Sch 1);	The area of new floorspace exceeds 500 square metres.
(d) intensive fish farming;	The installation resulting from the development is designed to produce more than 10 tonnes of dead weight fish per year.
(e) reclamation of land from the sea.	All development.
2. *Extractive industry*	
(a) Quarries, open-cast mining, and peat extraction (unless included in Sch 1);	All development except the construction of buildings or other ancillary structures where the new floorspace does not exceed 1,000 square metres.

Schedule 2

(b) underground mining;	
(c) extraction of minerals by fluvial dredging;	All development.

(d) Deep drillings, in particular—
  (i) geothermal drilling;
  (ii) drilling for the storage of nuclear waste material;
  (iii) drilling for water supplies;
with the exception of drillings for investigating the stability of the soil;
	(i) In relation to any type of drilling, the area of the works exceeds one hectare; or
	(ii) in relation to geothermal drilling and drilling for the storage of nuclear waste material, the drilling is within 100 metres of any controlled waters.

(e) surface industrial installations for the extraction of coal, petroleum, natural gas, and ores, as well as bituminous shale.	The area of the development exceeds 0.5 hectare.
3. *Energy industry*	
(a) installations for the production of electricity, steam, and hot water (unless included in Sch 1);	The area of the development exceeds 0.5 hectare.
(b) installations for carrying gas, steam and hot water;	The area of the works exceeds one hectare.
(c) surface storage of natural gas; (d) underground storage of combustible gases; (e) surface storage of fossil fuels;	(i) The area of any new building, deposit or structure exceeds 500 square metres; or (ii) a new building, deposit, or structure is to be sited within 100 metres of any controlled waters.
(f) industrial briquetting of coal and lignite;	The area of new floorspace exceeds 1,000 square metres.
(g) installations for the processing and storage of radioactive waste (unless included in Sch 1);	(i) The area of new floorspace exceeds 1,000 square metres; or (ii) the installation resulting from the development will require the grant of an environmental permit under the Environmental Permitting (England and Wales) Regulations 2010 in relation to a radioactive substances activity described in paras 5(2)(b), (2)(c) or (4) of Part 2 of Sch 23 to those Regulations, or the variation of such a permit.
(h) installations for hydroelectric energy production;	The installation is designed to produce more than 0.5 megawatts.
(i) installations for the harnessing of wind power for energy production (wind farms);	(i) The development involves the installation of more than two turbines; or (ii) hub height of any turbine or height of any other structure exceeds 15 metres.
(j) installations for the capture of carbon dioxide streams for the purposes of geological storage pursuant to Directive 2009/31/EC from installations not included in Sch 1.	All development.
4. *Production and processing of metals*	
(a) Installations for the production of pig iron or steel (primary or secondary fusion) including continuous casting;	

(b) installations for the processing of ferrous metals—
  (i) hot-rolling mills;
  (ii) with hammers;
  (iii) of protective fused metal coats;	

(c) ferrous metal foundries;	

(d) installations for the smelting, including the alloyage, of non-ferrous metals, excluding precious metals, including recovered products (refining, foundry casting, etc);
(e) installations for surface treatment of metals and plastic materials using an electrolytic or chemical process;
(f) manufacture and assembly of motor vehicles and manufacture of motor-vehicle engines;
(g) shipyards;
(h) installations for the construction and repair of aircraft;
(i) manufacture of railway equipment;
(j) swaging by explosives;
(k) installations for the roasting and sintering of metallic ores.

The area of new floorspace exceeds 1,000 square metres.

5. *Mineral industry*
(a) Coke ovens (dry coal distillation);
(b) installations for the manufacture of cement;
(c) installations for the production of asbestos and the manufacture of asbestos-based products (unless included in Sch 1);
(d) installations for the manufacture of glass including glass fibre;
(e) installations for smelting mineral substances including the production of mineral fibres;
(f) manufacture of ceramic products by burning, in particular roofing tiles, bricks, refractory bricks, tiles, stoneware, or porcelain.

The area of new floorspace exceeds 1,000 square metres.

6. *Chemical industry (unless included in Sch 1)*
(a) Treatment of intermediate products and production of chemicals;
(b) production of pesticides and pharmaceutical products, paint and varnishes, elastomers, and peroxides;
(c) storage facilities for petroleum, petrochemical and chemical products.

The area of new floorspace exceeds 1,000 square metres.

(i) The area of any new building or structure exceeds 0.05 hectare; or
(ii) more than 200 tonnes of petroleum, petrochemical or chemical products is to be stored at any one time.

7. *Food industry*
(a) Manufacture of vegetable and animal oils and fats;
(b) packing and canning of animal and vegetable products;
(c) manufacture of dairy products;
(d) brewing and malting;
(e) confectionery and syrup manufacture;

The area of new floorspace exceeds 1,000 square metres.

(f) installations for the slaughter of animals;
(g) industrial starch manufacturing installations;
(h) fish-meal and fish-oil factories;
(i) sugar factories.

Schedule 2

8. *Textile, leather, wood, and paper industries*
(a) Industrial plants for the production of paper and board (unless included in Sch 1);
(b) plants for the pre-treatment (operations such as washing, bleaching, mercerization) or dyeing of fibres or textiles;
(c) plants for the tanning of hides and skins;
(d) cellulose-processing and production installations.

The area of new floorspace exceeds 1,000 square metres.

9. *Rubber industry*

Manufacture and treatment of elastomer-based products.

The area of new floorspace exceeds 1,000 square metres.

10. *Infrastructure projects*
(a) Industrial estate development projects;

The area of the development exceeds 0.5 hectares.

(b) urban development projects, including the construction of shopping centres and car parks, sport stadiums, leisure centres, and multiplex cinemas;

(i) The development includes more than 1 hectare of urban development which is not dwellinghouse development; or
(ii) the development includes more than 150 dwellings; or
(iii) the overall area of the development exceeds 5 hectares.

(c) construction of intermodal transshipment facilities and of intermodal terminals (unless included in Sch 1);

The area of the development exceeds 0.5 hectare.

(d) construction of railways (unless included in Sch 1);

The area of the works exceeds one hectare.

(e) construction of airfields (unless included in Sch 1);

(i) the development involves an extension to a runway; or
(ii) the area of the works exceeds one hectare.

(f) construction of roads (unless included in Sch 1);

The area of the works exceeds one hectare.

(g) construction of harbours and port installations including fishing harbours (unless included in Sch 1);

The area of the works exceeds one hectare.

(h) inland-waterway construction not included in Sch 1, canalization, and flood-relief works;

The area of the works exceeds one hectare.

(i) dams and other installations designed to hold water or store it on a long-term basis (unless included in Sch 1);

(j) tramways, elevated and underground railways, suspended lines, or similar lines of a particular type, used exclusively or mainly for passenger transport;

(k) oil and gas pipeline installations (unless included in Sch 1);
(l) installations of long-distance aqueducts;

(i) The area of the works exceeds one hectare; or,
(ii) in the case of a gas pipeline, the installation has a design operating pressure exceeding seven bar gauge.

(m) coastal work to combat erosion and maritime works capable of altering the coast through the construction, for example, of dykes, moles, jetties, and other sea defence works, excluding the maintenance and reconstruction of such works;

All development.

(n) groundwater abstraction and artificial groundwater recharge schemes not included in Sch 1;	
(o) works for the transfer of water resources between river basins not included in Sch 1;	The area of the works exceeds one hectare.
(p) motorway service areas.	The area of the development exceeds 0.5 hectare.

11. *Other projects*

(a) Permanent racing and test tracks for motorized vehicles;	The area of the development exceeds one hectare.
(b) installations for the disposal of waste (unless included in Sch 1);	(i) The disposal is by incineration; or (ii) the area of the development exceeds 0.5 hectare; or (iii) the installation is to be sited within 100 metres of any controlled waters.
(c) waste-water treatment plants (unless included in Sch 1);	The area of the development exceeds 1,000 square metres.
(d) sludge-deposition sites; (e) storage of scrap iron, including scrap vehicles;	(i) The area of deposit or storage exceeds 0.5 hectare; or (ii) a deposit is to be made or scrap stored within 100 metres of any controlled waters.
(f) test benches for engines, turbines, or reactors;	
(g) installations for the manufacture of artificial mineral fibres;	The area of new floorspace exceeds 1,000 square metres.
(h) installations for the recovery or destruction of explosive substances;	
(i) knackers' yards.	

12. *Tourism and leisure*

(a) Ski-runs, ski-lifts, and cable-cars and associated developments;	(i) The area of the works exceeds one hectare; or (ii) the height of any building or other structure exceeds 15 metres.
(b) marinas;	The area of the enclosed water surface exceeds 1,000 square metres.
(c) holiday villages and hotel complexes outside urban areas and associated developments;	The area of the development exceeds 0.5 hectare.
(d) theme parks;	
(e) permanent camp sites and caravan sites;	The area of the development exceeds one hectare.
(f) golf courses and associated developments.	The area of the development exceeds one hectare.

13. *Changes or extensions*

(a) Any change to or extension of development of a description listed in Sch 1 (other than a change or extension falling within para 21 of that Schedule) where that development is already authorized, executed or in the process of being executed;	Either (i) The development as changed or extended may have significant adverse effects on the environment; or (ii) In relation to development of a description mentioned in a paragraph in Sch 1 indicated below, the thresholds and criteria in Column 2 of the paragraph of this table indicated below applied to the change or extension (and not to the development as changed or extended):

Schedule 2

Paragraph in Sch 1	Paragraph of this table
1	6(a)
2(a)	3(a)
2(b)	3(g)
3	3(g)
4	4
5	5
6	6(a)
7(a)	10(d) (in relation to railways) or 10(e) (in relation to airports)
7(b) and (c)	10(f)
8(a)	10(h)
8(b)	10(g)
9	11(b)
10	11(b)
12	10(o)
13	11(c)
14	2(e)
15	10(i)
16	10(k)
17	1(c)
19	2(a)
20	6(c)

(b) any change to or extension of development listed in paras 1–12 of Column 1 in this table, where that development is already authorized, executed or in the process of being executed;	Either (i) The development as changed or extended may have significant adverse effects on the environment; or (ii) In relation to development of a description mentioned in Column 1 of this table, the thresholds and criteria in the corresponding part of Column 2 of this table applied to the change or extension are met or exceeded.
(c) development of a description mentioned in Sch 1 undertaken exclusively or mainly for the development and testing of new methods or products and not used for more than two years.	All development.

The present wording of para 13 reflects the decision of the High Court in *R (on the application of Baker) v Bath and North East Somerset District Council* [2009] EWHC 595 (Admin); [2010] 1 P & CR 4 where it was found that the old wording in the 1999 Regulations wrongly sought to limit consideration for the purpose of screening to the change or extension on its own rather than to the development as changed or extended.

The Schedules (particularly Sch 2) are very wide, and to some extent use somewhat obscure expressions, so that a good deal of legitimate disagreement may be involved in applying them to the facts of any particular case. In *R (Anne-Marie Goodman) v London Borough of Lewisham and Big Yellow Property Company Ltd* [2003] EWCA Civ 140; [2003] Env LR 140, the Court of Appeal had to consider

12.09

whether the authority correctly interpreted the expression 'urban development projects' in deciding that the development of a storage and distribution centre fell within the ambit of para 10(b) of Sch 2. In quashing a grant of planning permission for that development the Court of Appeal held that if an authority makes an understanding of expressions used in the Regulations which is wrong in law, the court may correct it. However, if the meaning in law is imprecise (as opposed to determining what the meaning was in the first place) a range of different meanings may be legitimately available. In such a case the court will only interfere if the planning authority goes outside the range of legitimate meanings. A recent illustration is *R (on the application of Crematoria Management Ltd) v Welwyn Hatfield BC* [2018] EWHC 382 (Admin) concerning crematoria facilities at a cemetery.

Identifying relevant Sch 2 projects

12.10 As already indicated the criteria for determining whether a Sch 2 project requires EIA is whether or not it is likely to give rise to significant effects on the environment by virtue of its nature, size, or location. With the exception of development which is located wholly or partly within a 'sensitive area', the first decision to be made is whether it meets or exceeds the threshold or criteria listed in column 2 of Sch 2. No such test, however, is provided for the development of land for any of the activities set out in column 1 of Sch 2, where the land is located mostly or partly within a 'sensitive area'. A 'sensitive area' includes land within an area of Special Scientific Interest, a National Park, the Broads, an Area of Outstanding Natural Beauty, World Heritage Sites, scheduled monuments, and land to which Nature Conservation Orders apply.

12.11 Most helpfully, Sch 3 of the Regulations sets out selection criteria that must also be taken into account in determining whether development is likely to have significant effects on the environment. Such criteria apply to all development within column 1 of Sch 2, and irrespective of whether the development takes place on land in a sensitive area.

12.12 The selection criteria set out in Sch 3 for screening Schedule 2 developments are as follows:

1. Characteristics of development
   The characteristics of development must be considered having regard, in particular, to—
   (a) the size of the development;
   (b) the cumulation with other development;
   (c) the use of natural resources;
   (d) the production of waste;
   (e) pollution and nuisance;
   (f) the risk of accidents, having regard in particular to substances or technologies used.
   (g) the risks to human health (for example, due to water contamination or air pollution).

Schedule 2

2. Location of development
   The environmental sensitivity of geographical areas likely to be affected by development must be considered, having regard, in particular, to—
   (a) the existing land use;
   (b) the relative abundance, quality, and regenerative capacity of natural resources in the area;
   (c) the absorption capacity of the natural environment, paying particular attention to the following areas:
       (i) wetlands:
       (ii) coastal zones;
       (iii) mountain and forest areas;
       (iv) nature reserves and parks;
       (v) European sites and other areas classified or protected under national legislation;
       (vi) areas in which there has already been a failure to meet the environmental quality standards, laid down in Union legislation and relevant to the project, or in which it is considered that there is such a failure;
       (vii) densely populated areas; and
       (viii) landscapes of historical, cultural, or archaeological significance.
3. Characteristics of the potential impact
   The potential significant effects of development must be considered in relation to criteria set out under paras 1 and 2 above, and having regard in particular to—
   (a) the magnitude and spatial extent of the impact (for example geographical area and size of the population likely to be affected);
   (b) the nature of the impact;
   (c) the transboundary nature of the impact;
   (d) the intensity and complexity of the impact;
   (e) the probability of the impact;
   (f) the expected onset, duration, frequency and reversibility of the impact;
   (g) the cumulation of the impact with the impact of other existing and/or approved development;
   (h) the possibility of effectively reducing the impact.

12.13 The Schedule identifies three broad criteria to be taken into account, namely: the characteristics of the development; the environmental sensitivity of the location; and the characteristics of the potential impact. The Secretary of State's view about the need for an EIA is expressed in the Planning Practice Guidance 'Indicative Screening Thresholds' (4-057-2070720). For example, referring to para 10(b) 'Urban Development Projects', the Secretary of State considers that an EIA is only likely to be required if:

(a) the area of the scheme exceeds 5 ha,
(b) 10,000 m² of new commercial floorspace is created, or
(c) the scheme would have significant urbanizing effects in a previously non-urban area (1,000 new dwellings).

Given the range of Sch 2 projects and the importance of locational factors, it is not possible to formulate criteria or thresholds which will provide a universal test of whether or not EIA is required. The most that the PPG says can be offered is a broad indication of the type or scale of development which is likely to be a candidate for assessment and, conversely, an indication of the sort of development for which EIA is unlikely to be necessary. The PPG does this by containing a link from PPG (4-057-2070720) to a table of 'Indicative Screening Thresholds' indicating when and when not EIAs are likely to be required, but it contains a warning that these thresholds should only be used in conjunction with the general guidance, and particularly that relating to 'sensitive locations'.

Who decides whether EIA is required?

12.14 Given the lack of a simple test for deciding whether or not EIA is required, particularly for Sch 2 development, on whom does the decision depend? In the first instance, the local planning authority may 'screen' an application for Sch 2 development to determine whether EIA is required. The determination is referred to as a 'screening opinion'. If an authority fails to screen a Sch 2 application with the result that no consideration is given as to whether the development is likely to have a significant effect on the environment by virtue of factors such as its nature, size, and location, the courts could quash a subsequent grant of planning permission if the grant is challenged timely. It seems that the Regulations do not expressly impose upon either the local planning authority or the Secretary of State a general obligation to consider whether EIA is required. But they will want to be on their guard.

12.15 The central issue in many cases will in fact be whether the proposed development is likely to have significant effects on the environment, etc. To answer that question, the authority must be sure that it has sufficient information to enable it to form a sensible judgment as to the likelihood of the proposed development having a significant effect on the environment. Full knowledge of the project's likely significant effect on the environment is, however, not required at this stage. Thus, the degree of information required at this stage will be less than that required at the later second stage once it has been decided that EIA is required, see: *R (on the application of Jones) v Mansfield DC* [2003] EWHC 7 (Admin). It is not sufficient that the environmental effect would be a factor in determining whether to grant permission. This was not in itself determinative as to whether the effects were likely to be significant, see: *R (on the application of Loader) v Secretary of State for Communities and Local Government* [2012] EWCA Civ 869; [2013] PTSR 406. Also, in *William Blossom v Derbyshire CC* [2011] EWHC 2566 (Admin); [2012] JPL 443. It was held that in deciding whether the effect was likely to be significant, it might have to be accepted that if permission were not to be granted, the position on the site could change, in which case comparison should be made between this as well as the existing position.

12.16 In *British Telecommunications plc and Bloomsbury Land Investments v Gloucester City Council* [2001] EWHC Admin 1001; [2002] 2 P & CR 33, it was pointed out that the Regulations required that screening was necessary when the proposed development was likely to have significant effects on the environment, not whether the development was likely to have significant adverse effects. It was held that there was no justification for treating the phrase 'significant effects' as though it was qualified by the word 'adverse'. For that reason, the High Court quashed a grant of planning permission for the redevelopment of the Blackfriars area of the city. The court thought that the wording used in the Regulations was essential as it gave the public an opportunity to form their own view as to whether the effects were adverse or beneficial.

12.17 A question raised at this stage is to what extent can the effect of the proposed development be reduced or controlled by conditions or by other public bodies such as the Environment Agency? It has been held that proper screening is of importance to the involvement of the public in environment assessment. This was emphasized by Sullivan J in *R (on the application of Lebus) v South Cambridgeshire DC* [2002] EWHC Admin 2009, where the proposed development was the erection of an egg-production unit. In that case the issue was the effect and relevance of proposed pollution and management control measures to the development. There, commenting on *British Telecommunications*, he said:

> Whilst each case will no doubt turn upon its own particular facts, and whilst it may well be perfectly reasonable to envisage the operation of standard conditions and a reasonably managed development, the underlying purpose of the Regulations in implementing the Directive is that the potentially significant impacts of a development are described together with a description of the measures envisaged to prevent, reduce and, where possible, offset any significant adverse effects on the environment. Thus the public is engaged in the process of assessing the efficacy of any mitigation measures.
>
> It is not appropriate for a person charged with making a screening opinion to start from the premise that although there may be significant impacts, these can be reduced to insignificance as a result of the implementation of conditions of various kinds. The appropriate course in such a case is to require an environmental statement setting out the significant impacts and the measures which it is said will reduce their significance.

After describing the approach of the Council, he concluded:

> ... In so far as one can discern the Council's reasoning, it was erroneous on the two grounds set out above: it was no answer to the need for an EIA to say the information would be supplied in some form in any event, and it was not right to approach the matter on the basis that the significant adverse effects could be rendered insignificant if suitable conditions were imposed. The proper approach was to say that potentially this is a development which has significant adverse environmental implications: what are the measures which should be included in order to reduce or offset those adverse effects?

12.18 It follows that the decision-maker must not put into separate compartments the development proposal and the proposed remedial measures and consider only the first when making a screening decision. Each case must be considered on its merits. Although some minor remedial measures can be discounted to be dealt with by standard conditions, any others should not be put off for later consideration. Remedial measures cannot be ignored or deferred at the screening stage in their entirety.

12.19 Both the *British Telecommunications* case and the *Lebus* case were considered by the Court of Appeal in *Bellway Urban Renewal Southern v Gillespie* [2003] EWCA Civ 400; [2003] Env LR 30. There the Secretary of State had considered that the proposed development relating to an area of contaminated land in a densely populated urban area was unlikely to cause significant effects on the environment and that therefore no EIA was necessary. He expressed himself satisfied that remediation of the land could be cured by conditions. The court held that in deciding whether EIA was necessary, the Secretary of State was not obliged to 'shut his eyes' to the remedial measures. As was said by Pill LJ in the *Bellway* case:

> The Secretary of State has to make a practical judgment as to whether the project would be likely to have significant effects on the environment by virtue of factors such as its nature, size, or location. The extent to which remedial measures are required to avoid significant effects on the environment, and the nature and complexity of such measures will vary enormously but the Secretary of State is not as a matter of law required to ignore proposals for remedial measures included in the proposals before him when making his screening decision. In some cases the remedial measures will be modest in scope, or so plainly and easily achievable, that the Secretary of State can properly hold that the development project would not be likely to have significant effects on the environment even though, in the absence of the proposed remedial measures, it would be likely to have such effects. His decision is not in my judgment pre-determined either by the complexity of the project or by whether remedial measures are controversial though, in making the decision, the complexity of the project and of the proposed remedial measures may be important for consideration.

12.20 The conclusion whether to adopt a positive or negative screening opinion (ie to require or not require an EIA) is a fact-sensitive judgment for the decision-maker, the Court will only intervene if there is an error of law. In *R (on the application of Hockley) v Essex County Council* [2013] EWHC 4051 (Admin) Lindblom J summarized the principles at [23]–[25]:

> 23. In *R. (on the application of Jones) v Mansfield District Council* [2004] Env. L.R. 21 Carnwath L.J., as he then was, emphasised (in paragraph 58 of his judgment) that 'the EIA process is intended to be an aid to efficient and inclusive decision-making in special cases, not an obstacle race', and that 'it does not detract from the authority's ordinary duty, in the case of any planning application, to inform itself of all relevant matters, and take them properly into account in deciding the case.'
>
> 24. In *R. (on the application of Bateman) v South Cambridgeshire District Council* [2011] EWCA Civ 157 Moore-Bick L.J. said (in paragraph 20 of his judgment) that it was important to bear in mind 'the nature of what is involved in giving a screening opinion'. A screening opinion, he said, 'is not intended to involve a

detailed assessment of factors relevant to the grant of planning permission; that comes later and will ordinarily include an assessment of environmental factors, among others'. Nor does it require 'a full assessment of any identifiable environmental effects'. What is involved in a screening process is 'only a decision, almost inevitably on the basis of less than complete information, whether an EIA needs to be undertaken at all'. The court should not, therefore, impose too high a burden on planning authorities in what is simply 'a procedure intended to identify the relatively small number of cases in which the development is likely to have significant effects on the environment ....'. In the light of the decision of the *European Court of Justice in Landelijke Vereniging tot Behoud van de Waddenzee v Staatssecretaris Van Landbouw, Natuurbeheer en Visserij* [2004] ECR I-7405 and the Advocate General's opinion in *R. (on the application of Mellor) v Secretary of State for Communities and Local Government* [2010] Env LR 18 Moore-Bick L.J. said (in paragraph 17 of his judgment) that a likelihood in this context was 'something more than a bare possibility .... though any serious possibility would suffice'.

25. In *R. (on the application of Loader) v Secretary of State for Communities and Local Government* [2012] EWCA Civ 869, Pill L.J., with whom Toulson and Sullivan L.JJ. agreed, said (in paragraph 31 of his judgment) that there was 'ample authority that the conventional *Wednesbury* approach applies to the court's adjudication of issues such as these'. That principle is firmly established in the domestic jurisprudence. For example, in *R. (on the application of Evans) v Secretary of State for Communities and Local Government* [2013] EWCA Civ 114) Beatson L.J. said (in paragraph 22 of his judgment) that the 'assessment of the significance of an impact or impacts on the environment has been described as essentially a fact-finding exercise which requires the exercise of judgment on the issues of "likelihood" and "significance"' (see also paragraph 40 of Laws L.J.'s judgment in *Bowen-West v Secretary of State* [2012] EWCA Civ 321). In *Jones v Mansfield* Carnwath L.J. said (at paragraph 61) that because the word 'significant' does not lay down a precise legal test but requires the exercise of judgment on planning issues and consistency in the exercise of that judgment in different cases, the function is one for which the courts are ill-equipped.

Holgate J added in *R (on the application of Birchall Gardens LLP) v Hertfordshrie County Council* [2016] EWHC 2794 (Admin); [2017] Env LR 17 at [66]–[67]: **12.21**

66. It is common ground that the analysis in paragraph 20 of the judgment of Moore-Bick LJ in *R (Bateman) v South Cambridgeshire District Council* [2011] EWCA Civ 157 continues to apply to the screening process under the 2011 Regulations (*Mackman v Secretary of State for Communities and Local Government* [2015] EWCA Civ 716; [2016] Env LR 6 at paragraph 7). A screening opinion does not involve a detailed assessment of factors relevant to the grant of planning permission; that comes later and will ordinarily include environmental factors. Nor does it include a full assessment of any identifiable environmental effects. It includes only a decision, almost inevitably on the basis of less than complete information, as to whether an EIA needs to be undertaken at all. The court should not impose too high a burden on planning authorities in relation to 'what is no more than a procedure intended to identify the relatively small number of cases in which the development is likely to have significant effects on the environment.'

67. The issues of whether there is sufficient information before the planning authority for them to issue a screening opinion and whether a development is likely to

have significant environmental effects, are both matters of judgment for the planning authority. Such decisions may only be challenged in the courts on grounds of irrationality or other public law error (*R (Jones) v Mansfield District Council* [2003] EWCA Civ 1408; [2004] Env L.R. 21 (paragraphs 14–18 and 52–55 and *R (Noble Organisation Ltd) v Thanet District Council* [2005] ECWA Civ 782; [2006] Env. L.R.8 paragraph 30).

12.22 In *R (on the application of Cairns) v Hertfordshire County Council* [2018] EWHC 2050 (Admin) Lang J gave short-shrift to the attempt to read across the CJEU judgment in *People Over Wind & Sweetman v Coillte Teoranta* [2018] PTSR 1668 to the EIA Regime (discussed in detail in Chapter 26). The Judge found at [28] that, unlike the Habitats Directive, the EIA Directive expressly requires 'the possibility of effectively reducing the impact' (transposed in England at para 3(h) of Sch 3 to the EIA Regulations 2017) to be taken into account when undertaking a screening assessment.

12.23 A developer may well decide EIA will be required for his proposed development and will submit an environmental statement with his application for planning permission. If the applicant states that the information he has submitted is intended to constitute an environmental statement for the purposes of the Regulations, then, unless the Secretary of State otherwise directs, the local planning authority is required to treat it as such and the statement is an essential part of the EIA of the development. If on the other hand, the applicant has not made it clear that the information submitted is an environmental statement for the purposes of the Regulations, and the local planning authority considers the development does not require EIA, none will be necessary, although the information given by the applicant may still be taken into account by the local planning authority in determining the application for planning permission.

12.24 It is also possible that a developer may, before submitting a planning application, be in doubt as to whether his proposed development requires EIA. In such cases, reg 6(1) provides that he may request the local planning authority 'adopt a screening opinion'. The request must be accompanied by a plan sufficient to identify the location of the land and a brief description of the nature and purpose of the development and its possible environmental effects. The authority may ask the developer for further information in order to formulate an opinion. Then, unless the authority and developer so agree to extend, the authority must give its opinion within three weeks of the request, and give clearly and precisely the full reasons for adopting that opinion. Should the local planning authority decide that EIA is required and the developer disagrees or the authority fails to give a screening opinion within the three-week period, the developer may request the Secretary of State to make a 'screening direction'. Should he then direct that EIA is required (but not otherwise) the Secretary of State must give a clear and precise statement of his full reasons for doing so.

12.25 It used to be the position that if the Secretary of State decided that EIA is not required, no reasons need to be given. However, in *R (on the application of Christopher Mellor) v Secretary of State for Communities and Local Government* [2009] EWCA Civ. 1201 following a ruling by the European Court of Justice, it was held that if an interested party asks, reasons must be given for the decision. Then with the consolidation of the Regulations the opportunity was taken to change the position and reg 5(5)(a) of the 2017 Regulations provides that where a local planning authority adopts a screening opinion or the Secretary of State makes a screening direction, they must 'state the main reasons for their conclusion with reference to the relevant criteria listed in Schedule 3'. If it is determined not to be EIA development they must 'state any features of the proposed development and measures envisaged to avoid, or prevent what might otherwise have been, significant adverse effects on the environment'. Also, the authority or the Secretary of State, as the case may be, must send a copy of the opinion or direction and a copy of the written statement to the person who proposes to carry out, or who has carried out, the development in question.

12.26 Yet another possibility is that a developer may submit an application for planning permission for development which could be a Sch 1 or 2 development without submitting an environmental statement. Where the local planning authority considers the application to be within Sch 1 or 2 of the Regulations it is required to proceed as if an application had been made to it under reg 6 requesting the authority to give a 'screening opinion' as to whether an EIA is required for the development. If the authority considers that it is so required, the applicant must within three weeks either provide an environmental statement or ask the Secretary of State for a screening direction. Since 15 January 2007 the publicity requirements have been strengthened to make them compliant with the publicity requirements of the Aarhus Convention.

12.27 In two situations the Secretary of State may have to deal with a development proposal which is not accompanied by an environmental statement. First, if an application for planning permission is called in for determination by the Secretary of State under s 77 of the 1990 Act and secondly, where an appeal is made to the Secretary of State under s 78 of the 1990 Act and in either case is not accompanied by an environmental statement and the development is considered by the Secretary of State to be a Sch 1 or 2 development. In both cases the Secretary of State will notify the applicant accordingly, who will then have three weeks to provide an environmental statement which, if not complied with, will result in the Secretary of State losing jurisdiction to deal with the application or appeal, save to refuse it.

12.28 Essentially, therefore, it is for the local planning authority to decide in the first place whether a proposed development falls within the descriptions of development set out in Schs 1 and 2 to the Regulations and, in the latter case, whether or not the development would be likely to have significant effects on the environment. It was held in *Berkeley v Secretary of State for the Environment* [2001] 2 AC 603 that that decision is only reviewable by the courts on traditional *Wednesbury* grounds or if there has been an error of law. That position was confirmed by the Court of Appeal in *R (on the application of Evans) v Secretary of State for Communities and Local Government* [2013] EWCA Civ 114; [2013] JPL 1027 notwithstanding the observation of the Aarhus Convention Compliance Committee in its December 2010 Report which expressed concern at the *Wednesbury* approach. Beatson LJ held at [38]:

> The Committee's view and concern is undoubtedly worthy of respect. But, even if it had reached the view that the *Wednesbury* approach does not enable the court to assess the substantive and procedural legality of the Secretary of State's decision, its view would have had no direct legal consequence.

12.29 In *R (Blewett) v Derbyshire CC* [2003] EWHC 2775 (Admin); [2004] Env LR 29, Sullivan J opined that:

> it was important that decisions on EIA applications are made on the basis of 'full information' but the Regulations are not based on the premise that the environmental statement will necessarily contain the full information. The process is designed to identify any deficiencies in the environmental statement so that the local planning authority has the full picture ... when it comes to consider the environmental information of which the environmental statement will be but a part.

EIA and permitted development rights

12.30 Because the majority of permitted development rights largely concern development of a minor nature, such development is unlikely to fall within Sch 1 or 2 of the Regulations. However, the General Permitted Development Order 2015 (GPDO) provisions insofar as they relate to Sch 1 or 2 development, provide that Sch 1 development is not permitted development. The GPDO also provides that Sch 2 development is not permitted development under the Order unless the local planning authority has adopted a screening opinion to the effect that EIA is not required. It should also be noted that the environmental assessment regime applies equally to a local development order made under s 61A of the 1990 Act.

12.31 If the authority's opinion is that environmental impact assessment is required, permitted development rights are withdrawn and a planning application accompanied by an environmental statement must be made. There are, however, a number of types of permitted development in the GPDO which are not subject to these restrictive provisions relating to Sch 2 development.

'Scoping opinions' and preparing an environmental statement

12.32 Before making a planning application, a developer may ask the local planning authority to give in writing an opinion as to the information to be provided in the environmental statement. The opinion so given is called a 'scoping opinion' (reg 15). The request for this opinion must include the same information as would be required to accompany a request to the local planning authority for a 'screening opinion'. Indeed, both requests may be made at the same time. This will include a plan indicating the proposed location of the development, a brief description of the nature and purpose of the proposal, and its possible environmental effects, giving a broad indication of their likely scale. The local planning authority may seek further information from the developer.

12.33 Where a scoping opinion is sought from a local planning authority, the authority must respond within five weeks of the request, failing which the developer may apply for one to the Secretary of State. There is, however, no provision for the Secretary of State to intervene if the developer and local planning authority disagree as to the content of a scoping opinion provided by the authority, though if the application for development is called in or goes to the Secretary of State by way of appeal, the Secretary of State will be in a position to form his own opinion on the matter at that stage.

12.34 Lastly, it should be noted that under the Environmental Information Regulations 2004 (SI 2004/3391), a number of public bodies must make environmental information already in their possession available to any person who requests it. This obligation is supplemented by 19 of the 2017 Regulations, under which the local planning authority is required to forward the environmental statement to any consultation body or to any other person directly affected by the development or with an interest in the application but is unlikely to become aware of it by site notice or local advertisement. The bodies under this obligation are statutory consultees under Art 18 and Sch 4 of the Development Management Procedure Order 2015 (DMPO) and those listed in reg 2(1) of the 2017 Regulations and include: any principal council for the area in which the land is situated; Natural England; and the Environment Agency.

Publicity requirements

12.35 By reg 23 an applicant for planning permission or subsequent consent, or an appellant, who submits an environmental statement in connection with an application or appeal, must ensure that a reasonable number of copies of the statement are available at the address named in the notices published or posted. A reasonable charge reflecting printing and distribution costs may be made to a member of the public for a copy of an environmental statement made available in accordance with reg 23.

12.36 On receipt of the application, the local planning authority must take a number of steps additional to those it is already required to take with any planning application, namely: publish the application and statement in accordance with the provisions set out in Arts 15 and 16 and Sch 3 of the DMPO; send copies of the statement and application to those consultation bodies who have not already received them from the applicant; send three copies of the statement and application to the Secretary of State; and place the statement and any related screening or scoping opinions or directions in Part I of the planning register. Similar publicity requirements are required for environmental statements which are submitted after a planning application.

12.37 It should be noted that the Environmental Information Regulations contain a very wide definition of environmental information. There are a limited number of exceptions to disclosure but those there are must pass an overriding test that 'in all the circumstances of the case, the public interest in maintaining the exception outweighs the public interest in disclosing the information'.

Consideration of EIA applications

12.38 The local planning authority should determine such applications within 16 weeks from the date of the receipt of the statement instead of the normal eight weeks prescribed for determining all other applications. If the local planning authority fails to make a determination after 16 weeks (or such further period as agreed with the applicant), the applicant may appeal to the Secretary of State against non-determination. Under reg 3 planning permission cannot be granted for EIA Development unless an EIA has been carried out in respect of that development. Further by reg 26(1) in respect of an application, appeal or subsequent consent for EIA Development the decision-maker must:

(a) examine the environmental information;
(b) reach a reasoned conclusion on the significant effects of the proposed development on the environment, taking into account the examination referred to in sub-paragraph (a) and, where appropriate, their own supplementary examination;
(c) integrate that conclusion into the decision as to whether planning permission or subsequent consent is to be granted; and
(d) if planning permission or subsequent consent is to be granted, consider whether it is appropriate to impose monitoring measures.

Environmental information, it will be recalled, means the environmental statement, including any further information, any representations made by any body required by the Regulations to be invited to make representations (the consultation bodies), and any representations made by any other person about the environmental effects of the development. 'Subsequent consent' captures discharge of conditions, see reg 2(1).

Publicizing determinations of EIA applications

12.39 Once the application has been determined, the local planning authority must, in addition to notifying the applicant, notify the Secretary of State and the public (by local advertisement or such other means which are reasonable in the circumstances). Under reg 30(1)(d) the planning authority or Secretary of State must also make available for public inspection a statement containing:

(i) details of the matters referred to in regulation 29(2) (the right to challenge, and the significant effects on the environment, conditions, mitigation measures, monitoring or reasons for refusal);
(ii) the main reasons and considerations on which the decision is based including, if relevant, information about the participation of the public; and
(iii) a summary of the results of the consultations undertaken, and information gathered, in respect of the application and how those results (in particular, in circumstances where regulation 58 applies, the comments received from an EEA State pursuant to consultation under that regulation) have been incorporated or otherwise addressed.

12.40 The requirements of the statement under the previous regulations were considered by the Court of Appeal in *R (on the application of Richardson) v North Yorkshire County Council* [2003] EWCA Civ 1860; [2004] 1 WLR 1920. There had been a clear failure to supply reasons in accordance with the forerunner of reg 30. The Court of Appeal found the appropriate remedy was an order for reasons to be supplied. However, in *Dover District Council v CPRE (Kent)* [2017] UKSC 79; [2018] 1 WLR 108 Lord Carnwath JSC disapproved of that approach at [48]:

> I find the distinction drawn between notification of the decision, and of the reasons on which it is based, artificial and unconvincing. In the regulations (as in the Aarhus Convention, which is now expressly referred to in the Directive) the provision of reasons is an intrinsic part of the procedure, essential to ensure effective public participation

However, his Lordship did say that he 'did not necessarily disagree' with the decision not to quash the decision, because the Council had granted permission on the basis of its officer's recommendation. In such circumstances, the proper inference is that the reasons for doing so are those set out in the officer's report (absent positive indications to the contrary).

Special cases

12.41 A number of modifications to the EIA regime described above apply in some special cases. These include local authorities' own development, development likely to have significant environmental effects in other Member States of the Community, and development which is the subject of an enforcement notice. In the last of these cases, the Secretary of State, in dealing with an appeal against an enforcement notice, may not grant planning permission for unauthorized EIA Development, unless an EIA has been carried out in respect of that development (reg 36) and a local planning authority has an express obligation to have regard to the 'need to secure compliance with the requirements and objectives of the Directive' in the exercise of their enforcement functions (reg 35).

C. JUDICIAL CHALLENGE

Scope

12.42 The question of whether there has been compliance with the Environmental Impact Assessment Regulations has been considered by the courts on many occasions. One early decision on the main application of the Regulations was in *R v Swale BC, ex p the Royal Society for the Protection of Birds* [1991] JPL 39. In rejecting the Royal Society's argument that the Town and Country Planning (Assessment of Environmental Effects) Regulations 1988 applied, Simon Brown J (as he then was) held that the decision whether any particular development was or was not within the scheduled descriptions was a matter exclusively for the planning authority, subject only to *Wednesbury* challenge. He considered that questions of classification were essentially questions of fact and degree, not of law; and that the court was not entitled upon judicial review to act effectively as an appeal court and to reach its own decision so as to ensure that EEC obligations were properly discharged. This subjective approach to the implementation of the Regulations in the United Kingdom could well mean the European Community Directive being interpreted differently in different Member States of the European Community. However, in *R (on the application of Goodman) v London Borough of Lewisham and the Big Yellow Property Company* [2003] EWCA Civ 140; [2003] Env LR 28. Buxton LJ held that if the authority reached an understanding of the expressions used in the Regulations that was wrong in law, the court had to intervene. It was not just a question of *Wednesbury* unreasonableness. Buxton LJ however accepted that the meaning in law might be sufficiently imprecise so that in applying it to the facts a range of different conclusions may be legitimately available. In such a case the role of the courts will be more limited as they will only be able to impose their own view if the planning authority went outside this range of legitimate meanings.

12.43 A difficult problem that has confronted the courts is whether a project is Sch 2 development where it does not meet the thresholds but is capable of forming part of a larger development which would meet those thresholds. In the *Swale* case, Simon Brown J suggested in deciding the impact of a development that a development project should not be considered in isolation if in reality it is to be regarded as an integral part of an inevitably more substantial development. But this was merely obiter, as was his later comment that 'the question whether the development is of a category described in either Schedule must be answered strictly in relation to the development applied for, and not for any development contemplated beyond that'.

12.44 That issue was raised directly in the case of *British Airports Authority Plc v Secretary of State for Transport, Local Government and the Regions* [2002] EWHC 1920

(Admin); [2003] JPL 610. There, the Secretary of State had called in two applications. One was for approval for reserved matters following the grant of outline planning permission for an industrial park, the other for an application for full planning permission for a link road. In granting planning permission, the Secretary of State had failed to consider whether the totality of the two schemes of development were in fact capable of constituting an integral site and part of a single development. Had he done so, and then reached the conclusion that they were not a single development, the decision would have been vulnerable to legal challenge on the basis of irrationality. As a consequence of the Secretary of State's omission, the question of whether provision of the link road was development requiring EIA had been effectively sidestepped.

12.45 The issue arose before the ECJ in *Ecologistas en Accion-CODA v Ayuntamiento de Madrid* [2009] PTSR 458. The case concerned the splitting of the Madrid ring-road project into a number of different projects all below the assessment threshold was an unlawful breach of the Directive. The ECJ found that:

> the purpose of the amended [EIA] directive cannot be circumvented by the splitting of projects and the failure to take account of the cumulative effect of several projects must not mean in practice that they all escape the obligation to carry out an assessment when, taken together, they are likely to have significant effects on the environment within the meaning of Article 2(1) of the amended directive

12.46 The mischief to be avoided is not simply an attempt to avoid assessment under the EIA Directive altogether, but also a situation where a single project has been presented as a smaller EIA development in order to make it easier to gain planning permission, as Richards LJ observed in *R (on the application of Larkfleet Ltd) v South Kesteven DC* [2015] EWCA Civ 887; [2016] Env LR 4 at [37]:

> It is true that the scrutiny of cumulative effects between two projects may involve less information than if the two sets of works are treated together as one project, and a planning authority should be astute to ensure that a developer has not sliced up what is in reality one project in order to try to make it easier to obtain planning permission for the first part of the project and thereby gain a foot in the door in relation to the remainder

Lang J at first instance [2014] EWHC 3760 (Admin); [2015] Env LR 16, held that the legal obligation was as follows (approved by Richards LJ on appeal at [52]):

> the starting point will always be the proposed development. However, the planning authority ought also to go on to consider whether there are other proposed developments in the vicinity and if so, whether they should be assessed jointly with the proposed development, as if they comprised a single Schedule 2 development. The test is whether they ought to be regarded 'as part of the same substantial development' (per Davis LJ in *Burridge*[1]) or whether the proposed

---

[1] *Burridge v Breckland DC* [2013] EWCA Civ 228

development is 'an integral part of an inevitably more substantial development' (per Simon Brown J. in *Swale*[2]).

12.47 Whilst in both *Burridge* (per Davis LJ at [44]) and in *Bowen-West v Secretary of State for Communities and Local Government* [2012] EWCA Civ 321; [2012] Env LR 321 (per Laws LJ at [45]) the question of the proper scope of the Environmental Statement was assessed as a question for the Court (rather than a *Wednesbury* standard), the Supreme Court refused permission to appeal in *Larkfleet* on the basis that 'this is essentially a factual dispute' (22 February 2016 per Lords Kerr, Carnwath and Hughes). It would therefore seem that unless confronted with a case of clear project-splitting (as in *Ecologistas*), the Court is unlikely to intervene on the proper scope of the ES.

Consequences of a breach of the EIA Regulations

12.48 At first the courts seemed reluctant to intervene where there had been failures to apply the Regulations but the courts now adopt a robust approach to the obligations imposed by the EIA regime which has resulted in a steady stream of litigation. In *Berkeley v Secretary of State for the Environment* [2001] 2 AC 603, the Secretary of State had granted planning permission for residential development on part of Craven Cottage, the home of Fulham Football Club. Lady Berkeley (a third party) moved under s 288 of the 1990 Act to quash the decision, one of the grounds being that no environmental statement had been required of the applicant and that the proposed development was or could have been an 'urban development project' requiring submission of an environmental statement pursuant to Directive 85/337/EC because it was likely to have significant effects on the environment. The Secretary of State conceded that there had been a failure, which was not deliberate, to consider whether an environmental statement was required before the application for planning permission was considered. However, despite holding that there had been a breach of the Regulations which had implemented the EC Directive into domestic law, the Court of Appeal refused to exercise the discretion to quash the grant of planning permission, holding that the objectives of the Directive had in substance been achieved by the procedure which had been followed. So, although the procedures adopted had been flawed, they were nevertheless sufficiently thorough and effective to enable the Inspector (following a public local inquiry) to make a comprehensive judgment on all environmental issues. Hence the absence of an environmental statement in the circumstances of the case was of no significant practical importance. The House of Lords, however, found otherwise. In quashing the grant of planning permission, their Lordships held that the court was not entitled retrospectively to dispense with the requirements of an EIA on the ground that the outcome would have been the same, or

---

[2] *R v Swale Borough Council ex p. RSPB* [1991] PLR 6

that the decision-maker had all the information necessary to enable him to reach a proper decision on the environmental issues.

12.49 The *Berkeley* approach now needs to be seen in light of subsequent jurisprudence in the Supreme Court which has rowed back from the absolutist position. Starting in *Walton v Scottish Ministers* [2012] UKSC 44; [2013] PTSR 51 Lord Carnwath JSC held that even when confronted with a breach of an EU law derived obligation 'the court would retain a discretion to refuse relief on similar grounds to those available under domestic law' at [133].

12.50 The issue arose again in *R(on the application of Champion) v North Norfolk District Council* [2015] UKSC 52; [2015] 1 WLR 3710 in which a breach of the EIA Regulations was established. The Supreme Court considered *Walton* in light of subsequent CJEU case law, in particular *Gemeinde Altrip v Land Rheinland-Pfalz* [2014] PTSR 311. Lord Carnwath JSC explained that the *Gemeinde* case was not inconsistent with the position adopted by the Supreme Court in *Walton*. The position has been strengthened yet further with the insertion of s 31(2A) of the Senior Courts Act 1981 which provides that a judicial remedy should not be granted if it is 'highly likely' that the decision would not have been 'substantially different', on which see *R (on the application of Goring-on-Thames Parish Council) v South Oxfordshire District Council* [2018] EWCA Civ 860; [2018] 1 WLR 5161 per Lindblom LJ at [47]. A person seeking to challenge a decision on the basis of a breach of the EIA Regulations needs therefore to explain why it is not 'highly likely' that the decision would not have been 'substantially different' if the error had not occurred.

12.51 A further complication raised by *Champion* is Lord Carnwath JSC's observation that it may be relevant in deciding whether to grant permission to proceed with judicial review to consider the failure of the claimant to challenge the alleged error at the time (eg a negative screening opinion) rather than at the stage of the grant of planning permission. In *R (on the application of Catt) v Brighton & Hove City Council* [2007] EWCA Civ 298; [2007] Env LR 32 the Court of Appeal held that a failure to mount a timeous legal challenge to the screening opinion was no bar to a challenge to a subsequent permission on the same grounds. Lord Carnwath JSC in *Champion* observed at [63] that:

> Although we have not been asked to review that decision, I would wish to reserve my position as to its correctness. I see no reason in principle why, in the exercise of its overall discretion, whether at the permission stage or in relation to the grant of relief, the court should be precluded from taking account of delay in challenging a screening opinion, and of its practical effects (on the parties or on the interests of good administration).

Purposive approach

12.52 In *R v North Yorkshire CC, ex parte Brown* [2000] 1 AC 397, the House of Lords seemed prepared to look more closely at the EC Directive itself, rather than the regulations implementing the Directive into domestic law. The case concerned an 'old mining permission'. Under s 22 of and Sch 2 to the Planning and Compensation Act 1991, owners of these permissions had to apply to the local planning authority for them to be registered. Once registered, the permission could then be made subject to conditions. A question arose as to whether the determination of the conditions by the local planning authority required an EIA to be made in accordance with Council Directive 85/337 EC. The House of Lords held that it did; that the determination of the conditions was a 'development consent' under the Directive, and that it was a 'decision of the competent authority or authorities which entitles the developer to proceed with the project'. Hence their Lordships upheld the decision of the Court of Appeal to quash the authority's determination. Following the House of Lords decision, changes to the Environmental Impact Regulations were subsequently made to bring applications to determine such conditions within domestic law (see Chapter 23).

12.53 In *R v Durham CC and Sherburn Stone Company Limited, ex parte Huddleston* [2000] JPL 1125, the question again for decision was whether the courts could intervene where the statutory regime for implementing the EC Directive on EIA in the United Kingdom enables a company to revive a mining permission by registering it with the mineral planning authority without providing an EIA.

12.54 In this case the Sherburn Stone Company Ltd was the holder of a dormant planning permission to extract minerals on a large site in County Durham. The applicant lived close by. Under s 22 of the Planning and Compensation Act 1991, because no quarrying had taken place in the two years prior to 1 May 1991, that permission, known as an old mining permission, was suspended pending registration of the permission with the mineral planning authority and the setting of conditions to which the permission was to be subject.

12.55 On 15 February 1999 Sherburn made an application for registration and submitted with it a scheme of conditions. The County Council thereupon informed Sherburn that an environmental statement was required; Sherburn took the view, however, that no environmental statement was required and, on 24 May 1999, wrote to the County Council stating that because the three-month period allowed by the 1991 Act had expired without it having determined the conditions to which the permission was to be subject, there was a deemed determination of those conditions as set out in the Sherburn application.

12.56 It will be recalled that in the *North Yorkshire County Council* case above, the House of Lords decided that a mineral planning authority's determination under s 22 of the 1991 Act was a development consent falling within Council Directive 85/337/EC and therefore required an EIA as part of the registration process. Their Lordships, however, felt it unnecessary to decide the validity of the deeming provisions relating to the conditions to be imposed in a permission in the event of the minerals planning authority failing to determine them within the three-month time limit for doing so. As a result of that decision, the County Council (acting on counsel's advice) moderated its stance and accepted that it could not of its own motion treat the Directive as effective or, therefore, the deeming provision as ineffective.

At an expedited hearing, however, the Court of Appeal reversed the decision of the High Court and gave direct effect to the Directive, so as to require an environmental assessment before the deeming provisions could apply. In the court's view, the applicant was entitled to complain that the state had not set up the requisite machinery to give him the opportunity which should have been afforded to him (namely his right to be consulted) if the Directive had been properly implemented. In *R (on the application of Wells) v Secretary of State for Transport Local Government and the Regions* [2004] Env LR 27 the European Court of Justice held that this was not giving the Directive the required horizontal direct effect and that, where there had been a failure to carry out an EIA, the member state is required to make good any harm caused by the failure and this could include the revocation or suspension of any consent granted.

12.57

Outline applications

Environmental impact assessment was also the key issue in the decision of the High Court in *R v Rochdale MBC, ex parte Tew* [2000] JPL 54. The case arose following the grant of outline planning permission by Rochdale MBC for a 'business park ... with associated and complementary retail, leisure, hotel and housing ...', with siting, design, means of access, and external matters to be treated as reserved matters. An illustrative master plan accompanied the site plan, with an indicative schedule of floor space being provided later. The outline application, in a form which is sometimes described as a 'bare' application, reserved all detailed matters for subsequent approval, was accompanied by an environmental statement and was subsequently supplemented by an ecological survey. Local residents applied for judicial review to quash the grant of permission, the main ground of challenge being that the developers had failed to provide the information required by the Assessment of Environmental Effects Regulations 1988 (now superseded by the 2017 Regulations) and that accordingly, the Council was not entitled to grant planning permission for the development.

12.58

There was no dispute that the development was Sch 2 development likely to have significant effects on the environment by virtue of factors such as its nature, size, or location. The objectors successfully contended that therefore no application for planning permission could be granted unless the applicant includes a description of the developments proposed, which must comprise, at a minimum, information as to the 'design and size or scale of the project' as well as data necessary to identify the main effects that the development was likely to have on the environment. Hence the environmental assessment had been based on an Illustrative Masterplan and Indicative Schedule of Uses, which was inadequate for the purposes of Sch 3.

12.59

Although Sullivan J held that such a generalized description of the development was insufficient to comply with the Regulations, he refused to go so far as to hold that it was not possible to make any application for outline planning permission for a development which fell within Sch 1 or Sch 2. The description of the proposed development must, however, be sufficient to enable the main environmental effects which the development is likely to have to be stressed and identified so as to enable mitigation measures to be taken to ameliorate any adverse effects.

12.60 The decision raised questions of how far it is possible to seek outline planning permission for development projects falling within Schs 1 or 2. Round 2 of this particular saga was to follow shortly. Instead of pursuing their right of appeal to the Court of Appeal (leave for which had been granted), the developers submitted an amended application for outline planning permission. Unlike the earlier 'bare' application, only details of landscaping, design, and external appearance of the buildings were to be reserved. In addition, a new environmental statement accompanied the application. It contained much more detail. In particular, it contained a Schedule of Developments which set out the details of the buildings and their likely environmental effects; and the master plan was no longer merely illustrative. The local planning authority had also imposed conditions which was to tie the outline permission for the business park to the documents which comprised the application. The outline permission was further restricted so that the development that could take place would have to be within the parameters of the matters assessed in the environmental statement. Reserved matters would also be restricted to matters that had previously been assessed in the environmental statement. In a challenge to the decision of the local planning authority to grant planning permission, the High Court held in *R v Rochdale MBC, ex p Milne* (2001) 81 P & CR 365 that the application satisfied the requirements of the Environmental Assessment Regulations.

12.61 The problem of outline applications and environmental assessment was again emphasized in *R v Waveney DC, ex parte Bell* [2001] PLCR 292, where the High Court quashed a grant of outline planning permission for new printing works because the document which had accompanied the application and which purported to be an environmental statement, contained no information about the design of the development.

12.62 In an attempt to deal with the problem of the extent to which an outline planning permission complies with the Directive and the Regulations, the Government in 2002 issued an aide memoire to local planning authorities giving advice as to the approach authorities should take in considering applications for outline planning permission. That advice was as follows:

(a) An application for a 'bare' outline permission with all matters reserved for later approval is extremely unlikely to comply with the requirement of the EIA Regulations.

(b) When granting outline consent, the permission must be 'tied' to the environmental information provided in the environment statement, and considered and assessed by the authority prior to approval. This can usually be done by conditions although it would also be possible to achieve this by a s 106 agreement. An example of a condition was referred to in *ex p Milne* (above): 'The development on this site shall be carried out in substantial accordance with the layout included within the Development Framework document submitted as part of the application and shown on (a) drawing entitled "Master Plan with Building Layouts".' The reason for this condition was given as 'The layout of the proposed Business Park is the subject of an EIA and any material alteration to the layout may have an impact which has not been assessed by that process.' (See paras 28 and 131 of the judgment.)
(c) Developers are not precluded from having a degree of flexibility in how a scheme may be developed. But each option will need to have been properly assessed and be within the remit of the outline permission.
(d) Development carried out pursuant to a reserved matters consent granted for a matter that does not fall within the remit of the outline consent will be unlawful.

It should also now be noted that the Planning and Compulsory Purchase Act 2004 provides for a development order to make provision as to applications for planning permission made to a local planning authority. Article 8 of the DMPO now provides for a design and access statement to accompany most planning applications, whether in outline or full.

12.63 The position on outline applications was clarified in *R (Barker) v Bromley LBC* [2006] UKHL 52; [2007] 1 AC 470 where the local planning authority had granted outline planning permission for a mixed use and leisure development at Crystal Palace Park, London. Although the development had proved controversial, the Council had not required an EIA at that stage. At a later committee meeting to determine an application for the approval of reserved matters, several members had then pressed for an EIA to be submitted by the developer. The reserved matters application had included an 18-screen multiplex cinema with 4,800 seats and a 950-space car park. Acting on legal advice that an EIA could only be carried out at the outline planning stage and that the Council could not require one at this later stage, reserved matters approval was duly granted. Thereafter, the appellant applied unsuccessfully to quash the decision by way of judicial review. She had, however, also sought from the court a declaration:

that the decision was unlawful by reason of the Council's
(a) failure, at all or properly, to consider the requirements imposed on it by the Environmental Assessment Directive; and/or
(b) misdirection of itself in law in deciding that it had no power to require an environmental assessment in accordance with the requirements of the Directive.

Thereafter protracted legal proceedings followed, as a result of which the developers were unable to implement the approval of the reserved matters within the relevant time limit, thus leading to the lapse of the outline planning permission. Although there was now no planning permission to be quashed, the appellant proceeded with her claim for a declaration.

12.64 When the case eventually reached the House of Lords, their Lordships agreed that a reference of the issues raised should be sought from the European Court of Justice. In its ruling, the European Court of Justice held that where the rules at issue provide that an EIA in respect of a project may be carried out only at the initial outline planning permission stage, and not at the later reserved matters stage, those rules were contrary to Arts 2(1) and 4(2) of the Directive. Accordingly, the United Kingdom had thus failed to fulfil its obligation to transpose those provisions into domestic law. A few weeks later, the House of Lords, after considering the ruling from the European Court of Justice, had no choice but to grant the appellant the declaration she had asked for.

12.65 In doing so the House of Lords expressed the current position to be that

> in the case of a Sch 2 development the authority had to decide at the outset whether an assessment was needed. If sufficient information was given at the outset it ought to be possible for the authority to determine whether an assessment which was to be obtained at that stage would take account of all the potential environmental effects that were likely to follow as consideration of the application proceeded through the multi-stage process.
>
> Where it did not become apparent until a later stage that the project was likely to have some significant effects on the environment, an assessment would have to be carried out at the reserved matters stage before consent was given for the development.

12.66 From 1 September 2008, that loophole identified by the European Court in the *Barker* case was closed by the Town and Country Planning (Environmental Impact Assessment) (Amendment) (England) Regulations 2008, SI 2008/2093 (consolidated in the 2017 Regulations).

12.67 So it is now possible for environmental assessment to be carried out at the reserved matters stage of an application, however that does not justify a more relaxed approach at the outline stage. Assessment at the reserved matters stage may be required where likely significant effects are subsequently identified which were not identifiable at the outline stage, or present by wrongly not identified or require a fresh assessment to reflect a change in circumstances. However, in *Frackman v Secretary of State for Communities and Local Government* [2018] EWCA Civ 9; [2018] Env LR 18, the Court of Appeal held that the *Barker* approach was not analogous to the exploratory and monitoring stage of a hydraulic fracturing (commonly known as 'fracking') project, per Lindblom LJ at [63]:

> The granting of planning permission for the exploration and monitoring works did not, and could not, pre-empt or pre-judge the determination of that future

application, if it were ever to be made. That possible future proposal would have to be considered on its own planning merits when the time came, in the light of the assessment contained in its own environmental statement. The purpose, and sole purpose, of the present project was to establish whether or not shale gas existed in a sufficient quantity and was capable, both technically and viably, of being extracted should planning permission later be granted for its extraction. If the appeals before the Secretary of State succeeded, and planning permission for the proposals before him were granted, there would not be any approval for the commercial extraction of gas.

Continuing at [75] to observe that:

Assessment must be complete. And to be complete, it must be timely. If a future project is truly separate from the project under consideration, the assessment of its likely significant effects in the environmental statement for the present project is both unnecessary and inappropriate. If it is also uncertain in its conception and content, an attempt to assess its effects in the environmental statement for the present project would also be futile and potentially misleading. Such an exercise would not be timely; it would be premature and untimely. One comes back then to the same basic point. If, in the future, a project emerges for the commercial production of shale gas on these two sites, it can only properly be the subject of assessment under the regime for EIA when it comes to be promoted as a real, not merely hypothetical, proposal in an application for planning permission.

13

STRATEGIC ENVIRONMENTAL ASSESSMENT

A. INTRODUCTION	13.01	C. PREPARATION OF	
B. DETERMINATIONS OF THE		ENVIRONMENTAL REPORT	13.14
RESPONSIBLE AUTHORITY	13.11		

A. INTRODUCTION

In addition to Council Directive 85/337/EC The Assessment of the Effect of Certain Public and Private Projects on the Environment, now implemented in the United Kingdom as far as possible within normal town and country planning procedures (see Chapter 12), a later Council Directive 2001/42 EC, on the Environmental Assessment of Plans and Programmes Directive, has now been similarly implemented through normal town and country planning procedures. **13.01**

Whereas Directive 85/337 dealt with the environmental assessment of projects, Directive 2001/42 deals with the environmental impact of plans and programmes. Although the later Directive does not use the term 'strategic environmental assessment', this is the term likely to be used to describe the environmental assessment which complies with it. **13.02**

The Directive was brought into effect on 20 July 2004 by the Environmental Assessment of Plans and Programmes Regulations, SI 2004/1633. The departure of the United Kingdom from the European Union in 2019 is not (at least in the short-term) anticipated by the Government to change the operation of the SEA regime. This is because the Government has published the Environmental Assessments and Miscellaneous Planning (Amendment) (EU Exit) Regulations 2018 (SI 2018/1232), under the provisions of the European Union (Withdrawal **13.03**

Act) 2018, which is intended to ensure the SEA regime 'will continue to operate as [it] did before the date we leave the EU'.

13.04 The rationale behind the strategic environmental assessment is that whilst major projects likely to have an impact on the environment must be assessed under Directive 85/337/EEC, that assessment takes place at a stage when options for significant change are often limited. Decisions on the site of a project or on the choice of alternatives may already have been taken in the context of plans for a whole sector or geographical area. The strategic Environmental Assessment Directive plugs the gap by requiring the environmental assessment of a broad range of plans and programmes to be assessed, so that they can be taken into account when plans are being prepared and accepted.

13.05 The requirement for environmental assessment applies, in particular, to any plan or programme prepared for agriculture, forestry, fisheries, energy, industry, transport, waste management, water management, telecommunications, tourism, town and country planning, or land use, which sets the framework for future development consent of projects listed in Annex I or II to Council Directive 85/337/EC on the Assessment of the Effects of Certain Public and Private Projects on the Environment, as amended by Council Directive 97/11/ EC; and to any plan or programme which, in view of the likely effect on sites, has been determined to require an assessment pursuant to Arts 6 or 7 of Council Directive 92/43/EC on the Conservation of Natural Habitats and of Wild Flora and Fauna, as last amended by Council Directive 97/62/EC (Reg 5(1) to (3); Art 3.2 of the Directive).

13.06 In *R (on the application of Buckinghamshire CC) v Secretary of State for Transport* [2014] UKSC 3; [2014] 1 WLR 324 the Supreme Court held that a command paper setting out the Government proposals for a high-speed rail project was not a plan or programme setting the framework for future development consents as it did not constrain the decision-making process of the authority responsible. Setting a framework implied more than mere influence per Lord Carnwath JSC at [41]. What is required is that the plan or programme must 'operate as a constraint on the discretion of the authority' per Lord Sumption at [123]. Following *Buckinghamshire*, in *R (on the application of HS2 Action Alliance Ltd) v Secretary of State for Transport* [2014] EWCA Civ 1578; [2015] PTSR 1025, the Court of Appeal found that safeguarding directions issued by the Secretary of State, which ensured that no new building up the route of HS2 prejudiced its delivery, did not 'set the framework for future development'.

13.07 In the same way as the system of environmental impact assessment for specific projects may influence the decision on whether or not to grant planning permission for the project or perhaps the scope of any permissions granted, the system of strategic environmental assessment may influence the form and content of a plan or programme before it is adopted. Neither system is able to dictate to the decision-maker any particular outcome. However, in the same way as the system of environmental impact assessment for specific projects prevents the relevant authority from granting planning permission for development when an assessment required by the Regulations is required but has not been carried out, reg 8 prevents the adoption or submission for adoption of a plan or programme for which strategic environmental assessment is required before the completion of that assessment.

13.08 In the field of town and county planning, the Directive has a particular impact on regional strategies (now repealed), the spatial development strategy for London, and local development documents and local development plans. Although the provisions of the Directive are required to be applied to plans and programmes and to any modifications to them where formal preparation began after 21 July 2004, they will also normally apply to plans and programmes whose formal preparation began before that date, if they have not been adopted or submitted to a legitimate procedure leading to adoption by 21 July 2006.

13.09 Because the retroactive provision of the Directive affected many plans in the course of preparation, the Government published in advance of the bringing into force of the Directive, *A Practical Guide to the Strategic Environmental Assessment Directive: Guidance for Planning Authorities*. This was done in order to help authorities become familiar with its requirements and to prepare for them.

13.10 The Directive, and accordingly the Regulations, do not apply to plans and programmes whose sole purpose is to serve national defence or civil emergency, or to financial or budget plans and programmes. An exception is also made for plans and programmes that determine the use of a small area at local level and for minor modifications, if the authority responsible for preparing the plan or programme has determined that the plan or programme is unlikely to have significant environmental effects.

B. DETERMINATIONS OF THE RESPONSIBLE AUTHORITY

13.11 Regulation 9 requires the responsible authority, the authority by which or on whose behalf it is prepared to determine whether or not a plan, programme, or modification is likely to have significant environmental effects. In making this determination the authority is required to take into account the criteria specified in Sch I to the Regulations, and the views of the 'consultation bodies'. Schedule I is as follows:

Criteria for determining the likely significance of effects on the environment

1. The characteristics of plans and programmes, having regard, in particular, to:
    (a) the degree to which the plan or programme sets a framework for projects and other activities, either with regard to the location, nature, size, and operating conditions or by allocating resources;
    (b) the degree to which the plan or programme influences other plans and programmes including those in a hierarchy;
    (c) the relevance of the plan or programme for the integration of environmental considerations in particular with a view to promoting sustainable development;
    (d) environmental problems relevant to the plan or programme; and
    (e) the relevance of the plan or programme for the implementation of Community legislation on the environment (for example, plans and programmes linked to waste management or water protection).
2. Characteristics of the effects and of the area likely to be affected, having regard, in particular, to:
    (a) the probability, duration, frequency, and reversibility of the effects;
    (b) the cumulative nature of the effects;
    (c) the transboundary nature of the effects;
    (d) the risks to human health or the environment (for example, due to accidents);
    (e) the magnitude and spatial extent of the effects (geographical area and size of the population likely to be affected);
    (f) the value and vulnerability of the area likely to be affected due to:
        (i) special natural characteristics or cultural heritage;
        (ii) exceeded environmental quality standards or limit values; or
        (iii) intensive land use; and
    (f) the effects on areas or landscapes which have a recognized national, Community or international protection status.

13.12 Regulation 10 enables the Secretary of State to require a responsible authority to provide him with relevant documents. It also enables him to direct that a particular plan or programme is likely to have significant environmental effects. In the latter case, any determination to the contrary made under reg 9(1) by a responsible authority ceases to have effect. If a responsible authority has not made any determination under that provision, the Secretary of State's direction relieves it of the duty to do so.

13.13 Regulation 5 provides that where the first formal preparatory act of a plan or programme is after 21 July 2004, the responsible authority shall carry out, or secure the carrying out of, an environmental assessment in accordance with Part 3 of the Regulations during the preparation of the plan or programme and before its adoption. The plans or programmes to which this provision is made to apply include those prepared for town and country planning or land use which set the framework for future development projects listed in Annex I or II to Council Directive 85/337/EEC (see Chapter 12). The regulation is also made to apply to plans or programmes which, in view of the likely effect on sites, have been determined to require an assessment pursuant to Arts 6 or 7 of the EC Habitats Directive.

C. PREPARATION OF ENVIRONMENTAL REPORT

13.14 Under Part 3 of the Regulations, an environmental assessment requires the responsible authority to prepare an environmental report. Regulations 12(2) and (3) provide as follows:

> (2) The report shall identify, describe, and evaluate the likely significant effects on the environment of:
> (a) implementing the plan or programme; and
> (b) reasonable alternatives taking into account the objectives and the geographical scope of the plan or programme.
> (3) The report shall include such of the information referred to in Sch II to these Regulations as may reasonably be required, taking account of:
> (a) current knowledge and methods of assessment;
> (b) the contents and level of detail in the plan or programme;
> (c) the stage of the plan or programme in the decision-making process; and
> (d) the extent to which certain matters are more appropriately assessed at different levels in that process in order to avoid duplication of the assessment.

13.15 The information referred to in reg 12(3) above and set out in Sch 2 is as follows:

1. An outline of the contents and main objectives of the plan or programme, and of its relationship with other relevant plans and programmes.
2. The relevant aspects of the current state of the environment and the likely evolution thereof without implementation of the plan or programme.
3. The environmental characteristics of areas likely to be significantly affected.
4. Any existing environmental problems which are relevant to the plan or programme including, in particular, those relating to any areas of a particular environmental importance, such as areas designated pursuant to Council Directive 79/409/EEC on the conservation of wild birds and the Habitats Directive.
5. The environmental protection objectives, established at international, community or Member State level, which are relevant to the plan or programme and the way those objectives and any environmental considerations have been taken into account during its preparation.

6. The likely significant effects on the environment, including short-, medium-, and long-term effects, permanent and temporary effects, positive and negative effects, and second, cumulative and synergistic effects, on issues such as:
   (a) biodiversity;
   (b) population;
   (c) human health;
   (d) fauna;
   (e) flora;
   (f) soil;
   (g) water;
   (h) air;
   (i) climatic factors;
   (j) material assets;
   (k) cultural heritage, including architectural and archaeological heritage;
   (l) landscape; and
   (m) the inter-relationship between the issues referred to in sub-paragraphs (a) to (l).
7. The measures envisaged to prevent, reduce, and as fully as possible offset any significant adverse effects on the environment of implementing the plan or programme.
8. An outline of the reasons for selecting the alternatives dealt with, and a description of how the assessment was undertaken including any difficulties (such as technical deficiencies or lack of know-how) encountered in compiling the required information.
9. A description of the measures envisaged concerning monitoring in accordance with reg 17.
10. A non-technical summary of the information provided under paras 1 to 9.

13.16 Part 3 also provides that every draft plan or programme for which an environmental report has been prepared and its accompanying environmental report shall be made available for consultation. As soon as is reasonably practicable after the preparation of the relevant documents, the responsible authority is required to:

(a) send a copy of those documents to each consultation body;
(b) take such steps as it considers appropriate to bring the preparation of the relevant documents to the attention of the persons who, in the authority's opinion, are affected or likely to be affected by, or have an interest in the decisions involved in the assessment and adoption of the plan or programme concerned, required under the Environmental Assessment of Plans and Programmes Directive ('the public consultees');
(c) inform the public consultees of the address (which may include a website) at which a copy of the relevant documents can be viewed, or from which a copy may be obtained; and

(d) invite the consultation bodies and the public consultees to express their opinion on the relevant documents, specifying the address to which, and the period within which, opinions must be sent.

13.17 The period referred to in para (2)(d) above must be of such length as will ensure that the consultation bodies and the public consultees are given an effective opportunity to express their opinion on the relevant documents.

13.18 The main consultation bodies in England referred to in (a) above are defined in reg 4 as being the Countryside Agency; the Historic Buildings and Monuments Commission (English Heritage); English Nature; and the Environmental Agency.

13.19 Regulation 8 prevents the adoption or submission for adoption of a plan or programme for which environmental assessment is required before the completion of that assessment.

13.20 Part 4 of the Regulations deals with the procedures to be followed after the adoption of a plan or programme which has been subject to environmental assessment. In particular, it requires the person by whom the plan or programme has been prepared to give notice of its adoption and to make it and other specified information available for inspection. In addition, the Regulations require the person who prepared the plan or programme to monitor the significant environmental effects of the implementation of the plan or programme with a view to identifying, at an early stage, unforeseen adverse effects and being able to undertake appropriate remedial action.

13.21 Special provision is made in the Regulations for dealing with cases where draft plans and programmes prepared in the United Kingdom are likely to have significant effects on the environment in other Member States; and where draft plans and programmes prepared in another Member State are likely to have significant effects on the environment in any part of the United Kingdom.

13.22 The first case to come before the courts in this area was *R (on the application of Howsmoor Developments Ltd and others) v South Gloucestershire Council* [2008] EWHC 262 (Admin). There, an unsuccessful attempt was made to quash a developments brief adopted by the Council, on the ground that it did not comply with regs 8 and 12 and with government guidance on sustainable appraisal and strategic environmental assessment. The court held that the challenge amounted to an attempt to give the Directive a retrospective effect by submitting policies developed before the effective date of the Directive to the new regime.

13.23 More recently, in *City and District Council of St Albans v Secretary of State for Communities and Local Government* [2009] EWHC 1280 (Admin); [2010] 1 JPL

Strategic Environmental Assessment

70 the applicant authorities successfully claimed that the Secretary of State had made no proper assessment of alternative development proposals as was required by Part 2 of the Regulations, before the adoption of the regional spatial strategy for the East of England. The environmental report prepared in accordance with the Regulations had failed totally to identify the reasonable alternatives proposed by the authorities.

13.24 Similarly in *Save Historic Newmarket Ltd v Forest Heath DC* [2011] EWHC 606 (Admin); [2011] JPL 1233 it was held that the environmental report had failed to inform the consultees why alternative locations had been rejected. It was held that the report had to enable members of the public potentially affected by the plans to understand why the proposals were said to be environmentally sound and it was clear from Art 5 that those likely to be affected had to be presented with an accurate picture of the reasonable alternatives to the policies proposed and why they were not considered to be the best option.

13.25 In *Heard v Broadland DC* [2012] EWHC 344 (Admin); [2012] Env LR 23 Ouseley J held that the duty is not only to assess alternatives but to explain the reasons for selecting the alternatives dealt with, however obvious 'non-starters' are not required to be assessed, see [66]–[71]. The rejection of 'obvious non-starters' notwithstanding the 'low' threshold for assessment was upheld by the Court of Appeal in *Chalfont St Peter Parish Council v Chiltern District Council* [2014] EWCA Civ 1393 per Beatson LJ at [75].

13.26 In *R (on the application of Friends of the Earth) v Welsh Ministers* [2015] EWHC 776 (Admin); [2016] Env LR 1 Hickenbottom J held at [12] that the Directive is 'expressly procedural in nature' and does not 'impose any substantive duties on the relevant authority: it rather seeks to improve the quality of decision-making for development by requiring the authority to assess the potential environmental effects of a particular plan or programme before its adoption'. Hickenbottom J summarized the law at [88], as follows:

   i) The authority's focus will be on the substantive plan, which will seek to attain particular policy objectives. The EIA Directive ensures that any particular project is subjected to an appropriate environmental assessment. The SEA Directive ensures that potentially environmentally-preferable options that will or may attain those policy objectives are not discarded as a result of earlier strategic decisions in respect of plans of which the development forms part. It does so by imposing process obligations upon the authority prior to the adoption of a particular plan.

   ii) The focus of the SEA process is therefore upon a particular plan—i.e. the authority's preferred plan—although that may have various options within it. A plan will be 'preferred' because, in the judgment of the authority, it best meets the objectives it seeks to attain. In the sorts of plan falling within the scope of the SEA Directive, the objectives will be policy-based and almost certainly multi-stranded, reflecting different policies that are sought to be pursued. Those policies may well not all pull in the same direction. The choice of objectives, and the weight to be given to each, are essentially a matter for the authority subject to (a) a particular factor being afforded particular enhanced weight by statute or policy, and (b) challenge on conventional public law grounds.

iii) In addition to the preferred plan, 'reasonable alternatives' have to be identified, described and evaluated in the SEA Report; because, without this, there cannot be a proper environmental evaluation of the preferred plan.

iv) 'Reasonable alternatives' does not include all possible alternatives: the use of the word 'reasonable' clearly and necessarily imports an evaluative judgment as to which alternatives should be included. That evaluation is a matter primarily for the decision-making authority, subject to challenge only on conventional public law grounds.

v) Article 5(1) refers to 'reasonable alternatives *taking into account the objectives... of the plan or programme...*' (emphasis added). 'Reasonableness' in this context is informed by the objectives sought to be achieved. An option which does not achieve the objectives, even if it can properly be called an 'alternative' to the preferred plan, is not a 'reasonable alternative'. An option which will, or sensibly may, achieve the objectives is a 'reasonable alternative'. The SEA Directive admits to the possibility of there being no such alternatives in a particular case: if only one option is assessed as meeting the objectives, there will be no 'reasonable alternatives' to it.

vi) The question of whether an option will achieve the objectives is also essentially a matter for the evaluative judgment of the authority, subject of course to challenge on conventional public law grounds. If the authority rationally determines that a particular option will not meet the objectives, that option is not a reasonable alternative and it does not have to be included in the SEA Report or process.

vii) However, as a result of the consultation which forms part of that process, new information may be forthcoming that might transform an option that was previously judged as meeting the objectives into one that is judged not to do so, and vice versa. In respect of a complex plan, after SEA consultation, it is likely that the authority will need to reassess, not only whether the preferred option is still preferred as best meeting the objectives, but whether any options that were reasonable alternatives have ceased to be such and (more importantly in practice) whether any option previously regarded as not meeting the objectives might be regarded as doing so now. That may be especially important where the process is iterative, i.e. a process whereby options are reduced in number following repeated appraisals of increased rigour. As time passes, a review of the objectives might also be necessary, which also might result in a reassessment of the 'reasonable alternatives'. But, once an option is discarded as not being a reasonable alternative, the authority does not have to consider it further, unless there is a material change in circumstances such as those I have described.

viii) Although the SEA Directive is focused on the preferred plan, it makes no distinction between the assessment requirements for that plan (including all options within it) and any reasonable alternatives to that plan. The potential significant effects of that plan, and any reasonable alternatives, have to be identified, described and evaluated in a comparable way.

ix) Particularly where the relevant plan sets a framework for future projects (e.g. a core planning strategy), it may be appropriate and indeed helpful to have an SEA process that is iterative. If so, the appraisal has to evaluate the extant options at each stage in a comparable way. As part of an iterative SEA process, options which may be capable of achieving the objectives may be discarded on the way; but such options cannot be discarded without being subjected to an SEA Directive -compliant assessment.

x) Although an SEA process that is iterative may be particular appropriate for some framework-setting plans and programmes, it is by no means mandatory. The authority may adopt a non-SEA process to identify those options which meet the objectives. That non-SEA process may itself be iterative.

xi) The objectives an authority sets for plans caught by the SEA Directive are likely to be particularly broad and high level, as well as multiple and varied. An assessment as to whether the objectives would be 'met' by a particular option is therefore peculiarly evaluative; but an option will meet the objectives if, although it may not be (in the authority's judgment) the option that best meets the objectives overall (i.e. the preferred option), it is an option which is capable of sufficiently meeting the objectives such that that option could viably be adopted and implemented. That, again, is an evaluative judgment by the authority, which will only be challengeable on conventional public law grounds. However, whilst allowing the authority a due margin of discretion, the court will scrutinise the authority's choice of alternatives considered in the SEA process to ensure that it is not seeking to avoid its obligation to evaluate reasonable alternatives by improperly restricting the range options it has identified as such.

xii) The authority has an obligation to give outline reasons for selecting (i) its preferred option over the reasonable alternatives, and (ii) the alternatives 'dealt with' in the SEA process. Alternatives 'dealt with' include both (i) reasonable alternatives (which must be dealt with in the SEA process) and (ii) other alternatives (which need not, but may, be dealt with in that process). The reasons that are required are merely 'outline'. The authority need only give the main reasons, so that consultees and other interested parties are aware of why reasonable alternatives were chosen as such (including, in appropriate cases, why other options were *not* chosen as reasonable alternatives)—and, similarly, why the preferred option was chosen as such.

13.27 In *No Adastral New Town Ltd v Suffolk Coastal DC* [2015] EWCA Civ 88; [2015] Env LR 28 the Court of Appeal held that prior deficiencies in the sustainability appraisal could be cured by subsequent examination and public consultation per Richards LJ at [59].

13.28 In *Ashdown Forest Economic Development LLP v Wealden District Council* [2015] EWCA Civ 681; [2016] PTSR 78 the Court of Appeal considered whether a planning authority had lawfully considered alternatives to a 7 km buffer zone to a Special Area of Conservation. Richards LJ held at [42] that:

> the identification of reasonable alternatives is a matter of evaluative assessment for the local planning authority, subject to review by the court on normal public law principles, including *Wednesbury* unreasonableness. In order to make a lawful

assessment, however, the authority does at least have to apply its mind to the question. A fundamental difficulty faced by the Council in the present case, and not satisfactorily addressed in Mr Edwards's submissions, is that there is in my view no evidence that the Council gave *any* consideration to the question of reasonable alternatives to the 7 km zone. If the Council had formed a judgment that it was not appropriate to 'drill down' into the plan as far as the specific details of policy WCS12 for the purpose of identifying alternatives, or that there were no reasonable alternatives to the 7 km zone, then it would be in a relatively strong position to resist the appellant's claim. But in the absence of any consideration of those matters, it is in a very weak position to do so.

14

CONDITIONS

A. THE GENERAL POWER	14.05	E. REMOVING CONDITIONS PREVIOUSLY ATTACHED	14.76
B. SPECIFIC POWERS TO IMPOSE CONDITIONS	14.36	F. RETROSPECTIVE PLANNING APPLICATIONS	14.78
C. CHALLENGING AN INVALID CONDITION	14.69	G. DURATION OF PLANNING PERMISSIONS	14.81
D. EFFECT OF AN INVALID CONDITION	14.70		

14.01 Almost all planning permissions that are granted are granted subject to conditions. It often happens that the problem with decisions relating to land use is not over the question of whether the development should be permitted at all, but on what terms it should be permitted. Conditions may be imposed, therefore, not only to enhance the quality of the development but to ameliorate any adverse effects that might otherwise flow from the development. In order to assist local planning authorities in the exercise of their power, extensive advice has been given to them by the Secretary of State. The latest policy advice is contained within paras 54–55 of the NPPF.

14.02 Section 70(1) of the 1990 Act provides that in dealing with an application for planning permission, a local planning authority:

(a) ... may grant planning permission, either unconditionally or subject to such conditions as they think fit; or
(b) ... may refuse planning permission.

14.03 In addition to the power to impose such conditions as the authority think fit and without prejudice to the generality of that power, the Act gives the authority power to impose a number of specific conditions on the grant of planning permission.

14.04 An analysis of the definition of development contained in s 55 of the 1990 Act, whether it be operational development or a material change of use, will show that development is essentially a process; and a process which is begun and completed, so that with the full implementation of that process the planning permission authorizing it is spent. The fact that development is a process allows a local planning authority to impose, by way of conditions, restrictions which not only define the limits of what is authorized on the completion of the process, but also to control the way in which the process itself is carried out. Examples of the latter include conditions relating to hours of work, noise levels, and access to the site during the construction process, the erection of protective fencing around trees, and the provision of adequate space on site for the parking of vehicles, equipment, and materials of the contractors.

A. THE GENERAL POWER

14.05 Although couched in the widest of all possible terms, the power to impose conditions is not unlimited.

14.06 In *Pyx Granite Co Ltd v Ministry of Housing and Local Government* [1958] 1 QB 554 Lord Denning said at 572:

> Although the planning authorities are given very wide powers to impose 'such conditions as they think fit', nevertheless the law says that those conditions, to be valid, must fairly and reasonably relate to the permitted development. The planning authority are not at liberty to use their powers for an ulterior object, however desirable that object may seem to them to be in the public interest.

The law was later restated in this form by the House of Lords in *Fawcett Properties Ltd v Buckingham CC* [1961] AC 636.

14.07 In *Newbury DC v Secretary of State for the Environment* [1981] AC 578, the House of Lords were required to consider again the validity of a condition imposed under the general power now given by s 70(1) of the 1990 Act. According to their Lordships, conditions must comply with the following tests:

(a) They must be imposed for a planning purpose and not for an ulterior one.
(b) They must fairly and reasonably relate to the development permitted.
(c) They must not be so unreasonable that no reasonable authority could have imposed them.

Those tests were recently affirmed by *Elsick Development Co Ltd v Aberdeen City and Shire Strategic Development Planning Authority* [2017] UKSC 66; [2017] PTSR 1413 per Lord Hodge at [28].

14.08 Although the legal tests for the validity of a condition have been laid down in the *Newbury* case, the NPPF sets out a six-fold test the conditions should meet. This is that conditions should be enforceable, precise, reasonable in all respects as well as being necessary to make the development acceptable in planning terms, directly related to the development and, fairly and reasonably related in scale and kind to the development.

Imposed for a planning purpose

14.09 Like all statutory powers, a power can only be exercised for the purpose for which it is given. Conditions which are imposed for some ulterior purpose, therefore, are not exercised within that power. One of the leading cases in this area is *R v Hillingdon LBC, ex p Royco Homes Ltd* [1974] QB 720. Here, the applicant was able to obtain an order of *certiorari* to quash a grant of planning permission which had been made subject to ultra vires conditions.

14.10 The planning permission in question had permitted the development of land for residential purposes. It had been granted subject to two conditions which had required that the dwellings approved by the permission be designed to conform to space and heating standards laid down by the Department of the Environment for local authority housing, and that they be constructed at a cost which did not exceed the relevant cost yardstick for such housing. A further two conditions required the dwellings be first occupied by persons on the housing waiting list of the authority, and that for a period of 10 years from the date of first occupation they be occupied as the residence of a person who occupied by virtue of a tenure which would not be excluded from the protection of the Rent Act 1968 by any provision of s 2 of the Act. In the High Court, Lord Widgery CJ was in no doubt that the latter two conditions were ultra vires the authority and, although he considered that the first two conditions did not have a clear badge of ultra vires upon them, was unable to sever one set of conditions from the other because they had all been designed for a single purpose. Furthermore, he held that since the conditions were fundamental to the planning permission, the planning permission fell with the invalid conditions. Although the Lord Chief Justice considered the conditions to be ultra vires because they were unreasonable, Bridge J based his finding of ultra vires upon improper motive, namely, the attempt by the authority to transfer on to the shoulders of the applicant a duty (of housing people in need) which Parliament had placed upon the authority as a housing authority.

14.11 In 1987, Brent London Borough Council sought to impose a condition in a planning permission for residential development which provided that '25 per cent of the units the construction of which is hereby permitted shall not, without the written consent of the council, be occupied for a period of 10 years from the date that they were first occupied, otherwise than by a tenant or tenants on a periodic tenancy'. The reason for the condition was expressed to be 'to ensure that new residential developments contribute to meeting the needs of the borough's residents for low-cost housing and to offset the decline in the level of rental housing in the borough'. In discharging the condition, the Secretary of State considered that it did not serve a planning purpose, did not fairly relate to the permitted development, and was an unreasonable interference with a landowner's normal rights. He also had serious doubts about its legality ([1988] JPL 222).

14.12 The application of the first of the three *Newbury* tests was considered in *R v Bristol CC, ex p Anderson* [2000] PLCR 104. There, the Court of Appeal held that a condition in the grant of planning permission for the erection of flats to be occupied by students, which required the prior approval of the Council of a management agreement which included a prohibition on students residing on the site from keeping motor vehicles, did fulfil a planning purpose. Allowing an appeal from a decision of the High Court quashing the grant of planning permission given by the Council, the Court held that the management agreement was necessary to enable the student development to operate effectively and consonantly with the interests of nearby residents and others.

Fairly and reasonably relate to the permitted development

14.13 This test was first approved in *Pyx Granite Co Ltd v Ministry of Housing and Local Government* [1958] 1 QB 554, where the courts had to consider the validity of conditions attached to a grant of planning permission for quarrying for a limited period. The conditions in question limited the hours each day within which quarrying should be carried on, and required that all plant and machinery be removed from the site when no longer required and that the site be left in a tidy condition. The Court of Appeal, upholding the legality of the conditions, made it clear that they would have been quashed if they had not fairly and reasonably related to the development permitted. Although the case eventually reached the House of Lords, their Lordships held for the company on another ground, which relieved them of having to express an opinion on the validity of the conditions.

14.14 The principle was accepted by the House of Lords, however, in *Fawcett Properties Ltd v Buckingham CC* [1961] AC 636. There, the local planning authority had granted planning permission for the erection of cottages in the green belt subject to a condition that 'the occupation of the houses shall be limited to persons whose employment or latest employment is or was employment in agriculture … or in forestry, or in an industry mainly dependent upon agriculture and including also the dependants of such persons'. Fawcett Properties Ltd then purchased the properties and asked for a declaration that the condition was ultra vires. The House of Lords refused to grant the declaration, holding that the condition fairly and reasonably related to the permitted development.

14.15 In granting permission, the authority had recognized that agricultural workers need to live close to their place of work. The purpose of the authority in imposing the condition (now known as an agricultural occupancy condition) was to prevent the cottages being occupied by commuters, which would have infringed its policy of preserving green belt land from development.

14.16 In *British Airports Authority v Secretary of State for Scotland* [1980] JPL 260, the Scottish Court of Session took the view that a condition attached to a grant of planning permission for development at Aberdeen Airport which restricted the hours between which aircraft might take off or land, fairly and reasonably related to the development permitted. A clear case where there was no connection between the condition and the development permitted was seen in *Newbury DC v Secretary of State for the Environment* [1981] AC 578. There, planning permission had been granted for a period of 10 years for a change in the use of hangars previously used for the storage of civil defence vehicles, to use for the storage of synthetic rubber. The permission was subject to a condition that at the end of the 10-year period the hangars should be demolished. The House of Lords held that the Secretary of State had been right to quash an enforcement notice requiring the removal of the hangars after the expiry of the permission on the ground that the occupiers were entitled to use the hangars for storage during their occupancy without relying upon the grant of planning permission. Their Lordships, however, went on to express (as obiter) their further view that had the planning permission been in operation, the condition would have been ultra vires as it did not fairly and reasonably relate to the development permitted. It is difficult to see how on the facts their Lordships could have arrived at any other conclusion. The planning permission which was given related to the use of the property for a 10-year period. The requirement to demolish the hangars at the end of the period in no way restricted the quality or the nature of that use. The essential nexus between the permission without the condition and the condition was not just tenuous but non-existent. A condition will not be relevant to the permitted development if it seeks to control something not created by the proposed development.

14.17 In the *Newbury* case the House of Lords, whilst recognizing that it would be unusual for a condition requiring the demolition of a building to fairly and reasonably relate to a permission granted for a change of use, considered that, exceptionally, a condition might do so. The question of whether a particular condition could be described as exceptional was considered in *Delta and Design and Engineering Ltd v Secretary of State for the Environment and South Cambridgeshire DC* [2000] JPL 726.

14.18 In that case planning permission had been granted for a change of use of a listed building, Newton Hall. A condition attached to the permission required the demolition of an adjacent barn. The local planning authority considered that the change of use would have an adverse effect on the character of the Hall and its setting, but that effect could be offset in part, by an improvement to the setting of the building by the demolition of the barn. The company had sought the removal of the condition. Following the refusal of the local planning authority to do so, the company appealed unsuccessfully to the Secretary of State. It then appealed to the High Court to quash the decision of the Inspector, but again unsuccessfully. One of the grounds of appeal to both the Secretary of State and the High Court was that the condition did not reasonably relate to the permitted development and was therefore ultra vires. In overturning the decision of the High Court and quashing the Inspector's decision, the Court of Appeal held that the Inspector determining the appeal had failed adequately to address the question of whether the desirable action of enhancing the setting of Newton Hall had fairly and reasonably related to the change of use which the permission had granted. In addition, the trial judge at first instance had been wrong to decide that issue himself, which was a duty imposed on the Inspector as decision-maker, subject only to interference by the court on the well-established grounds identified in the *Newbury* case. Furthermore, in deciding the issue of lawfulness of the condition, his reasoning was contrary to the *Newbury* case. On the facts the court found great difficulty in seeing how the condition which the Council sought to impose could be said to relate fairly and reasonably to the permitted development.

14.19 However, this case does not rule out the possibility that occasion may arise where planning permission for a change of use of land or buildings could lawfully include a condition requiring the demolition of ancillary buildings, but it would require a much clearer and closer relationship between the change of use and the demolition of the building than that which occurred in the *Delta* case in order to be justified.

14.20 In a more recent case, *Tarmac Heavy Building Materials Ltd UK v Secretary of State for the Environment, Transport, and the Regions* [2000] PLCR 157, land had been used prior to 1 July 1948 and subsequently, for the manufacture of ready mixed concrete for which purpose a concrete batching plant had been erected. In 1952 planning permission had been granted for sand and gravel extraction on the land subject to a condition that at the completion of working, 'all building, huts or other structures on the site ... should be removed from the site'. The local planning authority considered that the implementation of that condition required that on the cessation of working, the concrete batching plant should also be removed. Following the service of an enforcement notice which required removal of the concrete batching plant, the Secretary of State rejected an appeal by Tarmac and upheld the notice. In subsequent proceedings, however, the High Court held that the condition could not possibly be said to fairly and reasonably relate to the permission granted in 1952 and quashed the decision of the Secretary of State. In *Menston Action Group v City of Bradford MDC* [2016] EWCA Civ 796 per Lindblom LJ at [14] 'to construe the condition as requiring "betterment" of that kind would be to ignore at least one of the three fundamental principles recognized in the House of Lords' decision in *Newbury*'.

Not be unreasonable

14.21 It will be recalled that in *R v Hillingdon LBC, ex p Royco Homes Ltd* [1974] QB 720, the Lord Chief Justice considered that the imposition of conditions which gave to the occupiers of houses erected under a planning permission rights to security of tenure was ultra vires because they were unreasonable. A further example of a condition held to be void because it was unreasonable occurred in *Hall & Co Ltd v Shoreham-by-Sea UDC* [1964] 1 WLR 240 (CA). There, the company had been granted planning permission for industrial development subject to a condition requiring it to construct an ancillary road over the entire frontage of the site at its own expense and to give a right of passage over it to persons proceeding to and from adjoining properties. The Court of Appeal held the condition to be unreasonable because its effect was to require the company to construct and dedicate a public road at its own expense. A similar view was taken in *City of Bradford Metropolitan Council v Secretary of State for the Environment* [1986] JPL 598 (CA) where it was held that a condition which required a highway maintainable at public expense to be widened by the applicant was manifestly unreasonable and ultra vires.

It is now quite clear that a condition in a planning permission which requires the developer to carry out or fund a public function of a local planning authority as a price for getting that permission is unlawful. This is so, irrespective of whether the initiative for the imposition of the condition comes from the local planning authority or, as it did in *City of Bradford Metropolitan Council v Secretary of State for the Environment* from the applicants themselves. In such circumstances, however, it would now be possible for an applicant to fund that function by the parties entering into what has for long been known as a s 106 obligation. **14.22**

Another case which fell four-square within the situation considered in *Hall & Co Ltd v Shoreham-by-Sea UDC* was *MJ Shanley Ltd v Secretary of State for the Environment* [1982] JPL 380. Here, the company had proposed to the local planning authority that if it was granted planning permission for residential development for 10 acres of land in the green belt, it would lay out a further 40 acres of land for recreational purposes and then, having done so, would donate the 40 acres to the public as public open space. The proposal having met with a favourable response from the authority, the company proceeded to buy additional land, but was then surprised when the authority refused to grant the planning permission. The company appealed to the Secretary of State who, in upholding the authority's refusal, held that a condition requiring the provision of 40 acres of open space would be invalid and unenforceable. On a subsequent application by the company to quash the decision of the Secretary of State, Woolf J supported the view taken by the Secretary of State of the invalidity of the condition. **14.23**

Other tests of the validity of conditions

Apart from the three tests laid down in *Newbury DC v Secretary of State for the Environment* [1981] AC 578 for the validity of a condition, it seems that a condition may also be void because it is either uncertain or unenforceable. In addition, it was thought at one time that a condition could not take away existing use rights. **14.24**

Uncertain conditions

14.25 A condition may be void for uncertainty if it can be given no meaning at all, or no sensible or ascertainable meaning. A condition which is merely ambiguous will not fail for uncertainty, though the courts may be required to resolve the ambiguity. The courts of course, are frequently required to construe ambiguous language in other areas of law, so have no difficulty in doing so in planning law. In *Fawcett Properties Ltd v Buckingham CC* [1961] AC 636, it was agreed that the condition limiting occupation of houses to workers (or the dependants of workers) in agriculture or forestry, or industries mainly dependent upon agriculture or forestry, could mean that a retired sheep farmer from New Zealand or a retired furrier from London would qualify, but not a telephone operator from Chalfont St Giles. The House of Lords held that in the context agriculture meant agriculture in the locality and so on, so that the condition was not void for uncertainty.

14.26 In *Alderson v Secretary of State for the Environment* [1984] JPL 429 the Court of Appeal applied *Fawcett Properties Ltd v Buckingham CC* in reversing a decision of the High Court that a condition attached to a planning permission which limited the occupation of premises to persons employed locally in agriculture was void, because the word 'locally' had no ascertainable meaning. Although it was said on behalf of the respondents that some authorities preferred to spell out a precise boundary to the area in which the agriculture was being carried on, the court held that the word locally had a perfectly intelligible meaning even though some doubtful cases might arise.

14.27 In *David Lowe & Sons Ltd v Musselburgh Corporation* 1974 SLT 5, the Scottish Court of Session was required to construe a grant of planning permission for residential development of three agricultural sites subject to a condition that:

> The sites are approved for the burgh's estimated future local authority and private housing needs over the next 20 years which cannot be accommodated within the existing burgh boundaries, in the proportion of one private house to four local authority houses.

Although one judge thought that it was a statement of the reason why planning permission was granted rather than a condition, the condition was held to be void on the ground that it was not capable of any certain or intelligible interpretation.

Unenforceable conditions

14.28 There are a number of instances where the Secretary of State has discharged a condition in a planning permission on the ground that it is unenforceable. It seems that in law such a condition may also be invalid. It is likely that in most cases a legal challenge to a condition alleging uncertainty would need to be based on the grounds of *Wednesbury* 'unreasonableness' (ie perversity).

14.29 A condition may be unenforceable on the ground that the local planning authority has no power to secure compliance with the condition. In *British Airports Authority v Secretary of State for Scotland* [1980] JPL 260, a condition was imposed in the grant of permission for development at Aberdeen Airport concerning the flight path of aircraft taking off and landing at the airport. The condition was concerned with matters over which the applicants had no control, since statutory authority to prescribe the direction of flight or aircraft lies with the Civil Aviation Authority. Since there were no steps the applicants could take to secure the result required by the condition for that additional reason, the authority was held to have no power to impose it under the relevant statutory provisions.

14.30 A condition would only be unenforceable if, for example, it required 'a landscape scheme to be submitted for the approval of the local planning authority', since it does not require a scheme to be actually approved by the authority. So too is it difficult to see how a condition that the development should be completed by a given date can be enforced since, once the time limit has expired, it is too late to require compliance with the condition.

Existing use rights

14.31 At one time it was thought that a condition in a planning permission could not take away existing use rights. In *Allnatt London Properties Ltd v Middlesex CC* (1964) 15 P & CR 288, planning permission had been granted for the demolition and replacement of industrial buildings forming part of a factory complex. The permission was granted subject to a condition that the replacement buildings were to be used only in conjunction with the main factory and, for the first 10 years, only by persons or firms who at the date of the permission occupied industrial premises in Middlesex. The purpose of the condition was to restrain any further influx of industrial development into the county without inhibiting the rebuilding of existing industrial premises. The effect of the condition, however, was to restrict for 10 years the number of potential purchasers of the company's property. Glyn-Jones J held that the condition was void. The company had a right to continue with the existing use of the factory complex and that right could not be taken away without compensation.

14.32 It was perhaps unfortunate that no appeal was made from this decision. A planning permission granted without conditions would also, if implemented, take away existing use rights without compensation. The owner would have the option not to implement the permission and to retain existing use rights, or to do so and lose them. Logically, it should make no difference where the planning permission has a condition attached to it.

14.33 The authority of *Allnatt London Properties Ltd v Middlesex CC* was not to last too long. In *Kingston-upon-Thames RLBC v Secretary of State for the Environment* [1973] 1 WLR 1549, planning permission had been granted to rebuild a station subject to a condition that land to the south of the station should be used for car-parking. When the condition was not complied with the authority served an enforcement notice. On appeal, the Secretary of State discharged the condition, because the land was being used to carry the electric traction cable and, on the authority of *Allnatt London Properties Ltd v Middlesex CC*, that right could not be taken away without compensation. The local planning authority then sought to challenge the Secretary of State's decision. The Divisional Court allowed the appeal and returned the case to the Secretary of State for reconsideration. In considering *Allnatt London Properties Ltd v Middlesex CC*, Lord Widgery CJ considered it correctly decided but for the wrong reason. The defect in the condition was that it did not reasonably relate to the development permitted. Bridge J, on the other hand, considered the decision to be wrong. He referred to the power of the local planning authority to regulate the use of land other than land in respect of that for which planning permission is granted, the exercise of which must encroach on the existing use rights of that other land. So long as a condition in a planning permission fairly and reasonably relates to the development permitted, the effect on existing use rights in no way affects its validity.

14.34 Reaffirmation of the principle was given in *Peak Park Joint Planning Board v Secretary of State for the Environment* [1980] JPL 114 where, after calling in an application for development for his own decision, the Secretary of State granted planning permission for the development but refused to impose certain conditions (as sought by the authority) on the ground that they would have affected existing use rights and were ultra vires. In a challenge to that decision, Sir Douglas Frank QC, sitting as a Deputy High Court Judge, held that the Secretary of State was wrong to hold that the conditions would be ultra vires because they derogated from existing use rights and he remitted the matter back to him for further consideration. In *Evans v Basingstoke and Deane BC* [2013] JPL 229 permission was granted for improvements to be carried out to an existing watercress processing plant. Because of environmental concerns that the increase in production could lead to pollution, a condition was imposed on the new development but this did not apply to the existing works as it was considered that this was not legally possible. The High Court held that the LPA had erred in law as a restrictive condition could be imposed on the use of the existing buildings if there was a possibility that the extension would lead to an increase in the use of the original buildings.

The need for precision

14.35 As stated earlier, Circular 11/95 contains a number of suggested models of acceptable conditions for use by local planning authorities in appropriate circumstances. The list is not exhaustive and authorities need to show care in the wording of other conditions if they are to be effective for the purposes intended. This can be difficult. In *R v Ealing LBC, ex p Zainuddin* [1995] JPL 925, the local planning authority had granted planning permission for a mosque, subject to a condition that no ceremonial gatherings or acts of worship should take place except within the buildings. The owners erected merely the frame of the building, with no roof and no sides, and then proceeded to hold a gathering of 1,500 devotees. The High Court held that the owners had not been in breach of the condition and granted judicial review of the authority's decision to serve a breach of condition notice. Then in *Telford and Wrekin* [2013] JPL 832 a condition was imposed on a planning permission that before the garden centre opened, details of the proposed type of goods to be sold should be submitted to and agreed in writing. It was held that this wording did not require that only those products could be sold. The court accepted that clearly the intention of the condition was to restrict sales only to certain products but this was not what the condition stated.

B. SPECIFIC POWERS TO IMPOSE CONDITIONS

Although specific powers to impose conditions are given to local planning authorities, it seems that their use should be subject to the same limitations as is the use of the general power, namely, that they must be imposed for a planning purpose, be fairly and reasonably related to the permitted development, and not be manifestly unreasonable. The following specific powers are given to authorities. **14.36**

Regulating other land

Section 72(1)(a) of the 1990 Act provides that a condition may be imposed on the grant of planning permission: **14.37**

> for regulating the development or use of any land under the control of the applicant (whether or not it is land in respect of which the application was made) or requiring the carrying out of works on any such land, so far as appears to the local planning authority to be expedient for the purposes of or in connection with the development authorised by the permission.

An example of its use would be where an owner of land applies for planning permission to erect a dwellinghouse with cesspit arrangements for the disposal of sewage. The authority may grant permission subject to a condition that the owner lays a sewer under adjoining land in his control to connect the dwellinghouse to the public sewer system. For the condition to be imposed, the land must be under the 'control' of the applicant. This requirement does not necessarily require the applicant to own an estate or interest in the land. In *George Wimpey & Co Ltd v New Forest DC* [1979] JPL 313, Sir Douglas Frank QC held that the question of whether land was in the applicant's control became a question of fact and degree for the Secretary of State and depended upon whether the control was of a degree and kind sufficient to satisfy him that the condition could be complied with.

14.38 In a ministerial decision in 1988, the Secretary of State in an appeal against an enforcement notice, considered ultra vires on the grounds of unreasonableness a condition in a grant of planning permission for a change of use of three floors of the old Derry and Toms building in Kensington High Street, London, from 'retail use' to 'use for exhibition purposes and ancillary restaurant'. The condition required that: 'The loading or unloading of vehicles visiting the premises, including those delivering fuel, shall not be carried out otherwise than from within the curtilage of the building.' The Secretary of State considered that the condition was dependent upon the action of others, such as the police or the highways authority, and since it purported to regulate use of the public highway, was unreasonable.

14.39 Similarly, in a ministerial decision [2001] JPL 241, the Secretary of State discharged a condition in a grant of planning permission for a change of use from a petrol filling station to a car sales showroom that 'there shall be no deliveries or collections of vehicles to and from the application site by car transporters', because deliveries to and from the site might well take place by persons who were not necessarily the occupiers of the appeal site.

14.40 It would be otherwise, however, if it were within the power of the beneficiary of the permission to comply with the condition. In *John & Joseph Davenport v Hammersmith & Fulham LBC* [1999] JPL 1112, planning permission had been granted to Joseph Davenport for the retention of a building in connection with the use of land for motor vehicle repairs. A condition in the planning permission prohibited vehicles which had been left with or in the control of the applicant being parked in the access road to the premises. The access road, which was a cul-de-sac, was a vehicular highway owned by the Borough Council. Following non-compliance with the condition, the Council served a breach of condition notice and then, subsequently, prosecuted the Davenports for non-compliance with that notice. Following their conviction, the Davenports appealed by way of case stated to the Queen's Bench Divisional Court. Central to the appeal was whether the condition prohibiting the parking and storage of vehicles could lawfully be imposed under s 70(1). The Divisional Court held that it could, since although the condition did not require that the Davenports should have control of the land in question, the condition was one that they were able to comply with, namely to ensure that they did not use the access road for the parking of vehicles left with them or which were within their control. So, too, would a condition in a planning permission for a change of use to a 'taxi information and booking office' which sought to prevent the collection of passengers from the taxi office.

14.41 A not uncommon condition imposed in planning permissions for new uses sited in busy town centre locations which meets the test of validity is 'no vehicles which are in the control of XYZ at [address of XYZ], shall be left or parked in the following "named" streets'.

Grampian-type conditions

14.42 The ability of a local planning authority to impose conditions under the general power to do so over land not under the control of the applicant was again raised in *Grampian Regional Council v City of Aberdeen DC* (1984) 47 P & CR 633. In this case planning permission had been made for a change of use of land from agricultural use to industrial use. The applicants had appealed to the Secretary of State for Scotland against non-determination of the application within the statutory time limit, and he had delegated the determination of the appeals to a reporter (Inspector) who took the view that traffic to and from the site would constitute such a hazard as to justify the refusal of planning permission. He considered that the hazard would be removed if an existing road could be closed, but concluded that it would not be competent to grant planning permission subject to a condition requiring the closure of the road since it did not lie wholly within the power of the first respondents to secure the closure, since any closure order that they might make would require confirmation by the Secretary of State under s 198(1) of the Town and Country Planning (Scotland) Act 1972, and might not necessarily be given. He accordingly dismissed the appeals. The First Division of the Inner House of the Court of Session allowed an appeal by the first respondents, holding that, while a condition requiring something to be done that was not within the control of the first respondents would be incompetent, a condition requiring that no development be commenced until the road had been closed would be competent. The appellants appealed, contending that the imposition on the grant of planning permission of any negative condition related to the occurrence of an uncertain event was unreasonable and, therefore, invalid and that in any event it was undesirable that there should be prolonged uncertainty as to whether the development would be able to go forward or not.

14.43 In dismissing the appeal the House of Lords held that there was a crucial difference between a positive and a negative type of condition in that the latter was enforceable while the former was not; that the reasonableness of any condition had to be considered in the light of the circumstances of the case and that in the present case, where the proposals for development had been found by the reporter to be generally desirable in the public interest, it would have been not only not unreasonable but highly appropriate to grant planning permission subject to the condition in question; that, moreover, it was impossible to view such a condition as unreasonable and not within the scope of s 26(1) of the Town and Country Planning (Scotland) Act 1972 if regard was had to s 198(1), from which it was reasonable to infer that it was precisely that type of condition that had been envisaged by the legislature when enacting s 26(1). (Note that ss 26(1) and 198(1) of the Scottish Act were identical to ss 29(1) and 209(1) of the Town and Country Planning Act 1971, now ss 70(1) and 247(1) of the 1990 Act.)

14.44 Since the *Grampian* case, the imposition of negative conditions (known colloquially as *Grampian*-type conditions) has risen in popularity, particularly with regard to highway works necessary on other land before any development on the application land can begin. Indeed, any condition that prohibits the commencement of development until some specified step has been taken is usually now referred to as a *Grampian* condition. Their utility, however, was restricted by policy advice that such conditions should not be imposed where such works are unlikely to be done within a reasonable period.

14.45 In *Jones v Secretary of State for Wales* (1990) 88 LGR 942, the Court of Appeal upheld that advice holding that it was unlawful for a local planning authority to grant planning permission subject to a condition which prevented development until some obstacle had been removed, unless there was a reasonable prospect of that obstacle being removed within the time limit imposed by the permission. The decision was purportedly based on the *Grampian* case, where it was said that the question whether a condition was unreasonable depended upon the circumstances of the case.

14.46 This approach was taken by the Secretary of State in *British Railways Board v Secretary of State for the Environment* [1994] JPL 32, where he took the view that, as a matter of law, a *Grampian* condition could not be validly attached to a permission unless there was a reasonable prospect of it being fulfilled. The House of Lords, however, held that the mere fact that a desirable condition appeared to have no reasonable prospects of fulfilment did not mean that planning permission must necessarily be refused. Their Lordships went on to hold that *Jones v Secretary of State for Wales* was wrongly decided.

14.47 Lord Keith, after referring to the earlier decision in *Grampian* and the Court of Appeal decision in *Jones*, said:

> The owner of the land to which the application related might object to the grant of planning permission for reasons which might or not be sound on planning grounds. If his reasons were sound on planning grounds no doubt the application would be refused. But if they were unsound, the mere fact that the owner objected and was unwilling that the development should go ahead could not in itself necessarily lead to a refusal. The function of the planning authority was to decide whether or not the proposed development was desirable in the public interest. The answer to that question was not to be affected by the consideration that the owner of the land was determined not to allow the development so that permission for it, if granted, would not have reasonable prospects of being implemented. That did not mean that the planning authority, if it decided that the proposed development was in the public interest, was absolutely disentitled from taking into account the improbability of permission for it, if granted, being implemented. For example, if there were a competition between two alternative sites for a desirable development, difficulties of bringing about implementation on one site which were not present in relation to the other might very properly lead to the refusal of planning permission for the site affected by the difficulties and the grant of it for the other. But there was no absolute

rule that the existence of difficulties, even if apparently insuperable, had to necessarily lead to refusal of planning permission for a desirable development. A would-be developer might be faced with difficulties of many different kinds, in the way of site assembly or securing the discharge of restricted covenants. If he considered that it was in his interests to secure planning permission notwithstanding the existence of such difficulties, it was not for the planning authority to refuse it simply on their view of how serious the difficulties were.

14.48 The law relating to the imposition of a *Grampian* condition seems from the cases to be that it is not ultra vires to impose a negative condition even though there is no reasonable prospect of it being fulfilled within the time limit of the permission; but that the fact that it is unlikely to be fulfilled within that period is material to whether or not one should be imposed. Put another way, there is no absolute rule that the existence of difficulties, however impossible they may appear to be, must necessarily lead to the refusal of planning permission for what would otherwise be acceptable development. The decision-maker must consider all relevant circumstances and the likelihood of the condition being fulfilled within the time limit of the permission is merely one of the factors to be taken into account. However, it should be noted that the PPG (21a-009-20140306) advises that 'such conditions should not be used where there are no prospects at all of the action in question being performed within the time-limit imposed by the permission'. In *Gladman Developments Ltd v Secretary of State for Communities and Local Government* [2017] EWHC 2768 (Admin); [2018] PTSR 616 Supperstone J found at [54]:

> Further, in the light of the inspector's finding as to the lack of evidence as to the effectiveness of the proposed mitigation measures, I agree with Mr Bowes that the reasonableness of the condition that the claimant now suggests it would have accepted is questionable.

Permission granted for a limited period

14.49 Section 72(1)(b) of the 1990 Act provides that a condition may be imposed on the grant of planning permission:

> for requiring the removal of any buildings or works authorised by the permission, or the discontinuance of any use of land so authorised, at the end of a specified period, and the carrying out of any works required for the reinstatement of land at the end of that period.

In order for the life of a planning permission to be limited to a term of years, it is necessary to impose an express condition in the permission requiring the authorized use of the land to be discontinued or the removal of any authorized building or works, etc at the end of some stated period. The dangers of not doing so are seen in *I'm Your Man Ltd v Secretary of State for the Environment* [1999] PLCR 109, where the local planning authority had granted planning permission in 1995 for the use of buildings for sales, exhibitions, and leisure activities for a temporary period of seven years. No express condition was imposed which required that use to cease at the expiration of that period. Before the expiration of the seven years, however, the owners applied for planning permission for the permanent use of the premises for those purposes. On appeal against the refusal of the local planning authority to grant planning permission for permanent use, it was argued that despite the fact that the 1995 permission was expressed to be for a temporary period, the permission was in effect a permanent permission. On dismissal of the applicants' appeal to the Secretary of State, the applicants successfully applied to the High Court for the decision to be quashed. It was held that the temporary period identified in the 1995 permission was a 'limitation' rather than a condition, and that local planning authorities had no power to impose a limitation on a grant of planning permission. This could only be done by way of a development order. Accordingly, the permission granted in 1995 was effectively a permanent permission.

14.50 It is quite clear that the grant of planning permission in the same terms as the development proposed in the application for permission cannot be treated as imposing a condition on the permission. The decision by the courts that a limitation in the description of the development does not operate as a condition of the planning permission could have a significant impact in other cases. A planning permission granted for the use of a holiday cottage between April and September each year, for example, would not prevent its unrestricted residential use throughout the year, unless an appropriate condition was imposed on the permission limiting the occupancy to its use during that period as a holiday cottage. Similarly, a planning permission granted for the erection of a retail building with a specified amount of selling space would not prevent a subsequent increase in the amount of floor space used within the building for that purpose (Ref: APP/W1715/X/03/P120801).

14.51 In a ministerial decision in April 2004 (Ref: APP/J 2210/X/03/1134471) an Inspector held that a grant of planning permission for the continued use as an occasional caravan camp in accordance with the application for planning permission, would not prevent the use of the land as a caravan site throughout the year, since the wish to restrict occupancy in this way had not been expressed as a condition of the permission.

14.52 In another ministerial decision (Ref: APP/D0515/X/1124089), planning permission had been granted for the use of a site as an airport and parachute drop zone using one light aircraft. An Inspector allowed an appeal against the refusal of a lawful development certificate for the use of a second light aircraft. The planning permission had contained a limitation to one aircraft, but this would only be controlled by way of a condition. Furthermore, an increase in the number of aircraft from one to two could not be described as development.

14.53 The kind of planning permission authorized by s 72(1)(b) is called a 'term consent' or 'a permission granted for a limited period'. It has several advantages in practice. First, where land is awaiting redevelopment, planning permission can be granted for a limited period for development which would not otherwise be allowed, such as for a charity shop in an area zoned for residential development. In such cases, the temporary permission is normally sought by the applicant himself. Secondly, where there have been strong objections to proposed development, the term consent enables the parties to 'have a trial run', so that it becomes clear during the currency of the term whether or not the objections made were well founded. If not, at the end of the term, another planning permission without a similar condition can be granted.

A somewhat unusual example of such a condition being imposed occurred in 1994, when consent (for three years) was granted for the retention of a fibreglass fish attached to the side extension of a dwellinghouse on land in Norbury, London SW16. The local planning authority had served an enforcement notice requiring its removal on the ground that its presence was detrimental to the amenity of nearby residents. It appeared that the fibreglass fish was a reproduction of a marlin caught by the appellant in the Pacific Ocean, and he wished to retain it as a work of art commemorating this achievement. The appellant had earlier attracted some notoriety by placing at various times on or near the appeal site, a military tank, a self-propelled gun, a large replica Spitfire, and an assortment of smaller items, some lit up at night. All had attracted traffic and activity and media attention to the site. **14.54**

In dealing with the planning merits of the case, the Inspector concluded that the presence of unauthorized developments at the appeal site, including the fish, had caused demonstrable harm to residential amenity and traffic safety in the area. He felt, however, that there was insufficient evidence available for him to come to a proper view of the extent to which that harm was attributable to the presence of the fish and to assess the future impact of the fish alone. In the circumstances, he decided to grant planning permission for the fish on a temporary basis, thus giving a proper opportunity for the impact of the fish alone to be tested. **14.55**

Subsequently the local planning authority was to seek a 'planning injunction' against the occupier requiring him, inter alia, to remove the replica Spitfire. This was the subject of further proceedings in *Croydon LBC v Gladden* [1994] JPL 723 (see Chapter 20). **14.56**

Where a term consent has been granted, planning permission is not normally required to revert to the previous use. Section 57(2) of the 1990 Act deals with the right to revert in these terms. **14.57**

> Where planning permission to develop land has been granted for a limited period, planning permission is not required for the resumption, at the end of that period, of its use for the purpose for which it was normally used before the permission was granted.

The effect of these provisions was considered in *Smith v Secretary of State for the Environment* [1983] JPL 462. It is clear that if a landowner has been granted a term consent no planning permission is required to return to the last normal use of the land, if this last use had been lawful. So, the provision requires no account to be taken of any use of land begun in contravention of planning control. Thus, if a term consent has been granted to change from a use of land which has been begun in contravention of planning control, the owner cannot under the section revert to that use at the end of the term without a grant of planning permission. It would be otherwise, of course, if the previous contravening use had become immune from enforcement action by virtue of the time limits now laid down in the Act for the taking of enforcement action.

Requiring the development to be commenced

14.58 Section 72(3) of the 1990 Act provides that where:

(a) planning permission is granted for development consisting of or including the carrying out of building or other operations subject to a condition that the operations shall be commenced not later than a time specified in the condition; and

(b) any building or other operations are commenced after the time so specified, the commencement and carrying out of those operations do not constitute development for which that permission was granted.

14.59 It should be noted that the provision only applies to building or other operations. Furthermore, the provision is concerned with the commencement of such development, not its completion.

14.60 In practice little use has ever been made of this statutory power. Since 1968 its purpose has been met by new mandatory conditions relating to the commencement of development which have been imposed in most planning permissions granted since April 1969. These provisions are now to be found in ss 91 to 95 of the 1990 Act, to which reference is made later. Indeed, the effect of s 72(4) is that subsection (3) applies only in the case of commencement conditions not governed by ss 91 and 92.

Limiting the benefit to a particular person

14.61 It may sometimes be appropriate to confine the benefit of a planning permission to a particular person. The power to do so derives from the wording of s 75(1) of the 1990 Act which provides:

> Without prejudice to the provisions of this Part [of the 1990 Act] as to the duration, revocation or modification of planning permission, any grant of planning permission to develop land shall (except insofar as the permission otherwise provides) enure for the benefit of the land and of all persons for the time being interested in it.

Specific Powers to Impose Conditions

In *Knott v Secretary of State for the Environment and Caradon DC* [1997] JPL 713, the District Council had granted planning permission for the erection of a dwelling subject to a condition that the 'permission should enure solely for the benefit of Mr & Mrs Knott'. The assumption had been that the condition controlled both the initial construction of the dwelling and its subsequent occupation for the benefit of the Knotts and them alone. The High Court thought otherwise, however, holding that once the permission had been implemented by the construction of the house and its occupation by the Knotts, the condition did not prevent persons other than the Knotts from occupying the dwelling. The effect of this judgment is that unless a person is the subject of a condition (such as an agricultural occupancy condition) which limits occupancy to a special class of persons, so that occupancy by a person not in that class is a material change of use, no planning permission is required for occupancy by any other person. Perhaps what the local planning authority should have done was to impose a condition limiting the occupation of the dwelling when completed solely to the Knotts.

14.62 Let no one say that planning law is dull. In the aftermath of the decision of the High Court, the District Council, after taking into account the views of the Secretary of State that the grant of planning permission could be said to have been grossly wrong, decided to make a revocation order to annul the permission and a discontinuance order requiring removal of the uncompleted dwelling. Both orders were then confirmed by the Secretary of State.

14.63 However, the Council then became aware that the dwelling was being constructed outside the boundaries of the application site and, mindful of the obligation to pay compensation for loss caused by the revocation and discontinuance orders, decided to issue an enforcement notice under s 174(2) of the 1990 Act on the ground that there had been a breach of planning control. If effective, this could, of course, have relieved the District Council of any compensation liability.

14.64 The applicants then applied to the High Court for relief by seeking a declaration that the Council's resolution to take enforcement action was contrary to law, and *certiorari* to quash the enforcement notice. In *R v Caradon DC, ex p Knott* (2000) 80 P & CR 154, Sullivan J granted the relief that had been sought.

14.65 The High Court held that the Council had not taken the decision to issue the enforcement notice in order to secure any planning objective, that having been achieved by the revocation and discontinuance orders. Furthermore, Sullivan J held that under the doctrine of estoppel, the Council was barred from taking enforcement action. Compensation for the revocation and discontinuance orders was settled, although the Council itself undertook the remedial works.

14.66 Personal planning permissions are comparatively rare, because if it is thought desirable to avoid a perpetuation of a use of land, a term consent can best achieve that purpose. The power is a statutory recognition, however, that planning permission may be granted in circumstances where permission would otherwise be refused. A personal planning permission may sometimes be granted on hardship grounds, and may sometimes be linked to a term consent.

14.67 Sometimes a personal planning permission may result from service of an enforcement notice issued by the local planning authority. One such case concerned contravening development of an industrial nature located in a rural area. In quashing the enforcement notice the Secretary of State granted a temporary and personal planning permission for a period of two years for the contravening development in order to allow the owner to search for an alternative location for his business during that period.

Specifying the use to which a building may be put

14.68 Mention has previously been made of s 75(2) and (3) of the 1990 Act which provides that:

> (2) Where planning permission is granted for the erection of a building, the grant of permission may specify the purposes for which the building may be used.
> (3) If no purpose is so specified, the permission shall be construed as including permission to use the building for the purpose for which it is designed.

The question is sometimes asked whether, if a building is demolished, the existing use rights associated with the building's previous lawful occupation survive to benefit the land itself or the use is extinguished with the building's demolition. The matter is not entirely free from doubt, but it is considered that the demolition ends a chapter in the land's planning history and that a new chapter is then commenced. The result, of course, is that as with the abandonment of a use, the land cannot be used for any purpose without the grant of planning permission, save for those activities and uses that are not development.

C. CHALLENGING AN INVALID CONDITION

14.69 The validity of a condition may be challenged following an appeal from a decision of the Secretary of State against an adverse decision by a local planning authority on a planning application. It may also follow an appeal to the Secretary of State against an enforcement notice alleging a breach of condition. It may also be challenged as a defence to a prosecution for failure to comply with a breach of condition notice; by an application for a certificate as to the lawfulness of proposed operations or uses; and of course, by an application for a declaration in the High Court.

D. EFFECT OF AN INVALID CONDITION

Where a condition is held to be invalid, the question arises whether the condition can be severed from the planning permission so that the permission survives shorn of its invalidity, or whether the condition cannot be severed so that the whole planning permission is void *ab initio*. 14.70

In *Hall & Co Ltd v Shoreham-by-Sea UDC* [1964] 1 WLR 240, a condition which required the company effectively to dedicate a road to the public at the company's expense was held to be invalid. The local planning authority had argued that if the condition was void, then the whole planning permission was a nullity. The Court of Appeal was persuaded by that argument because the invalid condition was fundamental to the whole of the planning permission. The suggestion in this and later cases was that if the invalid condition was incidental or trivial then it could be severed from the permission; if it were fundamental then the whole permission fell. 14.71

In *Allnatt London Properties Ltd v Middlesex CC* (1964) 15 P & CR 288, a condition was held to be void because it took away existing use rights. In argument, the local planning authority was unable to give any grounds on which a reasonable planning authority could have refused planning permission assuming the condition to be void. Not surprisingly, therefore, the court held that the permission could stand free of the condition. Since the authority would have been prepared to grant the permission in the absence of the condition, the impugned condition was clearly not one which was fundamental to the permission, so that the test to be applied may well be whether the local planning authority would have been prepared to grant planning permission in the absence of the condition. 14.72

The trivial/fundamental dichotomy was eventually supported by the House of Lords in *Kent CC v Kingsway Investments (Kent) Ltd* [1971] AC 72. Here the House of Lords held that conditions in an outline planning permission requiring details of proposals to be submitted to and approved by the authority before any work began and that the permission should cease to have effect after the expiration of three years unless within that time notice of approval of the detailed proposals had been given, were valid. Their Lordships went on, however, to consider the position if they had found otherwise. According to their Lordships, if the invalid conditions are unimportant, incidental, or merely superimposed on the permission, then the permission might endure. If the conditions are part of the structure of the permission, then the permission falls with it. 14.73

In *R v St Edmundsbury BC, ex p Investors in Industry Commercial Properties Ltd* [1985] 1 WLR 1168 (Div Court) it was said (obiter) that if a condition requiring the developer of a superstore to provide three independent retail units was invalid, it could be severed from the permission. 14.74

14.75 A more recent example of non-severability occurred in *Fisher v Wychavon DC* [2001] JPL 694, where planning permission had been granted for a residential caravan, subject to a condition that that use be discontinued not later than 'F' years from the date of the permission. The permission had been issued some 13 years earlier and it was unclear as to what was intended by the 'F' in the condition. The Court of Appeal refused to apply a blue line to strike out all reference to what was a temporary consent so as to leave a consent which was permanent, and so upheld a decision of the High Court that the planning permission was of no effect. So, an applicant challenging the validity of a condition has to be aware that a successful challenge may result in the whole permission being held to be invalid.

E. REMOVING CONDITIONS PREVIOUSLY ATTACHED

14.76 Under s 73 of the 1990 Act an application may be made to the local planning authority for the development of land without complying with conditions subject to which a planning permission was granted. On an application the authority must only consider the question of the conditions, and it may decide that the permission shall be subject to the same conditions as were previously imposed, that the permission should be granted subject to different conditions, or that permission should be granted unconditionally. There is a right of appeal to the Secretary of State and a right of challenge in the normal way to the courts on a point of law. Jurisdiction in all cases is limited to the conditions and decisions relating to those conditions.

14.77 A successful application under s 73 results in a fresh grant of planning permission, see: *London Borough of Lambeth v Secretary of State for Communities and Local Government* [2018] EWCA Civ 844; [2018] 2 P & CR 17 per Lewison LJ at [19]. However, in considering whether to grant a fresh planning permission, the local planning authority can only consider the question of conditions subject to which the earlier planning permission was granted. An authority can, if it so wishes, impose new conditions in the fresh planning permission, subject to the conditions being those which it could have lawfully imposed upon the earlier permission and which do not amount to a 'fundamental alteration' to the proposal put forward in the original application, see: *R v Coventry City Council, ex parte Arrowcroft Group plc* [2001] PLCR 113. In *Finney v Welsh Ministers* [2018] EWHC 3073 Sir Wyn Williams confirmed that 'a variation pursuant to section 73 can be lawful notwithstanding that it may necessitate a variation to the terms of the planning permission which preceded the section 73 application' at [39], removing the uncertainty which followed the observation to the contrary by Collins J in *R (Vue Entertainment Ltd) v City of York Council* [2017] EWHC 588 (Admin) at [14]. In *Lawson Builders Ltd v Secretary of State for Communities and Local Government*

[2015] EWCA Civ 122; [2015] PTSR 1324 the Court of Appeal held that s 73 only applies to development to be carried out and is not retrospective per Pitchford LJ at [22]–[24]. Guidance on the s 73 process can be found in the PPG (Flexible Options for Planning Permissions).

F. RETROSPECTIVE PLANNING APPLICATIONS

14.78 Section 73A of the 1990 Act provides for an application to be made to a local planning authority for planning permission for development which has already been carried out. This procedure applies not only to development carried out without planning permission, but to development carried out without complying with some condition subject to which planning permission was granted. It would seem that a developer must implement the permission and breach the condition before making an application under the section.

14.79 An application for planning permission under s 73A is in all respects, apart from the fact that development will have commenced, a conventional planning application. In dealing with it the local planning authority must have regard to the provisions of the development plan, so far as material, and to any other material considerations. Hence if the trigger for a s 73A application arises not from the fact that development has been undertaken without planning permission, but that there has been a breach of a condition subject to which an earlier planning permission was granted, the local planning authority in considering the merits of the application, is not required to confine its attention to the appropriateness of the conditions (see *Brenda Wilkinson v Rossendale BC* [2002] EWHC 1204 (Admin); [2003] JPL 82). The authority's role is to consider the planning merits of permitting the development to continue, and under what conditions, if any.

14.80 It is not possible, however, to make an application under either s 73 or 73A of the 1990 Act for permission for the 'removal' of a condition, since the removal of a condition does not amount to development.

G. DURATION OF PLANNING PERMISSIONS

14.81 Prior to 1969, one of the risks a local planning authority faced in granting planning permission was that the permission might never be implemented. This could be important in practice where development had to be restricted because of inadequate infrastructure. For example, a planning permission given to A (but not implemented) might prevent planning permission being given later to B because the existing infrastructure might not support both developments. In 1968, power was given to local planning authorities to impose conditions which it was thought

Conditions

would alleviate that problem. The statutory provisions are now to be found in the 1990 Act as amended by the Planning and Compulsory Purchase Act 2004.

Full planning permissions

14.82 Section 91 of the 1990 Act provides that every planning permission granted, or deemed to be granted, shall be subject to the condition that the development to which it relates must be begun not later than the expiration of:

(a) three years beginning with the date on which the permission is granted or ... deemed to be granted; or
(b) such other period (whether longer or shorter) beginning with that date as the authority concerned with the terms of planning permission may direct.

14.83 The period of three years mentioned in para 14.82 at (a) above was reduced from five years by s 51 of the Planning and Compulsory Purchase Act 2004.

14.84 The period mentioned in para 14.82 at (b) above is to be the period which the authority considers appropriate having regard to the provisions of the development plan and to any other material considerations.

14.85 The section further provides that if planning permission is granted without such a condition, it shall be deemed to have been granted subject to the condition in para 14.82 at (a) above. Exceptionally, if legal proceedings are brought to challenge the validity of a grant of planning permission (or a deemed grant of permission) the time limit for beginning the development is to be taken to be extended by one year.

14.86 The above provisions do not, for reasons which are in most cases self-evident, apply to:

(a) any planning permission granted by a development order or local development order;
(b) any planning permission granted under s 73A for development carried out before the grant of that permission;
(c) any planning permission granted for a limited period;
(d) any planning permission granted for the winning and working of minerals (which is subject to special provisions relating to the commencement of the development);
(e) any planning permission granted by an enterprise zone scheme;
(f) any planning permission granted by a simplified planning zone scheme; and
(g) any outline planning permission (which is subject to special rules).

14.87 It should be noted that the standard three-year period may be varied at the discretion of the local planning authority or on appeal by the Secretary of State. This power to vary may be useful where it is desired to phase the commencement of large-scale development over a prolonged period of time.

14.88 The existence of time-limits with which development must be begun imposes pressure on the developer to do so, since s 93(4) provides that development carried out after the date by which the condition requires it to be carried out shall be treated as not authorized by the permission. In other words, if the condition is not complied with, the benefit of the permission will be lost. This may be of little consequence to the landowner, who may reapply for planning permission which, if granted, will contain a like condition. The problem arises, however, where there has been a change in planning policy by the local planning authority since the first grant of permission, which results in the renewal application being refused. In such a case land which had a value which reflected the right to develop will no longer have that value. It will often be important, therefore, to ensure that development is begun by the date specified in the condition. If it is, then the planning permission will be kept alive. If not, then the permission will be lost.

14.89 This is of particular importance in view of s 38(6) of the Planning and Compulsory Purchase Act 2004. In *Kirkman v Secretary of State for Wales* [1995] EGCS 127, developers found to their cost that although in 1988 the local planning authority was prepared to grant planning permission for residential development, in 1992, as a result of what is now s 38(6), the dominance of the provisions of the development plan as a material consideration was sufficient to justify a later refusal.

14.90 Section 56 of the 1990 Act prescribes the activities that constitute compliance with the requirement that the development must be begun. It provides that development shall be taken to be begun on the earliest date on which any 'material operation' (previously called a 'specified operation') comprised in the development begins to be carried out. 'Material operation' is defined in s 56(4) to mean:

(a) any work of construction in the course of the erection of a building;
(aa) any work of demolition of a building;
(b) the digging of a trench which is to contain the foundations, or part of the foundations, of a building;
(c) the laying of any underground main or pipe to the foundations, or part of the foundations, of a building or to any such trench as is mentioned in para (b);
(d) any operation in the course of laying out or constructing a road or part of a road;
(e) any change in the use of any land which constitutes material development.

14.91 In the context of para (e), material development means any development other than:

(a) development for which planning permission is granted by a general development order for the time being in force and which is carried out so as to comply with any condition or a local development order limitation subject to which planning permission is so granted;
(b) development of a class specified in para 1 or 2 of Sch 3;
(c) development of any class prescribed for the purposes of this subsection.

14.92 It is also provided that if the development consists both of the carrying out of operations and a change of use, the development of land shall be taken to be initiated by the commencement of the operations or the carrying out of the change of use, whichever is the earlier. It is clear that great care must be taken to ensure compliance with the section.

14.93 In *High Peak BC v Secretary of State for the Environment* [1981] JPL 366, Courtdale Developments Ltd wished to exploit a planning permission with a time-limit for commencement of development within a five-year period, and so, within that time, the company arranged for a mechanical digger to dig a trench of the requisite width and depth to contain foundations. It had then proceeded to fill in the trench with the earth which had been excavated. The trench had been dug in order to keep the planning permission alive but back-filled to prevent animals and children falling into it. The Queen's Bench Divisional Court held that the company's action in digging the trench was an operation under what is now s 56(4) of the 1990 Act so that the permission had not expired.

14.94 In *South Oxfordshire DC v Secretary of State for the Environment* [1981] JPL 359, trenches had been dug which appeared to fulfil the requirements of what is now s 56(4), but they had not been dug for the development to which the planning permission related. Accordingly, the Secretary of State did not consider that that was sufficient to comply with the provisions, a conclusion which Woolf J was prepared to accept.

14.95 In *Malvern Hills DC v Secretary of State for the Environment* [1982] JPL 439, an enforcement notice had been served by the local planning authority on a company alleging a breach of planning control. The Court of Appeal was required to decide whether or not marking out with pegs the line of part of a proposed road constituted a 'specified operation'. The pegs had been placed in position so that a road could be constructed with machines which would be guided by the pegs. This was part of an overall operation, namely the laying out of a road. The pegging-out was intended to allow the engineering plant and machinery to follow the line of the roadway during its construction. If it did constitute a specific operation, the planning permission was still alive and there would be no breach. A divided court held that the work was a specified operation and found that, contrary to the view of the authority, the Secretary of State had not erred in law in so finding.

14.96 In this case the company had always believed that the condition which required the development to be begun by a set date had been complied with and so proposed to continue with the development despite its dispute with the authority. The local planning authority, who thought otherwise, had not only served an enforcement notice on the company requiring the cessation of all construction work on the site, but also a related stop notice. Now, under s 186 of the 1990 Act, compensation is payable for loss suffered due to the service of a stop notice if it is quashed on the ground that the matters alleged in the enforcement notice do not constitute a breach of planning control. Following a dispute over the amount of the company's loss, compensation was eventually determined by the Lands Tribunal, which awarded the company £42,562.

14.97 In a more recent case (*Commercial Land Ltd v Secretary of State for Transport, Local Government, and the Regions and Royal Borough of Kensington and Chelsea* [2002] EWHC 1264 (Admin)), the court held that the question of whether certain material operations were comprised in the development could not necessarily be answered by comparing them with approved plans. If there were differences, they might not be fatal.

14.98 It is now well known that the threshold for claiming that development has been begun is a very low one. A recent example of this can be seen in *R (on the application of Brent LBC) v Secretary of State for Communities and Local Government* [2008] EWHC 1991 (Admin) where the issue concerned the construction of an access road by a process known as 'Perma Zyme' which involved adding a chemical to soil to create a bonded layer of material which was capable of forming a road surface. This was held to be within s 56.

14.99 In the early 1990s the courts began to require that in addition to the need for a start to be made to the development in question, there had to be a continuing intention at that time to carry out the development for which the planning permission had been granted. As expressed in a number of cases, there had to be an 'earnest of intention to develop', failing which the act of starting the development would be 'colourable'.

14.100 The application of a colourability test is one which would always be extremely difficult to apply. Could, for example, the intention with regard to the carrying out of the development be passed on from the developer who obtained planning permission to another? Many developers of course undertake a specified operation prior to the likely expiry of a planning permission in the expectation of completing the development at a later date. On the other hand, a developer without the necessary finance to complete the development may carry out a specified operation in the hope of being able to raise the finance subsequently, or to dispose of the land to somebody who can. Intention is unlikely to be limited in application to the recipient of a planning permission, in the same way that a personal planning permission is limited to the recipient.

14.101 Issues of colourability now, however, no longer need to be considered in England following the lead given in a Scottish case. In *East Dumbartonshire Council v Secretary of State for Scotland and MacTaggart & Mickel Ltd* [1999] 1 PLR 53, the Inner House of the Court of Session (the equivalent of the English Court of Appeal) held, interpreting equivalent statutory provisions in Scottish legislation to those in England, that planning legislation does not impart into the relevant provisions of the Planning Acts any test of intention. The court held that

Parliament had laid down precisely what was required to be done on the site to keep the planning permission alive, and that was all that was required, no more and no less. In the *East Dunbartonshire* case the court rejected the need for a subjective intention test and ruled that the test was an objective one. The objective test was satisfied by first considering whether the work done was done in accordance with the planning permission and secondly whether it was material in the sense of not being *de minimis*.

14.102 One did not have to wait long to see whether English courts would follow the Scottish decision. In *Riordan Communications Ltd v South Bucks DC* [2000] JPL 594 Mr David Vaughan QC, sitting in the High Court as a Deputy Judge, considered that the unanimous decision of the Inner House in the *East Dumbartonshire* case was, if not actually binding upon him, a decision which should be treated with such a high degree of respect as to make little difference to a judge of first instance in England. There is, the Deputy Judge considered, 'no justification in the terms or the structure of the legislation for the ill-defined requirement that some operation should be carried out with some particular intention'. The approach taken in the *East Dunbartonshire* case that the question must be approached objectively and not subjectively has now been followed by the Court of Appeal in *Staffordshire CC v Riley* [2002] PLCR 75.

14.103 But indeed an approach that has far wider implications than the requirements imposed by s 56 is what is called the *Whitley* principle, namely the principle that the operations to which the planning permission relates are the operations which it authorizes, not those which contravene the conditions of the permission. In *F G Whitley & Sons Co Ltd v Secretary of State for Wales* [1990] JPL 678, planning permission had been granted for mineral extraction, subject to a number of conditions, including one which provided that no working should take place except in accordance with a scheme to be agreed with the local planning authority or, in the absence of agreement, by the Secretary of State. The developers were unable to reach agreement with the local authority. In an attempt to prevent the permission expiring, the developers carried out work on the site. An enforcement notice was served in relation to those works and was upheld by the Secretary of State. In a subsequent judicial challenge to the notice, Woolf LJ said:

> As I understand the effect of the authorities to which I am about to refer, it is only necessary to ask a single question: are the operations (in other situations the question would refer to development) permitted by the planning permission read together with its conditions? The permission is controlled by and subject to the conditions. If the operations contravene the conditions they cannot properly be described as commencing the development authorised by the permission. If they do not comply with the permission they constitute a breach of planning control and for planning purposes will be unauthorised and thus unlawful.

His Lordship went on to say that works carried out under a planning permission could never qualify as 'development to which it relates' unless the works were also carried out in compliance with the conditions subject to which the permission was granted. Hence for example, works carried out before a condition precedent had been satisfied do not save a permission which would otherwise be time-expired. It should be emphasized that the *Whitley* principle is one of general application and is not applicable only to conditions relating to time.

14.104 A similar view of the law was taken in *Handoll and Suddick v Warner, Goodman & Streat, Cook, and East Lindsey DC* [1995] JPL 930, where the High Court took the view that 'works which do not comply with the permission and any conditions to which it is subject do not constitute the implementation or commencement of a planning permission'. This is of course a principle of general application. It applies to a condition precedent, a commencement condition, or a limitation. The principle was applied in somewhat different circumstances in *Handoll*, where planning permission had been granted for a bungalow subject to an agricultural occupancy condition. In the event the bungalow was built 90 feet away from where it should have been built. When the new owners decided they wanted to use the land for dog kennels they were told by the authority of the condition. Since this was the first they knew of the condition they decided to sue the solicitors who had acted for them for negligence. The defendants raised a preliminary point as to whether any loss had been suffered by the claimants, it being contended that as the bungalow had not been built in accordance with the planning permission, namely on the land for which planning permission had been granted, it was not subject to the agricultural condition imposed by the authority. The Court of Appeal accepted that contention. So, because the particular planning permission had not been implemented, the conditions imposed on that planning permission were unenforceable.

14.105 Similarly in *Wycombe DC v Williams* [1995] 3 PLR 19, the High Court held that where a development does not comply to a material extent with a planning permission, a condition which was attached to development the subject of that planning permission cannot be applied to the unauthorized development that was carried out. It appears, however, that the decision in *Handoll* would have no application where the difference between the approved development and the development which was carried out falls within the normal tolerances or minor variations inherent in the laying-out and construction process.

14.106 It is, however, with regard to commencement conditions that the principle has had its greatest impact. In this connection the *Whitley* principle was applied in *Oldham MBC v Roland Bardsley (Builders) Ltd* [1996] JPL B119, where planning permission had been granted subject to conditions relating to the fencing of trees and the provision of a drainage scheme and emergency access, all of which were to be in accordance with a scheme approved by the authority. None of the conditions had been met, but development had been begun within the period specified in the planning permission for doing so. In granting an application for judicial review of a decision of the authority, the High Court held that the authority had been given wrong advice by their Director of Environmental Services to the effect that the permission had not expired when in fact, under the law, the site operations undertaken within the period for so doing were unauthorized and unlawful. Within a few days of that decision the Court of Appeal in *Daniel Platt Ltd v Secretary of State for the Environment and Staffordshire CC* [1996] JPL 349 showed no inclination to depart from the *Whitley* principle.

14.107 The courts have, however, recognized limited exceptions to this general principle. In *Agecrest Ltd v Gwynedd CC* [1998] JPL 325 conditions of a planning permission required a number of schemes to be submitted and approved before development could commence. Subsequently however, the local planning authority agreed that the development could commence without full compliance with those conditions. The High Court held that the authority had a discretion in the way in which it dealt with such conditions and that the work did amount to a start of the development. Further in *R v Flintshire CC, ex p Somerfield Stores Ltd* [1998] EGCS 53, a condition in a planning permission required a study to be made and approved by the Council of projected traffic generation and highway effects and of the implications of the development before the development commenced. The study had been carried out with the full knowledge and co-operation of the Council and the highway authority. However, the developers had made no actual application to the Council for approval of the study, nor was there a record of the Council communicating approval to the developer. Nevertheless, the High Court refused an application for judicial review to quash the Council's decision not to consider taking enforcement action against the development, holding that the general principle had to be applied with common sense and with regard to the facts of the particular case. In the instant case it would have been unreasonable for the Council to have decided that the planning permission had not been implemented.

14.108 In *Leisure Great Britain plc v Isle of Wight CC* [2000] PLCR 88 the court considered that any exception to the general *Whitley* principle should be on a clearly identifiable basis and not simply because the court considered it unfair on the merits to apply the general principle. The exceptions are therefore essentially limited to circumstances where the developer has done all he can do to meet the condition; where approval had subsequently been given so that work done before the expiry date of the permission was lawful; where the local planning authority had agreed that development could commence without full compliance with the condition; where the condition has in substance been complied with but the formalities, including written notice of approval, have not been completed before work started; or where enforcement action in respect of operations carried out in breach of the condition cannot be taken because it would be irrational to do so (in the *Wednesbury* sense) or unlawful to do so because of immunity from enforcement action by the passage of time.

14.109 In *R (Hart Aggregates Ltd) v Hartlepool Borough Council* [2005] EWHC 840 (Admin) Sullivan J argued that a further distinction had to be made between conditions which (a) prohibited development taking place before certain action had been taken (true conditions precedent); and (b) conditions which merely required certain matters to be agreed before the commencement of the development. In the case of (a) it could be argued that since this was a breach of a condition precedent the breach amounted to unauthorized development and not a breach of condition. In the case of (b), the commencement of development before the condition has been fulfilled, is simply a breach of the condition and therefore commencement operations save the permission though of course the condition has still been breached. The problem with this pragmatic distinction is that it will be difficult in practice to separate the two. In this regard Sulllivan J suggested at para 67 that a difference could be drawn between a case where no details whatsoever had been submitted (and so the permission had not been implemented at all) and a case where the failure had been limited to a failure to obtain approval for one particular aspect of the development (where the development has been implemented but there has been a breach of a planning condition against which enforcement action can be taken). He returned to this distinction in *Rastrum v Secretary of State for Communities and Local Government* [2009] EWCA Civ 1340 where it was held that works commenced after it was too late to submit details did not save a permission even though it was too late to take enforcement action against the works themselves. The Court of Appeal has approved the approach taken by Sullivan; see *Greyfort Properties v Secretary of State for Communities and Local Government* [2011] EWCA Civ 908.

Outline planning permissions

14.110 The provisions relating to the duration of planning permission are slightly modified with regard to outline planning permission. Section 92(2) of the 1990 Act now provides that where outline planning permission is granted for development consisting in or including the carrying out of building, or other operations, it shall be granted subject to conditions to the effect:

(a) that, in the case of any reserved matter, application for approval must be made not later than the expiration of three years beginning with the date of the grant of outline planning permission; and
(b) that the development to which the permission relates must be begun not later than—
  (i) omitted by s 51 of the Planning and Compulsory Purchase Act 2004;
  (ii) the expiration of two years from the final approval of the reserved matters or, in the case of approval on different dates, the final approval of the last such matter to be approved.

14.111 Again, it is provided that the standard period of three years or two years mentioned in the section may be varied at the discretion of the local planning authority or, on appeal, by the Secretary of State.

14.112 In addition, in the condition which requires applications for approval of reserved matters to be made within three years (para 14.110 at (a) above), the local planning authority may specify separate periods in relation to separate parts of the development. This flexibility can be particularly useful where the proposed development is on a large scale and is of a mixed nature.

14.113 It is important to remember that in order to keep the planning permission alive, the final approval of all reserved matters, whether given by the local planning authority or by the Secretary of State on appeal, must result from an application or applications for approval made to the authority within three years from the date of the grant of outline planning permission. If a landowner applies within the three-year period for approval of reserved matters and approval is not given, he cannot submit further applications for approval of matters reserved by that permission, unless they are also submitted within three years of the date of the grant of the outline permission. A landowner may submit any number of applications for approval of reserved matters within the three-year period. One application, however, need not cover every reserved matter requiring approval. A landowner may wish to submit a series of applications, each for the approval of specific reserved matters. For example, he may wish to obtain approval of matters relating to layout, siting, design, and external appearance before applying for the approval of matters relating to landscaping. All such applications, however, must be submitted within the specified three-year period if the permission is to be kept alive.

14.114 It seems from the case of *Etheridge v Secretary of State for the Environment and Torbay BC* [1984] JPL 340, that a later grant of full planning permission (ie where all details have been approved) may act as an approval of details of development which had been reserved in an earlier outline permission. For this to happen, it appears that the full planning permission must approve exactly those matters (but not necessarily all of them) which, in respect of the land to which they related, would have had to have been approved on an application for approval of reserved matters. Furthermore, the fact that full planning permission may relate to only part of the land covered by the earlier outline permission, does not affect its validity in relation to the whole of the site, as was made clear in *R v Secretary of State for the Environment, ex p Bilton* (1975) 31 P & CR 154.

14.115 It should be noted that local planning authorities sometimes grant planning permission subject to conditions on matters that require the prior approval of the authority before development can be commenced. If those matters are not matters that come within the definition of 'reserved matters', s 92 has no application to that matter. Hence the condition would be subject to s 91.

Extending time conditions

It was held by the High Court in *R v Secretary of State for the Environment, ex p Corby BC* [1995] JPL 115, that the power available to a developer under s 73 of the 1990 Act to apply to the local planning authority for planning permission for the development of land without complying with a condition imposed on the grant of a previous planning permission could, subject to subsection (4) of that section, be used with regard to conditions imposed requiring the submission of applications for approval of reserved matters to be made within a specified period, in addition to a condition requiring commencement of the development within a specified period. 14.116

Subsection (4) of s 73 provides: 14.117

> This section does not apply if the previous planning permission was granted subject to a condition as to the time within which the development to which it related was to be begun and that time has expired without the development having been begun.

In other words the section could only be used if the permission was still alive and capable of implementation. The Planning and Compulsory Purchase Act 2004 however, further limited the right under s 73 of the 1990 Act to seek a change to a condition imposed in a previous planning permission, by taking away that right where the condition sought to be changed was a condition relating to time. A new subsection (5) of s 73 now provides: 14.118

> (5) Planning permission must not be granted under this section to the extent that it has effect to change a condition subject to which a previous planning permission was granted by extending the time limit in which:
> (a) a development must be started;
> (b) an application for approval of reserved matters (within the meaning of section 92) must be made.

The effect of the changes made by the 2004 Act is significant. In particular it reduces the life of a planning permission to three years (or five in the case of an outline planning permission). Furthermore, the effect of adding subsection (5) to s 73 means that once planning permission has been granted for development, no condition as to time is capable of being altered. If a developer finds that existing time conditions in a planning permission cannot be met, he must submit another application for planning permission for that development, which he may do at any time, even where the time limits for commencement imposed in the earlier planning permission have not expired. Any subsequent application will of course be dealt with by the authority in the same way as any other application, namely by having regard to the development plan so far as material and to any other material considerations.

However the Town and Country Planning (General Development Procedure) (Amendment) (England) Order 2009 created a procedure whereby permissions that are about elapse can be kept alive by a simplified procedure. This is now to 14.119

be found in Art 20 of the Development Management Procedure Order 2015 (DMPO). It applies only to planning permissions which are extant both on 1 October 2010 and at the date of application, and have not yet been commenced. It also applies to listed building and conservation area consents. Outline permissions can also be extended under this power, provided they are extant both on 1 October 2010 and at the date of application, and have not yet commenced. The power to extend does not apply to any permissions granted after the measure comes into force. This is because local planning authorities already have discretion under ss 91 and 92 of the 1990 Act to grant planning permissions for longer periods if they are satisfied that there are good planning reasons for doing so.

Completion notices

14.120 The provisions considered so far operate to secure that, as far as possible, development is begun within the period stipulated in the permission. The provisions do not secure that the development once begun will actually be completed. Accordingly, s 94 of the 1990 Act provides that if the local planning authority is of opinion that the development will not be completed within a reasonable period, it may serve a completion notice on the owner and occupier of the land and any other person who in the opinion of the local planning authority will be affected by the notice, stating that the planning permission will cease to have effect at the expiration of a further period (being not less than 12 months) after the notice takes effect. A completion notice will only take effect after confirmation by the Secretary of State who, before confirming the notice, must give a person on whom the completion notice was served and the authority an opportunity of appearing before, and being heard by, an Inspector appointed for that purpose. A completion notice cannot be served until the period allowed for the commencement of the development has passed. In the case of a full planning permission, this will normally be after five years, a period which has now been reduced to three years under the changes to the life of planning permissions introduced by the 2004 Act.

14.121 Section 95(4) provides that if a completion notice takes effect, the planning permission referred to in it shall become invalid at the expiration of the period specified in the notice. Section 95(5) then goes on to provide that the previous subsection shall not affect any permission so far as development carried out under it before the end of the period mentioned in that subsection is concerned. Now, since planning permission is granted for development and not for a series of stages in the development process, that provision appears to mean that once a completion notice has taken effect, any act of development which has taken place in the process of partially implementing the permission will be development undertaken without planning permission, and thus be liable to enforcement notice procedure. So if, for example, planning permission has been granted for the erection of a two-storey building and only the ground floor has been built by the time a completion notice takes effect, no planning permission would exist for the single-storey building. It would be otherwise, however, if, as happened in another context in the case of *F Lucas & Sons Ltd v Dorking & Horley RDC* (1964) 62 LGR 491, a grant of planning permission for the erection of a number of houses could be constructed as a grant of a number of mini planning permissions, each of which authorized the construction of an individual house.

14.122 An alternative view is that a completion notice has no effect on that part of the development which has been completed, but renders nugatory that part of the development uncompleted. Whichever is the better view, it is clear that the completion notice does not guarantee completion of a part-finished development. It is for that reason that completion notices are so rarely used.

14.123 The interpretation of s 95(5) has now been considered by the courts. In *Cardiff City Council v National Assembly for Wales and Malik* [2006] EWHC 1412 (Admin); [2007] 1 P & CR 9, a completion notice had been served following the partial construction of a garage for which planning permission had been granted. Although the completion notice had been confirmed by the National Assembly, no further work to the garage had been carried out. Consequently, the City Council served an enforcement notice requiring demolition of that part of the garage which had been constructed and the removal of the resultant debris. The owner appealed against the enforcement notice and an Inspector appointed by the National Assembly recommended that the appeal should fail and the enforcement notice upheld. The Inspector had included that s 95(5) was 'slightly ambiguous', taking the view that its effect was not to save permission for a partially completed development, but to withdraw permission for the garage development. Since the part-built structure did not now have planning permission, its erection and retention was a breach of planning control.

14.124 The National Assembly, however, took a different view of s 95(5) from the Inspector. Accordingly, it allowed the appeal and quashed the enforcement notice. On appeal by the City Council against the National Assembly's decision, the High Court held that where development in respect of which planning permission has been granted is not completed, despite the service of a completion notice, works carried out prior to the expiry of the completion notice remain development authorized by the planning permission.

14.125 The effect of this decision is that a local planning authority can do little, save using its power to serve a revocation or discontinuance order, to deal with partially-built structures however unsightly and detrimental to the visual amenity of an area they may be. What is more, they can remain so ad infinitum without any prospect of enforcement action.

14.126 Evidence given by the Department of the Environment to the Environment Committee of the House of Commons in June 1997 disclosed that there had only been 21 cases in the five years from 1992 to 1997 where the confirmation of completion notices had been sought from the Secretary of State. Most of the cases involved housing development. In one case, however, a completion notice had been confirmed where planning permission had been granted for a shopping development in 1988, but by 1994 only the car park had been constructed. The Department's evidence gave no details for that period of non-contested cases, that is cases where there had been compliance with the completion notice without the need for the Secretary of State's confirmation of it.

15

THE CONSTRUCTION, SCOPE, EFFECT, AND LIFE OF A PLANNING PERMISSION

A. CONSTRUCTION OF A PLANNING PERMISSION	15.01	F. PLANNING AND HIGHWAYS	15.42
B. SCOPE OF A PLANNING PERMISSION	15.16	G. PLANNING PERMISSION AND ACTIONS IN NUISANCE	15.47
C. EFFECT OF A PLANNING PERMISSION	15.28	H. PLANNING PERMISSION AND ACTIONS FOR NEGLIGENCE	15.53
D. PUBLIC RIGHTS OF WAY AND DEVELOPMENT	15.40	I. PLANNING PERMISSION AND ACTIONS IN DECEIT	15.58
E. INTERFERENCE WITH EASEMENTS AND OTHER INTERESTS OR RIGHTS	15.41	J. LIFE OF A PLANNING PERMISSION	15.63

A. CONSTRUCTION OF A PLANNING PERMISSION

15.01 Doubts may arise about the precise construction of a grant of planning permission. The construction will occasionally involve looking not only at the notification of the decision but also behind the notification at the application for planning permission stage.

15.02 The rule established by the courts is that if the planning permission is on the face of it a complete and self-contained document, not incorporating by reference any other document, the planning permission will stand on its own. If, on the other hand, the planning permission incorporates other documents, such as the application for planning permission, then those documents should be taken into account in construing the permission.

15.03 In *Miller-Mead v Minister of Housing and Local Government* [1963] 2 QB 196, the Court of Appeal held that a planning permission runs with the land and cannot be cut down by reference to the application pursuant to which it was granted. The reason for the court taking that view was that the permission may come into the hands of people who have never seen the application and who must, therefore, rely on the actual words used in the grant. The decision ignored the fact that applications for planning permission (and also the grant) must be entered by the local planning authority in a planning register which is available for public inspection at all reasonable times.

15.04 Although ideally an applicant for planning permission should be able to see the precise terms of the permission from the permission itself (i.e. the notification of the decision to grant), the decision in *Miller-Mead v Minister of Housing and Local Government* could have created difficulties for the many local planning authorities who expressly link the grant of permission to the application to which it related. Indeed, six weeks later, in *Wilson v West Sussex CC* [1963] 2 QB 764, the Court of Appeal had to consider a grant of planning permission which said: 'The council hereby permit the following development, that is to say ... in accordance with the plan and application No ... submitted to the council on ...'.

15.05 Although the court thought that the incorporation of the 'relevant correspondence' into the permission was a very unfortunate practice, it held that where the permission specifically incorporates the terms of the application for planning permission, it was proper, and indeed necessary, to refer to the terms of the application in construing the permission.

15.06 A few years later, in *Slough Estates Ltd v Slough BC (No 2)* [1971] AC 958, the House of Lords confirmed the later view of the Court of Appeal that it was proper to look at the application if it were incorporated in the permission itself.

15.07 In *Manning v Secretary of State for the Environment* [1976] JPL 634, planning permission had been granted for a limited period for the erection of a riding school, to be used by a private riding school together with disabled riders. The reason for the grant of the permission was that it would enable facilities for disabled riders to be provided. Later, towards the end of that period, an application was made for the renewal of the permission. The permission, when granted, referred to 'continued use of indoor riding school'. A dispute then arose over whether the later permission was to be construed as widely as the first and include the use, not only for the disabled but for the general riding school as well, or whether (as the local planning authority had maintained) the use was limited to disabled persons only. The claimant, contending that it was not so limited, obtained a declaration to that effect in the High Court. The Court of Appeal, upholding the decision of the High Court, held that in this case it was relevant not only to look at the planning permission, but also at the previous history, the previous application and the previous permission.

15.08 Although it is better to restrict the scope of this decision to the interpretation of 'renewal applications', it is significant that Stephenson LJ thought that because documents such as applications for and grants of permission were rarely drafted by lawyers, they should in his view 'be given a tolerant view'.

15.09 It also seems that, unless incorporated in the permission, it is not permissible to look at the resolution of the authority, or of the appropriate committee of the authority, in order to construe the permission. In *R v West Oxfordshire DC, ex parte Pearce Homes Ltd* [1986] JPL 523 the planning committee of the authority adopted a resolution that planning permission be granted subject to the execution of an agreement under the then s 106 of the 1990 Act. Details of the resolution were then notified to the applicants by letter. Subsequently, the applicants were refused permission for the development on the ground that the site had now been scheduled by the Secretary of State under the Ancient Monuments and Archaeological Areas Act 1979. In an application for judicial review of the authority's decision to refuse planning permission, the company alleged that the resolution had the effect of granting the planning permission it was seeking, or alternatively that if it did not then permission had been granted by the subsequent letter.

15.10 Refusing the application, Woolf J held that, ordinarily, to decide what planning permission had been granted, all it was necessary to do was to look at the actual notification of the decision. Normally one could not look at the resolution except to determine other issues, such as whether or not an officer had authority to notify the grant of planning permission. He went on to hold that the letter subsequent to the resolution did not amount to a grant of planning permission. It had simply anticipated that a grant would be made once an agreement had been completed.

15.11 In *Wivenhoe Port Ltd v Colchester BC* [1985] JPL 396, the Court of Appeal favoured the view that, if it were necessary to do so, it was appropriate to look at the application *as an aid* to the construction of a planning permission. The reason for this approach was the recognition that a grant of planning permission is made in response to an application, and that the permission granted cannot purport to grant something outside the terms of the application.

15.12 In later cases, *Oakimber Ltd v Elmbridge BC* (1991) 62 P & CR 594 and *Staffordshire Moorlands DC v Cartwright* (1991) 63 P & CR 285, the Court of Appeal held that the terms of a planning permission had to be construed in the factual context of the application on which it was based. More recently, in *R v Secretary of State for the Environment, ex p Slough BC* [1995] JPL 135, Schiemann J considered that there was a strong public interest in the court taking a grant of planning permission as granting what it purported to grant, though where the permission was not prima facie clear, or where an application was expressly incorporated in the permission, different considerations arose. The mere recital of the application number at the top of the permission did not incorporate the application into the planning permission. In order to do that, words such as 'in accordance with the plans and application' would be necessary. The decision of the High Court was subsequently upheld by the Court of Appeal [1995] EGCS 95. According to the court the general rule was that, in construing a planning permission, regard might be had only to the permission itself, including the reasons stated for it. Since the breach of planning control might lead to criminal sanctions, the court felt that the public should be able to rely on a document that was plain on its face without having to consider whether there was any discrepancy between the permission and the application.

15.13 The law in this field has now been helpfully summarized by Beatson LJ in *Telford & Wrekin Council v Secretary of State for Communities and Local Government* [2013] EWHC 79 (Admin) at [33]:

> ... I first summarise my understanding of the effect of the authorities put before me on the construction of a planning permission (and of the conditions in it):
> (1) As a general rule a planning permission is to be construed within the four corners of the consent itself, i.e. including the conditions in it and the express reasons for those conditions unless another document is incorporated by reference or it is necessary to resolve an ambiguity in the permission or condition: *R. v Ashford DC* [1998] P.L.C.R. 12 at 19 (Keene J); *Carter Commercial Developments v Secretary of State* [2002] EWCA Civ 1994 at [13] and [27] (Buxton and Arden LJJ); *Sevenoaks DC v First Secretary of State* [2004] EWHC 771 *(Admin)* at [24] and [38] (Sullivan J); *R. (Bleaklow Industries) v Secretary of State for Communities and Local Government* [2009] EWCA Civ. 206 at [27] (Keene LJ); *R. (Midcounties Co-operative Limited) v Wyre Forest DC* [2010] EWCA Civ. 841 at [10] (Laws LJ).
> (2) The reason for the strict approach to the use of extrinsic material is that a planning permission is a public document which runs with the land. Save where it is clear on its face that it does not purport to be complete and self-contained, it should be capable of being relied on by later landowners and members of the public reading it who may not have access to extrinsic material: *Slough Estates v Slough Borough Council* [1971] A.C. 958 at 962 (Lord Reid); *Carter Commercial Developments v Secretary of State* at [28] (Arden LJ); *R. (Bleaklow Industries) v Secretary of State for Communities and Local Government* [2009] EWCA Civ 206 at [27]) (Keene LJ); *Barnett v Secretary of State* [2009] EWCA Civ 476 at [16]–[21] (Keene LJ, approving Sullivan J at first instance); *R. (Midcounties Co-operative Limited) v Wyre Forest DC* [2010] EWCA Civ 841 at [10] (Laws LJ).
> (3) It follows from (2) that in construing a planning permission:
>   a. the question is not what the parties intended but what a reasonable reader would understand was permitted by the local planning authority, and
>   b. Conditions must be clearly and expressly imposed, so that they are plain for all to read.
> (4) As well as the cases cited at (2), see *Sevenoaks DC v First Secretary of State* [2004] EWHC 771 (Admin) at [38] and [45] (Sullivan J).
> (5) Conditions should be interpreted benevolently and not narrowly or strictly (see *Carter Commercial Development Ltd v Secretary of State for the Environment* [2002] EWHC 1200 (Admin) at [49], per Sullivan J) and given a commonsense meaning: see *Northampton BC v First Secretary of State* [2005] EWHC 168 (Admin) at [22] (Sullivan J).

(6) A condition will be void for uncertainty only 'if it can be given no meaning or no sensible or ascertainable meaning, and not merely because it is ambiguous or leads to absurd results': *Fawcett Properties v Buckingham County Council* [1961] A.C. 636, 678 per Lord Denning. In Hulme's case Elias LJ stated this was an application of the benevolent construction principle.

(7) If there is ambiguity in a condition it has to be resolved in a common sense way, having regard to the underlying planning purpose for it as evidenced by the reasons given for its imposition: *Sevenoaks DC v First Secretary of State* [2004] EWHC 771 (Admin) per Sullivan J at [38] accepting the submission at [34].

(8) There is no room for an implied condition in a planning permission. This principle was enunciated in *Trustees of Walton on Thames Charities v Walton and Weighbridge District Council* (1970) 21 P. & C. R. 411 at 497 (Widgery LJ), in the following terms: 'I have never heard of an implied condition in a planning permission and I believe no such creature exists. Planning permission enures for the benefit of the land. It is not simply a matter of contract between the parties. There is no place, in my judgment, within the law relating to planning permission for an implied condition. Conditions should be express, they should be clear, they should be in the document containing the permission.' This principle also precludes implying an obligation by way of an addition to an existing condition: *Sevenoaks DC v First Secretary of State* [2004] EWHC 771 (Admin) at [45] (Sullivan J).

(9) Where planning permission containing conditions has been granted in a decision by an inspector allowing an appeal, and a condition is ambiguous, it is possible to construe it in the context of the decision letter as a whole: *Hulme's* case at [13(a)]. Doing this does not involve impermissible 'implication' from an extrinsic source, but is best described as a question of 'construction': *Hulme's* case at [37]. In *Hulme's* case, Elias LJ stated (at [37]) that even 'if it can be described as an implied condition it is very different in nature from that envisaged in the *Trustees of Walton* case.'

(10) In the context of what suffices to exclude the operation of the Use Classes Order 1987:

a. A grant of planning permission for a stated use is a grant of permission only for that use, but could not, in itself, be sufficient to exclude the operation of the UCO because if it did, the operation of the UCO would be curtailed in a way which could not have been intended: *Dunoon Developments Ltd v Secretary of State for the Environment* [1992] J.P.L. 936 at 107 (Sir Donald Nicholls V-C)

b. In general, to exclude the operation of the UCO, it is necessary for the local planning authority to do so by the imposition of a condition in unequivocal terms: *Carpet Decor (Guildford) Ltd v Secretary of State for the Environment* [1981] J.P.L. 806 at 808 (Sir Douglas Frank QC).

Those principles need to now be read in light of the judgment of the Supreme Court in *Trump International Golf Club Scotland Ltd v Scottish Ministers* [2015] UKSC 74; [2016] 1 WLR 85 at [31]–[36], in which Lord Hodge JSC held that planning permissions and conditions were not in a special category when it comes to using implication as a technique of interpretation. However, his Lordship observed at [35] that the court 'will exercise great restraint in implying terms

15.14

into public documents which have criminal sanctions'. Accordingly, in *Lambeth London Borough Council v Secretary of State for Communities and Local Government* [2018] EWCA Civ 844; [2018] 2 P & CR 17 the Court of Appeal declined to imply a condition excluding the sale of food to give effect to the intention of the planning authority. A similarly cautious approach was adopted in *Government of the Republican of France v Royal Borough of Kensington & Chelsea* [2017] EWCA Civ 429; [2017] 1 WLR 3206. That said, the courts are willing to show a degree of flexibility to resolve a plain error by a process of construction. For example, in *Newark & Sherwood District Council v Secretary of State for Communities and Local Government* [2013] EWHC 2162 (Admin) Stephen Morris QC (sitting as a Deputy High Court Judge) found that a reference within a condition to a turbine being 'three-bladed' when the application was 'two-bladed' could be resolved by construction.

15.15 As to the exclusion of the Use Classes Order 1987 by condition, the last word is now to be found in *Dunnett Investments Ltd v Secretary of State for Communities and Local Government* [2017] EWCA Civ 192; [2017] JPL 848 in which the Court of Appeal found that a condition which stated that a property could be used for 'no other purpose whatsoever, without express planning consent from the Local Planning Authority first being obtained' was sufficiently clear to exclude the operation of the UCO. On this particular topic, see further: B Garbett, 'Implied Conditions in Planning: Are We Losing the Way?' [2017] 1 JPL 2.

B. SCOPE OF A PLANNING PERMISSION

15.16 Although, as stated, the grant of planning permission cannot purport to grant something outside the terms of the application, this does not mean that the grant must replicate precisely what has been applied for.

15.17 In *Bernard Wheatcroft Ltd v Secretary of State for the Environment* [1982] JPL 37 an application for planning permission had been made for 'approximately 420 dwellings on 35 acres of land'. Permission was refused. On appeal, the Inspector recommended the appeal be refused, but indicated that if it were possible to restrict the area to 25 acres and for the number of dwellings to be reduced to 250, then such development would not be objectionable. In accepting his Inspector's recommendation that the appeal be dismissed, the Secretary of State considered he had no power to grant planning permission for development on a smaller site and with houses at a lower density than that which was indicated on the original application form. In granting an application made to the High Court to quash the Secretary of State's decision, Forbes J held that it was permissible to grant planning permission subject to a condition that only a reduced development was to be carried out, provided that the result did not differ substantially from the development proposed in the original application. This was an aspect to which the Secretary of State had failed to have regard. What clearly cannot be done is to consider an amendment to an application which would have the effect of altering its whole character.

15.18 The main criterion to which the Secretary of State (or indeed a local planning authority) must have regard is whether the development would be so changed that it would in substance be no longer what was applied for and that to grant planning permission would be to deprive those who should have been consulted on the changed development of the opportunity of such consultation. In a later case, *Wessex Regional Health Authority v Salisbury DC* [1984] JPL 344, Glidewell J upheld the decision of an Inspector to refuse planning permission for residential development. The appellants had invited the Inspector, during an appeal against a refusal of planning permission by the local planning authority, to consider the argument that if 48 houses were too many, but 37 were acceptable, he could grant planning permission subject to a condition limiting the number to 37. The Inspector decided that 48 houses was too many and dismissed the appeal. He also took the view that in the circumstances a reduction in number from 48 to 37 differed substantially from the development proposal and should rightly form the basis of a fresh application.

15.19 The principle has had ramifications in other situations which have not led to litigation. In the aftermath of the decision in *Bernard Wheatcroft Ltd v Secretary of State for the Environment*, the Secretary of State had to consider an application by the National Coal Board to exploit what became known as the Vale of Belvoir coalfield.

15.20 The National Coal Board had applied for planning permission to construct and work three mines at Hose, Saltby, and Asfordby, and to tip spoil adjacent to those three sites. The Inspector had recommended the grant of permission for all three mines, but that permission be refused for the proposed spoil tips at Hose and Saltby.

15.21 After considering the report the Secretary of State concluded that the development of the mine at Hose was environmentally unacceptable. In addition, before tipping at any of the sites could be contemplated, the possibility of other methods of spoil disposal should be further examined. So, had there been acceptable proposals for the disposal of spoil, the Secretary of State would have been prepared to grant planning permission for the development of the mines at Asfordby and Saltby.

15.22 The National Coal Board had submitted, however, one application for planning permission covering all the underground coal extraction in Leicestershire, together with the three mine complexes and three spoil tips, thus opting to stand or fall by a strategy of developing the whole coalfield as one project. In his decision letter the Secretary of State said:

> in those circumstances the granting of planning permission for only part of the development would be in effect granting a permission for development which is significantly different in kind from the proposal which was the subject of the application. This may be a point which the Board would wish to bear in mind in future.

15.23 In a later case, *Breckland DC v Secretary of State for the Environment* (1992) 65 P & CR 34, the local planning authority sought to quash the decision of an Inspector whereby he had allowed an appeal for a 16-pitch gypsy caravan site in Norfolk. The case is believed to be the first to come before the courts where an amendment of a planning application by an Inspector involved the enlargement of the application site. The effect of the amendment was to increase the application site by 50 per cent, bringing it nearer to three nearby residences and increasing the number of pitches. In quashing the Inspector's decision Mr David Widdicombe QC, sitting as a Deputy Judge, considered that the legal validity of an enlargement might be harder to justify than a reduction. He thought the test of validity of the action was derived from *Bernard Wheatcroft Ltd v Secretary of State for the Environment* but it was an exercise of discretion which could only be challenged within the *Wednesbury* rules. He held that the parish council and local residents were deprived of the opportunity to be consulted on the proposed amendment, and it was *Wednesbury* unreasonable of the Inspector to hold that the amendment did not substantially alter the proposal. The decision to allow the amendment was unreasonable and therefore invalid.

Split decisions

15.24 A variant of the principle in *Bernard Wheatcroft Ltd v Secretary of State for the Environment* [1982] JPL 37 is the development of what may be called the 'split decision', whereby planning permission is granted not for reduced development as in *Wheatcroft*, but for only part of the land the subject of the application, whilst being refused for the remaining part.

15.25 An example is a ministerial decision involving the North Wiltshire District Council, where an application had been made for the erection of 11 detached houses on land at Tetbury Hill, Malmesbury. In default of the decision within the prescribed period, the applicants had appealed to the Secretary of State. About half of the site was included within the 'limits of development' for the town of Malmesbury as identified on the proposals map in the Malmesbury local plan. The remainder of the site lay outside the limits. The Inspector took the view that that part of the development which lay within the limits of development boundary would be acceptable, but not that which lay outside. Although the applicants had objected at the inquiry to the making of a split decision, the Inspector dismissed the appeal and refused planning permission for development of that part of the site which lay outside the limit of development boundary, but at the same time allowed the appeal and granted planning permission for the erection of dwellinghouses in respect of that part of the application site which lay inside the boundary. For obvious reasons, the grant of planning permission was a grant of outline planning permission, with approval of details relating to siting, design, external appearance, means of access, and landscaping being reserved for the approval of the local planning authority.

15.26 The legality of the practice of giving a split decision on an application for planning permission has not often been tested in the courts, but it is thought that the principle to be applied would be the same as that in the *Wheatcroft* case, namely, whether it would be unreasonable to grant permission which would be substantially different from the development applied for.

15.27 Issues of severability were considered by the courts in *Johnson v Secretary of State for Communities and Local Government* [2007] EWHC 1839 (Admin) where it was pointed out that s 79(1)(b) of the 1990 Act clearly allows part of an application to be permitted and part to be refused. The court felt that the real question to be applied was whether the partial grant of planning permission would give rise to material considerations, including a change in the balance of planning considerations, or to a need for representations which have not been considered.

C. EFFECT OF A PLANNING PERMISSION

15.28 Until the decision of the Divisional Court in *Petticoat Lane Rentals Ltd v Secretary of State for the Environment* [1971] 1 WLR 1112, it had always been assumed, but with only slender authority for so doing, that the implementation of a planning permission destroyed the old use to which the land had previously been put. The case concerned a site which had been cleared after having been bombed during the Second World War. It had been leased to a company, which used it to let out stalls to street traders every day of the week. In 1963, planning permission had been granted for a new commercial building on the site supported on pillars. The open ground floor was to be used as a car-parking and loading area ancillary to the commercial use of the building. Under the terms of the permission that area could continue to be used for market trading on Sundays, when the ground floor would not be needed for that ancillary car-parking use. Almost immediately after the building had been constructed, market traders began to use the ground floor not only on Sundays but on every day of the week.

15.29 Almost inevitably the local planning authority served an enforcement notice on the company alleging the making of a material change of use without permission and requiring the discontinuance of weekday trading. The company appealed. After a public inquiry, the Secretary of State upheld the notice on the grounds that any existing use rights had been extinguished with the implementation of the permission. The Divisional Court held, dismissing an appeal by the company, that, where an area of open land was developed by the erection of a new building over the whole site, the land as such was merged into the new building and a new planning unit was created with a new use; and that any use to which the new building was put thereafter was a change of use which, if not authorized by the planning permission, could be restrained by planning control.

15.30 In so holding, the court relied heavily on one of its earlier decisions, namely *Prossor v Minister of Housing and Local Government* (1968) 67 LGR 109 (Div Court). This was a case of a petrol service station on a main road where the occupier sought and obtained planning permission to rebuild the petrol station. He was given such permission and an express condition was attached to the permission to the effect that no retail sales other than the sale of motor accessories should be carried on the site. In fact, having let the establishment, the occupier began to exhibit second-hand cars for sale on the site, which was clearly a breach of the condition if the condition was effective. It was argued in favour of the occupier that he was enabled to do that because there was a continuing and unbroken use of the land for the sale of second-hand cars, and in his contention the fact that he had had a new and inconsistent planning permission and had implemented it did not destroy that right. Lord Parker CJ, having dealt with a number of arguments not relevant to the present appeal, put the matter thus:

> Assuming ... that there was at all material times prior to April 1964 [the date of the rebuilding] an existing use right running on this land for the display and sale of motor cars, yet by adopting the permission granted in April 1964, the appellant's predecessor, as it seems to me, gave up any possible existing use rights in that regard which he may have had. The planning history of this site, as it were, seems to me to begin afresh on 4 April 1964, with the grant of this permission, a permission which was taken up and used, and the sole question here is: has there been a breach of that condition?

15.31 Although in the *Prossor* case the use of the land for the display of second-hand cars had been expressly prohibited by a condition of the planning permission, the court in *Petticoat Lane Rentals Ltd v Secretary of State for the Environment* thought that to be irrelevant. According to Widgery LJ, the fact that there was an express prohibition was no more than an indication of the fact that the draftsman of the permission had found it easier to express his wishes in that way.

15.32 Although the court in the *Petticoat Lane Rentals Ltd* case was unanimous in holding that the existing use of the land had been extinguished by the erection upon it of a new building, both Bridge J and Lord Parker CJ drew a distinction between, on the one hand, a case where land formerly open and not built upon had been used for a certain purpose and subsequently the land itself had been built upon; and on the other hand, a case where open land had been used, that land had subsequently been embodied in the curtilage of a site developed by building for other purposes, but the building had not extended over all the land used for the former purpose. It is quite clear that in the latter situation, the local planning authority could, by express condition, exclude the right to continue the former use of the land not built upon. Without such a condition being imposed, however, the position is far from clear.

15.33 The decision in *Prossor v Minister of Housing and Local Government* was considered by the House of Lords in *Newbury DC v Secretary of State for the Environment* [1981] AC 578. One of the three main issues to be determined in that case was whether the company concerned, having been granted planning permission to change the use of hangars for the storage of civil defence vehicles to use for the storage of synthetic rubber, could subsequently contend that no permission was necessary on account of existing use rights. In deciding that there was no bar to the right of the company to do so, their Lordships referred to the *Prossor* case. Relating that case to the facts before him, Viscount Dilhorne felt that *Prossor's* case was not sustainable on the basis that obtaining and taking up planning permission in itself prevents reliance on existing use rights. He went on:

> If, however, the grant of planning permission, whether it be permission to build or for a change of use, is of such a character that the implementation of the permission leads to the creation of a new planning unit, then I think that it is right to say that existing use rights attaching to the former planning unit are extinguished. It may be that in the *Prossor* case the erection of the new building created a new planning unit. If it did, and it is not very clear from the report, then in my view that case was rightly decided.
>
> It is clear that in this case the grant of the planning permission in May 1962 did not create a new planning unit and so, in my opinion, [the company] were not precluded from relying on the existing use rights attaching to the site.

15.34 The idea that the implementation of a planning permission may lead to the creation of a new planning unit was echoed by Lord Fraser of Tullybelton in the *Newbury* case when he said:

> The only circumstances in which existing use rights are lost by accepting and implementing a later planning permission are, in my opinion, when a new planning unit comes into existence.

15.35 The relevance of a new planning unit was again considered, this time by the Court of Appeal, in *Jennings Motors Ltd v Secretary of State for the Environment* [1980] JPL 521. There, land had been used for many years for the repair and maintenance of vehicles and the sale and hire of cars. In 1975, a new single-storey building was erected without planning permission on a small part of the site to replace an existing building. The new building was used for vehicle repair and servicing. Eventually the local planning authority served an enforcement notice which required not the demolition of the building, but the discontinuance of the use to which the building had been put. The occupiers appealed against the notice and, after an inquiry, the Inspector concluded that the planning unit was the site as a whole, and that the use could be carried on anywhere within the site, thus the appeal should be allowed. The Secretary of State, however, upheld the enforcement notice on the ground that when the new building was erected a new planning history was commenced in respect of it for which there had been a material change of use from 'no use'. The Divisional Court upheld the Secretary of State's decision, but on appeal by the occupiers the Court of Appeal allowed the appeal, holding that the erection of a new building on part of a whole site does not in itself constitute a new planning unit or a new chapter in the planning history and, accordingly, the Secretary of State had erred in law in holding that development had taken place.

15.36 The decision in the *Jennings* case was concerned with the question of whether an established use survived within the new building. It did not determine the question of whether the implementation of a planning permission on part of a site created a new planning unit or introduced a new chapter in planning history as regards the rest of the site.

15.37 This latter aspect was considered subsequently by the Divisional Court of the Queen's Bench Division in *South Staffordshire DC v Secretary of State for the Environment* [1987] JPL 635. Apart from preferring the term 'new chapter in planning history' to that of 'new planning unit', the court considered that established use rights on the rest of a site would survive implementation of planning permission to erect a building on another part of the site, unless the development which took place was inconsistent with the established use.

15.38 Unfortunately, the cases subsequent to the *Petticoat Lane Rentals Ltd* case, such as *R (on the application of Alpha Plus Group Ltd) v Royal Borough of Kensington and Chelsea* [2007] EWHC 2840 (Admin) have not succeeded in resolving the problem there identified of the effect of implementing a planning permission which affects only part of the original planning unit, on the existing use rights of the part of the unit not affected by the development. Certainly, *Pioneer Aggregates (UK) Ltd v Secretary of State for the Environment* [1985] AC 132, suggests that existing use rights on an undeveloped portion of a site may remain extant when development of only a part of it is carried out. Until this problem is resolved, a person applying for planning permission to develop part of his land should consider restricting his application to that part only, leaving the authority to restrict the existing use rights of the other part by condition, if they should consider this to be necessary. Otherwise, it might be difficult to maintain that the grant of permission and its implementation for the part has led to the creation of a smaller planning unit carved out of the old so that the existing use rights in what is left of the old still remain.

15.39 The risks that can be run by applying for planning permission to develop the whole of a parcel of land when the application could be limited to only part is seen in *Wiggins v Secretary of State for the Environment, Transport, and the Regions* and *Slough BC* [2001] PLCR 365. There, part of a parcel of land was being lawfully used for the crushing of concrete. In 1995 the claimant had sought planning permission for that activity to be carried out on the whole of the site. Permission was granted but made subject to a condition requiring the use of the land to be discontinued by 1998. When this did not occur, the authority took enforcement action in respect of the whole site. An Inspector's refusal to allow an appeal against the enforcement notice was subsequently upheld in the High Court. In what may be seen as a somewhat unconvincing decision, the court held that if the planning permission was strictly unnecessary because it covered the same site and gave permission only for the activities which could in any event be continued, the existing use rights could not be extinguished. But if planning permission is required, different considerations apply. It was not possible to split the decision and say, because it was not needed for one part, the use of that part could continue. The reality in this case was that permission was required to continue the use of the two parts and that was a different site from one part of the parcel on its own.

D. PUBLIC RIGHTS OF WAY AND DEVELOPMENT

Under s 247 of the 1990 Act the Secretary of State may, by order, authorize the stopping up or diversion of any *highway*, if satisfied that it is necessary to do so in order to enable development for which planning permission has been granted to be carried out. A more limited power is given to local planning authorities by s 257 to make orders authorizing the stopping up or diversion of any *footpath or bridleway* in order to enable development for which planning permission has been granted to be carried out. The grant of planning permission does not in itself authorize the stopping up or diversion of rights of way and if those rights are obstructed before any order has been made, the development cannot proceed until the obstruction has been removed. It should be emphasized that the grant of planning permission does not guarantee that any order will be made under these provisions. No assumption should be made that merely because planning permission has been granted, an order will invariably be made or confirmed under these provisions.

15.40

E. INTERFERENCE WITH EASEMENTS AND OTHER INTERESTS OR RIGHTS

Sections 203–206 of the Housing and Planning Act 2016 provide the power to override easements and other rights. These provisions are largely the same as the former provisions of s 237 of the Town and Country Planning Act 1990, the purpose of which was explained by Dyson J in *R v City of London Corporation and*

15.41

Royal Mutual Insurance Society, ex parte Mystery of the Barbers (1997) 73 P & CR 59 at [64]:

> The statutory objective which underlies section 237 of the 1990 Act is that, provided that work is done in accordance with planning permission, and subject to payment of compensation, a local authority should be permitted to develop its land in the manner in which it, acting bona fide, considers will best serve the public interest. To that end, it is recognised that a local authority should be permitted to interfere with third party rights. A balance has to be struck between giving local authorities freedom to develop land held for planning purposes, and the need to protect the interests of third parties whose rights are interfered with by local authority development. Section 237(1) is the result of the balancing exercise. Parliament has decided to give local authorities the right to develop their land and to interfere with third party rights, but on the basis that work is done in accordance with planning permission (with the protection inherent in the planning process), and that third parties affected are entitled to compensation under section 237(4).

F. PLANNING AND HIGHWAYS

15.42 The development of land frequently requires the development site to be linked to an adjoining highway, or improvements to be made to the surrounding highway network. Not surprisingly, it is felt that the cost of such work should fall not on the highway authority but upon the developer. Section 278 of the Highways Act 1980, therefore, provides that if a highway authority is satisfied that it would be of benefit to the public for the authority to enter into an agreement with any person (who will normally be the developer) for the carrying out of highway works, the authority may do so on terms that that person pay the whole or part of the cost. Such agreements are independent of the system of planning obligations created under s 106 of the 1990 Act. Normally, agreements under s 278 are entered into by the Highways Agency on behalf of central government.

15.43 The discretion given to a highway authority to enter into a s 278 agreement is not unlimited. In *R v Warwickshire CC, ex p Powergen plc* [1998] JPL 131, the local planning authority for the area had refused to grant planning permission to Powergen for a supermarket on the site of a former power station. Satisfactory development would have required the widening of an existing highway and bridge over a canal, together with other minor highway works. Powergen appealed against the refusal of planning permission to the Secretary of State who, after the holding of a public local inquiry at which evidence on highway aspects had been submitted by the County Council as highway authority, decided to allow the appeal and grant outline planning permission for the development. The permission was subject, however, to a condition requiring the carrying out of prescribed highway works, including the widening of the bridge over the canal.

15.44 In order for the condition to be satisfied, Powergen then sought from the County Council as highway authority an agreement under s 278 of the Highways Act 1980, which the Council then refused to enter into on the ground that the works would not satisfactorily minimize the risk of accidents.

15.45 On an application for judicial review the High Court quashed the decision of the County Council not to enter into a s 278 agreement. Forbes J held that where the benefit to the public of the proposed highway works in respect of which a s 278 agreement had been sought, had been fully considered and determined during the planning process because the works had formed a detailed and related aspect of the application for which planning permission had been properly obtained, the highway authority's discretion to enter into the agreement was necessarily limited to matters likely to be of a relatively minor nature. Accordingly, he held that the County Council's refusal to enter into a s 278 agreement was *Wednesbury* unreasonable. That decision was then upheld by the Court of Appeal ([1998] JPL 131). According to the Court of Appeal, the County Council as highway authority had no option but to co-operate in implementing the planning permission by entering into a s 278 agreement. Accordingly, although the highway authority's 'approval or consent' was still required before the condition could be satisfied, such approval or consent could not be unreasonably withheld.

15.46 Whether approval or consent is unreasonably withheld will, of course, depend upon the particular circumstances of each case. In *R v Cardiff CC, ex p Sears Group Properties Ltd* [1998] PLSCS 92, the highway authority had not objected to development proposed subject to the developer entering into a s 278 agreement. Accordingly, the planning permission had been granted. Then, owing to local government reorganization, both the local planning authority and the highway authority had changed. The new highway authority then decided to review the traffic implications of the proposed development and decided that before completion of the s 278 agreement, the developer should submit for consideration an updated traffic impact analysis. In an unsuccessful challenge to that decision, the High Court considered that the wish of the highway authority to see whether there had been a change in circumstances since the planning permission was granted which would justify them not entering into s 278 agreement was not unreasonable in the *Wednesbury* sense. For a further discussion of s 278 of the 1980 Act and *Powergen,* see: T Graham, 'The Powergen Case and the Emperor's New Clothes' [2018] 7 JPL 741.

G. PLANNING PERMISSION AND ACTIONS IN NUISANCE

15.47 Where planning permission is given for the development of land and subsequently implemented, the question whether the use of the land amounted to an actionable nuisance is decided by reference to the neighbourhood following implementation of the permission and not as it was before implementation of the permission. In *Gillingham BC v Medway (Chatham) Dock Co Ltd* [1993] QB 343, a local authority unsuccessfully brought proceedings for a declaration and injunction that the defendants' operation of their premises around the clock as a commercial port amounted to a public nuisance because of noise and vibration from heavy vehicular traffic using residential roads leading to the port. The court held that the grant of planning permission for the use of the premises as a commercial port operating 24 hours a day changed the character of the residential area, and that the question of nuisance fell thereafter to be decided by reference to a neighbourhood with that development or use and not as it was previously.

15.48 Prior to the *Gillingham* case, it had been generally assumed that the grant of planning permission, if implemented, did not take away the rights of owners affected by the development to sue in the tort of nuisance for any loss suffered. The effect of the *Gillingham* case, however, was to call that assumption into question, particularly where the planning permission granted was for major development which had the effect of altering the character of the immediate neighbourhood. Did the decision mean that thereafter, where planning permission for development has been implemented, the question of whether it amounted to a nuisance was to be considered by reference to the character of the neighbourhood with the development; or was the decision to be interpreted to mean that no action in nuisance could be brought following the implementation of any planning permission? In *Wheeler v JJ Saunders Ltd* [1995] JPL 619, the Court of Appeal confined the implications of the *Gillingham* case to the former interpretation, in holding that where planning permission had been granted and implemented for building a row of 20 pens each of which was capable of containing 20 pigs close to a row of holiday cottages, the owner of the cottages could sue for actionable nuisance caused by smell.

15.49 In another case, *Hunter v Canary Wharf Ltd* [1996] 1 All ER 482, the Court of Appeal shed further light on the extent to which a grant of planning permission for development gives immunity from an action based on nuisance resulting from that development.

15.50 The claimants had claimed from Canary Wharf damages in nuisance for television interference caused to their homes by the presence of the Canary Wharf tower, and from the London Docklands Development Corporation, damages in nuisance resulting from dust created by the construction of link roads in the area. One of the defences raised, which was tried as a preliminary issue, was whether, once a local planning authority had balanced the interests of the community against those of individuals and granted planning permission for development, members of the community had a claim in nuisance with respect to structures built in accordance with that permission.

15.51 Even though the views expressed by the Court of Appeal were *per curiam*, the court came down firmly in favour of the view that, whilst the question of whether a nuisance exists falls to be decided by reference to the character of the neighbourhood after the development has been implemented, implementation of the permission does not in itself grant an immunity from nuisance actions. Although the case finally went to the House of Lords on appeal, the argument that a grant of planning permission should be a defence to proceedings in nuisance under existing law was not pursued.

15.52 In *Watson v Croft Promo-Sport* [2009] EWCA Civ 15 the Court of Appeal reiterated the proposition that 'planning permission as such does not affect the private law rights of third parties' but accepted that the implementation of planning permission may 'so alter the nature and character of the locality as to shift the standard of reasonable user which governs the question of nuisance or not'. The Court however refused to overturn the conclusion of the judge that the grant of planning permission for a motor circuit had not altered the nature of the locality which remained essentially rural. The Supreme Court in *Coventry v Lawrence* [2014] UKSC 13; [2014] AC 822 has now held in a case concerning speedway and stock car racing that as a general principle the benefit of a grant of planning permission would be of no assistance to a defendant in a nuisance claim. Lord Neuberger PSC stated that it would be wrong in principle that through a grant of planning permission a planning authority should be able to deprive a property owner of a right to object to what would be otherwise be a nuisance. However, it was accepted by the court that the grant of planning permission could be relevant in determining whether a nuisance had been caused. Thus, the fact that the planning authority considered that a certain noise level was acceptable after 8.30am could support a conclusion that such a noise level after that time was not a nuisance. An Act of Parliament can authorize actions which result in a nuisance and so provide a defence of statutory authority. In this regard the Planning Act 2008 grants such a defence to a nuisance claim against any development granted planning consent for 'nationally significant infrastructure projects'; see Chapter 28.

H. PLANNING PERMISSION AND ACTIONS FOR NEGLIGENCE

15.53 It would seem that no action for negligence will lie against a local planning authority as a result of a grant of planning permission to another. In *Ryeford Homes Ltd v Sevenoaks DC* [1990] JPL 36, the High Court held that in exercising its regulatory planning functions the local planning authority did not have that sufficiently special relationship or a sufficient 'proximity' to owe an individual landowner any duty of care. The correctness of that approach was reinforced by the decision of the House of Lords in *Murphy v Brentwood District Council* [1991] 1 AC 398, in relation to a local authority's exercise of its building control functions.

15.54 There have been a number of more recent cases, in some of which the courts have held local authorities liable for loss caused to others by the conduct of their officers, under the doctrine of *Hedley Byrne & Co v Heller & Partners Ltd* [1964] AC 465. In *Welton v North Cornwall DC* (CA, 17 July 1996) the court upheld an award against the Council of £34,000 damages, where the Council's environmental health officer had, in the purported exercise of his powers under public health legislation, negligently and unreasonably required the owner of a restaurant to carry out substantial alterations and modifications to his kitchen. Again, in *Lambert v West Devon BC* [1997] JPL 735, the Borough Council was held liable for negligent advice given by a building control officer to the owner of a building and then acted upon, that he could proceed to carry out work to a building, even though the owner's application to amend an existing grant of planning permission for work to the building had not yet been determined by the Borough Council. In both these cases the officers responsible for the negligent misstatements had stepped well outside the boundaries of their duties.

15.55 The difficulty in holding planning authorities liable for the negligence of their officers and servants has been underlined, however, in other recent cases. In *R v Chung Tak Lam v Borough of Torbay* [1998] PLCR 30 the Court of Appeal upheld a decision of the High Court dismissing a claim against the Borough alleging negligence, nuisance, and breach of duty in granting planning permission to a neighbour which had caused the claimants damage when the permission was implemented. It was held that no private law right of action for breach of statutory duty existed in respect of any statutory duties imposed on the Borough by the relevant statutory regimes under which their officers had acted, and that no additional claim for breach of the common law duty of care lay in the circumstances of the case.

15.56 In *Haddow v Secretary of State for the Environment* (1998) 95(7) LSG 33 the High Court dismissed a claim against the Secretary of State (and at the same time a related action against Tendring District Council), seeking damages in respect of alleged misstatements by an officer from the Department of the Environment and by an officer of the Council respectively. The claimant contended that she had received misleading advice that she should amend a planning application so that a direction made by the Secretary of State that the proposed development required environmental impact assessment could be withdrawn. In his judgment, Peter Lever QC, sitting as a Deputy Judge, quoted with approval part of the judgment of Collins J in the High Court in *Chung Tak Lam*, where he said:

> It seems to me that it would be wholly detrimental to the proper process of considering planning applications if the local authority, in addition had to have regard to the private law interests of any persons who might be affected by the grant of

permission, and to ask itself in each case whether it had properly had regard to the individual rights of those concerned. If it were potentially liable to actions in negligence in those circumstances, it seems to me that the carrying out of its important functions in the public interest would be likely to be adversely affected.

In dismissing the claim, the Deputy Judge held, inter alia, that the claimant had not shown a relationship with the Secretary of State which gave rise to a duty of care, or that the Secretary of State had assumed responsibility to her in the giving of advice, or that what his officer had said had been wrong. Likewise, he found that the officer of the Council had not assumed any responsibility to the claimant and that there had been no duty of care and so no breach of duty on his part.

15.57 The courts have not gone so far as to allow local planning authorities to shelter behind a general blanket of immunity in respect of anything done in the exercise of their planning functions. In *Kane v New Forest DC* [2001] EWCA Civ 878; [2002] 1 WLR 312, the Court of Appeal held that the authority owed a duty of care to a pedestrian injured following the negligent construction of a footpath which emerged onto the highway at a dangerous place. In subsequent proceedings, the authority was held to be in breach of that duty. For a further discussion of the *Kane* case see: A Samuels, 'Is the Local Planning Authority Liable for a Defective Design?' [2003] 12 JPL 1514.

I. PLANNING PERMISSION AND ACTIONS IN DECEIT

15.58 In dealing with all matters, a local planning authority should act with integrity and even-handedness. Any failure to do this may make the authority liable in damages in an action based on the tort of deceit, as indeed happened in *Slough Estates plc v Welwyn Hatfield DC* [1996] 2 PLR 50.

15.59 The case concerned two major shopping centres. One was called the Howard Centre and was built by the claimant, Slough Estates, in Welwyn Garden City. The other, called A1 Gallerias, was located only a mile away from the Howard Centre and was built on land in respect of which the defendant council were head-leaseholders.

15.60 In response to concern expressed by Slough Estates that the area did not have the capacity to support two retail developments, the Council agreed that in order to reduce competition which would affect the Howard Centre, it would enforce a 'tenant mix agreement' made with the developers of A1 Gallerias whereby the occupants of that centre would be restricted to 'leisure' retailing.

15.61 Subsequently, however, the Council resolved not to enforce the terms of the tenant mix agreement; but it failed to inform Slough Estates that it had done so, with the result that Slough Estates continued with its construction of the Howard Centre. Worse still, the Council decided to keep the decision to relax enforcement of the terms of the tenant mix agreement to itself and to pretend to other parties, including particularly Slough Estates, that the agreement was still in force and that it was their intention to enforce it.

In the words of May J:

> From July 1987 [the council] were nursing a lie and had set themselves a time bomb.... Thereafter there was a policy to tell lies about the tenant mix agreement if it was necessary to do so. The lies were watered down wherever possible, but they were conscious lies.

15.62 May J proceeded to find for the claimants and to award them agreed damages believed to be £29.75m against the Council in respect of the loss the company had suffered as a result of the Council's deceit.

J. LIFE OF A PLANNING PERMISSION

15.63 Once granted, planning permission will continue in force until one of the following events deprives it of its effectiveness:

(a) Where the development authorized by the permission has been carried out and completed. Here the permission is spent. The benefit of the permission has been accepted and the development which has been carried out in accordance with the terms of the permission becomes part of the existing use rights in the land. Where a personal planning permission has been granted, the benefit of the permission will cease on the death of the person concerned.

(b) Where planning permission has been granted subject to a condition imposed under ss 91 and 92 of the 1990 Act requiring development to be begun within a specified period, and the development has not been begun within that period, development carried out after the end of that period is to be treated as not authorized by the permission.

(c) Where planning permission is revoked under s 97 of the 1990 Act. This provision empowers a local planning authority to revoke or modify any planning permission to develop land granted on an application under Part III of the Act at any time in the case of permission for the carrying out of building or other operations, before the operations are completed and, in the case of permission for a change of use, before the change of use has taken place. The revocation or modification, however, will not affect any building or other operations carried out before the coming into force of the revocation or modification order. Unless an order is unopposed it will not come into effect until confirmed by the Secretary of State. The revocation or modification of a planning permission entitles any person interested in the land to claim compensation from the local planning authority under s 107 of the 1990 Act for any expenditure, loss, or damage incurred in carrying out work rendered abortive by the revocation or modification, and any other loss or damage sustained which is directly attributable to the revocation or modification. In calculating the latter head of claim, the value of any other planning permission granted or likely to be granted for the development of the land must be taken into account. The willingness of the local planning authority, therefore, to grant an alternative permission to the one to be revoked or modified will reduce the compensation payable and may, at the same time, lead to the order being unopposed.

Where the development permitted by a planning permission has been carried out and completed, the local planning authority cannot serve a revocation or modification order. Under s 100 of the 1990 Act, however, the authority can require that any use of land should be discontinued, or that conditions should be imposed on the continuance of a use of land, or that any buildings or works should be altered or removed. Any such discontinuance order is required to be confirmed by the Secretary of State. As with revocation or modification orders, compensation must be paid to any person who has suffered damage in consequence of the order under s 115 of the 1990 Act.

(d) Every planning permission for the winning and working of minerals or the deposit of mineral waste is made subject to a condition limiting the duration of the permission to 60 years (Sch 5(1) to the 1990 Act).

(e) Where more than one planning permission has been granted in respect of land, and the carrying out of the development authorized by one permission makes it impossible to carry out the development authorized by another. This may extend beyond cases where the implementation of the planning permission makes it physically impossible to implement another. In *Pilkington v Secretary of State for the Environment* [1973] 1 WLR 1527 the owner of land was granted planning permission to build a bungalow on part of the land, site B. It was a condition of the permission that the bungalow should be the only house to be built on the land. He built the bungalow. Later the owner discovered the existence of an earlier permission to build a bungalow and garage on another part of the same land, site A. That permission contemplated the use of the rest of the land as a smallholding. He began to build the second bungalow and was then served with an enforcement notice alleging a breach of planning control. The Divisional Court held that the two permissions could not stand in respect of the same land, once the development sanctioned by the second permission had been carried out. The effect of building on site B was to make the development authorized in the earlier permission incapable of implementation. The bungalow built on site B had destroyed the smallholding: and the erection of two bungalows on the site had never been sanctioned.

15.64 In *Pioneer Aggregates (UK) Ltd v Secretary of State for the Environment* [1985] AC 132, Lord Scarman thought the *Pilkington* decision was a common-sense decision and correct in law.

15.65 Mere incompatibility of the planning permission with another planning permission already implemented may thus invalidate it. It may of course also arise where, because once one planning permission has been implemented, it is physically impossible to implement the other.

15.66 The decision in the *Pilkington* case was also considered and followed by the Court of Appeal in *Staffordshire CC v NGR Land Developments Limited and Roberts* [2003] JPL 56.

15.67 It should be noted that although existing use rights may be abandoned, it is not possible to abandon a planning permission. In *Pioneer Aggregates (UK) Ltd v Secretary of State for the Environment* [1985] AC 132, the respondent company, after a long period of non-user, had resumed the use of land for mining operations. The local planning authority alleged that the resumption constituted development and served an enforcement notice on the company requiring the use to be discontinued. The issue reached the House of Lords which held that there was no general rule of law that a planning permission which is capable of being implemented according to its terms can be abandoned. Their Lordships thought that the clear implication of what is now s 75(1) of the 1990 Act was that only the statute or the terms of the permission itself could stop the permission enduring for the benefit of the land and for all persons for the time being interested therein.

15.68 The principle that a valid permission capable of implementation could not be abandoned by the conduct of the owner or occupier was followed in *Camden LBC v McDonald's Restaurants Ltd* (1992) 65 P & CR 423. The case concerned property used as a restaurant between 1972 and 1987. In December 1987 the Secretary of State had granted planning permission for a single storey rear extension which had never been implemented. Between 1987 and 1991 when McDonald's had taken a lease of the premises, the property had either remained vacant or been used as a bookshop. When McDonald's sought to implement the permission to build the extension, the local planning authority maintained that the permission had lapsed. In granting declarations that the planning permission for the extension was valid and subsisting and that the ground floor of the premises could lawfully be used for restaurant purposes, the Court of Appeal held that one had to 'look back at the permission ... and see whether in fact the development there contemplated can now be carried out'. Here the premises were still in existence and it remained physically possible to build the extension.

15.69 The authority had also claimed that the use of the premises as a bookshop fell within Class A1 of the Use Classes Order and that it would not be lawful to change the use of the premises back from A1 to A3 without planning permission. The court held, however, that the permission for the extension was for operational development, not a grant of permission for a material change of use.

16

DEVELOPMENT BY THE CROWN, STATUTORY UNDERTAKERS, AND LOCAL AUTHORITIES; PUBLIC WORKS ORDERS

| A. THE CROWN | 16.01 | C. LOCAL AUTHORITIES | 16.10 |
| B. STATUTORY UNDERTAKERS | 16.05 | D. PUBLIC WORKS ORDERS | 16.30 |

A. THE CROWN

16.01 For many years planning legislation did not bind the Crown. This resulted from the application of a fundamental principle of the constitution that the Crown was not bound by statute unless expressly stated to be so, or bound by necessary implication.

16.02 In June 1992 the Government decided, as part of a policy outlined in the Citizen's Charter, progressively to remove any immunities which sheltered departments and Crown bodies from regulations, inspection, and enforcement requirements placed on others and to bring to an end the exemptions now granted to the Crown under planning legislation. This has now been done by the provisions of Part 7 of the Planning and Compulsory Purchase Act 2004, so that subject to a number of important modifications, from 7 June 2006 the Planning Acts now bind the Crown. The Planning Acts are the Town and Country Planning Act 1990, the Planning (Listed Building and Conservation Areas) Act 1990, and the Planning (Hazardous Substances) Act 1990. The modifications to a number of provisions in the Planning Acts are intended to take account of the unique character of the Crown.

16.03 Fuller details of these changes to the law are to be found in Circular 02/2006, 'Crown Applications of the Planning Acts' issued by the Department for Communities and Local Government.

16.04 Almost every area of planning law has been affected as a result of making the Planning Acts apply to the Crown. The changes which have been brought into force by a mass of subordinate legislation are too numerous to include most of them within the context of this book. The main areas of planning law which have been modified to meet the special needs of the Crown are concerned with national security, enforcement, and permitted development rights and use Classes.

(a) *National security*

The Planning Acts provide that planning inquiries should normally be held in public. In this way, oral and documentary evidence can be heard or seen by those attending the inquiry. These provisions, however, are now to be modified in cases where the public disclosure of information would relate to national security or to the security of any premises or property, and the disclosure of this information would be contrary to the national interest. In such cases it is provided that the Attorney-General may appoint a person to represent the interests of those who would be prevented from being able to hear or inspect such material. Where that is done, the Secretary of State may require the person or persons prevented from seeing the sensitive material to pay the fees and expenses of the person appointed by the Secretary of State.

(b) *Urgent Crown development*

Where the appropriate authority certifies that the development is of national importance, and that it is necessary that the development is carried out as a matter of urgency, the appropriate authority may, instead of making an application for planning permission to the local planning authority, make it instead to the Secretary of State. Where the appropriate authority proposes to take this course, it must publish in one or more newspapers circulating in the locality of the proposed development a notice describing the proposed development and stating its intention to make an application to the Secretary of State. The appropriate authority must also provide the Secretary of State with all necessary documentation, including if required, an environmental statement.

The Secretary of State may then require the authority to provide further information; make documents or other material available for inspection by the public and publish a notice to that effect; and consult the local planning authority and such other persons as are specified in a development order. Thereafter, the application is in effect treated as if it were a called in application. Furthermore, to speed up the decision-making process, the Inquiry Procedure Rules have been amended to shorten the time periods for the raising of various procedures required by the rules.

(c) *Enforcement*

Although the Crown may be subject to enforcement action, the Act provides that it should remain immune from prosecution for any offence under the Planning Acts. However, a local planning authority, before taking any step for the purposes of enforcement in relation to Crown land must first obtain the consent of the appropriate authority for the purpose of enforcement. These steps include entering land; bringing proceedings; and the making of an application, but not the service of a notice or the making of an order (other than a court order).

(d) *Trees: enforcement*
Parallel to the other provisions of the Planning and Compulsory Purchase Act 2004 which made the Crown subject to the Planning Acts, the Act amends the 1990 Act to prohibit the Crown from doing any act to a tree in a conservation area which might be prohibited by a tree preservation order, unless it serves notice of its intention to do so on the local planning authority and either the authority consents, or if the authority has not responded within six weeks, and it carries out the work between six weeks and two years from the date of the notice.

(e) *Old mining permissions*
The Planning and Compulsory Purchase Act 2004 modifies s 22 and Sch 2 to the Planning and Compensation Act 1991 to allow Crown bodies holding old mining permissions (ie, those granted between 1943 and 1948) the opportunity to register such permissions and apply for the determination of new conditions on the same terms as applied to other old mining permissions.

B. STATUTORY UNDERTAKERS

16.05 The expression 'statutory undertakers' is defined in s 262(1) of the 1990 Act to mean:

> persons authorised by any enactment to carry on any railway, light railway, tramway, road transport, water transport, canal, inland navigation, dock, harbour, pier or lighthouse undertaking or any undertaking for the supply of hydraulic power and a relevant airport operator ...

16.06 In addition, for the purposes of some of the Act's provisions, the term may be deemed to include other bodies such as the Civil Aviation Authority, postal service providers, telecommunications operators, public gas transporters, and water and sewerage undertakers.

16.07 Statutory undertakers wishing to develop land must normally apply for planning permission to do so to the local planning authority. Modifications to the normal procedures are made in relation to applications for the development of 'operational land' of such bodies.

16.08 Operational land in relation to statutory undertakers is defined in s 263 of the 1990 Act to mean:

(a) land which is used for the purpose of carrying on their undertaking; and
(b) land in which an interest is held for that purpose.

One important modification to planning procedures is that where an application for planning permission for the development of operational land comes before the Secretary of State, as with an appeal against an adverse decision by the local planning authority or because the application has been called in under s 77 of the 1990 Act, the Secretary of State is required to act in relation to the appeal or called-in decision jointly with the appropriate Minister; that is, the Minister responsible for the operations of the particular statutory undertaker.

16.09 Apart from this modification, planning permission for certain development of statutory undertakers is granted under various Classes of the General Permitted Development Order. Much of that permitted development is extensive in character. In other cases, legislation requires development by statutory undertakers to be authorized by a government department. In such cases, s 90(1) of the 1990 Act provides that the department concerned may, in granting that authorization, direct that planning permission for the development shall be deemed to be granted, subject to such conditions as may be specified. The value of this procedure is that it enables the authorizing department to consider all matters relating to the proposed development at the same time, many of which may not be related to the land-use matters, such as the significance of the proposed development to the strategic functions and responsibilities of the industry concerned.

C. LOCAL AUTHORITIES

16.10 Local authorities, like statutory undertakers, need to obtain planning permission for any development they propose to carry out. As with statutory undertakers, certain development by local authorities is permitted development under the various classes of the General Permitted Development Order. Furthermore, where other legislation requires development by a local authority to be authorized by a government department, s 90(1) of the 1990 Act provides that the department concerned may, in granting the authorization, direct that planning permission for the development be deemed to be granted.

16.11 There are other special provisions, however, which apply to other development. Section 316 of the 1990 Act empowers the Secretary of State to make regulations governing development of land of 'interested planning authorities' and the development of any land by interested planning authorities jointly with any other persons. The current regulations are the Town and Country Planning General Regulations 1992, SI 1992/1492. The Regulations revoke and replace regulations made in 1976 which had been subject to much criticism.

16.12 Section 316(6) defines an 'interested planning authority' in relation to any land as meaning 'any body which exercises any of the functions of a local planning authority in relation to that land; and for the purposes of this section land is land of an authority if the authority has an interest in it'. In short, the term will embrace any body acting as a local planning authority, such as a county planning authority with regard to a county matter, or any other authority such as an urban development corporation to which planning powers have been transferred.

16.13 The requirements of the Town and Country Planning General Regulations have always been regarded as fundamental and strict, and a failure to comply with them has been regarded by the courts as fatal. Many of the cases, whilst still relevant to the current statutory provisions, turn on the interpretation of the old 1976 Regulations and the provisions of the 1990 Act, before amendments were made to that Act by the Planning and Compensation Act 1991. In *Steeples v Derbyshire County Council* [1985] 1 WLR 256, Webster J held that the failure to place notices in the planning register as required by the Regulations rendered the deemed grant of planning permission ultra vires and void. In *R v Lambeth LBC, ex p Sharp* [1987] JPL 440 (CA), the authority proposed to construct a floodlit synthetic athletics track with seats for 1,100 spectators in some six acres of parkland. Among a number of irregularities committed by the authority in the process of obtaining deemed planning permission for the development was a failure in a newspaper advertisement required by the Regulations to specify the period within which objections to the proposed development should be made to the authority. Croom-Johnson LJ granted *certiorari* to quash the deemed grant of permission. Unanimously upholding that decision, the Court of Appeal held that the breach of the Regulations had been fundamental.

16.14 A few months later in the High Court in *R v Doncaster MDC, ex p British Railways Board* [1987] JPL 444, Schiemann J followed the approach of the Court of Appeal in the *Lambeth* case and quashed a resolution of the authority to carry out development involving the building of a superstore in the town centre, in the light of a host of irregularities in the procedures followed by the authority.

16.15 The process by which authorities were in effect able to grant planning permission to themselves has been subject to much criticism. In this area local planning authorities were seen by many to be partial to their own development proposals. The stakes are high, since the value of a grant of planning permission can be considerable. This is particularly so where development proposals were made for under-used, county council-owned playing fields. Until the law was changed by the Planning and Compensation Act 1991, such development proposals were determined not by the district council as local planning authority for their area but by the county council as the owner of the playing fields.

16.16 The problem however was best seen with regard to the growth in the desire for superstores and hypermarkets. Although it is no part of the planning system to protect commercial interests from competition, the effect of such development on shopping outlets in existing town centres is something which must be taken into account in deciding whether they should be allowed. The problem becomes acute in cases where there are a number of proposals for superstore development in the same area, since the greater the number, the greater the impact on the existing centre.

16.17 Frequently because of this impact, there could be general agreement between authorities and developers that the number of superstores in any area should be limited. When this was followed by a number of applications for such development by different developers, the question of which one was to be preferred has often posed a difficult decision for the authority. To meet this difficulty, a local planning authority might fail to issue a decision within the prescribed period for doing so, in the hope that at least one of the applicants would appeal to the Secretary of State against the non-determination of the application, and that other applications not determined would be called in by the Secretary of State. It is he who would then make the decision, after holding a composite local inquiry into all the applications and the question of bias would not arise.

16.18 The main difficulty arose, however, when one of the proposed sites for this development was on land in which the local planning authority had an interest. Inevitably if an authority dealt with the application in which it had an interest for planning permission and proceeded to grant planning permission for the development it would be difficult for the authority to avoid a suggestion of bias.

16.19 The test of bias originally applied by the courts was whether a reasonable man would consider that there was a real likelihood of bias. However, the correct test to be applied in judging an authority's actions was outlined in *R v Sevenoaks DC, ex p Terry* [1985] 3 All ER 226. In that case, the Council as local planning authority had granted planning permission to a company called Fraser Wood Properties in respect of a site known as the Old Post Office Yard for the purpose, inter alia, of erecting a supermarket. The Council had, on an earlier date, approved a recommendation that an offer by Fraser Wood to purchase a lease of the site should be accepted and the officers were authorized to take all necessary action. The formal agreement between the Council and Fraser Wood was not entered into until after the date on which planning permission was granted. In an application for judicial review of the Council's decision, the applicant contended that the planning permission was void on the grounds that the Council had fettered the discretion of the planning committee and further, or alternatively, that the Council gave to reasonable people the appearance that they regarded themselves as committed to the development.

16.20 Dismissing the application, Glidewell J said in relation to these situations:

> ... but it is not uncommon for a local authority to be obliged to make a decision relating to land or other property in which it had an interest. In such a situation, the application of the rule designed to ensure that a judicial officer does not appear to be biased would, in my view, often produce an administrative impasse. In my judgment, the correct test to be applied in the present case is for the court to pose to itself

the question: had the district council before 5 January 1982 acted in such a way that it is clear that, when the committee came to consider Fraser Wood's application for planning permission, it could not exercise proper discretion? ... if the answer to the question is No, it is in my judgment neither necessary nor desirable for the court to go further and consider what the opinion of a reasonable man would be.

16.21 The issue again arose for determination in the Queen's Bench Division in *R v St Edmundsbury BC, ex p Investors in Industry Commercial Properties Ltd* [1985] 1 WLR 1168 (Div Court). There the Council's planning committee had granted outline planning permission to J Sainsbury plc for the erection of a supermarket on land owned by the Council. The applicants for relief had applied for judicial review to quash the Council's decision. The circumstances which gave rise to their application were that at the meeting at which the committee had considered the matter, the committee had before it seven applications for supermarkets in respect of six sites, one of which was made on the applicants' behalf. Each of the applications was refused, save for that made by Sainsbury's for a supermarket on land owned by the Council, who had entered into a contract to sell a 125-year lease of the site to Sainsbury's in the event of planning permission being obtained. The applicants contended that the Council had thereby fettered itself from proper exercise of its discretion and that the decision in favour of Sainsbury's had given rise to the inference of bias.

16.22 Refusing the application and applying the dictum of Glidewell J in *R v Sevenoaks DC, ex p Terry*, Stocker J held that the test of what a hypothetical reasonable man would apprehend had no application in determining the validity of an administrative decision such as the grant of planning permission. The sole test was whether, despite its interests or its previous actions, the planning authority genuinely and impartially exercised its discretion, since there were many cases in which a local authority's own interests and land were likely to be affected by a favourable planning decision made by it. Accordingly, once a planning authority's decision was found or conceded to be fair there was no requirement to pose some further test by which the decision might be impugned as unlawful or void, either by reference to what the reasonable man would suspect or by reference to whether viewed through some other eyes, such as those of the judge, there was a real likelihood of bias.

16.23 However the position is different when a member of the planning committee or an officer has a personal interest in the outcome, as opposed to the planning authority having a particular policy. In this regard it is important to distinguish between the situation where there has been a predetermination of the application because of an inflexible policy and a case of bias. The legal test for bias has now been laid down in a non-planning case by the House of Lords in *Porter v Magill* [2002] 2 AC 257, where Lord Hope of Craighead said: 'The question is whether the fair-minded and informed observer, having considered the facts, would conclude that there was a real possibility that the tribunal was biased.'

16.24 The test was applied by Richards LJ in a planning context in *Georgiou v Enfield LBC* [2004] LGR 497 where he thought it was necessary to consider, 'Whether, from the point of view of the fair-minded and informed observer, there was a real possibility of bias in the sense of approaching the decision with a closed mind and without impartial consideration of all relevant planning issues'.

16.25 New procedures introduced in 1992, were intended to alleviate the disquiet caused by the operation of the old statutory provisions. The main features of the Regulations are as follows.

(a) A local planning authority must make an application to itself for planning permission to develop land within its area. Local planning authorities can therefore continue to grant themselves planning permission for development carried out by them, such as schools or local authority housing, and will also be able to grant themselves permission for development undertaken jointly with another person, such as a joint venture with a housing association where the authority's interest is significant. Circular 19/92 suggests that the authority's level of financial commitment could be a useful test of whether the interest is significant or not. If, however, the permission is personal to the authority, the permission will not survive if the land is sold on for private development.

(b) For development proposed to be carried out on local authority owned land by other parties, planning permission now has to be sought from the responsible development control authority (thus a county council which is, for example, seeking to dispose of land with planning permission has to apply to the district council, unless the development is a 'county matter'; and the district council has to apply to the county council for development which is a 'county matter').

(c) Local planning authorities which now have to make a planning application to themselves or to another local planning authority will be subject to broadly the same statutory procedures as other applicants.

(d) Applications are required to be publicized as prescribed by a development order in the same way as applications from the public.

(e) In order to avoid a conflict of interest, reg 10 provides that:

> Notwithstanding anything in s 101 of the Local Government Act 1972 (arrangements for the discharge of functions by local authorities), no application for planning permission for development may be determined
> (a) by a committee or sub-committee of the interested planning authority concerned if that committee or sub-committee is responsible (wholly or partly) for the management of any land or buildings to which the application relates; or
> (b) by an officer of the interested planning authority concerned if his responsibilities include any aspect of the management of any land or buildings to which the application relates.

The effect of this regulation is that where there is a conflict of interest, the decision may only be made by the full council.

(f) An important amendment to the general rule, however, was made in the Town and Country Planning General (Amendment) Regulations 1998. Generally, planning permission enures for the benefit of the land. Regulation 9 of the Town and Country Planning General Regulations 1992 provide that where a planning authority grants itself planning permission for its own development, the permission enures only for the benefit of the authority or, in the case of joint development, the authority and any other person specified in the application for planning permission as the joint developer. The effect of the amendment is to exclude from the ambit of reg 9 those planning authorities which are the sole local authority for their area, so that they may grant themselves permission which enures for the benefit of the land.

In England, the councils in question are a district council in an area where there is no county council; a county council in an area where there is no district council; and a council of a London borough.

16.26 Despite these new provisions, allegations of bias continue to be made. An example, but one in which the allegations were not established, is to be found in *R v Canterbury CC, ex p Springimage Ltd* [1995] JPL 20, where the court applied the test set out in *R v Sevenoaks DC, ex p Terry*.

16.27 Allegations of bias may arise also not from the authority's ownership of land proposed to be developed, but from the position of members of the authority responsible for making decisions. In *R v Secretary of State for the Environment, ex p Kirkstall Valley Campaign* [1996] 3 All ER 304, an urban development corporation had granted planning permission for retail development of land belonging to a rugby club. It was claimed that because of the private interests of three members of the Council and an officer of the Council in the decision taken, it was tainted by bias. In an application for judicial review to quash the decision to grant planning permission, the High Court held that the principle that a person was disqualified from participating in a decision if there was a real danger that he would be influenced by a pecuniary or personal interest in the outcome was of general application and not limited to judicial or quasi-judicial bodies or proceedings. Where members had an interest, it had to be declared and the member concerned could not participate in the decision unless it was remote or insignificant. In this case, the court refused to grant judicial review of the decision on the ground that the personal interest of members had either disappeared by the time the decision was made, or that it was too remote.

16.28 Difficult problems arise with the application of the test for bias set down in *Porter v Magill*. Members of a planning committee are entitled and expected to have views on planning issues and are more than likely to have expressed them. It is acknowledged therefore, that one has to accept the need to be 'cognizant of the practicalities of local government'. The test set out in the Court of Appeal in *Persimmon Homes Teeside Ltd v R (on the application of Lewis)* [2008] EWCA Civ

746 is whether committee members have made the decision with closed minds, or that the circumstances in which they made it give rise to such a real risk of closed minds, that the decision ought not in the public interest be upheld.

16.29 However s 25 of the Localism Act 2011 (the 2011 Act) has changed the law on 'predetermination' by making it clear that if a councillor has given a view on an issue, this does not show that the councillor has a closed mind on that issue, so that if a councillor has campaigned on an issue or made public statements about their approach to an item of council business, he or she will be able to participate in discussion of that issue in the council and to vote on it if it arises in an item of council business requiring a decision. Quite apart from the possibility of judicial challenge, individual councillors were also subject to compliance with the Model Code of Conduct set out by the Secretary of State under the provisions of Part 3 of the Local Government Act 2002 and could be subject to complaints to the Standards Board for England, which had the power to disqualify the member concerned, to suspend them from office (or from a particular role in the Council), or to reprimand them. Chapter 5 of the 2011 Act has provided for the abolition of the Standards Board and Model Code of Conduct. It has been replaced by a statutory duty to promote and maintain high standards of conduct and a power for authorities to adopt voluntary codes of conduct. The new Act also provides for the establishment and maintenance of a register of members' and co-opted members' interests. It is a criminal offence to fail, without reasonable excuse, to comply with obligations imposed by regulations to register or declare personal interests, or to take part in council business when prevented from so doing by such regulations.

D. PUBLIC WORKS ORDERS

16.30 Until 1992, a private Act of Parliament was the normal method used to obtain powers to construct public works such as the provision of railways, tramways, inland waterways, ports, and harbours. Such Acts would often be required because of the need for the promoters of the development to obtain powers to compulsorily acquire the land on which the development was to take place; to obtain immunity from actions in nuisance or other torts which would otherwise be available to those affected by the development; and to extinguish public or private rights of way likely to be interfered with by the development.

16.31 As far as development control was concerned, under subordinate legislation where the Act specifically designated the nature of the development and the land upon which it was to be carried out, the development was 'permitted' under the Order. Hence the private Act procedure was in effect determining questions of development control, without the promoters of that development being required to obtain express planning permission from the local planning authority or Secretary of State.

16.32 During the 1980s, the procedures for obtaining these powers came to be increasingly criticized. An increase in the number of schemes being proposed led to considerable pressure on parliamentary time. In addition, it was felt that the procedures themselves were archaic and not the most suitable way of examining effectively this kind of proposal. In particular, the process ignored the development of the planning inquiry system and the role it played in assessing the impact of major proposals which involved the development of land.

16.33 In 1992, following a report of the Joint Committee on Private Bill Procedure, the Government introduced in Part I of the Transport and Works Act 1992 ('the 1992 Act'), an entirely new procedure allowing the Secretary of State to make orders for the authorization of transport and other works and the making of related provisions.

16.34 Under s 1 of the 1992 Act the Secretary of State is given power to make orders relating to the construction or operation of railway; tramway; trolley vehicle system; or a system using a mode of guided transport prescribed by order made by the Secretary of State under s 2 of the Act. Guided transport systems currently prescribed under s 2 include aerial cableway; lift; magnetic levitation; monorail; road-based with cable or rail guidance; road-based with side guidance and track-based with side guidance.

16.35 In addition, under s 3 of the 1992 Act the Secretary of State is given power to make orders relating to the construction or operation of inland waterways and the carrying out of prescribed works which interfere with rights of navigation in inland and territorial waters.

The content of Works Orders

16.36 Works Orders contain provisions very similar to those previously found in private Acts of Parliament. Section 5 of the 1992 Act, together with Sch 1, provides that they may include provisions such as the application, modification, or exclusion of other statutory provisions: the carrying out of civil engineering or other works; the acquisition of land, whether by compulsion or agreement; the creation and extinguishment of rights over land; the abrogation and modification of agreements relating to land; the protection of the property or interests of any person; the charging of tolls, fares, and other charges; the making of bye-laws and their enforcement; the payment of rates; the submission of disputes to arbitration; and the imposition of requirements to obtain the consent of the Secretary of State.

16.37 Although a Works Order will not in itself grant planning permission for any development involved in implementing the proposals, planning permission may be deemed to be granted by the Secretary of State at the time of making the Order; likewise, the Order may also have effect to grant consent to the compulsory purchase of land and to consent required under the Planning (Hazardous Substances) Act 1990.

The procedure for applying for a Works Order

16.38 Any body with power to promote or oppose Bills in Parliament has the power to apply for a Works Order. This includes private individuals as well as corporations. Under s 7 of the 1992 Act, applications must be made in accordance with rules made by the Secretary of State. The present rules are the Transport and Works (Applications and Objections Procedure) (England and Wales) Rules 2006, SI 2006/1466 and provide for the submission of a draft Order with the application, a memorandum explaining the powers sought, a statement as to the status of the applicant, an affidavit stating that the prior consultation and notification procedure required by rules have been followed, a list of consents, permission, or licences which have been sought, the appropriate fee, an environmental statement similar to that required by the Town and Country Planning (Environmental Impact Assessment) Regulations 2011, plans etc, of the proposed works, particulars of how the works are to be funded, and an estimate of the length of time the works are expected to take. The applicant must also state whether he seeks a decision from the Secretary of State that planning permission should be deemed to be granted for any development proposed.

16.39 Provision is also made under s 10 for allowing objections to be made to a draft Order. Under s 11, the Secretary of State may hold a public inquiry for the purposes of an application for a Works Order. The Transport and Works (Inquiry Procedure) Rules 1992, SI 1992/2817 prescribe the procedure to be followed in connection with public local inquiries held under s 11 of the Act. The Secretary of State is indeed obliged to hold such an inquiry if objections to the Order are received from statutory objectors such as local authorities, or landowners whose land is proposed to be acquired. Otherwise, objectors may have to be content with the opportunity to appear before and be heard by a person appointed by the Secretary of State by way of a hearing.

Schemes of national significance

16.40 Although for most Works Orders, parliamentary approval will not be required for the proposals contained in them, it is otherwise where, in the opinion of the Secretary of State, the application relates to proposals which are of national significance. Under s 9 of the 1992 Act, such proposals must be approved by both Houses of Parliament.

16.41 Where the Secretary of State takes the view that a proposal in an application for a Works Order is of national significance, he would normally place a motion before Parliament asking for approval of the proposal before any public local inquiry is held into objections. The purpose of this process is that it enables Parliament to decide at an early stage whether it wishes to endorse the need for the project, leaving questions of detail to be dealt with at the inquiry. The Secretary of State has a residual power, however, to refer a proposal in a Works Order back to

Parliament for further consideration after the holding of a public local inquiry so that any earlier resolution by Parliament may be modified before the Order is made by him.

So far it is believed that few proposals in applications for a Works Order have been subject to the s 9 process. In July 1996 it was used in connection with the Central Railway Works Order. That order contained proposals for the construction of a railway between Leicester and the Channel Tunnel via Rugby on a dismantled railway alignment to link with the existing Chiltern line, and then on to Olympia in London and Ashford and Folkestone. **16.42**

The 'draft' Order contained powers for Central Railway to build and operate the railway and terminals, to acquire land compulsorily, to create new accesses to motorways and other roads, and temporarily or permanently to stop up or divert streets and footpaths. The draft Order also sought to disapply parts of public general legislation, including the regulating regime for licensing and track access in the Railways Act 1993. **16.43**

The motion to approve, brought first in the House of Commons, was rejected by 172 votes to seven. If the draft Order had been approved by both Houses, the proposals would then have been considered at a public inquiry, with the final decision on whether to approve the Order then being made by the Secretary of State. **16.44**

Throughout the proceedings the Government maintained a neutral stance, unwilling to either support or damn the proposals. According to the Minister for Railways and Roads, for the Government to support such a scheme, 'they would need to be persuaded that the merits of the proposal were so overwhelming as to justify unequivocal support'. Without Government support, therefore, any scheme of national significance is unlikely to receive parliamentary approval and thus proceed further. **16.45**

Planning permission

Quite apart from the s 9 process, where any proposals in a Works Order involve the development of land, planning permission must of course be obtained before these proposals can be implemented. Applicants for a Works Order may decide to seek express planning permission from the local planning authority. Given the scale and nature of proposals contained in a Works Order, however, it is much more likely that applicants for an Order will seek the involvement of the Secretary of State. **16.46**

The power of the Secretary of State to grant planning permission for any development involved in the implementation of proposals in an Order is contained in subsection (2A) of s 90 of the 1990 Act which provides: **16.47**

> On making an order under sections 1 or 3 of the Transport and Works Act 1992 which includes provision for development the Secretary of State may direct that

planning permission for that development shall be deemed to be granted, subject to such conditions (if any) as may be specified in the direction.

16.48 This power of the Secretary of State to grant 'deemed' planning permission when making a Works Order is facilitated by a provision in the regulation for the making of an application for a Works Order requiring the applicant to state if he wishes the Secretary of State to grant deemed planning permission for development proposed in the Order. He must also identify in the application any matters which he is content should be reserved for subsequent approval by the local planning authority.

16.49 Although the power contained in subsection (2A) above is expressed in permissive terms and the Secretary of State may in theory withhold deemed planning permission when making an Order, it is inconceivable that he would do so given the importance of the planning issues to most applications for a Works Order. Indeed, during the debate on the 1992 Act in the House of Commons, an unqualified assurance was given on behalf of the Secretary of State that where an application for planning permission was sought as part of the Order, the Secretary of State would determine the Works Order and the deemed planning permission at the same time.

16.50 It should be noted, however, that the Secretary of State's power to grant planning permission under s 90(2A) of the 1990 Act does not circumvent the need to obtain listed building consent where the development proposed will affect a listed building.

16.51 Another method of providing for development of national importance is by use of hybrid Bill procedure. Such Bills are usually introduced in Parliament by the government of the day. They have both a private and a public aspect in that their provisions affect particular classes of people as well as others generally. Hence parliamentary procedure requires the Bill to comply with elements of the procedures for private Bills, as well as complying with the usual provisions for public Bills. This method of legislation is not in fact often used and, as explained in Chapter 28, there are now other controls regarding the need for consents to major projects.

17

PLANNING AGREEMENTS; PLANNING OBLIGATIONS; AND THE COMMUNITY INFRASTRUCTURE LEVY

A. INTRODUCTION AND ENABLING POWERS	17.01	F. APPEALS	17.37
B. PLANNING OBLIGATIONS	17.17	G. AMENDMENT OF PLANNING OBLIGATIONS	17.39
C. PLANNING OBLIGATIONS (THE DETAILED REGIME)	17.21	H. THE SECRETARY OF STATE'S POLICY	17.40
D. CREATION OF PLANNING OBLIGATIONS	17.25	I. REFORMING PLANNING CONTRIBUTIONS	17.60
E. MODIFICATION AND DISCHARGE OF PLANNING OBLIGATIONS	17.32	J. THE COMMUNITY INFRASTRUCTURE LEVY	17.63

A. INTRODUCTION AND ENABLING POWERS

Planning obligations are a development from the power first given to local planning authorities by s 34 of the Town and Country Planning Act 1932 to enter into planning agreements with landowners for regulating the development or use of their land. From that Act, the power found its way into the Town and Country Planning Act 1947; and thence into the Town and Country Planning Act 1971 as s 52. On the consolidation of planning legislation in 1990, s 52 of the 1971 Act was replaced by s 106 of the Town and Country Planning Act 1990 as the new statutory authority for the power to enter into planning agreements. Now, following the passing of the Planning and Compensation Act 1991, the original s 106 of the 1990 Act has been replaced in its entirety by new ss 106, 106A, and 106B which have been inserted into the 1990 Act in its place. The replacement sections also introduced new arrangements and new terminology. From 25 October 1991, the power to enter into a 'planning agreement' under the 1990 Act was repealed and replaced by the power to enter into a 'planning obligation'.

17.01

17.02 It should be emphasized that the current statutory provisions relating to planning obligations do not affect planning agreements entered into under either s 52 of the Town and Country Planning Act 1971, or the original s 106 of the 1990 Act (now repealed). These agreements may continue to play a part in regulating the use and development of land.

17.03 Section 52 of the 1971 Act and the original s 106 of the 1990 Act provided that a local planning authority could enter into an agreement with any person interested in land in its area for the purpose of restricting or regulating the development or use of the land, either permanently or during such period as may be prescribed by the agreement. It further provided that an agreement made under this section with any person interested in land could be enforced by the local planning authority against persons deriving title under that person in respect of that land as if the local planning authority were possessed of adjacent land and as if the agreement had been expressed to be made for the benefit of such land.

17.04 As subsequently amended by later legislation, a local planning authority's power under s 52 to enter into a planning agreement was extended to enable it to require a landowner not only to refrain from carrying out works on the affected land, but also to require him to do so.

17.05 As regards the exercise of these powers following their initial introduction in 1932, there is evidence that they provided a useful mechanism for controlling development in advance of the preparation by a local planning authority of a development plan for its area. Once that point had passed, however, the need for such agreements largely disappeared. Indeed, it has been estimated that in the 25 years up until 1968, no more than 500 agreements were made. In the 1970s, however, the position began to change dramatically, and there was evidence that the statutory provision was being used in a way quite unconnected with its original purpose. Local planning authorities saw the statutory provision as an opportunity for obtaining a 'planning gain' for their community. In some cases, the grant of planning permission was made conditional upon the applicant entering into a planning agreement. So, no agreement, no planning permission. In return for the grant of planning permission, the developer would be expected to enter into an agreement to provide some public benefit, which might or might not be related to the development for which planning permission was to be granted. He might, for example, be required to contribute towards the provision of infrastructure or the restoration of a nearby listed building, or to provide public amenities such as open spaces or community centres. For the most part planning agreements were sought and obtained for a proper and legitimate planning purpose. For example, it might take the form of a requirement that the applicant should pay for improvements to a nearby (off-site) road junction to accommodate traffic to be generated by the development; or that he should pay for a new sewer which would be needed if the development was to take place; or that after the building authorized by the planning permission had been erected, existing buildings on the site should be demolished; all constitute examples of planning agreements entered into for a legitimate planning purpose.

17.06 Occasionally, however, planning agreements were sought for purposes which could be considered of doubtful legality. Examples might include a requirement that the applicant provide new roads or sewers in excess of that required to serve the additional demand generated by the particular development in question; or that he be allowed an increase in the density or plot ratio normally permitted in return for the dedication of land as open space or as a footpath.

17.07 It will be seen that the use of planning agreements linked to the grant of planning permission raised both moral and legal issues. It raised a moral issue where used by a local planning authority to circumvent the general principle that landowners are entitled to planning permission for the development of their land unless there is a substantial planning objection to the development, by the addition of a requirement that they should contribute something in return for that entitlement. It raised a legal issue in the sense that there is vagueness and uncertainty over the extent of authorities' power to require a planning agreement to be entered into as part of a 'planning permission package'. It is not surprising, therefore, that from the beginning of the 1970s, commentaries on the use of s 52 agreements were sometimes characterized by such terms as 'the sale of planning permissions' or 'cheque-book planning'; and in severe cases, their use was regarded by developers as little short of blackmail.

17.08 On the other hand the system was not universally disliked by developers. The giving of a public benefit was often seen as a small price to pay in return for a grant of planning permission, and often enabled development which would otherwise have been controversial to be more readily accepted by the community. This may explain why so few attempts were made to challenge such agreements in the courts. The question of planning gain was raised in *Westminster Renslade Ltd v Secretary of State for the Environment* [1983] JPL 454. The appellant developer had sought planning permission for comprehensive development involving offices, car parks, a bridge, a new station, and a transport interchange at Feltham railway station in Hounslow. On appeal, the Inspector upheld the decision of the local authority to refuse permission, on the ground, inter alia, that the plans did not show sufficient provision for car-parking that would be under public control. In the High Court, Forbes J, quashing the decision, held that the Inspector was not entitled to treat the provision of publicly controlled car parks as a valid material consideration in determining the appeal. According to Forbes J, if a developer freely chose to give away his rights because he considered it more likely he would be granted planning permission if he did so, it might be legitimate to take into account what the developer was providing as planning gain. But it was not right to say that planning permission could be refused unless a landowner took on a burden which should more properly be shouldered by the local planning authority. The decision suggested that if there is a genuine planning objection to proposed development, but that objection could be overcome by some action taken by the developer, then that was a legitimate consideration to be taken into account by the authority. For example, if lack of infrastructure is the sole reason for refusing planning permission for development, but the developer agrees to provide it himself or to meet the cost of providing it, that is a proper consideration to be taken into account. If, on the other hand, the authority is seeking a contribution from the developer towards the provision of public facilities (as by requiring the dedication of open space) which the authority is required to provide, that is not a proper consideration to be taken into account.

17.09 So prolific became the use made of planning agreements to obtain planning gain from a developer, that policies covering the matter began to be contained in development plans.

17.10 In *Richmond upon Thames LBC v Secretary of State for the Environment* [1984] JPL 24, an application was made for planning permission for the addition of an entrance hall and offices to an existing building in Richmond. The local planning authority had refused planning permission, because, inter alia, the development proposed did not provide adequate planning advantages as required by the development plan for the area. The relevant policy in the plan stated that 'all office developments will normally be required to provide planning advantage which is considered most appropriate to the site'.

17.11 On appeal, the Inspector felt unable to regard the development-plan policy requirement of planning gain as a prerequisite for the grant of planning permission as being a valid reason for its refusal. It seems that the Inspector took the view that in the light of a then recently published report by the Property Advisory Group on the subject of planning gain, the development plan policy might not be a valid policy. In the High Court, Glidewell J held that if that were the case it was a view the Inspector was not entitled to take. In the exercise of the court's discretion, however, he decided not to quash the decision.

17.12 Whatever the limits of the power to enter into a planning agreement, they could not be used to fetter the exercise by a local planning authority of their statutory powers.

17.13 In *Windsor & Maidenhead RBC v Brandrose Investments Ltd* [1983] 1 WLR 509, a developer and the local planning authority entered into a s 52 agreement under the Town and Country Planning Act 1971, whereby the developer undertook to demolish existing buildings and redevelop the site on which the buildings stood. The authority then granted the developer outline planning permission to develop its property along the lines contemplated in the agreement. But then later, the authority designated land as a conservation area pursuant to what is now s 69 of the Planning (Listed Buildings and Conservation Areas) Act 1990, which included the developer's land. This meant that buildings in the conservation area could not be demolished without the authority's consent. When the developer started to demolish in accordance with the permission and the agreement, the authority sought an injunction restraining it from proceeding with the demolition. The Court of Appeal held that a s 52 agreement could not fetter an authority's discretion in the exercise of its statutory powers and the agreement could not bind the authority not to exercise their powers to designate a conservation area, even though the effect of so doing might be to frustrate the purposes of the agreement.

17.14 Nevertheless, the legal contours within which planning agreements operate remained far from certain. In *R v Gillingham BC, ex p Parham Ltd* [1988] JPL 336 (Div Court), a comparison was made between the powers of a local planning authority to impose conditions in a grant of planning permission, and the power of an authority to enter into statutory planning agreements. In the view of the court, an agreement had to satisfy two of the three requirements for the imposition of a valid condition as set out in the decision of the House of Lords in *Newbury DC v Secretary of State for the Environment* [1981] AC 578. First, since the power to enter into a statutory agreement was given by planning legislation, an agreement could only be entered into for a planning purpose, not an extraneous one. Secondly, as with the exercise of all public law powers, the power has to be exercised reasonably in accordance with *Wednesbury* principles (*Associated Provincial Picture Houses Ltd v Wednesbury Corporation* [1948] 1 KB 223). In the view of the court, however, it was not necessary that the purposes of a statutory planning agreement should 'fairly and reasonably be related to the permitted development'.

17.15 In *R v Wealden DC, ex p Charles Church (South East) Ltd* [1989] JPL 837, it was again held that the test of a fair and reasonable relationship to the development proposed did not apply to the making of statutory planning agreements. If that was correct, then no legal fetter existed on the power of the local planning authority to seek planning gain, other than the test of reasonableness and the knowledge that if the authority attempted to extract too much in the way of gain, the Secretary of State on appeal might grant planning permission without any planning agreement at all. If, on the other hand, the courts were to decide that a planning agreement must fairly and reasonably relate to the permitted development, the advantages of a planning agreement as opposed to the imposition of conditions in the planning permission becomes otiose, apart from the fact that a condition cannot require monetary payments to be made by a developer whereas a developer may agree to do so via a planning agreement; and the fact that it was easier for an authority to enforce the terms of a planning agreement (by an injunction) than it is to enforce compliance with a condition (by an enforcement notice or breach of condition notice).

17.16 The precise legal contours within which planning applicants operated continued to be in doubt. In *R v Plymouth City Council, ex p Plymouth and South Devon Co-operative Society* [1993] JPL 1099 (a case concerned with planning obligations and referred to later), the Court of Appeal held that the test of materiality for the purpose of s 70(2) of the 1990 Act was, as with a condition imposed in a grant of planning permission, that (a) it had to serve a planning purpose; (b) it had to relate fairly and reasonably to the development permitted; and (c) it had to be not *Wednesbury* unreasonable. Yet in *Good v Epping Forest DC* [1994] JPL 372 (a case concerned with planning agreements) the Court of Appeal accepted that planning agreements could be valid even though they went beyond what could be required by condition. Indeed, Ralph Gibson LJ, who gave the leading judgment, said:

> ... it is not surprising that section 52 agreements might go to matters beyond those that fairly and reasonably relate to the development ... because there would be little point in enacting section 52 ... if section 52 agreements were confined to those matters which could be dealt with by way of conditions.

B. PLANNING OBLIGATIONS

17.17 One of the many problems associated with planning agreements was that only the developer and local planning authorities could be parties to them. A developer was not obliged to enter into an agreement when applying for planning permission and if a local planning authority decided to hold out for one, he could only appeal against non-determination of the application or its refusal, whichever was the case. The Inspector or the Secretary of State could then conclude, however, that permission could only be given if there was an agreement to meet some requirement that could not be met by the imposition of a condition. In such cases, the only action the Inspector could take was to grant permission without any agreement being made or to refuse permission altogether.

17.18 Accordingly, the Government decided that there should be statutory provision to enable a developer to give a unilateral undertaking (which would be binding on him and on successors in title) to carry out certain works or to do whatever the undertaking may specify. The advantage of such an undertaking, which would be enforceable by the local authority, was that it would not be necessary for the local planning authority to agree its terms. In considering the related planning application or appeal, the authority or the Secretary of State respectively would be required to have regard to the terms of any unilateral undertaking offered by the developer before or during the course of appeal proceedings.

17.19 The Government also decided to amend the law concerning the extent to which s 52 agreements could be discharged or modified. A party to such an agreement could apply to the Lands Tribunal for the agreement (or part of it) to be discharged if it was obsolete, but there was no provision for appeal against an agreement which, while not obsolete in legal terms, no longer had utility or validity for planning purposes. For example, an individual might have bought land which enjoyed planning permission for residential development but was subject to a s 52 agreement to maintain access to a community building beyond the site. If in the time that had elapsed since the permission was granted and the agreement made, a different access to the community building had been provided across other land, the need for the planning agreement in connection with the residential permission would have disappeared. Furthermore, the Lands Tribunal had no jurisdiction either to modify or discharge a *positive* covenant contained in a planning agreement.

Accordingly, the Government legislated to enable a party entering into or giving the new planning obligation to apply to the local planning authority for the obligation (or part of it) to be discharged on the ground that its planning purpose had ended or was no longer relevant, so that the permission would become (to that extent) unencumbered. 17.20

C. PLANNING OBLIGATIONS (THE DETAILED REGIME)

Section 106 of the Town and Country Planning Act 1990 merely replaced s 52 of the Town and Country Planning Act 1971 in the consolidating legislation. 17.21

Section 12 of the 1991 Act, however, replaced s 106 of the 1990 Act with new ss 106, 106A, and 106B. The new s 106 amended the law relating to 'planning agreements' by enabling a developer to enter into a 'planning obligation', which could be *either* agreed with the authority, or by the developer giving a unilateral undertaking. The section also provided for planning obligations to include positive obligations. The new provisions, however, did not affect planning agreements entered into on or before 25 October 1991. These agreements continue to be governed by the old law. 17.22

The new s 106A of the 1990 Act enabled a person bound by a planning obligation to apply to the local planning authority for its modification or discharge, and the new s 106B enabled a person bound by an obligation to appeal to the Secretary of State where the local planning authority refuses or fails to determine an application for its modification or discharge. 17.23

Reservations as to whether the system of planning obligations recovers for the community a satisfactory share in the benefits arising from the development of land led the Government to propose a further and parallel system to planning obligations called planning contributions. It seems that under the system of planning obligations only 6 per cent of all planning permissions brought any contribution to the cost of supporting infrastructure. However, the proposal for 17.24

'planning contributions' has been abandoned and a new system of Community Infrastructure Levies (CILs) introduced by the Planning Act 2008. The new system of CILs and its relationship with planning obligations is dealt with in paras 17.65–17.80.

D. CREATION OF PLANNING OBLIGATIONS

17.25 Section 106 of the 1990 Act provided that any person interested in land in the area of a local planning authority could, by agreement or otherwise, enter into an obligation (defined as 'a planning obligation'). The section provided that such obligation could restrict the development or use of land in some specified way; require specified operations or activities to be carried out in, on, under, or over land; require the land to be used in some specified way; or require a sum or sums to be paid to the authority on a specified date or dates or periodically. It is interesting to note that the section set out in rather more detail than did the old provisions the purpose of a planning obligation. The obligation could provide for money payments to be made, either of a specific amount or by reference to a formula, and require periodical payments to be paid indefinitely or for a specific period. There is no specific requirement, however, that the payments relate to the land itself or to the development which is to be carried out. Wide as s 106 is drafted it is not unlimited. In *R (on the application of Khodari) v Kensington & Chelsea LBC* [2017] EWCA Civ 333; [2018] 1 WLR 584 the Court of Appeal found a requirement in a planning permission that a property developer enter into an obligation that future occupiers of a building would not apply for a residential parking permit was not capable of being a planning obligation under s 106 because it did not relate to 'the land' in which the person making the agreement was interested.

17.26 It will be apparent that it was open to a developer to agree with a local planning authority to enter into a planning obligation. Such agreement, however, is no longer essential. It could be, therefore, that after negotiation with a developer the local planning authority declined to accept a planning obligation offered by the developer. Under these provisions, however, on an appeal to the Secretary of State against the refusal of planning permission (or perhaps an appeal against non-determination of an application), the Secretary of State was able, at the same time as granting planning permission, to accept under s 106 an undertaking by the developer to which the local planning authority was not a party but which, when accepted by the Secretary of State, is enforceable by the authority against the party giving it and any of its successors in title. It should be noted, however, that there is no power for the Secretary of State, or any other person, to enforce the obligation.

17.27 It is normal practice for a planning obligation to be made before the grant of the planning permission to which it relates unless there are exceptional reasons for doing otherwise. In addition, the obligation will state it will not come into operation until planning permission has been granted.

17.28 The section provided also that in the event of a breach of any requirement in a planning obligation to carry out any operations, the local planning authority could enter the land and carry out the operations and recover the cost of doing so from the person against whom the obligation was enforceable. The authority was also given the power to enforce the obligation by injunction. The section further provided that a planning obligation could not be entered into except by way of a deed (presumably to ensure enforceability should there be an absence of consideration from the authority); that the deed should state that the obligation is a planning obligation for the purposes of the section; that it identified the land concerned; that it identified the person entering into the obligation and stated his interest; and that it identified the authority by whom the obligation was enforceable. Under the section a planning obligation could be unconditional or subject to conditions. It could also impose restrictions or requirements for an indefinite or specified period, thus enabling, for example, an obligation to end when a planning permission expired.

17.29 Following the cases of *R v South Northamptonshire DC, ex p Crest Homes plc* [1995] JPL 200 (CA) and *Wimpey Homes Holdings Ltd v Secretary of State* [1993] JPL 919, it seems that a planning obligation expressed in positive terms to transfer land would not be within s 106, as it would not directly impose any restriction on the development or use of land. A requirement to transfer land could, it seemed, be imposed indirectly under s 106, by means of an obligation restricting the use or development of land until such a transfer occurs.

17.30 A problem arose, however, if a s 106 obligation or agreement sought to transfer land to a person who is not a party to it. In *Jelson Ltd v Derby City Council* [2000] JPL 203, it was considered that whilst the provisions of s 106 were based in public law, it took effect subject to the ordinary rules of contract. One of the key contractual rules arises from s 2 of the Law of Property (Miscellaneous Provisions) Act 1989. The section requires, inter alia, a contract for the sale of land to be in writing and to be signed by or on behalf of each party to the contract. In the *Jelson* case, the company had agreed to transfer land to the Council's then undisclosed nominee housing association. Because the s 106 agreement lacked the signature of the intending 'purchaser' it was held to have fallen foul of s 2 of the 1989 Act. The court held, however, that apart from the agreement to transfer the land, the agreement remained in effect between the parties. It would seem from *Waltham Forest LBC v Oakmesh Ltd and Family Mosaic Housing* [2009] EWHC 1688; [2010] JPL 249 that, where there is an obligation to build on land, the obligation must clearly identify the land. In this case the court interestingly granted a mandatory order for works to be carried out.

17.31 Section 106 also provided that a planning obligation shall be a local land charge for the purposes of the Local Land Charges Act 1975. If, therefore, it is not registered as a local land charge, it remains binding upon a bona fide purchaser of the land for value, but such purchaser will be entitled under the Act to compensation for non-registration.

E. MODIFICATION AND DISCHARGE OF PLANNING OBLIGATIONS

17.32 Under the pre-1991 law, any person wishing to secure the modification or discharge of a restrictive covenant entered into as part of a s 52 agreement, could apply to the Lands Tribunal under s 84 of the Law of Property Act 1925. This procedure was considered to be unsatisfactory, since, as previously stated, the discharge or modification of positive covenants in an agreement was outwith the jurisdiction of the Lands Tribunal; and in determining whether or not to allow discharge or modification of restrictive covenants, the courts have taken the view that a restrictive covenant such as one not to build on land is not necessarily obsolete because planning permission has since been granted for the development of that land.

17.33 Accordingly, it was decided that, since covenants are entered into exclusively for a planning purpose, the jurisdiction of the Lands Tribunal should not apply to planning obligations. Section 106A of the 1990 Act, therefore, provided that any person against whom a planning obligation was enforceable at any time after the 'relevant period', can apply to the local planning authority by whom the obligation was enforceable for the obligation to be modified in some specified way or to be discharged. The 'relevant period' was such period as may be prescribed by the Secretary of State, or a period of five years from the date the obligation was entered into. No 'relevant period' has ever been prescribed.

17.34 Where an application is made to a local planning authority to modify or discharge a planning obligation, the authority could determine that the obligation should continue to have effect without modification; or if the obligation no longer serves a useful purpose, that it should be discharged; or if the obligation continued to serve a useful purpose but would serve that purpose equally well if it had effect subject to the modifications specified in the application, that it should have effect subject to those modifications.

17.35 The correct approach to s 106A is set out by Richards LJ in *R (on the application of The Garden and Leisure Group Ltd) v North Somerset Council* [2003] EWHC 1605 (Admin); [2004] 1 P & CR 39 at [28]:

> there are four essential questions to be considered: what is the current obligation? what purpose does it fulfil? is it a useful purpose? and if so, would the obligation serve that purpose equally well if it had effect subject to the proposed modifications?

Mr Elvin lays stress on the words 'equally well' and describes them as ordinary English words importing a principle of equivalence. Section 106A involves a precise and specific statutory test and does not bring in the full range of planning considerations involved for example in an ordinary decision on the grant or refusal of planning permission.

In *R (on the application of Mansfield District Council) v Secretary of State for Housing, Communities and Local Government* [2018] EWHC 1794 (Admin); [2018] JPL 1334 the High Court resolved a conflicting approach in the case law by finding that an obligation did need to serve a useful *planning* purpose, simply a 'useful purpose'. Garnham J arrived at that view for four reasons at [30]–[38]. First, s 106A itself contained no qualification to the expression of 'useful purpose'. Secondly, the practitioner's text, the *Planning Encyclopaedia*, suggested no such qualification. Thirdly, reading-in the word 'planning' invited debate about what constituted a planning consideration in that context, and therefore led to uncertainty. Finally, there was no reason why, as a matter of principle, the precise character of the useful purpose served by the obligation should determine whether the local authority had the power to discharge it. The critical question was whether the obligation served some useful function, the absence of which made the maintenance of the obligation pointless.

17.36 Planning agreements are often used to ensure the provision of affordable housing (an estimated 50 per cent involve affordable housing) but changing economic circumstances may mean that the development becomes economically unviable. The consequence may be that the development will not go ahead unless the authority agrees to a modification. Section 7 of the Growth and Infrastructure Act 2013 has therefore made special provision for the applications and appeals to modify or discharge affordable housing elements of s 106 agreements. This has been done by inserting three new sections, ss 106BA, 106BB, and 106BC, into the 1990 Act. These provisions will lapse on 30 April 2016 unless the Secretary of State uses his power to amend the date by affirmative order. The new provisions provide for a special procedure for applications to vary an 'affordable housing requirement' contained in a planning obligation and defines that term. Basically, if it can be shown that the affordable housing requirement means that the development is not economically viable, the authority must modify or discharge the agreement so that the development becomes economically viable. The authority may not modify the agreement in a way which makes it more onerous but this only applies to the first application and in the case of subsequent applications the only requirement is that the modification should not make the development economically unviable. The effect of these sections was considered by the High Court in *Medway Council v Secretary of State for Communities and Local Government* [2016] EWHC 644 (Admin). However, that is likely to be of only historic interest as these sections were repealed by the Growth and Infrastructure Act 2013.

F. APPEALS

17.37 Section 106B of the 1990 Act provides a right of appeal to the Secretary of State when a local planning authority fails to determine an application for the discharge or modification of a planning obligation within the prescribed period for so doing, or determined that a planning obligation should continue to have effect without modification. On an appeal, the Secretary of State has the same powers in relation to the application as had the local planning authority. Where an appeal was made under these provisions, the applicant or the authority is given an opportunity of appearing before and being heard by a person appointed by the Secretary of State for that purpose. If, however, an application is made to vary or discharge the obligation before the relevant period has expired and the local planning authority refuses, there is no statutory right of appeal. There is no obligation on the local planning authority to discharge a planning obligation and in *R (on the application of Millgate Developments Ltd) v Wokingham BC* [2011] EWCA Civ 1062; [2012] JPL 258 it was held by the Court of Appeal that a Planning Inspector's refusal to discharge a development company's unilateral undertaking to make contributions to a local authority's infrastructure was not unlawful, even where the Inspector had determined that the contributions were unnecessary, since the undertaking remained a valid contribution for planning purposes.

17.38 The statutory provisions enabled the Secretary of State to make regulations governing applications to a local planning authority to modify or discharge a planning obligation and appeals to the Secretary of State when such applications are refused or not determined. The regulations make provision with regard to the form and content of applications and appeals, notification of, and publicity for applications, determination of applications, and determination of appeals by persons appointed by the Secretary of State.

G. AMENDMENT OF PLANNING OBLIGATIONS

17.39 It seems clear that the parties to a s 106 obligation may amend the obligation by agreement. What is not clear is whether a s 106 agreement can be used to amend an existing s 52 agreement. In *R v Merton LBC, ex parte Barker* [1998] JPL 440, Latham J held, without deciding the issue, that the question seemed to him to be 'at the very least arguable'.

H. THE SECRETARY OF STATE'S POLICY

17.40 In order to seek to prevent the kind of abuse with planning obligations that had arisen in the case of planning agreements, the policy of the Secretary of State expressed in Circular 1/97 was to require a fair, open, and reasonable negotiation of planning obligations, so that the obligations enhanced the quality of the development and enabled proposals to go ahead which might otherwise be refused. In particular, the Circular advised that local planning authorities should not seek a contribution through a planning obligation unless it was relevant to planning; directly related to the proposed development; fairly and reasonably related in scale and kind to the proposed development; and reasonable in all other respects.

17.41 That policy became known as the 'necessity test'. In two landmark cases, the House of Lords considered the proper approach to planning gain.

R v Plymouth City Council, ex p Plymouth and South Devon Co-operative Society (1994) 67 P & CR 78

17.42 In 1992, the market leaders in the food retailing business, J Sainsbury plc and Tesco Stores Ltd, were each granted planning permission by Plymouth City Council, the local planning authority for the city, for the erection of a superstore on the city's outskirts. Both permissions were dependent upon the companies entering into an agreement under s 106 of the 1990 Act as amended whereby each company covenanted to provide, or provide funding for, various projects which formed no part of the development itself. In particular, J Sainsbury plc agreed to provide the city with a tourist information centre, an art gallery display, and a birdwatching hide. The company also agreed to make contributions towards the development of the city's park-and-ride facilities and a much-needed increase in the city's crèche provision for working mothers. The total cost to the company of meeting these and other covenants was to be in excess of £3.6 million. Tesco Stores Ltd too agreed that it would provide, following the grant of planning permission, a variety of benefits not directly related to the development for which the company had applied.

17.43 Not surprisingly, the third major food retailer present in the area, the Plymouth and South Devon Co-operative Society, sought (albeit unsuccessfully) both in the High Court and the Court of Appeal to challenge the Council's decision. The Society had found itself faced with two competitors, whereas previously it had expected that there would, at most, be only one.

17.44 It will be recalled that s 70(2) of the 1990 Act provides that in determining an application for planning permission, the local planning authority 'shall have regard to the provision of the development plan, so far as material to the application, and to any other material consideration'. The Society's case was that the City Council had acted unlawfully by taking into account immaterial considerations, namely, the offers by the other two food retailers to provide some or all of the community benefits. The Society argued that in order for a benefit to be taken into account it had to be 'necessary', that is, needed in order to overcome what would otherwise be a planning objection to the development or some harm which would flow from it. Both the High Court and the Court of Appeal rejected the Society's argument. A unanimous Court of Appeal [1993] JPL 1099 held that the test of materiality was (as with a condition imposed in a grant of planning permission by the *Newbury* case) three-fold, namely, it had to serve a planning purpose; it had to fairly and reasonably relate to the development permitted; and it had to be not *Wednesbury* unreasonable. The Court of Appeal held that all the benefits offered by Sainsbury's and Tesco met that three-fold test.

17.45 The decision of the Court of Appeal was thought by many as likely to have far-reaching consequences. It would seem that in determining applications for planning permission, a local planning authority could take into account any benefit (including those not necessary for the development to proceed) provided that it fairly and reasonably relates to the permitted development. The benefit no longer had to be one whose absence would justify the refusal of planning permission. The decision suggested that the advice contained in the then Circular 16/91 was, at best, inaccurate. At worst, it indicated an avenue whereby the test laid down in the Circular could be circumvented by a developer anxious to secure planning permission from a local planning authority which is itself anxious to obtain a contribution from developers to meet the cost of other socially desirable benefits. Above all, despite a judicial statement in the case that planning permission cannot be bought or sold, it raised the spectre that this indeed could happen, particularly in those cases where the scales between a grant or refusal of planning permission were evenly balanced.

Tesco Stores Ltd v Secretary of State for the Environment
[1995] 1 WLR 759

17.46 Here both Tesco Stores Ltd and Tarmac Properties Ltd sought planning permission to build a retail store on the outskirts of Witney in Oxfordshire. Following a public inquiry into both proposals, the Inspector recommended permission for Tesco but not for Tarmac. Contrary to those recommendations the Secretary of State refused Tesco's application but granted Tarmac permission.

17.47 At the public inquiry, the County Council had argued that full private funding for a new road to the west of the town (the West End Link Road) had to be provided if a superstore was to be built on either of the proposed sites. Tesco was willing to provide such funding if it was permitted to develop its site.

17.48 The Secretary of State considered that, given the distance between the link road and the proposed store, the relationship between them was tenuous. Using the tests of reasonableness set out in Circular 16/91, the Secretary of State did not consider that the link road was necessary to enable any of the superstore proposals to go ahead, or was otherwise so directly related in scale to any of the proposed developments that they might not be permitted without it. Full funding of the link road was not, according to the Secretary of State, fairly and reasonably related in scale to any of the proposed developments. Furthermore, given that the increase in traffic using the link road as a result of building the superstore might be less than 10 per cent, it would be unreasonable to seek even a partial contribution from developers towards the cost.

17.49 Tesco applied under s 228 of the 1990 Act for the Secretary of State's decisions to be quashed. It argued that its offer to fund the link road was a material consideration which the Secretary of State should have taken into account and that he had erred in applying the tests. In particular, he had applied an inappropriate test of necessity. This challenge was upheld in the High Court but rejected by the Court of Appeal.

17.50 In the High Court the learned Deputy Judge, following the *Plymouth* case, held that although the offer of full funding went beyond what was 'necessary', it was a material consideration because it was fairly and reasonably related to the proposed development. Although the tests in *Newbury DC v Secretary of State for the Environment* [1981] AC 578 (which had been applied to planning obligations in the *Plymouth* case) were silent on the question of scale, the Secretary of State should have had regard to the Tesco offer. The Court of Appeal, however, held that he had indeed done so, but because the Secretary of State had found that there was only a tenuous connection between the link road and the proposed development, he must have concluded that the offer of full funding was material but had given it no weight, which he was entitled to do. Steyn LJ said that it was not open to the Secretary of State to dilute the *Newbury* requirements but, in the exercise of his wide statutory discretion, he could adopt a more stringent policy. However, Steyn LJ considered that the Secretary of State had done this, but that his reasoning could not easily be reconciled with the decision in the *Plymouth* case, which he considered 'obliquely destroyed the core of the Circular' and 'became perilously close to emasculating the principle that planning permission may not be sold and bought'.

17.51 In the House of Lords, their Lordships upheld the decision of the Court of Appeal that the Secretary of State had not erred in law in dismissing Tesco's application for a retail store and in granting permission to Tarmac for similar development. According to their Lordships, the test to be applied in determining whether a planning obligation was a material consideration was whether it had some connection with the proposed development which was not *de minimis*. If that connection was established, the planning obligation had to be taken into account by the local planning authority. Their Lordships went on to say that once the link was established, the weight to be given to the planning obligation was a matter for the decision-maker, subject only to the obligation not to act unreasonably in the *Wednesbury* sense and to have regard to established planning policies. In the *Tesco* case their Lordships agreed that the Secretary of State had taken into account Tesco's offer to fund the link road but had given the offer little weight, as he was entitled to do.

17.52 One effect of the House of Lords judgment was to show that there was no requirement that in order for a planning obligation to be within 'the law', it had to be necessary in order to enable the development proposed to proceed. In practice, the decision meant that local planning authorities had the same freedom to consider, but then still decline to follow, a government policy statement on planning obligations as they had on any other matter.

17.53 Although it was recognized in the *Tesco* case that the Secretary of State's policy was a lawful policy, it was nevertheless more restrictive than the law. Ministerial policy is of course a material consideration to be taken into account in the determination of planning permissions. If local planning authorities decide to give that policy little weight, however, and to seek or accept additional benefits outside the scope of that policy, they have no need to fear that courts would interfere simply because they did not follow that advice. No policy could control the scope of an obligation a developer is prepared to offer in an attempt to seek planning permission, other than the public law tests of relevance to the development proposed and *Wednesbury* unreasonableness.

17.54 However, the tests in Ministerial policy have now been given a statutory basis as a result of the introduction of the scheme of CILs. Section 223 of the Planning Act 2008 gives the Secretary of State very wide powers to make regulations including provisions as to how s 106 obligations can or cannot be used. Regulation 122(2) of the Community Infrastructure Regulations 2010 places into law for the first time the Government's policy tests on the use of planning obligations. From 6 April 2010 it has been unlawful for a planning obligation to be taken into account when determining a planning application for a development, or any part of a development, that is capable of being charged the levy, if the obligation does not meet all of the following tests:

(a) necessary to make the development acceptable in planning terms;
(b) directly related to the development; and
(c) fairly and reasonably related in scale and kind to the development.

17.55 These provisions have been considered a number of times by the courts. In *Telford & Wrekin Borough Council v Secretary of State for Communities and Local Government* [2013] EWHC 1638 (Admin) Turner J at [88] held that the purpose of reg 122 was 'to inhibit developers from "buying" planning permission with the promise of wide ranging largesse'. In *R (on the application of Welcome Break Group Ltd) v Stroud District Council* [2012] EWHC 140 Bean J held at [50] that the *Tesco* approach (above) remained good law. In *R (on the application of Working Title Films Ltd) v Westminster City Council* [2016] EWHC 1855 (Admin) Gilbart J considered that where there was a breach of policy countervailing benefits could be considered as 'necessary' at [25]. Regulation 122 does not however prohibit the developer entering into an obligation, simply that it cannot form a reason for granting permission if it offends reg 122, see *R (on the application of Millgate*

Development Ltd) v Wokingham Borough Council [2011] EWCA Civ 1062. As a consequence of *Millgate*, planning obligations often include a so-called 'blue pencil' clause providing that any obligations found to be in breach of reg 122 do not continue to bind the developer. Care needs to be taken not to leave out of account matters which should not be excluded under reg 122, as in *Amstel Group Corporation Ltd v Secretary of State for Communities and Local Government* [2018] EWHC 633 (Admin) per Lang J at [66].

There were a number of other problems associated with the system of planning obligations. One problem arose from the fact that development within the area of one local planning authority may also have consequences for adjacent land which is in the area of another local planning authority. The harmful effects can be diluted, removed, or compensated for by the use of a s 106 obligation as regards land within the area of the local planning authority in which the development is to take place. It is more difficult, however, to provide like benefits by a s 106 obligation for land in the area of another local planning authority when that authority is not the body granting the permission. **17.56**

A second problem could occur when a developer had entered into a s 106 obligation, whereby the developer has agreed to contribute to the road infrastructure costs associated with development for which planning permission was being granted. Subsequently, another developer applies for planning permission for nearby land, and benefits from the road infrastructure provided previously by the first developer. The result is that the road infrastructure costs which should be shared equitably between both developers, are in fact borne by the developer who applied for planning permission first. How this problem could arise can be seen by the facts of *R (on the application of Lichfield Securities Ltd) v Lichfield DC and Christopher JN Williams* [2001] PLCR 519. The issue in that case flowed from an agreement made under s 106, whereby a developer agreed to pay to the local planning authority a contribution towards the cost of improvements to the local highway network. A second developer wishing to develop adjacent land then sought details from the local planning authority as to the methodology of calculation and as to the amount of contribution which the first developer was being required to pay under the s 106 agreement, on the ground that this would affect the amount of its own contribution. Being dissatisfied with the local planning authority's response the second developer successfully obtained from the Court of Appeal judicial review of the authority's decision as being procedurally unfair. Although the case was not directly on the point, the system did not allow a local planning authority to require a developer to make a contribution in the case of a benefit that has already been provided by another developer's planning obligation. **17.57**

As will be seen, the CIL is designed to meet these problems of 'pooled contributions'. However, as can be seen from the judgments of the Supreme Court in *Elsick Development Co Ltd v Aberdeen City & Shire Strategic Development Planning Authority* [2017] UKSC 66; [2017] PTSR 1413 there must be more than a 'trivial' **17.58** connection between the development and the relevant infrastructure contribution per Lord Hodge at [52].

17.59 In addition, it should be mentioned that, quite independent of s 106, where off-site highway works are required in order to enable development to proceed, s 278 of the Highways Act 1980 requires the developer to enter into an agreement with the highway authority that it will either carry out the highways work itself, or pay the cost of doing so to the highway authority.

I. REFORMING PLANNING CONTRIBUTIONS

17.60 The operation of the system of planning obligations has shown not only a distinction between case law and ministerial policy, but a lack of clarity about the sort of contributions that could be sought or offered. In addition, it was found that some agreements take an unacceptably long time to negotiate and it often involves substantial legal costs. The Government decided therefore, that the old system should be overhauled and a new system called 'planning contributions' introduced which would retain some elements of the old but provide greater transparency, predictability, and accountability.

17.61 Accordingly, ss 46 to 48 of the Planning and Compulsory Purchase Act 2004 provided an alternative to planning obligations whereby developers make contributions towards services and facilities relating to their proposed development. Thereafter there were to be two different forms or methods for developers' contributions in place of one, and both of these were known as planning contributions.

17.62 In 2007, however, the Government announced that its intention was to abandon the proposal to institute the planning contributions system provided in the 2004 Act. Instead it proposed the creation of a new Planning Gain Supplement to sit alongside planning obligations. This was to take the form of the Community Infrastructure Levy.

J. THE COMMUNITY INFRASTRUCTURE LEVY

17.63 Section 205 of the Planning Act 2008 authorizes the Secretary of State to make regulations to provide for the establishment of a Community Infrastructure Levy. The purpose of supplementing the existing scheme of planning obligations according to the Government, is to capture more planning gain to finance additional investment; to make the planning charge-setting process simpler and more certain; to provide a fairer means of securing contributions from developers for infrastructure; and to encourage regions and local authorities to plan positively for housing and economic growth.

17.64 The 2008 Act sets out the bare bones of the structure and basic machinery for the calculation and charging of CIL, leaving the detailed provisions to be filled in by statutory instruments to be made by the Secretary of State. It prescribes that the charging authorities will in the main be the authorities responsible for the production of local development plans for their area. Under s 208(3) of the 2008 Act the liability to pay CIL will arise upon the start of the development. Under subsection (4) anyone may be able to assume responsibility for the levy, though this must be done in accordance with the regulations. Development liable to the levy is defined in the Act 'as anything done by way of or for the purpose of the creation of a new building, or anything done to or in respect of an existing building'. Under s 209, the regulations may specify certain works or changes of use which are not to be treated as development or that the creation of or anything done to an existing structure will be treated as development.

17.65 The liability to pay the levy is to be calculated upon the commencement of development. The regulations must thus make provision for determining when development is to be treated as commencing. In the case of outline planning permission this will not be the date when it is granted, but when all necessary matters reserved by the permission have been approved.

17.66 Section 211 of the 2008 Act requires a charging authority which proposes to charge CIL to issue a document to be known as a charging schedule. This schedule would set out for the authority's area the rates, or other criteria, by reference to which the amount payable is to be calculated. Subsection (2) of the section requires charging authorities, in setting the CIL rates, to have regard (in the manner and to the extent specified by the regulations) to (a) the actual and expected costs of infrastructure; (b) matters specified by CIL regulations relating to the economic viability of development (such as the economic effects of planning permission or of the imposition of CIL); and (c) the actual and expected sources of funding for infrastructure.

17.67 A charging schedule has to be examined and approved. Section 212 of the 2008 Act provides that before the schedule is approved, it first has to be examined. This must be done by a person appointed for that purpose by the charging authority. That person must be independent of the authority and have the appropriate qualifications and experience. Persons who have made representations about the draft will have the right to be heard at this stage. On completion of the examination the examiner may approve the charging schedule. Only if the examiner does so may the charging authority proceed to approve the schedule. Then, once published, the charging schedule will come into effect. In one of the few challenges to an adoption of a charging schedule in *R (Fox Strategic Land and Property Ltd) v Chorley BC* [2014] EWHC 1179 (Admin); [2014] JPL 1152, Linblom J (as was) concluded that an authority did not need to adduce evidence concerning the effect of a future requirement in a development plan policy upon the viability of residential development.

17.68 Lastly, one should mention that the 2008 Act also contains, inter alia, provisions requiring charging authorities to prepare lists of projects which they propose will be funded by CIL and to circumscribe the circumstances where CIL can be spent on projects which are not listed. And of course, the Act repeals those statutory provisions in the 1990 Act which provided for the scheme of planning contributions.

17.69 CIL came into force on 6 April 2010 through the Community Infrastructure Levy Regulations 2010 (SI 2010/948) (now subsequently amended, most recently in 2018).

17.70 Local authorities are required to spend the CIL funds on the infrastructure needed to support the development of their area and they will decide what infrastructure is needed. CIL is intended to focus on the provision of new infrastructure and should not be used to remedy pre-existing deficiencies in infrastructure provision unless those deficiencies will be made more severe by new development. CIL can be used to increase the capacity of existing infrastructure or to repair failing existing infrastructure, if that is necessary to support development.

17.71 Using new powers introduced in the Localism Act 2011, the Government will require charging authorities to allocate a meaningful proportion of CIL revenues raised in each neighbourhood back to that neighbourhood. The intention is to ensure that where a neighbourhood bears the brunt of a new development, it receives sufficient money to help it manage those impacts. Charging authorities will be able to use funds from CIL to recover the costs of administration, with the Regulations permitting them to use up to 5 per cent of their total receipts on administrative expenses to ensure that the overwhelming majority of revenue from CIL is directed towards infrastructure provision.

17.72 The Planning Act 2008 provides a wide definition of the infrastructure which can be funded by CIL, including transport, flood defences, schools, hospitals, and other health and social care facilities. This definition should allow CIL to be used to fund a very broad range of facilities such as play areas, parks and green spaces, cultural and sports facilities, district heating schemes, and police stations and other community safety facilities. The Regulations rule out the application of CIL for providing affordable housing.

17.73 Charging authorities wishing to charge CIL must produce a charging schedule setting out the rates in their area. Charging schedules will be a new type of document within the folder of documents making up the local authority's local development framework in England, sitting alongside the local development plan in Wales and the London plan in the case of the Mayor's levy. In each case, charging schedules will not be part of the statutory development plan.

17.74 The 2011 Act limits the binding nature of the examiners' reports on CIL rates. Previously, an examiner scrutinized a council's rates, and all changes that they request were binding, including the rates set for specific areas or types of development.

Under the new provisions examiners are only able to ensure councils do not set unreasonable charges.

17.75 CIL is intended to provide infrastructure to support the development of an area rather than to make individual planning applications acceptable in planning terms. So, it is not to replace the system of planning obligations. There will still be some site specific impact mitigation requirements without which a development should not be granted planning permission. Therefore, the Government considers there is still a legitimate role for development specific planning obligations to enable a local planning authority to be confident that the specific consequences of development can be mitigated. However, in order to ensure that planning obligations and CIL can operate in a complementary way and the purposes of the two regimes are clarified, the Regulations scale back the way planning obligations operate.

17.76 One way of achieving this objective, as already noted, is that the Government's policy have been put on a statutory basis, as long as the development or part of the development is capable of being charged CIL whether there is a local CIL in operation or not.

17.77 The Regulations on the local adoption of CIL, restrict the local use of planning obligations to ensure that individual developments are not charged for the same items through both planning obligations and CIL. Where a charging authority sets out that it intends to fund an item of infrastructure via CIL then that authority cannot seek a planning obligation contribution towards the same item of infrastructure.

17.78 On the local adoption of CIL or nationally after a transitional period of (originally) four years (but ultimately extended to 6 April 2015), the Regulations restrict the local use of planning obligations for pooled contributions towards items that may be funded via CIL. This is because CIL is the Government's preferred vehicle for the collection of pooled contributions. Pooled contributions may still be sought from up to five separate planning obligations for an item of infrastructure that is not locally intended to be funded by CIL. For provision that is not capable of being funded by CIL, such as affordable housing, local planning authorities are not restricted in terms of the numbers of obligations that may be pooled.

17.79 There has been limited case law concerning the CIL regime, however some cases have clarified the correct application of the regime. In *Hillingdon LBC v Secretary of State for Communities and Local Government* [2018] EWHC 845 (Admin) the High Court held that a demand notice was invalid where it failed to give details of the surcharges imposed or the rights of appeal. In *R (Orbital Shopping Park Swindon Limited) v Swindon BC* [2016] EWHC 448 (Admin); [2016] PTSR 736 Patterson J quashed liability and demand notices which calculated CIL liability by amalgamating two separate planning applications into one. In order to benefit from the exemptions at reg 40 of the CIL Regulations, a developer had to show the building was actually in a lawful use on the relevant date, it was not sufficient to show that the building could have been put to a lawful use at that time, see: *R (Hourhope Ltd) v Shropshire Council* [2015] EWHC 518 (Admin); [2015] PTSR 933 and *R (Giordano Ltd) v London Borough of Camden* [2018] EWHC 3417. On a related note, CMG Ockelton (sitting as a Deputy Judge) found in *R(Shropshire Council) v Secretary of State for Communitie and Local Government* [2019] EWHC 16 (Admin) that, in order to benefit from the 'self build' exemption at reg 67, the self-builder needed to serve the commencement notice in the prescribed form, email to the authority indicating the commencement date was insufficient to benefit from the exemption.

17.80 In October 2016, 'A New Approach to Developers Contributions' was published by Liz Peace, reviewing the CIL regime following a commission by the Government, commonly referred to as 'the Peace Review'. The Government's response was published in the Housing White Paper 'Fixing our Broken Housing Market' (Cmd 9352). The Peace Review made a number of recommendations some of which were taken up by the Government, including (i) introduction of a Strategic Infrastructure Levy, (ii) CIL indexation to be linked to house prices, and (iii) removing pooling restrictions in certain circumstances.

17.81 In December 2018, the Government published draft amending regulations (the Community Infrastructure Levy (Amendment) (England) Regulations 2019). The key proposed changes are: (i) creating a financial penalty for failing to serve a commencement notice, rather than losing the entire CIL relief, (ii) removing the pooling restrictions, and (iii) exempting Starter Homes from CIL liability. The consultation closed on 31 January 2019.

18

APPEALS; STATUTORY REVIEW; JUDICIAL REVIEW; THE OMBUDSMAN

A. APPEALS	18.01	H. POWER TO CORRECT DECISION LETTERS	18.73
B. NATURAL JUSTICE OR FAIRNESS	18.17	I. AWARD OF COSTS	18.79
C. WRITTEN REPRESENTATION PROCEDURE	18.39	J. STATUTORY REVIEW	18.93
D. HEARINGS	18.44	K. JUDICIAL REVIEW	18.117
E. LOCAL INQUIRIES	18.49	L. THE REQUIREMENT OF STANDING	18.121
F. MAJOR INFRASTRUCTURE PROJECTS	18.64	M. THE NEED FOR EXPEDITION	18.124
G. TIME WITHIN WHICH THE SECRETARY OF STATE IS REQUIRED TO TAKE DECISIONS	18.70	N. THE PLANNING COURT AND THE CRIMINAL JUSTICE AND COURTS ACT 2015	18.127
		O. THE REMEDY	18.130
		P. THE ROLE OF THE OMBUDSMAN	18.131

A. APPEALS

From most decisions of local planning authorities there is an appeal to the Secretary of State and from him to the courts on a point of law. In determining an appeal, the Secretary of State may allow the appeal, dismiss it, reverse, or vary any part of the decision of the local planning authority and generally deal with the appeal as if it were before him in the first instance, see s 79 of the 1990 Act. **18.01**

The main right of appeal is that given by s 78 of the 1990 Act, which provides for an appeal against the refusal of planning permission or a grant of planning permission subject to conditions. **18.02**

The s 78 machinery is also available where the local planning authority has failed to give a decision on an application for planning permission within the period **18.03** prescribed for so doing, or appeals against the refusal of any consent, agreement, or approval required by a grant of planning permission subject to conditions, or against the refusal of any approval required under a development order.

18.04 Advice on the procedures for handling appeals under s 78 is given in a document published by the Planning Inspectorate titled *Procedural Guide—Planning Appeals (England)* (27 July 2018).

18.05 Other appeal machinery exists in relation to enforcement notices, listed buildings and conservation area consents, listed building enforcement notices, certificates of lawfulness of existing or proposed use or development, tree preservation orders, and advertising consent.

18.06 It should be noted that the Planning Act 2008 has amended the 1990 Act to allow the Secretary of State to require that s 78 appeals must now be accompanied by such information as is prescribed by a development order. The power is made to extend also to appeals to the Secretary of State under s 195 (lawful development appeals), appeals under s 174 (enforcement notices), and appeals under s 21 of the Planning (Listed Buildings and Conservation Areas) Act 1990 (see Arts 36 and 37 of the Development Management Procedure Order 2015 (DMPO).

18.07 It sometimes happens that a local planning authority may consider that for one reason or another an application for planning permission is invalid. This may occur, for example, if an authority considers insufficient detail has been submitted by the applicant for the authority to determine the application. The question then arises as to whether the Secretary of State has jurisdiction to entertain an appeal by the applicant as a result of the authority's non-determination. In two decisions, the Court of Appeal has decided that he had. In *Geall v Secretary of State for the Environment* [1999] JPL 909 the court held that an Inspector can decide whether an application was or was not valid. Thus, if he decides the application is invalid, he must (on behalf of the Secretary of State) refuse to entertain the appeal. In *R v Secretary of State for the Environment, ex p Bath and North Somerset DC* [1999] 1 WLR 1759, the Court of Appeal applied the principle to listed building applications and held that a local planning authority was required by statute to determine an application. The right of appeal to the Secretary of State was available even when the authority had formed the opinion that the application was invalid, and the applicant was entitled to have the opinion of the Secretary of State on the question of its validity.

18.08 When an application for planning permission is determined, the applicant is told, in addition to the decision, a summary of policies and proposals in the development plan relevant to the discussion. This duty was emphasized by the High Court in *R (Wall) v Brighton and Hove DC* [2004] EWHC 2582. The applicant is also told that he must give notice of appeal to the Secretary of State within a period of six months or, where there are extraordinary circumstances, such longer period as the Secretary of State may allow.

18.09 A notice of appeal, made by completing a form obtainable from the Secretary of State, should be accompanied by a copy of such of the following documents as are relevant to the appeal:

(a) the application made to the local planning authority which has occasioned the appeal;
(b) all plans, drawings, and documents sent to the authority in connection with the application;
(c) all correspondence with the authority relating to the application;
(d) any notices or any certificates provided to the authority in accordance with the provisions of a development order made under s 65 of the Act;
(e) any other plans or drawings relating to the application which were not sent to the authority;
(f) the notice of the decision or determination if any; and
(g) if the appeal relates to an application for approval of reserved matters, the application for outline planning permission, the plans submitted with that application, and the outline planning permission granted.

An applicant must also send a copy of the notice of appeal, and of any such plans or drawings mentioned in para (e) as accompany it, to the local planning authority on the same date as he gives notice to the Secretary of State. A new requirement of the 2015 Order is that appellants must also accompany their appeal form with a 'full statement of case' and a draft statement of common ground. A definition of 'full statement of case' is to be found within Annex J to the *Procedural Guide* (referred to above).

18.10 The Secretary of State is not bound to entertain the appeal, though the occasions on which he has not done so are thought to be rare. Under s 79(6) of the 1990 Act, if the Secretary of State is of the opinion that, having regard to the provisions of ss 70 and 72(1) of the Act and the development order, planning permission could not have been granted by the local planning authority or could not have been granted by the authority otherwise than subject to the conditions imposed, he may decline to determine the appeal. This might occur, for example, where the local planning authority has been directed by the Secretary of State to refuse planning permission or to impose conditions on any permission granted.

18.11 Furthermore, s 79(6A) of the 1990 Act provides that if at any time before or during the determination of an appeal it appears to the Secretary of State that the appellant is responsible for undue delay in the progress of the appeal, he may give the appellant notice that the appeal will be dismissed unless the appellant takes within the period specified in the notice such steps as are specified in the notice for the expedition of the appeal. Then, if the appellant failed to take those steps within that period, the Secretary of State could dismiss the appeal without any consideration of its merits.

18.12 Before determining an appeal under s 78, the Secretary of State is required by s 79(2), if either the applicant or the local planning authority so desire, to afford to each of them an opportunity of appearing before and being heard by, a person appointed by the Secretary of State for that purpose. However, from 2009 the right to have an appeal determined by way of a public inquiry or hearing has been removed by the amendment to s 79(3). The Planning Inspectorate ('PINS') now determines the mode by which an appeal is to be determined. In accordance with s 319A(6) of the 1990 Act the Secretary of State has published 'criteria that are to be applied' when determining the mode of appeal within Annex K of the *Procedural Guide*. In *North Norfolk District Council v Secretary of State for Housing, Communities and Local Government* [2018] EWHC 2076 (Admin) the High Court rejected a challenge to PINS' decision to determine a re-opened appeal by way of written representations, illuminating the wide statutory discretion now afforded to PINS in this respect.

18.13 Although in law the decision made on appeal is that of the Secretary of State, the majority of appeal decisions are made by Inspectors, that is, by members of the Department's Planning Inspectorate, standing in the shoes of the Secretary of State. In 1968 it was established that more than 90 per cent of the recommendations made by Inspectors to the Minister were accepted by him. It was decided, therefore, to give Inspectors the power to make decisions on behalf of the Minister. These cases are sometimes referred to as 'transferred cases'. Given originally for a limited class of development and a limited range of appeals, the power has been gradually extended and now by the Town and Country Planning (Determination of Appeals by Appointed Persons) (Prescribed Classes) Regulations 1997, SI 1997/420, applies to all planning appeals (in England) (with the exception of appeals by statutory undertakers relating to the development of operational land), and to development for which an environmental statement is required. Recent changes now allow Inspectors to determine appeals against refusals of listed building consent, listed building enforcement notices, appeals against a refusal of hazardous substances consent, appeals relating to mineral permissions under the Environment Act 1995, appeals concerning tree preservation notices, and enforcement notice appeals requiring environmental assessment. In addition, under the 1990 Act the Secretary of State has the power to recover the jurisdiction to decide an appeal from an Inspector in any other particular case. These cases are known as 'recovered' cases.

18.14 The criteria for recovering jurisdiction, which were set out by the Secretary of State in three Parliamentary statements: 'recovery criteria' (30 June 2008); 'neighbourhood planning' (9 July 2015); and 'onshore oil and gas' (16 September 2015). In addition, other cases may merit recovery because of the particular circumstances.

Not every case recovered by the Secretary of State for his own decision necessarily involves the Secretary of State personally making the decision. It will often be made by a senior official in the decision branch of the Department, acting for the Secretary of State. Recovered cases which are likely to be referred personally to the Secretary of State include: **18.15**

(a) developments of major importance with more than local significance which prompt 'substantial regional and national controversy';
(b) developments that raise 'important or novel issues of development control';
(c) schemes to which another Government Department has raised major objections or has an interest in;
(d) proposals of major significance for the delivery of climate change and energy efficiency policies;
(e) residential developments of more than 150 homes or on sites of more than five hectares that affect government objectives to balance between housing demand and supply.

In *R (on the application of Gleeson Developments Ltd) v Secretary of State for Communities and Local Government* [2014] EWCA Civ 1118; [2014] PTSR 226 the Court of Appeal held that the Secretary of State had no implied power to withdraw a decision issued by an inspector in the absence of a valid direction recovering jurisdiction. The Court of Appeal also dealt with the requirements for a valid direction under Sch 6, para 3(1) of the Town and Country Planning Act 1990. **18.16**

B. NATURAL JUSTICE OR FAIRNESS

It is a long-established principle that in the interval between the decision of the local planning authority and the decision of the Secretary of State (or Inspector), the Secretary of State should not 'listen to one party behind the back of the other'. In short, the decision-maker is required by the rules of natural justice 'to hear both sides' and not be biased. This duty to observe the rules of natural justice is today usually referred to by the courts as a duty to act fairly. **18.17**

One of the earliest cases to establish this was *Errington v Minister of Health* [1935] 1 KB 249 (CA), where the local authority had made a draft clearance order under housing legislation. Objections had been made to the order and a local inquiry held. After receiving the Inspector's report, the Minister had entered into correspondence with the authority and the Inspector, and an official of the Ministry and officers of the local authority had visited and conferred on the site. Subsequently, the Minister had confirmed the order. The objectors then successfully claimed that in hearing further evidence of one party (the local authority) behind the backs of the others (the objectors) the Minister had been guilty of a breach of natural justice and that his decision should not be allowed to stand. **18.18**

18.19 A landmark example is *Fairmount Investments Ltd v Secretary of State for the Environment* [1976] 1 WLR 1255. In this case the applicants owned a number of houses within an area declared to be a clearance area under the Housing Act 1957. The local planning authority had subsequently made a compulsory purchase order for the purpose of demolishing the houses which it considered to be unfit for human habitation. The applicants, who contended that the houses could be rehabilitated without demolition, objected to the order and an inquiry was duly held. At the inquiry the authority published documents showing the reasons for the order and a summary of the principal grounds of unfitness. This emphasized settlement but did not suggest that it was a continuing problem. The summary did not refer to the foundations of the applicant's property nor did it suggest that they were defective and at the inquiry no reference was made to the foundations. Following the inquiry, the Inspector had visited the houses in question. In his report he had stated that the settlement in all the houses appeared to be due to the foundations 'not having been taken deeply enough into the clay'. He concluded that because of that it was his opinion that 'satisfactory rehabilitation would not be financially viable'. Following his report, the Secretary of State had confirmed the order.

18.20 In quashing the Secretary of State's decision, the House of Lords held that the decision had been made in breach of the rules of natural justice. It had been based on an opinion formed by the Inspector about the adequacy of the foundations which had not formed part of the authority's case and which the applicants had not been given an opportunity to refute. In the words of Lord Russell of Killowen, the applicants had not had 'a fair crack of the whip'.

18.21 Unfortunately, the application of the duty to act fairly in taking administrative decisions must remain uncertain both as regards its extent and scope. With thousands of appeal decisions to be made each year, administrators require something more concrete on which to base the conduct of the inquiry process than sporadic judicial decisions. Accordingly, the power to make rules under what is now s 9 of the Tribunals and Inquiries Act 1992 has been exercised to make rules for the conduct of appeals. In the field of s 78 appeals, the existence of statutory rules now means that appeals have to be conducted within the discipline of both the common law duty to act fairly and the statutory rules. The statutory rules however, also perform a second function. They provide a timetable for action, so that once an appeal has been made, any delay in proceeding with it is reduced to a minimum. Administrators know that if they comply with the statutory rules, they are not likely to infringe the duty to act fairly. But unfortunately, it does occasionally happen. The following cases are examples.

18.22 In *Hambledon & Chiddingfold Parish Councils v Secretary of State for the Environment* [1976] JPL 502, it was said that although compliance with the Inquiry Procedure Rules did not mean *ipso facto* that there must have been compliance with the rules of natural justice, a complainant attempting to show otherwise faced a heavy burden of proof.

18.23 In *Granada Theatres Ltd v Secretary of State for the Environment* [1976] JPL 96, it was held that taking into account petitions and letters not disclosed to the applicants was a breach of the rules of natural justice.

18.24 In *Hudson v Secretary of State for the Environment* [1984] JPL 258, it was held that the Inspector had erred in not giving the parties an opportunity to deal with a matter of substance which had influenced his decision.

18.25 In *Simmons v Secretary of State for the Environment* [1985] JPL 253, the Inspector was seen by the appellant in discussion with the chairman of the planning committee of the local planning authority after the close of the inquiry. Although the Inspector was totally absolved from any bias, the decision was quashed as being contrary to natural justice.

18.26 In *Furmston v Secretary of State for the Environment* [1983] JPL 49, the Secretary of State submitted to judgment and paid the applicant's costs where it was alleged the Inspector had discussed the applicant's development proposal with a representative of the District Council before the site meeting and with a representative of the County Council after the site meeting, without any representative of the applicant being present. Although in later correspondence with the applicant the Secretary of State had said that the discussion with the County Council representative had been about the District Council's lack of co-operation in forwarding documentation to it, the applicant pursued his challenge because he considered that justice must not only be done but seen to be done. In fact, the Secretary of State had nothing to lose by submitting to judgment; an identical planning application to the district planning authority having by then been granted.

18.27 In *Second City (South West) Ltd v Secretary of State for the Environment* (1990) 61 P & CR 498, the Secretary of State had dismissed an appeal against a refusal of planning permission for residential development. In his decision letter, the Secretary of State had referred to the site as being 'outside the village fence of Backwell as identified on the Woodspring Rural Areas Local Plan' which was on deposit, and where development would not be allowed. Because the applicants had not been given an opportunity to deal with this aspect, the High Court quashed the Secretary of State's decision.

18.28 In *Cadbury Schweppes Pension Trust Ltd v Secretary of State for the Environment* [1990] EGCS 86, an Inspector refused to relax a condition in a planning permission granted for mixed industrial and office use in adherence to a local policy statement for the provision of on-site car-parking. Because the applicant had not been given an opportunity to comment on the point or to show that it was fallacious the High Court quashed the decision.

18.29 A somewhat unusual case is *Rockhold Ltd v Secretary of State for the Environment* [1986] JPL 130, where three applications for planning permission had been made for the same site. Each had gone to appeal and different Inspectors had rejected the appeals for different reasons. The applicants had challenged the decision made by the last Inspector on a number of grounds, but in particular that the decision of an Inspector ought to be consistent with earlier decisions. Forbes J held that although Inspectors ought generally to be consistent in their decisions, each Inspector was free to exercise his own judgment on matters of planning merit and this he had done. After the decision had been given, however, the appellants learnt that the Inspector who had determined the appeal had also acted as a field officer (planning) for a local amenity group, the Chiltern Society. His responsibilities there included the vetting of planning applications within the area covered by the Society. Although an appeal to the Court of Appeal from the decision of Forbes J was pending, the appellants sought and obtained leave to apply for judicial review of the Inspector's decision. One reason for so doing was that if an appeal under what is now s 288 of the 1990 Act were to succeed, it would not automatically follow that a fresh inquiry would be held. Another reason was that the additional ground of attack on the decision (namely the *appointment* of the Inspector) might not fall within the ambit of that section. The judicial review proceedings were subsequently abandoned, but only after the Court of Appeal had agreed (contrary to its normal practice) to quash the Inspector's decision by a consent order.

18.30 In *R (on the application of Ortona Ltd) v Secretary of State for Communities and Local Government* [2008] EWHC 3207 (Admin); [2009] JPL 1033, the High Court quashed a decision of the Secretary of State where it was shown that the Inspector who had made the decision to refuse planning permission for development in Cromer had until 2003 been employed in the planning department of the Norfolk County Council and had been responsible for the transport policies at issue in the appeal. Collins J quashed the decision holding that a reasonable, informed observer would take the view that there was a possibility of bias.

18.31 In another case, resolved without resort to the courts, the Inspector, accompanied by his architectural assessor, had, prior to the opening of a local inquiry into the applications for planning permission for the redevelopment of Limehouse Basin in London's East End, visited the site both on foot and by helicopter. The helicopter was, however, provided by the local planning authority and a representative of the authority had been present on the visit.

18.32 At the opening of the inquiry objectors to the application asked the Inspector to withdraw on the ground that there had been a breach of natural justice. The Inspector refused their request, but in turn offered them an opportunity to accompany him on a site visit by helicopter. This offer was accepted by some objectors but without prejudice to their rights, which they then pursued by asking the Secretary of State to intervene and remove the Inspector. This the Secretary of State duly did.

18.33 In a letter to the parties, the Secretary of State said he was satisfied that the Inspector did not in fact do anything on his original site visits which could in any way have resulted in unfairness to any of the parties at the inquiry; but he concluded that, in all the circumstances, the best course would be for him to close the inquiry and begin proceedings afresh, with a new Inspector and assessor.

18.34 The law does not require that Inspectors should deny themselves all social intercourse with the parties involved. In *Cotterell v Secretary of State for the Environment* [1991] JPL 1155, after a site visit, the Inspector had gone to a public house in the company of representatives of both sides. Before leaving the assembled company, the appellants' representative had offered to buy another round of drinks but this had been refused. In the event the Inspector remained in the pub with the other side for a further 20 minutes whilst they consumed another round of drinks bought by the Inspector. Refusing an application to quash the Secretary of State's decision to uphold the local planning authority's refusal to grant planning permission for development, the learned Deputy Judge held that, bearing in mind the occasion started with everyone together and that the appellants' representative left the others alone, it fell on 'the right side of the line'.

18.35 In *Fox v Secretary of State* [1993] JPL 448, the High Court refused to quash a decision of the Secretary of State upholding the local planning authority's decision to refuse the appellant planning permission for residential development. The Inspector who conducted the inquiry had travelled to the appeal site in the company of the authority's planning officer and another witness. It appears that before doing so, the Inspector had given the appellant assurances that he would not discuss the case during the journey; assurances which had been accepted by the appellant, who had travelled to the site on his own.

18.36 The court took the view that in all the circumstances, a reasonable man would not have thought that anything might have taken place during the car journey which might have affected the Inspector's impartiality. Hence, there had been no breach of natural justice. The Judge added, however, that he doubted the wisdom of the Inspector asking an unrepresented appellant whether he objected to him travelling without the appellant in a car with the Council's witnesses.

18.37 The requirements for natural justice in planning appeals were reviewed and re-stated in *Hopkins Developments Ltd v Secretary of State for Communities and*

Local Government [2014] EWCA Civ 470; [2014] PTSR 1145 per Jackson LJ at [62]:

i) Any party to a planning inquiry is entitled (a) to know the case which he has to meet and (b) to have a reasonable opportunity to adduce evidence and make submissions in relation to that opposing case.
ii) If there is procedural unfairness which materially prejudices a party to a planning inquiry that may be a good ground for quashing the Inspector's decision.
iii) The 2000 Rules are designed to assist in achieving objective (i), avoiding pitfall (ii) and promoting efficiency. Nevertheless the Rules are not a complete code for achieving procedural fairness.
iv) A rule 7 statement or a rule 16 statement identifies what the Inspector regards as the main issues at the time of his statement. Such a statement is likely to assist the parties, but it does not bind the Inspector to disregard evidence on other issues. Nor does it oblige him to give the parties regular updates about his thinking as the Inquiry proceeds.
v) The Inspector will consider any significant issues raised by third parties, even if those issues are not in dispute between the main parties. The main parties should therefore deal with any such issues, unless and until the Inspector expressly states that they need not do so.
vi) If a main party resiles from a matter agreed in the statement of common ground prepared pursuant to rule 15, the Inspector must give the other party a reasonable opportunity to deal with the new issue which has emerged.

Beatson LJ in a concurring judgment added some valuable additional considerations at [84]–[87], which were applied in relation to the position of a 'Rule 6' party in *Preston New Road Action Group v Secretary of State for Communities and Local Government* [2018] EWCA Civ 9; [2018] Env LR 18. In *Barlow v Secretary of State for Communities and Local Government* [2019] EWHC 146, Andrews J held at [11] that the entitlement to procedural fairness extended to all parties entitled to appear not simply to the main or 'Rule 6' parties. Building on Jackson LJ's criteria (i) in *Hopkins,* Andrews J provided further guidance at [58] to determine whether someone has had a 'reasonable opportunity' to respond to new evidence.

18.38 In *Broadview Energy Developments Ltd v Secretary of State for Communities and Local Government* [2016] EWCA Civ 562; [2016] JPL 1207 the Court of Appeal were very critical of the practice of a local MP contacting the Minister (including in the House of Commons tea room) without the other parties knowing. Disagreeing with Cranston J (who had formerly been an MP and solicitor general) Longmore LJ held at [29] that:

> …. I would not endorse that part of the judge's judgment in which he said that lobbying of Ministers by MPs was part and parcel of the representative role of a constituency MP with its implication that such lobbying was permissible even when the Minister is making a quasi-judicial decision in relation to a controversial planning application. MPs should not, with respect, be in any different position from other interested parties. Whether the failure of the Minister to say (politely) that he could not listen to what Mrs Leadsom had to say constitutes, on the facts of this case, a material breach of the rule of natural justice or gives rise to the appearance of bias is, of course, a somewhat different matter.

On the facts however, the appeal was dismissed.

C. WRITTEN REPRESENTATION PROCEDURE

18.39 At one time a decision on whether an appeal proceeded by written representation procedure, a hearing, or a public local inquiry was taken by the parties themselves. This has now changed following a new s 319A being added to the 1990 Act by the Planning Act 2008. The purpose of the new section is to require the Secretary of State to determine the procedure by which certain proceedings under the 1990 Act should be considered appropriate. The regulations, the Town and Country Planning (Determination of Appeal Procedure) (Prescribed Period) (England) Regulations 2009, SI 2009/454, prescribe that this must be done within seven working days of a valid appeal. He must also notify the appellant and the local planning authority of what procedure has been selected and publish the criteria that are to be applied in determining the appeal method.

18.40 In the case of all three different procedures the Secretary of State has made regulations governing their r conduct. The procedure for the conduct of written representation procedure is now governed by the Town and Country Planning (Written Representation Procedure) (England) Regulations 2009, SI 2009/452.

18.41 These regulations comprise two parts. Part 1 provides for an expedited procedure, which will only apply to suitable householder appeals. 'Householder appeals' and householder applications are defined in Art 37(8) and Art 2(1) of the DMPO and reg (2)1 of the Written Representation Regulations. The intention of introducing the expedited procedure for written representation appeals is to provide a 'fast track' appeal process leading to a determination of such appeals within eight weeks.

18.42 The procedures covered in Part 2 of the Regulations are to apply to non-householder appeals, or to householder appeals which the Secretary of State considers should not proceed under the expedited procedure.

18.43 As emphasized earlier, in addition to compliance with the statutory rules, the decision-maker must also comply with the common law duty to act fairly. In *Jory v Secretary of State for Transport, Local Government, and the Regions and Asia House and Westminster City Council* [2002] EWHC 2724 (Admin); [2003] JPL 549, the High Court quashed the decision of an Inspector to grant planning permission for residential development after he had considered with the developer and the City Council the conditions subject to which the planning permission had been granted; but had not considered them with local residents who had appeared at the Inquiry and who had objected to the development. The most recent example is *Ashley v Secretary of State for Communities and Local Government* [2012] EWCA Civ 559; [2012] JPL 1235 where an application was made to quash a successful appeal against the refusal of planning permission, on the basis that the objector had not had the opportunity to address new evidence in the form of a noise report submitted by the developer in written representations. The noise report had been submitted on the last day of the six-week period set by the Regulations and had been relied upon by the Inspector. The Court of Appeal overturned the grant of permission holding that the Inspector had failed to comply with the rules of natural justice. The objector should have been given an opportunity to comment on the new evidence. The old rules allow for the submission of representations after the six weeks but guidance issued by the Inspectorate strongly advises against allowing the submission of representations outside the six-week period. The new wording of the guidance is fortunately not so dogmatic and is more flexible.

D. HEARINGS

18.44 As an alternative to the written representation procedure or the formal local inquiry the Secretary of State may determine that the appeal be dealt with by a more informal procedure, namely a hearing. The procedure is now, however, governed by formal rules, the Town and Country Planning (Hearings Procedure) (England) Rules 2000, SI 2000/1626. A hearing is likely to be suitable where the development is small-scale; there is little or no third party interest; complex legal, technical, or policy issues are unlikely to arise; and there is no likelihood that formal cross-examination will be needed to test the opposing cases. Where a hearing takes place, the Inspector takes a more active role in the proceedings by leading a discussion rather than by following the more formal procedures of the local inquiry. The proceedings are more relaxed than those of a local inquiry. An interesting example of the more relaxed procedures is that under r 12(1), the Inspector can, if he thinks one or matters may be more satisfactorily resolved, under certain conditions, adjourn the hearing to the appeal site and if this is done it removes the need for a site inspection under r 12(2). These informal proceedings do not, however, absolve an Inspector from the duty to act fairly and to ensure that he takes into account all the information available to him before making his decision.

18.45 A reminder of the danger that the more relaxed atmosphere of non-inquiry procedures could lead not to a 'full and fair' hearing but to a less than thorough examination of the issues, so that the vigorous examination essential to the determination of difficult questions would be diluted, was given in *Dyason v Secretary of State for the Environment and Chiltern DC* [1998] JPL 778. There, the Council had refused the applicant planning permission to carry out alterations to existing buildings to provide a single-storey building for ostrich breeding. Dyason appealed to the Secretary of State who held a hearing as opposed to a public inquiry.

In advance of the hearing, Dyason submitted a business plan to the Inspector. During the hearing he called an expert to give his opinion on the business plan. The expert had not seen the business plan in advance and he explained to the Inspector that he could offer no assistance as he had not seen it. No opportunity was given for a short adjournment to enable the expert witness to consider it. Evidence was given by an expert witness on behalf of the Council, however, about similar development elsewhere. Refusing planning permission, the Inspector said in his decision letter that the evidence of the Council's witness that the proposed floor space would be approximately double that which was reasonably necessary 'had not been disputed'.

18.46 Allowing the appeal and quashing the Inspector's decision, the Court of Appeal considered the Inspector had not given the applicant's business plan the consideration it deserved and that the Inspector should have adjourned the hearing to allow the applicant's expert witness to see the plan so that he could comment upon it.

18.47 In coming to the conclusion that a fair hearing did not occur and that the decision must be quashed, Pill LJ said:

> Planning permission having been refused, conflicting propositions and evidence will often be placed before an Inspector on appeal. Whatever procedure is followed, the strength of a case can be determined only upon an understanding of that case and by testing it with reference to propositions in the opposing case. At a public local inquiry the Inspector, in performing that task, usually has the benefit of cross-examination on behalf of the other party. If cross-examination disappears, the need to examine propositions in that way does not disappear with it. Further, the statutory right to be heard is nullified unless, in some way, the strength of what one party says is not only listened to by the tribunal but is assessed for its own worth and in relation to opposing contentions.
>
> There is a danger, upon the procedure now followed by the Secretary of State of observing the right to be heard by holding a 'hearing', that the need for such consideration is forgotten. The danger is that the 'more relaxed' atmosphere could lead not to a 'full and fair' hearing but to a less than thorough examination of the issues. A relaxed hearing is not necessarily a fair hearing. The hearing must not become so relaxed that the rigorous examination essential to the determination of difficult questions may be diluted. The absence of an accusatorial procedure places an inquisitorial burden upon an Inspector.

18.48 The *Dyason* case was considered by Keene J (as he then was) in *Croydon LBC v Secretary of State for the Environment* [2000] PLCR 171. What that case established he said, '... is that, when there is an informal hearing which, as a matter of procedure, normally excludes cross-examination, the Inspector has to play an enhanced role in order to resolve conflicts of evidence. In addition, such an Inspector must not arrive at a finding adverse to a party without having put the point to the party in question or his witness ... '

E. LOCAL INQUIRIES

18.49 Local inquiries, it is said, are most suited to complex development proposals and to cases which generate substantial third-party representation, or where it is desirable to cross-examine those giving evidence.

18.50 The procedure followed at a local inquiry held under s 78 is regulated substantially by the common law rules of natural justice and by the Town and Country Planning (Inquiries Procedure) (England) Rules 2000, SI 2000/1624 or the Town and Country Planning (Determination by Inspectors) (Inquiries Procedure) (England) Rules 2000, SI 2000/1625. Both sets of Inquiry Procedure Rules deal with the procedure to be followed before, during, and after an inquiry. Both sets also deal with the procedure where an inquiry is held by the Secretary of State in connection with listed buildings appeals, and conservation area consent appeals. The former set of rules apply when the Secretary of State is to make the decision after considering a recommendation of the Inspector (recovered cases), the latter set when the Inspector is making the decision on behalf of the Secretary of State (transferred cases).

18.51 Because most appeals where a local inquiry is held are determined by Inspectors, the latter set of rules (SI 2000/1625) are dealt with below in some detail. Mention has already been made that the statutory rules impose a discipline on the parties to ensure that the inquiry process is conducted as efficiently and effectively as possible, which in turn should lead to speedier decisions.

18.52 Under the present rules all the major stages in the appeal process are programmed to take place from what was then called the 'starting date'. This is the date of the Secretary of State's written notice to the applicant and the local planning authority that it is his intention to cause a local inquiry to be held. In short, the starting date is the trigger for all subsequent stages of the inquiry process, so that the period between acceptance of the appeal and the inquiry itself is used to advantage.

Transferred cases (SI 2000/1625)

18.53 *Procedure before the inquiry*

(a) On receiving the relevant notice from the Secretary of State that an inquiry is to be held, the local planning authority must inform the Secretary of State and the appellant in writing of the name and address of any statutory party who made representations to them. Statutory parties are the owners of the land or a tenant of an agricultural holding to which the application relates, who made representations to the local planning authority within 21 days of being served with a notice of the application as required by the General Development Procedure Order or, in a case to which the Environmental Impact Assessment Regulations apply, adjoining owners or occupiers (see r 4(1)).

Local Inquiries

(b) The Secretary of State must notify the name of the Inspector to every person entitled to appear at the inquiry (r 5(1)).

(c) No later than six weeks after the starting date, the local planning authority must send two copies of its statement of case to the Secretary of State, and a copy of its statement to any statutory party (r 6(1)). The rule requires the Secretary of State then to send a copy of the local planning authority's statement of case to the appellant. Likewise he must send a copy of the appellant's statement of case to the local planning authority (see para (e) below). Under the Rules, a statement of case means a 'written statement which contains full particulars of the case which a person proposes to put forward at an inquiry and a list of any documents which that person intends to refer to or put in evidence'. According to the ministerial guidance, it is helpful if the parties provide with their statement the data, methodology, and assumptions used to support their submission.
Inquiries procedure

(d) If the Secretary of State or any local authority has previously given to the local planning authority a direction restricting the grant of planning permission for which application was made, or the Secretary of State or any other Minister of the Crown or government department or local authority has expressed, in writing, to the local planning authority, the view that the application should not be granted either wholly or in part, or should be granted only subject to conditions, the local planning authority must include the terms of any direction; and any views expressed or representations made on which it intends to rely in its submission at the inquiry, in its statement of case (r 4(1)).

(e) No later than six weeks after the starting date, the appellant must send two copies of its statement of case to the Secretary of State, and another copy to all statutory parties (r 6(3)). In addition, the Secretary of State may require *any other person* who wishes to appear at an inquiry to send him, within four weeks of being required to do so, three copies of its statement of case. A copy of that statement must also be sent to any statutory party (r 6(6)).

Statements of case prepared under this rule are referred to colloquially as 'rule 6 statements'. It is also provided in r 6(5) that the appellant and local planning authority may each require the other to send them a copy of any document, or of the relevant part of any document, referred to in the list of documents comprised in that party's statement of case.

(f) Where the Inspector considers it desirable to do so, he may hold a pre-inquiry meeting at not less than two weeks' written notice to the appellant, the local planning authority, any statutory party, and any other person entitled to appear or whose presence at the inquiry appears to the Inspector to be desirable. Pre-inquiry meetings must be held where it is expected that the inquiry will last for eight days or more, unless the Inspector considers it unnecessary to do so (r 7). Its purpose is to encourage the parties to prepare for the inquiry and avoid wasting time at the inquiry with matters which are not relevant nor in dispute. Pre-inquiry meetings may deal with such matters as: the clarification of issues, nature of evidence to be submitted, exchange of proofs of evidence, presentation and numbering of plans and documents, normal sitting hours of the inquiry, its likely duration, order of presentation of cases or issues, and facilities available (telex, photography, secretariat, etc).

18.54 It should be noted too, that the Inspector may not later than 12 weeks after the starting date send to the appellant, the local planning authority, and any statutory party a written statement of the matters which appear to him to be likely to be relevant to his consideration of the appeal. Such a statement is usually served in advance of any pre-inquiry meeting (r 7).

> (g) Unless a lesser period of notice is agreed, the Secretary of State must give not less than four weeks' written notice of the date, time, and place for the holding of the inquiry to every person entitled to appear (r 10).

18.55 The Rules also provide that the date fixed by the Secretary of State shall be, unless he considers it impractical, not later than 20 weeks after the starting date. In exercise of that duty, it is the practice of the Secretary of State to give the principal parties (the appellant and local planning authority) one refusal to the date offered by him for the commencement and ongoing consideration of the inquiry. In *R v Secretary of State for the Environment, Transport, and the Regions, ex p Borough of Kirklees* [1999] JPL 882, the Council sought unsuccessfully to challenge the decision of the Secretary of State to impose a second date for the inquiry, after the Council had refused the first date offered. The Council's main ground for challenging the Secretary of State's decision had been the difficulty it faced in obtaining locally based counsel (there were others available in Birmingham and London) and the lack of availability of expert witnesses over that time. The court held that judicial review, a remedy of last resort, should rarely be permitted to progress the sort of application made by the Council, where there was recourse to the Inspector, who had the power to arrange matters at the inquiry in order to accommodate the unavailability of expert witnesses.

It should also be noted that the Secretary of State may require the local planning authority to serve notice of the inquiry on specified persons or classes of persons; publish notice of the inquiry in one or more newspapers circulating in the locality; and post a notice in a conspicuous place or places near to the land (r 10).

Procedure during the inquiry

18.56 (h) Those entitled to appear at the inquiry include the appellant, the local planning authority, and if they are not the local planning authority, the county or district council in whose area the land is situated, statutory parties, and any other person who has served a statement of case (r 11(1)). In addition, the rule also provides that nothing in r 11(1) 'shall prevent the Inspector from permitting any other person to appear at an inquiry, and such permission shall not be unreasonably withheld' (r 11(2)). The latter part of this rule allows the Inspector to permit any person who can make a contribution to the determination of the appeal to appear at the inquiry. Any person entitled or permitted to appear may do so on his own behalf or be represented by any other person.

(i) Where the Secretary of State has given the local planning authority a direction restricting the grant of planning permission or the Secretary of State or any other Minister or any government department or local authority has expressed in writing to the local planning authority the view that the application should not be granted, the appellant may, not later than four weeks before the date of the inquiry, apply to the Secretary of State for a representative of the Secretary of State, Minister, department, or other body concerned to be made available at the inquiry. The rule provides that the representative shall give evidence and be subject to cross-examination to the same extent as any other witness, but that the representative of a Minister or government department shall not be required to answer any question which in the opinion of the Inspector is directed to the merits of government policy (r 12).

(j) A person entitled to appear at an inquiry who proposes to give, or to call another person to give, evidence at the inquiry by reading a proof of evidence must send copies of the proof to the Inspector and any statutory party together with a written summary. No written summary, however, is required where the proof of evidence proposed to be read contains no more than 1,500 words. Where a copy of a proof of evidence is sent to the Inspector in accordance with the rule (with or without a summary) this must normally be done no later than four weeks before the date fixed for the holding of an inquiry; and copies of that proof and any summary must be sent at the same time to the other party and to any statutory party. Where a written summary is so provided, only the summary is to be read at the inquiry, unless the Inspector permits or requires otherwise (r 14).

(k) The Rules, as now amended, also provide that the local planning authority and the appellant shall jointly prepare an agreed statement of common ground which should be sent to the Secretary of State and any statutory party not less than six weeks after the start of the appeal process (r 15). The statement is to contain agreed factual information about the subject of the appeal. The purpose of this is to save inquiry time on matters which are not in dispute.

(l) Except as is otherwise provided in the Rules, the procedure at an inquiry is determined by the Inspector. He will begin by identifying what in his opinion are the main issues to be considered at the inquiry and any matters on which he requires further explanation from those entitled or permitted to appear.

The Rules provide that, unless the Inspector determines otherwise, the local planning authority shall begin and the appellant shall have the right of final reply; and that other persons entitled or permitted to appear shall be heard in such order as the Inspector may determine. The appellant, the local planning authority, and statutory parties are entitled to call evidence and to cross-examine persons giving evidence, but any other person appearing may do so only to the extent permitted by the Inspector. Where a person gives evidence at an inquiry by reading a summary of his evidence (which is the norm), his statement of evidence may be tendered in evidence and the person cross-examined on it as if the statement were given orally. The Inspector may allow the local planning authority (or the appellant or both of them) to alter or add to any submissions made in their rule 6 statement, but must give (if necessary by adjourning the inquiry) the other party, and any statutory parties, an adequate opportunity of considering the fresh submission. If any person appearing or present at an inquiry, behaves in the opinion of the Inspector in a disruptive manner, he may be required by the Inspector to leave (r 16).

(m) Rule 17 (1) provides that the Inspector may make an unaccompanied site visit before or during the inquiry without giving notice of his intention to do so. Inspectors often visit the site on their own before the commencement of the inquiry. In addition, the rules provide that the Inspector may during an inquiry or after its close inspect the land in the company of the appellant, the local planning authority, and any statutory party. Under rule 17(2)(b), if so requested by the appellant or the planning authority, the Inspector must make such an inspection before or during the inquiry. In *R (on the application of Payne) v Secretary of State for Communities and Local Government* [2011] JPL 767 Burton J held that to comply with an equivalent rule for hearings the Inspector must actually enter onto the land and it is not enough, as in this case, to remain on the pavement outside the house which was the subject of the appeal. The reason for site visits is to enable the Inspector visually to assess the impact of the proposed development on the immediate surroundings. No discussion of the merits of an appeal is allowed during a site inspection.

Procedure after the inquiry

18.57 (n) The Rules provide that if, after the close of the inquiry, the Inspector proposes to take into consideration any new evidence or any new matter of fact (not being a matter of government policy) which was not raised at the inquiry and which he considers to be material to his decision, he shall not come to a decision without first notifying the persons entitled to appear at the inquiry who appeared at it of the matter in question; and affording them an opportunity within three weeks of the date of notification of making representations to him in respect of it or of asking for the reopening of the inquiry (r 18).

The genesis of this provision is to be found in the notorious *Chalk Pit* case in 1961. There, the owners of land in Essex applied for planning permission to develop land by quarrying chalk. The local planning authority refused the application on the ground that it would affect crops and livestock on neighbouring land. The owners appealed against the refusal to the Minister of Housing and Local

Government, who appointed an Inspector to hold a local inquiry. Although the Inspector recommended that the appeal be rejected, the Minister allowed it and granted planning permission. It then became known that after the Inspector had made his recommendations, the Minister had had discussions with the Ministry of Agriculture, Fisheries, and Food, who had convinced him that with proper safeguards the quarrying could be carried out without adversely affecting the neighbouring land. Adjacent landowners then applied to the High Court to set aside the Minister's decision. In *Buxton v Minister of Housing and Local Government* [1961] 1 QB 278, the court held that the statutory review procedure available under the Act to challenge the decision of the Minister was only available to a person aggrieved by that decision, and that Buxton (one of the neighbours affected) did not have the necessary standing to challenge the Minister's decision because he had not been aggrieved in the legal sense. Although the authority of that decision has since been progressively much weakened, the landowners, having been defeated on a preliminary issue, secured detailed consideration of the problem by the Council on Tribunals, which led to a subsequent special report by the Council and the adoption of their proposals to amend the Inquiry Procedure Rules in the manner indicated above. This particular provision, however, has not been a fertile field of litigation. This is because Inspectors (and also the Secretary of State in recovered cases) are meticulously careful to ensure that they do not take into account new evidence or new issues of fact in breach of the Rules. The distinction between 'fact' to which the rule applies, and 'opinion' to which it does not, is discussed in para 18.62 below.

(o) The Inspector is required to notify his decision and his reasons for it, in writing, to all persons entitled to appear at the inquiry who did appear, and to any other person who, having appeared at the inquiry, had asked to be notified of the decision (r 19).

The obligation to state reasons for the decision has given rise to much litigation. In the much cited case of *Re Poyser and Mills' Arbitration* [1964] 2 QB 467, it was held that reasons must be adequate and intelligible and deal with the substantial points that have been raised. The obligation to give reasons was not met where they were scanty, uninformative, and unintelligible.

Fortunately, the most important of the subsequent cases on this aspect have been considered by the House of Lords in *South Bucks DC and anor v Porter (No 2)* [2004] UKHL 33; [2004] 1 WLR 1953. There, Lord Brown summarized the judicial authorities governing the proper approach to a reasons challenge in the planning context as follows: **18.58**

> The reasons for a decision must be intelligible and they must be adequate. They must enable the reader to understand why the matter was decided as it was and what conclusions were reached on the 'principal important controversial issues', disclosing how any issue of law or law or fact was resolved. Reasons can be briefly

stated, the degree of particularity required depending entirely on the nature of the issues falling for decision. The reasoning must not give rise to a substantial doubt as to whether the decision-maker erred in law, for example by misunderstanding some relevant policy or some other important matter or by failing to reach a rational decision on relevant grounds. But such adverse inference will not readily be drawn. The reasons need refer only to the main issues in the dispute, not to every material consideration. They should enable disappointed developers to assess their prospects of obtaining some alternative development permission, or, as the case may be, their unsuccessful opponents to understand how the policy or approach underlying the grant of permission may impact upon future such applications. Decision letters must be read in a straightforward manner, recognising that they are addressed to parties well aware of the issues involved and the arguments advanced. A reasons challenge will only succeed if the party aggrieved can satisfy the court that he has genuinely been substantially prejudiced by the failure to provide an adequately reasoned decision.

It is of course also necessary to show in a successful judicial challenge for a failure to state reasons that the appellant's interests have been substantially prejudiced by that failure. In the House of Lords in *Save Britain's Heritage v Number 1 Poultry Ltd* [1991] I WLR 153, Lord Bridge said:

> Whatever may be the position in any other legislative context, under the planning legislation, when it comes to deciding in any particular case whether the reasons given are deficient, the question is not to be answered *in vacuo*. The alleged deficiency will only afford a ground for quashing the decision if the court is satisfied that the interests of the applicant have been substantially prejudiced by it. This reinforces the view I have already expressed that the adequacy of reasons is not to be judged by reference to some abstract standard. There are in truth not two separate questions: (1) were the reasons adequate? (2) if not, were the interests of the applicant substantially prejudiced thereby? The single indivisible question, in my opinion, which the court must ask itself whenever a planning decision is challenged on the ground of a failure to give reasons is whether the interests of the applicant have been substantially prejudiced by the deficiency of the reasons given. Here again, I disclaim any intention to put a gloss on the statutory provisions by attempting to define or delimit the circumstances in which deficiency of reasons will be capable of causing substantial prejudice, but I should expect that normally such prejudice will arise from one of three causes. First, there will be substantial prejudice to a developer whose application for permission has been refused or to an opponent of development when permission has been granted where the reasons for the decision are so inadequately or obscurely expressed as to raise a substantial doubt whether the decision was taken within the powers of the Act. Secondly, a developer whose application for permission is refused may be substantially prejudiced where the planning considerations on which the decision is based are not explained sufficiently clearly to enable him reasonably to assess the prospects of succeeding in an application for some alternative form of development. Thirdly, an opponent of development, whether the local planning authority or some unofficial body like *Save*, may be substantially prejudiced by a decision to grant permission in which the planning considerations on which the decision is based, particularly if they relate to planning policy, are not explained sufficiently clearly to indicate what, if any, impact they may have in relation to the decision of future applications.

Recovered cases (SI 2000/1624)

18.59 Where the Secretary of State has used his power to recover jurisdiction over the determination of the appeal, the Inspector, instead of determining the appeal himself, will usually make recommendations to the Secretary of State as to how the appeal should be determined. The procedure is regulated by the Town and Country Planning (Inquiries Procedure) Rules 2000, SI 2000/1624 and, of course, by the duty to act fairly. The Inquiries Procedure Rules relating to recovered cases differ from those applicable to transferred cases in a number of ways.

18.60 Apart from the necessary differences (particularly in terminology) resulting from the position of the Secretary of State and the complex nature of the planning issues involved, the most significant change in these rules from the rules relating to transferred cases is that relating to the close of the inquiry. Rule 17 provides that after the close of the inquiry, the Inspector must make a report in writing to the Secretary of State which must include his conclusions and his recommendations or, if he makes no recommendations, his reasons for not doing so. Before he determines the appeal, the Secretary of State may take into account new evidence or new matters of fact. He may also, however, decide to differ from the Inspector on a matter of fact. The latter situation can only occur, of course, in recovered cases where the Secretary of State is considering the Inspector's report prior to making his decision. Accordingly, if the Secretary of State does decide to:

(a) differ from the Inspector on any matter of fact mentioned in or appearing to him to be material to a conclusion reached by the Inspector; or
(b) take into consideration any new evidence or new matter of fact (not being a matter of government policy),

and is for that reason disposed to disagree with a recommendation made by the Inspector, he shall not come to a decision at variance with that recommendation without first notifying the persons entitled to appear at the inquiry who appeared at it of his disagreement and reasons for it; and affording them an opportunity of making written representations to him or (if the Secretary of State has taken into consideration any new evidence or new matters of fact, not being a matter of government policy) of asking for the reopening of the inquiry. This must be done within three weeks of the Secretary of State's notification (r 17(5)).

18.61 The rules which impose obligations on the Secretary of State to give the parties an opportunity to make further representations are concerned with matters of fact or new evidence or new matters of fact, not statements of opinion or the planning merits. The distinction has caused difficulty in the past, particularly in recovered cases.

18.62 In *Lord Luke v Minister of Housing and Local Government* [1968] 1 QB 172 the Inspector in his report to the Minister had made two statements. The first was that the site of the proposed development was clearly defined behind walls. The second was that a well-designed house would add to the charm of the setting. He accordingly recommended that the appeal be allowed. In his decision letter, however, the Minister said he accepted the Inspector's findings of fact, but could not accept the Inspector's conclusions or recommendation. He considered the proposed development would lead to sporadic development in open countryside. He then dismissed the appeal, without giving the appellant the opportunity to make further representations. The appellant argued that in disagreeing with the second statement of the Inspector, the Minister had differed from him on a finding of fact. Although the High Court upheld the appellant's contention, the Court of Appeal held that the Minister's difference of opinion with the Inspector was not on a finding of fact, but on a question of opinion on the planning merits of the proposed development, and that he was not obliged to give the appellant a further opportunity to make representations.

18.63 In *Pyrford Properties Ltd v Secretary of State for the Environment* (1978) 36 P & CR 28, the policy of the local planning authority was to restrict office development in its area, though exceptions were to be made for 'local firms'. The appellants were a firm with international ramifications, but the business had started in the locality. On an appeal against the refusal of planning permission, the Inspector had found that the appellants were and remained a local firm and recommended that the appeal be allowed. In his decision letter upholding the authority's refusal to grant planning permission, however, the Secretary of State said that he agreed with the Inspector's findings of fact but not his conclusions that the firm remained a local firm. Quashing the Secretary of State's decision for failing to comply with the relevant procedural rule by providing the appellants with an opportunity to make further representations, Sir Douglas Frank QC, sitting as a Deputy Judge of the High Court, recognized that it was not easy to draw from the *Lord Luke* decision any firm rules for distinguishing findings of fact from expressions of opinion on the planning merits, unless it were that the former depended on evidence of an existing state of affairs and the latter upon a subjective opinion of what would result from the proposed development.

F. MAJOR INFRASTRUCTURE PROJECTS

18.64 For many years concern has been expressed at the time taken to determine appeals into major development projects.

18.65 Apart from development which may be authorized by parliamentary Bills or by public Works Orders, most proposals for major infrastructure projects have been dealt with through the normal planning processes. Usually the application is called in for decision by the Secretary of State who then holds a public local inquiry into the proposal.

18.66 Although relatively infrequent, public inquiries at which such projects are considered are long, protracted, and expensive. Inquiries into projects which have lasted more than 180 sitting-days, in addition to the inquiry into the Heathrow Airport Terminal 5 proposal which itself lasted 524 sitting-days, include Stansted, Sizewell B Nuclear Power Station, and Hinkley Point Nuclear Power Station.

18.67 In addition to the main purpose of the inquiry, other related proposals linked to the project may also have to be considered. For example, the Terminal 5 inquiry involved the consideration of 21 planning applications, six highway orders, two transport and works applications, five Acquisition of Land Act 1981 orders, three applications under the Civil Aviation Act 1982 and Airports Act 1986, one scheduled monument order, and three unopposed stopping up/diversion orders.

18.68 There is also the further difficulty that such developments are rarely the consequence of specific proposals in a development plan, and may be in areas where there is an absence of specific national policy guidance. However, this is far less likely to be the case now that the Localism Act 2011 has introduced National Policy Statements.

18.69 Accordingly in July 2001, the Government announced new measures to govern the planning process for the determination of applications for planning permission for such projects. These measures have now been introduced by the Planning Act 2008 (see Chapter 28).

G. TIME WITHIN WHICH THE SECRETARY OF STATE IS REQUIRED TO TAKE DECISIONS

18.70 The Secretary of State has never previously been subject to a time limit for the making of a decision on a planning issue which has come to him by way of appeal. Now, s 55 and Sch 2 of the Planning and Compulsory Purchase Act 2004 require him to prepare a timetable within which he should come to a decision in dealing with called in applications and appeals for which he has recovered jurisdiction. The descriptions of decisions to which the Schedule applies are specified in the Town and Country (Timetable for Decisions) (England) Order 2005, SI 2005/205. Under these provisions the Secretary of State must inform the parties of the timetable to be applied to decisions made by him on called-in applications and 'recovered' appeals.

18.71 At this stage he may vary the standard timetable. He may also later revise the timetable if events occur that prevent the set timetable from being met. If the Secretary of State fails to meet the timetable, he must give reasons for that failure.

18.72 The provisions require the Secretary of State to prepare an annual report to Parliament on his performance under these provisions.

H. POWER TO CORRECT DECISION LETTERS

18.73 Sections 56 to 59 of the Planning and Compulsory Purchase Act 2004 introduced new provisions in planning law where the Secretary of State or an Inspector issue a decision document which contains a 'correctable error'.

18.74 The provisions define a correctable error as one which is contained in any part of the decision document, but which is not part of any reasons for the decision. It has been suggested that this power is in the nature of a 'slip rule'.

18.75 The correction power may be exercised either where the Inspector or Secretary of State has written to the applicant to explain the error and to say he is considering making the correction, or he has been requested to do so by any person. In the former case, the applicant had originally to agree to the correction. Following the Planning Act 2008, the consent of the applicant and, if different, the owner of the land, is no longer required.

18.76 A formal correction notice specifying the error to be corrected or the notice of a decision not to correct an error in the decision letter (as the case may be) must then be sent by the Inspector or Secretary of State to the applicant, the owner of the land in respect of which the decision was made, the local planning authority and, if the correction was sought by any other person, to that person.

18.77 The effect of issuing a notice correcting an error is that the original decision is taken not to have been made, but is replaced for all purposes by the correct decision and one which becomes effective on the date that the correction notice was issued. The statutory period for challenging the decision, therefore, operates from that date. Where a decision has been made not to correct an error, the statutory period is not affected.

18.78 An early example of the use of this power to issue a corrected decision letter was one issued in June 2006, when it was used to correct two errors in a decision letter which had referred to dates as occurring in the year 2007, instead of 2006.

I. AWARD OF COSTS

18.79 Occasionally, particularly following an inquiry, one or even both of the major parties involved will seek to recover from the other side their costs incurred in pursuing the appeal. In England and Wales, the award of costs is governed by s 250(5) of the Local Government Act 1972, and is applied to planning appeals and other proceedings under the 1990 Act by s 320(2) and Sch 6 to the 1990 Act. Section 250(5) empowers the Secretary of State to 'make orders as to the costs of the parties at the inquiry and as to the parties by whom the costs are to be paid, and every such order may be made a rule of the High Court on the application of any party named in the order'. The purpose in making an order as to costs a rule of the High Court is to enable a party to sue and be sued on an award. Similar provisions are to be found in s 89 of the Planning (Listed Buildings and Conservation Areas) Act 1990.

18.80 Prior to 1986, the Secretary of State's powers to make an award of costs were limited to local inquiries. The power has since been extended to cover all appeals, whatever the procedure adopted. In addition, Inspectors have now been given the right to exercise the Secretary of State's power to award costs. Inspectors also have the power to initiate an award of costs.

18.81 The principles on which the power to award costs is exercised are based substantially on the general principles set out by the Council on Tribunals in 1964 in its *Report on the Award of Costs at Statutory Inquiries* (Cmnd 2471).

18.82 The award of costs in planning appeals is not routine. The view is taken that the award of costs should not necessarily follow the decision on the planning merits of the appeal, so that the appellant would be awarded costs if his appeal was successful and would have costs awarded against him if he was unsuccessful. Instead, costs of a planning appeal will normally be borne, therefore, by the party that incurs them.

18.83 Before the Planning and Compensation Act 1991, the Secretary of State was able to make an award of costs against a party, requiring that party to pay the costs of another party, only where an inquiry or hearing had taken place. He had no power to do so where an inquiry or hearing had been cancelled as a result of the appellant abandoning the appeal or the local planning authority abandoning its case. The abandonment of an appeal by the appellant, or an objection to the development by the authority, could lead to the party not at fault incurring considerable costs preparing for the appeal which had then been aborted. Accordingly, the Planning and Compensation Act 1991 introduced a new power into the 1990 Act giving the Secretary of State the ability to make an award of costs where an inquiry or hearing has been arranged, but is then cancelled and does not take place.

18.84 The criteria the Secretary of State uses in exercising his power to award costs, both in relation to cases where an appeal or hearing has taken place and where it has not, are now set out in the PPG (16-027-20140306 onwards) which deals with (i) the general approach, (ii) how to make an application for costs, (iii) non-exhaustive examples of behaviour which may lead to an award of costs, and (iv) costs in compulsory purchase and analogous orders.

18.85 The test of reasonableness for an Inspector in dealing with an application for costs is different from that where the courts examine the reasonableness of the decision. For an Inspector, unreasonable means what it means in the ordinary sense of the word, see: *Manchester City Council v Secretary of State for the Environment*

[1988] JPL 774. For the courts, unreasonableness means unreasonableness in the *Wednesbury* sense.

18.86 The following is a brief summary of the criteria for awards of costs on grounds of unreasonable behaviour contained in the PPG.

18.87 Appellants are at risk of an award of costs against them on procedural grounds in circumstances where there is:

- resistance to, or lack of cooperation with the other party or parties in providing information, discussing the application or appeal, or in responding to a planning contravention notice;
- delay in providing information or other failure to adhere to deadlines;
- only supplying relevant information at appeal when it was requested, but not provided, at application stage;
- introducing fresh and substantial evidence at a late stage necessitating an adjournment, or extra expense for preparatory work that would not otherwise have arisen;
- prolonging the proceedings by introducing a new ground of appeal or issue;
- not completing a timely statement of common ground or not agreeing factual matters common to witnesses of both principal parties;
- failing to attend or to be represented at a site visit, hearing, or inquiry without good reason;
- providing information that is shown to be manifestly inaccurate or untrue;
- deliberately concealing relevant evidence at planning application stage or at a subsequent appeal;
- withdrawal of an appeal without good reason.

And on substantive grounds in circumstance where:

- the development is clearly not in accordance with the development plan, and no other material considerations such as national planning policy are advanced that indicate the decision should have been made otherwise, or where other material considerations are advanced, there is inadequate supporting evidence;
- the appeal follows a recent appeal decision in respect of the same, or a very similar, development on the same, or substantially the same site where the Secretary of State or an Inspector decided that the proposal was unacceptable and circumstances have not materially changed in the intervening period;
- in enforcement and lawful development certificate appeals, the onus of proof on matters of fact is on the appellant. Sometimes it is made plain by a recent appeal decision relating to the same, or a very similar development on the same, or substantially the same site, that development should not be allowed. The appellant is at risk of an award of costs, if they persist with an appeal against

an enforcement notice on the ground that planning permission ought to be granted for the development in question;
- lack of cooperation on any planning obligation.

Planning authorities are at risk of an award of costs against them on procedural grounds as a consequence of: **18.88**

- lack of cooperation with the other party or parties;
- delay in providing information or other failure to adhere to deadlines;
- only supplying relevant information at appeal when it was previously requested, but not provided, at application stage;
- not agreeing a statement of common ground in a timely manner or not agreeing factual matters common to witnesses of both principal parties;
- introducing fresh and substantial evidence at a late stage necessitating an adjournment, or extra expense for preparatory work that would not otherwise have arisen;
- prolonging the proceedings by introducing a new reason for refusal;
- withdrawal of any reason for refusal or reason for issuing an enforcement notice;
- failing to provide relevant information within statutory time limits, resulting in an enforcement notice being quashed without the issues on appeal being determined;
- failing to attend or to be represented at a site visit, hearing, or inquiry without good reason;
- withdrawing an enforcement notice without good reason;
- providing information that is shown to be manifestly inaccurate or untrue;
- deliberately concealing relevant evidence at planning application stage or at subsequent appeal;
- failing to notify the public of an inquiry or hearing, where this leads to the need for an adjournment.

And on substantive grounds as a consequence of:

- preventing or delaying development which should clearly be permitted, having regard to its accordance with the development plan, national policy and any other material considerations;
- failure to produce evidence to substantiate each reason for refusal on appeal;
- vague, generalized, or inaccurate assertions about a proposal's impact, which are unsupported by any objective analysis;
- refusing planning permission on a planning ground capable of being dealt with by conditions risks an award of costs, where it is concluded that suitable conditions would enable the proposed development to go ahead;
- acting contrary to, or not following, well-established case law;
- persisting in objections to a scheme or elements of a scheme which the Secretary of State or an Inspector has previously indicated to be acceptable;

- not determining similar cases in a consistent manner;
- failing to grant a further planning permission for a scheme that is the subject of an extant or recently expired permission where there has been no material change in circumstances;
- refusing to approve reserved matters when the objections relate to issues that should already have been considered at the outline stage;
- imposing a condition that is not necessary, relevant to planning and to the development to be permitted, enforceable, precise, and reasonable in all other respects, and thus does not comply with the guidance in the National Planning Policy Framework on planning conditions and obligations;
- requiring that the appellant enter into a planning obligation which does not accord with the law or relevant national policy in the National Planning Policy Framework, on planning conditions and obligations;
- refusing to enter into pre-application discussions, or to provide reasonably requested information, when a more helpful approach would probably have resulted in either the appeal being avoided altogether, or the issues to be considered being narrowed, thus reducing the expense associated with the appeal.
- not reviewing their case promptly following the lodging of an appeal against refusal of planning permission (or non-determination), or an application to remove or vary one or more conditions, as part of sensible on-going case management.
- if the local planning authority grants planning permission on an identical application where the evidence base is unchanged and the scheme has not been amended in any way, they run the risk of a full award of costs for an abortive appeal which is subsequently withdrawn

18.89 Statutory consultees, other parties, and interested parties are also at risk of costs, as set out in the PPG, although awards against them are rare.

18.90 Applications for award of costs should normally be made to the Inspector at the inquiry. Later claims will be entertained only if the party claiming costs can show good reason for not having made the claim earlier. If an award of costs is made, the parties will endeavour to agree the amount to be recovered. If agreement is not possible, either party can refer the matter for determination to the Supreme Court Taxing Office. An application is a two-stage process. The first stage requires an application to have the costs award made an order of the High Court. This act will enable the party in whose favour the award has been made to sue upon it if necessary. It also enables the party to claim interest on the amount of the award from that date. The second stage involves applying to the Taxing Office to commence assessment proceedings. Under the Civil Procedure Rules, an award of costs under s 250(5) of the Local Government Act 1972 is assessed on what is known as the 'standard basis'.

It was held in *R v Secretary of State for the Environment, ex p North Norfolk DC* [1994] EGCS 131, that the Inspector must give clear and intelligible reasons for a decision on costs, just as he must do on the issues in the appeal. **18.91**

Most awards of costs are made against local planning authorities. In *R v Secretary of State for the Environment, ex p Wakefield MBC* (1998) 75 P & CR 78, the High Court held that there was an evidential threshold which, if reached, was likely to put a planning authority beyond the risk of finding that it had been guilty of unreasonable conduct. What was required of the authority, it was said, was a 'sufficient evidential basis', that is, evidence not lacking in substance, which is capable of belief and which, if accepted, would be capable of making good the planning authority's objection. Section 2 of the Growth and Infrastructure Act 2013 has broadened the powers of the Secretary of State to award costs and to recover his own costs. Costs now can be recovered in part as well as in full and in the case of all appeal procedures not just local inquiries. The power also applies even if the inquiry or hearing has not taken place but costs have still been incurred as when the hearing or inquiry is cancelled. **18.92**

J. STATUTORY REVIEW

The 1990 Act contains a number of provisions under which the decision of the Secretary of State may be challenged in the courts. The procedures are often referred to as proceedings for statutory review, in order to distinguish them from judicial review proceedings which are normally available to a person wishing to question the validity of a public authority's actions. **18.93**

Section 288 of the 1990 Act provides the only means whereby a person may question the validity of a decision made by the Secretary of State on an appeal under s 78 with the permission of the High Court. This is because s 284(1) prescribes that, except insofar as may be provided by this part of the Act, the validity of any decision on an appeal under s 78 'shall not be questioned in any legal proceedings whatsoever'. Once a decision has been made on a s 78 appeal, therefore, whether it be a transferred or recovered case, the decision can only be questioned by using the machinery available under s 288. **18.94**

Section 288(1) provides: **18.95**

> If any person—
> (a) is aggrieved by any order to which this section applies and wishes to question the validity of that order on the grounds—
>   (i) that the order is not within the powers of this Act, or
>   (ii) that any of the relevant requirements have not been complied with in relation to that order; or

(b) is aggrieved by any action on the part of the Secretary of State to which this section applies and wishes to question the validity of that action on the grounds—
  (i) that the action is not within the powers of this Act, or
  (ii) that any of the relevant requirements have not been complied with in relation to that action,
he may make an application to the High Court under this section.

18.96 In the context of appeals relating to decisions under the 1990 Act, it should be noted that in addition to appeals under s 78 of the 1990 Act, s 288 also covers other matters such as decisions relating to:

(a) revocation and modification orders (s 97);
(b) discontinuance orders (s 102);
(c) tree preservation orders (s 198);
(d) orders defining Areas of Special Advertisement Control (s 221(5));
(e) discontinuance, prohibition, and suspension orders in respect of mineral workings (paras 1, 3, 4, and 6 of Sch 9);
(f) decision on planning merits of called in applications (s 77);
(g) decision of Secretary of State to confirm completion notice (s 95);
(h) decision on appeal ground (a) on enforcement appeals (s 177);
(i) any decision of Secretary of State on a purchase notice (s 141);
(j) any decision on appeal in respect of certificate of lawfulness of existing use or development or certificate of lawfulness of proposed use or development (s 195);
(k) any decision made by Secretary of State in respect of tree preservation orders;
(l) appeals against refusal of express consent or the issue of a discontinuance notice in the field of advertisement control; and
(m) from 2015, a costs order.

18.97 For claims made on or after 26 October 2015 an application for permission to proceed with a planning statutory review 'must be made before the end of the period of six weeks beginning with the day after the date the order is confirmed, or the date on which the action is taken' (s 288(4B)). An application under the section must be made within six weeks from the date on which the action is taken. In *Griffiths v Secretary of State for the Environment* [1983] 2 AC 51, it was held that time begins to run from the date the Secretary of State takes an irreversible step in relation to the decision, as by typing, signing, and dating the decision letter, and not when it is received by the appellant. Also, in *Stainer v Secretary of State for the Environment* [1994] JPL 44 it was held that Christmas Day and bank holidays counted in the calculation of the six weeks, however does not include the last day if that is a day on which the court office is closed rather includes the next day on which the court office is open, see: *Calverton Parish Council v Nottingham City Council* [2015] EWHC 503 (Admin); [2015] PTSR 1130. The time limit to make the application within six weeks means precisely six weeks, and there would appear to be no discretion available to the court to extend the period.

18.98 It had generally been thought that the period to file a claim form under s 288 could not in any circumstances be extended. However, in recent years the correctness of absolute statutory preclusions has been doubted, see *R (Adesina) v Nursing and Midwifery Council* [2013] EWCA Civ 818. In *Croke v Secretary of State for Communities and Local Government* [2019] EWCA Civ 54, *Adesina* was applied to the planning context by Lindblom LJ, who found at [40] that the Court retained a discretion to extend time to file a s 288 claim 'in exceptional circumstnaces on human rights grounds'.

18.99 Not everyone may use s 288 to challenge the Secretary of State's decision. The section gives the right to 'any person aggrieved'. That clearly includes the appellant and the local planning authority. The position of others, particularly third parties, is less clear. The leading authority on the term 'person aggrieved' is now to be found in the decision of the Supreme Court in *Walton v Scottish Ministers* [2012] UKSC 44; [2013] PTSR 51. Lord Reed JSC held at [86] that persons who made 'objections or representations as part of the procedure which proceeded the decision being challenged'. Furthermore, Lord Reed held at [87] that there are circumstances where a person who has not participated may, nonetheless, be considered a 'person aggrieved':

> .... for example an inadequate description of the development in the application and advertisement could have misled him so that he did not object or take part in the inquiry .... Ordinarily, however, it will be relevant to consider whether the applicant stated his objection at the appropriate stage of the statutory procedure, since that procedure is designed to allow objections to be made and a decision then to be reached within a reasonable time, as intended by Parliament.'

Walton was applied by Supperstone J in *Crawford-Brunt v Secretary of State for Communities and Local Government* [2015] EWHC 3580 (Admin); [2016] JPL 573 to find neighbouring landowners to a development site did not have standing to bring a challenge under s 288. See also: *Norman Brunt v Secretary of State for Communities and Local Government* [2018] EWHC 2910 (Admin).

18.100 The decision of the Secretary of State under s 288 may be challenged either on the ground that 'the action is not within the powers of this Act' or, that 'any of the relevant requirements have not been complied with'. 'Relevant requirements' means any requirements of the Act or of the Tribunals and Inquiries Act 1992, or of any order, regulations, or rules made under either Act (s 288(9)). It includes, therefore, as the case may be, not only a failure to comply with the main Town and Country Planning Inquiry Procedure Rules but also the Town and Country Planning (Enforcement) (Inquiry Procedure) Rules; the Town and Country Planning (Enforcement) (Notices and Appeals) Regulations; the Town and Country Planning (Control of Advertisements) Regulations; and the Town and Country Planning (Appeals) (Written Representations Procedure) Regulations where these are relevant. Where a challenge is made on the grounds that the relevant requirements have not been complied with, the person aggrieved must, if he is asking for the order to be quashed, also show that he has been substantially prejudiced by the failure to comply with those requirements.

18.101 Traditionally, the two grounds of challenge available are referred to as substantive ultra vires and procedural ultra vires. In practice, however, there is some overlap, since allegations that there has been a breach of natural justice (as opposed to a breach of the Inquiry Procedure Rules) may properly be regarded as being outside the powers of the Act rather than a failure to comply with any relevant requirements.

18.102 Section 289 of the 1990 Act provides for appeals to the High Court against decisions of the Secretary of State on enforcement appeals. Since 1991 however, appeals under this section can only be brought with the consent of the High Court and any further appeal to the Court of Appeal, only with the consent of the Court of Appeal or the High Court. Under this provision application to the High Court for leave to bring appeal proceedings must be made within 28 days after notice of the decision of the Secretary of State has been given to the applicant.

18.103 The principles upon which planning decisions will be quashed by the courts have been stated on many occasions, particularly by Forbes J in *Seddon Properties Ltd v Secretary of State for the Environment* (1981) 42 P & CR 26 and approved by the Court of Appeal in *Centre 21 v Secretary of State for the Environment* [1986] JPL 915. Although the application made in *Seddon* was a challenge of a Secretary of State's decision, the principles laid down in the case apply equally to decisions of Inspectors. The principles summarized by Forbes J were:

(1) The Secretary of State must not act perversely. That is, if the court considers that no reasonable person in the position of the Secretary of State, properly directing himself on the relevant material, could have reached the conclusion that he did reach, the decision may be overturned; see, for example, *Ashbridge Investments Ltd v Minister of Housing and Local Government* [1965] 1 WLR 1320, per Lord Denning MR and Harman LJ at pp 1326 and 1328. This is really no more than another example of the principle enshrined in a sentence from the judgment of Lord Greene MR in *Associated Provincial Picture Houses Ltd v Wednesbury Corporation* [1948] 1 KB 223 at p 230: 'It is true to say that, if a decision on a competent matter is so unreasonable that no reasonable authority could ever have come to it, then the courts can interfere.'
(2) In reaching his conclusion the Secretary of State must not take into account irrelevant material or fail to take into account that which is relevant; see, for example, again the *Ashbridge Investments* case *per* Lord Denning MR at p 1326.
(3) The Secretary of State must abide by the statutory procedures, in particular by the Town and Country Planning (Inquiries Procedure) Rules 1974 [now the Inquiries Procedure Rules 2000]. These rules require him to give reasons for his decision after a planning inquiry, and those reasons must be proper and adequate reasons that are clear and intelligible and deal with the substantial points that have been raised, *Re Poyser and Mills' Arbitration* [1964] 2 QB 467.

(4) The Secretary of State in exercising his powers which include reaching a decision such as that in this case must not depart from the principles of natural justice: *per* Lord Russell of Killowen in the *Fairmount Investments* case.

More recently, the principles have been re-stated by Lindblom J (as he was) in *Bloor Homes (East Midlands) Ltd v Secretary of State for Communities and Local Government* [2014] EWHC 754 (Admin); [2017] PTSR 1283 at [19]: **18.104**

(1) Decisions of the Secretary of State and his inspectors in appeals against the refusal of planning permission are to be construed in a reasonably flexible way. Decision letters are written principally for parties who know what the issues between them are and what evidence and argument has been deployed on those issues. An inspector does not need to 'rehearse every argument relating to each matter in every paragraph': see the judgment of Forbes J in *Seddon Properties Ltd v Secretary of State for the Environment* (1978) 42 P & CR 26, 28.

(2) The reasons for an appeal decision must be intelligible and adequate, enabling one to understand why the appeal was decided as it was and what conclusions were reached on the 'principal important controversial issues'. An inspector's reasoning must not give rise to a substantial doubt as to whether he went wrong in law, for example by misunderstanding a relevant policy or by failing to reach a rational decision on relevant grounds. But the reasons need refer only to the main issues in the dispute, not to every material consideration: see the speech of Lord Brown of Eaton-under-Heywood in *South Bucks District Council v Porter (No 2)* [2004] 1 WLR 1953, 1964B–G.

(3) The weight to be attached to any material consideration and all matters of planning judgment are within the exclusive jurisdiction of the decision-maker. They are not for the court. A local planning authority determining an application for planning permission is free, 'provided that it does not lapse into *Wednesbury* irrationality' (see *Associated Provincial Picture Houses Ltd v Wednesbury Corpn* [1948] 1 KB 223) to give material considerations 'whatever weight [it] thinks fit or no weight at all': see the speech of Lord Hoffmann in *Tesco Stores Ltd v Secretary of State for the Environment* [1995] 1 WLR 759 , 780F–H. And, essentially for that reason, an application under section 288 of the 1990 Act does not afford an opportunity for a review of the planning merits of an inspector's decision: see the judgment of Sullivan J in *Newsmith Stainless Ltd v Secretary of State for the Environment, Transport and the Regions (Practice Note)* [2001] EWHC Admin 74 at [6]; [2017] PTSR 1126, para 5 (renumbered).

(4) Planning policies are not statutory or contractual provisions and should not be construed as if they were. The proper interpretation of planning policy is ultimately a matter of law for the court. The application of relevant policy is for the decision-maker. But statements of policy are to be interpreted objectively by the court in accordance with the language used and in its proper context. A failure properly to understand and apply relevant policy will constitute a failure to have regard to a material consideration, or will amount to having regard to an immaterial consideration: see the judgment of Lord Reed JSC in *Tesco Stores Ltd v Dundee City Council (Asda Stores Ltd intervening)* [2012] PTSR 983, paras 17–22.

(5) When it is suggested that an inspector has failed to grasp a relevant policy one must look at what he thought the important planning issues were and decide whether it appears from the way he dealt with them that he must have

misunderstood the policy in question: see the judgment of Hoffmann LJ in *South Somerset District Council v Secretary of State for the Environment (Practice Note)* [2017] PTSR 1075, 1076–1077; (1992) 66 P & CR 83 , 85.

(6) Because it is reasonable to assume that national planning policy is familiar to the Secretary of State and his inspectors, the fact that a particular policy is not mentioned in the decision letter does not necessarily mean that it has been ignored: see, for example, the judgment of Lang J in *Sea & Land Power & Energy Ltd v Secretary of State for Communities and Local Government* [2012] EWHC 1419 (QB) at [58].

(7) Consistency in decision-making is important both to developers and local planning authorities, because it serves to maintain public confidence in the operation of the development control system. But it is not a principle of law that like cases must always be decided alike. An inspector must exercise his own judgment on this question, if it arises: see, for example, the judgment of Pill LJ *Fox Strategic Land and Property Ltd v Secretary of State for Communities and Local Government* [2013] 1 P & CR 6, paras 12–14, citing the judgment of Mann LJ in *North Wiltshire District Council v Secretary of State for the Environment* (1992) 65 P & CR 137, 145.

18.105 Many applicants for statutory review (and judicial review) mistakenly assume that the courts are entitled to substitute their own judgment on the planning merits for that of the decision-maker; or they assume that a court is entitled to interfere with the decision of an Inspector or local planning authority on the basis that the decision-maker has given insufficient weight, or too much weight, to a particular material consideration or to a part or parts of the evidence. As was said in *Tesco Stores v Secretary of State for the Environment* [1995] 1 WLR 759 (HL) at 780, 'if there is one principle of planning law more firmly settled than any other, it is that matters of planning judgment are within the exclusive province of the local planning authority or the Secretary of State'.

18.106 The courts will only intervene to quash a decision on recognized legal principles (see *City of Edinburgh v Secretary of State for Scotland* [1997] 1 WLR 1447 (HL)). One of the recognized grounds on which the courts may quash a decision is on grounds of *Wednesbury* unreasonableness. As stated above the *Wednesbury* principle, as it is known, is founded on the decision of the Court of Appeal in *Associated Provincial Picture Houses Ltd v Wednesbury Corporation* [1948] 1 KB 223.

18.107 The case was not about town and country planning, but its importance lies in the control of administrative discretion generally. Although text books have been written on the meaning and application of the principle, the essence of it is that administrators should not make discretionary decisions which are so unreasonable that no reasonable person, properly understanding the law, would make them. For a decision to be quashed on *Wednesbury* grounds, therefore, it is necessary to show that the decision made was perverse or irrational. It has been said that the threshold to be overcome by a person alleging unreasonableness, is to show that the decision 'defies comprehension' or 'borders on absurdity'. The threshold is a high one. Many attempts to quash decisions on this ground have failed because the decision-maker was able to show that the decision under challenge was within the scope of reasonable responses available to any reasonable decision-maker.

18.108 Another ground on which the courts may quash a decision is where the Secretary of State or an Inspector misconstrues or misapplies a planning policy in reaching a decision. The exact relationship between the courts and the planning authorities in interpreting policy has been clarified by the Supreme Court in the Scottish decision of *Tesco Stores v Dundee City Council* [2012] UKSC 13; [2012] PTSR 983. The Supreme Court made it clear that the meaning of a policy is a matter of law for the Courts to decide. Lord Reed (who gave the main judgment) at [17]–[19] however stated that the application of policy was a matter for the decision-maker (and could only be challenged on the grounds that it was irrational or perverse) 'planning authorities do not live in the world of Humpty Dumpty—they cannot make the development plan mean what they would like it to mean'.

18.109 It should also be noted that just as questions of weight are exclusively for the decision-maker, so too are findings of fact. The courts will not intervene unless there is simply no evidence at all to support the findings, or the findings are irrational or perverse in the narrow (*Wednesbury*) sense. The Supreme Court adopted the same approach to the construction of national planning policy issued by the Secretary of State in *Hopkins Homes Ltd v Secretary of State for Communities and Local Government* [2017] UKSC 37; [2017] 1 WLR 1865.

18.110 A question is sometimes asked as to whether there is a duty on the decision-maker to consider whether, and to what extent, any detriment or objection he may find as likely to arise from proposed development could be dealt with by the use of appropriate conditions. The question has been considered by the courts on a number of occasions, particularly in *M J Shanley v Secretary of State for the Environment* [1982] JPL 380 and *Marie Finlay v Secretary of State* [1983] JPL 802. The latter decision was confirmed by the Court of Appeal in *Topdeck Holdings Ltd v Secretary of State* [1991] JPL 961 where, it was said:

> An Inspector should not have imposed upon him an obligation to cast about for conditions not suggested before him. He emphasised 'obligation'. If, of his own motion, he wished to impose a condition, then, different considerations would arise, including perhaps the reopening of the appeal.

The court then went on to further consider what an Inspector should do in regard to a condition which was neither requested, nor more significantly, offered. According to Mann LJ, (who agreed with the views expressed by Forbes J in the *Marie Finlay* case):

> If a party to an appeal wanted the appeal to be considered on the basis that some condition could cure the planning objection put forward, then it was incumbent on the appellant to deal with that condition at the inquiry. Unless such a condition has been canvassed, the Secretary of State was not at fault in not imposing such a condition.

18.111 In *National Anti-Vivisection Society v First Secretary of State* [2004] EWHC 2074 (Admin) Collins J held at [32] that the approach of *Top Deck* was one of general application and not confined to its own facts. See also *Gladman Developments Ltd v Secretary of State for Communities and Local Government* [2017] EWHC 2768 (Admin); [2018] PTSR 616 in relation to mitigating the impacts of a development on air quality by Grampian condition. It is now usual in the case of public inquiries for the Inspector to ask the parties if they wish to suggest conditions to be imposed in any grant of permission, if that should be his decision. This will generally result in the local planning authority suggesting appropriate conditions to which the applicant may or may not agree.

18.112 A similar approach is applied where an Inspector may not have before him all the information he considers necessary to arrive at a proper decision. Although it is not possible to lay down general rules in such circumstances, it was said in *John Taylor v Secretary of State for Wales* [1985] JPL 792 that:

> an Inspector has no duty to seek to put the parties' own representations in order to give them assistance. However, if an Inspector came to a conclusion that he was unable to come to a fair decision on the issue on the basis of the material before him … [he was not] … necessarily entitled to sit back and hold that because of a lacuna which could easily be filled, the party had failed to fulfil a burden placed upon him.

18.113 Section 288(5) of the Act provides that:

> On any application under this section the High Court—
> (a) may … by interim order suspend the operation of the order or action, the validity of which is questioned by the application, until the final determination of the proceedings;
> (b) if satisfied that the order or action in question is not within the powers of this Act, or that the interests of the applicant have been substantially prejudiced by a failure to comply with any of the relevant requirements in relation to it, may quash that order or action.

18.114 Despite the wording of the subsection, the courts have held that they have a residual discretion not to quash a decision where an application is made under the section, see: *Simplex GE (Holdings) Ltd v Secretary of State for Communities and Local Government* [2017] PTSR 1041. As Purchas LJ held in *Simplex*, where an error of law is established the decision should be quashed unless the decision-maker 'would necessarily have reached the same conclusion if he had not acted on the erroneous factor'.

18.115 Where a decision of the Secretary of State is quashed under these provisions, its effect is to leave the appeal outstanding, so that a further lawful decision has then to be made. Where a decision is quashed by the courts, both sets of Inquiry Procedure Rules require the Secretary of State to give those who were entitled to appear at the inquiry and who duly did so, the opportunity to make further comments on the case following the court's decision. The action taken by the

Secretary of State will depend upon the defect that caused the original decision to be quashed. An unintelligible decision letter can be corrected by the issue of an intelligible decision letter and an oversight in the drafting of a condition cured by the making of the necessary correction to the condition, so long as the parties concerned have been given the opportunity to make further representations before the Secretary of State proceeds to make a fresh decision. A failure to allow the parties to comment on new matters of fact taken into account after the close of the inquiry or to ask for the inquiry to be reopened, can be cured by giving them that opportunity or by reopening the inquiry. In *Kingswood DC v Secretary of State for the Environment* [1988] JPL 248, it was held that following the quashing of a decision, the Secretary of State was obliged to deal with the matter *de novo* with a clean sheet, and that he had to have regard to the development plan and to any other material considerations, and thus to any further material considerations arising after the date of the original decision. For an insightful analysis on this issue, see: J Maurici QC and M Seitler, 'The status and Legal Effect of a Quashed Appeal Decision in Planning Law' [2018] 5 JPL 492–506.

18.116 The procedures for making a challenge under s 288 are set out in Part 8 of the Civil Procedure Rules 1998 and Practice Direction 8C. In *Secretary of State for Communities and Local Government v Bovale and Herefordshire DC* [2009] EWCA Civ 171; [2009] 1 WLR 2274 the Court of Appeal ruled that, while an individual judge had wide powers of case management, he had no power to make what were in substance practice directions.

K. JUDICIAL REVIEW

18.117 As already indicated, an appeal to the High Court under s 288 of the 1990 Act will normally follow upon a refusal by a local planning authority to grant planning permission for development or to grant it subject to conditions; a subsequent appeal being made to the Secretary of State against the authority's decision; and then the determination of that appeal by the Secretary of State. As has also been seen, the statutory review procedure provided for in s 288 is available only to a 'person aggrieved' by the decision of the Secretary of State and to the local planning authority concerned. As interpreted by the courts, a 'person aggrieved' may include not only the applicant or appellant, but a third party such as a neighbour. The ability of a third party, however, to make a legal challenge under s 288 to the grant of planning permission for development is dependent upon the applicant for planning permission appealing in the first instance to the Secretary of State against the authority's decision. If the applicant for planning permission should be happy with the local planning authority's decision on the application and does not appeal to the Secretary of State however, the judicial remedy that can follow a s 288 appeal is not available to them.

18.118 Owing to the unavailability of s 288 in those circumstances, any third party wishing to challenge as ultra vires the decision of a local planning authority to grant planning permission for development must generally use the alternative procedure known as 'judicial review' which is available under the provisions of s 31 of the Senior Courts Act 1981 and Part 54 of the Civil Procedure Rules. Under these rules an 'application for judicial review' has become a 'claim for judicial review' and it follows that an applicant is now known as a claimant. New terminology has also been introduced for some of the remedies which may be sought by judicial review. An order of *mandamus*; an order of prohibition; and an order of *certiorari* have become respectively a mandatory order; a prohibiting order; and a quashing order.

18.119 The procedure for obtaining judicial review of a planning decision is in two stages. First, a claimant must make an application to the Planning Court, which is a specialist part of the High Court, for permission to proceed with the claim. By CPR r 54.5(5) 'where the application for judicial review relates to a decision made by the Secretary of State or local planning authority under the planning acts, the claim form must be filed not later than six weeks after the grounds to make the claim first arose'. The rationale for a permission filter is a recognition that public bodies are vulnerable to actions by busybodies and meddlers and that some filter is necessary to prevent them being harassed by such people. Permission is determined by a single Judge on the papers. If permission is refused, an applicant can renew their application at an oral hearing unless the initial Judge records the claim 'totally without merit' CPR r 54.12(7). In those circumstances, an applicant can seek permission from the Court of Appeal. Whereas in the past applications for judicial review were generally made without notice being served on any other party, the present claim for judicial review must now be served on the defendant and any person whom the claimant considers to be directly affected by the claim. This gives the defendant and those directly affected by the claim the opportunity to put before the court summary grounds of defence before permission to proceed is given. As long as the applicant can show that he has an arguable case and that he has the necessary standing required to seek judicial review, permission to apply will normally be granted. In addition to the Court rules, regard should be had to the *Administrative Court Judicial Review Guide* (July 2018).

18.120 Another requirement is the recent introduction of a pre-action 'protocol' for judicial review. This requires a letter to be sent by the claimant to the defendant setting out the main facts and issues before the claim for permission to proceed with judicial review is formally lodged. The protocol requires that the defendant should send a letter of response to the claimant within 14 days. The procedure is to give a public authority the opportunity to act upon the claimant's concerns and so lead to a settlement.

L. THE REQUIREMENT OF STANDING

A claimant must have 'a sufficient interest in the matter to which the application relates'. This is a requirement of both s 31 of the Senior Courts Act 1981 and Part 54 of the Civil Procedure Rules 1998. It impacts not only on the application for permission stage, but also on the second stage when permission to proceed has been granted and the court is considering the substantive merits of the application. The precise nature of the standing required to seek and obtain judicial review has given rise to much litigation. In *R v Inland Revenue Commissioners, ex p National Federation of Self-Employed and Small Businesses Ltd* [1982] AC 619, the House of Lords held that 'standing' was not just a preliminary issue to be determined only at the permission stage, but was also a substantial issue to be considered at the actual application stage as part of the merits of the case. In *R v Foreign Secretary, ex p World Development Movement Ltd* [1995] 1 WLR 386, the Divisional Court applied the *Inland Revenue* case, holding that since standing went to 'jurisdiction', it was not to be treated merely as a preliminary issue, but had to be considered against the legal and factual context of the whole case, and that the merits of the challenge were the important, if not the dominant, factor in considering standing. Rose LJ held that factors to be considered included vindicating the rule of law, the importance of the issue raised, the likely absence of any other responsible challenger, and the nature of the relief sought. His Lordship also considered as relevant to the case the prominent role of the applicants in giving advice, guidance, and assistance on questions of overseas aid. — 18.121

Although neither of these cases involved planning issues, notable cases in this field where applicants have been held to have the necessary standing have included *Covent Garden Community Association Ltd v Greater London Council* [1981] JPL 183 (an incorporated body of local residents) and *R v Inspectorate of Pollution, ex p Greenpeace Ltd (No 2)* [1994] 4 All ER 329 (CA). In a more recent case, *R v Cotswold DC, ex p Barrington Parish Council* [1997] EGCS 66, the High Court held that despite the fact that the parish was situated some distance from the development site, the Parish Council had sufficient standing, as it was bona fide concerned about the increased through traffic which would go through the parish if redevelopment of the site went ahead. On the other hand, in *R v North Somerset DC and Pioneer Aggregates (UK) Ltd, ex p Garnett* [1997] JPL 1015, the High Court held that the applicants for judicial review had no standing when they lived three miles away from the development site, had no rights over the land, did not themselves object to the application for planning permission, had no commercial interest, and had no statutory rights to be consulted on the application. — 18.122

Overall, in deciding whether to grant permission, the courts are more concerned with the merits of the claim rather than academic or arid challenges. The — 18.123

Government expressed concern that applications for judicial review can be used as a delaying tactic and in a consultation paper, 'Judicial Review: Proposals for Further Reform', issued in September 2013, proposed tightening the rules on standing so as to restrict access to the courts. However, whilst this proposal was not taken forward, changes to the permission and substantive stage were introduced. Section 31 of the Senior Courts Act 1981 was amended by the Criminal Justice and Courts Act 2015 to include new ss 2A–2C:

(2A) The High Court—
   (a) must refuse to grant relief on an application for judicial review, and
   (b) may not make an award under subsection (4) on such an application,
   if it appears to the court to be highly likely that the outcome for the applicant would not have been substantially different if the conduct complained of had not occurred.
(2B) The court may disregard the requirements in subsection (2A)(a) and (b) if it considers that it is appropriate to do so for reasons of exceptional public interest.
(2C) If the court grants relief or makes an award in reliance on subsection (2B), the court must certify that the condition in subsection (2B) is satisfied.
(3C) When considering whether to grant leave to make an application for judicial review, the High Court—
   (a) may of its own motion consider whether the outcome for the applicant would have been substantially different if the conduct complained of had not occurred, and
   (b) must consider that question if the defendant asks it to do so.
(3D) If, on considering that question, it appears to the High Court to be highly likely that the outcome for the applicant would not have been substantially different, the court must refuse to grant leave.
(3E) The court may disregard the requirement in subsection (3D) if it considers that it is appropriate to do so for reasons of exceptional public interest.
(3F) If the court grants leave in reliance on subsection (3E), the court must certify that the condition in subsection (3E) is satisfied.

M. THE NEED FOR EXPEDITION

18.124 In addition to having the necessary standing to bring a claim for judicial review, it used to be a requirement of Part 54 of the Civil Procedure Rules that an application for permission to proceed must be made 'promptly', and in 'any event not later than three months from the date when the grounds for the application first arose'. In addition, s 31(6) Senior Courts Act 1981 provides that the court may refuse to grant permission to proceed or any relief sought on the claim where there has been 'undue delay' in making it, on which see *Gerber v Wiltshire Council* [2016] EWCA Civ 84; [2016] 1 WLR 2593 and the highly unusual case of *R (on the application of Thornton Hall Hotel Ltd) v Wirral MBC* [2018] EWHC 560 (Admin); [2018] PTSR 954 (which resulted in the quashing of a planning permission six years after it had been issued).

18.125 The courts had begun to get concerned that whereas an applicant for statutory review of a planning decision given by the Secretary of State must take action in the courts within six weeks of the decision, the claimant for judicial review of a planning decision by a local planning authority would normally have three months in which to take appropriate action as long as the claimant acts promptly. Indeed, in what might be termed judicial legislation, a number of decisions of the High Court, some sustained on appeal by the Court of Appeal, held that the normal period for bringing a claim for judicial review should also be six weeks. The new practice was however universally criticized, being eventually considered by the House of Lords in *R v Hammersmith and Fulham London Borough Council, ex p Burkett* [2002] UKHL 23; [2002] 1 WLR 1593. The question to be considered was whether the time limit for commencing proceedings ran from the date of a resolution to grant planning permission or the grant of planning permission itself. Their Lordships held that time ran from the date of the grant for the reason that a mere resolution to grant planning permission created no legal rights. With regard to the replacement of the three-month time limit by a six-week rule, their Lordships considered that the legislative three-month limit could not be contracted by a judicial policy decision.

18.126 The Civil Procedure (Amendment No 4) Rules have now brought consistency between the two remedies of statutory review and judicial review by amending r 54.5 of the Civil Procedure Rules so that a claim form for an application for review of a planning decision must be filed within six weeks of the date when the grounds for the application first arose. In shortening the time limit the new rule has also dropped the need to act 'promptly'.

N. THE PLANNING COURT AND THE CRIMINAL JUSTICE AND COURTS ACT 2015

18.127 In July 2013 a 'planning fast track' system was introduced in the Administrative Court. The aim being to ensure that the most important planning cases were heard quickly before specialist judges. The Civil Procedure (Amendment No 3) Rules have now amended the Civil Procedure Rules to establish a new Planning Court within the High Court. A new Section II is inserted into Part 54 of the Civil Procedure Rules to provide for planning-related judicial reviews and statutory challenges to be dealt with in a specialist list forming the Planning Court:

18.128 A Planning Court claim means a judicial review or statutory challenge which
   a) involves any of the following matters—
      1. planning permission, other development consents, the enforcement of planning control and the enforcement of other statutory schemes;
      2. applications under the Transport and Works Act 1992;
      3. wayleaves;

    4. highways and other rights of way;
    5. compulsory purchase orders;
    6. village greens;
    7. European Union environmental legislation and domestic transpositions, including assessments for development consents, habitats, waste and pollution control;
    8. national, regional or other planning policy documents, statutory or otherwise; or
    9. any other matter the judge appointed under rule 54.22(2) considers appropriate; and
  b) has been issued or transferred to the Planning Court.

18.129 This reform has been followed up by the Criminal Justice and Courts Act 2015. The Act amends s 288 to require permission of the High Court to proceed with a planning statutory review, in line with s 289 and judicial review. A new subsection (4C) is inserted into s 288 so that the order or action challenged can be suspended, but this does not apply to an application questioning the validity of a tree preservation order. The requirement for permission also applies to other planning statutory reviews, for example challenges to development plan documents under s 113 of the Planning and Compulsory Purchase Act 2004. The Act also amends s 12 of the Administration of Justice Act 1969 to provide for a 'leap frog' appeal from the High Court and the Upper Tribunal to the Supreme Court if a point of law of general importance is involved.

O. THE REMEDY

18.130 A claim for judicial review may be used to secure a mandatory order, a prohibiting order, or a quashing order. It may also be used to secure an injunction or a declaration. The procedure is flexible, in that although the applicant must specify in his application for permission the particular remedy or remedies he seeks, the court may decide to grant some other remedy allowed for by the order if it considers it more appropriate to do so. Judicial review, it must be emphasized, is not an 'appeal' from a decision of a public authority, but a review of the manner in which the decision is made. It deals with the legality or validity of the decision, not as an appeal to the Secretary of State, on whether the decision is right or wrong. For that reason, the court cannot substitute its own decision for that being challenged.

P. THE ROLE OF THE OMBUDSMAN

18.131 The administration of government services, whether carried out by central or local government, may sometimes lead to complaints by citizens which the courts are either unable to deal with because no legal rights of the citizen have been infringed, or because where they have been, the courts are ill-equipped to provide an adequate remedy. As a result, Parliament has set up two public sector Ombudsman systems to help the citizen. First, the Parliamentary Commissioner Act 1967 established the Parliamentary Commissioner for Administration (colloquially known as the Parliamentary Ombudsman) to receive and investigate complaints against Central Government Departments. Secondly, the Local Government Act 1974 established two Commissions for Local Administration, one for England and one for Wales, the membership of which consists of Local Commissioners (colloquially known as Local Government Ombudsmen) to receive and investigate complaints against local government.

18.132 Although a number of important differences exist in the way in which the Parliamentary and Local Government Ombudsmen operate, their jurisdictional remit (though held in relation to different tiers of government activity) is the same, namely to investigate complaints by members of the public who claim to have 'suffered injustice in consequence of maladministration'. In addition, the maladministration must have occurred in connection with the exercise of the 'administrative functions' of the Department or authority concerned.

18.133 The role of public service Ombudsmen has been considered by the Law Commission in its publication, *Remedies against Public Bodies*. In a Scoping Report, the Commission said:

> The ombudsmen are intended in general to provide a cost-free and more informal method of dealing with grievances against the state [than the courts]. It has been said that the ombudsmen may in some ways be a better long-term complaints resolution mechanism where public bodies are concerned, on the grounds that they are more able to deal with the systemic nature of some public law disputes and are able to provide feedback to public bodies to enable them to improve their working practices and policies.

18.134 Neither the Parliamentary Commissioner Act 1967 nor the Local Government Act 1974 attempted to define the meaning of the word 'maladministration', though in the debate in the House of Commons during the passage through Parliament of the Parliamentary Commission Act 1967, the Lord President of the Council defined it as covering 'bias, neglect, inattention, delay, incompetence, inaptitude, perversity, turpitude, arbitrariness and so on'. It has been said that the greatest part of this ten-point catalogue is the 'and so on'. In *R v Local Commissioner for Administration, ex p Bradford MDC* [1979] QB 287, Lord Denning MR described the term as 'open-ended'. In truth, the catalogue has proved to be the working basis upon which the Ombudsmen proceed.

18.135 In 1993, the Parliamentary Ombudsmen gave other examples of acts or omissions he considered were likely to fall within the term maladministration. They were:

— rudeness (though that is a matter of degree);
— unwillingness to treat the complainant as a person with rights;
— refusal to answer reasonable questions;

— neglecting to inform a complainant on request of his or her rights or entitlement;
— knowingly giving advice which is misleading or inadequate;
— ignoring valid advice or overruling considerations which would produce an uncomfortable result for the overruler;
— offering no redress or manifestly disproportionate redress;
— showing bias whether because of colour, sex, or any other grounds;
— omission to notify those who thereby lose a right of appeal;
— refusal to inform adequately of the right of appeal;
— faulty procedures;
— cavalier disregard of guidance which is intended to be followed in the interest of equitable treatment of those who use a service;
— partiality; and
— failure to mitigate the effects of rigid adherence to the letter of the law where that procedure results in manifestly inequitable treatment.

18.136 Two important limits in the jurisdiction of the Parliamentary and Local Government Ombudsman must also be mentioned. First, both Ombudsmen are prohibited from questioning the merits of any decision taken without maladministration in the exercise of a discretion vested in the Department or in the authority, as the case may be. This means that a member of the public cannot complain to the Ombudsman merely because he considers the body concerned should have reached a different decision to the one it did reach. Maladministration must always be present, therefore, before the Ombudsman can issue an adverse report. Secondly, both Ombudsmen are prohibited from investigating cases where the person aggrieved has or had a remedy in any court of law, or a right of appeal, reference, or review before any tribunal.

18.137 This provision is an attempt to provide a demarcation line between the remit of the courts and the remit of the Ombudsman. It is not a rigid demarcation line, however, since a proviso in both the Parliamentary Commissioner Act 1967 and the Local Government Act 1974 allows the Ombudsman to investigate a complaint if satisfied that in the particular circumstances it is not unreasonable to expect the complainant not to pursue his legal remedies or rights of appeal.

18.138 In *R v Commissioner for Local Administration, ex p Liverpool CC* [2001] 1 All ER 462 (CA), Henry LJ indicated that the circumstances where it might be appropriate for the Ombudsman to exercise discretion to investigate where judicial review might be available were where, having regard to the weaknesses of the coercive fact-finding potential of judicial review, it would be difficult, if not impossible, for the complainants to obtain the necessary evidence to bring judicial review proceedings; where the complainants are unlikely to have the means to pursue a remedy through the courts; and where the Ombudsman's investigation and report are able to provide a just remedy when judicial review may fail to do so.

In two substantial ways the Parliamentary and the Local Government Ombudsman **18.139** schemes differ. First, access to the Parliamentary Ombudsman can only be obtained via a Member of the House of Commons, whereas access by members of the public to the Local Government Ombudsman is direct. Secondly, whereas the Parliamentary Ombudsman is usually successful when he finds maladministration and injustice in persuading the Central Government Department concerned to provide the remedy he has sought for the injustice suffered by the complainant, in some 5 per cent of cases where the Local Government Ombudsman has sought a remedy from the authority for injustice suffered by the complainant, the authority concerned has declined to provide it.

The statistics show that complaints of injustice suffered through maladministra- **18.140** tion made against the Secretary of State are rare. This is not the position, however, with regard to complaints made to the Local Government Ombudsmen against local authorities exercising their functions. The Annual Report of the Commission for Local Administration in England for 2017/18 shows that, although there was a fall in the number of complaints received in the year compared with the previous year, 12 per cent related to 'planning and development', as in the previous year. The lowest proportion of complaints upheld related to 'planning and development' at 41 per cent.

Among a selection of financial remedies obtained by Local Government **18.141** Ombudsmen for complainants over the past few years have been the following:

(a) Failure to inform a purchaser that planning permission had been granted for an extension to neighbouring property—£7,800 for reduction in market value; £878 agents' fees; and £250 for time and trouble.
(b) Failure to deal with noise nuisance; complainant forced to take own legal action—£2,000 for having to endure nuisance; £13,000 and contribution to complainants' legal costs.
(c) Failure to ensure developer complied with a planning condition requiring foul/surface water drainage—£8,067 for replacement kiln and £8,220 for reinstating building.
(d) Failure to confirm a compulsory purchase order preventing service by owner of business premises of blight notice—£6,500 for delay and uncertainty plus £250 for time and trouble.
(e) Failure to inform and consult on pedestrianization proposal—£38,729, being half the costs incurred by the complainants in connection with the public local inquiry.
(f) Not adequately dealing with complaints regarding the continuing development of a nearby industrial estate which had polluted a watercourse and affected the complainant's farming activities—£26,926 to cover a number of separate categories of harm identified by the Ombudsman.

(g) Failure to deal properly with an application for planning permission for two neighbouring sites in that the authority failed to advertise proposed development affecting the setting of a listed building, failed to notify English Heritage, and failed to advertise the application as a departure from the provisions of the development plan—£40,000 to the owner of one site in return for his entering into a s 106 agreement not to implement the planning permission and £35,000 each to two other complainants.

(h) The redesignation of land by the authority from community to retail use and an invitation to tender for a lease advertised. Complainant company awarded lease but application for planning permission subsequently refused. Compensation of £14,937 awarded, being half the company's costs associated with preparing planning application.

(i) Failure to assess properly the merits of an amended application for the erection of a detached garage, resulting in the depreciation of a neighbour's property—£18,000.

(j) Granting planning permission having formed an incorrect view of the nature of the proposed development, resulting in the diminution of value of a neighbour's property—£10,000.

(k) Taking into account irrelevant considerations in granting planning permission for a forestry contractor's yard; not applying s 54A, ignoring the previous decision of the Inspector following an appeal against an earlier refusal—£10,000, being the loss in value of the complainant's home.

(l) Approval of detail for large dwelling given contrary to provisions of development plan—£15,000 to complainant for depreciation in value of his property.

(m) Misleading advice as to right to restore farmhouse. Subsequent enforcement action and farmhouse had to be demolished—£70,686 to cover demolition and other costs.

(n) A local planning authority gave conflicting decisions as to whether development had commenced within the period of five years required by a condition in the grant of planning permission. Authority later issued lawful development certificate accepting that it had—£17,692 to cover complainants' financial losses (fees for legal advice, LDC application fee, and interest lost because sale of land delayed).

(o) Misleading advice given to Council by officers over planning status of land, leading to the grant of planning permission and loss in value of a neighbour's property—£25,000 being the loss suffered by the neighbour as a result.

(p) Failure to consider on a reserved matters planning application, the impact of a block of flats on a neighbour's cottage—£37,500 being the loss in value of the cottage.

(q) Failure of Council to secure the payment of a deposit from a developer to ensure that links to a private road were brought up to an adequate standard—£16,250.

(r) Failure to deal with an application to erect a mobile telephone mast within the statutory time-scale, resulting in planning permission being given by default—£66,442 in total to four complainants in respect of the devaluation of their properties.

A remedy may be other than financial. These include the taking of mitigation measures such as erection of walls, fences, acoustic barriers, the construction of flues, the taking of action under other legislative codes, such as environmental protection legislation, seeking relocation of development, or the enforcement of s 106 obligations. It should however be noted that a local authority has a discretion whether to accept the Local Government Ombudsman's recommendation, see: *R (on the application of Nestwood Homes Developments Ltd) v South Holland District Council* [2014] EWHC 863 (Admin); [2014] BLGR 354.

18.142

19

HUMAN RIGHTS

A. THE HUMAN RIGHTS ACT 1998	19.01

A. THE HUMAN RIGHTS ACT 1998

The substantive provisions of the Human Rights Act were brought into force on 2 October 2000. Its purpose was to incorporate into domestic law the provisions of the European Convention on Human Rights. The main features of the Act are: **19.01**

(a) So far as it is possible to do so, primary and subordinate legislation, whenever passed, must be read and given effect to in a way which is compatible with the Convention.

(b) Public authorities are forbidden to act in a way which is incompatible with Convention rights. If they should do so, 'the victim' of that act may proceed directly against the authority concerned in the courts.

(c) Although the courts have not been given the power to strike down legislation which is incompatible with Convention rights, they may make a declaration of incompatibility. Any legislative provision declared by the courts to be incompatible with the Convention, however, does not necessarily make the decision unlawful. Although s 6(1) of the Act provides that it is unlawful for a public authority to act in such a way that is incompatible with a Convention right, the provision is disapplied in cases where the authority could not have acted differently because of the wording of the Act of Parliament. This means that a declaration of incompatibility does not affect the validity, continuing operation, or enforcement of that provision in any particular case, nor is it binding upon the parties. Any declaration of incompatibility would of course be of great symbolic significance, which it would be impossible for the Government to ignore. Accordingly, the Act provides a 'fast track' procedure which enables the Secretary of State to amend statutes by way of statutory instrument.

The main Convention rights that are likely to be relevant to land-use controls are set out in Art 1 of Protocol 1 and Arts 6 and 8 of the Convention. The following are the more important extracts from those Articles:

Article 1 of Protocol 1

Every natural or legal person is entitled to the peaceful enjoyment of his possessions. No one shall be deprived of his possessions except in the public interest.

Article 6(1) of the Convention

(1) In the determination of his civil rights and obligations or of any criminal charge against him, everyone is entitled to a fair and public hearing within a reasonable time by an independent and impartial tribunal established by law ...

Article 8 of the Convention

(1) Everyone has the right to respect for his private and family life, his home and his correspondence.

(2) There shall be no interference by a public authority with the exercise of this right except such as is in accordance with the law and is necessary in a democratic society in the interests of national security, public safety or the economic well-being of the country, for the prevention of disorder or crime, for the protection of health or morals, or for the protection of the rights and freedoms of others.

19.02 Since 1966, it has been possible for individuals, after exhausting all domestic law remedies, to petition the European Court of Human Rights directly to complain that they have suffered from an infringement of their rights under the Convention. This right has not been affected by the Human Rights Act.

19.03 In the past, the European Court of Human Rights has considered a number of complaints from individuals under this procedure. The following are three of the most important cases affecting land use decided by the European Court.

19.04 In *Bryan v United Kingdom* [1996] JPL 386 (ECHR) the applicant had been served with an enforcement notice and after exhausting all domestic remedies, unsuccessfully alleged a breach by the United Kingdom of Art 6(1) of the Convention insofar as he had not received in the determination of his civil rights 'a fair and public hearing ... by an independent and impartial tribunal'. The Court held that although the review by an Inspector did not of itself satisfy the requirements of Art 6, the procedures and safeguards of judicial review available to him were sufficient compliance with the Convention.

19.05 In *Buckley v United Kingdom* [1996] JPL 1018 (ECHR), the applicant had been refused planning permission for the siting of a caravan on her own land. She alleged, inter alia, a breach of Art 8 of the Convention, which protects a person's rights to respect for his home. It was held that Art 8 did not go so far as to allow an individual's preference as to his place of residence to override the general interest;

and that since the regulatory framework within which the decision was made contained adequate procedural safeguards protecting the applicant's interest, there had been no violation of Art 8.

19.06 In *Chapman v United Kingdom* (2001) 33 EHRR 329 (and other related cases), the European Court of Human Rights had to consider whether there had been a breach of Art 8 of the Convention as a result of action taken by the local planning authority, by way of injunctions and enforcement notices, to require the complainant to cease occupation of a caravan on her land. Although the Court held that the measures taken constituted an interference with her rights under Art 8(1), it also found the interference to have been 'in accordance with law' and that it pursued a legitimate aim of protecting 'the rights of others' through preservation of the environment. There had therefore been no breach of Art 8.

19.07 Given the views expressed by many commentators on the likelihood that some of the main principles of planning legislation would be found to be incompatible with the Convention, it was understandable that following the incorporation of the Convention into domestic law, some litigation would follow.

19.08 The most significant of these cases gave rise to the landmark decision of the House of Lords in what have become known as the *Alconbury* decisions. Four applications had been made to the High Court for declarations that the planning process in each case was not compatible with Art 6(1) of the Convention. The *Alconbury* case itself involved an appeal against a refusal of planning permission recovered by the Secretary of State under ss 78 and 79 of the 1990 Act. Two of the other cases involved decisions by the Secretary of State to call in applications for planning permission under s 77 of the 1990 Act for determination by himself. The fourth case involved the proposed use by the Secretary of State of highway orders and related compulsory purchase orders in connection with a scheme to improve the A34/M4 road junction. In all four cases the Divisional Court of the Queen's Bench Division was prepared to grant the declarations of incompatibility sought.

19.09 Appeals were pursued in three of the four cases. With the consent of the parties involved and the Divisional Court, the conjoined appeals were 'leapfrogged' to the House of Lords. The fourth case was not appealed since it did not raise any different issue. On 9 May 2001 the House of Lords in *R (on the application of Alconbury Developments Ltd) v Secretary of State for the Environment, Transport and the Regions; R (on the application of Holding & Barnes) v Secretary of State for the Environment, Transport and the Regions*; and *Secretary of State for the Environment, Transport and the Regions v Legal and General Society Ltd* [2001] 2 WLR 1389 unanimously allowed all three appeals from the Divisional Court's decision.

19.10 The House of Lords agreed that the determination of administrative matters such as planning decisions involved the determination of 'civil rights and obligations' within the meaning of the Convention and that, in challenging them, people were entitled to the protection of Art 6. The Secretary of State had not claimed that in dealing with a called in application or a recovered decision, he was acting as an independent tribunal and, for that reason, he could not be seen to be impartial. According to the House of Lords, the Divisional Court had erred in concluding that Art 6 prohibited the Secretary of State from being both a policy-maker and a decision-maker. The question for the courts was whether there was sufficient judicial control to ensure a determination by an independent and impartial tribunal subsequently. There was no requirement that this should constitute a rehearing by way of an appeal on the merits. What was required was that there should be a sufficient review of the legality of the decision and the procedures that were followed. None of the judgments of the European Court of Human Rights required that the courts should have 'full jurisdiction' to review policy or the overall merits of a planning decision. The European Court of Human Rights had recognized that planning decisions fell into a specialized area. As in the *Bryan* case, the European Court had recognized that in planning matters it was necessary to have regard to such matters as the subject matter of the decision appealed against, the way in which the decision was arrived at, and the content of the dispute, including the desired and actual grounds of appeal. In each of the cases there would be a public inquiry before an Inspector. The inquiry would be an occasion for the exploration of facts including the need for and desirability of the development. The inquiry would be regulated by rules to ensure fairness in the procedure, and there would be opportunities for judicial review after the eventual decision of the Secretary of State. Accordingly, in the cases before their Lordships, there had in principle been no violation of Art 6 of the Convention. The scope of judicial review was sufficient to comply with the standards set by the European Court.

19.11 Although the basic features of the British planning process thus appear to have survived relatively unscathed by the incorporation of the Convention into domestic law, the clean bill of health given to it in the *Alconbury* judgment by the House of Lords did not necessarily mean that all aspects of the planning process were compatible with the Convention. Some aspects may yet be found to be in breach, so imposing on the Government an obligation to make appropriate changes. In addition, the incorporation of the Convention into British domestic law has no doubt been a peripheral influence on some of the ways in which planning decisions are made. It must be borne in mind, however, that under Art 8 planning authorities, in exercising their powers under it, are entitled to have regard to what 'is necessary in a democratic society in the interests of ... the economic well-being of the country ... the protection of health or morals ... or for the protection of the rights and freedoms of others'. Likewise, under Art 1 of Protocol 1 a person may not be deprived of his possessions 'except in ... the general interest'. The decision-maker will frequently, therefore, be called upon to strike a balance between interference with a landowner's rights and the wider public issues such as harm to the environment. In this context, the European Court of Human Rights has accepted the principle that within that legitimate area of discretion given to the decision-maker, a 'margin of appreciation' should be allowed in a state's favour.

The application of the Act

19.12 The effect of these provisions is to strengthen the influence of proportionality as a factor to be taken into account by the decision-maker. He will frequently have to strike a balance between landowners' rights and wider public concerns, such as harm to the environment. In those cases, the degree of interference must be proportionate to the harm. In the Court of Appeal in *Lough v First Secretary of State* [2004] 1 WLR 2557 Pill LJ spelt out the approach to be followed in considering Art 8 and Art 1 of the First Protocol:

> Recognition must be given to the fact that Article 8 and Article 1 of the First Protocol are part of the law of England and Wales. That being so, Article 8 should in my view normally be considered as an integral part of the decision maker's approach to material considerations and not, as happened in this case, in effect as a footnote. The different approaches will often, as in my judgment in the present case, produce the same answer but if true integration is to be achieved, the provisions of the Convention should inform the decision maker's approach to the entire issue. There will be cases where the jurisprudence under Article 8, and the standards it sets, will be an important factor in considering the legality of a planning decision or process.

He went on to say:

> The question whether the permission has 'an excessive or disproportionate effect on the interests of affected persons' is a question which has routinely been posed by decision makers both before and after the enactment of the 1998 Act ...

and

> it is important to emphasise that the striking of a fair balance lies at the heart of proportionality.

19.13 Yet cases challenging planning decisions continue to come before the courts. They include the following:

(a) In *R (on the application of Vetterlein) v Hampshire CC and Hampshire Waste Services Ltd* [2002] PLCR 289, the claimants who were 'third parties' challenged the local planning authority's decision to grant planning permission for the construction of a waste incinerator. The court held that though it was appropriate in some circumstances to look beyond the claimants' front doorstep, there was no reasonable and convincing evidence that the claimants' quality of life was so directly affected by the incinerator as to engage Art 8. Furthermore, even if Art 6 entitled the claimants to a fair and public hearing, the opportunity given to the claimants to make detailed representations during the public consultation process and to address the committee had fulfilled that requirement.

(b) In *Lafarge Redland Aggregates Ltd v Scottish Ministers* 2001 SC 298, the Scottish Court of Session had to consider the extent of the requirement under Art 6 to provide a decision within a reasonable time. It held that the failure of the Scottish Ministers to determine an application for planning permission made in 1991 for a 'super quarry' on the Isle of Harris was a breach of Art 6. The delay which had occurred after the application had been called in was described by the court as one of 'scandalous proportions'.

(c) In *South Bucks DC v Porter (No 1)* [2003] UKHL 26, the House of Lords had to consider the implications of the Human Rights Act 1998 on the use of injunctions under the provisions of s 187B of the 1990 Act. The case (and other linked cases) concerned the use of injunctions against gypsies to secure their removal from land where there had been a breach of planning control. In spelling out the factors which needed to be considered, the House emphasized the duty under the Human Rights Act to act in accordance with the Convention. Proportionality required not only that the injunction be appropriate and necessary for the attainment of public interest objectives, but that it did not impose an excessive burden on the individual whose private interests were at stake. This case is considered more fully in Chapter 20 (Enforcement).

19.14 Not unexpectedly, cases continue to be brought before the courts on human rights grounds particularly with regard to the decisions of local planning authorities and third party rights.

19.15 It would seem beyond doubt that in the case of the determination of planning applications, a local planning authority is not an independent and impartial tribunal for the purposes of Art 6, in the same way as it was accepted in the *Alconbury* case that the Secretary of State was not. As with *Alconbury*, the question of whether Art 6 was engaged with regard to local planning authority decisions, will depend very much upon the authority's decision-making procedures and the extent to which any defects in them can be cured by the High Court's power of review. These procedures will often involve the rights of third parties. The following cases have addressed this problem.

19.16 In *R (on the application of Kathro) v Rhondda Cynon Taff CBC* [2002] PLCR 304, a distinction was made between the decision-making powers of a local planning authority and that of the Secretary of State. In that case it was acknowledged that where an authority (which is not an independent and impartial tribunal) has to determine a disputed issue of fact, the control exercised by the domestic courts might not be sufficient to ensure compliance with Art 6.

19.17 In *R (Adlard) v the Secretary of State for Transport, Local Government, and the Regions* [2002] JPL 1379, the Court of Appeal had to consider a challenge to the Secretary of State's decision not to call in an application for planning permission for the redevelopment of Fulham Football Club. The local planning authority had previously resolved to grant planning permission, but in doing so, had not given objectors to the development the opportunity to voice their objections at an oral hearing. The question for the court to decide was whether that had been a breach of their rights under Art 6. In considering that question the court considered some earlier High Court decisions. Those were:

(a) *Friends Provident Life and Pensions Ltd v the Secretary of State for Transport, Local Government and the Regions and ors* [2002] JPL 958. The claimant sought to challenge the local planning authority's grant of planning permission for a large shopping centre in Norwich. It argued that the Secretary of State's failure to call in the application was a breach of Art 6. The High Court considered that there was no reason why Art 6 should not extend to the administrative decision-making power, provided it directly affected their rights. On the facts however, the court considered that the issues in dispute 'did not give rise to the type of investigation of fact which required the safeguards attaching to a public inquiry before an independent Inspector, which would then ensure that the determination of [the claimant's] civil rights was Art 6 compliant'.

(b) *R (on the application of Cummins) v Camden LBC* [2001] EWHC Admin 116. Here, the High Court held that Art 6 was not engaged by the formulation and preparation of development plan policies.

(c) *R (Aggregate Industries UK Ltd) v English Nature* [2003] Env LR 3. In this case the claimants had challenged the decision of a local planning authority to grant planning permission for the redevelopment of a leisure centre. It was claimed that the decision and the failure of the Secretary of State to call in the application for his own determination were in breach of their Art 6 rights. The court decided that a claim that an objector's civil rights had been infringed had to be both significant and evidenced; and that the impact on 'view' was most unlikely to meet such a test.

19.18 In the *Adlard* case, the Court of Appeal, having considered the above three cases, went on to conclude that although in each case the objectors had been given limited opportunities to make their submissions, nothing in them suggested that oral hearings were necessary to satisfy Art 6. It also concluded that the statutory planning scheme as a whole was plainly compliant with Art 6. However, the court would not rule out that an oral hearing might be necessary in an 'exceptional' case. Also of interest is the decision in *Thomas v Bridgend CBC* [2012] JPL 25 where the Court of Appeal held that the exclusion of compensation rights for the depreciation of property in providing a new relief road, was not proportionate. The court therefore interpreted s 19(3) of the Compensation Act 1973 so as to provide for compensation.

19.19 Other cases where the courts have had to consider human rights issues include:

(a) *Bovis Homes Ltd v New Forest District Council* [2002] EWHC 483 (Admin), where the High Court held that Art 6 did not apply to the local plan process because civil rights were not directly affected by that process.

(b) *Re James Stewart's Application v Planning Appeals Commission* (2003 [NI 149]), where the Northern Ireland Court of Appeal accepted that generally the absence in law of a right to compensation for planning restrictions was not incompatible with Convention rights.

19.20 In the *David Lough* case, the Court of Appeal held that the diminution in the value of land did not *of itself* constitute a loss contemplated by human rights law, since it does not affect the peaceful enjoyment of possessions. However, it might demonstrate the loss of privacy or amenity which would be a human rights issue.

19.21 Emphasis on the need for a local planning authority, in taking enforcement action, to consider and weigh up both the harm to the environment and the needs of those affected by such action was recognized by the High Court in *R (on the application of O'Brien and O'Brien) v Basildon DC* [2006] EWHC 1346 where, on an application for judicial review, it quashed a decision by the authority to use its powers under s 178 of the 1990 Act to enter and remove the applicants' caravans from land in the green belt in order to secure compliance with the enforcement notice. The authority had failed to do so.

19.22 In considering the effect of the Human Rights Act on the planning system it should be recalled that before the Human Rights Act became law, the Government assessed the implications of the Act for the planning process and decided that no changes were required in order to avoid successful challenges under it. Post-*Alconbury*, that confidence has not changed. In an answer to a parliamentary question in the House of Commons on 15 October 2001, a Parliamentary Under-Secretary of State said: '[We] do not consider that there is any need on Human Rights Act grounds for changes to the appeals system generally or specifically in relation to third party objectors.'

20

ENFORCEMENT OF PLANNING CONTROL

A. INTRODUCTION	20.01	I. STOP NOTICES	20.109
B. PLANNING CONTRAVENTION NOTICES	20.07	J. BREACH OF CONDITION NOTICES	20.138
C. ADDITIONAL RIGHTS OF ENTRY ON PROPERTY	20.13	K. INJUNCTIONS	20.152
D. TEMPORARY STOP NOTICES	20.17	L. REVERSION TO EARLIER USE	20.168
E. ENFORCEMENT NOTICES	20.25	M. CERTIFICATES OF LAWFULNESS OF EXISTING USE OR DEVELOPMENT (CLEUDS) AND CERTIFICATES OF LAWFULNESS OF PROPOSED USE OR DEVELOPMENT (CLOPUDS)	20.169
F. ISSUE OF ENFORCEMENT NOTICES	20.40		
G. CONTENT OF ENFORCEMENT NOTICES	20.56		
H. APPEALS AGAINST ENFORCEMENT NOTICES	20.70		

A. INTRODUCTION

20.01 The Agricultural Land (Removal of Surface Soil) Act 1953 provides that where the removal of surface soil from agricultural land constitutes development, it is an offence to do so without planning permission. Subject to that sole exception, to carry out the development of land without planning permission does not constitute a criminal offence. Nevertheless, there has to be some sanction to ensure that unauthorized development can be prevented. The sanction provided by the law is mainly imposed by the enforcement notice machinery contained in Part VII of the Town and Country Planning Act 1990. Under this machinery, once an enforcement notice takes effect, the development which is unauthorized must cease or be removed. If it is not, then, and only then, is a criminal offence committed of failure to comply with the enforcement notice.

20.02 The law relating to enforcement notices has been strengthened over the years on numerous occasions, the most major being in 1991. Under the Planning and

Compulsory Purchase Act 2004, the Crown has been made subject to enforcement action and a new 'temporary' stop notice procedure has been introduced. Also, the Localism Act 2011 ('the 2011 Act') has introduced a new means of taking enforcement action against a breach of planning control when the time limits have expired and the breach has been concealed. The 2011 Act also contains new provisions concerning applications for retrospective planning permission, where an enforcement notice has been issued. Finally, the 2011 Act has introduced a totally new procedure whereby binding assurances about non-enforcement can be made.

20.03 The provisions of Part I of the Planning and Compensation Act 1991 supplemented and amended the enforcement provisions contained in Part VII of the 1990 Act. The amendments, which strengthened and improved the enforcement of general planning control, were based on the recommendations made in a report by Robert Carnwath QC (as he then was), *Enforcing Planning Control*, published by the Department of the Environment in April 1989.

20.04 According to Baroness Blatch, Parliamentary Under-Secretary of State at the Department of the Environment, in introducing the 1991 Act in the House of Lords in November 1990, the report showed that there was a small minority of people who were determined contraveners of planning regulations. Acknowledging this, Baroness Blatch said:

> it is those people who bring the system into disrepute; and it is their damaging and unwelcome activities ... which the enforcement amendments are intended to deter or, failing that, to remedy through increased penalties; new methods of enforcing planning conditions; and improved powers of local authority officers to enter private land for enforcement purposes.

20.05 Part I of the 1991 Act supplemented the provisions of the 1990 Act by providing a new procedure for local planning authorities to obtain information relating to suspected breaches of planning control (planning contravention notices); for enforcing planning conditions (breach of condition notices); and for obtaining injunctions to restrain breaches of planning control (planning injunctions). The remainder of Part I of the 1991 Act amended the 1990 Act to alter the time limits on the taking of enforcement action; to provide for greater flexibility in the drafting and service of enforcement notices; to revise the power of the Secretary of State on appeal; to extend the power of a local planning authority to execute works required by an enforcement notice; to increase the penalties for non-compliance with an enforcement notice; to revise the provisions relating to stop notices; to provide for a new certificate of lawful use or development; and to give authorities greater rights of entry to property for enforcement purposes.

20.06 Despite the changes which were made to the enforcement provisions by the 1991 Act, concern continued to be expressed with regard to those who disregarded planning legislation. In December 2001, the Government accepted that 'Effective action needs to be taken against those who try wilfully to avoid planning controls ... Where planning regulations are broken, there is a perception—often accurate—that they are not being sufficiently enforced.' Accordingly, a 'temporary' stop notice procedure was introduced by the 2004 Act.

B. PLANNING CONTRAVENTION NOTICES

In deciding whether or not to serve an enforcement notice, the local planning authority must, as far as possible, be sure of its facts. Accordingly, s 324 of the 1990 Act gave a power to local planning authorities to enter land, subject to at least 24 hours' notice of intention to do so, for the purposes of surveying it in connection with the service of notices, including enforcement notices. In addition, s 330 enables a local planning authority to demand information from the occupier of land as to his interest. The Carnwath report recommended that there should be a new optional statutory procedure, not only to enable authorities to obtain information, but to secure co-operation from an owner without recourse to enforcement action. This was done by the Planning and Compensation Act 1991, which inserted ss 171C and 171D into the 1990 Act providing for the service of planning contravention notices. Under s 171C(1), where it appears to the local planning authority that there may have been a breach of planning control in respect of any land, the authority may serve a notice to that effect (called a 'planning contravention notice') on any person who is the owner or occupier of the land or has any other interest in it, or who is carrying out operations on the land or using it for any purpose. Where a notice is served, s 171C(2) provides that the notice may require the recipient to give such information as may be specified in the notice about any operations being carried out on the land, any use of the land, and any other activities being carried out on it, and any matter relating to conditions or limitations subject to which any planning permission has been granted in respect of the land. In addition, s 171C(3) provides that, without prejudice to the generality of s 171C(2), the notice may require the recipient, so far as he is able to do so, to state whether or not the land is being used for any purpose specified in the notice, or whether any operations, or activities specified in the notice are being or have been carried out on the land; to state when any use, operations, or activities began; to give the names and addresses of any persons known to him to use or have used the land for any purpose or to be carrying out or have carried out any operations, or activities on the land; to give any information in his possession as to any planning permission for any use or operations or any reason for planning permission not being required for any use or operations; to state the nature of his interest (if any) in the land and the name and address of any other person known to him to have an interest in the land.

20.07

20.08 Under s 171C(5), a planning contravention notice must inform the recipient of the likely consequences of his failure to respond to the notice and, in particular, that enforcement action may be taken. In addition, the recipient must also be informed that in the event of enforcement action being taken, failure to respond to the notice may affect his entitlement to compensation in the event of a stop notice also being served. It should be noted that the service of a planning contravention notice in no way prejudices other action the planning authority may wish to take in respect of a breach of planning control, including the service of a temporary stop notice. If a local planning authority is already in possession of all the information necessary, it may decide to take enforcement action without the earlier service of a planning contravention notice.

20.09 Subsection (1) of s 171D provides that if any person fails to comply with any requirement of a planning contravention notice within a period of 21 days, he shall be guilty of a criminal offence. The section goes on to provide that if at any time after conviction that person continues to fail to comply with any requirement of the notice, he may be convicted of a second or subsequent offence, thereby ensuring that the requirement is eventually complied with. Under s 171D(3), it is a defence for a person charged with an offence to prove that he had a reasonable excuse for failing to comply with a requirement in the notice. In addition to the above, a person is guilty of an offence if the information he gives in response to a planning contravention notice is false or misleading in a material particular, or he recklessly makes a statement which is false or misleading in a material particular.

20.10 Under s 171C(4), a planning contravention notice may give notice of a time and place at which any offer which the recipient of the notice may wish to make to apply for planning permission, or to refrain from carrying out any operations or activities, or to undertake remedial works, and any representations which he may wish to make about the notice, will be considered by the authority. The authority must give the recipient an opportunity to make any such offer or representations, in person, at a specified time and place.

20.11 It will be seen that the refusal of the person served with a planning contravention notice to make an offer (as opposed to providing the information required by the notice) is not a criminal offence. The recipient of the notice may well decline to do so without fear of any penalty. Hence, there must be considerable uncertainty as to the extent to which an offer would be made to the local planning authority by that 'small minority of determined contraveners' mentioned by Baroness Blatch.

20.12 In the first case to consider this new provision, *R v Teignbridge DC, ex p Teignmouth Quay Co Ltd* [1995] 2 PLR 1, the procedure was described as 'intrusive and if properly served, [the] compliance was mandatory'. The court went on to grant judicial review to quash the notice, on the ground that the local planning authority's inquiries before service were not sufficient on their own to satisfy the minimal statutory requirements before which the notice could be served.

C. ADDITIONAL RIGHTS OF ENTRY ON PROPERTY

20.13 The rights of local planning authorities in the 1990 Act to enter on land did not distinguish between the power to enter land for the purposes of investigating a breach of planning control and other powers to enter land for planning purposes, such as in connection with development plan preparation; the consideration of applications for planning permission; or the making, for example, of a revocation or modification order. It was often difficult, therefore, for a local planning authority to obtain the precise information needed in order to take formal and effective enforcement action. Mention has been made above of the powers now available to a local planning authority under the 1990 Act to obtain information by means of the 'planning contravention notice'. In addition, however, the 1991 Act introduced into the 1990 Act three new sections, ss 196A, 196B, and 196C, in order to give local planning authorities more specific rights of entry onto land to be exercised where enforcement action is foreseen.

20.14 Subsection (1) of s 196A provides that any person duly authorized in writing by a local planning authority may at any reasonable hour enter land to ascertain whether there is or has been any breach of planning control on land; to determine whether any of the powers conferred by the Act on a local planning authority should be exercised; to determine how any such power should be exercised; and to ascertain whether there has been compliance with any requirement arising from earlier enforcement action in relation to the land. The power of entry given by this subsection is subject to the proviso that there must be reasonable grounds for entering the land for any of those purposes. In the case of any building used as a dwelling-house, the section provides that admission to the building shall not be demanded 'as of right', unless 24 hours' notice of the intended entry has been given to the occupier of the building. It would appear that this 24 hours' notice is not necessary if the authority wishes to enter upon land adjoining a dwellinghouse or on land within its curtilage.

20.15 If entry in accordance with these provisions is refused, s 196B(1) provides that if it is shown to the satisfaction of a justice of the peace, on sworn information in writing, that there were reasonable grounds for entering any land for the purposes of ascertaining whether there has been a breach of planning control or for determining whether enforcement action should be taken, and that admission to the land has been refused, or a refusal is reasonably apprehended, or the case is one of urgency, the justice may issue a warrant authorizing any person duly authorized in writing by the local planning authority to enter the land. It should be noted that the warrant authorizes entry onto the land in question on one occasion only, and entry must be within one month from the date of issue of the warrant, and at a reasonable hour, unless the case is one of urgency.

20.16 Section 196C of the 1990 Act contains provisions which are supplementary to ss 196A and 196B discussed above. All the provisions in s 196C replicate provisions previously found in the 1990 Act, being applicable to the exercise of rights of entry for a whole range of planning purposes. The section groups those supplementary provisions in one section to be exercised in connection with the enforcement of planning control.

D. TEMPORARY STOP NOTICES

20.17 Section 52 of the Planning and Compulsory Purchase Act 2004 has added greatly to the powers for a local planning authority to deal with breaches of planning control which may have been disclosed, either by the service of a planning contravention notice, or otherwise. Section 52 introduced into the 1990 Act new ss 171E to 171H. Those new sections give a local planning authority a new wide discretionary power to serve a temporary stop notice to halt what it considers to be breaches of planning control for a period of up to 28 days. The provisions enable authorities to service the notice without waiting until an enforcement notice can be formally served. Its use can prevent the intensification of a use or other form of development believed to be unlawful whilst further action is being considered. A temporary stop notice has an immediate effect from the time a copy is displayed on the land with an accompanying statement as to its effect, though it may be withdrawn by the authority before the 28 days have expired. A second temporary stop notice may also be issued in respect of the same activity, but only if the authority has first taken some other enforcement action in relation to the breach of planning control constituted by the activity required to be stopped by the earlier notice. Section 171E(3)(c) requires the authority to set out the reasons for issuing the notice but there is no right of appeal to the Secretary of State. Temporary stop notices are free-standing, in the sense that unlike ordinary stop notices, they do not depend on an enforcement notice being served.

20.18 There are restrictions on the issuing of a temporary stop notice. It is provided by the new s 171F of the 1990 Act that a temporary stop notice should not prohibit the carrying out of any activity which has been carried out for at least four years, unless it is an activity consisting of or incidental to operational development or to the deposit of refuse. In addition, a temporary stop notice cannot be issued to prohibit the use of a building as a dwellinghouse. However, that provision allows the Secretary of State, by regulation, to prescribe any other activity which cannot be prohibited by a temporary stop notice. That power has been used to prescribe the circumstances in which a temporary stop notice cannot prohibit the stationing of caravans. The effect of the Town and Country Planning (Temporary Stop Notices) (England) Regulations 2005 was that a temporary stop notice cannot prohibit the stationing of a caravan on land where it was stationed on the land immediately before the issue of the temporary stop notice; and it is occupied at that time by a person as his main residence. However, those Regulations were revoked on 4 May 2013 (SI 2013/830).

In *R (Wilson) v Wychavon DC and anor* [2007] EWCA Civ 52, the Court of **20.19**
Appeal held that a statutory provision prohibiting the use of a temporary stop notice in the case of a dwellinghouse but not in the case of a caravan discriminated against gypsies, but that the need to weigh up the risk of harm to caravan dwellers against the protection of the environment made it compatible with their human rights under Art 14 of the Convention.

The new sections provide that the notice must be in writing; prohibit the carrying **20.20**
on of the activity; set out the reasons for issuing the notice; and be served on the person who the authority thinks is carrying on the activity, a person who is the occupier, and a person who has an interest in the land.

A copy of the notice and statement of the effect of the notice must also be displayed by the authority on the land. **20.21**

The provisions make it an offence to contravene a temporary stop notice (which **20.22**
includes causing or permitting the contravention of a notice). It is punishable on summary conviction or on indictment to an unlimited fine. In determining a fine the court has to have regard to any financial benefit which has accrued to the person in consequence of the offence.

In certain cases the compensation may be payable by the local planning authority **20.23**
to the owner of an interest in the land to which the notice serves, where that person has suffered loss or damage directly attributable to the prohibition effected by the notice. The right to compensation is limited, however, to cases where the temporary stop notice is withdrawn by the authority, or the activity specified in the notice has been authorized by planning permission, a development order, or a local development order, or a certificate of lawful use or development in respect of the activity is granted under s 191 of the 1990 Act.

Since being introduced, the temporary stop notice has proved a popular enforcement tool for local planning authorities, with over 530 being issued in the first **20.24**
year. They have been used successfully to stop a wide variety of unauthorized development, including: damage to listed buildings, trees, wildlife sites, unauthorized landfill, quarrying, tipping, processing and storage of waste, clay extraction, building new houses, flats, garages, barns, gypsy sites, access roads, and engineering and building works.

E. ENFORCEMENT NOTICES

Time limits on enforcement action

Under subsection (2) of s 171A of the 1990 Act, enforcement action may be taken **20.25**
by the issue of an enforcement notice or by the service of a breach of condition notice. Such enforcement action may only be taken in relation to a breach of planning control, defined in s 171A(1) as carrying out development without the

required planning permission, or failing to comply with any condition subject to which planning permission has been granted.

20.26 The Planning and Compensation Act 1991 made important amendments to the 1990 Act with regard to the time limits for the bringing of enforcement action by a local planning authority. Under the old law, where the breach of planning control was the carrying out without planning permission of operational development, no enforcement action could be taken after the end of a period of four years from the date the operations were completed. No change was made in that provision, save that the period is now made to run for four years from the date on which the operations were substantially completed. A question may arise as to when an operation is *substantially* completed, particularly in the case of a dwellinghouse. In *Sage v Secretary of State for the Environment, Transport and the Regions and Maidstone BC* [2003] UKHL 22; [2003] 1 WLR 983, the Court of Appeal had held that a dwellinghouse was not substantially completed if what still remained to be done amounted to development under s 55(1) of the 1990 Act.

20.27 If that had remained the law, it would have meant that works which might still be needed to make the dwellinghouse fit for habitation, such as the putting in of an internal staircase, would not prevent the building from being regarded as substantially completed. This is because of s 55(2) of the 1990 Act which provides that works for the maintenance, improvement, or other alteration of a building which affect only the interior of the building or which do not materially affect its external appearance do not involve the development of land.

20.28 The House of Lords, however, thought otherwise. Lord Hobhouse, who gave the main speech, thought that any work carried out by way of completing an incomplete structure, would not be work for the maintenance, improvement, or other alteration of the building. In short, his Lordship restricted the operation of s 55(2) to a building which had already been completed, not to one that remained uncompleted. According to Lord Hobhouse, one had to adopt a holistic approach to determine whether building works had been substantially completed. He observed that where an application for planning permission was made for a single operation, it was made in respect of the whole of that operation. The concept of a full planning permission required a detailed building of a certain character; if an operation was not carried out both externally and internally fully in accordance with the planning permission then the whole operation was unlawful.

20.29 In *First Secretary of State v Chelmsford BC* [2003] EWHC 2800 (Admin); [2004] JPL 1074, the High Court applied *Sage* in holding that the bringing onto land of two static caravans and their bolting together did not amount to a substantial completion of the development and was therefore unlawful. The holistic approach required by Lord Hobhouse in *Sage* meant that substantial completion had not occurred until after the subsequent application of cladding to the structure, which in itself would not have required planning permission. In *Fidler* *v Secretary of State for Communities and Local Government* [2010] EWHC 143 (Admin); [2010] JPL 915 the appellant had built a dwelling in the green belt without planning permission. It had been hidden from public view by being surrounded by walls of straw bales. Forbes J held that the Inspector was entitled to find that the straw bales and tarpaulins formed part of the totality of the operational development in the holistic sense accorded by the authority of the *Sage* decision and so the building was not substantially completed until they were removed. However, from *Adargh Glass Ltd v Chester City Council* [2009] EWHC 745; [2009] Env LR 34 it would seem that where there is a large, complex development made up of several distinct elements it may not be necessary for the whole project to be completed before any element becomes immune. The onward appeal in *Fidler* was withdrawn following the handing down of the *Welwyn* judgment in the Supreme Court (discussed later).

20.30 Under s 171B(2) (as under the previous law), no enforcement action can be taken in relation to a change of use of any building to use as a single dwellinghouse if the use had subsisted for more than four years. That includes breaches of condition which result in a new dwellinghouse, see: *Arun District Council v First Secretary of State* [2006] EWCA Civ 1172; [2007] 1 WLR 523. It should be emphasized, however, that the immunity from enforcement action applies to a change in the use of any building to use as a single dwellinghouse, and it matters not that the change of use may be a breach of condition intended to prevent such a change. For the purposes of enforcement action, the Secretary of State has taken the view that in order to establish that a building has been used as a single dwellinghouse, it must be shown that for the four-year period ending with the taking of enforcement action, the building must comprise a self-contained independent unit of accommodation, containing all the facilities normally associated with a dwelling behind a single, lockable door. In *Moore v Secretary of State* (1999) 77 P & CR 114 it was said that the distinctive characteristics of a dwellinghouse were to be its ability to afford to those who use it the facilities required for day-to-day private domestic existence.

20.31 The Supreme Court has held in *Welwyn Hatfield Council v Secretary of State for Communities and Local Government* [2011] UKSC 15; [2011] 2 AC 304 that where there had occurred an unauthorized erection and use of a building as a dwellinghouse, the use had not become lawful, even though four years had elapsed since the dwellinghouse use had commenced. The erection and use of the building as a dwellinghouse had been concealed for four years. No enforcement action had been taken as the permission had been granted to build a hay barn and the building, which was used as a dwellinghouse, had been built to look like a hay barn. It was therefore held that no change of use of the building had taken place on which the four-year rule could apply. Although the dwellinghouse had been disguised to look like a barn, it had always been intended that it would be used as a dwellinghouse. The argument that the building once completed had a nil use and so a change of use had taken place was rejected. The strange result is that in a case where it is too late to take enforcement action against the building operation, it cannot be argued that the use as a dwellinghouse is equally lawful. Yet the logic of the Supreme Court would seem to suggest that no material change of use has taken place and so it would seem to follow that the use, though not permitted, was not unauthorized development. In *Sumner v Secretary of State for Communities and Local Government* [2010] EWHC 372 (Admin); [2010] JPL 1014 Collins J found that where a building, constructed in breach of planning legislation, was immune from enforcement action because the enforcement time limit had expired, that did not mean that the use of the building was to be regarded as lawful. He found that the use of the building was not ancillary to its construction as s 171B of the Town and Country Planning Act 1990 drew a distinction between operational development and change of use. This does leave the law in a rather confused state.

20.32 In *Welwyn*, the Supreme Court also held that positive and deliberately misleading false statements by an owner, which successfully prevented discovery before the time limits elapsed, could override the statutory immunity from enforcement. Section 124 of the 2011 Act amends the 1990 Act and allows enforcement action to be taken against a breach of planning control when the time limits for taking action have expired and the breach has been concealed. In order to use these powers, the local planning authority must apply to the magistrates' court for a 'planning enforcement order' within six months of the day on which the apparent breach came to the authority's knowledge. If an order is granted, the authority has one year to take enforcement action. A magistrates' court may make the order only if satisfied, on the balance of probabilities, that the apparent breach, or any of the matters constituting the apparent breach, has (to any extent) been deliberately concealed. The magistrates' court must also consider that it is just to make the order in all the circumstances. In *Jackson v Secretary of State for Communities and Local Government* [2015] EWCA Civ 1246; [2016] QB 811 the Court of Appeal held that the *Welwyn* principle survived the legislative amendments at s 124 of the 2011 Act. Accordingly, a local authority can still take enforcement action on the basis of positive deception notwithstanding that the criteria in the planning enforcement order regime have not been made out in a given case.

20.33 Where the contravening development involved some other material change of use or breach of condition, it used to be the case that since 1964 there was no time limit on the period within which an enforcement notice could be served. This was changed by the 1991 Act. Section 171B of the 1990 Act now provides that in the case of any other breach of planning control (ie other than operational development or a change of use of any building to use as a single dwellinghouse), no enforcement action may be taken at the end of a period of 10 years beginning with the date of the breach. If there has been a material change of use, the change becomes lawful even if the actual use changes but keeps within one of the classes of the Use Classes order. The subsequent changes did not amount to development and therefore did not stop time running; see *R (on the application of Harbidge) v Secretary of State for Communities and Local Government* [2012] EWHC 1128 (Admin).

So the position now can be summed up as follows: **20.34**

Unauthorized operations	Time limit of four years
Unauthorized change of use of building to a dwellinghouse use	Time limit of four years
Other unauthorized material change of use or breach of condition	Time limit of 10 years

The rationale of the four- and 10-year periods of immunity is that, throughout the relevant period of unlawful use, the local planning authority, although having the opportunity to take enforcement action, has failed to do so and consequently it would be unfair and/or could be regarded as unnecessary to permit enforcement. It follows therefore that in order to become lawful, a use must have continued actively throughout the four- or 10-year period to the extent that enforcement action could have been taken against it at any time. Consequently, if any significant period of dormancy occurs in the use of the land, the immunity period required will recommence when the use is reactivated. This is considered in more detail in para 20.182. **20.35**

A further important change should also be noted. Under the old law, where an enforcement notice had been issued and was subsequently held to have been defective, further enforcement action had to be taken before the period of immunity commenced. Now under s 171B(4)(b) if an enforcement notice is held to be defective, the authority is given a further four years from the taking of the previous enforcement action (or purported action) in which to issue another effective enforcement notice in respect of the same breach. **20.36**

The purpose of this 'second bite' provision is to remove the protection given to developers whereby under the old law they were able to avoid enforcement action by establishing that a technical error had been made in the enforcement notice; and during the period they were doing so, the time for service was continuing to run and eventually expired, leaving it too late for another enforcement notice to be issued. In *Jarmain v Secretary of State for the Environment, Transport and the Regions* [2000] JPL 1063, it was held that it was not necessary for the actual breach of development control to be described in the same way in both enforcement notices. The subsection could not be used to cover two different physical developments or two different changes of use, but it could be used to cover the same actual breach of development control, even though they were described in different ways. Accordingly, the Court of Appeal dismissed an appeal from a decision of the High Court which had held that where the first enforcement notice **20.37** had described incorrectly the breach of planning control as being the siting on land of a 'mobile home', the subsection enabled the authority to issue a further enforcement notice which described the breach as the erection of 'a single storey building' on the land.

20.38 In *Fidler v First Secretary of State for the Environment and Reigate and Banstead BC* [2003] EWHC 2003 (Admin); [2004] 1 PLR 1 it was said that where a second bite notice goes wider than the earlier notice, as for example by including land and uses outside those specified in the first notice, or does not describe more accurately that which had been wrongly described in the earlier notice, the later notice is more than a mere correction of a technicality. It thus falls outside the range of circumstances at which s 171B(4) was aimed.

20.39 The exceptions to this 'second-bite provision' are in those cases where an appeal against a previous enforcement notice has succeeded on any of the grounds in 174(2) (a), (c), or (d), or planning permission has since been granted for the matter in question. In those circumstances it clearly would not be open to the local planning authority to take enforcement action. However, in *R (on the application of Romer) v London Borough of Haringey* [2006] EWHC 3480 (Admin); [2007] JPL 1354, it was held that the second bite provision could apply to a case where the earlier enforcement notice incorrectly identified the site and wrongly described the alleged breach. This liberal approach was followed in *R (on the application of Lambrou) v Secretary of State for Communities and Local Government* [2013] EWHC 325 (Admin); [2014] JPL 538 where it was held that s 171B(4) could apply to purported enforcement action even if the first notice had been found to be erroneous or had failed in its purpose, as long as the intention behind the later enforcement notice was broadly the same.

F. ISSUE OF ENFORCEMENT NOTICES

20.40 Under s 172 of the 1990 Act, a local planning authority may *issue* an enforcement notice where it appears to it:

(a) that there has been a breach of planning control; and
(b) that it is expedient to issue the notice, having regard to the provisions of the development plan and to any other material considerations.

The provision in para (b) above is, of course, to be read in conjunction with s 38(6) of the Planning and Compulsory Purchase Act 2004 (see Chapter 3), which gives the development plan a position of primacy over other material considerations where a determination has to be made under the planning Acts. Once issued, a copy of the enforcement notice is now required to be *served*. Subsection (2) of s 172 provides that a copy shall be served:

(a) on the owner and occupier of the land to which it relates; and
(b) on any other person having an interest in the land, being an interest which, in the opinion of the authority, is materially affected by the notice.

20.41 The term 'owner' in s 172(2) causes few problems. Section 336(1) of the 1990 Act defines an owner as:

> ... a person, other than a mortgagee not in possession, who, whether in his own right or as trustee for any other person, is entitled to receive the rack rent of the land or, where the land is not let at a rack rent, would be so entitled if it were so let.

The Act, however, does not define the term 'occupier'. The term has, therefore, given rise to some litigation, particularly over the question of whether caravan dwellers come within the term. In *Munnich v Godstone RDC* [1966] 1 WLR 427, it was considered that they did not. In *Stevens v Bromley LBC* [1972] Ch 400, it was considered that they did. In a later case, *Scarborough BC v Adams* [1983] JPL 673, caravan dwellers were again held to be occupiers and entitled, therefore, to be served with a copy of the enforcement notice. In *Stevens*, it was held that the question of whether a caravan dweller was an occupier was one of fact and degree in every case. There would be many cases where it would be difficult to decide on which side of the line it fell, but exclusive occupation and a degree of permanence were factors to be taken into account. Whether a person is an occupier and therefore has a right to be served with an enforcement notice may be critical, since s 174 of the 1990 Act allows a person who occupies the land to which a notice relates by virtue of a licence, a right of appeal to the Secretary of State against the notice.

20.42 Where a person entitled to be served with a copy of an enforcement notice is not served, the position can be quite complicated. At one time, the position was that if an enforcement notice was challenged in the courts on the ground that a person required to be served with a notice had not been served, the court had no option but to quash the notice. This led to a practice known as 'shuffling of interests', whereby, after the local planning authority had made enquiries about the nature of a person's interest in land prior to the service on him of the enforcement notice, that person transferred his interest to a friend or relative, so that when the notice was eventually served it was served on a person who was not the owner of an interest in the land, and was not served on the person who had now become the owner. Similar transfers sometimes took place between associated 'one-man' companies.

20.43 To meet this difficulty, the 1968 Act introduced a number of new provisions into the law. One, which is now found in s 176(5) of the 1990 Act, provides that where it would otherwise be a ground for determining an appeal in favour of the appellant that a person required to be served with a copy of the enforcement notice was not served, the Secretary of State may disregard that fact if neither the appellant nor that person has been substantially prejudiced by the failure to serve him.

20.44 This may meet the case of a transfer made between spouses prior to service of a copy of the enforcement notice. But it is not likely to meet the case of an innocent purchaser who may know nothing of the notice and is unable, therefore, to appeal to the Secretary of State before the notice has taken effect. Accordingly, a further change in the law was made which is now found in s 285 of the 1990 Act. Normally, the validity of an enforcement notice cannot be questioned in the courts on any of the grounds on which a person may bring an appeal against it to the Secretary of State (see below). Since one of the grounds of appeal to the Secretary of State is that copies of the enforcement notice were not served on those required to be served by the Act, this provision would, by itself, mean that a person not served would be unable to question the legality of the notice if he were subsequently prosecuted under s 179(6) to (8) of the Act for a failure to comply with the notice.

20.45 Accordingly s 285 provides that the embargo on questioning the validity of an enforcement notice shall not apply to proceedings brought under s 179(6) to (8) of the 1990 Act against a person who:

  (a) has held an interest in the land since before the enforcement notice was issued ...;
  (b) did not have a copy of the enforcement notice served on him ...; and
  (c) satisfies the court—
    (i) that he did not know and could not reasonably have been expected to know that the enforcement notice had been issued; and
    (ii) that his interests have been substantially prejudiced by the failure to serve him with a copy of it.

20.46 Despite those elaborate provisions, however, it may still be possible for a person to be bound by an enforcement notice of which he has no notice. The saving provisions of s 285 do not anticipate that a local planning authority might choose not to prosecute under s 179(6) to (8) but to exercise its powers under s 178(1) to enter the land and to carry out the work which is required to be done by the enforcement notice. In *R v Greenwich LBC, ex p Patel* (1985) 51 P & CR 282, the applicant sought by way of judicial review an order of prohibition against the local planning authority prohibiting it from entering his land and demolishing a shed which had been erected on the land by his wife without the grant of planning permission. The enforcement notice had been served on the applicant's wife as the person 'owning the land'. It was in fact owned by the applicant. There had been no appeal against the notice to the Secretary of State. Earlier, it appears, the applicant's wife had been refused planning permission to erect the shed on the land which she had stated she owned; and an appeal against the refusal had been dismissed by the Secretary of State. The applicant claimed he first knew of the notice when his wife received a letter from the local planning authority informing her of its intention to enter the land and demolish the shed.

20.47 In withholding the relief applied for, the Court of Appeal refused to hold that the failure to serve the enforcement notice in accordance with what is now s 172(2) rendered it a nullity. According to the Court of Appeal, Parliament has expressly provided machinery to deal with circumstances where an enforcement notice has not been served on a person who should have been served. In doing so, it felt able to distinguish the Scottish case of *McDaid v Clydebank DC* [1984] JPL 579, where the Court of Session had seemingly held to the contrary. In that case, however, the local planning authority had erred in that it had been aware of the identity of the owner but had still failed to serve him. In the *Patel* case, the Court of Appeal found that there had been no deliberate disregard of the statutory requirement by the local planning authority; nor had it failed to show due diligence. Furthermore, there was no reason to suppose that the applicant had suffered any real prejudice.

20.48 The Scottish case shows that despite the changes made in 1968, there may still be situations where the failure to serve an enforcement notice in accordance with the provisions of s 172(2) will render the notice a nullity. For that to happen, however, it appears that not only must the owner or occupier have been prejudiced by the failure to serve the notice on him, but there must also have been some malfeasance on the part of the authority.

20.49 Subsection (3) of s 172 of the 1990 Act also provides a strict time limit for service of copies of the enforcement notice. According to the subsection, the service of the notice shall take place:

(a) not more than 28 days after its date of issue; and
(b) not less than 28 days before the date specified in it as the date on which it is to take effect.

20.50 The importance of this provision is that s 173(8) of the 1990 Act provides that any enforcement notice must specify the date on which it is to come into effect; after which date no appeal will lie to the Secretary of State.

20.51 Two key dates, therefore, are the date when the enforcement notice is issued (ie, made by the authority) and the date specified in the notice as the date on which it is to come into effect. The effect of s 172(3) is to ensure that within that time period all copies of an enforcement notice that have to be served are served within 28 days of the date of its issue, and that any recipient of a copy of such an enforcement notice has it in his possession for at least 28 days before it comes into effect.

20.52 The purpose of the first period is to overcome a problem that sometimes used to arise when an enforcement notice was served on different persons on different days. In *Bambury v Hounslow LBC* [1966] 2 QB 204, enforcement notices were served on three occupiers of land on 22 August 1964. Each notice required the unauthorized development to be discontinued within 28 days from the date on which the notice took effect. All stated that the notice should take effect on the expiration of 28 clear days after service of the notice.

20.53 Then on 8 September 1964 a further enforcement notice in similar terms was served on the owner. On appeal to the High Court the enforcement notices were quashed. The occupiers successfully contended that there could not be two dates for the coming into force of the same enforcement notice. If there were two separate dates, there were in effect two separate enforcement notices, neither of which had been served as required by the law on both the owners *and* occupiers of the land to which they related.

20.54 Under the 1990 Act provisions, the procedure is commenced not when the enforcement notice is served by the authority, but when it is *issued* by it; and it enables the authority to serve *copies* of the notice, on persons required to be served, on any number of different dates, so long as all persons are served within the time span set out in s 172(3).

20.55 The purpose of the second period is to give the recipient of the notice a minimum period of 28 days in which to decide whether or not to appeal against the notice. If he decides not to appeal, the notice takes effect on the date stated. If, however, he decides to appeal against the notice to the Secretary of State, s 175(4) provides that subject to any order made under s 289(4A) (on which see para 20.103), the enforcement notice shall be of no effect pending the final determination or withdrawal of the appeal.

G. CONTENT OF ENFORCEMENT NOTICES

20.56 Section 173(1) of the 1990 Act provides that an enforcement notice shall state:

(a) the matters which appear to the local planning authority to constitute the breach of planning control; and
(b) the paragraph of s 171A(1) within which, in the opinion of the local planning authority, the breach falls.

20.57 Following the judgment in *Copeland BC v Secretary of State for the Environment* (1976) 31 P & CR 403 where a building had been erected otherwise than in accordance with approved plans, an enforcement notice may be served alleging that the building as a whole had been built without planning permission.

20.58 The 1990 Act originally provided that an enforcement notice should 'specify' the matters alleged to constitute the breach. By requiring the notice now to 'state' these matters, the drafters of the 1991 Act hope that notices will be less likely to be challenged as being a nullity because the breach has not been specified correctly. In addition, the effect of subsection (2) of the new s 173 is that as long as the recipient of an enforcement notice understands from the notice what the matters are which the local authority considers to be a breach of planning control, the notice is not to be regarded as defective on the ground that it did not state the breach with sufficient clarity or particularity.

It seems from the decision in *Westminster City Council v Secretary of State for the Environment and Aboro* [1983] JPL 602 that it is not necessary to specify in an enforcement notice the use from which it is alleged there has been a material change of use, though it is usual to do so. Furthermore, in *McCarthy v Secretary of State for the Environment, Transport and the Regions* [1999] JPL 993, the High Court held that an enforcement notice could lawfully be served in relation to part of a planning unit, provided the question of the materiality of the change of use was considered by reference to the whole of the planning unit.

20.59

Having stated the breach of planning control, subsections (3) and (4) of section 173 then require the notice to specify the steps which the authority requires to be taken, or the activities which the authority requires to cease, in order to achieve, wholly or partly, any of the following purposes:

20.60

(a) remedying the breach by making any development comply with the terms (including conditions and limitations) of any planning permission granted in respect of the land, by discontinuing any use of land or by restoring the land to its condition before the breach took place; or
(b) remedying any injury to amenity which has been caused by the breach.

Subsection (5) provides the following examples of what an enforcement notice may require:

(a) the alteration or removal of any building or works;
(b) the carrying out of any building or other operation;
(c) any activity on the land not to be carried on except to the extent specified in the notice;
(d) the contour of a deposit of refuse or waste materials on land to be modified by altering the gradient or gradients of its sides.

In addition, where an enforcement notice is issued in respect of a breach of planning control consisting of demolition of a building, the notice may require the construction of a 'replacement building', as similar as possible to the demolished building.

20.61

By virtue of s 173(11), if the notice could have required any buildings or works to be removed or any activity to cease, but does not do so, or requires the construction of a replacement building, and the notice is complied with, planning permission is deemed to be granted for the buildings, works, activity, or replacement building. While a notice can require positive building works, in *Lipsen v Secretary of State for the Environment* [1976] P & CR 95 (Div Court), it was established that an enforcement notice cannot require a former use to be revived. The notice can only require that the activities which amount to a material change of use should cease.

20.62

This is a very important provision where there has been a breach of planning control and the local planning authority decides to 'under-enforce'. If the notice has been complied with, planning permission is granted for that development which

20.63

has not been enforced against. The section does not grant planning permission for development not enforced against in the notice, but is limited to producing the effect of a grant of permission for that development. Hence, as held in *Sparkes v Secretary of State for the Environment, Transport and the Regions* [2000] PLCR 279, the provision does not allow conditions to be imposed on that unenforced development.

20.64 In *Murfitt v Secretary of State for the Environment* (1980) 40 P & CR 254 and *Somak Travel v Secretary of State for the Environment* (1988) 55 P & CR 250, the principle was established that an enforcement notice can properly require the undoing or removal of any incidental operational development where it forms an integral part of the development enforced against. This is so even though the operational development may by itself not constitute a breach of planning control. So that, for example, where hard-standings and sheds are an integral part of an unauthorized use, an enforcement notice can require them to be removed as part of the cessation of that unauthorized use. The principle also applies to operational development which by itself is immune from enforcement action by virtue of the four-year rule or development which has been carried out as permitted development. In *Kestrel Hydro v Secretary of State for Communities and Local Government* [2016] EWCA Civ 784 the Court of Appeal confirmed that *Murfitt* and *Somak Travel* remained good law in a case concerning a Private Members' Club for adults engaging in naturist pursuits and sexual activities. When a local planning authority took enforcement action in respect of an unauthorized change of use of land, the notice could require the cessation of the unauthorized use and the removal of any building works that facilitated, and were integral to, that use.

20.65 Having stated what has to be done to remedy the breach, the notice must also specify the period at the end of which the steps required to be taken must be taken or any activities required to cease must cease. In this connection, s 173(9) provides that a notice may specify different periods for the taking of different steps or activities.

20.66 An enforcement notice must specify such additional matters as may be prescribed, and regulations may require every copy of an enforcement notice to be accompanied by an explanatory note giving information about rights of appeal. Indeed, reg 4 of the Town and Country Planning (Enforcement Notices and Appeals) Regulations, SI 2002/2682 requires that the explanatory note should contain a copy of ss 171A to 177 of the 1990 Act, or a summary including information as to the right of appeal and of the recipient's duty to give his grounds of appeal. In addition, the Regulations require the local planning authority to specify details of all policies and proposals in the development plan relevant to the decision to issue the notice; the fee payable for any deemed application for planning permission; and a requirement for the Secretary of State to notify the appellant and the local planning authority when he considers he has received all the documents required to enable him to entertain the appeal.

20.67 The new provisions in the 1990 Act relating to the steps which the recipient of the notice must take to remedy the breach were redrafted by the 1991 Act in order to give local planning authorities greater flexibility in the choice of those steps including, if the authority wish, the power to 'under-enforce'.

20.68 It should also be noted that local planning authorities are now given the power to withdraw an enforcement notice issued by them, or waive, or relax any requirement of an enforcement notice, including, in particular, power to extend the time specified in the notice for compliance with it (s 173A(1)). When using this power, however, the authority must give notice of its exercise to every person served with a copy of the enforcement notice.

20.69 Where an enforcement notice is withdrawn, the local planning authority may issue another, and that other may be more onerous than the notice which was withdrawn (*Manchester City Council v McLoughlin* (*The Times*, 5 April 2000).

H. APPEALS AGAINST ENFORCEMENT NOTICES

20.70 Section 174(1) of the 1990 Act provides that:

> A person having an interest in the land to which an enforcement notice relates or a relevant occupier may appeal to the Secretary of State against the notice, whether or not a copy of it has been served on him.

20.71 It should be noticed that the persons entitled to appeal under s 174(1) are not coterminous with the persons who are required to be served with a copy of the notice under s 172(2). The right of appeal to the Secretary of State is restricted to those having an interest in the land and relevant occupiers. A 'relevant occupier' is a person who:

(a) on the date on which the enforcement notice is issued, occupies the land to which the notice relates by virtue of a licence; and
(b) continues so to occupy the land when the appeal is brought.

It would seem that the term relevant occupier would include a person entitled to a right of way over the land.

20.72 An appeal must be made by notice in writing to the Secretary of State before the specified date (ie, the date specified in the notice as the date on which it is to take effect). Failure to appeal by that date may be fatal for any person wishing to do so, since, as was confirmed by the Court of Appeal in *Howard v Secretary of State for the Environment* [1975] QB 235, the Secretary of State has no jurisdiction to extend that date. After that date if no appeal has been made the enforcement notice will come into effect and must be complied with, unless of course, the notice is itself a nullity. It is therefore very important that those entitled to appeal do so within the time limits.

20.73 Section 174(2) provides that an appeal may be brought on any of the following grounds:

(a) that, in respect of any breach of planning control which may be constituted by the matters stated in the notice, planning permission ought to be granted or, as the case may be, the condition or limitation concerned ought to be discharged. [However, s 123 of the 2011 Act amends s 174 of the Town and Country Planning Act 1990 so that if a retrospective planning application has been made, but an enforcement notice has been issued after the date of the application but before the time for making a decision has expired, the developer cannot then appeal against the enforcement notice on this ground];
(b) that those matters have not occurred;
(c) that those matters (if they occurred) do not constitute a breach of planning control;
(d) that, at the date when the notice was issued, no enforcement action could be taken in respect of any breach of planning control which may be constituted by those matters;
(e) that copies of the enforcement notice were not served as required by s 172;
(f) that the steps required by the notice to be taken, or the activities required by the notice to cease, exceed what is necessary to remedy any breach of planning control which may be constituted by those matters or, as the case may be, to remedy any injury to amenity which has been caused by any such breach; or
(g) that any period specified in the notice in accordance with s 173(9) falls short of what should reasonably be allowed.

20.74 It will be seen that ground (a) relates to the merits of the development, grounds (b) to (e) to questions of law or fact or mixed questions of law and fact, and grounds (f) and (g) to remedial measures required to be taken by the notice. The relationship between grounds (a) and (f) have been considered a number of times recently. In *Ioannou v Secretary of State for Communities and Local Government* [2014] EWCA Civ 1432; [2015] 1 P & CR 10 the Court of Appeal held that if an alternative scheme fell outside that which could be permitted under a ground (a) appeal then it could not be permitted pursuant to a ground (f) appeal. In *Miaris v Secretary of State for Communities and Local Government* [2016] EWCA Civ 75; [2016] JPL 784 the Court of Appeal held that a planning decision-maker could not determine the planning merits of a future scheme under a ground (f) appeal (in the absence of a ground (a) appeal).

20.75 The real purpose of setting out the grounds of appeal in s 174(2) is not merely to list the likeliest grounds on which an appeal would want to be brought. Its significance lies in the restrictive provisions of s 285(1) of the 1990 Act. That subsection provides:

> The validity of an enforcement notice shall not, except by way of an appeal under Part VII, be questioned in any proceedings whatsoever on any of the grounds on which such an appeal may be brought.

20.76 The effect of this provision is to prevent the validity of the notice being challenged on any of the grounds specified in s 174(2) except by way of appeal to the Secretary of State. It prevents a person from questioning the validity of the notice on those grounds by way of proceedings for judicial review or (save for the one exception previously mentioned) in proceedings brought against that person for a failure to comply with the enforcement notice. The provision, however, does not prevent a person from questioning the validity of the notice by judicial review or by way of defence to a prosecution for failure to comply with the notice on grounds not specified in s 174(2). A person is not precluded, therefore, from challenging the legality of an enforcement notice other than by way of appeal, if he can show the notice to be a nullity, on which see *Miller-Mead v Minister of Housing and Local Government* [1963] 2 QB 196 (see later). In *South Hams District Council v Halsey* [1996] JPL 761 it was held that for an enforcement notice to be a nullity, the notice has to be defective on its face. This would occur, for example, if a person could show that the notice failed to specify the date on which it was to take effect; failed adequately to state the matters alleged to constitute the breach; failed to identify the land affected; failed to specify the steps required to be taken to remedy the breach as occurred in *Tandridge DC v Verrechia* [2000] QB 318); or failed to state a compliance period. For an example of this latter deficiency, see [2000] JPL 549 where an Inspector treated six enforcement notices as nullities where no period for compliance had been stated.

20.77 Likewise, in *R (Lynes and Lynes) v West Berkshire DC* [2002] EWHC 1828 (Admin); [2003] JPL 1137, the High Court granted a declaration that an enforcement notice (and an associated stop notice) were nullities where the enforcement notice had stated that it was to take effect 'immediately', since this failed to specify the 'period for compliance' required by s 179(3).

20.78 In *Clive Payne v the National Assembly for Wales and Caerphilly County Borough Council* [2006] EWHC 597 (Admin); [2007] JPL 117, the High Court allowed an appeal against the decision of the National Assembly for Wales (and remitted the matter to the National Assembly for redetermination) to uphold an enforcement notice where an Inspector had varied the terms of the notice which he had considered to be a nullity. However, in *Trott v Broadland District Council* [2011] EWCA Civ 301 it was pointed out by Sullivan LJ that today the courts are unwilling to make fine distinctions between errors that make an enforcement notice a nullity and errors which only go to validity and can be corrected on appeal.

20.79 In order to avoid the Secretary of State being unable to consider an appeal against an enforcement notice because, perhaps due to postal delays, the notice of appeal was not received before the date on which the enforcement notice was expressed to take effect, s 174(3) provides that an appeal shall be made either by giving written notice to the Secretary of State before the date specified in the notice as the date on which it is to take effect, or by sending such notices to him in a properly addressed and prepaid letter posted to him at such time that, in the ordinary course of post, it would be delivered to him before that date.

20.80 As a general principle of law, a person given a right of appeal on certain specified grounds (as with enforcement notice appeals) is the person who has to make good those grounds and on whom the onus rests. In *Nelsovil v Minister of Housing and Local Government* [1962] 1 WLR 404 (Div Court), it was held that where an appeal against an enforcement notice is made the burden of proof is on the appellant, recently applied by Holgate J in *Distinctive Properties (Ascot) Ltd v Secretary of State for Communities and Local Government* [2015] EWHC 729 (Admin); [2015] JPL 1083.

Appeal procedure

20.81 As already stated, an appeal must be made by notice in writing to the Secretary of State, before the date specified in the notice as the date on which it is to take effect. In order to determine the appeal properly, however, the Secretary of State needs to know the grounds upon which a person is appealing against the notice, as well as the facts upon which the appeal is based. He will also need to know the reason why the authority served the notice in the first place. Prior to the Local Government and Planning (Amendment) Act 1981, it was difficult for the Secretary of State to move to a speedy determination of the appeal if the parties concerned failed to provide this information, and in the absence of a power to make regulations requiring this to be done, his only course was to determine the appeal without that information. The 1981 Amendment Act resolved much of this difficulty by reformulating the obligation on the appellant to specify his grounds of appeal and to give the Secretary of State the power to make regulations with regard to enforcement notice appeals.

20.82 Section 174(4) and (5) of the 1990 Act now provides:

> (4) A person who gives notice under sub-section (3) shall submit to the Secretary of State, either when giving the notice or within the prescribed time, a statement in writing—
> (a) specifying the grounds on which he is appealing against the enforcement notice; and
> (b) giving such further information as may be prescribed.
> (5) If, where more than one ground is specified in that statement, the appellant does not give information required under sub-section (4)(b) in relation to each of those grounds within the prescribed time, the Secretary of State may determine

the appeal without considering any ground as to which the appellant has failed to give such information within that time.

Under s 175(1) of the 1990 Act the Secretary of State may by regulations prescribe the procedure which is to be followed on appeals under s 174 and, in particular, but without prejudice to the generality of this subsection, may—

(a) require the local planning authority to submit, within such time as may be prescribed, a statement indicating the submissions which it proposes to put forward on the appeal;
(b) specify the matters to be included in such a statement;
(c) require the authority or the appellant to give such notice of such an appeal as may be prescribed; and
(d) require the authority to send to the Secretary of State, within such period from the date of the bringing of the appeal as may be prescribed, a copy of the enforcement notice and a list of the persons served with copies of it.

20.83 Under these provisions the Secretary of State has made the Town and Country Planning (Enforcement Notices and Appeals) Regulations 2002, SI 2002/2682. These regulations require the appellant to specify (in addition to his grounds of appeal) the facts upon which the appeal is based. He must do this within 14 days of being required to do so. In practice, if the appellant has not supplied this information within one week of the end of the 14-day period, the Secretary of State sends a warning letter to the appellant setting out the powers of the Secretary of State at the end of that period. Section 176(3) provides that the Secretary of State:

(a) may dismiss an appeal if the appellant fails to comply with s 174(4) within the prescribed time; and
(b) may allow an appeal and quash the enforcement notice if the local planning authority fails to comply with any requirement of regulations made by virtue of paras (a), (b), or (d) of s 175(1) within the prescribed period.

Furthermore, s 174(5) provides that:

if where more than one ground is specified in that statement, the appellant does not give information required under sub-section (4)(b) in relation to each of those grounds within the prescribed time, the Secretary of State may determine the appeal without considering any ground as to which the appellant has failed to give such information within that time.

20.84 Under these provisions the local planning authority can also be required to provide information relevant to the appeal, and if it fails to do so, the Secretary of State is empowered to allow the appeal and quash the notice.

20.85 It will be seen that enforcement notice machinery contains a rigorous timetable within which each particular stage must be completed. In particular, the recipient of the notice has to ensure:

(a) that if he wishes to appeal he does so before the enforcement notice takes effect;
(b) that if he does appeal he specifies his grounds and the facts upon which each ground of appeal is based and in any event within 14 days of being required to do so; and

(c) that in the event of the enforcement notice taking effect he takes, within the period or periods stated in the notice, the steps required by the notice to be taken to remedy the breach of planning control.

For its part, the local planning authority has to ensure:

(a) that copies of the notice are served on those required to be served within 28 days of issue by the authority;
(b) that each recipient is in possession of a copy of the notice for at least 28 days before it takes effect; and
(c) that if an appeal is made against the notice, it provides the Secretary of State, within the period prescribed for doing so, with the information required to be provided under the Regulations.

20.86 Under s 175(3), the Secretary of State used to be required, if either the appellant or the local planning authority so desired, to give to each of them an opportunity of appearing before, and being heard by, a person appointed by the Secretary of State for the purpose. However, since 2009 in England and 2014 in Wales, that right has been removed. Parties may indicate the mode of determination they would like but ultimately the process is now determined by the Planning Inspectorate. Where an inquiry is held the procedure is governed by the Town and Country Planning (Enforcement) (Inquiries Procedure) (England) Rules 2002. Other rules apply to appeal proceedings dealt with by hearings or written representations.

20.87 It has been estimated that evidence is given on oath in about half the cases involving appeals based on grounds (c), (d), or (e) of s 174(2).

20.88 Section 177 of the 1990 Act provides that on determination of an appeal under s 174, the Secretary of State may:

(a) grant planning permission in respect of the matters stated in the enforcement notice as constituting a breach of planning control, whether in relation to the whole or any part of those matters or in relation to the whole or any part of the land to which the notice relates;
(b) discharge any condition or limitation subject to which planning permission was granted;
(c) determine whether, on the date on which the appeal was made, any existing use of the land was lawful, any operations which had been carried out in, on, over, or under the land were lawful or any matter constituting a failure to comply with any condition or limitation subject to which planning permission was granted was lawful and, if so, issue a certificate under s 191.

20.89 Indeed, s 177(5) used to provide that where an appeal against an enforcement notice is made, the appellant shall be deemed to have made an application for planning permission in respect of the matters stated in the enforcement notice as constituting a breach of planning control. Accordingly, the Secretary of State had power to grant planning permission, even though no appeal has been made on ground (a) of s 174(2), that planning permission ought to be granted for the matter alleged to be a breach of planning control. However, s 123 of the 2011 Act has amended s 177(5) so that the Secretary of State may only grant planning permission when allowing an enforcement appeal if the appeal was made under ground (a) and only ground (a) appeals result in a deemed application for planning permission. Under the section and the appropriate regulations, the planning application fee must be paid at the time written notice of appeal is given to the Secretary of State or within such period as is specified by the Secretary of State. If the appropriate fee is not paid, the deemed application, or the appeal to the extent to which it is based on ground (a) of s 174(2), will lapse. This latter provision is intended to overcome the problem where in the past the Secretary of State could quash the enforcement notice on the ground that planning permission for the contravening development should be granted, but was unable to grant planning permission because no planning application fee had been paid. That in effect left the planning status of the land in 'limbo'; without any planning permission existing for the development which had taken place, and enforcement powers being no longer available.

20.90 A further limitation on the power of the Secretary of State to grant planning permission under s 177 in respect of any matter stated in the enforcement notice to constitute a breach of planning control, is that with the 'deemed' application which relates to development for which environmental assessment is required, the Secretary of State is precluded from granting planning permission unless an environmental statement has been submitted.

The power to vary

20.91 As the statistics show, many enforcement notices, although upheld by the Secretary of State, are varied by him on appeal. Power to do this is given by s 176(1) of the 1990 Act, which provides that on an appeal under s 174 the Secretary of State may:

(a) correct any defect, error, or misdescription in the enforcement notice; or
(b) vary the terms of the enforcement notice,
if he is satisfied that the correction or variation will not cause injustice to the appellant or the local planning authority.

20.92 It seems that the power given to the Secretary of State under para (a) above allows him to alter the substance of an enforcement notice in order to enable him to give effect to the determination of one of the statutory grounds of appeal. The power given to him under para (b) above allows him to give effect to its substance by overcoming a defect in form and thus failing on a technicality. In *Ahmed v Secretary of State for Communities and Local Government* [2013] EWHC 2084

(Admin); [2014] 2 P & CR 11 an enforcement notice required the complete demolition of a new building and the reconstruction of the former building. The High Court held that on appeal the Inspector had erred in law in not considering an obvious alternative course of using the power to vary the terms of the enforcement notice so that it complied with the grant of planning permission for a smaller building which was time-expired.

20.93 The powers of the Secretary of State under this provision are limited. An enforcement notice must tell the recipient clearly what he has done wrong and what he must do to remedy it. If it fails to do this, the notice is a nullity and beyond correction. The best known consideration of the scope of this power was by Lord Denning MR in *Miller-Mead v Minister of Housing and Local Government* [1963] 2 QB 196 (CA) where he said, at p 221:

> The Minister has power… to correct any informality, defect or error in the enforcement notice if he is satisfied that the informality, defect or error is not a material one. This seems to me to be wider than the 'slip rule'. I think that it gives the Minister a power to amend, which is similar to the power of the court to amend an indictment. He can correct errors so long as, having regard to the merits of the case, the correction can be made without injustice. No informality, defect or error is a material one unless it is such as to produce injustice. Applied to misrecitals, it means this: if the misrecital goes to the substance of the matter, then the notice may be quashed. But if the misrecital does not go to the substance of the matter and can be amended without injustice, it should be amended rather than that the notice should be quashed or declared a nullity. In this way the legislature has disposed of the proposition that there must be a 'strict and rigid adherence to formalities'.

20.94 The statutory provisions considered by Lord Denning have been significantly reformulated in s 176(1) to reflect the construction placed by him on the earlier statutory provisions, and also to restrict the power of correction or variation to cases where this can be done without injustice to the authority as well as to the appellant. The power is often used to delete from an enforcement notice land falling outside the planning unit, to alter the steps required to remedy the breach, and to extend the time for compliance with the notice. Equally in *R (Howells) v Secretary of State for Communities and Local Government* [2009] EWHC 2757 (Admin); [2010] JPL 741 it was accepted that there was a power to extend or increase the requirements of a notice and to enlarge the area shown on the plan attached. This can of course only be done if it would not cause injustice and is required in order to remedy the breach of planning control. It cannot be used, however, to turn a nullity into a valid enforcement notice.

20.95 The difficulties of expressing to the recipient of the notice in clear terms what must be done to remedy the breach is best seen in *Kaur v Secretary of State for the Environment* [1990] JPL 814. In that case the notice had required, inter alia, the removal of a mansard roof. On appeal, the Inspector considered the wording could have been clearer and amended it to require the reinstatement of a pitched roof the design of which was required to be 'first agreed with the local planning authority'. Sir Frank Layfield QC, sitting as a Deputy High Court Judge, held that the notice did not thus tell the recipient with reasonable certainty what steps had to be taken to remedy the breach. In that case the unacceptable clause was the requirement that the reinstatement be agreed with the local planning authority. It is possible, however, for an Inspector dealing with an appeal to vary such a requirement and introduce certainty in place of uncertainty about what needs to be done, as, for example, requiring reinstatement to conform as nearly as possible with a specified photograph.

20.96 The terms of an enforcement notice (and thus the power to vary) cannot require action to be taken beyond that of remedying the breach. It cannot be used to bring to an end an existing lawful use. In *Mansi v Elstree DC* (1964) 15 P & CR 153 the Divisional Court remitted to the Minister for variation a notice which required the discontinuance of sales of goods from premises, where it was clear that there was an established use for retail sales of produce from a garden nursery, and this use would have been lost if the notice in its original form had been upheld. A more recent example of the application of the *Mansi* principle can be seen in the case of *John Kennelly Sales Ltd v Secretary of State for the Environment* [1994] 1 PLR 10.

20.97 It also seems that an enforcement notice cannot prevent the subsequent implementation of development permitted by the General Permitted Development Order. This is because s 181(2) provides:

> ... any provision of an enforcement notice requiring a use of land to be discontinued shall operate as a requirement that it shall be discontinued permanently, *to the extent that it is in contravention of Part III* [our emphasis]; and accordingly the resumption of that use at any time after it has been discontinued in compliance with the enforcement notice shall to that extent be in contravention of the enforcement notice.

Development permitted by the General Permitted Development Order is not in contravention of Part III of the 1990 Act. Accordingly, it cannot be required to be discontinued as part of an enforcement notice. In *Duguid v Secretary of State for the Environment, Transport and the Regions* (2001) 82 P & CR 6, the Court of Appeal upheld a decision of the High Court which held that where an enforcement notice had required a use of Sunday markets to cease, this notice did prevent the owner from holding no more than 14 such markets in one calendar year as is permitted under the GPDO.

20.98 Problems may arise in protecting existing use rights from the effect of an enforcement notice. The approach to that problem has been set out by Duncan Ouseley QC, at that time sitting as a Deputy Judge in *Kinnersley Engineering Ltd v Secretary of State for the Environment, Transport and the Regions* [2001] JPL 1082, in the following way:

> Given that existing use rights are to be protected, the question of whether it is necessary to spell those out in the enforcement notice depends on how obvious it is

that the enforcement notice can and will be construed so as to protect them, in the context of a criminal prosecution. It needs to be remembered that subsequent landowners are also bound by the notice, and concern over its interpretation may affect dealings with them.

In my judgment, the key issue is whether it is obvious that the existing use rights [as found by the Inspector] would be protected.

In *R (on the application of Reid) v Secretary of State for Transport, Local Government and the Regions* [2002] EWHC 2174 Sullivan J followed the same approach.

20.99 Where the Secretary of State determines to allow the appeal he may quash the enforcement notice. He may also give any directions necessary to give effect to his determination on the appeal.

20.100 From the decision of the Secretary of State on appeal against an enforcement notice, the appellant or the local planning authority or any other person having an interest in the land may, as rules of court provide (under s 289 of the 1990 Act), appeal to the High Court against the decision on a point of law or require the Secretary of State to state and sign a case for the opinion of the High Court. The application must be made within 28 days. Furthermore, where the court is of the opinion that the decision was erroneous in point of law, it cannot set aside or vary the decision. The remedy is to remit the matter to the Secretary of State with the opinion of the court for rehearing and determination by him.

20.101 Because appellants have sometimes used the litigation process to delay or frustrate the implementation of an enforcement notice by submitting unmeritorious appeals, the Planning and Compensation Act 1991 introduced subsection (6) into s 289 of the 1990 Act. The subsection introduced an entirely new 'leave' requirement, by providing that:

No proceedings in the High Court shall be brought… except with the leave of that court and no appeal to the Court of Appeal shall be so brought except with the leave of the Court of Appeal or of the High Court.

In *Wendy Fair Markets Ltd v Secretary of State for Communities and Local Government* [1996] JPL 649 the Court of Appeal held that this subsection on appeals could not be evaded by using s 16 of the Senior Courts Act 1981. This ruling has been followed in *Walsall BC v Secretary of State for Communities and Local Government* [2013] EWCA Civ 370; [2013] JPL 1183 and affirmed again in *Binning Property Corp Ltd v Secretary of State for Housing, Communities and Local Government* [2019] EWCA Civ 250. It follows that if leave to bring an appeal is refused by the High Court under s 289 there is no ability to appeal against that decision, absent 'misconduct or unfairness' see Lindblom LJ in *Binning* at [26].

This provision applies equally to a local planning authority, as it does to the recipient of an enforcement notice. Under the Civil Procedure Rules, this action must be taken within 28 days of the Secretary of State's decision (unless the period is extended by the court for good reason). The 28-day period for appealing to the High Court under s 289 against a decision on an enforcement notice appeal should not be confused (which it often is) with the six-week period for appealing under s 288.

20.102 Section 175(4) provides that where an appeal is brought under s 174, the enforcement notice shall be of no effect pending the final determination or withdrawal of the appeal. In *London Parachuting Ltd v Secretary of State for the Environment* (1985) 52 P & CR 376, it was held that this meant final determination of the appeal by the Secretary of State. Once this determination had been made, the enforcement notice, if upheld, was required to be obeyed. In *R v Kuxhaus* [1988] QB 631 (CA), however, the court disapproved of that decision, holding (with reluctance) that where an appeal was made to the court, this had the effect of further suspending the operation of the enforcement notice until the court had finally determined the matter. This decision meant, therefore, that it was possible to frustrate the effect of an enforcement notice for a considerable length of time by pursuing an appeal to the Secretary of State, then beyond that to the courts. At that stage, it was not uncommon for the appellant then to withdraw the appeal.

20.103 To deal with this problem, the Planning and Compensation Act 1991 inserted subsection (4A) into s 289 of the 1990 Act (the section which deals with appeals to the High Court against enforcement notices). The effect of the subsection is that where an appeal is made to the courts against the decision of the Secretary of State in relation to an enforcement notice, the High Court or Court of Appeal may order that the notice shall have such effect or have effect to such extent as may be specified in the order, pending the final determination of the proceedings and any rehearing and determination by the Secretary of State. This provision will thus allow the courts, in dealing with the enforcement notice appeal, to decide whether, pending the determination of the appeal, the appellant should be made to comply with the enforcement notice and, if so, to what extent, or whether the notice should continue to be of no effect.

20.104 Although in determining an appeal against an enforcement notice, the Secretary of State has power to quash an enforcement notice, the powers of the court in dealing with an appeal are limited to remitting the matter to the Secretary of State with the opinion of the court for his rehearing and redetermination. There is no power available to the court, therefore, to quash or set aside an enforcement notice. In *R (Perrett) v Secretary of State for Communities and Local Government* [2009] EWCA Civ 1365; [2010] 2 All ER 578 the Court of Appeal held, in a complicated case where five enforcement notices were served with regard to the same farm building complex, that on remitting all five to the Secretary of State, he was not obliged to hear all five appeals *de novo* or to allow a party to open up grounds that had not yet been raised. Richards LJ said that the Secretary of State had a wide discretion to decide just what matters should be dealt with following a successful challenge and could decide to confine himself to the grounds on which the notice was quashed.

20.105 It appears that a decision made by the Secretary of State to allow an appeal against an enforcement notice on any of the grounds mentioned in (c) to (e) in s 174 of the 1990 Act is capable of giving rise to an estoppel *per rem judicatam* or to 'issue estoppel'. In *Thrasyvoulou v Secretary of State for the Environment* [1990] 2 AC 273, a number of enforcement notices alleging breaches of planning control had been issued in 1981. On appeal, an Inspector had decided that no material change of use had taken place. Following a second batch of enforcement notices issued in 1985, an Inspector hearing the appeals decided that he was not bound by the decision reached by the earlier Inspector in relation to the 1981 notices. The House of Lords held that there was an important distinction between an issue raised by an appeal against an enforcement notice on ground (a) of what is now s 174(2) of the 1990 Act, where the question is whether planning permission should be granted, and the issues raised by grounds (b) to (e). In the former case the public have a right to attend an inquiry and be heard as objectors, whereas in the latter case they have no *locus standi* as objectors, although they may be heard as witnesses of fact. Their Lordships thought that Parliament must have intended the determination of any issue arising under what are now grounds (c) to (e) of s 174(2) in favour of an appellant to be conclusive. Any such determination gives rise to an estoppel *per rem judicatam*. Such 'cause of action' estoppel will arise whenever the determination of the ground decided in favour of the appellant on an appeal against one enforcement notice can be relied on in an appeal against a second enforcement notice which is in the same terms and is directed against the same alleged development as the first.

20.106 In related proceedings the House ruled that where on one enforcement notice appeal an Inspector had ruled that land was immune from enforcement proceedings (because the use had been established before 1964), a second Inspector on a subsequent enforcement notice appeal was bound by issue estoppel to accept the ruling.

20.107 In *Porter v Secretary of State for Transport* [1996] 3 All ER 693 (CA) it was said that for issue estoppel to arise the four criteria that had to be established were:

(a) The issue in question must have been decided by a court or tribunal of competent jurisdiction.
(b) The issue must be one which arises between parties who are parties to the decision.
(c) The issue must have been decided finally and must be of a type to which an issue estoppel can apply.
(d) The issue in respect of which the estoppel is said to operate must be the same as that previously decided.

The *Thrasyvoulou* principle was again applied by the Court of Appeal in *Hammond v Secretary of State for the Environment and Maldon DC* [2001] EWHC Admin 1172. **20.108**

I. STOP NOTICES

At one time one of the difficulties with the enforcement of planning control was that a person could begin to develop without planning permission and, when an enforcement notice was served, use delaying mechanisms (including the right of appeal) to postpone its operation whilst at the same time continuing with the development. The effects of this were two-fold. First, where the development involved the erection of a building, the Secretary of State, in determining the appeal, might be less likely to require the demolition of a building which had been completed than one in the early stages of erection; secondly, the adverse environmental effects of the unauthorized development could continue for a longer period than necessary if the enforcement notice were finally to take effect. **20.109**

Stop notices must be distinguished from temporary stop notices which are dealt with in para 20.18. **20.110**

The statutory provisions relating to stop notices are now contained in s 183 of the 1990 Act. Subsection (1) of that section provides: **20.111**

> (1) Where the local planning authority consider it expedient that any relevant activity should cease before the expiry of the period for compliance with an enforcement notice, they may, when they serve a copy of the enforcement notice or afterwards, serve a notice (in this Act referred to as a 'stop notice') prohibiting the carrying out of that activity on the land to which the enforcement notice relates, or any part of that land specified in the stop notice.

Subsection (2) of s 183 defines 'relevant activity' to mean any activity specified in the enforcement notice as an activity which the local planning authority requires to cease and any activity carried out as part of that activity or associated with that activity. This provision makes it clear that a stop notice may be directed not merely to an activity specified in an enforcement notice as an activity the authority require should cease, but also to any use of land which is ancillary to its main use.

It should be noted that a stop notice may now be served on a person at the same time as the person is served with an enforcement notice, thus reversing the decision in *R v Southwark LBC, ex p Murdoch* (1990) 155 JP 163, that a local planning authority had no power to serve an enforcement notice and stop notice simultaneously. **20.112**

A stop notice cannot, however, be served where the enforcement notice has taken effect, presumably because thereafter, the failure to comply with the enforcement **20.113** notice is itself a criminal offence. The stop notice is given teeth by virtue of s 187(1) of the 1990 Act which provides for a criminal sanction if any person contravenes, or causes or permits the contravention of, a stop notice; and he may thereafter be convicted of a second or subsequent offence under the section. The Legal Aid, Sentencing and Punishment of Offenders Act 2012 made the fine for a contravention of a stop notice unlimited. The 1991 Act amendment also requires the court in imposing a fine to have regard to any financial benefit which has accrued or is likely to accrue to the wrongdoer in consequence of the offence. In *David Lewis v Three Rivers DC* [2013] EWHC 3250 (Admin); [2014] JPL 636 it was held that different charges for a breach of a stop notice can be brought for repeated breaches committed over a period of time rather than bringing one charge relating to repeated breaches over a period of time.

20.114 Cases have arisen where the imposition of criminal penalties has not prevented an activity being continued in breach of a stop notice. Accordingly, the Government had proposed in November 1996 a change in the law to give local planning authorities the power to take physical steps to ensure compliance with a stop notice, such as preventing access to the site by any person in pursuance of the activity prohibited by the notice (by, for example, placing a barrier across the site entrance), and to enter land and confiscate any equipment or material being used by a person in pursuance of a prohibited activity. The new powers were to be linked to the prosecution of a stop notice offence under s 187 of the 1990 Act and so would be available only where a person has been convicted of an offence and the court has made an order authorizing the authority to take those steps. However, it would seem that there are no immediate proposals to implement such a change.

20.115 Under s 183(6) the stop notice may be served by the local planning authority on any person who appears to them to have an interest in the land or to be engaged in any activity prohibited by the notice.

20.116 Section 183(4) of the 1990 Act provides that a stop notice shall not prohibit the use of any building as a dwellinghouse. Prior to the 1991 Act, this exclusion applied also to the use of land as the site for a caravan occupied by any person as his main residence. Because of the potential harm to local amenities caused by unauthorized residential caravan sites, the 1991 Act removed the prohibition against service with regard to caravans.

20.117 In addition, s 183(5) prohibits the use of a stop notice to prohibit the carrying out of any activity if that activity has been carried out (whether continuously or not) for a period of more than four years ending with the service of the notice. Prior to the 1991 Act, a stop notice could not be used to prohibit the carrying out of any activity on land begun more than 12 months earlier unless it was, or was incidental to, building, engineering, mining, or other operations, or the deposit of refuse or waste materials. Although the 1991 Act extended the limitation period for service of a stop notice from 12 months to four years, it has maintained the right of a local planning authority to serve a stop notice within that (now) extended period, for activities amounting to operational development or the deposit of refuse or waste, or activities incidental thereto. The general extension of the time limit from 12 months to four years reflects more, however, the fact that a use of land may at first be seen to be non-objectionable, but may become otherwise because of intensification.

Service of stop notices

A stop notice must refer to the enforcement notice to which it relates and have a copy of that notice annexed to it. It must also specify the date on which it will take effect. Before the Planning and Compensation Act 1991, the date on which a stop notice was specified to take effect was not to be earlier than 3 and not later than 28 days from the date of service. The purpose of giving 3 days' grace before the stop notice took effect was to cushion those affected from losses incurred by having to bring work to an immediate standstill. It was believed, however, that some activities, such as the depositing of waste, mineral extraction, etc, could be sufficiently damaging to require them to be stopped immediately. Accordingly, the 1991 Act amended the 1990 Act by substituting a provision to allow a stop notice to specify an earlier date than 3 days for its coming into effect, if the authority considers there are special reasons for so doing and a statement of those reasons is served with the stop notice. A stop notice will cease to have effect where the enforcement notice to which it relates is withdrawn or quashed, or the period for compliance with the enforcement notice has expired, or the local planning authority withdraws it. **20.118**

Compensation for loss due to stop notices

Local planning authorities have often claimed they are deterred from serving stop notices because of the risk they run of having to pay compensation to the person on whom the notice is served, if he is successful in an appeal to the Secretary of State against the related enforcement notice. In fact the liability to pay compensation is much restricted, compensation only being payable if the enforcement notice is quashed on grounds other than that planning permission ought to be granted for the development to which the notice relates; or where the authority decides to withdraw the stop notice; or it is varied on appeal so that the matter alleged to constitute a breach of planning control is no longer included in the notice. **20.119**

Section 186(2) of the Act provides that when a stop notice is first served, a person who has an interest in or who occupies the land to which the notice relates shall not be entitled to compensation in respect of any loss or damage directly attributable to the prohibition contained in the notice as of right. In *International Traders Ferry Ltd v Adur DC* [2004] EWCA Civ 288; [2004] 2 PLR 106, it was held that the interest referred to in the subsection was a legal or equitable interest. As **20.120** regards whether an occupier qualified under this provision, the correct approach was to follow that laid down in *Stevens v Bromley LBC* (CA) (see para 20.41) with regard to a person's entitlement to be served with an enforcement notice.

20.121 Despite attempts to explain the statutory provisions in earlier Circulars, local planning authorities remained confused by the provisions relating to compensation. Accordingly, the Planning and Compensation Act 1991 amended the 1990 Act by substituting a new subsection (5) of s 186 to clarify the circumstances in which compensation is not to be payable where a stop notice ceases to have effect. It is now provided that no compensation is payable in respect of any prohibition in a stop notice of any activity which, at any time when the notice is in force, constitutes or contributes to a breach of planning control. In addition, it should be noted that under various other statutory provisions (eg planning contravention notices in s 171C of the 1990 Act; or the power to require information about interests in land under s 330 of the 1990 Act), a person may be required to provide a local planning authority with relevant information. If that person fails to provide that information, or otherwise fails to co-operate with the local planning authority when responding to the notice, no compensation is payable in respect of any loss or damage which could otherwise have been avoided. The justification for this provision is that the local authority should not be liable if insufficient information has been given to it to enable it to decide whether to take enforcement action, and if it does so, to draft the notice with complete precision.

20.122 The philosophy behind the compensation provisions is that no compensation should be payable merely because the landowner and the local planning authority have taken a different view on whether or not planning permission for development should be granted. The correct procedure for the landowner is to submit an application for planning permission to the local planning authority and, on refusal, to appeal to the Secretary of State. If he develops first, is served with an enforcement notice and related stop notice, and then the enforcement notice is quashed solely on the ground that planning permission for the development should be granted, no compensation for loss due to the stop notice is payable. The owner is the victim of his own actions. Compensation becomes payable, therefore, where for some reason other than the merits of the development proposed, the local planning authority has, in the view of the Secretary of State, made a mistake.

20.123 Mention has already been made (in 14.95) of the case of *Malvern Hills DC v Secretary of State for the Environment* (1983) 46 P & CR 58 (CA), where compensation had to be paid for loss caused by service of a misconceived stop notice. Another example occurred in *Sample (Warkworth) Ltd v Alnwick DC* (1984) 48 P & CR 474. Here, an enforcement notice was quashed on the ground that there had been no breach of planning control. The award made (of £3,122) included rent for temporary accommodation, the cost of idle time of workmen, and for additional work necessary to rectify deterioration caused by delay in completing the development.

Execution of works required by enforcement notices

20.124 Under s 178 of the 1990 Act as originally enacted, if any steps which an enforcement notice required to be taken *other* than the discontinuance of a use of land had not been taken, the local planning authority was entitled to enter the land and take those steps and recover from the owner of the land any expenses reasonably incurred in doing so. It was felt that the inability of authorities to use this power to secure the discontinuance of a use was a serious obstacle to their efforts to secure the cessation of illegal uses of land. Hence, the Planning and Compensation Act 1991 strengthened s 178 of the 1990 Act by removing that disability. Under the current provision, a local planning authority can enter land where *any steps* which an enforcement notice required to be taken have not been taken within the period for doing so and recover the expenses of so doing from the owner of the land.

20.125 Note that it may sometimes happen that the owner is prevented from taking the steps required to be taken by the notice because some other person (such as a tenant) has an interest in the land. In such cases, s 178(4) allows the owner to apply to the magistrates' court for an order under the Public Health Act 1936 that that other person should permit those steps to be taken.

Offence where enforcement notice not complied with

20.126 Under s 179 of the 1990 Act, where, at any time after the end of the period for compliance with an enforcement notice, any step required by the notice to be taken has not been taken, or any activity required by the notice to cease is being carried on, the person who is then the owner of the land is in breach of the notice and guilty of an offence. However, s 125 of the 2011 Act has created a procedure whereby the local planning authority can give a binding assurance to a person that they will not be prosecuted. This is done by inserting a new s 172A into the 1990 Act which provides that a local planning authority can give a person a letter explaining that they were obliged to serve the enforcement notice on that person but giving an assurance that the person is not at risk of being prosecuted in connection with the matters relating to the enforcement notice that are specified in the letter. The letter should further explain that, if the authority subsequently wishes to withdraw the assurance in full or part, the authority will first give the person a letter specifying a future time for the withdrawal that will allow the person a reasonable opportunity to take any steps necessary to avoid any risk of prosecution. An assurance given (so far as not withdrawn) is binding on any person with power to prosecute.

20.127 Prior to the Planning and Compensation Act 1991, the person guilty of the offence of noncompliance with the notice was the person who was the owner of the land in respect of which the enforcement notice had been served. Where the person responsible for non-compliance was a subsequent owner, the original owner was entitled to have the subsequent owner brought before the court in any prosecution. Under a new s 179, it is now the owner of the land at any time after the end of the period for compliance with the notice who has primary responsibility for securing compliance with the notice. The section recognizes, however, that the owner of the land may not be responsible for the failure to comply with an enforcement notice if, for example, another person (such as a tenant) occupies the land and is responsible for non-compliance. The section provides too that a person who occupies the land or has an interest in it (other than the owner) must not carry out any activity on it which is required by the notice to cease. If he should do so, the section makes this a criminal offence. It is also made clear that when an owner of land is in breach of an enforcement notice he shall be guilty of an offence, and he may be guilty of a second or subsequent offence if he continues in breach.

20.128 The section provides that where a person charged with non-compliance with an enforcement notice has not been served with a copy of it, and the notice is not contained in the statutory register of enforcement and stop notices kept under s 188 of the 1990 Act, it shall be a defence for him to show that he was not aware of the existence of the notice.

20.129 The maximum penalty that a magistrates' court may impose on a person guilty of non-compliance with an enforcement notice was increased under the Planning and Compensation Act 1991 from £2,000 to £20,000, and from 2012, the fine which may be imposed is unlimited following an amendment brought by the Legal Aid, Sentencing and Punishment of Offenders Act 2012. In addition, however, in determining the amount of any fine to be imposed on a convicted person, the court (whether the offence was tried summarily or on indictment), must now have regard to any financial benefit which has accrued or is likely to accrue to that person in consequence of the offence.

20.130 If a person is prosecuted for failure to comply with an enforcement notice, he cannot, at that stage, challenge the earlier decision to issue the enforcement notice on the ground that the decision to do so was ultra vires. In *R v Wicks* [1997] 2 All ER 801, the defendant had been prosecuted for failure to comply with a notice. He had appealed to the Secretary of State against the notice, but unsuccessfully. He had not taken the opportunity to raise any questions about the validity of the notice on his appeal to the Secretary of State, or by way of judicial review. The House of Lords held he was not now entitled to raise in a criminal prosecution the question of whether the notice was ultra vires on the grounds of bad faith, perversity, and irrelevant considerations. It is otherwise, however, in a prosecution for failure to comply with a breach of condition notice (see para 20.150). On a prosecution for failure to comply an enforcement notice, the court cannot go 'behind' the enforcement notice and consider whether what the defendant had done was not in breach of planning control. Thus, in *Kirklees MDC v Angus Heron* [2011] EWHC 2393 (Admin); [2012] JPL 466 it was argued that what was being alleged (storage) as a breach of planning control was in fact ancillary to the primary business and so not a development. The Magistrates' Court therefore held the defendant not guilty. Langstaff J held that the effect of s 285 of the 1990 Act is that the Magistrates cannot go behind the requirements of a valid notice.

20.131 It is not uncommon, once an enforcement has come into effect, for an occupier of land to proceed to lodge an application for planning permission for the contravening development which is the subject of the enforcement notice. Then, on prosecution for failure to comply with the notice, the occupier will ask for the criminal proceedings to be adjourned pending determination of the application for planning permission and/or any subsequent appeal. Magistrates have been advised not to adjourn such proceedings save in wholly exceptional circumstances. In *R v Beaconsfield Magistrates, ex p South Buckinghamshire DC* (1993) 157 JP 1073 (Div Court), Staughton LJ said:

> As a general rule, magistrates should ... proceed to hear and determine the guilt or innocence of the defendant, notwithstanding that a planning application has recently been presented. If the defendant has a defence or claims to have a defence, it should be tried and determined whether he is guilty or not. If he does not have a defence and does not claim to have one, he should be convicted ... other than in exceptional cases ... Where the fate of the planning application is expected to be determined shortly, the magistrates should also deal with sentence in such cases and not adjourn them. They can, of course, take into account in considering the severity or lenience of any penalty the fact that a planning application is pending....
>
> I do not think that the magistrates are absolutely deprived of all discretion in such a case where compassionate circumstances exist. Section 179(5) of the Town and Country Planning Act 1990 provides that if after a person has been convicted he does not as soon as practicable do everything in his power to secure compliance with the enforcement notice, he should be guilty of a further offence. Thus a conviction has the effect that the defendant, besides being guilty of failing to comply with the notice in the first place, becomes liable to a fine of up to £200 for each day after that. The magistrates were entitled to consider the effect that the sub-section would have on Mrs K and Mrs S. They had outstanding planning applications which had not yet finally been determined. If they were convicted and did not thereafter comply with the previous enforcement notices they were liable to a daily fine. Bearing in mind the particular circumstances of the ladies, their age, means, state of health and the substantial period of time when the local authority had taken no action consequent on the breach of the enforcement notices, the justices were entitled to take a very unusual course in the wholly exceptional circumstances of the case.

20.132 Since the decision in the *Beaconsfield Magistrates* case, the courts have had to consider the impact of the Human Rights Act 1998 and in particular its effect on the use of injunctions to supplement criminal sanctions for non-compliance with an enforcement notice. There is now no doubt that in exercising their powers, the courts cannot now avoid the consideration of planning issues. Referring to the judgment of Simon Brown LJ in *South Bucks DC v Porter* [2002] 1 WLR 139, which was approved by the House of Lords [2003] UKHL 33, Silber J in *South Cambridgeshire DC v Flynn* [2006] EWHC 1320 identified the approach taken by both the Court of Appeal and the House of Lords in the *Porter* case as follows:

> ... the court need not shut its mind to the possibility of the planning authority itself coming to reach a different planning judgment in the case.... (Simon Brown LJ)
>
> Nor need the court refuse to consider ... the possibility that a pending or prospective application for planning permission may succeed since there may be material to suggest that a party previously unsuccessful may yet succeed.... (Lord Bingham)
>
> If the court thought that there was a real prospect that an appeal against an enforcement notice or a fresh application by the Defendant for the requisite planning permission might succeed, the court could adjourn the injunction application until the planning situation had become clarified. But where the planning situation is clear and apparently final the court would, in my opinion, have no alternative but to consider the injunction without regard to the merits of the planning decisions (Lord Scott)

Once an enforcement notice, always an enforcement notice

20.133 Even though an enforcement notice may have been complied with, it continues to have effect as against any subsequent unauthorized development covered by the notice. Section 181(1) of the Act provides that:

> Compliance with an enforcement notice, whether in respect of—
> (a) the completion, removal or alteration of any buildings, or works;
> (b) the discontinuance of any use of land; or
> (c) any other requirements contained in the notice,
> shall not discharge the notice.

20.134 This provision ensures that once a person has taken the steps required to be taken by the notice, the enforcement notice will continue to bite if the unauthorized development is recommenced. So too, a breach of condition notice is not discharged by compliance with its terms.

20.135 The only limitation on this rule is that provided by s 180 of the 1990 Act, which provides that where, after the service of a copy of an enforcement notice or a breach of condition notice, planning permission is granted for any development carried out before the grant of that permission, the notice shall cease to have effect insofar as it is inconsistent with that permission.

20.136 The rule applies equally to a temporary planning permission as to a planning permission not so time-limited. In *Cresswell v Pearson* (1998) 75 P & CR 404 the High Court held that where by virtue of s 180, an enforcement notice ceased to have effect because of the later grant of planning permission for a limited period, the enforcement notice did not revive at the end of that period, per Brooke LJ at 408. The court held that the proviso in s 180(1) that the enforcement notice 'shall cease to have effect' was clear and that there was no question of the notice going into suspended animation for the duration of the permission. Lewison J came to the same conclusion in *Fowles v Heathrow Airport Limited* [2008] EWHC 219 (Ch) at [90], albeit observing that is was 'somewhat surprising'. Furthermore, there is no requirement that the conditions attached to the subsequent grant of permission have been complied with in order for s 180 to operate, see: *London Borough of Havering v Secretary of State for the Environment* (1983) 45 P & CR 258. The relevant question is formulated by Lindblom J in *R (Rapose) v London Borough of Wandsworth* [2010] EWHC 3126 (Admin); [2011] JPL 600 at [29]:

> For the purposes of the present case the critical words in section 180, as Mr Taylor has submitted, are 'so far as'. These words make it clear, among other things, that it is not necessarily a completed development to which section 180 relates. In my judgment, the main question to be considered here is not, as the Council appeared at least originally to contend, whether the 2003 planning permission did or did not permit the unauthorized extension to be retained on its own, but whether there are elements of development common to both the permission and the enforcement notice. As Mr Taylor submitted, if there is fabric which forms part of that which the planning permission approved, the enforcement notice cannot thereafter be relied upon to attack that much of the development. Conversely, however, the enforcement notice continues to be effective against so much of the fabric as is not approved by the planning permission.

The approach of Lindblom J in *Rapose* was followed by Gilbart J in *Goremsandu v Secretary of State for Communities and Local Government* [2015] EWHC 2194 (Admin).

20.137 In circumstances where s 180 bites however, the local planning authority would be able to issue a further enforcement notice if the breach of planning control continued beyond the limited period for which the permission was granted.

J. BREACH OF CONDITION NOTICES

20.138 Under s 171A of the 1990 Act, failure to comply with any condition or limitation subject to which planning permission has been granted constitutes a breach of planning control. Accordingly, an enforcement notice may be served specifying the steps to be taken to remedy the breach.

20.139 In 1989, evidence was given to the review of enforcement procedure conducted by Robert Carnwath QC that the enforcement notice procedure was insufficiently flexible to secure the enforcement of conditions. The view was expressed that '... enforcement action was very rarely an efficient means of dealing with breaches of conditions relating to the period of construction of a project on such things as noise or working hours, since a stop notice would be too drastic in most cases and enforcement is too slow and unsure'. It was thought that there was a need for a summary remedy which would enable conditions to be enforced without enabling the merits to be reopened through the full panoply of an enforcement notice appeal.

20.140 Accordingly, the Planning and Compensation Act 1991 introduced a new s 187A into the 1990 Act to give local planning authorities a new procedure for the summary enforcement of a breach of a condition or a limitation subject to which a planning permission has been granted. The procedure provides local planning authorities with an additional and independent method of dealing with breaches of a condition or limitation as an alternative to the service of an enforcement notice under s 171A or obtaining an injunction from the courts, in order to secure compliance with a condition.

20.141 The new s 187A applies where planning permission for the carrying out of any development of land has been granted subject to conditions; and any of the conditions are not complied with. In such cases subsections (1) and (2) of s 187A empower a local planning authority to serve a notice (called a breach of condition notice) on any person who is carrying out or has carried out the development, or any person having control of the land, requiring him to secure compliance with such of the conditions as are specified in the notice. The notice, which the authority has power to withdraw, must specify the steps which the authority considers ought to be taken, or the activities which the authority considers ought to cease, to secure compliance with conditions specified in the notice. In this context, the word 'conditions' is expressed to include limitations.

20.142 In *Nourish v Adamson* [1998] JPL 859 (Div Court), it was held that where it could be shown that a person was, at the relevant time, the owner of the land, the burden of proof then lay on that person to show that although he was the owner, he did not have the control which one would normally expect an owner to have, namely the ability to secure compliance with the notice.

20.143 Under s 187A(7), the breach of condition notice must specify the period allowed by the authority for compliance with it, which must be not less than 28 days from the date of service of the notice, or that period as extended by any further breach of condition notice served by the authority on that person.

20.144 Then, if at the end of that period any of the conditions specified in the notice are not complied with and the steps specified in the notice have not been taken, or the activities specified have not ceased, the recipient of the notice will be in breach and be guilty of an offence. Furthermore, if at any time after conviction the recipient of the notice continues to be in breach of the notice, he may be convicted of a second or subsequent offence, thereby ensuring that eventually he ceases to be in breach.

20.145 There have been a number of recent cases resulting from prosecutions for non-compliance with a breach of condition notice.

20.146 In *East Hampshire DC v SLV Building Products Ltd* [1996] (Lands Tribunal), the company successfully argued before magistrates that it had not been in breach of a condition in a planning permission which had restricted use of 'working machinery' to specified hours, by using a 'forklift truck' on the site outside those hours. In an appeal by the Council by way of case stated, the High Court upheld the justices' findings.

20.147 In *John [and Joseph] Davenport v Hammersmith & Fulham LBC* [1999] JPL 1122 the appellants had been convicted by the magistrates of a failure to comply with a breach of condition notice. The condition had been imposed on a grant of planning permission for the retention of two buildings in connection with the use of land for motor vehicle repairs. The condition provided that 'No vehicles which have been left with or are in the control of the applicant shall be stored or parked in Tasso Road'. The notice had been served on John Davenport as being 'a person having control of the land'. On appeal, by way of case stated, the High Court quashed his conviction, holding that the condition did not regulate the use of the land subject to the planning permission, but the use of Tasso Road, over which he had no control.

20.148 It should be noted that no right of appeal to the Secretary of State is provided where this new procedure is used. This is because the merits of the condition are not in issue. If the recipient does not comply with the notice, a criminal prosecution in the magistrates' court for being in breach of the notice should follow. The local planning authority will, of course, have to prove all the elements in the offence, though s 187A(11) recognizes a defence that the recipient took all reasonable measures to secure compliance with the conditions specified in the notice; or if he was served with the notice as the person having control of the land, that he no longer had control.

20.149 Judicial review may be sought, however, if in issuing a breach of condition notice the local planning authority has acted outside its statutory powers. In *R v Ealing LBC, ex p Zainuddin* [1995] JPL 925, the High Court quashed a breach of condition notice relating to the attendance of 1,500 people at a ceremony to lay a foundation stone for a mosque, which had been issued on the basis that the event was in breach of the conditions in a grant of planning permission that 'no religious or ceremonial gatherings or acts of worship shall take place within the site except within the building'. The High Court held that there had been no breach of the condition where the meeting of devotees had taken place at a time when only the frame of the building existed. The condition should of course have provided that no gatherings should take place within the building and its curtilage before it was completed.

20.150 In *R v Wicks* [1997] 2 All ER 801, the House of Lords held that it was not open to the recipient of an enforcement notice to challenge the validity of the notice in criminal proceedings taken against him for non-compliance with the notice.

It would seem that different considerations apply where the proceedings relate to non-compliance with a breach of condition notice. In *Alfonso Dilieto v Ealing LBC* [1998] PLCR 212, the Divisional Court of the Queen's Bench Division held that in a prosecution for the non-compliance with a breach of condition notice, the magistrates had jurisdiction to consider the validity of the notice where a challenge to it had been based on the ground that since the contravention of the condition had been begun more than 10 years previously, the breach of condition notice had been issued out of time. Dilieto had been convicted by the Ealing justices for failure to comply with a breach of condition notice. On appeal against conviction by way of case stated, the Council had argued that following the decision in *Wicks*, the magistrates could decide whether the notice was a nullity in the sense of its being invalid on its face, but could not decide whether it was invalid on the ground raised by the appellant. The Council claimed that in order to challenge the breach of condition notice, the appellant should have moved to have the notice quashed by way of judicial review. In the Divisional Court however, Sullivan J refused to accept that the approach of the House of Lords in *Wicks* as regards enforcement notices was equally applicable in the case of breach of condition notices. One of the reasons he gave for taking that view was that whereas s 174 contains elaborate provisions for enabling a person to appeal to the Secretary of State against an enforcement notice, there were no equivalent provisions with regard to breach of condition notices. He also pointed to the likelihood that Parliament could not have intended a person wishing to show the breach of condition notice had been served more than 10 years after the breach of the condition to have no right of appeal whatsoever. To hold otherwise, he thought, would enable a planning authority unsure of whether enforcement would be out of time to sidestep the issue by serving a breach of condition notice.

20.151 The decision in *Dilieto*, whilst clearly welcome, leaves unclear what other points of law can now be raised before magistrates as a defence to a prosecution for failure to comply with a breach of condition notice. Sullivan J in the *Dilieto* case thought that allegations that a breach of condition notice had been served in bad faith, or for improper purposes, or on the basis of irrelevant considerations, were matters better suited to judicial review rather than to magistrates' courts. However, on the same day as judgment was given in the *Dilieto* case, the House of Lords gave judgment in *Boddington v British Transport Police* [1999] 2 AC 143 in which, in a case which was not concerned with planning issues, their Lordships appeared to draw a lesser demarcation line than that drawn in *Dilieto* between the grounds of challenge that could or could not be taken in magistrates' court proceedings. In particular, the Lord Chancellor, Lord Irvine of Lairg, referring to the charges of inconsistencies in magistrates having to deal with difficult points of administrative law, thought that magistrates should not be underestimated and that 'the practical risks of inconsistency are probably exaggerated'. It thus remains to be seen how far magistrates' courts will be able to deal with the whole range of legal challenges that can be made where invalidity is alleged on a prosecution for non-compliance with a breach of condition notice.

K. INJUNCTIONS

From the early days of planning control, injunctions have occasionally been used by local planning authorities as an aid to enforcement. One of the earliest cases in this area was *Attorney-General v Bastow* [1957] 1 QB 514, where the Attorney-General, at the relation of the local planning authority, obtained an injunction restraining the defendant from using land or causing or permitting it to be used as a caravan site contrary to the terms of an enforcement notice. The defendant had continuously disregarded the notice and been prosecuted and convicted on a number of occasions for that offence. **20.152**

A year later, in *Attorney-General v Smith* [1958] 2 QB 173, the Attorney-General, again at the relation of the local planning authority, was granted an injunction restraining the defendant from using or causing or permitting to be used as a caravan site, any land within the boundaries of the authority without the prior grant of planning permission. The evidence was that the defendant, by moving caravans from one unauthorized site to another, was using the machinery of the Planning Act not for the purpose of making genuine applications for planning permission, but for the purpose of delay in order to evade the provisions of the Act for as long as possible. The need for local authorities to obtain the fiat of the Attorney-General in order to pursue such cases is now no longer needed. Section 222 of the Local Government Act 1972 provides: **20.153**

> Where a local authority consider it expedient for the promotion or protection of the interests of the inhabitants of their area ... they may prosecute or defend or appear in any legal proceedings and, in the case of civil proceedings, may institute them in their own name.

This power was used on a number of occasions. Reference has previously been made to the case of *Bedfordshire CC v Central Electricity Generating Board* [1985] JPL 43. Another case, where a local planning authority obtained an injunction to restrain a contravening use against which enforcement notice proceedings had been taken, was *Westminster City Council v Jones* [1981] JPL 750. In this case, the local authority acted to prevent the operation of an amusement arcade causing nuisance and disturbance in a residential area. The defendant had known when he took a lease of premises that he needed planning permission for the new use but he had elected to proceed before he had got the permission or before he took adequate steps to ascertain the authority's attitude. The authority had served both an enforcement notice and a stop notice on the defendant; and a summons for failure to comply with the latter was shortly due to be heard. Rather than wait just **20.154** under one month for the criminal proceedings to be heard, however, the court was prepared to grant the injunction asked for.

20.155 In certain cases it was shown possible to obtain an injunction to restrain a threatened or actual breach of planning control even before an enforcement notice or stop notice was served. This was achieved in *Southwark LBC v ML Frow* [1989] JPL 645 where property had originally been used by members of the same family as two informal flats. Minor and superficial building works had taken place and the property was being prepared for occupation as nine bedsit flats. The owner was contacted and told that a planning application was required, but that it was likely that such an application would be refused. Additionally, he was informed that enforcement action was being considered and that the units should not be occupied.

20.156 It needed to be established whether a material change of use had occurred, and whether enforcement and stop notices could be served. However, the use as bedsits was dependent upon occupation and thus the authority could not serve the notices as no change of use had yet occurred. As the premises began to become occupied, it became imperative that further occupation be prevented, although allowing the existing tenants to remain. It was the authority's opinion that full occupation of the building as bedsits was undesirable owing to the effect of adjoining neighbours, the extremely poor quality of the accommodation itself, and possible traffic implications in an already heavily parked and trafficked area.

20.157 As the use, usefulness, and legality of using enforcement notices and stop notices were in doubt, and as the warnings and advice to the owner were being ignored, an injunction was sought and obtained.

20.158 The report *Enforcing Planning Control* in 1989 considered that injunctions had proved a useful back-up to the statutory system in difficult cases. In the view of Robert Carnwath QC there were doubts about the circumstances in which the remedy was available, particularly the extent to which it was available to restrain an actual or threatened breach of planning control *before* it had become a criminal offence following service of an enforcement notice or stop notice.

20.159 The review recommended that an authority should be able to apply for an injunction in respect of any breach or threatened breach of planning control, whether or not an enforcement notice or stop notice has been served. Such a remedy could be used in urgent cases where there was a serious threat to amenity and time was of the essence; or as a back-up for other remedies where they had failed to secure the termination of a breach. Accordingly, the Planning and Compensation Act 1991 introduced s 187B into the 1990 Act, to give local planning authorities an express right in planning law to obtain from the High Court or a county court an injunction. The section provides that where the authority '... consider it necessary or expedient for any actual or apprehended breach of planning control to be restrained by injunction, they may apply to the court for an injunction, whether or not they have exercised or are proposing to exercise any of their other powers under this Part'. The authority does not have to pursue other means of enforcement, including criminal prosecution under s 179 or 187A of the 1990 Act, before seeking injunctive relief under s 187B.

20.160 The use of the power to seek an injunction to remedy a breach or threatened breach of planning control under the statutory powers has been considered by the Court of Appeal in two decisions given on the same day. In *Croydon LBC v Gladden* [1994] JPL 723, it was held that the power enabled the court to issue a mandatory injunction requiring an occupier to remove a replica Spitfire aeroplane from the garden of a dwellinghouse. In *Runnymede DC v Harwood* [1994] JPL 724 the court granted an injunction which sought to restrain an occupier from using his land for the storage of motor vehicles contrary to the requirements of an enforcement notice. If the court were to have withheld injunctive relief it would have given temporary planning permission for the continuance of an activity for which the local planning authority had consistently refused permission. It was held that s 187B of the 1990 Act was much wider than the power previously available to a local planning authority. It was no longer necessary to show that criminal penalties were not enough to deter the defendant from infringing planning law. So, an injunction might be sought, for example, in order to prevent the occupation of dwellinghouses where the developer has not complied with a condition in the grant of planning permission that an access road to the dwellings be provided before the dwellings are occupied. Furthermore, in *Connors v Reigate and Banstead BC* [2000] JPL 1178 (CA), it was said that there was no necessity for an authority to show either that there was a nuisance or a risk of irreparable harm. Its function was to uphold planning procedures and to ensure that those who wished to develop land should not pre-empt the statutory procedures which Parliament has laid down.

20.161 The scope of an injunction may be particularly useful where there are difficulties in ascertaining precisely who has the power to remedy the breach. In *Hillingdon LBC v Guinea Enterprises Ltd (and 15 others)* [1997] JPL B11, the court granted an injunction to restrain unauthorized aggregate reprocessing on land in the green belt. The injunction was sought in the following wide terms:

> The defendants (save for the trustees and the neighbours), any person controlling, administering, financing, holding shares in or otherwise subscribing to or connected with the defendant companies or the servants or agents of such persons and any successor in title to any interest in the land be restrained from conducting whether by themselves, with others, or through any company tipping, crushing or exporting waste etc. on the land or on any other land designated as Green Belt in the Borough and that all plant be removed from the land.

20.162 In *South Cambridgeshire DC v Persons Unknown* (Times Law Reports, 11 November 2004), the Court of Appeal agreed that an injunction could be granted to restrain persons unknown from perpetrating identified breaches of planning control at an identified site.

20.163 In *Kettering BC v Perkins* [1999] JPL 166, the court accepted that although there is a general rule that injunctions should be as precise as possible, it is not an absolute rule, and since the statutory scheme to control land use does not always admit of absolute precision, injunctions under s 187B may be granted in extensive terms. Indeed, in *Wealdon DC v Nelson James Krushandal* [1999] JPL 174 the Court of Appeal dismissed an appeal against the granting of an injunction which prohibited the stationing of a mobile home on any land in the area of the District Council.

20.164 An important decision by the House of Lords in *Kirklees MBC v Wickes Building Supplies Ltd* [1993] AC 227, that an injunction granted to enforce the law did not need to be supported by an undertaking in damages, further encourages the use of this provision.

20.165 As a result of the Human Rights Act 1998, the use of injunctions to control breaches of planning law has been considered and clarified by the House of Lords. In the landmark case of *South Bucks DC v Porter* [2003] UKHL 26; [2003] 2 AC 558, the House of Lords set out the cornerstone of the court's powers to grant an injunction under s 187B of the 1990 Act. In doing so, the House of Lords approved the approach taken in the Court of Appeal by Simon Brown LJ. The House had to consider a number of related cases concerning gypsies, who had challenged the grant of injunctions made against them by the High Court which required them to cease the use of land in the green belt for the stationing of caravans. Applications for planning permission had been made but refused. In dismissing an appeal by the Council from a decision of the Court of Appeal to remit the matter back to the High Court for reconsideration, the House of Lords accepted that the following principles governed the grant of an injunction. These principles have subsequently been summarized in the following propositions:

(a) The court has a discretion as to whether an injunction should be granted. This discretion should be exercised with due regard to the purpose for which it was conferred, here to restrain actual threatened breaches of planning control. This is an original and discretionary, not a supervisory jurisdiction. The power exists mainly to permit abuses to be curbed and urgent solutions provided where these are called for.

(b) The court need not examine matters of planning policy or judgment that are the exclusive preserve of the authorities administering the planning regime.

(c) Nevertheless the court is not obliged to grant relief because a planning authority considered it necessary or expedient to restrain a planning breach.

(d) The court should have regard to all the circumstances, including the personal circumstances of the family, and the availability of other suitable accommodation. Particular attention should be given to the position of members of the gypsy community, their needs and their lifestyle, together with any shortage of pitches or appropriate sites in the relevant area. Genuine absence of appropriate alternative accommodation makes the interference potentially more serious and, depending on other factors, may require greater justification.

(e) Having regard to section 6 of the Human Rights Act 1998 and Art 8 of the European Convention on Human Rights and Fundamental Freedoms, the court should only grant an injunction where it is just and proportionate to do so.

In the *Porter* case the Court of Appeal reversed the judge's decision because he had not taken account of non-planning considerations (which included their right to family life under Art 8 of the European Convention on Human Rights). The House of Lords upheld the Court of Appeal's decision. With regard to the last of these propositions, Lord Scott had observed:

> The hardship likely to be caused to a Defendant by the grant of an injunction to enforce the public law will always, in my opinion, be relevant to the court's decision whether or not to grant the injunction. In many, perhaps most, cases the hardship prayed in aid by the Defendant will be of insufficient weight to counterbalance a continued and persistent disobedience to the law. There is a strong general public interest that planning control should be observed and, if not observed enforced. But each case must depend upon its own circumstances.

20.166 One of the best commentaries on s 187B of the Act is contained in the heading of the law report of the decision of Gray J in *Aylesbury Vale District Council v Florent, Florent and Oxford Gun Company* [2007] EWHC 724 (QB); [2008] JPL 70. It reads:

> Whilst s.187B of the Act was couched in wide terms, permitting an injunction to be granted as the court thought appropriate, and conferring a broad discretion upon the court, it was clear that the court had to take into account the likely effect of the injunction or any penalty for its infringement on the human rights of the defendant and, secondly, that the court had to be satisfied that the injunction was sufficiently necessary for the legitimate aim of protecting the environment to justify overriding the defendants' rights. Articles 6 and 1 to the First Protocol to the European Convention on Human Rights were engaged in the present case. However, it was not only the human rights of the Florents which had to be considered, but those of residents affected by the shooting noise under Arts 8 and 1 to the First Protocol ... the court had to bear in mind in addition the other statutory remedies available to a planning authority. When deciding whether to grant interlocutory injunctive relief, it was legitimate for the court to take account of such matters as the nature of the occupation of the site, the degree and flagrancy of the breach of planning control, the planning history of the site, the planning objections received and the conduct of the defendants as well as health and safety considerations.

20.167 For a further detailed and comprehensive review of the development of this area, see the Court of Appeal decision in *Basildon District Council and others v Equality and Human Rights Commission* [2009] EWCA Civ 13; [2009] JPL 1074.

L. REVERSION TO EARLIER USE

20.168 When an enforcement notice has taken effect, a question may arise as to what use the land can henceforth be put. Section 57(4) of the 1990 Act provides that where an enforcement notice has been issued in respect of any development of land, planning permission is not required for the use of that land for the purpose for which it could lawfully have been used if that development had not been carried out. In other words, where an enforcement notice takes effect, a landowner may revert to the use for which it could have been used immediately before the use complained of in the enforcement notice, provided that the use was lawful (see *Young v Secretary of State for the Environment* [1983] JPL 677 (CA)).

M. CERTIFICATES OF LAWFULNESS OF EXISTING USE OR DEVELOPMENT (CLEUDS) AND CERTIFICATES OF LAWFULNESS OF PROPOSED USE OR DEVELOPMENT (CLOPUDS)

20.169 The report by Robert Carnwath QC, *Enforcing Planning Control*, recommended that a new single procedure be introduced to replace the former 'established use' certificate provisions in ss 191 to 196 of the 1990 Act and the provisions in s 64 of the 1990 Act that enabled a local planning authority to determine whether a proposal to carry out operations on land or make any change in the use of land was development and, if so, whether an application for planning permission in respect of the development was required. The Planning and Compensation Act 1991, however, established not one but two new procedures. First, a procedure to enable anyone who wishes to do so to apply to the local planning authority to determine whether *existing* operational development on land or an *existing* use of land, or any other matter constituting a failure to comply with any condition or limitation subject to which planning permission has been granted, was lawful, and, if so, to be granted a certificate to that effect. Secondly, a procedure to enable anyone who wishes to ascertain whether any *proposed* operational development or use of land would be lawful, to apply similarly to the local planning authority for a determination of this question, and, if it would be, to obtain an appropriate certificate to that effect. As with the old s 64 procedure, neither of the two procedures gives a local planning authority power to answer a general question as to what use or operational development would be lawful for an owner to carry out on his land.

20.170 Furthermore, the local planning authority is not entitled to consider the planning merits of any application.

Certificate of lawfulness of existing use or development (CLEUD)

20.171 The main purpose of this certificate procedure is to simplify and modernize the old provisions in the 1990 Act which enabled the owner of land to obtain from the local planning authority a certificate of established use which granted him immunity from the subsequent enforcement action. That procedure originated in the Town and Country Planning Act 1968 when it was decided to change the rule that any development that had taken place more than four years previously should be immune from enforcement action, to a rule which limited that immunity to development of an operational nature and a change of use of any building to use as a single dwellinghouse. Furthermore, the 1968 Act provided that any other change of use was not to acquire immunity from enforcement action by the passage of time. Thereafter, enforcement action could be taken at any time. The changes made to the law by the 1968 Act created many problems. The position was that any change of use made on or before 31 December 1963 without a grant of planning permission continued to be immune from enforcement notice procedure, whereas a change of use made on or after 1 January 1964 could, apart from the one exception mentioned above, never acquire that immunity. Although immediately after 1968 it may not have been too difficult to prove the precise date on which a change had actually taken place, the difficulty of doing so was bound to increase with the passage of time and the frequency with which property is bought and sold. Hence the 1968 Act introduced a procedure for an owner to obtain an 'established use' certificate. The certificate was a procedural innovation designed to assist a vendor to sell his property with the aid of something like a guarantee that no enforcement notice would be served in respect of the use stated in the certificate.

20.172 Unfortunately, many owners of land did not apply, preferring to wait until the land was sold or doubts were raised about the lawfulness of the existing use. By 1991, as 1964 became more remote, it became progressively more difficult to operate the established use certificate procedure satisfactorily. Reliable evidence as to the state of affairs in 1964 was difficult to obtain, with the result that many applications for such certificates, which had to be decided on the basis of a 'balance of probabilities', were considered to be unsatisfactory. The decision to phase out the established use certificate procedure was linked, of course, to the change in the law made by the 1991 Act relating to the period when immunity from enforcement action was acquired.

20.173 The 1991 Act amended the 1990 Act by substituting new ss 191 to 194. Subsection (1) of s 191 provides that if any person wishes to ascertain whether any existing use of buildings or other land is lawful; any operations which have been carried out in, on, over, or under land are lawful; or any other matter constituting a failure to comply with any condition or limitation subject to which planning permission has been granted is lawful; he may apply to the local planning authority specifying the land and describing the use, operations, or other matter.

20.174 Subsections (2) and (3) of s 191 specify the circumstances in which development or the failure to comply with a condition is to be regarded as lawful. Under s 191(2), operations are lawful at any time if no enforcement action may then be taken in respect of them (whether because they did not involve development or require planning permission or because the time for enforcement action had expired or for any other reason) and they do not constitute a contravention of any of the requirements of any enforcement notice then in force.

20.175 Under s 191(3) any matter constituting a failure to comply with any condition or limitation subject to which planning permission has been granted, is lawful at any time if the time for taking enforcement action in respect of the failure has then expired and it does not constitute a contravention of any of the requirements of any enforcement notice or breach of condition notice then in force.

20.176 Subsection (4) of s 191 provides that if, on an application under this section, the local planning authority is provided with information satisfying it of the lawfulness at the time of the application of the use, operations, or other matter described in the application, or that description as modified by the local planning authority or a description substituted by it, it must issue a certificate to that effect; and in any other case it must refuse the application.

20.177 The onus of proving the lawfulness of an existing use or development appears to rest with the applicant. The courts have held in *Gabbitas v Secretary of State for the Environment* [1985] JPL 630 that the relevant test of the evidence on such matters is 'the balance of probability'. Moreover, the courts have held that the applicant's own evidence does not need to be corroborated by 'independent' evidence in order to be accepted. If the local planning authority has no evidence of its own, or from others, to contradict or otherwise make the applicant's version of events less than probable, there is no good reason to refuse the application, provided the applicant's evidence alone is sufficiently precise and unambiguous to justify the grant of a certificate 'on the balance of probability'. This principle applies equally to enforcement notices where the ground of appeal is made under s 174(2)(d).

20.178 It should be noted that, as with the old certificates of established use, the local planning authority has no discretion as to whether or not to issue a certificate. It should be emphasized that the issue of a certificate under these provisions neither creates nor removes rights. It is merely a declaration, binding upon the authority, that certain existing rights attach to a given property. If the applicant can satisfy the local planning authority of the lawfulness of development carried out, he will be entitled to be issued with the certificate. Once issued, s 191(6) provides that the lawfulness of any use, operations, or other matter for which a certificate is in force shall be conclusively presumed. It will not, therefore, be possible for the authority to take enforcement action against any use, operations, or other matter specified in the certificate. Thus in order to ensure that a high degree of precision is achieved in describing the particular lawful use or development specified in the certificate, s 191(5) provides for a certificate to specify the land to which it relates, describe the uses, operations, or other matter in question (including, if appropriate, the relevant use Class), give the reasons for determining the use, operations, or other matter to be lawful, and specify the date of the application for the certificate.

Many problems seem to have been caused by the certificate of lawful use or development procedure, although for the most part they have involved the application to particular cases of general planning law principles. However, in *Panton and Farmer v Secretary of State for the Environment, Transport, and the Regions and Vale of White Horse DC* [1999] JPL 461, guidance was given by the High Court on the approach a decision-maker should follow in considering an application. This was first, to ask and answer the question, 'When did the material change of use specified in the application occur?' To be lawful, this would need to be before 1 July 1948, by 31 December 1963, or at a date at least 10 years prior to the current application. Secondly, if the material change of use took place prior to those dates, has the use specified in the application been lost by operation of law in one of the three possible ways, namely by abandonment, the formation of a new planning unit, or by way of a material change of use, be it by way of implementation of a further planning permission or otherwise? Thirdly, if he is satisfied that the description of the use specified in the application does not properly describe the nature of the use which resulted from the material change of use, the decision-maker must modify/substitute each description so as properly to describe the nature of the material change of use which occurred. The *Panton and Farmers* decision was considered by the Court of Appeal in *Secretary of State for the Environment, Transport, and the Regions v Thurrock BC* [2002] EWCA Civ 226; [2002] 2 PLR 43. The case involved a challenge to an Inspector's decision to allow an appeal against an enforcement notice served by the Borough Council on the ground that service of the enforcement notice was time-barred. It was unclear, however, if the Inspector had considered whether the change of use had been carried on for the whole 10-year period ending with the date of the enforcement notice. The Court of Appeal considered that the Inspector had wrongly interpreted *Panton* in thinking that if the use enforced against had first commenced before the 10-year period, it could only be held to be unlawful if the use had been abandoned during that period. In the court's view it was only when lawful use rights had been acquired, that the use could be lost by abandonment, replacement by a different use, or extinguishment following the formation of a new planning unit. **20.179**

In the *Thurrock* case, the Court of Appeal considered that the rationale of immunity from enforcement was that throughout the whole of the ten-year period of unlawful use the local planning authority, although having the power to take enforcement action, had failed to do so. So, if at any time during the relevant period the authority would not have been able to take enforcement proceedings in respect of the breach (because for example, the unlawful use had temporarily **20.180** ceased), then any such period could not count towards the 10-year period which gives rise to the immunity.

20.181 The effect of the decision in the *Thurrock* case therefore, is to require a far more stringent test of immunity than had previously been thought following the decision in *Panton and Farmer*. In particular, the decision means that if an unlawful use ceases and is then recommenced, the 10-year period required for immunity begins with the act of the recommencement. For an unlawful use to obtain immunity from enforcement it has to be exercised continually and without significant interruption for the whole of the 10-year period.

20.182 The *Thurrock* test, if applied literally, would mean that any period of dormancy occurring during the relevant period cannot count towards the rolling period of years which gives rise to the immunity from enforcement proceedings. It will, therefore, be of interest to see to what extent a minimal interruption in an unlawful use during the claim period is held to be within the *Thurrock* principle. A short period of inactivity may be regarded as part of a continuing use; a longer period not. What constitutes a short period for these purposes must be a question of fact and degree for the decision-maker in every case. In *Thurrock* the Court of Appeal considered that a factory's weekend break or a closure for the summer holidays would not be sufficient to constitute a break in the 10-year period. No doubt, further judicial guidance on this issue can be expected, and many borderline cases are expected to arise. See for example *Swale Borough Council v First Secretary of State* [2005] EWCA Civ 1568; [2006] JPL 886.

20.183 In *Miles v the National Assembly for Wales* [2007] EWHC 10 (Admin) the High Court held that the 10-year period of immunity had not been met when the use of land for motorcycling activity had been interrupted by an outbreak of foot and mouth disease for which the applicant had not been responsible. The interruption had lasted 18 months.

20.184 The decision in *Thurrock* indicates that it is wrong to assume that a material change of use is a once and for all event. Now, in order to have a 10-year period of immunity, an owner must demonstrate that the use has been carried on continuously throughout the 10-year period, during which the local planning authority could reasonably, if it had so wished, have taken enforcement proceedings.

20.185 However in the case of conditions it would seem that even if there has been a continuous breach for more than 10 years, immunity can be lost if there follows a period when there is no breach and then a subsequent new breach of the condition. This occurred in the case of *Ellis v Secretary of State for Communities and Local Government* [2009] EWHC 634 (Admin); [2010] 1 P & CR 21, where planning permission for a house in the green belt had been granted subject to a condition that it be occupied only by people employed in agriculture or forestry and their dependants. It had always been occupied in breach of that condition, apart from some brief periods when it was unoccupied. During one such period the previous owner applied for a certificate of lawfulness in relation to the occupancy of the house by a person who did not comply with the occupancy condition, on the basis that the breach had begun more than 10 years earlier. The High Court, applying *Nicholson v Secretary of State for the Environment and Maldon District Council* (1998) 76 P & CR 191, upheld a rejection of the certificate on the grounds that the crucial question was whether the relevant breach of planning control still subsisted at the date of the application. As with determining whether a material change of use has taken place, in determining whether a use is lawful, it is important to identify the correct planning unit, which is a material consideration; see *R (on the application of Sellars) v Basingstoke and Deane BC* [2013] EWHC 3673 (Admin); [2014] JPL 643.

20.186 As with the statutory provisions for CLOPUDs, s 193(7) provides that a certificate once issued may be revoked by a local planning authority.

20.187 Lastly, it was held in *R v Epping Forest BC, ex p Philcox* [2000] PLCR 57 that if a certificate of lawful use or development is issued in respect of a limited area of land, it is within a local planning authority's power to subsequently issue another certificate covering a larger area of land than that covered by the earlier certificate.

20.188 The principles to be applied when considering an CLEUD application were summarized by *R (Flint) v South Gloucestershire Council* [2016] EWHC 2180 (Admin); [2017] JPL 310 per HHJ Wacksman QC at [29]–[30]:

> 29 The importance of precision in defining in the certificate the use found to be lawful has been emphasised by the courts on a number of occasions. Both counsel referred me to the leading authorities. In *Broxbourne Borough Council v Secretary of State for the Environment* [1980] QB 1, the Divisional Court stated that otherwise the authority may be precluded from preventing a use for which planning permission would not have been granted because the certificate had been issued in terms wider than were necessary. It was also observed that precision is of assistance to a prospective purchaser. Where it is wider than necessary, it will be quashed, as it was in *R v Sheffield City Council ex p Russell* (1994) 68 P&CR 331. There the certificate relating to clay pigeon shooting was quashed because there was no evidence that the shooting took place on an exclusive daily basis which was otherwise than for recreational purposes of those using the land.
>
> 30 It is not a requirement of law, however, that in all cases a certain degree of particularisation is required. What is an appropriate level of detail will vary from cases to case and is a matter of judgment for the decision maker based on the evidence (see *R v Thanet District Council ex parte Tapp* [2001] EWCA Civ 559, *Hillingdon v Secretary of State for Communities and Local Government* [2008] EWHC 198 (Admin) and *R (North Wiltshire) v Cotswold District Council* [2009] EWHC 3702 (Admin)). However, it is wrong in law to include in the certificate some of the particularity but not all of it (see *Main v Secretary of State for Communities and Local Government* (1998) 77 P&CR 300).

Certificate of lawfulness of proposed use or development (CLOPUD)

20.189 Although this certificate is authorized by Part VII of the 1990 Act, it has little to do with enforcement, except insofar as a certificate under s 192 may prevent enforcement action from being taken. Reference has been made to this certificate in Chapter 8.

21

LISTED BUILDINGS AND CONSERVATION AREAS

A. INTRODUCTION	21.01	H. LISTED BUILDING PURCHASE NOTICES	21.93
B. LISTED BUILDINGS	21.02	I. CERTIFICATES OF IMMUNITY	21.94
C. WHAT CAN BE LISTED	21.23	J. LISTED BUILDINGS IN NEED OF REPAIR	21.98
D. THE PROTECTION	21.45	K. BUILDING PRESERVATION NOTICES	21.113
E. BUILDINGS IN ECCLESIASTICAL USE AND MONUMENTS	21.49	L. CONSERVATION AREAS	21.130
F. LISTED BUILDING CONSENT	21.56	M. RECENT CHANGES	21.149
G. LISTED BUILDING ENFORCEMENT NOTICES	21.77		

A. INTRODUCTION

PPS5 'Planning for the Historic Environment' introduced a new administrative approach to the historic environment by creating the concept of 'heritage assets'. The National Planning Policy Framework ('NPPF') defines a 'heritage asset' as follows: A building, monument, site, place, area or landscape identified as having a degree of significance meriting consideration in planning decisions, because of its heritage interest. It includes designated heritage assets and assets identified by the local planning authority (including local listing). **21.01**

The NPPF explains that:

> The value of a heritage asset to this and future generations because of its heritage interest. The interest may be archaeological, architectural, artistic or historic. Significance derives not only from a heritage asset's physical presence, but also from its setting. For World Heritage Sites, the cultural value described within each site's Statement of Outstanding Universal Value forms part of its significance.

The concept of significance, whilst not mentioned in the legislation itself, has been held to be a relevant determining factor in assessing whether the statutory tests are met, see: *Catesby Estates Ltd v Steer* [2018] EWCA Civ 1697; [2018] JPL 1375 per Lindblom LJ at [30].

B. LISTED BUILDINGS

21.02 The law relating to listed buildings and conservation areas is now contained in the Planning (Listed Buildings and Conservation Areas) Act 1990. The Government's policies on the conservation of the historic environment are set out within the NPPF and Planning Practice Guidance ('PPG').

21.03 Listed building control is a special form of control applicable to buildings of special architectural or historical interest. This specific form of control, which is exercised over the development of land, is intended to prevent the unrestricted demolition, alteration, or extension of a listed building without the express consent of the local planning authority or the Secretary of State. The control does not depend upon whether the proposed activity constitutes development under s 55 of the Town and Country Planning Act 1990. It extends to any works for the demolition of a listed building, or for its alteration or extension in any manner likely to affect its character as a building of special architectural or historic interest.

21.04 It may not always be clear whether works to a listed building constitute the demolition or alteration of a building. Whether work amounts to demolition or alteration of a listed building has to be considered in the context of the whole of the listed building. Following the decision of the House of Lords in *Shimizu (UK) Ltd v Westminster City Council* [1997] JPL 523, partial demolition will generally be regarded as an alteration rather than demolition. In that case the Lands Tribunal (which was dealing with an issue of compensation arising from the refusal of listed building consent) was held to have correctly decided that the removal of internal chimney breasts on five floors of a listed building constituted not works of demolition but an alteration to the building.

21.05 Despite the decision in *Shimizu*, problems can still arise where part only of a listed building is to be demolished. The substantive demolition of a listed building, or any significant part of it, should be treated similarly to total demolition of the building. As pointed out in *Sullivan v Warwick DC and Wilson Bowden Developments Ltd and English Heritage* [2003] EWHC 606 (Admin); [2003] JPL 1545, in deciding whether the demolition of part of a listed building was significant, it was necessary to look not merely at the physical scale of the demolition, but also the quality of that part of the building to be demolished and its contribution to the character of the listed building as a whole.

21.06 The appropriate classification of works to a listed building as demolition or alteration may impact upon whether notice needs to be given to the Royal Commission on Historic Monuments (which is required before a listed building can be demolished); whether an application for listed building consent for works to the listed building is needed; and if it is, whether notice needs to be given to specified amenity bodies. It also has implications for work done to non-listed buildings within conservation areas where consent is required for the demolition of a building (see para 21.133).

21.07 It should be emphasized that whilst the total demolition (or in some cases partial demolition) of a listed building is subject to listed building control, works for the alteration or extension of a listed building is subject to listed building control only if the work affects the character of the building as a listed building. In a ministerial decision in 1972 the Secretary of State decided that the painting in yellow of the front door of a dwelling in the historic Georgian Royal Crescent in Bath amounted to unauthorized work altering the character of a listed building and was subject, therefore, to listed building control. But in *Windsor and Maidenhead RBC v Secretary of State for the Environment* [1988] JPL 410, the Secretary of State had taken the opposite view in finding that painting the Georgian stucco of a listed building in black, was not an alteration and was therefore outside listed building control. The High Court, however, held that having regard to the meaning of the word 'alteration' in ordinary language, and having regard to the relevant statutory provisions, repainting was capable of being an alteration. It also held that the critical question in such a case was whether or not repainting in that case affected the character of the building as one of special architectural or historic interest. This was a matter for the Secretary of State to decide. It seems, therefore, that simple cleaning work to a listed building would not normally require listed building consent. This is probably true also of repainting unless the repainting was of a different colour and so affected its character as a building of special architectural or historic interest. In a ministerial decision in 1989, it was held that the removal of the original-type of glass forming the top glazed panels showing the word 'Telephone' in maroon on a white background on a number of listed telephone kiosks in Cheltenham, and their replacement with panels showing the word 'Phonecard' in white on a green background, affected their character as buildings of special architectural or historical importance.

21.08 The law relating to listed building control is found in the Planning (Listed Buildings and Conservation Areas) Act 1990 ('the LBCA Act 1990') and the Planning (Listed Buildings and Conservation Areas) Regulations 1990, SI 1990/1519 (although now Wales has a separate set in the Planning (Listed Buildings and Conservation Areas) (Wales) Regulations 2012). The LBCA Act 1990 has recently been amended by the Enterprise and Regulation Reform Act 2013 and related subordinate legislation.

21.09 Under s 1 of the LBCA Act 1990, the Secretary of State for Culture, Media, and Sport is required to compile lists of buildings of special architectural or historic interest or approve, with or without modifications, such lists compiled by the

Historic Buildings and Monuments Commission for England (known generally as English Heritage) or by other persons or bodies of persons. Furthermore, s 1(4) provides that before compiling, approving, or amending any list, the Secretary of State shall consult with the Commission in relation to buildings situated in England and with such other persons or bodies of persons as appear to him appropriate as having special knowledge of, or interest in, buildings of special architectural or historic interest.

21.10 The Secretary of State for the Department for Culture Media and Sport in 2010 issued a document entitled 'Principles of Selection for Listing Buildings' which sets out the following criteria that will be used when assessing whether a building is of special interest and therefore should be added to the statutory list:

— *Architectural interest*: To be of special architectural interest a building must be of importance in its architectural design, decoration, or craftsmanship; special interest may also apply to nationally important examples of particular building types and techniques (eg, buildings displaying technological innovation or virtuosity) and significant plan forms;

— *Historic interest*: To be of special historic interest a building must illustrate important aspects of the nation's social, economic, cultural, or military history and/or have close historical associations with nationally important people. There should normally be some quality of interest in the physical fabric of the building itself to justify the statutory protection afforded by the listing.

21.11 When making a listing decision, the Secretary of State may take into account the extent to which the exterior contributes to the architectural or historic interest of any group of buildings of which it forms part. This is generally known as group value. The Secretary of State will take this into account particularly where buildings comprise an important architectural or historic unity or a fine example of planning (eg squares, terraces, or model villages) or where there is a historical functional relationship between a group of buildings. If a building is designated because of its group value, protection applies to the whole of the property, not just the exterior.

21.12 In considering whether a building is of special architectural or historic interest the Secretary of State may take into account the desirability of preserving, on the grounds of its architectural or historic interest, any feature of the building containing a man-made object or structure fixed to the building or forming part of the land and comprised within the curtilage of the building. The desirability of preserving such a feature is a factor which would increase the likelihood of the building being listed. However, in the absence of any other aspects of special architectural or historic interest, such features will justify the listing of the building only if they are of themselves of sufficient interest to render the building of special interest. The provision can be used for a variety of features; examples could include a finely panelled 16th-century room, a fireplace, and over-mantel that has been introduced from another building, or an elaborate plaster ceiling. This provision cannot be used to preserve in situ anything that is not a fixture, such as furniture or paintings.

The document then indicates the general principles that follow from the application of these criteria: **21.13**

(a) *Age and rarity*: The older a building is, and the fewer the surviving examples of its kind, the more likely it is to have special interest. The following chronology is meant as a guide to assessment; the dates are indications of likely periods of interest and are not absolute. The relevance of age and rarity will vary according to the particular type of building because for some types, dates other than those outlined below are of significance. However, the general principles used are that:
— before 1700, all buildings that contain a significant proportion of their original fabric are listed;
— from 1700 to 1840, most buildings are listed;
— after 1840, because of the greatly increased number of buildings erected and the much larger numbers that have survived, progressively greater selection is necessary;
— buildings of less than 30 years old are normally listed only if they are of outstanding quality and under threat.

(b) *Aesthetic merits*: The appearance of a building—both its intrinsic and architectural merit and any group value—is a key consideration in judging listing proposals, but the special interest of a building will not always be reflected in obvious external visual quality. Buildings that are important for reasons of technological innovation, or as illustrating particular aspects of social or economic history, may have little external visual quality.

(c) *Selectivity*: Where a building qualifies for listing primarily on the strength of its special architectural interest, the fact that there are other buildings of similar quality elsewhere is not likely to be a major consideration. However, a building may be listed primarily because it represents a particular historical type in order to ensure that examples of such a type are preserved. Listing in these circumstances is largely a comparative exercise and needs to be selective where a substantial number of buildings of a similar type and quality survive. In such cases, the Secretary of State's policy is to list only the most representative or most significant examples of the type.

(d) *National interest*: The emphasis in these criteria is to establish consistency of selection to ensure that not only are all buildings of strong intrinsic architectural interest included on the list, but also the most significant or distinctive regional buildings that together make a major contribution to the national historic stock. For instance, the best examples of local vernacular buildings will normally be listed because together they illustrate the importance of distinctive local and regional traditions. Similarly, for example, some buildings will be listed because they represent a nationally important but localized industry, such as shoemaking in Northamptonshire or cotton production in Lancashire.

(e) *State of repair*. The state of repair of a building is not a relevant consideration when deciding whether a building meets the test of special interest. The Secretary of State will list a building which has been assessed as meeting the statutory criteria, irrespective of its state of repair.

21.14 It should be noted that economic factors cannot be taken into account in deciding whether or not to list a building. In March 1997 the Government confirmed its view that the rule was a sound one. Such matters as the cost of maintenance of a listed building or the cost of repairs to it, or whether the building should be allowed to be converted to a more economic use are, however, matters to be taken into account as material considerations in considering applications for listed building consent.

21.15 Buildings are classified in grades to reflect their relative architectural and historic interest. Buildings of historic interest may justify a higher grading than would otherwise be appropriate:

— Grade I buildings are of exceptional interest;
— Grade II* buildings are particularly important buildings of more than special interest;
— Grade II buildings are of special interest, warranting every effort to preserve them.

About 2.5 per cent of listed buildings are in Grade I; 5.5 per cent in Grade II*; and 92 per cent in Grade II (unstarred).

21.16 The significance of grading is that the more important the grade the more difficult it may be to obtain listed building consent to carry out work to the building. The grade also affects the availability of obtaining financial assistance for repairs to the listed building.

21.17 There are about 372,000 entries in the statutory lists in England, but since a single list entry may include more than one building (as in the case of a group of terraced housing), over 500,000 individual buildings are thought to be protected as listed buildings. About 9,000 are classified as Grade I and 19,000 buildings are classified as Grade II*. Domestic buildings account for 38 per cent of all buildings, with agricultural buildings accounting for just over 12 per cent.

21.18 Occasionally listed buildings have their status withdrawn because they have been demolished; they have lost their qualifying features through alteration, fire, etc; their architectural or historic merits prove to have been misjudged; or they have been listed in error. In 1988 for example, a building at Sea Palling, Norfolk, was added to the lists as a 16th-century house. It had in fact been built in the preceding five years. The roof had come from an old barn; lintels and doors from a demolition site; and the bressummers over the inglenook fireplaces from a scrapyard. For authenticity, the owner had built in some settlement. It was subsequently claimed that the building deserved to be listed on grounds of its rarity and eccentricity if not antiquity! In addition, a building may be deleted from a list following demolition, with or without listed building consent.

21.19 Needless to say, it is very rare for consent to be granted for the total demolition of a Grade I listed building. With regard to the other grades, figures show that in 1997/98, consent for the total demolition of a Grade II* listed building was given in only two cases; and total demolition of a Grade II (unstarred) listed building in 56 cases. In 1997, a total of 327 buildings were removed from the list during the year; that figure included those removed following the grant of consent for their demolition.

21.20 There is still no statutory provision requiring consultation with either the local planning authority or the owner or occupier of a building before it is added to a statutory list. However, following concern at the lack of any formal procedures for the public to be made aware that a building was being considered for listing, the Secretary of State announced in March 1995 that there would be public consultation on recommendations for listing made as a result of English Heritage's thematic studies of post-war and other building types. In August 1995, the Secretary of State announced that the consultation procedure would be extended to proposals to spot-list individual post-war buildings. The present practice can be found on English Heritage's website and involves the owner and the local planning authority being consulted about a proposal that a building should be listed. Once a building is listed however, the Department writes to the owner. This is in the nature of an early warning, because local planning authorities are required formally to notify owners and occupiers that a building has been included in a statutory list as soon as they receive notification of that fact from the Department. Authorities must also register the buildings as a local land charge. No formal machinery exists at this stage for an owner or occupier to challenge the inclusion of a building in a list. There is no right of appeal.

21.21 There is, however, an informal mechanism to challenge the listing of a building. If an owner or occupier makes representations to the Department, the matter is referred to a different Inspector from the one who made the original recommendation. A second opinion is obtained, and the Department may in the light of that second opinion decide that the building should not be listed after all.

21.22 Some buildings that are listed under s 1 of the LBCA Act 1990 are also protected as a scheduled monument under the provisions of s 1 of the Ancient Monuments and Archaeological Areas Act 1979 (see Chapter 22). By virtue of s 61 of the LBCA Act 1990, however, most of the listed building control provisions of that Act are disapplied to buildings that are also scheduled monuments.

C. WHAT CAN BE LISTED

21.23 Under s 1(5) of the LBCA Act 1990, a listed building means a building which for the time being is included in a list compiled or approved by the Secretary of State under the section. It will be recalled that under s 336(1) of the 1990 Act, a building 'includes any structure or erection, and any part of a building, as so defined, but does not include plant or machinery comprised in a building'. Listed buildings can therefore include such objects as lampposts, water troughs, cranes, bridges, tunnels, and urinals.

21.24 The definition of a building to include part of a building implies that every part of that building may be listed. Thus, listed building status extends to the interior of the building as much as to its exterior. The recent case of *Dill v Secretary of State for Communities and Local Government* [2018] EWCA Civ 2619 illustrates that the word 'buildings' within the Act includes listed items (in that case relating to two limestone piers).

21.25 Section 91(1) of the LBCA Act 1990 provides also that except insofar as the context otherwise requires, the word 'building' in the Act shall have the same meaning as given to it in the Town and Country Planning Act 1990. The effect of these two provisions (as was recognized by the House of Lords in *Schimizu (UK) Ltd v Westminster City Council* [1997] JPL 523) is that it gives the Secretary of State the power not only to list a building, but to list part of a building; so that where a part is listed, the part becomes the listed building. Section 1(5) of the LBCA Act 1990 amplifies that definition by providing that the following shall be treated as part of a building:

(a) any object or structure fixed to the building;
(b) any object or structure within the curtilage of a building which, although not fixed to the building, forms part of the land and has done so since before 1 July 1948.

21.26 The effect of para (a) is to enable control to be applied to both internal and external features of a building which are part of its historic fabric or of architectural interest, such as wall panelling, chimney-pieces, and wrought-iron balconies.

21.27 The effect of para (b) is to exclude from control any free-standing buildings erected within the curtilage of a listed building after 1 July 1948, unless, of course, the building has been listed in its own right. The Enterprise and Regulatory Reform Act 2013 has amended s 1(5) to allow in England the description of a listing to exclude objects or structures as being part of the building. The listing may also now make clear that any part or feature of the building is not of special architectural or historic interest.

21.28 A problem may arise with regard to para (a) as to precisely what is covered by the term 'object or structure fixed to the building'. The problem was considered by the House of Lords in *Debenhams plc v Westminster City Council* [1987] AC 396. There, the respondents owned a hereditament comprising two separate buildings on opposite sides of a street but joined by a footbridge over and a tunnel under the street. One of the buildings (the Regent Street building) was listed in its own right. The other building (the Kingly Street building) was not listed. A dispute arose as to whether the respondents could claim listed building exemption from rates under the General Rate Act 1967 for the period the hereditament had been unoccupied. The magistrate had held that the respondents were not entitled to the listed building exemption because the Kingly Street building was not a listed building. The respondents contended that the whole hereditament was listed because the Kingly Street building was a 'structure fixed to a [listed] building'. The House of Lords, in supporting the magistrates' view that the respondents were not entitled to the exemption, held that the term 'structure fixed to a [listed] building', only encompassed a structure which was ancillary and subordinate to the listed building itself and which was either fixed to the main building or within its curtilage, as, for example, the stable block of a listed mansion house or the steading of a listed farmhouse. The fact that one building was subordinate to another for the commercial purposes of the occupier or that a completely distinct building was connected to a listed building to which it was not subordinate, did not make the building a structure fixed to a listed building.

21.29 The *Debenhams* decision was followed in a later case, *Watts v Secretary of State for the Environment* [1991] JPL 719, where a successful challenge was made to the decision of the Secretary of State to dismiss an appeal against a listed building enforcement notice in respect of the demolition of part of a garden wall in order to provide a vehicle access. The question for the High Court to consider was whether the wall was subject to listed building control as being a 'structure fixed to a [listed] building' within the meaning of what is now s 1(5)(a) of the LBCA Act 1990. The facts were that in 1985, the adjacent Bix Manor House and adjoining barn had been specifically listed, but other buildings within the curtilage of the Manor House and the garden wall were not specifically referred to. At the date of the listing, the section of the wall now demolished had formed part of the curtilage of an adjacent property separate from the Manor in terms of both ownership and physical occupation. In quashing the decision of the Secretary of State and remitting the matter to him for further consideration, the court held that although historically and physically the wall had been associated with Bix Manor, at the time of listing, the part of the wall demolished was ancillary to another separate (unlisted) building and not a structure ancillary to Bix Manor. The structure was not, therefore, subject to listed building control. In *Secretary of State for the Environment, Transport, and the Regions v Skerritts of Nottingham* [2000] JPL 789, the Court of Appeal held that a stable block standing in the grounds of a hotel fell within the curtilage of the hotel and was accordingly listed.

21.30 In determining whether a structure is within the curtilage of a listed building, one should take into account the historic independence of the building; the physical layout of the principal building and any other buildings; evidence of common ownership now and at the date of listing; whether the structure forms part of the land; and their use or function past or present. In addition, it is necessary to consider the 'principal and ancillary' test formulated in the *Debenhams* case and the extent to which the structure has some degree of functional subordination to the building.

21.31 The significance of the 'list description' was considered by the House of Lords in *City of Edinburgh Council v Secretary of State for Scotland* [1997] 3 PLR 71. It would seem that every part of a listed building is in law equally 'listed', so that listing may protect the interior of a building as much as its exterior, regardless of any special architectural or historic interest which any particular part may have. It is, of course, common for the Secretary of State to provide a description of each building listed. That description, however, does no more in law than provide an aid to its identification, and any features not noted in the description are also part of the listing.

21.32 It should also be noted that in *Richardson Development Ltd v Birmingham City Council* [1999] JPL 1001 it was held that s 1(5)(a) allows a structure fixed to the land to be treated as part of the listed building, even though the structure was erected after the date of listing. However, it would, of course, be subject to the principle enunciated in the *Debenhams* case that it should be both fixed to the listed building and be ancillary to it.

21.33 A further difficulty concerns the extent to which control may be exercised over 'objects' fixed to a listed building. In 1989 the Secretary of State announced that in the light of legal advice, the statue of the *Three Graces*, believed to have been carved by Canova in 1817, which for many years had stood in a temple in Woburn Abbey, was subject to listed building control as being an 'object' fixed to a listed building. He had decided, however, not to take listed building enforcement action to secure its return to the temple.

21.34 Then in 1990, he announced that in the light of further information he had received, the better view was that the *Three Graces* was not part of the listed building and therefore not subject to listed building control ([1991] JPL 401). The Secretary of State's view was that the test to be applied was (as Lord Mackay had stated in the *Debenhams* case) the same test as applied at common law to decide whether an article was a fixture.

21.35 It appeared that the statue was installed in the *tempietto* in 1819 and remained there until 1872, when it was removed for exhibition at the Royal Academy. It was returned to Woburn Abbey in 1973 and remained installed in the *tempietto* until 1985. In that year it was sold and removed from Woburn Abbey. In his decision the Secretary of State said that the common law test, although easily stated, was not so easily applied. As regards the degree of annexation, the Secretary of State found it not to be great. The plinth on which the statue had stood had not been fastened to the floor in such a way as to make removal of the statue, which was freestanding, particularly difficult.

21.36 As regards the purpose of annexation, the Secretary of State said he now took the view, on further consideration, even accepting that the *tempietto* was specifically built or modified to house the statue, that this did not of itself mean that the statue became part of the building. According to the Secretary of State, he considered that even if the degree of annexation, looked at in isolation, could have been sufficient to satisfy the relevant test (which he doubted), the purpose of annexation in this case was not such as to make the statue part of the building. He thought that if the position was judged objectively, and without regard to the way in which the owners had regarded and treated the statue, it seemed that the object or purpose of installing the statue in the *tempietto* was not to dedicate it to the land or to incorporate it into the land, but to show off the statue. That, he felt, was consistent with the treatment of the *Three Graces* by the 'owners' of the land and the statue, and by the Revenue authorities, on the deaths of the 11th and 12th Dukes, when such owners chose to treat the statue as a chattel and not as a fixture. Accordingly, the Secretary of State decided that the weight of the arguments brought the scales firmly down against the *Three Graces* being a fixture at the time of listing in 1961. Free from the restrictions which would otherwise have prevented the statue being sold had it been regarded as part of the listed building, it was subsequently sold for £7.6m to the Victoria and Albert Museum and the National Gallery of Scotland who share its display.

21.37 It will be seen that in coming to the decision he eventually reached, the Secretary of State applied a two-fold test: first, the degree to which the object is attached or annexed to the building and secondly, the purpose of annexation. Clearly the first test must be satisfied for the second to need to be considered.

21.38 Then a little later, in [1991] JPL 1101, the Secretary of State decided that an 18th-century sundial, which had rested on a listed terrace but without being fixed to it, had not become part of the land and was not subject, therefore, to listed building control.

21.39 The question of how far works of art can be regarded as objects fixed to a listed building, however, continues to cause difficulty. A few years ago, in a ministerial decision, [1995] JPL 241, an Inspector quashed enforcement notices served by Westminster City Council requiring the return and reinstatement in a listed building in New Bond Street, London W1 of a bronze sculpture by Henry Moore; a painting, *Spirit of Architecture*, by Ben Nicholson; a heraldic clock by

Christopher Ironside; and an iron sculpture by Geoffrey Clarke entitled *The Complexities of Man*. The Inspector found that all four works were commissioned to be enjoyed in their own right and to be part of a fitting-out scheme by the tenant of the building, Time-Life, ongoing into occupation. He concluded, therefore, that all the works of art enforced against were chattels and not fixtures under the common law relating to fixtures. Hence, they were not fixed to the listed building and were not part of it. The decision was in fact subsequently quashed by the High Court with the consent of both parties. This arose because the Inspector had incorrectly considered the question of whether the items were fixtures at the date on which the building was listed, rather than the date the objects were placed in the building. Subsequently, following a further inquiry, the Secretary of State decided to uphold the enforcement notices which had required the works of art to be returned to the building ([1999] JPL 292).

21.40 In another ministerial decision at [1995] JPL 256, issued just two months earlier, the Secretary of State for Wales had accepted his Inspector's recommendation in upholding enforcement notices served by the Montgomeryshire District Council, which required the return to Leighton Hall, Welshpool, of three ormolu bronze chandeliers and a carillon clock which had been removed from the Hall without listed building consent. In *Kennedy v Secretary of State for Wales* [1996] 1 PLR 97, the High Court refused to quash the Secretary of State's decision holding that the definition of a fixture was the same for listed building legislation as it was for any other area of law. On the question of whether a chattel or an article was a fixture, a clear test had to be applied, namely the degree to which it was annexed to the building and then, if it is found to be annexed, the purpose for which it was put there. Following the decision, the dealer to whom the clock had been sold refused to return it to Leighton Hall, but after the County Council obtained an interim injunction requiring compliance with the enforcement notice, he duly did so.

21.41 A reminder of the way in which listed building control can impact upon the content of a listed building can be seen in another ministerial decision [1999] JPL 1145, where the Secretary of State upheld enforcement action taken by Harborough District Council to secure the reinstatement in Noseley Hall, Noseley, Leicestershire, a Grade II* listed building, of seven paintings in the style of the Italian painter, Pannini. In dealing with the degree to which the paintings could be said to be annexed to the Hall, the Secretary of State accepted the Inspector's conclusions that 'the fixing of the seven Panninis with mirror plates and screws and the similar fixing, or the possible embedding of the large Pannini into the mantel plaster, provided a sufficient degree of connection to the building to meet the first test'.

21.42 The Secretary of State also accepted the Inspector's conclusions with regard to the second test, namely the purpose of annexation. The Inspector found that that purpose had been to enhance the 'beauty of the study by the careful matching of pictures with the interior architecture'. Accordingly, the Panninis were integrated into the internal decor of the study in the early 18th century and thereby became part of the building. They were therefore to be regarded as fixtures and as such had to be regarded as part of the listed building.

At the listed building enforcement notice appeal the owners also sought listed building consent to the removal of the seven Panninis, in the event of the Secretary of State finding that they were indeed objects fixed to a listed building. This application was, perhaps not surprisingly, refused. **21.43**

A further enforcement notice served by the District Council with regard to two 18th-century paintings of a Galloway Mare entitled 'Ring Tail', was quashed by the Secretary of State on the recommendation of his Inspector, on the ground that whilst the use of several plates and supporting blocks provided a sufficient degree of annexation to pass the first test, they failed the purpose test in that the paintings had not been installed 'for the purposes of creating a beautiful room as a whole' and lacked any symbiotic relationship with the interior of the hall. **21.44**

D. THE PROTECTION

The special control over listed buildings is secured in the main by a criminal sanction. Section 7 of the LBCA Act 1990 provides that subject to the following provisions of the Act, no person shall execute or cause to be executed any works for the demolition of a listed building or for its alteration or extension in any manner which would affect its character as a building of special architectural or historic interest, unless the works are authorized. Section 9 provides that if a person contravenes s 7 he shall be guilty of an offence. It is a defence to the prosecution, however, to prove all the following matters: **21.45**

(a) that works to the building were urgently necessary in the interests of safety or health or for the preservation of the building;
(b) that it was not practicable to secure safety or health or, as the case may be, to preserve the building by works of repair or works for affording temporary support and shelter;
(c) that the works carried out were limited to the minimum measures immediately necessary; and
(d) that notice in writing justifying in detail the carrying out of the works was given to the local planning authority as soon as reasonably practicable.

Following changes introduced by the Planning and Compensation Act 1991, the maximum fine on summary conviction for executing, or causing to be executed, without listed building consent, any works for the demolition of a listed building or for its alteration or extension in a manner affecting its character as a building of special architectural or historic interest, or for the failure to comply **21.46** with any conditions attached to listed building consent to carry out works to a listed building, has been increased from £2,000 to £20,000. In determining the amount of any fine, however, the court is required to have regard to any financial benefit which has accrued or appears likely to accrue to the wrongdoer in consequence of the offence. This extends a requirement previously applicable only where a person was convicted on indictment. In addition, the maximum term of imprisonment on conviction on indictment has been increased from six months to two years.

21.47 There is no doubt that the courts use the enhanced powers now available to them. In a Welsh case in 1998, the owners of a listed building (Grade II) had pleaded guilty to the partial demolition of the building one day after it had been listed. In fining the owners £200,000, based on the likely profit to them of redeveloping the site, the judge described the owner's conduct as a 'cynical commercial act'. In another case, magistrates fined a development company £10,000 for gutting a 19th-century house (listed Grade II) and for removing all period features, in order to convert the building into bedsits. The offences were described as being 'serious and flagrant'.

21.48 The offence is an offence of strict liability, so that the prosecution does not have to prove that the defendant was aware that the building was a listed building in order to establish criminal liability. A consequence of this is that the intent or state of mind or motives of a person are irrelevant to the issue of guilt. In other words, it is an offence in which there is technically speaking no *mens rea*. However, a person's intention, state of mind, motives, and knowledge may be relevant to the punishment, if not to the issue of innocence or guilt (*R v Wells Street Metropolitan Stipendiary Magistrate, ex p Westminster City Council* [1986] 1 WLR 1046 (Div Court)).

E. BUILDINGS IN ECCLESIASTICAL USE AND MONUMENTS

21.49 It has been estimated that nearly 15,000 listed buildings are in religious use, 13,000 of them being churches of the Church of England. Of the buildings listed Grade I, well over a third are Anglican parish churches.

21.50 Section 60(1) and (2) of the LBCA Act 1990, however, provides that ecclesiastical buildings which are for the time being used for ecclesiastical purposes are not subject to ss 3, 4, 7 to 9, 47, 54, and 59 of the Act. These relate to listed building control, including building preservation notices, restrictions on works of demolition, alteration, or extension, compulsory acquisition of buildings in need of repair, urgent preservation works by a local authority, English Heritage, and the Secretary of State, and offences in relation to intentional damage. Section 75 of the Act provides that ecclesiastical buildings which are for the time being used for ecclesiastical purposes are not subject to s 74 of the Act which relates to the control of demolition of buildings in a conservation area. These exemptions are commonly collectively referred to as the 'ecclesiastical exemption'.

21.51 It follows that although ecclesiastical buildings can be listed under s 1 of the LBCA Act 1990, no criminal offence can be committed under s 9 for unauthorized works for the demolition, alteration, or extension of an ecclesiastical building which is for the time being used for ecclesiastical purposes or would be so used but for the works. Some limited control over unauthorized work to ecclesiastical buildings, however, has been recognized following the decision of the House of Lords in *Attorney-General v Howard United Reform Church Trustees, Bedford* [1976] AC 363. In that case their Lordships decided that the exemption applies to the alteration or extension of a listed building, which is used and will continue to be used for ecclesiastical purposes, but does not apply to the total demolition of a church, as it would then be impossible for the building to be used any longer for ecclesiastical purposes.

21.52 In 1984, following general concern over the 'ecclesiastical exemption', the Department of the Environment issued a consultation paper inviting comments on whether the exemption should be maintained. Following consideration of the responses to the paper, it was decided in general to retain the exemption. The Housing and Planning Act 1986, however, introduced a new provision to give the Secretary of State power to make orders for restricting or excluding the operation of s 60(1) to (3) in relation to ecclesiastical buildings in particular cases. These provisions are now contained in s 60(5) and (6) of the LBCA Act 1990.

21.53 Further consultation papers on the scope of the ecclesiastical exemption then followed in March 1989 and February 1992. Finally, in July 1994, the Government announced that as from 1 October 1994 it would use its powers to bring religious bodies within the normal secular controls over both internal and external works to their listed buildings, except for those bodies who have an approved control system of their own which conforms with a Government Code of Practice. Those bodies which have approved control systems, such as the Church of England, the Church in Wales, the Roman Catholic Church, the Methodist Church and the Baptist Union of Great Britain, the Baptist Union of Wales, and the United Reformed Church continue, therefore, to benefit from exemption from listed building control. After 1 October 1994, however, all other religious bodies were made subject to normal listed building and conservation controls.

21.54 The relevant subordinate legislation giving effect to the above, the Ecclesiastical Exemption (Listed Buildings and Conservation Areas) Order 1994, SI 1994/1771, did, however, somewhat reduce the scope of the exemption. Under the Order, the exemption applies only to buildings whose primary use is as a place of worship, and to objects or structures attached to their exterior or within their curtilage to the extent that they are not listed in their own right. It is also provided that special arrangements apply to cathedrals of the Church of England. In that case the exemption covers not only the cathedral itself and buildings, but objects or structures which are located within an area designated by the Secretary of State after consultation with the Cathedrals Fabric Commission for England and which fall within a Precinct indicated by the Commission under the Care of Cathedrals Measure 1990. The special arrangements also cover places of worship elsewhere within the precinct and tombstones elsewhere within the precinct which are not listed in their own right.

21.55 Following a further review the present law is to be found in the Ecclesiastical Exemption (Listed Buildings and Conservation Areas) Order 2010, effective from 1 October 2010, which prospectively revokes and replaces the 1994 Order from 1 October 2010. The 2010 Order amends the law:

- to ensure that, apart from in a small number of special cases, all buildings subject to the Ecclesiastical Exemption are covered by the control mechanisms of the relevant exempt denomination; and
- to reduce instances of 'dual control', where both denominational and local authority controls apply, by extending the Ecclesiastical Exemption to cover separately listed buildings and structures fixed to or in the curtilage of exempt church buildings, where they themselves constitute ecclesiastical buildings for the time being in use for ecclesiastical purposes.

F. LISTED BUILDING CONSENT

21.56 Listing is not intended to 'mothball' a building or to ensure it is retained 'in aspic'. The philosophy behind listed building control is that as far as possible a listed building should be retained in use, and that where changes to it are necessary to enable it to be used, those changes should, as far as possible, respect and retain the quality and characteristics of the building.

21.57 Under s 8 of the LBCA Act 1990, works for the alteration of a listed building are authorized if:

(a) written consent for their execution has been granted by the local planning authority or the Secretary of State; and
(b) they are executed in accordance with the terms of the consent and of any conditions attached to it.

The section also provides that:

Works for the demolition of a listed building are authorized if—
(a) such consent has been granted for their execution;
(b) notice of the proposal to execute the works has been given to the Royal Commission;

(c) after such notice has been given either—
  (i) for a period of at least one month following the grant of such consent, and before the commencement of the works, reasonable access to the building has been made available to members or officers of the Royal Commission for the purpose of recording it; or
  (ii) the Secretary of the Royal Commission, or another officer of theirs with authority to act on their behalf for the purposes of this section, has stated in writing that they have completed their recording of the building or that they do not wish to record it; and
(d) the works are executed in accordance with the terms of the consent and of any conditions attached to it.

21.58 It will be seen that works for the demolition, alteration, or extension of a listed building can only be authorized by a specific grant of listed building consent. This is so even though the works do not constitute development, as in the case of works for the maintenance, improvement, or other alteration of a building which affect only the interior of the building or which do not materially affect its external appearance. It will often happen, however, that before development or redevelopment can take place, both listed building consent and planning permission will be required. In such cases, both may be applied for at the same time. Sometimes, however, an applicant will wish to establish the planning position first, before applying later for listed building consent. Whichever method is adopted, the local planning authority is required, in considering whether to grant planning permission for development or listed building consent for any works, to have special regard to the desirability of preserving the building or its setting or any features of special architectural or historic interest which the building possesses (s 66(1) and s 16(2) of the LBCA Act 1990). This provision has been considered twice in recent years by the Court of Appeal. In *East Northamptonshire District Council v Secretary of State for Communities and Local Government* [2014] EWCA Civ 137; [2015] 1 WLR 45 the Court of Appeal held that a decision maker must give 'considerable importance and weight' to the desirability of preserving a listed building per Sullivan LJ at [29]. However, in *Jones v Mordue* [2015] EWCA Civ 1243; [2016] 1 WLR 2682 the Court of Appeal found that there was no need to recite that 'considerable importance and weight' had been applied to the statutory objective per Sales LJ at [27]–[28].

21.59 Where redevelopment of land requires the demolition of a listed building, the submission of an application for consent to demolition prior to the making of an application for planning permission for the redevelopment must be almost unknown, since the absence of any development proposals for a replacement building could be a material consideration in determining the application for listed building consent.

Procedure for obtaining listed building consent

21.60 The procedure for obtaining listed building consent is set out in s 10 of the LBCA Act 1990 and in the Planning (Listed Buildings and Conservation Areas)

Regulations 1990, SI 1990/1519. Application must be made to the local planning authority on a form obtainable from the authority, and must be accompanied by sufficient particulars to identify the building to which it relates, including a plan; such other plans and drawings necessary to describe the proposed works; and such other particulars as may be required by the authority. It is not possible for an owner to make an application for 'outline' listed building consent; he is required to give sufficient details to enable the impact of the works on the building to be assessed at this one stage. The degree of detail required to be submitted is primarily a matter for the local planning authority. If insufficient detail had been provided, the authority may either refuse the application for that reason or treat the application as invalid for failure to comply with the section. However, under s 17(2) of the LBCA Act 1990, the local planning authority may still decide to grant listed building consent on the information in its possession but subject to a condition reserving specified details of the proposed works for their subsequent approval.

21.61 Section 10(4) provides that an application for listed building consent (of such description as is specified) must be accompanied by a statement setting out the design principles and concepts that have been applied to the works, as well as a statement about how issues relating to access to the buildings have been dealt with.

21.62 Section 10(3) allows the Secretary of State to specify consultation requirements in respect of both listed building and conservation area consents. This power has now been strengthened by the Planning and Compulsory Purchase Act 2004 by allowing the Secretary of State to impose a duty on consultees to respond, within a fixed period, which mirrors the requirement now imposed on consultees to planning applications.

21.63 Under s 19 of the LBCA Act 1990 there is a procedure for varying or discharging conditions which have previously been attached to a listed building consent. The section, however, gives the right to apply for variation or discharge of the conditions to any 'person interested in a listed building'. It seems that the purpose of this restriction is to prevent 'third parties' seeking an alteration to the earlier consent, where they would have no responsibility for carrying out the work if the conditions were to be varied or discharged.

21.64 The application form must include certificates similar to those required by the Development Management Procedure Order (DMPO) in relation to applications for planning permission made by persons other than the owner of the land to which the application relates. In addition, the Regulations require local planning authorities to publish in a local newspaper circulating in the locality a notice regarding the application, display a site notice for 21 days on or near the land to which the application relates, and take into account any representations received as a result before determining the application.

21.65 Under s 15(5) of the LBCA Act 1990, the Secretary of State has power to direct local planning authorities to notify specified persons of any applications for listed building consent and the decision taken by the authority on them. Extensive use has been made of this power. The previous Directions issued under this power have now been consolidated into the 'Arrangements for Handling Heritage Applications Directions 2015' which came into force on 15 April 2015. The Directions require notification to Historic England for works to Grade I or II* listed buildings and relevant works to Grade II (unstarred) listed buildings. Works involving the demolition of a listed building or alterations require notification to: the Society for the Protection of Ancient Buildings, the Ancient Monuments Society, the Council for British Archaeology, the Georgian Group, the Victorian Society, and the Twentieth Century Society, as appropriate.

21.66 Within the Greater London area, local planning authorities are required to notify English Heritage of all applications for works to Grade I and Grade II* listed buildings; all applications for works to Grade II unstarred railway and underground stations; theatres, cinemas, bridges across the Thames; as well as many other works; and works to listed buildings owned by a local planning authority, where the application is not made by the authority.

21.67 The obligation of the local planning authority to comply with these directions does not affect the provisions in s 13 of the LBCA Act 1990 under which a local planning authority is required to notify the Secretary of State of any application for listed building consent which it proposes to grant. The purpose of the provision is to enable the Secretary of State to call in any applications for listed building consent for his own determination. The Secretary of State, however, is empowered under s 15 of the LBCA Act 1990 to direct that notification to him shall not apply to a specified application. He also has power to withdraw that exemption from notification in individual cases. Slightly different notification arrangements apply within Greater London.

21.68 The 2015 Directive contains a direction absolving local planning authorities from the obligation under s 13 to notify the Secretary of State of certain applications for listed building consent which they are proposing to grant. The absolution from the need to notify reflects the growing number of applications that are made as the number of listed buildings increases, and the fact that many of the applications relate to minor works to Grade II (unstarred) listed buildings.

21.69 The absolution extends, therefore, to applications for listed building consent to carry out works for the demolition, alteration, or extension of a Grade II (unstarred) listed building outside the Greater London area, unless the application proposes the carrying out of works for the demolition of a principal building or works for alteration of a principal building which comprise or include the demolition of a principal external wall of the principal building; or the demolition of all or a substantial part of the interior of the principal building.

Determination of applications

21.70 Unless the Secretary of State has exercised the right to call in the application for his own determination, the local planning authority is free to determine it after having considered any representations received. As with applications for planning permission, there is a right of appeal to the Secretary of State if the application is not determined within eight weeks (s 20(2) of the LBCA Act 1990). As previously stated, s 16(2) of the LBCA Act 1990 provides that, in considering whether to grant listed building consent, the local planning authority must have special regard to the desirability of preserving the building or its setting or any features of special architectural or historic interest which it possesses. Furthermore, in deciding whether or not to grant listed building consent, it appears now to be an undisputed proposition that the quality of any replacement buildings may be a material consideration to be taken into account (see the speech by Lord Bridge of Harwich in *Save Britain's Heritage v Number 1 Poultry Ltd* [1991] 1 WLR 153(CA)). Likewise, in *Richmond-upon-Thames LBC v Secretary of State for the Environment* (1978) 37 P & CR 151 and in *Kent CC v Secretary of State for the Environment* [1995] JPL 610, it was held that the nature or appearance of a replacement building is a material consideration in determining whether consent should be given for the demolition of a building (in the *Richmond* case of an unlisted building within a conservation area). It should also be noticed that s 38(6) of the Planning and Compulsory Purchase Act 2004 does not apply to decisions on applications for listed building consent, since there is no statutory requirement to have regard to the provisions of the development plan.

Conditions

21.71 Section 16(1) of the LBCA Act 1990 provides that listed building consent may be granted subject to conditions. Section 17(1) provides that without prejudice to this general power, listed building consent may be granted subject to conditions with respect to:

(a) the preservation of particular features of the building, either as part of it or after severance therefrom;
(b) the making good, after the works are completed, of any damage caused to the building by the works; and
(c) the reconstruction of the building or any part of it following the execution of any works, with the use of original materials so far as practicable and with such alterations of the interior of the building as may be specified in the conditions.

In addition, s 17(3) provides that listed building consent for the demolition of a listed building may be granted subject to a condition that the building shall not be demolished before:

(a) a contract for the carrying out of works of redevelopment of the site has been made; and

(b) planning permission has been granted for the redevelopment for which the contract provides.

The purpose of this condition is to ensure that a listed building is not demolished prematurely before redevelopment is ready to take place. It should also be noted that (as with planning permission) listed building consent enures for the benefit of the land. Section 16(3), however, allows the authority to impose a condition limiting the consent to a specified person or persons.

21.72 There is no power to grant a temporary listed building consent, but as with the grant of planning permission, listed building consents must include time limits. Section 18(1) of the LBCA Act 1990 provides that every listed building consent shall be granted subject to a condition that the work to which it relates must be begun not later than the expiration of (a) three years beginning with the date on which the consent is granted; or (b) such other period (whether shorter or longer), being a period which the authority considers appropriate having regard to any material considerations. By subsection (2), if the authority fails to grant consent subject to such a condition, the consent is deemed to be granted subject to the three-year time period. Under changes made in 2003 to the Listed Buildings Regulations, where a local planning authority grants listed building or conservation area consent where conditions have been attached, it must provide a reason for granting the consent.

Listed building consent for work already executed

21.73 As in the case of general planning control under Part III of the 1990 Act which allows, by virtue of s 73A, a retrospective application to be made for planning permission to retain buildings or works or continue the use of land, s 8(3) of the LBCA Act 1990 enables a retrospective application to be made for listed building consent after work to a listed building has taken place. Such applications must be made in the same way as any other application for listed building consent. It should be noted, however, that the work is only authorized from the actual date the consent is given, so that a prosecution for executing or causing to be executed works for the demolition of a listed building or for its alteration or extension in a way which would affect its character can still be taken.

Appeals

21.74 Where a local planning authority refuses to grant listed building consent or grant consent subject to conditions, the applicant may appeal to the Secretary of State within a period of six months.

21.75 The appeal procedures correspond closely with those for ordinary planning appeals under s 78 of the 1990 Act.

21.76 It should be noted that the appeal procedure provides an owner with one of the few opportunities he has to object formally to the listing. Under s 21(3) of the LBCA Act 1990, among the grounds on which an appeal may be brought is the ground that the building concerned is not of special architectural or historic interest and ought to be removed from any list compiled or approved by the Secretary of State. In determining the appeal, the Secretary of State may, if he thinks fit, remove the building from the list.

G. LISTED BUILDING ENFORCEMENT NOTICES

21.77 As well as taking criminal proceedings for unauthorized works to a listed building, a local planning authority may, under s 38 of the LBCA Act 1990, issue a 'listed building enforcement notice'. Because of the existence of the criminal offence, there is no necessity for the related stop notice procedure as exists with general planning control. It should be noted that whereas criminal liability under the Act is imposed on any person who executes or causes to be executed work to a listed building which is unauthorized, enforcement action can be taken under s 38 irrespective of whoever carried out the works. This could include therefore a previous owner. Since there is no limitation period for the serving of a listed building enforcement notice, the sins of a previous owner may well be visited upon the present owner (see *Brown v First Secretary of State* [2003] EWCA Civ 665; [2003] JPL 1536).

21.78 As well as specifying the alleged contravention, a listed building enforcement notice must require such steps as may be specified in the notice to be taken within such period as may be specified in the notice:

(a) for restoring the building to its former state; or
(b) if the authority considers that such restoration would not be reasonably practicable or would be undesirable, for executing such further works specified in the notice as it considers necessary to alleviate the effect of the works which were carried out without listed building consent; or
(c) for bringing the building to the state in which it would have been if the terms and conditions of any listed building consent which has been granted for the works had been complied with.

21.79 It seems that a listed building enforcement notice can be served in respect of a listed building which has been demolished, so long as a substantial part of it is available for rebuilding. In *R v Leominster DC, ex p Antique Country Buildings Ltd* [1988] JPL 554 a 'cruck barn', a Grade II listed building with a timber frame which had been erected before 1620, was dismantled without listed building consent having been obtained. Some 70 to 80 per cent of the barn's timbers had been sold by the owner in a condition which rendered them suitable for re-erection elsewhere. The intention of the purchasers had been to export the timbers to the United States, where they would be reassembled. On the question of whether a local planning authority had power to serve a listed building enforcement notice requiring the cruck barn to be re-erected on its original site notwithstanding that the building had been demolished, the High Court held that where the components of a building were substantially extant, its restoration was possible and could lawfully be required by the local planning authority.

21.80 Such action would not be an option, however, if a listed building were demolished and, like Humpty Dumpty, it was not possible to put its parts together again. If a listed building were accidentally demolished, as has occurred when a motor vehicle demolished a listed telephone kiosk ([1990] JPL 444), enforcement action would not be available to the local planning authority. In this particular case, the accident had totally destroyed the kiosk, which was lost forever.

21.81 The *Leominster* case also established that a listed building enforcement notice could be served on the owners of the disassembled parts of the listed building, though the ownership of 70 to 80 per cent of the component parts was thought to be a necessary threshold for this to be possible. The case also recognizes that although a building may be separated from the land on which it stood so that it is no longer attached to it, it retains its status for the purposes of the Act. The court in *R (Judge) v First Secretary of State* [2005] EWCA Civ 1155 again recognized that listed building consent can be granted for the removal of a listed 'statue' and its re-erection at a particular spot elsewhere.

21.82 As with the enforcement procedure for general planning control, there is a right of appeal against the notice to the Secretary of State. The appeal procedures are similar. Two important differences, however, should be mentioned. First, there is no four-year limitation period for the issuing of a listed building enforcement notice similar to that which exists for operational development in general planning control. Secondly, the grounds of appeal to the Secretary of State can include the ground 'that the building is not of special architectural or historic interest'.

21.83 Section 25 of the Planning and Compensation Act 1991 made various amendments to the LBCA Act 1990. As far as possible, the amendments mirror amendments made by the 1991 Act in the field of the enforcement of general planning control. The main amendments were as follows:

(a) The power of a local planning authority to withdraw a listed building enforcement notice before it has taken effect was extended to include a power to withdraw a notice after it has taken effect.
(b) In order to prevent appeals against listed building enforcement notices being invalidated owing to postal delays, it was provided that an appeal may be validly made if sent to the Secretary of State in a properly addressed and prepaid letter posted to him at such time that, in the ordinary course of post, it would be

delivered to him before the date specified in the notice as the date on which it is to take effect.

(c) Section 39(3) of the LBCA Act 1990 provides that 'where ... an appeal is brought the listed building enforcement notice shall ... be of no effect pending the final determination or withdrawal of the appeal'. In *R v Kuxhaus* [1988] QB 631 (a decision on the related s 175(4) of the 1990 Act) the Court of Appeal held that the words 'final determination' meant that the enforcement notice was suspended not only up to the time the decision of the Secretary of State had been given on appeal, but until any appeal from his decision to the courts had been decided. This meant that an owner could delay having to comply with the enforcement notice by appealing to the Secretary of State and then to the courts before withdrawing his appeal to the courts at the last moment. In that way, the owner was able to use the procedure to continue to use his land in contravention of planning control for a longer period than would otherwise have been the case.

21.84 In order to prevent unnecessary appeals from decisions of the Secretary of State to the High Court, many of which are withdrawn before trial, the 1991 Act made two changes to s 65 of the LBCA Act 1990. First, a new subsection (3A) provides that:

> in proceedings brought by virtue of this section, the High Court or, as the case may be, the Court of Appeal may ... order that the listed building enforcement notice shall have such effect, or have effect to such extent as may be specified in the order, pending the final determination of those proceedings and any rehearing and determination by the Secretary of State.

21.85 The effect of this provision means that a listed building enforcement notice may not necessarily be suspended by the taking of legal proceedings. Under s 65(3A), the court is given the power to decide the effect of the enforcement notice during the period before it comes to a final judgment on the appeal.

21.86 Schedule 3 to the 1991 Act made a further change to s 65 of the LBCA Act 1990, by substituting within it a new subsection (5). The new subsection provides that:

> No proceedings in the High Court shall be brought by virtue of this section except with the leave of the court and no appeal to the Court of Appeal shall be so brought except with the leave of the Court of Appeal or of the High Court.

This provision in relation to listed building enforcement notices replicates a similar provision introduced by the 1991 Act in relation to the enforcement of general planning control.

21.87 On an appeal against a listed building enforcement notice, the Secretary of State has power to correct any 'misdescription' in the notice, so long as he is satisfied that the correction or variation will not cause injustice to the appellant or the local planning authority. Before 1991, his power to correct a notice on appeal was limited to the correction of any 'informality, defect or error in the notice'.

21.88 Where the steps required to be taken by a listed building enforcement notice have not been taken, it is provided that the person who is the current owner of the land is the person in breach of the notice. This, of course, may not be the same person as the owner on whom the notice was served.

21.89 Where an owner of land has not taken the steps required to be taken by the listed building enforcement notice within the prescribed time, he is guilty of an offence. If at any time after conviction he still does not take those steps, he may be guilty of a second or subsequent offence.

21.90 As previously mentioned, the maximum penalty for failure to comply with a listed building enforcement notice was increased on summary conviction from £2,000 to £20,000. In addition, however, in determining the amount of any fine, the court is required to have regard to any financial benefit which has accrued or appears likely to accrue to the wrongdoer in consequence of his offence.

21.91 A local planning authority has express power to apply to the court for an injunction where it considers it necessary or expedient to restrain any actual or apprehended breach of listed building control. The power is available whether or not the authority has exercised or is proposing to exercise any of its other powers under the LBCA Act 1990. Furthermore, where the rules of court so provide, an injunction may be issued against persons whose identity is unknown.

21.92 Under s 88 of the LBCA Act 1990, the various authorities are given power to enter land at any reasonable time for certain specified purposes connected with listed building control. These purposes include ascertaining whether a breach of listed building control has taken place and whether a listed building is being maintained in a proper state of repair. The 1991 Act provided an opportunity to bring together in one section of the LBCA Act 1990 all the statutory provisions authorizing 'rights of entry' to land in relation to listed building control. However, the 1991 Act, by adding a new s 88A to the LBCA Act 1990, also strengthened the power of the authorities to obtain information needed for a proper discharge of their listed building control functions. The section now allows a local planning authority, the Secretary of State or, in Greater London, the Historic Buildings and Monuments Commission for England, to enter on land for any of the purposes set out in s 88 of the 1990 Act under the warrant of a magistrate without prior notice. The applicant for a warrant must show to the satisfaction of the magistrate that there are reasonable grounds for entering the land for any of the purposes set out in s 88, and that admission to the land has been refused (or refusal is reasonably apprehended), or the case is one of urgency.

H. LISTED BUILDING PURCHASE NOTICES

21.93 If listed building consent has been refused or granted subject to conditions, an owner of land may serve on the council of the district or London borough in which the land is situated a notice, called a listed building purchase notice, requiring the council to purchase his interest in the land. In order to do so, however, he must be able to show that the land has become 'incapable of reasonably beneficial use'. The statutory provisions, which are contained in ss 32 to 37 of the LBCA Act 1990 are similar to the provisions in Part VI of the 1990 Act which enable the owner of an interest in land to serve a purchase notice where an application for planning permission to develop land is refused or granted subject to conditions.

I. CERTIFICATES OF IMMUNITY

21.94 At one time, one of the difficulties that occurred with listed building control was that a landowner might apply for and obtain planning permission for the redevelopment of land on which there stood a building of some architectural or historic interest, but one not protected by inclusion in the lists. The planning permission obtained was often an outline permission, which left the landowner with the obligation to obtain approval of reserved matters before the redevelopment could actually be commenced. Then, before approval of reserved matters had been obtained, the building would be added to a list compiled or approved by the Secretary of State. Since this would generally mean the redevelopment could not then take place, or at best could not take place in the way originally envisaged, the landowner might have spent a considerable sum of money in preparing the plans, etc needed for detailed approval which would then be wasted.

21.95 To meet this difficulty, s 6 of the LBCA Act 1990 provides that where an application has been made for planning permission for any development involving the alteration, extension, or demolition of a building, or planning permission has been granted for such development, any person may apply to the Secretary of State for a certificate stating that he does not intend to list the building.

21.96 Once a certificate is issued, the building cannot be listed for a period of five years or be the subject of a building preservation notice made by the local planning authority during that period (para 21.108). If a certificate should not be granted, the building will almost certainly be added to the list. Although the law does not require that step to be taken, a failure to add it to the list at the same time as the decision is taken not to issue a certificate might well lead to the building's immediate demolition.

21.97 A good example of the certificate procedure occurred in 1992, when the Secretary of State issued a certificate in relation to buildings in the South Bank Centre, including the Hayward Gallery, the Queen Elizabeth Hall, the Purcell Room, and associated walkways.

J. LISTED BUILDINGS IN NEED OF REPAIR

21.98 There is no general obligation placed on the owner of a listed building to keep it in repair. However, under s 54 of the LBCA Act 1990, local authorities have power to execute any works which appear to them to be urgently necessary for the preservation of listed buildings in their area. Before doing so, they must give the owner of the building not less than seven days' notice in writing of their intention to do so. Such a notice can also be served in respect of the unused part of a partly occupied listed building, and the works executed may consist of or include works for providing temporary support (such as scaffolding or props) for the building.

21.99 Under s 55 of the LBCA Act 1990, a local authority may recover the expenses incurred by it in carrying out such work. In such cases, the authority is required to give notice to the owner, who can make representations to the Secretary of State that 'some or all of the works were unnecessary for the preservation of the building'. The Secretary of State may then determine to what extent the representations are justified and, in consequence, the amount the authority can require the owner to pay. Representations may also be made on the ground that the amount sought to be recovered is unreasonable or would cause hardship, or that in the case of works for affording temporary support or shelter, the temporary arrangements have continued for an unreasonable length of time. In *R v Secretary of State for Wales, ex p City and County of Swansea* [1999] JPL 524, it was held that, subject to those statutory defences, a defaulting owner is liable to pay the cost of work that was necessary to preserve the building, provided that the local planning authority reasonably thought that the work was urgently necessary.

21.100 These provisions do not apply to ecclesiastical buildings or to scheduled monuments. The arrangements are subject to some modification in the case of listed buildings in Greater London, where the Historic Buildings and Monuments Commission for England has a similar power.

Compulsory purchase of listed buildings in need of repair

21.101 Under s 47 of the LBCA Act 1990, the Secretary of State may authorize a local authority (or English Heritage in Greater London) to acquire compulsorily any listed building (other than an ecclesiastical building or ancient monument) where it appears to him that reasonable steps are not being taken for the building's proper preservation.

21.102 A condition precedent to the exercise of this power is the service on the owner of the building of a 'repairs notice' under s 48, specifying the works which the authority considers reasonably necessary for the proper preservation of the building and explaining that if the works required by the notice are not carried out compulsory purchase proceedings may be taken.

21.103 In *Robbins v Secretary of State for the Environment* [1989] 1 WLR 201, the House of Lords rejected the argument that a repairs notice could only require the carrying out of works that were necessary for the proper preservation of a building as it subsisted at the date on which the notice was served. It was there held that the notice could require the owner to restore the building to the condition it was in at the date the building was listed, though not before it was listed.

21.104 Should the notice contain any items which are invalid because they require works to be done which are not for preservation, the notice remains valid and the invalid items may simply be disregarded. There is no right of appeal against the repairs notice. If the owner complies with it the authority need do no more. If, however, after two months from the date of service of the notice, reasonable steps have not been taken for properly preserving the building, the authority may commence compulsory purchase proceedings. If the authority proceeds to do so, two special points should be noted. First, the compulsory purchase has to be authorized by the Secretary of State, who may not do so unless satisfied that it is expedient to make provision for the preservation of the building and to authorize its compulsory acquisition for that purpose. Hence, in objecting to the compulsory purchase order, the owner may claim that the building is not of special architectural or historic interest and should not be preserved, or that the work specified in the repairs notice is unnecessary for the preservation of the building. Secondly, any person having an interest in the land may apply within 28 days of service of notice of the order to a magistrates' court for an order staying further proceedings on the compulsory purchase order; and if the court is satisfied that reasonable steps have been taken for properly preserving the building, the court must order a stay.

21.105 The Secretary of State may also use the powers available under s 48 to local planning authorities. In 1992, the Secretary of State served a repairs notice on the owners of the former St Ann's Hotel in The Crescent, Buxton, a Grade I listed Georgian building. Following dissatisfaction with the lack of any significant progress being made to repair the building, and in order to halt any further deterioration through neglect and indecision, the Secretary of State later used his powers under s 48 of the LBCA Act 1990 to serve a compulsory purchase order on the owner. The building was subsequently purchased, however, by the local planning authority. With the help of funding from the National Lottery, the County Council, and the District Council, the external part of the buildings in the Crescent have now been fully restored. Another example of the power being used by the Secretary of State was the commencement of compulsory purchase proceedings for Apethorpe Hall, a Grade I listed country manor house in the village of Apethorpe, Northamptonshire. The proceedings followed the service of a repairs notice on the owner which was not complied with.

21.106 Some light has been shed on the use of listed building repair notices by a published report of growing antiquity ([1992] JPL 609). The report, based on a survey of local planning authorities in England, shows that over a six-year period between 1984 and 1990, local planning authorities authorized the issue of 287 listed building repair notices. That step alone led the owners of 125 buildings affected either to commence repairs to the building or to sell it on for others ready to do so. Of the 162 repair notices that were actually served by local planning authorities, repairs were started by the original owner in 87 cases, though in 14 of the cases the repair work did not begin until the compulsory purchase order inquiry stage had been reached.

Compensation

Where a listed building is compulsorily acquired as part of the normal process of land acquisition for public purposes, compensation is assessed on the normal market value basis. By s 49 of the LBCA Act 1990, for the purposes of assessing compensation for the compulsory acquisition of a listed building, it is to be assumed that listed building consent would be granted for any works for the alteration or extension of the building. No assumption may be made, however, that listed building consent would have been granted for works for the demolition of the building, apart from any works for the purposes of the limited development of any class specified in Sch 3 to the 1990 Act. It will, of course, still be possible for an owner to claim that, but for the acquisition, listed building consent would have been granted for the demolition of the building and planning permission granted for redevelopment of the land. **21.107**

Where a listed building in need of repair is acquired in order to preserve it, and it can be shown that the building was deliberately allowed to fall into disrepair for the purposes of justifying its demolition and the development or redevelopment of the site or adjoining site, the local authority may acquire the building at a substantially lower price. In order for this to happen, s 50 of the LBCA Act 1990 requires the compulsory purchase order to contain an application for a 'direction for minimum compensation', and the Secretary of State must include such a direction in the order when confirmed by him. Where a direction for minimum compensation is made, compensation for the acquisition is to be assessed on the basis that it is to be assumed that, but for the acquisition, listed building consent would *not* be granted for any works for the demolition, alteration, or extension of the building other than works necessary for restoring it to and maintaining it in a proper state of repair; and that planning permission would *not* be granted for any development or redevelopment of the site. **21.108**

The owner of an interest in the land subject to a direction for minimum compensation may appeal to the Secretary of State against the direction at the time he appeals against the compulsory purchase order. Alternatively, he may apply to the magistrates' court for an order that the direction be not included in the order on the ground that the building has not been deliberately allowed to fall **21.109** into disrepair for the purposes of justifying demolition and the development or redevelopment of the site.

21.110 In the report referred to in the previous section, it is disclosed that there has been a final decision about minimum compensation by the Secretary of State in only six cases. He confirmed the order for minimum compensation in three cases. In three cases the Secretary of State rejected the order for minimum compensation but this did not affect the case for acquisition; and in these cases, the order was in any event confirmed by the Secretary of State.

21.111 Two further minimum compensation cases were taken to the magistrates' court. In one, the magistrates rejected the claim for minimum compensation although the owner had previously been refused listed building consent to demolish. The compulsory purchase order was one of those already cited which were subsequently confirmed by the Secretary of State. In another case, the authority was successful in convincing the magistrates that a direction for minimum compensation should be included in the compulsory purchase order but the Secretary of State ultimately rejected the compulsory purchase order entirely. In five cases the issue was never resolved because the owner's action obviated the need to pursue compulsory purchase; the other cases remained ongoing.

21.112 More recently, in December 1994, the Secretary of State confirmed a compulsory purchase order for the acquisition of a Grade II listed building in Alton, Hampshire ([1995] JPL 641). The order, which contained a direction for minimum compensation, followed service by the local planning authority of two 'urgent works notices' under s 54 of the 1990 Act, then a repair notice under s 48 of the Act. The owner had earlier applied to the magistrates' court to have the direction for minimum compensation removed but this had been refused. The Secretary of State took the view that he could only differ from the finding of the court if the owner had been able to produce evidence not then available.

K. BUILDING PRESERVATION NOTICES

21.113 If it appears to a local planning authority that a building in its area, which is not a listed building, is of special architectural or historic interest and it is in danger of demolition or of alteration in such a way as to affect its character as a building of such interest, it may, under s 3 of the LBCA Act 1990, serve on the owner and occupier a 'building preservation notice', stating that the building appears to it to be of special architectural or historic interest and that it has requested the Secretary of State to consider adding it to a statutory list. The notice must also explain its effect. A building preservation notice cannot be served if a certificate of immunity is in operation.

21.114 The effect of the notice is to apply to the building most of the provisions of the Act relating to listed buildings, so that it becomes a criminal offence to execute or cause to be executed works for the demolition of the building or for its alteration or extension in a manner which would affect its character as a listed building without listed building consent.

21.115 A building preservation notice remains in effect for six months from the date of its service (though it may be renewed), unless it has previously lapsed through the inclusion of the building in a statutory list, or the earlier notification by the Secretary of State to the authority that he does not intend to so include it. If the Secretary of State gives notice that he does not intend to include the building in a list compiled or approved by him, no further building preservation notice may be served within the following 12 months.

21.116 Once the notice has lapsed, all proceedings arising from the application of listed building control will also lapse, save for any criminal liability under ss 9 (execution of works to a listed building without consent) or 43 (penalties for non-compliance with a listed building enforcement notice).

21.117 A fetter on the exercise by the local planning authority of its power to issue a building preservation notice is that under s 29 of the LBCA Act 1990 compensation must be paid for any loss or damage which is directly attributable to the effect of the notice if the building is not subsequently listed by the Secretary of State. The compensation may include any sum for which the applicant has become liable in respect of any breach of contract caused by the requirement of the notice.

21.118 Building preservation notices should be distinguished from what is known as 'spot listing'. This occurs when an approach is made to the Secretary of State by a local authority (or other body or person), without any service of a building preservation notice, to have a building added to the statutory lists. It is claimed that the listing process, which may take months or years when done as part of a general or thematic survey of buildings of architectural or historic interest, can be completed within 24 hours by the spot listing method. Statistics show that of 3,574 buildings added to the statutory lists in 1990, 1,330 (37.2 per cent) were added as a result of spot listing, whereas only 49 (1.3 per cent) were added following service of a building preservation notice. In evidence given by English Heritage to the Committee of Public Accounts of the House of Commons in November 1992, it was disclosed that over 2,500 requests for spot listing were made each year, and that in 50 per cent of cases recommendations for listing were made. In the year 2006/07 353 buildings were added to the statutory lists as a result of spot listing.

Buildings threatened by development proposals

21.119 Public concern for the preservation of buildings has led to increasing problems when proposals are made for the development of land which includes a building which is not protected by listing. An application for planning permission may generate considerable public pressure for the preservation of existing buildings on the land, which, if achieved, would prevent the development proposed going ahead. Faced with an application for planning permission which generates such pressure, the local planning authority may decide to serve a building preservation notice. As stated, however, if the building is not subsequently listed, the local planning authority will be liable to pay compensation for any loss or damage suffered. If, on the other hand, the building is then listed, the application for planning permission may merely have served the purpose of alerting people's attention to the need to preserve the buildings on the site, with unfortunate results for the applicant.

21.120 It must be recognized that the act of listing may well diminish the landowner's prospects of developing or redeveloping the site and the possible loss of its value for that purpose. In *Amalgamated Investment & Property Co Ltd v John Walker & Sons Ltd* [1976] JPL 308, the parties had entered an agreement for the sale and purchase of a disused warehouse. The purchase price of £1,700,000 reflected the potential of the site for redevelopment. On the day after contracts were exchanged, the Secretary of State added the building to the statutory list. As a result, the market value of the property (with no redevelopment potential) was no more than £200,000. The purchasers thereupon sought rescission of the contract on the ground of common mistake, claiming that the parties believed at the time of the contract that the property was capable of development, or alternatively, that the listing had frustrated the purposes of the contract so that it was void and of no effect and ought not to be enforced. Refusing the application, the Court of Appeal held that loss must lie where it fell; that the only mistake made was one relating to the expectations of the parties and that a risk of listing was inherent in the ownership of all buildings. Although this case was concerned with which of the two parties should bear the loss, it illustrates the loss that any owner may suffer as the result of a building being listed.

21.121 In these circumstances, it is not surprising that an owner wishing to redevelop land on which stands a non-listed building, may decide first to demolish the building, and then to apply for planning permission for redevelopment. In this connection, although the definition of development now includes the demolition of buildings, the demolition of any building other than a dwellinghouse is excluded from the definition of development by virtue of s 55(2)(g) of the 1990 Act; and in relation to dwellinghouses, demolition of most is permitted development under the General Permitted Development Order. It should however be noted, that demolition of a building in a conservation area requires 'conservation area consent'.

21.122 The effect of listing on the value of an owner's interest in land helps to explain why penalties for contravention of listed building control may reflect the benefit obtained by the wrongdoer and why the law contains provisions relating to the payment of minimum compensation where listed buildings in need of repair are compulsorily acquired in order to secure their preservation.

Historic parks and gardens

21.123 Since 1984 nearly 1,600 parks and gardens of 'special historic interest' in England have been identified by English Heritage through its Register of Parks and Gardens. The main purpose of the Register is to identify and draw attention to the best historic parks and gardens which constitute an important part of the cultural heritage of England.

21.124 Like listed buildings, sites on the Register are listed in three grades, namely those of exceptional historic interest (Grade I); those of great historic interest (Grade II*); and those of special historic interest (Grade II).

21.125 Unfortunately, however, unlike listed buildings, sites on the Register have no special statutory protection, so that there are no additional powers available to control development and work done to them beyond normal planning powers.

21.126 However, Art 18 and para (s) to Sch 4 of the DMPO requires local planning authorities to consult Historic England before granting planning permission for development affecting Grade I or II* historic parks and gardens on their Register.

Historic battlefields

21.127 Since 1991 English Heritage (or Historic England as it is now known) has started to compile a Register of Historic Battlefields, selection being based on the political significance of the engagement, its military historical significance, or its biographical significance. As with historic parks and gardens, no special statutory protection is given to the 43 registered historic battlefields sites currently on the Register although, as with historic parks and gardens, the fact that they are on the Register should be a material consideration in determining applications for planning permission which affect them.

World Heritage Sites

21.128 There is no special control exercised over World Heritage Sites as such. Inclusion in the World Heritage List is essentially honorific and leaves the existing rights and obligations of owners, occupiers, and planning authorities unaffected. A prerequisite for World Heritage Site status is, however, the existence of effective legal protection and the establishment or firm prospect of management plans to ensure a site's conservation and preservation. In the United Kingdom, legal protection is achieved through listing and scheduling and their associated controls, by the establishment of conservation areas, by the designation of World Heritage Sites as Art 2(3) land in the GPDO and by the outstanding international importance

21.129 There are 31 World Heritage Sites in the United Kingdom. Twenty-six are cultural heritage sites, four natural heritage sites and there is one mixed site, namely, St Kilda. The sites are: Blaenavon Industrial Landscape (2000); Blenheim Palace (1987); Canterbury Cathedral, St Augustine's Abbey, and St Martin's Church (1988); Castles and Town Walls of King Edward in Gwynedd (1986); City of Bath (1987); Cornwall and West Devon Mining Landscape (2006); Derwent Valley Mills (2001); Durham Castle and Cathedral (1986); Frontiers of the Roman Empire (1987, 2005, 2008); Gorham's Cave Complex (2016); Heart of Neolithic Orkney (1999); Historic Town of St George and Related Fortifications, Bermuda (2000); Ironbridge Gorge (1986); Liverpool—Maritime Mercantile City (2004); Maritime Greenwich (1997); New Lanark (2001); Old and New Towns of Edinburgh (1995); Palace of Westminster and Westminster Abbey including Saint Margaret's Church (1987); Pontcysyllte Aqueduct and Canal (2009); Royal Botanic Gardens, Kew (2003); Saltaire (2001); Stonehenge, Avebury and Associated Sites (1986); Studley Royal Park including the Ruins of Fountains Abbey (1986); The English Lake District (2017); The Forth Bridge (2015); Tower of London (1988); Dorset and East Devon Coast (2001); Giant's Causeway and Causeway Coast (1986); Gough and Inaccessible Islands (1995, 2004); Henderson Island (1988) and St Kilda (1986, 2004, 2005).

L. CONSERVATION AREAS

21.130 Under s 69 of the LBCA Act 1990, every local planning authority must from time to time determine which parts of its area are areas of special architectural or historic interest, the character or appearance of which it is desirable to preserve or enhance, and shall designate those areas as conservation areas. It would appear that in deciding to designate such an area, a local planning authority can consider as one entity the whole of an area which gives rise to special architectural or historic interest and that not every part of that area need have in it something of special architectural or historic interest. In *R v Canterbury City Council, ex p Halford* [1992] 2 PLR 137, the High Court held it could only interfere with a decision to designate if there had been an infringement of the *Wednesbury* principles. Designation cannot be used simply as a pretext to prevent the demolition of a specific building (*R (on the application of Arndale Properties Ltd) v Worcester City Council* [2008] JPL 1583). However, the decision of Ouseley J in *Trillium (Prime) Property GP Ltd v Tower Hamlets LBC* [2011] EWHC 146 (Admin) shows that, where the existence of an unlisted building is an important factor in determining that an area has a special character that is worth preserving or enhancing, a threat to that building can be a proper reason for making a conservation area designation.

21.131 Designation of a conservation area by a local planning authority gives the authority considerable additional powers over the development and use of land in the area. In *R v Surrey CC, ex p Oakimber Ltd* [1995] EGCS 120 it was held that the authority had a broad discretion to determine which parts of its area were of special architectural or historic interest with a character or appearance which should be preserved or enhanced. In rejecting a challenge to the designation of land at Brooklands, Surrey, the High Court held that there was no obligation on the local planning authority to look at each piece of land in a proposed conservation area in isolation. The authority was entitled to consider, as an entity, the whole of an area which gave rise to special architectural or historic interest.

21.132 Land in a conservation area may not be included in a simplified planning zone (s 87(1) of the 1990 Act).

21.133 It will be seen that whilst listing procedures focus upon the protection of individual buildings, designation of conservation areas focuses upon conservation policies for particular areas. The designation of a conservation area has the following particular consequences:

(a) Under s 71 of the LBCA Act 1990, the local planning authority must from time to time formulate and publish proposals for the preservation and enhancement of such areas.
(b) Under s 72 of the LBCA Act 1990, in the exercise with respect to any buildings or other land in a conservation area of any powers under any of the provisions of the Planning Acts or Part I of the Historic Buildings and Ancient Monuments Act 1953, 'special attention should be paid to the desirability of preserving or enhancing the character or appearance of that area'.

21.134 This provision is derived from s 277(8) of the Town and Country Planning Act 1971. Its scope was first considered by the courts in *Steinberg v Secretary of State for the Environment* (1988) 58 P & CR 453, where the main issue for decision was whether the Inspector, in allowing an appeal against the decision of the local planning authority to refuse planning permission to erect a two-storey house in a conservation area, had correctly applied s 277(8) of the Town and Country Planning Act 1971. In his decision letter the Inspector had said that from his observations of the site and its surroundings and from representations received, he considered the main issue to be decided was whether the proposal would constitute overdevelopment of the site and whether the proposed development would harm the character of the conservation area. In quashing the decision, the High Court held that the Inspector had misdirected himself on a point of law. The duty imposed by s 277(8) was 'to pay special attention to the desirability of preserving or enhancing the character or appearance of the conservation area'. The court held that there was a world of difference between what the Inspector had defined for himself—whether the proposed development would 'harm' the character of the conservation area—and the need to pay special attention to the desirability of preserving or enhancing the character or appearance of the area. Harm was one thing, preservation or enhancement another. The concept of avoiding harm was essentially negative, the underlying purpose of s 277(8) essentially positive.

21.135 The *Steinberg* decision was later considered by the High Court in *Unex Dumpton Ltd v Secretary of State for the Environment* [1990] JPL 344. According to the court, the duty under s 277(8) did not relieve the Secretary of State or his Inspector of the need to consider whether harm would be caused by proposed development in a conservation area or if so, whether the benefits of the proposed development would outweigh that harm. Important though the provisions of s 277(8) were, they were only one of the material considerations that had to be taken into account and only required that 'special attention' be paid to the matters set out in s 277(8).

21.136 The *Steinberg* decision was also considered by the Court of Appeal in *Ward v Secretary of State for the Environment* [1990] JPL 347. There, the Court held, inter alia, that by failing properly to consider whether proposed development in a conservation area would preserve or enhance the area, the Inspector had fallen short of the statutory requirement imposed by s 277(8). Although the Court of Appeal appeared to endorse the *Steinberg* principle, its application continued to give rise to difficulties. It seems that the positive duty imposed by s 277(8) is a material consideration in determining planning applications. It is, however, merely one material consideration, though one given a certain pre-eminence by the section. It may be, for example, that the decision-maker, having paid special attention to the desirability of preserving or enhancing the character or appearance of the conservation area, may decide nevertheless that the application should be refused because of insuperable highway objections.

21.137 This approach was confirmed when the meaning of the provision was further considered by the House of Lords in *South Lakeland DC v Secretary of State for the Environment* [1992] 2 AC 141. There, their Lordships had to consider a decision by an Inspector to allow an appeal against a refusal of outline planning permission for the erection of a new vicarage on a site within a conservation area. The Inspector had allowed the appeal and granted planning permission for the development on the ground that, provided the proposed vicarage did not cause harm 'to the character of the conservation area', it would not damage the appearance of the village. The local planning authority then successfully applied to quash the Inspector's decision on the ground that he had failed to discharge the duty imposed on him by s 277(8) of the Town and Country Planning Act 1971 to pay special attention to the desirability of 'preserving or enhancing' the character or appearance of the conservation area.

21.138 The Secretary of State appealed to the Court of Appeal which reversed the decision of the High Court on the ground that the Inspector had indeed discharged his duty under s 277(8) by his finding that, since the character and appearance of the conservation area would not be harmed by the development, the area's character and appearance would remain preserved. The planning authority appealed to the House of Lords.

21.139 In his speech dismissing the appeal, Lord Bridge of Harwich approved the interpretation placed upon the provision by Mann LJ, in the Court of Appeal, in which he said:

> In seeking to resolve the issue I start with the obvious. First, that which is desirable is the preservation or enhancement of the character or appearance of the conservation area. Second, the statute does not in terms require that a development must perform a preserving or enhancing function. Such a requirement would have been a stringent one which many an inoffensive proposal would have been inherently incapable of satisfying. I turn to the words. Neither 'preserving' nor 'enhancing' is used in any meaning other than its ordinary English meaning. The court is not here concerned with enhancement, but the ordinary meaning of 'preserve' as a transitive verb is 'to keep safe from harm or injury; to keep in safety, save, take care of, guard': *Oxford English Dictionary*, 2nd ed. (1989), vol. 12, p. 404. In my judgment character or appearance can be said to be preserved where they are not harmed. Cases may be envisaged where development would itself make a positive contribution to preservation of character or appearance. A work of reinstatement might be such. The parsonages board never advocated the new vicarage on that basis. It was not a basis which the Inspector was invited to address but importantly he did not have to address it because the statute does not require him so to do. The statutorily desirable object of preserving the character or appearance of an area is achieved either by a positive contribution to preservation or by development which leaves character or appearance unharmed, that is to say, preserved.

21.140 After agreeing with the construction placed upon the provision by Mann LJ, Lord Bridge concluded:

> We may, I think, take judicial notice of the extensive areas, both urban and rural, which have been designated as conservation areas. It is entirely right that in any such area a much stricter control over development than elsewhere should be exercised with the object of preserving or, where possible, enhancing the qualities in the character or appearance of the area which underlie its designation as a conservation area under s 277. But where a particular development will not have any adverse effect on the character or appearance of the area and is otherwise unobjectionable on planning grounds, one may ask rhetorically what possible planning reason there can be for refusing to allow it. All building development must involve change and if the objective of s 277(8) were to inhibit any building development in a conservation area which was not either a development by way of reinstatement or restoration on the one hand ('positive preservation') or a development which positively enhanced the character or appearance of the area on the other hand, it would surely have been expressed in very different language from that which the draftsman has used.

21.141 It is now settled law that preserving the character or appearance of a conservation area can be achieved not only by a positive contribution to preservation, but also by development which leaves the character or appearance of the area unharmed.

21.142 Lastly, the wording of s 72 also suggests that where an application is being made for the demolition of an unlisted building in a conservation area (see (h) below), the local planning authority must consider details of the replacement development (if any) or the treatment of the land, before it can discharge its duty under the section. In fact, it is not uncommon for an authority in granting conservation area consent for demolition, to tie the demolition to redevelopment of the site. This is in order to prevent the site lying vacant and detracting from the character and appearance of the area. The wording of the condition will be such as to ensure that demolition does not take place until a contract for the carrying out of works of redevelopment has been entered into and planning permission received for the redevelopment for which the contract provides.

21.143 Under s 73 of the LBCA Act 1990, the local planning authority must give publicity to any applications for planning permission where the development would, in the opinion of the authority, affect the character or appearance of a conservation area. Under reg 5 of the Planning (Listed Buildings and Conservation Regulations) 1990, the local planning authority must publish in a local newspaper circulating in the locality in which the land is situated and display on or near the land for not less than seven days, a notice indicating the nature of the development proposed and stating where a copy of the application, and all plans and other documents submitted with it may be open to inspection, for a period of 21 days. The local planning authority must send a copy of the notice to the Commission. The Secretary of State has power, after consultation with the Commission, to make a direction modifying the requirement. The effect of a direction (contained in Circular 01/01 as regards advice on the handling of heritage sites) is to restrict, inter alia, the requirement of notification to the Commission to development of a site of more than 1,000 square metres or the construction of any building more than 20 metres in height above ground level.

21.144 Under the provisions of Art 4 of the General Permitted Development Order, directions are often made in relation to specified classes of development in conservation areas, thus restricting permitted development rights under the order in those areas.

21.145 Land in a conservation area is within the definition of Art 2(3) land in the General Permitted Development Order. The significance of this is that the permitted development in such areas is not as wide as development which is permitted by the Order in respect of non-Art 2(3) land.

21.146 Under the provisions of s 211 of the 1990 Act, a person proposing to cut down, top, or lop a tree in a conservation area (other than a tree already protected by a tree preservation order) is required to give six weeks' prior notification to the local planning authority of his intention to do so. The purpose of this provision is to enable the authority to make a tree preservation order if it considers it necessary to do so. Under Part III of the Town and Country Planning (Trees) Regulations 1999, however, s 211 is not to apply to trees which are dying, dead, or dangerous; to work necessary to prevent or abate a nuisance; work in accordance with a felling licence or a forestry dedication or approved plan of operations; work in compliance with a statutory obligation; or work to a tree whose diameter does not exceed 75 millimetres. If, however, the cutting down or uprooting of a tree is for the sole purpose of improving the growth of other trees, the exemption applies to trees not exceeding 100 millimetres. The diameter of a tree for these purposes is to be ascertained by measurement, over the bark of the tree, at a point 1.5 metres above the natural ground level. A special rule applies to multiple-stemmed trees if they are to qualify as small trees under this exception.

21.147 Under Part 4 of the Town and Country Planning (Control of Advertisements) (England) Regulations 2007, SI 2007/783, the local planning authority may submit to the Secretary of State for his approval an order designating the whole or part of a conservation area as an area of special control of advertisements (see Chapter 24). In such cases stricter control is exercised over the display of advertisements.

21.148 Under s 74 of the LBCA Act 1990, the *demolition* of all unlisted buildings in conservation areas was controlled by the need for 'conservation area consent'. Demolition without consent was a criminal offence. As a consequence of the decision in *R (SAVE Britain's Heritage) v Secretary of State for Communities and Local Government* [2011] EWCA Civ 334; [2011] PTSR 1140 both conservation area consent and planning permission were required for the demolition of most buildings in a conservation area. To avoid this duplication the Enterprise and Regulation Reform Act 2013 has repealed the need for conservation area consent (although it still applies in Wales). In order to retain the same level of protection (that the need for conservation area consent provided), the 2013 Act (by inserting a new s 196D) has also made it an offence to fail to obtain planning permission for the demolition of a building in a conservation area or to be in breach of a condition or limitation imposed on a grant of permission for demolition. The 2013 Act has also put in place similar defences to prosecutions to those that were available against prosecution for not having conservation area consents. Also, just as there was no time limit on enforcing conservation area consents, there is no time limit on the service of enforcement notices for a breach of planning control by the demolition of a building in a conservation area. Finally, it should be noted that the permitted development rights for demolition of buildings have been removed from Part 31 of the GPDO by the Town and Country Planning (General Permitted Development) (Amendment) (England) (No 3) Order 2013 now incorporated into Part 11 of the 2015 GPDO.

M. RECENT CHANGES

21.149 The Enterprise and Regulation Reform Act 2013 has also made three important additions to the law. These are as follows.

Heritage partnership agreements

21.150 Section 60(2) of the Enterprise and Regulation Reform Act 2013 inserts new ss 26A and 26B into the LBCA Act 1990 which provide that a LPA may make a heritage partnership agreement with any owner of a listed building situated in England. Such agreements are similar to planning agreements which are explained in Chapter 17. The heritage agreement can grant listed building consent for the execution of works to alter or extend the building but it cannot be used to grant consent for demolition of the building. The agreement can also be used to specify works which the parties consider do not require listed building consent because they would not affect the character of the building. Section 26B makes various supplemental provisions for the review, termination, and variation of agreements and for consultation and publicity. There is a power to make regulations and the Planning (Listed Buildings and Conservation Areas) (Heritage Partnership Agreements) (England) Regulations 2014 (SI 2014/550) have been made which set out in further detail the procedures for heritage partnership agreements.

Listed building consent orders

21.151 Section 60(3) of the 2013 Act has inserted new ss 26C and 26D into the LBCA Act 1990 which allow the Secretary of State and a LPA to make consent orders that grant listed building consent for works of any description short of demolition. In both cases the order may impose conditions on the consent. These provisions are similar to the provisions set out in ss 59 to 61D of the 1990 Act in respect of development orders and local development orders. The Planning (Local Listed Building) (Consent Orders) (Procedure) Regulations 2014 (SI 2014/551) provide for the procedures for the preparation and revocation of local listed building consent orders. They also provide for when compensation can be claimed if an order is withdrawn.

Certificates of lawfulness

21.152 Previously there was not a statutory mechanism under which a person could test whether any proposed works required listed building consent because the works would affect the character of the listed building, unlike the position with development control whereby under s 191 of the 1990 Act a person could seek a certificate of lawfulness of an existing use or development. Section 61 of the 2013 Act inserts a new s 26H into the 1990 Act which mirrors s 191. An application can now be made to the LPA describing the proposed works. Where a certificate is granted the lawfulness of the works is conclusively presumed provided the works are carried out within ten years of the date of issue of the certificate. As with certificates of lawfulness of existing use or development, it is a criminal offence to make false or misleading statements in applying for a certificate and there are rights of appeal against refusals or non-determinations. The Planning (Listed Buildings) (Certificates of Lawfulness of Proposed Works) (England) Regulations 2014 (SI 2014/552) set out the detailed procedures for applications, appeals, and revocations. The provisions were considered in *R (on the application of the Government of the Republic of France) v Royal Borough of Kensington & Chelsea* [2017] EWCA Civ 429; [2017] 1 WLR 3206. The Court of Appeal held that s 26H could only be used to apply for a certificate that proposed works to a listed building would not effect its character as a building of special architectural or historic interest, it could not be used to certify whether a listed building consent had been implemented and thus whether proposed works were lawful. Accordingly, the scope of the s 26H certificates are considerably more narrow than the Certificates of Proposed Lawful Use or Development available under s 192 of the Town and Country Planning Act 1990, on which, see further: A Bowes, 'The Narrow Scope of Certificates under the Planning (Listed Buildings and Conservation Areas) Act 1990 s.26H' [2017] 9 JPL 905.

22

ANCIENT MONUMENTS AND AREAS OF ARCHAEOLOGICAL IMPORTANCE

A. SCHEDULED MONUMENTS	22.02	D. PROTECTION UNDER	
B. ANCIENT MONUMENTS	22.08	PLANNING LEGISLATION	22.13
C. AREAS OF ARCHAEOLOGICAL IMPORTANCE	22.11		

Statutory protection of ancient monuments has existed since 1882. Today the protection is secured in varying degrees by the Ancient Monuments and Archaeological Areas Act 1979 ('the 1979 Act'). Section 61(7) of the 1979 Act defines a 'monument' as meaning: **22.01**

(a) any building, structure, or work, whether above or below the surface of the land, and any cave or excavation;
(b) any site comprising the remains of any such building, structure, or work or of any cave or excavation; and
(c) any site comprising, or comprising the remains of, any vehicle, vessel, aircraft, or other moveable structure or part thereof which neither constitutes nor forms part of any work which is a monument within para (a) above,

and any machinery attached to a monument shall be regarded as part of the monument if it could not be detached without being dismantled.

A. SCHEDULED MONUMENTS

The degree of protection given to a monument under the 1979 Act depends upon whether it is classified as a 'scheduled monument' or as an 'ancient monument'. Under the Act the Secretary of State is required to compile and maintain a 'schedule of monuments'; hence a 'scheduled monument' is defined in terms of inclusion within that schedule. A monument can only be included in the schedule where it appears to the Secretary of State to be of national importance (s 1 of the Act). An 'ancient monument', on the other hand, is defined in wider terms than a scheduled **22.02** monument and means any scheduled monument and 'any other monument which in the opinion of the Secretary of State is of public interest by reason of the historic, architectural, traditional, artistic, or archaeological interest attached to it'.

22.03 The Act gives the greatest degree of protection to monuments which are scheduled monuments. Under s 2 of the Act, a criminal offence is committed where a person executes or causes or permits to be executed prescribed works to a scheduled monument without first having obtained 'scheduled monument consent' for the works. The works referred to in the section include demolition, destruction, or damage to a scheduled monument, removing or repairing a scheduled monument or any part of it, altering or adding to it, or flooding or tipping operations on land in, on, or under which there is a scheduled monument. Scheduled monument consent may be granted subject to conditions.

22.04 Under s 3 of the 1979 Act, the Secretary of State may make an order granting scheduled monument consent for the execution of works of any class or description specified in the order. The order currently in force is the Ancient Monuments (Class Consents) Order 1994, SI 1994/1381. As with the GPDO in relation to the development of land, this Order removes the need for an express application to be made for scheduled monument consent where the work involved is of a minor nature.

22.05 Section 5(1) of the 1979 Act provides that where any works are urgently necessary for the preservation of a scheduled monument, the Secretary of State may enter the site and carry out these works, but normally at his own expense.

22.06 At present there are thought to be about 19,700 entries in the schedule of monuments in England, representing about 23,000 individual monuments subject to protection. These include ecclesiastical ruins, megalithic monuments, crosses and inscribed stones, as well as famous sites such as Stonehenge, the Tower of London, and Hadrian's Wall. The Historic Buildings and Monuments Commission for England (known as Historic England), has embarked on a resurvey programme, which is expected to result eventually in significant additional numbers being given protection by the Secretary of State as scheduled monuments.

22.07 One difficulty with the provisions relating to the scheduling mechanism is that the definition of the term 'monument' presupposes some definable and identifiable entity. It is difficult, therefore, to schedule 'general urban debris' from an earlier age which may be spread over a large area. For that reason, few monuments have been scheduled in urban areas.

B. ANCIENT MONUMENTS

22.08 The 1979 Act also contains powers for the protection of 'ancient' monuments. As previously indicated, the term 'ancient monument' includes all scheduled monuments, but is not restricted merely to that category.

Under the Act, the Secretary of State is given power to acquire compulsorily any ancient monument for the purpose of securing its preservation. In addition, he is given power to acquire an ancient monument by agreement or by gift. **22.09**

As an alternative to acquisition of an ancient monument, the Secretary of State may by s 12 of the 1979 Act be constituted its guardian. Guardianship provides a means whereby the Secretary of State can assume responsibility for maintaining an ancient monument where the owner or occupier is unable or unwilling to do so, but without disturbing the existing ownership of the monument. Where an ancient monument is taken into guardianship, a duty is placed on the guardian to maintain the monument, for which purpose he is given control and management powers. An obligation is also placed on the guardian to permit public access to the monuments under his guardianship. **22.10**

C. AREAS OF ARCHAEOLOGICAL IMPORTANCE

In addition to the powers relating to scheduled and ancient monuments, s 33 of the 1979 Act provides for the designation by the Secretary of State of what are called 'areas of archaeological importance'. Areas designated include the historic centres of Canterbury, Chester, Exeter, Hereford, and York. Designation, however, does not protect the site from damage or destruction. Its purpose is merely to allow time for a site which is threatened by development proposals to be excavated and recorded. Under s 35 of the Act, it is a criminal offence for any person to carry out or cause or permit to be carried out on the designated land any operation involving disturbance of the ground, flooding or tipping, without first having served a notice of that operation (called an 'operations notice') on the local authority in whose area the land is situated. The notice must be served at least six weeks before the operation is due to commence. After receiving an operations notice, the local authority or other investigating authority (such as a university archaeological unit) may enter and inspect the site, observe any operations, and carry out excavations. An authority can only carry out excavations, however, if within four weeks of service of the operations notice it has itself given notice of its intention to carry out excavations. In such a case, the authority is given four months and two weeks from the end of the six-week period to carry out the excavation, during which period no operation involving disturbance of the ground, etc (ie development) can be carried out. Thus, under these provisions, development can be delayed for a maximum period of six months. **22.11**

Although more relevant to the field of movable artefacts, s 42(4) of the 1979 Act also contains a provision making it a criminal offence for a person to use a metal detector in a protected place without consent. A protected place means any place which is either the site of a scheduled monument or any monument in the **22.12** ownership or guardianship of the Secretary of State or situated in an area of archaeological importance.

D. PROTECTION UNDER PLANNING LEGISLATION

22.13 Ancient monuments and sites of archaeological interest may also be protected under town and country planning legislation. Development plans may contain policies for the protection of ancient monuments and sites of archaeological interest and the effect of development on a scheduled monument may be a material consideration to be taken into account in determining applications for planning permission.

22.14 By paragraph 185 of the NPPF plans should set out a 'positive strategy for the conservation and enjoyment of the historic environment, including heritage assets most at risk through neglect, decay or other threats'. This strategy should take into account:

a) the desirability of sustaining and enhancing the significance of heritage assets, and putting them to viable uses consistent with their conservation;
b) the wider social, cultural, economic and environmental benefits that conservation of the historic environment can bring;
c) the desirability of new development making a positive contribution to local character and distinctiveness; and
d) opportunities to draw on the contribution made by the historic environment to the character of a place.

22.15 Archaeological remains identified and scheduled as being of national importance should normally be earmarked in development plans for preservation. The desirability of preserving an ancient monument and its setting is a material consideration in determining planning applications whether the monument is scheduled or unscheduled. (See *Hoveringham Gravels Ltd v Secretary of State for the Environment* [1975] QB 754 (CA).) Where the proposed development would affect a monument which is not a scheduled monument, the authority may impose a condition in a grant of planning permission placing an embargo on any development taking place until specified archaeological facilities have been provided.

22.16 In addition, NPPF (para 187) states that:

Local planning authorities should maintain or have access to a historic environment record. This should contain up-to-date evidence about the historic environment in their area and be used to:
a) assess the significance of heritage assets and the contribution they make to their environment; and
b) predict the likelihood that currently unidentified heritage assets, particularly sites of historic and archaeological interest, will be discovered in the future.

22.17 As an alternative to the imposition of conditions in the grant of planning permission, s 106 of the Town and Country Planning Act 1990 has enabled a person interested in land, by agreement or otherwise, to enter into an obligation for the purpose of restricting the development or use of land. It has not been uncommon under this provision for developers to provide not only archaeological facilities on the site, but also the funding of those facilities.

22.18 In addition to the statutory provisions protecting ancient monuments described above, it should be emphasized that voluntary co-operation between archaeologists and developers for the protection of ancient monuments and archaeological sites has become a well-established practice in the United Kingdom.

22.19 This co-operation has been formalized in a voluntary Code of Practice drawn up by the British Property Federation and the Standing Conference of Archaeological Unit Managers. Experience has shown that this voluntary co-operation is preferable when the objective sought is physical preservation—particularly where it concerns the preservation of buried remains in situ. Thus, where development of land is to be allowed, it may be possible to minimize damage to a monument by raising ground levels under the proposed new buildings, by using foundations which minimize any damage, or by sealing archaeological remains underneath the new buildings in order to secure their preservation for the future. Where preservation in situ is not possible, however, the only acceptable alternative may be archaeological excavation for the purposes of 'preservation by record'. Preservation by record is a general term used to describe the process of documentation by means of photographic record, written report and, where appropriate, the display of the important artefacts/remains which have been uncovered in the course of an excavation.

22.20 An example of this co-operation may be seen in the dispute over the remains of the Rose Theatre, in Southwark, London, where it is believed two of Shakespeare's plays received their first performance. The remains of the theatre were discovered in the course of preliminary works connected with redevelopment. Despite requests to do so, the Secretary of State refused to exercise his powers under the 1979 Act to make the site a scheduled monument, which had he done so, would have then required scheduled monument consent to be obtained before the redevelopment could proceed.

22.21 Under the existing law, compensation for loss of development value of land is not payable where loss results from a site being made a scheduled monument. If, however, planning permission for development of land has been granted and the development is then frustrated because the site is subsequently scheduled, compensation for loss of development value becomes payable. In *R v Secretary of State for the Environment, ex p Rose Theatre Trust Co* [1990] 1 QB 504, an action was brought challenging the decision of the Secretary of State not to make the site and remains of the theatre a scheduled monument. Refusing an application for judicial review to quash the decision, the High Court held that the risk that compensation might be payable was a relevant factor for the Secretary of State to consider in coming to his decision. The court also found that in deciding whether or not to exercise his powers, the Secretary of State was entitled to take into account the developer's desire to co-operate in preserving the remains. As a result of this co-operation, the developers agreed at a cost to themselves of over £10m, to redesign their proposed development in order to protect the site, to remove all piling from the area, to contain remains of the theatre footings, and to provide sufficient headroom over the remains to allow for their future display. Following the development of the Rose Court building, which included those proposals, the Secretary of State decided to include the site of the remains in the schedule of ancient monuments.

22.22 A potential future new development is the new concept of a 'conservation covenant' proposed by the Law Commission in its paper 'Conservation Covenants' (Law Com No 349) published in March 2013 for consultation. The proposal was to create an agreement between landowner and a conservation body to ensure the conservation of natural or heritage features on the land. It is described as private and voluntary arrangement made in the public interest, which continues to be effective after the land changes hands. For a full analysis of the proposal see: N Pratt, 'Analysing Conservation Covenants' [2014] 12 JPL 1310 and B Holligan, 'Narratives of Capital Versus Narratives of Community: Conservation Covenants and the Private Regulation of Land Use' [2018] 30(1) J Env L 55. Following consultation, the Law Commission recommended introducing a new statutory scheme of conservation covenants in England and Wales. In this scheme, a conservation covenant would:

- be formed by the agreement of two parties: a landowner (a person with a freehold estate or leasehold estate of more than seven years), and a responsible body drawn from a limited class of organizations;
- be able to contain both restrictive and positive obligations;
- be capable of binding the landowner's successors in title (that is, all subsequent owners) after he or she has disposed of the land; and
- be made for the public good.

22.23 The Government responded positively to the Law Commission's proposal on 28 January 2016 and, again, within the Government's 25-year Environment Plan: 'A Green Future: Our 25-year Plan to Improve the Environment'. Published in January 2018, the Plan suggests (at p.62) that the Government will:

> [work] with landowners, conservation groups and other stakeholders we will review and take forward the Law Commission's proposals for a statutory scheme of conservation covenants in England.

23

MINERALS

A. INTRODUCTION	23.01	D. INTERPRETATION OF	
B. OLD MINING PERMISSIONS	23.03	MINING PERMISSIONS	23.32
C. MINING PERMISSIONS GRANTED BETWEEN 1948 AND 1982	23.13		

A. INTRODUCTION

Because of the particular nature and effect of mineral working, special provisions **23.01** have been considered necessary to control its environmental effects. Following the report of the Stevens Committee on Planning Control over Mineral Working in 1976, the Government decided to implement many of the report's recommendations, which it did in the Town and Country Planning (Minerals) Act 1981. The main features of that Act, which have now been incorporated in the 1990 Act, were as follows:

(a) It established 'mineral planning authorities' to be responsible for all planning control over mineral working, including the service of enforcement notices and stop notices. Since the winning and working of minerals is a 'county matter' under Sch 1 to the Town and Country Planning Act 1990, the mineral planning authority (MPA) will be the county planning authority except in respect of a site in a metropolitan district or London Borough or other unitary authority, when it will be the local planning authority (s 1(4) of the 1990 Act).

(b) It amplified the definition of development to bring within its scope activities relating to mineral working which may not previously have been regarded as being included within the definition (s 55(4) of the 1990 Act).

(c) It provided that owners of 'mineral rights' should be notified of applications for planning permission for the mining and working of minerals in the same way as other owners are required to be notified (s 65 of the 1990 Act and General Development Procedure Order).

(d) It authorizes the MPA, in a grant of planning permission for mineral working, to impose both 'restoration' and 'aftercare' conditions. A restoration condition secures that any or all of subsoil, topsoil, and soil-making materials are replaced after the completion of the mineral working and the site contoured in an appropriate manner. An aftercare condition imposes an obligation to bring the land back to a required standard where the land is to be restored to agricultural, forestry, or amenity use after the working has ceased (para 2, Sch 5 to the 1990 Act). An aftercare condition, which can only be used in conjunction with a restoration condition, becomes operative after the restoration condition has been complied with. Aftercare may also be secured by the imposition of a condition in the planning permission requiring the subsequent approval by the MPA of an 'aftercare scheme'.

(e) It made every planning permission for mineral working subject to a time limit upon its life. Where the MPA fails to impose a time limit, a 60-year time limit is deemed to be imposed. The 60-year time limit is also made to apply to existing planning permission granted before 22 February 1982 and to run from that date (paras 1–6 of Sch 5 to the 1990 Act). The reason for the imposition of a 60-year time limit on the life of a mineral planning permission was due to the need to avoid paying compensation to landowners for the imposition of a restriction on the life of the permission. It would seem from *Earthline Ltd v West Berkshire Council* [2003] JPL 715 (CA) that the power given by subsequent legislation to amend the conditions subject to which a mineral planning permission is subject does not give the local planning authority the power to amend the condition relating to the life of the permission.

(f) It imposed a duty on the MPA to review every site in its area of current or former mineral working to determine whether it should revoke or modify a planning permission; order the discontinuance of a use or the alteration or removal of buildings; prohibit the resumption of mining and the working of minerals; or order the suspension of mineral working (s 105 of the 1990 Act). Section 105 of the 1990 Act has now been repealed; but has been replaced by the further provisions of s 96 of the Environment Act 1995 (see para 23.15).

(g) It authorized the MPA to prohibit by order the resumption of mineral working which had not been carried on for at least two years and where it appeared to it that the resumption of such development was unlikely (paras 3 and 4, Sch 9 to the 1990 Act). Any order made may impose requirements to alter or remove plant, etc and restoration and aftercare conditions.

(h) It authorized the MPA to suspend by order the winning and working of minerals where the development has begun but has not been carried on for at least 12 months, and it appears that a resumption was likely. The order must specify a period during which specified steps must be taken for the protection of the environment (paras 5 to 10, Sch 9 to the 1990 Act). The purpose of this provision is to secure the temporary restoration of the site before mineral working is resumed.

(i) Where a local planning authority revokes or modifies planning permission, compensation becomes payable where any person has incurred expenditure in carrying out work rendered abortive by the revocation or modification or has otherwise sustained loss directly attributable to that restoration or modification. The Act authorizes the Secretary of State to make regulations which in some circumstances will reduce the amount of compensation for which MPAs will be liable when revoking or modifying a planning permission for mineral working, or making a discontinuance order relating to such development or making a prohibition or suspension order under the Act (s 116 of the 1990 Act). The relevant regulations are now the Town and Country Planning (Compensation for Restrictions on Mineral Working and Mineral Waste Depositing) Regulations 1997, SI 1997/1111.

The provisions in the 1981 Act for a review and updating of conditions did not work well in practice. MPAs were reluctant to risk incurring compensation liabilities, which were difficult to assess, in advance of using their order-making powers. The shortcomings of the 1981 Act were recognized in due course, when further fundamental legislation was enacted. **23.02**

B. OLD MINING PERMISSIONS

Towards the end of 1990 concern began to be expressed over old permissions for mineral working, granted before 1946 under a then legislative scheme known as interim development orders (IDOs). Under the Town and Country Planning Act 1947, permissions granted under IDOs before 22 July 1943 ceased to be effective on 1 July 1948. However, where consent for development had been granted on or after 22 July 1943, permission for that development (insofar as it had not been carried out before 1 July 1948) was deemed to be granted under the 1947 Act and no fresh application was needed. The existence of such permissions led to the following problems: **23.03**

(a) Unlike planning permission granted after the 1947 Act came into force, there was no requirement that such permissions be registered. Hence, many people (including local planning authorities) were ignorant of the existence or the precise details of a permission.
(b) Because such permissions were not registered, long dormant workings could be reactivated without warning.
(c) The permissions were frequently indefinite in duration and were not subject to the type of conditions that are normally attached to present-day permissions aimed at protecting the environment, such as conditions relating to hours of work, noise, vibrations, and dust emissions.
(d) The extension of existing works covered by these permissions could have a significant adverse impact on the environment and amenity.

To meet these problems, s 22 and Sch 2 of the Planning and Compensation Act 1991 introduced new procedures for dealing with permissions for the winning and working of minerals or the depositing of mineral waste originally granted under IDOs. They are referred to in the Act as 'old mining permissions'. The main effect of these provisions was that a landowner or mineral owner with planning permission for development consisting of the winning and working of minerals or involving the depositing of mineral waste authorized by interim development orders made after 21 July 1943 could, within six months of the new provisions being brought into operation, apply to the MPA to have the permission registered. If no application for registration of the permission was made by 1 May 1991, therefore, the permission ceased to have effect and no compensation was payable. Any dispute about the validity of the permission in respect of which the application to **23.04** register was made, had to be determined by the Secretary of State. It is believed that 508 applications were made for the registration of interim development order permissions. They have often involved the resolution of disputed issues of fact and, on occasions, where it could be shown that all parties have proceeded on the basis that there was in existence a planning permission, the concept of the 'presumption of regularity', as propounded in *Calder Gravel Ltd v Kirklees MBC* (1989) 60 P & CR 322, has been applied.

23.05 The next stage was to settle suitable conditions. In *R v North Yorkshire County Council, ex p Brown* [1999] JPL 616, Lord Hoffmann (at 619) set out precisely the procedure required by Sch 2 to the 1991 Act to be followed. He said:

> Once the application for registration had been granted, the owner of the land became entitled to apply to the mineral planning authority to determine the conditions to which the permission was to be subject: para 2(2). The application had to be made (subject to any agreed extension) within 12 months of the grant of registration or the determination of an appeal against its refusal: para 2(4)(b). If no application was made within such period, the permission ceased to have effect. The land owner was required in the first instance to propose his own conditions, but the mineral planning authority was entitled (subject to an appeal to the Secretary of State) to include 'any conditions which may be imposed on a grant of planning permission for development consisting of the winning and working of minerals or involving the depositing of mineral waste': para 2(1)(a). These words plainly confer a very wide discretion to impose conditions for the protection of the environment, subject of course to any policy guidance which may be given by the Secretary of State. In addition, the mineral planning authority was required to impose a condition that working should cease not later than 21 February 2042: para 2(1)(c).

> The schedule gave the mineral planning authority three months in which to determine the conditions. If it failed to do so, it was treated as if it had determined that the permission was to be subject to the conditions set out in the application: para 2(6)(b). Once the conditions had been finally determined, the conditions were required to be registered (para 3(2)) and the old permission had effect as if it had been granted subject to those conditions: section 22(2).

> In the period before the final determination of the conditions, section 22 distinguishes between what is sometimes called a 'dormant permission', where in the period of two years before 1 May 1991, no development had been carried out to any substantial extent on the land to which the permission related, and a permission by virtue of which extraction had been going on. In the case of a dormant permission, no extraction could take place until the conditions had been finally determined: section 22(3). In the case of an active permission, the owner could continue to operate as before, subject to having to comply with the conditions when they were determined or to cease operations if the permission lapsed on account of his failure to apply for their determination.

23.06 This distinction between dormant and active conditions, therefore, was intended to prevent the reactivation of dormant permissions without proper planning conditions; avoid applicants having to prepare and submit schemes of conditions too far in advance of their need to work the site; ensure that schemes that are prepared and submitted are appropriate to the circumstances pertaining at the time; and ensure that the workload for both applicants and MPAs is more evenly spread.

23.07 The purpose of these provisions was to ensure that eventually the extent and terms of old mining permissions were publicly known; that where old mining permissions are being implemented, conditions imposed on the permissions ensure that operational activity complies with modern standards; and that operations cannot be recommenced on sites which have recently been lying dormant without first proving the validity of an old mining permission and having conditions relating to operating and restoration aspects attached to it.

23.08 The provisions have given rise to much litigation. In the *North Yorkshire* case their Lordships held that Council Directive 85/337 EC, the Assessment of the Effects of Certain Public and Private Projects on the Environment, applied to the determination by the Council under s 22 of the 1991 Act of the conditions attached to an old mining permission, since that decision was the equivalent of a 'decision of the competent authority or authorities which entitles the development to proceed'. Accordingly, since the Council had not considered whether environmental assessment was required at that time, the Court of Appeal had been right to reverse the decision of the High Court and quash the determination of the conditions.

23.09 Two further cases should be mentioned. In *R v Peak District National Park Authority, ex p Blacklow Industries Ltd* [2000] JPL 290, the applicants applied for *certiorari* to quash a determination by the minerals planning authority in respect of an application made to the authority under Sch 13 of the Environment Act 1995 for the determination of conditions to which a 1952 planning permission was to be subject. The authority had determined the application in the absence of an environmental impact assessment. Days later the authority, in the light of the decision of the court in the North Yorkshire County Council case, wrote to the applicants to say that it had made its determination without prejudice to its view that in the absence of an environmental impact assessment it had no jurisdiction to determine the application and its decision was therefore a nullity. Granting the order, the High Court held that since the determination was a public document, it was right that it should be made public that the determination was of no legal effect.

23.10 In *R v Somerset CC, ex p Morris & Perry (Gurney Slade Quarry) Ltd* [2000] 2 PLCR 117, the County Council as the mineral planning authority for the area, had given the applicants notice of its determination of the conditions to which old planning permission was to be made subject, after the expiration of an extended period to which the applicant and authority had earlier agreed in writing. Accordingly, by virtue of Sch 2, para 2(6) of the 1991 Act, that had the effect of the authority being treated as having determined that the permission was to be subject to the conditions put forward by the applicants. Thus, owing to non-compliance with the strict time limits or extensions agreed in writing, the conditions were significantly less stringent than environmental considerations might otherwise justify or require.

23.11 It should be noted that under the Planning and Compulsory Purchase Act 2004, the Crown is to be entitled to register old mining permissions and to apply for the determination of new conditions to be attached to them.

23.12 However, notwithstanding the measures taken in the Town and Country Planning (Minerals) Act 1981 and in the Planning and Compensation Act 1991 relating to old mineral permissions, concern continued to be expressed about the adequacy of planning controls over development involving mineral working.

C. MINING PERMISSIONS GRANTED BETWEEN 1948 AND 1982

23.13 The changes to the law relating to mineral working made by the Town and Country Planning (Minerals) Act 1981 and by the Planning and Compensation Act 1991 in relation to old mining permissions (see para 23.03) left unaffected those planning permissions for mineral working which had been granted between 1948 and 1982.

23.14 By the early 1990s it had become clear that many of the provisions of the 1981 Act had not worked well. In March 1992 the Government issued a consultation paper which proposed a number of reforms, both for mineral planning permissions granted between 1948 and 1982 and for those granted after 1982. The overall aim of the proposals for the 1948–82 permissions was to establish a 'level playing field' for mineral operators regardless of the date of their permissions. As things were, holders of modern permissions and of 'reformed' IDO permissions granted between 1943 and 1948 were seen to be at a disadvantage compared to others.

23.15 The Government's proposals have been given effect to by the Environment Act 1995, s 96 and Schs 13 and 14. These provide for an 'initial review' and updating of permissions granted between 1948 and 1982 and 'periodic reviews' of *all* mineral permissions thereafter. Permissions granted between 1948 and 1982 are known as 'old mineral planning permissions' to distinguish them from 'old mining permissions' referred to earlier. The provisions related to England, Wales, and Scotland. The work was to be carried out in two stages.

23.16 Schedule 13 provided for an initial review and updating of mineral sites where the predominant planning permission for minerals development was granted after 30 June 1948 and before 22 February 1982 (one of the principal commencement dates of the Town and Country Planning (Minerals) Act 1981).

The scheme of the initial review was as follows: **23.17**

— The Schedule makes a distinction between 'dormant' sites and 'active' sites. A dormant site is one where no substantial development has been carried out in the period beginning on 22 February 1982 and ending on 6 June 1995. No further mineral development can be carried out on dormant sites until a new scheme of conditions has been submitted to, and approved by the MPA.
— Active sites have to be reviewed in two successive phases, each of three years. A Phase I site is an active site where the mineral permission was granted after 30 June 1948 and before 1 April 1969. A Phase II site is a site where the mineral permission was granted after 31 March 1969 and before 22 February 1982.
— By 31 January 1996, every MPA had to prepare a list (known as the 'first' list) of all dormant and active Phase I and Phase II mineral sites in their area. MPAs were required to advertise that the list had been prepared, and to notify owners. If a site had been omitted from the list, landowners had to apply within three months for the inclusion of their land within the list, failing which the mineral permission ceased to have effect. In addition, the list had to specify in respect of active Phase I sites the date by which an application for approval of new conditions had to be submitted to the MPA. If applications were not submitted by that date, then again the mineral permission ceased to have effect.
— By 31 October 1998, every MPA had to prepare a list (known as the 'second' list) of all active Phase II sites in their area. Preparation of this list meant in effect taking the first list of active Phase II sites, but incorporating in the second list specific dates for the submission by landowners of applications for approval of new conditions. As with the first list, a failure to do so meant the mineral permission ceasing to have any effect.
— No compensation was payable for loss suffered from the imposition of new conditions for a dormant site. For active sites, compensation is payable for loss suffered from the imposition of new conditions, only if the new conditions restrict working rights and, in the opinion of the MPA, the effect of the more restrictive conditions would prejudice to an unreasonable degree the economic viability of the operation or the asset value of the site.

Schedule 13 then provides that the owner of any land or mineral which forms part of a dormant Phase I or II site may apply to the MPA to determine conditions to which the relevant planning permissions relating to the site are to be subject. The MPA must then proceed to determine the conditions to which the planning permission is to be subject. If the MPA does not do this within three months of receiving the owner's application, the planning permission becomes subject to the conditions proposed by the owner. **23.18**

In the case of *R v Oldham MBC and Pugmanor Properties Ltd, ex p Foster* [2000] JPL 111, Keene J described the duty of the MPA. The list it had to compile was a **23.19** list of mineral sites, not a definitive list of relevant planning permissions. It only had to consider whether a relevant planning permission or permissions exist in respect of a given site, it need not identify those permissions in the list. Under the schedule, the MPA's duty was to determine conditions to which each relevant planning permission relating to the site is to be subject, as there may be more than one permission relating to the site.

23.20 Schedule 14 provides for a subsequent and ongoing review by the MPA of all planning permissions for mineral development, including of course, old mining permissions which would have been reviewed under the 1991 Act. The scheme of periodic reviews is that they should take place every 15 years from the date of either a previous review, or, if no revision has taken place, from the date of the latest mineral permission relating to the site. When the scheme is in operation, MPAs will be required to give owners 12 months' notice of the date by which an application for approval of new conditions must be submitted to them. If no such application is made by that date, the permission will cease to have effect. Section 10 of and Sch 3 to the Growth and Infrastructure Act 2013 have amended Sch 14 to give MPAs in England a discretion as to whether or when to carry out a review but the review date must not be earlier than the previous dates by which reviews had to be carried out.

23.21 It should be noted that MPG14: The Environment Act 1995: Review of Mineral Planning Permissions, explained in great detail the requirements introduced by the Environment Act for the initial and periodic reviews of mineral planning permissions.

23.22 The application of the Environment Act 1995 to mineral planning permissions has attracted some litigation. In *Dorset CC v Secretary of State for the Environment, Transport, and the Regions and Rothchild Estates Ltd* [1999] JPL 633, the High Court refused an application by the MPA to quash a decision of the Secretary of State allowing an appeal by Rothchild Estates against the MPA's decision not to include its land in the 'first list' of mineral sites. The MPA had unsuccessfully argued that the development of part of the site for housing rendered the mineral permission incapable of implementation; and that since the permission was no longer valid it could not be registered.

23.23 In *R v North Lincolnshire Council, ex p Horticulture and Garda Products Sales (Humberside) Ltd* [1998] Env LR 295, the applicants for judicial review had first learnt of the exclusion of their land from the first list of mineral sites after the three-month period for them to seek its inclusion had passed. The applicants had not been at fault; neither indeed had the North Lincolnshire Council who had inherited the list from the Humberside Metropolitan Borough Council under local government reorganization, and who had omitted the site from the first list in breach of statutory duty. The North Lincolnshire Council considered that it had no power to extend the three-month period or to otherwise remedy the omission from the first list and its consequences. The High Court held that it could only intervene if the MPA had acted unlawfully, and refused the application.

23.24 It should also be noted that although the *North Yorkshire* case referred to earlier in this chapter involved the legislation relating to pre-1948 mineral permissions contained in the Planning and Compensation Act 1991, the reasoning in the *North Yorkshire* case must apply equally to determinations of conditions attached to mineral permissions granted between 1948 and 1982 which are governed by Sch 13 to the Environment Act 1995 and to conditions attached to permissions subjected to periodic review under Sch 14. However, the Secretary of State was clearly concerned about the impact of the decision given by the Court of Appeal in that case and no doubt feared, rightly as it turned out, that the House of Lords would dismiss an appeal from the Court of Appeal's decision. In anticipation that this might happen, therefore, the Secretary of State announced that he was drafting on a contingent basis, regulations under s 2(2) of the European Communities Act 1972 to adopt the review procedures of both the 1991 and 1995 Acts to enable requirement of environmental impact assessment in appropriate cases. He duly did so, and amendments to the Town and Country Planning (Environmental Impact Assessment) (England and Wales) Regulations 1999 were made by SI 2000/2867, which came into force on 15 November 2000. The amendments provide that the Regulations should impact upon applications to determine the conditions to which a planning permission is to be subject, in the same way as they apply to applications for planning permission. The amendments also introduced into the main regulations a change in terminology. The Regulations use the word ROMP, which is clearly an acronym derived from 'Registration of Old Mining (or Mineral) Permissions'. The provisions regarding ROMPs can now be found in Part 9 of the Environmental Impact Assessment Regulations 2017.

23.25 A ROMP may be a ROMP application or ROMP development. A ROMP application means an application to an MPA to determine the conditions to which a planning permission is to be subject under:

(a) para 2(2) of Sch 2 to the 1991 Act (registration of old mining conditions);
(b) para 9(1) of Sch 13 to the 1995 Act (review of old mineral planning permissions); or
(c) para 6(1) of Sch 14 to the 1995 Act (periodic review of mineral planning permissions).

ROMP development is development, which is yet to be carried out, and which is authorized in a planning permission in respect of which a ROMP application has been or is to be made.

23.26 A number of other cases, some involving the application of environmental impact assessment on mineral permissions, are dealt with in Chapter 13. See generally also recent cases of *R v Hammersmith and Fulham LBC, ex p CPRE; R v Durham*

CC and Sherburn Stone Company Limited, ex p Huddleston; and *R v Rochdale MBC, ex parte Tew (CA)*.

23.27 ROMP applications continued to constitute a problem. It seems that the 2000 Regulations were not retrospective. These regulations were applied only to those applications which sought determination of conditions reviews after 15 November 2000. In March 2000 informal guidance was provided which advised that, for applications for determination of new conditions which pre-dated 15 November 2000, MPAs and mineral operators would need to apply the principles of the 2000 Regulations voluntarily. In the majority of cases the requested information has been supplied and new conditions have been determined.

23.28 Many applications for new mineral operating conditions (made before 15 November 2000) remained undetermined for a variety of reasons. The delay meant that some mineral operations could continue under old permissions. For a little while, therefore, operations at active sites could continue with little or no mitigation of the environmental impacts.

23.29 This problem, however, was remedied by the Environmental Impact Assessment (Mineral Permissions and Amendment) (England) Regulations 2008, SI 2008/1556. The Regulations came into force on 22 July 2008. They applied the 1999 Environmental Impact Assessment Regulations, with modifications, to ROMP applications made before 15 November 2000 which are undetermined on 22 July 2008 ('undetermined ROMP applications'). They also make provisions which apply to all ROMP applications. The 1999 Regulations have now been consolidated and partially revised by the Town and Country Planning (Environmental Impact Assessment) Regulations 2017, which came into force on 30 November 2017.

23.30 The 1999 Regulations were also modified so that screening opinions must be provided for all undetermined ROMP applications as soon as reasonably practicable on or after 22 July 2008 and acceptance of the screening opinion or an application for a screening direction should be made in writing within three weeks of the screening opinion.

23.31 Regulation 10 of the 1999 Regulations (now reg 15 of the 2017 Regulations) was modified so that scoping opinions must be provided for all undetermined ROMP applications as soon as reasonably practicable after screening. Acceptance of the scoping opinion or an application for a scoping direction from the Secretary of State should be made in writing within three weeks of the scoping opinion. Regulation 11 of the 1999 Regulations (now reg 16 of the 2017 Regulations) was modified to make similar provision in relation to scoping directions for applications which have been called in for determination by the Secretary of State, and for appeals to the Secretary of State. Mineral planning authorities or the Secretary of State must warn applicants or appellants of the consequences of not providing

D. INTERPRETATION OF MINING PERMISSIONS

Planning permissions granting mining rights can give rise to difficult questions of interpretation and in particular the meaning of 'working and winning' of particular minerals. The problem arises because in the course of getting at a particular mineral it is inevitable that other minerals will be exposed. In *Secretary of State for Communities and Local Government v Bleaklow Industries Ltd* [2009] EWCA Civ 206; [2009] 2 P & CR 21, the Minister of Housing and Local Government in 1952 granted planning permission for the extraction of fluorspar and barytes on a site in Derbyshire ('the 1952 permission'). It was agreed that the permission had two limbs: the first granted permission for the winning and working of fluorspar, the second for the working of limestone which was won in the course of working fluorspar by turning over old spoil dumps, by open-cast working and by underground mining. The Court of Appeal held that working and winning had distinct meanings. 'Winning', as used in the 1952 permission, referred to the process of achieving access to the desired mineral, so that it could then be worked, and 'working' referred to the process of removing the desired mineral from its position in the land. When fluorspar was contained in a vein embedded in limestone, 'winning' would consist of obtaining access to the vein and 'working' would describe the process of extracting the fluorspar from the vein. So, in this case the first limb of the 1952 permission authorized the working of limestone when it was won in the process of *working* fluorspar but there was no express permission to work limestone which had been *won* in the course of winning fluorspar. So, the winning and working and subsequent export from the site of any limestone severed in order to win fluorspar or barytes was not permitted. This decision has since been applied in *R (on the application of High Peak Spar Ltd) v Secretary of State for Communities and Local Government* [2009] EWHC 3719 (Admin).

23.32

24

THE CONTROL OF OUTDOOR ADVERTISEMENTS

A. INTRODUCTION	24.01	E. FLY-POSTING	24.31
B. DEEMED CONSENT	24.15	F. DEVELOPMENT AND THE DISPLAY OF ADVERTISEMENTS	24.37
C. EXPRESS CONSENT	24.22		
D. AREAS OF SPECIAL CONTROL (ASC)	24.25		

A. INTRODUCTION

The source of the power to control advertisements is found in ss 220 to 225 of the Town and Country Planning Act 1990 (the 1990 Act). Section 220 gives the Secretary of State power to make regulations for restricting or regulating the display of advertisements, so far as it appears to him to be expedient in the interests of amenity or public safety. The present regulations are the Town and County Planning (Control of Advertisements) (England) Regulations 2007, SI 2007/783 (the Regulations). The Regulations update and improve the arrangements for controlling outdoor advertisements and make the control more responsive to rapidly changing forms of advertising. Circular 03/2007 further explains the legislation and provides guidance for local planning authorities and advertisers to help ensure that the system operates effectively. The latest Regulations also coincide with the creation of a database to enable local planning authorities to input and extract details of prosecutions and formal cautions against advertisers who unlawfully display advertisements alongside motorways and trunk roads. The database will also include details of persons guilty of fly-posting. It is hoped that this information will help to track down persistent offenders and ensure that fines reflect the seriousness of the offence. **24.01**

The power to control advertisements can only be exercised in the interests of amenity or public safety. As the content of an advertisement can only be considered from these aspects, the control cannot be used as an instrument **24.02** of censorship. Regulation 3(4) makes this clear by providing that 'unless it appears to the local planning authority to be required in the interests of amenity or public safety, an express consent for the display of advertisements shall not contain any limitation or restriction relating to the subject matter, content, or design of what is to be displayed'. Under reg 3(1) of the Regulations, the local planning authority in exercising its powers is required to take into account:

(a) the provisions of the development plan, so far as they are material;
(b) and any other relevant factors.

It should be noted that the provisions of s 38(6) of the 2004 Act do not apply to advertisement control as the duty to take into account the development plan is imposed by the regulations and not by the 1990 Act. Hence, policies in the development plan cannot be considered by themselves to be decisive.

24.03 The Regulations further provide that without prejudice to the generality of para (1)(b)—

(a) factors relevant to amenity include the general characteristics of the locality, including the presence of any feature of historic, architectural, cultural, or similar interest;
(b) factors relevant to the public safety include:
  (i) the safety of persons using any highway, railway, waterway, dock, harbour, or aerodrome (civil or military);
  (ii) whether the display of the advertisement in question is likely to obscure, or hinder the ready interpretation of, any traffic sign, railway signal, or aid to navigation by water or air;
  (iii) whether the display of the advertisement in question is likely to hinder the operation of any device used for the purpose of security or surveillance or for measuring the speed of any vehicle.

It is also provided that in taking account of factors relevant to amenity, the local planning authority may, if it thinks fit, disregard any advertisement that is being displayed.

24.04 Section 224 of the 1990 Act contains provisions relating to enforcement. Under the section, the regulations may make provision to enable the local planning authority to require the removal of any advertisement displayed in contravention of the regulations, or the discontinuance of the use for the display of advertisements of any site which is being so used in contravention of the regulations. In addition, s 224(3) provides that if any person displays an advertisement in contravention of the regulations he shall be guilty of an offence and liable on summary conviction to a fine of such amount as may be prescribed, not exceeding level four on the standard scale. In the case of a continuing offence, the maximum fine now specified in reg 30 is one tenth of level four on the standard scale for each day during which the offence continues after conviction.

24.05 In *Kingston upon Thames RBC v National Solus Sites Ltd* [1994] JPL 251, the Queen's Bench Divisional Court held that where different posters, each advertising goods, were displayed on an advertising hoarding on different sites without consent, each display constituted a single and separate offence under the Control of Advertisement Regulations. The decision greatly increases the maximum sentence a court may impose where an authority lays multiple informations in respect of each advertisement poster.

24.06 In addition to the powers given to local planning authorities under s 224 of the 1990 Act, s 225 empowers local planning authorities to remove or obliterate any placard or poster displayed in contravention of any regulations made under s 220. It should be noted, too, that Private Acts promoted by local authorities may vary or extend the powers available to authorities under s 225 of the Act as, for example, the London Local Authorities Act 1995 which, inter alia, gives the relevant local authorities power to require the occupier of premises to remove signs other than advertisements on the surface of any building, fence, or other structure or erection. The same Act also amends subsections (3) to (5) of s 225 so as to require a person displaying a placard or poster in contravention of the regulations made under s 220 to remove it within two days.

24.07 The control of advertisements system under the 1990 Act covers a wide range of advertisements and signs. The last amendments to the definition of the word 'advertisement' in s 336(1) of the 1990 Act were made by s 24 of the Planning and Compensation Act 1991. As amended, the definition (with the amendments in italics) now reads:

> advertisement means any word, letter, model, sign, placard, board, notice, *awning, blind*, device or representation, whether illuminated or not, in the nature of, and employed wholly or partly for the purposes of, advertisement, announcement or direction, and (without prejudice to the previous provisions of this definition) includes any hoarding or similar structure used, *or designed*, or adapted for use, *and anything else principally used, or designed or adapted principally for use*, for the display of advertisements, and references to the display of advertisements shall be construed accordingly.

24.08 The purpose of each of the amendments was as follows:

(a) *Awning, blind.* These words brought two additional methods of displaying advertisements within the statutory definition. Before this amendment was made, it was not clear whether awnings and blinds on which an advertisement was displayed, but held in place by metal supporting arms secured to the wall of a building, were to be treated solely as an outdoor advertisement or whether, independent of the provisions in the Act granting deemed planning permission for advertisements displayed in accordance with the Advertisement Regulations, planning permission was needed for any development that they might involve. The amendment means that awnings and blinds can now be treated solely as an outdoor advertisement.

(b) *Or designed.* The purpose of this amendment was to make it clear that the definition of 'advertisement' includes hoardings and similar structures (such as rotating poster-panels) designed for use for the display of advertisements, even though no actual display is presently taking place.

(c) *And anything else principally used or designed or adapted principally for use.* The purpose of this amendment was to extend the definition of 'advertisement' so that it includes objects such as gantries, pylons, or free-standing drums often found in shopping precincts.

24.09 So far there has been little litigation on the meaning of the word 'advertisement'. In two linked cases, however, *Great Yarmouth BC v Secretary of State for the Environment* and *Newport BC v Secretary of State for Wales* [1997] JPL 650, spaceflower lighting equipment had been placed on the top of amusement centres. Although free-standing, the equipment could project a beam of light skywards to produce an image, generally a flower, on the base of any cloud cover. Its purpose was to announce the holding at the centre of certain leisure activities. The respective local planning authorities had invited the owners of the amusement arcades to apply for express consent to the display of an advertisement. On refusal of their applications, the owners appealed to the Secretary of State, who declined to entertain the appeals on the ground that no advertisement was being displayed. In quashing the Secretary of State's decision to refuse to entertain the appeals, the High Court held that he had proceeded on the basis that an advertisement had to have a tangible or physical presence. That was not necessary in the case of 'a sign', the Deputy Judge calling in aid the biblical description of what appeared in the sky at the time of the nativity.

24.10 The cases highlighted the changing nature of advertisement technology and the possible difficulty of bringing some forms within the existing system of advertising control. In *Butler v Derby City Council* [2005] EWHC 2835 QBD (Admin), Sullivan J referred to the narrow meaning of the term advertisement as usually applying to the display of 'material which promotes a product or service'. Then, referring to the definition of the term in s 336(1) of the 1990 Act he said:

> If the word 'advertisement' had stood alone in s 336(1) I would not have given it such a narrow meaning. However, the fact that Parliament felt it necessary to add the words 'announcement or direction' suggests that it was recognized that advertisement might be given too narrow a meaning which might be harmful to the interests of amenity or public safety. Parliament therefore made it clear beyond any doubt that 'advertisement' was to be given a very broad meaning for the purposes of the Act.

24.11 Note that for the purposes of the Regulations, the term advertisement does not include anything employed wholly or as a memorial or as a railway signal; or as a placard or other object borne by an individual or an animal.

Exclusions from control

Regulation 4 prohibits the display of advertisements unless the display had either 'deemed consent' (Part 2 of the Regulations) or 'express consent' (Part 3 of the Regulations), but excluding advertisements to which reg 1(3) applies. Regulation 1(3) specifies in Sch 1 to the Regulations cases to which Parts 2 and 3 are not to apply, provided that the display complies with the particular conditions and limitations considered by the Schedule to be relevant to the advertisement displayed. Schedule 1 has the following nine Classes, each of which has its own conditions and limitations which have to be complied with if the display is to be excluded from advertising control. They are: **24.12**

CLASS A	An advertisement displayed on enclosed land.
CLASS B	An advertisement displayed on or in a vehicle normally employed as a moving vehicle.
CLASS C	An advertisement incorporated in the fabric of a building. [Note: It was this particular provision in earlier advertising regulations that allowed without the need for consent, the word 'OXO' to be incorporated within the fabric of the building on the south bank of the River Thames occupied by the manufacturers of that commodity. For many years, tourists were advised that one could obtain within the building, 'the cheapest square meal in London'.]
CLASS D	An advertisement displayed on an article for sale or on the container in, or from which, an article is sold.
CLASS E	An advertisement relating specifically to a pending parliamentary, European parliamentary, or local government election or a referendum under the Political Parties, Elections, and Referendums Act 2000.
CLASS F	An advertisement required to be displayed by standing orders of either House of Parliament or by any enactment of any condition imposed by any enactment on the exercise of any function.
CLASS G	A traffic sign.
CLASS H	(a) Country's national flag. (b) The flag of the Commonwealth, the European Union, or the United Nations. (c) The flag of any English county. (d) The flag of any saint.
CLASS I	An advertisement displayed inside a building.

Reference should be made to each Class of the Schedule for other particular limitations from this exclusion from control. **24.13**

The scheme of control

Advertisements subject to control by the Regulations fall into two main groups, namely, advertisements for which deemed consent is granted by the Regulations and advertisements which require express consent from the local planning authority or the Secretary of State. **24.14**

B. DEEMED CONSENT

24.15 Under reg 6 (and Sch 3), deemed consent is granted for the display of the following broad categories of advertisements subject to stated conditions and limitations and the power of the local planning authority to serve a discontinuance notice:

Class 1	Functional advertisement of government apartments and their agencies, local authorities, public transport undertakers, statutory undertakers, and Transport for London. (The overall size of advertisements within the Class may not exceed 1.55 square metres in area.)
Class 2	Miscellaneous advertisements relating to the premises on which they are displayed (eg advertisements relating to professions, businesses, or trades carried on in premises).
Class 3	Miscellaneous temporary advertisements (eg advertisements relating to the sale or letting of premises).
Class 4	Illuminated advertisements on business premises.
Class 5	Other advertisements on business premises. [Note In *Addison Lee Ltd v Westminster City Council* [2012] EWHC 152 (Admin); [2012] JPL 969 the High Court held that the display of an advertisement on cigarette bins, publishing a mini cab service, was not a deemed consent when the advertisement had no relationship to the business carried on in the premises.]
Class 6	An advertisement on a forecourt of business premises.
Class 7	Flag advertisements.
Class 8	Advertisements on hoardings.
Class 9	Advertisements on highway structures.
Class 10	Advertisements for neighbourhood watch and similar schemes.
Class 11	Directional advertisements.
Class 12	Advertisements inside buildings.
Class 13	Advertisements on sites used for the preceding 10 years for display of advertisements without express consent. [Note: The application of Class 13 was considered by the Court of Appeal in *R (on the application of Clear Channel UK Ltd) v Hammersmith and Fulham LBC* [2009] EWCA Civ 2142; [2010] JPL 751 where it was held that a digital display advertising hoarding that allowed images to be displayed at intervals did not enjoy deemed consent when it replaced a static display. Then in *Winfield v Secretary of State for Communities and Local Government* [2012] EWCA Civ 1415; [2013] 1 WLR 948 it was held that an Inspector had correctly found that time stopped running when the advertisements were taken down because of a threat of enforcement. It was also held that there was still a break, if the structure on which the advertisement was placed remained in place.]
Class 14	Advertisements displayed after expiry of express consent.
Class 15	Advertising on balloons.
Class 16	Advertisements on telephone kiosks.

24.16 The deemed consent granted for the display of the advertisements in the above Classes, as well as being granted subject to the conditions and limitations stated in each Class, is also subject to what are referred to as the standard conditions.

The standard conditions (set out in Sch 2 to the Regulations) are: **24.17**

1. No advertisement is to be displayed without the permission of the owner of the site or any other person with an interest in the site entitled to grant permission.
2. No advertisement shall be sited or displayed so as to—
    (a) endanger persons using any highway, railway, waterway, dock, harbour, or aerodrome (civil or military);
    (b) obscure, or hinder the ready interpretation of, any traffic sign, railway signal, or aid to navigation by water or air; or
    (c) hinder the operation of any device used for the purpose of security or surveillance or for measuring the speed of any vehicle.
3. Any advertisement displayed, and any site used for the display of advertisements, shall be maintained in a condition that does not impair the visual amenity of the site.
4. Any structure or hoarding erected or used principally for the purpose of displaying advertisements, shall be maintained in a condition that does not endanger the public.
5. Where an advertisement is required under these Regulations to be removed, the site shall be left in a condition that does not endanger the public or impair visual amenity.

The other conditions and limitations to which the deemed consent may be subject relate to such matters as size of the advertisement, size of characters or symbols on the advertisement, area and height of the advertisement, and its position. **24.18**

The deemed consent to the display of the above Classes of advertisements may be restricted in two ways. First, under reg 7, the Secretary of State, if satisfied upon a proposal made to him by the local planning authority that the display of advertisements of any class or description (other than Class 12 or 13) should not be undertaken in any particular area or in any particular case without express consent, may direct that the consent granted by the regulations for that class or description shall not apply in that area or case, for a specified period or indefinitely. **24.19**

In the past the Secretary of State has issued directions with regard to estate agents' noticeboards in a number of conservation areas within Central London. Similar directions had been made in relation to the display of advertisements in the Royal Borough of Kensington and Chelsea, Westminster City Council, Charwood Borough Council, and the City of Bath. The directions have meant that before displaying 'for sale' or 'to let' notices in those areas, specific consent for the display must to be obtained. The directions were granted to protect the visual amenity of residential areas of special quality from persistently high numbers of estate agents' boards and because it was felt that there was no other effective way of controlling them. **24.20**

24.21 Secondly, under reg 8, a local planning authority may serve a notice on the advertiser as defined in reg 2(1) requiring the discontinuance of the display of an advertisement, or the use of a site for the display of an advertisement for which there is deemed consent, if it is satisfied that it is necessary to do so to remedy a substantial injury to the amenity of the locality or a danger to members of the public. There is a right of appeal against the notice to the Secretary of State.

C. EXPRESS CONSENT

24.22 Unless an advertisement requiring consent has deemed consent for its display under reg 6, express consent is required. An application for express consent is made to the authority on whom it falls to determine it. The authority may then refuse consent, or grant consent, in whole or in part, subject to the standard conditions and to such additional conditions as they think fit. Regulation 14 provides that an express consent shall be subject to the condition that it expires at the end of such period as the local planning authority may specify; or where no period is satisfied, a period of five years. The Regulations give a right of appeal to the Secretary of State against a decision of the authority on an application for express consent.

24.23 The reason for having a fixed period of consent is that there can be no guarantee that whilst the effects of a particular advertisement display on amenity and public safety may be acceptable at the time express consent is granted, subsequent changes to the built environment may make the continued display of the advertisement unacceptable. To save the trouble of advertisers having to apply for express consent at the end of the five-year period, such advertisements are given the benefit of deemed consent for their continued display (Class 14). Similarly, because documentary evidence may not be available to show a grant of express consent for an advertisement on a site used for the display of advertisements within the past 10 years the same deemed consent provisions apply (Class 13).

24.24 Consequent upon the changes made to the 1990 Act by the Planning and Compensation Act 1991 and the Planning and Compulsory Purchase Act 2004, the Regulations now give to a local planning authority the same powers to decline to determine an application for express consent to the display of an advertisement as it has to decline to determine an application for planning permission.

D. AREAS OF SPECIAL CONTROL (ASC)

24.25 Under s 221 of the 1990 Act, the Advertisement Regulations may make different provision with respect to different areas. In particular, the Regulations may make special provision with respect to conservation areas, areas defined as experimental areas, and areas defined as areas of special control (ASCs).

24.26 An experimental area is an area prescribed for a period, for the purpose of assessing the effect on amenity or public safety of advertisements of a prescribed description.

24.27 As regards ASCs, regs 20 and 21 provide more detailed provisions. The local planning authorities are required to advertise any proposal to designate or modify them and to consider any representations they receive. If they then decide to proceed, a formal ASC Order is submitted for the Secretary of State's consideration. He may decide to approve the submitted Order; to approve it with specified modifications; or not to approve it. If an Order is fully or partly approved, the local planning authority must advertise the approval and its effective date. There are special transitional provisions for advertisements already displayed on the date a new Order comes into force. Orders must be reviewed at least every five years, though noncompliance with that duty is not infrequent.

24.28 As regards such areas, designation as such has the following four main practical effects:

(a) there is a greater restriction on general advertising hoardings; and
(b) certain classes of advertisement which normally benefit from deemed consent may now require the express consent of the local planning authority.

24.29 The purpose of requiring the Secretary of State's approval is to ensure that nationally applicable standards are applied in determining what areas are subject to this stricter control. It is believed that about 50 per cent of the area of England and Wales has been designated as areas of special control.

24.30 In November 2000, following concern over the current operation of the ASC regime, the Government asked local planning authorities to undertake a review of ASCs in their area in order to satisfy themselves that their extent remains appropriate and necessary. The legislative scope of the ASC regime was to remain unchanged.

E. FLY-POSTING

24.31 There is no formal definition of 'fly-posting' in the 1990 Act or the Control of Advertisement Regulations 1992. It is, however, generally considered to apply to advertisements displayed on buildings and street furniture without the consent of the owner, contrary to the provisions of the regulations. It is often used indiscriminately to promote records, musical, or other events and market products such as food, drink, and clothing as well as business cards displayed in telephone boxes. Fly-posting is notoriously difficult to control, let alone eradicate. The reasons for this include: the time and resources necessary to identify who carried out the fly-posting, visiting the site, collecting evidence and revisiting the site to confirm whether the posters have been removed; the difficulties in prosecuting unincorporated organizations such as political groups; the low level of fines imposed and costs awarded; and the minimal deterrent effect of a successful prosecution.

24.32 It would appear that the very nature of the problem prevents the planning system from obtaining more effective control over fly-posting. In December 1998, the Government published an independent research report on the issue which recommended a number of changes to existing legislation and revised/updated guidance to local planning authorities in the form of a Good Practice Guide. In response, the Government amended s 224(5) of the 1990 Act to provide that the guilt of the owner or occupier may be excluded only by reason that the advertisement was displayed without his knowledge; or that he took all reasonable steps to prevent the display or, after the advertisement had been displayed, to secure its removal.

24.33 Furthermore, the Government amended s 225 of the 1990 Act to allow local authorities to remove placards or posters where they consider them to be in contravention of the Control of Advertisement Regulations.

24.34 Lastly, in an attempt to control the worst excesses of fly-posting, s 43 of the Anti-Social Behaviour Act 2003 provides for a local authority to issue a 'penalty notice' on any person the authority has reason to believe has committed a 'relevant offence' in the area of the authority. The Act makes the display of an advertisement in contravention of the Control of Advertisements Regulations one of the relevant offences. A proviso that may meet enforcement difficulties however, is that a penalty notice relating to fly-posting can only be given to a person if the authority believes that he personally affixed or placed the advertisement in position against or on the land.

24.35 The Localism Act 2011 ('the 2011 Act') has reformed the law relating to fly-posting. Section 127(1) inserts five new sections. A new s 225A allows a local planning authority to remove any display structure in their area which, in their opinion, is used for the display of illegal advertisements. A new s 225C allows local planning authorities to take action against persistent fly-posting on 'surfaces'. They may serve an action notice on the owner or occupier of the land where the surface is situated if it is known or can be discovered. If not, they may fix the notice to the surface. The action notice requires the owner or occupier to take specified measures to prevent or reduce the frequency of the unauthorized advertisements. Then a new s 225E modifies the notice procedure for statutory undertakers. If a notice under s 225C is served on a statutory undertaker, it can serve a counter-notice on the local planning authority specifying alternative measures which would have the same effect as the notice in dealing with fly-posting.

Also a new s 225F allows local planning authorities to take action against signs (graffiti) which it considers to be detrimental to the amenity of the area or offensive. **24.36**

F. DEVELOPMENT AND THE DISPLAY OF ADVERTISEMENTS

Where the display of advertisements in accordance with the Regulations involves the development of land, s 222 of the 1990 Act provides that planning permission for that development shall be deemed to be granted and that no application shall be necessary for that development under Part III of the Act. **24.37**

25

TREES, HEDGEROWS, AND HIGH HEDGES

| A. THE PROTECTION OF TREES | 25.01 | C. THE PROTECTION OF HEDGEROWS | 25.20 |
| B. COMPENSATION | 25.19 | D. THE CONTROL OF HIGH HEDGES | 25.34 |

A. THE PROTECTION OF TREES

Cutting down a tree does not appear to be development within s 55 of the 1990 Act; hence it is not subject to general development control. The Act contains provisions, however, to secure the preservation and planting of trees. Under s 197 of the 1990 Act, a duty is imposed on a local planning authority to ensure, whenever it is appropriate, that in granting planning permission for development adequate provision is made by the imposition of conditions, for the preservation or planting of trees. Indeed, in *St Vincent Housing Association v Secretary of State for Communities and Local Government* [2011] EWHC 3339 (Admin); [2012] JPL 845 it was held that if permission was granted for dwellings which would be overlooked by trees, this could lead to consent to cut down or cut back the trees. **25.01**

Under s 198, if it appears to a local planning authority that it is expedient in the interests of amenity to make provision for the preservation of trees or woodlands in its area, it may for that purpose make a tree preservation order with respect to such trees, groups of trees, areas of trees, or woodlands as may be specified in the order. In particular, the order may make provision for prohibiting the cutting down, topping, lopping, uprooting, wilful damage, or wilful destruction of trees except with the consent of the local planning authority, and for securing the replanting of any part of a woodland area which is felled in the course of forestry operations permitted by or under the order. **25.02**

25.03 The PPG (36-029-20140306), advises that 'area classification' (the so-called 'area order') should only be used in emergencies, and then only as a temporary measure until the trees within the area can be assessed properly and reclassified with a view to their replacement with individual or group classification where appropriate.

25.04 The Act does not contain a definition of the word 'tree'. According to Lord Denning MR in *Kent CC v Batchelor* (1976) 33 P & CR 185 (CA), a 'woodland' tree 'ought to be something over seven or eight inches in diameter'. Lord Denning's observations in the case, however, were obiter, and in a later case, *Bullock v Secretary of State for the Environment and Malvern Hills DC* [1980] JPL 461, it was said that the word 'tree' should bear its ordinary meaning and that what is or is not a tree is not to be defined by any particular diameter. This approach has been recently followed in *Palm Developments Ltd v Secretary of State for Communities and Local Government* [2009] EWHC 220 (Admin); [2009] 2 P & CR 16 where Cranston J held that a woodland tree preservation order could apply to protect saplings and extend to all trees in a woodland, even those which were planted or grew after the order was made. He pointed out that, unlike the Forestry Act 1967 and the protection given to trees in conservations areas by the Town and Country Planning (Trees) Regulations 1999 for trees in conservation areas, the law on tree preservation orders imposed no limit on the size of the trees that could be protected. He also held that there was also nothing illogical in tree preservation orders applying to future trees. As the purpose of a woodland tree preservation order was to safeguard the woodland as a whole, which depended on regeneration or new planting, it had to extend to trees which grew or were planted after the order was made. On the other hand, it would seem that a tree preservation order cannot apply to bushes, hedges, or shrubs and that if a hedgerow is made subject to such an order, then only the 'trees' in the hedgerow will be protected. The approach in *Palm Developments* was approved by the Court of Appeal in *Distinctive Properties (Ascot) Ltd v Secretary of State for Communities and Local Government* [2015] EWCA Civ 1250; [2016] 1 WLR 1839 per Sir David Keene at [42].

25.05 A tree preservation order cannot prohibit the cutting down, uprooting, topping, or lopping of trees which are dying or dead or have become dangerous, or where the cutting down, uprooting, topping, or lopping is in compliance with any obligations imposed under an Act of Parliament, or is necessary for the prevention or abatement of a nuisance or which is necessary in order to carry out development for which full planning permission has been granted. In order to trigger the exception relating to nuisance, the nuisance must be one which is actionable in law. There must be present some actual or imminent damage, not merely 'pure encroachment' of roots or branches into or over adjoining land. Furthermore, in considering the application of the exception, the possibility of alternative engineering solutions to abate or prevent the nuisance (such as underpinning of the neighbouring land) must be disregarded. However, if the owner could abate or prevent the nuisance by cutting down, uprooting, topping, or lopping the offending tree, to be within the exception the work must be the minimum necessary to do so (*Perrin v Northampton BC* [2007] EWCA Civ 1353; [2008] 1 WLR 1307). Note too that the order cannot prohibit work carried out in compliance with a tree felling licence (ss 15 and 198 of the Forestry Act 1967), or a forestry dedication plan or operations or covenant approved by the Forestry Commission (s 200 of the 1990 Act) during open-cast coal mining.

25.06 The 1990 Act provides for the enforcement of tree preservation orders. If any person, in contravention of a tree preservation order, cuts down, uproots, or wilfully destroys a tree, or wilfully damages, tops, or lops a tree in such a manner as to be likely to destroy it, he shall be guilty of an offence. A defendant shall on conviction be liable to an unlimited fine which may reflect the financial benefit which has accrued or is likely to accrue to him in consequence of the offence. In *Maidstone BC v Mortimer* (1980) 43 P & CR 67 (Div Court), it was held that the offence is an absolute offence and that proof of knowledge by the accused of the existence of an order is not required. The penalties may indeed be heavy. In one case ([1991] JPL 101), a property company was fined £50,000 for breach of a tree preservation order and ordered to pay the local authority's costs in the sum of £2,250. Under s 206 of the 1990 Act, if any tree is removed, uprooted, or destroyed in contravention of a tree preservation order the owner (unless the local planning authority dispenses with the requirement) must plant another tree of appropriate size and species in the same place as soon as he reasonably can. In such cases, the tree preservation order will then apply to the replacement tree. Similarly, if a tree is cut down because it is dead, dying, or dangerous, the landowner is under a duty to replace it.

25.07 If a landowner fails to comply with the requirements of this part of the Act, it provides that the local planning authority may serve a notice on the owner of the land, within four years of the failure, requiring him to plant a tree or trees of such a size as may be specified in the notice. There is a right of appeal against the notice to the Secretary of State. Once the notice has taken effect, the local authority may enter the land and take the steps required by the notice.

25.08 The Legal Aid, Sentencing and Publishing of Offenders Act 2012 and Localism Act 2011 made changes to s 206 of the 1990 Act. The main changes were as follows:

(a) removing the cap on the level of fine for a breach of s 206(1); and
(b) introducing a six-month period in which a prosecution under s 206(4) must be brought. The date runs from the date on which knowledge of evidence to justify proceedings under s 206(4) came into the prosecutor's knowledge. However,

that must not exceed three years from the date of the offence. Section 206(4C)–(4D) provide for the process for the prosecutor to do that. Those provisions do not apply in Wales.

Present changes to the law, made and prospective

25.09 The Town and Country Planning (Tree Preservation) (England) Regulations 2012 (SI 2012/605) provide for use of a standard application form for applications for consent under a tree preservation order. The explanatory notes provide that the new Regulations:

- i) include a new much shorter, simpler model form of TPO. This will be easier for authorities to administer and the general public to understand;
- ii) give all new TPOs immediate provisional effect (there will be no need to make a special direction to give them effect immediately, as at present);
- iii) reduce the administrative burden of authorities when notifying people of the making of new TPOs by requiring the service of copies only on the owner and occupier of the land on which the trees are situated and anyone else entitled to cut the trees;
- iv) qualify the scope of exempted works (particularly in respect of dead, dying and dangerous trees) and clarify the requirement for prior notification;
- v) introduce a default period of two years for consent of approved works;
- vi) remove the power to vary or revoke a consent to carry out work to a tree protected by a TPO (this is rarely used and only applies to TPOs made before 2 August 1999);
- vii) adopt one system, using conditions, to secure necessary replacement planting where consent is given to remove any tree protected by a TPO (so simplifying the system); and
- viii) provide a common system for compensation claims arising out of the refusal of consent or imposition of conditions, based on the current provisions that apply only to TPOs made after 1999.

As has been seen, if someone is aggrieved by a local authority's decision on their application to fell or prune a protected tree, or by its failure to make a decision, they have the right of appeal to the Secretary of State. Similar rights of appeal also apply in relation to notices enforcing replanting requirements, known as tree replacement notices. About 750 TPO appeals are made to the Secretary of State each year. The majority are determined on the basis of an exchange of written representations with a few being the subject of informal hearings. Even those appeals which follow the written route take an average of around 26 weeks from start to decision. In many cases the appeal is not a review of the merits of the local authority's decision but involves consideration of new information which is submitted by the parties with the appeal or even at a later stage. The result is that the case before the Secretary of State may differ significantly from that originally considered by the local planning authority.

25.10 A purpose of the new Regulations was to make the process more efficient and accessible to those using the system. This is to be achieved by introducing a fast track procedure for dealing with TPO appeals (including appeals against tree replacement notices). The appeal decision will be made on the basis of the application originally made to the local planning authority, together with any third party comments received at that time and following a visit to the site by an appointed Inspector. Where appropriate, the appeal will be handled by an Inspector with suitable arboricultural expertise.

25.11 The Regulations provide that an order shall specify the trees, groups of trees, or woodlands to which it relates and indicate their position by reference to a map. Where the order relates to a group of trees, the number of trees in the group must be specified. Once the authority has made the order, but before confirming it, a copy of the order must be served on the persons interested in the land affected, with a notice stating the reasons for making the order and a statement that objections or other representations may be made to the authority within 28 days. A copy of the order must also be made available for inspection, free of charge, at all reasonable hours, at the offices of the authority.

25.12 After having considered any objections or representations made in respect of the order, the authority may then confirm it, which it may do with or without modifications, with notice of confirmation being given to persons interested in the land affected by the order. Under the Regulations, a 'person interested' in relation to land affected by an order means every owner and occupier of the land and every other person whom the authority knows to be entitled to fell any of the trees to which the order relates or to work by surface working any materials in or under the land. Furthermore, land affected by the order includes adjoining land.

25.13 The order will not take effect until confirmed by the authority, though under s 201 of the Act, the local planning authority may include in the order a direction that it shall take effect immediately, in which case it remains in force for a period of six months or until the order is confirmed, whichever is the earlier. There is no right of appeal to the Secretary of State against the making of the order. Once the order is confirmed, it cannot be questioned in any legal proceedings whatsoever, except by way of application made within six weeks to the High Court under s 288 of the 1990 Act.

25.14 Any order made can be varied or revoked by the local planning authority. The person seeking consent must make an application to the authority identifying the tree or trees to which it relates, the work for which consent is sought and stating his reasons for making the application. The authority may then grant consent, either unconditionally or subject to conditions as the authority think fit, or refuse consent. In granting consent, the authority may require, by a direction given in writing, a replacement tree to be replanted. The direction may include requirements as to species, number of trees per hectare, the preparation of the land prior to planting, and the erection of fencing necessary to protect newly planted trees.

25.15 The applicant may appeal to the Secretary of State against the refusal of the authority to grant consent, or its failure to make a determination within the prescribed eight-week period.

25.16 As previously mentioned, protection is also given to trees which are not subject to a tree preservation order but which are located in a conservation area. Special provisions also apply to the Crown following the Planning and Compulsory Purchase Act 2004 which has made the Crown subject to the Planning Acts.

25.17 Until recently, the law concerning tree preservation orders has been contained in s 192 and Sch 8 of the 1990 Act, together with regulations made under powers given in the Act. It was decided, however, to transfer many of the provisions found in the body of the Act directly into regulations made thereunder. This was done under the following provisions of the Planning Act 2008:

> Section 192 and Schedule 8 which is introduced by this section, make amendments to provisions in TCPA 1990 concerning tree preservation orders. In short, they provide for the transfer of provisions from tree preservation orders into regulations.
>
> Subsections (2) to (6) of section 192 repeal various provisions of TCPA 1990 which set out provision that may be included in tree preservation orders, including:
> (1) provision prohibiting works to trees without the consent of the local planning authority;
> (2) exemptions which allow works to protected trees without consent;
> (3) provision regulating applications for consent to carry out works to trees, and appeals;
> (4) provision for the payment of compensation for loss or damage caused by tree preservation orders.
>
> Subsection (7) of section 192 enables these deleted provisions of TCPA 1990 to be replaced by provision included in regulations. For this purpose, it inserts seven new sections into the Act. New section 202A makes general provision about the regulations, which would be subject to the negative resolution procedure. New sections 202B to 202G contain additional details about the sort of provision that may be contained in the regulations. In particular, the regulations may include provision about: the form of tree preservation orders; the procedures to be followed where tree preservation orders are to be confirmed; the prohibited activities in relation to trees; applications for consent to carry out works to trees; powers to give consent to works subject to conditions; applying the tree preservation order to trees planted under a condition; appeals against decisions to refuse consent; entitlement to compensation following decisions on applications for consent; and the keeping of public registers containing information on tree preservation orders.
>
> Schedule 8 makes further amendments needed to give effect to the transfer of provisions from tree preservation orders to regulations.
>
> Section 193 makes transitional provisions about tree preservation orders. The regime set out in tree preservation regulations will apply to trees identified in an existing order in place of the existing provisions.

25.18 These provisions came into force in England on 6 April 2012 and the 2012 Regulations were made pursuant to s 202A and apply to England.

B. COMPENSATION

Part 6 of the 2012 Regulations makes provision for compensation if a person has suffered loss or damage caused or incurred in consequence of the refusal of any consent required by an order, or by the grant of consent subject to conditions, compensation shall be payable by the authority. In order to claim compensation, the claim must be made within 12 months of the date of the authority's decision (or the Secretary of State's on appeal). Furthermore, no claim may be made if the loss or damage amounts to less than £500. In addition, reg 24(4) now provides that no compensation shall be payable in respect of any loss of development value or other diminution in the value of land resulting from the refusal of consent or conditional grant. **25.19**

C. THE PROTECTION OF HEDGEROWS

The Regulations

In 1994, a report by the Institute of Terrestrial Ecology revealed that between 1990 and 1993, an annual average of 3,600 kilometres of hedgerows in England and Wales were removed or destroyed. As a result, the Government took powers in s 97 of the Environment Act 1995 to enable it to protect important hedgerows, but left the detailed arrangements for doing so to be set out in regulations. This has now been done by the Hedgerows Regulations 1997, SI 1997/1160 which came into force on 1 June 1997. **25.20**

The Regulations make no attempt to define the term 'hedgerow'. It should be noted however, that the *Oxford English Dictionary* defines a hedgerow as 'a row of bushes forming a hedge with the trees, etc growing out of it'. **25.21**

It has been estimated that the Regulations are at most likely to protect only about 20 per cent of existing hedgerows. One of the reasons for this is that protection afforded by the Regulations applies only to 'important' hedgerows, though in order to facilitate their protection the Regulations apply to a far wider class of hedgerows. **25.22**

By reg 3, the Regulations are to apply to any hedgerow growing in, or adjacent to, any common land, protected land, or land used for agriculture, forestry, or the breeding or keeping of horses, ponies, and donkeys, if the hedgerow has a continuous length of 20 metres or more, or meets another hedgerow at each end. **25.23**

'Protected land' for this purpose means land managed as a nature reserve pursuant to s 21 of the National Parks and Access to the Countryside Act 1949 and **25.24** land notified as an area of special scientific interest under s 28 of the Wildlife and Countryside Act 1981.

25.25 The Regulations, however, do not apply to any hedgerow within the curtilage of, or making a boundary of the curtilage of, a dwellinghouse.

25.26 Before removing a hedgerow to which the Regulations apply, the owner must first notify the local planning authority that he proposes to do so. The form of notice is set out in Sch 4 to the Regulations and is called a 'hedgerow removal notice'.

25.27 The following activities may, however, proceed without *any* prior notification to the authority:

(a) removal to allow necessary or reasonable access, either in place of an existing opening or where none is available;
(b) removal to give assistance in emergencies;
(c) removal for national defence purposes;
(d) development authorized by planning permission; or for which planning permission is deemed to have been granted, except for most of the classes of development for which planning permission is granted under Art 3 of the General Permitted Development Order;
(e) work undertaken by drainage authorities and authorized by legislation for the purpose of flood defence or land drainage;
(f) work to prevent the spread of, or ensuring the eradication of, a plant or tree pest notifiable under plant health legislation;
(g) proper management practice such as normal trimming, coppicing, and laying; and
(h) work carried out by the Secretary of State of his functions with respect to highways for which he is the highway authority.

25.28 Following the receipt of a hedgerow removal notice and after consulting with the parish council in England or any community council in Wales within whose area the hedgerow is situated, the local planning authority may give to the owner written notice that the hedgerow may be removed, or serve on the owner a notice called a 'hedgerow retention notice' indicating that the hedgerow may not be removed. If no hedgerow retention notice has been served by the authority within 42 days of the receipt by the authority of a hedgerow removal notice, the owner is free to proceed to carry out the work proposed in that notice.

25.29 It is a requirement of the Regulations that unless a hedgerow retention notice has been served, the removal of a hedgerow must be carried out in accordance with the proposal specified in the hedgerow removal notice, and be completed within two years of the date that notice was served on the authority.

Limitation on control

25.30 Although notice of proposed removal of a hedgerow is required to be given for a wide class of hedgerow, reg 5(6) provides that a local planning authority:

(a) shall not give a hedgerow retention notice in respect of a hedgerow which is not an 'important' hedgerow;
(b) shall give such a notice in respect of an 'important' hedgerow unless satisfied, having regard in particular to the reasons given for its proposed removal in the hedgerow removal notice, that there are circumstances which justify the hedgerow's removal.

25.31 The definition of an 'important' hedgerow is thus crucial to the authority's exercise of the power to prevent its removal. Regulation 4 states that a hedgerow is 'important' if it, or the hedgerow of which it is a stretch:

(a) has existed for 30 years or more; and
(b) satisfies at least one of the criteria listed in Part II of Sch 1 to the Regulations.

25.32 The criteria listed in Part II of Sch 1 are too extensive to be quoted *in extenso* in this work, but they all relate to hedgerows which have some archaeological or historical significance or are important to wildlife or landscape qualities.

25.33 The Regulations also contain provisions which make contravention of a number of the regulations a criminal offence (reg 7); require replacement of any hedgerow removed in contravention of the Regulations (reg 8); provide for appeals against hedgerow retention notices to the Secretary of State (reg 9); require the local planning authority to maintain records (reg 10); allow for enforcement by way of injunction (reg 11); and provide for rights of entry (regs 12 to 14). There are also further provisions for hedgerows owned by local planning authorities (reg 15) and on ecclesiastical property (reg 16).

D. THE CONTROL OF HIGH HEDGES

25.34 In the last few years, concern has been expressed over the way in which high hedges (often containing Leylandii) on private property can cause a nuisance to neighbouring properties.

25.35 An attempt to deal with this has been made by the provisions of Part 8 of the Anti-Social Behaviour Act 2003. Under the Act, if it is not possible for people to settle their hedge dispute amicably, either of the parties can refer their dispute to the local authority. For this to be done:

(a) the hedge in question must be formed wholly or predominantly of a line of two or more evergreen or semi-evergreen trees or shrubs; and
(b) must rise to a height of more than two metres above ground level.

In addition:

(a) the hedge must act, to some degree, as a barrier to light or access; and
(b) because of its height, adversely affect the complainant's reasonable enjoyment of their domestic property.

25.36 Domestic property is defined as a dwelling or garden or yard used or enjoyed wholly or mainly in connection with a dwelling.

25.37 In each case the authority (who may charge a fee to be paid by the complainant) must consider initially whether the complaint is justified. If it does so, it can decide the action that should be taken in order to remedy the adverse effect. This is done by the authority serving a 'nuisance notice'. The notice, however, cannot require the hedge to be reduced to a height of less than two metres above ground level, or indeed, require it to be removed altogether.

25.38 Power is given to the authority to specify in the notice the 'initial action' which must be taken before the end of the compliance period; as well as any preventative action it is considered should be taken after the end of the compliance period where the hedge remains on the land.

25.39 The Act provides for a right of appeal by the owner or occupier of the land affected to appeal to the Secretary of State. The High Hedges (Appeals) (England) Regulations 2005 (SI 2005/711), deals with the procedure for appeals. The appeal must be made within 28 days of issue of the remedial notice. The Secretary of State may then appoint a person to hear and determine the appeal on his behalf. He may on appeal quash the remedial notice, vary it, or himself issue a notice where none was issued by the local authority.

25.40 If the hedge owner fails to comply with a remedial notice, he will be liable on conviction in the magistrates' court to a level three fine (up to £1,000). In addition, the local authority would have default powers to go in and do the required work and recover the cost of so doing from the hedge owner.

26

CONSERVATION OF NATURAL HABITATS AND PROTECTED SPECIES AND BIODIVERSITY

| A. THE HABITATS REGULATIONS 2017 | 26.02 | B. CASE LAW | 26.13 |

Another impact made on domestic planning law by the country's membership of the European Community has arisen from the need to implement the terms of Council Directive 79/409/ EC on the Conservation of Wild Birds and Council Directive 92/43/EC on the Conservation of Natural Habitats and of Wild Fauna and Flora. **26.01**

A. THE HABITATS REGULATIONS 2017

The obligations under these Directives are now implemented by the Conservation of Habitats and Species Regulations 2017 (SI 2017/1012). The Regulations apply to sites that are designated as Special Areas of Conservation (SACs) under the Habitats Directive and also to sites classified as Special Protection Areas (SPAs) under the EC Council Directive on the Conservation of Wild Birds. The Habitats Directive applies a common protection regime to SACs and SPAs, and they are referred to collectively in the Regulations as 'European sites'. As with the SEA and EIA regimes, the draft Conservation of Habitats and Species (Amendment) (EU Exit) Regulations 2019, published under the provisions of the European Union (Withdrawal Act) 2018, appear to suggest the Habitats regime will continue for some time after the UK's exit from the European Union. **26.02**

Regulation 63 provides: **26.03**

> A competent authority, before deciding to undertake, or give any consent, permission or other authorisation for, a plan or project which—
> (a) is likely to have a significant effect on a European site in Great Britain (either alone or in combination with other plans or projects), and

(b) is not directly connected with or necessary to the management of the site, shall make an appropriate assessment of the implications for the site in view of the site's conservation objectives.

The regulation provides that for the purposes of the assessment, the competent authority shall consult the relevant nature conservation body and, if it considers it appropriate, take the opinion of the general public, by such steps as it considers appropriate.

26.04 Circular 06/2005 'Biodiversity and geological conservation' sets out the approach to be followed in the consideration of development which may affect a European site. The PPG (8-011-20140612) sets out that Defra is working on replacement advice, so the Circular appears to remain in force in the meantime. The National Planning Policy Framework draws attention in Chapter 15 of to the duty to protect the natural environment and to conserve and enhance biodiversity and further the conservation of habitats and species of principal importance. Applying the Circular (para 99) in *Bagshaw v Wyre Borough Council* [2014] EWHC 508 (Admin), Stewart J found that a planning authority had failed to ascertain the presence or otherwise of protected species prior to the grant of permission and so quashed the permission.

26.05 The competent authority (normally the local planning authority or Secretary of State) may agree to the plan or project only after having ascertained that it will not adversely affect the integrity of the European site. Regulation 64, however, provides that:

(1) If the competent authority is satisfied that, there being no alternative solutions, the plan or project must be carried out for imperative reasons of overriding public interest (which, subject to paragraph (2), may be of a social or economic nature), it may agree to the plan or project notwithstanding a negative assessment of the implications for the European site or the European offshore marine site (as the case may be).
(2) Where the site concerned hosts a priority natural habitat type or a priority species, the reasons referred to in paragraph (1) must be either—
  (a) reasons relating to human health, public safety or beneficial consequences of primary importance to the environment; or
  (b) any other reasons which the competent authority, having due regard to the opinion of the European Commission, considers to be imperative reasons of overriding public interest.

26.06 If the local planning authority intends to grant planning permission despite a negative assessment of the implications for a European site, the authority must first notify the Secretary of State, who thus may use his power to call in the application. By reg 70 the assessment provisions are also made to apply to the grant of planning permission on an application under Part III of the 1990 Act, or an appeal under s 78, or where it follows from the service of the purchase notice, enforcement notice, or discontinuance order.

26.07 Regulation 71 requires the review of existing planning permissions which have not been fully implemented and which are likely significantly to affect a designated SPA or classified SAC; and if necessary, the taking of appropriate action.

26.08 The duty to review applies to any planning permission or deemed planning permission except that granted by development order or by virtue of the adoption of, or alterations to, a simplified planning zone scheme. The duty does not apply to a permission where the development has been completed, or which is granted for a limited period that has expired, or which was subject to a time condition relating to commencement and that time has elapsed without the development having begun.

26.09 Under reg 72, where the competent authority ascertains that the carrying out or continuation of the development would adversely affect the integrity of a European site, it must consider whether any adverse effects could be overcome by a planning obligation made under s 106 of the 1990 Act and, if so, invite those concerned to enter into such an obligation. If no such obligation is entered into, the competent authority must proceed to use its powers under the 1990 Act either to revoke or modify the planning permission or require the discontinuance of a use or the removal of buildings or works so as to overcome the adverse effects.

26.10 The Regulations prevent the GPDO permitting development rights which adversely affect the integrity of European site or offshore marine site without written notification from the planning authority. Regulation 75 provides:

> It is a condition of any planning permission granted by a general development order made on or after 30th November 2017, that development which—
> (a) is likely to have a significant effect on a European site or a European offshore marine site (either alone or in combination with other plans or projects), and
> (b) is not directly connected with or necessary to the management of the site, must not be begun until the developer has received written notification of the approval of the local planning authority under regulation 77 (approval of local planning authority).

26.11 Regulation 76 provides for the opinion of the appropriate nature conservation body to be sought that the development is not likely to have the effect mentioned in reg 75(a) and that such opinion shall be conclusive of that question for the purpose of relying on the planning permission granted by the order. Alternatively, reg 77 provides that a person intending to carry out development in reliance on the permission granted by the order may apply in writing to the local planning authority for their approval (with the appropriate fee), which the authority must then consider after taking into account any representations made by the appropriate nature conservation body.

26.12 Regulations 80–83 deal with local development orders, neighbourhood development orders, simplified planning zones, and enterprise zones coming into force on or after 30 November 2017.

B. CASE LAW

26.13 The status of a site as an SPA can have unusual consequences. In *R (Medway DC) v Secretary of State for Transport, Local Government and the Regions* [2002] EWHC 2516 (Admin); [2003] JPL 583, the Secretary of State, in a consultation paper on airport development in the South East, had omitted to include Gatwick Airport as a possible site for expansion. This was because it had been agreed in 1979 that no second runway would be built there before 2019. The High Court held that it was irrational not to include Gatwick as a possible site for expansion since if Cliffe in Kent, the site of an SPA which was included as a possible site for airport expansion were to be chosen for the expansion, it would have significant adverse effects for the SPA. It was necessary to include Gatwick in the consultation paper because of the obligation to consider alternatives before giving any grant of planning permission where there would be adverse effects on the SPA.

26.14 The duty under reg 63 to assess the implications of development for European sites has given rise to other litigation. In *Hart District Council v Secretary of State for Communities and Local Government* [2008] EWHC 1204 (Admin); [2008] 2 P & CR 16, an unsuccessful challenge was made to the decision of the Secretary of State to allow appeals by the District Council against the Council's decision to refuse planning permission for residential development in the Thames Basin Special Protection Area. It was claimed that mitigation reasons could as a matter of law be considered at the screening stage. The court considered this to be correct. *Hart* was expressly approved by the Supreme Court in *R (Champion) v North Norfolk District Council* [2015] UKSC 52; [2015] 1 WLR 3710.

26.15 However, the approach in *Hart* has now been held to be contrary to the Directive by the CJEU in *People Over Wind v Teoranta* [2018] PTSR 1668. The case concerned a challenge to cable being laid which was necessary to connect a wind farm to the electricity grid. Planning permission was granted for the windfarm, subject to various conditions, including one which required the development to be 'managed in accordance with a Construction Management Plan, which shall be submitted to, and agreed in writing with, the planning authority prior to commencement of development'. The claimants argued that the laying of the cable would have an adverse effect on the Nore pearl muscle (an Annex II species present in two SACs). The laying of the cable did not require permission but would be required if the project required an appropriate assessment. The screening opinion concluded that without protective measures the development was a potential for adverse effects, but that taking into account sedimentation of gravels, there would be no adverse effect and thus no appropriate assessment was required. The CJEU found that approach to be in breach of Art 6(3) of the Habitats Directive, in particular at [40]:

In the light of all the foregoing considerations, the answer to the question referred is that Article 6(3) of the Habitats Directive must be interpreted as meaning that, in order to determine whether it is necessary to carry out, subsequently, an appropriate assessment of the implications, for a site concerned, of a plan or project, it is not appropriate, at the screening stage, to take account of the measures intended to avoid or reduce the harmful effects of the plan or project on that site.

26.16 A further discussion of the *People Over Wind* case can be found in S Tromans QC and V Hutton, 'Mitigation Measures and Appropriate Assessments: A Change in the Wind from Luxembourg: People Over Wind v Teoranta' [2018] 8 JPL 896 and A Bowes, 'Re-thinking Mitigation at the Screening Stage' [2018] 8 JPL 893. There is no prescribed form for an appropriate assessment and the obligations at reg 63 are not especially onerous. Accordingly, the effects of the judgment are perhaps not that significant. Moreover, in *R (Langton) v Secretary of State for Communities and Local Government* [2018] EWHC 2190 (Admin) Sir Ross Cranston distinguished *People Over Wind*, finding that the licensing conditions were not 'mitigation' rather were 'integral features of the project' at [157]. Interestingly, that was the submission of Natural England. Whilst mitigation may be considered as part of an appropriate assessment, the CJEU confirmed in *Grace & Sweetman v An Bord Pleanala* [2018] Env LR 37 that compensatory measures must not be considered as part of an appropriate assessment under Art 6(3). Rather, those kinds of measures fell to be considered within an assessment under Art 6(4) (ie whether there exist imperative reasons of overriding public importance).

26.17 In *R (on the application of Lewis) v Redcar and Cleveland Borough Council* [2007] EWHC 3166 (Admin); [2008] JPL 1156 the High Court upheld the manner in which the Council had considered and granted planning permission for development in an SPA, and that it was not invalidated by any breach of what was then reg 48 of the 1984 Regulations.

26.18 Other cases of relevance to this area are *ADT Auctions Ltd v Secretary of State for the Environment, Transport and the Regions* (2000 WL 389632) and *Buglife v Thurrock Thames Gateway Development Corporation* [2008] EWHC 475 (Admin); [2008] Env LR 31.

26.19 The Conservation of Habitats and Species Regulations 2017 also set out a system of strict protection for European Protected Species (EPS) which include in Britain great crested newts and all species of bat, otter, and dormice. Article 12(1) of the Habitats Directive requires member states to establish a system of strict protection for EPS by prohibiting the deterioration or destruction of their breeding sites and resting places. Further, s 40 of the Natural Environment and Rural Communities Act 2006 imposes a duty on all public authorities in England and Wales to have regard in the exercise of their functions, to the purpose of conserving diversity. Article 16(1) of the Habitats Directive permits member states to derogate from the requirements of Art 12 for imperative reasons of overriding interest provided that there is no satisfactory alternative and the derogation is not detrimental to

Conservation of Natural Habitats and Protected Species and Biodiversity

the maintenance of the populations of the species concerned at a favourable conservation status in their natural range.

26.20 Regulation 43 of the 2017 Regulations transposes the above requirements by making it a criminal offence to carry out the prohibited activities without a licence unless a licence has been granted. Licences are granted by Natural England; see s 78 of the Natural Environment and Communities Act 2006. So, while the effect on an EPS is clearly a material consideration, the actual licensing is not carried out by the local planning authority. However, reg 9(3) of the 2017 Regulations provides that a competent authority (in substance any public body) in exercising any of its functions must have regard to the requirements of the Habitats Directive insofar as those requirements are affected by the exercise of those functions. This clearly covers a local planning authority carrying out its planning functions. The exact relationship between the development control system and the licensing by Natural England has recently been considered by the Supreme Court in *R (Morge) v Hampshire CC* [2011] UKSC 2; [2011] 1 WLR 268.

26.21 Previously, in *R (on the application of Woolley) v Cheshire East BC* [2009] EWHC 1227 (Admin); [2010] Env LR 5 it was held that a local planning authority's duty under the Regulations to have regard to the requirements of Directive 92/43 in the exercise of its functions was not satisfied where it simply noted the existence of the Directive and referred to the need for a licence. Equally it would not have been sufficient had the authority also made it a condition of any planning permission that such a licence be obtained. Instead the authority had to engage with the provisions of the Directive and consider whether the derogation requirements within it might be met. HH Judge Waksman QC held that this meant that if it was clear that a licence would not be granted the planning authority should refuse permission.

26.22 In *Morge* Hampshire CC granted planning permission for a rapid bus service, which would run along the route of an old railway line which had become an ecological corridor for flora and fauna. Natural England had objected on the grounds of the impact on bats but withdrew their objection when it was found that the site contained no roosting bats though it was used by bats foraging for food. The Supreme Court held that the duty of the local planning authority is limited to that set out in reg 9(3) of the Regulations and the LPA does not have to consider whether Natural England would grant or refuse a licence. Ward LJ in the Court of Appeal had laid down that if the planning committee had concluded that Natural England would not grant a licence or was uncertain, it must refuse permission. While if it thought it was likely that a licence would be granted the committee could grant planning permission. If it was uncertain either way it must refuse permission. The Supreme Court basically held that this would be wrong in principle as the primary responsibility for ensuring compliance with the Directive was vested in Natural England. Planning permission should only be refused under the Directive if the proposed development would both be likely to offend Art 12(1) and be unlikely to be licensed pursuant to the derogation powers. A grant of planning permission is no longer a defence to a prosecution for not having a licence and so if planning permission is granted but a licence refused Natural England could enforce the Directive by bringing a criminal prosecution. For a further discussion on *Morge* see: L Warren, 'Bats or Buses: A Battle for a Beeching Cast-off—R. (on the application of Morge) v Hampshire CC' [2011] 13(3) Env L R 205; J Lowther, 'Determining the Meaning of "Disturbance" for European Protected Species' [2011] 23(2) J Env L 319; and G Nardell and P Simpson, 'A Disturbance in the Law? Implications of Recent Case Law on the Species Protection Provisions of the Habitats Directive' [2011] 9 JPL 1155.

The approach of the Supreme Court in *Morge* has since been followed in *R (on the application of Prideaux) v Buckingham CC* [2013] EWHC 1054; [2013] Env LR 32 and *William Walton v Scottish Ministers* [2012] UKSC 44; [2012] PTSR 51. This approach means that planning authorities will to some extent have to second guess whether Natural England would consider that a licence is required and if so whether a licence would be granted. In *Elliot v Secretary of State for Communities and Local Government* [2012] EWHC 1574; [2013] Env LR 5, Keith J held that the Secretary of State was entitled to consider that a licence would be granted on the grounds that Natural England were not objecting to the proposed development. A similar approach was taken in *Prideaux*. **26.23**

The requirements for a planning authority under the Regulations were neatly summarized by Jay J in *Wealden District Council v Secretary of State for Communities and Local Government* [2017] EWHC 351 (Admin); [2017] Env LR 31 at [44]: **26.24**

i) the consideration of whether there are likely significant effects is a 'trigger' for an appropriate assessment: *R. (Champion) v North Norfolk* DC [2015] 1 WLR 3710 at paragraph 41; *Ashdown Forest Economic Development LLP v Wealden District Council & Anor* [2015] EWCA Civ 681 at paragraph 12; *R (Mynydd y Gwynt) v. Secretary of State for Business Energy and Industrial Strategy* [2016] EWHC 2581 at paragraph 20;

ii) where there is a risk of significant adverse effects to a protected site, there should be an appropriate assessment; and such a risk exists 'if it cannot be excluded on the basis of objective information that the plan or project will have significant effects on the site concerned'; and 'in case of doubt as to the absence of significant effects such an assessment must be carried out': the *Waddenzee* case (Case C-127/02) [2004] ECR-1 7405 at paragraph 44; *R (Hart District Council) v. SSCLG* [2008] 2 P&CR 16 at paragraph 78; *Mynydd y Gwynt* [although this should now be seen in light of *People Over Wind* (above)];

iii) 'appropriate' is not a technical term but means that the assessment should be appropriate to satisfy the responsible authority that the project will not adversely affect the integrity of the site concerned, to a 'high standard of investigation'; and this issue is a matter of judgment for the authority: *Champion*, at paragraph 41; *Mynydd y Gwynt* , at paragraph 20;

iv) in respect of the second stage the competent authority must be certain that the plan or project in question will not adversely affect the integrity of their site concerned: Waddenzee at paragraphs 56–57. There should be 'no reasonable scientific doubt' remaining as to the absence of such effects (paragraph 59); *Sweetman and others v An Bord Pleanála* (Case C-258/11) [2014] PTSR 1092 at paragraphs 45–49;

v) this involves a 'strict' precautionary approach: *Smyth v. Secretary of State for Communities and Local Government* [2015] EWCA Civ 174 at paragraph 61;

vi) the appropriate assessment 'cannot have lacunae and must contain complete, precise and definitive findings and conclusions capable of removing all reasonable scientific doubt as to the effects of the works proposed on the protected site concerned': *Sweetman* at paragraph 44;

vii) a third party alleging that there was a risk that cannot be excluded on the basis of objective information must produce credible evidence that there was a real as opposed to hypothetical risk that must have been considered: *Boggis v. Natural England* [2009] EWCA Civ 1061 at paragraph 37;

viii) a decision-maker discharging its duties under the Habitats Directive and the Habitats Regulations should give the views of a statutory consultee considerable weight (*Ashdown Forest Economic Development LLP v SSCLG, Wealden District Council* [2014] EWHC 406 (Admin) at paragraph 110). However, that advice is not binding and it does not have to be given such weight if cogent reasons can be given for departing from it: see *R (Akester) v. DEFRA* [2010] EWHC 232 (Admin) at paragraph 112; *Wealden DC v. SSCLG* [2016] EWHC 247 (Admin) at paragraphs 91 and 95; *DLA Delivery v. Lewes District Council* [2015] EWHC 2311 at paragraph 32; *Mynydd y Gwynt* at paragraph 20.

27

REMEDIES FOR ADVERSE PLANNING DECISIONS

A. COMPENSATION FOR RESTRICTIONS ON DEVELOPMENT 27.01
B. COMPENSATION FOR THE REVOCATION OR MODIFICATION OF PLANNING PERMISSIONS UNDER SECTION 97 OF THE 1990 ACT 27.08
C. COMPENSATION FOR DISCONTINUANCE OF A USE OR THE ALTERATION OR REMOVAL OF BUILDINGS OR WORKS UNDER SECTION 102 OF THE 1990 ACT 27.14
D. PURCHASE NOTICES 27.16

A. COMPENSATION FOR RESTRICTIONS ON DEVELOPMENT

27.01 The general principle of allowing compensation to owners who suffer loss through the exercise by a planning authority of its statutory powers to control development was recognized in early legislation.

27.02 Thus the Housing, Town Planning etc Acts of 1909 to 1925 gave a right to compensation, with certain exceptions, for any injurious affection to an owner's interest in land due to the making of a town planning scheme. The Town and Country Planning Act 1932 also gave a right to compensation for injurious affection to land due to the coming into operation of any provisions in a town planning scheme, or the doing of any work under it, which infringed or curtailed the owner's legal rights.

27.03 These earlier Acts were concerned, however, with the effects of the coming into operation of a 'town planning scheme'. But when, under the Town and Country Planning Act 1947, the town planning scheme was replaced by the much more flexible 'development plan' and planning permission became obligatory for all forms of 'development', the right to compensation (if any) became related to the actual decision taken by the planning authority in any particular case and not to the provisions of the development plan.

27.04 By 1990, the law provided for the payment of compensation for adverse planning decisions in two distinct situations:

(a) planning decisions restricting development other than 'new development' (contained in the now repealed s 114 of the 1990 Act); and

(b) restrictions on new development where land has an 'unexpended balance of development value' (Part V of the 1990 Act).

27.05 In 1991, the Government decided, in the Planning and Compensation Act 1991, to repeal the right to compensation in both cases.

27.06 As regards (a) in para 27.04, the repeal was made retrospectively to apply to cases where the relevant application for planning permission was made on or after 16 November 1990. It was considered that the payment of compensation for restriction on development other than new development (often referred to as development within the 'existing use of land') was regarded as outdated and gave rise to abuse by stimulating applications for planning permission simply in order to obtain compensation for any refusal. According to the Government, the opportunities for developers to exploit the right to compensation under s 114 of the 1990 Act were a matter of concern, particularly in conservation areas in parts of central London where property prices were high. The purpose in making the repeal of s 114 retrospective to 16 November 1990 (the day following publication of the original 1991 Bill) was to prevent a flood of applications for planning permission being made in order to elicit payment of compensation before the law had been changed.

27.07 With regard to the repeal of the provisions for the payment of compensation for restrictions on new development, (b) in para 27.04, the view taken by the Government was that the number of successful claims had become very small, whilst the cost of administrative work in examining potential claims and in recovering any compensation paid where planning permission was subsequently granted for development was no longer justified.

B. COMPENSATION FOR THE REVOCATION OR MODIFICATION OF PLANNING PERMISSIONS UNDER SECTION 97 OF THE 1990 ACT

27.08 Where an order revoking or modifying a planning permission has been made, s 107 of the 1990 Act provides for the payment of compensation by the local planning authority under the following heads:

(a) expenditure in carrying out work which is rendered abortive by the revocation or modification; or
(b) loss or damage otherwise sustained which is directly attributable to the revocation or modification.

27.09 For the purposes of these provisions, any expenditure incurred in the preparation of plans for the purposes of any work, or upon other similar matters preparatory to it, are to be taken to be included in the expenditure incurred in carrying out that work. No compensation, however, can be paid for any work carried out before the grant of the permission which has been revoked or modified.

27.10 Compensation will include any depreciation in the value of an interest in the land. The measure of compensation will be the amount by which the value of the claimant's interest, with the benefit of the original planning permission, exceeded the value of that interest with the planning permission revoked or modified under the order. Values are based on the rules in s 5 of the Land Compensation Act 1961, so far as applicable, and it must be assumed that planning permission would be granted for development falling within paras 1 and 2 of Sch 3 to the 1990 Act. The section has been modified in its application to development consisting of the winning and working of minerals.

27.11 The Act also provides that where planning permission for the development of land has been granted by a development order and that permission is withdrawn, whether by the revocation or amendment of the order or by the issue of directions, and on a subsequent application for planning permission for that development the application is refused, or is granted subject to conditions (other than those previously imposed by the development order), the provisions of s 107 are to apply as if the planning permission granted by the development order had been expressly granted under the Act and then revoked or modified by an order under s 97 (s 108).

27.12 Section 108 further provides, however, that where planning permission granted by development order is withdrawn by revocation or amendment of the order, compensation will only be payable if the subsequent application for planning permission is made within 12 months of the date on which the revocation or amendment became operative.

27.13 The main purpose of this provision is to ensure that a right to compensation does not exist in perpetuity simply because a type of development was once permitted development under a development order. However, a one-year period of grace is allowed to provide compensation for a person who was in the process of undertaking a development for which permission under a development order was then withdrawn, and who may already have incurred expenditure in reliance on that permission.

C. COMPENSATION FOR DISCONTINUANCE OF A USE OR THE ALTERATION OR REMOVAL OF BUILDINGS OR WORKS UNDER SECTION 102 OF THE 1990 ACT

27.14 Any person who suffers loss in consequence of such an order, either through depreciation in the value of his land, or by disturbance, or by expense incurred in complying with the order, is entitled, under s 115 of the 1990 Act, to compensation from the local planning authority, provided his claim is made within 12 months.

27.15 Compensation for depreciation in the value of land will be assessed in accordance with the rules in s 5 of the Land Compensation Act 1961, subject to a reduction in respect of the value to the claimant of any timber, apparatus, or other materials removed for the purpose of complying with the order.

D. PURCHASE NOTICES

27.16 Sections 137 to 148 of the 1990 Act contain provisions enabling the owner of an interest in land affected by a planning decision or order to require the purchase of that interest. This has sometimes been described as a form of 'compulsory purchase in reverse', since it is the owner who initiates the proceedings leading to the acquisition of his interest.

27.17 The Act provides that where, on an application for planning permission to develop any land, permission is refused or is granted subject to conditions, then if the owner of the land claims:

(a) that the land has become incapable of reasonably beneficial use in its existing state; and
(b) in a case where planning permission was granted subject to conditions or was modified by the imposition of conditions, that the land cannot be rendered capable of reasonably beneficial use by the carrying out of the permitted development in accordance with those conditions; and
(c) in any case, that the land cannot be rendered capable of reasonably beneficial use by the carrying out of any other development for which planning permission has been granted or for which the local planning authority or the Secretary of State has undertaken to grant planning permission,

he may, within 12 months from the date of the planning decision, serve on the council of the district or London borough in which the land is situated, a notice requiring that council to purchase his interest in the land.

27.18 There is no statutory definition of the term 'reasonably beneficial use' but, following the case of *R v Minister of Housing and Local Government, ex parte Chichester RDC* [1960] WLR 587 (Div Court), it seems that the test is not whether the land is less valuable to the owner than if developed in accordance with the owner's wishes. Rather, the test is whether the use is reasonably beneficial to the owner in all the relevant circumstances of the particular site. Use by a prospective owner may be taken into account, but only where there is evidence to conclude that there is in fact a prospective purchaser for the land in question. In *Wain v Secretary of State for the Environment* (1981) 44 P &CR 289 the Court of Appeal held that, if part of the land was capable of reasonable beneficial use, then the purchase notice could not be confirmed. In such a case presumably it would still be open to the owner to apply for planning permission for the area of land that was not capable of reasonably beneficial use and then serve another notice in respect of that land only. It was also held in *Balco Transports Services Ltd v Secretary of State for the Environment (No 2)* [1986] JPL 123 that a purchase notice could succeed even if the reason why the land was incapable of reasonably beneficial use was because of unlawful development (such as using land as a refuse tip or for sorting scrap) as long as it was now too late to take enforcement action.

27.19 The Secretary of State's policy guidance, contained in Circular 13/83, 'Purchase Notices', at para 13, says:

> In considering what capacity for use the land has, relevant factors are the physical state of the land, its size, shape and surroundings, and the general pattern of land-uses in the area; a use of relatively low value may be regarded as reasonably beneficial if such a use is common for similar land in the vicinity ... Profit may be a useful comparison in certain circumstances, but the absence of profit (however calculated) is not necessarily material: the concept of reasonably beneficial use is not synonymous with profit.

In *Colley v Canterbury City Council* [1992] JPL 925, the Court of Appeal expressed agreement with that approach.

27.20 For the purpose of determining what is a 'reasonably beneficial' use of the land, no account shall be taken of any prospective use of the land which would involve the carrying out of development other than any development specified in paras 1 or 2 of Sch 3 to the 1990 Act.

27.21 The council on whom a purchase notice is served shall, within three months of such service, serve a responding notice on the owner stating either:

(a) that the council is willing to comply with it; or
(b) that another local authority or statutory undertakers specified in the response notice have agreed to comply with it in their place; or
(c) that for reasons specified the council is not willing to comply with the purchase notice and has not found any other local authority or statutory undertakers who will agree to comply with it in its place, and that a copy of the

purchase notice and of the response notice has therefore been sent to the Secretary of State.

27.22 In cases (a) and (b) in para 27.21, the council on whom the purchase notice was served, or the other authority who has agreed to comply with it, as the case may be, will be deemed to be authorized to acquire the owner's interest in the land and to have served a notice to treat on him on the same date as the service of the response notice.

27.23 In case (c) in para 27.21 the council on whom the purchase notice is served must send a copy of it and its response notice to the Secretary of State together with its reasons for being unwilling to comply with it.

27.24 Before confirming, or taking any other action, the Secretary of State must give notice of his proposed action to the person who served the notice, to the local authority on whom it was served, to the local planning authority and to any other local authority or statutory undertakers who might be substituted for the authority on whom the notice was served. He must also afford to any of these persons or authorities the opportunity of a hearing if they so require.

27.25 After such hearing the Secretary of State may decide to take action available to him under the Act, other than that specified in his notice to the parties concerned.

27.26 The following courses of action are open to the Secretary of State:

(a) to confirm the purchase notice if satisfied that the land is in fact incapable of reasonably beneficial use;
(b) to confirm the notice, but to substitute some other authority or statutory undertakers for the authority on whom the notice is served;
(c) to refuse to confirm, on grounds that the necessary conditions are not fulfilled;
(d) instead of confirming the notice, to grant permission for the development in question, or to revoke or amend any conditions imposed;
(e) instead of confirming the notice, to direct that if a planning application is made, permission shall be given for some other form of development.

27.27 Where an owner of land which has a restricted use by virtue of a *previous* planning permission serves a purchase notice, the Secretary of State is not obliged to confirm the notice if he considers that the land ought to remain undeveloped in accordance with the previous planning permission or, as the case may be, remain or be preserved or laid out as amenity land in relation to the remainder of the larger area for which that previous planning permission was granted.

27.28 This provision was introduced by the Town and Country Planning Act 1968 to reverse the effect of the decision in *Adams & Wade Ltd v Minister of Housing and Local Government* (1965) 18 P & CR 60. There, planning permission had been granted for the development of part of an area of land subject to a condition which required the remainder to be preserved as amenity land for the benefit of

Purchase Notices

the part developed. Application was then made for permission to develop the amenity land, and when the application was refused the owner served a purchase notice claiming it to be incapable of reasonably beneficial use. The Minister's contention that, having had the benefit of the previous permission, the purchase order procedure could not be used to avoid the burdens of that permission was rejected, and his decision not to confirm the notice held to be invalid.

27.29 The provision which gives the Secretary of State power to refuse to confirm a purchase notice served in respect of amenity land is now found in s 142 of the 1990 Act. The power extends beyond the situation found in the *Adams & Wade Ltd* case, since it is expressed to cover not only cases where the preservation of amenity land is an express condition of a previous planning permission, but also where the application for the previous permission contemplated that the part not comprised in the development should be treated in that way.

27.30 In *White v Herefordshire Council* [2007] EWCA Civ 1207 it was held by the Court of Appeal that while there was no right to amend a purchase notice, an owner could serve more than one purchase notice. Whether there had been an implied withdrawal of an earlier notice would depend on the circumstances and the terms on which the owner served the second notice.

27.31 Purchase notices are rarely used. In 2010/11, only five purchase notices were referred to the Secretary of State, of which three were withdrawn. Any party aggrieved by the decision of the Secretary of State on a purchase notice may, within six weeks, make an application to the High Court on the grounds that either (a) the decision of the Secretary of State is not within the powers of the Act; or (b) the interests of the applicant have been substantially prejudiced by a failure to comply with any relevant requirements (ss 284 and 288).

27.32 The court has power to quash the Secretary of State's decision, in which case the purchase notice is treated as cancelled.

27.33 If, within nine months from the service of a purchase notice or six months from its transmission to the Secretary of State (if it ends earlier), the Secretary of State has neither confirmed the notice, nor taken any other action, nor notified the owner that he does not propose to confirm, the notice is deemed to be confirmed at the end of that period.

27.34 Where a purchase notice is confirmed, or deemed to be confirmed, the effect is that the authority on whom it was served will be deemed to be authorized to acquire the owner's interest compulsorily and to have served a notice to treat either on such date as the Secretary of State may specify, if he confirms the notice, or otherwise at the expiration of the period referred to in para 27.33 (s 143).

27.35 In the above cases (and also where a local authority confirms a purchase notice without reference to the Secretary of State) since notice to treat is deemed to have been served, the owner may, if necessary, take the requisite steps to secure the assessment of compensation and the acquisition of his interest in the land, as in any other compulsory purchase case.

27.36 The usual power to withdraw a notice to treat, under s 31 of the Land Compensation Act 1961, is not exercisable in these cases (s 143(8) of the 1990 Act).

27.37 Compensation for land acquired under a purchase notice will, in general, be assessed on the same basis as that of any other land compulsorily acquired.

27.38 Where, instead of confirming a purchase notice in respect of the whole or part of the land, the Secretary of State directs that planning permission should be given for some other form of development then, if the 'permitted development value' of the interest in the land (or part of it) is less than its 'Schedule 3 value', the owner may claim compensation equal to the difference, estimated in accordance with the rules of s 5 of the Land Compensation Act 1961, so far as applicable. Any dispute about the compensation will be determined by the Lands Tribunal.

27.39 'Permitted development value' means the value of the owner's interest calculated on the assumption that planning permission would only be given in accordance with the Secretary of State's direction. 'Schedule 3 value' means open market value on the assumption that planning permission would only be given for the forms of development specified in paras 1 and 2 of Sch 3 to the 1990 Act.

27.40 A purchase notice is also available in the case of the revocation or modification of a planning permission under s 97 or the discontinuance of a use or removal etc of buildings or works under s 102.

28

NATIONALLY SIGNIFICANT INFRASTRUCTURE PROJECTS

| A. ALTERNATIVE METHODS OF DETERMINING MAJOR PROJECTS | 28.09 | B. NATIONALLY SIGNIFICANT INFRASTRUCTURE PROJECTS | 28.13 |

For many years concern has been expressed at the time taken to make decisions about major development projects. **28.01**

Apart from development which may be authorized by parliamentary Bills or public Works Orders, most proposals for major development projects have been dealt with through the normal planning processes. Usually the application has been called in for decision by the Secretary of State who has then held a public local inquiry into the proposal. **28.02**

However, the term 'major inquiries' came to be used to describe particular inquiries into large projects where the standard procedures for an inquiry were not appropriate so that ad hoc procedures were then developed to deal with these projects. Furthermore, there was no precise definition of a major inquiry and it was not until 2002 that special procedure rules were created for the consideration of major infrastructure projects. Apart from the actual length of the inquiry, the term was normally applied to projects of national significance, such as airports, nuclear power stations, and the like. The need for such projects was often controversial and contested, so the policy context would often not be settled. In addition, the evidence supporting the project would often be complicated and scientifically complex. **28.03**

Although relatively infrequent, public inquiries at which such projects were considered were long, protracted, and expensive. Inquiries into projects which have lasted more than 180 sitting-days (in addition to the inquiry into the Heathrow Airport Terminal 5 which lasted 524 sitting-days), include airport development at Stansted, Sizewell B Nuclear Power Station, and Hinckley Point Nuclear Power Station. **28.04**

28.05 In addition to the main purpose of the inquiry, other related proposals linked to the project may also have to be considered. For example, the Terminal 5 inquiry involved the consideration of 21 planning applications, six highway orders, two transport and works applications, five Acquisition of Land Act 1981 orders, three applications under the Civil Aviation Act 1982 and Airports Act 1986, one scheduled monument order, and three unopposed stopping up/diversion orders.

28.06 There was also the further difficulty that such developments were rarely the consequence of specific proposals in a development plan, and were often in areas where there was an absence of specific national policy guidance.

28.07 There have been various attempts in the past to create procedures that, while ensuring that the need and location for such projects is proved and the views of objectors are taken into account, the whole process is not unduly protracted and expensive. The latest format is the creation by the Planning Act 2008 of an entirely new system of development consents for what are termed 'nationally significant infrastructure projects' (NSIPs). The ambitious objective is to achieve outcomes that are both faster and fairer, more efficient and more accountable, that ensure more timely delivery, and that improve the ability of communities and individuals to participate. The new system gave the responsibility for approving the projects to a new body called the Infrastructure Planning Commission. However, the Coalition Government has considered that such important decisions should be taken by the Secretary of State and the Localism Act 2011 ('the 2011 Act') has abolished the Commission and restored the responsibility for making the final decision to Government.

28.08 Before considering the new scheme it is necessary to consider in more detail the other existing methods of approving major developments that are used.

A. ALTERNATIVE METHODS OF DETERMINING MAJOR PROJECTS

28.09 There have for some time existed various methods for the authorization of such projects apart from the traditional planning inquiry. The Town and Country Planning Act 1968 created the device of the Planning Inquiry Commission. The genesis for this device was the need for a procedure which would enable alternative sites to be considered for important development where only a limited number of sites for such development were available and suitable. This mechanism is still available and is found in s 101 of the 1990 Act, but it has never been used. Other alternatives for securing authorization are private and hybrid Acts of Parliament. The private Bill procedure resembles a public inquiry in that after the second reading the Bill is committed to a small committee consisting of four members in the Commons and five members in the Lords that hears arguments and evidence put by the promoters and opponents of the Bill. The process is expensive, as the parties have to bear the expense of hiring advocates, expert witnesses, and parliamentary agents and also the preparation of documents. It can also take up much valuable parliamentary time. Furthermore, the members of the committee may not have the expertise to judge the arguments. It is now rarely used as a means of approving large projects. A hybrid Bill is a public Bill that may in certain respects affect private rights and interests. A good example of a hybrid Bill was the Channel Tunnel Rail Link Bill which authorized the construction of a new rail link between St Pancras and the Channel Tunnel and which, inter alia, affected the rights of property owners whose land had to be compulsorily acquired or were otherwise affected by the proposal. As with private Bills, a committee of each House is set up to hear arguments by those who allege their interests are injuriously or adversely affected by a hybrid Bill. However, unless the House has given an instruction to the contrary, the second reading of a hybrid Bill establishes its principle and removes from the promoters the onus of proving its expediency. So, as well as having the disadvantages of the private Bill procedure, it could be seen as unfair to objectors.

28.10 Furthermore authorization can also be given by ministerial order. Under s 59 of the 1990 Act a special development order can grant permission for development of land specified in the order. This has the advantage from the point of view of the promoters of the scheme that it obviates the need for a public inquiry but the procedure has not been used to authorize major projects except when the proposal has already been considered by a public inquiry. As explained in Chapter 2, in *Essex CC v Ministry of Housing and Local Government* (1967) 18 P & CR 531 it was held that a special development order was a purely administrative power and could not be challenged on grounds of procedural fairness.

28.11 Part I of the Transport and Works Act 1992 also enables the approval of infrastructure projects such as railway, tramway, and inland waterway schemes to be made by ministerial order. Such orders are made by statutory instrument, and do not involve any parliamentary procedure except in a case where a scheme is one of national significance. Before making the order, the Secretary of State can afford objectors a hearing and this will take the form of a public inquiry, the rules for which are very similar to planning inquiries. It seems that all the above procedures may continue to be used for major development projects not considered to be nationally significant.

28.12 However, under s 9 of the 1992 Act, in the case of schemes that the Secretary of State considers to be of 'national significance', the application including the draft order, the environmental statement, and the supporting documents are submitted to Parliament. Single debates are held in each House on a motion inviting the House to approve the proposals. The importance of this procedure is that, although a public local inquiry must be held in cases where a statutory objector makes a valid objection, there is a presumption that parliamentary approval has settled the case for, and the location of, the project. After the conclusion of the inquiry the Inspector reports to the Secretary of State who then determines whether to make or reject the order, after taking into account any objections that have not been withdrawn and the Inspector's report.

B. NATIONALLY SIGNIFICANT INFRASTRUCTURE PROJECTS

28.13 The Planning Act 2008 introduced a unified 'development consent' procedure for 'Nationally Significant Infrastructure Projects'. The Act provided the creation of 'National Policy Statements' to guide the Commission (now the Secretary of State) in its consideration of the particular project being considered. As previously stated, the 2011 Act has abolished the Commission and s 130 of the 2011 Act amends ss 5, 6, and 9 of the Planning Act 2008 to require House of Commons approval of national policy statements and material amendments to existing national policy statements. House of Commons approval is required in addition to complying with the existing consultation, publicity and Parliamentary scrutiny arrangements in ss 7 and 9 of the Planning Act 2008. A draft national policy statement or amendment to an existing national policy statement ('a proposal') must be laid before Parliament and can only be designated if the House of Commons resolves within 21 sitting days that it should be proceeded with, or that period ends without the House of Commons resolving that it should not be proceeded with. A challenge to an NPS may be brought under s 13(1) of the Planning Act 2008 and may be brought within six weeks of being designated or published but may not be brought to impugn a draft statement, see: *R (Hillingdon LBC) v Secretary of State for Transport* [2017] EWHC 121 (Admin); [2017] 1 WLR 2166.

28.14 Whilst the main principles of these provisions are set out in the 2008 Act, as one would expect, the details have been set out in a series of subordinate legislation and Government guidance.

The meaning of 'nationally significant infrastructure projects'

28.15 The 2008 Act defines in s 14 the meaning of nationally significant infrastructure projects. This is done by reference to the following categories of projects and thresholds for each type of project as set out in ss 15 to 30 of the Act.

Section 15: Generating stations
This covers on-shore generating stations with a capacity of more than 50 megawatts or in the case of off-shore stations 100 megawatts.

Section 16: Electric lines

Lines within premises of the person responsible for its installation are excluded as are lines not expected to have a nominal voltage of more than 32 kilovolts.

Section 17: Underground gas storage

To be included the working capacity must be expected to be at least 43 million standard cubic metres or the maximum flow rate is expected to be at least 4.5 million standard cubic metres.

Sections 18 and 19: LNG facilities/gas reception facilities

Similar size limits as above are imposed on these facilities.

Section 20: Gas transporter pipelines

The construction of a pipeline meeting specified criteria and conveying gas to supply at least 50,000 customers.

Section 21: Other pipelines

The pipeline must be expected to be a cross-country pipeline requiring authorization under the Pipelines Act 1962 which crosses between England and Wales or is an oil or gas pipeline and the other end of it is in Scotland.

Section 22: Highways

Highways where the Secretary of State will be the highway authority for the highway, or the highway is to be constructed for a purpose connected with a highway for which the Secretary of State is (or will be) the highway authority. Improvement of a highway is only included if the Secretary of State is the highway authority for the highway, and the improvement is likely to have a significant effect on the environment. Alteration of a highway is only included if the alteration is to be carried out by or on behalf of the Secretary of State, and the highway is to be altered for a purpose connected with a highway for which the Secretary of State is (or will be) the highway authority.

Section 23: Airports

Construction or alteration of an airport that is expected to be capable of providing air passenger service for at least 10 million passengers per year, or air cargo transport services for at least 10,000 air transport movements of cargo aircraft per year.

Section 24: Harbour facilities

The construction or alteration of harbour facilities capable of handling: (a) in the case of facilities for container ships, 500,000 TEU ('TEU' means a twenty-foot equivalent unit); (b) in the case of facilities for ro-ro ships, 250,000 units; (c) in the case of facilities for cargo ships of any other description, 5 million tonnes; and

(d) in the case of facilities for more than one of the types of ship mentioned in paras (a) to (c), an equivalent quantity of material as prescribed.

Sections 25 and 26: Railways and rail freight interchanges

The construction or alteration of the railway must be part of a network operated by a person granted a licence under s 8 of the Railways Act 1993. This in effect covers Network Rail. Construction of railfreight interchanges are also included.

Sections 27 and 28: Dams and reservoirs and transfers of water resources

The construction or alteration of a dam or reservoir is included if the construction will be carried out by one or more water undertakers, and the volume of water to be held back by the dam or stored in the reservoir is expected to exceed 10 million cubic metres.

Section 29: Waste water treatment plants

The construction or alteration of a waste water treatment plant having a capacity exceeding a population of 500,000.

Section 30: Hazardous waste facility

The construction or alteration of a facility for the final disposal or recovery of hazardous waste, where the capacity is expected to be, in the case of the disposal of hazardous waste by landfill or in a deep storage facility, more than 100,000 tonnes per year and, in any other case, more than 30,000 tonnes per year.

Section 35ZA: Business and commercial projects

Section 26 of the Growth and Infrastructure Act 2013 has created a new section 35 which enables the Secretary of State to direct that certain commercial and business development requires consent under the nationally significant infrastructure regime contained in the 2008 Act, as well as retaining the existing power of the Secretary of State to direct that development in the fields of energy, transport, water, waste water or waste requires consent under the 2008 Act.

Development consent

28.16 It is important to understand that the new 'development consent' for nationally significant infrastructure projects is not a species of planning permission but an entirely new form of statutory consent for the whole project. Under s 33 of the 2008 Act the new development consent will override the need for any other consent or permission that would otherwise be required. Thus, where development consent is granted, consent is no longer required for listed building consent, conservation area consent, scheduled monument consent, pipeline construction authorization, gas storage authorization, or consent for the construction of generating stations.

The requirement for development consent clearly obviates the need for planning permission to be obtained for the same development. Section 131 of the 2011 Act has amended s 33 so that changes by the Secretary of State can be made to the type of consents that are needed or not needed.

It is therefore a form of one-stop consent which can also confer on developers certain rights for the purpose of facilitating the project including compulsory purchase powers, though in such a case the affected parties can require a hearing (see ss 92 and 120). It is, however, equally important to note that where a development consent is not needed the old consent regimes, as explained above, still apply. **28.17**

'Development' is given the same meaning as in s 55 of the 1990 Act but s 32 of the 2008 Act provides that certain other actions constitute development. Thus, under subsection 32(2) the conversion of a generating station to enable it to use gas or petroleum as a fuel source, starting to use a cavity or strata underground for the purposes of gas storage, and an increase in the permitted use of an airport come within the definition. Similarly, under subsection 32(3), works which would require listed building consent, conservation area consent, or works to or operations to ancient monuments are also to be taken to be development. This links to the fact that under s 33 consents under the other regimes are no longer required if development consent is required. **28.18**

Infrastructure Planning Commission

A major role in the new system was to be played by a new independent body called the Infrastructure Planning Commission. The Commission has been responsible for examining the first applications for development consents and would have been responsible for deciding the application when there had been in force a relevant national policy statement (NPS). Section 128 of the 2011 Act abolishes the Infrastructure Planning Commission and transfers its functions to the Secretary of State. The 2011 Act enables the Secretary of State to appoint an Inspector, or a panel of three to five Inspectors, to examine an application and make a recommendation to the Secretary of State as to the decision to be made on the application. These Inspectors will be drawn from a new Major Infrastructure Planning Unit formed within the Inspectorate. Schedule 13 to the 2011Act makes the necessary amendments in transferring functions and as stated enable examinations of the applications to be carried out by a single Inspector or a panel of up to five Inspectors, depending on the size and complexity of the application. To ensure that applications transfer from the Infrastructure Planning Commission to the Major Infrastructure Planning Unit without interruption, there is a new power of direction under s 129 of the 2011 Act which will enable the Secretary of State to specify how the transition should be dealt with on a case by case basis. These new provisions are not yet in force at the time of writing. **28.19**

National policy statements

28.20 National Policy Statements (NPS) provide the policy framework as to how applications should be decided. The abolition of the Commission will not change this. Section 5(5) of the 2008 Act allows for the NPS to identify suitable locations and may set out in relation to a specified description of development, the amount, type, or size of development of that description which is appropriate nationally or for a specified area. Under section 5 the NPS can also:

— set out the criteria to be applied in deciding whether a location is suitable (or potentially suitable) for a specified description of development;
— set out the relative weight to be given to specified criteria;
— identify one or more locations as suitable (or potentially suitable) for a specified description of development;
— identify one or more statutory undertakers as appropriate persons to carry out a specified description of development; and
— set out circumstances in which it is appropriate for a specified type of action to be taken to mitigate the impact of a specified description of development.

So, the NPSs can be very prescriptive as they can identify locations as suitable or unsuitable for a specified type of development. It should be noted that, unlike normal Government policies in Planning Policy Guidance and Planning Policy Statements, the policies in the NPS are binding as s 104(3) required the Commission to decide the application in accordance with any relevant NPS except in certain specific situations. This legal requirement now applies to the Secretary of State. So, in some respects the NPSs are like binding development plans. Also, the exceptions do not give much flexibility as they mainly apply only when the decision would be in breach of international or national law. On the other hand, s 104(7) did give the Commission some discretion as it allowed the commissioners to make a decision not in accordance with the NPS when satisfied that the impact of the proposed development would outweigh its benefits. So, it was at least theoretically possible that an application could be rejected on the grounds that the adverse local or other impacts outweigh the national benefits. With the abolition of the Commission, the Major Infrastructure Planning Unit will still have to apply the policies in the relevant NPS when making recommendations. However, in this regard it should be noted that s 106 of the 2008 Act, as amended, provides that in deciding whether to grant a development consent, the Secretary of State may disregard representations that relate to the merits of the policy set out in an NPS.

28.21 Under s 12 the Secretary of State may designate a statement as an NPS even though the statement was issued before s 5 had come into force. So existing policy statements, such as Planning Policy Statements and Guidance, can become NPSs. Under s 12, subsections (3) and (4), before an NPS can be designated the

Secretary of State must first carry out a sustainability appraisal. Sections 7 and 8 provide for consultation. The Act leaves it to the Secretary of State to decide what consultation and publicity is appropriate, but the Secretary of State must consult such persons, and such descriptions of persons, as may be prescribed. Where the proposals refer to a particular location as being suitable (or potentially suitable) for a specified type of development, the Secretary of State must ensure that there is suitable publicity for the proposal in that location. The Secretary of State must have regard to such responses to the consultation and publicity in deciding whether to proceed with the proposal. Also, under s 10, when the Secretary of State is either designating or reviewing an NPS this must be done with the objective of contributing to sustainable development. Section 130 of the 2011 Act has inserted a new s 6A into the 2008 Act. This provides that if the proposal is an amendment of an earlier proposal, further consultation need not be carried out if there has already been consultation and the amendments do not materially affect the policy. Where the amendments do materially affect the policy, the new s 6A(3) provides that it is sufficient for further consultation to be limited to the material amendments.

28.22 Under s 6 the Secretary of State is under a duty to review all or part of an NPS when considered appropriate to do so and the change materially affects the policy. In deciding when to review a national policy statement the Secretary of State must consider whether there has been a significant change in any circumstances on the basis of which any of the policy set out in the statement was decided and whether if the change had been anticipated at that time, any of the policy set out in the statement would have been materially different. Before amending an NPS the Secretary of State must carry out an appraisal of the sustainability of the policy set out in the proposed amendment and carry out consultation and publicity, subject to the changes introduced by the 2011 Act.

28.23 All proposed NPSs and amendments to NPSs must under s 9 be laid before Parliament and if, during the relevant period (to be specified by the Secretary of State in relation to the proposal) either House of Parliament makes a resolution with regard to the proposal, or a committee of either House of Parliament makes recommendations with regard to the proposal, the Secretary of State must lay before Parliament a statement setting out the Secretary of State's response to the resolution or recommendations. Section 130 of the 2011 Act has strengthened the role of Parliament by requiring House of Commons approval of NPSs and of material amendments to existing NPSs. A draft NPSs or an amendment to an existing NPS must be laid before Parliament and can only be designated if the House of Commons resolves within 21 sitting days that it should be proceeded with, or that period ends without the House of Commons resolving that it should not be proceeded with. So, the controls are similar to the negative procedure for statutory instruments where the statutory instrument will become law as long as there is not a negative resolution.

Applications for orders granting development consent

28.24 Part 5 of the 2008 Act sets out a pre-application procedure. Under ss 42 to 44 there is a duty to consult certain people and categories of people (to be prescribed in secondary legislation) about the proposed application. The consultees are to include certain local authorities and persons with rights over land and other prescribed persons. Section 46 provides that the applicant must give the Commission (now the Secretary of State) a copy of the consultation documents on or before commencing consultation under s 42, and under s 47 the applicant must prepare and publish a statement setting out how he proposes to consult local people about the proposed application. The applicant must consult with the relevant local authority before publishing such a statement, and the local authority must reply within 28 days. The consultation must be carried out in the manner set out in the statement and under section 49 of the Act, the applicant must consider any relevant responses he has received to the consultation and publicity, and take these into account before submitting an actual application. The detailed rules as to consultation, publicity and the form of an application are set out in the Infrastructure Planning (Applications: Prescribed Forms and Procedure) Regulations 2009 (SI 2009/2264). It should also be noted that the Infrastructure Planning (Environmental Impact Assessment) Regulations 2017 (SI 2017/572) impose environmental impact assessment requirements for applications for development consents.

28.25 Under s 51 of the 2008 Act the Secretary of State can give advice to an applicant, a potential applicant or others about applying for an order granting development consent or making representations about an application but any such advice cannot relate to the merits of any particular proposal. Schedule 13 para 10(1) of the 2011 Act has amended s 51 so that the Secretary of State can, by regulations, make provision for the giving of advice.

The examination of applications

28.26 Part 6 of the 2008 Act sets out how applications are to be decided once the pre-application stage is over. The Secretary of State must first accept the application and under s 55 the application can only be accepted if it complies with the statutory requirements, such as whether it is in the prescribed form and accompanied by the consultation report. Under s 60, once accepted, relevant local authorities must be informed by the Secretary of State and invited to submit by a specified deadline a report (called a local impact report) giving details of the likely impact of the proposed development on the authority's area.

28.27 The Act sets out the procedures for examination of an application. Once an application has been accepted, under s 61 the Secretary of State must decide whether the application should be handled by a panel or by a single appointed person (which is the term given to the Inspector) and there is power to switch from a single appointed person to a panel. Under s 65 a panel must consist of at least three persons. Decisions are made by majority voting but the chair has a casting vote.

28.28 Under s 88 there must be first an initial assessment of the principal issues arising on an application. Then a preliminary meeting must be held with the applicant and each interested party. The purpose of the meeting is to enable those present to make representations as to how the application should be examined and to discuss any other matter the examining authority wishes. The examining authority will then decide how the application is to be examined.

28.29 Section 87 provides that it is for the examining authority (a panel or a single appointed person) to decide how to examine an application. However, the Act makes clear that there is still to be some sort of public examination before coming to a decision but this is to be essentially an investigatory process, with the majority of the evidence being given in writing (see s 90) and then probed by direct questioning by the examining body with generally no adversarial cross-examination by opposing counsel unless the examining body consider this to be appropriate. It is intended that in examining applications greater use is to be made of written representations with less reliance on oral representations; and restrictions are placed on the use of cross-examination by interested parties at a hearing. Indeed, there is only to be a hearing where (under s 91) it is decided by the examining authority that this is necessary for the examination of an issue to receive oral representations, either to ensure the adequate examination of an issue, or so that an interested party has a fair chance to put their case. There is, however, an opportunity for what are termed 'open-floor hearings' (under s 93) where at least one interested party informs the examining authority of a wish to be heard within the specified deadline. Each interested party is entitled to make oral representations at an open-floor hearing. However, there is no right to question its own witnesses or other parties' witnesses and it is up to the examining authority to decide whether a person making an oral representation can be questioned by an interested party and the duration of an oral representation and/or questioning. The process by which the examining authority will come to make recommendations therefore resembles in many ways the 'examination in public' which has been used for some time to examine objections to development plans. Section 98 of the Act sets a timetable for examination of applications and decisions. A deadline of six months is stipulated for carrying out the examination procedure and a further three months is allowed for the examining authority to make the report to the Secretary of State.

28.30 The term 'interested party' is defined by s 102 (as amended by s 138(8) of the 2011 Act) and further details are set out in the Infrastructure Planning (Interested Parties and Miscellaneous Provisions) Regulations 2015 (SI 2015/462). References to the making of a representation include the giving of evidence and a representation is a relevant representation to the extent that it is a representation about the application. It must be made in the prescribed form and manner and be received within the prescribed deadline. Most importantly under s 106 of the 2008 Act it should not contain:

(a) material about compensation for compulsory acquisition of land or of an interest in or right over land;
(b) material about the merits of policy set out in a national policy statement; or
(c) material that is vexatious or frivolous.

The limited right provided for interested parties to have an oral hearing and to cross-examine has proved very controversial and it has been argued that this means that arguments over factual issues cannot be resolved by expert witnesses giving evidence and being cross-examined. The Government would argue that evidence can be tested where necessary by cross-examination by members of the examining authority conducting the inquiry and in special circumstances cross-examination by interested parties could be allowed.

28.31 At the conclusion of consideration of an application the Secretary of State will either grant or refuse consent. In doing so the order may grant development consent for associated development including the construction of dwellings. A statement of reasons must be given for granting or refusing consent and must be given to all interested parties and published.

The content of development consent orders

28.32 As well as imposing conditions as to how the development will have to be carried out (as in the case of ordinary planning permissions), under s 120 an order may make provision for ancillary matters. Schedule 5 to the Act contains a (non-exhaustive) list of those matters, which include provisions authorizing the compulsory acquisition of land, the creation, suspension, and extinguishment of rights over land, the stopping up of highways, the charging of tolls, and the payment of contributions and compensation. A consent order can require subsequent approval by the Secretary of State or another person such as a local authority of a matter connected with the development. This is akin to a planning condition requiring subsequent approval of details. This power has been increased by s 140 of the 2011 Act so that such approval can be required even if it could not have been made under the previous systems of regulation that the consent order has replaced.

28.33 In the case of compulsory acquisition under section 122 the decision-maker must be satisfied that the land:

(a) is required for the development to which the development consent relates;
(b) is required to facilitate or is incidental to that development; or
(c) is replacement land.

There must also be a compelling case in the public interest for the land to be acquired compulsorily.

Further, s 123 provides that the decision-maker can only authorize compulsory acquisition of land if the application for the order included a request for compulsory acquisition of the land to be authorized and all persons with an interest in the land consent to the inclusion of the provision. Procedures equivalent to those set out in the Acquisition of Land Act 1981 must also be followed. S115(1) permits applications for development consent to cover not just the nationally significant project itself but also 'associated development'. In *R (Innovia Cellophane Ltd) v Infrastructure Planning Commission* [2011] EWHC 2883 (Admin); [2012] PTSR 1132 Cranston J held that this would cover the building of accommodation for construction workers. The building of 'dwellings' is excluded from the definition of associated development but Cranston stated that this wording did not prevent the building of hostels and other forms of non-permanent accommodation which were not self-contained. Then in *David Gate v Secretary of State for Transport* [2013] EWHC 2937 Turner J stated that as the purpose of the new regime was to streamline the process of obtaining consent for national projects, it would be wrong to impose a narrow interpretation as to which projects came within its jurisdiction. **28.34**

Legal challenges

Legal challenges must be brought by way of a claim for judicial review. Section 118 provides that challenges can be made to: **28.35**

— an order granting development consent;
— a refusal of development consent;
— a decision of the Secretary of State not to accept an application for an order granting development consent;
— a decision in relation to an error or omission;
— a decision to change or revoke a development consent order; or
— anything else done, or omitted to be done, by the Secretary of State in relation to an application for an order granting development consent.

As with statutory challenges under the 1990 Act, there is imposed a six-week time limit in which a challenge must be brought. Thus, in the case of an order granting development consent, proceedings must be filed during the period of six weeks beginning with the day on which the order is published or, if later, the day on which the statement of reasons for making the order is published.

Duration and enforcement of development consent orders

The 2008 Act does not lay down any specific period but development must be commenced before the end of the period prescribed by the Secretary of State or such period set out in the order whether shorter or longer. Failure to begin development within time results in the order ceasing to have effect. Unusually, s160 makes it a criminal offence to carry out development (for which development **28.36** consent is required) without such a consent and it is also a criminal offence under s161 to breach the terms of the order granting consent. However, there is an equivalent of an enforcement notice in that under s 169, where a person has been found guilty of an offence under ss 160 and 161, the relevant local planning authority may serve a notice requiring the person to remove the unauthorized development and to return the land to its previous condition or to remedy the failure to comply with the terms of the order. There is also provision for the local planning authority to carry out the works itself and to charge for the costs where steps have not been taken to comply with an unauthorized development notice.

28.37 S115(1) of the 2008 Act permits applications for development consent to cover not just the nationally significant project itself but also 'associated development'. In *R (Innovia Cellphone Ltd) v Infrastructure Planning Commission* [2011] EWHC 2883 (Admin); [2012] PTSR 1132 Cranston J held that this could cover the building of accommodation for construction workers. The building of dwellings is excluded from the definition of associated dwellings but Cranston J held that this did not prevent the building of hostels and other forms of non-permanent accommodation which were not self-contained. Then in *David Gate v Secretary of State for Transport* [2013] EWHC 2937 Turner J said that the purpose of the new regime was to streamline the process of obtaining consent for national projects and it would be wrong to impose a narrow interpretation as to which projects came within its jurisdiction.

29

TOWN AND VILLAGE GREENS

A. INTRODUCTION	29.01	D. PROCEDURE	29.37
B. RIGHT TO APPLY	29.07	E. POST-REGISTRATION RIGHTS	29.41
C. DEFINITION	29.15	F. RECTIFICATION	29.46

A. INTRODUCTION

Land which has been registered as a village green under the Commons Registration Act 1965 or Commons Act 2006, is protected from any development or use, which would interfere with the recreational use of the land by the local inhabitants. Section 12 of the Inclosure Act 1857 provides that it is a public nuisance to do a number of things to a green, including 'interrupting the use or enjoyment of a green as a place of exercise or recreation'. Further, s 29 of the Commons Act 1876 provides that any 'encroachment or inclosure' of a village green is a public nuisance as well as a civil tort. As such, to have land registered as a village green represents a tremendous blight on the commercial value of the land. **29.01**

The justification for village greens is explained by Lord Hoffmann in *R v Oxfordshire County Council ex parte Sunningwell* [2000] 1 AC 335, at 349 as being that 'any legal system must have rules of prescription which prevent the disturbance of long-established de facto enjoyment'. Thus, where a landowner has acquiesced in the use of his land for informal recreation, for the fixed period, the law bars him from enforcing his absolute rights in the land, and grants rights to a limited class of society to use the land for lawful sports and pastimes. Village green law, as Patten LJ held in *Taylor v Betterment Properties (Weymouth) Ltd* [2012] EWCA Civ 250; [2012] 2 P & CR 3 at [36], is therefore 'traceable' to the general law of prescription but, as we shall see, is located within its own distinct sub-set of rights. **29.02**

The Report of the Royal Commission on Common Land (1958) (Cmnd 462), chaired by Sir Ivor Jennings (commonly known as 'the Jennings Report'), emphasized the importance of these open spaces, which were in danger of being **29.03** developed because of uncertainties about their status. The Jennings Report informed the policy of the Commons Registration Act 1965 which increased the protection to village greens. The Act classified greens into three classes (a), (b), or (c). Class (a) concerned 'land which had been allotted by or under any Act for the exercise or recreation of the inhabitants of any locality'. Class (b) concerned land 'on which the inhabitants of any locality have a customary right to indulge in lawful sports and pastimes'. Class (c) concerned land 'on which the inhabitants of any locality have indulged in such sports and pastimes as of right for not less than 20 years'. The scheme of the Act was to conduct a one-off nationwide inspection and registration of land, after which if not registered, the historic recreational use of these greens would no longer be protected. Commons Registration Authorities had until 31 July 1970 to register land as a Class (a) or (b) green. Class (c) greens, so called 'new greens' however, could come into effect after a period of 20 years use by the inhabitants of a 'locality'.

29.04 The scope of Class (c) greens was for many years after 31 July 1970, uncertain. The first litigation on new greens emerged in the 1990s, 20 years after the statutory-cut off in 1970. But it was not until the landmark decision of the House of Lords in *R v Oxfordshire County Council ex parte Sunningwell* [2000] 1 AC 335 that new greens became highly relevant to landowners, local authorities, residents and developers.

29.05 Lord Hoffmann's speech in *Sunningwell* settled a number of uncertainties in the law. First, that the subjective belief of users of the green as to their entitlement to use was not relevant. Accordingly, the decision of the Court of Appeal in *R v Suffolk County Council, ex parte Steed* (1998) 75 P & CR 102 was wrongly decided. Secondly, the phrase in the legislation, 'sports and pastimes', was a global term which meant that provided activity on the land satisfied either term, it counted towards the registration of a Class (c) green. Thus, Lord Hoffmann concluded at 357 that 'dog walking and playing with children were, in modern life, the kind of informal recreation which may be the main function of a village green'. Thirdly, the House of Lords held that toleration of users is not inconsistent with qualifying village green use. This important decision brought the concept of the village green into the modern world, and paved the way for 15 years of litigation, at the highest level, on this ancient legal concept.

29.06 Parliament has re-visited the legislation three times since 1965. First, via the Countryside and Rights of Way Act 2000, it legislated to loosen the area from which the users of the green could come from. Since then, qualifying users may come from either a 'locality' or a 'neighbourhood within a locality'. Secondly, Parliament passed the Commons Act 2006, the policy of which was to make it easier to register land as a new green. Finally, by the Growth and Infrastructure Act 2013, Parliament has heavily curtailed the right to make an application to register a new green where it cuts against the planning system via certain 'trigger events'. The Planning (Wales) Act 2015 extended similar restrictions to Wales.

B. RIGHT TO APPLY

29.07 The current scheme for registering new greens is provided at s 15 of the Commons Act 2006. Any person may apply to register land as a new green in one of two circumstances. The italicized phrases have developed into terms of art in the case law, and receive greater individual analysis later in this chapter under 'Definition' at para 29.15.

29.08 The first situation is where a *significant number* of the inhabitants of any *locality* or of any *neighbourhood within a locality*, have indulged *as of right*, in *lawful sports and pastimes* for a period of at least 20 years, and they continue to do so at the time of the application. In practice, this period comes to an end when the Commons Registration Authority date stamps the application form and allots the application a unique number.

29.09 The second situation is where a *significant number* of the inhabitants of any *locality* or of any *neighbourhood within a locality* have indulged *as of right* in *lawful sports and pastimes* for a period of at least 20 years, and ceased to do so before the time of the application, but after the commencement of s 15 (being 6 April 2007). An application must be made within one year of the qualifying use ceasing in England, or within two years if the land is in Wales.

29.10 Section 15(4) provided a period of five years in which to make an application, in the case of land ceasing to be used prior to the commencement of s 15. This subsection is no longer relevant as the five-year timeframe since 2007 has since elapsed. The five-year period of grace was held not to disproportionately interfere with the landowner's rights under Art 8 of the European Convention on Human Rights 1950 or Art 1 to the First Protocol by the Court of Appeal in *R (Newhaven Port & Properties Ltd) v East Sussex County Council* [2013] EWCA Civ 673; [2014] QB 282.

29.11 Following the recommendation of the Penfold Review into *non-planning consents* (July 2010) (accessed at <http://www.bis.gov.uk/penfold>) that the Government review the village green legislation in order to 'reduce the impact on developments that have received planning permission', the Government consulted on radical changes to the scheme of legislation. These resulted in Parliament amending the Commons Act 2006, via the Growth and Infrastructure Act 2013.

29.12 The right to apply to register land as a new green is now severely restricted. First, by s 15A which allows a landowner to deposit a statement, in a prescribed form, bringing to an end any qualifying use, preventing the use acquiring legal protection.

By s 15A(2) the statement does not however have the effect of preventing any period of qualifying use commencing.

29.13 Section 15C provides that the right to apply to register land under s 15 ceases to apply in England if an event specified in Sch 1A (or Sch 1B in Wales), known as a 'trigger event' occurs in relation to the land. The current trigger events are when:

- an application for planning permission in relation to the land which would be determined under s 70 of the Town and Country Planning Act 1990 is first publicized in accordance with requirements imposed by a development order by virtue of s 65(1) of that Act;
- an application for planning permission made in relation to the land under s 293A of the Town and Country Planning Act 1990 (an application for the development of Crown land) is first publicized in accordance with subsection (8) of that section;
- a draft of a development plan document which identifies the land for potential development is published for consultation in accordance with regulations under s 17(7) of the Planning and Compulsory Purchase Act 2004;
- a development plan document which identifies the land for potential development is adopted under s 23(2) or (3) of the Planning and Compulsory Purchase Act 2004; (note: land sitting within settlement boundaries where there was a 'presumption in favour of sustainable development' was found to engage this trigger event in *R (on the application of Cooper Estates Strategic Land Ltd) v Wiltshire Council* [2018] EWHC 1704 (Admin) per David Elvin QC (sitting as a Deputy Judge) at [58]–[69]);
- a proposal for a neighbourhood development plan which identifies the land for potential development is published by a local planning authority for consultation in accordance with regulations under para 4(1) of Sch 4B to the Town and Country Planning Act 1990 as it applies by virtue of s 38A(3) of the Planning and Compulsory Purchase Act 2004;
- a neighbourhood development plan which identifies the land for potential development is made under s 38A of the Planning and Compulsory Purchase Act 2004;
- a development plan for the purposes of s 27 or 54 of the Town and Country Planning Act 2004, or anything treated as contained in such a plan by virtue of Sch 8 to the Planning and Compulsory Purchase Act 2004, continues to have effect (by virtue of that Schedule) on the commencement of s 16 of the Growth and Infrastructure Act 2013 and identifies the land for potential development;
- a draft of a local development order under s 61A(2) of the Town and Country Planning Act 1990 which would grant permission for operational development of the land is first published for consultation in accordance with provision included (by virtue of para 1 of Sch 4A to that Act) in a development order made under s 59 of that Act;

- a proposed application for an order granting development consent under s 114 of the Planning Act 2008 in relation to the land is first publicized in accordance with s 48 of that Act;
- an application for such an order in relation to the land is first publicized in accordance with s 56(7) of the Planning Act 2008;
- a notice is published by virtue of s 6 of the Transport and Works Act 1992 that an application has been made under that section, in circumstances where the notice contains a statement that a direction for deemed planning permission in respect of the land under s 90(2A) of the Town and Country Planning Act 1990 is being applied for.

29.14 The right to apply to register land as a new green ceases to apply on the occurrence of any one of these actions in England (or Sch1B in relation to Wales), until a 'terminating event' occurs, such as the planning application is withdrawn. The terminating events are detailed in full at column 2 in the table in Sch 1A (or Sch1B in relation to Wales) to the Commons Act 2006. Section 16(4) Growth and Infrastructure Act 2013 provides that it does not matter whether the trigger event occurred before or after the commencement of the section, but by s 16(5) the amendments above do not apply to an application sent before the day on which the section came into force (25 April 2013).

C. DEFINITION

29.15 The test to be applied at s 15 of the Commons Act 2006 turns on five questions:

- Is there a qualifying locality or neighbourhood?
- Have lawful sports and pastimes been indulged in on the land?
- Has this been done as of right?
- And for 20 years?
- By a significant number of the relevant inhabitants?

Locality or neighbourhood within a locality

29.16 A customary right cannot be claimed for the public at large. Accordingly, a narrow class of the public must be shown to have used the land. This small class must come from either a 'locality' or a 'neighbourhood within a locality'.

29.17 A 'locality' means a unit '... recognizable by law'. *Ministry of Defence v Wiltshire County Council* (1995) 4 All ER 931 per Harman J at 937. Therefore, it may include boroughs, districts, parishes, or manors. The Court of Appeal in *Paddico (267) Ltd v Kirklees Borough Council* [2012] EWCA Civ 262; [2012] 2 P & CR 1 overruled Vos J's judgment at first instance that a conservation area amounted to a 'locality'. Sullivan LJ held that a conservation area did have legally significant boundaries, but they were not defined by reference to any 'community of interest on the part of the inhabitants' at [29]. In *Jones v NHS Property Services Ltd* [2018] EWCA Civ 721; [2018] 2 P & CR 15 the Court of Appeal found that small changes in the locality over the qualifying period were not important provided '[the locality] had existed in some clearly identifiable form throughout' at [72].

29.18 A 'neighbourhood within a locality' by contrast need not have been an administrative unit recognized by the law. The leading articulation of the concept is found in the judgment of Sullivan J in *R (Cheltenham Builders) v South Gloucestershire District Council* [2003] EWHC 2803 (Admin); [2004] 4 PLR 95 at [85]:

> I do not accept the defendant's submission that a neighbourhood is any area of land that an applicant for registration chooses to delineate upon a plan. The registration authority has to be satisfied that the area alleged to be a neighbourhood has a sufficient degree of cohesiveness, otherwise the word 'neighbourhood' would be stripped of any real meaning. If Parliament had wished to enable the inhabitants of any area (as defined on a plan accompanying the application) to apply to register land as a village green, it would have said so.

Thus, the users of the land must therefore be from a narrow class of the general public. In the event the land is registered, it is this narrow section of the public who will have the right to use the land for lawful sports and pastimes and not the public at large. In *Jones*, Lindblom LJ held that the assessment of whether a neighbourhood is 'cohesive' is 'a distinctly impressionistic and protean concept, which allows ample scope for differences of judgment' at [104].

Have lawful sports and pastimes been indulged in on the land?

29.19 Lord Hoffmann tells us in *Sunningwell* that the term 'lawful sports and pastimes' means a 'single composite class' of activity. It may be organized sports, but more likely, and just as relevant, the use may be confined to informal pastimes such as dog walking, running, or kicking a ball around. The position was endorsed a decade later by the Supreme Court in *R (Lewis) v Redcar & Cleveland Borough Council* [2010] UKSC 11; [2010] 2 AC 70. Lord Hope held at [85] that:

> ... it has been settled law that dog walking and playing with children count as lawful sports and pastimes. Since both activities can and do take place on almost any and every open space near centres of population, the scope for applying to register land as a village green is correspondingly wide. Owners of land are taken to be aware of this chapter of the law and of the need to take appropriate preventative steps if they see a risk of circumstances arising in which an application could be made and their land become registered as a village green.

29.20 Walking, jogging, and dog walking are amongst the most common claimed uses. The question is whether that use is of a character to point to village green use or, to the acquisition of lesser rights, such as a right of way. This dilemma was put to the High Court as part of a Part 8 claim by Oxfordshire County Council, who sought guidance on a number of issues in its capacity as Commons Registration Authority. The claim was motivated by Miss Catherine Robinson's application to register an area of land over the railway line from Port Meadow in North Oxford, known as the 'Trap Grounds', as a new green. Lightman J addressed the point in detail through three scenarios at first instance in the case of *Oxfordshire County Council v Oxford City Council* [2004] EWHC 12 (Ch); [2004] Ch 253 at [102]–[105]. In essence, Lightman J held that the key question was how the use would have appeared to the reasonable landowner. In the event of an ambiguity in the use (as to whether it should be referable to rights of way use or village green use) the matter should be resolved in favour of rights of way use, because the consequences for the land owner of a right of way over his land are less onerous than the land being registered as a village green. What this often comes down to is whether those who walk over the land do so in a transitory way (ie to get from A to B) or do so in a recreational way. This is a narrow taxonomy of use and leads to lengthy sessions of evidence at public inquiries (on which see later under 'Procedure' at para 29.35). In *R (on the application of Allaway) v Oxfordshire County Council* [2016] EWHC 2677 (Admin) Patterson J dismissed a suggestion that Lightman J was wrong in the *Oxfordshire* case that users of worn paths should be generally excluded from qualifying users at [51] and [56].

Has the use been 'as of right'?

Lord Hoffmann held in *Sunningwell* that use 'as of right' means *nec vi, nec clam, nec precario*. That is to say use without *force*, without *secrecy*, and without *permission*. In his speech, at 351A, Lord Hoffmann explained the rationale for the three 'vitiating circumstances' which prevent use maturing into a legal right: 29.21

> … each constituted a reason why it would not be reasonable to expect the owner to resist the exercise of the right—in the first case, because rights should not be acquired by the use of force, in the second because the owner would not have known of the user and in the third, because he had consented to the user, but for a limited period.

That approach was expressly approved by the Supreme Court in *Lewis*, when Lord Walker confirmed that as of right was 'sufficiently described by the tripartite test nec vi, nec clam, nec precario' at [20]. Accordingly, the Supreme Court overruled the finding in the Court of Appeal that a deference to the landowner, by inhabitants pausing their recreational activity to allow golf shots to be played, amounted to use that was not as of right. The deference of the local inhabitants could be taken to indicate that the inhabitants recognized that two uses can in practice co-exist. Lord Neuberger in *R (Barkas) v North Yorkshire County Council* [2014] UKSC 31; [2015] AC 195 explained at [14] that:

> … if a person uses privately owned land 'of right' or 'by right', the use will have been permitted by the landowner—hence the use is rightful. However, if the use of such land is 'as of right', it is without the permission of the landowner, and therefore is not 'of right' or 'by right', but is actually carried on as if it were by right—hence 'as of right'. The significance of the little word 'as' is therefore crucial, and renders the expression 'as of right' effectively the antithesis of 'of right' or 'by right'.

29.22 As to whether the use has been *nec vi*, Lord Rodger held in *Lewis* that the burden on the applicant is to demonstrate the use by local inhabitants has been 'peaceable' at [87]. It would not be peaceable to tear down fences which were erected by the landowner, nor would it be peaceable to continue to recreate on land upon which signs indicated that such use was prohibited. In *Winterburn v Bennett* [2016] EWCA Civ 482; [2017] 1 WLR 646 the Court of Appeal held that no further action was required by a landowner beyond erecting a suitably worded sign to render use contentious, on which see further N Pratt, 'Confrontation, Contentious Use and a West Yorkshire Chip Shop' [2016] 5 Conv 414. Whilst *Winterburn* was a private easement case, there is no principled basis on which to distinguish its reasoning from village green cases and indeed, the Court arguably went no further in *Winterburn* than it did in *Betterment Properties (Weymouth) Limited v Dorset CC* [2012] EWCA Civ 250; [2012] 2 P & CR 3. Thus, in *R (on the application of Cotham School) v Bristol City Council* [2018] EWHC 1022 (Admin) Sir Wyn Williams expressly applied the reasoning in *Winterburn* to a village green case. The question as to whether use has been *nec clam*, rarely arises. Use which is secret and not in plain sight will not qualify. Finally, use which is pursuant to a revocable permission will be *precario* use, and not counting towards registration of a new green. The permission may be express (in the form of a licence) or implied (in the form of charging for entry) but must be in the form of an 'overt act which is intended to be understood, and is understood, as permission to do something which would otherwise be an act of trespass' per Lord Walker in *R (Beresford) v Sunderland City Council* [2003] UKHL 60; [2004] 1 AC 889 at [75].

29.23 Lord Hoffmann found in *Sunningwell* at 359, that toleration of use is not inconsistent with use as of right. His Lordship explained that this was because new greens did not rely on a presumed grant or dedication for legally enforceable rights to emerge. As such, a balance must be struck between the interests of the landowner and the protection of long-established de facto enjoyment, which, in the case of new greens, Parliament has endorsed. This 'balance' of interests laid the ground for the appeal in *Beresford*, which took the toleration argument a step further. It was argued that mowing the grass and providing amenities amount to not just toleration, but an encouragement of use by the landowner, rendering the use by local inhabitants not *as of right*. The House of Lords did not agree and quashed the refusal to register the Sports Arena in Washington as a village green.

29.24 The House of Lords in *Beresford*, however, invited further argument on a narrow but important point as to whether the powers by which a local authority held land rendered recreational use otherwise than *as of right*. Lord Bingham held at [9] that recreational use pursuant to a statutory right to recreate was not use as of right as follows:

> After the House had reserved judgment at the conclusion of oral argument, however, the House became concerned to explore the possibility that, on the special facts

of this case, the inhabitants of the locality might have indulged in lawful sports and pastimes for the qualifying period of 20 years or more not 'as of right' but pursuant to a statutory right to do so. Such use would be inconsistent with use as of right.

This general articulation of principle has given rise to a frequent argument that the recreational use of a given piece of land has not been *as of right* but *by right*. This is premised on the principle of prescription law that use by long user cannot create a right to do something already authorized by the general law, as Sullivan J explained by the example of the acquisition of a right of way over a common to which s 193 of the Law of Property Act 1925 already granted rights to 'air and exercise' in *R v Secretary of State for the Environment ex parte Billson* [1999] QB 374 at 393–394.

29.25 With the principle established in relation to new greens, the next question is in what circumstances will use be *by right*. The *obiter* view of their Lordships in *Beresford* was that where land was held under s 164 of the Public Health Act 1875 or s 10 of the Open Spaces Act 1906 the inhabitants of the locality already enjoyed a right to use the land and were thus not users *as of right*. In both those circumstances a local authority is prevented from bringing the recreational use of the land to an end, without going through a formal process of appropriating the land to an inconsistent purpose via s 122 of the Local Government Act 1972.

29.26 In *Barkas* the *by right* principle was taken a stage further, to extend its application to land held under statutes which permitted the land to be put to several inconsistent uses besides just recreation, without the need for formal appropriation. As Lord Neuberger PSC explained at [23]:

> Section 12(1) [Housing Act 1985] and its statutory predecessors bestow a power on a local (housing) authority to devote land ... for public recreational use ... until the land is removed from the ambit of that section. Where land is held for that purpose, and members of the public then use the land for that purpose, the obvious and natural conclusion is that they enjoy a public right, or a publicly based licence, to do so.

The Supreme Court also resolved to expressly overrule the ultimate conclusion in *Beresford*. Holding that on the facts it was plain the city council had lawfully allocated the land for public recreation for an indefinite period and accordingly the House of Lords was wrong to conclude in those circumstances the public use of the land was 'as of right'. Furthermore, their Lordships disapproved of the finding in the *Beresford* case that there is a middle category of users between licensees and trespassers. As Lord Neuberger PSC held at [27]:

> As against the owner (or more accurately, the person entitled to possession) of land, third parties on the land either have the right to be there and to do what they are doing, or they do not. If they have a right in some shape or form (whether in private or public law), then they are permitted to be there, and if they have no right to be there, then they are trespassers. I cannot see how someone could have the right to be on the land and yet be a trespasser ... in other words a 'tolerated trespasser' is still a trespasser.

The decision of the House of Lords in *Beresford* is consequentially now bad law and should not be relied upon, per Lord Carnwath JSC in *Barkas* at [86] (with whom Lords Neuberger PSC, Reed, Hughes, and Lady Hale agreed). The issue remains as to the application of the Commons Act 2006 to publicly owned land. Lord Carnwath JSC rightly observed at [66] that land in public ownership is not exempt from registration, and went on to observe of the *Oxfordshire* case that:

> Although the land was in public ownership, it had not been laid out or identified in any way for public recreational use, and indeed was largely inaccessible …

It would therefore appear that land held by a local authority and used for lawful sports and pastimes is not exempt from registration. However, where that land has also been 'laid out [and] identified' for public recreation, the use by local inhabitants for lawful sports and pastimes will be *precario*, and therefore not registrable.

29.27 The application of the 'by right' principle has generated a debate amongst commentators. Austin-Baker and Mayfield argue that 'by right' is nothing more than a 'mythical beast', not a valid reason to refuse to register land as a new green (R Austen-Baker and B Mayfield, 'Uncommon Confusion: Parallel Jurisprudence in Town and Village Green Applications' (2012) 1 Conv PL 55). However, in a thorough analysis in response to Austen-Baker and Mayfield's article, Blohm explains the 'by right' doctrine is based on a sound principle in prescription law, that 'where a pre-existing right exists, an equivalent user "as of right" cannot' (L Blohm QC, 'The "By Right" Doctrine and Village Green Applications—a Response' (2014) 1 Conv PL 40, 44). The decision of the Supreme Court in *Barkas* has, it is submitted, now settled the law with regards to use pursuant to a public (as opposed to a private) right, by removing *Beresford*.

29.28 The remaining question is whether 'by right' sits outside the 'three vitiating factors' identified by Lord Hoffmann in *Sunningwell* and by the Supreme Court in *Lewis*, or whether it is best rationalized as a species of *precario* use, see: A Bowes, '"As of Right": The Current Conceptual Crisis in the Public Law of Prescription Post Barkas' [2013] 5 JPL 495 and A Bowes, '"As of Right": Where are We Now?' [2016] 2 JPL 123. In *Newhaven* Richards LJ at [86] appeared to accept 'by right' as a fourth 'vitiating factor' when making a distinction between bylaws, which he held to be implied revocable licences creating *precario* use, and the statutes in *Barkas*, which he found to render subsequent use 'by right'. In *Barkas* however, the Supreme Court appeared to conceive use pursuant to a statutory right as *precario* use rather than as a separate conceptual category of 'by right', see Lord Neuberger at [20] and Lord Carnwath at [51].

Continuous use for 20 years on the land

29.29 The use, to be of a qualifying character, must be demonstrated for a period of 20 years. It is not necessary, however, that the use be actually continuous, rather it

Definition

must be exercised with such frequency as to convey the manifestation of a public right: *Lewis* per Lord Walker at [33]–[34]. The recreational use of the land need not be the sole or even dominant use of the land. Ouseley J held in *R (Newhaven Port & Properties Ltd) v East Sussex County Council* [2012] EWHC 647 (Admin); [2012] 3 WLR 709 at [65] that:

> It was for the county council, guided by the inspector, to judge whether there was sufficient lawful use. It did not have to be non-stop. Breaks in use would not without more break continuity of use. The nature and level of use simply had to be that which, judged objectively would make a landowner aware that the public were asserting a right.

The High Court judgment was subsequently successfully appealed on different grounds: [2013] EWCA Civ 276.

29.30 Similarly, it is not a requirement to use every square inch of the land for it to be registered as a new green. As Lightman J held in *Oxfordshire* at [95] that:

> There is no mathematical test to be applied to decide whether the inaccessibility of part of the land precludes the whole being a green. The existence of inaccessible areas, e.g. ponds, does not preclude an area being held to be a green. It is to be borne in mind that section 22 of the 1965 Act for the purposes of the Act defines 'land' as including 'land covered with water'. Greens frequently include ponds. They may form part of the scenic attraction and provide recreation in the form of, e.g., feeding the ducks or sailing model boats. Further overgrown and inaccessible areas may be essential habitat for birds and wildlife, which are the attractions for bird watchers and others. In my view in a case such as the present the registration authority must first decide on a common sense approach whether the whole of the land the subject of the application was used for the 20-year period for the required recreational purposes. For this purpose it is necessary to have in mind the physical condition of the land during the relevant period. The physical condition can change. If the land was clear during the periods of qualifying user, the fact that it later became heavily overgrown is irrelevant. If any substantial part of the land by reason of its physical character has not been so used, then that part may not have become a green or part of a green and consequently the whole of the land may not be so registered. In such a situation the second question arises whether the remainder of the land satisfies the requirement and, if it does, the remainder is registrable. If the whole of the application land is not a green, it is still open to the registration authority to find that part or parts are a green. The availability of this alternative may save the registration authority from any temptation to strain its finding of fact on the first question to safeguard the existence of a green.

Lightman J's 'common sense' approach was followed by Sullivan J in *Cheltenham Builders* at [29]–[30]. The issue was taken to extreme in *Newhaven*, where the land in issue was a tidal-beach, only accessibly for a minority of the day. However, Ouseley J's following finding at [52] was expressly approved on appeal:

> The fact that lawful sports and pastimes cannot be engaged in over the whole of the registered land all the time, is not a reason for refusing to register all the land over which at times of the day, depending on the state of the tide, the public can and do engage as of right in lawful sports and pastimes ...

29.31 Finally, it is not a requirement that the land bear any particular characteristics to be a new green. Lord Scott in *Oxfordshire* offered an *obiter* and minority view that to be a new green, qualifying use for the fixed period was not sufficient, 'something more was required'. At [77] his Lordship explained that:

> In my opinion, the 'something more' would have been a quality in the land in question that would have accorded with the normal understanding of the nature of a town or village green, namely, an area of land, consisting mainly of grass, either in or in reasonable proximity to a town or village and suitable for use by the local inhabitants for normal recreational activities.

However, when Lord Scott's premise was deployed in *Newhaven*, Ouseley J rejected the notion in robust terms at [33] thus:

> I see no coherent legal basis for doing so. Parliament has chosen its words, on three occasions so as to exclude any notion of a requirement that the registered green be 'grassy' or 'traditional'. It has clearly eschewed the Royal Commission's definition. It has not attempted to incorporate any other, such as that for example, essayed by Lord Scott.

Ouseley J's reasoning was endorsed on appeal by Richards LJ: [2013] EWCA Civ 276; [2014] QB 186 at [42].

By a significant number

29.32 'Significant number' is not defined in the legislation. The case law tells us that the question is to be resolved from the point of view of the reasonable landowner. Lord Hope held in *Lewis* at [67] that the use by local inhabitants should be:

> ... of such amount and in such manner as would reasonably be regarded as being the assertion of a public right.

This follows Sullivan J's approach in *R v Staffordshire County Council, ex parte Alfred McAlpine Homes Ltd* [2002] EWHC 76 (Admin); [2002] 2 PLR 1 at [64] where he held that 'significant' was interpreted as follows:

> ... the number of people using the land in question has to be sufficient to indicate that their use of the land signifies that it is in general use by the local community for informal recreation, rather than occasional use by individuals as trespassers.

29.33 Further clarity was distilled from the decision in *R (on the application of Oxfordshire & Buckinghamshire Mental Health NHS Foundation Trust) v Oxfordshire County Council* [2010] EWHC 530 (Admin). HHJ Wacksman QC held that following the amendments to the Commons Registration Act 1965 affected by the Countryside and Rights of Way Act 2000, there was no longer a requirement that the users of the green were 'predominantly' from the locality or neighbourhood within the locality. The learned Judge held at [71] that 'it matters not that many or even most come from elsewhere'.

A long unresolved issue was that of 'spread'. Is it necessary for the users of the green to be evenly distributed across the neighbourhood or locality, or may the users be clustered around the green? Vos J in *Paddico (267) Ltd v Kirklees Metropolitan Council* [2011] EWHC 1606 (Ch) was not persuaded by the lack of a spread of users at [106(i)]: **29.34**

> ... I should say, in passing, that I was not impressed with Mr Laurence's suggestion that the distribution of residents was inadequately spread over either Edgerton or Birkby. Not surprisingly, the majority of the users making declarations lived closest to Clayton Fields with a scattering of users further away. That is precisely what one would expect and would not, in my judgment, be an appropriate reason for rejecting registration. None of the authorities drives me to such an illogical and unfair conclusion.

The issue of spread did not feature in the subsequent appeals in *Paddico*. The issue was however addressed by the Court of Appeal in *Jones v NHS Property Services Ltd* [2018] EWCA Civ 721; [2018] 2 P & CR 15 where Lindblom LJ comprehensively rejected the requirement to demonstrate a 'spread' of users across a qualifying locality or neighbourhood at [78]. As the Supreme Court refused permission to appeal on this ground, it therefore appears that the consideration of spread is now settled as an immaterial consideration.

Statutory incompatibility

In *R (on the application of Newhaven Port & Properties Ltd) v East Sussex County Council* [2015] UKSC 7; [2015] AC 1547 the Supreme Court considered whether the statutory duty on the statutory undertaker to 'maintain and support' Newhaven Harbour overrode s 15 of the Commons Act 2006 by implication such as to prevent registration. Lord Neuberger PSC found at [93] that s 15 of the Commons Act 2006 did not apply to land 'acquired by a statutory undertaker (whether by voluntary agreement or by powers of compulsory purchase) and which is held for statutory purposes that are inconsistent with its registration as a town or village green?'. However, at [101] the Court held that 'the ownership of land by a public body, such as a local authority, which has statutory powers that it can apply in future to develop land, is not of itself sufficient to create a statutory incompatibility'. **29.35**

Whilst the clash of duties was clear on the facts of Newhaven it was less clear in the co-joined appeals of *Jones v NHS Property Services Ltd* and *Lancashire County Council v Secretary of State for Environment, Food and Rural Affairs* [2018] EWCA Civ 721; [2018] 2 P & CR 15 which concerned land held by a local education authority and the National Health Service property company. The landowners in each appeal sought to rely on the application of that principle to land held by an education authority and the National Health Service, respectively. Lindblom LJ (with whom Jackson and Thirwall LJJ agreed) rejected that approach and found at [39] that the approach of Ouseley J in the Lancashire appeal to be 'essentially consistent' with the Supreme Court's decision in *Newhaven*. The tests of statutory incompatibility are set out by Lindblom LJ at [40] as follows: '(i) there must be **29.36** "specific" statutory purposes or provisions attaching to [the] particular land [subject to the application], (ii) Parliament must have conferred on the landowner powers to use the "particular land for specific statutory purposes with which its registration as a town or village green would be incompatible" and (iii), so as to "clearly impede", or "prevent" or "restrict" the exercise of any statutory power, or the discharge of any statutory duty, relating specifically to that particular land'. As such in a case where: (i) 'the statutory powers and duties relied upon were general in their character and content' (at [40]), (ii) 'there was no statutory obligation to maintain or use the land in question in a particular way, or to carry out any particular activities upon it' (at [40]), (iii) performance of those general duties 'might be or become more difficult or less convenient' but 'not that it would be prevented from carrying out any particular statutory function relating specifically to the land whose registration as a town or village green had been applied for' (at [40]) and (iv), performance of the 'relevant statutory purposes were capable of fulfilment through the county [landowner's] ownership, development and management of its property assets … without recourse to the land in question' (at [40]) the principle in *Newhaven* will not arise. In *R (on the application of Cotham School) v Bristol City Council* [2018] EWHC 1022 (Admin) Sir Wyn Williams rejected an attempt to extend the *Newhaven* principle to land held by an academy school with only limited land on which it could perform its statutory duties. The Court of Appeal also rejected an attempt to extend the principle to private landowners carrying on commercial operations in *TW Logistics Ltd v Essex County Council* [2018] EWCA Civ 2172; [2018] 3 WLR 1926. For further consideration of the case law on statutory incompatibility, see the discussion in A Bowes, 'Is Land in Public Ownership in a Special Category? A Consideration of the Law Post R (Lancashire CC) v SSEFRA' [2018] 9 JPL 973. However, it should be noted that in October 2018, the Supreme Court granted permission to appeal in the *NHS* and *Lancashire* cases to argue the statutory incompatibility point afresh, so the position may change following the hearing of those appeals on 16–17 July 2019.

D. PROCEDURE

29.37 The relevant legislation which deals with an application to a Commons Registration Authority in England which is not one within one of the seven 'pilot areas', is set out in the Commons (Registration of Town of Village Greens) (Interim Arrangements) (England) Regulations 2007 (SI 2007/457). Regulation 6(4) of those Regulations provides that:

> (4) The registration authority must not reject the application without giving the applicant a reasonable opportunity of dealing with—
> (a) the matters contained in any statement of which copies are sent to him under paragraph (3); and (b) any other matter in relation to the application

which appears to the authority to afford possible grounds for rejecting the application; and

(b) any other matter in relation to the application which appears to the authority to afford possible grounds for rejecting the application.

29.38 The Regulations provide no further amplification as to what procedure should be followed to determine the application. The Court of Appeal provided helpful guidance in *R (on the application of Whitmey) v Commons Commissioners* [2004] EWCA Civ 951; [2005] QB 282. Arden LJ held that a Commons Registration Authority must 'act reasonably' holding at [29] that where there is a serious dispute of fact:

> ... the authority may well properly decide, pursuant to its powers under section 111 of the 1972 Act, to hold an inquiry. We are told that it is the practice for local authorities so to do either by appointing an independent inspector or by holding a hearing in front of a committee. If the dispute is serious in nature ... it should proceed only after receiving the report of an independent expert (by which I mean a legal expert) who has at the registration authority's request held a non-statutory public inquiry.

29.39 Accordingly, in all but the most clear-cut of cases a Commons Registration Authority is best advised to convene a non-statutory public inquiry pursuant to its powers at s 111 of the Local Government Act 1972. The authority should appoint a lawyer, versed in the law of village greens, independent of the parties, to hear the evidence and provide a report and recommendation to assist the authority to determine the application. In *Somerford Parish Council v Cheshire East Borough Council* [2016] EWHC 619 (Admin) the High Court found that the Council should have held a public inquiry to resolve whether the application land was highways land.

29.40 Outside the pilot areas the procedure is set out within the Commons Registration (England) Regulations 2014. A notable difference between the pilot and non-pilot areas is the requirement to supply reasons for acceding to an application at reg 36(3)(a) within the pilot areas. However, in *Jones* the Court of Appeal found that outside the pilot areas, in the absence of an express duty to supply reasons, a common law duty to supply reasons arises, see [99]–[100].

E. POST-REGISTRATION RIGHTS

29.41 Section 10 of the Commons Registration Act 1965 provides that:

> The registration under this Act of any land as common land or as a town or village green, or of any rights of common over any such land, shall be conclusive evidence of the matters registered, as at the date of registration, except where the registration is provisional only.

Lord Hoffmann tells us in *Oxfordshire* that it is the act of registration which creates the positive rights for inhabitants [43], overruling *New Windsor v*

Mellor [1975] Ch 380, CA. His Lordship held the practical effect of s 10 was as follows [50]:

> In my view, the rational construction of section 10 is that land registered as a town or village green can be used generally for sports and pastimes. It seems to me that Parliament must have thought that if the land had to be kept available for one form of recreation, it would not matter a great deal to the owner whether it was used for others as well. This would be in accordance with the common law, under which proof of a custom to play one kind of game gave rise to a right to use the land for other games.

His Lordship held that registration of a new green does not have the effect of excluding the landowner from the land, rather 'he still has the right to use it in any way which does not interfere with the recreational rights of the inhabitants' at [51]. There must be give and take on the part of the landowner and that of the inhabitants. The matter was expressly addressed by the Supreme Court in *Lewis*, where Lord Brown said at [100] that the effect of registration was to record the rights of the inhabitants thus:

> ... preluding the owner from thereafter diminishing or eliminating such rights but not at the expense of the owner's own continuing entitlement to use the land as he has been doing.

29.42 As to the future, Lord Brown explains at [101]:

> ... in so far as future use by the locals would *not* be incompatible with the owner continuing in his previous use of the land, the locals can change, or indeed increase, their use of the land; they are not confined to the same 'lawful sports and pastimes', the same recreational use as they had previously enjoyed. But they cannot disturb the owner so long as he wishes only to continue in his own use of the land.

29.43 What then of a landowner who interferes with the recreational use of the registered green? Lightman J in *Oxfordshire* was of the opinion that the inhabitants would have a cause of action to seek an injunction to restrain the interference. The relevant local authority could issue an application for an injunction pursuant to their powers at s 222 of the Local Government Act 1972.

29.44 The criminal law prohibits more serious interferences with the recreational use of the land. Section 12 of the Inclosure Act 1857 for example prohibits:

> ... the laying of manure, soil, ashes, rubbish or other matter or thing thereon or *do any other act whatsoever* (whether willfully or not) to cause damage to a green or to impede the use or enjoyment thereof as a place of exercise or recreation.

Similarly, s 29 of the Commons Act 1876 creates a public nuisance for any encroachment or building or enclosure of a green. Any inhabitant of the parish, the parish council themselves or the District Council, may lay an information before the Magistrates to commence proceedings.

29.45 Post-registration is potentially fraught with problems. The first problem is one of communal rights, or 'local rights' as Lord Carnwath conceives them in *Barkas* at [53]. The proprietary right to use the land is that of the inhabitants of the relevant locality or neighbourhood within a locality. However, 'local inhabitants' are not a legal entity capable of holding a proprietary right collectively. Thus, as Clarke observes of the law of new greens 'the law struggles to find appropriate legal structures for the recognition and efficient regulation of land that is communally used' in A Clarke, 'Creating New Commons: Recognition of Communal Land Rights within a Private Property Framework' (2006) 59 *Current Legal Problems* 319. Secondly, as a Commons Registration Authority is not obliged to record upon registration the nature of lawful sports and pastimes, nor the relevant locality or neighbourhood from where the inhabitants came, how is a court, 20 years or so from registration, supposed to resolve the extent of the inhabitants' rights over the land? As the tension between the landowner's use of his land and the use of the land by local inhabitants is potentially great, the enforcement of inhabitants' rights would therefore appear to be set for much future litigation. In *TW Logistics Ltd v Essex County Council* [2018] EWCA Civ 2172; [2018] 3 WLR 1926 however, the Court of Appeal found that the landowner was 'entitled to continue his pre-existing activities as long as they do not interfere unduly with the recreational rights to which the registration gives rise' per Lewison LJ at [24] and Lindblom LJ at [108].

F. RECTIFICATION

29.46 Where land is registered and entered upon the register of town and village greens, the High Court has a power to 'rectify' the register. In the non-pilot areas, s 14 of the Commons Registration Act 1965 provides that the High Court may rectify the register, which would include deleting the land, if it is demonstrated the land was wrongly registered, or registered under a fraud, and it is just to so rectify. The 'correction' of registers for pilot areas is dealt with at s 19 of the Commons Act 2006. The key issues on a claim under s 14 of the Act will be (i) whether the land should have been registered and, (ii) whether it is not just to rectify the register.

Error of law

29.47 On appeal in *Paddico* [2012] EWCA Civ 262; [2012] 2 P & CR 1, Sullivan LJ at [12] adopted Vos J's formulation at first instance, which was:

(i) Whether the Land ought or ought not to have been registered as a TVG by the Council for the reasons it relied upon on [at the date of registration]?
(ii) If the Land ought not to have been registered, whether its registration can be supported on any of the alternative basis . . .

An application to the High Court will therefore have to demonstrate that not only was the reasoning wrong with reference to the law as it stood at the time, but that there is no alternative basis upon which the decision to register could be sustained.

Just to rectify?

29.48 The Act has no definition of 'justice'. The question therefore arises by what yardstick should it be said that it is 'just' to rectify the register? The question was addressed by the Supreme Court in the conjoined appeals in *Adamson v Paddico (267) Limited* and *Taylor v Betterment Properties (Weymouth) Limited* [2014] UKSC 7; [2014] AC 1072. Lady Hale, having analysed the various standards by which 'justice' could be judged, settled on the equitable doctrine of laches at [34] thus:

> The better analogy would therefore appear to be with the equitable doctrine of laches, which generally requires (a) knowledge of the facts, and (b) acquiescence, or (c) detriment or prejudice.

Knowledge of the facts is unlikely to be much of a problem, as the landowner at the time of an application to register would have had the opportunity to object, and any subsequent purchasers have the opportunity to consult the register. Acquiescence is unlikely to be fulfilled as Lady Hale held at [36] that a failure to object after registration will not go to establishing 'acquiescence'. Accordingly, the determination of whether it will be 'just' to rectify the register will turn on a balance of detriment or prejudice.

29.49 Lady Hale identified four categories of prejudice to be considered. First, there is the prejudice to local inhabitants, about which her Ladyship made the point at [38] that given they had been using the land under a mistake prejudice was unlikely to be suffered by them. The exceptions might be if practices, such as an annual cricket match, had grown up around the green being a village green. Secondly, is the prejudice to other individuals, but that is unlikely ever to be great per Lady Hale at [39]. Thirdly, is the prejudice to public authorities, this prejudice turns on whether the registration of the land as a village green has resulted in decisions being made, such as the allocation of housing on other sites at [40]. The fourth, and most important element is the prejudice to the fair determination of the case. The greater the lapse in time between the application and the claim in the High Court, the harder it will be to hear evidence from the relevant users of the land or access important written evidence at [41]–[42].

29.50 As Pratt observes the decision to use the doctrine of laches in assessing whether it is just to rectify the register, has tipped the scales firmly in favour of the landowner in a s 14 claim, in N. Pratt 'The Application of the Equitable Doctrine of Laches to the Rectification of the Town and Village Green Register' [2014] 6 JPL 588. With the new statutory restrictions on making an application (discussed above at para 29.11) and the *Paddico* decision, Pratt questions at 595 whether 'the environmental and social aims have been unduly subjugated beneath the economic aim in the sustainable development balance'.

INDEX

abandonment
 planning permission 15.67–15.69
 use, of 6.143–6.162
access
 demolition 21.57
 design and access statements 9.08–9.10
 high hedges 25.35
 highways 5.61, 5.68, 7.33
 listed buildings 21.57
 outline planning permission 9.14–9.15, 9.18
 public access obligation 22.10
account of profits 9.49
acknowledgment of receipt of planning applications 10.01–10.09
action area plans 4.28
adjacent land
 demolition 5.55–5.56
 material change of use 6.08–6.09
 tree preservation orders 25.03
administrative errors, recovered cases 18.16
administrative powers of Secretary of State
 advice 2.19
 appeals 2.21–2.23
 approval 2.20
 called in applications 2.24–2.33
 certificates of lawfulness of existing use or development, appeals against 2.23
 certificates of lawfulness of proposed use or development, appeals against 2.23
 circulars 2.55, 2.56, 2.60
 default powers 2.35–2.53
 Development Management Procedure Orders, directions on 2.31–2.34
 development plans 2.20, 2.35–2.53
 enforcement notices, appeals against 2.22
 guidance 2.19
 listed building consent 2.31
 Minerals Planning Guidance Notes 2.57
 Mineral Policy Statements, list of 2.57
 minor policy statements 2.55
 modifications to schemes 2.20
 Phelps Report 2.39–2.40
 planning permission 2.21, 2.23–2.38
 Planning Policy Guidance Notes (PPGs) 2.55–2.59
 Planning Policy Statements (PPSs) 2.55, 2.57
 policy control 2.20
 structure plans 2.20
 tree preservation orders, appeals against 2.23

advertising *see* advertising, control of outdoor; publicity and advertising
advertising, control of outdoor 24.01–24.37
 amenity 24.01–24.03, 24.23, 24.26
 appeals 18.05, 24.09, 24.22
 areas of special control (ASC) 24.25–24.30
 awnings 24.08
 blinds 24.08
 censorship 24.02
 classes 24.12, 24.15–24.16, 24.19, 24.28
 conditions 24.15–24.18, 24.22
 consent 18.05, 24.12, 24.14–24.24, 24.28
 conservation areas 21.147, 24.20, 24.25
 criminal offences 24.01, 24.04–24.05
 database, creation of a 24.01
 deemed consent 24.12, 24.14–24.23, 24.28
 definition of advertisement 24.07–24.11
 designed for advertisements, items which are 24.08
 development of plan 24.37
 development plans 24.02
 discontinuance notices 24.15, 24.21
 enforcement 6.102–6.103, 24.04–24.06
 estate agents in conservation areas 24.20
 exclusions 24.12
 experimental areas 24.25–24.26
 express consent 24.12, 24.14, 24.19, 24.22–24.24, 24.28
 fees for applications 9.51
 fines 24.01, 24.04
 fly-posting 24.01, 24.31–24.36
 General Permitted Development Order 7.46
 listed building consent 6.101
 material change of use 6.100–6.103
 normal use of land 6.100, 6.102
 obliteration 24.06
 persistent offenders 24.01
 planning permission 6.101, 24.37
 principally used or designed or adapted principally for use as advertisement 24.08
 public safety 24.01–24.02, 24.23, 24.26
 removal 6.103, 24.04, 24.06
 scheme of control 24.14
 scope 24.07
 Secretary of State 24.01, 24.09, 24.19–24.20, 24.29
 technology 24.10
 temporary buildings and uses 7.46
 transitional provisions 24.27

665

Index

advice 2.19, 9.62
affordable housing
   applications, determination of
      planning 11.125–11.133
   Community Infrastructure Levy 17.72, 17.78
   definition 11.130–11.131
   future eligible households, remaining at
      appropriate price for 11.132
   material considerations 11.125–11.133
   NPPF 11.130–11.131
   personal circumstances 11.126
   planning agreements 17.36
   policy 11.125–11.130
   procedure 11.133
   social rented housing, definition of 11.130
aggrieved persons 18.99
agreements *see* **planning agreements**
agriculture 6.10, 6.33–6.46
   allotments 6.43
   buildings 5.25, 5.27–5.29, 6.45, 7.47–7.52
   caravans on land 6.38
   classes of development 7.47–7.48
   cloches 5.26
   consultation 10.49
   definition 6.35–6.46
   fence posts 6.50
   fish farming 5.69–5.71, 5.78, 6.46
   gardens, extensions to 6.51–6.52
   General Permitted Development Order 7.47–7.52
   leisure plots 6.47–6.50
   material change of use 6.10, 6.33–6.52, 6.120,
      6.124–6.125, 6.134
   normal use of land 6.39
   operational development 6.34
   planning permission, notification to owners
      of 9.37–9.38, 9.40, 9.43
   primary or dominant use 6.120,
      6.124–6.125, 6.134
   security of tenure 9.37
   size 7.48
   value 1.10
airports 28.15
Alconbury **decisions** 19.08–19.11, 19.15, 19.22
allotments 6.43
alteration works
   building preservation notices 21.113–21.114
   compensation 27.14–27.15
   conservation areas 21.143
   ecclesiastical use and monuments, buildings
      in 21.50–21.51
   partial demolition as a structural alteration 5.60
alternative sites, existence of
   applications, determination of
      planning 11.82–11.88
   detailed consideration 11.86
   legal obligations to consider alternatives 11.88
   major infrastructure projects 28.09
   material considerations 11.82–11.88

   nationally significant infrastructure projects
      (NSIPs) inquiries 28.09
amendment of applications
   conditions 10.63
   limitations 10.61
   material change of use 10.63
   scope of applications 15.16
   third parties 10.61
ancient monuments 22.08–22.10
   archaeological facilities, provision of 22.15–22.17
   Code of Practice on voluntary cooperation 22.19
   compensation for loss of development value 22.21
   compulsory purchase 22.09
   conditions 22.15–22.17
   Conservation Covenants 22.22–22.23
   definition of monument 22.01, 22.08
   development plans 22.13, 22.15
   guardianship 22.10
   local development frameworks 22.14
   machinery attached to monuments 22.01
   material consideration 22.13
   national importance, archaeological remains
      of 22.15
   National Planning Policy Framework 22.14–22.16
   nationally significant infrastructure projects
      inquiries 28.18
   planning legislation 22.13–22.23
   preservation by record 22.19
   public access obligation 22.10
   regional spatial strategies 22.14
   scheduled monuments 22.02, 22.08, 22.21
   Secretary of State 2.09, 22.09–22.10
   voluntary cooperation 22.18–22.20
animals *see* **natural habitats and protected species,
   conservation of**
antennas 7.32, 11.109
anti-social behaviour *see also* **nuisance**
   fears of residents 11.104–11.105
   fly-posting 24.34
   high hedges 25.35
appeals 18.01–18.16 *see also* **enforcement notices,
   appeals against**
   acknowledgment of receipt of planning
      applications 10.02, 10.05, 10.08
   administrative powers 2.21–2.26
   advertising consents 18.05
   applications
      determination 11.62–11.68
      dismissed, where appeals have been 10.13
      fees 9.51, 9.55–9.56
      invalidity 18.07
      overlapping 10.19
      repeat 10.13–10.14, 10.16
   called in applications 18.04
   cancellation, costs of 18.83
   certificates of lawfulness of existing or proposed
      use or development 18.05, 20.177, 20.179
   climate change policies 18.15

Index

compulsory purchase 21.104
conditions 14.69, 14.76, 18.02–18.03, 18.10, 21.74
conservation area consent 18.05, 18.50
costs 18.79–18.92
delay 18.11
development orders, approvals under 18.03
dismissal, notice of 18.11
energy efficiency policies 18.15
enforcement 10.13
enforcement notices 20.39, 21.82–21.91
environmental impact assessments 18.13
fees for applications 9.51, 9.55–9.56
'full statement of case', definition of 18.09
Government departments, objections from other 18.15
guidance 18.04
hazardous substances consent 18.13
hearings 18.44–18.47
high hedges 25.39
householder appeals 18.41
important or novel issues of development control 18.15
Inquiry Procedure Rules 18.21–18.22
inspectors 18.12–18.14
judicial review 18.119, 18.125, 18.127–18.129
lawful development appeals 18.06
listed buildings 18.05, 18.07, 18.13, 18.50, 21.70, 21.74–21.76, 21.104
local inquiries 18.50–18.63
major importance which prompt substantial regional and national controversy, developments of 18.15
major infrastructure projects 18.64–18.69
material consideration, previous appeal decisions as a 11.62–11.68
mineral permissions 18.13
natural habitats and protected species, conservation of 26.06, 26.14
natural justice and fairness 18.21, 18.29
notice 18.08–18.09, 18.11
operational development 5.77–6.77
overlapping applications 10.19
Parliamentary and Local Government Ombudsmen 18.137
planning agreements 17.17
planning obligations 17.26, 17.37–17.38
previous decisions as a material consideration 11.62–11.68
public inquiries 18.12
recovered cases 18.13–18.16, 18.70
refusal of permission 18.02
repeat applications 10.13
residential developments affecting government objectives 18.15
reviews 18.94–18.97, 18.98, 18.102–18.103–18.104, 18.114–18.115
Secretary of State 18.01, 18.06–18.16
senior officials, decisions by 18.15

statutory undertakers 16.08
stop notices 20.119, 20.122
summaries of policies and proposals in development plans 18.08
time limits 18.03, 18.21, 18.70–18.72, 20.39, 21.82
transferred cases 18.13
tree preservation orders 18.05, 18.13, 25.07–25.10, 25.13, 25.15
twin-tracking 9.57–9.58
written representations 18.39–18.42
appearance 9.14–9.15, 9.18
applications for planning permission *see also* **determination of planning permission applications**
acknowledgment of receipt 10.01–10.09
amendments 10.61–10.63, 15.16
appeals
determination 11.62–11.68
dismissed, where appeals have been 10.13
fees 9.51, 9.55–9.56
invalidity 18.07
overlapping applications 10.19
repeat applications 10.13–10.14, 10.16
conservation areas, developments affect character or appearance of 10.45
consultation 10.48–10.56
content and form 9.01–9.12
county planning authorities, jurisdiction of 10.46
decline to determine applications, power to 10.10–10.25
design and access statements 9.08–9.10
development plans, developments not in accordance with 10.56–10.63
directory requirements 9.11
fees 9.50–9.56
form 9.01–9.12
highways, developments affecting 10.41
listed buildings, developments affecting the setting of 10.43–10.44
mandatory requirements 9.11
notification of owners 9.30–9.49
notification requirements 10.41–10.47
outline applications 12.58–12.67
outline planning permission 9.13–9.24
overlapping applications 10.18–10.21
parish and community councils 10.42
planning permission, construction of 15.04–15.08, 15.11–15.14
Planning Portal 9.06
planning register 9.64–9.66
present interests in land 9.30–9.31
pre-submission requirements 9.01–9.66
procedure on receipt by local planning authorities 10.01–10.63
publicity 10.26–10.40, 10.47
repeat applications 10.10–10.17
retrospectivity 10.22–10.25, 14.78–14.80

Index

applications for planning permission (*cont.*)
  same day, applications received on 10.21
  scope 15.15–15.26
  similar applications 10.10–10.12, 10.14, 10.18–10.19
  Standard Application Form 9.01–9.06, 9.38
  statutory undertakers 16.07
  third parties 9.30–9.31
  twin-tracking 9.57–9.58
  validation of applications 9.03–9.04, 9.07
architectural or historical interest *see* ancient monuments; conservation areas and conservation area consent; sites of archaeological interest; special architectural or historical interest; scheduled monuments
Areas of Outstanding Natural Beauty (AONB) 3.03, 7.20
areas of special scientific interest, areas of (ASSIs) 2.82, 25.20
art, works of 21.39–21.44
article 4 directions 7.06–7.11, 7.36
assembly and leisure 6.89–6.90, 7.36
awnings 24.08

bad faith 20.151
bad neighbour development 10.26, 10.33
Barlow Report 1.10, 1.13
battlefields 21.127
benefit to a particular person, limiting 14.61–14.67
betterment 1.07–1.08, 1.10–1.13, 1.16
bias
  default powers to revoke or modify planning permission 2.40, 2.44
  independent and impartial tribunal 19.04, 19.10, 19.15
  local authorities 16.15, 16.18–16.29
  Model Code of Conduct, abolition of 16.29
  natural justice or fairness 18.25–18.26, 18.30–18.38
  personal interests of committee members 16.23–16.24, 16.27–16.29
  real likelihood/possibility test 16.19, 16.22–16.24
  superstores and hyperstores 16.18–16.24
  test 16.19, 16.22–16.24
biodiversity 2.57
blinds 24.08
boundaries of roads 5.65–5.66
breach of condition notices 20.05, 20.138–20.153
  appeals 20.150
  bad faith 20.151
  burden of proof 20.142
  Carnwath Report 20.139
  criminal offences 20.144–20.150
  enforcement notices 20.134–20.140, 20.150
  injunctions 20.140
  judicial review 20.149, 20.151
  magistrates 20.151
  service 20.141, 20.143, 20.150–20.151
  stop notices 20.139
  time limits 20.25, 20.143
  validity of notices 20.150
Brexit 13.03
bridleways 15.39
Broads
  Broads Authority 2.90, 7.20
  conservation 2.90
  General Permitted Development Order 7.20
  simplified planning zones 2.82
brownfield land register 7.68, 9.26
builders' huts 7.39
building, definition of
  buildings operations 5.15–5.29
  caravans 5.23
  certificates of lawfulness 5.24–5.25
  chalets 5.20
  cloches on agricultural land 5.26
  coal hoppers and conveyors 5.16
  demolition 5.53–5.54
  erections 5.14–5.26
  fences 5.26
  gates 5.26
  marquees 5.21
  mobile cranes 5.18
  model villages 5.15
  permanence 5.15, 5.18–5.31
  physical attachment 5.15, 5.19, 5.21
  polytunnels on agricultural land 5.25, 5.27–5.29
  sculptures 5.25
  size 5.15, 5.19–5.20
  walls 5.26
building operations 5.12–5.39
  buildings, definition of 5.14–5.29
  demolition 5.40–5.60, 5.76
  extensions 5.32–5.35
  external appearance, material effect on 5.30–5.32, 5.36–5.39
  floodlights 5.37–5.38
  interior 5.30–5.33
  mezzanine floors 5.34–5.35
  not development, operations which are 5.30–5.39
  operational development 5.12–5.39, 5.75, 5.77
  other operations, definition of 5.75, 5.77
building preservation notices 21.113–21.129
  alterations 21.113–21.114
  certificates of immunity 21.113
  compensation 21.117, 21.119, 21.122
  criminal offences 21.114, 21.116
  demolition 21.113–21.114, 21.121
  development proposals, buildings threatened by 21.119–21.122
  duration 21.115
  extension 21.113–21.114
  historic battlefields 21.127
  historic parks and gardens 21.123–21.126
  lapse of notice 21.116
  listed buildings 21.113–21.129
  public pressure 21.119

Index

restrictions 21.117
Secretary of State, statutory listing by 21.113, 21.115, 21.117
special architectural or historical interest, preservation of buildings of 21.113, 21.118
spot listing 21.118
statistics 21.118
World Heritage Sites 21.128–21.129
building societies 6.61
buildings *see also* **building, definition of**
agriculture 6.45, 7.47–7.52
buildings operations 5.12–5.39
building preservation notices 21.113–21.129
outline planning permission 9.13, 9.16
purchase notices 27.40
removal 27.40
telecommunications 7.54–7.55
use, condition of specification of 14.68
burial grounds 6.30–6.31
bushes 25.04
business uses
amenity, detriment to the 6.72, 6.75
industrial process, definition of 6.73
light industry 6.74
material change of use 6.56, 6.72–6.75, 7.36
Use Classes Order 6.56, 6.72–6.75, 7.36

called in applications
administrative powers 2.24–2.33
appeals 18.04
Crown development 16.04
Development Management Procedure Orders, directions on 2.31–2.33
fair hearing, right to a 2.29
Government policy 18.04
guidelines 2.25
judicial review 2.26, 2.28–2.29
merits 2.25, 2.29
natural habitats and protected species, conservation of 26.06
oral hearings, right to 2.29
reasons 2.27
statutory undertakers 16.08
timetable 18.70
urgent Crown development 16.04
written representations 18.42
caravans
acknowledgment of receipt of planning applications 10.03–10.05
agriculture 6.38
building, definition of 5.23
discrimination 2.18
enforcement notices 20.41
intensification 6.104–6.106, 6.113
occupiers, definition of 20.41
site licences 10.03–10.05
stop notices 20.116
temporary stop notices 2.17–2.18

care, persons in single households receiving 6.82, 6.86
Carnwath Report 20.03, 20.07, 20.139, 20.158–20.159, 20.169
carrying out an activity without ascertaining whether it needs permission 8.17–8.21
cause of action estoppel 20.105
central government *see also* **Secretary of State**
applications for planning permission 11.27–11.61
consultation 1.06
delay 1.06
Government departments, objections from other 18.15
government policies as material consideration 11.27–11.61
highways 15.45
Homes England 2.75–2.77, 2.100
local authorities 16.10
organization of planning 2.01–2.63
policies 11.27–11.61
public control over land use, growth of 1.06
residential developments affecting government objectives 18.15
certificates of lawfulness of existing use or development (CLEUDs)
administrative powers 2.23
appeals 2.23, 18.05, 20.177, 20.179
applications 20.188
burden of proof 20.177
Carnwath Report 20.169
discretion 20.178
enforcement 20.05, 20.169–20.187
error 20.186
established use certificates 20.169, 20.171–20.172
evidence 20.177
guidance 20.179–20.182
immunity 20.171–20.172, 20.180–20.185
larger areas of land, issue of further certificates to cover 20.187
material change of use 20.171, 20.179, 20.184
merits of decisions 20.170
operational development 20.169
planning permission 8.02–8.08
purpose 20.171
rescission 20.186
revocation 20.186
sale of property 20.171
standard of proof 20.177
Thurrock test 20.180–20.184
certificates of lawfulness of proposed use or development (CLOPUDs) 8.02–8.08
administrative powers 2.23
appeals 2.23, 18.05
building, definition of 5.24–5.25
burden of proof 8.03
Carnwath Report 20.169
enforcement 20.05, 20.169–20.170, 20.189
false statements 8.04

Index

certificates of lawfulness of proposed use or development (CLOPUDs) *(cont.)*
  General Permitted Development Order 8.02, 8.08
  limitations 8.07
  material change of use 8.06
  merits of decisions 20.170
  operational development 20.169
  prescribed form 8.03–8.04
  revocation 20.186
  standing to apply 8.08
certificates of lawfulness of proposed works 21.152
chalets 5.20
change of use *see* material change of use
cheque book planning 17.07
churches 21.49, 21.53–21.55
CIL *see* Community Infrastructure Levy (CIL)
circulars 2.55, 2.56, 2.60
Citizen's Charter 16.02
City of London Corporation 2.98
clean air 11.73–11.75
clearances 1.02
CLEUDs *see* certificates of lawfulness of existing use or development (CLEUDs)
climate change 4.48, 18.15
CLOPUDs *see* certificates of lawfulness of proposed use or development (CLOPUDs)
coal hoppers and conveyors 5.16
coastal areas 1.10
colourability test 14.99–14.101
commencement of development
  commencement of developments 14.81–14.126
  completion notices 14.120–14.126
  duration of permissions and conditions 14.81–14.126
  expiry of permission 14.81–14.126
  extending time conditions 14.116–14.119
  full planning permission 14.82–14.109
  outline planning permission 14.110–14.115, 14.119
  requiring 14.58–14.60, 14.81–14.126
committees
  delegation 11.01–11.07, 11.09–11.14
  joint committees 4.64
  Model Code of Conduct 16.29
  personal interests 16.23–16.24, 16.27–16.29
common land *see* town and village greens
community care houses providing support for disabled and mentally disabled people 6.84
community councils *see* parish and community councils
community development 4.11
Community Infrastructure Levy (CIL)
  affordable housing, expenditure on 17.72, 17.78
  amending regulations (draft) 17.81
  calculation 17.64–17.65
  charging schedule 17.66–17.67, 17.73
  commencement of development 17.64–17.65
  creation 1.26
  demand notices 17.79
  development liable to the levy, definition of 17.64
  entry into force 17.69
  external costs borne by community 1.16
  infrastructure, expenditure on 17.70–17.77
  liability 17.64–17.65
  listing of projects 17.68
  Localism Act 2011 1.27, 17.71
  neighbourhood, expenditure on 17.71
  outline permission 17.65
  planning contributions 17.24, 17.63, 17.77–17.83
  planning gain 17.62, 17.63
  Planning Gain Supplement 17.62
  planning obligations 17.24, 17.54–17.55, 17.63–17.83
  pooled contributions, restrictions on 17.78
  review of (Peace Review) 17.80
community right to build 1.27, 7.65
community uses 6.56, 6.88–6.90, 7.36
compensation *see also* damages
  alteration of buildings 27.14–27.15
  ancient monuments 22.21
  article 4 directions 7.11–7.12, 7.36
  assessment 21.107, 27.15
  building preservation notices 21.117, 21.119, 21.122
  compensation/betterment problem 1.07–1.08, 1.10–1.13, 1.16
  compensation fund 1.13–1.15, 1.18
  compulsory purchases 1.22, 21.107–21.112, 21.122
  conditions 23.17
  conservation areas 27.06
  default powers to revoke or modify planning permission 2.47–2.53
  demolition of listed buildings 21.107–21.112
  depreciation in value 27.10
  development plans 27.03
  discontinuance of use 27.14–27.15
  easements and other interests or rights, interference with 15.41–15.42
  expenditure in compliance with work 27.08–27.09, 27.13–27.15
  General Permitted Development Order 7.11–7.12, 7.36
  historical background 27.01–27.02
  listed buildings 21.107–21.112, 21.122
  loss or damage 27.08
  minerals 23.01–23.02, 23.17, 27.10
  Parliamentary and Local Government Ombudsmen 18.141
  planning contravention notices 20.08
  planning permission 1.13, 1.17–1.18, 27.03, 27.06–27.07
  public control over land use, growth of 1.07–1.08, 1.10–1.16
  purchase notices 27.35–27.38
  refusal of planning permission 1.13, 1.17–1.18, 7.11
  removal of buildings 27.14–27.15
  restrictions on development 27.01–27.07

Index

revocation or modification of planning permissions 27.08–27.13
scheduled monuments 22.21
sites of archaeological interest 22.21
stop notices 20.08, 20.119–20.123
subsequent applications, time limit for 27.12
temporary stop notices 20.23
Town and Country Planning Act 1990 27.08–27.13
town planning schemes 27.02–27.03
tree preservation orders 25.19
value, loss of development 22.21
compensation/betterment problem 1.07–1.08
definition 1.07
development charges 1.13, 1.16
floating value 1.10, 1.12
industrial or commercial purposes, land zoned for 1.07
recovery of value of betterment 1.07
sale of land, deferment until 1.07
shifting value 1.10–1.11
Uthwatt Report 1.10–1.12, 1.14
completion notices 14.120–14.126
comprehensive development, areas of 3.06
compulsory purchase
ancient monuments 22.09
appeals against repair notices 21.104
compensation 1.22, 21.107–21.112, 21.122
deliberate disrepair, allowing 21.108–21.112
development plan documents 4.84
directions for minimum compensation 21.108–21.112
listed buildings 21.101–21.112
nationally significant infrastructure projects inquiries 28.17, 28.33–28.34
public works orders 16.30, 16.37
repairs notice, service of 21.102–21.105
schemes of national significance 16.43
Secretary of State 2.09, 21.104–21.105
concert halls 6.89–6.90
conditions 14.01–14.126
acknowledgment of receipt of planning applications 10.08
advertising, control of outdoor 24.15–24.18, 24.22
amendment of applications 10.37, 10.63
appeals 2.21, 14.69, 14.76, 18.02–18.03, 18.10
applications, determination of planning 11.27
benefit to a particular person, limiting 14.61–14.67
breach of condition notices 20.150
certainty 14.25–14.28
challenging invalid conditions 14.69
commencement of development, requiring 14.58–14.60, 14.81–14.126
conditions precedent 14.103–14.109
definition of development 14.04
demolition 21.71
development orders 7.02

discharge 10.37
duration of planning permissions 14.81–14.126
effect of invalid conditions 14.70–14.75
enforceable, conditions must be 14.08, 14.28–14.30
enforcement notices 20.88
existing use rights 14.31–14.34, 14.72
expiry of permission 15.66
extending time conditions 14.116–14.119
fact or degree, questions of 14.37
fairly and reasonably relate to development 14.13–14.20, 14.36
full planning permission 14.82–14.109
General Permitted Development Order 7.13–7.20
general power 14.05–14.35
Grampian-type conditions 14.42–14.48
imposed for a planning purpose 14.09–14.12, 14.36
Interim Development Order Permissions 2.67
life of a planning permission 15.66
limited period, permission granted for a 14.49–14.57, 14.66
listed buildings 21.60, 21.62–21.63, 21.71–21.72
material change of use 14.04, 14.18–14.19
material considerations 14.08
minerals 23.01–23.02, 23.17–23.20, 23.24–23.28
model conditions 14.01
necessary, conditions must be 14.01, 14.08
negative conditions 14.42–14.48
normal use of land 14.57–14.58
operational development 14.04
outline planning permission 9.17–9.18
particular person, limiting benefit to a 14.61–14.67
planning agreements 17.14–17.17
planning obligations 17.28
positive conditions 14.43
precision 14.08, 14.35
public functions, provision of 14.21–14.23
publicity 10.37
purchase notices 27.17
reasonableness 14.08, 14.13–14.23, 14.28, 14.36, 14.38, 14.42–14.48
refusal of permission 11.27
regulating other land 14.37–14.41
relevance to development 14.08, 14.13–14.20, 14.36
relevance to planning 14.08–14.12, 14.36
removal of conditions previously attached 14.76–14.77, 14.80
reserved matters 9.17–9.18
retrospective planning applications 14.78–14.80
reviews 18.110–18.111
scheduled monuments 22.03–22.04
severance 14.70–14.71, 14.74–14.75
simplified planning zones 2.83
specific powers 14.03, 14.36–14.68
tests 14.07–14.08, 14.24–14.35
time conditions, extending 14.116–14.119
tree preservation orders 25.01, 25.08, 25.19
trivial/fundamental dichotomy 14.72–14.73

conditions *(cont.)*
  uncertain conditions 14.25–14.28
  unenforceable conditions 14.08, 14.28–14.30
  Use Classes Order 6.91
  use of buildings, specifying 14.68
  void, invalidity having effect of making permission 14.70–14.75
  Wednesbury unreasonableness 14.28
conflicts
  development plan documents 4.78
  local authorities, conflicts of interest in 16.25
  planning permission 15.66–15.69
  policy 4.78
consent *see also* **conservation areas and conservation area consent; listing buildings and listed building consent**
  advertising, control of outdoor 18.05, 24.12, 24.14–24.24, 24.28
  alterations 21.57–21.58, 21.69
  demolition 21.57–21.59, 21.69, 21.148
  hazardous substances 16.37, 18.13
  scheduled monuments 22.03
  single consent regime 1.26
  term consent 14.53–14.57, 14.66
  time limits 21.72
  tree preservation orders 25.08, 25.14–25.15
conservation *see* **conservation areas and conservation area consent; listing buildings and listed building consent; natural habitats and protected species, conservation of**
conservation areas and conservation area consent 21.130–21.148
  advertisements, area of special control of 21.147, 24.20, 24.25
  alterations 21.143
  appeals 18.05, 18.50
  applications for planning permission 10.17, 10.20, 10.45
  building preservation notices 21.121
  character or appearance, affecting 10.45, 21.134–21.141
  conditions 21.62, 21.72
  consequences of demolition 21.133
  consolidating legislation 1.21–1.22
  demolition 5.48, 5.52, 21.148
    building preservation notices 21.121
    consent 21.148
    ecclesiastical use and monuments, buildings in 21.50
    notice 21.06
    pretext to prevent 21.130
    replacement developments, consideration of 21.142
  designation 2.09, 21.130–21.133
  discretion 21.130–21.131
  ecclesiastical use and monuments, buildings in 21.50
  estate agents, advertising by 24.20

fees for applications 9.53
  General Permitted Development Order 7.20, 21.144–21.145
  harm, consideration of 21.134–21.141
  local inquiries 18.50
  National Planning Policy Framework 21.01–21.02
  nationally significant infrastructure projects inquiries 28.16, 28.18
  newspaper advertisements 10.45
  notification requirements 10.45
  outline planning permission 9.16
  overlapping applications 10.20
  planning agreements 17.13
  Planning (Listed Buildings and Conservation Areas) Act 1990 1.21–1.22
  Planning Policy Statements 21.02
  preservation or enhancement of character or appearance 21.134–21.141
  publicity 10.45, 21.143–21.148
  repeat applications 10.17
  replacement developments, consideration of 21.142
  Secretary of State 2.09
  simplified planning zones 2.82, 21.132
  special architectural or historical interest, areas of 21.130–21.132
  Steinberg principle 21.134–21.136
  trees
    notice of cutting down, lopping or topping 21.146
    tree preservation orders 16.04, 21.146, 25.04, 25.15
  Wednesbury unreasonableness 21.130
Conservation Covenants 22.22–22.23
Conservation of Habitats and Species Regulations (Habitats Regulations) 2017 26.02–26.12
consolidating legislation 1.21–1.22
consolidation of undesirable uses 11.158
construction of a planning permission 15.01–15.14
  applications 15.04–15.08, 15.11–15.14
  correspondence 15.05, 15.10
  documents, taking into account 15.02, 15.05–15.14
  extrinsic evidence 15.04–15.08, 15.11–15.14
  planning register, inspection of 15.03–15.04
  renewal applications 15.07–15.08
  resolutions of planning authorities or committees 15.09–15.10
consultation
  agricultural land 10.49
  applicants, by 9.63
  applications 10.48–10.55
  central government, approval by 1.06
  Countryside Agency 13.18
  county planning authorities 10.51
  English Heritage 21.126
  English Nature 13.18
  Environment Agency 11.154, 13.18

fees 9.60–9.61
Greater London 2.99
hazardous substances, HSE and 10.48
Historic Buildings and Monuments Commission 13.18
informal planning advice, liability for negligent 9.62
listed buildings 21.20, 21.62–21.63
local authorities 9.59–9.62
local development orders 7.58
London, Mayor of 2.99
national amenity societies 10.53
nationally significant infrastructure projects inquiries 28.21–28.22, 28.24, 28.26
natural habitats and protected species, conservation of 26.03, 26.11
negligence 9.63
neighbourhood development orders 7.61
neighbours 10.26
number of consultations 10.55
parish councils 10.53
Planning Policy Statements 9.59
pre-submission requirements 9.59–9.63
public control over land use, growth of 1.06
publicity 10.26, 10.39
regional planning guidance 3.25
responses 10.52–10.55
Secretary of State 10.53–10.54
specialist bodies 10.48
strategic environmental assessments 13.16–13.18
time limits 10.06, 10.50, 10.52–10.54
very large developments, consultation on 1.27
content and form of planning applications 9.01–9.12
design and access statements 9.08–9.10
directory requirements 9.11
mandatory requirements 9.11
Planning Portal 9.06
Standard Application Form 9.01–9.06
validation of applications 9.03–9.04, 9.07
contravention notices *see* **planning contravention notices**
conveyancing 9.45
costs 18.79–18.92
appeals 18.79–18.92
applications 18.90
cancellation of appeals 18.83
criteria 18.84
examples of where parties are at risk of costs against them 18.87–18.89
late claims 18.90
planning agreements 17.60
planning obligations 17.60
reasonableness 18.85
reasons 18.91
Report on the Award of Costs at Statutory Inquiries 18.81
Secretary of State 18.79–18.84

standard basis 18.90
taxation of costs 18.90
unreasonable conduct, sufficient evidential basis for finding 18.92
Wednesbury unreasonableness 18.85
Countryside Agency, consultation of 13.18
county planning authorities and district planning authorities 2.64–2.66, 2.92–2.97
applications for planning permission 10.10–10.25
consultation 10.51
development control 2.92, 2.95–2.96
development plans, preparation and maintenance of 2.92, 2.94
division of responsibility 2.66, 2.93–2.97
functions 2.92
Greater London 2.64
joint planning boards 2.67
minerals local plans 2.94
regional strategies and Regional Planning Boards 2.94
restructuring 2.65
statistics 2.97
surveys 4.13–4.15
two-tier system 2.65–2.66
unitary authorities 2.65, 2.94
unitary development plans 2.94
waste local plans 2.94
covenants
Conservation Covenants 22.22–22.23
forestry 25.05
positive covenants 17.32
restrictive covenants 15.43–15.44, 17.32
Criminal Justice and Courts Act 18.129
criminal offences
advertising, control of outdoor 24.01, 24.04–24.05
alterations 21.45–21.46
archaeological importance, areas of 22.11–22.12
breach of condition notices 20.144–20.150
building preservation notices 21.114, 21.116
demolition 21.45–21.46
ecclesiastical use and monuments, buildings in 21.49–21.50
enforcement notices 20.01, 20.126–20.132, 21.77, 21.85–21.91
fears of residents 11.104
fly-posting 24.01, 24.31–24.34
fraud 2.40, 2.44, 9.49
hedgerows 25.33
high hedges 25.40
injunctions 20.158–20.160
listed buildings 21.45–21.48, 21.77, 21.85–21.91
metal detectors in protected places, offence of using 22.12
nationally significant infrastructure projects inquiries 28.36
planning contravention notices 20.09
planning permission, notification to owners of 9.44

Index

criminal offences (*cont.*)
  scheduled monuments 22.03
  stop notices 20.113–20.114
  surface soil, removal of 20.01
  temporary stop notices 20.22
  tree preservation orders 25.06–25.08
cross-examination 18.49, 28.29, 28.30
Crown 16.01–16.04
  Citizen's Charter 16.02
  enforcement 16.04, 20.02
  immunity 16.02–16.04
  national security 16.04
  old mining permissions 16.04
  Secretary of State, applications to the 16.04
  tree preservation orders 16.04, 25.16
  urgent Crown development 16.04
curtilage 6.12–6.32
  definition 6.12–6.14
  ecclesiastical use and monuments, buildings in 21.54–21.55
  extension of homes 7.25–7.27, 7.29–7.30
  fact or degree, matters of 7.29, 7.31
  gardens 6.13, 6.51
  General Permitted Development Order 7.22–7.32
  hedgerows 25.25
  incidental to enjoyment of dwelling house, uses which are 6.12–6.32
  listed buildings 21.12, 21.25, 21.28–21.30
  open land embodied in curtilage 15.31
  permitted development 7.23–7.28
  re-erecting houses or improvements 7.29–7.30
  satellite antennas 7.32
  temporary buildings and uses 7.40
custom housebuilding *see* **self-build and custom housebuilding**

damages 15.61, 15.65, 20.164 *see also* **compensation**
dams 28.15
death 15.66
deceit 15.61–15.65
decision letters, power to correct 18.73–18.78
declarations
  action for a declaration 8.09–8.16
  incompatibility, of 19.01
  judicial review 18.130
  material change of use 8.10
  nuisance 15.50
  originating summons 8.09–8.10
  planning permission 8.09–8.16
  scope of planning permission 8.09
decline to determine planning applications, power to 10.10–10.25
default powers to revoke or modify planning permission
  administrative powers 2.35–2.53
  bias 2.40, 2.44
  compensation 2.47–2.53
  development plans 2.35–2.53
  financial consequences, consideration of 2.47–2.53
  fraud 2.40, 2.44
  judicial review 2.43–2.45, 2.53
  material considerations 2.48
  national policy guidance 2.53
  Phelps Report 2.39–2.40, 2.43
  public interest 2.51
  revocation of planning permission 2.35–2.53
  standing 2.41–2.42, 2.45
  Town and Country Planning Act 1990 2.35–2.53
definition of development *see* **development, definition of**
delegation 11.01–11.14
Delivering a Fundamental Change consultation paper 1.23
demolition
  building operations 5.40–5.60, 5.76
  building preservation notices 21.113–21.114, 21.121
  buildings 5.53–6.55
  chalets 5.20
  compensation for demolishing listed buildings 21.107–21.112
  compulsory purchase for listed buildings 21.107–21.112
  conditions 21.71
  conservation areas 5.48, 5.52, 21.06, 21.50, 21.121, 21.148
  criminal offences 21.45–21.46
  current position 5.51–5.60
  development, definition of 5.40–5.60, 5.62, 5.64, 5.76
  dwelling houses 5.53–5.56
  ecclesiastical use and monuments, buildings in 21.50–21.51
  enforcement notices 21.79–21.80
  engineering operations 5.60, 5.62, 5.64
  environmental impact assessments 5.55, 5.60
  Environmental Impact Assessment Directive 5.55
  listed buildings 5.48, 5.52, 21.03–21.07, 21.57–21.59, 21.69
  compensation 21.107–21.112
  compulsory purchase 21.107–21.112
  conditions 21.71
  criminal offences 21.45–21.46
  deliberate disrepair, allowing 21.107–21.112
  enforcement notices 21.79–21.80
  grades 21.19
  notice 21.57, 21.65
  partial demolition 21.04–21.07
  permitted development, as 5.54
  recording of building 21.57
  repair 21.107–21.112
  restoration of buildings 21.79–21.80
  withdrawal of status 21.18–21.19
  notice 21.06, 21.57, 21.65
  operational development 5.40–5.60, 5.62, 5.64, 5.76

Index

partial demolition 5.60, 21.04–21.07
pretexts 21.130
prior approval 5.56–5.59
recording of building 21.57
repair, listed buildings in need of 21.107–21.112
replacement developments, consideration of 21.142
restoration/replacement of buildings 20.61–20.62, 21.79–21.80
Secretary of State, directions of 5.51–5.52, 5.55–5.56
structural alterations 5.60
use of buildings, specifying the 14.68
whole building, removal of 5.47–5.48
departure applications 10.56–10.60
depreciation in value 27.08–27.13
design principles and concepts, statements of 21.61
determination of planning permission applications 11.01–11.159
affordable housing 11.125–11.133
alternative sites, existence of 11.82–11.88
appeal decisions, previous 11.62–11.68
conditional permission 11.27
consolidation of undesirable uses 11.158
development plans 11.31–11.44
environmental information 11.159
fear of residents 11.104–11.109
financial circumstances 11.134–11.145
government policies 11.27–11.61
licensing control 11.156–11.157
material considerations 11.44–11.61
personal circumstances of applicants 11.110–11.119
piecemeal development, risk of 11.89–11.90
pollution control 11.146–11.155
precedent, creation of a 11.77–11.81
preservation of existing uses 11.91–11.103
previous appeal decisions 11.62–11.68
private interests, protection of 11.69–11.76
reasons 11.05
refusal of permission 11.27
development charges 1.13, 1.16–1.17
development corporations 2.100
development, definition of
appeals 18.11
central government, approval by 1.06
core definition 5.02
demolition 5.40–5.60, 5.62, 5.64, 5.76
development plans 1.04–1.05, 3.17–3.20
enforcement notices 20.79, 20.101
engineering operations 5.61–5.71, 5.75, 5.77–5.79
fair hearing, right to a 19.13
Human Rights Act 1998 19.13
local authorities 16.16
local inquiries 18.51
local plan tier 3.20
major infrastructure projects 28.01, 28.04
material change of use 5.02–5.10, 6.01–6.169
mining operations 5.72–5.75, 5.77

nationally significant infrastructure projects inquiries 28.01, 28.04, 28.16
natural justice or fairness 18.21
operational development 5.01–5.79
planning obligations 17.60
public control over land use, growth of 1.04
public inquiries 28.04
refusal of planning permission 10.02
simplified planning zones 2.86
structure plan tier 3.17–3.19
superstores and hyperstores 16.16
Development Management Procedure Order (DMPO)
administrative powers 2.31–2.34
called in applications 2.21–2.33
consultation 2.34
green belt 2.33–2.34
registers, maintenance of 2.13
scope 2.13
text App D
development of development plans 3.01–3.35
1947 system 3.04–3.10
1968 system 3.04, 3.10–3.28
2004 system 3.04, 3.29–3.33
comprehensive development, area of 3.06
content
changes 3.04
three generations of plans 3.04–3.33
defects in systems 3.08–3.10, 3.17–3.25
delay 3.17–3.20
Delivering a Fundamental Change 3.29–3.31
documents, content of development plan 3.35
first generation plans 3.05–3.10
form
changes 3.04
three generations of plans 3.04–3.33
fresh surveys, duty to carry out 3.07
Future of Development Plans 3.10
Greater London 3.14–3.15
historical background 3.01–3.04
irrelevant policies, examples of 3.19
land use planning 3.09, 3.12, 3.19
Local Development Plan Framework 3.30–3.32
Local Government Act 1992 3.04
local plan tier 3.11, 3.13, 3.16, 3.20–3.25, 3.28–3.30
Localism Act 2011 3.34–3.36
London boroughs 3.04, 3.14–3.15
metropolitan boroughs 3.04, 3.14–3.15
minerals local plans 3.28
object, denial of right to 3.21
old-style plans 3.04–3.10
Planning and Compulsory Purchase Act 1991 3.26–3.28
Planning and Compulsory Purchase Act 2004 3.04, 3.29–3.33
planning permission 3.01–3.02
population increases 3.08

Index

development of development plans (*cont.*)
public local inquiry system 3.31
purpose 3.01–3.06, 3.12–3.13
regional planning guidance
  (RPGs) 3.22–3.25, 3.32
regional spatial strategy, replacement with 3.32
regional strategies, abolition of 3.34–3.36
reorganization of local government 3.16
second generation plans 3.04, 3.10–3.28
single local plans 3.28
single structure plans 3.27
structure plan tier 3.11–3.13, 3.16–3.19, 3.24,
  3.27–3.28, 3.30, 3.32
surveys 3.05, 3.07
third generation plans 3.04, 3.29–3.33
three generations of plans 3.04–3.33
Town and Country Planning Act 1947 3.04–3.10
Town and Country Planning Act 1968 3.04,
  3.10–3.28
Town and Country Planning Act 1971 3.10–3.11
Town and Country Planning Act
  1990 3.10–3.11, 3.26
traffic, growth in 3.08
two-tier system 3.10–3.28
unitary authorities 3.04
unitary development plans 3.15, 3.24, 3.29
waste local plans 3.28
development orders *see also* **local development orders (LDOs)**
appeals 18.03
approvals 18.03
conditions 7.02
Localism Act 2011 7.04
negative procedure 2.13
neighbourhood development orders 7.04,
  7.61–7.66
planning permission 7.01–7.04
revision of revocation of order, completion
  after 7.60
special development orders 2.15–2.18
statutory instruments 2.13
development plan documents 4.26–4.58
adoption 4.56–4.58, 4.61
appraisal 4.45
climate change 4.48
community development 4.11
compulsory purchase 4.84
conflicts in policy 4.78
definition 4.26
Greater London 4.77
implementation 4.66
independent examination 4.49–4.55
inspectors' reports, binding nature of 4.56–4.58
joint committees 4.64
justified, effective and consistent with national
  policy requirement 4.61–4.55
legal challenges 4.67–4.76
legal significance 4.77–4.85

local development documents 4.22–4.30,
  23.31–4.48, 4.59, 7.58, 13.08
local development framework and schemes
  4.14–4.25, 4.45–4.48, 4.58
local development plan documents 4.01–4.02,
  4.18, 4.26–4.32, 4.48, 4.59–4.66
Localism Act 2011 4.01, 4.60
material considerations 4.26, 4.84
meaning of 4.85
miscellaneous provisions under PCPA Part 2
  4.60–4.66
modifications 4.56–4.58
National Planning Policy Framework 4.61
old system to new system, transfer of 4.86–4.89
Planning and Compulsory Purchase Act
  2004 4.01–4.91
  old system to new system, transfer
    of 4.86–4.89
  Royal Assent 4.87
  transitional provisions 4.79, 4.86–4.89
Planning Inspectorate 4.49–4.55
Planning Policy Statements 4.54
policies map 4.47
preparation 4.45–4.48
quashing plans 4.82
reasons for recommendations 4.55
regional spatial strategies 4.01
regional strategies 4.01
reviews 4.26
revision 4.63
revocation 4.62
scrutiny 4.45
soundness of plans 4.51–4.55
spatial planning documents, as 4.45
specification of development plan documents 4.45
structure plans 4.02
supplementary planning documents 4.27–4.32
surveys 4.12–4.15
sustainable community strategy 4.48
timetables 4.02
transitional provisions 4.79, 4.86–4.89
urban development corporations 4.65
Wales 4.90–4.91
withdrawal 4.57, 4.60
development plans *see also* **development of
  development plans; development plan documents**
administrative powers 2.20
adoption 2.20
advertisements 24.02
ancient monuments 22.13, 22.15
applications for planning permission 10.56–10.63,
  11.31–11.44
approval 2.20
changes to system 1.20, 1.23
compensation for restrictions on
  development 27.01–27.07
county planning authorities and district planning
  authorities 2.92, 2.94

Index

default powers 2.35–2.53
delay 1.04–1.05
departure applications 10.56–10.60
directions 10.56–10.63
  enforcement notices 20.40–20.41
  failure to comply with directions 10.63
  judicial review 10.63
maintenance 2.92, 2.94
major infrastructure projects 28.06
material considerations 11.31–11.35, 11.44
modification 2.20
national importance, archaeological remains of 22.15
nationally significant infrastructure projects inquiries 28.06
neighbourhood development plans, and 4.34, 4.43
not in accordance with plans, developments which are 10.56–10.63
outdated plans 1.05
planning agreements 17.09–17.11
planning gain 17.09–17.11
planning permission, grant of 10.56–10.63
policy control 2.20
preparation 2.92, 2.94
presumption in favour of plans 11.36–11.41
public control over land use, growth of 1.04–1.05
sites of archaeological interest 22.13, 22.15
special procedures 10.56
summaries of policies and proposals in development plans 18.08
Wales 4.90
devolution 1.23, 4.91
disabled and mentally disabled people, community care houses providing support for 6.84
discontinuance
  advertising, control of outdoor 24.15, 24.21
  compensation 27.14–27.15
  consolidation of undesirable uses 11.158
  enforcement notices 20.124
  minerals 23.01
  natural habitats and protected species, conservation of 26.06
  notice 24.15, 24.21, 26.06
  purchase notices 27.40
discrimination 11.51–11.53, 20.19
district planning authorities *see* **county planning authorities and district planning authorities**
documents *see* **development plan documents** 21.60
drinking establishments 6.69, 7.36
duration of planning permissions and conditions 14.81–14.126
  commencement of developments 14.81–14.126
  completion notices 14.120–14.126
  expiry of permission 14.81–14.126
  extending time conditions 14.116–14.119
  full planning permission 14.82–14.109
  life of a planning permission 15.66–15.72
  outline planning permission 14.110–14.115, 14.119

dwelling houses *see also* **housing**
  adjoining dwelling houses 5.55–5.56
  buildings adjoining dwelling houses 5.55–5.56
  definition 5.53, 7.23
  demolition 5.53–5.56
  General Permitted Development Order 7.23
  normal use of land 6.21
  residential uses 6.82–6.84
  single dwelling house as two or more separate houses 6.93–6.97
  Use Classes Order 7.36

easements and other interests or rights, interference with 15.40–15.44
EC law *see* **EU law**
ecclesiastical use and monuments, buildings in
  alterations 21.50–21.51
  approved control systems 21.53, 21.55
  churches 21.49, 21.53–21.55
  conservation areas 21.50
  consultation papers 21.52–21.53
  criminal offences 21.49–21.50
  curtilage, objects or structures within 21.54–21.55
  demolition 21.50–21.51
  dual control 21.55
  ecclesiastical exemption 21.50–21.55
  extensions 21.50–21.51
  fixtures 21.54–21.55
  hedgerows 25.33
  listed buildings 21.49–21.55, 21.100
  local authorities' power to carry out works 21.100
  repairs 21.100
  Secretary of State, powers of 21.52
  statistics 21.49
  tombstones 21.54
  unauthorized works 21.51
economic considerations *see* **financial and economic considerations**
effect of planning permission 15.27–15.38
  existing use rights 15.27–15.33, 15.37–15.38
  new planning units, creation of 15.33–15.37
  old use, destruction of 15.27–15.33, 15.37–15.38
  open land embodied in curtilage 15.31
  part of land, development of 15.37–15.38
EIAs *see* **environmental impact assessments (EIAs)**
electric lines 28.15
emergencies *see* **urgency**
enabling powers 17.01–17.16
energy 2.57, 18.15
enforcement 20.99–20.189 *see also* **enforcement notices**
  advertising, control of outdoor 6.103, 24.04–24.06
  appeals 10.13
  binding assurances of non-enforcement 20.02
  breach of condition notices 20.05, 20.138–20.153
  Carnwath Report 20.03

Index

enforcement (cont.)
  certificates of lawfulness of existing use or
      development 20.05, 20.169–20.187
  certificates of lawfulness of proposed use or
      development 20.05, 20.169–20.170, 20.189
  conditions 14.08, 14.28–14.30
  Crown 16.04
  development consent orders 28.36
  entry, right of 20.05, 20.13–20.17
  injunctions 20.05, 20.152–20.169
  Localism Act 2011 1.27, 20.02
  nationally significant infrastructure projects
      inquiries 28.36
  planning agreements 17.03
  planning contravention notices 20.07–20.12
  planning obligations 17.26, 17.33
  repeat applications 10.13
  stop notices 20.109–20.123
  temporary stop notice procedure 20.02, 20.17–20.24
  time limits 20.02, 20.05, 20.25–20.39
  Town and Country Planning Act 1947 1.20
  tree preservation orders 25.06
enforcement notices 20.25–20.107 *see also*
    enforcement notices, appeals against
  additional matters 20.66
  advertising, control of outdoor 6.102–6.103
  breach of condition notice 20.134–20.140, 20.150
  caravan dwellers 20.41
  carrying out an activity without ascertaining
      whether it needs permission 8.17–8.20
  content 20.56–20.70
  copies 20.54
  criminal offences 20.01, 20.126–20.132
  Crown 20.02
  defective notices 20.36, 20.58
  demolition 21.79–21.80
  development plans 20.40–20.41
  discontinuance 20.124
  entry into force, date of 20.50, 20.53
  entry, right of 20.46, 20.124
  errors 20.37–20.38, 20.58, 20.78,
      20.91–20.94, 20.100
  execution of works by local planning
      authorities 20.05, 20.124–20.125
  extension of time 20.02, 20.68
  failure to comply 20.01
  fines 20.129
  further enforcement notice 20.137
  Human Rights Act 1998 20.132
  injunctions 20.132, 20.154–20.157
  issue 20.40–20.55
  listed buildings 21.77–21.92
  Localism Act 2011 20.02
  material change of use 20.59, 20.62
  material considerations 20.40–20.41
  minerals 23.01
  natural habitats and protected species,
      conservation of 26.06
  occupiers 20.41, 20.53
  once an enforcement notice, always an
      enforcement notice 20.133–20.136
  one man companies 20.42
  operational development 20.64
  owners 20.41–20.42, 20.53
  penalties, increase in 20.05
  planning contravention notices 20.07
  planning register 9.66
  quashing notices 2.22, 20.42, 20.53
  replacement buildings after
      demolition 20.61–20.62
  retrospectivity 10.22–10.25, 20.02
  service 20.41–20.49, 20.53–20.55
  specification of breach 20.55–20.60, 20.67
  stop notices 20.109–20.112, 20.123
  temporary stop notices 20.17
  time limits 20.25–20.39, 20.49–20.52, 20.68
  time periods for works or termination of
      activities 20.65
  Town and Country Planning Act
      1990 20.01–20.03
  under-enforcement 20.63, 20.67
  validity 20.45
  variation 2.22
  withdrawal 20.68–20.69
enforcement notices, appeals against 20.70–20.108
  architectural or historical interest, buildings not of
      special 21.82
  burden of proof 20.80
  cause of action estoppel 20.105
  conditions 20.88
  correct, power to 20.91, 20.93–20.94
  criminal offences 21.77, 21.85–21.91
  declarations 20.77
  defects 20.92
  delay 20.79, 20.101
  demolition 21.79–21.80
  entry, power of 21.84–21.92
  errors 20.78, 20.91, 20.93–20.94, 20.100
  existing use rights 20.98
  explanatory note 20.66
  fees 9.51, 9.55, 20.89
  final determinations 20.102
  General Permitted Development Order 20.97
  grounds 20.73–20.76, 20.80–20.81, 20.92
  High Court, appeals to 20.100, 20.103
  immunity 20.106
  information, provision of 18.06, 20.84
  injunctions 21.91
  issue estoppel 20.105–20.108
  listed buildings 18.13, 21.82–21.91
  local authorities 2.22
  merits of development 20.73–20.74
  notice of appeals 20.72, 20.79, 20.81,
      20.85, 20.89
  nullity of notice 20.76–20.78
  oaths 20.87

Index

procedure 20.81–20.90
quashing enforcement notices 20.83–20.84, 20.104
questions of fact and law or mixed questions of law and fact 20.73–20.74
rehearings 20.100, 20.103
relevant occupiers 20.71
remedial measures 20.73–20.74, 20.96
restoration of buildings 21.79–21.80
reversion to earlier use 20.168
rights of way, persons with 20.71
Secretary of State 20.70–20.72, 20.76–20.100, 20.103–20.105
service 20.43, 20.46–20.47, 20.71
setting aside notices 20.104
specification of works 20.95
statistics 2.22
steps to be taken, specification of 21.78
suspension 21.83, 21.85
terms of notices 20.96
Thrasyvoulou principle 20.105–20.108
time limits 20.39, 20.55, 20.72, 20.77, 20.83–20.85, 20.100–20.101, 21.82
time periods for work 20.85
Town and Country Planning Act 1990 18.06
unmeritorious appeals 20.101
validity of notice 20.76–20.78, 20.93–20.94
vary, power to 20.91–20.108
withdrawal of appeals 20.102

engineering operations
boundaries of roads 5.65–5.66
burial grounds 6.30
definition 5.61–5.65
demolition 5.60, 5.62, 5.64
development, definition of 5.61–5.71, 5.75, 5.77–5.79
environmental impact assessments 5.67
fish farming 5.69–5.71, 5.78
highways, access to 5.61, 5.68
operational developments 5.61–5.71, 5.75, 5.77–5.79
other operations 5.75, 5.77–5.79
skills, requirement for engineering 5.61
waste or refuse, deposit of 5.63

English Heritage
consultation 21.126
historic battlefields 21.127
historic parks and gardens 21.123, 21.126
listed buildings 21.65
scheduled monuments 22.06

English Nature, consultation of 13.18
English Partnerships 2.75
Enterprise and Regulation Reform Act 2013
certificates of lawfulness of proposed works 21.152
heritage partnership agreements 21.150
key reforms summarized 1.30, 21.149
listed building consent orders 21.151

enterprise zone authorities
administration 2.79

designation orders 2.78–2.80
duration 2.80
Secretary of State 2.78
simplified planning schemes 2.79
superfast broadband 2.80
tax 2.78, 2.80

enterprise zones 26.12

entry, right of
additional rights 20.13–20.16
enforcement 20.05, 20.13–20.16 20.46, 20.124, 21.84–21.92
hedgerows 25.33
listed buildings 21.85–21.92
notice period 20.14
planning contravention notices 20.07, 20.13
planning obligations 17.28
reasonable grounds 20.14
refusal of entry 20.15
tree preservation orders 25.08
warrants 20.15

environment
applications for planning permission 11.159
authorizations 11.146, 11.154
biodiversity 2.57
clean air 11.73–11.75
climate change 4.48, 18.15
Environment Act 1995 1.23
Environment Agency 1.23, 11.154
European Convention on Human Rights 20.19
fracking 11.155
geological conservation 2.57
Human Rights Act 1998 19.06, 19.09, 19.11–19.12, 19.21
information 11.159
licensing 11.146
material considerations 11.159
mineral planning permissions, review and updating of 1.23
minerals 23.22, 23.24
National Park authorities, creation of 1.23
planning control 11.146–11.155
Planning Policy Statements 2.57, 11.150–11.151
prescribed processes 11.152
renewable energy 2.57
sustainable development 4.08
temporary stop notices 20.19

environmental impact assessments (EIAs) 12.01–12.67
see also **strategic environmental assessments**
Aarhus Convention 12.26
appeals 18.13
consequences of breach of EIA Regulations 12.48–12.51
consideration of applications 12.38
Directive 12.01–12.03, 12.42–12.53, 12.62–12.64
demolition 5.55, 5.60
direct effect 12.57
engineering operations 5.67
Environmental Agency 12.17, 13.18

679

Index

environmental impact assessments (EIAs) (*cont.*)
   environmental information 11.159, 12.05, 12.34, 12.37–12.41, 12.48, 12.58
   environmental statements 12.05, 12.38, 12.48, 12.58–12.61
   expert qualitative assessments 12.04
   expert quantitative assessments 12.04
   freedom of information 12.34, 12.37
   General Permitted Development Order 7.16, 12.30
   information 12.15
   inspection of documents 12.39–12.40
   judicial challenge 12.42–12.67
   judicial review 12.42
   local development orders 7.56
   major developments 1.20
   mandatory assessments 12.06
   minerals 12.52–12.53, 23.08, 23.24–23.29
   nationally significant infrastructure projects inquiries 28.24
   nature, size and location of projects 12.06, 12.08
   outline planning applications 12.58–12.67
   outline planning permission 9.23, 12.44, 12.58–12.64
   permitted development rights 12.30–12.31
   planning register 9.66
   pollution control 11.148
   procedure 12.05
   projects requiring EIAs 12.06–12.41
   public involvement 12.17
   public works orders 16.38
   publicity 12.26, 12.35–12.37, 12.39–12.40
   purposive approach 12.52–12.57
   reasons 12.24–12.25
   remedial measures 12.17–12.22
   reserved matters 12.62–12.64, 12.66–12.67
   Schedule 1 developments 12.06, 12.07, 12.26
   Schedule 2 developments 12.06, 12.08–12.14, 12.26, 12.43
   scoping opinions 12.32–12.34, 12.36
   screening directions 12.24–12.25
   screening opinions 12.14–12.22, 12.24–12.25, 12.30, 12.36
   sensitive areas 12.06, 12.08
   significant effects 12.15–12.22
   simplified planning zones 2.85
   special cases 12.41
   strategic environmental assessments 4.29, 13.01–13.26
   Wednesbury unreasonableness 12.42
   who decides whether EIA is required 12.14–12.29
error
   certificates of lawfulness of existing use or development 20.186
   decision letters, power to correct 18.73–18.78
   enforcement notices 20.37–20.38, 20.58, 20.78, 20.91–20.94, 20.100
   planning permission, notification to owners of 9.46–9.47

   recovered cases 18.16
   time limits 20.37–20.39
established use certificates 20.169, 20.171–20.172
estate agents in conservation areas 24.20
estoppel *see also* **estoppel by representation**
   cause of action estoppel 20.105
   enforcement notices 20.105–20.108
   issue estoppel 20.105–20.108
estoppel by representation 11.15–11.26
   legitimate expectations 11.22–11.26
   Local Government Ombudsman 11.21
   officers, by 11.15–11.26
   ostensible authority 11.16–11.17
EU law
   environmental impact assessments 12.01–12.03, 12.42–12.53, 12.53–12.57, 12.62–12.64
   Habitats Directive 13.05, 13.13, 26.01–26.03, 26.19–26.24
   minerals 12.52–12.53, 12.53
   strategic environmental assessments 4.30, 13.01–13.10, 13.13, 13.22
   Wild Birds Directive 26.01–26.03
European Convention on Human Rights 1.23, 7.61, 19.01, 19.03–19.11, 20.19
European protected species 26.19–26.24
European sites 26.02–26.17
European Union, UK departure *see* **Brexit**
excavation of sites 22.11
execution of works by local planning authorities
   ecclesiastical use and monuments, buildings in 21.100
   enforcement notices 20.05, 20.124–20.125
   expenses, recovery of 21.99
   Greater London 21.100
   listed buildings 21.98–21.100
   notice 21.98–21.99
   scheduled monuments 21.99
   temporary support 21.98–21.99
   urgent works 21.98–21.99
existing use, lawfulness of *see* **certificates of lawfulness of existing use or development (CLEUDs)**
existing use rights
   conditions 14.31–14.34, 14.72
   enforcement notices 20.98
   planning permission, effect of 15.27–15.33, 15.37–15.38
experts
   environmental impact assessments 12.04
   hearings 18.45–18.46
   local inquiries 18.53
   nationally significant infrastructure projects inquiries 28.30
   qualitative assessments 12.04
   quantitative assessments 12.04
expiry of permissions 14.81–14.126, 15.66
expropriation *see* **compulsory purchase**
extension works
   building preservation notices 21.114

buildings operations 5.32–5.35
curtilage 7.25–7.27, 7.29–7.30
ecclesiastical use and monuments, buildings in 21.50–21.51
gardens 6.51–6.52
General Permitted Development Order 7.25–7.27, 7.29–7.30
listed buildings 21.58
exterior
buildings operations 5.30–5.32, 5.36–5.39
listed buildings 21.07, 21.24, 21.26, 21.31
material effect on external appearance 5.30–5.32, 5.36–5.39
painting 7.33

fair hearing, right to a
Alconbury decisions 19.08–19.11, 19.15, 19.22
called in applications 2.29
civil rights and obligations 19.10, 19.17, 19.19
delay 19.13
Human Rights Act 1998 19.01, 19.04, 19.08–19.19, 19.22, 20.165–20.167
independent and impartial tribunal 19.04, 19.10, 19.15
injunctions 20.165–20.167
judicial review 19.04
oral hearings 19.17–19.18
personal circumstances 11.119
public hearings 19.13
fairness *see* **natural justice or fairness**
false or misleading statements
certificates of lawfulness of proposed use or development 8.04
planning contravention notices 20.09
planning permission, notification to owners of 9.44
time limits 20.32
farming *see* **agriculture**
fears of residents
anti-social behaviour 11.104–11.105
applications for planning permission 11.104–11.109
criminal offences 11.104
health, telecommunications antenna and 11.109
justified, whether fears are 11.106
material considerations 11.104–11.109
moral judgments 11.107
fees
advertisements, display of 9.51
appeals 9.51, 9.55–9.56
applications 9.50–9.56
certificates of lawful use of development 9.51
conservation areas 9.53
consultation 9.60–9.61
enforcement notices, appeals against 9.51, 9.55
hazardous substances 9.53
listed buildings 9.53
pre-submission requirements 9.50–9.56

reserved matters, approval of 9.51
Secretary of State, powers of 9.53–9.54
site visits to mining and landfill sites 9.54
fences 5.26, 6.50, 7.33
financial and economic considerations
applications for planning permission 11.134–11.145
Covent Garden approach 11.134–11.140
listed buildings–11.144, 21.13
local finance considerations, definition of 11.145
material considerations 11.45, 11.50, 11.134–11.145
personal circumstances 11.111–11.114
tree preservation orders 25.08
financial and professional services 6.61, 6.64–6.67, 7.36
fines
advertising, control of outdoor 24.01, 24.04
enforcement notices 20.129
fly-posting 24.31
high hedges 25.40
listed buildings 21.46–21.47, 21.90
stop notices 20.113
temporary stop notices 20.22
tree preservation orders 25.06, 25.08
fish farming 5.69–5.71, 5.78, 6.46
fixtures
annexation 21.35–21.37, 21.40, 21.42
ecclesiastical use and monuments, buildings in 21.54–21.55
listed buildings 21.12, 21.25, 21.28–21.29, 21.32–21.44
works of art 21.39–21.44
flood risk 2.57
floodlights 5.37–5.38
floor space 5.32–5.35
fly-posting 24.31–24.36
action notices 24.35
anti-social behaviour, penalty notices and 24.34
criminal offences 24.01, 24.31–24.34
definition 24.31
fines 24.31
Good Practice Guide 24.32
graffiti 24.36
Localism Act 2011 24.35
penalty notices 24.34
removal 24.33, 24.35
surfaces 24.35
food and drink, sale of 6.61, 6.68, 7.36
footpaths 15.39
forestry
dedications plans, operations or covenants 25.05
material change of use 6.10, 6.33–6.46
operational development 6.34, 7.43
tree preservation orders 25.05
fracking 11.155
fraud 2.40, 2.44, 9.49
freedom of information 12.34, 12.37

full planning permission, duration of and conditions 14.82–14.109
  colourability test 14.99–14.101
  commencement of developments 14.82–14.109
  comply with permission, works must 14.103–14.109
  conditions precedent 14.103–14.109
  expiry of permission 14.82–14.109
  intention 14.99–14.102
  material change of use 14.92
  material development 14.91
  material operations 14.90–14.95
  time limits 14.82–14.109
  variation of period for commencement 14.87
  Whitley principle 14.103, 14.106, 14.108
'full statement of case', definition of 18.09

gardens
  agriculture 6.51–6.52
  building preservation notices 21.123–21.126
  curtilage 6.13, 6.51
  extensions 6.51–6.52
  General Permitted Development Order 6.51–6.52
  historic parks and gardens 21.123–21.126
  incidental to enjoyment of dwelling house, uses which are 6.13
  material change of use 6.51–6.52
  planning permission 6.51–6.52
gas 28.15, 28.16
gates 5.26, 7.33
General Permitted Development Order (GPDO) 7.05–7.55
  advertisements 7.46
  agricultural buildings and operations 7.47–7.52
  Areas of Outstanding Natural Beauty 7.20
  article 4 directions 7.06–7.12, 7.36
  Broads 7.20
  certificates of lawfulness of proposed use or development 8.02, 8.08
  classes of development 7.05
  compensation 7.11–7.12, 7.36
  conditions on planning permission 7.13–7.20
  conservation areas 7.20, 21.144–21.145
  curtilage 7.22–7.32, 7.40
  demolition of buildings 5.54
  dwelling house, definition of 7.23
  enforcement notices 20.97
  entry into force 7.05
  environmental impact assessments 7.16, 12.30
  extension of homes 7.25–7.27, 7.29–7.30
  forestry buildings and operations 7.53
  gardens 6.51–6.52
  gates, fences, walls or other means of enclosure 7.34
  general considerations 7.06–7.21
  highways, access to 7.33
  immediate directions 7.08
  local authorities 16.10
  local development orders 7.56
  material changes of use 7.35–7.28
  minor operations 7.33
  National Parks 7.20
  natural habitats and protected species, conservation of 26.10
  non-immediate directions 7.08
  painting of exterior 7.33
  parts of orders 7.05, 7.22–7.55
  planning permission 2.13, 7.05–7.55
  prior approvals 10.17
  public works orders 16.31
  re-erecting houses or improvements 7.29–7.30
  refusal of planning permission 7.11
  rural areas 7.07
  scope 2.13
  Secretary of State 2.13–2.14
  statutory undertakers 16.09
  telecommunications 7.54–7.55
  temporary buildings and uses 7.38–7.46
  text App C
  Use Classes Order 6.91, 7.35–7.28
  withdrawal of planning permission 7.09, 7.14
  World Heritage Sites 7.20, 21.128
generating stations 28.15, 28.16, 28.18
geological conservation 2.57
government *see* central government; local authorities; Secretary of State
GPDO *see* General Permitted Development Order (GPDO)
graffiti 24.36
Greater London
  City of London Corporation 2.98
  consultation 2.99
  county planning authorities and district planning authorities 2.64
  development corporations 2.100
  development plans, development of 3.14–3.15
  development plan documents 4.77
  Greater London Assembly 1.23, 2.98, 2.100
  Greater London Authority Act 1999 1.23, 2.98
  large scale developments 2.99
  listed buildings 21.66, 21.69, 21.100
  local authorities' power to carry out works 21.100
  Localism Act 2011 2.100
  major infrastructure 2.99
  Mayor 2.98–2.100
  organization of planning 2.98–2.100
  planning permission 2.98–2.99
  refusal of planning permission 2.99
  Secretary of State, directions of 2.99
  spatial development strategy 2.98–2.99, 4.77
  strategic policies, development which may affect 2.99
  unitary development plans 3.15
green belt 2.82, 19.21
Growth and Infrastructure Act 2013
  changes to planning system 1.28
  objectives 1.29

Index

guardianship of ancient monuments 22.10
guided transport systems 16.34

habitats *see* **natural habitats and protected species, conservation of**
harbours 16.30, 28.15
hardship 11.111–11.114, 11.118, 14.65
hazardous substances
  appeals 18.13
  consent 16.37, 18.13
  consolidating legislation 1.21–1.22
  consultation 10.48
  fees for applications 9.53
  Health and Safety Executive 10.48
  nationally significant infrastructure projects inquiries 28.15
  Planning (Hazardous Substances) Act 1990 1.21–1.22
  public works orders 16.37
  Standard Application Form 9.05
  waste 28.15
health
  fears concerning telecommunications antenna 11.109
  public health 1.02
hearings 18.44–18.47 *see also* **fair hearing, right to a**
  appeals 18.44–18.47
  experts 18.45–18.46
  informal proceedings 18.44
  oral hearings 2.29, 19.17–19.18
  public hearings 19.13
  public inquiries 18.45
  rules 18.44
hedgerows 25.20–25.33
  architectural or historical interest, of 25.32
  criminal offences 25.33
  curtilage 25.25
  definition 25.21
  ecclesiastical property 25.33
  entry, right of 25.33
  Hedgerow Regulations 25.20–25.33
  important hedgerow, definition of 25.31–25.32
  injunctions 25.33
  limitations 25.30–25.33
  local planning authorities, owned by 25.33
  nature reserves 25.24
  notification of activities 25.26–25.28
  protected land, definition of 25.24
  removal notices 25.26–25.30
  retention notices 25.28–25.30
  special scientific interest, areas of 25.20
  statistics 25.20
  tree preservation orders 25.04
hedges *see* **hedgerows; high hedges**
helicopters, taking off and landing of 6.27–6.28, 7.46
heritage
  heritage partnership agreements 21.150

World Heritage Sites 7.20, 21.128–21.129
high hedges 25.34–25.40
  access, barrier to 25.35
  anti-social behaviour 25.35
  appeals 25.39
  compliance period 25.38
  criminal offences 25.40
  domestic property, definition of 25.36
  fines 25.40
  initial action 25.38
  Leylandii 25.34
  light, barrier to 25.35
  nuisance 25.34, 25.37
  reduction in height 25.37
  referral of disputes to local authorities 25.35–25.37
  remedial orders 25.37–25.40
highways 15.45–15.49
  access 5.61, 5.68, 7.33
  applications for planning permission 10.41
  boundaries 5.65–5.66
  central government 15.45
  costs of work 15.45–15.49
  discretion 15.45–15.49
  engineering operations 5.61, 5.64–5.66, 5.68
  General Permitted Development Order 7.33
  nationally significant infrastructure projects inquiries 28.15
  notification requirements 10.41
  Secretary of State, directions from 10.41
  section 278 agreements 15.45–15.49
  Wednesbury unreasonableness 15.48–15.49
historic battlefields 21.127
Historic Buildings and Monuments Commission, consultation of 13.18
historic parks and gardens
  building preservation notices 21.123–21.126
  English Heritage 21.123, 21.126
  grades 21.124
  planning permission, consultation of English Heritage before grant of 21.126
  Register of Parks and Gardens 21.123
historical background 1.01–1.27
  compensation for restrictions on development 27.01–27.02
  consolidating legislation 1.21–1.22
  development plans, development of 3.01–3.04
  legislative landmarks 1.21–1.26
  Localism Act 2011 1.27
  Planning Act 2008 1.25–1.26
  public control over land use, growth of 1.01–1.20
  Town and Country Planning Act 1990 1.21–1.22
historical interest *see* **conservation areas and conservation area consent; listing buildings and listed building consent; special architectural or historical interest**
home, right to respect for the 19.01, 19.05, 19.12, 20.165–20.167

Index

Homes England (previously Homes and Communities Agency) 2.75–2.77, 2.100
hospitals 6.80–6.81
hostels 6.79
hot food, sale of 6.61, 6.70–6.71, 7.36
hotels 6.79
housing *see also* dwelling houses
   affordable housing 11.125–11.133
   community care houses providing support for disabled and mentally disabled people 6.84
   housing action trusts 2.88–2.89
   insanitary housing conditions 1.02
   multiple occupation, houses in 6.82–6.84, 7.36
   planning policy statements 2.57
   public control over land use, growth of 1.02
   residential developments affecting government objectives 18.15
   self-build and custom housebuilding 11.160–11.162
   single dwelling house as two or more separate houses 6.93–6.97
   single households 6.82–6.86, 7.36
Housing and Planning Act 2016 1.32
housing land supply 11.120–11.124
human rights *see* **European Convention on Human Rights; Human Rights Act 1998**
Human Rights Act 1998 19.01–19.22
   Alconbury decisions 19.08–19.11, 19.15, 19.22
   application of Act 19.12–19.22
   declarations of incompatibility 19.01
   delay 19.13
   enforcement notices 20.132
   entry into force 1.23, 19.01
   environment 19.06, 19.09, 19.11–19.12, 19.21
   European Convention on Human Rights, implementation of 1.23, 19.01, 19.07, 19.11
   European Court of Human Rights 19.03–19.10
   exhaustion of local remedies 19.02, 19.04
   fair hearing, right to a 19.01, 19.04, 19.08–19.19, 19.22, 20.165–20.167
   fast-track procedure to amend statutes 19.01
   green belt 19.21
   home, right to respect for the 19.01, 19.05, 19.12, 20.165–20.167
   independent and impartial tribunal 19.04, 19.10, 19.15
   injunctions 19.13, 20.165–20.167
   judicial review 19.04, 19.10
   margin of appreciation 19.11
   neighbourhood development orders 7.61
   oral hearings 19.17–19.18
   peaceful enjoyment of possessions 19.01, 19.11, 19.12, 19.20
   proportionality 19.12–19.13
   public authorities 19.01
   public hearings 19.13
   third party rights 19.13–19.15
hybrid Bill procedure 16.51
hydrocarbon exploration *see* **fracking**

hypermarkets *see* **supermarkets, superstores and hypermarkets**
immunity
   building preservation notices 21.113
   certificates of lawfulness of existing use or development 20.171–20.172, 20.180–20.185
   Crown 16.02–16.04
   enforcement notices 20.106
   listed buildings 21.94–21.97
   negligence 15.60
   nuisance 15.50–15.55
   time limits 20.29–20.32, 20.35, 20.36
impartiality *see* **bias**
important or novel issues of development control 18.15
improvements 7.29–7.30
incidental to enjoyment of dwelling house, uses which are 6.10, 6.11–6.32
   burial grounds 6.30–6.31
   certificates of lawful use 6.32
   curtilage 6.12–6.32
   fact and degree, matter of 6.15–6.27
   gardens 6.13
   helicopters, landing and taking off of 6.27–6.28
   material change of use 6.10, 6.11–6.32
   reasonableness 6.18–6.27, 6.29
included within development, uses which are 6.92–6.99
independent and impartial tribunal 19.04, 19.10, 19.15
industrial development 11.113–11.114
industrial population, distribution of 1.10
industrial process, definition of 6.73
industrial uses
   general industrial 6.76
   informal planning advice, liability for negligent 9.62
   material change of use 6.56, 6.76–6.78, 7.36
   special industrial groups 6.77
   storage or distribution 6.78
   Use Classes Order 6.56, 6.76–6.78, 7.36
informal planning advice, liability for negligent 9.62
information
   enforcement notices 18.06, 20.84
   environmental impact assessments
      definition 12.05, 12.37, 12.38
      environmental statements 12.05, 12.38, 12.48, 12.58
      exceptions to disclosure 12.37
      freedom of information 12.34, 12.37
      material considerations 11.159
      significant effect 12.15
      special cases 12.41
   environmental information 11.159, 12.05, 12.34, 12.37–12.41, 12.48, 12.58
   environmental statements 12.05, 12.38, 12.48, 12.58

Index

freedom of information 12.34, 12.37
material considerations 11.159
outline planning permission 9.16
planning contravention notices 20.07–20.08
websites, publication on local authority 10.35
infrastructure *see* **Community Infrastructure Levy (CIL); Growth and Infrastructure Act 2013; Infrastructure Planning Commission; major infrastructure projects; nationally significant infrastructure projects (NSIPs) inquiries**
Infrastructure Planning Commission 1.26–1.27, 28.07, 28.13, 28.19–28.20
injunctions 20.152–20.169
breach of condition notice 20.140
Carnwath Report 20.158–20.159
criminal offences 20.158–20.160
damages, undertakings in 20.164
discretion 20.165–20.167
enforcement action 20.05, 20.152–20.169
enforcement notices 20.132, 20.154–20.157, 21.91
Enforcing Planning Control 20.158
fair hearing, right to a 20.165–20.167
hedgerows 25.33
home, right to respect for the 20.165–20.167
Human Rights Act 1998 19.13, 20.165–20.167
judicial review 18.130
limited period, permission for a 14.56
listed buildings 21.91
nuisance 15.50
personal circumstances 20.165–20.167
scope 20.161–20.163
statistics 20.169
stop notices 20.155–20.157
threatened or actual breaches 20.155–20.160
tree preservation orders 25.08
unknown persons 20.162
inland waterways 16.30, 16.35
inquiries *see* **local inquiries; nationally significant infrastructure projects (NSIPs) inquiries**
insanitary housing conditions 1.02
inspection *see also* **inspectors; environmental impact assessments (EIAs)**
planning register 9.64, 9.66
tree preservation orders 25.11
inspectors
appeals 18.12–18.14
development plan documents 4.56–4.58
local development orders 7.58
local inquiries 18.50–18.63
Localism Act 2011 4.56
procedure for transferred cases
after inquiries 18.57–18.58
before inquiries 18.53
during inquiries 18.56
recovered cases 18.13–18.14, 18.50, 18.59–18.63
reports, binding nature of 4.56–4.58, 7.58
transferred cases 18.13, 18.50, 18.53–18.58

intensification 6.104–6.114
Interim Development Order Permissions 2.67
interior
buildings operations 5.30–5.33
listed buildings 21.24, 21.26, 21.31
interruption of use 6.143–6.162
issue estoppel 20.105–20.108

joint committees 4.64
joint planning boards 2.67
judicial powers of Secretary of State
natural justice 2.63
preliminary determinations of law 2.62
quasi-judicial powers 2.63
judicial review 18.117–18.130
Administrative Court 18.119
appeals 18.119, 18.123, 18.127–18.129
breach of condition notice 20.149, 20.151
called in applications 2.26, 2.28–2.29
declarations 18.130
default powers to revoke or modify planning permission 2.43–2.45, 2.53
defence 18.119
delay 18.123
development plans 10.63
environmental impact assessments 12.42
expedition, need for 18.124–18.126
extension of time 18.124–18.126
fair hearing, right to a 19.10
Human Rights Act 1998 19.04, 19.10
injunctions 18.130
mandatory orders 18.120, 18.130
nationally significant infrastructure projects inquiries 28.35
Parliamentary and Local Government Ombudsmen 18.138
permission to proceed 18.117–18.120, 18.125
planning contravention notices 20.12
pre-action protocol 18.120
procedure 18.119, 18.130
prohibition 18.120, 18.130
quashing orders 18.120, 18.130
remedies 18.120, 18.130
repeat applications 10.14
reviews 18.93
service 18.119
standing 18.121–18.123
statutory review 18.119, 18.126
sufficient interest 18.121
terminology 18.120
third parties 18.117–18.120
time limits 18.124–18.126
justice *see* **natural justice or fairness**

Lake District Planning Board 2.67
landfill sites, visits to 9.54
Lands Tribunal 17.32–17.33
landscaping 9.14–9.15, 9.18

685

Index

lawful sports and pastimes 29.19–29.20
layout 9.14–9.15
LDOs *see* local development orders (LDOs)
leasehold interests 9.36
legal challenges to development plans 4.67–4.76
legislative powers of Secretary of State 2.12–2.18
   Development Management Procedure Order 2.13
   development orders 2.13
   General Permitted Development Order 2.13–2.14
   regulations and orders 2.12–2.13
   special development orders 2.15–2.18
   statutory instruments 2.12–2.13
   Town and Country Planning Act 1990 2.12
   Use Classes Order 2.13–2.14
legitimate expectations 11.22–11.26
leisure and assembly 6.89–6.90, 7.36
leisure plots 6.47–6.50
Leylandii 25.34
licensing
   applications for planning permission 11.156–11.157
   caravan sites 10.03–10.05
   control 11.157
   material change of use 11.157
   material considerations 11.156–11.157
   pollution control 11.146
   tree felling licences 25.05
life of a planning permission 15.66–15.72
light, barriers to 25.35
limited period, permission granted for a 14.49–14.57, 14.66
listed building consent orders 21.151
listing buildings and listed building consent 21.03–21.129 *see also* listed buildings in need of repair
   access to building 21.57
   administrative powers 2.31
   advertisements 10.43, 21.64
   aesthetic merits 21.13
   age and rarity 21.13
   already executed, works 21.73
   alteration 21.03–21.07, 21.45–21.46, 21.57–21.58, 21.69
   amenity societies, notification of 21.65
   annexation
      degree 21.35, 21.36, 21.40
      purpose 21.36–21.37, 21.42
   appeals 18.05, 18.07
      enforcement notices 18.13, 21.82–21.91
      local inquiries 18.50
      Secretary of State 21.70, 21.74–21.76
   applications for consent 21.64–21.70
   architectural interest, definition of 21.10
   architectural or historical interest, buildings of special 21.03, 21.09–21.12, 21.45
      appeals 21.76
      character 21.07
      criminal sanctions 21.45
      determination of applications 21.70

      enforcement notices 21.82
      Planning (Listed Buildings and Conservation Areas) Act 1990 1.21
   building preservation notices 21.113–21.129
   certificates of 21.94–21.97
   challenging listing 21.20–21.21
   character, alteration of 10.43–10.44, 21.07
   classification 21.15–21.19, 21.65–21.69
   compensation 21.122
   conditions on consent 21.60, 21.62–21.63, 21.71–21.72
   consent orders 21.151
   consolidating legislation 1.21–1.22
   consultation 21.20, 21.62–21.63
   criminal offences 21.45–21.48, 21.77, 21.85–21.91
   curtilage, objects or structures within 21.12, 21.25, 21.28–21.30
   definition of listed building 21.23–21.25
   demolition 5.48, 5.52, 21.03–21.07
      access to building 21.57
      conditions 21.71
      consent 21.57–21.59, 21.69
      criminal offences 21.45–21.46
      enforcement notices 21.79–21.80
      grades 21.19
      notice 21.57, 21.65
      partial 21.04–21.07
      recording of building 21.57
      restoration of buildings 21.79–21.80
      withdrawal of status 21.18–21.19
   design principles and concepts, statements of 21.61
   details of buildings 21.60
   drawings 21.60
   ecclesiastical use and monuments, buildings in 21.49–21.55
   economic factors 21.13
   enforcement notices 21.77–21.92
      appeals 18.13, 21.82–21.91
      architectural or historical interest, buildings not of special 21.82
      criminal offences 21.77, 21.85–21.91
      demolition 21.79–21.80
      entry, power of 21.84–21.92
      injunctions 21.91
      restoration of buildings 21.79–21.80
      Secretary of State, appeals to 21.82–21.84
      steps to be taken, specification of 21.78
      suspension 21.83, 21.85
      time limits 21.82
   English Heritage 21.65
   entry, power of 21.84–21.92
   extension 21.58
   exterior 21.07, 21.24, 21.26, 21.31
   fees for applications 9.53
   financial considerations 11.144
   fines 21.46–21.47, 21.90
   fixtures 21.12, 21.25, 21.28–21.29, 21.32–21.44

Index

annexation 21.35–21.37, 21.40, 21.42
  works of art 21.39–21.44
free-standing buildings 21.27
Grade I 21.15, 21.17, 21.19, 21.65–21.66
Grade II * 21.15, 21.17, 21.19, 21.65–21.66
Grade II 21.15, 21.19, 21.67–21.69
grades 21.15–21.19, 21.65–21.69
Greater London 21.66, 21.69
group value 21.10
historic interest, definition of 21.10
immunity 21.94–21.97
imprisonment 21.46
injunctions 21.85–21.91
intention 21.48
interior 21.24, 21.26, 21.31
list description 21.31
listed building consent orders 21.151
local inquiries 18.50
local land charges 21.20
London 21.66, 21.69, 21.93
material considerations 21.59, 21.70
mens rea 21.48
national interest 21.13
National Planning Policy Framework 21.01–21.02
nationally significant infrastructure projects
    inquiries 28.16, 28.18
newspaper advertisements 10.43, 21.64
notice
  consent, applications for 21.65–21.69
  demolition 21.57, 21.65
  listing, of 10.43–10.44
  publicity 10.43–10.44, 10.47, 21.64
objects fixed to buildings 21.33–21.44
orders 21.151
outline consent 21.60
outline planning permission 21.94
overlapping applications 10.20
partial demolition 21.04–21.07
parts of building 21.25
personal circumstances 11.115–11.117
Planning (Listed Buildings and Conservation
    Areas) Act 1990 1.21–1.22, 21.02
planning permission 10.43–10.44, 21.58–21.59,
    21.94–21.95
plans 21.60
principle and ancillary test 21.30, 21.32
Principle of Selection 21.10–21.13
procedure for obtaining consent 21.60–21.69
protection 21.45–21.48
public works orders 16.50
publicity 10.43–10.44, 10.47, 21.64
purchase notices 21.93
purpose of listing 21.56
recording of buildings 21.57
reform 21.149–21.144
removal from list 21.76
repeat applications 10.17
reserved matters, approval of 21.94

restoration of buildings 21.79–21.80
retrospective applications for consent 21.73
Royal Commission on Historic Monuments 21.06
scheduled monuments 21.22
second opinions 21.21
Secretary of State 21.09–21.11, 21.65, 21.70,
    21.74–21.76, 21.82–21.84
selectivity 21.13
settings, effect on 10.43–10.44
site notices 21.64
spot listing of Post-War buildings 21.20
statistics 21.17, 21.19, 21.21
steps to be taken, specification of 21.78
strict liability offences 21.48
temporary listed building consent 21.72
third parties 21.63
time limits 21.72, 21.82
urgent works 21.45
value, effect on 21.122
what can be listed 21.23–21.44
withdrawal of status 21.18–21.19
works of art 21.39–21.44

listed buildings in need of repair
appeals against repair notices 21.104
architectural or historic interest, claims that
    buildings are not of 21.104
compensation for compulsory
    purchase 21.107–21.112, 21.122
compulsory purchase 21.101–21.112
  appeals against repair notices 21.104
  compensation 21.107–21.112, 21.122
  deliberate disrepair, allowing 21.108–21.112
  directions for minimum
    compensation 21.108–21.112
  repairs notice, service of 21.102–21.105
  Secretary of State, authorization
    of 21.104–21.105
deliberate disrepair, allowing 21.108–21.112
demolition 21.107–21.112
  compulsory purchase 21.107–21.112
  deliberate disrepair, allowing 21.108–21.112
  directions for minimum
    compensation 21.108–21.112
directions for minimum
    compensation 21.108–21.112
ecclesiastical buildings 21.100
expenses, recovery of 21.99
Greater London 21.100
local authorities' power to carry out
    works 21.98–21.99
  ecclesiastical buildings 21.100
  expenses, recovery of 21.99
  Greater London 21.100
  notice 21.98–21.99
  scheduled monuments 21.99
  temporary support 21.98–21.99
  urgent works 21.98–21.99
notice 21.98–21.99, 21.102–21.106

Index

listed buildings in need of repair (*cont.*)
  repair notices 2.09, 21.102–21.105
  scheduled monuments 21.99
  Secretary of State 2.09, 21.104–21.105
  service of repair notices 21.102–21.105
  special interest test 21.13
  statistics 21.106
  stay of proceedings 21.104
  temporary support 21.98–21.99
  urgent works 21.98–21.99
LNG facilities 28.15
local authorities 2.64–2.97, 16.10–16.29 *see also* county planning authorities and district planning authorities
  appeals 2.23
  bias 16.15, 16.18–16.29
    Model Code of Conduct, abolition of 16.29
    personal interests of committee members 16.23–16.24, 16.27–16.29
    real likelihood/possibility test 16.19, 16.22–16.24
    test 16.19, 16.22–16.24
  Broads Authority 2.90
  conflicts of interest 16.25
  consultation 9.59–9.62
  delay 16.16
  enforcement notices, appeals against 2.22
  enterprise zone authorities 2.78–2.80
  execute works, power to 20.05, 20.124–20.125, 21.98–21.100
  General Permitted Development Order 16.10
  government departments, authorization by 16.10
  hedgerows owned by authorities 25.33
  Homes England 2.75–2.77
  housing action trusts 2.88–2.89
  interested planning authorities 16.11–16.12
  joint planning boards 2.67
  land in which local authority has interest 16.18–16.26
  listed buildings in need of repair 2.93–21.102
  Localism Act 2011 16.29
  Model Code of Conduct 16.29
  National Park authorities 2.68–2.69
  organization of planning 2.01–2.02, 2.64–2.97
  personal interests of committee members 16.23–16.24, 16.27–16.29
  playing fields 16.15
  public control over land use, growth of 1.03–1.05
  reorganization 1.20, 3.16
  standards, duty to promote and maintain 16.29
  superstores and hypermarkets 16.15–16.24
    bias 16.18–16.24
    delay 16.16
    land in which local authority has interest 16.18–16.22
    limits 16.16
    personal interests of committee members 16.23–16.24, 16.27

  Secretary of State, decisions by 16.16
  urban development corporations 2.70–2.74
  websites, publication on local authority 10.35
local community groups 7.04
local development *see* local development framework and schemes; local development orders (LDOs); local plans
local development documents *see* development plan documents
local development framework and schemes 4.14–4.21
  ancient monuments 22.14
  definition 4.22
  Delivering a Fundamental Change 3.30–3.31
  development plan documents 4.18–4.48, 4.58–4.66
    environmental impact assessment 13.08
    preparation 4.45–4.48
    revision 4.63
    saved plans 4.02
    transitional arrangements 4.88
    withdrawal 4.59–4.66
  development plans, development of 3.11, 3.13, 3.16, 3.20–3.25, 3.28–3.32
  environmental impact assessment 13.08
  Local Development Plan Framework 3.30–3.32
  matters to be included 4.18
  minerals 4.14
  non-development plan documents 4.20
  Planning and Compulsory Purchase Act 2004 4.14–4.21
  Planning Policy Statements 4.18, 4.22
  saved plans 4.02
  Secretary of State 4.21
  sites of archaeological interest 22.14
  statements of community involvement 4.18
  supplementary planning documents 4.18
  waste 4.14
local development orders (LDOs) 7.56–7.60
  approval 7.57
  completion of development after revision of revocation of orders 7.60
  consultation 7.58
  development plan documents 7.58
  environmental impact assessments 7.56
  General Permitted Development Order 7.56
  Habitats Regulations 2017 26.12
  inspector's reports, binding nature of 7.58
  Planning and Compulsory Purchase Act 2004 7.56
  planning permission 7.56, 7.61–7.66
  preparation 7.58–7.59
  procedure 7.56
  reasons, statements of 7.58–7.59
  restrictions 7.56
  revision of revocation of order, completion after 7.60
  Secretary of State 7.57, 7.59

Index

Local Government Ombudsmen *see* **Parliamentary and Local Government Ombudsmen**
local inquiries 18.49–18.63
  appeals 18.50–18.63
  close of inquiries 18.60
  conservation area consent appeals 18.50
  cross-examination 18.49
  delay 18.51
  development plans 3.31
  documents, copies of 18.53
  efficiency and effectiveness 18.51
  experts 18.53
  inspectors 18.50–18.63
  listed buildings appeals 18.50
  natural justice and fairness 18.50, 18.59
  new evidence or new matters of fact 18.60–18.62
  notice 18.53
  opinions 18.61–18.63
  parties
    persons entitled to appear 18.53–18.56
    statutory 18.53
  pre-inquiry meetings 18.53
  procedure 18.50, 18.53–18.58
  proofs of evidence, copies of 18.56
  reasons 18.57–18.58
  recommendations 18.59–18.62
  recovered cases 18.50, 18.59–18.63
  representatives of Secretary of State 18.56
  rule 6 statements 18.53
  rules 18.50–18.61
  Secretary of State 18.50, 18.52, 18.53–18.63
  service of notice 18.53
  site visits 18.56
  starting date 18.52
  statements of case 18.53
  statutory parties 18.53
  third party representation 18.49
  time limits 18.53
  transferred cases 18.50, 18.53–18.60
local land charges 17.31, 21.20
local nature partnerships 2.91
local planning authorities *see* **local authorities**
local plans
  abolition 3.30
  complexity 3.29
  content 3.28
  delay 3.20
  development plan documents 4.02, 4.18–4.48, 4.58–4.48, 4.88, 13.08
  development plans, development of 3.11, 3.13, 3.16, 3.20–3.25, 3.28–3.32
  Localism Act 2011 1.27
  mineral local plans 3.28
  neighbourhood development plans, and 4.39
  preparation 3.29
  review of 4.16
  rewriting policies, limits on 1.27
  single local plans 3.28
  tier 3.11, 3.13, 3.16, 3.20–3.25, 3.28–3.30
  waste local plans 3.28
local spatial management 2.57
Localism Act 2011
  Community Infrastructure Levy 1.27, 17.71
  community right to build 1.27
  cooperation 1.27
  development orders 7.04
  development plans, development of 3.34–3.36
  development plan documents 4.01, 4.60–4.66
  enforcement 1.27, 20.02
  fly-posting 24.35
  Greater London 2.100
  historical background 1.27
  Home and Communities Agency, limits of powers to outside London of 2.100
  local authorities 16.29
  local plans 1.27
  London Development Agency, abolition of 2.100
  National Policy Statements 18.68
  nationally significant infrastructure projects inquiries 1.27, 28.07
  neighbourhood development orders 7.61, 7.65
  neighbourhood development plans 1.27
  regional strategies 3.34–3.36
  retrospective applications 10.22
  very large developments, consultation on 1.27
locality qualifying as town or village green 29.16–29.18
London *see also* **Greater London**
  boroughs 3.04, 3.14–3.15, 4.13
  development plans, development of 3.04, 3.14–3.15
  listed buildings 21.66, 21.69, 21.93
  London Development Agency, abolition of 2.100
  Olympic Delivery Authority 2.74
  spatial development strategy 13.08
  strategic environmental assessments 13.08
  surveys 4.13

major developments *see also* **major infrastructure projects; nationally significant infrastructure projects (NSIPs) inquiries**
  appeals 18.15
  definition 10.32–10.33
  environmental impact assessments 1.20
  publicity 10.31–10.33, 10.36, 10.47
  regional and national controversy, developments of major importance which prompt substantial 18.15
major infrastructure projects 18.64–18.69 *see also* **nationally significant infrastructure projects (NSIPs) inquiries**
  ad hoc procedures 28.03
  alternative methods of determination 28.09–28.12
  alternative sites, consideration of 28.09
  appeals 18.64–18.69
  consent 1.26

Index

major infrastructure projects (*cont.*)
  definition 28.03
  delay 28.01, 28.04
  development plans 28.06
  evidence 28.03
  expense 28.01, 28.04, 28.09
  Greater London 2.99
  hybrid Acts 28.09
  ministerial orders, authorization of 28.10–28.11
  National Policy Statements 18.68
  national significance, schemes of 28.12
  objections 28.11–28.12
  Parliament, submission of schemes of national significance to 28.12
  Planning Act 2008 1.25–1.26
  Planning and Compulsory Purchase Act 2004 1.23
  Planning Inquiry Commission 28.09
  private Acts 28.09
  procedural fairness 28.10
  procedure 28.10
  public inquiries 18.65–18.69, 28.02–28.04, 28.11–28.16
  related proposals, consideration of rules 18.67
  Secretary of State 18.64, 28.02, 28.07, 28.11–28.12
  single consent regime 1.26
  special development orders 28.10
maladministration
  definition 18.134–18.135
  Parliamentary and Local Government Ombudsmen 9.62, 10.27, 18.132–18.136, 18.139–18.141
  third parties 10.27
margin of appreciation 19.11
markets 7.46
marquees as buildings 5.21
material change of use
  abandonment of use 6.143–6.162
  adjacent land, effect on 6.08–6.09
  advertising 6.100–6.103
  agriculture 6.10, 6.33–6.52, 6.120, 6.124–6.125, 6.134
  amendment of applications 10.63
  ancillary uses 6.117–6.142, 6.164–6.165
  applications for planning permission 11.148–11.159
  business uses 6.56, 6.72–6.75, 7.36
  carrying out an activity without ascertaining whether it needs permission 8.17–8.18
  certificates of lawfulness of existing use or development 20.171, 20.179, 20.184
  certificates of lawfulness of proposed use or development 8.06
  conditions 14.04, 14.18–14.19
  declaration, action for a 8.10
  definition 6.01–6.07
  development, definition of 5.02–5.10, 6.01–6.169, 14.04

  enforcement notices 20.59, 20.62
  exclusions from development 6.10–6.91
  fact and degree, question of 6.05–6.07
  forestry 6.10, 6.33–6.46
  gardens, extensions to 6.51–6.52
  General Permitted Development Order 7.35–7.28
  incidental to enjoyment of dwelling house, uses which are 6.10, 6.11–6.32
  included within development, uses which are 6.92–6.99
  industrial uses 6.56, 6.76–6.78, 7.36
  intensification 6.104–6.114
  interruption 6.143–6.162
  leisure plots 6.47–6.50
  licensing control 11.157
  mixed or composite use of land 6.136, 7.36
  off-site effects 6.08–6.09
  operational development 5.02–5.10
  planning permission 14.92
  planning unit 6.115–6.142, 6.163–6.169
  preservation of existing uses 11.91–11.94
  primary or dominant use 6.117–6.142, 6.164–6.165
  residential uses 6.56, 6.79–6.88
  retail business, change in type of 6.09
  same use Class, change of use within the 6.10, 6.53–6.91, 7.36
  shopping area uses 6.56, 6.59–6.71, 7.36
  single dwelling house as two or more separate houses 6.93–6.97
  social and community uses of non-residential kind 6.56, 6.88–6.90, 7.36
  subdivision of planning unit 6.163–6.169
  time limits 20.30–20.33
  Use Classes Order 6.10, 6.53–6.91, 7.35
  waste and refuse material, disposal of 6.98–6.99
material considerations 11.44–11.55
  affordable housing 11.125–11.133
  alternative sites, existence of 11.82–11.88
  ancient monuments 22.13
  appeal decisions, previous 11.62–11.68
  consolidation of undesirable uses 11.158
  default powers to revoke or modify planning permission 2.48
  development plans 4.26, 4.84, 11.31–11.35, 11.44
  enforcement notices 20.40–20.140
  environmental information 11.159
  fear of residents 11.104–11.109
  financial circumstances 11.45, 11.50, 11.134–11.145
  government policies 11.27–11.61
  licensing control 11.156–11.157
  listed buildings 21.59, 21.70
  National Planning Policy Framework 11.58
  'other material considerations', definition of 11.45–11.53
  personal circumstances of applicants 11.110–11.119
  piecemeal development, risk of 11.89–11.90
  planning obligations 17.44, 17.49–17.53

Index

Planning Policy Guidance Notes 2.59
Planning Policy Statements 2.59
pollution control 11.146–11.155
precedent, creation of a 11.77–11.81
preservation of existing uses 11.91–11.103
previous appeal decisions 11.62–11.68
private interests, protection of 11.69–11.76
race discrimination 11.51–11.53
sites of archaeological interest 22.13
social and economic considerations 11.45, 11.48, 11.50
mentally disabled people, community care houses providing support for disabled and 6.84
metal detectors in protected places, offence of using 22.12
metropolitan boroughs 3.04, 3.14–3.15
Mineral Policy Statements (MPSs) and Minerals Planning Guidance Notes (MPGs)
  administrative powers 2.56–2.67
  aims 2.56
  National Planning Policy Framework, replacement with 2.57, 11.58
minerals 23.01–23.32 *see also* **Mineral Policy Statements (MPSs) and Minerals Planning Guidance Notes (MPGs)**
  1948–1982, permissions granted between 23.13–23.31
  active sites, review of 23.17
  aftercare conditions 23.01
  appeals 18.13
  compensation 23.01–23.02, 23.17, 27.10
  conditions 23.01–23.02, 23.05–23.11, 23.17–23.20, 23.24–23.28
  county planning authorities and district planning authorities 2.94
  development, definition of 5.72–5.75, 5.77
  development plans, development of 3.28
  discontinuance orders 23.01
  dormant sites, review of 23.17
  duration of permission 15.66, 23.03, 23.05
  enforcement notices 23.01
  environment 1.23, 12.52–12.53, 23.08, 23.22–23.29
  interim development orders 23.03, 23.14
  interpretation of mining permissions 23.32
  list of active sites 23.17–23.23
  local development schemes 4.14
  local plans 2.94, 3.28
  mineral planning authorities 23.01–23.02, 23.17–23.31
  Minerals Planning Guidance 23.21
  mining, definition of 5.72–5.75
  mining operations 5.72–5.75, 5.77
  modification of planning permission 23.01
  notification of owners 23.01
  old mining permissions 16.04, 23.03–23.12
  operational developments 5.72–5.75, 5.77
  owners, notification of 23.01
  peat 5.72
  planning permission 1.23, 9.41, 23.01–23.32
  reactivation of workings 23.03
  Registration of Old Mining Permissions 23.03, 23.05, 23.11, 23.24–23.31
  regularity, presumption of 23.03
  removal or extracted from land, material 5.74
  restoration conditions 23.01
  resumption of workings 23.01
  review 23.01, 23.15–23.24
  revocation of planning permission 23.01
  screening directions 23.30–23.31
  screening opinions 23.30–23.31
  site visits 9.54
  Standard Application Form 9.05
  Stevens Committee 5.74, 23.01
  stop notices 23.01
  time limits 23.01, 23.03
  working and winning 23.03, 23.32
minor operations 7.33
misrepresentation 9.49
mistake *see* **error**
mixed or composite use of land 6.136, 7.36
mobile cranes 5.18
model villages as buildings 5.15
modification *see* **revocation or modification**
monuments
  ancient monuments 2.09, 22.01, 22.02, 22.08–22.10, 28.18
  ecclesiastical use and monuments, buildings in 21.49–21.55, 21.100, 25.33
  Historic Buildings and Monuments Commission, consultation of 13.18
  scheduled monuments 21.22, 21.99, 22.02–22.07, 22.21, 28.16
morality 11.107, 17.06–17.07
motor sports 7.46
moveable artefacts 22.12
MPGs *see* **Mineral Policy Statements (MPSs) and Minerals Planning Guidance Notes (MPGs)**
MPSs *see* **Mineral Policy Statements (MPSs) and Minerals Planning Guidance Notes (MPGs)**
multiple occupation, houses in 6.82–6.84, 7.36

national controversy, major developments causing 18.15
national heritage *see* **heritage**
National Parks
  environment 1.23
  General Permitted Development Order 7.20
  joint planning boards 2.67
  local authorities 2.68–2.69
  Secretary of State 2.69
  simplified planning zones 2.82
  Wales 2.69
National Planning Policy Framework (NPPF)
  affordable housing 11.130–11.131
  ancient monuments 22.14–22.16

Index

National Planning Policy Framework (NPPF) (*cont.*)
  conservation areas 21.01–21.02
  development plan documents 4.51
  housing land supply 11.120–11.124
  introduction of 2.57
  listed buildings 21.02
  material considerations 11.58
  Mineral Policy Statements (MPSs) and Minerals Planning Guidance Notes (MPGs) 2.57, 11.58
  natural habitats and protected species, conservation of 26.04
  Planning Policy Guidance Notes 2.57, 11.58
  Planning Policy Statements 2.57, 11.58
  revised version 4.10
  sites of archaeological interest 22.14
  sustainable development 4.08
National Policy Statements
  Localism Act 2011 18.68
  major infrastructure projects 18.68, 28.13, 28.19–28.23
  nationally significant infrastructure projects inquiries 28.13, 28.19–28.23
national security 16.04
national significance *see* **nationally significant infrastructure projects (NSIPs) inquiries; schemes of national significance**
nationally significant infrastructure projects (NSIPs) inquiries 28.01–28.36
  ad hoc procedures 28.03
  airports 28.15
  alternative methods of determination 28.09–28.12
  alternative sites, consideration of 28.09
  ancient monuments 28.18
  applications for orders granting consent 28.24–28.25
  change of circumstances 28.22
  compulsory purchase 28.17, 28.33–28.34
  conservation area consent 28.16, 28.18
  consultation 28.21–28.22, 28.24, 28.26
  contents of development consent orders 28.32–28.34
  criminal offences 28.36
  cross-examination 28.29, 28.30
  dams 28.15
  definition 28.15
  delay and expense 28.01, 28.04
  development consent orders 28.13, 28.16–28.20, 28.24–28.25, 28.31–28.36
  development, definition of 28.16
  development plans 28.06
  electric lines 28.15
  enforcement of development consent orders 28.36
  environmental impact assessments 28.24
  evidence 28.03, 28.30
  examination of applications 28.26–28.31
  experts 28.30
  gas reception facilities 28.15
  gas storage 28.15, 28.16
  gas transporter pipelines 28.15
  generating stations 28.15, 28.16, 28.18
  harbour facilities 28.15
  hazardous waste facilities 28.15
  highways 28.15
  Infrastructure Planning Commission 1.26–1.27, 28.07, 28.13, 28.19–28.20
  interested party, definition of 28.30
  judicial review 28.35
  legal challenges 28.35
  listed building consent 28.16, 28.18
  LNG facilities 28.15
  Localism Act 2011 1.27, 28.07
  Major Infrastructure Planning Unit 28.19–28.20
  National Policy Statements 28.13, 28.20–28.23
  nuisance 15.55
  open-floor hearings 28.29
  Parliament, laying before 28.23
  pipelines 28.15, 28.16
  planning permission 28.16
  pre-application procedure 28.24
  public examination 28.29
  publicity 28.21–28.22, 28.24
  railways and rail freight interchanges 28.15
  remove development, notice to 28.36
  representations, prescribed forms for 28.30
  reservoirs 28.15
  scheduled monument consent 28.16
  Secretary of State 1.27, 28.07, 28.13, 28.15–28.16, 28.19–28.36
  sustainable development 28.21–28.22
  time limits 28.13, 28.29, 28.35
  underground gas storage 28.15
  waste water treatment plants 28.15
  water resources, transfer of 28.15
natural habitats and protected species, conservation of 26.01–26.24
  appeals 26.06, 26.14
  Areas of Outstanding Natural Beauty 2.82, 7.20
  areas of special scientific interest, areas of 2.82, 25.20
  Broads 2.82, 2.90, 7.20
  called in applications 26.06
  consultation of nature conservation bodies 26.03, 26.11
  discontinuance notices 26.06
  enforcement notices 26.06
  enterprise zones 26.12
  European protected species 26.19–26.24
  European sites 26.02–26.17
  General Permitted Development Order 26.10
  Habitats Directive 13.05, 13.13, 26.01–26.03, 26.19–26.24
  Habitats Regulations 2017 26.02–26.12
  hedgerows 25.24
  local development orders 26.12
  local nature partnerships 2.91
  National Planning Policy Framework 26.04

Index

nature reserves 25.24
neighbourhood development orders 26.12
planning obligations 26.09
planning permission 26.01, 26.03, 26.06–26.17
Planning Policy Statements 26.04
public opinion 26.03
purchase notices 26.06
reviews of planning permissions 26.07–26.08
Secretary of State, notification to 26.06
simplified planning zones 26.08, 26.12
Special Areas of Conservation 26.02–26.17
Special Protection Areas 26.02–26.17
Wild Birds Directive 26.01–26.03
natural justice or fairness 18.17–18.38
  appeals 18.21–18.22, 18.29
  bias 18.25–18.26, 18.30–18.38
  burden of proof 18.22
  delay 18.21
  Inquiry Procedure Rules 18.21–18.22
  judicial powers of Secretary of State 2.63
  local inquiries 18.50, 18.59
  public inquiries 18.21–18.22
  rectification 29.48–29.50
  reviews 18.101, 18.103–18.104
  Secretary of State 18.19–18.20, 18.26–18.27, 18.32–18.35
  timetable 18.21
  written representations 18.42
nature reserves 25.24
necessity 17.41, 17.44, 17.49–17.52
negligence 15.56–15.60
  consultation 9.63
  immunity 15.60
  informal planning advice, liability for negligent 9.62
  negligent misstatements 15.57–15.59
  proximity 15.56
neighbourhood *see also* neighbourhood development orders
  bad neighbour development 10.26, 10.33
  Community Infrastructure Levy 17.71
  expenditure 17.71
  neighbourhood development plans 1.27
  nuisance 15.50–15.55
  qualifying as town or village green 29.16–29.18
neighbourhood development orders 7.61–7.66
  community right to build orders 7.65
  consultation 7.61
  European Convention on Human Rights 7.61
  Habitats Regulations 2017 26.12
  Human Rights Act 1998 7.61
  local community groups 7.04
  Localism Act 2011 7.61, 7.65
  neighbourhood areas
    all or part of areas 7.57
    designation 7.64
  neighbourhood forums 7.04, 7.61
  parish councils 7.04, 7.61

permitted developments 7.63
planning permission 7.57
procedure for making 7.66
referenda 7.61, 7.64
revocation 7.62
neighbourhood development plans 4.33–4.44
  concept of 4.33
  conformity with local plans 4.39
  development plans, and 4.34, 4.43
  examination of 4.38–4.40
  legal challenges to 4.42
  making of 4.35–4.43
  modification of 4.44
  referendum on 4.41, 4.43
Neighbourhood Planning Act 2017 1.33
neighbours, consultation with 10.26
new planning units, creation of 15.33–15.37
non-residential institutions 6.88
normal use of land
  advertising 6.100, 6.102
  agriculture 6.39
  conditions 14.57–14.58
  dwelling houses 6.21
  interruption of use 6.147
  temporary uses 7.44
notification of planning permission applications to owners 9.30–9.49
  account of profits 9.49
  agricultural holdings 9.37–9.38, 9.40, 9.43
  certification requirements 9.38–9.49
  conveyancing 9.45
  criminal offences 9.44
  errors 9.46–9.47
  false or misleading statements 9.44
  form 9.34
  fraudulent misrepresentation 9.49
  leasehold interests 9.36
  minerals 9.41
  novel or important issues of development control 18.15–18.16
  owner, definition of 9.36
  prescribed date 9.33–9.34
  representations 9.35, 9.42
  reserved matters 9.46
  service 9.35, 9.42
  Standard Application Form 9.38
  subsequent purchasers 9.45
  time limits 9.35, 9.42
NPPF *see* National Planning Policy Framework (NPPF)
NSIPs *see* nationally significant infrastructure projects (NSIPs) inquiries
nuisance 15.50–15.55 *see also* anti-social behaviour
  declarations 15.50
  defence of statutory authority 15.55
  high hedges 25.34, 25.37
  immunity from actions 15.50–15.55, 16.30
  injunctions 15.50

Index

nuisance (*cont.*)
  nationally significant infrastructure projects 15.55
  neighbourhood, reference to the 15.50–15.55
  notices 25.37
  public works orders 16.30
  tree preservation orders 25.05
nursing homes, definition of 6.80

objections
  denial of right to object 3.21
  development plans, development of 3.21
  major infrastructure projects 28.11–28.12
  public inquiries 16.39, 28.11–28.12
  public works orders 16.39
obsolescence 17.19–17.20, 17.32
occupiers 20.41, 20.53, 20.71
offences *see* **criminal offences**
off-licences 6.65
off-site effects 6.08–6.09
old mining permissions 23.03–23.12
  conditions 23.05–23.11
    active 23.06–23.07
    dormant 23.06–23.07
  consent 23.03
  Crown 16.04
  duration 23.03, 23.05
  EIA Directive 23.08
  interim development orders 23.03, 23.14
  presumption of regularity 23.03
  reactivation of workings 23.03
  registration 23.03, 23.05, 23.11
  time limits 23.03
  winning and working 23.03
old-style plans 3.04–3.10
old use, destruction of 15.27–15.33, 15.37–15.38
Olympic Delivery Authority (ODA) 2.74
ombudsmen *see* **Parliamentary and Local Government Ombudsmen**
open land 6.62 *see also* **town and village greens**
open views, preservation of 11.69
operational development 5.01–5.79
  agriculture 6.34
  ancillary basis 9.13
  appeals 5.77–5.79
  building operations 5.12–5.60, 5.75–5.76
  certificates of lawfulness of existing use or development 20.169
  certificates of lawfulness of proposed use or development 20.169
  conditions 14.04
  demolition 5.40–5.60, 5.62, 5.64, 5.76
  development, definition of 5.01–5.79, 14.04
  enforcement notices 20.64
  engineering operations 5.61–5.71, 5.75, 5.77–5.79
  forestry 6.34, 7.43
  material change of use 5.02–5.10
  mining operations 5.72–5.75, 5.77

  other operations
    definition 5.75–5.79
    restrictions 5.75
  outline planning permission 9.13
  planning permission 5.01, 9.13
  single process 5.06–5.10
  use of land 5.03
  waste materials, deposit of 5.78
operational land 16.07–16.08
oral hearings 2.29, 19.17–19.18
organization of planning
  central government 2.01–2.63
    Greater London 2.98–2.100
  local authorities 2.01–2.02, 2.64–2.97
  Secretary of State 2.02–2.63
outdoor advertisement control *see* **advertising, control of outdoor**
outline planning applications 12.58–12.67
outline planning permission *see also* **permission in principle**
  access 9.14–9.15, 9.18
  appearance 9.14–9.15, 9.18
  applications 9.13–9.24
  buildings 9.13, 9.16
  commencement of development 14.110–14.115, 14.119
  Community Infrastructure Levy 17.65
  conditions 9.17–9.18, 14.110–14.115, 14.119
  conservation areas, erection of buildings in 9.16
  Delivering a Fundamental Change 9.24
  duration 14.110–14.115, 14.119
  environmental impact assessments 9.23, 12.44, 12.58–12.64
  environmental statements 12.60–12.61
  expiry of permission 14.110–14.115, 14.119
  extension of time 14.119
  grant of outline permission 9.14
  landscaping 9.14–9.15, 9.18
  layout 9.14–9.15
  listed buildings 21.94
  minimum threshold of information 9.16
  operational development on ancillary basis 9.13
  outline 9.18
  outline applications 12.58–12.67
  pre-submission requirements 9.13–9.24
  redlining 9.23
  reform 9.24
  reserved matters 9.13–9.22, 14.112–14.115
  scale 9.14–9.15, 9.18
  scope 9.18
  time limits 14.110–14.115, 14.119
overlapping applications 10.18–10.21
  appeals 10.19
  conservation area consent 10.20
  listed building consent 10.20
  same day, applications received on 10.21
  similar applications 10.18–10.19
  time limits 10.19

owners
  definition 9.36, 20.41
  enforcement notices 20.41–20.42, 20.53
  minerals 23.01
  planning permission, notification to 9.33–9.49

painting 7.33
parish and community councils
  applications for planning permission 10.42
  consultation 10.53
  neighbourhood development orders 7.04, 7.61
  notification requirements 10.42
  planning permission 10.42
parks *see* historic parks and gardens; National Parks
Parliamentary and Local Government Ombudsmen 18.131–18.142
  administrative functions 18.132
  appeals 18.137
  compensation 18.141
  courts or tribunals, availability of remedies from 18.136–18.138
  creation 18.131
  estoppel by representation 11.21
  informal planning advice, liability for negligent 9.62
  judicial review, availability of 18.138
  jurisdiction 18.132, 18.136
  Law Commission 18.133
  limits on jurisdiction 18.136
  maladministration 9.62, 18.132, 18.134–18.136, 18.139–18.141
  merits of decisions 18.136
  mitigation measures 18.142
  remedies 18.141–18.142
  statistics 18.140
  third parties 10.27
part of land/buildings
  development 15.37–15.38
  listed buildings 21.25
  planning permission 15.23–15.26, 15.37–15.38
  severance 15.26
  split decisions 15.23–15.26
pastimes, lawful 29.19–29.20
Peace Review 17.80
peaceful enjoyment of possessions 19.01, 19.11, 19.12, 19.20
Peak Park Joint Planning Board 2.67
peat 5.72
periodical payments 17.25
permanence of buildings 5.15, 5.18–5.31
permission in principle
  appeal, right of 7.71
  brownfield land register 7.68, 9.26
  consultation 7.72
  exclusions 7.74, 9.27
  grant of 7.69, 7.74, 9.27
  guidance 7.73
  introduction of 9.25

  permission in principle stage 7.67, 7.69, 9.27
  technical details consent stage 7.67, 7.70, 9.28
permitted development *see* General Permitted Development Order (GPDO)
personal circumstances of applicants
  affordable housing 11.126
  applications, determination of planning 11.110–11.119
  fair hearing, right to a 11.119
  finances 11.111–11.114
  hardship 11.111–11.114, 11.118
  industrial development 11.113–11.114
  injunctions 20.165–20.167
  listed building consent 11.115–11.117
  material considerations 11.89–11.90
personal interests of committee members 16.23–16.24, 16.27–16.29
Phelps Report 2.39–2.40, 2.43
piecemeal development, risk of 11.89–11.90
pipelines 28.15, 28.16
planning agreements
  affordable housing 17.36
  amendment 17.39
  appeals 17.17
  cheque book planning 17.07
  conditions 17.14–17.17
  conservation areas 17.13
  costs 17.60
  development plans 17.09–17.11
  discharge 17.19–17.20
  enforcement 17.03
  fettering of statutory powers 17.12
  legitimate planning purpose 17.05
  materiality, test of 17.16
  modification 17.19
  moral and legal issues 17.06–17.07
  obsolescence 17.19–17.20, 17.32
  planning gain 17.05, 17.08–17.11
  planning obligations 17.01–17.02, 17.16–17.20, 17.22, 17.39
  restrictive covenants 17.32
  sale of permission 17.07
  Secretary of State, policy of 17.40
  shopping centres and superstores 17.42–17.59
  Wednesbury unreasonableness 17.14–17.16
Planning and Compensation Act 1991 1.22
Planning and Compulsory Purchase Act 2004 1.23–1.24
planning conditions *see* conditions
Planning (Consequential Provisions) Act 1990 1.21–1.22
planning contravention notices 20.07–20.12
  Carnwath Report 20.07
  compensation 20.08
  criminal offences 20.09
  definition 20.05
  enforcement notices 20.07
  entry, power of 20.07, 20.13
  failure to comply 20.09

Index

planning contravention notices (*cont.*)
  failure to respond, consequences of 20.08
  false or misleading information 20.09
  information 20.07–20.08
  judicial review 20.12
  offers, making 20.10–20.11
  quashing notices 20.12
  reasonable excuse for failure to comply 20.09
  service 20.07–20.08
  stop notices 20.08
  temporary stop notices 20.08
planning contributions
  Community Infrastructure Levy 17.24, 17.63, 17.68, 17.77–17.83
  planning obligations
    appeals 17.37
    Community Infrastructure Levy 17.24, 17.63, 17.68
    Secretary of State 17.40–17.41, 17.42, 17.45, 17.48
  pooled contributions, restrictions on 17.78
Planning Court 18.127
'planning fast track' system 18.127
Planning for a Sustainable Future White Paper 1.25
planning gain 17.05, 17.08–17.11, 17.62, 17.63
Planning (Hazardous Substances) Act 1990 1.21–1.22
Planning Inquiry Commission 28.09
Planning Inspectorate 4.49–4.55
Planning (Listed Buildings and Conservation Areas) Act 1990 1.21–1.22
planning obligations 17.17–17.83
  amendments by agreement 17.39
  appeals 17.26, 17.37–17.38
  breach 17.28
  Community Infrastructure Levy 17.24, 17.54–17.55, 17.62–17.83
  conditions 17.28
  costs 17.60
  creation 17.25–17.31
  definition 17.01
  delay 17.60
  discharge 17.23, 17.32–17.38
  enabling powers 17.01–17.16
  enforcement 17.26, 17.33
  enter into land and carry out operations, power to 17.28
  external costs borne by community 1.16
  Lands Tribunal 17.32–17.33
  local land charges 17.31
  material consideration 17.44, 17.49–17.53
  modification 17.23, 17.32–17.39
  money payments 17.25
  natural habitats and protected species, conservation of 26.09
  necessity test 17.41, 17.44, 17.49–17.52
  periodical payments 17.25
  planning agreements 17.01–17.02, 17.16, 17.17–17.20, 17.22

  amendment 17.39
  appeals 17.17
  conditions 17.17
  costs 17.60
  discharge 17.19–17.20
  modification 17.19
  obsolescence 17.19–17.20, 17.32
  restrictive covenants 17.32
  Secretary of State, policy of 17.40
  shopping centres and superstores 17.42–17.59
planning contributions
  appeals 17.37
  Community Infrastructure Levy 17.24, 17.63, 17.68
  Secretary of State 17.40–17.41, 17.42, 17.45, 17.48
  Planning Gain Supplement 17.62
  pooled contributions 17.58
  positive covenants, discharge or modification of 17.32
  reasonableness 17.44, 17.48, 17.51
  reform 17.60–17.62
  restrictive covenants 17.32
  Secretary of State 17.40–17.63
  shopping centres and superstores 17.42–17.59
  time of creation 17.27
  Town and Country Planning Act 1990 17.01, 17.21–17.22
  transfer of land 17.29–17.30
  unilateral undertakings 17.18, 17.22, 17.26
  useful purpose, obligations serving a 17.34–17.35
  Wednesbury unreasonableness 17.44, 17.51
planning permission *see also* **applications for planning permission; conditions; outline planning permission**
  abandonment of permission 15.67–15.69
  account of profits 9.49
  administrative powers 2.21, 2.23–2.30, 2.35–2.38
  advertising, control of outdoor 6.101, 24.37
  agricultural holdings 9.37–9.38, 9.40, 9.43
  appeals 2.21, 2.23
  applications 15.04–15.08, 15.11–15.14
  bias 2.40, 2.44
  called in applications 2.24–2.30
  carrying out an activity without ascertaining whether it needs permission 8.17–8.21
  cases of doubt 8.01–8.21
  certificates of lawfulness of proposed use or development 8.02–8.08
  certification requirements 9.38–9.49
  colourability test 14.99–14.101
  commencement of development 14.81–14.126
  compensation 1.13, 1.17–1.18, 2.47–2.53, 27.03, 27.06–27.13
  completion of development 15.66
  comply with permission, works must 14.103–14.109
  conflicts of permissions 15.66–15.70

Index

construction of a planning permission 15.01–15.14
continuance in force 15.66
conveyancing 9.45
correspondence 15.05, 15.10
criminal offences 9.44
death of persons concerned 15.66
declaration, actions for a 8.09–8.16
default powers to revoke or modify planning permission 2.35–2.53
development charges 1.13
development orders 7.01–7.04
development plans 2.35–2.53, 3.01–3.02, 10.56–10.63
documents, taking into account 15.02, 15.05–15.14
duration 14.81–14.126, 15.66–15.72
effect of planning permission 15.27–15.38
errors 9.46–9.47
existing use rights 15.27–15.33, 15.37–15.38
expiry 14.81–14.126, 15.66
extrinsic evidence 15.04–15.08, 15.11–15.14
false or misleading statements 9.44
financial consequences, consideration of 2.47–2.53
form 9.34
fraud 2.40, 2.44, 9.49
gardens 6.51–6.52
General Permitted Development Order 2.13, 7.05–7.55
granting permission, ways of 7.01
Greater London 2.98–2.99
intention 14.99–14.102
judicial review 2.43–2.45, 2.53
leasehold interests 9.36
life of a planning permission 15.66–15.72
limited period, permission for a 14.49–14.57
local development orders 7.56–7.54
material change of use 14.92
material considerations 2.48
material development 14.91
material operations 14.90–14.95
minerals 1.23, 9.41, 15.66, 23.01–23.32
national policy guidance 2.53
nationally significant infrastructure projects inquiries 28.16
natural habitats and protected species, conservation of 26.01, 26.03, 26.06–26.17
neighbourhood development orders 7.61–7.66
new planning units, creation of 15.33–15.37
notification 9.33–9.49
old use, destruction of old 15.27–15.33, 15.37–15.38
open land embodied in curtilage 15.31
operational developments 5.01
owners, notification to 9.33–9.49
parish and community councils 10.42
part of land 15.23–15.26, 15.37–15.38
partial implementation 14.121–14.125
permission in principle *see* **permission in principle**
Phelps Report 2.39–2.40, 2.43
planning register, inspection of 15.03–15.04
previous planning permission, restricted use due to 27.27–27.29
public interest 2.51
public works orders 16.31–16.39, 16.46–16.51
purchase notices 27.40
refusal 1.13, 1.17–1.18, 2.21
renewal applications 15.07–15.08
reserved matters 9.46
resolutions of planning authorities or committees 15.09–15.10
revocation or modification 2.23, 2.35–2.53, 15.66, 27.08–27.13, 27.40
sale of permission 17.07
scope 15.15–15.26
severance 15.26
simplified planning zones 2.83
special development orders 2.15–2.18, 7.03
split decisions 15.23–15.26
standing 2.41–2.42, 2.45
time limits 14.82–14.109
Town and Country Planning Act 1947 1.13, 1.17–1.18
Town and Country Planning Act 1990 2.35–2.53
variation of period for commencement 14.87
Whitley principle 14.103, 14.106, 14.108
Planning Policy Guidance Notes (PPGs) 2.55–2.56 *see also* **Mineral Policy Statements (MPSs) and Minerals Planning Guidance Notes (MPGs)**
administrative powers 2.55–2.56
aims 2.56
ancient monuments 22.16
material considerations 2.59
National Planning Policy Framework, replacement with 2.57, 11.58
simplified planning zones 2.87
sites of archaeological interest 22.16
Wales 2.58
Planning Policy Statements (PPSs) *see also* **Mineral Policy Statements (MPSs) and Minerals Planning Guidance Notes (MPGs)**
administrative powers 2.55, 2.57
ancient monuments 22.14–22.16
biodiversity 2.57
conservation areas 21.02
consultation 9.59
development plan documents 4.54
flood risk 2.57
geological conservation 2.57
historic environment 2.57
housing 2.57
list of PPSs 2.57
local development framework and schemes 4.18, 4.22
local spatial management 2.57
material considerations 2.59

Index

Planning Policy Statements (PPSs) *(cont.)*
  National Planning Policy Framework, replacement with 2.57, 11.58
  natural habitats and protected species, conservation of 26.03
  pollution control 2.57, 11.150–11.151
  renewable energy 2.57
  rural areas 2.57
  sites of archaeological interest 22.14–22.16
  strategic environmental assessments 13.09
  supplementary planning documents 4.31
  sustainable development 2.57
  sustainable economic growth 2.57
  waste management 18.39–18.42
Planning Practice Guidance Suite 2.60–2.61
planning register
  applications for planning permission 9.64–9.66
  Development Management Procedure Order 2.13
  enforcement notices 9.66
  environmental impact assessments 9.66
  inspection 9.64, 9.66
  minerals 23.24–23.31
  parts 9.65
  pre-submission requirements 9.64–9.66
  simplified planning zones 9.66
  stop notices 9.66
planning unit 6.115–6.142, 6.163–6.169, 15.33–15.37
playing fields 16.15
pollution control
  amenity 11.153
  applications, determination of planning 11.146–11.155
  authorizations 11.146, 11.154
  Environment Agency 11.154
  environmental impact assessments 11.148
  licensing 11.146
  material considerations 11.146–11.155
  NPPF 2.57, 11.150–11.151
  Planning Policy Statements 2.57
  prescribed processes 11.152
population increases 3.08
ports and harbours 16.30
positive covenants, discharge or modification of 17.32
PPGs *see* **Planning Policy Guidance Notes (PPGs)**
PPSs *see* **Planning Policy Statements (PPSs)**
precedent, creation of a 11.77–11.81
preliminary determinations of law 2.62
preservation of existing uses
  applications, determination of planning 11.91–11.103
  fair chance test 11.95–11.96N
  material change of use 11.91–11.103
  reasonable possibility test 11.95
  reasonable probability test 11.97–11.98, 11.101
pre-submission requirements 9.01–9.66
  consultation
    applicants, by 9.63

  local planning authorities 9.59–9.62
  content and form 9.01–9.12
  fees 9.50–9.56
  notification of owners 9.30–9.49
  outline planning permission 9.13–9.24
  planning register 9.64–9.66
  twin-tracking 9.57–9.58
previous appeal decisions as material consideration 11.62–11.68
primary or dominant use 6.117–6.142, 6.164–6.165
prisons 6.81
private Acts 16.30–16.33, 16.36–16.38, 16.51
private interests, protection of
  amenity 11.72, 11.76
  applications, determination of planning 11.69–11.76
  clean air 11.73–11.75
  open views, preservation of 11.69
  public interests, overlapping 11.69–11.70
procedural fairness 28.10
professional and financial services 6.61, 6.64–6.67, 7.36
prohibition 18.120, 18.130
proportionality 19.12–19.13
proposed use or development, certificates of *see* **certificates of lawfulness of proposed use or development (CLOPUDs)**
proposed works, certificates of lawfulness of 21.152
protected species *see* **natural habitats and protected species, conservation of**
proximity 15.56
public control over land use, growth of 1.01–1.20
  approval by central government 1.06
  Barlow Report 1.10, 1.13
  clearances 1.02
  compensation/betterment problem 1.07–1.08, 1.10–1.14, 1.16
  compensation fund 1.13
  consultation 1.06
  delay 1.04–1.05
  development plans 1.04–1.05
  discretion 1.03
  historical background 1.01–1.20
  insanitary housing conditions 1.02
  local authorities 1.03–1.05
  public health 1.02
  schemes
    approval by central government 1.06
    failure of schemes 1.09
    implementation 1.06
    preparation 1.03–1.05
    time limits 1.03–1.05
  Scott Report 1.10, 1.13
  total development value of UK land 1.14
  Town and Country Planning Act 1947 1.13–1.20
  Uthwatt Report 1.10–1.14
public functions, condition of provision of 14.21–14.23
public hearings 19.13

Index

public inquiries *see also* local inquiries; nationally significant infrastructure projects (NSIPs) inquiries
  appeals 18.12
  delay and expense 28.04
  duration 18.66, 28.04
  hearings 18.45
  linked projects 28.05
  major infrastructure projects 18.65–18.69, 28.02–28.04
  national security 16.04
  natural justice or fairness 18.21–18.22
  objections 16.39, 28.11–28.12
  public works orders 16.32, 16.39
  rules 18.21–18.22
  schemes of national significance 16.44
public interests, overlapping 11.69–11.70
public pressure and opinion 21.119, 26.03
public works orders 16.30–16.51
  compulsory acquisition 16.30, 16.37
  contents of orders 16.36–16.37
  environmental impact assessments 16.38
  General Permitted Development Order 16.31
  guided transport systems 16.34
  hazardous substances consent 16.37
  hybrid Bill procedure 16.51
  inland waterways 16.30, 16.35
  listed building consent 16.50
  nuisance actions, immunity from 16.30
  objections 16.39
  planning permission 16.31–16.39, 16.46–16.51
  ports and harbours 16.30
  private Acts 16.30–16.33, 16.36–16.38, 16.51
  procedure 16.32, 16.38–16.39
  public inquiries 16.32, 16.39
  railways 16.30, 16.34
  reserved matters 16.48
  rights of way, extinguishment of public or private 16.30
  schemes of national significance 16.40–16.45, 16.51
  Secretary of State, authorization of 16.33–16.34, 16.46–16.50
  standing to apply 16.38
  tramways 16.30, 16.34
  trolley vehicle systems 16.34
publicity and advertising 10.26–10.40
  applications for planning permission 10.26–10.40, 10.47
  bad neighbour development 10.26, 10.33
  changes to applications 10.37
  conditions, discharge or amendment of 10.37
  conservation areas 10.45, 21.143–21.148
  consultation 10.26, 10.39
  departure applications 10.57
  development plans 10.58
  duplication of publicity and notice requirements 10.47
  environmental impact assessments 12.26, 12.35–12.37, 12.39–12.40
  environmental statements 12.35–12.36
  levels of publicity 10.29
  listed buildings 10.43–10.44, 10.47, 21.64
  major developments 10.31–10.33, 10.36, 10.47
  nationally significant infrastructure projects inquiries 28.21–28.22, 28.24
  neighbours, consultation with 10.26
  newspaper advertisements 10.30–10.31, 10.38, 10.43, 10.45, 21.64
  notice requirement 10.27–10.34, 10.47
  para 2 applications, developments specified in 10.29–10.30
  quashing permission for failure to comply 10.40
  reserved matters, approval of 10.37
  service of notices 10.31
  site notices, display of 10.30–10.31, 10.34
  summary of requirements 10.36–10.40
  third parties, notification of 10.26–10.27
  time limits 10.30–10.31, 10.34, 10.37–10.38, 10.40
  websites, publication on local authority 10.35
purchase notices 27.16–27.40
  amenity land 27.27–27.28
  buildings, removal of 27.40
  cancellation 27.32
  compensation, assessment of 27.35–27.38
  conditions 27.17
  confirmation of notices 27.34, 27.38
  definition 27.16
  discontinuance of a use 27.40
  implied withdrawal 27.30
  listed buildings 21.93
  natural habitats and protected species, conservation of 26.06
  notice to treat 27.22, 27.34–27.36
  permitted development value 27.38–27.39
  planning permission, revocation or modification of 27.40
  previous planning permission, restricted use due to 27.27–27.29
  reasonably beneficial use 27.17–27.18, 27.21, 27.26
  responding notice 27.21
  schedule 3 value 27.38–27.39
  second notice, service of 27.30
  Secretary of State, actions of 27.23–27.25, 27.29–27.32
  service 27.17, 27.30, 27.33–27.35
  statistics 27.31
  time limits 27.17, 27.21, 27.33
  withdrawal 27.30

quashing orders 18.120, 18.130
quasi-judicial powers 2.63

race discrimination 11.51–11.53, 20.19
railways and rail freight interchanges 16.30, 16.34, 16.42–16.45, 28.15

Index

reasonably beneficial use 27.17–27.18, 27.21, 27.26
reasons
   adequate and intelligible reasons 18.57–18.58
   appeals 11.62–11.63
   applications, determination of planning 11.05
   called in applications 2.27
   costs 18.91
   development plan documents 4.55
   environmental impact assessments 12.24–12.25
   local development orders 7.58–7.59
   local inquiries 18.57–18.58, 18.60
   notification 18.57
   recovered cases 18.60
   stop notices 20.118
   timetable, failure to meet the 18.71
   transferred cases 18.57–18.58
rebuilding or replacement
   demolition 20.61–20.62, 21.79–21.80
   enforcement notices 20.61–20.62, 21.79–21.80
   General Permitted Development Order 7.29–7.30
   listed buildings 21.79–21.80
   minerals 23.01
   tree preservation orders 25.06–25.09
recording of sites/buildings 21.57, 22.11
recovered cases 18.13–18.16, 18.50, 18.59–18.63
redlining 9.23
refuse, deposit of 5.63, 6.98–6.99
regional and national controversy, developments of major importance which prompt substantial 18.15
regional planning guidance (RPGs)
   consultation 3.25
   development plans, development of 3.22–3.25, 3.32
   preparation 3.25
   regional spatial strategy, replacement with 3.32
regional strategies
   abolition 3.34–3.36
   ancient monuments 22.14
   county planning authorities and district planning authorities 2.94
   development plan documents 4.01
   Localism Act 2011 3.34–3.36
   Regional Planning Boards 2.94
   regional spatial strategy 3.32, 4.01, 22.14
   sites of archaeological interest 22.14
   strategic environmental assessments 13.08
   sustainable development, cooperation over 3.34
registration *see* **planning register; town and village greens**
remedies *see also* **compensation; declarations; injunctions**
   account of profits 9.49
   adverse planning decisions 27.01–27.40
   damages 15.61, 15.65, 20.164
   enforcement notices 20.73–20.74, 20.96
   environmental impact assessments 12.17–12.22
   exhaustion of local remedies 19.02, 19.04
   high hedges 25.36–25.40
   judicial review 18.120, 18.130
   mandatory orders 18.120, 18.130
   Parliamentary and Local Government Ombudsmen 18.141–18.142
   prohibition 18.120, 18.130
   purchase notices 26.06, 27.16–27.40
   quashing orders 18.120, 18.130
removal
   advertising, control of outdoor 6.103, 24.04, 24.06
   compensation 27.14–27.15
   fly-posting 24.33, 24.35
   hedgerows 25.26–25.40
   nationally significant infrastructure projects inquiries 28.36
   purchase notices 27.40
renewable energy 2.57
repairs, listed buildings in need of
   appeals against repair notices 21.104
   architectural or historic interest, claims that buildings are not of 21.104
   compensation for compulsory purchase 21.107–21.112, 21.122
   compulsory purchase 21.101–21.112, 21.122
   deliberate disrepair, allowing 21.108–21.112
   demolition 21.107–21.112
   directions for minimum compensation 21.108–21.112
   ecclesiastical buildings 21.100
   expenses, recovery of 21.99
   Greater London 21.100
   local authorities' power to carry out works 21.98–21.100
   notice 21.98–21.99, 21.102–21.106
   repair notices 21.102–21.105
   scheduled monuments 21.99
   Secretary of State, authorization of 21.104–21.105
   service of repair notices 21.102–21.105
   special interest test 21.13
   statistics 21.106
   stay of proceedings 21.104
   temporary support 21.98–21.99
   urgent works 21.98–21.99
repeat applications 10.10–10.17
   appeals 10.13–10.14, 10.16
   changes in relevant circumstances 10.12
   conservation area consent 10.17
   decline to determine planning applications, power to 10.10–10.17
   discretion 10.15
   enforcement appeals 10.13
   judicial review 10.14
   listed building consent 10.17
   more than one similar applications, refusal of 10.13
   notice of decision to decline consideration of applications 10.16

Index

prior approvals under GPDO 10.17
Secretary of State, appeals to 10.14, 10.16
similar applications 10.10–10.12, 10.14
time limits 10.12–10.13, 10.16
replacement *see* **rebuilding or replacement**
reserved matters
  approval 10.37
  conditions 9.17–9.18
  definition 9.22
  environmental impact assessments 12.62–12.64, 12.66–12.67
  fees for applications 9.51
  listed buildings 21.94
  outline planning permission 9.13–9.22, 14.112–14.115
  planning permission
    notification to owners 9.46
    outline 9.13–9.22, 14.112–14.115
  public works orders 16.48
  publicity 10.37
reservoirs 28.15
residential institutions 6.80–6.81
residential uses
  care, persons in single households receiving 6.82, 6.86
  community care houses providing support for disabled and mentally disabled people 6.84
  dwelling houses 6.82–6.84
  hospitals 6.80–6.81
  hostels 6.79
  hotels 6.79
  material change of use 6.56, 6.79–6.88
  multiple occupation, houses in 6.82–6.84, 7.36
  nursing home, definition of 6.80
  prisons 6.81
  residential institutions 6.80–6.81
  secure residential institutions 6.81
  single households 6.82–6.86, 7.36
  students 6.84
  Use Classes Order 6.56, 6.79–6.87
restoration *see* **rebuilding or replacement**
restrictions on development, compensation for 27.01–27.07
restrictive covenants 15.43–15.44, 17.32
resumption of use after abandonment 6.148–6.162
retail business
  material change of use 6.09
  shopping area uses 6.56, 6.59–6.71, 7.36
  supermarkets, superstores and hypermarkets 16.15–16.24, 16.27, 17.42–17.59
  wholesale cash and carry 6.63
retrospectivity
  decline to determine planning applications, power to 10.22–10.25
  enforcement notices 10.22–10.25, 20.02
  listed buildings 21.73
  Localism Act 2011 10.22–10.25

planning applications 14.78–14.80
reviews *see also* **statutory reviews**
  development plan documents 4.26
  natural habitats and protected species, conservation of 26.07–26.08
  surveys 4.12–4.14
revocation or modification
  administrative powers 2.35–2.38
  certificates of lawfulness of existing use or development 20.186
  certificates of lawfulness of proposed use or development 20.186
  compensation 27.08–27.13
  default powers 2.35–2.53
  development plan documents 4.60–4.66
  life of a planning permission 15.66
  local development orders 7.60
  Mineral Policy Statements (MPSs) and Minerals
  minerals 23.01
  planning agreements 17.19
  planning permission 2.23, 2.35–2.53, 15.66, 27.08–27.13, 27.40
  purchase notices 27.40
  restrictive covenants 17.32
  tree preservation orders 25.14
right of entry *see also* **entry, right of**
  bridleways 15.39
  diversion 15.39
  enforcement notices 20.71
  extinguishment 16.30
  footpaths 15.39
  private rights of way 16.30
  public rights of way 15.39, 16.30
  public works orders 16.30
right to a fair hearing *see* **fair hearing, right to a**
roads *see* **highways**
RPGs *see* **regional planning guidance (RPGs)**
rural areas
  article 4 directions 7.07
  General Permitted Development Order 7.07
  Planning Policy Statements 2.57
  Scott Report 1.10
  sustainable development 2.57

sale of land, deferment of payment until 1.07
same use Class, change of use within the 6.10, 6.53–6.91
satellite antennas 7.32, 11.109
saved plans 4.02
scale 9.14–9.15, 9.18
scheduled monuments 22.02–22.07
  ancient monuments 22.02, 22.08
  compensation 22.21
  conditions 22.03–22.04
  consent 22.03
  criminal offences 22.03
  definition 22.02, 22.07
  English Heritage 22.06

701

Index

scheduled monuments (*cont.*)
  listed buildings 21.22, 21.99
  local authorities' power to carry out works 21.99
  nationally significant infrastructure projects inquiries 28.16
  repairs 21.99
  resurvey programme 22.06
  Secretary of State 22.02–22.06
  sites of archaeological interest 22.21
  statistics 22.06
  urgent works 22.05
schemes of national significance 16.40–16.45
  compulsory acquisition 16.43
  hybrid Bill procedure 16.51
  Parliament, approval by 16.40
  public inquiries 16.44
  railways 16.42–16.45
  Secretary of State 16.40–16.41
scope of planning permission 15.15–15.26
  amendments to applications 15.16
  applications, scope of 15.15–15.26
  part of land, grants of permission over 15.23–15.26
  severance 15.26
  split decisions 15.23–15.26
  Wednesbury unreasonableness 15.22
  scoping opinions 12.32–12.34, 12.36
Scotland
  burial grounds 6.30
  devolution 1.23
  primary legislation 2.05
  Scotland Act 1998 1.23
  Scottish Parliament 1.23, 2.05
Scott Report 1.10, 1.13
screening directions 12.24–12.25, 23.30–23.31
screening opinions
  environmental impact assessments 12.14–12.22, 12.24–12.25, 12.30, 12.36
  minerals 23.30–23.31
  significant effects 12.16–12.22
sculptures 5.25
SEAs *see* **strategic environmental assessments (SEAs)**
second generation plans 3.04, 3.10–3.28
Secretary of State
  administrative powers 2.19–2.62
  advertising, control of outdoor 24.01, 24.09, 24.19–24.20, 24.29
  ancient monuments 2.09, 22.09–22.10
  appeals 18.01, 18.06–18.16
  archaeological importance, areas of 22.11
  article 4 directions 7.10
  building preservation notices 21.113, 21.115, 21.117
  climate change policies 18.15
  Communities and Local Government, for 2.04, 2.09
  completion notices 14.120–14.125
  compulsory purchase orders 2.09, 21.104–21.105
  conservation areas, designation of 2.09
  consultation 10.53–10.54
  costs 18.79–18.84

  Crown 16.04
  decision letters, power to correct 18.73–18.78
  demolition 5.51–6.52, 5.55–6.55
  Department of National Heritage 2.09
  Development Management Procedure Order 2.13
  ecclesiastical use and monuments, buildings in 21.52
  energy efficiency policies 18.15
  enforcement notices 20.70–20.72, 20.76–20.100, 20.103–20.105
  enterprise zone authorities 2.78
  fees for applications 9.53–9.54
  General Permitted Development Order 2.13–2.14
  Government departments, objections from other 18.15
  Greater London 2.99
  hierarchy 2.10
  highways 10.41
  historic buildings 2.09
  housing action trusts 2.88
  important or novel issues of development control 18.15
  judicial powers 2.62–2.63
  legislative powers 2.12–2.18
  listed buildings 21.09–21.11, 21.65, 21.70, 21.74–21.76, 21.82–21.84, 21.104–21.105
  local development orders 7.57, 7.58–7.59
  local development plans 4.59
  local development schemes 4.21
  local inquiries 18.50, 18.52, 18.53–18.63
  major importance which prompt substantial regional and national controversy, developments of 18.15
  major infrastructure projects 18.64, 28.02, 28.07, 28.11–28.12
  Ministers of State, assistance from 2.07–2.08
  National Park authorities 2.69
  nationally significant infrastructure projects inquiries 28.07, 28.13, 28.15–28.16, 28.19–28.36
  natural habitats and protected species, conservation of 26.06
  natural justice or fairness 18.19–18.20, 18.26–18.27, 18.32–18.35
  organization of planning 2.02–2.68
  Parliamentary Under-Secretaries, assistance from 2.07
  planning agreements 17.40
  planning obligations 17.40–17.59
  political responsibility, statement of 2.03
  public works orders 16.33–16.34, 16.46–16.50
  purchase notices 27.23–27.25, 27.29–27.32
  reasons, statements of 7.59
  recovered cases 18.15
  regulations and orders 2.12–2.13
  representatives 18.56
  residential developments affecting government objectives 18.15
  reviews 18.93–18.116

Index

scheduled monuments 22.02–22.06
schemes of national significance 16.40–16.41
Scottish Parliament 2.05
senior officials, decisions by 18.15
special development orders 2.15–2.18
statutory instruments 2.12–2.13
superstores and hyperstores 16.16
supplementary planning documents 4.29
timetable for reaching decisions 18.70–18.72
urban development corporations 2.71–2.72
Use Classes Order 2.13–2.14
Welsh Assembly 2.06
secure residential institutions 6.81
self-build and custom housebuilding 11.160–11.162
Self-Build and Custom Housebuilding Act 2015 1.31, 11.160
senior officials, decisions by 18.15
severance 14.70–14.71, 14.74–14.75, 15.26
shopping area uses
building societies 6.61
display windows 7.36
drinking establishments 6.69, 7.36
financial and professional services 6.61, 6.64–6.67, 7.36
food and drink 6.61, 6.68, 7.36
hot food, sale of 6.61, 6.70–6.71, 7.36
material change of use 6.56, 6.59–6.71, 7.36
off-licences 6.65
open land 6.62
solicitors' offices 6.66
Use Classes Order 6.56, 6.59–6.71, 7.36
visited by members of the public 6.63, 6.65–6.67
wholesale cash and carry 6.63
shrubs 25.04
simplified planning zones (SPZs)
adoption 2.83
approval 2.83
Areas of Outstanding Natural Beauty 2.82
Broads 2.82
completion of development, delay in 2.86
conditions on planning permission 2.83
conservation areas 2.82, 21.132
duration 2.86
enterprise zone authorities 2.79
environmental impact assessments 2.85
general schemes 2.84
green belt 2.82
Housing and Planning Act 1986 2.81
national parks 2.82
natural habitats and protected species, conservation of 26.08, 26.12
planning permission 2.83
Planning Policy Guidance Notes 2.87
planning register 9.66
special scientific interest, areas of 2.82
specific schemes 2.84
statutory framework 2.87
Town and Country Planning Act 1990 2.81, 2.83

single dwelling house as two or more separate houses 6.93–6.97
single households 6.82–6.84, 7.36
single local plans 3.28
single structure plans 3.27
site notices 10.30–10.31, 10.34, 20.21, 21.64
site visits 9.54, 18.56, 25.10
sites of archaeological interest 22.11–22.21
archaeological facilities, provision of 22.15–22.17
Code of Practice on voluntary cooperation 22.19
compensation for loss of development value 22.21
conditions 22.15–22.17
criminal offences 22.11–22.12
development plans 22.13, 22.15
excavation and recording of sites 22.11
local development frameworks 22.14
material consideration 22.13
metal detectors in protected places, offence of using 22.12
moveable artefacts 22.12
national importance, archaeological remains of 22.15
National Planning Policy Framework 22.14
operations notice 22.11
Planning Policy Guidance Notes 22.16
Planning Policy Statements 22.14–22.16
preservation by record 22.19
regional spatial strategies 22.14
scheduled monuments 22.21
Secretary of State 22.11
time limits 22.11
voluntary cooperation 22.18–22.20
social and community uses of a non-residential kind
assembly and leisure 6.89–6.90, 7.36
concert halls 6.89–6.90
material change of use 6.56, 6.88–6.90, 7.36
non-residential institutions 6.88
Use Classes Order 6.56, 6.88–6.90, 7.36
visited by members of the public 6.88
social considerations 11.45, 11.48, 11.50
social housing *see* **affordable housing**
solicitors' offices 6.66
spatial development strategy 2.98–2.99, 4.77
special architectural or historical interest *see also* **sites of archaeological interest**
appeals 21.76
archaeological importance, areas of 22.11–22.12
architectural interest, definition of 21.10
building preservation notices 21.113, 21.118
character 21.07
conservation areas 21.130–21.132
criminal sanctions 21.45
enforcement notices 21.82
hedgerows 25.32
historic battlefields 21.127
Historic Buildings and Monuments Commission, consultation of 13.18
historic environment 2.57

special architectural or historical interest (*cont.*)
   historic interest, definition of 21.10
   historic parks and gardens 21.123–21.126
   listed buildings 21.03, 21.09–21.12, 21.45
     appeals 21.76
     character 21.07
     criminal sanctions 21.45
     determination of applications 21.70
     enforcement notices 21.82
   Planning (Listed Buildings and Conservation Areas) Act 1990 1.21
   Planning Policy Statements 2.57
   Town and Country Planning Act 1947 1.13, 1.20
Special Areas of Conservation (SAC) 26.02–26.17
special development orders 2.15–2.18, 7.03
Special Protection Areas (SPAs) 26.02–26.17
special scientific interest, areas of (ASSIs) 2.82, 25.20
split decisions 15.23–15.26
sport 7.46, 29.19–29.20
spot listing 21.20, 21.118
SPZs *see* **simplified planning zones (SPZs)**
Standard Application Form 9.01–9.06, 9.38
standards, duty to promote and maintain 16.29
statements of community involvement 4.16, 4.18
statutory authority, defence of 15.55
statutory instruments 2.12–2.13
statutory reviews 18.93–18.116
   aggrieved persons 18.99
   appeals 18.94–18.97–18.98, 18.102–18.103–18.104, 18.114–18.115
   conditions 18.110–18.111
   fresh decisions 18.114–18.115
   grounds of challenge 18.101
   judicial review 18.93
   natural justice 18.101, 18.103–18.104
   policy, misapplication of 18.108
   procedure 18.116
   quashing decisions 18.103–18.106, 18.114–18.115
   relevant requirements, compliance with 18.100
   scope 18.97
   Secretary of State 18.93–18.116
   standing 18.99
   substitution of judgment 18.105
   third parties 18.99
   time limits 18.97–18.98
   ultra vires
     procedural 18.101
     substantive 18.101
   Wednesbury unreasonableness 18.106–18.107, 18.109
statutory undertakers 16.05–16.09
   appeals 16.08
   applications 16.07
   called-in decisions 16.08
   definition 16.05–16.06
   General Permitted Development Order 16.09
   operational land 16.07–16.08

Stevens Committee 5.74, 23.01
stop notices 20.109–20.123
   appeals 20.119, 20.122
   breach of condition notice 20.139
   caravan sites 20.116
   compensation 20.09, 20.119–20.123
   criminal offences 20.113–20.114
   distinguished from temporary stop notices 20.110
   enforcement notices 20.109–20.112, 20.123
   extension of time limits 20.117
   fines 20.113
   injunctions 20.155–20.157
   minerals 23.01
   physical steps to enforce compliance, right to take 20.114
   planning contravention notices 20.08
   planning register 9.66
   reasons 20.118
   relevant activity, definition of 20.111
   revision 20.05
   service 20.112–20.120
   time limits 20.117, 20.118
strategic environmental assessments (SEAs) 13.01–13.26
   Brexit and 13.03
   consultation 13.16–13.18
   Countryside Agency, consultation of 13.18
   Directive on SEA 4.30, 13.01–13.10, 13.22
   English Nature, consultation of 13.18
   Environmental Agency, consultation of 13.18
   Habitats Directive 13.05, 13.13
   Historic Buildings and Monuments Commission, consultation of 13.18
   local development documents 4.29, 13.08
   local development plans 13.08
   London, spatial development strategy for 13.08
   notice 13.20
   Practical Guide to the SEA Directive, A 13.09
   preparation of reports 13.14–13.26
   regional strategies 13.08
   reports, preparation of 13.14–13.26
   responsible authority
     determinations of the 13.11–13.13
     preparation of reports 13.14–13.26
   scope 13.05
   significant environmental effects 13.11–13.12, 13.15, 13.20–13.21
   supplementary planning documents 4.19, 4.30
structure plans
   abolition 3.30, 3.32
   administrative powers 2.20
   content 3.28
   delay 3.17–3.19
   development plans, development of 3.11–3.13, 3.16–3.19, 3.24, 3.27, 3.30, 3.32
   development plan documents 4.02
   first generation plans 3.17
   regional strategies, replacement 4.02

Index

saved plans 4.02
single structure plans 3.27
tier 3.11–3.13, 3.16–3.19, 3.24, 3.27, 3.30, 3.32
students 6.84
supermarkets, superstores and hypermarkets
  bias 16.18–16.24
  delay 16.16
  land in which local authority has interest 16.18–16.22
  limits 16.16
  local authorities 16.15–16.24
  personal interests of committee members 16.23–16.24, 16.27
  planning obligations 17.42–17.59
  Secretary of State, decisions by 16.16
supplementary planning documents 4.19, 4.27–4.32
surface soil, offence of removal of 20.01
surveys 4.12–4.15
  county councils 4.13–4.15
  development plan documents 4.12–4.15
  development plans, development of 3.05, 3.07
  district councils 4.13–4.15
  Local Planning Regulations 4.12
  London boroughs 4.13
  Planning and Compulsory Purchase Act 2004 4.12–4.15
  reviews, matters to be included in 4.12–4.13
  scheduled monuments 22.06
  two-tier systems 4.13
sustainable community strategy 4.48
sustainable development
  A Better Quality of Life – a Strategy for Sustainable Development for UK 4.07
  community involvement 4.11
  cooperation 3.34
  definition 4.06, 4.08
  economic role 4.08
  environmental role 4.08
  National Planning Policy Framework 4.08
  nationally significant infrastructure projects inquiries 28.21–28.22
  objectives 4.07–4.08
  Planning and Compulsory Purchase Act 2004 4.03–4.11
  Planning Policy Statements 2.57
  presumption in favour of sustainable development 4.09
  regional strategies 3.34
  rural areas 2.57
  social role 4.08

tax 2.78, 2.80
technical details consent 7.67, 7.70, 9.28
telecommunications
  antenna 7.32, 7.55, 11.109
  General Permitted Development Order 7.54–7.55
  health fears, antenna and 11.109

temporary buildings and uses 7.38–7.46
  advertisements 7.46
  builders' huts 7.39
  casual use on temporary basis 7.41–7.45
  clay pigeon shooting 7.46
  curtilage 7.40
  General Permitted Development Order 7.38–7.46
  helicopters landing and taking off 7.46
  markets 7.46
  motor sports 7.46
  normal use of land 7.44
  permanent intermittent use, change to 7.41–7.45
  war games 7.46
temporary stop notice procedure 20.02, 20.17–20.24
  breach 20.22
  caravans, siting of 20.18–20.19
  compensation 20.23
  criminal offences 20.22
  discrimination 20.19
  display on land 20.21
  distinguished from stop notices 20.110
  enforcement 20.02, 20.17–20.24
  environment 20.19
  European Convention on Human Rights 20.19
  fines 20.22
  free-standing, as 20.17
  planning contravention notices 20.08
  popularity 20.24
  restrictions 20.18
  service 20.20, 20.23
  time limits 20.17
  writing 20.20
temporary support of listed buildings 21.98–21.99
third generation plans 3.04, 3.29–3.33
third parties
  amendment of applications 10.61–10.62
  applications for planning permission 9.30–9.31, 10.61–10.62
  conditions 21.63
  Human Rights Act 1998 19.13–19.15
  judicial review 18.117–18.120
  listed buildings 21.63
  Local Government Ombudsman 10.27
  local inquiries 18.49
  maladministration 10.27
  publicity 10.26–10.27
  reviews 18.99
time limits
  acknowledgment of receipt of planning applications 10.02–10.09
  annual reports 18.72
  appeals
    decision-making 18.70–18.72
    enforcement notices 20.39, 20.55, 20.72, 20.77, 20.83–20.85, 20.100–20.101
    failure to give decisions 18.03
    natural justice or fairness 18.21
    recovered appeals 18.70

Index

time limits (cont.)
  archaeological importance, areas of 22.11
  breach of condition notices 20.25, 20.143
  called in applications 18.70
  caravan site licences 10.03–10.04
  concealment 20.31–20.32
  conditions 21.63
  consultation 10.06, 10.50, 10.52–10.54
  decision letters, power to correct 18.77
  decision-making, timetables for 18.70–18.72
  defective enforcement notices 20.36
  development plans 4.02
  enforcement notices 20.02, 20.05, 20.25–20.39, 20.49–20.52, 20.68
    appeals 20.39, 20.55, 20.72, 20.77, 20.83–20.85, 20.100–20.101
    errors 20.37–20.38
    expiry of time limits 20.02, 20.68
    listed buildings 21.82
  extension
    acknowledgment of receipt of planning applications 10.02
    enforcement notices 20.02, 20.68
    judicial review 18.124–18.126
    outline planning permission 14.119
    stop notices 20.117, 20.118
  false statements 20.32
  full planning permission 14.82–14.109
  immunity from enforcement action 20.29–20.32, 20.35–20.36
  judicial review 18.124–18.126
  list of time periods for enforcement action 20.34
  listed buildings 21.72, 21.82
  local development documents, preparation of 4.02
  local inquiries 18.53
  material change of use 20.30–20.33
  minerals 23.01
  nationally significant infrastructure projects inquiries 28.13, 28.29, 28.35
  natural justice or fairness 18.21
  outline planning permission 14.110–14.115, 14.119
  overlapping applications 10.19
  planning permission
    notification to owners 9.35, 9.42
    outline 14.110–14.115, 14.119
  publicity 10.30–10.31, 10.34, 10.37–10.38, 10.40
  purchase notices 27.17, 27.21, 27.33
  reasons for failure to meet the timetable 18.71
  recovered appeals 18.70
  refusal of planning permission, delay treated as 10.02
  repeat applications 10.12–10.13, 10.16
  reviews 18.97–18.98, 18.126
  revision of timetable 18.71
  second bite provision 20.36–20.39
  Secretary of State 18.70–18.72

  site notices, display of 10.31, 10.34
  stop notices 20.117, 20.118
  substantial completion 20.25–20.29
  temporary stop notices 20.20
  variation of timetable 18.71
Town and Country Planning Act 1947 1.13–1.18, 1.20
Town and Country Planning Act 1990
  compensation for revocation or modification of permission 27.08–27.13
  consolidation 1.21–1.22
  default powers to revoke or modify planning permission 2.35–2.53
  enforcement notices 18.06, 20.01–20.03
  entry into force 1.22
  historical background 1.21–1.22
  Planning and Compulsory Purchase Act 2004 1.24
  planning obligations 17.01, 17.21–17.22
  public control over land use, growth of 1.13–1.20
  scope 1.21
  Secretary of State for the Home Department 2.12
  simplified planning zones 2.81, 2.83
  text App A
town and village greens
  continuous use for 20 years 29.29–29.31
  definition, test for 29.15
  lawful sports and pastimes 29.19–29.20
  locality or neighbourhood qualifying as 29.16–29.18
  rectification of register
    error of law 29.47
    'just' to rectify 29.48–29.50
    power of 29.46
  registration
    error of law 29.47
    procedure 29.37–29.40
    rectification 29.46–29.50
    right to apply 29.07–29.14
    rights after 29.41–29.45
    statutory incompatibility 29.35–29.36
  regulatory development 29.01–29.06
  'significant number' of users 29.32–29.34
  use 'as of right' 29.21–29.28
traffic, growth in 3.08
tramways 16.30, 16.34
transferred cases 18.13, 18.50, 18.53–18.58
transport see also Community Infrastructure Levy (CIL); infrastructure; major infrastructure projects; nationally significant infrastructure projects (NSIPs) inquiries
  guided transport systems 16.34
  helicopters, taking off and landing of 6.27–6.28, 7.46
  inland waterways 16.30, 16.35
  railways and rail freight interchanges 16.30, 16.34, 16.42–16.45, 28.15
  traffic, growth in 3.08
  tramways 16.30, 16.34

Index

trolley vehicle systems 16.34
tree preservation orders 25.02–25.19
  adjoining land 25.12
  administrative powers 2.23
  amenity 25.02
  appeals 2.23, 18.05, 18.13, 25.07–25.10,
    25.13, 25.15
  area classifications 25.03
  bushes 25.04
  compensation 25.19
  conditions of consent 25.01, 25.08, 25.19
  confirmation of orders 25.12–25.13
  consent 25.08, 25.14–25.15
  conservation areas 16.04, 21.146, 25.04, 25.15
  copies 25.09
  criminal offences 25.06–25.08
  Crown 16.04, 25.16
  definition of tree 25.04
  duration 25.13
  financial benefit accruing to convicted persons,
    having regard to 25.08
  fines 25.06, 25.08
  forestry dedication plans or operations or
    covenants 25.05
  future trees 25.04
  group classification 25.03
  guidance 25.03
  hedges 25.04
  injunctions 25.08
  inspection of orders 25.11
  interested persons, definition of 25.12
  nuisance, abatement of a 25.05
  planting trees, condition of 25.01
  reform 25.09–25.18
  replacement trees, replanting of 25.06–25.09
  revocation 25.14
  shrubs 25.04
  site visits 25.10
  Town and Country Planning Act 1947 1.13
  tree felling licences 25.05
  tree replacement notices 25.06–25.09
  variation 25.14
trolley vehicle systems 16.34
twin-tracking 1.23, 9.57–9.58

ultra vires 18.101
under-enforcement 20.63, 20.67
underground gas storage 28.15
undertakers *see* **statutory undertakers**
unitary authorities 2.94, 3.04
unitary development plans (UDPs)
  abolition 3.30
  county planning authorities and district planning
    authorities 2.94
  development 3.15, 3.24, 3.29
  Greater London 3.15
  metropolitan areas 3.15

urban areas, public control over 1.10
urban development corporations (UDCs)
  development plan documents 4.60–4.66
  functions 2.70–2.72
  local planning authorities 2.71
  Olympic Delivery Authority 2.74
  Secretary of State 2.71–2.72
  winding up 2.73
Urban Regeneration Agency 2.75–2.76
urgency
  called in applications 16.04
  Crown 16.04
  electronic communications code operators 7.54
  listed buildings 21.45, 21.98–21.99
  local authorities' power to carry out works 21.98–21.99
  national importance, developments of 16.04
  scheduled monuments 22.05
  Secretary of State, applications to the 16.04
  time periods for inquiries, shortening of 16.04
  tree preservation orders 25.03
use *see also* **material change of use; Use Classes
    Order (UCO)**
  abandonment 6.143–6.162
  conditions specifying use 14.68
  consolidation of undesirable uses 11.158
  demolition 14.68
  destruction of old use 15.27–15.33, 15.37–15.38
  incidental to enjoyment of dwelling house, uses
    which are 6.10, 6.11–6.32
  intensification 6.104–6.114
  interruption of use 6.143–6.162
  operational developments 5.03
  preservation of existing uses 11.91–11.98, 11.101
  public control over land use, growth of 1.01–1.20
Use Classes Order (UCO)
  ambit of 6.91
  business uses 6.56, 6.72–6.75, 7.36
  conditions 6.91
  entry into force 6.54
  General Permitted Development Order 6.91,
    7.35–7.28
  industrial uses 6.56, 6.76–6.78, 7.36
  material change of use 6.10, 6.53–6.91, 7.35
  not included in a particular class, uses 6.57
  parts of Order 6.56
  residential uses 6.56, 6.79–6.87
  same use Class, change of use within the 6.10,
    6.53–6.91, 7.36
  scope 2.13
  Secretary of State 2.13–2.14
  shopping area uses 6.56, 6.59–6.71, 7.36
  single, defining use 6.55
  social and community uses of a non-residential
    kind 6.56, 6.88–6.90, 7.36
  sui generis use 6.57–6.58, 6.83
  text App B
Uthwatt Report 1.10–1.14

value
  agricultural value 1.10
  compensation
    compensation/betterment problem 1.07–1.08, 1.10–1.14, 1.16
    depreciation in value 27.08–27.13
    development value, compensation for loss of 22.21
    floating value 1.10, 1.12
    listed buildings 21.122
    permitted development value 27.38–27.39
    purchase notices 27.38–27.39
    schedule 3 value 27.38–27.39
    scheduled monuments, loss of development value and 22.21
    shifting value 1.10–1.11
    total development value of UK land 1.14
views, preservation of open 11.69
village greens *see* **town and village greens**

Wales
  development plans 4.90–4.91
  devolution 1.23, 4.91
  Government of Wales Act 1998 1.23
  independent examination 4.90
  legislative powers 2.06
  local development plans 4.90
  National Park authorities 2.69
  Planning and Compulsory Purchase Act 2004 4.90
  Planning Policy Guidance Notes 2.58
  Secretary of State 2.06
  Wales Spatial Plan 4.90
  Welsh Assembly 1.23, 4.90–4.91
walls 5.26, 7.34
waste
  county planning authorities and district planning authorities 2.94
  deposit 5.63, 5.78
  development plans, development of 3.28
  engineering operations 5.63
  hazardous waste 28.15
  local development schemes 4.14
  local plans 2.94, 3.28
  material change of use 6.98–6.99
  nationally significant infrastructure projects inquiries 28.15
  operational developments 5.78
  Planning Policy Statements 2.57
  sustainable 2.57
  water treatment plants 28.15
water
  resources, transfer of 28.15
  treatment plants 28.15
way, rights of *see* **right of entry**
websites, publication on local authority 10.35
***Wednesbury* unreasonableness**
  conditions 14.28
  conservation areas 21.130
  costs 18.85
  environmental impact assessments 12.42
  highways 15.48–15.49
  planning agreements 17.14–17.16
  planning obligations 17.44, 17.51
  reviews 18.106–18.107, 18.109
  scope of planning permission 15.22
wholesale cash and carry 6.63
wild animals and birds *see* **natural habitats and protected species, conservation of**
works of art 21.39–21.44
World Heritage Sites 7.20, 21.128–21.129
written representation procedure 18.39–18.42
  appeals 18.39–18.42
  called-in applications 18.42
  expedited procedure 18.40–18.42
  fairly, duty to act 18.42
  householder appeals 18.40
  householder applications 18.40
  non-householder appeals 18.42